ON
STAGE

*Selected Theater Reviews
from The New York Times
1920-1970*

Edited and Introduced by
BERNARD BECKERMAN
and HOWARD SIEGMAN

ON
STAGE

Preface by John Houseman

AN ARNO PRESS BOOK
published in cooperation with
QUADRANGLE / The New York Times Book Co.

Contents

The date line after each review gives the year, month and day,
in that order, when it was printed in *The New York Times*

Introduction

This is a valuable book — valuable for the material it contains and for the manner in which it has been selected and presented. To their hundreds of representative play-reviews "reflecting the highlights of fifty theatrical seasons" Bernard Beckerman and Howard Siegman have added a brief, pragmatic history of the New York stage from 1920 to 1970 reconstructed in terms of what seemed to them its most "significant" theatrical events. Inevitably one has personal reservations — things one feels might have been left out and things one hates not to see included. But by their own standards the editors' choices are conscientious and comprehensive and the tone of their survey is informed and objective.

Leafing gratefully through the riches of this nostalgic anthology I found myself reflecting that it could have been compiled in no other city than New York during this particular half-century and from the columns of no other paper than the *New York Times*. At the time this collection begins the *Times* was one of a dozen dailies published in New York City: today it is the only full-sized newspaper available to that town's many million readers. But long before it had assumed its present monopoly the *Times* had come to occupy a special position in our lives. Through its various departments, it has directly influenced the cultural developments of its time; for the theatre in particular it has also become its official historian. For all but the specialized researcher it is in the faded, crumbling back-issues or from the micro-filmed projections of the *New York Times* that authoritative information is obtained regarding the success or failure of theatrical ventures in America over the past half-century. And this information can, in the main, be relied on as solid, temperate and complete.

Each of the reviews that make up this collection is the

independent creation of a newspaperman of individuality and taste. If collectively they seem to represent the middle range of the enlightened public opinion of their day, this is precisely what they were intended to do. Over the years the drama reviewers of the *New York Times* were chosen less for their theatrical expertise or for the depth and brilliance of their esthetic perceptions than for their ability to report their reactions in readable form to readers of average education and moderately sophisticated tastes: they were expected to combine sincerity, credibility and a certain experience with a sensible and normal Everyman's point of view about the theatre.

The first reviews reprinted in this collection are mostly by Alexander Woollcott who for all his acerbic brilliance was a man of conventional and even sentimental tastes. His successor, Stark Young — the finest and most impassioned judge of theatrical productions we have ever had in this country — lasted for one year, no more. He was followed by a veteran of whom I know nothing and then, in 1926, by Brooks Atkinson whose tenure lasted for more than thirty years and who is, in consequence, responsible for most of the material collected here.

In Atkinson the *New York Times* found its ideal drama reviewer. With characteristic scruple, he was inclined to refer to himself as a "reporter," rather than a critic. A literate man of intense sincerity, a conservative artistically, with an increasingly open mind, he remained surprisingly untarnished by his prolonged contact with the gritty realities of Show Business. Eager to lend his support to whatever he considered valuable and progressive in an art-form of which he had become — by journalistic accident — the nation's most powerful figure, he exerted a consistently benificent influence on the American theatre of his time. He had his avowed prejudices and enthusiasms and he was sometimes slow to accept original talent (having villified the first three Brecht plays he reviewed he later became an admirer and virtually saved THE THREEPENNY OPERA from still-birth). He was an ardent champion of the Federal Theatre of the W.P.A. in the mid-thirties; twenty years later he was among the first to recognize and encourage the new Off-Broadway productions that were sprouting out of the ruins of the collapsing commercial system. In the third decade of his tenure his unabated enthusiasm and sense of responsibility for the American theatre was still driving him to cover store-front theatres and out-of-town performances that no first-string New York drama reviewer had ever attended before. In that sense these reports of his are far more than routine accounts of the outstanding successes of his day.

For that very reason it is well to remember when reading his pieces, and those of his predecessors and successors, that though many of their judgements have, in this volume's editors' words, "stood up remarkably well", these men are, by the very nature of their journalistic function, reporters rather than critics. Written in desperate haste (on the presses ninety minutes after the fall of the curtain) as part of a weekly grind that averaged five to six shows a week for months on end, they supply the raw material from which critics, in the perspective of time, will one day write the significant history of those most vital, variegated and wonderful years in the American theatre.

John Houseman

The Passing -
and Everlasting - Show

During the half-century stretching from 1920 to 1970 *The New York Times* has conscientiously chronicled the fortunes of the New York stage. Not only have its critics reviewed all the significant, and many of the insignificant, productions of the era, amounting to more than 21,000 works, but its drama reporters have tracked down the smallest bits of news pertaining to theatrical affairs and personalities. Its Sunday section on the arts has examined the main trends in theater and permitted the reviewer to amplify his daily remarks. Taken together, the play reviews, news items, and theatrical reports constitute a kaleidoscopic prospect of the American stage.

In 1971 *The Times* and Arno Press undertook the formidable task of gathering and publishing this mass of theatrical material. The result was an exhaustive and fascinating compendium collected into ten volumes which provide the scholar with an irreplaceable storehouse of information and offer the layman a full range of reviews and commentary. The present single volume, based on the comprehensive collection, provides the reader with more than four hundred representative play reviews, reflecting the highlights of fifty theatrical seasons. Any sort of selection is bound to exclude someone's favorites. Indeed, an entire book of reviews would hardly suffice to convey the brilliance of some decades. But even in a collection of this limited scope, the reader will discover the richness of these theatrical years.

Two criteria guided the choice of reviews. First, the selection is intended to reflect the total range of productions available to the playgoer. In a few instances, this has necessitated the inclusion of a review which covers a play no longer important but of a type popular in an earlier time. In their entirety, therefore, the reviews compose a history of the American stage from 1920 to 1970.

Secondly, the reviews are intended to include the most significant individual productions and all the major dramatists, actors, directors, designers, composers, and choreographers of the time. The frequency with which a particular personality appears is a rough index of his or her importance in the American theater. Significance rather than quantity has been the hallmark. For example, Owen Davis, who probably wrote more plays than any other single American playwright, is only represented by reviews of *Icebound* (1923) and *Ethan Frome* (1936) while Thornton Wilder, who wrote less than half a dozen full length plays is represented by reviews of *Our Town* (1938), *The Skin of Our Teeth* (1942), and *The Matchmaker* (1955).

Inevitably a certain distortion is bound to creep into the collection. Classic plays, for instance, are represented in far greater numbers than are popular comedies and melodramas. Yet since the production of a classic often serves as the culmination of an actor's career, the inclusion of its review can not be neglected. In general, then, reviews of routine entertainment appear in far lower proportion in this collection than the entertainment itself did on stage. Thus, the collection reflects the topography of the theatrical years between 1920 and 1970 but naturally emphasizes the peaks.

The men who wrote the reviews were a varied lot of journalists, critics, and writers, some of whom had personal experience in the theater. First in importance was the drama critic himself. In 1920 he was only one of fifteen reviewers who wrote for daily newspapers in New York. In 1970 the *Times* reviewer all but stands alone as the decisive voice in the fortunes of a production. As back-up men for the drama critic were second string critics and reporters who covered premieres when more than one play opened on the same night, as frequently occurred in the twenties. These were the writers who produced the many unsigned reviews in the collection.

Nine men filled the post of drama critic for *The New York Times* between 1920 and 1970. Alexander Woollcott, who had assumed the post in 1914, remained until 1922. He was succeeded by John Corbin who returned to a job that he had filled twice before, in 1903 and from 1917-1919. This time he only remained through the 1923-1924 season. Stark Young covered productions for 1924-1925. At the beginning of the 1925-1926 season no reviewer is listed, but in the course of the year Brooks Atkinson assumed the post which he held uninterruptedly until 1942. In 1946 he returned as critic and remained until 1960, to become the single most influential dramatic critic that has ever written about the American stage. Between Atkinson's two tours of duty, Lewis Nichols filled the position. Since Atkinson retired, the position has been occupied successively by Howard Taubman (1960-1965), Stanley Kauffmann (1966), Walter Kerr (1966-1967), and Clive Barnes (1967-present). To them all the theater owes a considerable debt. Reading their reviews fifty, forty, thirty years after they were writing, one is struck by the durability of their judgment and the keenness of their perceptions. Under the pressure of early deadlines, often having no more than an hour in which to compose their reviews, they recorded American stage history faithfully and mirrored its events accurately. Through their eyes, the reader can share the past at the same time as he discovers how the past became the present.

*   *   *

At a special matinee on February 3, 1920, a hybrid cast drawn from two Broadway shows gave the first performance of Eugene O'Neill's *Beyond the Horizon.* The next day Alexander Woollcott, *The New York Times* critic, hailed the play as a "memorable tragedy" with "greatness in it." So general was this response that the play began a continuous run on March 9th. Somewhat more than three months later, on the evening of June 22nd, Florenz Ziegfeld presented his annual edition of the *Follies,* the fourteenth in the line. Like its predecessors, this huge and fast-moving revue proved once again how accurately Mr. Ziegfeld could "hit the popular mark" by combining the pulchritudinous pageantry of beautiful girls with the spontaneous buffoonery of comics such as Fanny Brice, Eddie Cantor, W. C. Fields, and Ray Dooley. Both *Beyond the Horizon* and the *Follies* were immensely successful, the first unexpectedly, the second predictably so. But similar though their popularity was, as productions they represented two quite opposing traditions in the American theater.

By its very nature, theater is a show place where imaginary

games are played. It is also a hallowed hall where human drama is enacted. "Show" and "play" suggest frivolous appeal, superficial but scintillating entertainment that temporarily catches the customer's fancy. This side of theater is cultivated by show business. "Drama" has a darker sound. It suggests art; it is concerned with primal experience and demands concentrated attention. This side is fostered by "groups," "ensembles," "guilds," in short, by art organizations committed to the creation of "serious" drama. The *Follies,* flamboyant and trendy, was show business in high style. *Beyond the Horizon,* a personal statement on fatality in human decision, was particularly significant not only because its author initiated a new standard of drama in the United States but even more so because his was the first voice from the art theater to catch the ear of the public at large.

By the end of the nineteenth century the once common stock company had all but disappeared. It was replaced by a progressively more centralized system of packaging and distributing entertainment. No longer did the audience rely on an independent troupe of players headed by a manager who was himself a player. Instead, a town was only one stop on what came to be known in show business as the road. Stars, building productions around their individual talents, could tour the country indefinitely as O'Neill's father did for twenty years in the role of the Count of Monte Cristo. The profits from doing so were enormous, so enormous in fact that businessmen soon ousted stars as managers. By 1905 the road was in the hands of such theatrical producers as Marc Klaw, A. L. Erlanger, Charles Frohman, and the Shubert brothers, who selected or assembled plays and controlled their distribution. Although operating out of New York, where shows were cast, rehearsed, and first presented, the producers actually depended on the road for the greater part of their profit. This had considerable effect on the kind of show they selected. They tended to pick scripts that would appeal to the populace as a whole, thus perennially underestimating popular taste.

But even while these men were strengthening their hold on the stage, contrary forces were at work. Centralization, though it initially meant that a uniform product could be shipped to every town and city in the nation, eventually led to a deterioration of standards. As costs of production and transportation mounted, expenditures outran income. Shows became shoddy; this in turn contributed to a further decline of the road. More decisive and more devastating in its effect on touring, however, was the spreading popularity of the motion picture which provided finished entertainment at low prices. Even in its silent form, the "movies" by 1918 had begun to draw audiences away from the theater. But when sound was added to image in 1927, the decline became precipitous.

In the intervening years the American commercial theater enjoyed a last fling of prosperity. It was a decade when the United States became aware of itself as a world power. New York, the center of American sophistication, assimilated anew all the varied cultures that thronged its streets and passed through its ports. Its theater, now cut off from the hinterland and confined to the metropolis, underwent a rate of expansion rare in the annals of show business.

The sheer quantity of activity was astonishing. There were 127 new shows produced in 1905. By 1915, the figure had risen slightly to 133 and by 1920, to 144. But in 1924-1925, despite the collapse of the road, the number leaped to 228, and kept going up, year by year, to 255 in 1925-1926, to 263 in 1926-1927, and finally to a high of 264 new productions in 1927-1928.

This growth, though primarily achieved through commercial production, did include a parallel growth in non-commercial theater. From the beginning of the century dedicated people, both on and off the stage, had tried to infuse artistic purpose into the helter-skelter dealings of show business. Some thought this could be done by upgrading the work of playwrights, and so they hailed the arrival of any dramatist of serious intent. In 1906, for example, the mantle fell on William Vaughn Moody, whose play, *The Great Divide,* seemed to promise so much for the future. Concurrently at Harvard Professor George Pierce Baker was encouraging new playwrights, a number of whom later transformed American drama. Others placed stress on organizing acting groups to produce unconventional European plays in the most advanced style of the day. In 1909 a coterie of thirty wealthy citizens promoted an ambitious and costly plan to establish an *art* theater based on the European repertory model. They erected a magnificent playhouse, the New Theatre on Central Park West, equipping it with the latest stage machinery. Sparing no expense, they mounted ten productions the first year. But in the end this sort of patronage, which proved so effectual in sustaining grand opera, was ineffective in encouraging serious theater. Within two seasons the New Theatre closed, leaving the cause of non-commercial theater to more modest and less professional groups which came into existence during the First World War. One, the Provincetown Players, ushered in the works of Eugene O'Neill. Another, the Washington Square Players, operated for several seasons, offering European plays infrequently performed by the commercial theater. In 1918 this group disbanded, but not without having spawned a successor, the Theatre Guild.

Naturally, not all the serious work in drama was produced by "art" theaters. There were commercial managers like Arthur Hopkins who were responding to the same contemporary currents in drama as the art theaters. They, too, offered unusual works by new dramatists and venerable classics in experimental styles. Nor were the "art" theaters themselves entirely able to keep aloof from commercal considerations. Indeed, as soon as they presented a play that won popular attention, they were caught in the dilemma of whether or not to exploit its commercial success. Since these theaters were usually in financial straits, economics rather than principle determined the answer. Therefore, it turned out that in practice the non-commercial stage was often swept into the commercial whirlpool while commercial producers not infrequently pursued artistcs ends. Nevertheless, no matter how much these two kinds of theatrical production overlapped in practice, in intent and method of operation, they were quite distinct.

Most characteristic of commercial producing is its one step operation. The goal is short term, namely, to get a show — one particular show — on stage. Operating through what is called the combination system, the producer assembles the talents and resources needed to create one effect. He is not encumbered by people who are almost but not quite suited for the play at hand. Sometimes inventively, sometimes ineptly, often ruthlessly, he searches out the ideal person for a particular task. He does not develop talent; he buys it. When he is fortunate and skillful, the result can be a highly polished, dazzling show. It is duplicated and triplicated, sold to films, and reproduced throughout the world. Based on a pay-as-you-go reality, such a commercial show is perpetuated as long as it sells and discarded as soon as it loses money.

Not so the art theater. First and foremost, it is guided by a philosophy, usually an artistic one, though sometimes one that is also political and social. Normally its resources are slight; they reside in the availability and energies of actors and writers welded together by a common objective. This kind of theater seeks artistic and economic continuity. It does not produce one play, but a series of plays. Because the work is communal, each script has to be fitted to the existing group. What may be lost in the fitting, it is believed, will be compensated for in the harmony of the whole. By the very nature of its long range views, the art theater tends to explore new writers, new plays, and new modes of performance. Eventually, both because of its innovative nature and its obligation to sustain a permanent organization, it requires some form of subsidy, whether through the beneficence of a private patron, like Otto Kahn or the subvention of a public agency such as the National Endowment for the Arts.

In the fifty years between 1920 and 1970, these contrasting ways of making theater have been continuously at work. They have shaped, colored, defined American stage history. From one point of view this stage history is cyclical. Men and women of immense talent appear: a John Barrymore, an Ina Claire, a Jed Harris, an Orson Welles. They burst upon the scene, astonish audiences, and then too often, while they are still at their peak, leave the stage or the stage leaves them. So too with art theaters. They arise, make an impact, die when their promise seems greatest. Again and again the process is repeated. Groups and individuals, imbued with new ideas, struggle to bring them to fruition, only to find that they cannot remain together long enough to reach full growth. In the meantime, whatever distinctive performances they are able to create receive the flattery of imitation by amateur and professional theaters around the globe.

From another point of view, however, the American stage reveals not so much a history of growth, promise, and premature decay, but of a continuing shift from one kind of theater to another. After 1928, there was a radical drop in the amount of theatrical production in New York. As a business, the stage became far more risky. Vast sums could be made, but at increasingly disadvantageous odds, a condition that still persists. Production and real estate costs continue to soar, further discouraging investment. Only productions that run a year or more are profitable. Consequently, the strictly commercial producer relies almost solely on musical theater, family comedy, and, occasionally, the thriller. In rare cases, he may circumvent the commercial system by utilizing a non-profit foundation as a sponsor of esoteric imports for limited runs. This is exactly how David Merrick brought the memorable production of *Marat/Sade* (1965) to Broadway. In short, the producer needs a non-commercial device to make a serious commercial production feasible, a truth to which Joseph Papp is testifying so successfully in the early seventies.

Fortunately, commercial contraction is being partly offset by non-commercial expansion. Gradually, the long-held American tradition that the theater is show business and should pay for itself is yielding to the recognition that theater is an art, and an art that deserves to be subsidized. The story of this struggle, filled as it is with setbacks, is nonetheless more happy than sad. In the twenties, what subsidy there was came from a handful of wealthy people who sustained the new art theaters. In the thirties the federal government provided work relief for theater artists just as it did for laborers. In the fifties charitable foundations assumed some of the responsibility for spurring and supporting regional theaters which are the old art theaters in a new setting. By the end of the sixties federal, state, and municipal aid to the arts became an accepted principle. New performing groups, partly underwritten by public monies, have come into existence. More significantly, permanent theatrical institutions have been founded. For the most part, they are administrative organizations such as the Repertory Theater of Lincoln Center, the New York Shakespeare Festival, and the Tyrone Guthrie Theatre of Minneapolis. They may or may not have permanent performing companies, but they do have continuity of administration, and they do receive direct or indirect support from public and private sources. In addition, there are many less institutionalized organizations: commune theaters (the Open Theatre), minority theaters (the Negro Ensemble Company), university theaters, street theaters, etc. All receive some sort of subvention.

In the course of this non-commercial expansion, theatrical horizons have broadened. The traffic between Broadway and off-Broadway and even off-off-Broadway is heavy; newspaper critics cover all the offerings. Actors take round trips between New York and resident theaters in New Haven, Los Angeles, and Houston. New productions spring from loft and basement, university and storefront. All this activity has not yet stimulated another creative outpouring such as the stage knew in the twenties. It remains to be seen what the variety of groups, the contribution of public funds, and the elevation of theater from show business to art will have on audiences of the future.

Meanwhile, looking back on the half-century of achievement represented by the reviews in this collection, one is struck by the richness and variety of the best work. It is the property of neither art nor commerce alone. Interestingly enough, it is at those times when an art theater turned commercial or a commercial producer absorbed the influence of the art theater that the finest plays have come to life. Stylistically and genetically *Death of a Salesman* was an extension of the energies released by the Group Theatre, and *Oklahoma!* under the banner of a commercialized Theatre Guild linked the realistic style of spoken drama to a ballet-derived choreography within the frame of a musical style half operatic, half popular in character.

Through all changes the American stage has remained eclectic. No Ibsen, no Chekhov dominates it. It is impossible to point to a decade and say it is marked by any one style. Instead, side by side there is Eugene O'Neill and George Gershwin, the high style of Jane Cowl and the earthy vitality of Bert Lahr, the frivolity of Ziegfeld's *Follies,* the hilarity of Kaufman and Hart, and the wistful magic of Tennessee Williams. From the overflowing cornucopia of the nineteen twenties to the more abstemious table of the forties and fifties on to the bewildering smorgasbord of the sixties, the playgoer in New York has had a remarkable bill of fare.

At the conclusion of every season *The New York Times* publishes annual statistics on the number of productions presented
during the year together with a count of performances given by
each. It generally divides the data into two broad categories: the
type of sponsor (off-Broadway, Theatre Guild, foreign presentations, etc.) and the genre of the show. From time to time the
sub-divisions in these categories may alter, especially in the case
of the sponsors who change from year to year. The listings under
the genres, however, remain remarkably constant. There is the
principal listing of "Dramatic Productions" ("Plays" after 1941),
and then "Musicals," "Revues," "Revivals," and "Miscellaneous." Together they sum up the varied fare of the New York
stage.

"Dramatic Productions" include tragedy, comedy, melodrama,
farce, and any other sort of spoken drama in their premiere
presentation. Productions of Shakespeare, Chekhov, and others
are relegated to the category of "Revivals." To describe all the
kinds of plays produced between 1920 and 1970 is clearly
impossible, but it is possible to point out certain familiar types.
Comedy, especially domestic character comedy, embedded in
middle-class life and displaying elements of farce and satire, has
long been a mainstay of the American theater. From George S.
Kaufman to Neil Simon, this genre has accounted for some of
the most popular and enduring shows on Broadway. Allied to
domestic comedy is a type of domestic comedy in which the style
of character comedy and the idiosyncratic wisecrack mix in esoteric surroundings as in *Mr. Roberts* (1948) and *The Teahouse
of the August Moon* (1953). Comedies of manners and outright
farces have also had their day, but have never been so central
to the New York stage as the more domesticated type.

Melodrama is also a frequent visitor to the stage. Although
it can take a variety of shapes, on Broadway it often appeared
and still appears in tales of mystery and terror. From *The Bat*
(1920) to *Angel Street* (1941) to *Child's Play* (1970), the
shrouded house, the murderous hand, the unexpected denouement are traditional thrills of the drama. If pure melodrama
turns up less frequently in live drama in recent decades, it is
because film and television have taken over much of the casual
entertainment that had at one time been the sole province of

the stage. The melodramatic touch, however, is an inevitable element of dramatic life. Like a vegetable dye, it can combine and color many other substances. It is often a prominent feature of plays that otherwise realistically dramatize life, whether it be the world of a big city newspaper in *The Front Page* (1928) or the back street of the slums in *Dead End* (1935). It can even mix with comedy as it does in *Arsenic and Old Lace* (1941).

Of all the kinds of plays covered by the heading "Dramatic Productions," serious drama, sometimes graced with the appellation tragedy, has been among the most distinctive yet troublesome residents of the stage. Whenever the condition of the American theater is discussed in somber tones, its deficiencies in "serious drama" are invariably proclaimed. Serious drama is considered to be large in purpose, sober in accent, and lasting in effect. It is regarded as financially hazardous though esthetically rewarding. In the last fifty years, its health has been the barometer of the state of the American theater. Eugene O'Neill is perhaps the serious dramatist par excellence although *Ah, Wilderness!* (1933) proved he could shape a domestic comedy as well as the best of the light-penned humorists. Comic writing in the United States, however, even by masters such as George S. Kaufman, Neil Simon, or Philip Barry at his best, has always occupied a secondary status; it is seldom treated with the respect that the comedy of a George Bernard Shaw or a Somerset Maugham receives. Consequently, it is mainly through the achievements of the "serious" playwrights that the American drama has earned much of its distinction. Eugene O'Neill, Tennessee Williams, Arthur Miller, and Edward Albee have won international recognition and produced an international dramatic literature through the scope of their aspirations, the starkness of their vision, and the power of their greatest works.

These writers have yet to be succeeded by others of equal stature. This may be partially due to the esthetic revolution that theater has undergone. As a young writer, O'Neill tested the bounds of the stage, exploring an enormous range of subjects and styles in an effort to stretch the dimensions of the art. But in later years he, like most of the serious writers, accepted the limitations of realism and worked within a narrow compass of dramatic form. In the sixties, however, a host of young dramatists began to question the conventions of the theater, twisting and inverting the medium in order to make it express something that it did not do in the past and that cinema does not do in the present. Much of their stimulus has come from abroad by way of the works of Bertolt Brecht, Samuel Beckett, and Harold Pinter. Among Americans, Jean-Claude van Itallie (*America Hurrah*, 1966) and Arthur Kopit (*Indians*, 1969) represent experimental and epic approaches that have reached large audiences.

Less wedded to experimentation and more committed to social statement was the work of new black dramatists. For many years black actors, directors, and writers tried to create their own theater. It was, however, with the movement toward black consciousness that black theater emerged as a many-voiced, autonomous expression of a people's struggle. Off-Broadway and in black communities throughout the country new theaters came into existence. Tied to the political and economic emancipation of the black people, writers for these theaters treated the stage as a weapon for defining black identity in its conflict with the white world. Among these writers are Imamu Amiri Baraka (LeRoi Jones) and Ed Bullins. At the same time, black dramatists have fully entered the arena of commercial production. Among those who have gained favorable receptions on Broadway are Lorraine Hansberry, Ossie Davis, and Melvin Van Peebles.

The New York Times listing for the next major category of entertainment provides a clue to the changing nature of the genre. Plays with song and dance were listed as "Musical Comedies" until 1931; such is the label for Jerome Kern's *Show Boat*. Some uneasiness as to whether the term musical comedy truly describes the changing form is evident between 1932 and 1944. During these years, the statistician keeps nervously shifting the category. It is "Musical Shows" some years, "Musical Comedies" others, until 1944 when the simple solution is reached of calling these productions "Musicals." And it was precisely during those years that composers and librettists expanded the medium of the musical, a work half-way between the spoken play and operetta, and transformed it into a distinctive genre with a peculiarly American stamp.

As a theatrical entertainment, the musical is quite young, not having separated itself from operetta to assume a distinct individuality until the 1890's. At first, it consisted of a loose arrangement of songs, dances, and jokes hung upon a slender thread of a comic, often improbable, plot. Spectacular settings and production numbers were artfully distributed through the evening. From these popular origins, still evident in the twenties, the musical developed into a rich harmony of story, music, and dance capable of a wide range of emotional tonality. While still predominantly comic, the musical increasingly treated serious and even tragic subjects. Indeed, in the sixties serious drama on Broadway was more likely to be found in musicals like *Fiddler on the Roof* (1964) and *Man of La Mancha* (1965) than in spoken plays.

During its years of artistic growth, however much the musical responded to the varied currents of the American theater, its production remained the province of the commercial producer, and in fact could only have been created by a combination system able to assemble the specialized talents needed to bring so complex a form to the stage. Often this kind of theater utilizes a collage of plots taken from books and plays, music derived from classical and popular example, dancing based upon balletic, modern, and vaudeville forms, all fused into a whole by the collaborative genius of composer, lyricist, librettist, choreographer, and director. Collaboration is so essential that most of the major works of the musical stage are the products of writing teams: George and Ira Gershwin, Rodgers and Hart, Rodgers and Hammerstein, and Lerner and Loewe among others. In only a few men was the ability to write both words and music joined, most notably in the cases of Cole Porter, Irving Berlin, and Frank Loesser.

Akin to the musical but quite distinctive in type is the "Revue." It consists of an alternating sequence of comic and dramatic sketches, songs, monologues, and production numbers (dances and displays). Although having many features of vaudeville, the revue, as it came to perfection in the twenties, was distinguished from vaudeville by a unifying style or concept. The Ziegfeld revues were renowned for their elaborate production numbers displaying beautiful girls while the Dietz and Schwartz revues were most celebrated for intimacy and wit. By contrast revues of the thirties, such as *Pins and Needles,* were often marked by a running theme of social satire. In general, the revue with its topical flavor and glittering spectacle proved to be the meeting ground between sophisticated Broadway and popular theater.

In its heyday during the twenties and thirties, the American revue brought together and nurtured some of the richest talents the American theater has ever produced; most of the major American comedians and musical artists enlivened the revue stage at one time or another. In later decades, revues became somewhat more specialized, often containing the work of a single composer or exhibiting the style of a small ensemble. Moreover, where once the revue was the kind of production that presented artists at the peak of their powers, in recent years it is often the channel through which fresh talent wins a hearing. In that respect, Leonard Sillman's series of *New Faces* and revues such as *From the Second City* represent the later style, just as the Ziegfeld *Follies* and *The Band Wagon* embodied the earlier.

The persistent category of "Revivals" reflects the peculiar emphasis that the New York theater has always placed on new plays. Hence, any new production of an established work was treated in a separate category. This attitude is essentially commercial; it regards the presentation of an old play, whether by Shakespeare or by Henrik Ibsen as economically questionable. Yet however much the commercial producer may regard a revival with wary esteem, season after season has offered a smattering of Shakespearean plays and modern classics. Over the years the importance of revivals to the American theater has changed somewhat. Certain of the art theaters, such as the Civic Rep or APA, concentrated on the production of classics, a responsibility now inherited by the institutional theaters. At the same time, celebrated actors or daring directors have occasionally taken time from presenting new works to undertake a revival; John Barrymore's *Hamlet* (1922) and Ruth Gordon's all-star production of *A Doll's House* (1937) were just such special offerings. Lastly, visitors from abroad brought plays of their native theater to New York, and more often than not what they brought was classified as revivals. Probably the most famous of these visits was that of the Moscow Art Theatre in 1923. In instances such as this, the foreign troupe proved an ally of the art theater movement by revealing the heights that a carefully trained ensemble could reach if given support and continuity.

What did not fall into the preceding four categories was lumped under "Miscellaneous." Among the most recurring miscellany was the one-man or one-woman show. A variety of performers proved to be enduring adornments of the stage in highly specialized offerings; Ruth Draper, in her dramatic sketches, was probably most notable. But this type of performance includes the singing of Marlene Dietrich (1969), the character monologue of Hal Holbrook as Mark Twain (1959), and the mime of Marcel Marceau (1966). Dramatized readings such as *Don Juan in Hell* (1951) also fall into this category. Less easily defined but frequently included under this anomalous umbrella are those quondam ice spectacles, puppet shows, and otherwise uncatalogued performances that have irregularly caught the attention of the American public.

To create so rich a confection of shows, to stir or attempt to stir so varied an audience as New York provided required a range of talent and an exuberance of energy seldom assembled in one city. The reviews in this book describe not only the content of the shows but convey an impression of all those personalities who dominated the stage. It is of the playwrights and actors one reads most, but in becoming centralized, the New York theater became the nexus of a host of professionals drawn from the entire globe. Directors, designers, composers, and choreographers all set their seal upon the image that is the American theater.

Well before 1920 the American stage doted on its stars, but whereas the star was once his own manager and headed his own company, by the twenties he had become an independent performer, likely to circulate from one management to another. A rearguard of stars endeavored to maintain the old stock system in some modified form and, in a few cases, that of the team of Sothern and Marlowe particularly, they succeeded in doing so on a modest level. Eva Le Gallienne who reached stardom in *Liliom* (1921) followed European example in trying to create a company dedicated to low-priced repertory. But for the most part, stars neither expected to be — nor cared to be — members of continuing troupes.

In the twenties performers worked frequently, played a variety of roles, and seldom remained in one show indefinitely. The road called occasionally and the movies beckoned. But usually there was little temptation for speaking actors to run to Hollywood. Nor was there television to compete for their services. Instead, Broadway provided abundant opportunity for a large number of leading and secondary players to bring experience and maturity to the stage. Moreover, as a consequence of the Actors' Equity strike of 1919, the performers were sharing in the growing theatrical prosperity of the decade.

Out of this lively setting emerged a host of musical and dramatic stars. Alfred Lunt and Lynn Fontanne, Katharine Cornell and Walter Huston, Fanny Brice and Beatrice Lillie came into prominence at the same time that established stars like Otis Skinner and Minnie Maddern Fiske continued to perform regularly, retaining their old fans and attracting new ones. A step behind were the young performers, ready to burst upon the scene, people like Spencer Tracy, Edward G. Robinson, Barbara Stanwyck, and Bette Davis. But with the arrival of talking pictures, the situation changed drastically. Not only was there a decrease in the number of shows, but the ripening talent of the theater, the stars-to-be, were drawn to the cinema, paid sums they could not earn in the theater and rocketed to a fame they could hardly imagine. Few returned to the stage.

The star system of the past thus suffered a severe blow. With rising costs and decreasing production, the stars found that if a show were to make a profit, they had to commit themselves to longer and longer runs, thus affording the performer less opportunity to act in different kinds of plays. And as the older stars aged, there were fewer and fewer players who could fill their shoes. As soon as talent showed itself, it was wafted off to the films and then later, to the television studio. The result was a curious contradiction. Economics demanded the star, but the star found it harder and less desirable to continue. Yet so unpredictable is history that in the sixties and seventies the stage has seen a strange reversal. Film stars who were no longer box-office draws, such as Lauren Bacall and Alexis Smith, returned to the stage to discover a new stardom.

Film and television, nevertheless, were not the only challenges faced by the star system. Intrinsic to the art theatre movement has always been the ideal of an acting ensemble. Each new organization has felt obliged to form a company of actors in which there were to be no stars but only fellow players. The Theatre Guild made a somewhat half-hearted stab in that direction. It was an offshoot of the Guild, however, the Group Theatre, that dedicated itself unreservedly to molding an ensemble, using the Moscow Art Theatre as a model. For a time it seemed as though the Group would be able to hold a core of actors together, but soon personal differences and economic pressures led to its dissolution. This failure shook but did not destroy the ideal of an ensemble. In fact, the ideal has grown stronger in the face of repeated demonstrations that a performing ensemble can not long survive in the United States. Instead of admitting defeat, new groups such as the Living Theatre and the Performance Group have insisted that not only must the members of the performing ensemble share artistic and political ideas, but they must be prepared to share a life style and, in effect, become a collective.

The American stage has not resolved this fundamental conflict between the star and the ensemble. The turbulent and overflowing world of performance that nurtured the stage star no longer exists. Only here and there, often by chance, does a major new personality appear, but when that happens, more rapidly than ever he or she is captured by the mass media. Meanwhile, collectives show great instability. Their work often lacks individuality, subsiding into a common denominator of performance at the very time that their bold aims cry for unusual skill and artistry. In the process, the personal power that a star radiates to a living audience has become a rare commodity, so rare that when it is for sale, as in the case of Katharine Hepburn's appearance in *Coco* (1969) or Ruby Keeler's appearance in the revival of *No, No, Nanette* (1970), it creates a unique kind of excitement.

The weakening of the star system, that is, of the actor's impact on the stage, has been counteracted by a strengthening of the

director's position. Originally the director had also been the
producer. He assembled the cast, arranged for the scenery, and
hired the playhouse. For David Belasco, at the turn of the century, there was no distinction between producing and directing.
Likewise, the people who founded the various art groups did not
differentiate between managing a show and staging it. Actually, it
was not until 1925 that *The New York Times* listed the name of
the director in a play's credits. By the thirties, however, a very
clear distinction was being formed between the producer, responsible for the entire show, and the director whom he hired.
By the sixties it was the rare producer who, like Harold Prince,
reserved the directing of a show for himself.

Concurrently with this development, the director became a
specialist. Margaret Webster was the authority on Shakespearean
production in the forties. George Abbott became known for his
racy maneuvering and crisp rhythm in comedy, Harold Clurman
for his sensitive evocation of lower middle class life, José Quintero for his O'Neill touch. Particularly in those productions that
stressed the acting ensemble, the director became Big Daddy,
guide and confessor, whose concept often became the hallmark
of the show. Elia Kazan, and even more so Lee Strasberg, molded
personalities and released pent-up talents. Peter Brook orchestrated the actors as elements of an elaborate dramatic metaphor.
The director, in effect, became the star who styled a production
and imposed a unifying personality upon it.

The expanded role of the director was matched by the expanded role of the choreographer. He is the last significant artist
to gain a foothold on the theatrical ladder. As an independent
creator, the choreographer makes an appearance in *Oklahoma!*
(1943). In that one production Agnes de Mille assimilated ballet
and modern dance into the Broadway musical, setting the style
for a generation to come. She was succeeded by a throng of
classically trained dancers who made dance an integral part of
the dramatic action until in *West Side Story* (1957) dance superseded song as the dominant feature of a show. Finally, it became
increasingly common in the sixties for choreographers such as
Jerome Robbins and Gower Champion to take full charge of
directing a musical as Robbins did for *Fiddler on the Roof*
(1964) and Champion for *Hello Dolly!* (1964).

All these events coincided with the rise of the scenic designer. In the experimentation that accompanied the growth of the art theater, the designer changed from being primarily a scene painter to becoming an architect of space. But there were limitations to the extent to which men like Robert Edmond Jones and Lee Simonson could experiment. They were bound by the proscenium stage and the world of photographic illusion. They were also bound by the prevalence of realistic drama with its stress on interior decoration rather than architecture. Not until the sixties did the new non-proscenium stages begin to appear in sufficient numbers so as to create new demands in stage design. The expansion of regional theater and the extensive use of open spaces for performance offered fresh possibilities to the designer. No longer merely a decorator, he had the opportunity to become an environment engineer. For *Acropolis* (1969) and *The Serpent* (1970) he shaped not only the world for the performer but also for the audience, defining the way it would see the play and redefining the very act of playgoing.

By the end of the sixties the audience found this act of playgoing, like all acts of city life, rather formidable. Throughout history, theater has always been an urban creature. Whether in classical Athens, Shakespearean London, or golden Paris, it thrived as the city thrived. No wonder is it then that the New York stage has undergone its severest trials at the very time that New York itself has suffered massive dislocations, nor is it especially prophetic to see the future of the first in the fortunes of the second. It is encouraging, therefore, to witness that in the struggle for survival the city recognizes the theater as one of its remarkable institutions, giving support where it can and fostering theatrical construction where possible. With the early seventies has come the completion of several new playhouses in the midtown district. In a way their opening symbolizes the renewal of New York stage life and may indeed signal a new burst of theatrical creativity.

Bernard Beckerman and *Howard Siegman*

From Business
to Art: 1920-1929

In the third decade of the twentieth century, the American theater came of age. Although in the first twenty years of the century some American playwrights had produced worthy plays which were realistic depictions of life, the majority of plays were sentimental comedies and dramas of dubious merit, florid melodramas, and importations or adaptations of popular foreign works. The theatre flourished, but there was a dearth of quality, particularly in the work of the playwrights.

In the decade of 1920-1929, however, the New York theater surged forward in a burst of energy, creativity, and talent. Within this relatively short period native playwrights, actors, directors, and designers were acknowledged, praised, and often emulated throughout the world. Foreign playwrights, actors, and productions were welcomed by admiring New York audiences who were becoming increasingly cosmopolitan. New techniques and concepts were explored and developed by the creative artists. The American composers, lyricists, and librettists broke away from many of the European conventions and began to produce a musical theater still deemed the most outstanding in the world. Of course, popular casual entertainment and sentimental and romantic drama still flourished, but now an art theatre was being created and, in many instances, the popular and the artistic were one and the same: the most distinguished plays and productions were often enormous box-office successes, and the popular comedies and musicals were often artistic triumphs.

Just prior to the beginning of the decade, two professional art theaters, The Theatre Guild and The Provincetown Players, began producing in New York. The Theatre Guild was to become the most prestigious theatrical management in the United States, producing plays by Eugene O'Neill, Sidney Howard, Maxwell

Anderson, Robert Sherwood, S. N. Behrman, Philip Barry, Bernard Shaw, and many of Europe's most celebrated playwrights. The Provincetown Players produced plays by, among others, Susan Glaspell, Paul Green, and Eugene O'Neill, including his early success *The Emperor Jones*. O'Neill moved to Broadway under commercial auspices with his plays *Beyond the Horizon* in 1920, *Anna Christie* in 1921, and *The Hairy Ape* in 1922. Later in the decade, The Theatre Guild would present his *Marco Millions, Strange Interlude,* and *Dynamo,* in addition to many productions of plays by Shaw including *Heartbreak House, Saint Joan,* and *Pygmalion*. In the twenties, The Guild also presented such European works as Molnár's *Liliom* and *The Guardsman,* Andreyev's *He Who Gets Slapped,* Capek's *R.U.R.,* and Ibsen's *Peer Gynt*. In addition to Eugene O'Neill, several American playwrights were given sensitive and skilled productions by The Guild. Sidney Howard's *The Silver Cord, They Knew What They Wanted,* and *Ned McCobb's Daughter;* Elmer Rice's *The Adding Machine,* and S. N. Behrman's early plays *The Second Man* and *Meteor* were all offered during the decade.

The twenties also produced outstanding comic writers. George S. Kaufman, either alone or in collaboration, wrote seventeen comedies during this period, among them the delightful *Dulcy, The Royal Family,* and the books for two Marx Brothers musicals, *The Cocoanuts* and *Animal Crackers*. George Kelly tellingly satirized American society in *The Torchbearers* and *The Show-Off*. Ben Hecht and Charles MacArthur created their riotous *The Front Page* and Philip Barry's sophisticated and lucid drawing-room comedies *Holiday* and *Paris Bound* added lustre to the Broadway scene. Robert Sherwood, Claire Kummer, Rachel Crothers, and Arthur Richman also produced graceful and witty plays during the twenties.

In 1926, one of the leading young actresses, Eva Le Gallienne, left Broadway and formed her Civic Repertory Theatre on Fourteenth Street. Outstanding productions of Chekhov, Ibsen, and Shakespeare were presented at popular prices, helping not only to advance the taste of the theater-going public but also to make available good theater to eager audiences who could not afford the Broadway scale of prices. On Broadway, its finest actor, John Barrymore, appeared as Hamlet and Richard III; later his per-

formance as Hamlet in London would convince the British public
that America could produce great classical acting. During the
decade, Lionel Barrymore was seen as Macbeth, Walter Hampden as Cyrano de Bergerac and David Warfield as Shylock. Julia
Marlowe and E. H. Sothern also appeared in their own production of *The Merchant of Venice*. Both Ethel Barrymore and Jane
Cowl were seen as Juliet in this period, and Miss Cowl was also
acclaimed for her Cleopatra. In 1923, Stanislavsky and the Moscow Art Theatre appeared in repertory, and in the same year the
legendary Eleanora Duse was seen in some of her greatest roles;
both companies had a profound influence not only upon the
audience but also upon the members of the theatrical profession.

By 1920, Maude Adams had already retired from the New
York stage, but other great stars from an earlier era such as Mrs.
Fiske, George M. Cohan, Otis Skinner, and Laurette Taylor
appeared throughout the decade. Such celebrated actors as Lynn
Fontanne, Alfred Lunt, Helen Hayes, Judith Anderson, Jeanne
Eagels, and Ruth Gordon all attained stardom in the twenties.
In 1925, Noel Coward made his first appearance on the New
York stage in his own play *The Vortex*. The careers of the three
Barrymores, Jane Cowl, Margaret Anglin, Walter Huston, Ina
Claire, and Pauline Lord flourished as the decade offered them
unlimited opportunities to perfect their art.

The musical theater in New York also thrived. Along with
operettas of Sigmund Romberg and Rudolf Friml, musical
comedies and revues by a host of new composers and lyricists
flooded the stage with invention, gaiety, and melody. Their
popular songs were known and sung all over the world, for
international celebrity was granted to New York's musical theater even before the decade's playwrights were acclaimed by
foreign critics and audiences. With spectacular décor and ravishing show-girls, the lavish revues of the era — the *Follies* of
Florenz Ziegfeld, the *Scandals* of George White, and the *Vanities*
of Earl Carroll — gave pleasure to thousands and employment
to such inimitable talents as Fannie Brice, Will Rogers, W. C.
Fields, Eddie Cantor, and Willie and Eugene Howard. The
ebullient Al Jolson was the most important star on the musical
stage during the period, and Marilyn Miller reigned as the undis-
puted queen of musical comedy in such productions as *Sunny,*

Sally, and *Rosalie.* Ruby Keeler achieved stardom in Gershwin's *Show Girl* late in the twenties, and Evelyn Laye, a glamorous prima-donna, captivated American audiences in Noel Coward's operetta *Bitter Sweet.* The comic abilities of Bert Lahr, Fred Stone, Leon Erroll, Charles Winninger, Bobby Clark, Ed Wynn, Edna May Oliver, and the four Marx Brothers were widely acclaimed. The French singer, Irene Bordoni, brought sophistication and wit to the musical stage, particularly when singing Cole Porter's equally sophisticated and witty songs. The brilliance and charm of Fred and Adele Astaire's dancing made them eminent favorites during the decade in such successes as *Funny Face* and *Lady, Be Good.* In 1924, two young and bewitching visitors from England, Beatrice Lillie and Gertrude Lawrence, began their dazzling American careers. Dennis King, equally at home on the dramatic and the musical stage, sang the romantic leads in three major musical offerings of the decade: *Rose Marie, The Vagabond King,* and *The Three Musketeers,* and became the matinée idol of the age. In 1927, Jerome Kern and Oscar Hammerstein's *Show Boat* arrived, and the musical theater took a giant step forward.

Although the motion-pictures offered strong competition, the theater was still a major provider of entertainment in New York during the decade of 1920-1929. During this time, the number of productions presented on Broadway ranged from a low of 145 in 1920 to a high of 264 in 1928. When these seasons are compared with the Broadway season of 1970, during which a grand total of 34 productions were presented on Broadway, one realizes how shocking has been the decline of commercial theatrical activity. Of the approximately two thousand productions reviewed in *The New York Times* during the twenties, exactly one hundred have been chosen for inclusion in this volume, a number that can merely hint at the excitement and diversity of the decade's theater.

1920 - 1929

Eugene O'Neill's Tragedy

BEYOND THE HORIZON, a tragedy in three
acts and six scenes, by Eugene O'Neil.
At the Morosco Theatre.

Robert Mayo	Richard Bennett
Andrew Mayo	Edward Arnold
Ruth Atkins	Helen MacKellar
Captain Dick Scott	Max Mitzel
Mrs. Kate Mayo	Mary Jeffery
James Mayo	Erville Alderson
Mrs. Atkins	Louise Closser Hale
Mary	Elfin Finn
Ben	George Hadden
Mr. Fawcett	George Riddell

The fare available for the New York
theatregoer is immeasurably richer and
more substantial because of a new play
which was unfolded yesterday afternoon
in the Morosco Theatre—an absorbing,
significant, and memorable tragedy, so
full of meat that it makes most of the
remaining fare seem like the merest
meringue. It is called "Beyond the
Horizon," and is the work of Eugene
O'Neill, son of that same James O'Neill
who toured the country for so many
years in the heroics of "The Count of
Monte Cristo."

The son's advent as a dramatist has
been marked by several preliminaries in
the form of one-act plays, done by the
Washington Square Players and by the
Provincetown folk at their little theatre
in Macdougal Street, but "Beyond the
Horizon" is the first of his long plays
to reach the stage, and even this one
comes not for a continuous engagement,
but for a series of special matinees. It
is presented at the Morosco by John D.
Williams with a cast chosen from his
own "For the Defense" company, eked
out by borrowings from the "Storm"
cast at Mr. Broadhurst's theatre. This
amalgam, while rather conspicuously
imperfect in one rôle, is for the most
part admirably suited to the work in
hand, player after player rising gratefully and spontaneously to the opportunities afforded by a playwright of real
power and imagination.

The only reason for not calling "Beyond the Horizon" a great play is the
natural gingerliness with which a reviewer uses that word—particularly in
the flush of the first hour after the fall
of the final curtain. Certainly, despite a
certain clumsiness and confusion involved in its too luxurious multiplicity of
scenes, the play has greatness in it and
marks O'Neill as one of our foremost
playwrights, as one of the most spacious
men to be both gifted and tempted to
write for the theatre in America. It is
a play of larger aspect and greater force
than was "John Ferguson," a play as
vital and as undiluted a product of our
own soil as any that has come this way
since the unforgotten premiére of "The

Great Divide." In its strength, its
fidelity, its color, its irony, and its piti-
lessness, it recalls nothing quite so much
as one of the Wessex tales of Thomas
Hardy. As to whether it will be, or
could be, popular—well, that lies not
within the province of this reviewer (nor
the wisdom of anybody) to say.

"Beyond the Horizon" rehearses the
tragedy of a man whose body and mind
need the open road and the far spaces,
but who, by force of wanton circumstance and the bondage of a romance
that soon burns itself out, is imprisoned
within the hill-walled boundaries of a
few unyielding acres, chained to a task
for which he is not fitted, withheld
from a task for which he was born. He
fails, and his failure distils a poison for
all about him. He sinks, amid wretched
and disheartening poverty, into con-
sumption, and the life in him wanes before your eyes, through scene after
scene written with splendid art and a
cunning knowledge of that plague, with
its alternating psychology of hope and
depression. At the end, he crawls out
of the farmhouse to die in the open road,
his last glance straining at the horizon
beyond which he had never ventured,
his last words pronouncing a message of
warning from one who had not lived in
harmony with what he was.

The accompanying and minor tragedy
is that of the brother, a sturdy, generous, earth-bound fellow, born to till those
very acres, and sure to go wrong if he
ever left the clean earth and the work
amid things of his own creation. So in
the Hardyesque irony of the O'Neill
mood, it is this brother whom Fate and
his own character drive out into the
lonely open. The measured tread of
Fate can be heard among the overtones
of this remarkable tragedy.

O'Neill is not only inexorable in the
working out of his play to its sadden-
ing conclusion, but a bit intractable in
the matter of its structure, a bit unyielding both to the habits of the average audience and the physical limitations of the average playhouse. The
breaking of his final act into two scenes,
mark of a chronic looseness of construction, is distinctly dissipative in its effect
and his scenario calls for two pretentious exteriors which the very palpable
draperies (painted in the curiously inappropriate style of a German post card)
do not provide very persuasively.

If the play itself has a certain awkwardness and if its mere mounting is
sometimes clumsy, the cast, at least, is
uncommonly fine. As the home-bound
wanderer, Richard Bennett plays with
fine eloquence, imagination, and finesse
—a performance people will remember as
they remember his John Shand in

"What Every Woman Knows." Save for an occasional Farnumesque posture, trailed from the "Storm," Edward Arnold plays the brother with tremendous force and conviction. Then Helen McKellar proves herself a first-rate actress as the woman, while Louise Closser Hale darts (like a trout for a fly) at the best part that has come her way since Prossy bridled in "Candida." Then Erville Anderson, as the old father —well, there are riches in this performance as there are in this play which make the reviewer "yearn for the open spaces" of the Sunday newspaper. Q. V.

Alexander Woollcott   1920 F 4.

Another Ervine Play.

JANE CLEGG, a play in three acts, by St. John Ervine. At the Garrick Theatre.

Henry Clegg....................Dudley Digges
Jane Clegg................Margaret Wycherly
Johnnie.......................Russell Hewitt
Jennie.............................Jean Bailey
Mrs. Clegg....................Helen Westley
Mr. Morrison..................Erskine Sanford
Mr. Munce....................Henry Travers

It is seldom that our stage—or, for that matter, any stage—produces a play as perfectly as "Jane Clegg" has been produced by the Theatre Guild, as the fourth and most satisfying of its contributions to the current season. This is the naturalistic domestic drama, written by the Irish playwright, St. John Ervine, whose "John Ferguson" set the Theatre Guild up in business. It was first staged in Manchester by Miss Horniman's company nearly seven years ago and it is not quite clear why its American production was deferred so long, for "Jane Clegg" is an expertly written and absorbingly interesting play.

It unfolds in three acts of steadily increasing momentum the story of a slow-thinking but strong and resolute woman who works out to her own satisfaction her theory that there is no sense in living with a man who isn't loyal. She is deaf to the churchly sentiments snapped at her by her errant husband's fretful but doting mother. The old dame piously announces that a woman should take a man for better or worse.

"It isn't right to ask a woman to take a man for worse," says Mrs. Clegg, "or a man to take a woman."

Her discovery of her husband's first infidelity catches her at a disadvantage, with two little children to shelter and no money at all. But the next time she has inherited and held fast to a little pot of money and the end of the play sees her holding wide the door for Mr. Clegg's permanent departure.

It is all very quietly unfolded, with a good deal of the studied calm of which your modern dramatist is so proud, and a good deal, too, of the persuasive lifelikeness which is a fairly recent achievement in the theatre—that same lifelikeness, for instance, which was so marked an element in the strength of "The Rise of Silas Lapham," but which vanished utterly when that Howells novel was wrenched and coarsened into a play.

The rôle of the husband in "Jane Clegg" affords Mr. Ervine a chance to create another sample of his kind of villiany, a new, kickable, whelpish kind, the villainy of the very weak. Like the coward in "John Ferguson" is the "absolute rotter" whom Jane has made the mistake of marrying, and the part is played by the same Dudley Digges, who now so revels in the pusillanimity and selfishness of Henry Clegg that you can hear the fascinated audience growing restless all around you—restless with nothing more nor less than the itch to shake him.

His is a completely satisfying performance, as is that of Margaret Wycherly as the wife, and Henry Travers as little Mr. Munce, the conscientious and rather plaintive bookie, to whom Mr. Clegg has incurred a debt of twenty-five pounds. Miss Wycherly's portrait of Jane Clegg is forcefully, reticently, spontaneously presented, with the most delicate of shadings and a deft suggestion throughout of all that is going on in the mind of the determined but inarticulate woman. As she moves through the play you can see her thinking it out, thinking it out.

It is a trifle invidious to single out those three from a company which acquits itself so well throughout, for the very children are well-managed and there is a capital performance as the old woman by Helen Westley—even Helen Westley, who after "Jane Clegg" may hold high the head at which, on previous occasions, we have felt constrained to hurl a few bricks.

Alexander Woollcott   1920 F 25.

Barrymore as Gloster.

THE TRAGEDY OF RICHARD, III., by Shakespeare. At, the Plymouth Theatre.

King Henry VI...................Arthur Row
Queen Margaret................Rosalind Ivan
Edward, Prince of Wales..Burford Hampden
Duke of York.............Marshall Vincent
Duchess of York..........Mrs. Thomas Wise
Edward.....................Reginald Denny
George....................E. J. Ballantine
Richard III..................John Barrymore
Edward.......................Mary Hughes
Richard....................Helen Chandler
Children of Clarence,
      Helen Chandler, Lois Bartlett
Earl of Warwick..........Walter Ringham
Duke of Buckingham...........Leslie Palmer
Duke of Norfolk.........Robert Whitehouse
Earl of Derby...........George De Winter
Lord Hastings.................Lewis Sealy
Cardinal Bourchier...Montague Rutherford
Earl of Westmoreland....Robert Whitehouse
Lord Clifford...........Stanley Warmington
Lord Rivers..............William J. Keighley
Lord Grey.....................Denis Auburn
Sir James Tyrrell..........John M. Troughton
Sir Richard Ratcliff....Montague Rutherford
Sir William Catesby....Stanley Warmington
Sir James Blount.........Malcolm Barrett
Sir William Brakenbury..William J. Keighley
The Lord Mayor of London..Isadore Marcil
First Murderer................Tracy Barrow
Second Murderer............Cecil Clovelly
Richmond................Raymond Bloomer
Queen Elizabeth........Evelyn Walsh Hall
Lady Anne...................Helen Robbins

On Saturday night at the Plymouth, before an alert, critical, honest, expectant audience, that stood at the end to cheer incontinently while the curtain rose and fell, John Barrymore appeared as Richard the Third. It was his first performance in a Shakespearean rôle and marked a measurable advance in the gradual process of bringing his technical fluency abreast with his winged imagination and his real genius for the theatre. Surely it was the highest point yet reached in that rapid, unexpected ascent which began four years ago with the production of Galsworthy's "Justice," and which has been unparalleled in the theatre of our time.

Fortified by backgrounds and trappings of great beauty, aided (if you care to use the word) by a company that is somewhat short of so-so, Mr. Barrymore held his first audience riveted until a few minutes before 1—an extraordinary feat in itself. There must needs be a deal of pruning, for, of course, the production will have to be lopped off here and there to make it fit the habit of our less leisurely audiences. The vexing questions of what to cut and what to spare will have to be determined, not by the intrinsic worth of the various materials, but by their effectiveness, when refracted through the wildly assorted media that chance to be assembled in Mr. Barrymore's support—if you care to use the word.

The text is one especially prepared and selected by an unnamed hand—a choice of sixteen abreviated scenes from the third part of "Henry the Sixth," and from "The Tragedy of Richard the Third." The adaptor followed the latter day fashion of nobly flouting the once favored concoction by Colley Cibber, yet accepted readily enough the Cibber theory that something rather radical was needed to build a suitable piece about the bent figure of Shakespeare's Gloster. Not that he utterly spurned old Cibber's handiwork, for one of Cibber's lines was evidently too great a temptation and was accordingly retrieved from the scrapheap of a version that served, in its time, for more than a century of limping Richards.

Beginning, as the Plymouth version does, with the stirring, groping boyhood of Richard, when the lad, embittered by his wanton deformity, stands hesitant at the crossroads where part the paths to good and evil—this grouping of the material permits that visible growth and change to a poisonous, dank, sin-rotted soul, spinning his plans from the throne of England, like some black and incredibly malignant spider. It is the progressive change which Mansfield so reveled in and which makes a living thing of Barrymore's Richard.

If Richard is worth playing at all, he is worth playing for all the greatness there is in him. After all, he has a titanic quality, a suggestion of a Lucifer defying creation, a Heaven-challenging giant standing outside and above the pygmy mortals with whose destinies he toys so lightly. He is more than inhuman: there must be a touch of the superhuman, and it is a Richard of such stature that Barrymore, in his new-found and still developing power, creates for us. Such a Richard can give a special accent and meaning to the diablerie and inner amusement of the midway scene, to the "Now is the Winter of our discontent," speech and to all its sardonic sequence, as far as the climax of that extraordinary wooing of the Lady Anne, even as far as the acceptance of the crown. When the dissolution comes, it takes the form of no ordinary man's repentence and misgivings, but rather is it the tottering of a mind that has overreached itself. Long before the tent scene, which is none too impressively managed at the Plymouth, before even the cursing of Richard by his mother, the king is streaked with madness—a mental disintegration that is revealed at first as by flashes of fitful and distant lightning.

All in all, a magnificent achievement. It ranks with Ada Rehan's Katherine and Forbes Robertson's Hamlet in this playgoer's Shakespearean experience. He would be tempted to call it great acting were it not for the obviously contradictory fact that John Barrymore is alive, very much alive and disgracefully young, and were it not also for the danger that twelve older and better playgoers would then rise and say in freezing tones: "Ho, ho, I guess you never saw So-and-So play Richard in Upper Tooting in 1869." But there, a fig for them. It is a great performance.

Of the investiture one may speak as heartily. Some of the scenes are of incomparable loveliness. All of them are rich and right—the work of an unerring artist of the theatre, Robert Edmund Jones. We are all always absurdly haunted by the fear that Mr. Jones is about to overstep himself, to import, for instance, a fantastic quality and an enervating prettiness into a Plantagenet play. But Mr. Jones's precision as an artist is as sure as his imagination is boundless. He is always right.

In the work of both Mr. Barrymore and Mr. Jones, it is difficult and quite unnecessary to say where they left off and where Arthur Hopkins began. Mr. Hopkins will probably have to shoulder alone the burden of responsibility for a rag-tag-and-bobtail company, of which half the players are intolerable and the other half are—well, tolerable. The most creditable work is done by E. J. Ballantine as Clarence, with further assistance that is passable by Mrs. Thomas Wise as the Duchess of York, Burford Hampden as the son of Henry, Mary Hughes as the princeling slaughtered in the Tower, Leslie Palmer as Buckingham, Stanley Warmington doubling as Clifford and Catesby, Evelyn Walsh Hall as Elizabeth, Cecil Closelly as the second murderer, and William J. Keighley as Brakenbury. The company is scarcely comparable with the one supporting Sothern and Marlowe. Perhaps we haven't enough players for two Shakespearean companies.

No account of the première of "Richard III." would be complete that did not speak of the electric atmosphere with which the house was charged—the sense of a great occasion. The combination of Arthur Hopkins, John Barrymore, and the Plymouth Theatre, with such precedents as "Redemption" and "The Jest" put into the mind of the playgoers, has recaptured for the New

York stage a certain festive glamour that has been missing since Augustin Daly died. The feeling found expression when, just before the curtain rose on the third act, the other members of the famous clan, their work around town cleaned up, entered the royal box. There was thunderous applause, a great craning of necks, nudging of ribs and beaming of faces. Not far from the stage sat the blessed Tom Wise, there, no doubt, to applaud Mrs. Wise and to remember, possibly a time when he and the star of the evening appeared together in a piece called " Uncle Sam ", an obscenely worthless enterprise in which, as we recall, Mr. Barrymore sat in an arbor and embroidered. That was something less than nine years ago, and it may have run through Mr. Wise's head that a good deal had befallen his erstwhile partner in that time. Speaking of growth and change.

Alexander Woollcott   1920 Mr 8

Hampden's Hamlet.

HAMLET, at the Lyric Theatre.
Claudius ....J. Harry Irvine
Hamlet ....Walter Hampden
Polonius ....Allen Thomas
Horatio ....William Sauter
Laertes ....Ernest Rowan
Rosencranz ....Raymond Sovey
Guildenstern................Jerome Colamor
Osric ....Le Roi Operti
Priest ....Richard Roselle
Marcellus ....John William Baker
Bernardo ....G. T. Hamilton
Francisco ....Laurence Langdon
Reynaldo ....Franklin Thorne
Player King ....G. F. Hannam-Clark
Player Queen........Elsie Herndon Kearns
First Page ....Cicely Barcham
Lucianus.....................Maxwell Ryder
Prologue ....Katherine Haden
First Grave Digger...........Allen Thomas
Second Grave Digger......Frank G. Spencer
Gertrude ....Mary Hall
Ophelia ....Beatrice Maude
Ghost of Hamlet's Father....Richard Abbott

Having dropped like a hot penny that mongrel and monstrous contraption " George Washington," Walter Hampden has resumed at the Lyric Theatre his performance of " Hamlet," a creditable achievement which commands the respect of his generation in the theatre. Both press and public have been responsive enough to it to give him at least a sense of satisfaction, but thus far those chronically myopic lords of the theatre who control the bookings have failed to prepare for it such a tour as it deserves. It has found its way into town now only by riding in on the back of a predestined failure. The production is chiefly satisfying in that it approaches " Hamlet " freshly and fearlessly, as though Mr. Hampden had found its musty script in some delving of his own and staged it as he would any other play, so that it is done without pomposity and with none of the paralysis of ritual. The appropriate and ingenious settings and most of the company are as before—with the addition, notably, of an excellent Polonius

contributed by Allen Thomas and a pollid Ophelia by Beatrice Maude.

Mr. Hampden's performance as the sweet prince has been lauded to the skies by some of his contemporaries. There has been, in some quarters, a disposition to hail him as the best Hamlet of our time. If, in this connection, the undefined phrase "our time" includes the period in which Forbes-Robertson's performance was visible in the American theatre, it would seem to this reviewer that some memories have been ungratefully short. If "our time" means merely yesterday and today, the praise can hardly be said to be extravagant. In that event, they are not saying much.

This Hamlet at the Lyric is unquestionably the best we have—but not quite the best we might have. To its performance is brought a royal presence, a rich and well-trained voice and a commanding intelligence. There is abundant force in it, even after the dissipating effect of a disposition to somewhat restless and semaphoric gesture. But among Mr. Hampden's considerable equipment as an actor, a sure sense of comedy seems to this playgoer to be lacking. The humor that makes Hamlet winning, the enriching and deepening humor, is absent. The impishness is there in full force, achieved by a sort of mechanical mockery. But Hamlet's roving, mutinous, lovable sense of fun, his enormous appreciation, are not there. This leaves the play still inexhaustibly interesting but it robs the tragedy of its pathos and poignancy, despoils it of its overtones. You could not possibly be bored by Walter Hampden's Hamlet but probably your heart would not be greatly wrung by it either.

Alexander Woollcott 1920 Mr 17.

ZIEGFELD FOLLIES OF 1920, a revue in two acts and twenty-five scenes. Dialogue, lyrics and music by Irving Berlin, Victor Herbert, Gene Buck, Dave Stamper, James Montgomery, Joseph McCarthy, Harry Tierney, George V. Hobart and W. C. Fields. At the New Amsterdam Theatre.
Principals: Eddie Cantor, Fanny Brice, Bernard Granville, John Steel, Mary Eaton, Charles Winninger, W. C. Fields, Van and Schenck, Carl Randall, Jack Donohue, Ray Dooley, De Lyle Alda, Moran and Mack, Jerome and Herbert, Lillian Broderick, Jane Carroll, Olive Cornell, Doris Eaton, Olive Vaughn, Florence Ware, Jessie Reed, Helen Shea.

The unfolding of Mr. Ziegfeld's annual contribution to the gayety of the Summer season took place last night at the New Amsterdam Theatre amid the scenes which have come to be associated with that momentous happening. " The Follies of 1920 " is a huge and fast-moving revue, somewhat less characteristically Ziegfeldian than some of its predecessors—several of the earlier entertainments have excelled it from the standpoint of beauty—but well stocked with talented performers and holding its own bravely until the final eleven-forty curtain. It is a good "Follies," with all the traditions which are associated therewith.

The niche filled by the annual Ziegfeld production has become one so permanent and definite that an account of the entertainment calls for a description of its contents rather than an appraisal thereof. As a producer of revenues of this kind Mr. Ziegfeld stands alone, and his ability to hit the popular mark has been so long a matter of record that it is no longer even to be marvelled at. Mr. Ziegfeld not only keeps pace with but anticipates, the trend of the times in revues. The new show follows the prevailing mode in inclining more and more to drapes and away from mere scenery, it departs a bit from the Ziegfeldian tradition in offering a minimum of fine vistas, and—though it be heresy —it seemed last night to make a bit less of the Ziegfeld girls than has been the custom of the past.

It is in its principals that the new show is strongest. Of "book" there is comparatively none this year—James Montgomery had been expected to provide that feature, but the exigencies of "Follies" construction demanded that most of the cast aside at the last moment—but there are some good scenes for all that. The talented Ray Dooley, for example, is hilariously funny in a skit which depends entirely upon her own gifts as a comedienne. Fanny Brice, working harder and more often than she ever did before in her life, is quite at her most comical—which, it must be admitted, is hilarious enough. Charles Winninger, shamefully treated in the matter of material, extracts much from little, and Carl Randall, Jack Donahue, W. C. Fields, Van and Schenck, Mary Eaton (a "Follies" newcomer), and John Steel are among the others who contrive to make the revue what it is.

It begins with the chorus boys this year, but gets rapidly to a scene called "Creation" in which a girl posed in mid-air provides a striking figure. Later, in a Ben Ali Haggin picture, the unadorned feminine form came in for still further attention. Between these episodes there were paraded the succession of scenes which make up the "Follies"—many of them quite good to look at, and all filled with the things which are Ziegfeld.

It was Mr. Ziegfeld himself who led forth Eddie Cantor at a late hour, the comedian having been unprogrammed. The Cantor-Ziegfeld ovation was perhaps the greatest of the evening. Mr. Cantor sang a pair of characteristic songs characteristically. Miss Brice, among other things, offered variants of her vampire and ballet numbers, as well as a "Florodora" number, and figured amusingly in a reminiscent automobile skit headed by W. C. Fields.

A youth named Jack Donahue contributed some eccentric dancing which met deserved approval, and Carl Randall danced both eccentrically and otherwise with vast success. The Messrs. Van and Schenck, appearing in various disguises, offered the harmony which has brought them fame, and Ray Dooley, as aforesaid, swept all before her in a skit in which she impersonated a squalling infant. John Steel, whose voice was one of the hits of last year's show, again won the vocal honors, even though he did not sing so well as a year ago. And there is also Bernard Granville, whom some people care for and others do not.

A theatre scene, with audience facing audience, is perhaps the outstanding novelty of the production.

1920 Je 23

The Bat

You know the mystery stories that Mary Roberts Rinehart writes for relaxation when she is tired of Tish and Aggie and cannot, for the moment, think of any more hospital romances to stage against a background of diet kitchens and clinical thermometers. The scheme is to coop up a handful of miscellaneous people, as on a boat or in a quarantined house, and there to let loose theft and arson and murder, to the accompaniment of crashing lights, mysterious knockings and sliding panels. The general impression created is of a madhouse just before the end of the world, the while the finger of suspicion moves steadily along the list of characters, reading from left to right. She is happiest when a sharp-tongued, self-possessed woman with iron gray hair is present to dominate the scene, especially if a comic maid servant can also attend, to scream and fall downstairs at inappropriate intervals and appear at the climax in curl-papers and a flowered kimona, muttering "Drat the man!"

THE BAT, a melodrama in three acts, by Mary Robert Rinehart and Avery Hopwood. At the Morosco Theatre.

Lizzie	May Vokes
Miss Cornelia Van Corder	Effie Ellsler
Billy	Harry Morvil
Brooks	Stuart Sage
Miss Dale Ogden	Anne Morrison
Dr. Wells	Edward Ellis
Anderson	Harrison Hunter
Reginald Beresford	Kenneth Hunter
Richard Flemming	Richard Barrows
An Unknown Man	Robert Vaughan

Mrs. Rinehart has taken one of these stories—in book form it was called "The Toll of the Secret Room" or "The Circular Staircase" or some such thing —and turned it into a play, with the assistance of her old-time collaborator, Avery Hopwood. His touch is nowhere recognizable in the result and probably all he brought to the joint product was a consultant's special knowledge of the stage, its tricks and its manners. As an expert with a growing reputation he appears to have been called in merely to keep an eye on her the while she wildly wrote her play. No doubt he called his part of the work the watch on the Rinehart.

Their new piece is called "The Bat" and it arrived last night at the Morosco Theatre, where it was competently staged and mounted by that same firm, Wagenhals & Kemper, that gave us their "Seven Days" some years ago and their "Spanish Love" just the other evening.

"The Bat" is a wild mystery melodrama, considerably wilder than any seen in these parts for a long time, and it is quite thoroughly interesting. If it were only half as complicated and fantastically improbable its tinkerers would doubtless fret themselves sick in the effort to make it as plausible and genuinely exciting as some of its forerunners have been, but it is so far past that point that it becomes a sort of mad game to the "button, button, who's got the button" antics of which it is very easy to surrender one's idle attention.

Those great folks who, in their effort to escape the perplexities and strains of their burdensome days, turn to detective stories of only the most unreal and preposterous sort would have the time of their lives at "The Bat," which is no end of fun if you let yourself go.

The perfect Rinehart servant is present in the person of the changeless May Vokes, whose performance, strongly reminiscent of Miss Dooley's carrying-on as the baby in the "Follies," would protrude fom any ordinary play but is quite all right amid the didoes in progress at the Morosco.

The perfect Rinehart heroine should be 58 years old and have a tart tongue. Something of the tang and acridity of Lucile Watson is needed. Indeed, Miss Watson herself would be a boon to "The Bat"; but in her absence the part is passably managed by the seasoned Effie Ellsler.

Then, of course, Harrison Hunter, in the guise of a detective, and Edward Ellis, as a mannerly crook, keep the piece from being too startlingly unlike other melodramas of our time. There should be a word for a fine bit of violent work by Stuart Sage, who plays one of those Rinehart nephews, the kind that get patted on the back and married off in time for the final chapter.

All these, and for that matter the others, serve acceptably in a piece that amounts almost to a travesty on the mystery melodrama of its day and is immensely amusing if you don't pucker your brow and take it seriously, if you don't keep saying: "Come, come, that's a bit thick" or embarrass everybody by asking questions like: "After all, why was the missing necklace and the head of the decapitated doctor put in the old Fleming punch bowl?"

Alexander Woollcott   1920 Ag 24

'THE FIRST YEAR' IS JOYOUS.

Simple, human and joyous is "The First Year." A scant idea of how good it is may be gleaned from the fact that enthusiastic reports of its merit had preceded it to the Little Theatre last night, and that it nevertheless managed to be about ten times as good as any one had dared hope. It is the work of Frank Craven, who has long been noted as a wooer of the homely chuckle, and who, some six or seven seasons ago, wrote a human little comedy called "Too Many Cooks," which gave delight to a lot of people, and which also gave promise of better things to come.

THE FIRST YEAR, a comedy in three acts by Frank Craven. At the Little Theatre.
Grace Livingston..............Roberta Arnold
Mr. Livingston...............William Sampson
Mrs. Livingston..............Maude Granger
Dr. Anderson....................Tim Murphy
Dick Loring................Lyster Chambers
Thomas Tucker...............Frank Craven
Hattie........................Leila Bennett
Mr. Barstow..................Hale Norcross
Mrs. Barstow.............Mercelta Esmonde

"The First Year," like "Too Many Cooks," is made up of the little things. There are two score of places in the new play at the Little which will strike a responsive chord in the breast of almost any one. Mr. Craven's specialty is the observant touch, the humor of recognition—"promptings of memory" Booth Tarkington called them. They come out time and again in "The First Year," and they are so good that it seems a particular shame that Mr. Craven has felt it necessary to broaden his humor even the slightest. In ninety-nine plays out of a hundred the broadening touches would pass unnoticed; it is only in a play so nearly flawless as "The First Year" that they stand out.

But this is a cavilling point in a play which provides so rare an evening in the theatre as does "The First Year." It is all quite simple and easy and even undramatic—Mr. Craven, for example, has not even troubled to carry over any suspense from his first act to the second, and for years and years and years the aspiring playwright has been told that this is something he must do if he would have a success. Yet Mr. Craven has not done it—and here is the most enjoyable comedy of the year.

All that he does in the first act is to woo and win a girl, and all that he does in the second is to quarrel with her. The second act, incidentally, is almost continuously hilarious—out of the serving of a dinner by an inexperienced maid Mr. Craven extracts, and legitimately, enough laughs to last the ordinary play for three acts. The progress of the quarrel between the young couple is natural and unforced—as skillful a piece of writing as has been done in a long time. In the final act, to be sure, they come together again—not without just a bit of mechanics on Mr. Craven's part, to be sure—but one even forgives him the expedient of the little child.

Mr. Craven is the harassed youth of the proceedings—a plodding, unromantic chap who is carried from the seventh heaven of happiness to the depths of despair, and back again. He gives a performance of rare humor, not unmixed with pathos. The remainder of the cast has been wisely chosen, doubtless by Winchell Smith, who had a directing hand in the proceedings. William Sampson has his best rôle of many years as a father who is always two jumps behind the conversation, and Roberta Arnold, although it required an act to become accustomed to her, gave a skillful performance as the wife. Tim Murphy yields just a bit to the temptation to overplay the rôle of a village doctor; Lyster Chambers is an interesting near-villain, and Leila Bennett plays a negro maid just about as well as it could be done. Miss Bennett it was who played the drab mountain girl of the now forgotten "Thunder." Like Mr. Craven, she has redeemed her promise.

1920 O 21

The Emperor Jones

The New O'Neill Play.

THE Provincetown Players began their new season in Macdougal Street last week with the impetus of a new play by the as yet unbridled Eugene O'Neill, an extraordinarily striking and dramatic study of panic fear which is called "The Emperor Jones." It reinforces the impression that for strength and originality he has no rival among the American writers for the stage. Though this new play of his is so clumsily produced that its presentation consists largely of long, unventilated intermissions interspersed with fragmentary scenes, it weaves a most potent spell, thanks partly to the force and cunning of its author, thanks partly to the admirable playing of Charles S. Gilpin in a title rôle so predominant that the play is little more than a dramatic monologue. His is an uncommonly powerful and imaginative performance, in several respects unsurpassed this season in New York. Mr. Gilpin is a negro.

The Emperor Jones is a burly darky from the States who has broken jail there and escaped as a stowaway to what the program describes as "a West Indian island not yet self-determined by white marines." There, thanks a good deal to the American business philosophy he had picked up as a half-preoccupied porter listening wide-eyed in the smoking rooms of the Pullman cars back home, he is sufficiently bold, ingenious and unscrupulous to make himself ruler within two years. He has moved unharmed among his sullen subjects by virtue of a legend of his invention that only a silver bullet could harm him—this part of the play, at least, is *not* Mr. O'Neill's invention — but now, when he has squeezed from his domain just about all the wealth it will yield, he suspects it would be well for him to take flight. As the play begins, the measured

sound of a beating tom-tom in the hills gives warning that the natives are in conclave there, using all manner of incantations to work up their courage to the point of rebellion.

The hour of Emperor Jones has come, and nightfall finds him already at the edge of the distant forest, through whose trackless waste he knows a way to safety and freedom. He has food hidden there and, anyway, his revolver carries five bullets for his enemies and one of silver for himself in case he is ever really cornered.

It is a bold, self-reliant adventurer who strikes out into the jungle at sunset. It is a confused, broken, naked, half-crazed creature who, at dawn, stumbles blindly back to his starting place, only to find the natives calmly waiting there to shoot him down with bullets they have been piously molding according to his own prescription.

The forest has broken him. Full of strange sounds and shadows, it conjures up visions of his own and his ancestral past. These haunt him, and at each crisis of fear he fires wildly into the darkness and goes crashing on through the underbrush, losing his way, wasting all his defense, signaling his path, and waking a thousand sinister echoes to work still more upon his terrible fear.

It begins with the rattle of invisible dice in the darkness, and then, as in a little clearing, he suddenly sees the squatting darky he had slain back home in a gamblers' quarrel. He plunges on, but only to find himself once more strangely caught in the old chain gang, while the guard cracks that same whip whose stinging lash had goaded him to another murder. Then, as his fear quickens, the forest fills with old-fashioned people who stare at him and bid for him. They seem to be standing him on some sort of block. They examine his teeth, test his strength, flex his biceps. The scene yields only to the galley of a slave ship, and his own cries of terror take up the rhythmic lamentation of his people. Finally, it is a race memory of old Congo fears which drives him shrieking back through the forest to the very clearing whence he had started and where now his death so complacently awaits him.

From first to last, through all the agonizing circle of his flight, he is followed by the dull beat, beat, beat of the tom-tom, ever nearer, ever faster, till it seems to be playing an ominous accompaniment to his mounting panic. The heightening effect of this device is much as you might imagine.

The Provincetown Players have squanderously invested in cushions for their celebrated seats and a concrete dome to catch and dissolve their lights, so that even on their little stage they can now get such illusions of distance and the wide outdoors as few of their uptown rivals can achieve. But of immeasurably greater importance in their present enterprise, they have acquired an actor, one who has it in him to invoke the pity and the terror and the indescribable foreboding which are part of the secret of " The Emperor Jones."

Alexander Woollcott 1920 N 7

HEARTBREAK HOUSE, a comedy in three acts by George Bernard Shaw. At the Garrick Theatre.

Ellie Dunn.................Elizabeth Risdon
Nurse Guinness.................Helen Westley
Captain Shotover.................Albert Perry
Lady Utterword.................Lucille Watson
Hesione Hushabye.............Effie Shannon
Mazzini Dunn.................Erskine Sanford
Hector Hushabye.....................Fred Eric
Boss Mangan.....................Dudley Digges
Randall Utterword.............Ralph Roeder
The Burglar.................Henry Travers

The New Shaw Play.

With the first production on any stage of the new Shaw play called " Heartbreak House," the Theatre Guild recorded last evening its most ambitious effort and, all things considered, its most creditable achievement. At the Garrick this brilliant comedy is superbly mounted and, with one fairly insignificant exception, wisely and richly cast. An admirable play has been added to the season's rather scanty list and overnight that list has quite doubled in cerebral values.

" Heartbreak House," despite the doldrums of tedium into which its second act flounders toward the end, is quite the larkiest and most amusing one that Shaw has written in many a year, and in its graver moments the more familiar mood of Shavian exasperation gives way to accents akin to Cassandra's. Of course that second act seems the more wearing because of our habit and disposition to a lunch-counter tempo, even in the theatre, but inasmuch as the Theatre Guild is not permitted to tamper with the sacred text, it is too bad that its company should feel so oppressed by it.

A good many of last evening's blurred impressions can be traced to players so uneasily conscious of the play's unwonted length that they rattled nervously through their pieces. It will all go better when the conclusion is forced upon them that a mumbled scene may save time, but is the last device in the world to ward off boredom.

Heartbreak House is Shaw's Bunyanesque name for cultured, leisured England (or Europe, for that matter) before the war—as distinguished from that part of leisure England called Horseback Hall, wherein the stables are the real centre of the household, and wherein, if any visitor wants to play the piano, he must upset the whole room, there are so many things piled on it.

The play is his picture of the idly charming but viciously inert and detached people who dwell in Heartbreak House, using their hard-earned (by some one else) leisure to no purpose. They are loitering at the halfway station on the road to sophistication. They have been stripped of their illusions and pretense, but instead of using this freedom to some end they sit around naked and doing nothing, except, perhaps, catching moral colds.

The moral of the piece is spoken by Captain Shotover. It is always possible to find the clear, honest eyes of Bernard Shaw peering out from behind the thin disguise of one of his characters, and it is tempting in this comedy to identify him at times with this disconcerting and slightly mad old mariner whom the natives suspect of an ability to explode dynamite by looking at it. Captain Shotover is sick of a languid reliance on an overruling Providence. One of the casual ways of Providence with drunken skippers is to run them on the rocks. Not that anything happens, he hastily explains. Nothing but the smash of the drunken skipper's ship on the rocks, the splintering of her rotten timbers, the tearing of her rusty plates, the drowning of the crew like rats in a trap.

"And this ship that we are all in?" asks the heroic Hector. " This soul's prison we call England?"

" The Captain is in his bunk," retorts Captain Shotover, " drinking bottled ditch-water, and the crew is gambling in the forecastle. She will strike and sink and split. Do you think the laws of God will be suspended in favor of England because you were born in it?"

No wonder the agitated Hector asks what he should do about it.

" Learn your business as an English man," replies the Captain, tartly.

" And what may my business as an Englishman be, pray?"

" Navigation—Learn it and live, or leave it and be damned."

But just then the war visits Heartbreak House in the guise of an air raid that sounds from a distance like Beethoven. It enraptures some, alarms others, exhilarates everybody, kills a burglar and a business man who had hidden too near the Captain's store of dynamite, destroys the rectory and passes on, leaving Heartbreak House not greatly changed, and with no firmer foundations than it had had before.

First honors in the cast must go to Henry Travers as the very Shavian burglar who serves so admirably the indisposition of Heartbreak House toward community service; to Effie Shannon as Mrs. Hushabye; to Elizabeth Risdon as Ellie Dunn; to Dudley Digges (who also directed the production) as Boss Mangan, and to Erskine Sanford as the gentle Mazzini Dunn.

Albert Perry as Captain Shotover, one of the most delightful characters Shaw ever invented, and Fred Eric as Hector Hushabye seem to have the right quality and undertsanding, but last night they forfeited a good deal of what is in their scenes by missing their right rhythm wth almost painful regularity. Here was a defect you felt would pass. It seems probable, too, that Lucile Watson will be very useful around the premises as soon as she has been persuaded to speak distinctly enough for you to catch at least the drift of her remarks. After all, Shaw never yet wrote a scene that could be expounded in dumb-show. About Ralph Roeder in the rôle of Randall, however, it seems unlikely that anything can be done.

The air raid which jounces "Heartbreak House" out of its purely conversational vein is capitally managed at the Garrick and both the settings, by Lee Simonson, are rich and beautiful. Indeed, they are almost too handsome. Somehow, a lovely investiture of a Shaw play seems a little incongruous—like perfuming the board room in a bank. The austerity of his text seems to chafe against the Simonson opulence as Shaw himself might rebel disgustedly at any *étalage de luxe.*

Alexander Woollcott   1920 N 11

The New Ziegfeldism.

SALLY, a musical comedy in three acts. Book by Guy Bolton, lyrics by Clifford Grey, music by Jerome Kern and Victor Herbert. At the New Amsterdam Theatre.

" Pops "	Alfred P. James
Rosalind Rafferty	Mary Hay
Sascha	Jacques Rebiroff
Otis Hooper	Walter Catlett
Mrs. Ten Broek	Dolores
Sally	Marilynn Miller
" Connie "	Leon Errol
Colonel Travers	Phil Ryley
Blair Farquar	Irving Fisher
Jimmie Hooper	Stanley Ridges
" Babe "	Alta King
Fluff	Betty Williams
Tot	Barbara Dean
Kitty	Vivian Vernon
Pickles	Gladys Montgomery
Bobby	Mary McDonald
Richard Farquar	Frank Kingdon
Billy Porter	Wade Boothe
Harry Burton	Jack Barker
Ivan	Earl Barroy

By processes of their own, which are made up partly of secret service and partly of premonition, the connoisseurs of musical comedy seemed to know in advance that "Sally," the new Ziegfeld production, would be worth going a long way to see. At least five or six times as many of them as could be housed at the New Amsterdam made a valiant effort to get into that theatre last evening for the New York premiere, and only those who were left outside were in any way disappointed. It is an amusing and tuneful diversion, this " Sally." It unleashes Leon Errol in his most comical mood, and the spirited and beguiling Marilynn Miller is like a jewel in its lovely setting. But above all it bears witness to the fact that the annual production of the " Follies " does not exhaust the energy and talent of a producer who knows a little more than any of his competitors the secret of bringing beauty to his stage.

It can be imagined that with his own namesake launched on its tour of the richer cities Mr. Ziegfeld, on turning his attention to this provision of an occasion for Miss Miller, he sent for the tireless Guy Bolton and that fount of melody, Jerome Kern, and bade them put together a pretty little piece after the pattern and in the modest manner of " Irene." Then, from sheer force of habit, he began to enroll comedians and dancers as for some pretentious revue, told Professor Urban to spare no pains and so gather about him such a splendor of curtains and settings and costumes as few theatres in the world dare dream of. The result is the gay frolic which was romped last evening on the New Amsterdam's stage.

Also, to judge from the result, he must have told his song writers and comedians that a little vulgarity would not be amiss, for " Sally " is one of these pieces wherein, amid all the profusion of beauty and incongruous daintiness, you keep coming on an occasional jest that belongs in a lower grade of burlesque show.

Mr. Errol is at his best. It was, if memory serves, the hero of "The Egoist" of whom the neighbors said: "He has a leg." So has Leon Errol. It is the right one and all last evening it kept refusing to support him in the manner to which he had been accustomed. Naturally it hampers him in his earnest effort to dance a Russian ballet all by himself. The pitchings and tossings of this zany, the antics of him are beyond description, but they are of no common order. They have style and charm and whimsicality.

So has Marilynn Miller, whose sprightly dancing and tonic freshness have enchanted us all before this, but who seemed to feel that her elevation to stardom called for a greater show of effort. Whereupon, for this occasion, she appears to have gone searching about and returned with a voice. She is singing now as never before.

Then there is the stately Dolores and the captivating Mary Hay (who is a treat to the eye in her Russian costume) and one Walter Catlett, very fresh from his London triumphs. He is like a curious blend of Ed Wynn and Eddie Cantor. To say that he reminds you of each and creates a nostalgia for both would be an unfair thrust and yet the truth lies somewhere within it.

But strangely enough, it is of none of these, not of Urban nor Jerome Kern, not of Leon Errol, not even of Marilynn Miller that you think first as you rush for the subway at ten minutes to mid-

night. You think of Mr. Ziegfeld. He is that kind of producer. There are not many of them in the world.

Alexander Woollcott   1920 D 22

At the Belasco Theatre.

DEBURAU, a play in four acts and six scenes, from the French of Sacha Guitry, adapted by Granville Barker. At the Belasco Theatre.

Jean Gaspard Deburau........Lionel Atwill
Marie Duplessis ....Elsie Mackay
Monsieur Bertrand ......Bernard A. Reinold
Robillard ....Hubert Druce
Laurent ....Joseph Herbert
Laplace ....Rowland Buckstone
Justine ....Margot Kelly
Madame Rebard ...,......Pauline Merriam
Clara ....Marie Bryar
Honorine ....Isabel Leighton
Clement ....Edmund Gurney
The " Barker ".................Sidney Toler
The Money Taker...........Helen Reimer
The Unknown Lady.........Lylia Burnand
A Journalist ....St. Clair Bayfield
The Lady with the Lorgnette....Eden Gray
Madame Rabouin...........Rose Coughlan
The Young Man ....John Roche
Maid ....Sallie Bergman
Master Charles ....Georgia Ryan
Charles Deburau ....Morgan Farley
A Doctor ....John L. Shine
The Prompter ....Fred Bickel
Scene Shifter ....Robert Roland
Duchess ....Pauline Merriam
A Sweetheart ....Hope Sutherland
A Lover ....Marinos Byron
Titine ....Mildred Call
Alexandre ....Edward Maurelly
A Gentleman ....Edwin Noel
Another Gentleman.............Nick Morris

One who is as fond of Sacha Guitry's "Deburau" as he might be of a dear, familiar song went, last evening, half hopeful, half apprehensive, to see its first New York performance and found that to the occasion offered by this excellent and appealing play Mr. Belasco had risen fully. Now, in what little retrospect the first hour after the final curtain affords, it seems to him that this production is the most creditable Belasco achievement yet witnessed by the theatre which bears his name. The fragrance, the glamour and the wistfulness of a quaint and singularly beautiful Parisian play have been caught and held there for American audiences.

Jean-Gaspard Deburau was one of the most celebrated of those early nineteenth century pantomimists who wrought such a sublimation from the once-Italian Pierrot that that poor moon-faced, moon-struck clown became a symbol of all human aspirations and human frailty. Just as Sacha Guitry in his own way is following in the steps of his distinguished father, so Deburau was succeeded one day at the Theatre des Funambules by his son. This abdication and succession, indeed, all the curious arc which a player's life describes, is traced in this play at the

Belasco—a drama of an actor, by an actor, for an actor. Taking as his pliant and inviting material the story of this half-forgotten mummer who had his little hour up a Parisian side-street some four-score years ago, the younger Guitry has written a bitter-sweet comedy which is itself the comedian's credo and apology, a study of the illusions and the ironies, the hurts and the compensations, the truths and the pretenses which make up the pageant of the theatre.

It seemed almost certain that much of the beauty of this play would of necessity hold its own in any adversity of translation and performance, but there were two especial points of doubt which must have been in many minds as the first curtain rose last evening. What had the skillful but sometimes capricious Granville Barker done to Guitry's free verse in his capacity as adter? And what of Deburau himself, an inexhaustible rôle and one as all important in this play in his honor as Hamlet is in "Hamlet"? Here, if ever there was one, was a rôle that seemed to have been written for Richard Mansfield. What would Lionel Atwill do with it?

On the first question it is possible after the first hearing to make only a halting and indecisive answer. To make a quaint play quainter, to fasten all minds to the reminder that it is a retrospective, fondly archaeological romance of a make-believe world, to set for it something of the minuet's pace, Mr. Barker, apparently in memory o' "Prunella," has thrown the free Guitry text into occasionally ingenious rhymed verse, sometimes even into the mincing step of the rhymed couplet. This is a process which gives the play something and takes away more, a little more than it gives. It slackens its movement, chills something of its ardor, makes faintly fanciful its scenes of heartache and longing. Of all the talents which met last evening at the Belasco, Mr. Barker's was the least.

But of Mr. Atwill's part, there need be no hemming and hawing in the answer. He brings to the rôle of Jean-Gaspard Deburau a performance of distinguished beauty, one full to the brim of charm and eloquence and understanding, equipped for it with just such a fine, resonant, old-time voice as this old-time play hungers for and just such a mask as the Pierrot of Pierrots should have. He stands, an arresting and impressive figure at the centre of as competent and shrewdly chosen a company as Guitry himself could have asked.

This company is without notable deficiencies anywhere and to name those who help most is to run through a long list that leads off with a youngster named Morgan Farley, who acquits himself handsomely as the younger Deburau and with an old-timer named Rose Coghlan, who was received last evening like a dowager queen on a state occasion and who acknowledged the hullabaloo of greeting by playing with all the relish in the world. Then let us applaud the fine gusto of Sidney Toler as the barker of the Funambules and Edmund Gurney as the chief drunkard of the Fufus, now long since gone, one and all, to their reckoning. But mostly one wants to applaud Mr. Belasco for the fastidious and generous and affectionate production he has given to a play which must have had a very special appeal to him. For once in a way all that is best in him as a producer is peculiarly suitable to the piece in hand. What fun he must have had rebuilding the Funambules, summoning to its portals Georges Sand and the young Chopin and all the great folk of that day and showing them in its auditorium with the old oil lamps a-flicker and all the scene a hubbub of color and whispering and smothered laughter.

It is the old, old score against Mr. Belasco that in his time he has busied himself overmuch with the cheaper and more negligible stuff of the stage, but it would be comparatively easy to defend in argument the position that at least he has always risen to the level of what good plays have chanced his way. It would be easier than ever now that " Deburau " has come to town.

Alexander Woollcott　1920 D 24

1921

The Critic as Artist.

THE GREEN GODDESS, a play in four acts by William Archer. At the Booth Theatre.
The Raja of Rukh............George Arliss
Watkins....................Ivan F. Simpson
Major Antony Crespin......Herbert Waring
Lucilla ....Olive Wyndham
Dr. Basil Traherne..........Cyril Keightley
Lieutenant Denis Cardew...Herbert Ransome
The High Priest............David A. Leonard
The Temple Priest............Guilo Bachia
An Ayah....................Helen Nowell

William Archer, celebrated as the advance man for the Ibsen plays in the English-speaking theatre and generally known throughout his own country and ours as one given to much lecturing and pamphleteering on the subject of how plays should be written, decided years ago that he himself could never write one. Apparently, however, he reconsidered, and last evening a play of his received its New York première at the Booth Theatre. This was " The Green Goddess," which owes a good deal to a characteristic and velvet-footed performance by George Arliss, and still more to an uncommonly rich and fastidious production by that interesting though intermittent man of the theatre, Winthrop Ames.

As for the play itself, it was a sore disappointment to all those professional folk who gathered at the Booth last evening in the lively hope of saying to one another in the smoking room: " Ho! Ho! This fellow Archer who thinks he knows so much! Well, he may know the theory! Ho! Ho!" For in " The Green Goddess " the veteran critic has tossed off a pragmatically successful melodrama, a thriller that really thrills.

He has attempted nothing more—nor less—than a suave and mannerly hair-raiser, and while his play will not touch your heart nor quicken your mind, it is practically certain to have a most agitating effect upon your scalp.

His fable, an inevitably interesting one even when less adroitly handled, belongs in that long and honorable tradition of imperial tales which pose against an ominous background of brown or yellow (but in either event hostile) people, a handful of marooned and imperiled folk belonging to what, however it may annoy Mr. Chesterton, is most easily described as the Anglo-Saxon race. Such peril in such isolation has all the concentrating effect of a spotlight, and it is in such a light that the events of " The Green Goddess " are, whisperingly unfolded, along with considerable hanky-panky of shifting lights and tinkling cymbals.

The goddess in question is the six-armed deity of a dynasty (doubtless Dravidian) which has retreated like a lost cause to some inaccessible reaches of the Himalayas. Into the clutches of her current rajah there fall (from a misguided airplane) two British officers and the wife of one of them, and the succeeding scenes concern themselves with the effort of the rajah to retain the lady and the efforts of these prisoners to get word across the snows to India. How, finally, the word is sent and how British bombing planes come booming over the rajah's little domain just as the tortures are beginning—that is the substance of " The Green Goddess." Whether or not they arrive in the nick of time, it would be grossly improper and highly unnecessary to report.

Mr. Archer has built his play fairly well and written it smoothly and then had the immense good fortune to fall into the hands of Mr. Ames, who, for some reason or other, was minded to emerge from his quasi-retirement and devote himself to an exceptionally handsome and silken production of this play. It is all good looking and the scene in the rajah's palace which reveals the dim blue distance of the snowclad Himalayas is one of those stage pictures which are getting to be quite everyday occurrences in our theatre, but which would have evoked considerable excitement and no little essay writing a few seasons ago.

" The Green Goddess " provides Mr. Arliss with the kind of work in which he is most happy. With his countenance at once gentle and diabolic, with his cat-like tread and with his uneasy but sinister hands, he seems to have been roaming our stage all his days in wistful quest of a play about a rajah with richly encrusted garments, a sardonic humor and an evil heart. Now he has found it, and it has the look and sound of a vehicle likely to trundle him as far and as comfortably as did " Disraeli."

After Mr. Arliss (and, of course, Mr. Ames), the one who helps " The Green Goddess " most is Ivan Simpson. He is still in service, but he has risen from valeting Rollo of the one wild oat to being a rajah's little gentleman, and this giddy ascent has stirred him into giving a capital performance. Olive Wyndham, Cyril Keightley, Herbert Waring (who accompanied Mr. Arliss to this country years ago in the tour of Mrs. Patrick Campbell)—all these are useful members of the company at the Booth, but it is Mr. Simpson who matters most in making " The Green Goddess " what it unmistakably is—good entertainment.

Alexander Woollcott 1921 Ja 19.

The Return of Our Peg.

PEG O' MY HEART, a comedy in three acts by J. Hartley Manners. At the Cort Theatre.

" Jerry "	A. E. Matthews
Alaric	Percy Ames
Hawkes	George Riddel
Brent	Thos. A. Braldon
Jarvis	George Sydenham
" Michael "	Michael
Mrs. Chichester	Maud Milton
Ethel	Greta Kemble Cooper
Maid	Mildred Post
" Peg "	Laurette Taylor

The New York run of " Peg o' My Heart " which, absurdly enough, was interrupted in the late Spring of 1914, was resumed last evening with a good many changes in the cast, but none of these matters much so long as Laurette Taylor continues in the rôle of Margaret O'Connell. She does. Therefore the Cort Theatre is once more full of laughter and the playgoer has another chance to sit down before one of the finest characterizations in comedy which has graced the American stage in our time. Peg with her bundles and her dog Michael under her arm, Peg with her tousled red hair, her gusty laugh, her skating walk and her fugitive smile, her wonderful, wistful smile—our Peg is back in Forty-eighth Street, and that thoroughfare seems a more cheerful place on that account.

Other cities in the land which saw other Pegs when Mr Manners's comedy was in the heyday of its first success bore up splendidly under the substitution and even professed to prefer their own; but it is to be hoped and believed that the announcement of any other comédienne's intent to play the part in New York would be received with hisses, petitions, injunctions, bricks and other expressions of displeasure.

It is a trifle late in the day to declare that " Peg o' My Heart " is not by a long shot the finest comedy ever staged in this town, and there is certainly no news value in the observation that it contains one of the happiest and most delightful rôles for the exhibition of Miss Taylor's fine art. To one seeing the play again after seven years it seems as though that rôle had somehow mellowed and sweetened with the years, and as though a hundred and one new touches of warmth and laughter had been added to it. One fancies Miss Taylor forever and forever recreating it, but perhaps this is just an illusion wrought by her skillful suggestion of always seeming to be playing the part for the first time in her wide-eyed and gratified existence. Probably the uncon-

verted will be moved to ask coldly whether, after all these years, it is still in her to look like the harum-scarum heroine of this " comedy of youth." The answer is a vehement affirmative. Miss Taylor appears to be in what is commonly known as the pink.

Of the newcomers to the company—newcomers to its New York performance, that is—there should be special mention of Greta Kemble Cooper as the glacial Ethel, and A. E. Matthews, the suave English comedian, who, after playing Jerry for 1,037 times in London and on tour, has come to the Cort in that singularly thankless rôle of the affable Baronet who spends most of his time doubled up with laughter at the ways of that comical Peg. The exact number of days Mr. Matthews has served in his indeterminate sentence to the part is derived from the program, which is full of such figures, but which says nothing whatever about the figure of Michael, who has become sadly bloated since that night in 1912 when, slim and frisky, she made her first appearance on any stage.

Alexander Woollcott   1921 F 15

Mr. Jones in " Macbeth."

MACBETH, a play in three acts, by William Shakespeare; music by Robert Russell Bennett. At the Apollo Theatre.

Duncan	J. Sayre Crawley
Malcolm	E. J. Ballentine
Donalbain	Burford Hampden
Macbeth	Lionel Barrymore
Banquo	Sidney Herbert
Macduff	Raymond Bloomer
Lennox	Alfred Shirley
Ross	Lionel Hogarth
Menteith	Herbert Jaap
Angus	Bernard Savage
Caithness	Haviland Chappell
Fleance	Mary Hughes
Siward	John Washburn
Seyton	Guy Cunningham
Boy	Helen Chandler
Doctor	Henry Vincent
Messenger	Harry Winston
An Old Man	Albert Shrubb
Porter	Frank Sylvester
First Murderer	Stuart Black
Sergeant and Second Murderer	
	Lawrence Cecil
Lady Macbeth	Julia Arthur
Lady Macduff	Helen Robbins
Gentlewoman	Marguerita Sargent
First Witch	Eleanor Hutchison
Second Witch	Nina Lindsey
Third Witch	Doris Fellows

The most willing and most expectant audience of the current season assembled last evening at the Apollo Theatre for the première of " Macbeth," which, properly enough, they looked forward to as the natural successor of " Richard the Third," which had been given a year before with the same imprint and with much the same talents or the same inheritance.

Here was another Shakespearean tragedy produced by Arthur Hopkins, produced for its own sake and as a separate masterpiece, rather than any mere part and parcel of some stockroom répertoire. Here was another

Barrymore to play the leading rôle. And here was the extraordinary and still experimental Robert E. Jones to robe and light and color it and give it background. It bade fair to be a first night of great memories. That audience dispersed quietly a little before midnight suffering chiefly from shock.

Shocked they were to find that it was within human power to rob that swift tragedy of so much of its excitement and of every atom of its baleful nightmare quality. Shocked that Lionel Barrymore, while often good and occasionally very good, should never once have brushed greatness in all the length and breadth of the play. Shocked, above all, that Mr. Jones, for all the three or four high moments of great beauty that he achieves, should have indulged in such impish antics of decoration as to become the star of "Macbeth," a "Macbeth" that will be talked of till the cows come home—as an oddity.

It seems a little derogatory of the playwright's and the players' art to come away from any revival of "Macbeth" gibbering chiefly of the decor, yet it would be rank affectation to pretend that any other part of last evening's proceedings commanded such interest as the didos of Mr. Jones. All that he has done for this revival represents an earnest effort to break away from the conventional two-dimension settings. But, for the most part, he has done this in such fashion as to make you feel a little wistful for the battered backdrops of Robert Mantell.

Of his Inverness, which resembles a giant molar tooth pitched rakishly in space, and of his blasted heath, with the three weirdest sisters in the history of Shakespearean production, which suggests nothing so much in all this world as the lodge room of the Ku Klux Klan, Poughkeepsie Chapter, it is easy to make fun. Only one attitude is easier. That is to lie down before them and sigh in the manner of the twenty lovesick maidens at the feet of Bunthorne.

Consider, for instance, that blawsted heath in detail. The curtain rises on a black-curtained stage of infinite depth and height. Glaring down on the centre are three five foot masks of dull silver. The eyes of these masks focus on a ring around which stand three indeterminate figures in crimson crepe. These red and midnight hags wear masks of bronze through which their girlish voices drone something inaudible to the fifth-row ears. And the play is under way. Startling? Decorative? Memorable? Yes. But of the scene's own atmosphere of supernatural soliciting, of storm and portent and dread—not an atom.

And so it goes throughout, with pleasant interludes when only a silvery forestage is used and there are other peaks of beauty, as when the blood-robed king and his blood-robed queen stand in a pool of light with nothing but blackness all around them. But for the most part these satisfying moments are interrupted by the spectacle of Mr. Jones laboring on to the stage with all manner of cubistic props to stand askew and rivet the unaccustomed eye.

Perhaps on the seventh or eighth visit to this production one may become so habituated to its new idiom that one can give undivided and even stimulated attention to the tale they tell and the

way they tell it. Such a playgoer would meet a Macbeth curiously and perhaps deliberately suggestive of yokelry, a genial-looking fellow of somewhat monotonous speech, but fine and barbaric in build and so intelligent an actor even at his second or third best as to command respect. He would meet a Lady Macbeth, as played by Julia Arthur, who is fragile, tremulous, sweet voiced, feminine—not at all convincing in the great first act, but better far thereafter. He would find all the lesser parts left to a far stronger company than served as a broken reed for the Barrymore Richard to lean upon. He would note especially the Malcolm of E. J. Ballantyne and the onlooker in the sleepwalking scene as played by Marguerita Sargent.

Those collectors of old programs and theatre memories who like to know how this and that was done at each revival may jot down in their notes that this time the dull and dubious passage of the wounded sergeant is played; that the lewd jesting of the porter is given in full (probably for the first time in many a year); that Banquo in person comes back to haunt Macbeth at the feast, and that the beautiful scene of the murder of Macduff's wonderful son is actually played, and beautifully played, too.

But after all, the loveliest sight that the revival afforded was just the sight of Ethel Barrymore sitting in the royal box, and the moment of highest enthusiasm in the evening was the moment when she entered it.

Alexander Woollcott   1921 F 18

A Theatre Guild Success.

LILIOM. a play in a prologue and seven scenes, by Franz Molnar. Adapted by Benjamin F. Glazer.

Marie	Hortense Alden
Julie	Eva Le Gallienne
Mrs. Muskat	Helen Westley
" Liliom "	Joseph Schildkraut
Four Servant Girls	Frances Diamond Margaret Mosier Anne de Chantal Elizabeth Parker
Policemen	Howard Claney Lawrence B. Chrow
Captain	Erskine Sanford
Plainclothes Man	Gerald Stopp
Mother Hollunder	Lilian Kingsbury
" The Sparrow "	Dudley Digges
Wolf Berkowitz	Henry Travers
Young Hollunder	William Franklin
Linzman	Willard Bowman
First Mounted Policeman	Edgar Stehli
Second Mounted Policeman	George Frenger
The Doctor	Robert Babcock
The Carpenter	George Frenger
First Policeman of the Beyond	Erskine Sanford
Second Policeman of the Beyond	Gerald Stopp
The Richly Dressed Man	Edgar Stehli
The Poorly Dressed Man	Philip Wood
The Old Guard	Walton Butterfield
The Magistrate	Albert Perry
Louise	Evelyn Chard

The Theatre Guild has made the old Garrick the most important and the most eventful theatre in America, and

It added measurably to the renown of that reclaimed playhouse last evening with the fifth and final production of its adventurous season. This was its wise and beautiful presentation of a wise and beautiful play—an odd, fantastic comedy written by that same Molnar who gave us "The Devil" long ago, and in later years "The Phantom Rival." It is called "Liliom," and the year has brought us no play more interesting, none more truly worth going to see.

In its way, a quizzical and airy and light-hearted way, it says the brave and bracing thing which Gorky said in "Night Lodging"—that down in the very dregs of humanity the spark that is divine lives on, waiting to be kindled into flame. "Liliom" lets you look into the soul of a dirty bum, lets you follow it beyond the grave and back to earth again and leaves you uplifted. There are such scenes of human squalor in it as Gorky might have written, but now and again there are dancing lights that Barrie might envy, and at times a cathedral hush settles over the play for those out front who have a prayer in their hearts.

The hero of our story is a shiftless young ne'er-do-well and bully of Budapest. His Hungarian neighbors call him Liliom, or the Lily, much as one of Mr. Chevalier's costers would have called his English cousin a Daisy. He is the pet and pride of a rowdy merry-go-round, where he works intermittently as bouncer, and he takes the kronen of the stray servant girls who fall victims to his charms.

Liliom is caught in his first highway robbery and stabs himself with the stolen knife he had brought along for the heart of the paymaster whose satchel he was after. You think things look pretty black for him in Magistrate's Court on high, but they see through him up there. They know how he came to beat that girl he lived with down below, how he came to plan the paymaster's murder, how he came to kill himself. They know what scalding repentance is in his heart though he is too much of the cocky old Liliom to admit it or make any plea for himself. You should see the swaggering jauntiness of him as he starts to serve his fifteen years in the purifying fires of the penetential plains, for he carries with him the promise that after that sentence has been served, he can go back to earth with a chance to do one good deed there.

Fifteen years later you see him hovering hopefully at the door of the home his wife and their little girl have made for themseelves below—the little girl he had never seen. He has even pinched a star out of Heaven and brought it down for her delight. He is hungry to claim her, to talk with her, to take her in his arms. But he finds her happy in some legend of his goodness and his bravery, and he has become too decent a chap to spoil it all by speaking. So, though it wrings his heart, he goes slouching away in silence. His hour on earth has been spent, and he has not enjoyed it at all, and probably he can-

not think of any good deed he has done there. But you know better. And so, you suspect, does that Magistrate in the First Court beyond.

Lee Simonson has mounted the play with reticence and beauty and imagination and nuderstanding. There are beauty and understanding in the performance as directed by Frank Reicher, as played by all the company, more especially as played by Joseph Schildkraut, the young actor who gave some faint promise of what he could do in a hopeless misadventure called "Pagans," which a few people saw at the Princess earlier in the season. It is a graphic and spirited and finely dramatic performance which he brings to "Liliom." He was invited by the Guild to play the rôle. There is no American actor to whom such an invitation is not an honor, none of such quality or such position that he could not afford to accept it.

Alexander Woollcott 1921 Ap 21

Mr. Maugham Much Magnified.

THE CIRCLE, a comedy in three acts, by W. Somerset Maugham. At the Selwyn Theatre.

Arnold Champion-Cheney, M. P..	
	Robert Rendel
Footman	Charles L. Sealy
Mrs. Shenstone	Maxine MacDonald
Elizabeth	Estelle Winwood
Edward Luton	John Halliday
Clive Champion-Cheney	Ernest Lawford
Butler	Walter Soderling
Lord Porteous	John Drew
Lady Catherine Champion-Cheney.	
	Mrs. Leslie Carter

The Selwyn Theatre proudly played host last evening to a searching, malicious and richly entertaining comedy called "The Circle." It is the work of that facile Englishman, W. Somerset Maugham, and the only reason for not announcing it forthwith as the best thing he ever wrote is the fact that once upon a time he wrote a book called "Of Human Bondage." At any rate, it is his best play, more satisfying even than "Our Betters." It says much more and says it just as well.

The Selwyns have cast it in the grand manner, assembling quite a jubilee company for this, their first venture in staging a high comedy from overseas. In casting "The Circle," they seem to have proceeded on the principle that a producer should either get just the right player for each part, or, failing that, then at any rate some one ever so celebrated. In summoning Mr. Drew to the rôle of Lord Porteous, they have had the good fortune to find an actor who was both—not only famous but fit.

The circle of the play's title is that described by the whirligig of time—the circle made by history in its pernicious habit of repeating itself. Here Maugham tells once more the favorite Victorian story of the wife who wrote a distracted note of farewell, fastened it to her pincushion and decamped with her lover to the Riviera or some such charitable spot on a kindly continent. But, in his malicious, modern way, he tells it in the cruel perspective of thirty years. He reintroduces the recreant pair after they have grown chill and gray and wrinkled in each other's company. He brings them back to serve as a horrible example for a younger woman who is minded to write just such another note for her own pincushion.

Then, with an ironic gleam of satisfaction in his eye, he has wrought a final scene just to show that the horrible example is wasted on the younger generation as is so often the way with horrible examples — and with younger generations. As the last curtain falls the young sinners are on their way and the old sinner, incorrigible sentimentalists, both, are trying hard not to show their inner sympathy and satisfaction.

The senior runaways are played by Mr. Drew and Mrs. Leslie Carter—the latter returning to us after a long absence—for a good many seasons have slipped away since her last appearance here on one of her excursions into vaudeville. It was a thunderous welcome, a royal greeting which was her portion when she swept onto the stage last evening as the painted, dissolute Lady Kitty, come simpering and smirking back to England after an indecorous exile of thirty years.

It is a rôle rich enough in acrid comedy to tempt a Marie Tempest into confessing her years, but Mrs. Carter was never greatly admired in comedy, even by those who would hear no criticism of her in the bosom beating rôles Mr. Belasco used to assign her in the old days. She enters into the Maugham play with considerable gusto, but now and again she takes a scene that calls for a delicate rapier and belabors it with a sledgehammer. She ranges from pretty good to pretty bad.

Mr. Drew, as has been said, is capital as Lord Porteous and Ernest Lawford has a rôle after his own heart in the abandoned husband, who so greatly enjoys the absurd spectacle which the years have wrought out of the friend and the wife who betrayed him. The part is tinged with a fine malice and some of this the deft and shrewd Mr. Lawford forfeits by a too contiuous gentleness, but, with this one half-smothered kiss, only a hearty round of applause should be his portion.

However, "The Circle" as written and as played at the Selwyn, reaches its highest and most perfected moments in the scenes which are left to Estelle Winwood as the young wife and to John Halliday as the breezy fellow from the Malay States who wants to run away with her—and, incidentally, who does. These two could hardly be better and theirs is the power if not the glory.

Which about sums it up, except to say that Mr. Rendel is rather a handicap as the young husband, that Mr. Drew made a happy speech, that Lionel and Ethel Barrymore occupied one stage box and Irvin Cobb the other, and that the members of the audience were so intent on looking at one another that a lot of time was lost in persuading them to sit down and look at the play. When, finally, they were beguiled into doing this for a time, they seemed to like it. Indeed, "The Circle" will prove a genuine test of the burning question as to whether or not folks intend to go to the theatre this season. If they wont go to "The Circle" they wont go to anything.

Alexander Woollcott   1921 S 13

Ibanez and Mr. Skinner.

BLOOD AND SAND, a play in four acts, from the novel of the same name by Blasco Ibanez, adapted by Tom Cushing. At the Empire Theatre.

Garabato	John Rogers
A Room Attendant	Edward Norris
Dr. Ruiz	Louis Calvert
Alvarez	F. D. Dalton
Juan Gallardo	Otis Skinner
Don Jose	William Lorenz
Antonio	Guy Nichols
Encarnacion	Octavia Kenmore
Senora Josefina	Edna Vaughn
Rosario	Madeline Delmar
Juanillo	Fred Verdi
Pepe	Martin Broder
Doña Sol	Catherine Calvert
El Nacional	Romaine Callender
Marques De Miura	Chas. N. Greene
Condesa De Torrealta	Shirley Gale
Dona Sarasate	Cornelia Skinner
Monsenor	Claude Gouraud
Don Ernesto	James Church
Dona Luisa	Eleanor Seybolt
Dona Emilia	Genevieve Delaro
A Servant	Robert Brinton
Pedro	Victor Hammond
Senora Angustias	Clara T. Bracy
Mariana	Devah Morel
A Picador	William Gaylord
A Priest	Carlos N. Gray
El Fuentes	Nathan Edward
An Attendant	Kenneth Kipling

The Empire Theatre, with the legend, "Charles Frohman Presents," still eloquent upon its program, recognized the new season last evening by opening its doors. The play was "Blood and Sand," a four-act piece contrived by a new playwright from the fairly celebrated novel which Blasco Ibanez wrote about the rise and fall of a bull-fighter. The wild, tempestuous, hot-blooded young torrero is played by the veteran Otis Skinner.

Those of us who remained chill and unimpressed by "The Four Horsemen of the Apocalypse," even at the time when it was considered distinctly bad form to be bored by that war novel, never explored enough further in the works of the famous Spanish novelist to read "Blood and Sand," and so cannot report now as to the fidelity of this dramatization by Tom Cushing. One coming fresh to the play, however, finds it a somewhat diffused but tolerably interesting piece with a singularly touching and dramatic scene just before the fall of the final curtain. It is a play which depends a little on such Spanish flavor as an American producer can impart to it when he tries hard. And depends heavily on the actor summoned to the rôle of El Gallardo.

It is probable that Otis Skinner, in all his forty-odd years on the stage, was never called upon to face a more difficult task than the one which taxes all his considerable resources in this new play. The matador could hardly be more dismayed by the bulls charging at him in the arena at Madrid than the actor in his sixties who sees coming toward him such a wild, horned rôle as that of the lusty Juan in "Blood and Sand." This stormy "boy," this magnificent "beast," this "splendid animal," about whom the populace and the ladies of Madrid rave so ardently in the Ibanez imagination and the Cushing script—here is a rôle that must have given Mr. Skinner pause.

But he is a canny actor who knows his craft better than most and who can fabricate a youth he has not. His success in this parlous business is really extraordinary. You cannot help admiring the skill and the gulle of the actor even if you must admit that the illusion is never really wrought from the play's beginning to the play's end.

Madeline Delmar gives an eloquent and moving performance as the little Andalusian wife whom the great torrero leaves behind him when he becomes famous. Then Catherine Calvert is picturesque and telling as Dona Sol, the grand lady of Madrid, who picks the bull fighter up for a few weeks of amusement and then drops him in favor of a symbolist poet from Paris. When Juan has fought his last fight and they carry him, mutilated and dying, into the little chapel off the arena he thinks the woman kneeling beside his litter is the lovely Dona Sol, come back to him. It is only his wife, but she knows he is dying, and she holds her tongue in love and mercy.

This little moment at the end of the play seemed worth all the rest to some of us, but there were those present last evening who were profoundly affected when, in an earlier scene, the wounded torrero defiantly removed the bandage from his injured leg. It was a little too much for two members of the audience, who promptly swooned away and had to be carried out. One of them was a dramatic critic.

Alexander Woollcott   1921 S 21

The Return of "Peter Grimm."

THE RETURN OF PETER GRIMM, a play in three acts, by David Belasco. At the Belasco Theatre.

Peter Grimm.................David Warfield
Frederik.....................John Sainpolis
James Hartman...........George Wellington
Andrew MacPherson........Joseph Brennan
Rev. Henry Batholommey......William Boag
Colonel Tom Lawton........John F. Webber
Willem.....................Richard Dupont
Kathrien....................Miriam Doyle
Mrs. Batholommey............Marie Bates
Merta.....................Marie Reichardt
The Clown.................David Malcom

David Belasco began the new season at his own theatre last evening with a flawless revival of that beautiful and moving play which he wrote for David Warfield's use ten years ago and more. In memory, "The Return of Peter Grimm" has seemed an admirable work and the recent attempts of a score of scribblers to capitalize the world's renewed interest in spiritualism have only added to its lustre. Seen again last evening at the theatre where it was first presented to New York, its great tenderness seemed undiminished and its curious spell unbroken. It is difficult to recall any play by an American author or any

performance by an American actor since Jefferson which has been so rich in loving kindness.

It is easy enough to sit down before "The Return of Peter Grimm" and cluck over its many and manifest imperfections. One could wish, for instance, that the return of the stubborn old florist could be managed with less obvious hanky-panky of spotlights and waves of darkness and all such didos of the impassioned machanician. One could wish, too, that some of Peter's messages could have less of the Sunday-school leaflet flavor to them. Indeed, it may be easy to quarrel with the play and its production at a dozen points, but it is not so easy when you have just come from the theatre and the spell of the play is still strong upon you.

"The Return of Peter Grimm" is by all odds the best play that has fallen to Mr. Warfield's lot since he was drafted from the old Weber and Field's Music Hall nearly twenty years ago. His portrait of Mynheer Grimm, as extraordinary in detail as it is in effect, has been simplified and perfected till it is a thing of beauty and immeasurably richer than the slap-dash work which is done in most of our helter-skelter theatres.

Mr. Belasco may be described as the American producer who takes his time, and "The Return of Peter Grimm," as written by him, as played by Mr. Warfield, as cast and staged now in its welcome revival, expresses at a hundred and one points his inner belief that a play is like a meerschaum pipe—something to be fussed with and coaxed and puttered over with plenty and plenty of time.

It is pleasant to find Marie Bates back in her old rôle as the parson's wife who never would forgive that mean old Dutchman for leaving her nothing but a silly miniature. And to find other players back in their places when, after ten years, the curtain was rung up again on "The Return of Peter Grimm."

Of course it is another boy who gets the message now from the old Dutchman, another youngster who rides off at last on Peter's shoulder, shrilling happily the song about Mr. Rat having gone to town to buy his niece a wedding gown. Richard Dupont is the impressive name of the actor chosen to play Willem, and no doubt he is a fortunate choice, but it is at this point that we miss something of the singular charm which the first performances had back in 1911.

The memory of little Percy Helton's beautiful playing as Willem haunted the play last night. But that was ten years ago, and since then little Percy Helton has grown up and played love scenes and gone off to the wars. It would be treason to a fond memory to suggest for one moment that this new boy is as good. But he is good enough—good enough certainly to help mark "The Return of Peter Grimm" as something to be counted by all theatregoers as among the blessings of the new season.

Alexander Woollcott   1921 S 22

FRANZ SCHUBERT IN A PLAY.

Composer's Tuneful Melodies Also In 'Blossom Time' at Ambassador.

BLOSSOM TIME, a musical comedy in three acts; adapted by Dorothy Donnelly from the original of A. M. Willner and H. Reichert; music by Franz Shubert; additional numbers by Sigmund Romberg and H. Berte. At the Ambassador Theatre.

Mitzi	Olga Cook
Bellabruna	Zoe Barnett
Fritzi	Dorothy Whitmore
Kitzi	Frances Halliday
Mrs. Kranz	Ethel Branden
Greta	Emmie Niclas
Baron Franz Schober	Howard Marsh
Franz Schubert	Bertram Peacock
Kranz	William Danforth
Vogl	Roy Cropper
Kupelweiser	Paul Ker
Von Schwind	Eugene Martinet
Binder	Lucius Metz
Erkmann	Perry Askam
Count Sharntoff	Yvan Servais
Hansy	Irving Meis
Novotny	Robert Paton Gibbs
Ilose	Mildred Kay
Mrs. Coberg	Erba Robeson
Waiter	Howard A. Berman
Dancer	Burtress Deitch
Four Guests	Gotham City Four

After jazz, what? They tried a new answer on Broadway last evening, when "Blossom Time" was produced at the Ambassador with music by a genius who was born when George Washington was yet President of the United States, and who died at 31 of starvation in Vienna, soon after the Garcias and Malibran had sung the first grand operas in New York.

Franz Schubert himself was the new play's central figure, so sincerely and tenderly portrayed by Bertram Peacock that the actor's curtain call after the second act surpassed any in the piping days of "Pirates" and "Gondoliers," while William Danforth, with his old "Mikado" smile, was father of the three daughters of the house that gave name to the Viennese original of "Drei Mädel Haus."

There were those in the audience who knew the music; among them Reinald Werrenrath, who has sung Schubert's "Thine Is My Heart" and "My Springtime Art Thou," or Mischa Elman, who has played the "Musical Moment" and "Marche Militaire." The immortal melodies, of a beauty that often lies near to tears, were perhaps necessarily sophisticated a bit by successive adapters, even at certain points "syncopated," for Broadway.

Since Mozart's "Impresario," however, no classic music has been more kindly treated in translation to the modern stage, and the place of a classic original text was taken by an innocent story of unrequited love of the composer.

"I am only a musician," Mr. Peacock apologized on his entrance at 8:35, and twenty minutes later the house had twice encored Schubert's "Serenade," just as it later recognized and redemanded many lyrics more.

Few at first caught the "Unfinished Symphony's" most striking theme as that of a Viennese waltz song recurring throughout the new score. But Miss Donnelly's deft adaptation took care of that, when at Schubert's poor lodging in the last act, one of the characters asked, "Why did you never 'finish' the symphony," and the composer, glancing at a charming heroine, answered, "Because I lost my inspiration."

Miss Olga Cook was the pretty Mitzi, more or less unknown to history, and Howard Marsh as the Baron Franz Schober, with a neat presence and tenor voice, sang—alas! shouted, too—but at any rate sang with fervor the songs of passionate longing that illuminate "Blossom Time" like pictures in a Christmas book. The pair deserved their cordial reception, but so did many of the little company in old Vienna gaieties of the Prater promenade and the double wedding at the Crown jeweller's house.

In the ensembles, led with a vigor proportioned to the tropical weather of last night by Oscar Radin from the enlarged orchestra pit, there were heard Zoe Barnett as a prima donna of those days, Dorothy Whitmore and Frances Halliday as Mitzi's marrying sisters, Lucius Metz and Perry Askam as the two bridegrooms, Roy Cropper, Paul Ker and Eugene Martinet as comrades of Schubert and the Baron about town.

There also were Ethel Brandon as the mother of the three maidens, Emmie Niclas as a sympathizing servant, Robert Paton Gibbs as Novotny of the secret police, Yvan Servais as Schubert's first patron, who paid good "pre-war" money for a song, and little Burtress Deitch, who danced at other folks' weddings, just as Schubert played there.

A certain quiet tempo of the talk, as well as the songs, seemed to please the audience as a novelty. True, the Count Sharntoff demanded of his prima donna, "Who is Mr. Beethoven—your lover," and she replied "O no, dearie, not yet"; but dialogue and plot in no way fell under her remark earlier, "O la la, what a burlesque."

Half a dozen of Schubert's love songs like "flowers in their place" in proper love scenes, delighted old Broadway. And the one "great" composer born in Vienna, the "creator of German song," left a legacy of more than 400 such songs from 100 poets at his most untimely death. His "adapters" have done service to his memory for musicians today.

1921 S 30

The New O'Neill Play.

ANNA CHRISTIE, a play in four acts by Eugene G. O'Neill. At the Vanderbilt Theatre.

Johnny the Priest	James C. Mack
First Longshoreman	G. O. Taylor
Second Longshoreman	John Hanley
A Postman	William Augustin
Chris. Christopherson	George Marion
Marthy Owen	Eugenie Blair
Anna Christopherson	Pauline Lord
Mat Burke	Frank Shannon
Johnson	Ole Anderson
Three Sailors, Messrs. Reilly, Hansen and Kennedy.	

The Vanderbilt Theatre, best known to those threading the maze of Broadway as the house where the jaunty

"Irene" held forth for two long seasons, was given over last evening to entertainment of a startlingly different sort—a heavily freighted, seagoing play by the man who wrote "The Emperor Jones" and "Beyond the Horizon." This was the piece called "Anna Christie," fostered and produced by Arthur Hopkins in his continuing direction of the career of that most gifted and interesting actress Pauline Lord. She gives a telling performance in a rich and salty play that grips the attention with the rise of the first curtain and holds it fiercely to the end.

This is the play which in an earlier form was once called "Chris," and under that title was tentatively produced at Atlantic City a good two years ago. It might be misleading, however, to suggest that the play which came to town last evening was the result of nothing more than the ordinary retouching to which the new pieces tested on the Jersey shore are so often subjected before they are deemed safe for exhibition in New York. What we have at the Vanderbilt is the play Eugene O'Neill wrote after he had torn "Chris" to pieces and thrown most of them away.

More specifically what we have at the Vanderbilt is a play about a boastful, sentimental, rambunctious Irish stoker who tumbles headlong in love with the daughter of a Swedish bargee and then finds, from her own heroic confession, that she has come east from no pastoral girlhood but direct from a raided brothel in St. Paul. An old story, as you see, but it is the essence of O'Neill's new play and remains its chief source of interest, for all the literary scenic effects with which it is offset, for all the great bales of atmosphere and the salt of the seaspray with which it is set off.

Somewhere along the ambushed highway that leads from Atlantic City to New York, this play was known for a time as "The Old Davil," which is the big Swede's name for the sea he has always feared and cursed. It was to hide her from the sea and its sorrows that he had packed his motherless daughter off to Minnesota years before; it was the sea which, when she came in time to know it, swept her mind clean and put the spirit in her that made her stand up and tell the agonizing truth to that roaring Irishman of hers. But in this play the part enacted by the sea seems a little forced, a thing of painted canvas, a factor less present and less potent than O'Neill may be guessed to have meant it to be.

"Anna Christie" might be described as a work which towers above most of the plays in town, but which falls short of the stature and the perfection reached by Eugene O'Neill in some of his earlier work. The earlier work had established him as the nearest thing to a genius America has yet produced in the way of a playwright, and, though this "Anna Christie" of his has less directness and more dross and more moments of weak violence than any of its forerunners, it is, nevertheless, a play written with that abundant imagination, that fresh and venturesome mind and that sure instinct for the theatre which set this young author apart—apart from a lot of funny little holiday workers in cardboard and tinsel.

Mr. Hopkins has done well by "Anna Christie." The choice of the difficult Pauline Lord for the central rôle was an inspiration and those genuine and multitudinous cheers which followed the third act last night were for her. The choice of Frank Shannon for the love-smitten stoker was also happy—a shot in the dark, probably. George Marion as old Chris is life-like enough, in all conscience, but a bit too tedious and diffuse in performance. Let there now be a final cheer for Eugenie Blair as a sodden old waterfront courtesan who slouches through the first act and out of the play to its great impoverishment. And let nothing that has been set down here be misread as a suggestion that "Anna Christie" is a play that the adult playgoer can afford to miss. By way of reassuring the timorous, it might even be explained that somehow O'Neill has managed a jovial ending. That, however, is part of the dross aforesaid.

Alexander Woollcott   1921 N 3

E.H.SOTHERN ACTS SHYLOCK

Julia Marlowe Portia in Notable Revival of "The Merchant of Venice."

THE MERCHANT OF VENICE, play in five acts, by William Shakespeare. At the Century Theatre.

Duke of Venice	Frank Peters
Prince of Morocco	Albert Howson
Prince of Arragon	France Bendtsen
Antonio	Sydney Mather
Bassanio	Frederick Lewis
Salanio	S. Frank Howson
Salarino	Jerome Collamore
Gratiano	V. L. Granville
Lorenzo	Vernon Kelso
Shylock	E. H. Sothern
Tubal	James Hagen
Launcelot Gobbo	Rowland Buckstone
Old Gobbo	William Adams
Leonardo	Harold Webster
Balthazar	Carolyn Ferriday
Portia	Julia Marlowe
Nerissa	Alma Kruger
Jessica	Lenore Chippendale

For the fourth week of their Shakespeare season at the Century Theatre, E. H. Sothern and Julia Marlowe brought out "The Merchant of Venice" last night. With the rearrangement of many scenes and liberal cutting the famous double comedy of the pound of flesh and the three caskets was brought within a four-hour limit and moved swiftly along. Long waits between the changing scenes, the thing hardest to bear to many a Shakespearean revival, have been eliminated, while there is here a successful blending of the simplicity of the old theatre and the stage devices of the new. The production attains a dignity and a directness admirably suited to the spacious speech of "Good Queen Bess's glorious days."

The only new thing in the recurring productions of "The Merchant of

Venice " is each actor's conception of Shylock. There has been a tendency to show a softer side of this famous figure of the old stage. Mr. Sothern's Shylock is a cruel Shylock, untouched by any consideration save his revenge. He is powerful of will and unbroken even at the end. He leaves the scene of the trial with his shoulders back and a sneer for the mocking of Gratiano. On the other hand, there is little emphasis on the old man's love for his daughter.

With this grim old story is bound up the beautiful story of Portia and the three caskets. Shakespeare lavished on it some of his finest poetry. If " Hamlet " has become to the modern audience a string of familiar quotations, " The Merchant of Venice " has become a chain of fine speeches. This is where Miss Marlowe comes in. Her charming voice and faultless diction are the great things in listening to this Shakespearean revival.

Mr. Sothern and Miss Marlowe have taught the others to speak " trippingly on the tongue." It is worth the journey to the Century to hear what the English language really is when the lines of the greatest glory of our literature are well spoken. Frederick Lewis as Bassanio was especially good in the picture, as was Miss Kruger as Nerissa. The short bit of the Prince of Aragon who chose the silver casket was well done by Mr. Bendtsen. Lorenzo not only spoke well to Jessica but sang well to her too, although they were not allowed to tell each other about " On such a night as this," presumably because on such a night as last night it was quite late.

1921 N 22

1922

Andreyev in Thirty-fifth Street.

HE WHO GETS SLAPPED, a play in four acts by Leonid Andreyev. At the Garrick Theatre.

Tilly	Philip Leigh
Polly	Edgar Stehli
Briquet	Ernest Cossart
Mancini	Frank Reicher
Zinida	Helen Westley
Angelica	Martha Bryan Allen
Estelle	Helen Sheridan
Francois	Edwin R. Wolfe
He	Richard Bennett
Jackson	Henry Travers
Consuelo	Margalo Gilmore
Alfred Bezano	John Rutherford
Baron Regnard	Louis Calvert
A Gentleman	John Blair
Wardrobe Lady	Kathryn Wilson
Usher	Charles Cheltenham
Conductor	Edwin R. Wolfe
Pierre	Philip Loeb
A Sword Dancer	Renee Wilde
Ballet Master	Oliver Grymes
Thomas	Dante Voltaire
A Snake Charmer	Joan Clement
A Contortionist	Richard Coolidge
A Riding Master	Kenneth Lawton
A Juggler	Francis G. Sadtler

The Theatre Guild emerged, flushed and triumphant, last night from the most daring of all its encounters with plays—its gallant adventure in staging " He Who Gets Slapped," by Leonid Andreyev. They have taken this baffling, tantalizingly elliptical tragedy out of the Russian and brought it to life on their stage in Thirty-fifth Street, where you may find it now, alive in its every moment and abrim with color and beauty.

To the mind of the average, plainspoken American playgoer much of it lies just out of reach, like a line of verse half remembered, like a piece of half familiar music coming a little muffled through a wall. But it has things in it that belong to the theatre of all the world, and the Guild engaged imagination and a sense of beauty to work on its unfolding. To all those who greatly enjoyed " Liliom " it may be recommended—recommended with a feeling that they may not find it satisfying, but that they can scarcely afford to go without seeing it.

The scene of this play is the greenroom, or whatever they call it, of a French circus—a circus in such a city, say, as Lyons, or, better still, Marseilles. In the midway off the ring its tale is told—with its clowns and bareback riders and animal tamers as the puppets dancing to the tugs of a most brooding Fate.

Into this fantastic, bespangled world out of the other world which they know of only vaguely as " out there " comes, mysteriously, humbly, appealingly, a nameless gentleman who is known ever after to them and to you as He. Out there a false wife and a false friend have hurt him past all endurance and, a little mad, perhaps, he throws away a great name and seeks refuge in the circus, seeks and finds sanctuary behind the white face and grinning mask of the clown—the clown who gets slapped. How he finds there, too, the loveliness of little Consuelo, the equestrienne, and how, too, he finds, through her, that, after all, there is no real refuge on this earth—all this is set forth in the fitful and sometimes perverse antics of Andreyev's genius.

It is set forth for New York in what seems to an unequipped judge to be an inelastic but endurable translation. It has been most beautifully mounted by the Guild's gifted young scene designer from Harvard, Lee Simonson. His lively sense of the dramatic and the pictorial have been matched, for once, by a kindred spirit in the direction of the play, for Robert Milton has done an uncommonly good job in the articulation of this intractable play. He has had a wisely chosen cast to work with.

To list all those who help would be to give many names already familiar to those who ponder much over theatre programs—names such as those of Frank Reicher, Helen Westley, Louis Calvert and John Blair. There might be a special word for Edwin R. Wolfe and there must be one for one English actor who always plays a minor rôle in Thirty-fifth Street and always plays it flawlessly. That is Henry Travers. Which leaves the remaining space for some inadequate comment on the work of Richard Bennett and Margalo Gillmore.

Mr. Bennett plays the rôle of He—plays it with his customary artfulness and understanding and perhaps with a

little more than that, a little more summoned to meet a great opportunity. It
is an admirable and a strengthening
performance. But those of us who suspect that there is more mockery and
more of heartache in this fey fellow
than Mr. Bennett finds there would
rather suspend judgment until we could
see it played by some one else—by John
Barrymore, for instance, or, better still,
by Ben Ami. A year ago Arthur Hopkins announced that he was going to
present Ben Ami in this play. It might
have been written for him.

Of Miss Gillmore as Consuelo it is
difficult to speak with a decent moderation. It is one of those perfect performances of which incorrigible young
playwrights dream in their hall bed-
rooms, which is why they so often weep
at rehearsals. On other nights, in other
plays, we have all seen this young
actress fumble and falter and blurr a
scene entrusted to her. As Consuelo, no
one could ask that a tone, a look, a
gesture be altered. Or so it was last
evening. It was an unbroken enchantment and it had the sparkle of morning
sunlight on a fountain. It was a true
occasion for the ink-stained wretches
who can write verse.

Alexander Woollcott 1922 Ja 10

By the Authors of "Dulcy."

TO THE LADIES! A comedy in three acts
by George S. Kaufman and Marc Connelly. At the Liberty Theatre.

Elsie Beebe	Helen Hayes
Leonard Beebe	Otto Kruger
John Kincaid	George Howell
Mrs. Kincaid	Isabel Irving
Chester Mullin	Percy Helton
Tom Baker	Robert Fiske
A truckman	J. J. Hylan
Another truckman	Albert Cowles
The toastmaster	William Seymour
The politician	William F. Canfield
The photographer	Alfred Falk
The stenographer	Norma Mitchell
The barber	John Kennedy
The bootblack	Paolo Grosso

The two new playrights who gave us
"Dulcy" have advanced further along
their road in the new piece called "To
the Ladies," which is now to be seen at
the Liberty Theatre. It is a wise and
merry and artful comedy, lacking altogether the little note of superciliousness
which sounded every now and again
through the laughter of their earlier
piece.

Its first New York performance was
an occasion of genuine and quite uproarious jollification, and it is full to the
brim of things that will tickle mortals
of all sorts and conditions. George
Tyler has started it on its way with a
good company—a company which,
probably through nervousness rather im-
perilled the best qualities of the play
last evening, in the first two scenes at
least.

"To the Ladies" is really an anecdote
guilefully and humorously tweaked and
twirled into a man's size three-act play.
It leads up to a single scene which, for
caustic and quite devastating humor,
has not often been approached by American playwrights. That scene is a stage

version of that astounding institution,
the American banquet.

In it these incorrigible authors tilt
with infinite relish at many of our civilization's smugnesses and pomposities,
but what they are chiefly after is that
unbelievable human perversity, the after-
dinner speech, the thing which all men
year and itch to make and which no
man ever really wanted to hear.

Mr. Kaufman and Mr. Connelly have
outdone themselves in this scene, which
they have most craftily worked into the
very stuff and substance of their play,
and it has been skilfully produced.

That banquet is the one attended by
Leonard Beebe, the complacent young
blockhead whom the authors have invented as a becoming background for
their little heroine. Beebe is the handsome lad, who, having gone down to
Mobile to attend his aunt's funeral,
meets this heroine at a dance and woos
her. It is not until after their marriage that she finds out he is the kind
of young man who goes into the title-
guessing contests in the evening newspapers, and that therefore, if he is ever
to amount to anything, she will have to
manage it for him somehow. The play
follows her campaign in this matter,
and it is attended by many skirmishes
and many agonies, the kind of everyday
agonies that keep life agitating in your
own home. It is a piece written on the
observation that all men who have, as
a matter of fact, amounted to anything,
have been married men, and on the
theory that that can hardly have been a
coincidence.

All through the first two scenes the
adroit and winning Helen Hayes to
some extent and Otto Kruger to a fearful extent, took sledgehammers to the
little playfulnesses of the Messrs. Kauf-
mann and Connelly. In particular, Mr.
Kruger would not express mild surprise
by anything less than a running broad
jump or a slight embarrassment by
anything short of a spasm of St. Vitus's
dance. But thereafter the performance
abated considerably and it was greatly
aided by the work in little rôles of
Isabel Irving, William Seymour, William F. Canfield and Norma Mitchell.
Miss Irving plays with sly humor, but,
all in all, the most perfect performance
in the cast is given by George Howell,
as the bland employer.

Alexander Woollcott 1922 F 21

Eugene O'Neill at Full Tilt.

THE HAIRY APE, a play in eight scenes,
by Eugene G. O'Neill. At the Provincetown Theatre.

Robert Smith	Louis Wolheim
Paddy	Henry O'Neill
Long	Harold West
Mildred Douglas	Mary Blair
Her Aunt	Eleanor Hutchison
Second Engineer	Jack Gude
A Guard	Harry Gottlieb
A Secretary	Harold McGee

The little theatre of the Province-
townsmen in Macdougal Street was
packed to the doors with astonishment
last evening as scene after scene unfolded in the new play by Eugene O'Neill.
This was "The Hairy Ape," a bitter,

brutal, wildly fantastic play of nightmare hue and nightmare distortion. It is a monstrously uneven piece, now flamingly eloquent, now choked and thwarted and inarticulate. Like most of his writing for the theatre, it is the worse here and there for the lack of a fierce, unintimidated blue pencil. But it has a little greatness in it, and it seems rather absurd to fret overmuch about the undisciplined imagination of a young playwright towering so conspicuously above the milling, mumbling crowd of playwrights who have no imagination at all.

"The Hairy Ape" has been superbly produced. There is a rumor abroad that Arthur Hopkins, with a proprietary interest in the piece, has been lurking around its rehearsals and the program confesses that Robert Edmond Jones went down to Macdougal Street and took a hand with Cleon Throckmorton in designing the eight pictures which the play calls for. That preposterous little theatre has one of the most cramped stages New York has ever known, and yet on it the artists have created the illusion of vast spaces and endless perspectives. They drive one to the conclusion that when a stage seems pinched and little, it is the mind of the producer that is pinched and little. This time O'Neill, unbridled, set them a merry pace in the eccentric gait of his imaginings. They kept up with him.

O'Neill begins his fable by posing before you the greatest visible contrast in social and physical circumstance. He leads you up the gangplank of a luxurious liner bound for Europe. He plunges you first into the stokers' pit, thrusting you down among the men as they stumble in from the furnaces, hot, sweaty, choked with coal dust, brutish. Squirm as you may, he holds you while you listen to the rumble of their discontent, and while you listen, also, to speech more squalid than even an American audience heard before in an American theatre. It is true talk, all of it, and only those who have been so softly bred that they have never really heard the vulgate spoken in all its richness would venture to suggest that he has exaggerated it by so much as a syllable in order to agitate the refined. On the contrary.

Then, in a twinkling, he drags you (as the ghosts dragged Scrooge) up out of all this murk and thudding of engines and brawling of speech, to a cool, sweet, sunlit stretch of the hurricane deck, where, at lazy ease, lies the daughter of the President of the line's board of directors, a nonchalant dilletant who has found settlement work frightfully interesting and is simply crazy to go down among the stokers and see how the other half lives aboard ship.

Then follows the confrontation—the fool fop of a girl and the huge animal of a stoker who had taken a sort of dizzy romantic pride in himself and his work as something that was real in an unreal world, as something that actually counted, as something that was and had force. Her horrified recoil from him as from some loathsome, hairy ape is the first notice served on him by the world that he doesn't belong. The remaining five scenes are the successive blows by which this is driven in on him, each scene, as written, as acted and as intensified by the artists, taking on more and more of the nightmare quality with which O'Neill seemed possessed to endow his fable.

The scene on Fifth Avenue when the hairy ape comes face to face with a little parade of wooden-faced churchgoers who walk like automata and prattle of giving a "Hundred Per Cent. American Bazaar" as a contribution to the solution of discontent among the lower classes: the scene on Blackwell's Island with the endless rows of cells and the argot of the prisoners floating out of darkness; the care with which each scene ends in a retributive and terrifying closing in upon the bewildered fellow—all these preparations induce you at last to accept as natural and inevitable and right that the hairy ape should, by the final curtain, be found dead inside the cage of the gorilla in the Bronx Zoo.

Except for the rôle of the girl, which is pretty badly played by Mary Blair, the cast captured for "The Hairy Ape" is an exceptionally good one. Louis Wolheim, though now and then rather painfully off the beat in his co-operation with the others, gives a capital impersonation of the stoker, and lesser parts are well managed by Harry O'Neill as an Irish fireman dreaming of the old days of sailing vessels, and Harold West as a cockney agitator who is fearfully annoyed because of the hairy ape's concentrating his anger against this one little plutocrat instead of maintaining an abstract animosity against plutocrats in general.

In Macdougal Street now and doubtless headed for Broadway, we have a turbulent and tremendous play, so full of blemishes that the merest fledgling among the critics could point out a dozen, yet so vital and interesting and teeming with life that those playgoers who let it escape them will be missing one of the real events of the year.

Alexander Woollcott 1922 Mr 10

THE TRUTH ABOUT BLAYDS. A play in three acts by A. A. Milne. At the Booth Theatre.

Oliver Blayds	O. P. Heggie
Isobel	Alexandra Carlisle
Marion Blayds-Conway	Vane Featherstone
William Blayds-Conway	Ferdinand Gottschalk
Oliver Blayds-Conway	Leslie Howard
Septima Blayds-Conway	Frieda Inescort
A. L. Royce	Gilbert Emery
Parsons	Mary Gayley

The audience that assembled with decorous expectancy at the Booth Theatre last evening found there an engrossing new play by Alan Alexander Milne. They found too that Winthrop Ames, a little elated at having triumphed in the warm bidding for it that followed its success in London, had fairly spread himself in the business of mounting and casting it. "The Truth About Blayds" is a wise, finely wrought English comedy that is as well played in America as any one could ask.

Indeed, it would repay Mr. Milne to slip on to a boat at Southampton one of these fine Spring days that are coming and pay his American friends a little visit. He would find those friends more numerous than he suspects and he ould see that on two of his best plays—this new one and " The Dover Road "—the American theatre is putting forth its best effort.

" The Truth About Blayds " has more of irony and less of ' Milne's buoyant vein of nonsense than any other of his plays that have passed this way. Its dominant figure—an overshadowing figure that is seen but briefly and that only in the first act—is the towering Oliver Blayds. Blayds, the great Victorian poet, the admired of Victoria, the chum of Meredith and Whistler—Blayds, the dean of them all, who lives long enough to find his name as sacrosanct as Hardy's—Blayds confesses in the courage of his last hours that all the poetry on which his fame rested was written by another man.

It had been poured out in the fecund youth of this true poet when the two were needy youngsters together in an Islington garret full seventy years before. How Blayds had inherited the mass of priceless manuscript, how once he had been tempted to publish a little of it as his own, and how, ever after, his years were conditioned by that first unconsidered theft—all that is brought out after his great funeral is over.

The rest of the play, the major part of the play, deals with this discovery and with the panicky casuistry of all the children and grandchildren who had become the great man's appendages while he lived grandly on and on. How, after much struggle, they decide never to tell the truth about Blayds, and how at last they even succeed in deluding themselves as to what really was the truth about Blayds—that is the substance of the new Milne play.

When Milne decided that his first act should usher Blayds out of the world and that the other two should watch the explosion of his confession in its effect on the Blayds household he boldly committed himself to a form which was bound to give his play a diminishing interest. It was inevitable that the first act should be the most telling of the three, and it must be admitted that after the grand old fraud has tottered off to his well-earned grave you miss him terribly about the play.

But there is no scene in all that remains which is not written with a keen humor and a sure dramatic instinct. " The Truth About Blayds " reinforces a dawning suspicion that this young Mr. Milne is the happiest acquisition the English theatre has made since it captured Shaw and Barrie.

O. P. Heggie is Blayds, a vital and dominant performance. Alexandra Carlisle is excellent in the rôle that commands the play which Blayds has made his magnificent withdrawal from the world. It is a long while since Ferdinand Gottschalk (who seems to have es-

caped from the cast of " Captain Applejack ") has been so thoroughly at home as he is in the rôle of William Blayds-Conway, one of the great man's most contented reflectors. And that whimsical young English comedian who overplayed so shockingly when he first ventured on our stage and who learned better so quickly, this Leslie Howard should be immediately placed under contract to play nothing but Milne plays as long as they both shall live. Howard and Milne look rather alike, by the way. To say nothing of the complete letter-writer, Gilbert Emery, who is also in the cast.

The one scene is the design of Norman-Bel Geddes. It is a singularly beautiful decoration, and if it were to be used for all other stage drawing rooms for the next ten seasons, no one would have any right to complain, except, possibly, Robert Edmond Jones.

Alexander Woollcott 1922 Mr 15

"ABIE'S IRISH ROSE" FUNNY.

Anne Nichols's Little Human Comedy Heartily Received at Fulton.

ABIE'S IRISH ROSE. A Comedy in Three Acts. By Anne Nichols. At the Fulton Theatre.

Mrs. Isaac Cohen..........Mathilde Cottrelly
Isaac Cohen..................Bernard Gorcey
Dr. Jacob Samuels............Howard Lang
Solomon Levy..............Alfred Weisman
Abraham Levy...........Robert B. Williams
Rosemary Murphy............Marie Carroll
Patrick Murphy....................John Cope
Father Whalen.................Harry Bradley
Flower Girl....................Dorothy Grau

" Abie's Irish Rose " vindicated her middle name, at least, by coming to the Fulton last night after a merry war and temporary truce between the play's author, Anne Nichols, and its first producer elsewhere, Oliver Morosco. Judge Julian Mack in the Federal Court yesterday, at the request of Mr. Morosco as plaintiff, adjourned hearing on an injunction application until June 1.

Miss Nichols, whose play is still running with two companies in San Francisco and Los Angeles—ten weeks in the latter city alone—organized the New York production on her own account, contending that Mr. Morosco's option had been too long delayed. She feared, in effect, that " Abie's Irish Rose " might be mistaken for a mere California poppy if it were much longer withheld from Broadway.

An " all-star " cast was billed in the piece under Miss Nichols's own direction. The veteran Mathilde Cottrelly was among the players last night, as were also Marie Carroll, John Cope, Alfred Weisman, Bernard Gorcey, Howard Lang, Harry Bradley, and, as Abie himself, Robert Williams.

Why the play must sooner or later have been meant for New York was fairly easy to see when the curtain rose on old Solomon Levy's big apartment in the Bronx. It was far more clear when the last curtain fell on a Christmas Eve

in the thrice-married Able's and Rosemary's tiny flat " one year later." Fell,
for instance, on Mme. Cottrelly as the
kindly Jewish neighbor, cooking, against
her will, a ham; on John Cope as the
Irish grandfather and Alfred Weisman
as the Jew who also " wanted grandchildren "—as Mr. Gorceley had said,
he " always talked wholesale "—and
finally on Harry Bradley and Howard
Lang as the priest and the rabbi, and
on " the family."

Able was a Romeo, heir to · riches in
New York, but with the ghetto in his
blood; Rose, a Juliet, with the blarney,
an heiress in California. This Able and
Rose had met " over there " in France
in the war; had been " married good
and tight by a nice little Methodist
minister," and, when cast off as "unwelcome strangers," just lived and loved,
" not wisely, but well." Perhaps this
Irish Rose is a hybrid, but handsome
Abie, too, was a bit of a Virginia
rambler.

A highly sophisticated Summer audience took the little comedy very heartily,
laughing uproariously at its juggling
with some fundamental things in human
life and at some others, not so fundamental, but deeply cherished, as lifelong
feelings are wont to be. The New York
scenes sagged on the lines in the play's
first act as did the Brooklyn Bridge
when the cables were being strung. The
Irish, in the person of big John Cope,
got the laughs going at the interrupted
wedding at old Levy's.

Miss Marie Carroll's Rosemary Mur-
phy-Levy, with a " Peg o' My Heart "
brogue, was girlish and charming as
she walked with her bridesmaids and
flower girl, a picture from her forgotten
days in " Oh Boy " or " Oh Lady,
Lady " down at the Princess. Robert
Williams, too, who told everybody
" You'l like her; she's a great girl,"
was himself a fine, likable lad as Abie
Levy, who " wasn't marrying a religion." It wasn't orange-blossom time,
so the knot was tied under " real California navy oranges." Small wonder
when Mr. Cope exclaimed, " Good God,
is she marryn· an A. P, A.? "

The play has its little sermon that
earned one of the heartiest · bits of applause last night. Priest and rabbi, it
appeared, also had met " over there."
" I gave the last rites to many Jewish
boys," said the fighting chaplain. " And
I to many of your Catholic lads," the
Jewish chaplain replied. " We're all
on the same road, I guess, even though
we do travel by different trains."

It takes two to make a quarrel, family or otherwise, fathers or sons. And
to make that quarrel up, it takes two—
but that would be telling. Rosebuds
and ramblers never grow singly. And
as the good priest said at last, " Sure,
Abie's a great boy." Personally, we
hope to be present at little Rebecca
Rachel and Patrick Joseph Levy's second birthday, if not their Hudson-Ful-
ton centennial.

1922 My 24

The Hippodrome Outdoes Itself.

BETTER TIMES, an extravaganza in three
acts and sixteen scenes, by R. H. Burnside. Music by Raymond Hubbell. At
the Hippodrome.
PRINCIPALS—Power's Dancing Elephants,
Patrick and Francisco, " Jacko," the Ginnett
family, Vasco, George Herman, Orlando and
his horses, Torbay, Long Tack Sam and his
troupe, Claudius and Scarlet, the Bell Brothers, Berlo Sisters, Marceline, Nanette Flack,
Frank Johnson, Fred McPherson, Lorna
Lincoln, Robert McClellan, Happy Lambert
and others.

For many weeks now passersby in
Forty-fourth and Forty-third Streets
have heard a hubbub of preparation
going on behind the closed doors of the
Hippodrome. Gay flutterings of many
colors have peeked through the open
windows Through them, too, have come
the sounds of hammers and saws at
work, of divers splashing, of horns and
elephants tuning up and snorting with
impatience. Then, with a pardonable
flourish, the doors were thrown wide on
Saturday night.

What was revealed there on the
largest· of our stages must have been a
source of some embarrassment to those
chroniclers of our theatre who have
lazily evaded the annual survey of the
Hippodrome program by simply and
amiably saying that each new one was
"bigger and better than ever." They
have squandered all their admiration
and have none left for this year, when
it happens to be true. The pageant of
1922 which, after profound cogitation,
has been called " Better Times," is, by
a considerable margin, the best-looking
and the most enjoyable of the entertainments which Charles Dillingham has
presented there in the many seasons of
his management.

This time he seems to have felt that
a little more taste and imagination
might not be wasted even in the Hippodrome, a little more freshness and ingenuity in the designing of the spectacles, a little more energy in combing
the side shows and tents of the world
for the best two-legged and four-legged
clowns and acrobats to entertain us.

Besides the familiar finale, when the
Hippodrome show always becomes suddenly amphibious; besides the annual
antics of .the elephants, one of which,
by the way, has been studying hard all
Summer and so learned a roguish
Spanish dance, with tambourine and all;
besides Jacko, that astounding and delightful crow which made its sensational
début there last year, there are many
new things to beguile the pilgrim.

There is, for instance, an eye-filling
pageant of fans which is rich with surprise and quite lovely in color and design. And there is an even more captivating ballet of snow-white figures that
emerge and vanish again, emerge and
vanish in the all-enveloping blackness
of the stage. And, lest the Hippodrome
should forget that it is after all a kind
of resident circus, there is a ballet
danced gaily and daintily by twenty
beautiful horses — Orlando's famous
troupe.

There should be a special word for one
·Torbay who has made an art out of that
old children's game—the little panto-

mine of shadows thrown by the night-light on the nursery wall. Most of us when commanded to perform this feat know how to make a swan arch its neck and dip for food. But Torbay can project all manner of romances and tragi-comedies on the wall, achieving little silhouettes which recall the Tenial illustrations for "Alice Through the Looking Glass" and some of the German nursery drawings of fifty years ago.

Then, too, there should be a word for an uncommonly spectacular troupe of Chinese gymnasts and another word for Claudius and Scarlet, who have made an agreeable life work out of playing old songs on the banjo and luring huge audiences into singing them. These were roared with great gusto on Saturday night and it was an amusing thing to hear such exponents of the latter-day ballads as Al Jolson and Irving Berlin and Elsie Janis warbling away with all their might at such old-time ditties as "The Little Brown Jug" and "My Daring Clementine."

Alexander Woollcott   1922 S 4

The New Richman Comedy.

THE AWFUL TRUTH, a comedy in three acts, by Arthur Richman. At Henry Miller's Theatre.

Daniel Leeson	Paul Harvey
Eustace Trent	George K. Barraud
Jayson	Lewis A. Sealy
Lucy Warriner	Ina Claire
Mrs. Leeson	Louise Mackintosh
Josephine Trent	Cora Witherspoon
Norman Satterly	Bruce McRae
Celeste	Kyra Alanowa
Rufus Kempster	Raymond Walburn

A bright, diverting little piece is this new work by Arthur Richman which was exhibited last evening at Henry Miller's Theatre. It is called "The Awful Truth," and it is about as ponderable and vital as those English comedies which the noblest Frohman of them all used to bring proudly over to the Empire Theatre each Autumn. But it has come to life under the deft and quickening touch of some director who has taste and wisdom and, in his own self, a strong sense of how high comedy should be played. Mr. Richman's piece is perfectly cast, graciously mounted and acted as delicately and suavely as he could possibly have asked. The program, with unaccustomed reticence, fails to say who the director was. Probably several hands coaxed and petted the little play into the gay and adroit thing we saw last night. Of those hands, the recognizable one is the fine Etruscan hand of Henry Miller.

On the strength of a charming and fragrant little comedy called "Not So Long Ago," Arthur Richman found a hearing for two other plays of his. One was a grave and somewhat acrid play called "Ambush," which the dourer of our critics made a great pother about, but which was indifferently presented by the Theatre Guild and indifferently supported by the public—quite properly, to our way of thinking. The other was "The Serpent's Tooth," a bit of dramatic shoddy given a momentary gleam of significance by the fine art of the incomparable Marie Tempest.

Now, behold him signing his name to a lighter-weight play—more artfully and more shrewdly written. Yet this, too, is cursed by his greatest weakness —implausibility. When Mr. Richman has invented his puppets and involved them in difficulties, he does not ask himself: "Would they really behave thus and so?" He just has them do whatever is convenient to him at the moment and washes his hands of them thereafter.

Thus shaky is the structure of "The Awful Truth," which is concerned with the efforts of a wayward and vexatious but frequently adorable woman to recapture the husband she had petulantly divorced some years before. It is scarcely Mr. Richman's fault that last night's audience could clearly foresee all that was to happen in his play ten minutes after it had started. This was because that excellent and reliable actor, Bruce McRae, was cast as the former husband, and it is one of the few immutable laws of the American theatre that the leading feminine rôle always marries Bruce McRae in the last act. Even this play in which she had already married him once was not allowed to be an exception.

That leading feminine rôle is played by Ina Claire—a captivating performance, spirited, discreet, sparkling, a bit of charming comedy, touched with the nicest banter and alight with a most delicate mockery. The scenes between her and Mr. McRae are a delight to watch. Excellent, too, is Paul Harvey as a large scow of a Westerner, a male Dulcy of the most oppressive and successful sort. Also George H. Barraud as a civilized fellow set up against him in contrast. But then there isn't a false note throughout. It makes one weep inwardly to think how many American plays, ranging from three to four times as good as this trifle by Arthur Richman, have fairly ached for the distinction his producer has imparted to "The Awful Truth."

Alexander Woollcott   1922 S 19

The Galsworthy Play.

LOYALTIES, a play in three acts, by John Galsworthy. At the Gaiety Theatre.

Charles Winsor	H. G. Stoker
Lady Adela	Cathryn Young
Ferdinand de Levis	James Dale
Treisure	Henry Carvill
General Canynge	Felix Aylmer
Margaret Orme	Jeannette Sherwin
Captain Ronald Dancy	Charles Quartermaine
Mabel	Diana Bourbon
Inspector Dede	Victor Tandy
Robert	Deering Wells
A Constable	Henry Morrell
Augustus Borring	Deering Wells
Lord St. Erth	Laurence Hanray
A Club Footman	Henry Morrell
Major Colford	Wilfrid Seagram
Edward Graviter	Henry Morrell
A Young Clerk	Deering Wells
Gilman	Victor Tandy
Jacob Twisden	Laurence Hanray
Ricardos	Henry Carvill

A festive and expectant audience awaited the new Galsworthy play last evening and found it good. This is the piece called "Loyalties," which was the single outstanding achievement of the last season in London, and which has been brought here with an excellent English company that is a faithful and uncannily accurate copy of the London original. It is an excellent play, far more artful and theatrically effective than most of Galsworthy's pieces—yet just as Galsworthian in its shrewd scrutiny of the human heart and in the hundred and one implications which reach far beyond the little limits of its story. It even takes on at times the aspect of a sly commentary on patriotism and the war. But enough of that.

What "Loyalties" is more obviously, however, is a latter-day retelling of "The Merchant of Venice"—a re-writing of that barbarous old play by a passionately impartial dramatist who is a very Bird Millman when it comes to balancing. Here once more is a haughty, embittered Jew, here the gabardine and the spit upon it, here the demand for a pound of the contemptuous gentile's flesh, here the trial. But, in the crisscross conflict of loyalties which Galsworthy recognizes is professional loyalty. And to so fair and square a play as he always feels obliged to write, he could admit no such shyster as Portia was. So this time the Jew gets his pound of flesh. But there comes thereafter a touch more Galsworthian than all the rest. The twentieth century Shylock gets his pound of flesh—and rather wishes he hadn't.

The Jew is young Ferdinand DeLevis, handsome, rich, spirited, race-conscious, venomous. At a fine old English house-party after the races, he misses from the wallet under his pillow a thousand pounds in notes. Sensitive and hot-tempered at all times, he feels that this is rather adding injury to insult. He has the notion that he is tolerated only for his money and that he doesn't propose to lose that. Indeed we are on DeLevis's side against all the rest. To an American audience, it is a little difficult to sympathize as much as Galsworthy would with the fastidious English gentry of the play, with their rising eye-brows, their lofty talk about the "esprit de corps that exists among gentlemen" and their shuddering distaste at DeLevis's vulgar desire to have his money back.

De Levis's private suspicions land squarely (and accurately) on Captain Ronald Dancy, a gallant and courageous officer whom their host and, indeed, all the other guests, have known since he was a kid. And later, when De Levis is stung to fury by being black-balled for a club in London, he spits out his accusation in public. Then follows one of those English defamation suits, with an upheaval of fresh evidence, Dancy's confession, De Levis's empty triumph, Dancy's suicide and all the sorry train of unhappiness and disgrace and regret.

The rôle of De Levis, created in London by an American actor named Ernest Milton, is played here by James Dale not quite so well, for all that it is almost a carbon copy, expression for expression, tone for tone, gesture for gesture. But it will serve, as will all

the other choices, some happier, some not so happy, which have filled out the cast at the Gaiety. There we have a smooth, creditable performance of a fine and engrossing play.

Alexander Woollcott 1922 S 28,

The Six Orphans.

SIX CHARACTERS IN SEARCH OF AN AUTHOR, a play in three acts from the Italian of Luigi Pirandello, translation by Edward Storer. At the Princess Theatre.

The Father	Moffat Johnston
The Mother	Margaret Wycherly
The Stepdaughter	Florence Eldridge
The Son	Dwight Frye
The Boy	Ashley Buck
The Little Girl	Constance Lusby
Mme. Pace	Ida Fitzhugh
The Manager	Ernest Cossart
The Leading Man	Fred House
The Leading Lady	Eleanor Woodruff
The Juvenile	Elliott Cabot
The Ingenue	Kathaleen Graham
The Character Woman	Maud Sinclair
The Third Actor	Jack Amory
The Fourth Actor	William T. Hays
The Third Actress	Leona Keefer
The Fourth Actress	Blanche Gervais
The Fifth Actress	Catherine Atkinson
The Stage Manager	Russell Morrison
The Property Man	John Saunders

Philosophical fooling and shrewd criticism on the art of the theatre mingle in the Italian play which Brock Pemberton is presenting in translation at the Princess. Imagine a playwright whose creative mind is haunted by six characters, the persons of a harrowing family drama, all urging insistently that they be given full and subtly shaded representation in the theatre. That is the normal condition of authentic creation; but as art consists in rigid elimination as well as in delicate emphasis, many of the aspirations of the six for self-expression have to be denied. Imagine next that the subject of their suffering is not sympathetic to the public, and that the only true and significant outcome is undramatic—not moving and inspiring, but static. That very often happens when a dramatist takes his real inspiration from life as it is actually lived, and in the supreme court of the manager's office he is nonsuited. There is no play.

But there are characters more live and vital than most of those that see the footlights. Imagine, finally, that these characters, still longing to live out their lives on the scene, go out in search of a more obliging author—and find a stage manager who has a company but no new play, only the stock stuff of a world somewhat deficient in new inspiration. Recognizing raw materials of interest and power, the enterprising business man undertakes to supply the place of author. It seems to him a positive windfall to be relieved of that insistent and obnoxious incident of production. He will allow the six characters to live out their own lives while a secretary takes down the dialogue and his company stands by preparing to assume the parts. Magnificent!

Those who look upon ordinary rehearsals as a madhouse will receive illumination. Instead of a single autho., long subdued in misery, the manager has his six orphans to contend with. The actors of his company, accustomed to have parts ruthlessly adapted to their personalities, are confronted each with a fury of unreason, demanding the absolute. For these characters, though the shadows of a dream, are "real" in the sense of being raw vitality unshaped to the necessities of art and the practical ends of the theatre. In the turmoil that ensues there is much satire on the foibles of player folk and managers and no little philosophy of dramatic art and dramatic criticism.

Margaret Wycherly is Mother in the roving dramatis personae and lends to the character genuine imagination and emotional power. Moffat Johnston is the garrulous father, eagerly philosophic and disquisitional. Florence Eldridge is the stepdaughter, overflowing with eager youth and charm. Throughout the production is able and highly competent. The audience last night, largely composed of folk of the theatre, rose to the novelty and humor of the idea and lingered long in applause after the brief three acts were over.

What the public will say to this rather slender and technical satire remains to be seen, but already it may be said that the season is indebted to Mr. Pemberton for one more exploration of strange fields and pastures new.

JOHN CORBIN.   **1922 O 31**

Jeanne Eagels.

RAIN, a play in three acts, by John Colton and Clemence Randolph; founded on W. Somerset Maugham's story, "Miss Thompson." At Maxine Elliott's Theatre.

Native Girl	Kathryne Kennedy
Native Policeman	Bhana Whitehawk
Natives	Oka Bunda, Llano Paulo
Ameena	Emma Wilcox
Private Griggs, U. S. M. C.	Kent Thurber
Corporal Hodgeson, U. S. M. C.	Harold Healy
Sergeant O'Hara, U. S. M. C.	Robert Elliott
Joe Horn	Rapley Holmes
Dr. McPhail	Fritz Williams
Mrs. McPhail	Shirley King
Mrs. Davidson	Catharine Brooke
Quartermaster Bates	Harry Quealy
Sadie Thompson	Jeanne Eagels
Rev. Davidson	Robert Kelly

It is a drama of altogether extraordinary grip and significance, of kaleidoscopic characters and chromatic passions, which John Colton and Clemence Randolph have fashioned out of Somerset Maugham's story "Miss Thompson."

The rain of the title descends on the South Seas, marooning a motley company in a hotel of Pago Pago. There is the landlord, a hedonist emancipated from Kansas and prohibition, who reads Nietzsche in a wicker chair and swigs home brew while his native wife cooks and serves, her ample mother-hubbard clutched by a brood of half-breed children. There are rollicking American marines and cockney British sailors. There are a traveling physician and his wife. Then there is Miss Thompson, a flashy and slangy good sort who is fleeing from the laws of California. Finally there is the Reverend Alfred Davidson, an American missionary who is bent on saving her soul.

The rain of the tropics which beats on the roof and drips copiously from the eaves is at once an irritant and a solvent. Under the spell of that long imprisonment the evil past lives again and new transgressions are engendered. Tropical languor mingle with fierce Northern passions of the spirit—and of the flesh.

Missionaries won't like this play, and perhaps not without reason. Davidson is of a type peculiarly abhorrent to the modern mood, especially in this metropolis. The gallery last night fairly booed and derided him. Yet he is no caricature, but rather a human being profoundly psychologized.

He is of the breed of the Pilgrim Fathers, with strong passions of the flesh held in leash only by a tyranny of the spirit, which he seeks to impose on all the world.

The natives of the South Seas, as no remarks to the intense delight of the audience, are so naturally depraved that he has had to show them what sin is. He does this by a species of blackmail, fining them whenever they are seen without trousers or mother hubbards, and by actually ruining any planter or trader who opposes him. The theocracy of Massachusetts lives again in the torrential tropics, the land of pineapple and palm.

But it is against his fellow American in distress that he now levels the justice of his God. Since "The Scarlet Letter" few searchings of that dark chamber where lust mingles with divine love have been as true and moving as this one. Under the impact of his fervor, the slangy, bedizened fugitive actually repents—consents to go back to San Francisco, though the crime for which she is wanted was in reality framed against her.

But in the long vigils of prayer, through which the culprit achieves a sort of sainthood, the missionary is undone. In the last scene Miss Thompson blazes forth in her cheap finery, fierce in her hatred of "all men." But the missionary has committed suicide, and for that she forgives him.

Miss Eagels, noted as a young actress of promise since her performance in "Daddy," rises to the requirements of this difficult rôle with fine loyalty to the reality of the character and with an emotional power as fiery and unbridled in effect as it is artistically restrained.

Among her sailor cronies she rollicks and drinks whisky with more than the swagger of the Bowery. Her conduct toward the gentle folk of the hotel party is a marvelous mingling of social awe and human arrogance. Her demeanor toward Davidson is subtly felt and inerrantly expressed in all the gamut of its tragic moods. The house, which missed the truth and fundamental understanding of the character of Davidson, fairly rose to Miss Eagels and acclaimed her.

The production was finely intelligent throughout, atmospheric in each individual character as in its suggestion of tropical luxuriance in heat and rain. The Davidson of Robert Kelley was properly vigorous and impassioned, yet modeled in every phase with spiritual comprehension. Rapley Holmes was an unfailing delight as the Nietzschean swigger of kawa. To Fritz Williams as the doctor fell the rôle of the confidant of one and all—a performance free from his earlier idiosyncracies and in the best manner of the admirable school in which he learned his art.

"Rain" is not a "pleasant" play, especially for the conventionally minded, but it is strikingly original in theme, true in characterization, vigorous in drama and richly colored with the magic of the South Seas.

JOHN CORBIN.　　　1922 N 8

A New Hamlet.

SHAKESPEARE'S HAMLET. At the Sam H. Harris Theatre.

Francisco	John Clark
Bernardo	Lark Taylor
Horatio	Frederick Lewis
Marcellus	E. J. Ballantine
Ghost of Hamlet's Father	Reginald Pole
Hamlet	John Barrymore
Claudius	Tyrone Power
Gertrude	Blanche Yurka
Polonius	John S. O'Brien
Laertes	Sidney Mather
Ophelia	Rosalind Fuller
Rosencrantz	Paul Huber
Guildenstern	Lawrence Cecil
First Player	Lark Taylor
Player King	Burnel Lundee
Second Player	Norman Hearn
Player Queen	Richard Skinner
Lucianus	Vadini Uraneff
A Gentlewoman	Stephanie D'Este
King's Messenger	Frank Boyd
First Grave Digger	Whitford Kane
Second Grave Digger	Cecil Clovelly
A Priest	Reginald Pole
Osric	Edgar Stehli
Fortinbras	Lowden Adams

The atmosphere of historic happening surrounded John Barrymore's appearance last night as the Prince of Denmark; it was unmistakable as it was indefinable. It sprang from the quality and intensity of the applause, from the hushed murmurs that swept the audience at the most unexpected moments, from the silent crowds that all evening long swarmed about the theatre entrance. It was nowhere—and everywhere. In all likelihood we have a new and a lasting Hamlet.

It was an achievement against obstacles. The setting provided by Robert Edmund Jones, though beautiful as his setting for Lionel Barrymore's "Macbeth" was trivial and grotesque, encroached upon the playing space and introduced incongruities of locale quite unnecessary. Scenically, there was really no atmosphere. Many fine dramatic values went by the board and the incomparably stirring and dramatic narrative limped. But the all important spark of genius was there.

Mr. Barrymore disclosed a new personality and a fitting one. The luminous, decadent profile of his recent Italian and Russian impersonations had vanished, and with it the exotic beauty that etched itself so unforgettably upon the memory, bringing a thrill of admiration that was half pain. This youth was wan and haggard, but right manly and forthright—dark and true and tender as befits the North. The slender figure, with its clean limbs, broad shoulders and massive head "made statues all over the stage," as was once said of Edwin Booth.

Vocally, the performance was keyed low. Deep tones prevailed, tones of a brooding, half-conscious melancholy. The "reading" of the lines was flawless—an art that is said to have been lost. The manner, for the most part, was that of conversation, almost colloquial, but the beauty of rhythm was never lost, the varied, flexible harmonies of Shakespeare's crowning period in metric mastery. Very rarely did speech quicken or the voice rise to the pitch of drama, but when this happened the effect was electric, thrilling.

It is the bad custom to look for "originality" in every successive Hamlet. In a brief and felicitous curtain speech Mr. Barrymore remarked that every one knows just how the part should be acted and he expressed pleasure that, as it seemed, he agreed with them all. The originality of his conception is that of all great Hamlets. Abandoning fine-spun theories and tortured "interpretations" he played the part for its prima facie dramatic values —sympathetically and intelligently always, but always simply. When thus rendered, no doubt has ever arisen as to the character, which is as popularly intelligible in the theatre as it has proved mysterious on the critical dissecting table.

Here is a youth of the finest intelligence, the tenderest susceptibility, with a natural vein of gayety and shrewd native wit, who is caught in the toils of moral horror and barbaric crime. Even as his will struggles impotently to master his external environment, perform the duty enjoined on him by supernatural authority, so his spirit struggles against the overbrooding cloud of melancholy.

If the performance had any major fault it was monotony, and the effect was abetted by the incubus of the scenic investiture. There was simply no room to play in. It may be noted as characteristic that the Ghost was not visible; the majesty of buried Denmark spoke off-stage while a vague light wavered fitfully in the centre of the backdrop. In one way or another the play within the play, the scene of the King at prayer and that of Ophelia's burial, all more or less failed to register dramatically.

The production came precious near to qualifying as a platform recitation. But even at that Mr. Barrymore might have vitalised more fully many moments. With repetition he will doubtless do so. The important point is that he revealed last night all the requisite potentialities of personality, of intelligence and of histrionic art.

The supporting company was adequate, but nothing more. The outstanding figures were the King of Tyrone Power and the Queen of Blanche Yurka. Neither Polonius nor the Grave Diggers registered the comedy values of their parts, a fact which contributed largely to the effect of monotony. But, strange to relate, the speaking of lines was uniformly good.

JOHN CORBIN.　　　1922 N 17.

1923

Russian High Comedy.

THE CHERRY ORCHARD, a comedy in four acts by Anton Tchekov, translated from the Russian by Jenny Covan. At Jolson's 59th Street Theatre.

Liuboff Andreievna Ranevskaya...
    Olga Knipper-Tchekhova
Anya .... Alla Tarasova
Varya .... Vera Pashennaya
Leonid Andreievitch Gaieff..
    Constantin Stanislavsky
Yermolai Alexeievitch Lopakhin..
    Leonid M. Leonidoff
Peter Sergeievitch Trofimoff
    Nikolai Podgorny
Boris Borisovitch Semyonoff-Pishtchik..
    Vladimir Gribunin
Charlotta Ivanavna........Maria Uspenskaya
Semyon Pantelevitch Yepikhodoff..
    Ivan Moskvin
Dunyasha .... Varvara Bulgakova
Firce .... Vassily Luzhsky
Yasha .... Nikolai Alexandroff
A Tramp............... Alexei Bondirieff
A Station Master............ Ivan Lazarieff
Post Office Clerk...........Lyoff Bulgakoff

The Moscow players proceeded last night from the lower depths of Gorky to the high comedy of Tchekhoff, revealing new artistic resources. Stanislavsky, Olga Knipper-Tchekhova, Moskvin, Leonidoff and half a dozen others entered with consummate ease into a rich variety of new characterizations. The stage management was less signal in its effects, but no less perfect. Yet for some reason " The Cherry Orchard " failed to stir the audience, even the Russian portion of it, as did " The Lower Depths " and even " Tsar Fyodor."

This is a play of comedy values both high and light. The milieu is that of the ancient landed aristocracy, beautifully symbolized by an orchard of cherry trees in full bloom which surrounds the crumbling manor house. Quite obviously, these amiable folk have fallen away from the pristine vigor of their race.

The middle-aged brother and sister who live together are unconscious, irreclaimable spendthrifts, both of their shrinking purses and of their waning lives. With a little effort, one is made to feel, even with a modicum of mental concentration, calamity could be averted. But that is utterly beyond their vacuous and futile amiability; so their estate is sold over their heads and the leagues of gay cherry trees are felled to make way for suburban villas.

Beneath the graceful, easy-going surface of the play one feels rather than perceives a criticism on the Russia of two decades ago. Here is a woman of truly Slavic instability, passing with a single gesture from heartbreak to the gayety of a moment, from acutely maternal grief for an only child long dead to weak doting on a Parisian lover who is faithless to her and yet has power to hold her and batten on her bounty. Here is a man whose sentiment for the home of his ancestors breaks forth in fluent declaiming, quasi-poetic and quasi-philosophic, yet who cannot lift a finger to avert financial disaster.

In the entire cast only one person has normal human sense. Lopakhin is the son of a serf who has prospered in freedom. He is loyal enough to the old masters, dogging their footsteps with good advice. But in the end it is he who buys the estate and fells the cherry trees for the villas of an industrial population. It is as if Tchekhoff saw in the new middle class the hope of a disenchanted yet sounder and more progressive Russia. The war has halted that movement, but indications are not lacking that it is already resuming.

With such a theme developed by the subtly masterful art of Tchekhoff there is scope for comedy acting of the highest quality. It is more than likely that the company seized every opportunity and improved upon it. But to any one who does not understand Russian, judgment in such a matter is quite impossible. Where effects are to be achieved only by the subtlest intonation, the most delicate phrasing, it fares ill with those whose entire vocabulary is da, da.

As an example of the art of the most distinguished company that has visited our shores in modern memory, this production of " The Cherry Orchard " is abundantly worth seeing. The play in itself is of interest as the masterpiece of the man who, with Gorky, has touched the pinnacle of modern Russian comedy. But if some Moscovite should rise up and tell us that in any season our own stage produces casts as perfect and ensembles as finely studied in detail, it would be quite possible to believe him.

JOHN CORBIN.   **1923 Ja 23**

SHAKESPEARE'S ROMEO AND JULIET.

At Henry Miller's Theatre.

Samson . . . . Bailey Hick
Gregory . . . . Frank Davis
Abram . . . . Edward Broadley
Balthasar . . . . .Richard Bowler
Benvolio. . . . . Vernon Kelso
Tybalt . . . . Louis Hector
Capulet . . . . Gordon Burby
Lady Capulet. . . . . Grace Hampton
Montague . . . . Lionel Hogarth
Lady Montague . . . . Lalive Brownell
Escalus. . . . . John Crawley
Romeo. . . . . Rollo Peters
Paris . . . . John Parrish
Peter . . . . Milfon Pope
Nurse to Juliet. . . . . Jessie Ralph
Juliet . . . . Jane Cowl
Mercutio . . . . Dennis King
An Old Man . . . . Neil Quinlan
Friar Laurence. . . . . Robert Ayrton
An Apothecary . . . . John Crawley

The play of "Romeo and Juliet" was produced last night. That is a statement much stranger than it may sound. Whoever was the inspiring genius of the occasion—the Selwyns, Jane Cowl and Frank Reicher together head the program—has perceived the fact that a play by Shakespeare, and this one in particular, is a thing of life and beauty; that laughing humor and gayety of the heart mingle in a multicolored skein with quick human passions tinged with foreboding and despair. And they know that the tempo of all this, though varied to suit the mood and the moment, is prevailingly swift—a river of singing shallows and darkly eddying pools that yet keeps a clear course to the sea. The result was an audience that reflected each mood, that smiled and thrilled at beauties unsuspected or long forgotten and departed, five minutes before midnight, in the inspiration of a great tragedy, and of great tragic acting.

It shall not be said, though the temptation is great, that every part was adequately acted. It is true, as we have so often been told, that the grand manner and the great tradition of the elder stage is no more. But it appears—what many have suspected—that ambitious youth and enthusiasm is a touchstone to which Shakespeare, the youngest of all dramatists if also the wisest, is ever quick to respond. This at least may be asserted, that from the first riotous encounter of Montagues and Capulets in the streets of Verona to the carnival of death in Juliet's tomb, every scene was played for its full worth by highly capable actors who knew just what they were about. Defects were noted by the observant, but only the carper found time to dwell on them.

The performance was equally notable for its vernacular quality, the accent of life in the living and for the eloquent intensity with which moments of supreme emotion were rendered. That is to say, it touched the two poles between which lies the rounded art of Shakespeare. These players have evidently listened to that youthful critic of acting, the Prince of Denmark. They spoke trippingly on the tongue, and continued to do so in the very tempest and whirlwind of passion.

The Romeo of Rollo Peters smiled at the jests of his comrades like the good fellow he was, yet touched both extremes of the scene in Friar Lawrence's cell, in which he measured his length on the floor and then rose to the pinnacle of joyous expectation. The Mercutio of Dennis King gossipped of Queen Mab and died in the arms of his friends to the equal admiration of the audience. That is a part that comes really as proof against failure as Hamlet is said to be. The Tybalt of Louis Hector, the Old Capulet of Gordon Burby, and the nurse of Jessie Ralph all deserved the high praise of the word adequate.

Of the Juliet it is difficult to write with moderation. Our reason, a priori, that it cannot be as good as it seems, but casts about rather helplessly to find flaws that are intrinsic. Miss Cowl's speech, though quite free from old mannerisms, is "modern" and at times colloquial—but so is the speech of Shakespeare, even in moments of torrential lyric beauty and of tragic suffering. The scene in which Juliet revolts from the nurse—"Ancient damnation, oh most wicked fiend !"—started with the familiar outburst but subsided into a tone of agonized self-communing. And one felt that the innovation was right. The moments of Juliet's extreme girlishness, the comedy of impatience with the nurse, Miss Cowl touched upon rather than exploited, yet if there was error one felt that it was on the right side.

The one thing essential to the part was always there and was denoted by means so simple and true that they defied analysis. There was youth to begin with, touched with the beauty and the mystery of great love. The balcony scene was as familiar as a caress, utterly ingenuous and impassioned; yet it positively sang with lyric exaltation. The potion scene ran the full gamut of womanly trepidation, grisly fear and heroic resolution. Never in modern memory has it been rendered with such virtuosity and at the same time with such simple conviction.

The ultimate scene in the tomb was perhaps the finest of all in its conception, as it was the most moving. For here Miss Cowl rose to that rare height where gesture is impotent and speech most effective when most subdued. It was a moment of absolute tragedy.

JOHN CORBIN.   1923 Ja 25

"ICE-BOUND" IS INTENSE.

Owen Davis's Grim Play of New England Is Finely Acted.

ICEBOUND, a play in three acts, by Owen
    Davis. At the Sam H. Harris Theatre.
Emma Jordan..............Lotta Linthicum
Henry Jordan.................John Westley
Nettie Jordan................Boots Wooster
Ella Jordan................Frances Neilson
Sadie Fellows.................Eva Condon
Orin Fellows..........Andrew J. Lawlor Jr.
Dr. Curtis..............Lawrence Eddinger
Jane Crosby...............Phyllis Povah
Judge Bradford..........Willard Robertson
Ben Jordan.................Robert Ames
Hannah................Edna May Oliver
Jim Jay................Charles Henderson

A fine performance and an unusually good play came together at the Sam H. Harris Theatre on Saturday night in "Ice-Bound," a New England character study that represents one more attempt on the part of the penitent Owen Davis to lift himself out of his past. Mr. Davis demonstrated in "The Detour" that he was willing and anxious to let bygones be bygones, and it is to his everlasting credit, when that play failed to meet with favor, that he did not issue a hot manifesto expressing his conviction that the public wanted nothing but bad plays, and that he was preparing to supply the demand. Instead he wrote "Ice-Bound."

It is a grim and nearly relentless play of the New England and the New Englanders that Owen Davis knows. It has an absorbing first act, followed by two acts that are only slightly less gripping. In the judgment of this reviewer it is not quite so fine a play as was "The Detour," but it is considerably more likely to be popular. Mr. Davis has seen to that, for he has sprinkled the play with a sardonic humor—somewhat the same sort of humor that plays over the surface of "Rain." There is, in fact, a vague kinship between this play and "Rain"—there is something of the same clash of character, the same pitting of a loose spirit against unbending tradition.

For the Jordans of "Ice-Bound" are

narrow, unforgiving, inhuman. Nature, as the younger and un-Jordanlike brother points out, has wisely keyed them in tune to their surroundings—they have been brought into the world half-frozen and bleak. Like the country, they are ice-bound. Living—within themselves, they grow narrower and meaner.

The first act, in which the family sits stiffly in the seldom-used parlor, while their mother lies dying upstairs, presents a graphic picture. You gather that the dying woman had been less of a Jordan than the others, and when the scapegrace younger son arrives you perceive that he is the only one of the lot who has taken after the mother. The play concerns itself with the cutting off of the typical Jordans in the old lady's will, and the eventual redemption of the erring son through a young woman who had been brought into the house some years before as a companion. All of which the old lady on her death bed had wisely foreseen and provided for.

The performance is excellent. In particular, Robert Ames and Phyllis Povah do splendid work as the family black sheep and the instrument of his redemption. John Westley, as the older son, gives the best performance of his career, and Edna May Oliver is amusing—although not always legitimately—as a maid. The youthful Andrew Lawlor fills a boy's rôle realistically, and there are other capable performances by Willard Robertson, Boots Wooster, Eva Condon and Lotta Linthicum.

To say nothing of Owen Davis.

JOHN CORBIN.   1923 F 12

The Harvard Prize Play.

YOU AND I, a comedy in three acts, by Philip Barry. At the Belmont Theatre.

Veronica Duane ....Frieda Inescort
Roderick White .... Geoffrey Kerr
Nancy White ......◄........ Lucile Watson
Maitland White ....H. B. Warner
Etta .... Beatrice Miles
G. T. Warren .... Ferdinand Gottschalk
Geoffrey Nichols .... Reginald Mason

The worst obstacle which the new comedy at the Belmont has to contend against is its reputation as a Harvard prize play. Callow youth and artificial cleverness have inhered in too many of its predecessors. In college comedy that remains at college, that is natural and right enough. In the setting of an older if not better world, the callowness and the artificiality are, as a rule, more evident than the youth and the cleverness.

"You and I" is an exception to this rule—a comedy which is technically good by professional standards and which has, besides, a genuine spirit of youth and a genuine cleverness—a facile abundance of quips and an unfailing felicity in the comedy of character. It is true that there is somewhat too much of the verbal play, too much of theatric cleverness. Another Harvard wit is on record

as not daring to be as funny as he could. Oliver Wendell Holmes knew the comedian's legerdemain of making half as much go twice as far. But though Mr. Barry is often beguiled he is never quite seduced. He has a situation to disclose of unusual freshness and human purport; and in the end he rounds up a satisfactorily workmanlike story.

The "You and I" of the play is the happily married couple as opposed to the solitary Ego of the creative talent. In marrying Nancy, Maitland White has foresworn his youthful love of painting to become a manufacturer of soap and perfumes. One business man in four, he believes, has a finer talent submerged in the mere money grubber. His son is similarly talented, thinks only of going to the Beaux Arts. And likewise this Roderick falls in love—throws over architecture for humdrum business and matrimony.

The play shows the father renouncing business and a good salary to take to painting in the attic, while the son renounces the Beaux Arts for fair Veronica. Beneath the resolute cleverness of the lines a domestic comedy emerges of genuine sentiment and charm. Just so, one believes, a business man of 43 would act if he suddenly picked up the canvas and the brushes abandoned in youth. And the portrait that resulted would be just this—somewhat stiff in the drawing but with a fulness of charm that made it worth $4,000 as the advertising symbol of soaps and perfumes. And a boy predestined to architecture would act precisely thus in the routine of office and factory, lingering for hours after luncheon to sketch plans for factory development.

The two women are drawn with equal freshness and distinctness of vision. Roderick's mother took her man from his talent without question—and lived to lead him back to it, though at the sacrifice of the material goods of life. His fiancée is of a more modern discernment and will, perceiving what a sacrifice she was exacting and bluntly refusing to accept it.

In all the recent contrasts drawn between the new generation with the older one, none has been as clear-eyed and at the same time as sympathetic as this one. Not so much can be said of the housemaid who does duty as artist's model. She is a quite preposterous creature of the comedy that was old a generation ago.

The prevailing affect of truthfulness would have been quite impossible except for the discretion of a really admirable company. H. B. Warner and Lucile Watson as Roderick's parents and Geoffrey Kerr and Frieda Inescort as the young folk hewed unfailingly to the line of character and situation, let Mr. Barry's quips fall as they might. Beatrice Miles showed capacities far beyond the scope of the pretentious housemaid. Ferdinand Gottschalk and Reginald Mason played minor parts with major distinction.

JOHN CORBIN.   1923 F 20

THE ADDING MACHINE, a play in seven scenes, by Elmer L. Rice. At the Garrick Theatre.

Mr. Zero	Dudley Diggs
Mrs. Zero	Helen Westley
Daisy Diana Dorothea Devore	Margaret Wycherly
The Boss	Irving Dillon
Mr. One	Harry McKenna
Mrs. One	Marcia Harris
Mr. Two	Paul Hayes
Mrs. Two	Therese Stewart
Mr. Three	Gerald Lundegard
Mrs. Three	Georgiana Wilson
Mr. Four	George Stehl
Mrs. Four	Edyth Burnett
Mr. Five	William M. Griffith
Mrs. Five	Ruby Craven
Mr. Six	Daniel Hamilton
Mrs Six	Louise Sydmeth
Policemen	Irving Dillon, Lewis Barrington
Judy O'Grady	Elsie Bartlett
Young Man	Gerald Lundegard
Shrdlu	Edward G. Robinson
A Head	Daniel Hamilton
Lieutenant Charles	Louis Calvert
Joe	William M. Griffith

New York last night was treated to the best and fairest example of the newer expressionism in the theatre that it has yet experienced. The verdict, of course, depends upon the personal reaction on the sensibilities of the observer.

He will see and hear, this observer, in "The Adding Machine," a Theatre Guild production at the Garrick—what starts out to be the short and simple annal of one of the great and glorious unsung of life, not too far above the submerged tenth, of a person, at times symbolical and at other times intensely personal, known simply as Mr. Zero.

For twenty-five years, day in and day out, excepting only national holidays and a week in the Summer, this Zero has added figures. Figures to right of him figures to left of him, volleyed and thundered from 9 to 5, six days a week, half Saturdays in July and August.

He married, this Zero, what must have been a sweet, moist-eyed, trusting bit of a girl, with infinite faith and pride in his tale of what lay just beyond this necessary beginning as a bookkeeper. But the days became weeks, the weeks became years, and the years decades—and still Zero is no further than his task of adding figures, and the little slip of a bride has become an ill-tempered, nagging, slovenly woman, bitter in her disillusionments and sharp with her tongue at him who is the cause of them.

Comes then, in the language of a great art, the twenty-fifth anniversary of Zero's career with the firm, of Zero still adding figures as he did a quarter of a century before. And at the close the day's work his employer appears, notifies him that adding machines are to be installed, machines so simple that they can be operated by high school girls and informs him gently but firmly that his services are no longer required.

For one mad moment all the figures he has ever added whirl madly in the Zero brain—and when he is again aware of the world he has stabbed his employer through the heart with a bill-file.

At his trial he becomes partly articulate—he tries to convey something of what the years of drudgery, endless, aimless drudgery, have done to him. He is sentenced to death and executed.

So far the larger part of his audiences will go hand i nhand with Mr. Rice, Mr. Moeller and Mr. Simonson, author, director and designer of last night's offering, and pronounce their work excellent. Mr. Rice, they will say, has written true dialogue, and Mr. Moeller has labored well to bring out the monotony and dullness and stupidity that are the life of the Zeio's of the world, and Mr. Simonson, be his methods ever so unorthodox, has created what not even the most orthodox of all can fail to understand.

The part of the fable just outlined runs through two of the play's three acts and four of its seven scenes. One of these early scenes, in particular, displayed a novelty and power that will long keep it in the memory of the beholder. It is simple enough—Zero and a female Zero are reading and checking figures to each other, in a dreary and monotonous sing-song, and as they work they think aloud and show their inmost, sacred selves, but theatrical as the device sounds in cold print, it was weirdly effective and gripping on the stage.

At the beginning of the play's third act and fifth scene at least some part of the audiences will not feel able to carry through. For one thing, this fifth scene, whatever its author's intent may have been, is coldly and gratuitously vulgar.

Some day a doctor's thesis will probably be written on that inward motive that drives the young expressionists to scenes in graveyards. (The father of them all, of course, had such a scene in "Fruehling's Erwachen." Despite the lack, at present, of an explanation, the fact of the inevitability of such scenes will have to be accepted. Mr. Rice's graveyard last night served as the locale for a scene almost literally from Mr. Schnitzler's "Reigen"—with, it seemed, no reason for the enactment of the scene save that the author willed it so. Certainly there was nothing in the behavior or thoughts of any of the characters that brought it on.

Past the inevitable expressionistic graveyard, the action moves to a pleasant spot in the Elysian Fields. Here Zero is given ample opportunity to catch up with some of the repressions and suppressed desires of his former life, but he turns his back on them at the last moment for fear of being considered not thoroughly respectable. What this scene, and the next and last, are meant to convey is vague, perhaps purposely. Certainly they were not offered as things of beauty by themselves.

At this writing, with the final curtain not yet decently cold upon an expressionist heaven dominated by a gigantic adding machine, the last act remains curious, vague blur, not, however, without excellent moments of satirical observation. It is, nevertheless, by far the weakest part of the play.

Expressionism, of course, is the modern definition for the method of production that covers all conceivable dramatic sins, and no one has a right to say to his brother what is and is not expressionism. To Messrs. Rice, Moeller and Simonson, obviously, it is the form of dramatic expression best conveying the illusion of reality in the presence of the obviously unreal.

The acting was excellent throughout. Helen Westley, without whom a Theatre Guild production is inconceivable, portrayed grandly the monster of a wife created by Zero and later destined to help push him to his earthly destruction. Dudley Digges as Zero lived the dumb, groping, plodding nature of the fellow. Margaret Wycherly played a female Zero with great restraint. Louis Calvert did nicely with an unobtrusive bit in the last scene.

Mr. Simonson's scenery is even more expressionistic than Mr. Rice's third act. In a courtroom scene, while Zero is tried, there is some excellent work by him. He shows us the Zero conception of justice, cold, inanimate, relentless, and the contrast between reality and unreality is heightened by the crooked bars and railings and walls. Mr. Simonson's, too, one suspects, is the effect of the whirling figures and the dashes of red that appear to Zero as his employer hands him his discharge for his faithful quarter century of labor.

Mr. Rice, it should be noted, is the author of "On Trial," an equally revolutionary play, so far as technique is concerned, of a few seasons ago.

1923 Mr 20

LA DONNA DEL MARE (THE LADY FROM THE SEA), a play by Henrik Ibsen in four acts. At the Metropolitan Opera House.

Ellida Wangel	Eleonora Duse
A Stranger	Memo Benassi
Dr. Wangel	Alfredo Robert
Boletta	Enif Robert
Hilda	Ione Morino
Ingstrand	Gino Fantoni
Arnholm	Ciro Galvani
Lyngested	Leo Orlandini

Perhaps because one had been forewarned by reports from London, the art of Eleonora Duse seemed strangely little affected by the lapse of two decades since her last appearance here. The statement is no mere echo of the loyal welcome extended by an audience that filled the vast Metropolitan Opera House —bursting the walls, the roof and the fire laws—and lingered full twenty minutes after "La Donna del Mare" was ended, clamoring to see her again and once again. Most of these enthusiasts heard very little and saw less. The press seats were fortunately well forward, within normal range of the stage.

It is true that Signora Duse's hair has the flashing gray of broken iron at the temples, and is quite white above the forehead. It is true that there are wide, faint circles beneath her eyes and that her marvelous hands, so eloquent in gesture, have more than their pristine slenderness. But the total impression is not so much of age as of the agelessness of an immortal spirit. Her cheeks have no more than their former spare softness, and her slow smile breaks out as of old in spiritual tenderness and sweetness. If she had not in her youth renounced the normal instruments of her art, the humble devices of make-up, the impression would have been that of an artistic vigor and of a beauty of face and form quite unexampled in one of her years.

And then there was the voice. If it has lost quality and power, few could have felt the fact because of the unique and penetrating joy it brought. It is the voice of a silver twilight, peopling an atmosphere Corot might have imagined with multitudinous accents of the human spirit. It is crepuscular in its plaintive repinings, as for a day that is dead—as also in its accents of a soul that struggles forward toward a glory of light beyond the far horizon. Many were present last night who welcomed Duse thirty years ago, when she ran the whole gamut from stark tragedy to comedy airily light. In that generation no voice has been heard even faintly resembling hers—nor is such a voice ever likely to be heard again.

The choice of Ibsen's "Lady From the Sea" for Duse's opening bill must be justified on other grounds than those of dramatic literature. Written in 1888, between "Rosmersholm" and "Hedda Gabler," it lacks the sombre atmospheric splendors of the one and the trenchantly dramatic characterization of the other. Anti-Ibsenites of yore denounced it as a mere study in incipient mental derangement. William Archer himself used it as an example of a theme and scenario hopelessly undramatic. Today interest in morbid psychology is more acute. It is possible that the younger generation will welcome the play as a remarkably convincing study of the sea-freedom complex. But even they can scarcely find it dramatically luminous.

As a medium for the art of Duse, nevertheless, "The Lady from the Sea" is amazingly, as it is unexpectedly, appropriate. Whatever of movement and development it contains transpires wholly in the realm of the spirit. Imprisoned within the narrow compass of Wangel's household, Ellida lives hectically, brain-sickly, remembering her stormy girlhood romance of the ocean. Every garment has a deep sea note—rich greens and blues of the bounding main, the foam white and the dead grey of the tempest. When The Stranger returns to claim her she denies him, shrinks from him. lives in a gruesome awe of him. The way in which this Ellida hovers behind Wangel, fluttering those fragile hands about his broad shoulders as if to snatch from him a sturdier resistence, yet peering beyond toward the peril that fascinates. is finely psychologic, superlatively eloquent. When the final test comes and Wangel tells her that she is free to follow her impulse or not as she chooses, all the effulgent silver of Duse's voice quivers with the joy of release and of the return to healthfulness. The "lady from the sea" is on the glad earth again.

The production, which Ibsen intended to be uncommonly picturesque, is bare to the point of crudeness. The supporting company is rather heavily Italianate and middle aged. Only the part of The Stranger stands out, Memo Benassi investing it with a thoroughly adequate spirit of youthful vigor and romance.

1923 O 30, 17:1

Walter Hampden.

CYRANO DE BERGERAC, a comedy in five acts by Edmond Rostand, English version by Brian Hooker. At the National Theatre.

Cyrano de Bergerac........Walter Hampden
Christian de Neuvillette.....Charles Francis
Comte de Guiche.............Paul Leyssac
Ragueaneau ....Cecil F. Yapp
Le Bret....................Ernest Rowan
Carbon de Castel-Jaloux...H. E. Humphrey
Ligniere ....William Sauter
Vicomte de Valvert.........Reynolds Evans
A Marquis.................Thomas F. Tracy
Second Marquis.............Joseph Latham
Montfleury............C. Norman Hammond
Bellerose..................Antonio Salerno
Jodelet.....................Le Rol Operti
Cuigy...................William H. Stevans
Brissaille.................Albert G. West
A Busybody................P. J. Kelly
A Musketeer............John Alexander
D'Artagnan..................Louis Polan
A Light Horseman...........Jay Fassett
The Porter..................Allen Thomas
A Man....................Marcel Dill
Another Man..............John E. Trevor
A Guardsman............Bernard Savage
A Citizen.................H. E. Humphrey
His Son....................Anthony Jochlin
A Pickpocket..............Cedric Weller
Betrandou the Fifer.........Allen Thomas
The Candle Lighter......Henry Fitzgerald
Roxane.................Caroll McComas
Her Duenna..............Ruth Chorpenning
Lise.....................Mary Hall
The Orange Girl..............Mabel Moore
A Soubrette............Margaret Barnstead
The Flower Girl......Elsie Herndon Kearns
A Comedienne...............Isabel Garland
Another Comedienne..........Anne Tonetti
Mother Marguerite de Jesus......Mary Hall
Sister Marthe.................Mabel Moore
Sister Claire.........Elsie Herndon Kearns
A Little Girl.

Walter Hampden opened his season of classical repertory at the National Theatre last night with a production of "Cyrano de Bergerac" thoroughly worthy of his ambition, which is the highest. An audience exceptionally intelligent and cultivated in the art of the drama followed his performance with rapt attention and breathless interest, rewarding him with genuine enthusiasm and liberal applause. It was an altogether auspicious beginning toward the repertory theatre we have so long lacked and longed for.

Rostand's "heroic comedy" is a classic—make no mistake about that. True, its essential artificiality can scarcely be exaggerated, its exploitation of the old romantic bag of tricks. But it would be equally difficult to exaggerate its charm for all who love humor and fancy, the thrill of vaillant deeds and the glamour of romantic love, enveloped in an atmosphere of poetic eloquence and shot through by the lightning flash of wit. The quarter of a century since its first production—by Coquelin in 1897 and by Richard Mansfield in 1898—has developed many new talents and brought many ephemeral changes in theatric taste; but it has only confirmed our first judgment, that we have here a French romantic comedy of the first water.

Mr. Hampden's Cyrano is an interpretation of great physical vigor, deep truth and intensity of passion. The scene of the duel, fought in the act of improvising a ballade—a palpable absurdity if ever there was one—has never been more convincingly rendered. This Cyrano really fenced, yet maintained the air of genuine improvisation. Long before the end of that rousing sword fight one was more than prepared to believe that the man was thoroughly capable of routing a band of one hundred hired assassins.

In the ensuing love passages Mr. Hampden's fine voice and his highly intelligent reading of poetic lines stood him in good stead. Defects of stage management, easily corrected, marred the balcony scene, but its romantic pathos was luminously rendered. One felt, and felt deeply, the passion that must utter itself even in the guise of a rival who reaped the reward—by the loved one's lips and her hand in marriage. In the final scene in which, in the hour of his death, Cyrano and Roxane discover their mutual love amid the falling leaves of Autumn, Mr. Hampden soared high in the region of tragic pathos.

In the lighter phases of the part, Mr. Hampden varied from excellent to adequate, at least in the judgment of some few of his audience. The scene of Cyrano's pretended fall from the moon, with its grotesque turns of fancy and its rough-and-ready humors, was a bit of bravura quite comparable to the scene of the duel-ballade. As a wit, this Cyrano wielded the broadsword rather than the rapier. The subtler play of humor, in which a smile outshone a tear or rhetorical bravery masked a bleeding heart, Mr. Hampden denoted but did not illumine—at least, I repeat, in the judgment of some few. He has many followers as intelligent as they are ardent in loyalty, who dwell on his indisputable versatility and admit few or no limitations to it.

The production, designed and supervised by Claude Bragden, is richly beautiful scenically and is finely thought out and expertly executed in most of the details of the acting. Cecil Yapp as Ragueneau and Paul Leyssac as de Guiche gave notably competent performance. Roxane is not a really good part and Carroll McComas missed some of its qualities of amiable and intelligent preciosity, but she was quite adequately charming and sympathetic.

Mr. Brian Hooker's blank-verse version of the play makes no pretension of literal fidelity. References to classic French poetry are freely rendered by analogous quotations from Marlowe and Shakespeare. The effect, if rather startling at first, is ultimately excellent. Especially admirable is the success with which Mr. Hooker has sought the dramatic word, the histronically effective phrase. And, withal, Rostand's fine wit and his richly poetic diction are admirably rendered. The version is more redolent of its original than any other we have been permitted to hear and speaks well for the discretion and taste of Mr. Hampden's management.

JOHN CORBIN.   1923 N 2

The Saint's Progress.

SAINT JOAN, a play in four acts and an epilogue, by George Bernard Shaw. Produced by The Theatre Guild; setting and costumes by Raymond Lovey. At the Garrick Theatre.

Robert de Baudricourt.......Ernest Cossart
Steward ....William M. Griffith
Joan ....Winifred Lenihan
Bertrand de Puleugy........Frank Tweed
The Archbishop of Rheims..Albert Bruning
La Tremouille................Herbert Ashton
Court Page..................Jo Mielziner
Gilles de Rais...........Waton Butterfield
Captain La Hire..........Morris Carnovsky
The Dauphin ....Philip Leigh
Duchesse de la Tremouille..Elizabeth Pearre
Dunois ....Maurice Colbourne
Dunois Page..................James Norris
Richard de Beauchamp....A. H. Van Buren
Chaplain de Stogumber.....Henry Travers
Peter Cauchon..............Ian Maclaren
Warwick's Page.............Seth Baldwin
The Insuisitor.........Joseph Macaulay
Canon D'Estivet..............Albert Perry
Le Courcelles............Waton Butterfield
Brother Martin Ladvenu..Morris Carnovsky
The Executioner..........Herbert Ashton
An English Soldier..........Frank Tweed
A Gentleman of 1920.......Ernest Cossart

"Saint Joan" is one of those Shaw plays, and they are among the best that improve as one looks back at them. In the three hours and a half of last night's performance, which lasted from a punctual 8 o'clock to a no less punctual 11:30, there seemed to be many backwater eddies in which the drama, the "chronicle play" as the program calls it, was lost in monotonously whirling words. Many of the Shavian stock of ideas and jokes walked again, particularly that favorite shillalah knocking of English imbecility. Out of the historic and heroic past, from within the very aura of a saintly presence, "topical allusions," reached forward to mite the humdrum world of today as glibly and irresponsibly as in a Gilbertain libretto. But these are only the contortions of the Sybil; they cannot permanently obscure the Sybil's inspiration.

This is no simple chronicle history, with its be-all and its end-all in merely historic events and personalities. It is, as Hogarth would have said, the Morality of a Saint's Progress. And, though it lacks the English painter's solidity of outline and his stanch actuality, it adds a touch of Celtic sympathy and fire, of philosophy, of intensely humanized imagination and of divination. This Joan is a simple country girl, homely and familiar as no other of her dramatic biographers has made her; but she is also the epic heroine of all sainthood. At 11:30 one begins to realize that the many lengthy discourses, even the seemingly stereotyped Shavian japes, all have their part in revealing to us how sainthood comes upon earth, how it truimphs—and it martyrized.

It comes from the hearts of the people, simple folk who are content with mere goodness and courage. We meet Joan at the Garrick as the result of the failure of certain hens to lay their accustomed eggs. It was thought to be a phenomenon related to the coming of the Maid of Domremy, and when the hens began to lay again the fact was of importance in procuring for her a horse and a helmet—the chance to lead the folk of France. Not that the great ones really believed. They perceived a personality of might, a spirit of flame, and made use of it to inspire armies hitherto defeated. From time to time, even among the great ones, this soul and that was touched to the vision, but always with a very human limitation. The priest remained always in bondage to the authority and the creed of his church, the soldier to the technique of his profession.

And so soon as Joan's great work was done, those whom she had profited most felt themselves most encumbered by her. The feudal Baron saw in the popular uprising which she headed the end of fealty to his order; the great prelate saw in it the end of the supremacy of the church. For Joan meant much more than the victory of France and the crowning of the Dauphin at Rheims. She meant the advent in the whole world of the force of Protestantism and Nationalism. And so the prelates and the Barons united to do away with her. The final words of this Joan, as she reappears in a dream among the mortal who have known her, are: "O God that madest this beautiful earth, when will it be ready to receive Thy Saints? How long, O God, how long!"

Certain passages in this curiously mingled play are of surpassing beauty. The initial scene of the eggs gives us a portrait of girlhood and sainthood blended which, in its very different way, is gracious and fine as anything in "Candida." A full half dozen of the men in the piece are as subtly and acutely characterized as the men of "Caesar and Cleopatra." The scene in which Joan first uplifts the sword of France before the altar thrills mightily with heroism of the spirit. Even the spoofing and topical gagging epilogue, in which a frock-coated top-hatted "Gentleman of 1920" talks with the spirits of Joan and of her associates of five centuries before, breathes a spirit and a philosophy which are of Shaw's best.

But the great triumph of the play is the scene of Joan's trial and burning. There the finest sympathy, the shrewdest intellectual intention, fuse with simple human feeling to produce really great drama. Nowhere else in Shaw is there a scene quite so true, so moving and uplifting. Yes, it is a play that gains mightily in retrospect.

The casting tops the Theatre Guild's previous best—a multitude of performances so variously and contrastingly fine as to defy brief commendation. The loan of Winifred Lenihan is superlative—with limitations. The "dangerous power" ascribed to the Saint, and her flaming spirit, are not always in full evidence. One believes in, but does not quite feel, her power of inspiring a whole nation and leading it to victory. But Joan's moods of frank girlhood, and of a sainthood patient and proud, are rendered with consummate simplicity and grace. Taken as a whole, it is a really great performance and one which, like the play, grows mightily in memory.

JOHN CORBIN.   **1923 D 29**

1924

From George M. to His Profession.

THE SONG AND DANCE MAN, a comedy in four acts by George M. Cohan; produced by George M. Cohan. At the Hudson Theatre.

Curtis.....................William Walcott
Charles B. Nelson............Frederick Perry
Joseph Murdoch...............Louis Calhern
John Farrell................George M. Cohan
Crowley...................William J. Phinney
Jim Craig.................Robert Cummings
Jane Rosemond...........Eleanor Woodruff
Mrs. Lane...................Laura Bennett
Leola Lane....................Mayo Methot
Freddie........................Al Bushee
Miss Davis............Mary Agnes Martin
Tom Crosby................John Meehan
Anna.........................Alice Beam

Devotees of the well-made play and sticklers for lifelikeness in the drama

will not find much to delight them in "The Song and Dance Man." Far from being the "Dramatic Comedy," which the program calls it, it is merely a theatric anecdote, and rather straggling at that. But all those greater hearts who love the theatre for the sheer glamour and fascination of it will take this offering to their bosoms.

The song and dance man whom Mr. Cohan impersonates is not at all a success. In the far hinterland he has gone from bad to worse, till the death of his dancing partner puts him down and out. But still he clings to his calling, believing in himself and dreaming always that he must eventually find fame on Broadway. Well, the caprice of fate takes him there, and he makes the acquaintance of the great ones of the theatre. But he is introduced to them not as an "actor" but as a hold-up man, for he has been rendered desperate by poverty and the destitution of old friends. So at last he gets his chance to show what he can do—and is an instant and utter failure. Mr. Cohan interpreted his curtain speech last night (as he will doubtless do hereafter) to show how bad this song and dance man was, and it was a delicious burlesque. But it was also just a little painful, for one had come to love the fellow for the warmth and loyalty of his heart and his unquenchable love of the footlights. There is just a little more than that in the evening. A song and dance girl, played by Mayo Methot, also gets her chance, and instantly makes good. After five years she is about to marry a famous illustrator and quit the stage. But in the hour of her decision the song and dance man turns up and tells his own experience. Having quit the stage and risen to a salary of fifteen thousand a year, the old lure proved too strong for him. Now again he is touring the tall timber. Once an actor, always an actor.

With all its dramatic crudities, "The Song and Dance Man" has moments, and not a few of them, that bring the heart up under the chin in spite of the manner of "Trelawney of the Wells." It is an honest, radiant tribute to a profession of many sorrows which cannot too often be told that the folk who give themselves to it are happy in having warm hearts and stanch loyalties.

JOHN CORBIN.   **1924 Ja 1,**

'KID BOOTS' FINE FIT FOR EDDIE CANTOR

Ziegfeld's Lavish Musical Comedy Is Also Much Benefited by Mary Eaton.

KID BOOTS, a musical comedy in two acts and eight scenes. Book by William Anthony McGuire, and Otto Harbach; music by Harry Tierney; lyrics by

Joseph McCarthy. Produced by Florenz
Ziegfeld. At the Earl Carroll Theatre.

Peter Pillsbury .... Harry Short
Herbert Pendleton............. Paul Everton
Harold Regan................ John Rutherford
Menlo Manville................. Harland Dixon
Miss Joyce,............... Madelyn Morrissey
Miss Huntington............. Katherine Stuart
Miss Brown..................,..... Diana Stegman
Miss Hoyt....................... Sonia Ivanoff
Miss Llewellen................. Yvonne Taylor
Miss Hughes................. Joan Gardner
Tom Sterling................. Harry Fender
Polly Pendleton................. Mary Eaton
First Golfer............ Morton McConnachie
Second Golfer................. Jack Andrews
First Caddie................. Dick Ware
Second Caddie................. William Blett
Third Caddie............,,....... Frank Zolt
Fourth Caddie................. Waldo Roberts
Fifth Caddie.................... Lloyd Keyes
Kid Boots...................... Eddie Cantor
Beth................................ Beth Beri
Carmen Mendoza............. Ethelind Terry
Jane Martin.................... Marie Callahan
Dr. Josephine Fitch........ Jobyna Howland
Randolph Valentine........... Robert Barrat
Federal Officer................. Victor Munroe
George Olsen and his orchestra.

With all of his accustomed profligacy,
if not more, Mr. Ziegfeld staged another
of his musical comedies last night at the
Earl Carroll Theatre, and called it "Kid
Boots." Mindful of the enormous vogue
of "Sally," the producer thereof took
good care to make one popular comedian
and one golden-haired dancer the central
figures in his new entertainment, and
the response of last night's audience
must have convinced him that he was
right.

It is Eddie Cantor and Mary Eaton
whom Mr. Ziegfeld thus pushed forward,
albeit it must be added that Mr. Cantor
has been forward these many seasons.
Of the two, of course, it is Mr. Cantor
upon whom the new entertainment leans
the more heavily. Here, certainly, is the
perfect show for the Cantor devotees—
which is only another way of saying
that it is the perfect show for the world
at large.

For it is Eddie Cantor, seeming a bit
more fervent and wide-eyed than he
ever has before, who makes "Kid
Boots" what it is. He is the most intense of the comedians—the light blazes
in his eye and communicates itself to
his audience, convincing them of his
passionate sincerity. In "Kid Boots"
he even strikes a respectable serious
note now and then, and he imparts an
unexpected subtlety to several scenes designed as broad comedy.

Cantor, in white face for most of the
distance, appears as a caddy master at
a Palm Beach golf club. In this capacity he gives a hilarious golf lesson
to Jobyna Howland, and then Miss Howland, conveniently made a doctor for
the purpose, gives Mr. Cantor a severe
electrical treatment—a reminiscent bit
for Cantor, of course, but none the less
comic. Some of the Cantor jokes have
also been heard before, but the art of
Cantor is such that one can enjoy an
old joke from his lips almost as much
as a new one. •

There are some other people in the
show, of course. Miss Eaton is lovely
to gaze upon, dances quite airly, and
was vociferously applauded by last
night's audience. Jobyna Howland is
amusing and Harland Dixon dances

even better than the last time. The
diminutive Marie Callahan, his partner,
also dances, and in addition reveals unexpected powers as a comedienne.

The experienced Messrs. Maguire and
Harbach, fashioners of the book, have
shrewdly arranged matters so as to give
Mr. Cantor half a dozen rich scenes.
For the rest they wisely kept their plot
in subjection. Mr. Tierney's score
seemed to contain several winners. All
in all, it is a goodly entertainment.

1924 Ja 1

COMEDIENNES STAR IN CHARLOT'S REVUE

**ANDRE CHARLOT'S REVUE OF 1924, a
revue in two acts and twenty-two scenes.
At the Times Square Theatre.**
PRINCIPALS — Beatrice Lillie, Gertrude
Lawrence, Jack Buchanan, Fred Leslie, Mar-
jorie Brooks, Robert Hobbs, Herbert Mundin,
Dorothy Dolman, Ronald Ward, Douglas Fur-
ber, Jill Williams and Peggy Willoughby.

With three of the most popular London revue comedians as its stars, an
English troupe came bravely to Forty-
second Street last night and presented
"Andre Charlot's Revue of 1924" at the
Times Square. Mr. Charlot, so far as
America has been permitted to learn, is
the foremost of the English revue producers—London's Mr. Ziegfeld, in other
words. The entertainment that he
brought to New York last night is frequently brilliant in idea, less rich than
American revue, and yet sufficiently
attractive to the eye, and particularly
fortunate in having Beatrice Lillie and
Gertrude Lawrence in its cast.

For Miss Lillie and Miss Lawrence are
the mainstays of this English revue—
comédiennes in two distinct and separate fields, and each excellent. Something of their fame had already been
brought to this shore by returning travelers, but no amount of advance description can take the edge off the enjoyment that is to be had from seeing
and hearing Miss Lillie sing "March
With Me," for example, or Miss Lawrence in the rendition of "I Don't
Know."

There is no one in New York quite
comparable to Beatrice Lillie. In appearance she is an exaggerated Lynn
Fontanne, and it is in burlesque that
she shines. The opening of the second
act found her as a fifty-year-old soubrette, still bent upon singing the giddy
ballades of her youth. And in "March
With Me," a bit of patriotism near the
finish, she rose to superb heights.

As for Miss Lawrence, she is invaluable in Mr. Charlot's comedy skits, and
she can do wonders with a fair-to-mid-
dling song. The third of the leading
players, Jack Buchanan, is a lengthy
gentleman with an amiable stage pres-

ence and first-rate dancing ability, but hardly remarkable otherwise.

Mr. Charlot has probably had the advantage of being able to select his numbers from the numerous revues that he has produced in London, and thus the piece assays high. It is a far more literate entertainment than any American revue—perhaps (terrible thought) it is a bit too literate for the general public.

A skit entitled "Inaudibility" turned out to be much funnier than any description of it would indicate, and there are three or four others equally entertaining. There are also, of course, a few dull ones. But, at least, it is English almost through and through—now and then some one woos a laugh by mentioning "Town Topics" or something else of the sort, but there is precious little concession to Times Square.

The music is swinging and the production moves rapidly, with nary an encore. The chorus, like the principals, is all English, and a little below the Ziegfeld-Music Box standard in appearance.

1924 Ja 10

THE MIRACLE,' FINE SPECTACLE, SHOWN

Reinhardt's Religious Pantomime Acted in Cathedral Setting at the Century.

BEAUTIFUL AS A PAGEANT

700 in Processions of Nuns and Throngs of Worshipers That Vibrate With Life and Color.

THE MIRACLE, a spectacular pantomime with music, in nine scenes, created and staged by Max Reinhardt. Book by Karl Vollmoeller; score by Engelbert Humperdinck; revised by Friedrich Schirmer. Scenery and costumes designed by Norman-Bel Geddes; produced by Morris Gest. At the Century Theatre.

Madonna................Lady Diana Manners
Sexton.....................Charles Peyton
Assistant Sexton..........David Hennessey
Old Sacristan................Elsie Lorenz
Old nun attendant.........Mrs. John Major
Mother of the nun.Claudia Carlstadt Wheeler
Grandmother of the nun.......Laura Alberta
The Nun...................Rosamond Pinchot
The Abbess.................Mariska Aldrich
A Peasant..................Louis Sturez
The Burgomaster............Lionel Braham
The Knight................Orville Caldwell
A Blind Peasant.......Rudolph Schildkraut
His Son.....................Schuyler Ladd
A Crippled Piper............Werner Krauss
The Archbishop................Luis Rainer
The Robber Count..........Lionel Braham
The Shadow of Death.........Luis Rainer
The Prince.................Schuyler Ladd
The Emperor..........Rudolph Schildkraut
Executioner................Lionel Braham

By JOHN CORBIN.

Max Rheinhardt's long delayed and much anticipated production of his famous religious pantomime was achieved last night, and with all good auguries. The cathedral into which the Century Theatre has been transformed by Norman-Bel Geddes is indescribably rich in color, unimaginably atmospheric in its lofty aerial spaces. The company of principals which Morris Gest has provided is of artists tried and true—in which category is now included Miss Rosamond Pinchot. But the feature of the performance which most impressed last night's audience was, that which has been least heralded. It was the noble band of seven hundred supernumeraries.

The truth seems to be that pantomime, even at its best, affords no great scope to histrionic ability of the first order. There were times when the dumb show seemed, in Hamlet's phrase, inexplicable. Even the program synopsis afforded no convincing explanation of the motives and meaning of The Piper, who figured as the active agent in the plot. Werner Krauss is an actor of prime reputation in Central Europe and he brought to bear a pantomimic talent of salient force and subtle intention. But the peculiar combination of beneficent purpose and maleficent effect which he is supposed to symbolize remained enigmatical. Rudolf Schildkraut, Lionel Braham, Schuyler Ladd and others performed simpler tasks more comprehensibly, but none of them won new laurels. Only the Madonna of Lady Diana Manners and Miss Pinchot's Nun made an impression that was indubitable and strong.

Crowd Scored at Every Turn.

The crowd scored at every turn—which is right enough in cathedral pantomime. The uniformed processions of nuns and the motley throngs of worshippers vibrated with life and color. Into an atmosphere of stately reverence and hushed religious awe they brought the surging vitality of mediaeval piety, the passion of religious conviction. They burst in at all the entrances of the auditorium, surged down the widened aisles and stormed the chancel on the stage.

The effect here was powerfully and beautifully augmented by Humperdinck's music, by voices from aloft in the cathedral clerestory, and by the far-away chiming of remarkably sweet-toned bells. Incense from swung censers lent perfume, while the smoke intensified the impression of atmospheric richness and depth. But in it all and through it all was the masterly magic of Reinhardt's manipulation of crowds.

It differed from that of Stanislavsky and his Moscow players in that it lacked the wider range of expression made possible by the elucidation of the spoken word; but by the use of dramatic attitude and significant gesture, the tossing of arms and the shuffle of multitudinous feet, universally varied murmurs and sudden concerted shouts, it produced an effect that was at times overwhelming, stupendous.

The Nun's Wanderings.

A similar masterhood was evident in the scenes of the Nun's wanderings in the outer world. Whether it was in fact the outer world, or only a cloistered dream of the libido, rioting ashamed in revels of the flesh, was not quite clear. The cathedral piers on the stage remained, as also the auditorium clerestory. But one followed the Nun through a dance of elves in a wood, interrupted by an incursion of huntsmen; through a Prince's nuptial feast and mock bridal procession; through revels in an imperial palace and the phantasm of an insane Emperor; through a proletarian revolution and the bloody orgies of a reign of terror. Everywhere the scene was multitudinously animated, vitalized, by the sweep of Reinhardt's imagination and his marvelous sense of detail.

As for Miss Pinchot, the outstanding impression of her performance was the naïf animal grace and the physical vitality which first attracted Reinhardt's attention. That is the primary and indispensable qualification for this marathon of parts. But the overtones were adequately varied, clear and strong. So far as pantomime goes, there was every evidence of a sound histrionic instinct, readily amenable to training. Her single vocal essay, a passionate utterance of the Lord's Prayer wrenched out of her in the depths of her misery, was both richly emotional and intelligently phrased.

Both the part and the performance of the Madonna were in striking contrast. For minutes together Lady Diana Manners stood in her stiff garments of brocade quite motionless against the cathedral pier, an embodiment of quiet, womanly grace. In the Madonna's living moments she walked with unconscious dignity and queenly repose among the assembled nuns. Yet the effect was vibrant, as if this creature of divine womanhood were indeed moving in an aura of the spirit.

The audience followed the performance with every evidence of intelligent interest and rapt attention. Probably because of the religious nature of scene and story, there was no great outburst of applause. Enthusiasm took the form of a series of calls at the close for those chiefly responsible for the production. Mr. Gest made a brief speech, referring to the public-spirited citizen or citizens who have encouraged him in this gigantic and thoroughly worthy artistic venture.

SCENIC MIRACLE WROUGHT.

Solid Gothic Cathedral Built Inside Big Century Theatre.

To provide setting for "The Miracle" a preliminary miracle was wrought in the Century Theatre. Inside the red and gold auditorium of the big playhouse on Central Park West has been set up the solid similitude of a Gothic Cathedral, its soaring columns and groined arches filling the stage and masking the interior of the house as far back as the balcony. The proscenium arch became the choir with the high altar set in the midst and surrounded by twenty 50-foot ton-weight columns in two semi-circular ranks, with their arches rising twenty feet higher and the dim religious light of eleven 40-foot-high stained glass windows splashing upon the scene their pools of deep blue and ruby red shot with green and yellow from the bright garments of the painted saints.

Between the columns are high grilled gates and beyond and around them all about the stage nine groups of lesser 50-foot columns with more stained glass windows forming the chapels of the ambulatory. Where the gilt pillars used to frame the stage on one side was built a solid tower rising to the roof and on the other a pulpit. Where, right and left, the ornate familiar boxes used to be, stand Gothic doors and a great rose window of stained glass. Cloisters sweep backward on either side, framing the house, and more stained glass windows look down from the balconies. Where the gilt dome used to be is a Gothic roof with swinging lanterns of stained glass.

Lined With a Cathedral.

Thus the theatre has been literally lined with a cathedral, not a mere contrivance of canvas and paint, but a solid structure of wood and iron and concrete and seeming stone. Where the stage floor was is the pavement of the chancel, reaching far forward into the auditorium, with broad steps where the first rows of orchestra seats used to be. The balcony rail is massed with banners and the sometime carpeted aisles wear the aspect of cold flagstones.

To work this transformation took the labor of 300 people for five months. Three and one-half months were spent building it piece-meal in three studios in various parts of the city. Six weeks have been required to set it up and all that time the theatre has been closed and full of scaffolds and the hammering of carpenters and builders. To build merely the high altar, thirty feet in height, cost the labor of twenty carpenters for a month and something like a million feet of lumber was consumed in the columns and doors and panels and arches. The mullions of the choir windows and the two great rose windows are made of laminated wood that used to give lightness to the wings and fuselages of war-time airplanes. The painted windows required 10,000 square feet of canvas and the cyclorama which closes the stage at the back and sides uses up 14,000 feet of black felt.

For the transformations which must take place in the dark and must suddenly give to the cathedral the similitude of a forest there are provided two 75-foot shafts, driven by electric motors of fifty horse-power. These motors are harnessed with 26,000 feet of steel cable to the movable scenery, which weighs 24,000 pounds. They send this weight aloft at the rate of a foot a second.

Seven hundred people all told are employed in the production, including fifty stage hands and forty electricians. In order to drill this multitude in the thousand seperate tasks which go to make up the massed effect, Max Reinhardt worked with twenty-two assistant stage managers rehearsing the company for seven weeks. For two weeks he has been rehearsing them in the theatre, directing his battalions from a scaffold like a ship's bridge, set in the midst of the auditorium.

Director Controls All Elements.

Beside him stood aids with megaphones. Posted about the house, on the stage, at all the entrances, in the galleries, underneath the stage, were other aids, each in charge of his separate cohort. From his high post the director controlled and co-ordinated all the elements which entered into the composition of his spectacle. The movable scenery, the light from a hundred points in the house, the organ in one gallery, the choir in the cloisters, the orchestra in another gallery, the bells, the great drums, the wind and thunder machines beneath the stage, the multitude of actors making entrances and exits all over the house, the principals on the stage—all had to be reached. His orders were passed by megaphone or telephone or signal to his subordinates, and thus gradually all this seeming chaos of men, women, material and machines were wrought into shape.

Nothing like it has ever been done in a New York theatre and probably nothing quite like it anywhere else in the world, though Reinhardt himself has produced "The Miracle" before. It has been done in Berlin and London in great arenas like Madison Square Garden. This time, a cathedral has literally been built for it and that cathedral, though it is inside a theatre, towers a hundred and ten feet from floor to roof-tree, a structure of seeming stone and solid wood and stained glass.

No exact figures of the cost can be given. Even Morris Gest, who has been the master builder, is unable to tell. His estimate runs around $600,000. Under Mr. Gest the organizer has been Max Reinhardt of Berlin and Salzburg. The architect of the cathedral is Norman-Bel Geddes, one of the youngest American stage designers.

1924 Ja 16.

Rachel Crothers Triumphs.

EXPRESSING WILLIE, a comedy in three acts by Rachel Crothers. At the Forty-eighth Street Theatre.

Minnie Whitcomb	Chrystal Herne
Mrs. Smith	Louise Closser Hale
Simpson	Douglas Garden
Reynolds	John Gerard
Willie Smith	Richard Sterling
Tallaferro	Alan Brooks
Dolly Cadwalader	Molly McIntyre
George Cadwalader	Warren Williams
Frances Sylvester	Marie Maddern
Jean	Laura Richards

By JOHN CORBIN.

A very wonderful thing happened last night at the Forty-eighth Street Theatre, a thing with scarcely a precedent in this or any season. The audience which assembled to welcome a new comedy by Rachel Crothers, produced by the Equity Players, was of exceptional distinction and had every reason to look for an evening of intelligent and well-mannered enjoyment; but few could have anticipated the perfect conjunction of play-writing, acting and stage management that unfolded itself as if by miracle. No dissentient voice was heard. The only approach to the unanimity of the verdict was at the first night of "The Swan." And this is a native comedy, written out of our own life by one of us.

When all due credit is allowed to her collaborators, the triumph rests with Miss Crothers. Hitherto she has generally pleased one by the felicity of her dialogue, amused one by her deftness in portraying character, touched and moved one by her power of feminine sentiment. Not often has a play of hers been rounded, complete. Last night every power seemed enlarged, intensified, perfected. The sallies of her wit took the audience by storm; it fairly shouted with laughter. The varied group of her characters was so subtly and saliently limned that half a dozen actors, long loved and honored, seemed lifted above themselves as by the touch of genius. And even while sides were still shaking with laughter, unaccustomed eyes took on the glamour of tenderness, of rapture at the perfection of humor that lies in perfect humanity.

It is not possible to relate just what it was all about. As well try to describe the variegated, gay and exquisite colorings of a butterfly's wing. There was an undertone of the new psychology, and it has never before seemed so profound, so convincing—or so derisible. The Willie who stood to be "expressed" (Richard Sterling) was a millionaire manufacturer of tooth paste, who had opened an Italian palace on Long Island and was in awe before the group of demi-fashionables and demi-fakes who flocked around him. His mother, racy of the Middle West (Louise Closser Hale) was shrewdly observant of his peril and deeply perplexed to find a remedy. Her best guess was to import a music teacher (Chrystal Herne) who had known Willie, and indeed loved him, in the early days out on the prairie.

But this Minnie Whitcombe and Miss Herne deserve a new paragraph; they could not, indeed, be adequately expressed in a long and leisurely essay. A starved soul, chained in slavery to the piano and its scales, she suddenly finds herself housed in grandeur, lapped in luxury and surrounded by folk whom, in the innocence of her heart, she takes to be the very real thing. A portrait painter, somewhat shrewder than the other guests if also more flamboyant, perceives the beauty of her face and soul and preaches to her the gospel of self-expression. What happens then is quite beyond words. For one thing, Miss Herne sits down at the piano and plays so well that one really believes she has suddenly come by the touch of musicianly greatness. As for the burgeoning that takes place in Minnie's soul, no one but a woman could divine it. No one but Miss Crothers could express it in the theatre so subtly, so unmistakably, with such a rapture of humor and tenderness.

It is Minnie who set forth to make Willie express himself, to the end that he may become worthy of her rival, the delectable obvious fake of an actress who is setting her cap for him. Merle Maddern plays this part with a cartoonist's vigor of line, yet with a satirical delicacy and truth that are unbelievable. The two women meet at midnight in Willie's bedroom, to Willie's vast embarrassment, and the contrast between the simple, preposterous innocence of one and the callous calculation of the other is at once soul-warming and hilarious.

For two acts it seemed all too good to be true, or at least to be sustained to the final curtain. But Miss Crothers accomplished the miracle. Her little comedy, at once so slight, so exquisite and so hilarious, ended in a blaze of glory.

One must at least mention the admirable work of Alan Brooks as the psychologic artist, of Molly McIntyre and of Warren William as calculating guests. As to Louise Closser Hale, anything said would be too little. Miss Crothers has given her a character of the first water and she renders it with the pristine humor of her Prossy in Shaw's "Candida," enhanced by the broader technique and the ripened feeling for life that have come in the intervening years.

1924 Ap 17

NEW MUSICAL PLAY 'ROSE-MARIE' DAZZLES

Arthur Hammerstein's Prodigal Production Has a Melodious Prima Donna, Mary Ellis.

ROSE-MARIE, a musical comedy in two acts and ten scenes. Books and lyrics by Otto Harbach and Oscar Hammerstein 2d; music by Rudolf Friml and Herbert Stothart. At the Imperial Theatre.

Sergeant Malone.............Arthur Deagon
Lady Jane.................Dorothy Mackaye
Black Eagle................Arthur Ludwig
Edward Hawley..............Frank Greene
Emile La Flamme........Edward Ciannelli
Wanda.......................Pearl Regay
Hard-Boiled Herman..........William Kent
Jim Kenyon....................Dennis King
Rose-Marie La Flamme.........Mary Ellis
Ethel Brander..................Lela Bliss

It is a magnificent musical play that Arthur Hammerstein last night brought to the Imperial Theatre. At a reasonably late hour, "Rose-Marie" was still speeding along to what seems certain to be one of the big musical successes of the new season.

There is a prodigal magnificence about the new production that almost takes the financial-minded beholder's breath away. This kind of thing, with two or three conspicuous exceptions, has hitherto been associated with revues. There is a seemingly endless array of costumes, tasteful, dazzling, colorful; there are platoons and platoons of chorus girls—75, the rapid calculators have it—tireless, graceful, beautiful; there are handsome sets and gorgeous draperies. There is, too, a plot, slightly less banally put forward than has been customary, and there is a select and capable array of principals.

So far as first honors in the production are concerned, they belong about in equal part to David Bennett, who staged the dances, and to Charles Le Maire, who designed the costumes. One of Bennett's ensemble numbers, having something or other to do with totem poles, evoked lusty and sustained cheering from all parts of the house. And Le Maire's costumes, as has been intimated above, were splendid and for the most part designed along unhackneyed lines.

"Rose-Marie" brings a new prima donna to the musical play stage in the person of Mary Ellis. Miss Ellis, lately of the strictly legitimate but formerly with the Metropolitan Opera House, has a voice of such quality as to place her at once among the two or three musical heroines whose voice is at least some part of their fortune. On the other hand, Miss Ellis seemed last night to show a tendency toward an unnatural cuteness that will probably disappear with further experience. She also, last night, had slight difficulties with the even sustenance of a French-Canadian accent with wh.ch the authors for no apparent reason saw fit to provide her.

William Kent bears, as they say, the comedy honors. It may well be that Mr. Kent is not funny and that his lines are without particular humorous appeal. Nevertheless, there is an active minority for which Mr. Kent is ever a source of near-hysterics, and it seems possible that a majority will be achieved through his work in the new piece.

Dennis King is the manly and tuneful

hero and Arthur Deagon is Sergeant Malone of the Northwest Mounted Police, to be sure, but nevertheless appealing and rich in entertainment value. Pearl Regay pleased greatly with eccentric and acrobatic dancing, and Dorothy Mackaye, in a stereotyped rôle, was charming and convincingly comical.

The score, in part made up of music above the average standard of musical plays, contained several tunes that will probably become nuisances before long.

1924 S 3

Triumph at the Plymouth.

WHAT PRICE GLORY, a play in three acts, by Maxwell Anderson and Laurence Stallings. Settings designed by Woodman Thompson; staged and produced by Arthur Hopkins. At the Plymouth Theatre.

Corporal Gowdy...............Brian Dunlevy
Corporal Kiper.............Fuller Mellish Jr.
Corporal Lipinsky.............George Tobias
First Sergeant Quirt..........William Boyd
Captain Flagg.................Louis Wolheim
Charmaine de la Cognac......Leyla Georgie
Private Lewisohn.............Sidney Elliott
Lieutenant Aldrich...............Faye Roope
Lieutenant Moore...............Clyde North
Lieutenant Schmidt........Charles Costigan
Gunnery Sergeant Sockkel..Henry G. Shelvey
Private Mulcahy...............Jack MacGraw
Sergeant Ferguson........James A. Devine
A Brigade Runner........John J. Cavanaugh
M. Pete de la Cognac..........Luis Alberni
Another Brigade Runner....Arthur Campbell
Brig. Gen. Cokeley.............Roy LaRue
A Colonel....................Keane Waters
A Captain..................William B. Smith
A Lieutenant.................Fred Brophy
Another Lieutenant........Thomas Buckley
A Chaplain....................John C. Davis
Town Mayor..................Alfred Renaud
Spike ....Keane Waters
Pharmacist's Mate ....Thomas Sullivan
Lieutenant Cunningham....J. Merrill Holmes
Lieutenant Lundstrom........Robert Warner

By STARK YOUNG.

Just a year ago Maxwell Anderson saw his "White Desert" win praise and pass too quickly off the stage through untoward circumstance. Last night at the Plymouth Theatre he and Laurence Stallings could feel nothing but satisfaction over their new play. "What Price Glory?" is something you can put your teeth into.

On the whole what is usually called the plot is hardly the main interest in this war play. The story, so far as it appears, is of the captain and the sergeant, old enemies with old scores to settle. The captain goes away on leave, the sergeant takes his sweetheart. When the captain returns he finds the girl's father demanding that the man who has deflowered her should wed her and pay him 500 francs. Chance turns the tide on the sergeant, and the captain is prevented from marrying off the pair only by the call to the front. In the dugout of the next act the

sergeant gets a start on the captain by acquiring a wound in the leg that might send him back to the town where the girl is. Alsation officers are captured, however, and the captain wins the staff's offer of a month off for his reward. The two arrived within a few minutes of each other in the girl's barroom and carry the struggle through till the call comes to go back to the front, revoking the month's leave.

The fundamental quality of "What Price Glory?" is irony. Irony about life and about the war, but iron so incontrovertible in its aspect of truth and so blazing with vitality as to cram itself down the most spreadeagle of throats. The chaos, the irrelevance, the crass and foolish and disjointed relation of these men's lives and affairs to the war shows everywhere, and the relation of the war to their real interests and affairs. This is a war play without puerilities and retorts at God and society, and not febrile and pitying, but virile, fertile, poetic and Rabelaisian all at once, and seen with the imagination of the flesh and mind together.

The irony of "What Price Glory?" culminates in the creation of Captain Flagg, the best drawn portrait in the realistic method that I have seen in years. In him the irony becomes superb. He is the true labor of war, the rough surface of the deep and bitter in human nature; he is intelligent, tender, brutal and right. He deserves much and wins little either from the world without or from within himself. He is a bum and a contemptuous hero. And he was played last night by Louis Wolheim with a security and a variety that I have never seen this actor achieve before, as well as with intelligence and a kind of husky wit.

The acting in the performance as a whole was above the average. In some places it needed more projection; it remained too much behind the footlights and too little toward the audience; it was too merely natural and not enough theatre. But in the main it went well. William Boyd as the sergeant rival to the captain played better and better as the acts went on. The scene where the captain and the sergeant stood at the bar and drank and quarreled over the girl was one of the best moments of this season; the stage managing also at this point, with the clearing away of the other persons to the far side of the stage and the pointing up of these two tragic, bitter and fantastic figures set there against each other, was perfect. Woodman Thompson's settings were fair but without a creative and dramatic relation to the play.

"What Price Glory?" is not one of those examples of the art of the theatre that discover a story, a pattern of action, that is in itself the very essence and expression of the play. It has not invented images of action or event that embody unescapably the dramatic idea, as the sleep-walking scene in "Macbeth," to take a lofty instance, does, or the great fables that survive the ages of men. It moves in the reverse direction—toward, that is, the creation and employment of character and dialogue for the dramatic purpose. And yet the proportions of story and war and talk and personality are perhaps part of the total idea behind the play. And the story has the advantage of being made cumulative, so that its heaviest weight and greatest tension fall where they should fall, in the final scene.

"What Price Glory?" lags somewhat in spots, no doubt; in the first and second acts it might well be shortened a little. But though it may have lagged, I for my part felt nothing of it, because of the sting and freshness of the writing, because of the speeches, the words and meanings and rhythms, like the beating of the pulse in your ears.

1924 S 6

Molnar and Theatre Guild Again.

THE GUARDSMAN, a comedy in three acts, by Franz Molnar. Directed by Philip Moeller; settings by Jo Mielziner; produced by the Theatre Guild. At the Garrick Theatre.

The Actor ....Alfred Lunt
The Actress, his wife........Lynn Fontanne
The Critic ....Dudley Digges
"Mama" ....Helen Westley
Liesl ....Edith Meiser
Creditor ....Philip Loeb
An Usher ....Kathryn Wilson

By STARK YOUNG.

The Theatre Guild began its season last night with a comedy of marriage and love among the artists. Molnar, who in the past has provided "Liliom" for the Guild and "The Devil" for George Arliss, not to speak of "The Swan" and other pieces that we have seen in New York, leaves us now with an amusing evening's entertainment to remember. "The Guardsman" is not important comedy or distinguished writing in any sense, and the performance at the Garrick is not distinguished. But the play is entertaining most of the time and often witty and full of clever contrivance.

Eleven years ago, in 1913 to be exact, this comedy, under the title of "Where Ignorance is Bliss," and adapted by Philip Littell, was given at the Lyceum Theatre and failed. To judge by the response of its new audience last night it may meet now with better success. Only in the second act, where the progress of the situation seemed to need marking into surer emphasis, did the interest drag.

An actor and his actress wife, after six months of marriage, have already come to troubled ways. He is jealous and suspicious; she has begun to play Chopin again, music whose melancholy and autumnal temper suits her mood and torments her husband, who dreads the end of everything between them after half a year, while May is still at hand and the leaves are not yet turned.

He has invented a test of his wife's fidelity. He walks beneath her window dressed as a guardsman and comes to visit her. In the second act there is a scene in the anteroom of her box at the opera in which she protests that she loves her husband, though she is not in love with him, and in the same breath leads on the passionate Prince. In the last act the actor returns unexpectedly from a supposed journey, and seems to find his wife on the point of a rendezvous. Behind the screen of his costume trunk he puts on the guardsman's uniform and confronts her. She has seen through the disguise from the start, by his kiss, by his liking his cigarettes, and, said more sweetly, by his ardent eyes. They malign one another's acting, they weep, and make it all up.

In the current of this story there are moments full of Molnar's particular brand of facile subtlety, never very profound anywhere, not in "Liliom," not in "The Swan" and not here in this comedy of the artist's temperament and domesticity, but cosmopolitan, easygoing and diverting. Into the performance of it last night a diverting and jolly quality permeated always. The slight depth of the dramatist's theme and treatment kept everything more or less at a certain level. The cosmopolitan and the distinguished, however, as well as the comic, might have been furthered by more elegance in the playing, more style and manner, more elaborate observation of the cynical and bland subtleties of the author's mood.

Lynn Fontanne portrayed the actress often delightfully, with now and again a kind of prima donna charm and no little technical fluency; she could heighten to advantage her whole performance and give it more brilliance and point. Alfred Lunt's actor was less convincing. His natural turn for cues and transitions often helped him out, but he fell a long way short of both Lynn Fontanne and Dudley Digges, who played the bachelor friend in a manner that was exactly right in every sense. Helen Westley abandoned herself vocally and visibly to a sharp and amusing sketch of Mama, the actress's more or less chaperon.

1924 O 14

Eugene O'Neill's Latest Play.

DESIRE UNDER THE ELMS, a play in three acts, by Eugene O'Neill. At the Greenwich Village Theatre.

Simeon Cabot....................Allen Nagle
Peter Cabot......................Perry Ivins
Eben Cabot......................Charles Ellis
Ephraim Cabot ....Walter Huston
Abbie Putnam...................Mary Morris
A Young Girl................Eloise Pendleton
An Old Farmer...........Romeyn Benjamin
The Fiddler................Macklin Marrow
A Sheriff.......................Walter Abel
An Old Woman.. ....Norma Millay
Deputies........,....Arthur Mack, William Stahl

By STARK YOUNG.

"Desire Under the Elms," the first play by Eugene O'Neill to be produced since "Welded," was presented last night at the Greenwich Village Theatre and proved to be as unlike that drama as it was unlike "The Hairy Ape" or "The Emperor Jones." "Desire Under the Elms" reverts in character to the earlier "Beyond the Horizon," though it exhibits by comparison a fine progress in solidity and finish. It has less sentiment than this older piece and more passion; it is better written throughout; it has as much tragic gloom and irony but a more mature conception and a more imaginative austerity.

"Desire Under the Elms" is essentially a story of solitude, physical solitude, the solitude of the land, of men's dreams, of love, of life. The God behind the existence created on this New England farm is a harsh God, who is alone and is not understood. The minds of the people in this story are shaken and tinged with loneliness, with thwarted passion, with the trivial, the intense, the drab exaltation and denial of life. Underneath this solitude desire works, the redemption through love.

The children of old Cabot hate him. The youngest, the son of the second wife, remembers his dead mother, worked to death, and sees her about the place, risen from her grave. The father brings home a third wife. The two older sons go away to California; the younger stays and thinks to avenge his mother. In time he and the young wife come to love each other.

A son is born, which old Cabot thinks is to be heir to the farm, leaving the second wife's son adrift in the world. While a dance in honor of the new-born child goes on in the kitchen, the father and son quarrel outside; the son believes his father when he hears that the woman wanted a son only to cheat him out of the farm. He reviles her. To prove to him that it was the love of him and not the desire for the farm that had driven her to him, she kills the child. He runs off for the sheriff. The father turns the live stock loose in the woods and plans to go away, but when he finds the money gone from its hiding place, he believes that God another time has willed that he stand by the farm. The son returns from the sheriff's, he falls at the knees of the woman, takes part of the blame on himself, and they go away together to prison.

Robert Edmond Jones's setting for "Desire Under the Elms" was profoundly dramatic. The end of a New England farmhouse with its overhanging elms was for all practical purposes built there on the stage, with a wall of actual stone coming down to the footlights; a scene that was realistic but at the same time strangely and powerfully heightened in effect.

The general performance of the play was usually adequate though not often on a level with the writing. Mary Morris, however, whose career as the fair Gertrude in "Fashion" last year was one of the flowers of the season's acting, played the wife in "Desire Under the Elms," with a new and suppressed method that deepened at times into an admirable poignancy and a kind of grim, thin poetry that seemed the exact truth of her lines. Charles Ellis, though his work in the earlier scenes was less successful or convincing, played with real poetry the passage where the boy is possessed with love for the woman and for his child. Walter Huston as the old man was everywhere trenchant, gaunt, fervid, harsh, as he should be in the part. In his ability to cover his gradations, to express the natural and convincing emotion, and to convey the harsh, inarticulate life embodied in this extraordinary portrait that Eugene O'Neill has drawn, Mr. Huston showed his talent and proved to be the best choice possible for the rôle.

The scene of "Desire Under the Elms" that best illustrates the highest quality of the play is that in which we see the dance going on, the father outside the house, the young wife and her lover in the upstairs room in each other's arms beside the child's cradle, a scene written with such poetry and terrible beauty as we rarely see in the theatre, a scene that for these qualities of poetry, terror and at the same time unflinching realism rises above anything that Mr. O'Neill has written.

1924 N 12

Love in the Valley.

THEY KNEW WHAT THEY WANTED, a comedy in three acts, by Sidney Howard. Settings and costumes by Carolyn Hancock; directed by Philip Moeller; produced by the Theatre Guild. At the Garrick Theatre.

Joe	Glenn Anders
Father McKee	Charles Kennedy
Ah Gee	Allen Atwell
Tony	Richard Bennett
The R. F. D.	Robert Cook
Amy	Pauline Lord
Angelo	Hardwick Nevin
Giorgio	Jacob Zollinger
The Doctor	Charles Tazewell
First Italian Mother	Frances Hyde
Her Daughter	Catherine Scherman
Second Italian Mother	Peggy Conway
Her Son	Thomas Scherman

By STARK YOUNG.

It is no reflection on the play to say that Pauline Lord walked away with "They Knew What They Wanted" last night at the Garrick, and created something in the theatre that ought to run to the season's end.

Sidney Howard, who has already shared this autumn with Edward Sheldon the honors of "Bewitched," writes now a romantic comedy. It is a gentle piece, successful in working its intentions, and very much what the author meant it to be. In a California valley, with the bare hills and the bright sun outside, Tony plans his wedding. He has seen a girl in Frisco, in a spaghetti palace; he has never dared visit her, but has written and proposed marriage. In a moment of fear lest she might not fancy so old a man as he is, he has substituted Joe's photograph for his own and sent that to her. He is a prosperous bootlegger; and too much of his own wine has made him unsteady on his feet when he starts to the train to meet the bride. Since nobody is at the train for her, she comes with the postman; Tony is brought in presently with his legs smashed from an automobile accident. Three months later, when Tony is mending and there is happiness all round, the doctor tells Joe that Amy is going to have a child. The two have not been alone together since that first night. Amy tells Tony everything, he keeps her by him. Joe goes away; every one has what he wants.

The weaker spot in the writing of the play is toward the last. The scene needs to be less soft and expected. Tony needs some more happily discovered things to say when he hears the facts about his wife and; when he makes the transition from rage and murder to the final forgiveness. For the rest of the comedy the bare telling cannot convey the kindly, glowing atmosphere and the sense of the children of songs and the vine and the sun that Mr. Howard achieves in the characters. The best writing in the play is in Joe's lines, with their sudden honesties and spurts of feeling; and the part of Amy as it is written is convincing and often touching. The night of the festa, with its singing and dancing and colored lanterns and sick man's whimsies, has plenty or color and warm, light romance.

"They Knew What They Wanted," however, would rest as a picturesque little play, made up pleasantly out of Western material and smoothly spun to its happy ending, if it were not for the playing that the Theatre Guild has found for it. Glenn Anders steps well out ahead of his past achievements. He understands exactly that kind of shiftless integrity in such a character as this Joe that he plays, a fellow who migrates along from place to place, sometimes talking for the I. W. W., sometimes in jail, sometimes in the orchards and vegetable farms, but honest throughout, and loose and kind, even tender when life comes near to him. Mr. Anders brings to the part his singular gift for a casual naturalness in his readings and inflections and for a varied tempo in his cues. Richard Bennett gave a performance of Tony that was too long dragged out at times, too obviously professional at times, and never imaginative, but a good, popular performance nevertheless, and well able to—hold the part and the scenes together.

Pauline Lord gave one of those instances of her work at its best that glorifies and makes pitiful the whole art of acting. Her playing last night had that shy pathos and intensity that we saw in her "Launzi" last year. She is an actress that, when she finds a part within her range, had in that part a range and perfection at the top of all the realism in our theatre. Last night she never missed a shading or a point; she had always a wonderful, frail power in the scene, and throughout her entire performance a kind of beautiful, poignant accuracy. And last but not least, her playing with the rest of the company was admirable and to be recommended all over town.

1924 N 25

ADELE ASTAIRE FASCINATES.

In Tuneful "Lady, Be Good" She Vividly Recalls Beatrice Lillie.

By STARK YOUNG.

LADY, BE GOOD!' A musical comedy in two acts and six scenes. Book by Guy Bolton and Fred Thompson, music by George Gershwin, lyrics by Ira Gershwin. Settings by Norman-Bel Geddes; staged by Felix Edwardes. At the Liberty Theatre.

Dick Trevor	Fred Astaire
Susie Trevor	Adele Astaire
Jack Robinson	Alan Edwards
Josephine Vanderwater	Jayne Auburn
Daisy Parke	Patricia Clarke
Bertie Bassett	Gerald Oliver Smith
J. Watterson Watkins	Walter Catlett
Shirley Vernon	Kathlene Martyn
Jeff	Cliff Edwards
Manuel Estrada	Bryan Lycan
Flunkey	Edward Jephson
Victor Arden	Victor Arden
Phil Ohman	Phil Ohman
Rufus Parke	James Bradbury

There is good news to spread among the mourners for Miss Beatrice Lillie's recent untimely departure from these parts. She returned last night, with an added freshness and a previously unrevealed dancing talent, in the piece called "Lady, Be Good" that came to the Liberty Theatre. But this time she calls herself Adele Astaire.

It should be explained, probably hastily, that it is a known fact that the Misses Lillie and Astaire are two different persons and that Miss Astaire is not exactly a newcomer. But Miss Astaire, in the opinion of at least one deponent, is as hilarious a comedienne as the gorgeous Miss Lillie. As recently as November, 1922, Miss Astaire was seen in the unlamented "Bunch and Judy," to set sail soon thereafter for London. And ever since then the penny posts have been full of the details of her two-year triumph abroad in, of all things, "Goodness Knows," with the title changed to "Stop Flirting" for no known reason.

But it is a different Adele Astaire whom last night's audience was privileged to see. When she left she was a graceful dancer—and she has returned, not only with all her glorious grace, but as a first-rate comedienne in her own right. Miss Astaire, in the new piece, is as charming and entertaing a musical comedy actress as the town has seen on display in many a moon.

Fred Astaire, too, gives a good account of himself in "Lady, Be Good," participates enthusiastically and successfully in most of Miss Astaire's dance offerings, and is allowed to win the hand in marriage of Miss Kathlene Martyn for the final curtain. A second hero, destined, the librettist intimates, to be Miss Astaire's lifelong mate, is Alan Edwards, recently of "Poppy," who again proves that he is one of the musical comedy stage's very best in one of its very worst assignments.

Walter Catlett, the leading comedian, manages to be consistently amusing almost all of the time, and Gerald Oliver Smith is allowed to deliver several at-

tractive nifties in a pleasant manner.
And there is further in the cast Cliff
Edwards, who plays a ukulele.

George Gershwin's score is excellent.
It contains, as might have been expected, many happy hints for wise orchestra leaders of the dancing Winter
that lies ahead and a number of tunes
that the unmusical and serious-minded
will find it hard to get rid of. The
lyrics, by Ira Gershwin, are capable
throughout and at moments excellent.

"Lady, Be Good" has exceptionally
handsome settings by Norman Bel-
Geddes. And there is an energetic chorus that dances excitedly and rythmic-
ally under the direction of Sammy Lee.

The book of the piece contains just
enough story to call Miss Astaire on
stage at frequent intervals, which thus
makes it an excellent book. But it
could have had a little more humor.

1924 D 2

'THE STUDENT PRINCE' BRINGS OUT CHEERS

Prodigious Operetta, Made From 'Old Heidelberg,' Is Magnificently Sung at Jolson's.

By STARK YOUNG.

THE STUDENT PRINCE (In Heidelberg),
an operetta in a prologue and four acts.
Book and lyrics by Dorothy Donnelly,
music by Sigmund Romberg. Settings
by Watson Barratt; staged by J. C.
Huffman; produced by the Shuberts. At
Jolson's Fifty-ninth Street Theatre.

First Lackey..............Frank Kneeland
Second Lackey............William Nettum
Third Lackey.............Lawrence Wells
Fourth Lackey............Harry Anderson
Von Mark................Fu ler Mellish
Dr. Engel................Greek Evans
Prince Karl Franz........Howard Marsh
Ruder...................W. H. White
Gretchen................Violet Carlson
Toni....................Adolph Link
Detlef..................Raymond Marlowe
Lucas...................Frederic Wolff
Von Asterberg...........Paul Kleema
Nicolas.................Fred Wilson
Kathie..................Ilse Marvenga
Lutz....................G orge Hassell
Hubert..................Charles W lliams
Grand Duchess Anastasia..Florence Morrison
Princess Margaret.......Roberta Beatty
Captain Tarnitz.........John Coast
Countess Leyden.........Dagmar Oakland
Baron Arnheim...........Robert Cal ey
Premier Dancer..........Martha Maso
Rudolph Winter..........Lucius Metz

"The Student Prince" is a prodigious
operetta. The play that was "Old Heidelberg" has been produced again in
musical form, and on a scale that never
would have been possible in the old
days. The production that came to Jolson's last night is richly scored and
magnificently sung, and merited even
the cheers that were sent across the
footlights by a friendly audience.

It is a romantic operetta of the old
school, this musical version of the play
that Richard Mansfield made famous,
and it is almost a perfect example of
its kind. The authors and the producers
have never for an instant been turned
aside from the business in hand. They
have told a simple romantic story with
all of the aid that music and singing
could bring to it, and they have out-
fitted it with a magnificent production.
Not even the comparative absence of the
comic element is of importance in "The
Student Prince"; the piece concentrates
so successfully upon its prime ingredients that nothing more is needed.

The simple story of the Prince of
Karlsburg and his love for a Heidelberg
barmaid lends itself perfectly to this
style of production—it requires a minimum of dialogue and so clears the decks
rapidly for the business of an operetta,
which is music. The score of this piece
is by far the best that Sigmund Romberg has done. The clicking heels of the
students and the high patent leather
boots of the court are not alone on the
stage of Jolson's; they are woven deep
into Romberg's music.

The high point of the evening is a
gorgeous court scene in the third act
(strangely enough, here is a musical
play in a prologue and four acts). Here
was a familiar enough operetta scene,
but the costumer and the producer have
taken even more than the customary advantage of it. Here, too, was the point
where the cheers burst forth for the
splendid voice of Howard Marsh. Mr.
Marsh and a blonde young person
named Ilse Marvenga are entrusted with
most of the singing, with Greek Evans
a prominent third. All three are excellent—Miss Marvenga is not without obstacles to overcome, but grows steadily
better as the evening progresses.

George Hassell, technically at the head
of the company, is somewhat swamped
by the largely musical nature of the
proceedings. Now and then, however,
he stirs a smile—and when he does so
it is tribute to his own powers, not the
librettist's. The latter, incidentally, was
Dorothy Donnelly, and she has done a
first-rate job for the purpose in hand.
Another who should be mentioned is the
veteran Adolph Link, who played a
single scene with mellow effectiveness.

The entire production is on the scale
that Jolson's Theatre demands—when
the Heidelberg students take possession
of the stage, in the first act, they are
some forty or fifty strong. And when,
all together, they sing one of those rousing drinking songs you are well aware
that something is taking place. Especially from the third row on the aisle.

1924 D 3

1925

PROCESSIONAL, a play in four acts by John Howard Lawson. Staged by Philip Moeller; settings and costumes by Mordecai Gorelick; produced by the Theatre Guild. At the Garrick Theatre.

Boob Elkins	Ben Grauer
Isaac Cohen	Philip Loeb
Sadie Cohen	June Walker
Jake Psinski	Charles Halton
Pop Pratt	William T. Hays
MacCarthy	Carl Eckstrom
Bill	Allan Ward
Phillpots	Donald Macdonald
The Sheriff	Redfield Clarke
A Man in a Silk Hat	William P. Canfield
Old Maggie	Patricia Barclay
Mrs. Euphemia Flimins	Blanche Frederici
Dynamite Jim	George Abbott
Rastus	Samuel D. Manning
Slop	Robert Collyer
Smith	Stanley Lindahl
Gore	E. F. Bliss
First Soldier	Lee Strasberg
Second Soldier	Stanley Lindahl
Third Soldier	Samuel Chinitz

By STARK YOUNG.

I found John Howard Lawson's "Processional" always interesting, good or bad as the scene in progress might be, I found it exciting, sometimes violently original, and sometimes moving and beautiful to an immense degree. To produce such a play took courage on the part of the Theatre Guild; in "Processional" there are challenges to convention, there are fresh effects to be attempted, there are instances of antagonisms, bad taste and crass thinking, none of which make the task of the producers easy. The Theatre Guild's end of it comes off only passably. To produce such a new piece properly would require months of experiment. A new style of acting is often needed and new methods and resources must be found to express the exact key of the writing. But the play itself last night at the Garrick could at least be followed throughout, and sometimes very well, and the varying quality of it discerned. It provided a strange experience in the theatre, and one rich in possibilities and not to be forgotten. The first act went off with a good speed and lively interest, the scenes following went less well, sometimes inexpertly and full of the amateur. The Ku Klux scene dropped into a poor tone indeed. The last act picked up and rose at length to deep and poetic tragedy. George Abbott as Dynamite Jim started off only so so; he improved for the scenes where the man returns after being strung to a tree and cut down and rescued. In this scene the blind man finds again his mother and the girl who is to bear him a child. Here Mr. Abbott was excellent, and June Walker as the girl equally good. Donald Macdonald played well the newspaper man. Blanche Frederici, from her first entrance to the last curtain, gave a strong, profound performance. She had a quietness and a certain brutal pathos such as are not often seen on the stage. And to me she was all the more remarkable for my having seen her once in a Northampton stock company do the best playing that I had ever seen in an Oscar Wilde comedy. The crowds last night were flat and without any quality of ensemble.

The style of the production, with Mr. Gorelick's satirical settings, and of the writing of the play must be encountered rather than described. It was a mixture of the serious, the vaudeville, the halls of jazz, a twisting and turning of the idea, great matter stirred up, passion and blood and revolution thrown into the air and brought down again to the rattle and sigh of drums and sliding horns, life stirred, shaken, dared, outraged, dreamed of and made beautiful, ending always in jazz. And in the course of it all America came in for a spanking, the land where thought cannot be followed to any conclusion, the land of idiotic, smug mottoes, of cheap ideals, flags, mother's day, mock freedom, hypocrisy and so on. Now and again the satire on our country was profound, as when the black man says that some day we may have a colored President, "a cultured nigger with a fine singing and speaking voice." Sometimes the theme was singularly imaginative, as when they speak of the jazz melody of a bad woman in a small town. It was America well spanked by a writer who seemed a poet, a genius, a college sophomore not yet grown up and a dramatic journalist by turns.

And yet it is out of this very rawness and jazz suddenness and nervous commotion in America that these best qualities in "Processional" arise and are propelled into such lively power. The story itself is out of America, these strikers in a coal mining town of Pennsylvania, this jazzing girl, daughter of a Jewish shopkeeper who lives off the miners and soldiers alike, this man hunt, this blood, this travesty of law, this hand of capitalism, the mother, the child to be born, and finally the general peace and easygoing, half-mocked spirit of forgiveness, and the jazz wedding; all these are taken from the American scene. And the characteristic action of mind on the author's part, the spasms of beauty and feeling, the relapses into irony and fooling, the nonsense, the silliness, the passion and poetry—all these are akin, pleasantly or spitefully, to the souls of our flags, jokes, ideals, raptures, pieties and half-spoken depths of feeling.

"Processional" marks an advance beyond Mr. Lawson's hotly debated "Roger Bloomer" two years ago; the new play is on the whole more sustained and more deeply cut. The best of "Processional" is in the last act. The love scene there is between the blind man who has come to take his mother away with him and the girl who is going to have a child is beautiful, moving dramatic writing, as fine as any I have heard in many years.

"Processional" is uneven, not on the whole very well produced, and as a play conceived with varying degrees of taste, intelligence, insight and imagination. But it is a feather in the Theatre Guild's cap. As a drama it throws off astonishing suggestions of living stuff; it is full of strong, wounded, indomitable life. However unequal it may be, it is always creative and streaked with genius. It has thrusts of poetic power.

It has, as "Roger Bloomer" had, a re-markable gift of pathos, a strange, fresh, young, robust, half brutal pathos unique in our drama. And whatever else it is, it is never anything but theatre.

1925 Ja 13

Mr. Arlen's "Green Hat."

THE GREEN HAT, a play in four acts, by Michael Arlen. Staged by Guthrie Mc-Clintic; produced by A. H. Woods. At the Broadhurst Theatre.

A Lady's Maid.................Antoinette Parr
An English Reporter............John Buckler
Manager of the Hotel Vendome,
                                    Gustave Rolland
Dr. Conrad Masters.............A. P. Kaye
Gerald Havele March.........Paul Guilfoyle
Napier Harpenden............Leslie Howard
Major Gen. Harpenden........Eugene Powers
Hilary Townshend.................Gordon Ash
Iris Fenwick, nee March..Katharine Cornell
Venice Pollen.............Margalo Gillmore
Lord De Travest................John Redmond
A Lady........................Jane Saville
Turner ....Harry Lilford
Sister Virginia............Gwyneth Gordon
Sister Clothilde.................Anne Tonetti
Madelaine ....Florence Foster
Truble ....Harry Barfoot

From the pages of a novel that has enjoyed vast popularity, Iris March and Napier Harpenden, chief characters of "The Green Hat," passed last evening at the Broadhurst to a play that has enjoyed no less popularity in the several cities where it has been seen. The frustrated young woman who flitted uncannily through the feverish pages of Mr. Arlen's book came to the stage, in the flesh, with a speaking voice, in the person of Katherine Cornell. And her performance was a vibrant one, teeming with emotion that was always just suppressed and expressed in a voice of strange, haunting timbre. Miss Cornell is perfectly cast in this part. The sympathy that Iris March summoned from the audience was a tribute chiefly to her acting. She is well supported by a cast of excellent actors. Indeed, Mr. Arlen's play has been equipped auspiciously. The humming personality of the fable, which is never quite revealed, passes across the footlights.

Although novels do not always walk on to the stage without leaving a vast deal of baggage in the wings, "The Green Hat" seems to have become a play without losing much of the original romance. Iris March and her neurotic brother, Gerald, are both here, represented in the essential incidents. And, as one of the lines puts it, "the Marches are let off from nothing." Napier Harpenden, who always loved Iris, is here also, ably played by Leslie Howard; and his father, too, facing Iris more than once. Hilary Townshend,

played by Gordon Ash, runs through the drama as a sort of moral standard against which the various incidents are measured. He, it appears, is rather more to the play than to the novel. And, finally, the wistful Venice Pollen is here, bewildered and generous, acted appealingly by Margalo Gillmore. Thus, none of the chief characters of the novel is missing, save the "first person singular," who originally told the story. That purely technical part could scarcely be represented on the stage.

If Mr. Arlen has managed quite adroitly to fit his novel to the theatre he has not done it perfectly. The drama is singularly wordy, the story moves on sometimes clumsily, and the third act, in particular, made up largely of long conversations between various sets of two characters, serves its dramatic purpose without heightening the effect on the audience. If the drama were less intelligently acted the piece-meal structure would destroy the illusion. And, as in the novel, one finds that the individual must yield a great deal in order to come under the spell of the drama. For it is a curiously unhappy story, crowded with bitter, futile people who fly out at one another in frequent bad temper and often are most enigmatic in what they say. They suffer. The fates pursue Iris unrelentingly. But why? Whose fault is it—theirs or the gods'? Mr. Arlen seems to blame the gods. The blame may be nearer at home, in the characters themselves, in their want of a sense of humor, in their want of ordinary willpower. Must we believe them the victims of circumstances? To enjoy the play it is necessary to believe that, to blame the gods and to answer with a gesture of despair the questions "What is love?" or "What is happiness?" that Iris now and then propounds.

If we grant this initial impulse, we may catch strange beauties in the four acts of "The Green Hat." The first act reveals the sitting-room of a hotel suite in Deauville, the morning after Boy Fenwick's unexpected death by falling from a window. It had been his wedding night with Iris March. And he died, Iris explains, "for purity." This is an exceptionally quarrelsome act, Gerald March, Napier, Hilary and Sir Maurice all shouting angrily at one another. Even Iris cannot keep them at peace. The second act, set ten years later in Napier's London flat, carries the story one peg further. Napier has just given a dinner to Venice, whom he is to marry shortly, and to relatives and intimate friends. After they have gone Iris appears unexpectedly. Napier finds that their childhood love is not dead. The third act in a Paris convent nursing home recounts the episode of Iris's illness there, and Napier's coming at the doctor's request. The last act in Sir Maurice's country home follows closely the last chapter in Mr. Arlen's novel. Here Iris and Napier defy the family and propose to run off together. Then Napier discovers that his wife, Venice, is with child, and he returns. Iris leaves madly in her motor. A crash and a flash of light indicate the rest.

This bare summary of the story makes no account of the beauty of the play. For that beauty is more properly a spell, a series of shades, or a light shadow. Beyond the movements of the characters and the abnormal glow of the dialogue is a subdued tone-quality that serves as unity. Much of this comes from the personality of Katharine Cornell. As she plays the part Iris March just misses the happiness, the release, that she is seeking. And the Venice Pollen whom Margalo Gillmore portrays shares in that blind groping for reality. Leslie Howard's acting in the part of Hilary Townshend serves as the wall beyond which this futile questioning and hunting cannot go. His playing is an able background to the mood of the drama. Mr. Arlen's story is sombre, brave and frequently touching. The acting preserves these qualities.

1925 S 16

The Super-Civilized.

THE VORTEX, a play in three acts, by Noel Coward. At the Henry Miller Theatre.

Preston	George Harcourt
Helen Saville	Auriol Lee
Pauncefort Quentin	Leo G. Carroll
Clara Hibbert	Jeannette Sherwin
Florence Lancaster	Lillan Braithwaite
Tom Veryan	Alan Hollis
Nicky Lancaster	Noel Coward
David Lancaster	David Glassford
Bunty Mainwaring	Molly Kerr
Bruce Fairlight	Thomas A. Braidon

For two acts and part of a third Noel Coward's play, "The Vortex," put on at Henry Miller's Theatre last evening, amused by its caricature of very languid, languorous moderns and sometimes bored by its excessive, pointless conversation. Then came a stirring climax, played most intensely and earnestly by Lilian Braithwaite and Mr. Coward himself, while the audience held its breath. This climax was a new mood for a somewhat shiftless play, no doubt the logical conclusion to the uneven course of the story, but, for all that, tacked on at the end.

Nevertheless, having written it sincerely, Mr. Coward played it in the same spirit; Miss Braithwaite matched his earnestness with her own. And as the final curtain dropped, the audience burst into a storm of applause and cheers, and did not stir until Mr. Coward expressed his gratitude. That was a moving last act, sputtering with emotion; it involved issues vital to our day. Obviously, this playwright, who knows the theatre with an actor's understanding, had said exactly what he believed. The audience rewarded him accordingly.

If one were required to describe precisely what happened in the course of three acts of "Vortex" one must needs reply, "Not much in volume." Many another

piece, better contrived, has packed more action into the same space. A silly mother loses her lover to her son's fiancée. And the boy confesses to taking drugs. Nothing more than this, except that mother and son, alarmed at the discovery of this mutual rottenness, cling to each other in despair, both afraid. But the general pointedness of the entire piece and the genuine tone of the climax both create a nervous tension uncommon in the theatre. The issues involved were shorn of qualification; again, the playwright had said exactly what he believed. The ovation at the end was a tribute to his directness.

Much has been written and spoken of the absurd, weary, worldly persons who people the play. They are truly "flowers of evil," nourished, as one line of the play expresses it, on a civilization that makes rottenness so easy. The first act discovers a group of them in the exotic receiving room of the Lancasters' flat in London. Pauncefort Quentin, enervated to the extreme, runs on with his ridiculous effeminate manners of the trifles that clutter his life. "My dear, you are too tiresome," he drawls now and then. Clara Hibbert, a singer, "with such a splitting headache," bores the company with her petty woes. And when Mrs. Lancaster appears with her lover, Tom Veryan, the assembly, in their own words, is "too priceless, really." Their poses, affectations, bare duplicities that perhaps the playwright intended for castigation, proved to be amusing for their absurdity. Mr. Coward has laid their silly vanities on thick.

When the audience began to wonder whether anything were to happen in this opening act, Mrs. Lancaster's son, Nicky, came in unexpectedly with the startling news of his betrothal to Bunty Mainwaring. Mrs. Lancaster's protest was quickly silenced by an appeal to her vanity. For Bunty, it appears, thought Mrs. Lancaster beautiful. To her that was sufficient introduction; and when Bunty appeared she was cordially received. And good feeling continued until Tom Veryan walked in. Bunty and Tom were old friends. The playwright, who is also an actor, did not let the significance of this meeting escape. Whatever surprise there might be about his drama was over at the end of Act I. The second act in the hall of the Lancasters' country home serves to break off Nicky's engagement and to restore Tom to the arms of Bunty, where he had been before. There is a hint, too, in this act, of Nicky's drug habit. This last act, in Mrs. Lancaster's bedroom, brings mother and son together for a bitter understanding.

Mr. Coward has poked fun at these drifting, well-mannered, insolent moderns, and has called them to account for their uncleanness in purely theatrical fashion. Ten persons comprise his play; only five of them are essential to his story. The others fell in the background of his canvas with various forms of hypochondria and megalomania, scandal, effeminate wrangles, small-talk, dancing, ma-jong, telephone calls and other pieces of stage business. Clara Hibbert, who is in this social group but not of it, serves as a mile-post, to point a moral finger at their indulgences.

Mr. Lancaster represents, in his brief appearances, the humiliating position of a husband surrounded by light-headed people and an unfaithful, empty wife. And Bruce Fairlight, the dramatist invited to the week-end party, shows merely how lost an intelligent man is in such company. In this way Mr. Coward lays the premises for his polemic against a tendency of the times. Whether such people exist as he has described them, in groups as in this one, to the degree his play suggests, is not the function of a newspaper report. But by judicious use of the lumber of the theatre he has based on them a sensational play.

As Mr. Coward and Miss Braithwaite share the responsibilities of the stirring climax, so they share most of the responsibility of the play. They are on the stage almost continuously. As Mrs. Lancaster Miss Braithwaite was droll in the pretenses and vanities of the first two acts. Her bored tones at the telephone and her wilting poses supplied farce as well as comedy. It was interesting to see the woman and the mother emerge from all this social froth in the last act. The emotions which she had buried beneath artificiality then became genuine. Mr. Coward's part spared him the affectations of the other people in the play. From the first he seemed direct. His theatrical grimaces at the piano at the close of the second act made that a good curtain. And his nervous, wrought-up playing in the final act virtually by itself put over the play. Miss Kerr made a hard Bunty Mainwaring. Mr. Carroll was capital as Pauncefort Quentin.

1925 S 17

'NO, NO, NANETTE' FULL OF VIGOROUS FUN

Charles Winninger Takes Comedy Honors in New Play With Many Agreeable Tunes.

NO, NO, NANETTE, a musical comedy in three acts. Book by Otto Harbach and Frank Mandel, lyrics by Irving Caesar and Otto Harbach, and music by Vincent Youmans. At the Globe Theatre.
Pauline ....Georgia O'Ramey
Sue Smith.....................Eleanor Dawn
Billy Early.................Wellington Cross
Lucille ....Josephine Whittell
Nanette ....Louise Groody
Tom Trainor...................Jack Barker
Jimmy Smith............Charles Winninger
Betty ....Beatrice Lee
Winnie ....Mary Lawlor
Flora ....Edna Whistler

It was not difficult last night at the Globe Theatre to understand why "No, No, Nanette," for the last twelve and more months has proved so popular with the natives of Chicago and points West, East, North, South. For the New York premiere of that merry musical comedy, imported practically intact after its many successful months in Chicago, showed that it is a highly meritorious paradigm of its kind.

There is to "No, No, Nanette," let it be stated for the benefit of those who assemble such statistical material, a plot, in which for the final curtain Nanette, the heroine, embraces Tom, the hero. There is a score, with more familiar quotations from itself—one refers to "I Want to Be Happy and "Tea for Two"—than even "Hamlet." And there is an energetic cast of well selected comedians.

First honors among last night's participants should go to Charles Winninger. Mr. Winninger is no stranger hereabouts in any form of the popular theatre that could be named. To last night's audience, however, without a dissenting shout that was audible, Mr. Winninger gave the best performance of his career in the not entirely unfamiliar musical comedy rôle of the husband who has some incidents in his life that are not exactly firesidish. Mr. Winninger was extremely mirth-provoking and it was a more than hardened theatregoer who was not moved to near hysterics by his every appearance.

Louise Groody, the featured player, appeared to better advantage than has been her lot in an unfortunate number of recent years. She was lithe, tuneful and personable, and the attendants at last night's opening were in sympathy with the hero's desire to lead her to lawful wedlock, though they were unconcerned with the details of the plot leading to that consummation.

Georgia O'Ramey, as ever, was funny but unsupplied with sufficient material for her great comedy gifts. Wellington

Cross was well received as Mr. Winninger's associate in the career of duplicity. Josephine Whittell was handsomely statuesque and sang well an interesting "blues" number in the last act. And a young woman named Mary Lawlor was loudly, if a bit too enthusiastically, welcomed on her contribution of acrobatic dancing to the piece.

It is full of much vigorous merriment and many agreeable tunes, this "No, No, Nanette." And of Charles Winninger, who contributes to it whole quarter hours as pleasing as any that recent musical shows have had.

1925 S 17

'THE VAGABOND KING' LAVISH AND TUNEFUL

Dennis King Shines Amid Friml's Melodies and Reynolds's Lovely Scenes and Costumes.

THE VAGABOND KING, an operetta in two acts and six scenes, based on Justin Huntly McCarthy's "If I Were King." Music by Rudolf Friml, book and lyrics by Brian Hooker and W. H. Post. Staged by Max Figman; produced by Russell Janney. At the Casino Theatre.

Rene de Montigny	Robert Craik
Casin Cholet	Leon Cunningham
Margot	Katherine Hayes
Blanche	Merle Stevens
Isabeau	Vivian Kelley
Jean De Loup	Marius Rogati
Hugette Du Hamel	Jane Carroll
Jehanneton	Mimi Hayes
Guy Tabarie	Herbert Corthell
Tristan L'Hermite	H. H. McCollum
Louis XI	Max Figman
Francois Villon	Dennis King
Katherine De Vaucelles	Carolyn Thomson
Thibaut D'Aussigny	Bryan Lycan
Captain of Scotch Archers	Charles Carver
An Astrologer	Leon Cunningham
Lady Mary	Olga Treskoff
Noel Le Jolys	Charles Vaughn Holly
Oliver Le Dain	Julian Winter
Tolson D'or	Earl Waldo
The Queen	Tamm Cortez
The Hangman	Jack Rose
First Courtier	Walter Cross
Second Courtier	John Mealey
Harlequin	Joseph S. Smith
Pirouette	Helen Grenelle

They have made a superfine musical play out of "If I Were King." The musical play is "The Vagabond King," which came last night to the Casino—and they are James Reynolds, who designed the loveliest scenes and costumes the town has seen in recent years; Rudolf Friml, who has provided a score in his own best tradition; Dennis King, as extravagantly picaresque and tuneful a person as Villon himself could have desired to be in a 1925 representation; Russell Janney, who has done the producing with a lavish and yet selective hand, and a well-trained and well-voiced chorus.

There was ample opportunity, of course, in the tale Justin Huntley McCarthy fashioned these long years ago for a picturesque, moving and poetic operetta. The most attractive of history's rogues, the most persuasive of its smooth-tongued scoundrels, is this Francois Villon, and never more appealing, in all his degradation, than when he lifts his brandied eyes from his depths to the countenance of a beautiful lady. So it was last night, and the first-night audience broke into manly and sympathetic cheers when Master Villon, king for a day, threw the gauntlet of battle into Burgundy's face. The rabble of Paris would save the day, and it did, for as stirring a third-act climax as can be found between here and Verdun.

Mr. King, as aforementioned, was manly, sympathetic, personable and tuneful. Carolyn Thomson, his lady, sang in a manner that indicated that hers have been associations beyond those of the musical stage, but her acting at times unfortunately indicated the same thing. Herbert Corthell and Bryan Lucan were sufficiently comical and villainous, respectively. And Max Figman acted well the part of the king who put his all on the chance that his kingdom might be saved by a mad man, as had been his sire's by a mad woman.

But it is to the production and to the music that most of the laurels for last night's triumph must be awarded. The play is a distinguished addition to last year's series of better-class musical successes, in large part because of the color schemes of Mr. Reynolds and the tunes of Mr. Friml.

1925 S 22

Glorifying Marilyn Miller

SUNNY, a musical comedy in two acts. Music by Jerome Kern and book and lyrics by Otto Harbach and Oscar Hammerstein 2d. Staged by Hassard Short; produced by Charles Dillingham. At the New Amsterdam Theatre.

Mile. Sadie	Helene Gardner
Bally Hoo	Charles Angelo
Tom Warren	Paul Frawley
Jim Deming	Jack Donahue
Bob Hunter	William Ladd
"Weenie" Winters	Mary Hay
Sam	Cliff Edwards
Siegfried Peters	Joseph Cawthorn
Harold Harcourt Wendell-Wendell	Clifton Webb
Sue Warren	Esther Howard
"Sunny" Peters	Marilyn Miller
Marcia Manners	Dorothy Francis
Magnolia	Pert Kelton
Jane Cobb	Jackie Hurlburt
Quartermaster	Louis Harrison
First Ship's Officer	Elmer Brown
Second Ship's Officer	Abner Barnhart
Ship's Captain	James Wilson
Diana Miles	Jeanne Fonda
Millicent Smythe	Joan Clement
Groom	Don Rowen

George Olsen and His Band.

For three hours, without interruption, Marilyn Miller and "Sunny" skipped gayly across the stage at the New Amsterdam last evening, for even the single intermission was enlivened with a jazz band concert. And when "Sunny" was not "glorifying" the particularly luminous beauty of Miss Miller, it was "glorifying" a certain standard of finesse and virtuosity in the composition of musical entertainment. For although this expansive entertainment sets no new limits to show humor, music or beauty, the performance has been skillfully pulled together, produced with a touch of glamour, and it never runs bare or dry. "Sunny" is cut to a familiar stage pattern; its distinction rests in the general excellence of all that it tries to do.

Perhaps this quality is nowhere better illustrated than in the case of Marilyn Miller, star by all the well-known portents of the theatre, but never to the exclusion of the production as a whole. Despite all the advantages success has put in her way, she retains on the stage an agreeable air of modesty and young beauty. She never presumes upon the good nature of either the audience or her associates on the stage. In this extravaganza she appears first in spangles on a white horse, queen of an English circus. The comedy carries her across the ocean, a stowaway, marries her to the angular and comic Jack Donahue in an opulent wedding scene aboard ship, and finally contrives obligingly enough to pair her off with Paul Frawley, who, theatregoers will remember, sings quite as well as he appears behind the footlights. Through this bizarre journey Miss Miller sings, dances very prettily, burlesques a bit, according to direction. All such business is quite apart from her personal charm. She never takes advantage of it.

The first act of "Sunny" keeps close to its story. The curtain rises upon a circus scene, crowded with men and women spectators, freaks, barkers, snake charmers, and the following scene involves a colorful circus parade, replete to the band. Successive settings take the piece through the byways of Southampton, on board an ocean liner at sea, to a fashionable resort in the South, through groves, fields, woods, to a final hotel ballroom, where the mistakes of the evening are pleasantly put to rights. The costumes are seldom the artificial ones of the show world; usually they represent the attire of well-dressed persons of real life, and even the men outdo in correctness the etiquette described on earlier pages of the program.

Like the star and the costumes, the music blends well with the general scheme. If none of it haunts the memory with exotic motives or unusual patterns, it is usually agreeable. The major song bears the title of the show, and turns up several times in the course of the evening. It wears well. Another, entitled "Do You Love Me?" which Miss Miller sings two or three times, has more character. The book contributes to the volatility of the entertainment without affording much humor. That staple of the musical stage has been left rather to the devices of Jack Donahue, eccentric dancer, and comedian in the jargon of the streets, and other principals of the cast.

Jack Donahue twists himself rhythmically into many ridiculous, angular positions and creates most of the merriment in "Sunny." The rest of the humor comes generally by way of satire and grotesque stupidities. The best of this sort is the number by Mary Hay and Clifton Webb, equipped respectively with a tiny parasol and a tremendous pair of "Oxford bags." In an entertaining, bland manner they work themselves into an absurd frenzy, which is all the more ridiculous because it is pointless. Marjorie Moss and Georges Fontana follow a similar scheme. Toward the end of this final act, Miss Moss enacts a frightened Spanish dancer of low intelligence, with all the manner but none of the illusion of that alluring wanton. Her imitation of typical Chaplin expressions, even to the portrayal of nausea before a moving curtain, is as subtle as it is enjoyable. With all these unobtrusive numbers smoothly fitted into the production, "Sunny" provides tasteful, unaffected entertainment, an appropriate background to set off the principal performer.   **1925 S 23**

Correction.

In the review of "Sunny," printed in these columns on Wednesday morning, confusion in names robbed Miss Pert Kelton of credit for one of the most amusing numbers in that production. The enthusiasm expressed for the burlesque Spanish dancing and the mimicking of Charlie Chaplin belongs entirely to her.

1925 S 27

Showing Up the Show Business

THE BUTTER AND EGG MAN, a comedy in three acts, by George S. Kaufman. Staged by James Gleason; produced by Crosby Gaige. At the Longacre Theatre.

Joseph Lehman................Robert Middlemass
Jack McClure.....................John A. Butler
Fanny Lehman................Lucille Webster
Jane Weston.....................Sylvia Field
Mary Martin...................Marion Barney
Peter Jones....................Gregory Kelly
Waiter ....Tom Fadden
Cecil Benham.................Harry Neville
Bernie Sampson...............Harry Stubbs
Peggy Marlowe................Eloise Stream
Kitty Humphreys.........Puritan Townsend
Oscar Fritchie.................Denman Maley
A. J. Patterson ....George Alison

Treason broke out in the Longacre Theatre last evening when George S. Kaufman's merry comedy, "The Butter and Egg Man," held up his own esoteric profession to ridicule and kept the audience laughing all the while. "Butter and egg men," it now appears, are credulous gentlemen of wealth, from out of town, who "stake a show." They begin as wealthy men; they come out as best they can. Mr. Kaufman's play records the adventures of one fresh from Chillicothe, Ohio (pop. 15,830), who, by the grace of Providence and an alert playwright, came out quite well enough. Furthermore, it appears now that "butter and egg men" increase by geometrical progression, for this piece multiplied them rapidly through the evening while the fortunes of young Peter Jones blew hot and blew cold. But finally, it now appears for the first time that the "show" business is not highly organized on intelligent bases, directed by experts who know what they are doing. The "show" business, one gathers, is something of a gamble.

The amusement that Mr. Kaufman's play affords comes as much from dialogue as from invention. As a matter of fact, both elements are in evidence in equal proportion. And if "The Butter and Egg Man" satirizes the theatrical business, the dialogue satirizes the argot of the business man no less. The patter is bright, abounding in "wise cracks," and the lines are highly charged with sardonic, ill-mannered humor. The structure of the play is quite as full of surprise and entertainment. Toward the end of the second act and all through the third the situation constantly changes. Mr. Kaufman has not spread his story thin.

When Peter Jones, in the hopeful, timid person of Gregory Kelly, enters the office of the Lehmac Production, Inc., in the first act, with a little more than $22,000 in the bank, eager to enter the theatrical business on the strength of two amateur productions back home, Joseph Lehman, his derby on his head, his feet on his desk, bellows—not unkindly—"Sit down, sweetheart!" Indeed, through the complexities of this ill-

omened theatrical venture, "sweetheart" is the customary sobriquet. Mr. Jones naturally hesitates, especially since he has not seen the production he is considering for investment. But when he hears the plot vagaries of the Lehmac production, involving a brothel as well as heaven, betrayal, reconciliation and other bromides of the trade, all described convincingly by Joe Lehman in his shirt sleeves—when young Mr. Jones hears all this and sees a friendly smile on the stenographer's comely countenance he writes his check for $20,000. And now, while Heaven smiles, he becomes a producer!

As a matter of fact, however, he becomes merely a "butter and egg man." After the first performance in Syracuse every one recognizes the show as a "flop." And so it might have been if Joe Lehman, irritable after that dismal performance, had not insulted his fair stenographer. In a moment of quixoticism Jones rushes to her defense, and before he knows it has taken an option on the entire production. With these transactions as background, the surprises of "The Butter and Egg Man" commence.

Mr. Kaufman keeps the ball always in the air. The office scene in the first act, with Lehman and his partner convincing Jones of the future to be had if their production, is pointed and amusing. The impromptu meeting of the managers, star, director and adviser in a Syracuse hotel room after the flat initial performance is filled with banter and stinging retort. And the last act, in the New York office again, with Jones, now the principal owner of a genuine "hit" (which the police threaten to advertise by censoring), reselling his interest to the original owners for $100,000, while an attorney in the next office waits with a suit for plagiarism—this final act reverses itself several times with hilarious plot development. What is sauce for the goose is sauce for the gander. And when the original owners come in with proposals to buy back the production, it is now young Jones who bellows, "Sit down, sweetheart!"

The performance is boisterous and hurried. As Joseph Lehman, Robert Middlemass enacted a bully as well as a business man, overbearing, irritable and blunt. Denman Maley made of the second "butter and egg man" a frightened, bewildered yokel, who sees a bad omen in the crowd at the box office of his theatre. And when he finds that he has more than trebled his investment he is quite as much confused. "I guess that teaches me a lesson," he exclaims philosophically. As Joe Lehman's cynical, bland wife ("Just a pal!" says Joe sardonically), Lucille Webster was derisive and maddening. Sylvia Field gave depth and gentleness to the part of the stenographer.

Gregory Kelly did not overplay either the stupidity or the exhilaration in the part of Peter Jones. In fact, sometimes in the last act he seemed to underplay it by not sharpening the point of his lines. By the time this last act came around the transmigration of his soul was complete. By that time he knew the "show" business thoroughly. "All you have to do," he told his partner, "is to give the public what it wants." "But how do you know what that is?" retorted this uncertain fellow. For a genuine producer that question was simple also. "They always want the same," said Peter Jones with final authority.

1925 S 24

No Cause for Alarm.

CRAIG'S WIFE, a play in three acts, by George Kelly. Settings by Sheldon K. Viele; staged by George Kelly; produced by Rosalie Stewart. At the Morosco Theatre.

Miss Austen	Anne Sutherland
Mrs. Harold	Josephine Williams
Mazie	Mary Gildea
Mrs. Craig	Chrystal Herne
Ethel Landreth	Eleanor Mish
Walter Craig	Charles Trowbridge
Mrs. Frazier	Josephine Hull
Billy Birkmire	Arling Alcine
Joseph Catelle	Arthur Shaw
Harry	J. A. Curtis
Eugene Fredericks	Nelan Jaap

Nothing is more imperative than a quiet, dispassionate view of George Kelly's new drama, "Craig's Wife," which was acted somewhat sententiously at the Morosco Theatre last evening. For those who take seriously Walter Craig's little polemic, in the closing act, about the new economic structure of society, and women of the new order who place security above love, honor and obedience—those who take this as seriously as Walter Craig intends it will find new cause for alarm in a much too terrifying era. Mr. Kelly will be remembered as author of two broad and merry comedies, "The Torch-Bearers" and "The Show-Off." In "Craig's Wife" he has written an earnest study of character which he seems to confuse with the problem play. In the leading part, Chrystal Herne gives a splendid portrayal of an incredibly selfish woman. The collapse of the Craig home in the final act appears rather to be the result of the woman's personal mendacity. There is no cause for social alarm!

In fact, all the matter of this play seems purely the substance of her character. Early in the first act Mrs. Craig explains to her recently affianced niece that not love but security is the true reason for marriage. For her own part, she is concerned with "fixing things" for herself, securing the house for her own safekeeping, assuring herself of well-being for the rest of her mortal existence. Succeeding events in the piece prove that she has spoken the truth. In the first place, she keeps the house

in order, making the servants use the back stairs to save wear on the front, refusing her husband permission to smoke in the living room, forever dusting, complaining and straightening the room. In the second place, she resists all neighborhood visiting. "They shall make no thoroughfare of my house," she insists. In the third place, as her husband's aunt declares, she is gradually isolating him from his friends and enmeshing him entirely within her own net of purposes. Yes, as the aunt puts it, she is "incredibly selfish."

If Mr. Craig doubts it when his aunt outlines the whole case meticulously, he soon discovers the full truth for himself. It seems that one of Craig's friends had shot his wife and himself just the night before the play opened. Craig had been at that house during the evening, and had left before the tragedy occurred. Inadvertently and quite innocently, Mrs. Craig involves him in the affair by secretly calling the telephone number of the house where the shooting took place. When the police come to investigate she protects herself with lies. She also protects herself against her husband by keeping silent about her strategical error. In discovering it, he thinks he discovers likewise that she has no respect for him as a man and husband. After several long and bitter colloquies her husband leaves her in possession of the house she has gradually made her own—safe, secure, warm and sheltered, but no longer bustling with self-confidence.

As this long summary of the drama must imply, Mr. Kelly has written this play as seriously as once upon a time Pinero and Jones were writing, and perhaps Ibsen, too; and as Brieux was writing when he hammered together the structure of "Accused." From the moment when Miss Herne walks on as Mrs. Craig, cold, impassive, indomitable and cruel, the play settles down to serious business. The story is told throughout in long dialogues between Mrs. Craig and her niece, Mrs. Craig and her husband's aunt, and Mr. and Mrs. Craig alone. Rarely are there more than two people in action on the stage at once. And in consequence, the drama is constantly irritating with long, mordant speeches that seem to further the purpose little if at all. Moreover, the subsidiary threads of the plot have not been too skilfully interwoven with the main theme. When Mr. Kelly abandons the police episode in the second act, after promising untold, unknown effects with it in the first, he seems to have swung a hammer to crush an eggshell.

At the close of the second act, Mr. Craig for the first time asserts his manhood within his own walls by wantonly smashing a little statue held sacred by his wife. He also flicks cigarette ashes and throws matches on the floor in a wild frenzy of masculine prerogative. Somehow the episode, a vital one to the themes, comes off purely as buffoonery.

In other words, Mr. Kelly has not built up this character study, joining cause to effect like the pseudo-philosopher in "Candide," smoothly and economically, with sure touch, with consistent control of his medium.

The response of the audience at the close of the performance, however, testified to his sincerity. For here is an American theme, equipped with all the machinery of American life, developed by a playwright who has given evidence before of his interest in the local scene for dramatic composition. And if he has not built his play with perfect skill, he has observed his subject matter accurately and transcribed it honestly in terms of the theatre. Mrs. Craig's concern with appearances, her terror of losing control of the situation and finding herself thrown out upon the world without means of support, her interest in her own future, her suspicions, her fear of neighbors prying within her house, her high-handed treatment of servants, her sense of the complexity of existence—all these traits have been accurately observed, and emerge in the performance. Perhaps they are typical of no particular place or period in civilized life. Despite their American cloak, they are essentially character. It is to Mr. Kelly's credit that he has discovered them in a drama.

Miss Herne's performance is a smooth, brittle character study. One feels in her acting a strong, malignant force sweeping through every scene. From beginning to end it seldom varies, a solid substance of smiling, overbearing, relentless duplicity. Mr. Trowbridge as Craig is affable and forceful. If his interpretation is less vital, it is no less intelligent; and it is consistently creditable. As a well-meaning, sentimental neighbor, Miss Hull is entertaining in the first act.

1925 O 13

INA CLAIRE RADIANT IN LONSDALE COMEDY

Roland Young and A. E. Matthews Also Play Flawlessly in Pleasant, Lively Drama.

THE LAST OF MRS. CHEYNEY, a comedy in three acts, by Frederick Lonsdale. Staged by Winchell Smith and Lewis Broughton; produced by Charles Dillingham. At the Fulton Theatre.

Charles ....A. E. Matthews
George ....Alfred Ayre
Lady Joan Houghton...........Nancy Ryan
Willie Wynton..................Lionel Pape
Lady Mary Sindley,.......Audrey Thompson
Maria ....Helen Haye
Mrs. Wynton..................Mabel Buckley
Lord Arthur Dilling..........Roland Young
Lord Elton....................Felix Aylmer
Mrs. Cheyney ....Ina Claire
Mrs. Webley..................Winifred Harris
William......................Henry Mowbray
Jim ....Edwin Taylor
Roberts ....Leslie Palmer

Ina Claire returned to town last night at the Fulton Theatre in "The Last of Mrs. Cheyney," which calls itself a comedy but which is really a pleasant melodrama sugared with typical paradigms of the newer English school of epigrammatical writing. The piece itself met with the obvious approval of a distinguished audience, and there was even more of an enthusiastic response to the flawless playing of Miss Claire, Roland Young and A. E. Matthews, her two leading associates.

Frederick Lonsdale is the author of the new play, which even now is playing in London with Gladys Cooper in the rôle that here is Miss Claire's. Mrs. Cheyney in it is an attractive young woman whose particular easiest way has been the development of a business association with a gang of crooks, without, happily, any impairment of the virtue required of the heroine of a Broadway comedy. Her enterprise and associations lead her as a guest to a country home at which are both a pompous and dull English lord who has offered her honorable marriage and a younger and cleverer English lord to whom marriage is only the remotest of the alternatives he has to suggest.

Through a change in the guest rooms —they are changed rather awkwardly and by Mr. Lonsdale—Mrs. Cheeney arrives at dead of night, on business bent, not in the room of a wealthy lady who owns pearls but of the younger of her suitors. He gives her her choice between exposure and what he now cynically no longer believes she could ever have regarded as her shame. She chooses exposure. Whereupon the elderly suitor at once withdraws his offer of marriage, in disgust, and the younger successfully presses his, in admiration. It is an interesting and fast-moving tale, well-developed, in terms of the theatre.

Miss Claire, Mr. Young and Mr. Matthews gave extremely excellent performances. All three have the quality of bestowing importance and dignity upon their most casual utterances, and there were utterances last night, from the text of Mr. Lonsdale, that were at the least most casual. The audience, in a state of happy admiration of the acting, was respectful even when things were banal and was loudly appreciative when something brilliant and clever and consequential was supplied to supplement the players' gift of importance and dignity. This was fortunately frequently the case.

Miss Claire was radiantly lovely and in supreme command of the impishness and slyness and cuteness that were in her rôle. Mr. Young, the younger and eventually successful suitor, was smooth in his phrasings and most engaging as a character who was not without his bounderisms. Mr. Matthews, a glorified and glamorous butler and the head of the crime syndicate with which Miss Claire allied herself, made quite plausible the author's assumption that all the women of the play should adore him, and brought the requisite cynicism and weariness to his interpretations.

An enjoyable evening is to be spent at the new play. Those who find pleasure in Mr. Lonsdale's fine writing and the run of his "Spring Cleaning" and "Aren't We All?" would indicate the existence of such an audience, will find almost an over-abundance of good things in "The Last of Mrs. Cheeney." To the others it will still remain engaging, a lively play with an interesting and well-told story and a cast headed by three of the most competent comedians in the English-speaking theatre.

1925 N 10

Ibsen in Revival.

THE MASTER BUILDER, a play in three acts, by Henrik Ibsen. For special matinees on Tuesdays and Fridays at Maxine Elliott's Theatre.

Knut Brovik	Sydney Machet
Ragnar Brovik	J. Warren Sterling
Kaia Fosli	Ruth Wilton
Halvard Solness	Egon Brecher
Aline Solness	Alice John
Doctor Herdal	William Raymond
Hilda Wangel	Eva Le Gallienne

In the second act of "The Master Builder," revived yesterday afternoon at Maxine Elliott's Theatre, Halvard Solness confesses that no corner of his character is safe from Hilda Wangel. And according to the same figure, no corner of "The Master Builder" is safe from Eva Le Gallienne, who plays Hilda in a transcendant performance, and who is ably supported by a company of actors quite worthy of their parts. There is little but the skill of actor and playwrighting to aid them in their task. The two settings serve the occasion sparingly, and the costuming (notably in the case of Miss Le Gallienne) does not enrich the illusion. Furthermore, this odd moment in the time schedule of the theatre is in no respect alluring. But the play comes off in a splendid performance; particularly throughout the final act, it is most exhilarating. A second performance will be given on Friday afternoon, and others will follow on succeeding Tuesdays and Fridays according to the response of the public.

"The Master Builder" belongs to the last four Ibsen plays, a group quite by themselves, more subjective and more searching than the two preceding groups. And of these four it is the best; as it is in many artistic respects the best of Ibsen plays. For although the dialogue is in prose, the theme is poetry, pulsating with emotion, regret, fear and resolution. Just how closely the symbolism interprets Ibsen's own life, no one can say too confidently. But the three stages in the master builder's career doubtless represent the three stages in Ibsen's career in the theatre; the character of Hilda Wangel recalls two or three young women who contributed to Ibsen's philosophy in much the same way; Solness's fear of the younger generation of builders may suggest Ibsen's own turn of mind at this period; and the duty-mad Aline follows closely Ibsen's conception of the unimaginative responsibilities of society. Behind the bare structure of the drama glows the passion of a philosophical poet who never got what he wanted. And apart from all this symbolism, "The Master Builder" is a play in its own right, chronicling the incident of an old man driven beyond his own powers by a mad, ecstatic young woman fresh from the mountains. It has the superb quality of establishing contact with the audience on universal principles; the playgoer can recognize in it whatever his own experience affords.

The story in itself is essentially a cruel one. Solness's great success as a builder has been costly in human happiness. The start came from the destruction by fire of his wife's family homestead on whose ruins he began to build rapidly. Thus, his career has cost his wife all the consolation of family heirlooms, and, in less degree, the consolation of two babies who died after the fire. Solness has drained also the life of Knut Brovik, formerly an architect, now in the master builder's employ; and he has successfully resisted the advancement of his fellow craftsman. During the space of the play, he lets Brovik die without the comfort of foreseeing his son's chance as a builder on his own; he cuts his wife to the quick with the vagaries of his temperament, and he casts off a devoted servant once her use has been superseded. Indeed, he finds no match for his own strength until the mad Hilda swoops down from the mountains, and drains him of life while she supplies the one impulse necessary to his progress as an inspired genius.

Miss Le Gallienne revealed every facet in the character of Hilda Wangel. Her entrance, knapsack in place, dressed in muddy tramping togs, was bold to the extreme. Sparing of gesture and mere artistry, she created a vibrant illusion of strength, directness and eerie perception. For the part of Hilda is not confined within the limitations of this workaday world, obedient to the rules governing phlegmatic characterization. When every one in the last scene mourns Solness as dead, she is still transfixed, gazing with ecstacy into the heights where for a moment he stood on the tower of his new house, high above the plain. For her, he has fulfilled his existence; the incident of death does not matter. Miss Le Gallienne's performance expressed that preternatural transcendance beyond the physical directions of the play.

As Halvard Solness, Mr. Brecher was no less direct and frank in his expression; and the exotic nuance of the part was no doubt considerably enhanced by the foreign touch to his accent. He portrayed Solness as a profound genius, subject to the injustices of his own personality, indifferent to everything save that which furthered his purpose. One could understand this man without wasting sympathy upon him; and also without conceding to him the license he demanded. For if Mr. Brecher's splendid performance missed in any detail, it was in not making the cruelties of Solness's career seem merely necessities.

Miss John was soft and gracious as the unhappy wife of the master builder; her acting had pity as well as pain. Miss Wilton made a frail bookkeeper, cast off impatiently by Solness when Hilda appeared. Mr. Sterling as the apprentice draftsman, and Mr. Machet played their parts quite as intelligently.

1925 N 11

Four Nuts in "The Cocoanuts."

Perhaps for the first time in their rough-and-tumble lives, the four Marx brothers kept respectable company last evening at the Lyric Theatre, where George S. Kaufman's new musical comedy, "The Cocoanuts," was put on. In a broad and spacious Florida hotel, decorated with the most exquisite taste, and in an airy patio, these low comedians associated on equal terms with people of refinement. For the new comedy is splendidly decked out with costumes of such brilliance that the eye fairly waters; with melodies by Irving Berlin; with Antonio and Nina de Marco for dancers; with Jack Barker and Mabel Witlee for singers; with clog-steppers, in sum, with the sublime beauty of a musical comedy set in Florida. Amid this opulent array the Marx brothers go through their antics as before.

THE COCOANUTS, a musical comedy in two acts and eight scenes. Book by George S. Kaufman, music and lyrics by Irving Berlin. Settings by Woodman Thompson; costumes by Charles Le Maire; staged by Oscar Eagle and Sammy Lee; produced by Sam H. Harris. At the Lyric Theatre.
Jamison.....................Zeppo Marx
Eddie........................Georgie Hale
Mrs. Potter...............Margaret Dumont
Harvey Yates..........Henry Whittemore
Penelope Martyn.........Janet Velie
Polly Potter..............Mabel Withee
Robert Adams..............Jack Barker
Henry W. Schlemmer.......Groucho Marx
Willie the Wop.............Chico Marx
Silent Sam.................Harpo Marx
Hennessy.................Basil Ruysdael
Frances Williams......Frances Williams

In the first act they seem rather thin against the splendor of the general comedy scheme, and only occasionally do they enact the rapid, organized buffoonery that was so painfully funny in these parts last season. In the second act, however, they rise to the surface. Groucho Marx keeps up a steady rattle of patter; Harpo goes through his lazy chicaneries and Chico performs once again at the piano.

At the same time that Florida is developing its land, to the annoyance of the rest of the civilized world, it is apparently developing a restful, colorful type of architecture and decoration. The first scene of "The Cocoanuts" represents the lobby of the hotel where all these revelries occur, on generous, restful lines. And for the first moments of the comedy, ladies and gentlemen of the chorus dance and sing here. Then the earnest, thin, not unkindly face of Groucho Marx, bearing the inevitable cigar, appears tentatively on the stairs, and the fun begins. Through the rest of the comedy the Marx brothers retain their familiar rôles—Groucho in the shabby cutaway, with the inadequate spectacles; Chico with the loud clothes and immigrant's accent; Harpo with the flaring wig, and the vulgar leers and grimaces far more effective than words; and Zeppo representing by contrast the decent young man.

And, as formerly, the voluble Groucho keeps up a heavy musketry of puns and gibes, twisting everything into the vulgar, unimaginative jargon of the shopkeeper. To him the eyes of his love "shine like the pants of a blue serge suit." When he steps down to the local jail to bail out a $2,000 prisoner, he finds a sale in progress and captures his prey for $1,900. And to him "jail is no place for a young man. There is no advancement." There are puns on a "poultry" $1,000, and a request to the lovers that they transfer their caresses to the "mushroom." Nothing is more amusing than the rapidity with which Groucho reduces everything to the stale bromides of the serious-minded merchant; and the speed with which he twists a burlesque probe for a missing shirt into a tailoring shop where he is measuring the victim for a suit of clothes and trying to sell him a pair of socks. All this with the seriousness of the instinctive man of business, bent upon doing his job well, and with such baffling twists in allusion that the audience is frequently three jumps behind him.

For the organized low comedy in which these brothers specialize, the current skit affords only one or two numbers, fewer than in their last appearance. Harpo shaking down his victims for watches and purses, stealing the detective's shirt from his chest and a guest's vest and coat from his back, or taking dictation on the cash register and calmly tearing the guest's mail into pieces and ripping up the telegrams as fast as they come—all these broad antics are particularly funny. In the first act the comedy is slow in starting, and is less loud and less funny than an expectant audience had hoped it to be. Throughout the second act the comedians are frequently on the stage and in good form. And yet the blatancy and fury of which they are capable do not reach the familiar extremes.

But "The Cocoanuts" surrounds them with better entertainment. Mr. Berlin's music is always pleasing. The number entitled "A Little Bungalow," sung by Miss Witlee and Mr. Barker, is especially melodious. The chorus number entitled "Five o'Clock Tea," runs swiftly with a charming theme. Most of the dance numbers, moreover, have an imaginative and elusive grace that are uncommon to the run of musical comedy. And Frances Williams sings the blues and shivers through a Charleston number.

According to the fashion of musical comedy, "The Cocoanuts" occasionally merges into ensemble numbers. At the close of the first act Groucho Marx, on the auctioneer's stand, conducts with all the enthusiasm of the development man and the sly candor of the comedian a sale of Florida real estate lots, some of them in the most exclusive residential district where no one lives at all. The second act resolves a probe into an old-time burlesque minstrel show with incidental clowneries and concludes with a garden fête with the skipjack comedians in ill-becoming Spanish vestments, with Chico "shooting" the piano keys and Harpo fooling languorously with the harp. One must not forget the brilliance of the patter and joking; it is never commonplace. Nor, as a matter of form, must one neglect to mention the existence of a plot.

1925 D 9

1926

Symbolism in an O'Neill Tragedy.

THE GREAT GOD BROWN, a play in a prologue, four acts and an epilogue, by Eugene O'Neill. Directed by Robert Edmond Jones; settings by Mr. Jones; produced by Macgowan, O'Neill & Jones. At the Greenwich Village Theatre.

William A. Brown	William Harrigan
His father	Milano Tilden
His mother	Clifford Sellers
Dion Anthony	Robert Keith
His father	Hugh Kidder
His mother	Eleanor Wesselhoeft
Margaret	Leona Hogarth
Cybel	Anne Shoemaker
Police Captain	Ellsworth Jones
Client	Seth Kendall

Some draftsmen, committeemen, &c.

By J. BROOKS ATKINSON.

What Mr. O'Neill has succeeded in doing in "The Great God Brown," now to be seen at the Greenwich Village Theatre, is obviously more important than what he has not succeeded in doing. He has not made himself clear.

But he has placed within the reach of the stage finer shades of beauty, more delicate nuances of truth and more passionate qualities of emotion than we can discover in any other single modern play. The symbolism inherent in all his plays is now carried to its ultimate conclusion; dramatic substance is spun into fragile bands of meaning; the abstract conflicts of life are transmuted and thrice refined. By use of masks, personalities are distinguished from appearances; two realities are murdered and lost, while one distorted image of a being, a surface mask, remains apparently immortal. From such piercing, critical probing of the soul is this drama constructed.

All this is patent in the current performance without being consistently intelligible. From the Olympian point of view, rather than the Broadway, one of Mr. O'Neill's chief signs of strength is his absorption in the ideal as opposed to the practical. It is not his fashion to bargain with his dreams in the interests of black and white playwrighting. And now that he has striven to increase the stature of drama so that it may catch the full richness of his emotion, he puts a responsibility upon his audience too great and far too flattering. For two acts "The Great God Brown" makes its esoteric points with translucent clarity, and meanwhile pours a flood of powerful feeling across the footlights. When the masks for each individual increase from one to two in the remaining acts, and quick shifts are made from one to the other or from mask to real flesh, and the play cuts loose entirely from reality, the result is quite bewildering. Mr. O'Neill will not blame his audience for begging the key to all this diffusion of figure; an an explanatory note in the program might easily make thorough understanding possible. Indeed, if every line in the play did not ring with passion and sincerity, the complexity of this mode of expression might engender impatience in the mind of the playgoer. Even now it will certainly give rise to choleric differences of opinion. But a playwright may do whatever he chooses; the audience can register only its approval or disdain. In the presence of so much genuine honesty of purpose, one willingly concedes Mr. O'Neill the benefit of the doubt and merely observes that "The Great God Brown" is in large part inarticulate.

To place within the limits of a newspaper review an intelligible account of the details of so involved a play is, of course, quite impossible. On the surface, "The Great God Brown" is a tragedy of love. Billy Brown loves Margaret. She, however, loves Dion Anthony, and marries him. It is Mr. O'Neill's contention that she loves not the real Dion Anthony, a sensitive, bruised being, but a distorted image of Dion, a mocking, cynical surface appearance represented by Dion's mask. Beyond these simple facts, the substance of "The Great God Brown" rests within the various personalities that come and go by clapping on or removing the masks. Only one of these personalities remains virtually constant—the mask of Dion that Margaret marries, and that she loves even when ultimately Billy Brown wears it. Once in the prologue Dion removes it in the ecstasy of passion; but Margaret recoils. She does not recognize him nor trust him again until he wears the appearance to which she is attached. Once long after their marriage Dion reveals his true self to her hungrily. But Margaret draws back affrighted. She never sees him unmasked again. Only a prostitute, the symbol of Mother Earth, sees Dion unmasked and keeps unmasked herself in his presence.

By such a device Mr. O'Neill multiplies the varieties of human emotion latent in his theme, and suffuses the whole in affecting tenderness. The contrasts between Dion seeking release for his soul agony in the sublime majesty of Scriptural instruction and Dion protecting himself with perverse cynicism in the presence of his wife are indescribably poignant. Complications set in, however, when Dion dies and wills his mask to Billy Brown, who has all these years cherished his love for Margaret. When Billy claps on Dion's mask, Margaret is quite deceived. And happier, for behind the familiar appearance is more warmth and youth than she had known in Dion. Up to this point, Billy has gone through the play unmasked. But now, in addition to Dion's mask, he fashions another mask representing himself in the familiar status of a successful business man. With bewildering versatility he changes from one to the other according to his absorption in business or domestic affairs, while the real Billy, in the flesh, unmasked, fades and finally dies. To recount further complications in this theme would confuse an already confused summary of the play. Mr. O'Neill has wrung every drop of passion from his drama and characterization.

In the larger sphere of form "The Great God Brown" is a work of art, with a beginning, a middle and an end, with character development, and with a penetrating criticism of life. By predicating the tragedy with a prologue that introduces the parents of the main characters, and by appending to it an epilogue that reveals Margaret as a middle-aged woman and her three boys now grown to maturity, Mr. O'Neill gives his play the sweep of universality and the continuity of successive generations. Nor is the play itself the chronicle of three individuals.

In the concluding act, when Billy Brown has breathed his last, an investigating policeman demands the victim's name, "Man," says Cybel conclusively. And "How d'yah sell it?" the policeman demands as the final words of the play. For Mr. O'Neill does not write in one key. In the dialogue, as well as in the characterization, he modulates his theme freely. From passages of winged poetry he shifts quickly to mordant irony; from the abstract he passes to the concrete without missing a beat. And the implications of "The Great God Brown" carry us far afield among the cruelest uncertainties of a pleading, sceptical mind. Obscure or clear, "The Great God Brown" is packed with memorable substance.

In a less sensitive performance, the play would be quite beyond human understanding. The principal actors have been all well chosen. The personal radiance of Miss Hogarth in the part of Margaret contrasts wonderfully with the phlegmatic countenance of her mask. Similarly in the part of Dion, Mr. Keith embuses his acting of the real man with an interior distress that sets off the surface mockery of his mask. Mr. Harrigan gives body to the part of Billy Brown. As Cybel, the prostitute and the symbol of Mother Earth, Miss Shoemaker plays with an extraordinary pity, understanding and gentleness.

1926 Ja 25

Melodrama of the Orient.

THE SHANGHAI GESTURE, a "melodrama of the Orient" in four acts, by John Colton. Staged by Guthrie McClintic; settings by Frederick W. Jones 3d; produced by A. H. Woods. At the Martin Beck Theatre.

Caesar Hawkins............Cyril Keightley
Lin Chi....................Conrad Cantzen
Prince Oshima............C. Henry Gordon
Poppy ....Mary Duncan
Mother Goddam..............Florence Reed
Ching Chang Mary..........Lquiè Emery
Ni Pau (Lost Petal).........John Bourdelle
Ex-Envoy Mandarin Koo Lot Foo,
                          Langdon Bruce
Sir Guy Charteris............McKay Morris
Sir John Blessington........Henry Warwick
Lady Blessington.......Eva Leonard Boyne
M.' Le Compte de Michet.
                      William Worthington
Mme. Le Comptesse de Michot,
                          Evelyn Wight
Mrs. Dudley Gregory........Vera Tompkins
Dudley Gregory.............Henry von Rhau
Don Querebro d'Achuna.C. Haviland Chappell
Donna Querebro d'Achuna..Margarita Orlova

By J. BROOKS ATKINSON

What little story Mr. Colton has for "The Shanghai Gesture," put on last evening at the Martin Beck, he spreads thin and unskillfully through four highly embellished acts. For the rest, he serves up a piquant sauce of life in the Shanghai underworld among the habitués of the licensed quarter, of white degeneracy and exotic excitations in general, with esoteric insinuations masquerading half-respectfully in the rich vestments of Chinese scenes. As the crafty Chinese Mother Goddam, keeper of the best-known house in the district, and clearing house for stupendous State and commercial secrets, Florence Reed plays the monotonous-voiced, sly Oriental in the idiom of the melodramatic stage. Bronchial troubles before the footlights and incidental music behind the scenes both contrived to make the play difficult to hear last evening. But after the showiest scenes the audience applauded enthusiastically, as though it had got what it expected and sought.

All the action of "The Shanghai Gesture" passes between noon and midnight on one Chinese New Year's Day at the "far-famed house" of Mother Goddam, 17 San Kaisu Road, Shanghai, China. That sobriquet she had picked up among the jolly tars of the American Navy and retained as evidence of her sense of humor. At the close of the second act the plot begins to emerge. After the fish course of a dinner given to Sir Guy Charteris, taiman of the British-China Trading Company, with all of the most respected people of the city as guests, Mother Goddam reminds him of one thing he had forgotten—that she is the woman who twenty years ago had lived with him, believing his purely conventional promises of marriage. In short, he had made her what she was that night.

For the time being Mother Goddam appears to have the upper hand and to be enjoying the full sweetness of a revenge planned for long, cruel twenty years. Alas! this venerable dowager of the licensed quarter has unwittingly smitten her own head. In the next act it appears that one of the revelers in her house that New Year's night is her own daughter by Sir Guy Charteris, and, for the time being, in the none too innocent company of Prince Oshima of Japan. And that is how it comes about that Mother Goddam kills her own daughter in a lurid final scene and brings the curtain down to a threnody of sobs and lamentations.

In the meantime, "The Shanghai Gesture" introduces as by-play the intimacies of such a background in the Orient. In the second act, as pièce de résistance of the dinner, a young English girl is sold to the highest bidder in a rabble of impatient junk-men, and Mother Goddam as auctioneer seems at that moment to plumb the nadir depths of depravity. Yet stay! Even this woman of professional evil retains her personal ideals. In the next act she washes her cheek, rather ostentatiously, where it has been kissed by Prince Oshima's unbridled and thoroughly intoxicated inamorata. In spite of these divertissments, however, "The Shanghai Gesture" never quite cloaks the barrenness of its plot and story. For most of the pyrotechnics go off all by themselves, with scant relation to the fable.

In costumes and scenery Mr. Colton's play has been richly adorned. "The Grand Red Hall of Lily and Lotus Roots" for the second act, "The Little Room of the Great Cat" for the third, and especially "The Green Stairway of the Angry Dragon" for the fourth, are lavish in their traditional gold ornaments, their regal panelings, their mosaics and Chinese reds. The series of latticed stairs and platforms in the final scene, climbing to dizzy heights above the stage, are beautifully designed and created. And the Oriental costumes, spangled and brocaded, fairly bewilder the eye. For so jejune a drama, the scenic investiture becomes sheer luxury.

Miss Reed's part has been written in one key of restraint, dignity and sly humor. Although she plays it faithfully throughout, four acts of this unrelieved even temper become rather tedious. As Sir Guy Charteris, Mr. Morris plays the cynical and jaded English degenerate according to formula. Miss Duncan goes through the maudlin scenes of her part as the sinful daughter with the familiar bravura. Mr. Gordon acts well the Japanese Prince. A large cast of hangers-on, dinner guests, coolies, servants and businesslike "apprentice mice" prove adequate to their incidental responsibilities.

1926 F 2

Barrie in Revival.

WHAT EVERY WOMAN KNOWS, a play in four acts, by Sir James M. Barrie. Staged by Lumsden Hare; revived by Lee Shubert and William A. Brady. At the Bijou Theatre.

John Shand	Kenneth MacKenna
Alick Wylie	Dennis Cleugh
David Wylie	Eugene Weber
James Wylie	Jack Terry
Maggie Wylie	Helen Hayes
Mr. Venables	Lumsden Hare
Countess de la Briere	Adelaide Prince
Lady Sybil Lazenby	Rose Hobart
Maid	Dora Micawber
Butler	Alfred Pinner
First Elector	A. O. Huhan
Second Elector	Vincent York
Third Elector	Harry Hatch

By J. BROOKS ATKINSON.

If the revival of Sir James M. Barrie's comedy, "What Every Woman Knows," mounted at the Bijou last evening, generally misses the crispness of so thoroughly Scotch a fantasy, Miss Hayes in the leading rôle makes adequate compensation by several moments of superlative poignancy. At the close of the third act, for instance, after the canny Maggie has boldly put all her eggs in one basket by manoeuvring a renegade husband into a fortnight with his hollow-pated and titled butterfly—at the close of this act Maggie's natural emotions overpower her for the first time. In such moments the naturalness of Miss Hayes's expression, always quite frank and fairly artless, proves thoroughly affecting; and once or twice the current revival makes this profound test of her talents. By experiencing the emotion herself she conveys it across the footlights in direct and equal proportion. These are moments of genuine beauty. Last evening the audience applauded enthusiastically these two or three scenes that are so moving in their tangle of womanly emotions and that are heightened perceptibly by Miss Hayes's acting.

Notwithstanding these deeply stirring scenes Miss Hayes is not yet quite up to the interpretation of so fullbodied a part. And although her abilities have broadened and taken firm root since her first diaphanous and fragile embodiments of Barriesque creation, this Maggie is a woman of tougher substance than Miss Hayes communicates. In brief, she is a woman of uncommon spirit. Consider the firm decisions her career requires of her when only her intuition and cosmic wisdom point the way. In the first place, she risks her chances of marriage on a boorish, poor-student railway-hand in the strangest of bargainings. At least twice in the remainder of the play she deliberately puts all her riches in a single leaky bottom and prays that her silly ship may ride out the cruelest gales. These incidents, as well as many sharp turns in the dialogue, portray Maggie as a high-spirited Scotch lassie, daring, proud and sometimes arrogant. In general Miss Hayes relies too much upon her extraordinarily appealing charm in the portrayal of so real and complex a personage. Her most appealing scenes transmute this same charm into a tenderness quite beyond description.

As John Shand, the obtuse and ambitious husband whose egotism blinds him to Maggie's superb wisdom, Mr. MacKenna misses the stiffness and almost militant pride upon which the drama largely depends. By his definition John emerges as rather too much a gentleman, too much a man of ordinary understanding. Certainly the enjoyment of the revival would be greatly enhanced by a rough, ambitious, thoroughly boorish Scotchman as humorless and stubborn as Barrie conceived him. Like Miss Hayes, Mr.

MacKenna proves most effective in the emotional scenes. When in the last act the light of truth begins to penetrate even his thick, well-nigh impervious breast, Mr. MacKenna's John Shand matches the playwright's conception perfectly. For in this scene John Shand resembles an ordinary man, responsive to ordinary appeals, and Mr. MacKenna plays him throughout the comedy in much the same spirit.

Of the remaining actors, Mr. Hare as Venables gives the most sympathetic interpretation. As David Wylie, the masterful butler, Mr. Weber is amusing and forceful. In general the performance needs molding and needs interpretation of the sly nuances of Sir James's peculiar humor. Although the production may be fairly described as serviceable, and last evening kept the audience generally entertained, it loses a good deal of the lustre of the playwright's composition.

In a sense, however, Barrie's plays are proved against acting, as the delight in reading them may indicate. For they fit the theatre neatly, they visualize action, and the dialogue glows throughout. Of course, what every man of common sense knows about "What Every Woman Knows", is that the dramatist's conception is obvious buncombe. For this comedy, written by a man, is no less than a libel on all mankind, yielding to women all the glorious achievements of the sterner, more hirsute sex. Worse: it reveals the men as oblivious of feminine guidance.

In spite of the obvious perversions of fact that one can scarcely regard with intellectual equanimity, and that as obviously strike to the very roots of our golden civilization, Sir James makes out a case not to be cast petulantly aside. And while the more flamboyant playwrights are indecently anatomizing their quivering souls in public, this tranquil, sentimental comedy proves more than commonly delightful. One hesitates to add that it is cheerful. Or that it is entertaining. For such direct qualities are no longer the fashion. Apparently "What Every Woman Knows" has not been played here in regular engagements since the Maude Adams revival of 1909. Even in the present mixed performance, it is piquant and enjoyable.

1926 Ap 14

Behind the Bright Lights.

BROADWAY, a "new play" in three acts, by Philip Dunning and George Abbott. Settings by Arthur P. Segal; staged by the authors; dances staged by John Boyle; produced by Jed Harris. At the Broadhurst Theatre.

Nick Verdis.....................Paul Porcasi

Roy Lane........................Lee Tracy
Lil Rice.....................Clare Woodbury
Katie...........................Ann Preston
Joe.....................Joseph Spurin-Calleia
Mazie Smith..................Mildred Wall
Ruby....................Edith Van Cleve
Pearl......................Martha Madison
Grace......................Molly Ricardel
Ann.......................Constance Brown
"Billie" Moore...............Sylvia Field
Steve Crandall.............Robert Gleckler
Dolph.......................Henry Sherwood
"Porky" Thompson..........William Foran
"Scar" Edwards..................John Wray
Dan McCorn................Thomas Jackson
Benny.......................Frank Verigun
Larry.....................Millard Mitchell
Mike........................Roy R. Lloyd

By J. BROOKS ATKINSON

In the uncertain shadows just behind the white lights, life moves with amazing speed, according to "Broadway," put on at the Broadhurst last evening. With an excellent cast, imaginatively directed, the co-authors of this exciting melodrama have caught the incongruities, the contrasts, the jealousies, ambitions and duplicities and have tossed them all together in blaring, ironic confusion. Their skill in keeping several themes singing all during the drama, the light as well as the malignant, suggests the composer; and their eye for the picturesque—well, perhaps this is the painter. Early in the first act an uptown gangster is fatally shot in the back. In the last act that victim's sweetheart murders the cowardly murderer. With free development such an incident in itself might do well enough for merchantable drama; all of us have paid for that much alone. But the authors of "Broadway" set it against a garish, strident background of cabaret singers, "hoofers," midnight parties, visiting gunmen from Chicago on a drunken spree, with a jazz band outside beating the appropriate tempo. The result is an exhilarating, madly colored melodrama, a kaleidoscope, spattered with the brightest pigments of local color.

Observing those unities of time celebrated by the students of drama, the authors tell their story simply in the private party room of the Paradise Night Club, New York City. When the curtain goes up the cabaret girls and the show "hoofer" are at rehearsal, all in bad temper and quarrelsome, all full of advice. Throughout the rest of "Broadway" this company of midnight entertainers make their entrances and exits, rushing to their dress-rooms, pulling hair and "wise-cracking" each other in the idioms of this pungent vicinity. One of the girls in the company, "Billie" Moore, serves the dramatic function of bringing the two threads of the story together. Roy Lane, the one male entertainer in the cabaret, has picked her, not only as his partner in a big "act" he is working up, but as his sweetheart, subject to the rules and regulations laid down by the marriage bureau. But Steve Crandall, known chiefly as a "big butter-and-egg man" from Florida, apparently has more success with her than the "hoofer." His presents are more lavish; his manners are far more elegant. However, the brightest members of the audience recognize him as a gunman, bootlegger and general tough long before he pulls a "rod" on his uptown competitor and shoots him through the back.

From this moment on the two stories travel in opposite directions. For a time Steve bulldozes the police, and, just as he is on the point of escaping to Canada, perhaps with the cabaret queen by his side, he is killed in revenge for his cowardly first-act murder. On the other hand, the "hoofer" makes rapid progress in his professional and personal career. While Steve lies dead in an adjoining office with the door securely locked, Roy Lane is flirting an offer from a vaudeville manager for his "act" with "Billie" Moore. The Broadway tempo never falters.

Effective though such contrast may be, hard and fleeting in its emotional appeal, the authors have not always managed it perfectly. Particularly in the first act, before the relationships have been firmly established, the transition from one theme to the other occasions a perceptible break in the continuity of the story. And no doubt many of the superfluous incidents and dialogue might be omitted to the advantage of the tale. By defining the important characters completely and by rushing the drama constantly, especially through the back-stage scenes, the authors, who are also the directors, give their play the illusion of motion even when it is not progressing at all. And the climax to the second act, a perfectly directed incident, has the effect of fusing the various elements of the play definitely. From that time on "Broadway" is firmly packed melodrama.

Although all the parts are played capitally, two of them emerge as excellent pieces of characterization. Mr. Tracy, seen last season in "The Book of Charm," and "Glory Hallelujah," squeezes his part dry. This "hoofer" becomes heroic as well as fatuous, tender and callous at the same time. And Mr. Glecker, seen in "A Man's Man" last year, makes Steve Crandall a sinister character not without a certain charm. As the cabaret girl in dispute between these two men, Miss Field also plays in more than one key. For if "Billie" Moore seems at first to be merely a sweet, young thing, Miss Field gives her uncommon spirit in the end. Conceived in terms of the theatre, written with a true sense of stage projection, "Broadway" makes every part thoroughly actable. None of the players fumbles his chance.

1926 S 17

AN AMERICAN TRAGEDY' SCORES A TRIUMPH

Dramatization of Dreiser's Novel Plays Finely Upon the Emotions and Has a Stirring Finish.

AN AMERICAN TRAGEDY, a play in a prologue and four acts, by Patrick Kearney, from the novel of the same name by Theodore Dreiser. Settings by Carolyn Hancock; staged by Edward Goodman; produced by Horace Liveright. At the Longacre Theatre.

Elvira Griffiths	Caroline Newcombe
Asa Griffiths	Frank Moran
Hester Griffiths	Olive Mercer
A Girl	Marian Florance
A Young Man	Sydney Coburn
Another Girl	Joan Brown
Another Young Man	Harry Arnold
Mrs. Samuel Griffiths	Grace Griswold
Bella Griffiths	Janet McLeay
Gilbert Griffiths	House Baker Jameson
Samuel Griffiths	Walter Walker
Clyde Griffiths	Morgan Farley
Sondra Finchley	Miriam Hopkins
Jill Trumbull	Sally Bates
Whiggam	Bert Wilcox
Roberta Alden	Katherine Wilson
Stuart Finchley	Philip Jones
Bertine Cranston	Martha Lee Manners
Harley Baggott	Jack Quigley
Dr. Glenn	Arthur Hughes
Mrs. Peyton	Violet Andrews
An Innkeeper	John Wheeler
A Deputy Sheriff	Sydney Coburn
Orville Mason	Albert Phillips
Alvin Belknap	Willard Dashiell
Ruben Jephson	Anthony Brown
Burton Burleigh	Bert Wilcox
Bailiff	Harold McCreery
Clerk of the Court	Frank Rutherford
Judge Oberwaltzer	Philip Wood

The dramatization of "An American Tragedy" begins slowly and somewhat uncertainly; it proceeds a bit jerkily until somewhere in the third act, when the emotional power of Dreiser's story begins to gain the upper hand. The fourth and final act plays upon the emotions frankly and magnificently. The play proceeds to a stirring finish, and last night's audience at the Longacre stayed in the theatre to indulge in the most outspoken enthusiasm of the season.

There are several scenes in the first two acts in which the story lives, but the necessity of condensation imposed a close-clipped style and an abrupt shifting of locale that made it a little difficult for the play to take complete hold. And just as the novel was almost entirely non-interpretive, so too was the play in these early scenes. In these stages, accordingly, the emotions were enlisted only momentarily. But with the tightening of the net around Clyde Griffiths the play required no one to speak for it. The final act, despite an abrupt shift of technique in the manner of its presentation, swept the play on to triumph.

Although it is, basically, the Dreiser story that provides the emotional tug, two of the high spots of this final act seem to have been the invention of Patrick Kearney, who made the dramatization. The act is in two scenes, courtroom and death house, although the use of the black-out enables the playwright to show a dozen or more moments. Mr. Kearney, unless the memory of this writer is faulty, must receive credit for Clyde's telegram to his mother in the West, which brings the scene to an effective end. And certainly his was the notion of bringing Sondra into the death house for a visit—an idea which might have turned out to be just theatrical, but which was positively stirring instead.

Previously, at the finish of the preceding act, Sondra had likewise been present, or just in the offing, when the District Attorney and his helper closed in on Clyde in the Adirondack camp. One who found these moments an unforgettable part of the novel likewise found them intensely moving at the Longacre last night, although regretting that the exigencies of the theatre made it impossible to show in more detail the inevitable approach of authority.

The considerable task of compressing the Dreiser novel within the limits of a play has been achieved by Mr. Kearney with considerable success—a bit more in the writing, perhaps, than in the stringing together. The play emerges copiously in a prologue and four acts—a dozen scenes in all. This episodic structure, as has been said, works against the play in the beginning—try as he may, Mr. Kearney is not always able to explain everything, and there is an occasional gap in the action. But as the play gains sweep structure no longer matters. In the final act, indeed, it no longer exists.

It is probable, in these cases of widely-read novels come to life, that the players face a more difficult task than the playwright. Morgan Farley, Katherine Wilson, Miriam Hopkins—these must needs be every one's idea of Clyde, Roberta and Sondra. All three are excellent. Mr. Farley makes Clyde eager, tremulous, sensitive. It is a bit hard to believe that he was a murderer, but it was equally hard to believe it of the Clyde of Mr. Dreiser. If undue stress has been laid herein upon the play as opposed to the novel, the seeker after information has only to disregard it. Without regard to anything that has gone before, "An American Tragedy" is a play to be seen.

1926 O 12

Bootlegging Bedlam.

OH, KAY! a musical comedy in two acts and five scenes; book by Guy Bolton and P. G. Wodehouse, music by George Gershwin, lyrics by Ira Gershwin; book staged by John Harwood; dances and ensembles staged by Sammy Lee; settings by John Wenger, produced by Alex A. Aarons and Vinton Freedley. At the Imperial Theatre.

Molly Morse	Betty Compton
Peggy	Janette Gilmore
The Duke	Gerald Oliver Smith
Larry Potter	Harland Dixon
Phil Ruxton	Marion Fairbanks
Dolly Ruxton	Madeleine Fairbanks
"Shorty" McGee	Victor Moore
Constance Appleton	Sacha Beaumont
Jimmy Winter	Oscar Shaw
Kay	Gertrude Lawrence
Revenue Officer Jansen	Harry T. Shannon
Mae	Constance Carpenter
Daisy	Paulette Winston
Judge Appleton	Frank Gardiner

By J. BROOKS ATKINSON.

Musical comedy seldom proves more intensely delightful than "Oh, Kay!" the new piece at the Imperial, with a serviceable book by Guy Bolton and P. G. Wodehouse, specialists in collaboration, and a rich score by George Gershwin. Usually it is sufficient to credit the sponors only the authors and the composer. But the distinction of "Oh, Kay!" is its excellent blending of all the creative arts of musical entertainment—the arts of staging no less than those of composing and designing. For half the enjoyment of the new musical play comes from the dancing, the comic pantomime and the drilling of a large company. Mr. Lee and Mr. Harwood have matched the authors at every turning with inventive and imaginative directing.

After two appearances in America as co-star in the English Charlot Revues, Gertrude Lawrence now appears as a principal in this new comedy. And the plot being what it is, she comes as the sister of a titled English bootlegger whose yacht hovers off our arid shores amid the excursions and alarums of Federal inspectors. ("The difference between a bootlegger and a Federal inspector," says the incriminating Victor Moore, "is that one of them wears a badge.") Most of us have heard Miss Lawrence singing various musical-hall tunes in good voice and excellent taste, with a wanton twinkle of comedy in her eyes. In her present rôle she gives expression to that mimic quality more

ever with a versatility barely indicated in the Charlot Revues in which Beatrice Lillie cut such uproarious capers. Miss Lillie, by the way, was among those present last evening. So obliging is the book of "Oh, Kay!" that Miss Lawrence may play not only the love-sick English lady but also the Cockney serving-maid who performs tricks on a long roll of French bread and affects a domestic slouch in her walk. As a low comedian she does not paint the Lillie, but she keeps the enjoyment varied and broad.

Most of this entertainment has to do with a cargo of forbidden liquor and as scurvy a lot of bad puns as ever scuttled a rum-runner. The supercilious duke, with the dapper Gerald Smith "up" on that part, and "Shorty" McGee, buffooned by Victor Moore, have concealed a shipment in the capacious cellar of Jimmy Winter, represented engagingly by Oscar Shaw. As it happens now and then on the musical stage, Jimmy Winter is facing the matrimonial firing-squad with a vixen fiancée whom he does not relish. And all this time a strange English lady seems vastly preferable. Well, things go from bad to worse until the wedding begins solemnly on the efflorescent terrace at Jimmy's luxurious Long Island villa. In the nick of time Federal inspectors, genuine as well as bogus, intervene on the side of law and love.

As the extemporaneous butler, battler or bottler (to speak from the book) Mr. Moore totters languidly through a long roulade of indiscriminate comedy, unseemly impertinence and a constant rattle of amusing "gags." Nothing since the Marx Brothers has been more hilarious than the offhand luncheon served clumsily by Miss Lawrence and Mr. Moore—a clatter of crockery on the stage and ominous sounds from the kitchen nearby. Through all this mixed comedy the diminutive Fairbanks twins wander charmingly, adding roses and honeysuckle to the construction of a "gag" or representing the bridegroom's happy youth.

"Oh, Kay!" bears out the implication of its title most conspicuously in the dancing and in the ordering of the chorus. Leading the footwork light brigade Mr. Dixon becomes wooden or supple according to need in a gauche potpourri of eccentric steps. And for the encore of "Clap Yo' Hands," the most pungent musical number, the chorus performs a cross between anatomical exercise and folk-dance, rapid and energetic.

Mr. Gershwin's score is woven closely into the fun of the comedy. Sometimes it is purely rhythmic, as in "Clap Yo' Hands" and "Fidgety Feet"; sometimes it is capricious as in "Do-Do-Do." Mr. Gershwin also composes in the familiar romantic vein of "Someone to Watch Over Me." In this plaintive number Miss Lawrence embellishes the song with expressive turns on the stage; she employs none of the artful rhetoric of musical comedy singing. For "Oh, Kay!" is the work of no individual. It is a group production to which every one has brought some appropriate decoration. When dramatic organizations pool their talents in this fashion we prattle with smug satisfaction about the universal development of the stage. Revue and musical comedy producers excel in such organized handicraft as a matter of course.

1926 N 9

THE CONSTANT WIFE, a comedy in three acts, by W. Somerset Maugham. Produced by the Charles Frohman Company at the Maxine Elliott Theatre.
Mrs. Culver..............Mabel Terry-Lewis
Bentley..................Thomas A. Braidon
Martha Culver...........Cora Witherspoon
Barbara Fawcett..........Jeanette Sherwin
Constance Middleton.......Ethel Barrymore
Marie-Louise Durham........Veree Teasdale
John Middleton, F. R. C. S..C. Aubrey Smith
Bernard Kersal..............Frank Conroy
Mortimer Durham.........Walter Kingsford.

The return of Miss Barrymore to light comedy is in itself a matter for huzzas; that she has been so fortunate. as to find a good one is a circumstance that calls for a clearing of the streets by the traffic squad, to be followed by the performance of at least a minuet. Her play, entitled "The Constant Wife," is the work of W. Somerset Maugham. It is a deft and sparkling comedy of no overwhelming importance, and its central rôle is so well suited to Miss Barrymore that it might have been written for her. In fact, it probably was.

One has but to consider Mr. Maugham's central notion to realize how completely Miss Barrymore makes the play and the part her own. Surrounded by friends and family who have learned that her husband is carrying on an intrigue with another woman, Miss Barrymore remains for an act or more in calm possession of that secret, as well as deep in enjoyment of the effect of such news upon the others. During all of this no word or phrase of Mr. Maugham's conveys to the audience that his heroine is undeceived; Miss Barrymore, however, is able to signal it in a dozen ways, quietly, subtly. Whether or not Mr. Maugham counted on it, it is advance information that serves to heighten expectation.

The eventual revelation of conditions is contrived for effective theatre; it is a plot turn of no consequence so far as the attitude of the wife is concerned. Perhaps it has been already forecast, in this summary, that the final situation finds the wife prepared to claim for herself the freedom that

had been taken by her husband. It is perhaps not an idea new in the theatre, but in the hands of Miss Barrymore it is pure gold. It was at this stage that the play rose to its high point, culminating on the triumphant note of the wife's departure. A departure not from the husband, it should be added, but for the merely temporary purpose of a romantic journey.

The captious may claim that it is a play on an old model, and this, indeed, it is. But it is a play written with wit and sprightliness—Mr. Maugham just about at his best. An early barrage of epigram is happily over and done with by 9 o'clock; at occasional moments thereafter Mr. Maugham is at slight pains to expound his thesis, but mainly he devotes himself to the business of writing a light comedy of a high order. It is the best play of its kind that has come from England in a long time.

Miss Barrymore, blossoming anew under the spur of good writing, looked her loveliest and played superbly—although no moment in the play called for anything that she has not done a dozen times before. Her company includes C. Aubrey Smith, who, minus those ample mustaches, returns from a long series of London comedies to render valiant service, particularly in the last act. Frank Conroy, as the lover, is likewise able, and not quite so much in the grip, this time, of that vague air of detachment.

And the play, it might be added, is at the Maxine Elliott Theatre.

1926 N 30

THE DESERT SONG, an operetta in two acts and eight scenes. Music by Sigmund Romberg, book by Otto Harbach, Oscar Hammerstein 2d and Frank Mandel. Libretto directed by Arthur Hurley; musical numbers staged by Robert Connolly; settings by Woodman Thompson; produced by Laurence Schwab and Frank Mandel. At the Casino Theatre.
Sid El Kar ....William O'Neal
Mindar ....O. J. Vanasse
Hassi ....Earl Mitchell
Benjamin Kidd...........Eddie Buzzell
Captain Paul Fontaine...........Glen Dale
Azuri ....Pearl Regay
Sergeant La Vergne........Albert Baron
Sergeant DuBassac.........Charles Davis
Margot Bonvalet.............Vivienne Segal
General Birabeau............Edmund Elton
Pierre Birabeau............Robert Halliday
Suzanne, His Ward.............Nellie Breen
Ethel ....Elmira Lane
Ali Ben Ali.....................Lyle Evans
Clementina...............Margaret Irving
Neri....................Rachel May Clark
Hadji ....Chas. Morgan

After a brief reversion to morality pageants, the Casino was reclaimed for operetta last night when Schwab and Mandel presented there what to date is probably their magnum opus, an elaborate musical show which seemed to have been especially devised for the fancy Moorish interior of the theatre. The title of the piece is "The Desert Song," and further news of it is that just before press time it seemed on its way to becoming a hit.

It appears that Otto Harbach, Oscar Hammerstein 2d, and Frank Mandel read the newspapers—or at least they did several months ago when the cable dispatches brought news of Riff uprisings in Northern Africa, and of the guerrilla warfare that was being waged there. Of such stuff they have fashioned an abundant plot, dealing with the supposed butterfly-chasing son of a French General who is in reality "The Red Shadow," leader of the insurgent natives, and of the girl he loves, who, seeing him at his home work, feels for him only a sisterly affection, but who falls victim to the lure of the mysterious rebel chief without knowing his real identity.

It is all floridly contrived, and executed in the grand, unstinting manner of the more affluent impresarios, but, by sheer weight possibly, it seems to be a little more important than the books of several kindred entertainments hereabout. It is something in the "Beau Geste" school, and assuredly merits this sultry title of "The Desert Song" more than it does the delicate "Lady Fair" by which it fist was known.

Two of the outstanding features of the evening were the excellent and sometimes rather imposing score which Sigmund Romberg has provided and the stirring and resonant male chorus, which provoked considerable enthusiasm. Romberg has contributed in "Ho" a number that in its sweep and pull seems a fitting successor to "The Song of the Vagabonds," which made the Casino rafters ring these many months. This is one of several which appear certain of enjoying their full measure of popular favor.

Vivienne Segal is the prima donna involved in these Riffish, though not raffish, proceedings. Last night she sang surely and truly and contributed definitely to the assets of the undertaking. The amusing Eddie Buzzell does well once he gets the chance, although he has an uphill battle through the first act.

There also is Pearl Regay, still doing sinuous dances and having difficulties with white men. The company is even larger than the orchestra, which overflows into the aisles, and most of its members perform the usual variety of tasks competently.

"The Desert Song" is, then, a large, slightly topheavy entertainment, providing full value for your money, and it seems sure of its niche among the local eye-and-ear hippodromes.

"The Dybbuk" in Hebrew.

THE DYBBUK (original version), a dramatic legend in three acts, by S. Ansky, with music by I. Engel; staged by E. Vachtangiv; presented in Hebrew by the Habima Players at the Mansfield Theatre.

First Batlan	Raikin Ben-Ari
Second Batlan	Benno Schneider
Third Batlan	Ben-Chaim
Meier	B. Tschemeritsky
Chonon	L. Warshawer
Hennoch	Benjamin Zemach
Messenger	A. Prudkin
Ascher	E. Winiar
Gnesia	Ch. Grober
Sender	D. Itkin
Lea	Anna Rovina
Friede	Tmima Yudelwitch
Gitel	Tamar Robins
Basia	F. Lubitsch
Refual	Aron Meskin
Berchik	S. Brook
Dvosia	Winiar-Katchur
Dreisel	Ch. Grober
Yachna	Chava Adelman
Nechuma	Anna Paduit
An Old Woman	Chana Hendler
Rivke	Elisheva Factorowitch
Elka	Ina Govinskaya
Menashe	Benjamin Zemach
Nacman	J. Bertonow
Mendel	Benno Schneider
Asrial	Naum L. Zemach
Michuel	Zwi Friedlander
Shameshon	B. Tschemerinsky

By J. BROOKS ATKINSON.

After the usual delays and postponements and the formality of Ellis Island probation, the Habima Players of Moscow have strung up their canvas scenery and set up their eccentric props in the Mansfield, where they acted "The Dybbuk" last evening. Almost exactly a year ago the Neighborhood Playhouse made this exotic play by Ansky a treasury of organized acting in an adaptation for the English stage. Next Thursday, incidentally, the Neighborhood players will put on "The Dybbuk" again. The Habima performance is described as the "original version"; the spoken tongue is Hebrew, or, as one of the soothsayers reported in the lobby, a Russian-Lithuanian dialect constructed upon Hebrew. In spite of an eager audience, to many of whom Hebrew was not an unfamiliar tongue, the spoken words obviously did not matter particularly last evening. For the attention was naturally focussed upon a highly stylized type of acting developed to a state of plastic perfection. We have all caught hints of it in other performances directed by the innumerable Moscovians now rummaging around this country. The direction of the Moscow Art Theatre Musical Studio had been tarred a little with the same brush. But no other performance in this city has been so bold in its stylization, so daring in its treatment of details and so skillful in evoking the latent moods of a production.

In order to describe it one must report some of the details. First of all, the make-up is extraordinary. Faces are painted with curious designs, in high colors, not unlike grotesque masks; mouths are pulled out of shape by daubs of grease-paint; eyes are rendered almost uncanny by circles and arches; noses are pulled to a sharp point. The black gowns of the chassidim are crudely smeared with white at the edges. All the benches and chairs used in the synagogue and at the wedding breakfast are off centre; the angular treatment of the property extends even to the unpretentious scenery. The actors move about the stage with grotesque motions, with absurd attitudes; the lines of the human figure are broken up by stooping or leaning heavily to one side. And the voices of the beggars, the professional prayer men and the choruses in general are individually unnatural, stressed and strained. Divided into its various parts, like the individual scores for a symphony, the production would be thoroughly unintelligible.

When all these separate parts are pulled together in a symmetrical performance the effect is astonishing—as unreal as the mystic legend of the play, as profound in its searching of the emotions, supple, resilient and varied. Sometimes the terminology of music is used most effectively in the discussion of this style of acting. And to some purpose in the present instance; for the direction of "The Dybbuk" employs stringed music off-stage and voices in chorus for the expression of the play. More and more until the last act (when the Tzadik attempts to cast out the spirit from Leah) runs into operatic treatment with chants, organized singing off stage and even the intonation of lines. Acted in this vein, the performance describes what we may vaguely term the "soul" of "The Dybbuk." It is a method extraordinarily beautiful when it is perfectly welded and polished; it would be disastrous in less talented hands.

Comparisons with the Neighborhood performance are inevitable after the spectacle of last evening. And comparisons show that the Neighborhood performance is a very good one indeed, and the legitimate offspring of the Habima. For when the Neighborhood players came to mount the piece, already famous in Hebrew and Yiddish, they employed as director David Vardi, once a member of the Habima troupe. They could not have done better; the stylized treatment is surely the authentic expression of this mystic drama. If the Habima are bolder in their construction of the elements of the performance, surer of touch, more expansive and more colorful, the Neighborhood production has obvious virtues. To the present reporter, at least, the lighting on the Grand Street stage was more imaginative, and the scenery more illuding. Oddly painted canvas, geometrical designs flung across the wings and rudely propor-

tioned altars in the Habima production doubtless have significance and purpose, but they do not stir the imagination.

The Moscow Theatre Habima was founded shortly after the 1905 revolution by N. L. Zemach for the acting of plays in Hebrew. It struggled through Tsarist persecutions in 1911 and Soviet disapproval in 1917. At that time it was championed by Maxim Gorky, Stanislavsky, Chaliapin and Nemirovitch-Dantchenko, whose names are all familiar in this country, and now it exists as a vigorous influence in the art of theatre expression. Several years ago with the Moscow Art Theatre we saw realism carried to the height of perfection. With the Habima we see a fresher method of group-acting, suited to dramas of a freer technique. Our stage may learn a good deal from it in the orchestration of producing.

1926 D 14

Craig's Mother.

THE SILVER CORD, a play in three acts, by Sidney Howard. Staged by John Cromwell; produced by The Theatre Guild. At the John Golden Theatre.
Hester .... Margalo Gillmore
David .... Eliot Cabot
Christina .... Elisabeth Risdon
Robert .... Earle Larimore
Mrs. Phelps .... Laura Hope Crews
Maid .... Barbara Bruce

By J. BROOKS ATKINSON.

After feeling his way around experimentally for several years, Sidney Howard has at last written a trenchant drama, "The Silver Cord," acted well at the John Golden Theatre last evening by a Theatre Guild cast. Having chosen a serviceable theme, he goes at it passionately and develops it by sheer force into a problem drama that demands an unequivocal answer of "yes" or "no," after the stimulating maner of George Bernard Shaw. When the curtain has come down you may begin to suspect that Mr. Howard has overdone his problem. But that is small matter. The point is that in the theatre "The Silver Cord" acts splendidly and blows up a vivid illusion. For the time being mother-love seems as sinister and malevolent as the middle-class morality of "Craig's Wife"—and vastly more entertaining.

Mr. Howard is writing of a mother's fierce determination to hold her two sons against all the world. The elder of them, David, has married abroad; the first scene depicts his home-coming with Christina, biologist as well as wife. The younger, Robert, is engaged to Hester, who is visiting her future mother-in-law. In the course of the three acts this Mrs. Phelps succeeds in turning Robert against Hester, and nearly separates David from his young wife. As Mrs. Phelps remarks: "The Chinese have always put filial love first, and they would be the most powerful nation in the world if they didn't smoke opium."

In the end, the alignment of forces—wife and sweetheart against mother and sons—raises this incident to the status of rationalization. On the point of leaving with Hester (who says she has made up her mind to marry an orphan) Christina tries the case as sententiously as a lawyer. In a long jeremiad, Shavian in its scientific reasoning, she accuses Mrs. Phelps of having duped her sons from the beginning into believing her a great woman. Quite ruthless in her candor she goes straight to the roots of this unnatural devotion. Then Mrs. Phelps pleads the case of mother-love with quite as much conviction. For a few stirring moments David struggles between devotion to his mother and the genuine love he feels for his wife; and then he follows Christina to the automobile, to New York and possibly to a career. If all this plain-speaking is enormously exhilarating in the theatre, it is because Mr. Howard enjoys the scene and lets himself go belligerently. The actors never let him down.

Mr. Howard is not too involved in his theme to have his little joke as he goes along and not too rational to eschew melodrama. For he writes a flavorsome dialogue that depicts character and holds the interest at the same time. Pitting the old generation against the new, in the persons of Mrs. Phelps and Christina, he plays with biology, with motherhood as a profession, with Omaha and New York, the Rockefeller Institute, vivisection and photographs of David as a baby. "Have you ever noticed how all babies look like Chief Justice Taft?" Hester inquires innocently. Through all this preliminary fooling, however, the conflicts of drama begin to emerge, and by the time of the second act "The Silver Cord" has run into hysterics and furious conversation.

Having been let down by Robert, Hester swears she will not stay in the house another moment. She rushes to the telephone to call a taxi. Mrs. Phelps pulls the telephone off the wall. At the end of this second act Hester, still beyond herself with grief and rage, tries to drown herself in the lake outside, and the two boys rush out to the rescue. "Boys, boys, come back for your overcoats!" Mrs. Phelps shouts at the window. "You'll catch cold in this weather!"

No doubt this conclusion to the second act is a bit thick, in spite of the fact that Mr. Howard has been laying emphasis upon the cruelty, selfishness and hypocrisy in Mrs. Phelps's character from the beginning. But it exemplifies as much as anything else his use of the theatre as a medium of expression. It is the sort of exaggeration that makes its point as realism. Sometimes "The Silver Cord" is verbose. But Mr. Howard is not the kind of literary playwright who depends upon dialogue entirely. Frequently he tells his story without a word—by unpacking a suitcase, moving around toilet articles, fussing with a baby pillow or exchanging flowers from table to piano.

The players make the most of their opportunity. In a excellently proportioned character portrait Mr. Cabot discovers the vascillating quality beneath the stolidity of David. Mr. Larimore does extremely well with Robert; he drenches the weakness of this boy in sympathy. Miss Risdon makes Christina a forthright sort of young woman, searching and courageous. Miss Gillmore quite surpasses herself with the poignant hysteria of Hester; that second-act scene in particular is a powerful one. Miss Crews does so well with the mother, often acting brilliantly with mere innuendoes, that it seems captious to complain of her too transparent frivolity. Sometimes she goes over to farce too generously for a drama.

The comedy has been excellently directed by John Cromwell. One enjoys in particular the fast pace of the acting.

1926 D 21

Presenting Beatrice Lillie.

OH, PLEASE! a farce revue in two acts. Libretto by Anne Caldwell and Otto Harbach, founded on a story by Maurice Hennequin and Pierre Veber, music by Vincent Youmans. Staged by Hassard Short; dances and ensembles arranged by David Bennett; settings and costumes by James Reynolds; produced by Charles Dillingham. At the Fulton Theatre.

Emma Bliss	Helen Broderick
Miss Fall River	Pearl Hight
Miss South Bend	Blanche Latell
Miss Topeka	Gertrude Clemens
Miss Walla Walla	Josephine Sabel
Jane Jones	Irma Irving
Dexter Lane	Nelson Snow
Buddy Trescott	Charles Columbus
Jack Gates	Nick Long Jr.
Nicodemus Bliss	Charles Winninger
Fay Follette	Kitty Kelly
Thelma Tiffany	Gertrude McDonald
Ruth King	Dolores Farris
Clarice Cartier	Cynthia MacVae
Lily Valli	Beatrice Lillie
Robert Vandeleur	Charles Purcell
Peter Perkins	Robert Baldwin
Dick Mason	Floyd Carder

By J. BROOKS ATKINSON.

Although a sort of musical comedy plot runs through the several scenes of "Oh, Please!" put on at the Fulton last evening, the program describes this production, not as a musical "extravaganza" but as a "farce-revue." For Beatrice Lillie, heretofore of "Charlot's Revue," is the principal player. And as all her admirers know, Miss Lillie, an incomparable comedian in the highly intelligent vein of Charlie Chaplin, has no patience with the stuffy sentimentalities and mawkish romance of the musical stage.

In the present skit she plays the utilitarian part of a frisky stage favorite who has broken the heart of a perfume manufacturer and has yielded her heart to him. When the plot betrays her for a few moments into warbling the usual love bathos with Charles Purcell at the usual close range she manages with some difficulty to keep a straight face. In such situations, however, she is ill at ease. For Miss Lillie is a comedian with the divine spark, a mimic of the highest skill, and everything she does is shot through with a piercing sense of humor. Fortunately, she has her revenge. Throughout the remainder of "Oh, Please!" as in the opening scenes, she ridicules every traditional staple of musical comedy, every one in the cast, every one in the audience, and nearly everything she does herself. The friendliest of first night audiences was completely captivated whenever she was on the stage—responsive to every meaningful flick of her eyelashes, every fleeting expression on her face.

Some day a scientist will explain once and for all the inscrutable secret of such brilliant humor and thus free us from the bondage of worshiping it blindly. In the meantime we must be content to enjoy it to the extreme and to marvel at its resourcefulness and amazing speed. In the stock situations of musical comedy, singing in the midst of chorus girls or chorus men, the object of their flamboyant stage courtesy, Miss Lillie remains ever so lightly detached. She is in it, but not of it. The burlesque is so quick, so nearly imperceptible, that the audience has no sooner caught her meaning before she is three or four paces ahead to something quite as subtle and effervescent. Once or twice she holds to her part in the comedy. As the heart-broken heartbreaker in the second act she conveys the sincerity of her affection by remaining grave. Singing "I Can't Be Happy" (while the scenes are being changed), she remains in a sombre mood. That passive quality is the extent of her musical comedy romance. In her next appearance, as a flouncy "girl of the old brigade," she is up to her old tricks again.

Being designed, one assumes, to praise Miss Lillie and not to bury her, "Oh, Please!" gives her free rein every now and then for the broad comedy scenes of which she is capable. In the last "Charlot's Revue" she impersonated the conventional concert artiste with her flowers and absurdly patronizing airs. Wrapped in a figured table covering, she elaborates this same burlesque in "Oh, Please!" to the limit of comedy. "Love me," she implores in a curiously thin, unsteady voice. And as she sings the chorus over and over again she strikes the most preposterous attitudes, tries all the chairs and couches in the room, pokes her head above a screen, clinging to the refrain as though mad. The hapless Charles Winninger is then involved; the banalities of "Love me" conclude with a ludicrous wrestling match on the forestage, the stupid song at last silenced. The clumsy, peripatetic "March With Me," by which Miss Lillie first became famous in New York, is not in the present revue, but she has revived "The Girls of the Old Brigade."

Well, there are other players, other talents and other incidents in Mr. Dillingham's florid production. As the California perfume manufacturer, depressed by a homely, chaste wife, Mr. Winninger brings a quality of humor and good nature well suited to Miss Lillie's. Mr. Purcell is the best, if not the only, singer in the cast; and he makes much of "I Know That You Know" and "Love and Kisses 'n' Everything." But the warm glorification of sentiment seems more than a little ridiculous in Miss Lillie's presence. One catchy, tricky tune, entitled "Nicodemus," and sung by Miss Lillie and Mr. Winninger, catches the exact spirit of the revue. For the most part the music is adequate without touching distinction.

At the opening of the second act "Oh, Please!" succumbs to a debauch of strutting and leaping, after the manner of modish productions. Toe-dancing, gymnastic exercises and dizzy whirls fill the stage; they are simply implausible. After "hoofing" vigorously for several moments, Mr. Long proceeds to jump over every one on the stage. Tomorrow night he will jump over the moon. The production is splendidly set by James Reynolds with extravagant costumes to match. Of course, Miss Lillie's original costumes do not always fit the general, glowing scheme. She fits nothing so perfectly as herself.

1926 D 22

'IN ABRAHAM'S BOSOM' A POWERFUL TRAGEDY

Range of Paul Green's Drama Runs From Infectious Gayety of Negro Race to Religious Ecstasy.

IN ABRAHAM'S BOSOM, "the biography of a negro," in seven scenes, by Paul Green. Settings by Cleon Throckmorton; directed by Jasper Deeter; produced by Provincetown Players. At the Provincetown Playhouse.

Bud Gaskins	Frank Wilson
Lije Hunneycutt	Thomas Mosley
Puny Avery	James Dunmore
Abraham McCranie	Julius Bledsoe
Colonel McCranie	L. Rufus Hill
Lonnie McCranie	H. Ben Smith
Goldie McAllister	Rose McClendon
Muh Mack	Abbie Mitchell
Douglas McCranie	R. J. Huey
Eddie Williams	Melvin Greene
Lanie Horton	Armithine Lattimer
Neilly McNeill	Stanley Greene

A sincere and powerful tragedy written with courage, understanding, logic and humor, was played last night by actors whose sincerity matched that of the author, and who added to that sincerity an unction and an instinctive and intense quality of dramatic action and speech equally admirable in the comic and the tragic passages. The play was "In Abraham's Bosom," by Paul Green, and the players were chiefly negroes, putting on the stage the phases of their own life in the turpentine country of North Carolina as the author, who belongs to that same country, has dramatized it for them.

For convincing faithfulness to that life and to the spirit of the drama it would be hard to imagine a better performance. The range runs all the way from the boisterous and infectious gayeyt of the race to the religious ecstasy and the madness of the hunted and baffled creature of mixed blood who is the central tragic figure. But they are all combined into a whole in which the bitterness which lies at the core of things is kept free of any accusing animus as between black and white. To begin with, the white man who writes the piece has seen the tragedy with deep sympathy for the blacks. For their part the negro players have played it in the spirit in which it is written. So that though it ends in the slaying of a white man by a black one, there can be no feeling of anything but pity for the victim of the furies who in his madness did the deed.

Julius Bledsoe played the part of that black man—a dreamer who is evermore being defeated and who wrecks his home, himself and family with his dreaming—with a forthrightness and conviction, with a range of eloquence and a power which were wholly admirable. He was especially impressive in the scene of religious exaltation when he prayed over the infant whom he dedicated to the saving of his people and in the mad scene after the murder his perfect solemnity in the situations of comedy contributed enormously to the effects produced by the others—especially Abbie Mitchell as an old woman and Armithine Lattimer as a sassy, giggling colored girl in the log cabin school scene where Bledsoe is the teacher. By the way, the setting of all the scenes is simple and good—the pine woods and the insides of the cabins. But the best scene of all is the scene of the murder, though it is only a simple drop with a snake fence and some trees against a pale night sky. The ghosts, which the crazed creature sees in this scene, are the best ghosts that this reviewer has seen on the stage in many moons.

The other negro players are all good and they take mighty good care of the comedy which is as essential to the drama as the tragedy both as a stage piece and as a representation of the life of the people of color whose lives for half a dozen generations have been led alongside the lives of the white people of our Southern States and whose quality is a part of the quality of this composite nation of ours. For instance, there are two turpentine hands in the first act. Their exchange of epithets and manual and verbal insults is done with the great spirit and fidelity—not to say enthusiasm. And there is the young man who plays the scapegrace son of the enthusiast—equally apt for a breakdown tune or for blubbery tears. Nor should the playing of the other tragic part—that of Abraham's wife—by Rose MacClendon go without praise. In the very last moment of the play she was very fine indeed—though she only looked it.

1926 D 31

Jazz Slayer Acquitted.

CHICAGO, a satirical comedy in a prologue and three acts, by Maurine Watkins. Staged by George Abbott; produced by Sam H. Harris. At the Music Box.

Roxie Hart	Francine Larrimore
Fred Casely	Carl Eckstrom
Jake	Charles A. Bickford
Amos Hart	Charles Halton
Sargeant Murdock	Charles Slattery
Martin S. Harrison	Robert Barrat
Babe	Arthur R. Vinton
Mrs. Morton	Isabelle Winlocke
Velma	Juliette Crosby
Liz	Dorothy Stickney
Billy Flynn	Edward Ellis
Mary Sunshine	Eda Heinemann
Moonshine Maggie	Feriki Boros
Go-to-Hell Kitty	Edith Fitzgerald
Bailiff	Carl De Mal
Judge Canton	Milano Tilden
Corbin	G. Albert Smith
Woman Reporter	Wilma Thompson
First Man Reporter	George Cowell
Clerk of the Court	Charles Kuhn
First Photographer	James E. Pall
Stenographer	Vincent York
Foreman of the Jury	G. W. Auspake
Reporters	Victor Wilbur, William Jack

By J. BROOKS ATKINSON.

After the curtain had been up a moment or two in "Chicago," at the Music Box last evening, Roxie Hart, stenographer, shot Fred Casely, a married Lothario, in her bedroom. That was by far the most exciting moment in the drama. For "Chicago" is not a melodrama, as the prologue indicates, but a satirical comedy on the administration of justice through the fetid channels of newspaper publicity—of photographers, "sob-sisters," feature stunts, standardized prevarication and general vulgarity. In the composition of her raucous lampoon, Miss Watkins has forgotten none of the "old hokum" or the blatant chicanery typical—it is alleged—of the trials of "beautiful murderesses." "Dancing feet" cause the downfall of Roxie Hart. Front-page publicity, rows upon rows of sentimental photographs and skillful acting at the trial save her lovely neck from the hangman's noose. Miss Watkins has spread the whole tawdry story through her comedy in racy dialogue and ludicrous situations.

If "Chicago" emerges in the performance, not as a firm, compact satire, deadly in its import, but rather as a generally diverting entertainment, the acting must bear most of the blame. In general, the piece is played heavily. And in particular it is played with a knowing smirk and with the tongue-in-the-cheek lest the audience believe the players duped by their lines. Who else should be duped? Of all the actors only Mr. Ellis, as the defending attorney, plays with the downright earnestness of a charlatan determined to pull the wool over the jury's eyes by the familiar sentimental and oratorical methods. In various degrees the other players regard the piece as a joke; Miss Larrimore does

so in particular. For the "devastating" effect that such journalistic satires properly covet, the performance must be hard, earnest and brittle. "Chicago" might well be one of the most stirring plays of the season.

Miss Watkins gathered her material as a newspaper reporter in Chicago; she has learned her craft at the knee of Professor Baker, pundit of the drama at Yale University. (In the halls of Academe, it is reported, "Chicago" was graded "98," or virtually perfect.) When Roxie Hart, the chief strumpet of this comedy, faces the police and the District Attorney after the murder, she naturally fears the worst. Miss Watkins has striven to show, by the method of satire, why no beautiful woman need quail before justice. With the arrival of the newspaper photographers, Roxie begins to perk up. And by the second act, set in the woman's ward of the county jail, she is in such a whirl of front-page publicity, of "mash" notes and presents, as she never dreamed of before. In the end, of course, she is booked for a long tour on the vaudeville stage. Just as she is on the point of announcing this news to the courtroom assembly, wild shots are heard outside. "Another murder!" the reporters shout gleefully. With a rush they leave Roxie in the moment of her triumph. As the curtain descends, the riff-raff of the courts and press are off again on a new cycle of three-ring criminal justice with "Gold Coast" Nellie blinking in the glare of the spotlight.

In spite of the melodramatic nature of the material, "Chicago" lacks the action one might expect. Miss Watkins is content to report and portray, and to develop the part of Roxie. Nothing is more amusing than Roxie's increasingly voracious appetite for the front-page, once she has felt the thrill of that monstrous institution, and her eleventh-hour device for holding the centre of the stage. When everything else fails to excite the reporters, when other, fresher murderesses roll in, Roxie stoops to feigned maternity. In a hushed voice she confides her womanly hopes to the press. A tenstrike! "Stork Hovers Over County Jail," explains the "sob-sister," stealing copy-desk thunder. From this time on Roxie's acquittal is assured.

What Chicago may think of this travesty is an interesting speculation. "Broadway" is no fit reprisal. Chicago newspaper correspondents were in the theatre last evening, for better or for worse.

1926 D 31

1927

Within the Cloiter.

THE CRADLE SONG, a comedy in two
acts, with an interlude in verse, from
the Spanish of Gregorio and Marie Martinez Sierra, translated into English by
John Garrett Underhill. Settings and
costumes by G. E. Calthrop; directed by
Eva Le Gallienne; produced by the Civic
Repertory Theatre. At the Civic Repertory Theatre.

Sister Sagario .... Ruth Wilton
Sister Marcelle ...... Beatrice de Neegaard
The Prioress .... Beatrice Terry
Sister Joanna .... Eva Le Gallienne
Mistress of Novices .... Mary Ward
The Vicaress .... Leona Roberts
Sister Tornera .... Margaret G. Love
Sister Inez .... Hilda Plowright
A Countryman .... Barlowe Borland
Sister Maria Jesus .... Chalee Hubbard
The Doctor .... Egon Brecher
Teresa .... Josephine Hutchinson
Antonio .... Hardie Albright

By J. BROOKS ATKINSON.

If Miss Le Gallienne's company at
the Fourteenth Street Theatre had
produced nothing else well this year,
the finely modulated performance of
"Cradle Song," put on last evening,
would still make the season distinguished. For this frail little comedy
by Martinez Sierra, with its scarcely
perceptible pathos and sentiment, becomes meltingly beautiful in the acting. None of the other dramas in Miss
Le Gallienne's variegated repertory demands quite the same delicacy in expression. Yet she and her actors suffuse "Cradle Song" with beauty.

If you must know what the play is
about, the matter is simple enough.
"Cradle Song" portrays two quietly
eventful days in a convent of enclosed
Dominican nuns in Spain. On the
first day a foundling is mysteriously
put in at the door. After flocking
around the basket and reading the letter inserted by an unnamed mother,
the good sisters agree to adopt it, and
the open-hearted physician, a bachelor,
offers to give it his name. On the
second day, represented in the second
and concluding act, the foundling has
blossomed into a radiant maiden who
this very day is to be married and
whisked across the water to America,
perhaps never to see her many mothers
again. Between the acts is an interlude of poetry recited before the curtain by Mr. Crawley. Nothing further happens in this wisp of a comedy
with its faint glow of romance.

With so little story to unfold, the
charm of "Cradle Song" accordingly
lies in the quality of the emotions portrayed. Within the shelter of this convent, life may not be turgid, but it is
full. And beneath the sober ritual of
courtesies and worship the sisters feel
as deeply as the screaming folk outside. Martinez Sierra has described a
wisely beneficent prioress who loves
her sisters and enjoys the high spirits
of the novices; a sour vicaress who is
forever detecting the works of the
devil in the slightest sparkle of good
nature; a physician who enjoys the
masculine privilege of shocking these
brides of the Lord, and many others
bred to the veil. When the foundling
is discovered, what shrieks of amazement from the novices! At first the
prioress does not know what course
to pursue. Is it wise to accept this
responsibility? Is it legal? When the
matter is put to vote, however, despite
the crabbed admonitions of the vicaress, every sister assents. Clearly it
is a rich gift, far beyond their wildest
expectations.

By the time of the second act they
have reared Teresa into maidenhood.
In the parlor of the convent they are
finishing her trousseau according to
the smartest fashions from Paris. Now
Martinez Sierra shows how deeply
they have cherished this child with so
many holy mothers. Antonio, the
young architect who is carrying Teresa swiftly away, comes to pay his respects to his mothers-in-law in assembly. In the midst of their talk, their
many domestic instructions to him,
their fervent blessings, the convent
bell summons them to the evening devotions. They rise obediently. Subdued in their talk, dignified in their
bearing, these sisters never give in to
their emotions. But the agony of the
parting nearly breaks them. Even the
vicaress snuffles a little. And as she
admonishes them to mind the pauses
in their prayers and to read them with
greater care than recently, the tears in
her throat nearly choke her speaking.
Miss Terry gives a splendid performance in the part of the prioress who
dominates this convent with wisdom
and sweetness. Miss Roberts expresses
well the crotchets of the vicaress and
also the downright, defiant affection.
Miss de Neergaard is amusingly
wicked as the sister who is never quite
serene under the veil. As the most
practical of the many vicarious mothers, Miss Le Gallienne plays with perhaps too much restraint. Miss Hutchinson, who first swept into fame last
year in "A Man's Man," gives a lovely performance as the foster-child of
a convent. As the physician Mr.
Brecher makes a good contrast in the
gruffness of his voice and manner.
The performance has been nicely attuned to its half-sacred, half-secular
theme.
Martinez Sierra is a Spanish poet,
novelist, dramatist, musician, actor,
and nearly everything else, including
manager of a theatre in Madrid. His
"Very Romantic Young Lady" was
produced at the Neighborhood Playhouse last Spring. "Cradle Song" was

written in 1911, and played here a matinees in 1921. It was successfully mounted in London early in the present season.

1927 Ja 25

Marriage, Love, &c.

SATURDAY'S CHILDREN, a comedy in three acts, by Maxwell Anderson. Settings by Jo Mielziner; staged by Guthrie McClintic; produced by the Actors' Theatre, Inc. At the Booth Theatre.
Florrie Sands..................Ruth Hammond
Willie Sands...................Richard Barbee
Mrs. Halevy.....................Lucia Moore
Bobby..........................Ruth Gordon
Mr. Halevy...................Frederick Perry
Rims O'Neil.....................Roger Pryor
Mrs. Gorlik....................Beulah Bondi

By J. BROOKS ATKINSON.

Beneath the mild manner and the irritatingly mild speaking of "Saturday's Children," put on at the Booth last evening, Mr. Anderson reveals a disquieting understanding of his innocent contemporaries in the first throes of married life. As co-author of "What Price Glory" and as author of "Outside Looking In" Mr. Anderson's mood was belligerent if not actively militant. In spite of the rough edgings of his present subject, however, he is sympathetic towards marriage, and he writes of it not only with lucidity but also with a graceful comic touch and a nice sense of the theatre. "Saturday's Children" is a tenuous drama on the most elementary of subjects; it is written from a delightful point of view. On the whole, it represents the rickety Actor's Theatre in one of its sturdier moments.

Prompted by a cosmically wise sister, full of original sin and a breaking heart, Bobby Halevy (female) traps Rims O'Neil (male) into a proposal. Not wantonly. In the first place she was in love with him and he was with her, and in the second place he gave every evidence of running off to South America on a business adventure. Posing as the cynosure of all snapping masculine eyes, Bobby indicated that she might marry another impetuous suitor. And so they are married. By the time of the second act, six months later, they have exchanged their tumultuous love for rent, grocery bills and visiting relatives not without disillusionment. Impulsively Bobby slams the front door, goes back to her job and takes a furnished room in a house so respectable that the doors must be left open upon gentlemen callers, and the landlady is more vigilant than a library policeman. When her husband defeats respectability in the last scene by slipping in at the window and

clamping a lock on the door from the inside, one assumes that "Saturday's Children" have seen their most unhappy days.

As this summary may indicate, Mr. Anderson has not built up a smashing plot to tear his characters into passionate shreds. He is concerned rather with the ethics and the truth of his topic. Bobby's scheming, vulgar sister, Florrie Sands, already a mother, represents what is cynically known as the practical point of view; she is as hard as Craig's malevolent wife. She it is who writes out the conversational formula by which Bobby trips up Rims's celibacy; and when Bobby's frail marriage-craft begins to rock dangerously, she it is again who advises Bobby to bind her husband securely forever with a baby. (Apparently Florrie is more active than Craig's wife.) Miss Hammond plays the part of Florrie well with all the cheap worldliness, the selfishness and the "baby talk" coquetry that she pours like oil upon all troubled waters without discrimination. Without pride or ideals, Florrie is, like Artemus Ward's drafted soldier, a "loathsome sight."

To supply contrast, and the wisdom of maturity, Mr. Anderson has written an engaging part in Bobby's father, Mr. Halevy, played by Mr. Perry. Halevy père, ripe in experience, is lazily amused at the spectacle of his daughter's married life, and also filled with pity. Not only a father but a grandfather, and a married man of long, honorable standing, he can supply the "low-down" or the "O'Neill" on the whole complex jumble of desires and frustrations. Mr. Perry gives the part all the quiet, humorsome charm with which Mr. Anderson has imbued it—a literary rather than dramatic creation.

As the sister of Florrie and the daughter of her father, Bobby bursts with the entire conflict of loyalties described in the play. Miss Gordon, once the gauche flapper of "Mrs. Partridge Presents" and last season the comic wife of "The Fall of Eve," acts this much more incisive part with a curiously subtle penetration. Her face wears the same comically vacant expression and occasionally her gestures recall the awkward arm-thrusts for which she was once famous. In spite of this comic equipment Miss Gordon manages to express Bobby as an earnest, deadly serious young lady who is determined to play fair with her husband and to sacrifice none of her ideals in the humdrum of domesticity. Miss Gordon conveys within a definitely limited range all the torture of a sincere matron who has come up hard against the wall of life. For all the hackneyed details of its conception, this is a noble little part. Miss Gordon keeps it in tune.

Mr. Pryor is frank in his description of Rims O'Neil. Miss Bondi edges the part of the lodginghouse keeper with delicious comedy. Frequently the playing is too soft in texture for a piece that leans toward theatrical weakness. The performance might well be much more robust. One suspects Mr. Anderson of being more a man of letters than a man of the theatre. As the reviewers invariably say upon such occasions, "Saturday's Children" profits quite as much as it loses by that weakness.

1927 Ja 27

"Rio Rita" Riot.

RIO RITA, a musical comedy in two acts. Book by Guy Bolton and Fred Thompson and music and lyrics by Harry Tierney and Joseph McCarthy. Settings by Joseph Urban; book staged by John Harwood; costumes designed by John W. Harkrider; staged and produced by Florenz Ziegfeld. At the Ziegfeld Theatre, Sixth Avenue at Fifty-fourth Street.

Padrone ....Juan Villasana
Reporter ....Al Clair
Roberto Ferguson............George Baxter
Carmen ....Helen C. Clive
Ed Lovett ....Robert Woolsey
Grim Gomez ....Fred Dalton
General Enrique Joselito Esteban.
                        Vincent Serrano
Raquel ....Gladys Glad
Conchita ....Marion Benda
Juanita ....Dorothy Wegman
Lolita ....Peggy Blake
Beppo ....Kay English
Rio Rita ....Ethelind Terry
Chick Bean ....Bert Wheeler
Dolly ....Ada-May
Jim ....J. Harold Murray
Sergeant McGinn ....Harry Ratcliffe
Sergeant Wilkins ....Donald Douglas
Davalos ....Alf P. James
Escanillo ....Pedro Rubin
Herminia ....Collette
Katie Bean ....Noel Francis
Montezuma's Daughter.....Katherine Burke

By J. BROOKS ATKINSON.

After a sufficient number of bystanders had been jostled along by the police, and a sufficient number of flash-light bombs had been touched off, and a sufficient number of necks had been twisted out of joint in an excited search for celebrities in the audience, Mr. Ziegfeld managed to pull back the curtains for "Rio Rita" last evening as the first production in his smart new theatre. The playhouse and the musical comedy provided a thoroughly enjoyable evening. In decorative showmanship Mr. Ziegfeld is the master of style. "Rio Rita" breaks no fresh trail into the hinterland of musical comedy; the book is commonplace enough and the humor will never hold both its sides with laughter. But for sheer extravagance of beauty, animated and rhythmic, "Rio Rita" has no rival among its contemporaries.

Much has been written about Mr. Urban's egg-shell design for the new theatre, and how low "gags" have been ex-

changed among the Broadway cognoscenti—"gags" of a deprecatory nature. "Departing from the usual custom," says a program note, "of erecting a theatre without regard to the kind or form of amusement that may happen to find its way within its walls, the Ziegfeld Theatre has been conceived for a definite purpose—a theatre to house the lighter forms of dramatic entertainment, opera comique and musical comedies and revues." For the wall and ceiling decorations of this ellepitical playhouse Mr. Urban has unfolded one of the most extravagant and bizarre cycloramas of imaginative designing to be found this side of fairyland. It is not only splendid but appropriate. According to Socrates (who, of course, is dead) beauty is perfection in usefulness. By the terms of that Athenian definition, the Ziegfeld Theatre is the divination of beauty in playhouses; for it fits the type of entertainment Mr. Ziegfeld proposes to foster there like tne proverbial glove. Indeed, it sets a standard. Mr. Ziegfeld must take care lest his productions on the stage prove inferior to the sweep of carnival beauty on the walls of his theatre.

It you are interested in the plot of "Rio Rita," you have a detective's job on your hands. Down in Mexico-land, where oil leases keep the Statesmen up all night, a certain bad man dubbed the Kinkajou had been up to something or other. Until 11 o'clock, when the present reporter departed this Mexican life, the bold villainies of the two-gun daredevil had not been clearly established. But that had not prevented inordinately beautiful dancing girls, or gringo cabaret girls, or Albertina Rasch dancers, or South-American troubadours or, for the matter, the original Central American Marimba Band (Nicaraguan hostages, perhaps?) from spinning across the stage, stamping their chic feet in unison or singing in chorus on any number of hot-blooded themes. In the most lustrous costumes —silver sombreros, blood-red shirts, fluffy ballet stuffs, embroidered velvet waistcoats—they whirled in squads, one on the heels of another, until the stage was as furious in its design as the wall decorations.

Meanwhile, Mr. Urban's scene portraits had painted the limitless space of Mexican outdoors and the evening warmth of a patio; and fine tapestries had masked the stage during the scene changes. The hippodromic proportions of "Rio Rita," splashed with bold brushfuls of color, were a feast to the eye.

Like the costuming, the casting is in the best of taste. As Rita (with whom life is "sweeta") Miss Terry sings of sweethearts or love or any other appropriate subject in a good voice that is notably well trained. And Mr. Murray, his collar reckleessly thrown open to display a manly throat, leads the Texas rangers in their "Vagabond

King" type of marching song. Miss May and Mr. Wheeler, equally adept in singing, "hoofing" and clowning, give a light touch to the production. For it is Miss May, in her topical jingles, who whispers the secrets of night-club closing, and concludes, for those who are in touch with the important news of the day, that one Browning "may be up a tree, but he can't shake Peaches down."

As a smart-Alec lawyer, Mr. Woolsey refuses "to give into his animal passions" by smoking Camels and generally conducts himself in that inoffensively droll fashion. According to the late tidings by special courier, Miss Francis, Miss May, Mr. Wheeler and Mr. Woolsey contribute one uncommonly amusing knockabout comedy skit late in the program.

Thus, "Rio Rita" packs the evening with lavish beauty—with beauty in detail as well as in general impression. Like a good architect, Mr. Ziegfeld looks to the soundness of his foundation before he starts piercing the clouds with super-structure. As the production is repeated it will no doubt settle down and cohere and move with greater speed than on its première.

Mr. Ziegfeld, no less than his patrons, was in a holiday mood last evening. Telegrammed to death with felicitions, he weakly displayed messages from President Coolidge, Mayor Walker and Eddie Cantor as evidence of the democracy of his friendships.

1927 F 3

Behind the Burlesque Scenes.

BURLESQUE, a comedy in three acts, by George Manker Watters and Arthur Hopkins. Settings by Cleon Throckmorton; staged and produced by Mr. Hopkins. At the Plymouth Theatre.

Bonny	Barbara Stanwyck
Jimmy	Paul Porter
Skid	Hal Skelly
Lefty	Charles D. Brown
A Fireman	Jack B. Shea
Mazie	Eileen Wilson
Gussie	Pauline Dee
Sylvia Marco	Ruth Holden
Bozo	Mitty DeVere
Harvey Howell	Ralph Theadore
Jerry Evans	Oscar Levant
A Walter	Wilkie Dodsworth
Stage Carpenter	Joseph Burton
Scotty	Jack B. Shea
Jack	Wilkie Dodsworth

By J. BROOKS ATKINSON.

With the production of "Burlesque" at the Plymouth last evening the native drama went behind the scenes of the show business again, as it did a year ago with "Broadway." For that is the fashion just now—to show us that honest emotions throb behind the tinsel and grease paint of the stage. If "Broadway" had not done the trick first, and with infinitely more skill in both drama and producing, "Burlesque" might not seem as clumsily written and staged as it does. Certainly it does not move with the brisk, flaming tempo of its brilliant predecessor. Its flair for genuine characterization, however, its picturesque mise-enscène and its comic dialogue, smelling of the pungent backstage theatre, should make it acceptable entertainment to the playgoer interested in the theatre.

Such panoramic dramas, as we have come to know them, do not require a firmly textured story. No exception to the rule, "Burlesque" weaves a picturesque course through the married life of a "low comic" and his wife. It is too familiar, in life and in the theatre, ever to seem novel. Skid, the principal comedian of a burlesque troupe, rises from the two-a-day to the glamour of the New York musical stage, under the tutelage of one Dillingham. He leaves his wife on the circuit. Without her in this wicked city he falls from grace until the bootleggers of New York and New Jersey groan from exhaustion and dismay. After one notorious party he loses his engagement. In the last act of "Burlesque" he is back in the circuit again in the affectionate care of his wife. During a "hoofing" scene, staged as such for the final scene of the play, they swear the eternal verities once more.

The story is admittedly commonplace and scattered. With the assistance of a grand performance by Hal Skelly as the "low comic" and Barbara Stanwyck as his wife ("head woman," as Moran and Mack would say of both the hoofer and the burlesque troupe), this comedy does better when it steers an unsteady, sometimes revealing course, among company managers, crowds of vindictive show-girls, gambling comedians and the usual big ranch man from the West.

In a dressing-room in the first act the "beef trust girl" and the new soubrette pull hair with a vengeance. In the drawing-room of a New York hotel suite several show folk dance riotously, and match sentimentalities on the wing. And in the last act of two scenes they rehearse to the blasphemous direction of a manager, and finally stage four or five scenes of their first-night performance. Through all this backstage huggermugger the story makes its way uncertainly. An audience largely composed of theatrical people relished the quips last evening excessively. "I've seen plenty of actors at the Friars and the Lambs," said the comedian disdainfully; "I'd rather work." And the provincial lady who wondered whether Klaw and Erlanger were really married. And the comedian who took so many bows that he bumped his knee and blacked his eye. These and other nicely polished gibes amused an expectant first night audience.

None of the details of dialogue or background matches the resourcefulness of the acting. As the comedian in question Mr. Skelly gives a glowing performance of fleeting character portrayal amid a whirl of eccentric make-ups and bits of hoofing and clowning. Trained on the circuit he speaks with authority of the putty-nose school of drama. Miss Stanwyck as his wife plays with genuine emotion and kicks her way skillfully through the chorus numbers. Miss Wilson as the soubrette and Mr. Brown as the company manager act their less conspicuous parts with a real tang. In the subordinate part of a cattle man Mr. Theadore gives a splendidly simple, frank, unembellished performance.

With a tighter, more symmetrical story and much firmer direction such actors could transform "Burlesque" into a swift instrument of acted drama. More and more the new plays prove that acting is generally more competent than playwriting. The essential idea of a play like "Burlesque" seems fascinating to any one who loves the theatre and the mad, irresponsible life that flows through the dressing rooms. But it requires more authoritative discipline, more versatility in showmanship, than the performance of "Burlesque" reveals. After properly rewarding the highly seasoned acting and confessing the lure of such theatrical material, one still leaves the theatre disappointed. "Burlesque" might have been far more incisive than it is.

1927 S 2

College Musical

GOOD NEWS, a musical comedy in two acts and nine scenes, by Laurence Schwab and B. G. DeSylva; music by Ray Henderson; lyrics by Lew Brown and Mr. DeSylva. Settings by Donald Oenslager; musical numbers staged by Bobby Connolly; directed by Edgar MacGregor; produced by Laurence Schwab and Frank Mandel. At Chanin's Forty-sixth Street Theatre.

Tom Marlowe	John Price Jones
"Beef" Saunders	John Grant
Bobby Randall	Gus Shy
Bill Johnson	Edwin Redding
"Pooch" Kearney	John Sheehan
Charles Kenyon	Edward Emery
Patricia Bingham	Shirley Vernon
Constance Lane	Mary Lawlor
Babe O'Day	Inez Courtney
Sylvester	Don Tomkins
Windy	Wally Coyle
Slats	Jack Kennedy
Millie	Ruth Mayon
Flo	Zelma O'Neal
The Band Leader	George Olsen

The Glee Club Trio,
    Bob Rice, Fran Frey and Bob Borger
The College Band...George Olsen's Orchestra

By J. BROOKS ATKINSON.

Co-education in America was considerably bucked up at the Forty-sixth Street Theatre last evening where "Good News" rah-rahed, joked, flirted and finally made an exciting end-run and a touchdown for "dear old (fill in name of)"——, in this instance, Tait College. Briefly, it is a ripping good show.

For once a musical play based upon undergraduate life and a football game has some resemblance to the disorderly, rhymeless scheme of things in American institutions of learning. Of course, the old staples of jealousy, misunderstanding and love's endearing young charms shape the plot for stage purposes. And the professor hated by every one for his nasty insistence upon rules and regulations turns out to be tenderhearted after all. True to stage form, he passes the captain of the football team on the eve of the Big Game. Tom Marlowe tosses the ball to Bobby Randall who sees the Main Chance and carries the pigskin across the goal line for a great Big Touchdown. Well, as Bobby Randall says on a less exciting occasion, "No matter how you slice it, it's still bologna." It also makes for rattling good entertainment in the theatre.

Every one in "Good News" is athaletic. The ushers wear the old jerseys, familiar in college life no less than twenty-five years ago; and George Olsen's nifty jazz orchestra begins the festivities with a sideline roar of "rah, rah, rah." Even before the curtain rose the adventuresome playgoers thus foresaw the Big Game of the Season.

What they did not foresee, perhaps, was a constantly fast entertainment with furious dancing, catchy tunes played to the last trombone squeal, endless light fooling by Gus Shy and Inez Courtney, excellent singing and genuine excitement in the last few scenes during the football game. Mary Lawlor, in the part of the misunderstanding young lady, is soft and charming, if rather too condescendingly coy. John Price Jones makes an inoffensively handsome football hero with an able singing voice. Edward Emery, late of "The Constant Nymph," is an extravagantly fine actor for a musical show; he makes the sour professor tenable. And one pert young freshman, Zelma O'Neal, dances herself into willing exhaustion to the snapping tune of "The Varsity Drag." In short, every one down to the transfixed Don Tomkins, a freshman, raises the known standards of college vitality considerably higher. "Good News" is what that label promises.

All that gossip has whispered about the chief studies of co-educational institutions turns out to be true in Dear Old Tait. Under the college arms of "Amor et Spes," these flaming youths just exist from one excitement to another. As in the old church anthem, they "laugh and sing.'' Crowds of them step rapidly and clap their hands in unison on the campus. Private life in the men's dormitory is one merry round of alarm-clock attachments, games, ill-kempt clothes and football signals. In affectionate groupings the sorority girls wander gracefully through the mystic rites of pajama parties; and the boys run in and out with no apparent embarrassment. Hear the impromptu football rallies in the campus. Hear the coach plead for the honor of the old college and the captain modestly depreciate his prowess.

If all this balderdash seems rather trying to the squeamish reader, be it known that the football scenes bear the authority of the Notre Dame coach. Doubtless it was Knute Rockne who steered the stage pontiffs accurately through the trying business of the locker-room scene. Observing the decencies of the stage, the coach curbs his traditionally profane tongue a trifle. But his whole-hearted abuse, the football team's dejection and the contempt of the old timer who knew players when players were players, have the ring of gridiron authenticity. Mr. Oenslager's settings for this and the other scenes are agreeable to contemplate.

Lively, humorous and skillfully staged, "Good News" fills the evening with solid pleasure.

1927 S 7

Negro Lithography.

PORGY, a play in four acts, by Dorothy and DuBose Heyward. Settings by Cleon Throckmorton; staged by Rouben Mamoulian; produced by The Theatre Guild. At the Guild Theatre.

Maria...........................Georgette Harvey
Jake..............................Wesley Hill
Lily.............................Dorothy Paul
Mingo............................R. J. Huey
Annie............................Ella Madison
Sporting Life....................Percy Verwayne
Serena...........................Rose McClendon
Robbins..........................Lloyd Gray
Jim..............................Peter Clark
Clara............................Mary Young
Peter............................Hayes Pryor
Porgy............................Frank Wilson
Crown............................George Moore
Crown's Bess.....................Evelyn Ellis
A Detective......................Stanley de Wolfe
Policemen..Hugh Rennie and Maurice McRae
Undertaker.......................Leigh Whipper
Scipio...........................Melville Greene
Simon Frazier....................A. B. Comathiere
Nelson...........................G. Edward Brown
Alan Archdale....................Edward Fielding
The Crab Man.....................Leigh Whipper
The Coroner......................Garrett Minturn

In spite of many obvious weaknesses in the texture of the performance, the dramatization of "Porgy," put on at the Guild Theatre last evening, turns out to be steadily interesting in the best tradition of the Guild. Originally "Porgy" was a crisp, vivid novel by DuBose Heyward. Transformed into a play it

is not crisp, and only spasmodically vivid; it is rather a chocolate-colored lithograph strip, splashed with color, disorderly, unwieldy, heavy and spontaneous by turns, yet always true. The performance matches both the strength and the weakness of this style of showmanship. But it represents the Theatre Guild off the beaten path of easy successes as it should be; and those who enjoy new American themes, honestly and authoritatively treated, will find "Porgy" worth their while.

The story of "Porgy" is simple enough. He is a negro mendicant, inhabitant of a squalid, brawling alley near St. Martin's Church in Charleston, S. C. By one of those odd streaks of fortune, typical of the rhymeless negro life, he finds himself sheltering Crown's notorious woman, Bess, while Crown is hiding from the law. Bess and Porgy get on surprisingly well. They successfully defeat Crown's attempt to wean Bess to himself again. They outwit the police and break down the opposition of pious women negroes in the alley. But fortune again separates them at the moment when, by all sound logic, their troubles should be finished. The play closes on a piteous scene in which Porgy tumbles into his goat cart and sets out for New York in search of his "woman," who, for all her vicious caprices, has become essential to his happiness.

In the novel Mr. Heyward managed skillfully to compress all the background and local color into the movement of his story. In the play he and his wife, Dorothy Hartzell Kuhns, resort to showmanship. With a cast of twenty-three characters, countless neighbors in the bustling alley, and nine fairly disjointed scenes, "Porgy" emerges as an ebony carnival of crap-shooting, murders, blaring picnics, comedy bits, passionate spirituals, a hurricane storm —a thread of story running timidly through a sprawling production. Sometimes it drifts away into tedium. Again the pace quickens, the action sharpens and negro life scampers panic-stricken into every corner of the alley. Visually it is picturesque. The acting and the singing are frequently eloquent. And as a bit of folk-life it catches the loyalties and superstitions of the negro in what their true value must be. If the Heywards have not made an articulate play, at least they have never sacrificed truth for showmanship.

Excepting a policeman or two, a detective and a lawyer, all the parts are negro, and are played by negro actors. Perhaps none of the white actors is particularly expressive; but, at any rate, it is amusing to see how trifling the white acting becomes against the turbulence of the negroes. Porgy is played by Frank Wilson, a letter carrier by trade, who acted beautifully in "In Abraham's Bosom." Rose MacClendon, a colleague in that former adventure, is also here. They are ably assisted by Wesley Hill as a full-spirited, full-blooded fisherman, Percy Verwayne as a suave New Yorker, Jack Carter as a domineering bully; A. F. Comathiere as a pompous negro shyster, Georgette Harvey as a bellowing, arms-akimbo alley oracle, and Evelyn Ellis as Bess, tormented by her sensual past.

In such acting there is life and spirit; it is lavish, animal and usually undisciplined. When the course of the drama requires discipline—as for grouping and pacing—the acting becomes subtly uneasy. Although the action sometimes flows into singing and swaying by the most natural transitions, the spirituals seem rather overdone. For the most part the direction appears to have made only the most elementary uses of a large and novel production. But for the curtain of one of the early scenes it rises to splendid theatrical generalship. Serena's room in the tenement is crowded with negroes swaying and singing graveyard melodies beside the covered body of the murdered crapshooter. Gradually the singing becomes more and more preternatural. In the violence of the religious orgy the lights are deliberately turned down until the stage is illuminated only from the front, and the pale wall behind quickly swarms with a myriad of dancing, swirling, leaping shadows. "Porgy" does not always live in the theatre as graphically as that scene expresses it.

1927 O 11

TAMING OF THE SHREW'
REVIVED IN 1927 DRESS

New Company at the Garrick Theatre Makes Shakespeare's Play a Good Show.

By J. BROOKS ATKINSON.

THE TAMING OF THE SHREW. Revival of Shakespeare's coedy in modern dress. Staged by H. K. Ayliff; prodced by The Garrick Players. At the Garrick Theatre.

A Lord	Berresford Lovett
Christopher Sly	C. H. Croker-King
Hostess	Engel Summer
Page	Teddy Jones
Huntsman	Thomas Donnelly
Valet	Robert Vivian
A Guest	Edla Frankau
Lucentio	Leslie Barrie
Tranio	Reginald Bach
Baptista Minola	Fothringham Lysons
Gremio	Maurice Cass
Hortensio	Gerald Hamer
Katherina Minola	Mary Ellis
Bianca Minola	Betty Linley
Biondelio	John McGovern
Petruchio	Basil Sydney
Grumio	Junius Matthews
Servant to Baptista	Mylom Merriam
Widow	Margaret George
Curtis	Maria Ouspenskava
Nathanial	Walter Speakman
Gregory	Richard Skinner
Tailor	Seldon Bennett
Pedant	Robert Vivian
Vincentio	Thomas Donnelly
Officer	John Turner

The considerable task of demonstrating the agelessness of Shakespeare, begun here a few seasons ago with the modern-clothes "Hamlet," was continued last night at the Garrick with an up-to-the-minute production of "The Taming of the Shrew." These productions are primarily exhibits of a producer's ingenuity, and it doesn't take so much ingenuity at that. One has but to comb the text for possible spots for interpolation—spots where the lines lend themselves to, or rather permit, the elaboration of the situation by means of a carpet sweeper, or an electric heater, or perhaps an automobile.

These little sundries furnish momentary pictorial amusement, but are likely to arouse an expectation great r than they can fulfill. The joke is soon over, but must necessarily be prolonged for the duration of the scene. The mere presence of modern dress is a less obtrusive factor; one is nowhere especially conscious of the clothes in the case of the production at the Garrick. But the other accessories, instead of proving the bard's agelessness, do rather the reverse. One strains to hear by what double entendre the presence of radio or revolver is justified; the amusement of the moment is matched by a consciousness of the trick.

This somewhat peevish complaint having been recorded, it may now be further remarked that in the main the new company at the Garrick has made "The Shrew" into a pretty good show. The major scenes of the play, in particular, proceed with spirit and interest, and if there is a flagging during some of the minor episodes it may be Shakespeare's fault. The question of who was going to marry Bianca certainly seemed gorgeously unimportant last night.

A good deal of the enjoyment is derived from the fact that Basil Sydney makes an excellent Petruchio. It is not detracting in the least from Mr. Sydney's performance to add

that Petruchio is not the most difficult of Shakespeare's leading parts;
both the character and the action are
simple in the extreme. Mary Ellis is,
of course, a beautiful Katherine—excellent in the rôle's occasional lighter
moments, such as the sun-and-moon
episode on the return trip to Padua,
but falling a little short of the fury
that should obsess her. There was,
too, the necessity for bridging the
sparsity of Katherina's lines by pantomimic rage, and this did not make
the task any easier.

One of the favorites of the evening
turned out to be Reginald Bach, an
English actor with a German name,
who played Tranio with a Cockney
accent and much comic spirit. There
was also Maria Ouspenskaya, who
never did catch up with the Moscow
Art Theatre again, playing Petruchio's cook and making of the rôle
an effective cartoon. And there
should be room for the news that
the cast also included an actor
named Fothringham Lysons.

The production marks the beginning of a new era at the Garrick—
the invading organization, dominated
by Mr. Sydney and Miss Ellis, announces that it is there to stay, with
a new play every month. And the
Garrick, it will be remembered, is
where the Theatre Guild began.

1927 O 26

SHOW BOAT, "an all American musical
comedy" in two acts, adapted from Edna
Ferber's novel of the same name. Book
and lyrics by Oscar Hammerstein 2d,
with music by Jerome Kern. Settings by
Josef Urban; dances arranged by Sammy
Lee; dialogue directed by Zeke Colvan;
costumes designed by John Harkrider;
produced by Florenz Ziegfeld. At the
Ziegfeld Theatre.

Windy ....Allan Campbell
Queenie ....Aunt Jemima
Steve ....Charles Ellis
Pete ....Bert Chapman
Parthy Ann Hawks ......Edna May Oliver
Cap'n Andy ....Charles Winninger
Ellie ....Eva Puck
Frank ....Sammy White
Rubber Face ....Francis X. Mahoney
Julie ....Helen Morgan
Gaylord Ravenal ....Howard Marsh
Vallon ....Thomas Gunn
Magnolia ....Norma Terris
Joe ....Jules Bledsoe
Dealer ....Jack Wynn
Gambler ....Phil Sheridan
Backwoodsman ....Jack Daley
Jeb ....Jack Wynn
La Belle Fatima ....Dorothy Denese
Old Sport ....Bert Chapman
Landlady ....Annie Hart
Ethel ....Estelle Floyd
Sister ....Annette Harding
Mother Superior ......Mildred Schewenke
Kim (child) ....Eleanor Shaw
Kim (as young woman) .....Norma Terris
Jake ....Robert Farley

Max ....Jack Daley
Man With Guitar ....Ted Daniels
Charlie ....J. Lewis Johnson
Lottie ....Tana Kamp
Dolly ....Dagmar Oakland
Old Lady on Levee ....Laura Clairon

The worlds of Broadway and Park
Avenue and their respective wives
put on their best bibs and tuckers
last night and converged at Mr. Ziegfeld's handsome new playhouse on
Sixth Avenue. There they milled
about elegantly in the lobby, were
pictured by flashlight photographers
and finally got to their seats and to
the business in hand. That was the
inspection of the newest offering
from the workshops of the maestro,
the much-heralded musical adaptation of Edna Ferber's novel, "Show
Boat."

From such remote centres of
theatrical omniscience as Pittsburgh,
Washington and Philadelphia had
come the advance word that it was
better than good—some reports even
extravagantly had it that here was
Mr. Ziegfeld's superlative achievement. It would be difficult to quarrel with such tidings, for last night's
performance came perilously near to
realizing the most fulsome of them.

All right, there you have it: "Show
Boat" is, with a few reservations in
favor of some of the earlier "Follies"
and possibly "Sally," just about the
best musical piece ever to arrive under Mr. Ziegfeld's silken gonfalon.
It has, barring perhaps a slight lack
of one kind of comedy, and an over-
abundance of another, and a little
slowness in getting under way—this
last due to the fact that it is
crammed with plot which simply
must be explained—about every in-
gredient that the perfect song-and-
dance concoction should have.

In its adherence to its story it is
positively slavish. The adaptation
of the novel has been intelligently
made, and such liberties as the demands of musical comedy necessi-
tate do not twist the tale nor dis-
tort its values. For this, and for
the far better than the average lyrics
with which it is endowed, credit Oscar Hammerstein 2d, who is rapidly
monopolizing the function of author
for the town's musical entertainments.

Then, too, "Show Boat" has an exceptionally tuneful score—the most lilting and satisfactory that the wily Jerome Kern has contrived in several seasons. Potential song hits were as common last night as top hats. Such musical recordings of amorous reaction as "You Are in Love," "I Can't Help Lovin' That Man," ' Do I Love You?" are sufficient for any show—to say nothing of "Old Man River," which Jules Bledsoe and a negro chorus make remarkably effective.

If these three contributions—book, lyrics and score—call for a string of laudatory adjectives, the production compels that they be repeated again—and with a short tiger. The colorful scenes on and around the showboat, plying its course along the Mississippi, that comprise the first act lend themselves well to a variety of effects and have been achieved with Mr. Ziegfeld's unimpeachable skill and taste.

In the second act the nine in r-ludes carry the spectator from the gaudy Midway Plaisance of the World's Fair to the sombre quiet of St. Agatha's Convent and then back to the new and mo ernized floating theatre, 1927 variety. The settings are all atmospherically perfect; the costumes are in the style of each of the periods and there is a finish and polish about the completed entity that caused even a first performance to move with unusual smoothness.

To recount in any detail the plot of a musical comedy usually is a silly and banal business; to tell Miss Ferber's large and clamorous public what happens to Magnolia and Gaylord Ravenal is unnecessary. But to tell them of the manner in which these characters and the many others of the best seller have been brought to life is something else again.

As Magnolia, Norma Terris appeared to be a revelation, even to the first nighters who had watched her work in previous dance-and-tune saturnalias. Her realization of Captain Andy's daughter seemed complete, even when she got around to imitating Ted Lewis and Ethel Barrymore in the final, or 11:45 P. M., scene. Howard Marsh, one of the more facial tenors, made a handsome and satisfactory Ravenal. Helen Morgan, who is among the town's most adept song saleswomen, was Julie, and purveyed two numbers in her distinctive style. As the dour and formidable New England mother, Parthy Ann Hawks, Edna May Oliver played with requisite austerity, although she did forget herself long enough to engage in a dance.

But the outstanding hit of the evening seemed to be reserved for Charles Winninger, who cut capers to his heart's content as Captain Andy.

He is in top form, and when Mr. Winninger is in top form he is an extremely waggish fellow. And in a moment during the "Show Boat's" performance when through the defection of an affrighted villain he is compelled to seize the stage and act out the remainder of the play himself, he is extraordinarily persuasive and convincing. Then there are the reliable Puck and White, presenting the low comedy specialties, and others too numerous to mention.

"Show Boat," as it should not be too difficult for the reader to ascertain by now, is an excellent musical comedy; one that comes perilously close to being the best the town has seen in several seasons. It must have afforded its producer, who has poured dollars into it by the thousands, a certain ironic satisfaction to hear the play's Chicago cabaret manager say with an air of finality, "No, I can't afford to take chances with amateurs with a $2,000 production on my hands." Mr. Ziegfeld can't afford to, either.

1927 D 28

1928

STRANGE INTERLUDE PLAYS FIVE HOURS

Eugene O'Neill's Melodrama Begins at 5:15, With Intermission at 7:40 for Dinner.

NINE   PICTURESQUE   ACTS

Old 'Aside' Used in Psychopathic Work That Combines Novel and Drama Techniques.

STRANGE INTERLUDE, a play in nine acts, by Eugene O'Neill. Staged by Philip Moeller; settings by Jo Mielziner; produced by the Theatre Guild. At the John Golden Theatre.
Charles Marsden.................Tom Powers
Professor Leeds.................Philip Leigh
Nina Leeds.....................Lynn Fontanne
Sam Evans......................Earle Larimore
Edmund Darrell.................Glenn Anders
Mrs. Amos Evans...............Helen Westley
Gordon Evans..................Charles Walters
Madeline Arnold...............Ethel Westley
Gordon Evans..................John J. Burns

By J. BROOKS ATKINSON.

Fresh, from the five hours of Eugene O'Neill's "Strange Interlude," performed at the John Golden last evening, one can soberly report that this nine-act drama at least maintains the interest to the end. It begins at 5:15, adjourns for dinner at 7:40, reconvenes at 9 and concludes at 11. Written by our foremost dramatist, acted intelligently by a notable troupe of actors, directed intelligently by Philip Moeller and sponsored by the Theatre Guild, "Strange Interlude" commands the respectful interest of the enthusiastic playgoer to whom experiment is never dull. All this one can earnestly report without believing that "Strange Interlude" is distinguished as a play or that Mr. O'Neill's combination of the novel and drama techniques is a permanent addition to the theatre.

By this time every sedulous theatregoer knows that in "Strange Interlude" Mr. O'Neill has introduced the old "aside" as an integral part of his psychopathic melodrama. His characters not only speak to each other in the normal dialogue of drama, but also utter their private thoughts in passing. When Nina Leeds accuses Charles Marsden of being "ghostless," for example, he speaks his private thought before he answers her statement publicly. "Ghostless? If she only knew!" Frequently these "asides" reveal a dramatic quality all their own. As often they seem fortuitous.

In the nine picaresque acts of his drama Mr. O'Neill records the sordid love affairs of a New England young woman whose betrothed was killed in the war. Thus denied the privilege of bearing a child by him, she succumbs to a morbid preoccupation in sex and gives herself gratuitously to promiscuous experiences. Finally she marries Sam Evans, a disarming weakling, but discovers that insanity is inherited in his family. Still eager to have a child, as much to satisfy her unwitting husband's pride as her own vanity, she takes their mutual friend, Edmund Darrell, as her lover. Believing himself a parent, and loved by his wife, Evans fairly blossoms with self-confidence and worldly success. In the meantime Darrell and Nina find themselves deeply and hopelessly in love.

The motives and incidents of "Strange Interlude" are far too complicated to be communicated in a fleeting newspaper review. And if one sometimes begrudges Mr. O'Neill the motives upon which he constructs his story one must at least concede him the ingenuity of his craftsmanship. The concluding acts describe the cross-purposes that torment the two lovers, the death of Sam Evans, and Nina's remarriage, not to Darrell, but to a pettifogging novelist who has always pursued her helplessly. Curiously enough Nina's illegitimately conceived son grows up in the image of her heroic fiancé who was killed years ago in the war; he repeats the triumphs of his mother's disembodied ideal, and her wish thus graphically becomes the father of her boy.

In the fable of "Strange Interlude" Mr. O'Neill has returned to the morbidness of his middle-period, a preoccupation with dark and devious human impulses, twisted and macabre. Nor does his point of view sweeten the unsavoriness of his material. Mr. O'Neill sets it down forcibly in all its rancor, hatred and despair. Even when the human motives are unselfish they are blighted by the selfish pestilence of others. In short, Mr. O'Neill does not illuminate his theme with pity or interpret its significance. Regarded purely as a story, "Strange Interlude" appears, at least to this observer, to lack dramatic distinction and originality. As in "Desire Under the Elms," one feels rather the mordant passion of the author, to whom these black forces have a strangely searching reality.

But, constructed of "asides" and in nine acts, "Strange Interlude" obviously is not to be approached purely as story. In spite of at least one forerunner, a piece entitled "Overtones," in which "asides" were essential to the drama, Mr. O'Neill's play has the novelty of an experiment. He pulls up his curtain on an expository "aside." He flings in "asides" generously throughout the first act. As the piece moves on they become less frequent as well as less subordinate. Long stretches of the drama run in the familiar conversational dialogue of the stage.

After the playgoer has become accustomed to having the characters mumble their private thoughts—for all the world like chants or prayers—he begins to search for their value. How much substance do they contribute to the drama? What fresh light do they reflect upon character? What do they express which cannot be conveyed vividly through the silent instrument of acting? What, in fine, distinguishes "Strange Interlude" from the old three-decker novel?

In the personal opinion of this reviewer, the answers to these questions must vary. When the "aside" merely elaborates the spoken thought it deadens the action until "Strange Interlude" looks like a slow-motion picture. And one irreverently suspects that there may be an even deeper thought unexpressed than the nickel-weekly jargon that Mr. O'Neill offers as thinking. Sometimes the "aside" is pure anti-climax after the speaking. When the "aside" shows contrast, and when it releases a smoldering passion that cannot burn in the normal dialogue, it is impregnated with the very stuff of drama. Even the pedant would not dispute its legitimacy, as no one disputed it in the entire history of drama until the naturalistic technique of the well-built play laid a deadly hand on playwrighting early in the century. Mr. O'Neill has restored the "aside" without giving it an entirely new meaning. He has not, one suspects, always used it wisely.

In the acting of this difficult and prolix chronicle drama the Guild company discloses rare mettle. Lynn Fontanne as Nina and Earle Larimore as Sam Evans play with admirable distinction and resourcefulness. More than any of the others they have mastered the technique of this strange play; and without upsetting the flow of drama they contrive to give their "asides" a true value. Meanwhile they describe two characters completely. One cannot speak too highly of their skill. As the other two chief characters, Tom Powers and Glenn Anders contribute admirable performances to a generally revealing performance. And without appearing precocious young Charles Walters conducts himself creditably as the son 12 years of age.

Limitations of space in the John Golden Theatre are said to be responsible for the indifferent lighting of Mr. Mielziner's utilitarian sets. Otherwise the Guild in a hospitable mood has lavished skill and patience—quite successfully—upon an exceedingly voluble play.

1928 Ja 31

In Newspaper English.

THE FRONT PAGE, a play in three acts, by Ben Hecht and Charles MacArthur. Staged by George S. Kaufman; settings by Raymond Sovey; produced by Jed Harris. At the Times Square Theatre.

Wilson	Vincent York
Endicott	Allen Jenkins
Murphy	Willard Robertson
McCue	William Foran
Schwartz	Tammany Young
Kruger	Joseph Spurin-Calleia
Bensinger	Walter Baldwin
Mrs. Schlosser	Violet Barney
Woodenshoes Eichorn	Jay Wilson
Diamond Louis	Eduardo Ciannelli
Hildy Johnson	Lee Tracy
Jennie	Carrie Weller
Molly Molloy	Dorothy Stickney
Sheriff Hartman	Claude Cooper
Peggy Grant	Frances Fuller
Mrs. Grant	Jessie Crommette
The Mayor	George Barbier
Mr. Pincus	Frank Conlan
Earl Williams	George Leach
Walter Burns	Osgood Perkins
Carl	Matthew Crowley
Frank	Gene West

By superimposing a breathless melodrama upon a good newspaper play the authors and directors of "The Front Page," shown at the Times Square last night, have packed an evening with loud, rapid, coarse and unfailing entertainment. Set in the press room of the Criminal Courts Building in Chicago, it stirs up reporters, criminals, politicians, wives and sweethearts into a steaming broth of excitement and comedy; and last evening an audience, obviously prepared to be delighted, hung on every line and episode until the end. Ben Hecht, novelist and dramatist and Chicago arbiter of taste, and Charles MacArthur, co-author of "Lulu Belle," have told a racy story with all the tang of front-page journalism, and George S. Kaufman has poured it on the stage resourcefully. Acted in the vernacular and in a lurid key by Lee Tracy, Willard Robertson, Osgood Perkins, Claude Cooper, Dorothy Stickney, George Barbier and many others—all welded into a seamless performance—"The Front Page" begins a new season noisily.

In the escape of a prisoner just on the eve of a political execution, and in the draggle-tailed characters involved, the authors have such a picturesque yarn to spin that their insistence upon thrusting bespattered conversation down the throats of the audience is as superfluous as it is unpleasant. No one who has ground his heels in the grime of a police headquarters press room will complain that this argot misrepresents the gentlemen of the press. And the Chicago scribes of "The Front Page," waiting impatiently for the hanging of Earl Williams while experimental sandbags are thumping on the gallows outside, are no cleaner of mouth than of linen. Wrangling at poker, leering over the political expediency of the execution, abusing the Sheriff and the Mayor insolently, they utter some of the baldest profanity and most slattern jesting that has ever been heard on the public stage. Graphic as it may be in tone and authenticity, it diverts attention from a vastly entertaining play.

The plot of "The Front Page" concerns Earl Williams's escape from jail on the eve of his hanging. For nearly an act he appears to be gone. In the fury of the excitement, when the press room is empty of all save Hildy Johnson of The Herald-Examiner, Williams feebly climbs in at the window and surrenders. But Hildy Johnson thinks fast. Instead of delivering Williams over to the police, who are searching for him far uptown, Johnson slams him into a roll-top desk and preserves him as a physical scoop for his newspaper. But even Walter Burns, the esoteric managing editor, cannot complete the kidnapping. Presently the police ferret out the mystery and only an eleventh-hour reprieve saves the neck of Earl Williams and saves Johnson and Burns from jail sentences.

After producing "Broadway" and "Spread Eagle," Jed Harris could not let such a plot cross the stage unembellished. And no stripped summary of "The Front Page" can convey the rowdy comedy of the pressroom, the whirr of the excitement, of nerves on edge, the apprehensive stupidity of the sheriff, the flatulence of the Mayor, the impatience of Johnson's fiancée who is ready to be married, the bewilderment of her mother caught up defenseless in the hurly-burly of a big newspaper yarn, the attempted bribery of the Governor's messenger and the ridiculousness of the inconsequential items telephoned to the desk while the man-hunt still prowls on. It is all here, down to the popular scrub woman and the policeman dispatched for sandwiches. Author and directors have accounted for every moment, tossed their story rapidly back and forth, and pulled down their curtains on the tensest episodes of all.

Such plays have little leisure for character development. Yet "The Front Page" denies the audience none of Hildy Johnson as he abandons newspaper work forever, blackens the character of his chief decisively, and finally juggles his impending marriage and a newspaper sensation through the rest of the play. Lee Tracy, one-time hoofer in "Broadway," acts the part vividly and impulsively. Willard Robertson, as the jaded sleuth for the Journal, plays admirably; and Osgood Perkins does as well by the managing editor. As Molly Malloy, a sinning sister of Clark Street, Dorothy Stickney gives one of her best performances. All the parts have been admirably cast. Equipped with a good script and directed with a sense of time and color, "The Front Page" keeps melodrama still the most able variety of current stage entertainment.

1928 Ag 15

A Tragedy of Submission.

MACHINAL, a play in two acts and ten "episodes," by Sophie Treadwell. Settings by Robert Edmond Jones; incidental music by Frank Harling; staged and produced by Arthur Hopkins. At the Plymouth Theatre.

A Young Woman	Zita Johann
A Telephone Girl	Millicent Green
A Stenographer	Grace Atwell
A Filing Clerk	Leopold Badia
An Adding Clerk	Conway Washburn
A Mother	Jean Adair
A Husband	George Stillwell
A Bellboy	Otto Frederick
A Nurse	Nancy Allan
A Doctor	Monroe Childs
A Young Man	Hal K. Dawson
A Girl	Zenaide Ziegfeld
A Man	Jess Sidney
A Boy	Clyde Stork
A Man	Clark Gable
Another Man	Hugh M. Hite
A Waiter	John Hanley
A Judge	John Waters
A Lawyer for Defense	John Connery
A Lawyer for Prosecution	James MacDonald
A Court Reporter	Otto Frederick
A Bailiff	John Hanley
A Reporter	Conway Washburn
Second Reporter	Hugh M. Hite.
Third Reporter	Hal K. Dawson
A Jailer	John Hanley
A Matron	Mrs. Charles Willard
A Priest	Charles Kennedy

By J. BROOKS ATKINSON.

From the sordid mess of a brutal murder the author, actors and producer of "Machinal," which was staged at the Plymouth last evening, have with great skill managed to retrieve a frail and sombre beauty of character. In superficial details the story resembles the Snyder and Gray murder case. But Sophie Treadwell, who is Mrs. W. O. McGeehan in private life, has in no sense capitalized a sensational murder trial in her strangely-moving, shadowy drama. Rather has she written a tragedy of submission; she has held an individual character against the hard surface of a mechanical age. And Zita Johann acts the leading part with a bewildered droop and a wistfulness that quite redeem the chief character from the commonness of the environment. Subdued, monotonous, episodic, occasionally eccentric in its style, "Machinal" is fraught with a beauty unfamiliar to the stage.

Throughout the rather commonplace story Miss Treadwell has kept the young woman pathetically individual. The first scene, treated expressionistically, discloses her in a business office, fumbling about her work, unhappy and afraid. She marries her giggling, complacent employer as the easiest way out of her private muddle. Successive episodes chronicle her career through marriage and motherhood. Once, vaguely pursuing some ideal, she falls in with an engaging adventurer; and now happy for the first time she takes him for her lover. In the last half of the play she is on trial for the murder of her husband. In conclusion, one scene shows her in prison on the eve of electrocution, and the last, played in darkness, reports bits of descriptive conversation and her frightened scream from the electric chair.

It is difficult by description to communicate the precise quality that distinguishes "Machinal" and that casts a subtly moving spell on the audience. Mr. Hopkins, as the producer and director, quite as much as Miss Treadwell, has isolated a fineness of spirit in the midst of shoddy externals. The husband's endless giggles and obese platitudes about success, the doctor's hurried, perfunctory observations in the sick room, the deadly average of the love scene, the impersonal hurry on all sides—all in contrast with the uncertainty of a human character, tell more of "Machinal" than its story. It is the tragedy of one who lacks strength; she is not adaptable; she submits. Events, people, circumstances stream by her, glib and optimistic, but they never relieve her loneliness. It is too much for her always. Wherever life touches her, it swamps her in mediocrity. Being the exposition of a character, stark and austere in style, "Machinal" makes no excuses for the tragedy it unfolds.

As the director Mr. Hopkins has kept it in a shade of monotone that does not produce the exhilaration we like in the theatre but that expresses the central character well. Personally and artistically Miss Johann represents the young woman in a studied, lucid performance. Without sentimentalizing the character, she conveys its frailty in the midst of a heedless world. As the husband, George Stillwell is amazingly true—simple and effortless in his fat,

mirthful smugness. And Clark Gable likewise plays the casually good-humored lover without a hackneyed gesture.

Excellent settings by Robert Edmond Jones, a warm, compelling ight effect by George Schaff as the concluding scene, contribute to the distinction of Mr. Hopkins's production. Yet still the precise quality of "Machinal" escapes definition in this ambiguous review.

1928 S 8

THE NEW MOON, a "romantic musical comedy" in two acts and twelve scenes. Book by Oscar Hammerstein 2d, Frank Mandel and Laurence Schwab and music by Sigmund Romberg. Dances arranged by Bobby Connolly; settings by Donald Oensinger; costumes designed by Charles Le Maire; produced by Schwab and Mandel. At the Imperial Theatre.

Julie.........................Marie Callahan
Monsieur Beaunoir.............Pacie Ripple
Captain Paul Duval........Edward Nell Jr.
Vicomte Ribaud...............Max Figman
Robert......................Robert Halliday
Alexander.......................Gus Shy
Besac........................Lyle Evans
Jacques.....................Earle Mitchell
Marianne...................Evelyn Herbert
Proprietor of the Tavern.....Daniel Barnes
Flower Girl...................Olga Albani
A Spaniard................Herman Belmonte
A Dancer.....................Edith Sheldon
Phillippe...................William O'Neal
Clotilde Lombaste...........Esther Howard
Fouchette....................Thomas Dale
Captain Dejean.................Lester Dorr
The Dancers............Rosita and Ramon
The Musicians......Hernandez Brothers Trio

Taking their story from the autobiography of an eighteenth-century French aristocrat, the fabricators of "The New Moon," which came up at the Imperial last evening, have produced an unusually pleasing musical comedy. Set to a full-bodied score by Sigmund Romberg, bedecked with flowing and brocaded costumes, sung, for the most part, beautifully, and acted with a grandeur that verges upon grandiloquence, it makes for generously romantic entertainment. Occasionally the political loyalties of the white-trousered tars, expressed chiefly by rhythmic thrusts of the arm and a tense look about the lips, seem too grim and fulsome for mugwump theatregoers. Let these flaming revolutionists swear their devotion with a bit less nobility. For the sake of sociability, let them have a frailty or two. The score, the singing, the costumes, the imaginatively directed dancing are pleasure enough.

Equipped with so stout a book, "The New Moon" approaches operetta. Oscar Hammerstein 2d, Frank Mandel and Laurence Schwab, authors in triplicate, have chronicled the daring adventures of one Robert Misson, whose carelessness with the lives of loyal subjects has made him an enemy of France. Disguised as a bondservant in the house of M. Beaunoir, right down here in our own New Orleans, Robert makes romantic love to his mistress, Marianne, and leads the revolutionists at the Chez Creole tavern. By manipulating the book quite honorably, the authors contrive his capture by the king's representative at a masked ball, put him in chains on the good ship New Moon, where his mistress follows loyally, arrange an attack by pirates, put him in command of the ship and find a way alternately to separate and join loving hearts until a late hour in the evening. It is not merely a good book; it is almost too good, and begins to weigh a little on the entertainment after the first act.

Painstaking as the authors have been, Mr. Romberg has caught the spirit of the operetta rather more intelligibly in his strong and virtuoso score. Deep, rushing, stirring, it is one of the best musical comedy scores written for many months. It is lyrically romantic in "Marianne," light and mischievous in "Gorgeous Alexander," sweetly tender in "Lover, Come Back to Me" and uncommonly beautiful in "Softly, as in a Morning Sunrise." In "Stouthearted Men" Mr. Romberg has composed one of those protean male choruses that every night assert manhood all through the theatrical district. Although the book occasionally gets out of hand, Mr. Romberg is always in command of his medium. Evelyn Herbert, an accomplished and altogether charming soprano; Robert Halliday and William O'Neal, baritones, do complete justice to Mr. Romberg's themes.

What the book lacks in humor the direction frequently supplies in droll antics among the players and the chorus. Gus Shy, who may be no wit but who is an obliging comic nevertheless, introduces a good deal of amusing mountebankery in the first act. In its naval manoeuvres and revolutionary defiance the direction is less original, but it is generally effective showmanship. Sweeping costumes, that show up well against Donald Oenslager's splendid sets, feast the eye even when the compositions are not fresh. And when Rosita dances her tango number the rainbow whirl of her flaring skirt is one of those memorable episodes that every good musical production affords.

In its occasional flings at philosophy "The New Moon" is sometimes less than profound. "A woman's friendship glitters like a false jewel and endures about as long," the misanthropic Phillippe mumbles sorrowfully. Such sadness is there in this romantic land of musical comedy. The dashing Robert Halliday, who sings well but converses a little like a train announcer, is less intellectual and more hearty. He is an opportunist. He can take a ship or a maidenly hand with complete dexterity.

1928 S 20

HOLD EVERYTHING, a musical comedy in two acts and nine scenes. Book by B. G. DeSylva and John McGowan and songs by Brown, DeSylva and Henderson. Settings by Henry Dreyfuss. Dances arranged by Jack Haskell and Sam Rose. Produced by Alex A. Aarons and Vinton Freedley. At the Broadhurst Theatre.

Marty	Buddy Horak
Mack	Harry Locke
Murf Levy	Harry Shannon
Pop O'Keefe	Edmund Elton
Norine Lloyd	Betty Compton
Betty Dunn	Alice Boulden
Gink Schiner	Bert Lahr
Sue Burke	Ona Munson
Toots Breen	Nina Olivette
Sonny Jim Brooks	Jack Whiting
Dan Larkin	Frank Allworth
Nosey Bartlett	Victor Moore
Bob Morgan	Robert O'Brien
The Kicker	Phil Sheridan

None of the more relentless playgoers need be coached on the plot of the droll prizefight musical comedy, "Hold Everything!" which spattered gore and humor on the boards of the Broadhurst last evening. Since the blond and sylph-like Jack Whiting, a most attractive musical comedy lead, plays the part of the contender, the fight remains modestly in the welterweight class. But otherwise the prizefight racket remains as "Ringside" and "The Big Fight" have already presented it—full of sinister gamblers, gushing young ladies, sweethearts, temptation, and a climactical scene behind the ropes.

Here the resemblances stop. For "Hold Everything!" employs the services of a motley crew of comedians —Victor Moore, who is always a trifle unsteady on the feet and in the neck, and speaks in a quavering voice; Nina Olivette, comedienne in the

Fanny Brice style, and Bert Lahr, a clown capacious in the mouth but enjoyably constricted above the eyebrows. As a pug who concludes his bouts more frequently on the nose than on the feet, Lahr supplies most of the uproarious comedy in this carnival. In company with Miss Olivette, who matches his clowning at every point, he dances, grimaces, rolls his eyes and sings with that sort of broad abandon that is instantaneously appreciated in the abdomen. "For two cents I'd knock you out myself!" screams the resourceful Miss Olivette. "You're mercenary," Lahr roars stupidly, "you're mercenary." In fact, so stupid is he in these days of advertising brilliance that he suffers the humiliating chagrin of having failed in his cigarette test. To his Philistine senses, they tasted like Meccas.

The book, which is annoyingly ubiquitous all evening, does badly by Mr. Moore's incomparable sense of comedy. He has scarcely a bright line to speak. Even with this textual disadvantage, however, Mr. Moore makes himself welcome whenever he flutters on the stage with a faint trace of alarm in his cherubic countenance. He has a brief intoxication scene; he wears a tight evening suit that does well by his aldermanic outerworks; he wears checks, and once, to be really funny, he wears no trousers at all. What pleasant humors he manages to squeeze out of an innocuous song entitled "Genealogy" attests to the superb skill of his style of comedy. "Hold Everything!" makes scanty use of one of our most ingratiating fools.

Being elaborate and rather threadbare, the book succumbs too frequently to the bland "I feel I owe you an explanations" and "Oh, there is something I wanted to tell yous" and "I do hope you understands." Let any book-maker beware of those revealing phrases. With a more sprightly and expert book "Hold Everything!" would be immeasurably more entertaining.

But Jack Whiting, once of "The Ramblers," and Ona Munson, recently of "Manhattan Mary," make an uncommonly pleasing couple in the leading parts. They dance beautifully; they make romance worth a jaded playgoer's while, and the gods are good to them before 11:15. Although the composers of "You're the Cream of My Coffee" seem to have strained their minds for musical originality, Mr. Whiting and Miss Munson sing it engagingly. Mr. Whiting sings by himself one of the best song numbers, "Footwork,"

surrounded by a chorus of reporters in—of all things—striped outing pants.

As the treacherous rich girl, Betty Compton is bright and dashing. Alice Boulden sings the principal song number, "Don't Hold Everything," so well that one is surprised that the production makes so little use of her ability. As finale to the first act a limber team of "hoofers" dance themselves breathless and the audience enthusiastic up and down a firmly constructed pair of steps. They and the chorus make the dancing of "Hold Everything!" more entertaining than the book and chorus.

1928 O 11

THIS YEAR OF GRACE, a revue in two acts and twenty scenes. Book, lyrics and music by Noel Coward. Staged by Frank Collins; dances and ensembles arranged by Max Rivers and Tilly Losch; produced by Arch Selwyn. At the Selwyn Theatre. PRINCIPALS—Beatrice Lillie, Noel Coward, Phyllis Harding, Madeline Gibson, Tommy Hayes, Florence Desmond, Sonnie Ray, Muriel Montrose, James Hepburn, G. P. Huntley Jr., Albertina Vitak, Marjorie Moss, Georges Fontana and others.

Through the successive light episodes of "This Year of Grace," which is now installed at the Selwyn, Beatrice Lillie, Noel Coward and their associated company have managed to retain a quality rarely found on the revue stage—a joyous gayety. Mr. Coward, who is a master of little things, has written the book, lyrics and music with grace, expertness and a neat sense of mocking humor. Although Miss Lillie has a more abundant talent than the present potpourri employs, she has never appeared so brilliant in pantomime and so unerring in satiric skill. Excellent dancing, simple trappings in the best of taste, an English company quite as light as its material, and, withal, a fine spirit of friendly gayety make "This Year of Grace" completely captivating. No wonder it has been enjoying a long engagement in London.

Whatever Mr. Coward has set his hand to glitters here. He has thumbed a large bundle of unpretentious subjects for satire and comedy—a tube station in London, sinful Paris of the 1890s, the eternal triangle as Barrie, Lonsdale and the French stage might present it, the brawling English seaside resort where no one really enjoys himself, the cloying love ballad of musical comedy. In one number, entitled "The Theatre Guide," he has made capsule parodies of three familiar plays—marvelously economical and wry bits of satire. Only one line suffices for "Any Civic Repertory Play." "Oh, the pain of it!" moans a sad woman clad in black. With such neat, well-laid strokes Mr. Coward cuts without letting blood. This, one feels, must be a medium more congenial to his talent than the full-length play.

Not since the days of "Charlot's Revue" has Miss Lillie appeared in a production so nearly worthy of her superb style of keen-edged comedy. All her preposterous sense of middle-class dignity makes grand merriment of ."The Bus Rush." As a channel swimmer, clad in the funniest bathing suit of modern times, handling photographers and the vulgar mob with the haughtiest condescension, Miss Lillie makes every moment burst with hilarity. Only those who have admired her in other productions can imagine what ridicule she packs into "Whoop, girls, up and at 'em" and "A-ding, a-ding, dong," as the refrains of two hackneyed ballads. . In company with Mr. Coward, whose talent in these ironic numbers is considerable, she dances a beflounced mazurka and impersonates the dangerous La Flamme, blazing queen of the Parisian Bohemia. "This Year of Grace" does not exploit Miss Lillie's genius completely. What opportunities it gives her she turns into unalloyed enjoyment.

Although Miss Lillie and Mr. Coward are the most conspicuous performers in this fast-flowing cartoon, they have many pleasant associates. The radiant Madeline Gibson sings and dances charmingly in the interludes. Georges Fontana and Marjorie Moss dance a waltz magnificently. And all the subsidiary players are equal to the little excursions into travesty with which this revue abounds.

Like the first "Charlot's Revue," "This Year of Grace" demonstrates the superiority of theatrical intelligence over the heavy opulence under which most revues are buried. Mr Coward and Mr. Cochrane have spared unnecessary decorations. The costumes are simple, but lovely in their radations of shading. The curtains are either frankly serviceable or painted with light-humored designs. Mr. Coward's ideas are never befogged by the staging. In one weird number, entitled "Dance Little Lady," the staring masks and the mechanized costumes disclose his

motive to perfection. Meanwhile, the production pirouettes gracefully and rapidly without an interruption. Mr. Coward has a remarkable flair for quick, sardonic fooling. "This Year of Grace" respects it and restores to our stage a gayety that has long been missing.

1928 N 8.

HOLIDAY, a comedy in three acts, by Philip Barry. Staged by Arthur Hopkins; settings by Robert Edmond Jones; produced by Mr. Hopkins. At the Plymouth Theatre.

Linda Seton	Hope Williams
Johnny Case	Ben Smith
Julia Seton	Dorothy Tree
Ned Seton	Monroe Owsley
Susan Potter	Barbara White
Nick Potter	Donald Ogden Stewart
Edward Seton	Walter Walker
Laura Cram	Rosalie Norman
Seton Cram	Thaddeus Clancy
Henry	Cameron Clemens
Charles	J. Ascher Smith
Delia	Beatrice Ames

With his marvelous gift for spinning, spiraling humors, Philip Barry keeps life gay through most of his new spindrift comedy, "Holiday," put on at the Plymouth last evening. For one act, in fact, he gives full rein to his scattered, mocking, fluffy fooling and to his characters who will not let the fun go out of their lives. Nothing could be grander amusement than that opening act. For no logical reason Mr. Barry also has a thesis on his hands—one so much of the Edith Wharton manner that it tags far behind his mischievous fun. Only the buoyancy of his point of view, the spurts of rippling dialogue and the shining verve of the acting bring "Holiday" safely through the solemnity of that fable.

What he is arguing is the emptiness of the rich, the solidly affluent life. All that stands between Johnny Case and the wealthy Julia Seton is his determination to keep free from the entangling alliances of social position. Having made his one killing in the stock market, he now insists upon retiring early in life when he can enjoy it, rather than late, when the spirit has run out. But to her strait-laced breeding, such a vagary damns him as an idler. There shall be no pariahs in her domestic life. And that, if you are interested, is the reason they break the engagement, and the reason her rebellious, smitten sister, now released from decent loyalty to a member of her own family, pulls on her cap and runs cheerfully after him.

Since, according to a crusted tradition, a playwright must have a story, let this one pass for what it is worth. For Mr. Barry it is hardly more than an excuse to push his favorite characters onto the stage and to uncork his matchless effervescence. What dialogue! It springs directly from the usual sources of polite banter; it does not eschew the lowly pun. Only a little rougher and disorderly, and it might be the Marx boys up to their old tricks. But Mr. Barry turns it neatly, flips it daintily into the pattern of his story, and for long periods lets it bounce back and forth between two characters like a tennis volley. Occasionally it seems a trifle self-conscious, as when the kin-spirits in worldly irreverence, led by Donald Ogden Stewart in person, sit down gravely while he discloses the secret of his fantastic success. Uusually it dances gayly without rhyme or reason and leaves only the impression of lightness when it has stopped. For if Mr. Barry does not scrupulously keep it in character, at least he keeps character in it.

For his chief character, the rebellious Linda Seton, such dialogue is a defense against the melancholy of her thoughts. It is no secret that Mr. Barry has drawn the part to suit Hope Williams, the ironically merry friend of the family in "Paris Bound" last year; and it will soon be no secret that Miss Williams is one of the most clear-headed comediennes we have. When Linda Seton finds the irresponsible Johnny one of kin in temperament and sits down to match nonsense with him, Miss Williams plays quietly with a sort of comic incandescence that is one of the superlative delights of this season. Through all the turns of the play she remains very much herself—boyishly awkward, but quick and sparkling. Whatever she may do with other characters, the style of the Linda Seton is definitely hers.

Having Arthur Hopkins as a producer for this play as well as "In a Garden" and "Paris Bound," Mr. Barry is in good hands. Casting and direction, as well as Robert Edmond Jones's settings, make the most of his comedy. All the acting gleams with light. Dorothy Tree as the reluctant Julia Seton lets the hardness of character break through the charm with great skill. Ben Smith as the blundering Johnny puts ruggedness as well as freshness into his part. In the minor part of despairing brother Monroe Owsley gives a splendid, true performance. Reclaimed from letters and shoved unceremoniously behind the footlights, Donald Ogden Stewart picks up the mood expertly. As the humorless father, Walter Walker, manages to keep a stock part humanly believable.

Mr. Barry is effortless with dialogue and characters. But pressing a story around them still keeps him uneasy. "Holiday" does not flow as graciously as "Paris Bound" and does not curl around ideas so amiably. But it has savor, fresh color and sunny merriment. Even when it is unhappily dramatic it is still a holiday in playmaking.

1928 N 27

EVA LE GALLIENNE
A WISTFUL PETER PAN

Gives a Buoyant Performance in Civic Theatre's Production of Barrie's Lovely Play.

PETER PAN, or THE BOY WHO WOULD NOT GROW UP, a play in five acts, by J. M. Barrie, with incidental music by John Crook. Directed by Eva Le Gallienne and J. Blake Scott; revived by the Civic Repertory Theatre. At the Civic Repertory Theatre.

Liza	Beatrice de Neergaard
Nana	J. Edward Bromberg
Michael Nicholas Darling	Vernon Jones
Mrs. Darling	Mary Ward
Wendy Moira Angela Darling	Josephine Hutchinson
John Napoleon Darling	Charles McCarthy
Mr. Darling	Donald Cameron
Tinker Bell	Herself
Peter Pan	Eva Le Gallienne
First Twin	David Vivian
Slightly	London Herrick
Ostrich	Harold Moulton
Tootles	Glesca Marshall
Curley	Alfred Corn
Second Twin	Henry Melvin
Nibs	Lester Salko
Captain Hook	Egon Brecher
Starkey	Sayre Crawley
Smee	John Eldridge
Blackman	Ted Fetter
Cecco	Harold Moulton
Cookson	Robert Ross
Tiger Lily	Jocelyn Gordon
Great Big Little Panther	J. Blake Scott
Mullins	Robert H. Gordon
Noodles	Walter Beck
Pirate	Lewis Leverett
A Tramp	Robert H. Gordon
A Cabman	Robert Ross

Peter Pan came back last night twenty-three years and a few weeks after his first venture out of Kensington Gardens into New York. With Peter came the whole Darling family, Nana, the dog-nurse, his gang of lost boys, his Red Skins, led by Tiger Lily, and his Pirate crew commanded by the redoubtable Captain Hook. Likewise, the wolves were there—the wolves that were fright-ened away by looking through your legs at them—and a most special and admirable Crocodile with the clock ticking inside him. Something was lacking that was Maude Adams, something elfin and piercing-sweet, expressed in double violin notes, something was lacking that was Ernest Lawford's lisp that so utterly disarmed the ferocious pirate cap-tain with his steel claw of a hand.

But Barrie's lovely, wistful, play-ful old piece about the children who flew out of the nursery window to the delights that children day-dream about had lost nothing essential of its magic because of the lapse of years and or because the Civic Re-pertory company were playing it in-stead of the company of Charles Frohman. Nothing was left undone and everything was well done, from the stage settings to the wag of Nana's tail. If Eva Le Gallienne lacked something of the sweet, keen wistfulness which Maude Adams gave the part of the boy who would not grow up, she was a gallant, buoy-ant, clean-cut figure, and gave Peter plenty of élan and boyish grace. She even expressed something of the aloofness of Peter—the boy who would not be mothered to the ruin of his boyhood—which was not with-in the compass of Miss Adams her-self.

Maude Adams wore russety tights, cross-gartered. Miss Le Gallienne wears the limit of bare legs. The dif-ference is only the difference in the costume conventions of the two periods. And it is the only serious difference between the dressing of the old Peter Pan and the new, though (of course) neither Pirates nor Redskins are copies of the Em-pire issue, and Miss Le Gallienne's production generally is her own, with many variations in detail from the New York original. Nothing could be better (for what it is) than the be-havior of the lost boys underground, when they are all in bed and Wendy is telling them Mrs. Darling's story. The Pirates are all that the heart of a boy—or a pacifical grown-up with lurking memories of lust for loot and slaughter—could desire.

Egon Brecher as Hook is a most egregious villain in red, even if he does not lisp or give such unction to the perfidious trap with "rich damp cake" that was to have got the chil-dren into his power. Nobody says "Stme-e-e-e" as it used to be said in the old days. But Smee is there and busy on the deck of the pirate ship—operating a sewing machine. John Eldredge plays the part, not without proper feeling. If one misses

the splash as the pirates go over-board, that perhaps is clinging over-much to a happy memory. And the surpassing excellence of the croco-dile may be counted as making up—in part—for the omission. Josephine Hutchinson's Wendy is a very serious Wendy—which is what Wendy must be above all things, and J. Edward Bromberg presents Nana with the right touch of comic caninity.

Last night the piece ran a bit too long. And it seemed that some of the dancing by the Red Skins might be omitted without notable loss and other business spared which the text and the context did not compel. The flying trick, by the way, was well managed and Miss Eva Le Gallienne's own dances in the character of the lightsome Peter were airily and ex-pertly executed.

1928 N 27

1929

STREET SCENE, a play in three acts, by Elmer Rice. Staged by the author; settings by Jo Mielziner; produced by William A. Brady, Ltd. At The Play-house.

Abraham Kaplan	Leo Bulgakov
Greta Fiorentino	Eleanor Wesselhoeft
Emma Jones	Beulah Bondi
Olga Olsen	Hilda Bruce
Willie Maurrant	Russell Griffin
Anna Maurrant	Mary Servoss
Daniel Buchanan	Conway Washburne
Frank Maurrant	Robert Kelly
George Jones	T. H. Manning
Steve Sankey	Joseph Baird
Agnes Cushing	Jane Corcoran
Carl Olsen	John M. Qualen
Shirley Kaplan	Anna Kostant
Filippo Fiorentino	George Humbert
Alice Simpson	Emily Hamill
Laura Hildebrand	Frederica Going
Mary Hildebrand	Eileen Smith
Charlie Hildebrand	Alexander Lewis
Samuel Kaplan	Horace Braham
Rose Moran	Erin O'Brien-Moore
Harry Easter	Glenn Coulter
Mae Jones	Millicent Green
Dick McGann	Joseph Lee
Vincent Jones	Matthew McHugh
Dr. John Wilson	John Crump
Officer Harry Murphy	Edward Downes
A Milkman	Ralph Willard
A Letter-Carrier	Herbert Lindholm
An Iceman	Samuel S. Bonnell
A Music Student	Mary Emerson
Marshall James Henry	Ellsworth Jones
Fred Cullen	Jean Sidney
An Old-Clothes Man	Joe Cogert
An Interne	Samuel S. Bonnell
An Ambulance Driver	Anthony Pawley

Still unwilling to write a conven-tional play according to the safe, stereotyped forms, Elmer Rice con-tents himself with writing an honest one in "Street Scene," put on truth-fully at the Playhouse last evening. If you disengage its story from its lithographic New York environment you must classify it as the drama of a crime of passion. When Frank Maurrant, a burly stagehand, finds his wife behind drawn blinds with Steve Sankey, a collector for the milkman, he kills both of them. Mr. Rice prepares for this violent scene in the first act, stages it in the second and discloses the consequences and some of its human significance in the last. Slight as this story is, unoriginal as it is, "Street Scene" has little more to say. Yet it manages to be generally interesting, frequently amusing and extraordinarily authentic until the final curtain.

For Mr. Rice has visualized it in terms of an average New York tenement house on the grimier edge of the middle class. And if the crime of passion stirs any emotions within you it is because Mr. Rice has succeeded in relating it to life and enlisting your sympathies for the tatterdemalions who troop along his average street, hang out of the windows on a hot Summer evening, gossip, quarrel, romance and make the best of their stuffy lot. Mr. Rice does not sentimentalize about them. He does not blame them for their prejudices and blunders and short tempers. Indeed, "Street Scene" constantly lacks a point of view. Mr. Rice has squandered all his talent on making each episode and character ring true.

He has observed and transcribed his material perfectly. Never did the phantasmagoria of street episodes seem so lacking in sketchy types and so packed with fully delineated character. No one with his eyes open on the streets of New York could miss the policemen, letter carriers, babies, janitors, doctors, the Jews, Swedes, Italians and Irish who pass up and down the dingy street, in and out of the seedy tenement door, or loiter on the steps to bear tales of wayward neighbors and muse over the imponderables of life. These obvious traits of our slummy life Mr. Rice has worked into his humane portrait—even to the exercising of the dog and the airing of night clothing in the faint sunlight of the listless city morning.

What distinguishes "Street Scene" from a host of synthetic forerunners is Mr. Rice's remarkable sense of character. Here are not merely the automatons of the giddy city streets, but the people—the intellectual Jew who runs on endlessly about the capitalistic classes, the Italian musician who dreams of the flowery land from which he came, the office girl who wants to move out to Queens, the pleasant woman who is quietly sacrificing her life to a sick mother, the

ruffian taxicab driver, the flirt, the school teacher, all brought into focus with telling strokes of character-portrayal.

Most of them are not smashing at the barriers that cramp their lives. Most of them are merely living. And Mr. Rice's flowing, somewhat sprawling drama, catches the primitive facts of child-birth on the third story, the chicken for soup, the petting after dark, the common hatred of the intellectual Jew—race prejudices, class morality, jolly, broad humor, sympathies, jealousies. Again, he expresses no point of view about such matters. For those who are interested, it is sufficient that he has completed his portrait with remarkable artistic integrity.

As his own director he has cast the parts quite as accurately. Leo Bulgakov's radical Jew, George Humbert's light-hearted Italian musician, Millicent Green's impudent chippie, Mary Servoss's tired Irish mother are excellent pieces of characterization. Some of the acting, like Beulah Bondi's malicious gossip and Erin O'Brien-Moore's office girl, have time and space enough for complete fulfillment. Excepting for a certain lack of restraint, Horace Braham's restless and sensitive young Jew is fine and true. Only the length of the cast prevents naming the boys, girls and the other neighbors who act creditably.

Whether or not an artist should have a more sentient point of view about his material is a question for the higher criticism rather than a newspaper review. Certainly "Street Scene" is not all of one piece. Furthermore, Mr. Rice's concluding philosophy which intelligently discusses the significance of this neighborhood incident, is nearly lost in the jumble of a street panorama. If you accept on its own terms this new play by the alert author of "Adding Machine" you will find it as vital, as fascinating, as comic, as the streets along which New York people live.

1929 Ja 11

The Price of Glory.

By J. BROOKS ATKINSON.

To report that "Journey's End," which was put on at Henry Miller's last evening, is an extraordinarily decent play is to pay it no left-handed compliment. For through all the anguish, terror, bravery and humors of this tremendously moving dug-out chronicle, R. G. Sheriff, the author, has kept the fundamental decency of his characters uppermost. Writing about it so soon after the deep emotion of the final curtain leaves the reviewer rather incapable of rendering a coherent report of all the fine qualities that lurk in this new war-play. Perhaps it is sufficient to remark that it is one of the most powerful and somberly beautiful dramas of recent times. Mr. Sheriff has not been lured off into the theatricality of trench life during a raid and a German bombardment. Such pyrotechnical episodes in "Journey's End" serve merely to illuminate individual and British character, and the play recovers some of the fine human beauty that has recently been lost in the turbulence of merely effective things.

As every one must know by this time, the young Englishman who has written the tragedy is not a professional playwright, but an insurance assessor. When he put together this Odyssey of strained nerves, death and comradeship at the front he was merely supplying the needs of an amateur acting organization with which he has been associated. But when, in the course of time Maurice Browne, one of the co-authors of "Wings Over Europe," put it on professionally in London, "Journey's End" speedily became the sensation of the season. Now Gilbert Miller has brought it to America about three months after its début and with a cast which, despite unfavorable tidings, acts it with memorable perfection. Just as Mr. Sheriff keeps the values of his play subdued, the black despair of the soldiers always looming in the background, so do the actors play with restraint, with simplicity and with great personal conviction.

It is the most unpretentious of stories. Into the sodden and mucky life of a British company at the front comes a young officer, Lieutenant Raleigh, scarcely out of school. He is overjoyed to be under the command of his old school hero, Captain Stanhope, who has been in the thick of the fighting for three dreary years. One of the fellow officers is an old schoolmaster, Lieutenant Osborne, paternal and able; another is a nerveless burgher, Lieutenant Trotter; and the last is a nerve-shattered weakling, Lieutenant Hibbert. Although others come in and out of the gloomy dug-out where all the action occurs and the grim roar of gunning, is seldom silent in the distance, "Journey's End" is principally an exposition of these officers of C Company under the dour circumstances of warfare.

Having come to the front line just on the eve of a German drive, they are in for it, and young Lieutenant Raleigh has his baptism of fire before he has hardly drawn a breath. You see young Raleigh and Osborne in the eight tense minutes before they lead an already doomed raid into the German lines; you see Osborne, fully conscious of his peril, making his private preparations and gallantly leading the conversation on familiar topics lest they become unnerved before they start. You hear, under all circumstances, the talk of home, and, for contrast, you listen to the humors of the sketchy mess table.

Not being a romantic, Mr. Sherriff does not spare you the heartbreaking realities of trench warfare; and not being a man of the theatre, he does not revel in bloodshed for its own sake. Lieutenant Osborne does not return from the raid. Lieutenant Raleigh is fatally wounded in the drive that follows the next morning. Such things Mr. Sherriff has woven into the texture of his narrative without exploiting their heroics. As a play, "Journey's End" may lack the form a more practiced hand might have given it; the division into scenes is more than a little arbitrary, and loses in emotion thereby, and it introduces its humors somewhat naïvely. But Mr. Sherriff comes into the theatre fresh. Above everything, you esteem the integrity of his characterization, his total lack of theatrical assumptions and the bare ruggedness of his dialogue.

Before the present company left London, they gave six performances at the Arts Theatre where they invited comparison with the original players. The comparison seems to have been invidious. But last evening their performance seemed, to this reviewer, a work of great beauty. As Lieutenant Osborne, Leon Quartermaine is endearingly manly and sympathetic. Derek Williams gives a winning portrait of the shy Lieutenant Raleigh whose spirit is touching and whose faith is unmovable. As Captain Stanhope, Colin Keith-Johnson is at once vigorous and profound. Victor Stanley makes a great deal of the cook's amiable blunders; and Henry Wenman is bluff, hearty and unimaginative as Lieutenant Trotter. This cast—all men—is as innocent of featured players as the handfull of British officers who have been tossed together by a common emergency. They share alike in the fortunes of the drama. And they keep uppermost the fundamental decency of Mr. Sherriff's writing.

1929 Mr 23

Revue, Pocket Edition.

THE LITTLE SHOW. An intimate revue in two acts and twenty-seven scenes. Lyrics by Howard Dietz and music mostly by Arthur Schwartz. Settings by Jo Mielziner; dances arranged by Danny Dare; produced by William A. Brady Jr. and Dwight Deere Wiman, in association with Tom Weatherly. At the Music Box.
PRINCIPALS—Clifton Webb, Fred Allen, Libby Holman, Helen Lynd, Bettina Hall, Romney Brent, Joan Carter-Waddell, John McCauley, Harold Moffet, Rainger and Carroll, Ernest Sharpe and others.

By J. BROOKS ATKINSON.

Most of the wit, humor and intelligence that somehow escape the musical stage has settled down pleasantly into "The Little Show," which rambled along in conversational tones at the Music Box last evening. It is unfailingly diverting. If that formal phrase appears to lack enthusiasm, be warned at the outset that the collectors of this pocket-edition revue have not sought to pain you with abdominal laughter or stimulate your gastric juices with wanton display. Having assembled several of the neatest entertainers in town, and put them to fooling with light and subtle materials, they have merely set about amusing you, and they have succeeded. Of course, that frenzied "Song of the Riveter" does seem to be intended seriously, although it lies close to travesty, and the humor has something more than a mere penchant for Anatole France's "la volupté." Otherwise, it is gay, sardonic, trifling and remarkably good fun.

Being completely off the beaten path, it turns up with novel ideas. You have no sooner recovered from the maudlin, sentimental theme song of our foremost hardware merchants ("Hammacher, Schlemmer, I love you—Always remember, Hammacher, Schlemmer") than you are witnessing the ingenious tragedy of deaf-mutes, cursing under their whiskers or talking low—which is at the height of the knees—or you are hearing about the hot-cross-bun designer who naturally works only one day a year. Most of these glib humors Fred Allen delivers in a flat voice like the wit of the senior dormitories. He is not merely an in-

gratiating comedian, but a deft one, with an extraordinary talent for making his points at a skimming pace. But "The Little Show" is not reduced to one mountebank. Clifton Webb is there with mincing steps and a nice touch of comedy, and the clownish Romney Brent radiates good humor as far as the eye can reach.

In fact, these three comedians have at their disposal the keenest sketch in the revue, "The Still Alarm," by George S. Kaufman, who can draw without smudging a line. It is the story of a horrible hotel fire as viewed from the eleventh floor by perfect gentlemen whose breeding remains with them to the end. While the two guests are bending over a series of house plans in the well-appointed apartment, the alert call-boy comes with a well-phrased message of alarm from the desk. There is no vulgar display of terror, rude haste, or selfishness. The deportment is flawless, at every point. In fact, when the floor grows hot and the smoke begins to roll in at the windows, good manners have triumphed so completely that the two guests are sitting down courteously, while the more artistic of the firemen starts to play on his violin the "little thing" he played so brilliantly at the Equitable holocaust.

Although "The Little Show" is most notable for its humors, it can dance and pipe as brightly as the rest. The dances staged by Danny Dare tap an amiable tattoo. For the more conventional balladry Joan Carter-Waddell is engaging and John McCauley pleasant, though too persistently winsome. There is the flaxen-haired Helen Lynd for gauche pranks to tunes, and there is the dark purple menace of Libby Holman in the blues. Being a small-gauged affair, "The Little Show" keeps all its people uncommonly busy. By providing them with excellent material, all in one light key, it keeps the intimacies always agreeable.

1929 My 1

Behind the Scene with Zigfield

SHOW GIRL, a musical comedy in two acts and fourteen scenes. Book by William Anthony McGuire from the novel by J. P. McEvoy; music by George Gershwin; lyrics by Ira Gershwin and Gus Kahn; dances staged by Bobby Connolly; ballets by Albertina Rasch; scenes by Joseph Urban; costumes designed by John W. Harkrider. Produced by Florenz Ziegfeld. At the Ziegfeld Theatre.

Snozzle ....Jimmie Durante
Virginia Witherby........Barbara Newberry
Steve ....Blaine Cordner
Premiere Danseuse ....Harriet Hoctor

By J. BROOKS ATKINSON.

Long after Mr. Ziegfeld's new musical spectacle, entitled "Show Girl," got under way at the Ziegfeld Theatre last evening, the flashlights were still popping outside, and the bustle and crackle of an eventful premiere kept the audience expectantly uneasy. For, using J. P. McEvoy's satiric novel of Broadway as the substance of the book, Mr. Ziegfeld was about to elevate the lithe and winsome Ruby Keeler to stardom and pluck the crack-brained trio of Clayton, Jackson and Durante out of night-club life and on to the musical stage. By wrapping them up in the lustrous splendor of his showmanship Mr. Ziegfeld makes them indisputably his and pieces together an interesting performance. But not without considerable effort. The task of blending materials that are episodic and individual makes "Show Girl" the least notable of the recent Ziegfeld productions.

Doubtless you recall Mr. McEvoy's effervescent novel of last season as the breathless and wryly amusing chronicle of Dixie Dugan's career on Broadway. Composed of telegrams and letters, scattered and spotty, with a satire of the greeting card business as a minor embellishment, Mr. McEvoy's novel seemed hardly suitable to the musical stage unless, as is the custom, the adapter straightway forgot it. But William Anthony McGuire, author of the dialogue, has been faithful in his fashion not only to the novel, but to the whole tradition of musical plays of backstage life. While this Dixie Dugan, in the fresh personality of Ruby Keeler, is on her way to fame on Broadway, you are constantly aware of banalities and awkward transitions. You miss the stately flow of the best Ziegfeld pageants.

Miss Keeler, being no Lucy Stone freebooter, appends the connubial "Jolson" to her signature in the program, and Mr. Jolson, sitting in Row C on the aisle last evening, rose in the audience toward the end of the performance and lifted up his voice in the general jubilee. It was a touching episode. As a tap-dancer and a singer Miss Keeler is an enjoyable performer herself, without pretensions or affectations.

For the last two seasons the three night-club rascals, headed by the mad and frenzied Jimmy Durante, have been threatening the musical stage. How to fit so rhymeless a trio of nonsense fabricators into anything more formal than a night-club racket has kept the pundits sitting up nights. Their transformation into "Show Girl" is not altogether sublime. When they transport their act intact and careen around the piano, Jackson strutting, Clayton hoofing and Durante bowing to the orchestra and breaking out into feverish and raucous songs, they recapture the excitement of their humors. Durante's sizzling energy can galvanize any audience. But when he is separated from that wonted "mowing mood of his and the "exubilance" of which he used to boast, he loses fire. His spluttering, insane material does not melt gracefully into a musical comedy book. His personality, however, batters its way through all barriers.

As usual, Mr. Ziegfeld has graced his production with beauty opulent in magnificence, yet soft as greensward. The expansive Joseph Urban has warmed his colors and painted designs with ample brushstrokes. Costumes worn with enviable poise sweep across the stage. The girls are as lovely as ever; and the Albertina Rasch ballet are more supple in sketches composed with more than the familiar imagination. In one number, entitled "An American in Paris," the lambent Harriet Hoctor dances an excellent ballet with the Albertine Rasch troupe.

Although Mr. Gershwin's spray of notes does not result in a first-rate score, it has moments of vividness or melody. "Do What You Do," as sung by Miss Keeler, and the "Harlem Serenade" are the most ingratiating compositions. Against these the raucous Jimmy Durante pits such ear-splitting harmonics as "Can Broadway Do Without Me?" and the zany "Jimmie, the Well-Dressed Man." It is not the most felicitous of combinations. Nor the best of the Ziegfeld productions. But the Summer months are not likely to yield anything so handsome.

1929 Jl 3

In the Roaring Forties.

STRICTLY DISHONORABLE, a comedy in three acts, by Preston Sturges. Settings by Raymond Sovey; staged by Brock Pemberton and Antoinette Perry; produced by Mr. Pemberton. At the Avon Theatre (formerly the Klaw).

By J. BROOKS ATKINSON.

Out of the slightly balmy civilization that has grown up around the more homelike and deferential speakeasies Preston Sturges has written a well-nigh perfect comedy in "Strictly Dishonorable," put on at the Avon last evening. After the sparkle of the first act we all held our collective breaths for fear the second act might destroy it. But the second act did not falter, nor the third; and by the time the final curtain had dropped on as well-turned a phrase as a gourmet could ask for, it was certain that a fresh talent for gay, bouyant comedy had come into the theatre. For no one could write such deft, amusing lines and describe characters with so much understanding who did not have genuine talent for the theatre. Those who had visited Mr. Sturges's "The Guinea Pig" last season were somewhat prepared for the rare enjoyment of the new comedy. Those who had not were taken completely by surprise.

Although Mr. Sturges is writing of a faintly delirious incident in a Forty-ninth Street speakeasy, he has the good taste to keep his characters neat and decent. Upstairs lives a judge whose mellowness does not come exclusively from the bottle, and Count di Ruvo, a Metropolitan Opera tenor of Italian grace and passion, whose old family retainer is the proprietor. While the judge is fortifying himself against the misery of going to bed by drinking, an old-fashioned, a surly youth from West Orange comes in with his fiancée, who, being new to the comforts of civilization, immediately warms up to the fragrance of speakeasy life.

Such is the informality of social life around the beautifully finished bar that presently "Strictly Dishonorable" is not only a rippling comedy but affecting romance with the dampening influence of West Orange safely beyond the door. Deserted by her churlish suitor at midnight, in a speakeasy inhabited by two gentlemen whom she has never seen before, and far away from home and mother in Mississippi, the young lady is tossed—practically chucked, in fact—upon the gallantry of the gentlemen. How her fate flutters from side to side through a long evening, how wildly her maidenly heart flutters, how cavalier a tenor can be, how paternal a disconsolate judge can be after office hours and how marvelously romance at midnight can alter the whole design of an innocent maiden's life—is the joy that will keep the Avon Theatre crowded during the bleak Winter ahead.

It is, as this grateful notice has already declared, a well-nigh perfect comedy. For Mr. Sturges has not only an extraordinary gift for character and dialogue, but for the flow and astonishment of situation. After a career squandered on the ordinary pabulum of the stage, you foresee none of the little pops and flourishes that keep this prank curling across the stage. But what tickles you most, perhaps, is the ease with which everything desirable can be arranged when the proper heads are put into play—how the unruly can be thrust out of the way, how the policeman can be coaxed on the side of virtue, how honor can be upheld and how readily hearts can be joined. Being on the side of gaiety, Mr. Sturges takes care to pick his characters pleasantly and to invest even the one policeman who appears twice with a thoroughly refreshing sense of humor. "But policemen never drink when they are on duty," the surprised young lady says over the champagne. "It just seems like never!" Patrolman Mulligan agrees.

Having fallen into appreciative hands, "Strictly Dishonorable" enjoys the splendors of a merry performance and direction. As the impulsive tenor Tullio Carminati, who was once associated with Duse, plays with rare grace and accomplishment, forbearing and alive. Muriel Kirkland, whose previous exploits on Broadway have been modest, conveys admirably all the winsome charm, bewilderment and mischief of the Mississippi baggage. As the gruff and tender-hearted judge, Carl Anthony acts with an infectious gleam of humor, enjoying both the humors and the responsibilities of every turn of fortune. Louis Jean Heydt as the West Orange civilian transforms the one ungrateful part in the play into a constant delight by the fine edge of his interpretation. Nor, in enthusiasm for the acting of the major parts, must one neglect the rather bulbous unction that William Ricciardi rubs into the part of the proprietor, or the chuckle in Edward J. McNamara's playing of the patrolman.

Excellent direction has pulled all the latent pleasantries out of their corners into the light where they can be enjoyed. "Strictly Dishonorable" is designed for enjoyment as a whole. Mr. Sturges has seen to that generously, keeping everything plausible and fresh.

1929 S 19

On the Tragedy of Remembrance.

BERKELEY SQUARE, a play in three acts and seven scenes, by John L. Balderston, suggested by Henry James's "A Sense of the Past." Staged by Leslie Howard. Settings by Sir Edward Lutyens, R. A. Produced by Gilbert Miller and Leslie Howard. At the Lyceum Theatre.

Maid	Irene Howard
Tom Pettigrew	Brian Gilmour
Kate Pettigrew	Valerie Taylor
Lady Anne Pettigrew	Alice John
Mr. Throstle	Tarver Penna
Helen Pettigrew	Margalo Gillmore
The Ambassador	Fritz Williams
Mrs. Barwick	Lucy Beaumont
Peter Standish	Leslie Howard
Marjorie Frant	Ann Freshman
Major Clinton	Charles Romano
Miss Barrymore	June English
Duchess of Devonshire	Louise Prussing
Lord Stanley	Henry Warwick
Duke of Cumberland	Robert Greig

By J. BROOKS ATKINSON.

If the story of "Berkeley Square," which was put on at the Lyceum last evening, is not without a certain awkwardness in the telling, it is because John Balderston, the author, an American newspaper correspondent in London, has put his hand to an extraordinary theme. You may feel pettishly in doubt about certain of the details, and you may be of two minds about the skill with which Mr. Balderston keeps his story in motion. But you will not be seriously disturbed; the reservations are technical only. For this exotic fable of a modern who, by some feat of supernaturalism, lives for a time in the midst of eighteenth-century London, is strangely absorbing and singularly touching in the first act and the last. Acted in its chief parts by such attractive, forthright players as Leslie Howard and Margalo Gillmore, it lives entirely by the necromancy of free imagination and makes one of the rarest evenings of the season. The plot comes from Henry James's "The Sense of the Past"; even James could not subdue it entirely. On its way to the stage it has turned up in two versions, both of which were played in London, and the script has been variously revised by J. C. Squire, editor of The London Mercury, and our own Marc Connelly. In fact, rumors have it that even others of no mean repute have been medicine-men in spite of themselves and have helped to put "Berkeley Square" in order for American audiences. They have not killed the patient; they have given us a play that casts a spell.

To describe it baldly, Peter Standish is an American of the 1928 vintage, living in an old Queen Anne house in Berkeley Square. For a brief time it is his privilege to take the place of his ancestor, Peter Standish, in London life of 1784. We see him in the second scene as a modern on the point of moving back, by some feat of unexplained magic, to the same house 145 years earlier. Excepting the last scene, the play then shows him mingling with the stream of life of that more formal day. What makes it all the more absorbing is that he is aware of the lapse of time and all that has happened during the intervening years. Accordingly, he is not of that period even when he is in it. Unlike all of the others save one, he knows what is going to happen. Although he tries to live according to the letter of their time, never anticipating in anything he does the things he knows are soon to happen, he does not wholly succeed.

If this exposition of the plot is at all lucid, you will understand the possibilities latent in Mr. Balderston's somewhat metaphysical theme. There is the amusement of watching Peter Standish entering timorously into a life to which he does not belong. In spite of himself he regards his contemporaries as walking corpses; there is something provocative and a little uncanny about his point of view. When he wants to amuse himself he confounds eighteenth century people with the epigrams of Oscar Wilde, and he astonishes them with his clairvoyance about the rude American colonies. His passion for baths perplexes them. His squeamishness about blowing his nose on the fingers offends them.

But Mr. Balderston does not toss away so remarkable a theme upon amusing trivia. What carries "Berkeley Square" beyond commonplaceness and gives it distinction as a work of art is the frustration of a very moving love affair woven into the pattern of the story. For according to the facts of eighteenth century life Peter Standish has to propose marriage to Kate Pettigrew, which he does. It is not long, however, before his twentieth century impostor has fallen in love genuinely with her sister Helen. By a dash of clairvoyance in her own nature Helen understands the hopelessness of their devotion. They love as human beings, but they meet as phantoms passing in time and space. Parting is inherent in their meeting; every heart-beat measures their doom. Although Mr. Balderston has not worked out this portion of the story completely, he has kept it on an exalted plane of preternatural tragedy.

In the limpid acting of Mr. Howard and Miss Gillmore it is a conflict fraught with great loveliness. Miss Gillmore is luminously beautiful as Helen, and she plays with a grace and lightness of touch and a sincerity that are enchanting. As Peter Standish, Mr. Howard plays with the neatness and delicacy of his finest work. Throughout the drama, in fact, Mr. Howard acts marvelously, clarifying the story constantly by the intelligence of his own performance. For what Mr. Howard understands, his audiences understand instantaneously, and he makes his transitions by the most intelligible means.

The subordinate rôles likewise are extremely well played. The dignity of Alice John as Lady Anne, the fearful earnestness of Valerie Taylor as her daughter, the charm and graciousness of Louise Prussing as the Duchess of Devonshire give depth to the story. Tarva Penna and Brian Gilmour are accomplished as mannered fops of the eighteenth century. Fritz Williams is as businesslike as ever as the American Ambassador of modern times.

These and the other several actors have been intelligently directed. And although "Berkeley Square" may not appeal to your reason, it will lay a strong hold on your imagination.

1929 N 5

'BITTER SWEET' HERE, WITTY AND BREEZY

Noel Coward's Artistic Operetta From London Is Composed of Musical Miniatures.

EVELYN LAYE IS RADIANT

Author Acts Many Roles in His Costume Romance—A Decorous Entertainment.

By BROOKS ATKINSON

BITTER SWEET, an operetta in three acts and seven scenes by Noel Coward. Settings and costumes by G. E. Calthrop and Professor Ernst Stern; staged by the author; dances arranged by Tilly Losch; Charles B. Cochran's production, presented by Florenz Ziegfeld and Arch Selwyn. At the Ziegfeld Theatre.

Parker	Trevor Glyn
Dolly Chamberlain	Audrey Pointing
Lord Henry	Patrick Ludlow
Vincent Howard	Max Kirby
The Marchioness of Chayne	Evelyn Laye
Sarah Millick	Evelyn Laye
Carl Linden	Gerald Nodin
Mrs. Millick	Isabel Ohmead
Mr. Hugh Devon	Tracy Holmes
Lady Devon	Kathlyn Lambelet
Sir Arthur Fenchurch	Charles Mortimer
The Marquis of Steere	Donald Gordon
Lord Edgar James	Richard Thorpe
Lord Sorrel	Hooper Russell
Mr. Vale	Leslie Bannister
Mr. Bethel	Anthony Neville
Mr. Proutie	Douglas Graeme-Brook
Jane	Winifred Talbot
Effie	Vesta Sylva
Piccolo	Peter Donald
Lotte	Zoe Gordon
Freda	Nancy Barnett
Hansi	Dorothy Debenham
Gussie	Sylvia Leslie
Manon (La Crevette)	Mireille
Captain August Lutte	Desmond Jeans
Herr Schlick	Charles Mortimer
Sari Linden	Evelyn Laye
Gussie	Sylvia Leslie
Lieutenant Tranisch	Louis Miller
Burley	Albert Chapman
The Marquis of Chayne	John Evelyn
Mr. Bethel	Anthony Neville
Mrs. Vale (Jane)	Winifred Talbot
Mrs. Proutie (Gloria)	Nancy Brown
The Duchess of Tenterton (Victoria),	Marjorie Raymond
The Duke of Tenterton	Donald Gordon
Lady Sorrel (Honor)	Isla Bevan
Lord Sorrel	Hooper Russell
Lady Edgar James (Harriet)	Audrey Pointing
Lady Devon	Jane Moore
Vernon Craft	Cunningham Glen
Cedric Ballantyne	Paul Spender-Clay
Bertram Sellick	Hugh Cuenod
Lord Henry Jade	George Woof Eddie
Accompanist	Lisbona

Mr. Coward is the master of little things, and the virtuosity of his talents amounts to genius. For what he describes as his operette, "Bitter Sweet," which was put on at the Ziegfeld last evening, he has written the book and the lyrics, composed the music, staged the production, and stopped just this side of acting all the parts. Although considerable showmanship has gone into the staging and the organization of the story, it is not a musical show in the rapid, flamboyant style to which we have become accustomed. But it is sheerly delightful by reason of the delicate perfection of the workmanship and the radiant splendor of Evelyn Laye, who has the principal rôle. It is a production composed of miniatures, each one neatly turned. It is charming; it is subtle and witty. By his mastery of little things Mr. Coward has mastered the artistry of musical entertainment in a refreshingly civilized style.

Although the plot of his costume romance is not highly inventive, Mr. Coward has managed to inform it with sufficient dramatic quality to carry the burden of his theme. When, in the first scene, the elderly Marchioness of Shayne surprises one of her party guests embracing the pianist, the story of her own high-spirited career begins. How, as a young lady of quality in 1875, she fell in love with her music teacher and ran off with him on the eve of the date set for her wedding to a gentleman of vast importance; how the music teacher became bandmaster in a Viennese café and she one of the hired dancing partners; how the bandmaster was slain in a duel with an officer who had kissed her; and how at length she returned to society as a famous singer and became the betrothed of the Marquis of Shayne—this is the burden of Mr. Coward's evening of song.

Although it is no great shakes as a story, it has more continuity than most books for musical productions, and it serves Mr. Coward's purpose admirably. For, again, his interest is in the style of romance. What you enjoy in "Bitter Sweet" is the skill with which he has turned out the usual set-pieces—investing the usual ceremonies ball with a native gayety and a compelling caprice, and enlivening Herr Schlick's café with a revelry that does not travesty its setting. Meanwhile, he introduces divertissements that have an air of reticent originality—a nice-mannered frolic amid the prospective bridesmaids, a droll, piquant song for the shameless ladies of the town in Vienna, and a wry caricature of the Oscar Wildettes. It is decorous entertainment, reveling in the billowing costumes of a grandiose age of style, and courting humor in the bouncing bustle.

Really, the details hardly matter. All that matters is the unity of style in the sundry materials of musical romance. What makes Evelyn Laye so rare a presence in the leading part is not merely her fragile beauty but the daintiness with which she acts and sings in the precise spirit of the play. As an actress she catches the ardor of the romantic love scenes of the first act; she trips through the dramatic episodes with a skill equal to Mr. Coward's composition. She has, moreover, a voice sweet in quality and full in tone—as competent for the warmth of such a piece as "Tell Me What Is Love" as it is for the girlishness of "The Last Dance" and the folk rhythms of the concluding "Zigeuner."

The cast of English players assembled for the American production includes many others of unusual skill—Gerald Nodin as the music teacher, Mireille as a saucy French café singer ("Life is very rough-and-tumble for the humble diseuse"), Sylvia Leslie, Zoe Gordon, Nancy Barnett and Dorothy Debenham as the audacious ladies of the town, Desmond Jeans as an imposing military captain, and a host of credible ladies and gentlemen of fashion.

If Mr. Howard, among his manifold activities, had found leisure to design and build the scenery, he might have had a more distinguished background for his innumerable cameos. His is not a devastating talent, but it has the texture of spun gold. And it draws out "Bitter Sweet" into a memorable pleasure.

1929 N 6

'RED RUST' IS GIVEN BY THEATRE GUILD

Studio Group of Younger Players Presents Soviet Drama at Martin Beck Theatre.

IT PROVES STIMULATING

Minimum of Propaganda Marks Absorbing Story of Swaggering and Villainous Revolutionist.

RED RUST, a play in three acts and eight scenes, from the Russian of V. Kirchon and A. Ouspensky, adapted by Virginia and Frank Vernon. Staged by Herbert J. Biberman; settings by Cleon Throckmorton; presented by the Theatre Guild Studio; produced by the Theatre Guild. At the Martin Beck Theatre.

Bezborodov	Lionel Stander
Lutikov	George Tobias
Andrei	Harry M. Cooke
Petrossian	Elliot Sullivan
Pimples	Lee Strasberg
Besseda	Albert Angell
Terekhine	Herbert J. Biberman
Voznesienski	Spencer Kimbell
Piotr	Lutha Adler
Supervisor	Charles Peyton
Vassili	Ackland Powell
Nina	Gale Sondergaard
Fenia	Florence House
Varvara	Virginia Berry
Lenov	William Challee
Lisa	Ruth Nelson
Fedor	Franchot Tone
Olga	Ruth Chorpenning
Youth	Joseph Kleima
Beggar	Thomas Fisher
Peddler	George Shoemaker
Mania	Eunice Stoddard
Loukitch	Curtis Arnall
Secretary	Charles Peyton
Zavialov	Harry Wilson
Nikolai	Boris Korlin

The Theatre Guild, probably the most powerful producing organization in what remains of the American theatre, last night made a happy return to the experiments of its earlier and less prosperous days when it introduced its studio at Martin Beck's handsome playhouse. This studio, composed of the younger element within the Guild, devoted its attention to a play from Soviet Russia, the second to have come to New York since the revolution. Its name was "Red Rust," and it may be described at the outset as being novel and almost continuously interesting and stimulating.

It is not, as one might assume from the fact that it was produced at the Moscow Proletarian Theatre in 1927, an out-and-out piece of propaganda. The Soviet régime, to be sure, is talked about in the light of its ambitions and aspirations, and the noble idealist who seems to represent communism at its theoretical best is the rather passive hero. But the play projects into the foreground so emphatically the villainous Terekhine, who has used the powers and opportunities granted him by the new freedom for his own lustful ends, that it seems almost at times to have been written by a couple of fellows who were not entirely satisfied with Russia's experiment.

This Terekhine has been an ardent revolutionist since 1917. One of the most thorough villains that have swaggered through Times Square in some months, his long service to the cause enables him to do pretty much as he pleases, or so he thinks. In his bestiality he keeps just within the flexible marriage laws, and it is not until he commits murder that affairs turn against him. Even then the murder is accepted as a suicide, and he at first gets off with a reprimand from the Commission of Control. But Fedor, the idealist, whose chief crime is that he has been born of bourgeois parents, is not satisfied, and eventually tracks down the real facts.

The hapless woman whose life Terekhine ruins is the patient, kindly Nina. Although he scoffs at marriage as "middle-class"—which seems to be the play's chief term of opprobrium for the conventions and customs of another time, or another land—he lives with her as her husband, while he has a wife and child in the country. His brutality and his torture are too much for her. She wants to die, but how? To commit suicide is plainly against the Soviet laws. Finally he provides the way out by killing her, with the result that he is caught up in the toils of the State.

If that plot were all of "Red Rust," it would indicate a highly melodramatic play, and probably not a very good one. While the suspicion remains that it is a better show than a play, there is considerably more to it than the foregoing account indicates. For one thing "Red Rust" has a stirring quality, and, even in dialogue, which in translation, sometimes sounds like parts of "The Front Page" crossed with Channing Pollock, it provides the invaluable essential of illusion. The people seem to be real Russians as often as they seem to be Theatre Guild actors, and you are conscious of the tremendous upheaval which that nation has experienced and from which it is creating its individual State and civilization.

As Terekhine, Herbert J. Biberman, who also staged the play understandingly, acts with great relish and unction. It is a part which demands those qualities. Gale Sondergaard plays a different sort of Nina from the one she was called upon to present in "Strange Interlude," and plays her with quiet skill. There are good performances by Ruth Chorpenning, Eunice Stoddard and Franchot Tone, as well by several lesser members of the large cast.

The production is simply but strikingly managed. Always in the back of the stage are the shadowy outlines of the Kremlin, while in front of it Lenin's tomb glows a dull red as a symbol of a new nation and, at the Martin Beck, of a provocative play from a land about which Americans hear much and know little.

1929 D 18

From Entertainment to Social Comment: 1930-1939

The excitement and diversity of the New York theater of the twenties continued throughout the next decade although the economic situation of the theater worsened. This was the decade of the depression; after the great Wall Street crash in 1929, theatrical managers found there was a shortage of money with which to finance their productions and, consequently, fewer attractions were offered on Broadway. Sound films had continued to lure away a vast portion of the theater audience, and radio now provided another and even more powerful source of competition. The movies were inexpensive (admission prices were as low as ten cents) and radio was free; the theatre (with admission prices as high as $4.40) now seemed a luxury to the general public.

This was a time of social ferment, and from the playwrights' and other theater artists' concern with vital issues emerged some of the most trenchant works of dramatic literature and some of the most exciting and vigorous theatrical organizations in the history of the American theater. One of the organizations was The Group Theatre, under the direction of Harold Clurman, Lee Strasberg, and Cheryl Crawford. .The Group Theatre, an offshoot of The Theatre Guild's Studio Company, within a short period rivalled its parent organization with impressive productions of *The House of Connelly* by Paul Green, the prize-winning *Men in White* by Sidney Kingsley (who would later create *Dead End*), and, more importantly, several plays by the decade's most promising discovery, Clifford Odets; among them were his *Awake and Sing!, Waiting for Lefty,* and *Golden Boy,* his most popular success. In 1939, The Group Theatre introduced another distinctive playwright to New York when it presented William Saroyan's *My Heart's in the Highlands.* Later that year, Saroyan would earn great praise and several awards for his *The Time of*

Your Life, presented by The Theatre Guild with Eddie Dowling in the leading role.

Older groups that did not respond to contemporary social problems faltered. In 1932, the financially hard-pressed Civic Repertory Theatre of Eva Le Gallienne, after having moved its successful production of *Alice in Wonderland* uptown to Broadway, ceased functioning; its Fourteenth Street headquarters were taken over by the radical Theatre Union and remained a popular-priced theater for the production of political plays such as *Stevedore* and *Black Pit.* In the mid-thirties the Federal Theatre was formed under the auspices of President Roosevelt's WPA and gave employment to thousands of theatrical workers, among them Orson Welles, who (with John Houseman) presented brilliant productions of Marlowe's *Dr. Faustus,* a Negro *Macbeth,* and Marc Blitzstein's *The Cradle Will Rock.* Welles and Houseman went on to form the Mercury Theatre and excited New York with their presentation of a modern-dress anti-fascist *Julius Caesar.*

The writer for the commercial theater also showed a new concern with social issues. Robert Sherwood provided such significant plays as *The Petrified Forest* and *Idiot's Delight.* S. N. Behrman's writing showed a new depth and range with his comedies of ideas, *Biography* and *End of Summer* (both with Ina Claire) and *Rain From Heaven* (with Jane Cowl), all produced by The Theatre Guild. During the thirties the Guild also presented the socially-conscious *They Shall Not Die* by John Wexley, *Both Your Houses* by Maxwell Anderson, *The Ghost of Yankee Doodle* by Sidney Howard, and the satirical "left of center" revue *Parade.* One of the most successful ventures of the decade was the Labor Stage's revue *Pins and Needles,* written by Harold J. Rome and performed by gifted members of the garment-workers' union. Along with Clifford Odets, the most important new playwright was another social critic, Lillian Hellman, who was acclaimed for her compelling plays *The Children's Hour* and *The Little Foxes.* Maxwell Anderson, who earlier in the thirties had given the stage two historical verse dramas, *Elizabeth the Queen* and *Mary of Scotland,* also dramatized the issue of social injustice in *Winterset.* The plea of Clifford Odets that "life should not be printed on dollar bills" was echoed in such disparate works as Anderson's *High Tor* and the Kaufman and Hart comedy *You Can't Take It With You.*

Some important plays and playwrights, it should be noted, seemed to remain aloof from the social ferment of the day. Eugene O'Neill produced his trilogy *Mourning Becomes Electra* and his nostalgic comedy *Ah, Wilderness!* while Thornton Wilder gave the stage one of the finest plays of the decade, *Our Town,* seemingly far removed from the troubled times. Some major comic writers produced lighter works which also seemed far removed from the pressures of the period: George S. Kaufman and Moss Hart satirized the lunacies of Hollywood in *Once in a Lifetime* and Alexander Woollcott and his coterie in *The Man Who Came to Dinner;* Noel Coward dazzled New York (with Gertrude Lawrence) in his own plays *Private Lives* and *Tonight at 8:30* and (with the Lunts) in *Design for Living;* and in 1939, a time of international crisis, the charming Lindsay and Crouse comedy *Life With Father* began its record-breaking run.

Contrary to the prevailing social commentary of the dramatic stage, the musical theater continued to be a source of unalloyed joy, full of color, wit, and melody. Even the political satires, *Of Thee I Sing* and *I'd Rather Be Right,* were good-natured spoofs rather than scorching attacks. In 1930, George and Ira Gershwin's *Girl Crazy* introduced the electrifying Ethel Merman to the legitimate stage where she has remained for four decades the most celebrated musical comedy star in the history of the American theater. Among the musical comedies in which she appeared during the thirties, most notable were those by Cole Porter: *Anything Goes, Du Barry Was a Lady,* and *Red, Hot and Blue!* In addition to Porter, the leading originators of musicals of the time were Richard Rodgers and Lorenz Hart, who created graceful and melodious presentations such as *On Your Toes, Babes in Arms,* and *The Boys from Syracuse,* and George Gershwin, whose opera *Porgy and Bess* was the most ambitious effort of the musical theater. In the same years the musical revue reached its peak with two works of Howard Dietz and Arthur Schwartz, *Three's a Crowd* and *The Band Wagon* (in which Fred and Adele Astaire appeared together for the last time on Broadway).

During the decade, the established stars (along with some

less familiar actors) enriched the stage with brilliant acting. Katharine Cornell appeared as Juliet and Saint Joan; Ruth Gordon was seen in *A Doll's House* and *The Country Wife;* the Lunts, Ina Claire, Eva Le Gallienne, Helen Hayes, Pauline Lord, Walter Huston, Jane Cowl, and Gertrude Lawrence all triumphantly continued their lustrous careers. Elisabeth Bergner made a sensational New York début in *Escape Me Never* while another great foreign actress, Alla Nazimova, was acclaimed for her performances in *Mourning Becomes Electra* and Ibsen's *Ghosts.* John Gielgud and Judith Anderson appeared in Guthrie McClintic's memorable production of *Hamlet,* and Maurice Evans became a star in New York with his appearances in *St. Helena,* the full-length *Hamlet,* and *Richard II.* Tallulah Bankhead at last found a part worthy of her talent and gave an unforgettable performance in *The Little Foxes,* as did the singer Ethel Waters in the non-musical *Mamba's Daughters.* Among the newer players, Burgess Meredith, Jules (later, John) Garfield, Julie Haydon, Margaret Sullavan, Montgomery Clift, and Uta Hagen attracted the most attention. Highly praised for its ensemble playing was The Group Theatre acting company which included Stella and Luther Adler, Morris Carnovsky, and J. Edward Bromberg. In its conscious effort to refine the art of acting, the Group Theatre set a standard for the generation that followed.

The theater of the thirties was sorely beset in many ways, but the quality, diversity, and creativity of the productions of the time were striking. From the reviews published during this period, ninety-four have been selected to represent this stimulating and provocative decade.

CHINA'S IDOL ACTOR REVEALS HIS ART

By J. BROOKS ATKINSON.

MEI LAN-FANG, in an Oriental program comprising five numbers, supported by his company of actors, dancers and musicians from Peking, with Miss Soo Yong as mistress of ceremonies. Presented for two weeks by F. C. Coppicus under the auspices of the China Institute in America. At the Forty-ninth Street Theatre.

Nothing an untutored Occidental can say about the art of Mei Lan-fang which was revealed at the Forty-ninth Street Theatre last evening will be of much importance except as guileless appreciation. For the drama of Peking, whence Mr. Mei and his actors come, has almost no point of similarity to the drama with which we are familiar; and the barrier of language is as nothing by comparison with the barrier of a completely exotic art. It is stylized, conventionalized and as old as the hills. It is, in fact, an arrested form of classical drama with virtually no striving after illusion and hardly a suggestion of realism. But it as beautiful as an old Chinese vase or tapestry. If you can purge yourself of the sophomoric illusion that it is funny, merely because it is different, you can begin to appreciate something of exquisite loveliness in pantomine and costume, and you may feel yourself vaguely in contact, not with the sensation of the moment, but with the strange ripeness of centuries. Perhaps you may even have a few bitter moments of reflecting that although our own theatrical form is enormously vivid it is rigid, and never lives so freely in terms of the imagination as this one does.

Mei Lang-fang, "Foremost of the Pear Orchard," is China's greatest actor of today. He has come here for a fortnight under the auspices of the China Institute of America, not as a commercial enterprise, but in the interests of cultural relations and good-will. To make his art intelligible, even remotely, for Western audiences, there is a mistress of ceremonies, Miss Soo Yong, who appears before the curtain before each playlet, explains the theme and directs attention to the conventions of the acting involved. Incidentally. Miss Yong speaks English with a clarity of diction rarely encountered among native speakers. Even with the assistance of her periodic expositions it is possible to have only the most general notion of what Mr. Mei and his actors are representing. And since the sketches are almost entirely lacking in tangible action, they serve chiefly as an additional reminder that the East and West cannot become twain on the basis of one evening's studious application in the theatre.

Mr. Mei plays female parts, for by virtue of an old tradition women have not until recently appeared on the Chinese stage, as they do, incidentally, in our own Chinese theatre in the Bowery. According to Miss Yong the usual term "female impersonator" does not accurately describe what the male actor of female parts is attempting to do. He is attempting rather to engender the imaginative image of an ideal woman. In one of the playlets, "The Suspected Slipper," Mr. Mei appears as Ying Chun, wife of a venerable general just returned to the wars and naturally uneasy about the reputation of his home. Even the Greek warriors had that domestic matter on their minds. In "The End of the 'Tiger' General" he is Fei Chen-o, a court lady, who avenges the honor of the royal family by slaying the invading rebel. In "The King's Parting With His Favorite" he is Yu Chi, the favorite concubine, bidding farewell to the king on his way to the wars.

How to describe a Chinese performance to those who have never seen one, either in the Orient or in the Chinese theatres of America, is a task to mock the midnight hour at which theatrical reviews are scribbled. To the weird, and to our Occidental ears, bruising tintinnabulation of a Chinese orchestra the performer enters, intones a preliminary recitative, and performs various ceremonial manoeuvres before proceeding to the dialogue of the playlet. In the case of Mr. Mei the speaking is in a convulsive falsetto, thrust against the teeth, and hardly more pleasant to the ears than the orchestra. Occasionally the action is intelligible once you are familiar with the theme of the play. For the most part it is buried deep in the traditions of Oriental theatrical artifice.

Mr. Mei is of average height, slender and extraordinarily graceful. He wears costumes and headdresses of the extravagant opulence familiar in Oriental artistry. His pantomime throughout is soft and gentle in the plasticity of its gesturing. He enters with a rippling rhythm which he maintains through various modulations in the formal scenes. He has delicately modeled hands; no doubt they are eloquent to those who understand the significance of the gestures. We call it stylized acting in the West. It is unreal and beautiful.

In other playlets there are ceremonial javelin duels, a feat of remarkable tumbling that represents the exorcizing of an evil spirit, and incidents of wand juggling not unlike the Oriental vaudeville turns. Although the stage is hung round with extravagantly decorated stuffs, there are few properties involved in the performances; and the property man, who was the chief ornament of "The Yellow Jacket," and who appears, bored and efficient, in the Chinese theatre in the Bowery, makes only one appearance in the program that was offered last evening.

But none of these details is of genuine significance. They merely hit the eyes of spectators unaccustomed to this display. And the chief impression is one of grace and beauty, stateliness and sobriety, of unalloyed imagination, and of living antiquity. Obviously, the theatre of Mei Lan-Fang does not mirror the thought of contemporary China. But it is not difficult to believe that it reflects something of the soul of the Chinese nation. If you can accept it on those terms you are as full of wonder as you are of bewilderment.

1930 F 17

NEW NEGRO DRAMA OF SUBLIME BEAUTY

Marc Connelly's "The Green Pastures" Excels as Comedy, Fantasy, Folklore, Religion.

By J. BROOKS ATKINSON.

From almost any point of view, "The Green Pastures," which was put on at the Mansfield last evening, is a play of surpassing beauty. As comedy, fantasy, folklore, religion, poetry, theatre—it hardly matters which. For occasionally there comes a time when those names hardly matter in comparison with the sublime beauty of the complete impression. And Marc Connelly has lifted his fable of the Lord walking on the earth to those exalted heights where utter simplicity in religious conception produces a play of great, emotional depth and spiritual exaltation —in fact the divine comedy of the modern theatre.

THE GREEN PASTURES, a "fable" in two acts and eighteen scenes, by Marc Connelly, suggested by Roark Bradford's Southern sketches, "Ol' Man Adam an' His Chillun." Staged by the author; settings by Robert Edmond Jones; produced by Laurence Rivers. At the Mansfield Theatre.

Mr. Deshee	Charles H. Moore
First Mammy Angel	Anna Mae Fritz
Archangel	J. A. Shipp
Gabriel	Wesley Hill
The Lord	Richard B. Harrison
Adam	Daniel L. Haynes
Eve	Inez Richardson Wilson
Cain	Lou Vernon
Cain's Girl	Dorothy Randolph
Zeba	Edna M. Harris
Cain the Sixth	James Fuller
Voice in Shanty	Josephine Byrd
Noah	Tutt Whitney
Noah's Wife	Susie Sutton
Shem	Milton J. Williams
Flatfoot	Freddie Archibald
Ham	Homer Tutt
Japheth	Stanleigh Morrell
Abraham	J. A. Shipp
Isaac	Charles H. Moore
Jacob	Edgar Burks
Moses	Alonzo Fenderson
Zipporah	Mercedes Gilbert
Aaron	McKinley Reeves
Pharaoh	George Randol
First Wizard	Emory Richardson
Head Magician	Arthur Porter
Joshua	Stanleigh Morrell
Master of Ceremonies	Billy Cumby
King of Babylon	Jay Mondayaye
Prophet	Ivan Sharp
High Priest	J. Homer Tutt
Hezdrel	Daniel L. Haynes

It has been suggested by Roark Bradford's volume of two years ago, entitled "Ol' Man Adam an' His Chillun," being the tales they tell about the time when the Lord walked the earth like a natural man. It has been best described as Uncle Remus's "Story of the Bible." In eighteen scenes it follows the chronicle of biblical history as ignorant religious negroes of the South might conceive it in childish terms of their personal experience. Beginning with a disarming vignette of a darky preacher teaching a class of negro children the main events of the Lord's creation, it moves swiftly into the fantastic comedy of a vision of heaven in terms of a fried-fish party, progresses to celestial drama of heart-breaking sincerity and concludes on a note of exhilarating faith. For everything that he has taken from Mr. Bradford's volume, Mr. Connelly contributes stuff of the finest imaginative splendor. You might not expect so much from an unpretentious negro fable. The beauty of the writing, the humility of the performance put the theatre to its highest use.

Mr. Connelly has made the transition from negro comedy to universal drama by the effortless process of increasing emphasis upon the enduring themes. At first you are delighted by the naive incongruities of the spectacle—the negro angels at their fried fish party, the tiny pickaninny in whose throat a fish bone gets lodged, the Lord in his private office cautioning Gabriel not to blow his horn, Noah blowing the steamboat whistle on the Ark, the elephants clambering up the gangplank. All through the play these magnificent strokes of imaginative comedy make "The Green Pastures" a rare piece of work.

But hardly has the fried fish party among the angels gotten under way before you realize that Mr. Connelly's play has nobler projects in mind. In fact, it has the Lord as its principal figure. Dressed in the formal garb of a parson, with his long coat and white tie, he is unpretentious. Even in his speech he is of humble origin. But straightway you perceive that he is a good man—the fusion of all the dumb, artless hopes of an ignorant people whose simple faith sustains them. He is a Lord of infinite mercy. There is a reverential moment when he creates the earth and rears up Adam in the sweetness of a new garden. There are moments of anxiety when, walking on the earth, he shakes his head sadly, and remarks, "Bad business. I don't like the way things are going at all." "What seems to be the main trouble?" he inquires of Noah. "Well, the chief trouble seems to be," Noah replies, "that the district is wide open." There are moments of rudely expressed glory when the Lord rewards Moses for his faithful service, and moments of wrath when

the Lord denounces the Babylonians. And more: there are moments when even the great Lord of creation suffers with the suffering of the world. "Being God is no bed of roses," he remarks wearily to Gabriel. He is a simple man, and a good man. In the end he is not above learning himself.

Probably this is the quality that exalts "The Green Pastures" into drama of great pith and moment. Putting the Lord on the stage in such simple terms that your imagination is stimulated into a transfiguring conception of sheer, universal goodness—that is Mr. Connelly's finest achievement. During the eighteen scenes he introduces harmonious material. The spirituals sung as chorals while the scenes are being changed carry the mood forward to the next episode. And Robert Edmond Jones, who has an imagination of his own, has designed settings that give the theme a vaulting impetus. But the Lord, walking humbly through Heaven and on the earth, telling folks to enjoy themselves, gives the play its divine compassion.

The cast and chorus include about ninety-five negro performers. Under Mr. Connelly's direction they have been molded into a finely tuned performance. Most of them appear on the stage too briefly to leave a personal impression. But the humbleness of Alonzo Fenderson as Moses and of Tutt Whitney as Noah, the rapt wonder of Daniel L. Haynes as Adam and the reverent comedy of Wesley Hill as Gabriel are performances of note. As the Lord, Richard B. Harrison has the part of greatest responsibility. He plays it with the mute grandeur of complete simplicity. This is a paternal and lovable creation. When, amid a thousand worries, he walks to the celestial window, looks about with an air of anxiety, orders the sun to be "a might cooler," and then remarks appreciatively, "That's nice," you believe in him implicitly. In fact, you believe in the entire play; it is belief incarnadined. Such things are truer than the truth.

1930 F 27

By J. BROOKS ATKINSON.

SHAKESPEARE'S HAMLET, in five acts and ten scenes. Settings by Herman Rosse; costumes by William Henry Matthews; presented by the Chicago Civic Shakespeare Society. At the Shubert Theatre.
Claudius .... William Courtleigh
Hamlet .... Fritz Leiber
Horatio .... John Burke
Polonius .... Philip Quin

Fritz Leiber's "Hamlet," which was acted at the Shubert last evening, has that uncommon quality of being not only a part but a play. It is the tragedy not only of a young man condemned to set an unjointed time to rights, but also of a brother and a sister, a witless old fool, a treacherous king and a faithless queen. For Mr. Leiber contends in the face of all stardom that Shakespeare is a dramatic poet telling here a story of great pith and moment, and that the actor's first duty is to make it intelligible. What he has accomplished in the lucidity and rapidity of staging, in the drive of a drama through many scenes and in the interpretation of the lines for their dramatic meaning—is a revelation in the producing of Shakespeare. For the expression of the tragedy as an organic unit, this is the most coherent Hamlet this courier has ever seen.

He approaches the part with the same blunt purpose as the play. His is a straightforward Hamlet—no muddy-mettled spouter of lines, but a character alert to all the relationships of the drama, clarifying the dialogue with simple gestures, waiting his time without slackening pace, keeping his diction clean and his mind on edge. He is, moreover, an actor of sufficient fullness to encompass the gusts of fury that at times sweep through the part, and to rise to the heights of a flagellating passion. Although he cuts through to the likeness of Hamlet he does not pluck out the heart of his mystery. For, after all, Hamlet is no normal person. The paralysis of will that gives the play its story, the hammering of the mind and the malignant brooding are the full measure of the character; and making no pretense to being a virtuoso Mr. Leiber does not squeeze the part dry. Applying common sense to the rôle, Mr. Leiber makes Hamlet an understandable character who appeals to the sympathies. But there is still more to this racked and pensive youth; there is a commanding nobility, and also a preternatural sensitivity to the whips and scorns of man's fortunes. Within the dramatic limitations he has set himself, Mr. Leiber does extraordinarily well.

Although his company is not all of a piece most of them are equal to their appointed tasks. Marie Carroll's child-like Ophelia puts this much-slandered part in its true perspective. All the attempts to lift this part into a cosmic significance seem as futile as they are in comparison with Miss Carroll's weak, bewildered, pathetic maiden who is caught up in a whirlwind beyond her comprehension. And the mad scene, which tries the souls of even the believers, becomes singularly affecting in the simplicity and the unostentatious design of Miss Carroll's acting. Virginia Bronson is a Queen of such excellent resolution and feeling that William Courtleigh's King seems to lack the royal authority. Nor does Philip Quin get all the bland humor in Polonius. The effeminate mannerisms of Rosencrantz and Guildenstern appear to be nothing but a distasteful truckling after illegitimate laughs. But the Laertes of Lawrence H. Cecil has admirable character, the Horatio of John Burke is to the point and the First Grave-Digger becomes a hearty low-comedy philosopher in the acting of Robert Strauss.

Mr. Leiber comes to New York under the auspices of the Chicago Civic Shakespeare Society with a repertory of seven plays, some of which, like "Twelfth Night," "As You Like It," "Richard III" and "King Lear," have almost faded from the New Yorker's memory. After completing a season of twelve weeks in Chicago he is now concluding a brief tour. Next year he will resume his activities in Chicago for the second of five guaranteed seasons.

The significance of his present engagement is, accordingly, more that of a Shakespearean festival than of individual plays. The productions are notably costumed. Herman Rosse has designed sets that make an ingenious compromise between scene suggestion and modernistic stylization, and they can be changed without interrupting the performance. On the whole, Mr. Leiber has got a remarkable enterprise well in hand. A man of great energy, he sets a high pace in the performances and whips his company straight through to the end. He stages Shakespeare for those who love the plays and who welcome an unusual opportunity to see them ably acted and produced.

1930 Mr 25

By J. BROOKS ATKINSON.

Panacea for Modern Complaints.

HOTEL UNIVERSE, a play by Philip Barry. Staged by Philip Moeller; setting by Lee Simonson; produced by the Theatre Guild. At the Martin Beck Theatre.

Ann Field	Katherine Alexander
Lily Malone	Ruth Gordon
Pat Farley	Glenn Anders
Tom Ames	Franchot Tone
Hope Ames	Phyllis Povah
Norman Rose	Earle Larimore
Alice Kendall	Ruthelma Stevens
Felix	Gustave Rolland
Stephen Field	Morris Carnovsky

Philip Barry, who has a neat talent for drawing room comedy, has gone off the deep end with his new drama, "Hotel Universe," which the Theatre Guild produced solemnly at the Martin Beck last evening. Off the deep end the water is turbid. Having assembled a group of modern valetudinarians on a fashionable veranda in Southern France Mr. Barry writes about them in a style that combines the dramatic methods of "The Cherry Orchard," "Strange Interlude" and "Mary Rose." It is an earnest venture, representing a talented young playwright in quest of solider substance than "Paris Bound" and "Holiday" contained. But froth gleaming with humor is a nobler invention than muddy-mettled prescribing for the soul. When Mr. Barry goes off the deep end in "Hotel Universe" he is soon over his head in what appear to be merely the shallows. The Guild has been there many times before.

His characters include the well-heeled worldlings who wear bruised hearts on gaudy sleeves. As his recent comedies have disclosed, such characters are invariably good for amusing conversation. So they are here for a half hour or more—rambling along aimlessly, making bitter gibes and trifling maliciously with the frailties of their friends. But such prattle is off the top of their minds. For they are disillusioned, bored, empty and futile, and at least four of them are potential suicides. All this Mr. Barry brings out in a pattern of an evening's disjointed conversation. Some of it stings. Some of it amuses. Some of it is preciosity.

All they need to develop their finest instincts and abilities for intelligent living are a restoration of faith and a clarification of mind. Each one of them has in his past the material for a wholesome present; each one has been in some way thwarted from the normal course of the things in which he believes. As it happens, they are guests of an eminent physicist who is commonly reputed to be out of his head. Walking in upon them unexpectedly, he casts a strange spell on them, talks not of the world but of the universe, of the infinity of time and space, the endlessness of life. Presently they are all caught up in the prescience of timeless things. Each one goes back in hallucination to the thing he cherishes most—the rich young vagrant to his first romance, the actress to her father, the Catholic to a priest, the Jewish banker to the tradesman who gave him his first job. Thus, restored to their true selves they are healed. What began as mordant jesting concludes in gayety and good spirits.

It may be a viable solution if you are touched by the illusion of the acting and the production. But if you remain disgruntled on the outside, "Hotel Universe" will sound like a competition of words, as credible in its moments of cynicism as it is in its eery raptures of faith. When the well-born discuss the emptiness of their lives and the sterility of existence, it is difficult to keep them from sounding sophomoric. Inevitably, the hackneyed phrases recur and give out an empty sound. And in "Hotel Universe" the protestations of faith are hardly better. They, too, are words. If the sickness of the soul goes no deeper than a choice of words, perhaps it is sufficient to prescribe words for healing. Mr. Barry has been lavish with words; they are arranged at times in purple patches. But they have little relation to life; and the tempest they whip up remains very comfortably inside the teapot.

Against one of Lee Simonson's vividly colorful settings the Guild has gathered a cast of familiar Guilders and notable visiting actors—Glenn Anders as an eminently tangible disciple of gloom; Earle Larimore as a clean-cut young man of finance; Franchot Tone as a likable mental wastrel; Phyllis Povah as a sensible young matron; Katherine Alexander as a forbearing hostess; Morris Carnovsky as the resonant old man.

In general, those who have the simplest parts give the most palatable performances. Miss Alexander and Miss Povah play straight to the point in parts that are not balmy, but Ruth Gordon is conspicuously miscast as the melancholy actress. The performance is frequently inaudible. As far as characterization is concerned, it remains very much on the surface. It is easier to make bricks without straw than it is to suffuse mental posturing with life.

1930 Ap 15

By J. BROOKS ATKINSON.

Generalities of a Genius.

UNCLE VANYA, a comedy in four acts by
Anton Chekhov, adapted by Rose Caylor.
Settings by Jo Mielziner; produced by Jed
Harris. At the Cort Theatre.

Marina .... Kate Mayhew
Michael Astroff.............. Osgood Perkins
Ivan Voinitski................. Walter Connolly
Sonia .... Joanna Roos
Alexander Serebrakoff........ Eugene Powers
Ilya Telegin................. Eduardo Ciannelli
Helena .... Lillian Gish
Mme. Voinitskaya............ Isabel Vernon
A Servant.................. Harold Johnsrud

Probably "Uncle Vanya," which
was acted at the Cort last evening,
is the least interesting of Chekhov's
major dramas. But like the others
it is eminently actable under sensitive direction. After a year's absence from Broadway Jed Harris
has returned to stage a luminously
beautiful performance of this intangible drama and to reawaken an
old confidence in his uncanny pre-
ceptions. Producing Chekhov requires more than anything else the
ability to translate limpness into
limpidity, and to see the high comedy where most observers see merely
the gloom of futility. With a cast
including such variegated talents as
those of Lillian Gish, Walter Connolly, Osgood Perkins, Joanna Roos,
Kate Mayhew and Eugene Powers,
Mr. Harris has succeeded brilliantly. The simple generalities of a
genius emerge as detached wisdom
and beauty, leavened with the humors of compassion.

"Uncle Vanya" is nearly self-contained. "The Cherry Orchard,"
"The Sea Gull" and to some extent
"The Three Sisters" constantly illuminate corners of life in general with
their random reflections upon many
things. "Uncle Vanya" is the germ
of these more expansive dramas. In
it you will find the ubiquitous country doctor, the pompous man of
learning, the radiant queen beloved
of all, the spinster who loves in vain,
the family drudge, the usual hanger-
on—and the petty embroils and the
malignant boredom. Thus, all the
familiar Chekhovian elements are
present.

Taken literally, the incidents of
their almost uneventful life would
mean boredom in the theatre as well
as in their lives. In the space of
four acts nothing happens except
that Uncle Vanya, in a fit of bad
temper, shoots twice at his blandly intellectual brother-in-law, and
misses. But the real drama lies in
Chekhov's awareness of the many
destinies that are silently following
inscrutable courses beneath the fabric of the story.

The big scenes, such as they are,
mutely dramatize nothing more dramatic than indifference. Thus, while
the intellectual potentate is discours-
ing in fulsome, classroom tones on a
project to sell an estate which is not
properly his and invest it in more
profitable securities, his daughter is
eating out her heart for a man that
does not love her, his wife is torn
between revulsion for him and alarm
about the affection the doctor bears
her, and his brother-in-law is in the
depths of despair over his unrequited
love and his wasted life altogether.

This sounds like either tragedy or
at least Muscovian despair. But to
Chekhov, who met all these situations on equal terms and sympathized
with them without dogmatic preaching, they are the comedy of life—
shaded, touched with melancholy, but
radiantly alive. So these actors play
"Uncle Vanya" with dignity and
precision and with a quietude that
last evening was at times merely inaudibility. It is the quintessence of
naturalism. The story flows so ef-
fortlessly, the lines are so rhymeless
and impulsive and the pace is so relaxed that you are scarcely aware
that an author and a director are
shaping the events of the evening.
This is the high comedy of stating
life accurately.

Although, judging by the storminess of the greeting at her entrance,
Lillian Gish is the star of the production, the performance has a unity
that takes no account of personality.
A coherent design in monotone, it
includes every part on equal terms.
Individually the parts are exquisitely
acted—Miss Gish, fragile and pliant,
as the young wife of a pretentious
scholar; Mr. Connolly, bungling and
childish as Uncle Vanya; Mr. Perkins, cynical and verbose as the
doctor; Miss Roos, young and lovely
as the daughter; the petulant pedantry of Mr. Powers as the professor;
the sweet patience of Miss Mayhew
as the nurse. They have the major
rôles; but the foolish humility of
Eduardo Ciannelli as the family pen-
sioner and the astringent intellectualism of Isabel Vernon as the mother
are quite as essential to the full composition.

To many theatregoers Chekhov is
still an enigma and a bore. In spite
of the ballyhoo of Chekhov up and
down Broadway and the belated recognition of a master hand, the drama
of ellipsis and inference is still, for
many people, completely undramatic.
But to those who have the patience
to listen Chekhov has pith and truth
to convey. Although "Uncle Vanya"
is not the best of his dramas this
finely-wrought production is full of
pale, tender beauty—and humor.

1930 Ap 16

By J. BROOKS ATKINSON.

Eva La Gallienne as Juliet.

SHAKESPEARE'S ROMEO AND JULIET, in four acts and twenty scenes. Settings and costumes designed by Aline Bernstein; staged by Eva Le Gallienne; revived by the Civic Repertory Theatre. At the Civic Repertory Theatre.

Escalus	Jacob Ben-Ami
Paris	Blake Scott
Montague	Harold Moulton
Capulet	Walter Beck
An old man	Joseph Kramm
Romeo	Donald Cameron
Mercutio	J. Edward Bromberg
Benvolio	Robert F. Ross
Tybalt	Robert H. Gordon
Friar Laurence	Sayre Crawley
Friar John	Joseph Kramm
Balthasar	Arnold Moss
Samson	Herbert Shapiro
Gregory	Robert Lewis
Peter	Burgess Meredith
Abraham	Lee Hillery
An apothecary	Howard da Silva
An officer	David Turk
Lady Montague	Mary Ward
Lady Capulet	Merle Maddern
Juliet	Eva Le Gallienne
Nurse to Juliet	Leona Roberts

Although Shakespeare described it as "Romeo and Juliet" the Civic Repertory performance, which was acted in Fourteenth Street last evening, is Juliet. For Miss Le Gallienne gives the finest and most elastic performance of her career in that rôle. During the last two or three years the superstition has grown up that Miss Le Gallienne is a better director than actress—a superstition largely fostered by her choice of occupations in her theatre. But her Juliet reveals her as an actress, not merely of intelligence which she has always been, but of scope and resilience, which she has become this season. Ardently girlish in the balcony scene, her Juliet grows steadily in dignity and command as the tragedy unfolds, and takes the terrors and resolutions of the potion scene with a new fullness of emotion. Miss Le Gallienne has always been mistress of fundamental details in acting. In this production, which is sometimes inaudible in the other parts, the clarity and sing of her diction are particularly enjoyable. But her greatest achievement is the acting of a romantic rôle with latitude and fluid grace.

Although the production as a whole is a work of mixed values it is the most ambitious venture that the Civic Repertory has made on the side of unalloyed beauty. Aline Bernstein, whose work is also steadily increasing in its imaginative authority, has designed a remarkable series of settings. One expansive device of several flights of stairs climbing into a blue background introduces the tragedy with three major acting levels. For the rest, a triangular structure, easily turned about, serves to suggest beautifully the balcony, the interior of Juliet's chamber and Friar Lawrence's cell. Splendidly lighted, especially for the balcony scene, these units of scenery make an ingenious compromise between concrete representation and conventional background, and they give the production an idealized splendor quite in harmony with the spirit of the play.

In these circumstances you might expect the performance to move briskly, but, particularly in the beginning, it is sluggish, and the long waits between the acts break the spell. There is, moreover, an overpowering suggestion of stair-climbing during the pageantry of the opening scenes. Part of the fault may be ascribed to Shakespeare, who got well into "Romeo and Juliet" before he touched on the essential problem of the drama, and whose poetry is here so sublimated that it forces little substance out of the characters. But part of the fault lies also in the amorphous staging which, for example, places the first meeting of Juliet and Romeo far in the background, where it is lost behind the ceremony of the dancing.

The performance improves steadily all through the evening. When it comes to the street brawl which is fatal to Mercutio it has pace and attack. What has seemed to be unsifted becomes lucid in this scene. And J. Edward Bromberg's Mercutio, which lacked character in the beginning, turns this duel and death into a species of clear-cut gallantry that is thoroughly moving. It is one of the best parts in Shakespeare, honored here in the observance of its valorous humor.

If Donald Cameron's Romeo had that much character, the performance of the tragedy might realize more consistently the beauties latent in it. But Mr. Cameron's portrait is hardly more than perfunctory. As the youth who falls in love with Juliet on the rebound from Rosaline this Romeo is a dull swain whose speaking of the lines is monotonous recitation. As the young man in the last act who suddenly comes through the mist of romance to the hard facts of reality Mr. Cameron takes a more tangible position in the performance.

Leona Roberts is capital as the bawdy nurse—plodding in her walk, mischievous in her humors and craftily amusing altogether. As Friar Lawrence, Sayre Crawley, who is still cursed with that tedious introductory speech, catches the fatherliness in that part. The other parts are variously played—some of them well, none of them badly. And although the performance as a whole is not perfect in its patterning, it has a fine texture and sometimes it resolves itself into scenes of living beauty. And Miss Le Gallienne's Juliet is no idle ornament hanging on the cheek of night, but a characterization in terms of imaginative acting.

1930 Ap 22

'LYSISTRATA' HERE WITH BROAD HUMOR

Aristophanes's Comedy Revived With Horse Play and Slapstick at 44th St. Theatre.

ITS DIALOGUE STILL RACY

Toned Down Since Production in Philadelphia—Memorable Flow of Color and Motion.

By J. BROOKS ATKINSON.

On second thought, the "Lysistrata," which was put on at the Forty-fourth Street last evening, does not come direct from Athens. Between Aristophanes and us stands Norman Bel Geddes, scene designer extraordinary, who produced this version for the Philadelphia Theatre Association several weeks ago, and whose bountiful scenery now sweeps up toward the flies in a Broadway playhouse. He has designed a magnificent production, imaginative, free, sculptural and colorful, and the concluding bacchanal, when viewed from the rear of the auditorium, is a memorable flow of color and motion.

ARISTOPHANES'S LYSISTRATA, a comedy in two acts in a new adaptation by Gilbert Seldes. Staged by Norman-Bel Geddes. Settings and costumes by Mr. Geddes. Incidental music by Leo Ornstein. Dances arranged by Doris Humphrey and Charles Weidman. Revived by the Philadelphia Theatre Association, Inc., under the management of Robert Sparks. At the Forty-fourth Street Theatre.

Lysistrata.............Violet Kemble Cooper
Kalonika....................Miriam Hopkins
Myrrhina...................Hortense Alden
First Athenian Woman........Ruth Garland
Lampito.....................Hope Emerson
First Old Man...................Ian Wolfe
Second Old Man..........Houston Richards
Third Old Man............Etienne Girardot
President of the Senate..Sydney Greenstreet
Clerk.......................Elliott Sullivan
A Herald from Sparta........Eric Dressler
Kinesias.....................Ernest Truax
First Young Man (Polydorus)..John Clearman
Second Young Man............George Cotton
Third Young Man............Clayton Irving
The Child..................James McCallion
Lycon....................Albert Van Dekker
Old women's chorus, old men's chorus, dancers, dwarf, young men's chorus, couriers, warriors, attendants, guards, populace.

If "Lysistrata" were "Antigone" or "Electra," this spacious edifice would be a masterful scene conception for the dignity of groupings and the declamation of Greek tragedy. But "Lysistrata" is horseplay, broader than a Second Avenue burlesque, full of rough-and-tumble, full of bawdry. The comic spirit could dance more freely if Mr. Geddes had spared the picture somewhat and tightened the performance. When he has experienced actors at his command—Violet Kemble Cooper, Ernest Truex, Sydney Greenstreet—Aristophanes triumphs over magnificence of scenery, for good actors know the craft of expression. But the pictorial quality of this "Lysistrata" is no unmixed dispensation for the younger actors. When the performance begins to sprawl, as it still does despite considerable cutting, you suspect that Mr. Geddes's setting is more on the side of the tragedians than the mountebanks.

But that is counsel of perfection, and "Lysistrata" is too hearty a comedy to be stared out of countenance by a promethean artist. Gilbert Seldes has written an English adaptation colloquial enough to be relished, and the sheer artlessness of the slapstick episodes makes them palatable and enjoyable even for the sciolists of Broadway. As every one must know by this time, "Lysistrata" is the story of the women of Greece who plot to conclude a tedious and ruinous interstate war by abstaining from love until their menfolk have made peace. Soldiers denied the consolations of domesticity grew less Martian and more reasonable politically.

So they do. As the most impetuous of the returned soldiers, Ernest Truex shows how shrewd Lysistrata has been, not only for Greece but for the craft of acting. For Mr. Truex is a capital actor, and the crowning episode of the story becomes enormously funny in his harum-scarum playing. Miriam Hopkins and Hortense Alden, as young women whose high resolves are foreign to their instincts, have a mischievous sense of humor that is likewise entertaining. Members of the constabulary were present last evening to safeguard the morals of Broadway art patrons. Although the police listened to some of the raciest conversation to be heard outside the marts of commerce, they wil' be relieved to know that it is tamer than what members of the Philadelphia Theatre Association heard when "Lysistrata" opened in that wellbred metropolis.

Since Fay Bainter, who played the leading part originally, has had other engagements to fulfill, Violet Kemble Cooper appears here as Lysistrata. It is one of her best performances. Her voice has strength enough to dominate so vast a scene; her diction is excellent. She gives the part authority and stature. Sydney Greenstreet, as the President of the Senate of the City of Athens, gives it amplitude. Although "Lysistrata" is a robust comedy, it is not sophisticated. Instead of cracking jokes, it pummels and grimaces, or splashes jars of water on a parcel of feeble old men. And, although the pace of the performance is slow and uneven, and lacking rhythm, it is a tempo not unsuited to the festival quality of the humors.

Those who expect a neat, brisk show will be disappointed. But those who still like to snort over the earthy japery of elementary comedy will find that the congenial version of "Lysistrata" has laughing matter of rare quality. Despite the fact that Mr. Geddes has not found the style best suited to the Aristophanes spirit, he has mounted an unusual production. From several different points of view, including that of enjoyment, it is one of the most interesting ventures of the season.

1930 Je 6

By J. BROOKS ATKINSON.

ONCE IN A LIFETIME, a comedy in three acts, by Moss Hart and George S. Kaufman. Staged by Mr. Kaufman; settings by Cirker & Robbins; produced by Sam H. Harris. At the Music Box Theatre.

George Lewis	Hugh O'Connell
May Daniels	Jean Dixon
Jerry Hyland	Grant Mills
The porter	Oscar Polk
Helen Hobart	Spring Byington
Susan Walker	Sally Phipps
Cigarette girl	Clara Waring
Coat check girl	Otis Schaefer
Phyllis Fontaine	Janet Currie
Miss Fontaine's maid	Marie Ferguson
Miss Fontaine's chauffeur	Charles Mack
Florabel Leigh	Eugenie Frontai
Miss Leigh's maid	Dorothy Talbot
Miss Leigh's chauffeur	Edward Loud
Bellboy	Payson Crane
Mrs. Walker	Frances E. Brandt
Ernest	Marc Loebell
Herman Glogauer	Charles Halton
Miss Leighton	Leona Maricle
Lawrence Vail	George S. Kaufman
Weisskopf	Louis Cruger
Meterstein	William McFadden
First page	Stanley Fitzpatrick
Second page	Edwin Mills
Three scenario writers	Kempton Race / George Casselbury / Burton Mallory
Rudolph Kammerling	Walter Dreher
First electrician	Jack Williams
Second electrician	John O. Hewitt
A voice pupil	Jane Buchanan
Mr. Flick	Harold Grau
Miss Chasen	Virginia Hawkins
First cameraman	Irving Morrow
The Bishop	Granville Bates
The sixth bridesmaid	Francis Thress
Script girl	Georgia MacKinnon
George's secretary	Robert Ryder

Having no visible reverence for Hollywood, Moss Hart and George S. Kaufman have written "Once in a Lifetime," which was acted at the Music Box last evening. It is a hard, swift satire—fantastic and deadly, and full of highly charged comedy lines. Since neither of the playwrights has ever visited Hollywood, it is no well-considered lucubration, but a rough-and-tumble burlesque, with a conventional story. Sometimes it drops into a false key of sobriety; and having been steadily convulsed by an extraordinarily comic first act, you have to readjust yourself to an easier pace through the rest of the piece. But the skinning of Hollywood is neat and complete. The good lines are hilariously funny. It is not the best skit with which Mr. Kaufman has been associated. But the gods of laughter know that it is good enough. As some one has already observed, no comic writer should ever be as funny as he can be.

If you know the form of theatrical satire you know already the general course of the story. Three small-time vaudeville performers set out for Hollywood as soon as the first talking picture has been shown on Broadway. Foreseeing the confusion of an industry that has made silent pictures exclusively, they hope to establish themselves as elocution teachers while the iron is hot. Their wild luck, their brazenness and the incompetence of talking-picture producers conspire to make them people of considerable influence before the play is over.

But that gives you little idea of the fun "Once in a Lifetime" contains. It tells you nothing of the bedlam that is Hollywood—the absurd pretentiousness of the Glogauer Studio, where uniformed pages are constantly parading around with ornate signs announcing Herman Glogauer's present location; the plight of the New York playwright, one of a shipment of sixteen, who has waited in his office for months without receiving a word of instruction, and finally breaks down from underwork; the wild turmoil of hiring and firing, putting names on doors with paint that is easily removable, and the travesty of a city in which even the waitress and bootblacks combine acting with their humble crafts.

Things happen so much on impulse that finally George Lewis, who used to be the best dead-pan feed in the vaudeville business, becomes general superviser of the Glogauer Studios by virtue of repeating another man's words to Herman Glogauer at the right moment. When Lewis has just completed his first production, he finds that he has produced the wrong script. He had had the right script in his hand when he began. But being annoyed by a draft, he had turned round to close the window, and then picked up the wrong script when he turned back. Upon such trifling accidents Hollywood fortunes depend—or at any rate Mr. Hart and Mr. Kaufman would have you think so.

Through all this higgledy-piggledy burlesque the authors scurry rapidly and maliciously, putting a poison barb on their lines. Mr. Kaufman has not only directed the performance skillfully, but he also makes his stage début as Lawrence Vail, the transplanted playwright. It is a part written less fantastically than the play, and Mr. Kaufman, who was doubtless unnerved last evening by the long salute of applause that greeted his appearance, had little fantasy to give them. By the time of his second appearance in the last act he had recovered.

The cast includes such enjoyable performers as Hugh O'Connell, who can beam and clown at the same moment; Jean Dixon, who can drench her lines in acid and also make an emotional incident count by the reticence of her acting; Spring Byington, who flutters gayly as the most widely syndicated movie critic in the world; Charles Halton, who keeps Herman Glogauer racing dizzily through the studio; Walter Dreher, who charges the expensive German director with a giddy temperament. It is all swift, shrieking and lethal. It is merciless and fairly comprehensive. If the fun lags a little during the middle sketches, it is only because the first act is so hilariously compact and because the best scenes all the way through are so outrageously fantastic.

1930 S 25

By J. BROOKS ATKINSON.

Vine Leaves in a Heap.

THE GREEKS HAD A WORD FOR IT, a play in three acts, by Zoe Akins. Settings by Livingston Platt; staged and produced by William Harris Jr. At the Sam H. Harris Theatre.

Schatze..........................Dorothy Hall
Jean.........................Verree Teasdale
Polaire.....................Muriel Kirkland
Waiter in night club............Jack Bennett
Louis Small....................Don Beddoe
Dey Emery..................Hardie Albright
Boris Feldman...........Ernest Glendinning
The Russian woman.........Helen Kingstead
Jones..........................Harold Heaton
Justin Emery..............Frederic Worlock
Stanton........................Gordon Stout
Waiter.........................John Walpole
Bellows......................Ethel Hamilton

What it is that "The Greeks Had a Word For," does not appear specifically in Zoë Akins's play of approximately that title, acted at the Sam H. Harris last evening. For with magnificent indifference to such a dull virtue as clarity, Miss Akins goes imposingly along through three loquacious acts, serving champagne freely, counting out $5,000 absentmindedly for trivial reasons, strewing her play with famous pianists, bankers, bankers' sons and three kept ladies. It is a strange discursion. One act interests you, although not without misgivings; the second alarms you by its daze and sluggishness, and then the third, which at last begins to give some heed to finding a conclusion, amuses you with some of the neatest dialogue Miss Akins has written. It is never a play with a theme or a sense of progression. Yet you are never willing to dismiss it as pointless. Somewhere Miss Akins has got hold of something. "The Greeks Had a Word For It," but they had many words. So has Miss Akins. They may not mean anything. Nevertheless, many of them are amusing.

All the action, says the program, is modern and "transpires in New York" during some very transpiring weather. Schatze, Jean and Polaire, who were once glorified by Ziegfeld, are now ladies of the town, with expensive tastes, considerable languor and a sense of which men to choose. During the course of the evening Polaire receives an honorable proposal of marriage from a banker's son, who, as you know, is a weakling. But Jean, who is an Italian blonde, and Italian blondes have lovely skin, manages to hoist herself up by her slipper straps and become the banker's bride. Not exactly the banker's bride, however. For just before the wedding ceremony in a private suite in the Ambassador Hotel she looks with envy upon her two sisters in sin who are just starting off on a harum-scarum adventure to Paris. She pulls off her wedding dress and joins them. Presumably, Justin Emery's wedding will be hampered somewhat by the lack of a bride.

Miss Akins does not vex herself with a story. She likes rather to luxuriate in comfortable surroundings, gazing at her characters through a golden mist. They are entertaining characters and Miss Akins constantly arranges them in droll situations. Of her three ladies Schatze is the practical one, alive to the responsibilities of her situation. Jean and Polaire spend most of their time verbally pulling each other's hair. Miss Akins's best achievement is the description of this trio, who hurl short and ugly words at each other, pass cutting insults, steal, scratch and insinuate, and yet remain loyal as a group against the rest of the world. It is a comic conception; Miss Akins has enlivened it with wryly humorous dialogue and considered it dreamily in terms of romantic adventure. But she never comes to grips with it. She postpones making decisions. You are interested and bored by turns.

Livingston Platt, scene designer, has taken pains to put these ladies of the town amid surroundings befitting their station. Luxury drenches the apartments where they bicker over their men. Dorothy Hall, Verree Teasdale and Muriel Kirkland are dryly entertaining as the three complaisant women.

Ernest Glendinning gives a thoroughly good performance as a celebrated pianist. In fact, good performances are the rule throughout, with Hardie Albright, Frederic Worlock and Don Beddoe in adjacent parts; and William Harris Jr. has directed with an obvious relish of his material. On the whole, there is more relish about the comedy than accomplishment. "The Greeks Had a Word For It" never fulfills its succession of promises.

1930 S 26

"GIRL CRAZY" A LIVELY AND MELODIOUS SHOW

George Gershwin's Music Set to Fresh and Amusing Lyrics by His Brother Ira.

When the first curtain arose on last night's antics at the Alvin, a large sign on the stage informed the audience that it was looking at Custerville, Ariz., a happy community which feminine wiles had not penetrated for more than fifty years. But since this was a musical comedy, that manless state obviously could not long endure. Before ten minutes had elapsed the personable Ginger Rogers had made her entrance, and from then on the young women principals and jazz coryphees came in droves. And, what with one thing and another, it all helped to make "Girl Crazy" what Broadway would call a lively and expert show. There is, then, fairly consoling news from Fifty-second Street this morning.

GIRL CRAZY, a musical comedy in two acts and eight scenes. Book by Guy Bolton and John McGowan, music by George Gershwin and lyrics by Ira Gershwin. Settings by Donald Oenslager; staged by Alexander Leftwich; dances and ensembles arranged by George Hale; produced by Alex A. Aarons & Vinton Freedley. At the Alvin Theatre.

Danny Churchill	Allen Kearns
Molly Gray	Ginger Rogers
Pete	Clyde Veaux
Lank Sanders	John Daley
Gieber Goldfarb	Willie Howard
Flora James	Eunice Healy
Patsy West	Peggy O'Connor
Kate Fothergill	Ethel Merman
Slick Fothergill	William Kent
Sam Mason	Donald Foster
Tess Parker	Olive Brady
Jake Howell	Lew Parker
Eagle Rock	Chief Rivers
Hotel Proprietor	Jack Classon
Lariat Joe	Starr Jones
The Foursome	Marshall Smith, Ray Johnson, Del Porter, Dwight Snyder.

Antonio and Renee Demarco.
"Red" Nichols and His Orchestra.
Al Siegal at the Piano.

Not the least important item in these tidings is the part played by the brothers Gershwin. George has written some good tunes, while Ira has provided tricky and ingratiating lyrics that should stimulate any ear surfeited with the usual rhyming insipidities of musical comedy. In one number, "Bidin' My Time," he has poked fun at the theme song school in verse; in all he has been fresh and amusing. And his brother has provided melody in "Embraceable You" and "But Not For Me," travestied the imperishable "Frankie and Johnnie" in "Sam and Delilah," and turned out several excellent rhythmic numbers, one of which, "I Got Rhythm," induces a veritable frenzy of dancing.

The book is serviceable, rather than distinguished. It gets its characters in and out of the proper entanglements and tears its hero and heroine apart at the end of the first act as every orthodox musical show libretto should. Set in the Southwest, "Girl Crazy" concentrates on affairs in a dude ranch. The ranch is run by a New York playboy who falls in love with an Arizona girl. Around the premises lurk a hardbitten pair of villains, who are alternately after somebody's $6,000 and the scalp of Willie Howard, who impersonates

Gieber Goldfarb, a Broadway taxi-cab driver forced by the exigencies of the story to become a sheriff addicted to impersonations of Maurice Chevalier, Eddie Cantor and George Jessel. That is not all, but you get the idea. What is important is that, with the music, dancing and some of the comedy, it does not matter more than it should.

The dancing combines intricacy and speed in the manner of the day, and is definitely one of the assets. Another is Ethel Merman, whose peculiar song style was brought from the night clubs to the stage to the vast delight last evening of the people who go places and watch things being done. Willie Howard is, as usual, Willie Howard; in several instances, particularly at the start of the show, he is funnier than he has been lately. He is, it may be recalled, in the rôle first intended for Bert Lahr, who was kept from joining the show by a previous contract. Assisting him in the comicalities of the evening is that gadfly merry-andrew, William Kent, who is permitted to be only moderately successful. The ingenue, Miss Rogers, is an oncoming young person of the type whom, at her first appearance, half of the audience immediately classifies as "cute."

The première performance was conducted by George Gershwin, and he got as much applause as any one on the stage. Under his baton were a pit-full of experts in syncopation, who contributed their share to making "Girl Crazy" an agreeable diversion which seems destined to find a profitable place among the luxuries of Times Square, if not the necessities.

1930 O 15

"THREE'S A CROWD" GAY AND TUNEFUL SHOW

By J. BROOKS ATKINSON.

THREE'S A CROWD, a revue in two acts and twenty-five scenes. Conceived and compiled by Howard Dietz, lyrics and music by Mr. Dietz, Arthur Schwartz and others. Staged by Hassard Short; settings by Albert R. Johnson; costumes designed by Kiviette; dances arranged by Albertina Rasch; produced by Max Gordon. At the Selwyn Theatre.
PRINCIPALS—Clifton Webb, Fred Allen, Libby Holman, Margaret Lee, Tamara Geva, California Collegians, Harold Moffett, Earl Oxford, Joan Clement, Lou Wood, Marybeth Conoly and others.

Those responsible for "Three's Crowd," and Howard Dietz seems to be chief among them, have put together a bright, smart and tasteful show. It has a pleasant lightness, a sort of unforced gayety, and, for the most part, a quizzical, knowing point of view. It has, to be sure, its valleys as well as its peaks—sometimes it seems to lose briefly its spontaneity of movement and once or twice it resorts rather distressingly to the obvious—but these depressions do not take long to negotiate. And when the show hits a high spot, it is a very high spot indeed.

Most heavily, of course, it all leans on the stars who have supplied its name, the Clifton Webb-Fred Allen-Libby Holman trio who contributed more than measurably to the success of the first "Little Show." Each of them is a leader, Mr. Webb of the dancing fraternity, Mr. Allen of the Broadway jokesmiths and Miss Holman of the lady torchbearers, and they have ample opportunity to demonstrate their talents. Mr. Webb also possesses a dry and peckish wit which is a valuable supplement to the magic of his agile feet. When he takes a bath before your very eyes, give a poisonous imitation of Rudy Vallee or glides gracefully through some tricky dance you find superior entertainment, as you do when the crack-voiced Mr. Allen appears in a hilarious travesty of the Byrd junket or the sultry Miss Holman intones the plaintive measures of a transatlantic song, "Body and Soul," which seems destined to duplicate its English popularity here.

The three receive excellent support, not only from the other entertainers, but also from Mme. Rasch, director of the dances, who has made a pleasant departure from music show routine, and Albert R. Johnson, in whose settings is a simplification that does not detract from their effectiveness, gayety or atmospheric correctness. The lighting of the show, which is important, too, is particularly good; in fact, one of the most striking numbers of this or any other revue is the "Body and Soul" dance which achieves a startling quality even more through its use of lights than through the poses of Mr. Webb and Tamara Geva, the Russian exotic. Among other assistants to the three stars is Margaret Lee, whose Tom Thumb caroling of a syncopated torch song, "All the King's Horses," deserves a word or two for itself, which it hereby gets.

It is pleasant to have Miss Holman and the Messers. Allen and Webb on Broadway again, and it is gratifying that they have returned in such an acceptable harlequinade. Although the applause from the Selwyn may have broken hearts over at "The Second Little Show" last night, it was merited and symptomatic of considerable real enjoyment on the part of the nabobs of New York's play set.

1930 O 16

By J. BROOKS ATKINSON

LEW LESLIE'S BLACKBIRDS OF 1930, a revue in two acts and twenty scenes. Book by Flourney Miller, and music and lyrics by Eubie Blake and Andy Razaf. Staged and produced by Mr. Leslie; special dances arranged by Al Richards; settings by Ward and Harvey; choral arrangements directed by Rosamond Johnson. At the Royale Theatre.
PRINCIPALS—Ethel Waters, Flourney Miller, Berry Brothers, Jazzlips Richardson, Buck and Bubbles, Mantan Moreland, Blue McAllister, Broadway Jones, Minto Cato, Neeka Shaw, Mercer Marquise, Cecil Mack's Choir, Eubie Blake and his orchestra and others.

When the black gals dance in the new edition of "Blackbirds," which appeared at the Royale last evening, you can forgive the comedians for being so silly and the song-smiths for having nothing on their minds. The diminutive black gals have hot feet; the buck dancers are whirling dervishes. In its mission of "glorifying the American Negro" this production puts its best dancing foot forward by letting the taller of the Berry brothers perform impossible rhythmic gyrations and Jazzlips Richardson wrack his body in devotion to his giddy name.

But there is little except pandemonium in the rest of Mr. Leslie's ambitious production to glorify the American Negro or the Broadway show shops. After the conventional opening scene on a Mississippi levee, when Broadway Jones and the Blackbird choir sing the rich harmonies of "Roll, Jordan," the music runs to tepid Tin Pan Alley tunes, bewailing those unkind fates that constantly force music hall songsters close to the footlights with pensive "memories of you." Even Ethel Waters, the vocal clown of the Negro stage, has nothing more original than "Lucky to Me" to lavish her sundry blandishments upon. Being short of tunes this "Blackbirds" sings each one of them over and

over again with the standard chorus girl manoeuvres at the end.

Even when they have no material at their disposal Negro comedians promise well. Black as the ace of spades, with those enormous white circles around their lips, they have questioning eyes which flutter and roll with comedy eloquence. Flourney Miller, tall and brutal, and Manton Moreland, his frisky satellite, are the comedians here, and their appearance is suitably raffish. But the skits they have to perform have little racial humor to enliven them, nor humor of any color. During the course of the evening this "Blackbirds" makes game of "The Last Mile," "The Green Pastures" and "All Quiet on the Western Front." From any point of view the travesties are pretty flat. In the case of "The Green Pastures" the travesty is elaborate, spectacular and pointless. When you consider all the energy that goes into these comedy numbers, you are amazed that the amusement can be so weak.

Whether Negro musical entertainments should remain faithful to Negro characteristics or should abide by the white man's formula for stage diversion is a question for the anthropologists to discuss quietly among themselves. Certainly even the best Negro shows we have are predominantly white in their direction. But the Negroes as entertainers have an exuberance that crops out in whatever they undertake. They dance with a matchless abandon. They strut and grimace with a contagious expression of high spirits. No arbitrary notions of propriety curb their eagerness to entertain. In the first edition of "Blackbirds" Mr. Leslie put their willingness to good use in colorful song numbers and ludicrous comedy sketches. Although he has staged the second edition more lavishly the material is slender. Not much remains except the willingness of his performers to give you a good time.

1930 O 23

By J. BROOKS ATKINSON.

Every Inch a Queen.

ELIZABETH THE QUEEN, a play in three acts, by Maxwell Anderson. Staged by Philip Moeller; settings and costumes designed by Lee Simonson; produced by the Theatre Guild. At the Guild Theatre.
Raleigh ....Percy Waram
Penelope ....Anita Kerry
Captain Armin................Philip Foster
Cecil ....Arthur Hughes
Bacon ....Morris Carnovsky

Essex	Alfred Lunt
Elizabeth	Lynn Fontanne
A Councillor	Charles Homer
Burghley	Robert Conness
The Fool	Barry Macollum
Mary	Mab Anthony
Tressa	Edla Frankau
Ellen	Phoebe Brand
Marvel	Royal Beal
A Man-at-Arms	John Ellsworth
A Courier	Charles Brokaw
A Captain of the Guards	Edward Oldfield
A Courtier	Robert Caille
A Herald	Vincent Sherman
Burbage	Whitford Kane
Heming	Charles Brokaw
Poins	Curtis Arnall

If Maxwell Anderson had made use of the theatre's artful tricks in "Elizabeth the Queen," which was acted at the Guild Theatre last evening, he might have written a showier play. But he could hardly have written the magnificent drama he has set down quietly on his own well-considered terms. It is a searching portrayal of character, freely imaginative in its use of history, clearly thought out and conveyed in dialogue of notable beauty. It is a drama of a dangerous love between a shrewish Queen and an ambitious young Lord Essex. Mr. Anderson has written it with the candor of an independent thinker who can say a wise thing as unobtrusively as he can make a glowing human statement. As Queen Elizabeth, Lynn Fontanne acts with a sterling grandeur that removes her completely from the company of all polite player-folk. This is acting of the very highest order—selfless, thorough, vigorous, luminously intelligent. The word "noble" has few friends these days. But it is a word that likes her; it explains somewhat the aura that she casts about this tormented Queen. So, noble it shall be for the transcendence of Miss Fontanne's acting.

The crisis in Mr. Anderson's play lies between love and policy. As far as he is concerned, Elizabeth and Essex love each other sincerely. But across their love the throne casts a sinister shadow. When, according to Mr. Anderson's version of history, Essex returns from Ireland, humiliated by his Queen and the victim of court intrigue, he means to capture the throne with his loyal army. Restored to each other they are lovers again. But his demand of an equal share of the throne strikes Elizabeth in the pride of her office. She throws him into the Tower. The last act, which tapers off somewhat after the crescendo of the second-act curtain, discloses Essex and Elizabeth parting on the hour of his execution. They are still lovers. But policy has triumphed over human emotion. Since both of them are of noble mind, neither one gives in. He goes to the executioner's doom. For her it is the doom of a great monarch.

Despite the parade of famous men and regal ceremony, of Sir Walter Raleigh, Francis Bacon and other court officials, there is in "Elizabeth the Queen" little drama of physical action. But the drama of the characterizations is quite as exciting, and the dialogue has a stimulating quality of its own. Without a suspicion of iconoclasm, Mr. Anderson has portrayed Elizabeth as a woman stormy of temperament, torn between natural tenderness and the brutality of office, sharp of tongue, quick-witted, decisive and wise. She can curse like a fishmonger's wife. She is blunt and precise in her State judgment. As personal fortunes turn against her she faces the world with bitter fortitude. And Essex is mettle worthy of a queen—audacious, proud with a great capacity for anger. Without thumbing the pages of old books for suitable anachronisms, Mr. Anderson has written of these two people in a prose that has pith and resiliency. He is not mannered; he is forthright. Between such folk there is no idle bandying of words.

Mr. Lunt and Miss Fontanne have long been favorites in this town. What is most remarkable about them is their capacity for being unspoiled. They still attack their work earnestly, giving it new fiber and increasing stature. "Elizabeth the Queen" finds them at the peak of their careers. As Lord Essex, Mr. Lunt is a person of extraordinary vitality; he acts with a vivid sense of character, and is enormously interesting into the bargain. With Miss Fontanne it is a case of transmutation, not merely of make-up, which masks her true features completely, but of voice, gesture and bearing. She is no artfully bedizened Queen of the theatre. She is every inch Queen Elizabeth.

All the parts are well played. Mr. Moeller's direction is evocation itself, and Mr. Simonson has drenched the play in regal beauty. We sorely need plays rich in character, thought and imagination. Mr. Anderson has written one.

1930 N 4

1931

By J. BROOKS ATKINSON.

Mr. Coward Still Going Along.

PRIVATE LIVES, a comedy in three acts, by Noel Coward. Staged by the author; settings by G. E. Calthrop; produced by Charles B. Cochran. At the Times Square Theatre.

Sybil Chase	Jill Esmond
Elyot Chase	Noel Coward
Victor Prynne	Laurence Olivier
Amanda Prynne	Gertrude Lawrence
Louise	Therese Quadri

Noel Coward's talent for little things remains unimpaired. In "Private Lives," in which he appeared at the Times Square last evening, he has nothing to say, and manages to say it with competent agility for three acts. Sometimes the nothingness of this comedy begins to show through the dialogue. Particularly in the long second act, which is as thin as a patent partition, Mr. Coward's talent for little things threatens to run dry. But when the time comes to drop the second act curtain his old facility for theatrical climax comes bubbling out of the tap again. There is a sudden brawl. Mr. Coward, in person, and Gertrude Lawrence, likewise in person, start tumbling over the furniture and rolling on the floor, and the audience roars with delight. For Mr. Coward, who dotes on pranks, has an impish wit, a genius for phrase-making, a subtlety of inflection and an engaging manner on the stage. Paired with Miss Lawrence in a mild five-part escapade, he carries "Private Lives" through by the skin of his teeth.

Take two married couples on their respective honeymoons, divide them instantly, and there—if the two leading players are glamorous comedians —you have the situation. As a matter of fact, it has a little more finesse than that. For Elyot Chase, who feels rather grumpy about his second honeymoon, and Amanda Prynne, who feels rather grumpy about hers, were divorced from each other five years ago. When they see each other at the same honeymoon hotel in France, they suddenly realize that they should never have been divorced. Their new marriages are horrible blunders. Their impulse is to fly away together at once. They fly. How rapturously they love and quarrel in a Paris flat, and how frightfully embarrassed they are when their deserted bride and bridegroom finally catch up with them, is what keeps Mr. Coward just this side of his wits' end for the remaining two acts.

For the most part it is a duologue between Mr. Coward and Miss Lawrence. Jill Esmond, as the deserted bride, and Laurence Olivier, as the deserted bridegroom, are permitted to chatter foolishly once or twice in the first act, and to help keep the ball rolling at the end. After the furniture has been upset. Thérèse Guadri, as a French maid, is invited to come in, raise the curtains and jabber her Gallic distress over unseemly confusion. But these are utilitarian parts in the major tour de force of Mr.

Coward and Miss Lawrence cooing and spatting at home.

Be it known that their passion is a troubled one. They coo with languid pleasure. But they are also touchy, and fly on the instant into feline rages. Mr. Coward's wit is not ostentatious. He tucks it away neatly in pat phrases and subtle word combinations and smartly bizarre allusions. Occasionally he comes out boldly with a flat statement of facts. "Certain women should be struck regularly like gongs," he declares. Acting just as he writes, he is crisp, swift and accurate. And Miss Lawrence, whose subtlety has not always been conspicuous, plays this time with rapidity and humor. Her ruddy beauty, her supple grace and the russet drawl in her voice keep you interested in the slightly wind-blown affairs of a scanty comedy. If Mr. Coward's talent were the least bit clumsy, there would be no comedy at all.

1931 Ja 28

Fleeing the Wimpole Street Ogre

By J. BROOKS ATKINSON.

THE BARRETTS OF WIMPOLE STREET, a play in three acts, by Rudolf Besier. Staged by Guthrie McClintic; settings and costumes designed by Jo Mielziner; produced by Katharine Cornell. At the Empire Theatre.

Doctor Chambers...............George Riddell
Elizabeth Barrett Moulton-Barrett,
                              Katharine Cornell
Wilson......................Brenda Forbes
Henrietta Moulton-Barrett.....Margaret Barker
Arabel Moulton-Barrett.........Joyce Carey
Octavius Moulton-Barrett......John Halloran
Septimus Moulton-Barrett..William Whitehead
Alfred Moulton-Barrett......Vernon Downing
Charles Moulton-Barrett......Frederick Voight
Henry Moulton-Barrett.........Basil Harvey
George Moulton-Barrett.......Leslie Denison
Edward Moulton-Barrett....Charles Waldron
Bella Hedley...............Dorothy Mathews
Henry Bevan................John D. Seymour
Robert Browning..............Brian Aherne
Doctor Ford-Waterlow......Oswald Marshall
Captain Surtees Cook..........John Buckler
Flush.............................Himself

If Rudolf Besier had been more inventive in the writing of "The Barretts of Wimpole Street," which was acted at the Empire last evening, he might have turned out a showier and stouter theatrical romance. But he could hardly have given us such genuine drama of a great love between two poets and the horror of a pious father's tyranny. It is the story of Elizabeth Barrett, the invalid, and an impetuous Robert Browning who bursts in upon her airless retreat, revives her by the excess of his own vigor and brings her to the fullness of her genius for life. But it is also the story of a cruel father whose austerity has filled a house with gloom and hatred and whose affection for his eldest daughter is dark and malignant.

After a long succession of meretricious plays it introduces us to Katharine Cornell as an actress of the first order. Here the disciplined fury that she has been squandering on catch-penny plays becomes the vibrant beauty of finely wrought character. Like Mr. Besier, Miss Cornell might be showier, but she could hardly be more discriminating, true and exalting. "The Barretts of Wimpole Street" is a triumph for her and the splendid company with which she has surrounded herself.

Mr. Besier's drama is a succession of scenes in Elizabeth Barrett's escape from her father. In the first act she is an invalid, imprisoned by her father's stern considerations. Reclining on her couch she reads and writes and receives callers. One of her visitors is Robert Browning, with whom she has been corresponding. He comes bounding into the room, all energy and fervent admiration, and before they have been together five minutes he is declaring his love like a man who means to have his way. She struggles against him, aware of the feebleness of her health. But the rest of the play is the chronicle of how Mr. Barrett's demoniac importunities frighten her more and more, and drive her into submitting to the great love she has for a fellow poet. After a third act, in which Browning appears only as an off-stage figure and manager, Elizabeth escapes, leaving Mr. Barrett dismal and lonely in the presence of ten children who hate him.

Mr. Besier does not specify the nature of Mr. Barrett's forbidding affection for his daughter. Sometimes he appears merely to represent parental possessiveness to the point of insanity. Suitors threaten his command of the things that are his. But in the last act his pleading with Elizabeth is certainly incestuous in impulse if not in fact; and then the cruelty of his household rule becomes a malady and a sinister threat. By this time Mr. Besier has thrust Robert Browning into the wings, losing the second most interesting of his character. If you are romantic you may have been hoping that this would be the love story of two poets who have left the record a transcendant devotion. But it is "The Barretts of Wimpole Street." What they suffer has greater significance in view of the two famous people it involves.

It has greatest significance in the acting of Miss Cornell. By the crescendo of her playing, by the wild sensitivity that lurks behind her ardent gestures and her piercing stares across the footlights she charges the drama with a meaning beyond the facts it records. Her acting is quite as remarkable for the carefulness of its design as for the fire of her presence. As Robert Browning, Brian Aherne has a dynamic force that fills the theatre whenever he enters. Charles Waldron is also an actor of rugged strength; as Mr. Barrett he is grim and resolute.

Guthrie McClintic has directed the performance with rare insight, varying the mood and keeping a loosely written play alive. Jo Mielziner's one set of a spacious room has beautifully captured the theme. Like Mr. Besier's play, everything about the performance is genuine.

1931 F 10

Beginning a New Era.

THE BAND WAGON, a revue in two acts, by George S. Kaufman and Howard Dietz, and music by Arthur Schwartz. Staged by Hassard Short; dances arranged by Albertina Rasch; settings by Albert R. Johnson; costumes by Kiviette and Constance Ripley; produced by Max Gordon. At the New Amsterdam Theatre.
PRINCIPALS—Fred and Adele Astaire, Frank Morgan, Helen Broderick, Tilly Losch, John Barker, Roberta Robinson, Philip Loeb, Francis Pierlot, Jay Wilson, Peter Chambers, Helen Carrington and others.

After the appearance of "The Band Wagon," which was staged at the New Amsterdam last evening, it will be difficult for the old-time musical show to hold up its head. George S. Kaufman and Howard Dietz have put the stigmata on stupid display by creating a thoroughly modern revue. It is both funny and lovely; it has wit, gaiety and splendor. Brilliantly written by Mr. Kaufman and Mr. Dietz, brilliantly staged by Hassard Short, brilliantly acted by the Astaires, Frank Morgan, Helen Broderick and Tilly Losch and brilliantly scored by Arthur Schwartz, it is a long step forward in the development of a civilized art of stage revues.

The authors are not unmindful of what they are doing. In the first number they travesty briskly all the set pieces of formula musical shows —the moonlight serenade, the blackout, the waltz number and the dance routine. "Nanette" lampoons the close harmony hokum; and in "Where Can He Be?" Miss Broderick laughs off the sleazy coquettishness of the hackneyed leading lady.

But "The Band Wagon" comes bearing gifts of its own. Nothing the Chauve-Souris has brought here surpasses the impish "Hoops" number that Fred and Adele Astaire sing and dance in their freshest style. A jovial stein song, "I Love Louisa," substitutes for the flamboyant old first-act finale a whirling merry-go-round flourish. In three extraordinary numbers Tilly Losch raises musical show dancing to the level of a fine art. One is a cloth-of-gold bit described as "The Flag." There is macabre splendor in "Dancing in the Dark." And the ballad of "The Beggar Waltz," with Fred Astaire, puts the revolving stage to use as an instrument of narrative beauty. Albert Johnson's gay settings, the smart costumes, the imaginative lighting give these decorative numbers a lean grace that is modern without being bizarre.

But the authors of "The Band Wagon" are satirists. Look to their sketches for the most malicious and expert wit of the season. "For Good Old Nectar" brings the old grads' cheering section into the college classroom and substitutes for the football hero the history champion. "The Pride of the Claghornes" turns topsy-turvy the most hallowed traditions of the South. "Pour Le Bain" applies cultured salesmanship to the marketing of bathroom appliances. There is a perverse lament for the business depression, and a skimming parody of a Fred Allen parody in "Three's a Crowd." No devastating wise-cracks, no smutty jokes, no heavy-handed gags and no laboriously assembled jests—the satire is adroit, informed and intelligent. You need not check your brains with your hat.

This wryly tempered fooling requires skillful performers. "The Band Wagon" has just that sort of band. Frank Morgan's dignified futility and his accurately pitched voice do as well by the grandiloquent Southern Colonel as the blandly esoteric announcer. Helen Broderick's venom is subdued and deadly. For several years the Astaires have been the most engaging pair of dancers on the musical stage. "The Band Wagon" is the best vehicle they have had. They ride it jauntily, and Fred Astaire has ripened into a comedian whose spirit is as breezy as his stepping.

Everything fits the rapid modern pattern of a sardonic stage revue. Arthur Schwartz's music has a nervous, stunning color, particularly for the "Dancing in the Dark" composition. And Albertina Rasch has designed dances for the chorus that completely avoid the old sentimental and gymnastic measures. In fact, "The Band Wagon" brings the revue stage up to date. After this the suffocating magnificence of formula showmanship will seem more lethal than ever.

1931 Je 4

Including Humor.

GEORGE WHITE'S SCANDALS, a revue in two acts and twenty-five scenes. Sketches by George White, Lew Brown and Irving Caesar, and songs by Mr. Brown and Ray Henderson. Settings by Joseph Urban; costumes designed by Charles LeMaire; staged and produced by Mr. White. At the Apollo Theatre.
PRINCIPALS—Rudy Vallee, Ethel Merman, Willie and Eugene Howard, Everett Marshall, Ray Bolger, Gale Quadruplets, Ethel Barrymore Colt, Loomis Sisters, Barbara Blair, Peggy Moseley, Ross MacLean, Jane Alden, Alice Frohman, Hazel Boffinger, Joan Abbott, Joanna Allen, Lois Eckhart and Fred Manatt.

By J. BROOKS ATKINSON.

Now that the hot weather has finally come, George White's show girls and clowns are stomping and bellowing in the eleventh edition of his "Scandals," which was mounted at the Apollo last evening. It is a first-rate show. For Mr. White has not only assembled an interesting troupe of trained seals but he has given them good tricks to perform. There is the celebrated Rudy Vallee, whose unassuming manner won over the Broadway cynics last evening. There is Willie Howard, who is more excitably funny than ever. There are Everett Marshall, an emigré from the opera, whose magnificent singing of a Negro fantasy drew a roar of "bravos," and Ray Bolger, whose rustic hoofing in the beloved Jack Donahue style also raised a shout. There are Ethel Merman, who is queen of the singing announcers, the Gale Quadruplets, who are grinning dancers, and a carload of what the competitive Mr. White denominates as "the most beautiful girls on the stage." Principals and chorus provide the liveliest company the town has had for some time.

In addition to his larks and mountebanks Mr. White has a show. Lew Brown and Ray Henderson have written a jovial score—"Life Is Just a Bowl of Cherries" and "Ladies and Gentlemen, That's Love" for the inexhaustible voice of Ethel Merman, who can draw herself up to a loud note with the hauteur of a real chantress; "This Is the Missus" with a chuckle of words and tune for Mr. Vallee's lucid voice, and "That's Why Darkies Were Born" for Mr. Marshall's ringing baritone. It is music-hall composing of quality; it is full of tunes and enjoyment; and the best score written since Schwartz's virtuoso improvisations for "The Band Wagon."

But, music or no music, the "Scandals" will be most popular for its comedy. Ray Bolger is an extraordinary toe-and-heel clown. He is lean and local in appearance, with an Adam's apple that something has been kind to, and he travesties the old soft-shoe dancing uproariously. For the second time in succession Willie Howard has material that he can stuff full of merriment. There is not a dull sketch in the lot. To see the stoop-shouldered Willie Howard, with his worried expression, appearing in a succession of flaring wigs and comic mustaches as a passionate Latin libertine, as a Continental quack who cannot remember whether he is endorsing yeast or bread on tonight's radio program, as a hot-tempered Spanish lover—why this, as the Bard of Avon put it, is excellent fooling. Mr. Howard screams, saws the air with his sharp fingers, rushes in alarm around the stage and intersperses with some of the blandest gleams ever shot across a footlight.

Mr. White has decked out his Forty-second Street festival with the proper accoutrements. In designing the settings Joseph Urban has made another pilgrimage through the unrealities. He has even found a new perspective for the regulation Empire State Building number. Charles Le Maire has given the costumes a dash of the smart and a pinch of the bizarre. Since neither Mr. Ziegfeld nor Mr. Carroll can exhaust the supply of pretty girls in this land of beauty prize-winners, Mr. White has found enough of them to keep you on the anxious seat. They dance, they sing and they look good-natured into the bargain.

In short, things look more cheerful in the theatre. Rudy Vallee has been transmuted from a lavendar myth to a likable reality. Willie Howard has been permitted to say, in his raucous east side accent, that he bagged the lion—he bagged him to go away. There is nothing like low comedy to relieve the imposing dullness of a big musical show.

1931 S 15

The Epic of The South

THE HOUSE OF CONNELLY, a play in two acts and six scenes, by Paul Green. Staged by Lee Strasberg and Cheryl Crawford; settings by Cleon Throckmorton; produced by the Group Theatre, Inc., under the auspices of the Theatre Guild. At the Martin Beck Theatre.

Big Sis ....Fanny De Knight
Big Sue ....Rose McClendon
Patsy Tate ....Margaret Barker
Will Connelly ....Franchot Tone
Jesse Tate ....Art Smith
Geraldine Connelly ....Stella Adler
Evelyn Connelly ....Eunice Stoddard
Robert Connelly ....Morris Carnovsky
Mrs. Connelly ....Mary Morris
Duffy ....J. E. Bromberg
Virginia Buchanan ....Dorothy Patten
Essie ....Ruth Nelson
Charlie ....Walter Coy
Jodie ....William Challee
Alec ....Clement Wilenchick
Ransom ....Philip Robinson
Reuben ....Clifford Odetts
Isaac ....Friendly Ford
Tyler ....Gerrit Kraber
Alf ....Robert Lewis
Henry ....Herbert Ratner

By J. BROOKS ATKINSON.

It is not, strictly speaking, a play that Paul Green has written in "The House of Connelly," which finally reached the stage at the Martin Beck last evening. In its utter simplicity of story and structure, in its flow and balance of mood, in its truth and sentience, it is more like a prose poem of the old South yielding to the new. And it is abidingly beautiful. Since the dimly remembered days of "In Abraham's Bosom" and "The Field God," Mr. Green, who is one of the most promising dramatists in the country, has been without a New York production. Now a new group of young actors, who call themselves the Group Theatre, have made their first public appearance under the sponsorship of the Theatre Guild, which has controlled the rights to "The House of Connelly" for two or three years. What beauties Mr. Green has imparted to his script these young actors have discovered. They play it with delicacy and tenderness, with imagination, with a remarkably affecting sincerity. As genuine as Mr. Green's fable of the South is the temper and limpidity of their playing.

Mr. Green is chronicling the transition of the South from a decaying aristocracy to working civilization. His Connellys are proud folk. Their lands have fallen into disuse. They are mortgaged on all sides. They live in reduced circumstances. Still they maintain their pride of family and tradition. But the new South is battering at their gates in the person of Jessie Tate, daughter of one of the tenant farmers. Active and eager, she sees how the house of Connelly can be strengthened and renewed by alert management of the plantation, and her enthusiasm fires young Will Connelly, the present heir of the name. It is a conflict not only between the new South and the old but concretely between aristocracy and the poor whites. All that Will has inherited is suspicious of her affection. But when the old blood has been devitalized the new cannot be denied. In the last scene Will and his tenant farmer's daughter become master and mistress of the house of Connelly.

As a drama "The House of Connelly" lacks scope and variety and richness, and sometimes Mr. Green has taken too much of his motivation for granted. Like the fable it is, it is too easily stated. But, being a

poet at heart, Mr. Green can transmute his fable into magnificence,
and he performs that feat of magic
repeatedly all evening. As his thread
of story spins along there are scenes
of humor, romance, foreboding and
terror. Again and again the simple
truth of its theme and the vibrancy
of its characters make "The House
of Connelly" an abiding experience
in the theatre. Although Mr. Green
may not have a dramatist's command of his subject, he has such
abundant understanding, such integrity of character and such magnetism of passion that you are likely
to remember the pure truth of his
prose poem long after you have forgotten a thousand craftsmanlike
plays about love, family and possession.

He has his match in these young
players. They are not only earnest
and skillful, but inspired. Although
the pace of their preformance may
seem a little self-consciously deliberate, they play like a band of musicians. Those best known are Margaret Barker, Franchot Tone, Rose
McClendon, Eunice Stoddard, Mary
Morris, J. E. Bromberg and Morris
Carnvosky.

But their group performance is too
beautifully imagined and modulated
to concentrate on personal achievements. There is not a gaudy, brittle
or facile stroke in their acting. For
once a group performance is tremulous and pellucid, the expression of
an ideal. Between Mr. Green's prose
poem and the Group Theatre's performance it is not too much to hope
that something fine and true has
been started in the American theatre.

1931 S29

MOURNING BECOMES ELECTRA, a trilogy
by Eugene O'Neill, consisting of HOME-
COMING, a play in four scenes; THE
HAUNTED, a play in five scenes, and THE
HAUNTED, a play in five scenes. Staged
by Philip Moeller; settings and costumes
designed by Robert Edmond Jones; produced by the Theatre Guild under the supervision of Theresa Helburn and Maurice
Wertheim. At the Guild Theatre.

HOMECOMING.

Seth Beckwith..............Arthur Hughes
Amos Ames.....................Jack Byrne
Louisa......................Bernice Elliott
Minnie....................,....Emily Lorraine
Christine.....................Alla Nazimova
Lavinia Mannon.................Alice Brady
Captain Peter Niles...........Philip Foster
Hazel Niles....................Mary Arbenz
Captain Adam Brant......Thomas Chalmers
Brig. Gen. Ezra Mannon..........Lee Baker

THE HUNTED.

Mrs. Josiah Borden........Augusta Durgeon
Mrs. Everett Hills..............Janet Young

Dr. Joseph Blake............Erskine Sanford
Josiah Borden.................James Bosnell
Everett Hills.................Oliver Putnam
Christine Mannon............Alla Nazimova
Hazel Niles....................Mark Arbenz

Peter Niles....................Philip Foster
Lavinia Mannon.................Alice Brady
Orin Mannon................Earle Larimore
A Chantyman.................John Hendricks
Captain Adam Brant.....Thomas Chalmers

THE HAUNTED.

Abner Small.................Erskine Sanford
Ira Mackel....................Oliver Putnam
Joe Silva.....................Grant Gordon
Amos Ames......................Jack Byrne
Seth Beckwith................Arthur Hughes
Peter Niles....................Philip Foster
Hazel Niles....................Mary Arbenz
Lavinia Mannon.................Alice Brady
Orin Mannon................Earle Larimore

By J. BROOKS ATKINSON.

Mr. O'Neill gives not only size but
weight in "Mourning Becomes Electra," which the Theatre Guild
mounted at its own theatre for the
greater part of yesterday afternoon
and evening. The size is a trilogy
that consumes six hours in the playing. The weight is the formidable
earnestness of Mr. O'Neill's cheerless
dramatic style. To him the curse
that the fates have set against the
New England house of Mannon is
no trifling topic for a casual dramatic discussion, but a battering
into the livid mysteries of life. Using
a Greek legend as his model, he has
reared up a universal tragedy of tremendous stature—deep, dark, solid,
uncompromising and grim. It is
heroically thought out and magnificently wrought in style and structure, and it is played by Alice Brady
and Mme. Nazimova with consummate artistry and passion. Mr.
O'Neill has written overwhelming
dramas in the past. In "Strange
Interlude" he wrote one almost as
long as this trilogy. But he has
never before fulfilled himself so completely; he has never commanded his
theme in all its variety and adumbra-
tions with such superb strength,
coolness and coherence. To this department, which ordinarily reserves
its praise for the dead, "Mourning
Becomes Electra" is Mr. O'Neill's
masterpiece.

As the title acknowledges, "Mourning Becomes Electra," follows the
scheme of the Orestes-Electra legend
which Aeschylus, Sophocles and
Euripides translated into drama in
the days of Greek classicism. Like
the doomed house of Atreus, this
New England family of Civil War
time is dripping with foul and unnatural murder. The mother murders the father. The son murders
his mother's lover. The mother
mercifully commits suicide. The
daughter's malefic importunities
drive the son to suicide. It is a family that simmers with hatred, sus-

picion, jealousy and greed, and that is twisted by unnatural loves. Although Mr. O'Neill uses the Orestes legend as the scheme of his trilogy, it is his ambition to abandon the gods, whom the Greeks humbly invoked at the crises of drama, and to interpret the whole legend in terms of modern psychology. From royalty this story of vengeance comes down to the level of solid New England burghers. From divinity it comes into the sphere of truths that are known. There are no mysteries about the inverted relationships that set all these gaunt-minded people against one another, aside from the primary mystery of the ferocity of life. Students of the new psychology will find convenient labels to explain why the mother betrays her husband, why the daughter instinctively takes the father's side, why the son fears his father and clings to his mother, why the daughter gradually inherits the characteristics of her mother after the deaths of the parents, and why the son transfers his passion to his sister. As for Mr. O'Neill, he has been chiefly concerned with the prodigious task of writing these modern plays.

And through three plays and fifteen scenes he has kept the rhythm of his story sculptural in its stark outline. The Mannon curse is inherited. For this fine New England mansion was built in hatred when the Mannons cast off the brother who had sinned with a French-Canadian servant. Her son, Captain Brant, comes back into their lives to avenge his mother's dishonor and he becomes the lover of Ezra Mannon's wife. From that point on "Mourning Becomes Electra" stretches out as a strong chain of murders and revenge and the house of Mannon is a little island walled round with the dead.

There are big scenes all the way through. Before the first play is fairly started the dance of death begins with Lavinia upbraiding Christine, her mother, with secret adultery. Christine plotting with Captain Brant to poison her husband on the night when he returns from the Civil War; Christine poisoning her husband and being discovered with the tablets by Lavinia as the climax to the first play; Lavinia proving her mother's guilt to Orin, her brother, by planting the box of poison tablets on the breast of her dead father and admitting her terrified mother to the chamber of death; Lavinia and Orin following their mother to a rendezvous with the captain on his ship and murdering him in his cabin; Lavinia forcing her brother to suicide and waiting panic-stricken for the report of his pistol; Lavinia in the last scene of the last play sealing herself up with this haunted house to live with the spectres of her dead—

all these are scenes of foreboding and horror.

Yet "Mourning Becomes Electra" is no parade of bravura scenes. For this is an organic play in which story rises out of character and character rises out of story, and each episode is foreshadowed by what precedes it. Although Mr. O'Neill has been no slave to the classic origins of his tragedy, he has transmuted the same impersonal forces into the modern idiom, and the production, which has been brilliantly directed by Philip Moeller, gives you some of the stately spectacle of Greek classicism. Lavinia in a flowing black dress sitting majestically on the steps of Robert Edmond Jones's set of a New England mansion is an unforgetable and portentous picture. Captain Brant pacing the deck of his ship in the ringing silence of the night, the murdered Mannon lying on his bier in the deep shadows of his study, the entrances and exits of Christine and Lavinia through doors that open and close on death are scenes full of dramatic beauty. To give you perspective on this tragedy Mr. O'Neill has a sort of Greek chorus in Seth, the hired man, and the frightened townsfolk who gather outside the house, laughing and muttering. Mr. O'Neill has viewed his tragedy from every side, thought it through to the last detail and composed it in a straikhtforward dialogue that tells its story without hysteria.

As Mr. O'Neill has mastered his play, so the actors have mastered their parts and so Mr. Moeller has molded the parts into a measured, fluent performance. Miss Brady, as Lavinia, has one of the longest parts ever written. None of her neurotic dramatics in the past has prepared us for the demoniac splendor of her Lavinia. She speaks in an ominous, full voice that only once or twice breaks into the splintery diffusion of articial climaxes. Lavinia has recreated Miss Brady into a majestic actress. As Christine, Mme. Nazimova gives a performance of haunting beauty, rich in variety, plastic, eloquent and imaginatively transcendant. Lee Baker as the Mannon father conveys little of the towering indomitability of that part and lets his death scene crumple into mediocrity. Earle Larimore plays Orin from the inside with great resource, elasticity and understanding. As Captain Brant, Thomas Chalmers has a solid bodv to his playing. There are excellently designed bits by Arthur Hughes and Erskine Sanford as townspeople. Philip Foster, and especially Mary Arbenz, give able performances as a brother and sister.

For Mr. O'Neill, for the Guild and for lovers of drama, "Mourning Becomes Electra," is, accordingly, an occasion for great rejoicing. Mr. O'Neill has set his hand to a tremendous story, and told it with coolness and clarity. In sustained thought and workmanship it is his finest tragedy. All that he fretted over in the past has trained him for this masterpiece.

1931 O 27

COUNSELOR-AT-LAW, a play in three acts and nine scenes, by Elmer Rice. Settings by Raymond Sovey; staged and produced by the author. At the Plymouth Theatre.

Bessie Green	Constance McKay
Henry Susskind	Lester Salkow
Sarah Becker	Malka Kornstein
A Tall Man	Victor Wolfson
A Stout Man	Jack Collins
A Postman	Ned Glass
Zedorah Chapman	Gladys Feldman
Goldie Rindskopf	Angela Jacobs
Charles McFadden	J. Hammond Dailey
John P. Tedesco	Sam Bonnell
A Bootblack	William Vaughn
Regina Gordon	Anna Kostant
Herbert Howard Weinberg	Marvin Kline
Arthur Sandler	Conway Washburne
Lillian Larue	Dorothy Dodge
An Errand Boy	Buddy Proctor
Roy Darwin	Jack Leslie
George Simon	Paul Muni
Cora Simon	Louise Prussing
A Woman	Jane Hamilton
Lena Simon	Jennie Moscowitz
Peter J. Malone	T. H. Manning
Johann Breitstein	John M. Qualen
David Simon	Ned Glass
Harry Becker	Martin Wolfson
Richard Dwight Jr.	David Vivian
Dorothy Dwight	June Cox
Charles Francis Baird	Elmer Brown

By J. BROOKS ATKINSON.

What Mr. Rice lacks as a showman he supplies as a dramatist of the highest integrity in "Counsellor-at-Law," which was acted at the Plymouth last evening. Any one, excepting Mr. Rice, will tell you that it is twice too long; it is completely unsifted. But Mr. Rice's accuracy of observation, his genius for dialogue and his understanding of the times in which he is living make "Counsellor-at-Law" a remarkably engrossing play. When the quality is superb a little prolixity and vagrancy among irrelevant matters is no great evil. As his own director Mr. Rice has cast Paul Muni in the chief part of a Jewish New York attorney. Mr. Muni gives one of those forceful and inventive performances that renew faith in the theatre. So long as Mr. Rice continues writing with such stunning fidelity, and directing his plays with such unobtrusive perfection, most of us will forgive him for writing much too much.

"Counsellor-at-Law" is the pattern of "Street Scene" applied to a New York attorney's office where representative troubles of a great metropolis hum over the telephone wires and are brought to the desk. Being an aggressive and shrewd person, George Simon has risen from the slums of the east side to the head of a powerful law office on Fifth Avenue, with clients of all the typical breeds. He is a good sort; he enjoys his work, he enjoys making money and takes pleasure in giving a helping hand to an old friend down on his luck. Such story as "Counsellor-at-Law" affords concerns the threat of his disbarment. For once, some years ago, Simon did conspire in the framing of a false alibi in the hope of saving a petty fourth offender from a life-term imprisonment. An old enemy among the beefsteak aristocracy of the profession has chanced upon this infected spot in a generally healthy career. How Simon saves his skin by discovering the infected spot in his opponent's career is the story of "Counsellor-at-Law," and an exciting, theatrical story once it gets started.

If you are a stickler for unalloyed fidelity, perhaps you can discover a trace of stage trickery in the solution of this perplexing narrative. But, like "Street Scene," "Counsellor-at-Law" does not depend on narrative alone for its portrayal of the human comedy of New York. Through the busy reception room of the Simon offices and through Mr. Simon's private office comic and tragic bits of New York hurry back and forth. Mr. Rice's dialogue glows with life; it is pithy, comic, and a deep revelation of character. And while the affairs of the Simon firm pour in over the telephone and through the door you become personally acquainted with clerks, embryo young lawyers, exonerated murderesses, gold-diggers, politicians, Union Square orators and disdainful people of high station. Having been a lawyer himself, Mr. Rice knows the formalities of the business, and being a dramatist, he knows how actively a lawyer's office illuminates the whole fabric of city life. And being the sort of hard thinker he is, he betrays by the tone of his cameo characterizations where his personal sympathies lie.

Although all the characters are clearly imagined and reported, the characterization of George Simon is the most complete, and the most significant as a fragment of New York. In his rise from the pavements Simon has not forgotten his neighborhood friends nor have his instincts changed. Having married a woman of considerable social standing, he aspires to be her equal in every respect. But his instincts for getting on in the world have not altered; he is still aggressive, a little grasping and shrewdly practical in the conduct of his business. Mr.

Rice's characterizations of people of breeding are on the edge of caricature; he has little of the warmth for them that he has for the less pretentious. But his portrait of George Simon is abundantly sympathetic; there is nothing evaded or omitted. In the playing of this part Mr. Muni is at the top of his form, less showily dynamic than usual, more lucid and precise. Life comes spurting and bubbling out of this part in the gusto of Mr. Muni's playing.

Although it is too late in the night to salute all the players according to their deserts, the cast is long and able. Anna Kostant as a private secretary whose affections are hopelessly entangled in her job, Constance McKay as a chattering switchboard operator, Louise Prussing as a lady of exalted station, J. Hammond Dailey as the man of all office work, Marvin Kline as the custodian of the Harvard Law School's honor, Jennie Moscowitz as the proud and sentimental mother of the boss—these are some of the actors who communicate best the flavor and humor of this animated law office scene.

1931 N 7

REUNION IN VIENNA, a play in three acts, by Robert E. Sherwood. Staged by Worthington Miner under the supervision of Theresa Helburn and Lawrence Langner; settings by Aline Bernstein; produced by the Theatre Guild. At the Martin Beck Theatre.

Kathie ....Mary Gildea
Laundryman ....Stanley Wood
Elena ....Lynn Fontanne
Dr. Anton Krug..............Minor Watson
Ilse ....Phyllis Connard
Emil ....Lloyd Nolan
Herr Krug....................Henry Travers
Frau Lucher................Helen Westley
Countess von Stainz.....Virginia Chauvenet
Count von Stainz.........Edward Fielding
Poffy ....Edouardo Ciannelli
Bredzi ....Bela Lublov
Strup ....Otis Sheridan
Torlini ....Bjorn Koefoed
Police Inspector............Murray Stevens
Chef ....Joseph Allen
Rudolph von Hapsburg.........Alfred Lunt
Baroness von Krett.......Cynthia Townsend
General Hoetzler............Frank Kingdon
Talisz ....Owen Meech
Sophia ....Justina Wayne
Koeppke ....William R. Randall
Valet ....Joseph Allenton
Bellboy ....Noel Taylor
Busboys.......Ben Kranz. Hendrik Booraem
Waiters..Charles E. Douglass, George Lewis

By J. BROOKS ATKINSON.

Between them Robert E. Sherwood and the Lunts have declared a lively holiday in "Reunion in Vienna," which the Guild mounted in fine fettle at the Martin Beck last evening. As the author, Mr. Sherwood has kept his sense of humor uppermost. As an unfrocked Habsburg prince, Mr. Lunt plays with extraordinary bounce and merriment. Miss Fontanne, as the mistress who is now the wife of a distinguished psychoanalyst, looks like a portrait by an old master—like Madame Récamier, in fact; and she plays with the willowy charm that has made her essential to the contentment of this country. The play may not be brilliant and the performance may be no piece of sustained coruscation. But Mr. Sherwood and the Lunts have kept the fun exuberant and the evening is heartily enjoyable.

It is the tale of a prince who steals back into his old country after ten years of banishment in search of the mistress he loved enduringly. In the meantime she has married a psychoanalyst of international fame, who has been striving, by the application of scientific reason, to exorcise the phantom of her prince. When word comes that the prince is returning to attend a royal reunion in Frau Lucher's hotel, the doctor advises her to go, to look at the prince, to laugh at him, and to reassure herself that he is no longer a part of her life. But the prince is as ardent, fantastic and persuasive as ever. She flies home to escape him. But he pursues her. He appeals to her husband's scientific enlightenment to settle their three-fold problem. It is giving the doctor a dose of his own medicine. At any rate, it concludes this madcap prank with a dash of romance, which is much more enjoyable than reason.

Mr. Sherwood's play is a garrulous piece that wavers unsteadily between burlesque and satire. It is a third over before the fun properly begins. But Mr. Sherwood has a very droll slant on his people and his situation and a great relish of comic outrageousness. He is no maker of crisp phrases. His humor consists in a robust enjoyment of the human comedy. How much of the fun is his, how much is Mr. Lunt's and how much the splendid direction of Worthington Miner it is impossible for the theatregoer to decide, since the three elements are perfectly blended. But when Mr. Lunt dashes into Frau Lucher's hotel in the second act, "Reunion in Vienna" puts on the broadest of grins. For this prince is a disarming rascal; he is coarse, sentimental and impulsive, and he is not too old for horseplay. Mr. Sherwood's gift is native. Mr. Lunt's is native, too. They translate this second act into fantastic, humorous romance, partly amorous and partly low comedy.

As the sweet and reasonable wife who still has a weakness for gayety, Miss Fontanne plays like a superb comedienne. She has glamour, poise and subtlety, and she has vitality enough for a frolic. In addition to the Lunts, "Reunion in Vienna" has two other Guild favorites and several good actors from other sources. Helen Westley is present as Frau Lucher, who they do say is really Frau Sacher of Vienna; and Miss Westley, slouching on the small of her back and puffing a cigar, roars like an imperial hag and arouses the customers. Henry Travers dodders around amusingly as a gossiping father-in-law, shaking his head in humorous despair. As the prophet of psychoanalysis, which, Mr. Sherwood declares, is Vienna's sole remaining industry, Minor Watson is articulate and good company.

There are two spirited sets by Aline Bernstein, one in the modern vein, one in the shabby royal. There are uniforms, violins and a concertina. When the Guild cuts loose, without intellectual reservations, it knows how to dispel the gloom. Mr. Sherwood has supplied the script. The Lunts supply the wine of comedy. Between them, they cut a capital caper.

1931 N 17

OF THEE I SING, a "new musical comedy" in two acts and eleven scenes. Book by George S. Kaufman and Morrie Ryskind, music by George Gershwin and lyrics by Ira Gershwin. Book staged by Mr. Kaufman; singing and dancing ensembles arranged by Georgie Hale; settings by Jo Mielziner; produced by Sam H. Harris. At the Music Box.

Louis Lippman	Sam Mann
Francis X. Gilhooley	Harold Moffet
Maid	Vivian Barry
Matthew Arnold Fulton	Dudley Clements
Senator Robert E. Lyons	George E. Mack
Senator Carver Jones	Edward H. Robins
Alexander Throttlebottom	Victor Moore
John P. Wintergreen	William Gaxton
Sam Jenkins	George Murphy
Diana Devereaux	Grace Brinkley
Mary Turner	Lois Moran
Miss Benson	June O'Dea
Vladimir Vidovitch	Sulo Hevonpaa
Yussef Yussevitch	Tom Draak
The Chief Justice	Ralph Riggs
Scrubwoman	Leslie Bingham
The French Ambassador	Florenz Ames
Senate Clerk	Martin Leroy
Guide	Ralph Riggs

What little dignity there may have been in politics and government has been laughed out of court by "Of Thee I Sing," a brisk musical comedy staged at the Music Box Saturday evening. It is the work of George S. Kaufman and Morrie Rys-

kind, as neat a pair of satirists as ever scuttled a national tradition; and it has George Gershwin's most brilliant score to sharpen the humor and fantasticate the ideas. For this loud and blaring circus is no jerry-built musical comedy, although occasionally it subsides into the musical comedy formula. And it is no idle bit of buffoonery, although occasionally it degenerates into the specious cleverness of Broadway. The authors have transposedt he charlatanry of national politics into a hurly-burly of riotous campaign slogans, political knavery, comic national dilemmas and general burlesque. They have fitted the dunce's cap to politics and government, and crowded an evening with laughter.

For half the evening they are blatantly attempting to elect John P. Wintergreen President of the United States on a maudlin platform of "Love." When the curtain goes up, after Mr. Gershwin's restless and echoing overture, you see a torchlight procession carrying illuminated sign-boards: "Vote for Wintergreen, A Man's Man's Man"; "Wintergreen, I Love You"; "Vote For Prosperity and See What You Get"; "Even Your Dog Likes Wintergreen"; "Wintergreen, The Flavor Lasts." Having a particularly bad political record the Republican party wants a platform of popular generalities, and having an attractive bachelor as its candidate it seizes upon "Love" as the magic watchword. It holds a bathing-beauty contest at Atlantic City to choose the President's bride.

The campaign is vulgar and furious. Campaign speeches are roared out in Madison Square Garden amid a caterwauling of prize-fight announcements while a comic wrestling match goes on in the foreground. The election results are flashed on an excited screen. There is heavy voting in the South for Jefferson Davis; heavy voting in California for Mickey Mouse, scattering votes here and there for light wines and beer, straight whisky, Walter Hampden and Mae West. America votes for what it likes best. After a good deal of such trumpery the President is elected; he is inaugurated and married at the same instant by a gymnastic Chief Justice; and as a climax to the second act he is saved from impeachment when the President's wife announces with pride that she is in a delicate condition. The Vice President proudly declares: "The United States has never impeached an expectant President." Whereupon the chorus sings "Posterity is just around the corner."

The book is long and complicated, heavily freighted with slanders and gibes; and before the evening is over you feel that it is becoming synthetic and unwieldy.

Being all in one strident key, it grows tiresome, for the authors are better satirists than story-tellers. They are also undiscriminating with their humors; they open their festivities with that unsavory bathroom joke. After developing a fantastic idea with the aid of Mr. Gershwin's full-bodied music neither are they above destroying it with a hard or shallow gag. And, at least to this commentator, the obstetrical horse-play that concludes the evening is a craftsman's device for rescuing a faltering story rather than a spontaneous comic idea. When the satire slides from politics to generalities—the second act of "Of Thee I Sing" loses most of its distinction.

But one detail of the story is pure inspiration. Treating the Vice President as a common nuisance is a source of constant hilarity. As Alexander Throttlebottom, Vice President of the United States, Victor Moore is pathetic and futile and vastly enjoyable in a satire that wants emotion generally. Even after they have nominated him, the campaign managers cannot remember his name. They mistake him for a waiter when he stumbles hopefully into the campaign headquarters and ask him to serve the pickles. Not knowing what to do with him, they finally ask him to keep out of sight until after the election. He is forgotten at the inaugural. The new government takes office without him. Finally he worms his frightened way into the White House in a crowd of nondescript tourists; and, talking with a White House lackey, he learns for the first time that the Vice President presides over the Senate. "Of Thee I Sing" is richest and ruddiest when Mr. Moore, full of good-will and bewildered innocence, teeters through the halls of statesmanship and tries to discover what place a Vice President has in the scheme of national affairs.

As the President, William Gaxton is dynamic and engaging, and very amusing in his parodies of Mayor Walker, although he itches to play snappy musical comedy. Lois Moran is a charming President's bride. Grace Brinkley is refulgent as an avaricious bathing beauty. As the French Ambassador, Florenz Ames has a subtlety that most of his colleagues lack.

There is dancing, both routine and inventive. There are lyrics done in Ira Gershwin's neatest style. There are settings by Jo Mielziner that adroitly convey the shoddiness of the political environment. Best of all, there is Mr. Gershwin's score.

Whether it is satire, wit, doggerel or fantasy, Mr. Gershwin pours music out in full measure, and in many voices. Although the book is lively, Mr. Gershwin is exuberant. He has not only ideas but enthusiasm. He amplifies the show. Satire in the sharp, chill, biting vein of today needs the warmth of Victor Moore's fooling and the virtuosity of Mr. Gershwin's music. Without them "Of Thee I Sing" would be the best topical travesty our musical stage has created. With them it has the depth of artistry and the glow and pathos of comedy that are needed in the book.

1931 D 28

1932

Philip Barry Speaks.

THE ANIMAL KINGDOM, a comedy in three acts and six scenes, by Philip Barry. Settings by Aline Bernstein; staged by Gilbert Miller; produced by Mr. Miller and Leslie Howard. At the Broadhurst Theatre.

Owen Arthur..................G. Albert Smith
Rufus Collier............Frederick Forrester
Cecelia Henry..................Lora Baxter
Richard Regan..............William Gargan
Tom Collier..................Leslie Howard
Franc Schmidt..................Betty Lynne
Joe Fisk..................Harvey Stephens
Daisy Sage..................Frances Fuller
Grace Macomber..................Ilka Chase

By J. BROOKS ATKINSON.

Philip Barry has written one of his best, "The Animal Kingdom," put on at the Broadhurst last evening. In the principal rôle Leslie Howard gives one of his richest performances. In fact, the news of the drama is uncommonly exhilarating this morning from nearly every point of view. For Mr. Barry has written a comedy that steps lightly straight into the face of problems for which you can have the greatest respect. Sometimes his cleverness intrudes a trifle upon a serious scene. Sometimes his characters seem rather blind to obvious ethical points. But it is no use pulling a long face over so superior a piece of work. Discussing the integrity of a group of cultivated moderns, Mr. Barry has preserved his own integrity as an artist and a believer, and illuminated his thesis with splendor. Mr. Howard and he are well mated. In both of them the light touch is instinctive.

They can communicate fervor and passion with the sincerest kind of dexterity.

It is not Mr. Barry's fashion to write as baldly as this report appears to indicate. He makes his points in spontaneous impulses of character. Above everything, he gives his characters spring and subtlety in gayety, and his dialogue has an iridescent sort of humor. In his telling the paralysis of social respectability is a long series of probabilities—concessions to good taste, compromises in the interests of kindliness, surrenders to expediency. The life of art is a priggish thing to describe in any form. Mr. Barry's artists do not escape priggishness altogether. Confronted with people of recognized standing, his artists do appear unhappily to be in the inferior position. But Mr. Barry's heart is with them, and his chief character believes in them and has all his pleasure in their company. They are the antidote to these charming people about whom Mr. Barry has written most of his plays.

Tom Collier marries the wrong woman. Just why it is hard to say. He is an engaging son of a wealthy aristocrat, a trifler on the surface but with abundant respect for honesty, and he is a quixotic publisher of books in which he believes. His art is the vicarious one of recognizing the truth in the artists with whom he deals. Probably he wants Cecelia Henry, and has to pay the price of marriage to have her; and he innocently believes that his marriage will not destroy a friendship of long standing with Daisy Sage, who is an artist. But it does. His marriage is the wrong thing for every one. Although it brings respectability into his social life, it separates him from the people who are his kind, and it poisons his own best instincts. Against his better judgment he publishes books to make money. Respectability creeps up on his style of living. As a married man he represents everything smug and spurious that once he held in contempt. When his old friends come to visit with him at his home he perceives that for him, at any rate, respectability is not the personal integrity in which he once believed. He abandons it. Leaving his wife, who has made her married life secure, he returns to the artist who has never demanded security from any one. She is the escape from the animal kingdom into the

higher one to which he has long been aspiring.

Leslie Howard is not only a winning performer but a conscientious artist. His portrait of Tom Collier is thorough and brilliant. The style is skimming. But the substance is solid. Mr. Howard's description of a sensitive young man who falls from the high estate of idealism is a dainty, skillful study in disintegration; it is moving without once being literal or pathetic.

He has an excellent company to sustain him. In the unpleasant part of the cunning wife, Lora Baxter is uncommonly discerning. As the friend of many years' standing Frances Fuller is reticent and splendid. As a butler who was once a pug, William Gargan brings a heartiness and exuberance much needed in a play of such fragile thinking and evocative emotion. Under Gilbert Miller's direction the subordinate actors are all as good as their parts.

In general, Mr. Miller has given the production an excellent appearance. Aline Bernstein's two settings, which are well lighted, have the quiet beauty and the life that the play requires. Mr. Barry's talent is finely tempered. Here he is writing of what he fervently believes. It is a sincere play, tender and amusing by turns; and it brings great loveliness into the theatre.

1932 Ja 13

"Yoshe Kalb" at The Folks.

A FINE CHASSIDIC DRAMA

Other Openings Include Isa Kremer at National and Boris Thomashefsky at Gaiety, Brooklyn.

Seven Yiddish theatres in Manhattan, Brooklyn and the Bronx began their seasons over the week-end, coincident with the Rosh ha-Shanah holidays.

Of major interest was the comeback of the Yiddish Art company, under the direction of Maurice Schwartz, at the Folks Theatre, with a fine Chasidic play, which is especially well suited to this troupe, steeped, as it is, in Jewish folklore. It is called "Yoshe Kalb," and is a dramatization of a novel of the same name by a young Polish writer of uncommon talent, I. J. Singer. The story it unfolds is of a powerful Chasidic rabbi, whose concerns are

very much of this world. Having
already buried three wives, in his
seventieth year he sets eyes on a
spirited young girl and determines
to make her No. 4. To satisfy the
proprieties, however, he must first
mafry off his young daughter, a
child of 15, and he arranges a match
between her and a boy who is so
deeply wrapped up in a Kabala
that the marriage cruelly wounds
him. He in turn hurts his wife by
his coldness, and she is too unknow-
ing to overcome it.

The girl whom the aged rabbi has
married, however, is a spitfire: she
won't have the old man, but she
falls in love with his ascetic son-in-
law and makes him return her passion. When she dies in childbirth,
the youth turns to a life of wandering to expiate his sin.

Portrayed in twenty-eight rapidly
moving vignettes, "Yoshe Kalb" encompasses many moods and colors.
There is an old woman's dance in
celebration of the wedding full of
serene dignity; a scene in a poor
man's synagogue racy and earthy; a
scene in which the old rabbi is rejected conveys genuine pathos. The
large cast is uniformly capable and
thoroughly immerses itself in the
material and spirit of the play.
Maurice Schwartz as the old rabbi
gives one of the best performances
he has rendered in several seasons.
Anna Appel, ritual bath attendant
and "barber"—she shaves the heads
of brides—is a powerful figure of
earth. Helen Zelinska as an idiot
reveals a vigor hitherto dormant in
her. Michael Rosenberg is a rambunctious fellow vital to his toes, and
Isadore Casher and Lazar Freed
acquit themselves more than creditably.

At the Downtown National Theatre
Isa Kremer made her début off the
concert stage in "The Song of the
Ghetto," by William Siegel, with
music by A. Olshanetsky.

Bravely weathering hackneyed situations and banalities of dialogue, and
sentimental ditties, which give her
no scope for her splendid gifts, Mme.
Kremer emerges as the great artist
she is when she is given the opportunity to do the folk songs for which
she has been known hitherto.

There are able players in the cast.
Miriam Fine has a charming voice,
Goldie Eisman is quite ingratiating,
Leon Gold and Muni Serebrov have
good natural voices and Yetta
Zwerling in her one rôle of the
harum-scarum she-who-gets-slapped
has a great deal of vitality.

Another opening took place in the
Bronx at the Prospect, where Jennie
Goldstein played the lead in Louis
Freiman's "The Common Law Wife."
In Brooklyn, Menasche Skulnik was
featured in "Mister Schlemihl," by
I. Rosenberg, at the Hopkinson;

Misha and Lucy German in H. Kal-
manovitch's "Mother and Mother-in-
Law," at the Liberty; Boris Thoma-
shefsky in "The End of the Russian
Tsar," at the Gayety, and Hymie
Jacobson and Miriam Kressin in "A
Girl Like You," by I. Lesh and S.
Secunda, at the Lyric.   W. S.

1932 O 3

DINNER AT EIGHT, a play in three acts
and eleven scenes, by George S. Kaufman
and Edna Ferber. Staged by Mr. Kaufman; settings by Livingston Platt; produced by Sam H. Harris. At the Music
Box.

Millicent Jordan	Ann Andrews
Dora	Mary Murray
Gustave	Gregory Gaye
Oliver Jordan	Malcolm Duncan
Paula Jordan	Marguerite Churchill
Ricci	Cesar Romero
Hattie Loomis	Margaret Dale
Miss Copeland	Vera Hurst
Carlotta Vance	Constance Collier
Dan Packard	Paul Harvey
Kitty Packard	Judith Wood
Tina	Janet Fox
Dr. J. Wayne Talbot	Austin Fairman
Larry Renault	Conway Tearle
The Bellboy	Robert Griffith
The Waiter	James Seeley
Max Kane	Samuel Levene
Mr. Hatfield	William McFadden
Miss Alden	Ethel Intropodi
Lucy Talbot	Olive Wyndham
Mrs. Wendel	Dorothy Walters
Jo Stengel	Frank Manning
Mr. Fitch	George Alison
Ed Loomis	Hans Robert

By BROOKS ATKINSON.

When George S. Kaufman and
Edna Ferber settle down to the writing of a play you can expect something not only skillful but solid.
Their "Dinner at Eight," which appeared at the Music Box Saturday evening, is an extraordinarily engrossing piece of work,
despite what seems to this column
to be an incomplete conclusion.
By examining as individuals a
group of people who are invited to
a small fashionable dinner Mr. Kaufman and Miss Ferber have designed
a New York microcosm in ten scenes,
somewhat after the manner of
"Grand Hotel." Written with a
great relish of the vagarious humanity involved in such a cycle, it is brilliantly directed by Mr. Kaufman and
vividly acted by an unexceptionable
company. Although it is lightened
with humor, it is a reflective drama,
detached and observant. Mr. Kaufman has had a hand in many slicker
plays; in "The Royal Family" Mr.
Kaufman and Miss Ferber wrote a
more exuberant comedy. But "Din-

ner at Eight" has a broader canvas, a warmer fund of sympathy and a wider point of view.

Mrs. Jordan of the fashionable New York Jordans is responsible for this many-sided episode in New York life. Lord and Lady Ferncliffe, bound for New York, have accepted by wireless an invitation to dine at her house. Whereupon she sits down to the telephone to invite as guests the people who are eligible, and the flurry of organizing a dinner gets under way. And here Mr. Kaufman and Miss Ferber begin to shape their drama. For "Dinner at Eight" goes skipping around the city to reveal the background of each of the invited guests. At dinner they will be an immaculate gathering revealing nothing of themselves. But while Mrs. Jordan is absorbed in the turmoil of organizing a dinner you acquire information of which she is quite unaware. She does not know, for example, that her husband is failing in business, and that he is stricken with heart disease that is numbering his days. She does not know that the flamboyant Dan Packard, whom she is inviting, is secretly acquiring the old family business that pays for her dinner, nor that Mrs. Packard has been relieving the boredom of her footless existence by a secret amour with Dr. Talbot. Nor does Mrs. Jordan know that the famous movie star, Larry Renault, is her daughter's lover, or that Renault, for all his pompous grandeur, is penniless and on the brink of suicide. She knows nothing of the tragic drama that is going on at that moment in her servants' hall. All this hidden anguish, which touches her vitally and gives her guests strange relationships, Mrs. Jordan has neither the time nor the ability to comprehend. But the authors have related it pungently in a series of splendidly written scenes.

They leave it uncompleted, I think. At the last moment Lord and Lady Ferncliffe break their engagement and remove the only reason there can be for such an imposing assembly. In the concluding scene, set in the Jordan drawing-room, all the guests save one dutifully gather, hear the news of the nobility's defection, chatter innocuously and drift off to the dining-room. There is a mute irony in this conclusion, more apparent to the authors than to the audience. For to at least one member of the audience this leaves the theatric situation hanging emptily in the air. Although critics have enormous license, as yet they have no authority to rewrite an author's play. But to this critic "Dinner at Eight" would be a much more piercing drama if Lord and Lady Ferncliffe did obediently keep their appointment and if the last scene, set in the dining-room, showed all the guests but one seated

at the table and prattling politely and vacuously on the rim of doom. Something concrete, something visually and audibly mordant is needed to sharpen "Dinner at Eight" at the end.

Both the acting and the production have a modern splendor that gives the play vitality in the theatre. There is not a slovenly stroke in the acting. Some of it has notable spirit and beauty. Constance Collier is remarkably volatile as an effervescent favorite of the stage. Conway Tearle plays the movie star with rugged, pathetic exactitude. Malcolm Duncan conveys the well-bred loneliness of Mr. Jordan with gallant reticence. Samuel Levene plays to the last uncanny inflection the part of a Broadway agent. As Mrs. Jordan, Ann Andrews has the style and fever of a lady of worldly fashion. and Marguerite Churchill brings rueful sincerity to the part of the panic-stricken daughter.

In designing the scenes, which are beautifully lighted and easily changed, Livingston Platt has found the lustre that properly accents the irony of this fable. "Dinner at Eight" is doubly ironic because the authors have kept scrupulously aloof. It is their most ambitious play. Although it ends weakly, it has abundant material. And, best of all, without being journalistic, it belongs heart and soul to the New York theatre of today.

1932 O 24

MUSIC IN THE AIR, "a musical adventure" in two acts and eleven scenes. Score by Jerome David Kern. Book and lyrics by Oscar Hammerstein 2d. Settings by Joseph Urban; costumes designed by John W. Harkrider; staged by Mr. Kern and Mr. Hammerstein, produced by Peggy Fears. At the Alvin Theatre.

Herman	Charles Belin
Tila	Mary McQuade
Dr. Walther Lessing	Al Shean
Sieglinde	Katherine Carrington
Karl Reder	Walter Slezak
Burgomaster	Marty Semon
Pflugfelder	Robert Williamson
Town Crier	Robert Rhodes
Heinrich	Cliff Heckinger
The Apothecary	George Bell
Widow Schreimann	Lydia Van Gilder
Priest	Paul Donah
Frau Pflugfelder	Gabrielle Guelpli
Hans	Edward Hayes
Cornelius	Reinald Werrenrath
Ernst Weber	Nicholas Joy
Uppmann	Harry Mestayer
Marthe	Dorothy Johnson
Frieda	Natalie Hall
Bruno	Tullio Carminati
Hulde	Desha
Stout Mother	Carrie Weller
Stout Father	Carl Edem
Stout Boy	George Dieter
Waiter	George Ludwig
Zoo Attendant	Alfred Russ

Herr Kirschner..............Alexis Obolensky
Frau Kirschener...................Ivy Scott
Sophie....................Kathleen Edwards
Assistant Stage Manager......Frank Dobert
Anna.........................Marjorie Main

By BROOKS ATKINSON.

At last the musical drama has been emancipated. In "Music in the Air," which was sung at the Alvin last evening, Jerome Kern and Oscar Hammerstein 2d have succeeded in telling a romantic story without recourse to the superannuated formula. What "The Cat and the Fiddle" gallantly began last season Mr. Kern and Mr. Hammerstein have now completed by composing a fable that flows naturally out of a full-brimming score. No precision dancing troupes; no knockabout comedians; no flamboyant song numbers; no grandiose scenic play—none of the hackneyed trumperies. Having a music box filled with tunes in all of his most alluring genres, Mr. Kern has found the way to sing them spontaneously, and Mr. Hammerstein has spun him a sentimental adventure that warms the vocal chords. Here are singers who can sing honestly, performers who can act beguilingly and here is an evening of heartening delight.

Grant the composer and author one premise. A musical play requires a curly-headed music master who lives preferably in Bavaria. So it is here. The music master is Dr. Walter Lessing, father of Sieglinde Lessing, who lives in a mountain village where apparently every one sings. Almost before the play has begun you thus listen to the Edendorf Choral Society, dressed in peasant costumes, singing "Melodies of May" and "I've Told Every Little Star" in the village schoolhouse, and chanting the prayer for the Edendorf Walking Club. From this scene "Music in the Air" progresses by natural stages to a musical publisher's office in Munich where a musical play is being written. How the disarming lovers of the country find themselves thrust into the sophisticated life of urban artists is the burden of Mr. Hammerstein's story. Without falling back into the cliché's of the trade he has written sentiment and comedy that are tender and touching. It is

an amusing story and an effortless piece of craftsmanship, and it provides a perfect setting for Mr. Kern's score.

As for Mr. Kern, he is in one of his most blissful moods. Melodies and chorals and waltzes flow out of his enchanted music box with only the most trifling interruptions. The innocence of "I've Told Every Little Star," the nostalgic sentiment of "Egern On the Tegern See" and the sweet rapture of "When Spring Is In the Air" represent Mr. Kern in his freshest vein. From Mr. Bennett's orchestration to Mr. Baravalle's command of the musicians you are in the hands of men who respect their art. And in Natalie Hall, Katherine Carrington, Reinald Werrenrath and Walter Slezak you have singers with trained voices. No musical play for some time has represented so high a standard of musical accomplishment.

In the face of so crowded a cast, and an avalanche of election news, it is impossible to salute properly all the fine performances. But nothing shall prevent a humble salaam before Al Shean. As the doddering old music master he knows how to touch the heart gently. Hullio Carminati's petulant playwright is another dryly amusing bit of artifice. Nicholas Joy, as the music publisher; Harry Mestayer, as an orchestra leader; Ivy Scott, as a producer's wife—all give nicely-tempered performances. In the zoo there are also excellent performances by a live elephant and an imitation dancing bear. All these divers and sundry have been wrapped up inside Mr. Urban's bountiful scenery. And the musical drama has come handsomely into its own.

1932 N 9

Eva and "Alice in Wonderland."

ALICE IN WONDERLAND, a play in two parts adapted by Eva Le Gallienne and Florida Friebus from "Alice in Wonderland" and "Through the Looking Glass" by Lewis Carroll; music by Richard Addinsell; devised and directed by Miss Le Gallienne; scenery and costumes, after Tenniel, by Irene Sharaff. At the Civic Repertory Theatre.

Alice ....Josephine Hutchinson
White Rabbit ....Richard Waring
Mouse ....Nelson Welch
Dodo ....Joseph Kramm
Lory ....Walter Beck
Eaglet ....Robert H. Gordon
Crab ....Landon Herrick
Duck ....Burgess Meredith
Caterpillar ....Sayre Crawley
Duchess ....Charles Ellis
Cheshire Cat ....Florida Friebus
March Hare ....Donald Cameron
Mad Hatter ....Landon Herrick
Dormouse ....Burgess Meredith
Two of Spades ....David Marks
Five of Spades ....Arthur Swensen
Seven of Spades ....Whitner Bissell
Queen of Hearts ....Joseph Schildkraut
King of Hearts ....Harold Moulton
Gryphon ....Nelson Welch
Mock Turtle ....Lester Scharff
Cook ....Howard da Silva
Red Chess Queen ....Leona Roberts
Train Guard ....Robert H. Gordon
Tweedledum ....Landon Herrick
Tweedledee ....Burgess Meredith
White Chess Queen ....Eva Le Gallienne
Humpty Dumpty ....Walter Beck
White Knight ....Howard da Silva

By BROOKS ATKINSON.

Since Eva Le Gallienne and Florida Freibus have a wholesome respect for "Alice In Wonderland" they have committed no violence. Their stage transcription, which was acted last evening at a dress rehearsal in Fourteenth Street, recaptures more of the innocent nonsense of the book than you would think possible. Inasmuch as the Oxford don wrote it for saucer-eyed reading rather than acting, do not blame the collaborators if they have not turned it precisely into a play. Rather have they related it in a frankly make-believe pageant of Tenniel scenes and Tenniel costumes to the wood notes wild of Richard Addinsell. No doubt the children will love it if their imaginations are still unfettered. But it is certain that their elders will love it with a nostalgic rapture for the days that no longer come. For Miss Le Gallienne's "Alice In Wonderland" is quite the most interesting variation the theatre has played on its main theme in some years. It is light, colorful and politely fantastic.

With that dithyrambic appreciation out of the way let this critical forum subside into straight reporting. To tell the fable of Alice touring Wonderland and stepping through the magic Looking Glass, Irene Sharoff has reproduced the Tenniel scenery on a cyclorama that unrolls across the rear of the stage. Some difficulty attends Alice's preliminary progress. To get her out of her comfortable British home, "Alice Through the Looking Glass" and "Alice in Wonderland" become a little confused. Although a telescopic table does shoot high into the air after Alice has drunk the magic elixir, the illusion of her diminuendo is not particularly satisfactory.

After that you are on safe wonderground again. For then the Wonderland inhabitants grow curiouser and curiouser, after the immortal style Tenniel created. In designing the costumes Miss Sharaff has reverenced the illustrations, adding to them colors that give the production a disarmingly lovely appearance. Through the pool of tears Alice patiently swims, trying to spare the sensibilities of the touchy Mouse; and then you meet in succession the Caterpillar, the Frog Footman, the Duchess, the bellicose Queen of Hearts, the Mock Turtle, the Red Chess Queen, Tweedledum and Tweedledee, the White Chess Queen, Humpty Dumpty, the White Knight and all the citizens of that perversely logical land. They speak the familiar words. They bark at Alice in the rudest fashion. To the notes of Mr. Addinsell's sympathetic score they sing an aria over Beautiful Soup, and the Walrus and the Carpenter appear as marionettes swaying solemnly above the walzing oysters.

Any one can see that as a stage production "Alice in Wonderland" and "Alice Through the Looking Glass" are too long. It is hard to sustain so fleeting and mad a mood. But the handiwork is sound and beautiful and the evening is uncommonly refreshing. For Miss Le Gallienne and Miss Friebus have solved for the stage the impenetrability of Lewis Carroll's book.

Shall we pronounce critical aphorisms over the overtones and nuances of the acting? We shall not. Let us content ourselves with reporting that under the gay foliage of the costumes the mummers are most satisflying. As Alice, Josephine Hutchinson is innocent without being precocious — a particularly well-bred Alice altogether. Some of the actors give their characters a terse definition. Sayre Crawley is especially biting as the Caterpillar. Joseph Schildkraut's raucous and rowdy Queen of Hearts, Harold Moulton's bland King of Hearts, Leona Roberts's Red Chess Queen and Howard da Silva's White Knight—all these parts recover the pith of their models in the acting. And Miss Le Gallienne, who does all the wire work in Fourteenth Street, makes an excellent White Chess Queen.

If you are a skeptic, prepare to shed your skepticism now. Alice and her voyageurs in Wonderland have crossed the footlights, as they did a half century ago, without surrendering their nationality. To a long history of interesting projects Miss Le Gallienne has now added the most original adventure of all. If the Oxford don had not grown tired of "Alice in Wonderland" long before he died, he would have enjoyed this guileless stage transcription.

1932 D 12

BIOGRAPHY, a comedy in three acts, by S. N. Behrman. Staged by Philip Moeller under the supervision of Theresa Helburn and Lawrence Langner; setting by Jo Mielziner; produced by the Theatre Guild as the second play of the fifteenth subscription season. At the Guild Theatre.

Richard Kurt ....Earle Larimore
Minnie ....Helen Salinger
Melchoir Feydak ....Arnold Korff
Marion Froude ....Ina Claire
Leander Nolan ....Jay Fassett
Warwick Wilson ....Alexander Clark
Orrin Kinnicott ....Charles Richman
Slade Kinnicott ....Mary Arbenz.

By BROOKS ATKINSON.

Although Mr. Behrman's new play, "Biography," is not as deep as a well nor as wide as a church door, it will serve. It is the somewhat nebulous story of a famous woman of the world who upsets one part of it by writing an intimate autobiography. Ina Claire plays the principal rôle. Unless memories are fading she has not appeared on the local stage since the crackling days of "Our Betters," and it is high time that that defect was remedied. For Miss Claire plays with dignity, wit, poise and dexterity, tossing off a line when a good phrase comes her way and loosing a warm flood of emotion when the play is in that mood. She is ably assisted by an excellent band of actors in a performance which, paradoxically enough, seems remote and tepid from a seat in the forward half of the theatre. Even the most urbane of comedies can sound half-hearted when a Theatre Guild first-night audience is disdainfully examining it.

Taking a hint from several familiar personages, Mr. Behrman is relating one chapter in the life of Marion Froude, an artist. Although she is a second-rate artist, she is famous for the celebrity of her sitters, many of whom are reputed to have been her lovers, also. Now when things are going badly, Richard Kurt, a belligerent magazine editor, persuades her to write her life-story for the news-stands. Simple as that sounds, it apparently involves her first girlhood lover, Leander Nolan, who is now running for United States Senator from Tennessee. Nolan imagines that his name,

connected with hers, will destroy his chances with the prudish electorate of his State. How this putative situation reacts upon Nolan, his fiancée, his prospective father-in-law, Richard Kurt and Marion Froude is the burden of a capital third act.

Mr. Behrman can write comedies that shine with the truth of character. Although "Biography" is not one of his most lucid, it is one of his maturest revelations of people. Especially when he has more than two of them together his comedy has a volatile spirit. Marion Froude, being "a big laissez-faire girl," brings them all together. Whether they are Bohemian, bourgeois or radical, they all find in her something that puts them at ease and makes them surrender. For she cannot find it in her heart to take sides against any one or for herself. Through her Mr. Behrman finds the common meeting-ground in characters who fly at each other's throats when she does not dominate the scene. Mr. Behrman's ideas are not clearly resolved, or perhaps they are deeply embedded. The play seems aimless and tenuous for half its length on that account. But when Mr. Behrman comes to grips with his people in the last act his characters stand fully revealed. It is a spectacle both comic and pitiable, for some of the characters are hypocrites, some of them are weaklings, some of them are passionately sincere, and one of them is kindly and wise. In his last act Mr. Behrman has taken his full measure as a modern playwright. He has a height and a depth, to say nothing of a skill, that few of his colleagues can encompass.

Under Philip Moeller's patient direction the actors give excellent portraits of character but the performance seems strangely attenuated. In addition to the radiant, heady acting of Miss Claire, "Biography" includes a splendid, headlong portrait of the radical young editor by Earle Larimore. As the Tennessee candidate for the Senate, Jay Fassett shows how a character can be developed from mere fatuousness to humble sincerity. Arnold Korff, who is out of the Reinhardt laboratory, brings comic richness to the subsidiary part of a Viennese melodist. Charles Richman is amusingly suave and supercilious as a pompous Southern editor; and Mary Arbenz plays well the part of his daughter.

The over-detailed duplex apartment in which all these lives are introspectively examined comes from Jo Mielziner's observant drawing-board. For Mr. Behrman has looked deep into the motives of a strange medley of characters. Sometimes it is possible to wish that he were blunter in the statement of his dramatic ideas.

1932 D 13

1933

DESIGN FOR LIVING, a play in three acts, by Noel Coward. Staged by the author; settings by G. E. Calthrop; produced by Max Gordon.   At the Ethel Barrymore Theatre.

Gilda	Lynn Fontanne
Ernest Friedman	Campbell Gullan
Otto	Alfred Lunt
Leo	Noel Coward
Miss Hodge	Gladys Henson
Mr. Birbeck	Philip Tonge
Photographer	Ward Bishop
Grace Torrence	Ethel Borden
Helen Carver	Phyllis Connard
Henry Carver	Alan Campbell
Matthew	Macleary Stinnett

By BROOKS ATKINSON.

Mr. Coward, who has a way of his own with musical romance and historical pageantry, has a way of his own with the familiar triangle. "Design for Living," which came to the Ethel Barrymore Theatre last evening, is the proof. It is a decadent way, if you feel obliged to pull a long moral face over his breezy fandango. It is an audacious and hilarious way if you relish the attack and retreat of artificial comedy that bristles with wit. Occasionally Mr. Coward appears to be asking you to look upon the volatile emotions of his characters as real, and that—if it is true—would be a pity. For he is the master of impudence and tart whimsy, of plain words that leap out of the dialogue like shafts of laughter. At least they do on the lips of his three chief actors. As Leo, he is the sharpest corner of his own triangle. As Otto and Gilda, Alfred Lunt and Lynn Fontanne complete this design for frivolous living. They are an incomparable trio of high comedians. And they give "Design for Living" the sententious acting that transmutes artificial comedy into delight.

What, with friends, acquaintances and servants, there are more than three characters in this triangle. Mr. Coward needs a few dull persons to victimize. But what he really enjoys is the bizarre nonsense of his three characters. One is a playwright. One is an artist. The third is a woman who is also an artist. Otto and Leo, who are close friends of very long standing both love her very much, and she loves them. To save herself from the complications of this singular situation she escapes from both and marries a sober art merchant who takes her to New York. But after a voyage around the world on a freighter the two wild oats turn up like Tweedledum and Tweedledee at her pent-house apartment. Their impudent gayety disarms her. After a stormy session with her husband, who knows the code of a gentleman, she returns to the exuberant disorder of her kind.

Unfortunately for the uses of artificial comedy, establishing this triangular situation involves considerable sobriety. All through the first act Mr. Coward writes as earnestly as a psychologist. Through a long stretch of the third act he surrenders to the patter of ordinary folk and, incidentally, to ordinary actors who can make little of the wrangling impertinence of their lines. When "Design for Living" sounds serious you wish impatiently that Mr. Coward would cut the cackle and come to the main business, which is his brand of satyr comedy. He touches that off with remarkable dexterity. Otto and Leo drinking themselves into silly merriment after Gilda has left them, Otto and Leo striding pompously around Gilda's penthouse in the last act, the fluff of worldly success and the vaudeville of telephone conversations suit Mr. Coward's skimming pen exactly. When he is in an impish mood, which is most of the time, he is enormously funny.

But the acting supplies the final brilliance. "Design for Living" is written for actors—in fact, for the three actors who are now most conspicuous in it. They are extraordinarily well balanced. Miss Fontanne, with her slow, languorous deliberation; Mr. Lunt, with his boyish enthusiasm; Mr. Coward, with his nervous, biting charity, create more variety in the acting than Mr. Coward has got into the parts. They enjoy this comedy as much as the audience does. Being under no solemn delusions about it, they make "Design for Living" an actors' lark.

It is one of the paradoxes of the theatre that the most trifling things are often the most priceless. Skill, art, clairvoyance about the stage, even erudition of a sort, have gone into this gay bit of drollery. It is highly diverting for the evening thereof.

1933 Ja 25

Men In White

By BROOKS ATKINSON.

Two years ago the Group Theatre actors upset the early autumnal complacence. Last evening, at the Broadhurst, they performed the same office by mounting the first engrossing play of the season, "Men in White," by Sidney Kingsley. Although Mr. Kingsley is not a medical man, he has written about the ideals and conflicts of loyalty of the medical profession with fervent convictions, disclosing uncommon familiarity with his subject. It is a good, brave play, despite a certain austerity in the writing and a slavish fondness for medical terms. And it is just the play to summon all the latent idealism from the young players of the Group Theatre. They play it with enkindling sincerity. After all these wretched weeks, Mr. Kingsley and the Group Theatre have opened the season of intelligent theatregoing. Let this forum express its admiration.

MEN IN WHITE, a play in three acts, by Sidney S. Kingsley. Staged by Lee Strasberg; settings by Mordecai Gorelik; produced by the Group Theatre in association with Sidney Harmon and James Ramsey Ullman, as the tenth new play of the 1933-34 theatrical season. At the Broadhurst Theatre.

Dr. Gordon .... Luther Adler
Dr. Hochberg .... J. Edward Bromberg
Dr. Michaelson............. William Challee
Dr. Vitale .... Herbert Ratner
Dr. McCabe .... Grover Burgess
Dr. Ferguson........... Alexander Kirkland
Dr. Wren .... Sanford Meisner
Dr. Otis .... Bob Lewis
Dr. Levine .... Morris Carnovsky
Dr. Bradley .... Walter Coy
Dr. Crawford .... Alan Baxter
Nurse Jamison........... Eunice Stoddard
Mr. Hudson .... Art Smith
James Mooney .... Gerrit Kraber
Laura Hudson .... Margaret Barker
Mr. Smith .... Sanford Meisner
Mrs. Smith .... Ruth Nelson
Dorothy Smith............. Mab Maynard
Barbara Dennin............ Phoebe Brand
Dr. Cunningham .... Russell Collins
First Nurse .... Paula Miller
Nurse Mary Ryan........ Dorothy Patten
Orderly .... Elia Kazan
Mr. Houghton............. Clifford Odets
Mr. Spencer............... Lewis Leverett
Mrs. D'Andrea....... Mary Virginia Farmer
Second Nurse................ Elena Karam

It is Mr. Kingsley's thesis that medicine is a ruthless master. Those who take the Hippocratic oath are embracing a religion. Young Dr. Ferguson, interne at St. George's Hospital, may become a brilliant surgeon if he works hard and selflessly at his profession for the next five or ten years. But the rich young lady to whom he is engaged looks forward to a marriage in which there may be pleasure as well as professional labor. With her wealth she can buy Ferguson's advancement. She might have done that. But while she is in the midst of preparations for the wedding Ferguson is ordered to assist in a critical operation to save the life of a nurse who has just been through an abortion. Ferguson is responsible for her calamity. This situation in all its torturing ramifications settles the question of loyalties more resolutely than any of the discussions could. Ferguson plunges back into medicine as a refuge. The young lady to whom he is engaged is now willing to take him on those ruthless professional terms.

Although this is Mr. Kingsley's first play to reach professional production, he has the gift of dramatic concreteness. "Men in White" abounds in scenes that have impact in the theatre. It dramatizes the hospital. It progresses from the interne's library to a patient's room, the director's room and the operating room. In most of the nine scenes some matter of human destiny is at stake. You may question the logic of the story. You may criticize the continuity and the writing. But "Men in White" has force in the theatre. It is warm with life and high in aspiration, and it has a contagious respect for the theme it discusses.

Under Lee Strasberg's thoughtful direction, all the acting is good. Some of it is excellent. J. Edward Bromberg's portrait of the paternal old surgeon rings true in every inflection and nervous tilt of the head. Morris Carnovsky's broken physician is finely detailed—reserved in accent and honest in effect. Alexander Kirkland as Ferguson, Margaret Barker as his fiancée, Phoebe Brand as the nurse play with a keen knowledge of their parts and their craft.

The production represents the theatre fully aware of its varied arts. Mordecai Garelik's sets are attractive, dramatic and practical. The lighting has a subordinate glamour all its own. After two years of real hardship, the Group Theatre is not only still in existence but still determined to keep the theatre in its high estate. This time they have a play worthy of their ambition, and they have adorned it with the most beguiling acting the town affords.

1933 S 27

AS THOUSANDS CHEER, a revue in two acts and twenty-three scenes, by Irving Berlin and Moss Hart. Staged and lighted by Hassard Short; dances arranged by Charles Weidman; settings by Albert R. Johnson; produced by Sam H. Harris as the third musical show of the 1933-34 theatrical season. At the Music Box.
PRINCIPALS — Marilyn Miller, Clifton Webb, Helen Broderick, Ethel Waters, Leslie Adams, Hal Forde, Jerome Cowan, Harry Stockwell, Thomas Hamilton, Hamtree Harrington, Peggy Cornell, Harold Murray, Charles Weidman and his dancers, and others.

By BROOKS ATKINSON.

No doubt some one will be able to suggest how "As Thousands Cheer" could be improved. But on the evidence disclosed Saturday evening at the Music Box, where the revue had its New York première, this column can only give its meek approval to every item on the program. Irving Berlin and Moss Hart, who wrote it in collaboration; Sam H. Harris, who has produced it in the pink of modern taste, and all the craftsmen who have contributed to it, have created a superb panorama of entertainment. By being topical it is a revue in the genuine meaning of that word. By being excellent in quality it is enormously exhilarating. Among the thousands who cheer, count this column as one of the noisiest. Let us all toss our sweaty nightcaps in the air.

In form it is a newspaper revue with columns of type streaming up and down the curtains and headlines introducing the various numbers. Under the banner line of "Franklin D. Roosevelt Inaugurated Tomorrow," for instance, you will discover what Mr. and Mrs. Hoover really think of Dolly Gann, Mellon, Stimson and their dynamic successors. "World's Wealthiest Man Celebrates 94th Birthday" reveals John D. Rockefeller Jr. trying to present Radio City to his father as a birthday gift, and running for his life as the curtains sweep together. There is a note on the baleful effect Noel Coward has upon hotel servants after they have been exposed to his mannerisms and macabre literary moods; and there is a domestic scene in Buckingham Palace to which the British object—possibly because it is the revue's only lapse from sententious brilliance. There is a great deal more of general current significance, and it is all crisply written, adroitly presented and wittily acted.

For the performers are off the show-shop's top shelf. Helen Broderick never misses a chance to put poison in the soup, nor does she waste a drop of acid. Whether she is Mrs. Hoover writhing with contempt or the Statue of Liberty thumbing her nose at foreign statesmen or Aimee Semple MacPherson teaming up with Mahatma Gandhi, Miss Broderick is the perfect stage wit. Ethel Waters takes full control of the audience and the show whenever she appears. Her abandon to the ruddy tune of "Heat Wave Hits New York," her rowdy comedy as the wife of a stagestruck "Green Pastures" actor and her pathos in a deep-toned song about a lynching give some notion of the broad range she can encompass in musical shows.

Clifton Webb, king of the decadent pants, sings and dances with a master's dexterity, and puts a keen point to all his sardonic sketches. His John D. Rockefeller Sr. and Mahatma Gandhi are masterpieces in miniature of topical parody. Marilyn Miller brings to the show not only the effulgence of her personality but a sense of humor as Joan Crawford and a chambermaid with literary delusions of grandeur. Among the secondary performers Leslie Adams has great relish of the humor involved in travestying Herbert Hoover and the King of England, and Hal Forde does a Ramsay MacDonald that is the subtlest caricature of the evening.

Nor does this exhaust the rich and bristling coffers of "As Thousands Cheer." Charles Weidman's dance arrangements are revelations of the comment this art can make on current affairs. The costumes designed by Varady and Irene Sharaff have meaning as well as beauty. Albert Johnson's settings testify to one of the keenest minds in that business, and Hassard Short's lighting and staging are among his best works. As for Mr. Berlin, he has never written better tunes or more sparkling lyrics; and Mr. Hart has never turned his wit with such economical precision. In these circumstances there is nothing a reviewer can do except cheer. Bravo and huzzas!

1933 O 2

AH, WILDERNESS! a play in three acts and seven scenes, by Eugene O'Neill. Staged by Philip Moeller; settings by Robert Edmond Jones; produced by the Theatre Guild as the first play of its sixteenth subscription season and the fourteenth new play of the 1933-34 theatrical season. At the Guild Theatre.

Nat Miller	George M. Cohan
Essie	Marjorie Marquis
Arthur	William Post Jr.
Richard	Elisha Cook Jr.
Mildred	Adelaide Bean
Tommy	Walter Vonnegut Jr.
Sid Davis	Gene Lockhart
Lily Miller	Edna Heinemann
David McComber	Richard Sterling
Muriel McComber	Ruth Gilbert
Wint Selby	John Wynne
Belle	Ruth Holden
Nora	Ruth Choppenning
Bartender	Donald McClelland
Salesman	John Butler

By BROOKS ATKINSON.

As a writer of comedy Mr. O'Neill has a capacity for tenderness that most of us never suspected. "Ah, Wilderness!" with which the Guild opened its sixteenth season last evening, may not be his most tremendous play, but it is certainly his most attractive. How much of it is autobiographical this column is not prepared to say just now, but obviously it is Mr. O'Neill's attempt to recapture past life of which he is fond. All the characters are beguiling; at least two of them are admirable and lovable. And toward them Mr. O'Neill's point of view is full of compassionate understanding.

As a Connecticut father of the year 1906, Mr. Cohan gives the ripest, finest performance in his career, suggesting, as in the case of Mr. O'Neill, that his past achievements are no touchstone of the qualities he has never exploited. On the whole, Mr. O'Neill's excursion into nostalgic comedy has resulted in one of his best works. His sources are closer to life than the tortured characters of "Mourning Becomes Electra." His mood is mature and forgiving. Now it is possible to sit down informally with Mr. O'Neill and to like the people of whom he speaks and the gentle, kindly tolerance of his memories.

In a large small-town of Connecticut in 1906 lives an ordinary American family. They are typical in their humors and vexations. They are average folk faced by average problems, and they have the strength to solve them. What concerns them most in "Ah, Wilderness!" is the youthful fervor of Richard, who is a senior in high school and a rebel. He reads Swinburne, Shaw, Wilde and Omar Khayyam, and his mother worries. He is an incipient anarchist; he hates capital and his father looks disturbed. He is also passionately in love with a neighbor's girl, and means to marry her. The scraps of Swinburne verse that he sends to her alarm her father, who forces her to break with Richard in good, melodramatic style. Being young and arrogant, Richard runs amok to spite her, and gets tight in the presence of a painted lady. His father and mother are sure that the world has come to an end. But the damsel manages to prove her devotion at a moonlit rendezvous on the beach and Richard is himself again. After everything has been settled naturally, the father and mother begin to remember that once they were young.

That, in brief, is the fact of the story. But it hardly communicates the warmth of pity that floods through the play. For undistinguished as the legend may be, Mr. O'Neill has given it distinction by the fervor of his emotion. He not only likes these burgher folk, but he understands them; and particularly in the last act in the scene between the son and the father he has caught all the love and anguish that such relationships conceal. The roistering scene in the back room of a small hotel bar is commonplace enough. Some of the domestic scenes are hackneyed, and the progress of "Ah, Wilderness!" lacks the drive of Mr. O'Neill's tragic war horses. But his recognition of the tortures of adolescence, and the petty despairs of small-town life, bring him closer to most of us than any of his other plays have done.

As a writer of comedy he is no gag buffoon. The lines that draw laughter from the audience cannot be detached from the play for isolated quotation. But his attitude toward his characters is lightened with a sense of humor. Part of the humor rebounds from the costumes of 1906—the flat straw hats, striped flannel trousers, long coats, high collars that the young blades wear in their frivolities, and the monstrous automobile garb needed for Fourth of July motoring. Part of the humor comes from the intellectual timidities that we persuade ourselves were typical of that day. Nat Miller falteringly talking sex to his son is one of the funniest episodes in this fable. There is an undercurrent of humor in all the dilemmas of the Miller children and in all the familiar jars of family life in the sitting-room and over the dinner-table. But if Mr. O'Neill's approach to Richard's torment of eager, youthful problems is not humorous it is fraught with humanity, and it is alternately poignant and disarming.

The Guild has risen to the occasion nobly. Mr. Moeller's direction is supple, alert and sagacious; and Robert Edmond Jones's settings recognize the humor in the stuffy refinement of 1906. As Nat Miller, the father, Mr. Cohan gives a splendid performance. Although that adjective is exact, it seems hardly enthusiastic enough for the ripeness and kindliness and wisdom of his playing. He is quizzical in the style to which we are all accustomed from him, but the jaunty mannerisms and the mugging have disappeared. For the fact is that "Ah, Wilderness!" has dipped deeper into Mr. Cohan's gifts and personal character than any of the antics he has written for himself. Ironic as it may sound, it has taken Eugene O'Neill to show us how fine an actor George M. Cohan is.

As Richard, Elisha Cook Jr. has strength as well as pathos. Mr. Cook can draw more out of mute adolescence than any other young actor on our stage. Marjorie Marquis is excellent as a troubled, normal mother. Gene Lockhart is capital as her amiable and bibulous brother. As the spinster who refused him sixteen years ago, Eda Heinemann is also uncommonly good. There are good performances of other parts by William Post Jr., Adelaide Bean, Walter Vonnegut Jr., Ruth Gilbert, Richard Sterling, John Wynne and Ruth Holden. And in spite of its dreadful title, "Ah, Wilderness!" is a true and congenial comedy. If Mr. O'Neill can write with as much clarity as this, it is hard to understand why he has held up the grim mask so long.

                              1933 O 3.

'Her Master's Voice.'

HER MASTER'S VOICE, a comedy in two acts and five scenes, by Clare Kummer. Staged by Worthington Miner. Production designed by Raymond Sovey. Incidental music by Miss Kummer. Produced by Max Gordon. At the Plymouth Theatre.

Queena Farrar .... Frances Fuller
Mrs. Martin .... Elizabeth Patterson
Ned Farrar .... Roland Young
Craddock .... Francis Pierlot
Aunt Min .... Laura Hope Crews
Mr. Twilling .... Frederick Perry
Phoebe .... Josephine Williams

By BROOKS ATKINSON.

Under the benevolent rule of the New Deal it is possible to have and to enjoy such a fluffy comedy as Clare Kummer's "Her Master's Voice," which was acted at the Plymouth last evening. Excepting "Amourette," which succumbed to several rare diseases a few weeks ago, Miss Kummer has not been represented in New York for some time. Roland Young and Laura Hope Crews, who play the principal rôles, have likewise been absent, shamelessly screening their art on the wind-swept lots of Hollywood. But now they are all back—and a good thing it is, too. For "Her Master's Voice" is just the sort of light and airy comedy about nothing in particular for these dextrous folks to trifle with.

Miss Kummer loves to spin her dialogues out of the crotchets of ordinary people. In this instance there is a young father who seems to have no talent for respectable labors, a young mother who is naturally somewhat worried, a petulant mother-in-law who puts into words the sort of truths that are unpleasant to hear, and a juggernaut aunt who is unaware of almost everything but who is confident of her ability to manage any one at all. What with the dislikes that family life inevitably breeds, the future looks black for a devoted young married couple for about two acts. But trust Miss Kummer to bring them through her artificial crises successfully. Everything is as right as rain in the end.

The story matters less than the dialogue. Miss Kummer has a rare gift for the elliptical humors of conversational sequence. Remarks that are not particularly amusing in themselves sound funny by reason of the unexpected direction they take. "Her Master's Voice" has a woeful scene halfway through when the comedy threatens to expire into mere friskiness. But presently Miss Kummer puts it to rights again with a connubial blunder that startles the proprieties of the well-bred people in her comedy. Before you are bored with them, every one is feeling as good-natured as possible and the curtain rings down. Miss Kummer's touch is as light and fragile as a puff-ball. It is amusing to see how gayly she avoids having nothing to say at all.

In the present instance she has actors whose touch is equally skimming. As the juggernaut aunt, Miss Crews is just pompous and literalminded enough to be the animated caricature of a Helen Hokinson drawing. Miss Crews has long been the mistress of this style of comedy. Mr. Young's subtle drolleries and nimble inflections of voice keep the part of the husband blandly mischievous. Elizabeth Patterson's calamity-ridden mother-in-law, Frances Fuller's earnest young wife, and Frederick Perry's neighborly good-fellowship round out a tickling performance under the sagacious direction of Worthington Miner.

The world in which Miss Kummer dwells is bright and pleasant, secure against the realities that vex most of us. Her people speak a bubbly brand of nonsense. It is good to hear it again.

1933 O 24

TOBACCO ROAD, a play in three acts, by Jack Kirkland, adapted from the novel of the same name by Erskine Caldwell. Setting by Robert Redington Sharpe; staged and produced by Anthony Brown. At the Masque Theatre.

Jeeter Lester	Henry Hull
Dude Lester	Sam Byrd
Ada Lester	Margaret Wycherly
Ellie May	Ruth Hunter
Grandma Lester	Patricia Quinn
Lov Bensey	Dean Jagger
Henry Peabody	Ashley Cooper
Sister Bessie Rice	Maude Odell
Pearl	Reneice Rehan
Captain Tim	Lamar King
George Payne	Edwin Walter

By BROOKS ATKINSON.

Since it is based on a novel, "Tobacco Road," which was acted at the Masque last evening, is not an organic play. Although Jack Kirkland has turned it into three acts, it is still Erskine Caldwell's novel at heart, which is to say that it is more like a soliloquy with variations than a dramatic character sketch. Under Mr. Caldwell's influence it is also one of the grossest episodes ever put on the

stage. Once the theatre used to be sinful. But now it is the novel that ferrets out the abominations of life and exposes them for sale in the marketplace. The men of letters have stolen the dramatists' crimson badge; and the theatre has never sheltered a fouler or more degenerate parcel of folks than the hardscrabble family of Lester that lives along the "Tobacco Road."

But that is not a full and disinterested report of the Masque Theatre's current tenant. For Mr. Caldwell is a demoniac genius—brutal, grimly comic and clairvoyant. No one has chronicled the complete degeneracy of the Georgia cracker with such inhuman detachment. He writes with the fiery sword. Although "Tobacco Road" reels around the stage like a drunken stranger to the theatre, it has spasmodic moments of merciless power when truth is flung into your face with all the slime that truth contains. That is why Mr. Caldwell's grossness cannot be dismissed as morbidity and gratuitous indecency. It is the blunt truth of the characters he is describing, and it leaves a malevolent glow of poetry above the rudeness of his statement.

"Tobacco Road" is the saga of Jeeter Lester, a good-for-nothing farmer who still lives on the land his father and grandfather farmed. But it is no longer his. Being lazy and dissolute, he has lost everything and now exists with his tatterdemalion family in the dirt and filth of a rickety shack. The Lesters are ragged, foul, starving and lazy. But still Jeeter preserves that fluency of talk and fecundity of crackbrained ideas and that animal sensuality which live in the lower darkness. Everything exists on the same plane of inhumanity. Even death leaves no impression upon life that is dead in everything save the body.

As Jeeter Lester, Henry Hull gives the performance of his career. For years Mr. Hull has been charming and trivial about many things and singularly obtuse about some others. But here is a character portrait as mordant and brilliant as you can imagine. Dressed in loathsome rags, untidily bearded and heavily wrinkled, Mr. Hull's Georgia cracker staggers through a whole gamut of emotions and passions — pungent, pathetic, horrible and gargantuanly comic.

The performance is shabbily directed. But it includes an excellent portrait of a headlong boy by Sam Byrd and a picturesque setting by Robert Redington Sharpe. Plays as clumsy and rudderless as "Tobacco Road" seldom include so many scattered items that leave such a vivid impression.

1933 D 5

1934

THEY SHALL NOT DIE, a play in three acts, by John Wexley. Staged by Philip Moeller (production committee: Theresa Helburn and Lee Simonson); settings by Lee Simonson; presented as the fifth play of its sixteenth subscription season by the Theatre Guild. At the Royale Theatre.

Cooley	William Lynn
Henderson	John L. Kearney
Red	Tom Ewell
St. Louis Kid	Fred Herrick
Blackie	Frank Woodruff
Deputy Sheriff Trent	Ralph Theadore
Jeff Vivian	Ralph Sanford
Lewis Collins	Bob Ross
Walter Colton	William Norton
Virginia Ross	Linda Watkins
Lucy Wells	Ruth Gordon
Luther Mason	Hale Norcross
Benson Allen	L. M. Hurdle
Roberts	George R. Hayes
Purcell	Alfred Brown
Walters	Bryant Hall
Warner	Grafton Trew
Heywood Parsons	Al Stokes
Roy Wood	Allan Vaughan
Andy Wood	Joseph Scott
Morris	Joseph Smalls
Moore	Frank Wilson
Killian	Eddie Hodge
Oliver Tulley	Robert Thomsen
Dr. Thomas	George Christie
Captain Kennedy	Frederick Persson
Sergeant Ogden	Ross Forrester
Mrs. Wells	Helen Westley
Russell Evans	Dean Jagger
Principal Keeper	Charles Henderson
Lowery	Carroll Ashburn
William Treadwell	Brandon Peters
Rev. Wendell Jackson	Fred Miller
Warden Jeffries	Leo Curley
Rokoff	Louis John Latzer
Cheney	St. Clair Bayfield
Nathan G. Rubin	Claude Rains
Johnny	Hugh Rennie
Mr. Harrison	Frank Wilson
Frank Travers	Douglas Gregory
Judge	Thurston Hall
Dr. Watson	Robert J. Lawrence
Attorney General Dade	Ben Smith
Seth Robbins	Harry Hermsen
Circuit Solicitor Slade	Carl Eckstrom

By BROOKS ATKINSON.

John Wexley, who once wrote a good play entitled "The Last Mile," and then a second one entitled "Steel," which was better than most people believed it to be, has now written one that will send a shiver of apprehension across the country. It is entitled "They Shall Not Die." It was played at the Royale Theatre last evening by one of the most stirring casts the Theatre Guild has assembled. It is Mr.

Wexley's declaration of his belief that the Scottsboro Negroes have been sentenced to die when grave doubt as to their guilt exists. Under Philip Moeller's resourceful direction it is a play of terrifying and courageous bluntness of statement —thoughtfully developed, lucidly explained and played with great resolution. None of the great causes of the last decade has received in the theatre such a calmly worded and overwhelmingly forceful defense as this. For once good works match the crusader's intentions.

Mr. Wexley does not mention Scottsboro by name. Perhaps that would be too incendiary, and no doubt he has not been able to tell the story with literal accuracy. But the Scottsville case of "They Shall Not Die" is too circumstantial to be mistaken for a playwright's folly. Beginning with a wild scene in the Cookesville jail, where nine Negroes, a few white boys and two white girls are kicked in by the sheriffs after a scuffle on a railroad train, it pushes on grimly through all the welter of statement and counter-statement to a brutal trial scene where a Jewish lawyer from New York stirs up a tornado of hatred in a Southern courtroom. Courtroom scenes are one of the theatre's most spurious products. But this one is masterly. Mr. Wexley has evaded nothing— Jew-baiting, sectionalism, political rancor, bloodlust or mob rule for Negroes. He has woven all these abnormal impulses into the dramatic pattern of his story. After the lawyer for the defense has made his appeal and the judge has charged the jury with religious sincerity, the jury is heard laughing riotously in the jury room. In those awful circumstances it is an inhuman sound. As the final curtain goes down, everyone realizes that guilt and innocence are not the great topics of discussion in that chamber of justice. Mr. Wexley has made his point like a working dramatist as well as a man of conviction.

Those who have been intimately associated with the Scottsboro case know better than this reviewer does how much latitude among the facts Mr. Wexley has assumed as a playwright. Many of the events that he dramatizes with so much confidence in the first act are open to dispute and much of the second act is subject to dramatic license. But readers of the newspapers know that Mr. Wexley has not been forced to invent the things that make his last act such an agonizing exposure of courtroom justice. The important features are matters of record. Mr. Wexley writes with the coolness of a man who has been deeply stirred. When the audience left the theatre last evening, it shared his feeling.

The cast is long. None of the parts, except that of the defense attorney, is showy or spacious. But the actors play with a sort of personal humility that communicates the strength of Mr. Wexley's conviction. As the defense attorney, Claude Rains does jeopardize his opening scene with histrionic flamboyancy. But in the court-room scene, which is the crucial one, the part catches up with him and he plays magnificently. Ruth Gordon and Linda Watkins play the parts of the two girls with admirable integrity. Helen Westley, Ben Smith, Thurston Hall, Erskine Sanford, Bob Ross, Frank Wilson are excellent. So are the others. So are Lee Simonson's settings. In short, the Theatre Guild has given Mr. Wexley invaluable assistance. For those with a social conscience "They Shall Not Die" is a tremendously powerful play.

1934 F 22

DODSWORTH, a play in three acts and fourteen scenes, by Sidney Howard, dramatized from Sinclair Lewis's novel of the same name. Staged by Robert B. Sinclair; settings by Jo Mielziner; produced by Max Gordon. At the Shubert Theatre.

Samuel Dodsworth.................Walter Huston
A Sales Manager.................Arthur Uttry
A Publicity Man.................Nolan Leary
A Secretary.................Alice Griswold
Henry E. Hazzard.................Charles Halton
Fran Dodsworth.................Fay Bainter
Thomas J. Pearson.................Harlan Briggs
Mrs. Pearson.................Ethel Jackson
Emily McKee.................Ethel Hampton
Harry McKee.................Mervin Williams
Two Traveling Gentlemen { Nick Adams
                        { William Morris
Clyde Lockert.................John Williams
An American Lady.................Beatrice Maude
Another American Lady.......Marie Falls
A Passenger.................Bert Gardner
His Wife.................Lucille Fenton
Edith Cortright.................Nan Sunderland
A Steward.................Charles Christensen
Another Steward.................Ivan Miller
A Barman.................Jay Wilson
A. B. Hurd.................Hal K. Dawson
Renee de Penable.................Leonore Harris
Arnold Israel.................Frederic Worlock
Kurt von Obersdorf.................Kent Smith
A Cashier.................J. H. Kingsberry
An American Mother.................Marie Falls
Her Daughter.................Betty Van Auken
A Tourist.................Frank W. Taylor
His Wife.................Myrtle Tannehill
"Junior".................Charles Powers
Information Clerk.................Ralph Simone
A Second Tourist.................Marie Mallon
Baroness von Obersdorf.Maria Ouspenskaya
Teresa.................Flora Fransioli

By BROOKS ATKINSON.

Among the virtues of "Dodsworth," which opened at the Shubert Saturday evening, place Walter Huston foremost. After wasting his fragrance on the motion-picture air for the last five years he has returned to remind us that he is one of the best actors our theatre has developed. We knew that before he slipped away. In "Mr. Pitt," "Desire under the Elms," "The Barker," "Elmer the Great," and "The Commodore Marries," he created characters that none of us is likely soon to forget. As Dodsworth the Middle Western automobile manufacturer from Sinclair Lewis's novel, he has a part that suits him perfectly. He overwhelms it with the strength of his personality. For without being the least bit studied or artful in his address Mr. Huston has a commanding presence that absorbs an audience completely and he has a power of direction that focuses interest upon the thought he is expressing. Even comedy by-play cannot divert you from the main issue of the scene he is acting. Once he prowls around a sleek hotel suite in his underwear and starched shirt—a grotesque spectacle—but what you remember is the thought of the scene. That gives some notion not only of his power but of his integrity.

For Mr. Huston is the most honest of actors—plain, simple, lucid, magnetic. Before "Dodsworth" is finished Mr. Huston acquaints you with every trait of this manufacturer's character. The stoop of his head, the strength and modesty of his walk, the heartiness of his comradely gestures, the frankness of his eyes, the thoughtful hesitation in a scene that bewilders him, the easy spontaneity of his manner when he is among friends, the rudeness of his voice when he is aroused —all these aspects of his playing reveal Dodsworth completely. Mr.

Huston understands him, and respects him, too. For in every situation Dodsworth behaves like an upright man. He has a native gift for the fundamental virtues of the manufacturer, father and husband. He has a decency of mind. Mr. Huston's acting of the part stirs your admiration and affection. How much of it is Huston and how much Dodsworth is a question that can be answered on the day after never. In the meantime it is enough to know that a broad-gauged and first-rate actor is now in town.

As a play, Mr. Howard's dramatization is an aimless chronicle. "Main Street" made a bad play; so did "Elmer Gantry." "Dodsworth" is the best of the three dramatic assaults upon the novels of the eminent Nobel Prizer. It opens with a coherent, highly stimulating first act that carries Dodsworth and his conceited wife from the familiar environment of Zenith to the strangeness of London. Drama critics who can read report that Mr. Howard has made no slavish transcription of the Lewis novel, which is the proper way to translate novels into plays. But even with the freedom he has assumed as a playwright, Mr. Howard has not succeeded in fusing the story or in keeping the drama from running down hill. The play is in fourteen scenes. In nettlesome dialogue it shows Mrs. Dodsworth running amuck among the cavalier graces of a Europe that intoxicates her empty-headed vanity. Although Mr. Howard is constantly aware of the revealing truths of character that the story supplies, he has not, in this reviewer's opinion, molded it into trenchant dramatic form. That is all the more surprising because Mr. Howard's greatest strength as a rule is his mastery of the theatre.

Most of the acting is excellent. Most of Fay Bainter's Mrs. Dodsworth is sensitive character portrayal. But what of that embarrassing scene in the last act when Miss Bainter drops character completely and indulges herself in a few maudlin moments of the blind staggers? The polite critical word for that sort of thing is bathos. Maria Ouspenskaya makes one of her rare and memorable appearances as a German countess. Although the scene is brief, this gifted actress burns it into the memory with the flame of her extraordinary artistry. Especially in the first act Nan Sunderland, who is also Mrs. Huston, gives an illuminating, lightly acted portrait of Edith Cortright. As the Parisian amoureux Frederic Worlock has saddled himself with a trying accent. In other parts there are excellent performances by Harlan Briggs, John Williams, Charles Halton and Kent Smith. All these actors have been intelligently directed by Robert Sinclair, and the entire performance is smothered in the only suit of dreary settings Jo Mielziner ever designed.

Thus, the random imperfections in the play and performance dull a good deal the enjoyment of a warm, expansive American theme. Mr. Huston's manly acting is its only clear expression. Having him back in town is an occasion for civic rejoicing.

1934 F 26

STEVEDORE, a play in three acts and ten scenes, by Paul Peters and George Sklar. Staged by Michael Blankfort and Irving Gordon; settings by S. Syrjala; produced by the Theatre Union. At the Civic Repertory Theatre.

Florrie	Millicent Green
Bill Larkin	Jack Hartley
Sergeant	Jack Daley
Bobo Valentine	Carrington Lewis
Rag Williams	Alonzo Fenderson
Angrum	Ray Yeates
Lonnie Thompson	Jack Carter
Joe Crump	G. I. Harry Bolden
Steve	Frank Gabrielson
Binnie	Georgette Harvey
Ruby Oxley	Edna Thomas
Sam Oxley	Al Watts
Uncle Cato	William C. Elkins
Jim Veal	Leigh Whipper
Blacksnake	Rex Ingram
Walcott	Dodson Mitchell
Mike	Robert Caille
Detective	Jack Williams
Lem Morris	Neill O'Malley
Marty Fox	Jack Williams
Al Regan	Frank Gabrielson
Charley Freeman	Irving Gordon
Mitch	Jack Hartley
Pons	Robert Caille
Cop	Jack Williams
Bertha Williams	Susie Sutton
Mose Venable	William C. Elkins
Nanny	Gena Brown
Sherman	Arthur Bruce

By BROOKS ATKINSON.

Having laid away "Peace on Earth," after a run of about four months, the militant Theatre Union has turned its attention to "Stevedore," which was put on at the Civic Repertory last evening. It is the work of Paul Peters and George Sklar, and it is a highly exciting, workmanlike drama of race riots in the South. Mr. Sklar was one of the authors of "Peace on Earth" and "Merry-Go-Round." Mr. Peters's roving career in the ranks of labor reads like a modern odyssey. If "Peace on Earth" could pay its way through a long engagement, "Stevedore" deserves a distinguished run, for it is a sound, mettlesome piece of dramatic writing. There is a ring of authenticity about the story and characterization. It has been ably staged by Michael Blankfort, graphically set with S. Syrjala's scenery and splendidly lighted. It is acted with tremendous gusto by a cast composed largely of Negro actors. If the Theatre Union is capable of stage work of this superior quality it will quickly make a place for itself in this town, not only as a labor group but as a vigorous producing organization. Between the audience and the play last evening was an extraordinarily interesting occasion.

"Stevedore" is a story of union problems and race riots along the huge docks of a Southern seaport. According to a program note, "it is based on incidents which occurred during the attacks on Negroes in East St. Louis in 1919, the Chicago attacks in 1919, the Dr. Sweet case in Detroit, the Bogalusa lumber strike, the New Orleans dock strikes, the Colorado bathing beach fight, the attack on the Camp Hill, Ala., share croppers and the similar attack at Tuscaloosa, Ala." Presumably, Mr. Peters knows some or all of these troubles at first hand. At any rate, with Mr. Sklar's assistance, he has turned this sort of material into a vigorous narrative and succession of variegated scenes. It is comic, brutish, hysterical and defiant, according to the temper of the episodes.

In a general way the story centres about Lonnie Thompson, a raw-boned Negro dock roustabout, who is framed for an assault upon a white woman chiefly because he is helping to organize a longshoremen's union. His escape from the police results through a series of inflammatory incidents in a race riot against all the Negroes living in his alley.

But "Stevedore" is remarkable chiefly for the lithographic color of its scenes and the broadness and keenness of its characterization. Scenes do not come much finer than the lazy noontime view of the Negroes singing, quarreling and laughing with animal enthusiasm on the dock, with the sun streaming down on the bales of cotton outside. No one could invent a scene like that. Nor is that all, for "Stevedore" describes in easy strokes the Negroes lounging about Bennie's neighborhood lunchroom or cringing there while the rioting whites hurl bricks through the windows. It shows them singing over the body of the old man who was killed, and it concludes with a stirring scene of resistance when the Negroes beat down a murderous invasion of their alley.

The white actors are good, particularly Dodson Mitchell as a fairly affable stevedore, Neill O'Malley as a labor organizer and Millicent Green as a back-alley strumpet. But the Negroes give their scenes a robustiousness and an earthiness that are wholly exhilarating. Whether it is the manliness of Jack Carter as Thompson, or the black brawniness of Rex Ingram as Blacksnake, or the broadbeamed callousness of Georgette Harvey as the lunchroom empress—it is acting with tang and bite and raciness, and the director has been wise enough not to discipline the nature out of it.

Many Negroes were in the audience last night, both downstairs and up. Their response to the lines and the incidents gave the play an entirely fresh meaning. If the drama seemed lively to the white audience it was a holiday for the galleries. Up there the roars of laughter and the jeers sounded like an Elks convention. For "Stevedore" comes into the theatre bursting with vitality. Although it has propaganda implications, it does not hamstring its characters with classroom ideas. The characters are as real and rich as the earth.

1934 Ap 19

WITHIN THE GATES, a play in two acts and four scenes, by Sean O'Casey. Staged by Melvyn Douglas; settings and costumes designed by James Reynolds; incidental music by Milton Lusk and A. Lehman Engel; dance arrangements by Elsa Findlay; produced by George Bushar and John Tuerk. At the National Theatre.

The Dreamer............Bramwell Fletcher
The Bishop.................Moffat Johnston
The Bishop's Sister.........Kathryn Collier
First Chair Attendant......Barry Macollum
Second Chair Attendant..John Daly Murphy
A Boy......................Alexander Lewis
The Atheist.................Morris Ankrum
The Policewoman......Jessamine Newcombe
The Young Man in Plus-Fours,
                              Ralph Sumpter
The Scarlet Woman........Miriam Goldina
First Nursemaid........Vera Fuller Mellish
Second Nursemaid..........Esther Mitchell
A Guardsman.................James Jolley
The Gardener................Barry Kelley
First Evangelist........Edward Broadley
Second Evangelist...........Arthur Villars
The Young Whore.............Lillian Gish
A Young Salvation Army Officer,
                              Byron McGrath
The Foreman................Ralph Cullinan
The Old Woman................Mary Morris
The Man in the Bowler Hat.Stanley G. Wood
The Man With the Stick.........Phil Bishop
The Man in the Trilby Hat...Charles Angelo
First Platform Speaker.......Gordon Gould
Second Platform Speaker...Dodson Mitchell
A Young Man.........Arthur Gould Porter
The Man in the Burberry......Charles Keane
Symbol of the Seasons....Margaret Mower
Woman Who Feeds the Birds..Ellen Larned

A group of down-and-outs, a chorus of young men and girls, Salvationists, strollers in the park, dancers, &c.

By BROOKS ATKINSON.

Let us face this thing boldly. Sean O'Casey has written a great play in "Within the Gates," which was staged at the National last evening. Being contemptuous of the petty depravities of the popular theatre, he has written a fantasy of Hyde Park, where he has imprisoned the full savor of life. When the text of "Within the Gates" was published last year, it seemed to many of us that Mr. O'Casey, who once wrote such biting plays as "Juno and the Paycock" and "The Plough and the Stars," had overreached himself in a poetic medium beyond his strength. But out of the dead print of the text a glorious drama rose last evening with songs and dances, with colors and lights, with magnificent lines that cried out for noble speaking. For Mr. O'Casey is right. He knows that the popular theatre has withered, and he also has the gift to redeem it with a drama that sweeps along through the loves and terrors of mankind. "Within the Gates" is a testament of Mr. O'Casey's abiding faith in life. Nothing so grand has risen in our impoverished theatre since this reporter first began writing of plays.

To people accustomed to the racy statements of the realistic drama it will be difficult to describe Mr. O'Casey's fantasy. It is set in Hyde Park and divided into four parts representing the seasons. There, amid the trees, flowers and benches, and in the shadow of the grim statue of a soldier, Mr. O'Casey discovers the people who represent the whole gamut of life— a poet, a Bishop, an atheist, a Salvation Army officer, unemployed, soap-box orators, nursemaids, soldiers, the tortured, ghastly train of the down-and-outs whose ominous, drum-beat monody is forever stealing through the park and striking terror in the hearts of the people loitering there.

If Mr. O'Casey has any specific story, it concerns the poet, the Bishop and the whore. Being sick in body and broken in heart, she is desperately in need of assistance. The Bishop can give her nothing but sanctimonious counsel. But the poet can give her understanding and share with her the few comforts that are his; and when the demoniac down-and-outs reach out for her the poet can drive them back by the force of his spiritual serenity. If there is a story in "Within the Gates," that is it.

But Mr. O'Casey is in search of many other things. Being a man of natural courage, he has opened the heart of "Within the Gates" to all the men who walk the earth and he has written fluid verses in which they can sing their affirmations and he has carved prose out of gold, Shakespeare and the Bible. Sitting in the park, he is aware of everything and he relishes it, for, among modern dramatists, he is the man who is completely alive. There is the low comedy of the street-corner philosophers. There is the timid middle-class propriety of the nursemaids. There is the selfish lust of the gardener and the slippery corruption of the young man in plus-fours. There is the venomous contempt and bitterness of the unemployed. Above all this, like the steam of the spring, hovers Mr. O'Casey's faith in the endurance of life. For God is his greatest character. By implication Mr. O'Casey has set all the fragments of Hyde Park life in universal perspective.

Dialogue is only a scratch on the surface of a play of this heroic stature. Being the theatre of spiritual magnificence, it needs all the glories of stage art, and it has them in this superb production. Last year "Within the Gates" was drably produced in London. Here George Bushar and John Tuerk, who deserve to be knighted, have given it a memorable production, directed with rare sensibility by Melvyn Douglas. The incidental music by Milton Lusk and A. Lehman Engel enkindles the drama as much as anything Mr. O'Casey has written. The songs have a purity of meaning; the chant for the down-and-outs is macabre. As the designer of the settings and costumes, James Reynolds has understood the problem of fantasy in all its ramifications, and endowed "Within the Gates" with a décor that lifts it into visual eminence. Elsa Findlay's dance arrangements are pitiably inadequate; they are twittering preciosities that should be flung out of the production instantly.

Fortunate in most of his collaborators, Mr. O'Casey is likewise fortunate in his actors, who have been splendidly directed. As the tortured young woman, Lillian Gish gives a performance instinct with the spirit of the drama. Never did an actress play a part with more sincerity or deeper comprehension. As the poet, whom Mr. O'Casey describes as the dreamer, Bramwell Fletcher brilliantly avoids the maudlin quagmires of the part. Moffat Johnston's bishop is a strong, clear, illuminating performance. As a slatternly old woman, Mary Morris plays superbly with a hint of the grand manner in tragedy. Ralph Cullinan has a voice that is perfect in tone for a play of this sort; as the foreman of the garden, he can impregnate a speech with the virtue of fantasy. John Daly Murphy gives a pungent performance as a park derelict. Phil Bishop introduces a hearty note of comedy as a querulous park sage. Byron McGrath's Salvation Army officer is soberly persuasive. In the long cast it would be hard to find a single actor who does not measure up to his part of the theme.

But all this merely reiterates the fundamental fact that Mr. O'Casey has written a great play. There is iron in its bones and blood in its veins and lustre in its flesh, and its feet rest on the good brown earth. In fact, it is a humbling job to write about a dynamic drama like "Within the Gates."

1934 O 23

THE CHILDREN'S HOUR, a drama in three acts, by Lillian Hellman. Settings by Aline Bernstine, executed by Sointu Syrjala. Staged and produced by Herman Shumlin at Maxine Elliott's Theatre.

Peggy Rogers ....Eugenia Rawls
Mrs. Lily Mortar ....Aline McDermott
Evelyn Munn ....Elizabeth Seckel
Helen Burton ....Lynne Fisher
Lois Fisher ....Jacqueline Rusling
Catherine ....Barbara Leeds
Rosalie Wells ....Barbara Beals
Mary Tilford ....Florence McGee
Karen Wright ....Katherine Emery
Martha Dobie ....Anne Revere
Dr. Joseph Cardin ....Robert Keith
Agatha ....Edmonia Nolley
Mrs. Amelia Tilford .....Katherine Emmet
A Grocery Boy ....Jack Tyler

By BROOKS ATKINSON.

If the author and the producer of "The Children's Hour," which was acted at Maxine Elliott's last evening, can persuade themselves to ring down the curtain when their play is over, they will deserve the admiration and respect of the theatregoer. For Lillian Hellman has written a venomously tragic play of life in a girls' boarding school—cutting in the sharpness of its dramatic style and in the deadly accu-

racy of the acting. In the last ten or fifteen minutes of the final act she tries desperately to discover a mettlesome dramatic conclusion; having lured "The Children's Hour" away from the theatre into the sphere of human life, she pushes it back among the Ibsenic dolls and baubles by refusing to stop talking. Please, Miss Hellman, conclude the play before the pistol shot and before the long arm of coincidence starts wabbling in its socket. When two people are defeated by the malignance of an aroused public opinion, leave them the dignity of their hatred and despair.

The point is that Karen Wright and Martha Dobie, headmistresses of a girls' boarding-school, are innocent. After many years of industry they have developed a country school with an enviable reputation. Among their students, however, is Mary Tilford, granddaughter of their chief patroness, and Mary is a diabolical adolescent. Miss Hellman has drawn that evil character with brilliant understanding of the vagaries of child nature. Purely as a matter of malicious vanity, Mary spreads the rumor that the headmistresses have an unnatural affection for each other. Horrified and convinced, her grandmother withdraws Mary from the school and warns the parents of other students. The scandal destroys the school and turns the two headmistresses into social exiles. To recover their self-respect, as well as the prestige of the school, they bring a libel action against Mrs. Tilford, but they cannot prove their innocence. That dazed and defeated situation seems to this correspondent to be the logical as well as the most overpowering conclusion to the play.

Having a lamentable respect for the theatre, Miss Hellman then pushes on into suicide and footlights remorse. She gilds the lily until it loses its freshness. For up to that moment "The Children's Hour" is one of the most straightforward, driving dramas of the season, distinguished chiefly for its unflinching characterization of little Mary. She is a vicious maid, but her strength and courage are tremendous. Her capacity for lying, cruelty and sadistic leadership is almost genius. That is the crucial character for two acts of the play. It has not only been ruthlessly drawn in the writing, but it is superlatively well acted by Florence McGee, who forces every drop of poison out of it. She plays it with as much spirit as a wildcat and considerably more craft and intelligence. In fact, you do not know whether to admire Miss McGee for her headlong acting or to fear the tyrannical part she is acting.

Nor is that the only piece of acting to admire in this piercingly directed production. Mr. Shumlin has chosen his actor. thoughtfully and directed them with a clear mind. Anne Revere's reticent Martha Dobie and Katherine Emery's broken Karen Wright are portraits of dramatic significance. Robert Keith plays the part of a manly fiancé with splendid decision, and Katherine Emery plays the sanctimonious patroness with womanly pride and genteel rectitude. As a supercilious and vile-tempered aunt, Alice McDermott gives an excellent performance. All the girls are well acted, especially Barbara Beals's overwrought little Rosalie.

In short, Miss Hellman has written and Mr. Shumlin has produced a pitiless tragedy, and both of them have daubed it with grease-paint in the last quarter of an hour. Fortunately, they can remove that blemish. Instruct the guardian of the curtain to ring down when the two young women are facing a bleak future. That will turn "The Children's Hour" into vivid drama.

1934 N 21

By BROOKS ATKINSON.

ANYTHING GOES, a musical comedy in two acts and nine scenes. Music and lyrics by Cole Porter. Book by Guy Bolton and P. G. Wodehouse and revised by Howard Lindsay and Russel Crouse. Staged by Mr. Lindsay; dances and ensembles arranged by Robert Alton; settings by Donald Oenslager; costumes designed by Jenkins; produced by Vinton Freedley. At the Alvin Theatre.

Bartender	George E. Mack
Elisha J. Whitney	Paul Everton
Billy Crocker	William Gaxton
Bellboy	Irvin Pincus
Reno Sweeney	Ethel Merman
Reporter	Edward Delbridge
First camera man	Neal Evans
Second camera man	Leslie Barrie
Sir Evelyn Oakleigh	Bettina Hall
Hope Harcourt	
Mrs. Wadsworth T. Harcourt,	Helen Raymond
Bishop Dodson	Pacie Ripple
Ching	Richard Wang
Ling	Charlie Fang
Snooks	Drucilla Strain
Steward	William Stamm
Assistant purser	Val Vestoff
First Federal man	Harry Wilson
Second Federal man	Arthur Imperato
Mrs. Wentworth	May Abbey
Mrs. Frick	Florence Earle
Reverened Dr. Moon	Victor Moore
Bonnie Letour	Vera Dunn
Chief officer	Houston Richards
Ship's drunk	William Barry
Mr. Swift	Maurice Elliot
Little boy	Billy Curtis
Captain	John C. King
Babe	Vivian Vance
The Foursome	Marshall Smith / Ray Johnson / Dwight Snyder / Dee Porter
The Ritz Quartette	Chet Bree / Bill Stamm / Neal Evans / Ed. Delbridge
The Alvin Quartette	Arthur Imperato / David Glidden / Richard Nealy / Stuart Fraser
Ship's Orchestra	The Stylists

By keeping their sense of humor uppermost, they have made a thundering good musical show out of "Anything Goes," which was put on at the Alvin last evening. They are Guy Bolton and P. G. Wodehouse, whose humor is completely unhackneyed; Cole Porter, who has written a dashing score with impish lyrics, and Howard Lindsay and Russel Crouse, who have been revising the jokes in person. After all, these supermen must have had a good deal to do with the skylarking that makes "Anything Goes" such hilarious and dynamic entertainment. But when a show is off the top shelf of the pantry cupboard it is hard to remember that the comics have not written all those jokes and the singers have not composed all those exultant tunes. If Ethel Merman did not write "I Get a Kick Out of You" and also the title song of the show she has made them hers now by the swinging gusto of her platform style.

Do you remember a pathetic, unsteady little man who answers to the name of Alexander Throttlebottom? Masquerading in the program as Victor Moore, he is the first clown of this festival, and he is tremendously funny. For it has occurred to the wastrels who wrote the book to represent him as a gangster disguised as a parson and to place him on a liner bound for Europe. Among the other passengers are a night-club enchantress, who sings with the swaggering authority of Ethel Merman, and a roistering man about town who enjoys the infectious exuberance of William Gaxton. There is also a lady of considerable breeding who can sing the soprano of Bettina Hall.

What a voyage! Last year Howard Lindsay staged a memorable comedy entitled "She Loves Me Not." What he learned there in the vein of theatre versatility he has generously applied to "Anything Goes," and the product is a rag, tag and bobtail of comic situations and of music sung in the spots when it is most exhilarating. Throttlebottom loks mighty absurd in those prelate's vestments. When his gangster blood comes through his disguise and his bewildered personality, comedy is the most satisfying invention of the human race. He calls his portable machine gun "My little pal putt-putt-putt" with a dying inflection. He muses on the advisability of bumping off an annoying passenger as if he were composing a wistful sonnet. Whatever he does, Mr. Throttlebottom, who is just as sweet under any other name, is the quintessence of musical comedy humor, and the authors of "Anything Goes" have given him the sort of thing he can do best.

As far as that goes, it suits William Gaxton, too. Following the lead of a madcap book, he is in and out of all sorts of disguises—a sailor, a Spanish nobleman with false whiskers just clipped off a Pomeranian, a fabulous public enemy. Through the show he fairly dances with enjoyment and high spirits, making every song sound good on his old Gaxiolaphone. When he sings with Miss Merman the composer ought to be very grateful for a pair of performers who can make every note burst with vitality and every line sound like a masterpiece of wit. "You're the Top" is one of the most congenial songs Mr. Porter has written. Mr. Gaxton and Miss Merman put their toes as well as their voices into it.

Although Miss Hall has a nicer talent, she plays the part of a girl of exalted station with winning good humor and she sings "All Through the Night" with the thrilling beauty of a trained artist. For minor diversion there is a foursome of dry-humored sailors for whom Mr. Porter has written a droll chanty. Count as items worth sober consideration a platoon of chorus girls whose dancing is also well-planned; a suit of Oenslager settings; a wardrobe of gowns by Jenkins—and a general good time. Guy Bolton and P. G. Wodehouse were always funny fellows. It does them no harm to be associated with Cole Porter, Howard Lindsay, Russel Crouse and a thundering good song-and-dance show.

1934 N 22.

ROMEO AND JULIET, Shakespeare's play in two acts and twenty-three scenes, arranged by Katharine Cornell. Staged by

Guthrie McClintic; settings by Jo Mielziner; dances directed by Martha Graham; incidental music by Paul Nordoff; revived by Miss Cornell for four and a half weeks. At the Martin Beck Theatre.

Escalus ....Reynolds Evans
Paris ....George Macready
Montague ....John Miltern
Capulet ....Moroni Olsen
An Old Man ....Arthur Chatterton
Romeo ....Basil Rathbone
Mercutio ....Brian Aherne
Benvolio ....John Emery
Tybalt ....Orson Welles
Friar Laurence ....Charles Waldron
Friar John ....Paul Julian
Balthasar ....Franklyn Gray
Sampson ....Joseph Holland
Peter ....David Vivian
Gregory ....Robert Champlain
Abraham ....Irving Morrow
An Apothecary ....Arthur Chatterton
Officer ....Irving Morrow
Guards ......Angus Duncan, Ralph Nelson
Lady Montague ....Brenda Forbes
Lady Capulet ....Irby Marshal
Juliet ....Katharine Cornell
Nurse ....Edith Evans
A Stret Singer ....Edith Allaire
Chorus ....Orson Welles
Citizens of Verona, Kinsfolk of both houses, Maskers, Watchmen and Attendants—Margaret Craven, Jacqueline De Wit, Lois Jameson Agnete Johansen. Ruth March, Pamela Simpson, Gilmore Bush, John Gordon Gage, William Hopper, Albert McCleery, Charles Thorne.

By BROOKS ATKINSON.

Having avoided Shakespeare until she believed herself ready to play him, Miss Cornell has hung another jewel on the cheek of the theatre's nights. Her "Romeo and Juliet," which she put on at the Martin Beck last evening, is on the high plane of modern magnificence. Probably no one expected anything less radiant from her resourceful workshops, where she and Guthrie McClintic prepare the dramas for her repertory. But the result is no less exalting to those who sit before the footlights, listen to the lines of Shakespeare's verse on the lips of modern actors and reflect the glow of Jo Mielziner's costumes and settings. For this is an occasion. When it is produced conscientiously and played with romantic and tragic candor "Romeo and Juliet" is a drama that drains the playgoer's emotions. In these circumstances all a reviewer can say is "Bravo!"

Being an actress who respects the drama above everything, Miss Cornell has been faithful to the text and taken pains to see that it tells a closely woven narrative. It is off in a rush; it hurries on through the ball to the sweet rapture of the balcony scene; and the tragedy it plumbs in the final tomb scene is the overpowering conclusion to a tremendous drama of idealized passions. Having a respect for the drama, Miss Cornell surrounds herself with superior actors. The Nurse of Edith Evans is a masterpiece. The Friar Laurence of Charles Waldron is brimming with fatherly affection and a good man's anxiety. As Romeo and Mercutio, Basil Rathbone and Brian Aherne, respectively, are not of first quality, in this reviewer's opinion, but they are able actors who do not let the drama down. Add to this Mr. McClintic's direction, which has an eye for stage grouping, and a sense of life throbbing through a spacious script, and Mr. Mielziner's brilliantly executed décor, and you have a "Romeo and Juliet" that will endure in the memory of our theatre.

Perhaps vitality is its fundamental motive. Certainly Miss Cornell's Juliet is vital. Looking especially lovely in the flowing vestments of a decorative period, she plays with an all-consuming fervor that takes the big scenes with the little and works them all into a pattern of star-crossed youthfulness. For girlishness there is the gayety of the evening festival and the ardor and vagrant mischief of the balcony scene. For tragedy there is the brave submission of that scene in the tomb. Since it is entirely a modern production of that style of its attack, Miss Cornell speaks her lines without declamation, and the singing in them comes more from the heart than the throat. There have been excellent Juliets within the last twelve years —one by Jane Cowl and another by Eva Le Gallienne. But Miss Cornell's is a complete re-creation— with the suppleness of an actress and the imperious quality of an artist who plays from within. Shakespeare has a vital servant in Miss Cornell.

Mr. Rathbone is a neat and tidy actor with an immaculate exterior. Within those limitations he plays a sufficient Romeo. The verse needs more virtuosity in speaking than he has at his command, for he is not always intelligible. When fortune goes against Romeo Mr. Rathbone can raise his voice in vigorous lamentation, but he lacks the emotional range to play the part all the way through. As Mercutio, Mr. Aherne is volatile and gay; it is, in fact, an enviable part and Mr. Aherne enjoys playing it. Perhaps that is its weakness, for he carries his exuberance to the point of scattering the character, and he speaks the Queen Mab lines in a casual style that loses the fancy of Shakespeare's verse.

Those are petty matters which a reviewer dislikes insisting upon in the presence of a fine performance of a heady drama. For there are no shabby patches in this "Romeo and Juliet." Orsen Welles's Tybalt, Moroni Olsen's Capulet, Irby Marshall's Lady Capulet and George Macready's Paris are instances of minor parts played with something better than minor authority. Miss Cornell has kept faith with her audiences by giving "Romeo and Juliet" a thoroughly sifted performance. She has kept faith with herself by acting Juliet with the humility of an artist who respects her material. Fortunately, she is a great actress, and that is why her Juliet is a deeply moving idealization of fate.

1934 D 21

RAIN FROM HEAVEN, a play in three acts, by S. N. Behrman. Staged by Philip Moeller; setting by Lee Simonson; production committee, Theresa Helburn and Mr. Simonson; produced by the Theatre Guild as the third offering of its seventeenth subscription season. At the Golden Theatre.

Joan Eldridge...............Hancey Castle
Mrs. Dingle...........Alice Belmore-Cliffe
Rand Eldridge.................Ben Smith
Hobart Eldridge...........Thurston Hall
Lady Violet Wyngate...........Jane Cowl
Hugo Willens.................John Halliday
Sascha Barashaev.........Marshall Grant
Phoebe Eldridge.................Lily Cahill
Clendon Wyatt...........Statts Cottsworth
Nikolai Jurin...................Jose Ruben

By BROOKS ATKINSON.

Out of the muddled tension of the contemporary world S. N. Behrman has spun a silken drawing-room comedy, "Rain From Heaven," with which the Theatre Guild celebrated Christmas Eve at the Golden. Under the rippling of the humor and the crackle of the wit it has a few sapient words to say about Fascism, Communism and Hitler's scourge of the Jews. Mr. Behrman is the ideal writer of comedy of manners because he never lets a joke go contrary to his principles and he does not create characters for a laugh. Lady Wyngate's house guests just outside London represent nearly every shade of cultivated intelligence of the Western World. For three acts they talk with captivating grace and polite anxiety about love, politics and the destiny of the human race. If Mr. Behrman wants to break a lance for any one of our aching causes he will have to bear down a good deal harder and post his principles on a placard where we can read them in literal words. But for sheer dexterity of style and decency of motive "Rain From Heaven" achieves an enviable perfection. Mr. Behrman has a gift that the theatre has never tarnished.

In "Rain From Heaven" he is neatly placing in opposition a group of characters who have a social resemblance but who represent antagonistic political points of view. Lady Violet Wyngate is a wealthy widow who has an instinct for championing lost causes. She is in love with an American aviation hero who, having just returned triumphantly from the Antarctic, is innocent of almost every problem of the day. Among her guests are a music critic who has been exiled from Germany for illegal blood content; a rich American who is fighting for a Fascist state to safeguard his property; a Russian exiled by the Communist dictatorship; a Rhodes scholar; a promising Jewish pianist; a tenacious American wife who does not love her husband, and her daughter, whose cross is that she is in love.

Without leading them on by inventing noisy dramatic crises, Mr. Behrman manages to turn his characters completely inside out. His gift for dialogue is so extraordinary that the process is marvelously engaging. "Rain From Heaven" is a play without action that gives the impression of skipping along at a giddy tempo. Although nothing of cosmic importance appears to be happening, the hostility of the ideas is so keen that at the concluding curtain Lady Wyngate's household of guests is quite transmogrified.

Ideas, stung by a little womanly guile, have closed the gates on every character in Mr. Behrman's cast. Although they are social equals, their principles, prejudices and experiences in the jangle of the contemporary world have shut them off from each other. In its bright, dainty and luminous way "Rain From Heaven" is tragedy in the parlor.

Mr. Moeller has directed an iridescent performance. As Lady Wyngate, Jane Cowl, who has been one of our recent absentees, gives an infinitely accomplished performance in which charm is seasoned with intelligence and compassion. John Halliday, who has likewise

been among the missing, returns to Broadway to play the exiled music critic like an actor and a gentleman. For avarice there is Thurston Hall, whose wholeness of character statement is an asset in any play; and for rueful good manners among Russian emigrés there is José Ruben, who is one of the best in the profession. As the wife with a serpent's cunning it is to be feared that Lily Cahill has a better figure than acting style. But that is the only rigid corner in the performance housed by a Lee Simonson setting. Mr. Behrman's comedy of manners is full of glints and graces. Doubtless it is wiser than a hurried theatregoer can appreciate on the basis of one holiday impression.

1934 D 25

ACCENT ON YOUTH, a comedy in thi acts, by Samson Raphaelson. Staged L Benn W. Levy; setting by Jo Mielziner; produced by Crosby Gaige. At the Plymouth Theatre.

Miss Darling.................Eleanor Hicks
Frank Galloway...........Ernest Lawford
Dickie Reynolds...........Theodore Newton
Linda Brown...........Constance Cummings
Steven Gaye..............Nicholas Hannen
Flogdell.....................Ernest Cossart
Genevieve Lang.............Irene Purcell
Chuck.....................William Carpenter
Butch...........................Al Moore

By BROOKS ATKINSON.

Being in a dressing-gown mood, Samson Raphaelson has written one of those comedies that dance on the border-line between the theatre and life, "Accent on Youth," which was put on at the Plymouth last evening. His principal character is a celebrated playwright; what happens in his private life becomes intricately involved with his talent for theatre technique. Since Molnar and Pirandello, and no doubt many others, have lifted gay baubles off that comedy counter, Mr. Raphaelson need not hesitate to look over the stock of goods himself. He is not the most versatile of playwrights, and "Accent on Youth" is frail and very much too long. But these comments are written by one who thoroughly enjoyed the first act and never lost interest in the less clear-headed improvisations that follow. The cast is excellent. The idea is full of comedy implications. Although Mr. Raphaelson is not the man to squeeze the most out of them, or to tell a fable without hesitating, he is light-fingered enough to keep the amusement sly and ingratiating. "Accent on Youth" is on the verge of becoming a genuinely captivating play.

In his early fifties Steven Gaye, famous for his comedies, has written the tragedy of an old man who loves a young girl. Although he is enthusiastic about it, he realizes that something is spurious in the construction. When he impulsively decides to abandon playwriting for good, and gives his young secretary notice, she takes her dismissal with ill grace. She blurts out that she is in love with him. As a man he is flattered and interested. But Steven has been a playwright too long not to have a detached interest in the problem of making life fit the theatre, and a large part of his interest in his secretary is the light she throws upon the problem of his play. By lifting his secretary's avowal intact he removes the one false note in his tragedy. He falls in love with her. Although she loves him, he is not without rivals. Through two less firmly written acts, Mr. Raphaelson records their varying fortunes with one foot in the theatre and the other reluctantly feeling around for the security of life.

If the story were all Mr. Raphaelson had to give, "Accent on Youth" might be less genial entertainment. But he has a facility for dropping comic lines into the dialogue occasionally, and he has refurbished the venerable comedy butler in the bumptious image of Ernest Cossart. Now, Mr. Cossart is as droll a clown as the theatre can offer. His figure is affably portly, his manner is mischievously grave, and his eyes dance with merriment. There are many scenes in which Mr. Cossart reclaims the play from prosiness by speaking the word "bizarre" so that it sounds funny, or by complimenting a guest on a recipe for biscuits. But none of them is quite so crack-brained as the scene in which he shows how he can touch his knuckles to the floor. A neat trick for those who can do it. Ernest Lawford also did it last evening, but when he bent down there was a woeful rip at the shoulder and a moment of polite anxiety.

Among other items, "Accent on Youth" offers Constance Cummings, better known on the screen than in the theatre. As the smitten secretary, she is not only glowing with youth but she is also an amiable actress. Nicholas Hannen plays

the dramatist with the skill of a mature actor. Irene Purcell as a capricious lady of the stage, Ernest Lawford as a comradely actor and Theodore Newton as an impetuous youth give able performances. As the director, Benn W. Levy has caught admirably the casual tempo of the script, but in collaboration with Mr. Raphaelson he could improve the performance by winnowing a half hour out of it.

The production is attractive, enclosed within a hospitable study designed by Jo Mielziner. Although Mr. Raphaelson's style is attenuated and frequently uncertain, "Accent on Youth" is attractive also. To lift one of his choicest lines, it may "not be a smash hit like a Eugene O'Neill drama, or a dismal failure like a Eugene O'Neill drama," but it is lightly good-humored and pleasantly insane.

1934 D 26

1935

THE PETRIFIED FOREST, a play in two acts, by Robert Emmett Sherwood. Staged by Arthur Hopkins; settings by Raymond Sovey; produced by Gilbert Miller and Leslie Howard, in association with Mr. Hopkins. At the Broadhurst Theatre.

A Telegrapher	Milo Boulton
Another Telegrapher	James Doody
Boze Hertzlinger	Frank Milan
Jason Maple	Walter Vonnegut
Paula	Esther Woodruff Leeming
Gramp Maple	Charles Dow Clark
Gabby Maple	Peggy Conklin
Alan Squire	Leslie Howard
Herb	Robert Porterfield
Mrs. Chisholm	Blanche Sweet
Mr. Chisholm	Robert Hudson
Joseph	John Alexander
Jackie	Ross Hertz
Ruby	Tom Fadden
Duke Mantee	Humphrey Bogart
Pyles	Slim Thompson
Commander Klepp	Aloysius Cunningham
Hendy	Guy Conradi
Sheriff	Frank Tweeddell
A Deputy	Eugene Keith
Another Deputy	Harry Sherwin

By BROOKS ATKINSON.

If it is not unethical to say so in the first sentence, Robert Sherwood's new show is a peach. He calls it "The Petrified Forest," and Leslie Howard appeared in it at the Broadhurst last evening. But be not deceived by the austerity of the title, for "The Petrified Forest" is a roaring Western melodrama with a few artful decorations of thought, sentiment and humor. Mr. Sherwood has been writing droll plays for nearly a decade; sometimes he has had difficulty in shaping them according to the theatre's image. But "The Petrified Forest" belongs close up to the footlights. Being pretty much in love with America, Mr. Sherwood has spun an exuberant tale of poetic vagabonds and machine-gun desperadoes; and Arthur Hopkins has drawn the tang of the open spaces into the direction. For literate melodrama, written by a man who is mentally restless in a changing world, "The Petrified Forest" is good, gusty excitement.

If it differs somewhat from conventional shooting shows, it is because Mr. Sherwood has taken an interest in his characters. They are collected around a gas station and lunchroom in the Eastern Arizona desert. Mr. Sherwood introduces them leisurely—Gabby Maple, whose mother is French and lives in France and who dreams of unimaginable beauties; Alan Squire, a disillusioned and futile intellectual who is on the road in search of something in which to believe; and at the point of several machine-guns Duke Mantee's gang, who are roaring down the road to the border and who drop in for a bite to eat. Jolted out of their complacence by the presence of these wild men, Mr Sherwood's characters indulge themselves in considerable astonishing autobiography. When the Sheriff's posse draws up, there is some excellent shooting and a desperate attempt to escape. But Mr. Sherwood has a little wistful heroism for his concluding scene and a few drops of sentiment that will do no theatregoer any harm.

As a matter of fact, Mr. Sherwood takes enormous pleasure in the company he is keeping. Even Duke Mantee, as you may have guessed, is a good egg according to his lights, and he leaves the gas station with one final shot and a pretty good impression. Meanwhile, Mr. Sherwood takes fair advantage of the situation by dropping a few sensible comments in the style of the crossroads philosopher—making a wry face at the American Legion, which will not like what he has to say, praising nature and ruminating over the state of the nation. All this he tells either in a vein of genial humor or with a bold literary flavor. If the talk sounds a little pretentious—no hard feelings, pal. It is good talk and Mr. Sherwood believes it.

At any rate, it sounds good as it slips off Leslie Howard's honeyed tongue. As the pensive intellectual who is passing through on foot Mr. Howard has things to say that might sound priggish if they were not beautifully spoken. But he has long been one of the finest of the theatre's breed, and this is one of his most winning performances, and it is a pleasure to take the part at his word. If a modern writer must die for the love of a newfound maid, let Mr. Howard do it just before the curtain comes down.

Under the benign influence of Mr. Hopkins's direction, all the actors are in fine fettle. Peggy Conklin gives her most perceptive performance to date as the gas-station dryad. Humphrey Bogart does the best work of his career as the motorized guerrilla. In the part of the garrulous old man of the desert Charles Dow Clark is vastly enjoyable. Blanche Sweet has a comic moment of character revelation as the resentful wife of a dull financier. Frank Milan as an amorous halfback and Walter Vonnegut as a pious Legionist give excellent performances. All the gangsters play with the braggart explosiveness of their breed.

Raymond Sovey has put a good roof over the drama. Mr. Sherwood and Mr. Hopkins have thought of everything else that is necessary. "The Petrified Forest" is an excellent vehicle for Mr. Sherwood's ideas and Mr. Howard's manifold gifts. In addition to that, it is a peach of a show, if it is not unethical to say so in the last sentence.

1935 Ja 8

ESCAPE ME NEVER! A play in three acts and eight scenes, by Margaret Kennedy. Settings and direction by Theodore Komisarjevsky; incidental music arranged by Leslie Bridgewater; produced by the Theatre Guild, in association with Charles B. Cochran, as the fourth play of its seventeenth subscription season. At the Shubert Theatre.

Sir Ivor McClean........Leon Quartermaine
Lady McClean................Katie Johnson
Fenella McClean...............Eve Turner
Woman Tourist...............Sh'ela Taylor
First Tourist.................Cyril Horrocks
Second Tourist................John Boxer
Caryl Sanger...............Griffith Jones
Butler.....................Bruno Barnabe
Herr Heinrich........William F. Schoeller
Gemma Jones...........Elisabeth Bergner
Sebastian Sanger............Hugh Sinclair
Walter.......................Peter Bull

First Spinster..................Joan Blair
Second Spinster.............Muriel Johnston
Mrs. Brown......................Joan Blair
Wilson.........................John Boxer
Petrova......................Nina Bucknall
Dresser....................Muriel Johnston
Pianist.....................Cyril Horrocks
Messenger....................William Mills
Miss Regan....................Susan Brown
First Man.......................Peter Bull
Second Man.....................John Boxer
Third Man.......................A. J. Felix
Stallkeeper.................Cyril Horrocks
Man........................Bruno Barnabe
Woman......................Muriel Johnston
Girl..........................Jane Vaughan

By BROOKS ATKINSON.

Whether Elisabeth Bergner is a great actress or not is difficult to determine on the basis of one evening at the theatre in her presence. But now that the curtain has just come down on her performance in "Escape Me Never!" it is a privilege to believe the best. She is the stuff of which angels are fashioned behind .the footlights. Margaret Kennedy has written for her a mediocre but sufficient companion piece to "The Constant Nymph." After a long career in London, it arrived last evening at the Shubert Theatre under the joint production of the Theatre Guild and Charles B. Cochran. As the bedraggled mate of one of the gypsy Sangers, Miss Bergner plays like a fiery particle in the theatre's firmament. She is slight and small, with flaxen hair; she has little of the imposing personal beauty of the conventional star, and she employs none of the theatre's aids to comeliness in make-up or costumery. But her acting has the insubstantiality of the breeze; it is light and spontaneous and gloriously free. If Congress is so omnipotent about immigration laws, surely it is powerful enough to make sure that Miss Bergner never again leaves this country except for a brief vacation.

In "The Constant Nymph," the Sangers were a bad lot, though endearing. They have not improved much in the present generation. The most gifted and unscrupulous of them, who is Sebastian and Hugh Sinclair simultaneously, takes up with a footless little wretch, Gemma Jones, who is Miss Bergner. The story is of Sebastian's cruelty and treachery and of Gemma's unearthly loyalty and devotion. Harum-scarum though she is, she has the wisdom of the ages. Although the gods are hard on her, she knows what they have planned for her and she does not rebel.

In spite of considerable loose storytelling, Miss Kennedy has recaptured a good deal of the wonder and vagabond rapture of "The Constant Nymph" characters. For Miss Bergner's purposes that is ideal. She translates Gemma into an inspired creature, who is half brat and half dryad. Sometimes she is only a gutter-snipe with common manners and an instinct for vulgar mockery. Sometimes she is pure spirit. It is impossible to tell what craft she has slipped into her characterization, for she dances through with incomparable buoyancy as though it were a fresh improvisation. No doubt Gemma Jones will be much the same character at tonight's performance. But those of us who were enkindled by its humor last evening and touched by its poignancy could swear that she had created it on the spur of the moment and could never recover the same impulses again.

Under Komisarjevsky's direction the fable is told with suppleness and eagerness. In the part of Sebastian Hugh Sinclair gives a magnificent performance that is quite equal to a searching occasion. In the less ingratiating parts of another Sanger and his sweetheart, Griffith Jones and Eve Turner give excellent performances; and the long cast includes Leon Quartermaine and William F. Schoeller, who are actors of mettle and experience. In addition to directing the performance, Komisarjevsky has designed the settings, some of which are imaginative, though some are only dull.

But by common consent this is Miss Bergner's occasion. "The soul of an artist" is a hackneyed phrase, but we can hardly escape it here, for her acting is lighted from within. When she appears on the stage, she is a free spirit, and she frees those who watch her from their memories of a world that is still blundering through the choked streets outside the theatre.

1935 Ja 22,

Waiting For Lefty

GROUP THEATRE SKETCHES, by Sanford Meisner, Florence Cooper, Bob Lewis, Clifford Odets, J. E. Bromberg, Walter Coy, Elia Kazan, Tony Kraber, Morris Carnovsky.
WAITING FOR LEFTY, play in six scenes, by Clifford Odets. Directed by Sanford Meisner and Clifford Odets. At the Civic Repertory Theatre.

Fatt.......................Morris Carnovsky
Joe.............................Art Smith
Edna..........................Ruth Nelson
Miller.......................Gerrit Kraber
Fayette..................Morris Carnovsky

Irv...........................Walter Coy
Florrie.....................Phoebe Brand
Sid...........................Jules Garfield
Clayton.....................Russell Collins
Clancy.......................Elia Kazan
Gunman.................David Korchmar
Henchman....................Alan Baxter
Secretary....................Paula Miller
Actor......................William Challee
Grady...................Morris Carnovsky
Dr. Barnes................Roman Bohnen
Dr. Benjamin.............Luther Adler
Agate Keller.............J. E. Bromberg
A man........................Bob Lewis
Voices in the audience....Herbert Ratner,
              Clifford Odets, Lewis Leverett

By BROOKS ATKINSON.

As actors in plays of conscious intellectual significance, the young people of the Group Theatre have been fumbling around without much success ever since they mounted "Men In White." But their afternoon program, consisting of random sketches and Clifford Odets's "Waiting for Lefty," which was repeated yesterday at the Civic Repertory Theatre, is an invigorating revelation of their skill and force as an acting company. For the first time in a good many months it is possible to write about them without fussy reservations. Like many other individuals and organizations, the Group Theatre is most stimulating when it is not competing with the entertainment business on Broadway, which is not interested in the studio craft of acting nor in the drama of social revolution.

Uptown the Group Theatre communicants are suspected of having no sense of humor. Nothing said between these column rules this morning is intended to suggest that they are native wits or mountebanks. But the fact remains that their bill of turns and improvisations is winningly good-humored. Their classroom presentation of the grave-digger scene from "Hamlet" is an amusing proof of the fact that words are less significant in the drama than acting styles and ideas of direction. In a nonsensical improvisation, labeled "Two Bums on a Bench," Mr. Bromberg and Mr. Carnovsky suggest that the written word is virtually superfluous, for they clown their way through an unintelligible comic sketch speaking nothing but gibberish. The most overpowering number in the preliminary program is entirely in pantomime to the off-stage music of the allegretto of Beethoven's Seventh symphony. What psychological effect the music has in the theatre this reporter is unable to explain on the spur of the moment. But without props, scenery or costumes Mr. Bromberg and two assistants translate their pantomimic surgical operation into a vivid silent drama. Among the other items there are parodies, slapstick bits and unblushing cowboy songs.

The dynamics of the program are the property of Mr. Odets's "Waiting for Lefty." His saga, based on the New York taxi strike of last year, is clearly one of the most thorough, trenchant jobs in the school of revolutionary drama. It argues the case for a strike against labor racketeering and the capitalist state by using the theatre auditorium as the hall where the taxi union is meeting. In four or five subordinate scenes, played with a few bare props in corners of the stage, the personal problems of several representative insurgents are drawn sharply. Mr. Odets is the author of "Awake and Sing!" which the Group Theatre expects to produce next week. "Waiting for Lefty" is soundly constructed and fiercely dramatic in the theatre, and it is also a keen preface to his playwriting talents.

His associates in the Group Theatre have never played with more thrust, drive and conviction. "Waiting for Lefty" suits them down to the boards. Incidentally, the progress of the revolutionary drama in New York City during the last two seasons is the most obvious recent development in our theatre. In addition to the Theatre Union, with its productions of "Stevedore" and "Sailors of Cattaro," there is the Artef band, which is playing "Recruits" in Yiddish as beautifully as the Habima troupe played "The Dybbuk." Now the Group Theatre gives its most slashing performance in a drama about the taxi strike. This program will be repeated at intervals this Winter.

1935 F 11

AWAKE AND SING! A play in three acts, by Clifford Odets. Staged by Harold Clurman; setting by Boris Aronson; produced by the Group Theatre. At the Belasco Theatre.

Myron Berger ....Art Smith
Bessie Berger ....Stella Adler
Jacob ....Morris Carnovsky
Hennie Berger ....Phoebe Brand
Ralph Berger ....Jules Garfield
Schlosser ....Roman Bohnen
Moe Axelrod ....Luther Adler
Uncle Morty ....J. E. Bromberg
Sam Feinschreiber ....Sanford Meisner

By BROOKS ATKINSON.

After experimenting with scripts

from several different hands, the Group Theatre has found its most congenial playwright under its own roof, Clifford Odets, whose "Awake and Sing!" was acted at the Belasco last evening. He has been for some time one of the Group actors, and he is the author of "Waiting for Lefty," the dynamic play in one act which has been done several times at special performances this Winter. Now he is writing in three acts a vigorous and closely matted drama of Jewish life in the Bronx, and nine members of the Group Theatre play it with stunning power. Having considerable power in his own right, Mr. Odets has written a drama that is full of substance and vitality; he is not afraid to tackle a big job. But it is necessary to add that he does not quite finish what he has started in this elaborately constructed piece. Although he is very much awake, he does not sing with the ease and clarity of a man who has mastered his score.

The home-life of his Bronx family is volcanic. His characters are drawn in several directions. Having brought up her family by force of her own character, Bessie Berger is a tyrant whose one ambition is to preserve her home. Under her roof she harbors a husband who is an amiable bungler and an aging father who is a student of revolution and a lover of the great arts. Her daughter is an unhappy and rebellious girl who creates the first crisis in the play by confessing that she is pregnant by a boy whose identity she will not reveal. Her son is a scatter-minded lad whose impulses are thwarted by his mother. For good measure, there is also a bitter neighborhood racketeer who is in love with the daughter and rebels against all his own impulses. These are the main characters. They are all excitable, restless and at loose ends; and they are generally flying at one another's throats.

Although Mr. Odets has a story to tell, his method is to infuse it with the development of his characters; the story cannot be dissociated for a moment from its people. In other words, he means to be a dramatist rather than a playwright. In this instance the defect of the method is the lack of clarity and simplicity in his writing. Although his dialogue has uncommon strength, his drama in the first two acts is wanting in the ordinary fluidity of a play. For two acts it is turbulent—packed with noisy, lunging humanity. In the last act Mr. Odets comes to at least two conclusions, and the daughter and son who have been dwelling in the dust awake and sing the melody of free people. When he succeeds in loosening the play from the bonds of his tense craftsmanship, Mr. Odets has the fervor and the skill in direct assertion that are the admirable qualities of "Waiting for Lefty." He may not be a master yet, but he has the ability to be one.

The Group Theatre actors play as if they felt at home inside Mr. Odets's Bronx saga. As the lonely, dreamy old man Morris Carnovsky plays with endearing gentleness; he is an actor of artistic eminence. Jules Garfield plays the part of the boy with a splendid sense of character development. As the daughter Phoebe Brand gives her most attractive performance. Stella Adler as the overbearing mother, Luther Adler as the half-malignant cigar-store lounger, J. E. Bromberg as a braggart garment vendor, Art Smith as the footless father and Sanford Meisner as a bloodless son-in-law give clearly imagined performances. Although Harold Clurman's direction seems to this reviewer to be overwrought and shrill, no one can complain that it is lacking in conviction.

So the Group Theatre batters its way on. To this student of the arts "Awake and Sing," in spite of its frenzy, is inexplicably deficient in plain, theatre emotion. There is something unyielding at the core of the play. Charge that comment off to the higher criticism. The pleasant news is that the Group Theatre has found a genuine writer among its own members and knows how to set his play to rattling on the boards.

1935 F 20

KIND LADY, a play in a prologue, three acts and an epilogue, by Edward Chodorov, with some assistance from George Haight. The play is based on a Hugh Walpole story called "The Silver Mask." Staged by H. C. Potter; setting by Jo Mielziner; produced by H. C. Potter and George Haight. At the Booth Theatre.

Mr. Foster .... Francis Compton
Mary Herries .... Grace George
Lucy Weston .... Irby Marshal
Rose .... Marie Paxton
Phyllis Glenning .... Florence Britton

Peter Santard ....Alan Bunce
Henry Abbott ....Henry Daniell
Ada ....Justine Chase
Doctor ....Alfred Rowe
Mr. Edwards ....Thomas Chalmers
Mrs. Edwards ....Elfrida Derwent
Aggie Edwards ....Barbara Shields
Gustav Rosenberg ....Jules Epailly

By BROOKS ATKINSON.

Since Grace George plays the leading part, it is easy to think well of "Kind Lady," which was acted with admirable skill at the Booth last evening. Edward Chodorov, who once wrote a raucous satire entitled "Wonder Boy," has adapted her play from a story by Hugh Walpole. Strictly speaking, it is mystery melodrama about a gang of clever rogues who hold a helpless lady captive in her own house and endeavor to seize her wealth. If it were directed and acted without finesse, it would scarcely disturb the Spring calm of Broadway. But H. C. Potter, of the rising young house of Potter & Haight, has cast it perfectly and directed it with infinite dexterity. The pitch is low; the performance is a study in ominous understatement. Beneath the well-bred quiet of the acting a story of subdued horror is told with agonizing suspense.

In case you are in the proper mood, imagine a wealthy, lonely lady with a kind heart who finds that her generosity has been imposed upon. She has befriended a cultivated vagrant who tries to interest her in his wretched family. His wife faints on her doorstep. The lady charitably takes her in. Presently, she finds that she is harboring a gang of thieves, who take over her house, cleverly disengage her from her friends and relatives and proceed to sell off her paintings and get control of her fortune.

In reviewing mystery plays it is customary not to give the plot away. But in the case of "Kind Lady" it is almost impossible to write anything without divulging essential information. For the natural story is the narrative of how the captive tries to win her freedom and how her captors keep her hidden away. Mr. Chodorov is a man of few words and impeccable literary taste. What makes "Kind Lady" exciting is the masque of austerity he uses to cover a torture tale.

Miss George is the gracious lady of our stage. As the warm-hearted victim of this play, her native reserve, her gentleness of manner and her gift for interior emotion turn her acting into a triumph of mettlesome subtlety. As the king of the thieves, Henry Daniell's bland and brazen good breeding is full of accomplished iniquity.

Against a skillfully gloomy setting by Jo Mielziner, Mr. Potter has assembled an excellent cast that includes Alan Bunce, Thomas Chalmers, Florence Britton, Elfrida Derwent, Irby Marshal and Francis Compton. They play in a style that is both casual and deliberate. Playgoers who relish sheer skill in theatrical statement will appreciate this astringent melodrama. Without once raising their voices, Mr. Chodorov and Mr. Potter have spun a yarn of crafty villainies.

1935 Ap 24

'At Home Abroad'

AT HOME ABROAD, a revue in two acts by Howard Dietz and Arthur Schwartz, with a bow to Raymond Knight. Scenery, costumes and direction provided by Vincente Minnelli; dances arranged by Gene Snyder and Harry Losee; dialogue staged by Thomas Mitchell; produced by the Shuberts. At the Winter Garden.
PRINCIPALS—Beatrice Lillie, Ethel Waters, Herb Williams, Eleanor Powell, Reginald Gardiner, Paul Haakon, Eddie Foy Jr., Vera Allen, Nina Whitney, James MacColl, Woods Miller, Six Spirits of Rhythm (Theodor Bonn, Douglas Daniels, Wilbur Daniels, Ernest Meyers, Virgil Scoggins and Leo Watson), Roy Campbell's Continentals, Sue Hasting's Marionettes and others but not wooden.

By BROOKS ATKINSON.

It is time to renew those old articles of faith in the theatre. Several nabobs of the stage, including Beatrice Lillie, have assembled the first accomplished revue of the season, "At Home Abroad," which was put on at the Winter Garden last evening. Howard Dietz and Arthur Schwartz, who have put words to music long before this, have supplied most of the material. Among the performers are Ethel Waters, Eleanor Powell, Paul Haakon, Herb Williams and Eddie

Foy Jr., whose talents are already familiar. What gives "At Home Abroad" its freshest beauty, however, is the scene and costume designing of Vincente Minnelli, who has also staged the production. Without resorting to opulence he has filled the stage with rich, glowing colors that give the whole work an extraordinary loveliness. Nothing quite so exhilarating as this has borne the Shubert seal before.

Under his direction the revue has such unity of appearance that it is more difficult than usual to pluck out the best numbers. The whole thing stirs with the life of superior stage entertainment. Count Miss Lillie as one of the chief ornaments. You will find her radiant comedy turning conventional glamour into humorous shoddy in several capital numbers—when she sings in mocking praise of Paree, when, as "Madcap Mitzi, the Toast of Vienna," she caricatures the stock musical comedy set piece, and when she performs with marvelous subtlety two excellent sketches written by Dion Titheradge. No one else can hover so skillfully between beauty and burlesque. When she appears in a stock number you always know which side she will take. But there is always the suggestion that Miss Lillie could be a music hall prima donna if her sense of humor were less brilliant.

Let us also speak a few words in praise of Ethel Waters, the gleaming tower of dusky regality, who knows how to make a song stand on tip-toe. Having sufficient appreciation of her talent the authors have written for her "Hottentot Potentate," which runs a high temperature, and "The Steamboat Whistle," which hails from Jamaica. Miss Waters can sing numbers like that with enormous lurking vitality; but she can also wear costumes. Mr. Minnelli has taken full advantage of that. He has set her in a jungle scene that is laden with magic, dressing her in gold bands and a star-struck gown of blue, and put her in a Jamaica set that looks like a modern painting. Miss Waters is decorative as well as magnetic.

The scheme of "At Home Abroad" is a travelogue. During the course of the evening Otis P. Hatrick, who is unsteady Herb Williams, and Henrietta Hatrick, who is Vera Allen, skip around the world. Not that the scheme is important. Every now and then it pauses long enough to let Eleanor Powell make your pulse beat with her tap-dancing, and Paul Haakon and Nina Whitney arouse your ad-

miration with the sweep of their dance duets. Although imitations have a bad reputation Reginald Gardiner redeems that art with a superb character study of the steam locomotive.

"At Home Abroad" is full of splendors, like the imaginative dance scheme entitled "The Lady With the Tap," where Miss Powell does her best work, and the seaside scene where Mr. Haakon dances with the grace of a young theatre god. The comedy is bright, shrewd and gay. The music is out of the best tune box, and Woods Miller sings the preludes like a gentleman. All this young Mr. Minnelli has wrapped up in a handsome package. . . . At last the season has begun.

1935 S 20

WINTERSET, a play in three acts, by Maxwell Anderson. Settings by Jo Mielziner; staged and produced by Guthrie McClintic. At the Martin Beck Theatre.

Trock	Eduardo Ciannelli
Shadow	Harold Johnsrud
Lucio	Morton L. Stevens
Piny	Fernanda Eliscu
Miriamne	Marge
Garth	Theodore Hecht
Esdras	Anatole Winogradoff
First Girl	Eva Langbord
Second Girl	Ruth Hammond
Hobo	John Philliber
Judge Gaunt	Richard Bennett
Carr	Billy Quinn
Mio	Burgess Meredith
Sailor	St. John Terrell
Radical	Abner Biberman
Policeman	Anthony Blair
Sergeant	Harold Martin
Two young Men	) Stanley Gould (Walter Holbrook

By BROOKS ATKINSON.

After having written in verse of heroes of history, Maxwell Anderson has gone one step further. In "Winterset," which was beautifully played at the Martin Beck last evening, he has written a verse tragedy of tatterdemalions along the East River waterfront. To report it with any sort of respectable decision a reviewer needs more time than there will be before the next edition. For "Winterset" is not all of a piece. There are moments in it when the verse seems superfluous or ostentatious, or when it seems actually to impede the drama. Before offering comment like that as final, however, one would like to be certain, for "Winterset" lives on a plane of high thinking, deep emotion and eloquent writing. It is packed with terror. It is a courageous poem to justice and integrity. In short, it is beautiful. Whether or not it is perfectly wrought does not seem to matter much at this moment.

There has been a legal murder. Some one has been convicted and executed for a pay-roll assassination he did not commit, and the gloomy ruin under one of the piers of Brooklyn Bridge is swarming with evil people who are determined to keep the secret buried. Trock, whose soul is blood-stained, is ready to kill every one else in the world lest his guilt be whispered. But the son of the man who was executed is walking the earth, bound that justice shall be done to his father's memory. He stumbles into the one human refuse heap where the evidence he needs is lurking. "Winterset" is the tragedy of his quest—of his love, his faith, his courage and his hatred of the world.

Some years ago Mr. Anderson wrote a stirring play in defense of Sacco and Vanzetti. The bitterness that lies deep in the souls of every one who believed in their innocence has shot "Winterset" through with ferocity against injustice. In some of the speeches that are screamed in a grimy, damp tenement basement on the waterfront it has ripened into poetry as hard as iron and as sharp as steel. Mr. Anderson is still raising his voice against the wickedness of society, and the tone is angry, rebellious and hot with scorn. With the romantic portions of his play he seems, in this reviewer's opinion, to be more self-conscious; and the tragedy concludes with an invocation that sounds formal and prolix. But when Mr. Anderson's personal convictions are engaged by the tragic story he is relating, he writes like a man inspired, and "Winterset" is a frightening drama laden with baleful significance. The emotion transcends the incidents that create it.

The production is a brilliant work of art. In the scene under the bridge Jo Mielziner has caught the remote majesty and immediate clutter of that vivid corner of the city; and his cheerless, barren tenement basement is a proper place for treachery and stealth. Mr. McClintic is up to this sort of thing and has collected actors worthy of high enterprise. As the judge whose mind has cracked under the strain of conscience Richard Bennett gives a memorable performance—gentle in

manner, kindly in tone, pathetically broken in mental process. As the little tenement girl who falls in love Margo's innocence of spirit and pleading tone of voice echo the theme of the tragedy. Burgess Meredith gives a sinewy performance as the son who is still on his father's mission. Mr. Meredith is the sort of actor who can put a solid foundation under a scene and a play.

Nor does that complete the bulletin of fine acting. Eduardo Ciannelli's cruel, sneering Trock is a vigorous portrait of malevolence. Harold Johnsrud as the Shadow, Theodore Hecht as the frightened accessory to the fact of the murder, Anatole Winogradoff as the pious patriarch, Anthony Blair as the comic policeman, Abner Biberman as the snarling radical—act like men who know their profession.

If the verse is not always lucid in its meaning, the actors are not blameless. Mr. Winogradoff does not speak clearly, and sometimes the words falter on Mr. Meredith's lips. But the poet in Mr. Anderson has not made full peace with the dramatist. He has not stretched the seams of his drama taut. At its best, however, his poetry is clean and piercing, and his tragedy a work of uncommon stature. Mr. Anderson and Mr. McClintic are well matched. They know how to make drama.

1935 S 26

THE TAMING OF THE SHREW, Shakespeare's comedy in two acts as arranged by Alfred Lunt and Lynn Fontanne. Staged by Harry Wagstaff Gribble; incidental score by Frank Tours; costumes designed by Claggett Wilson; settings by Carolyn Hancock; produced by the Theatre Guild, in association with John C. Wilson. At the Guild Theatre.

Christopher Sly........... ...Richard Whorf
A Lord.....................Lowell Gilmore
First Huntsman...............John Balmer
Second Huntsman............Gilmore Bush
Third Huntsman.............Winston Ross
Bartholomew ....William Clifford
Lucentio ....Alan Hewitt
Tranio............... Bretaigne Windust
Two Townswomen,
    Jacqueline De Witt Ernestine De Becker
Pantaloon ......;.............LeRoi Operti
Baptista ....Sydney Greenstreet
Gremio ....George Graham
Hortensio ....Barry Thomson
Bianca ....;,,Dorothy Mathews
Biondello ....George Meader
Petruchio ....Alfred Lunt
Grumio .. ..Horace Sinclair
Widow ....Doris Rich
Maid ....Jacqueline De Witt
Katherine ....Lynn Fontanne
Curtis..................Alice Belmore Cliffe
Nathaniel ....Gilmore Bush

Joseph ....Thomas Coley
Gregory ....William Gray.
Philip ....Winston Ross
Cook ....Stephen Sandes
Haberdasher.............S. Thomas Gomez
Tailor ....LeRoi Operti
A Pedant.................Robert Vivian
Vincentio ....David Glassford
Officer.................S. Thomas Gomez
A Prisoner...............Stephen Sandes
Horses......Harry Be Gar, Arthur Chester
Acrobats......Roy Rognan, George Snare,
                                Stuart Barlow
Dwarfs....John Ballas, Freddie Goodrow,
              Ray Holgate, Ray Schultz

By BROOKS ATKINSON.

Good friends, the tumult in Fifty-second Street last evening was Shakespeare. Alfred Lunt and Lynn Fontanne were pouncing on "The Taming of the Shrew" and playing it in the Guild Theatre like a game of ninepins. Most exceeding low, my friends, and most exceeding funny, for "The Shrew" is cabotinage and the Lunts have stuffed it with all the horseplay their barn loft holds. Beginning with the be-fuddled Christopher Sly induction, they have improvised a performance as the vagabond mummers of an ideal age might play it in a nobleman's courtyard. "Oh, this learning, what a thing it is," one of the characters says. Oh, this tumbling and revelry, how uproarious it is when pace is keen and the humor is midriff merriment. There is not a single grain of pedants' dust in this tan-bark version of "The Taming of the Shrew." Fifty-second Street is always a midway when the Lunts are appearing there.

Even in Shakespeare's time "The Taming of the Shrew" was a low tale for an afternoon of elementary fooling. Shakespeare and some unknown playmaker merely adapted it from a standard farce that had almost the same title and much the same mischief. The Lunts have drawn on both for this carnival junket—adding a band with drums, a troupe of tumblers, a cluster of midgets, a pair of comic horses and some fine songs set to good beer-garden music by Frank Tours.

If you complain that you cannot hear the lines nor decipher the Bianca plot, you are well within your rights. There is no time for clarity or exposition when the comedians are riding the whirlwind. Since he was an actor, Shakespeare will not object to a brace of good actors using his cluttered script for a public holiday. After all, lines are a nuisance. Pantomime is a sounder comedy medium. What you are offered by way of compensation is Richard Whorf's seedy Christopher Sly, who is as drunk as a waterfront stew, and a rag-tag and bobtail of prancing performers in a costume antic.

For Kate's father there is Sydney Greenstreet—corpulent, frightened, bewildered, hopeful. For Grumio, Horace Sinclair, who is a red-faced clown. For Biondello, George Meader, who can fill a song with joy. For Bianca, Dorothy Mathews; for Tranio, Bretaigne Windust; for Lucentio, Alan Hewitt, and for Curtis, Alice Belmore Cliffe, who looks jolly, and is.

For Petruchio and Katherine, well, here are the actors who have more gusto for every sort of stage hocus-pocus than any other performers on the American bulletin boards. Miss Fontanne is playing with a painful knee injury that doubtless handicaps her in the running broad jump and hundred-yard dash. But it does not curb the choler of ugly Kate. When she bellows from a room upstairs, the actors huddle in the corner and tremble. When she stamps on Petruchio's foot, he is stamped for all time. She is a pathetic creature when hungry, and a broken mare when Petruchio's training has exhausted her, and she is a lady of poise and breeding when in the last scene she teaches married women their duty.

As Petruchio, Mr. Lunt plays with incomparable bounce and humor, beaming with mischief, grimacing at the audience and vigorously driving the performance before him. The production is hung with gay settings by Carolyn Hancock and dressed in carnival trappings by Claggett Wilson. Mr. Gribble has directed the whole affair with the versatility and dispatch of a musical comedy ringmaster.

All Shakespeare needs at any time is actors. He has them here. Obviously, the Lunts have enjoyed devising this production. Audiences are always in luck when good actors are enjoying themselves.

1935 O 1

'Porgy and Bess,' Native Opera, Opens at the Alvin; Gershwin Work Based on Du Bose Heyward's Play

Todd Duncan and Anne Wiggins Brown in title rôles of "Porgy and Bess."

THE CAST.

PORGY AND BESS, "an American folk-opera" in three acts and nine scenes, based on the play, "Porgy," by Du Bose and Dorothy Heyward. Score by George Gershwin, libretto by Mr. Heyward, and lyrics by Mr. Heyward and Ira Gershwin. Staged by Rouben Mamoulian; scenery by Sergei Soudelkine; orchestra conducted by Alexander Smallens; produced by the Theatre Guild. At the Alvin Theatre.

Mingo.......................Ford L. Buck
Clara.......................Abbie Mitchell
Sportin' Life...............John W. Bubbles

Jake.......................Edward Matthews
Maria......................Georgette Harvey
Annie......................Olive Ball
Lily.......................Helen Dowdy
Serena.....................Ruby Elzy
Robbins,...................Henry Davis
Jim........................Jack Carr
Peter......................Gus Simons
Porgy......................Todd Duncan
Crown......................Warren Coleman
Bess.......................Anne Wiggins Brown
Detective..................Alexander Campbell
Two Policemen { ....Harold Woolf
             { ....Burton McEvilly
Undertaker.................John Garth
Frazier....................J. Rosamond Johnson
Mr. Archdale...............George Lessey
Nelson.....................Ray Yeates
Strawberry Woman...........Helen Dowdy
Crab Man...................Ray Yeates
Coroner....................George Carleton
Residents of Catfish Row, fishermen, children, stevedores, &c. The Eva Jessye Choir: Catherine Jackson Ayres, Lillian Cowan, Sara Dalgeau, Darlean Duval, Kate Hall, Altonell Hines, Louisa Howard, Harriet Jackson, Rosalie King, Assotta Marshall, Wilnette Mayers, Sadie McGill, Massie Patterson, Annabelle Ross, Louise Twyman, Helen R. White, Musa Williams, Reginald Beane, Caesar Bennett, G. Harry Bolden, Edward Broadnax, Carroll Clark, Joseph Crawford, John Diggs, Leonard Franklin, John Garth, Joseph James, Clarence Jacobs, Allen Lewis, Jimmie Lightfoot, Lycurgus Lockman, Henry May, Junius McDaniel, Arthur McLean, William O'Neil, Robert Raines, Andrew Taylor, Leon Threadgill, Jimmie Waters, Robert Williams, Ray Yeates.
Choral Conductor—Eva Jessye.
Children—Naida King, Regina Williams, Enid Wilkins, Allen Tinney, William Tinney, Herbert Young.
The Charleston Orphans' Band—Sam Anderson, Eric Bell, Le Verria Bilton, Benjamine Browne, Claude Christian, Shedrack Dobson, David Ellis, Clarence Smith, John Strachan, George Tait, Allen Tinney, William Tinney, Charles Williams, Herbert Young.

Dramatic Values of Community Legend Gloriously Transposed in New Form With Fine Regard for Its Verities.

By BROOKS ATKINSON.

After eight years of savory memories, "Porgy" has acquired a score, a band, a choir of singers and a new title, "Porgy and Bess," which the Theatre Guild put on at the Alvin last evening. Du Bose and Dorothy Heyward wrote the original lithograph of Catfish Row, which Rouben Mamoulian translated into a memorable work of theatre dynamics. But "Porgy and Bess" represents George Gershwin's longing to compose an American folk opera on a suitable theme. Although Mr. Heyward is the author of the libretto and shares with Ira Gershwin the credit for the lyrics, and although Mr. Mamoulian has again mounted the director's box, the evening is unmistakably George Gershwin's personal holiday. In fact, the volume of music he has written during the last two years on the ebony fable of a Charleston rookery has called out a whole brigade of Times Square music critics, who are quite properly the masters of this occasion. Mr. Downes, soothsayer of the diatonic scale, is now beetling his brow in the adjoining cubicle. There is an authoritative ring to his typewriter clatter tonight.

In these circumstances, the province of a drama critic is to report on the transmutation of "Porgy" out of drama into music theatre. Let it be said at once that Mr. Gershwin has contributed something glorious to the spirit of the Heywards' community legend. If memory serves, it always lacked glow of personal feeling. Being a fairly objective narrative of a neighborhood of Negroes who lived a private racial life in the midst of a white civilization. "Porgy" was a natural subject for theatre showmanship. The groupings, the mad fantasy of leaping shadows, the panic-stricken singing over a corpse, the evil bulk of the buzzard's flight, the screaming hurricane—these large audible and visible items of showmanship took precedence over the episode of Porgy's romance with Crown's high-steppin' gal.

Whether or not Mr. Gershwin's score measures up to its intentions as American folk opera lies in Mr. Downes's bailiwick. But to the ears of a theatre critic Mr. Gershwin's music gives a personal voice to Porgy's loneliness when, in a crowd of pitying neighbors, he learns that Bess has vanished into the capacious and remote North. The pathetic apprehension of the "Where's My Bess" trio and the manly conviction of "I'm On My Way" add something vital to the story that was missing before.

These comments are written by a reviewer so inured to the theatre that he regards operatic form as cumbersome. Why commonplace remarks that carry no emotion have to be made in a chanting monotone is a problem in art he cannot fathom. Even the hermit thrush drops into conversational tones when he is not singing from the topmost spray in a tree. Turning "Porgy" into opera has resulted in a deluge of casual remarks that have to be thoughtfully intoned and that amazingly impede the action. Why do composers vex it so? "Sister, you goin' to the picnic?" "No, I guess not." Now, why in heaven's name must two characters in an opera clear their throats before they can exchange that sort of information? What a theatre critic probably wants is a musical show with songs that evoke the emotion of situations and make no further pretensions. Part of the emotion of a drama comes from the pace of the performance.

And what of the amusing little device of sounds and rhythms, of sweeping, sawing, hammering and dusting, that opens the last scene early one morning? In the program it is solemnly described as "Occupational Humeresque." But any music hall would be glad to have it without its tuppence colored label. Mr. Mamoulian is an excellent director for dramas of ample proportions. He is not subtle, which is a virtue in showmanship. His crowds are arranged in masses that look as solid as a victory at the polls; they move with simple unanimity, and the rhythm is comfortably obvious.

Mr. Gershwin knows that. He has written the scores for innumerable musical shows. After one of them he was presented with the robes of Arthur Sullivan, who also was consumed with a desire to write grand. To the ears of a theatre critic there are intimations in "Porgy and Bess" that Mr. Gershwin is still easiest in mind when he is writing songs with choruses. He, and his present reviewer, are on familiar ground when he is writing a droll tune like "A Woman Is a Sometime Thing," or a lazy darky solo like "I Got Plenty o' Nuttin'," or made-to-order spirituals like, "Oh, de Lawd Shake de Heaven," or Sportin' Life's hot-time number entitled "There's a Boat That's Leavin' Soon for New York." If Mr. Gershwin does not enjoy his task most in moments like this, his audience does. In sheer quality of character they are worth an hour of formal music transitions.

For the current folk opera Sergei Soudeikine has prepared Catfish Row settings that follow the general design of the originals, but have more grace, humor and color. In the world of sound that Mr. Gershwin has created the tattered children of a Charleston byway are still racy and congenial. Promoting "Porgy" to opera involves considerable incidental drudgery for theatregoers who agree with Mark Twain that "classical music is better than it sounds." But Mr. Gershwin has found a personal voice that was inarticulate in the original play. The fear and the pain go deeper in "Porgy and Bess" than they did in penny plain "Porgy."

Exotic Richness of Negro Music and Color of Charleston, S.C., Admirably Conveyed in Score of Catfish Row Tragedy.

By OLIN DOWNES.

George Gershwin, long conspicuous as an American composer with a true lyrical gift and with original and racy things to say, has turned with his score of "Porgy and Bess" to the more pretentious ways of the musical theatre. The result, which vastly entertained last night's audience, has much to commend it from the musical standpoint, even if the work does not utilize all the resources of the operatic composer, or pierce very often to the depths of the simple and pathetic drama.

It is in the lyrical moments that Mr. Gershwin is most completely felicitous. With an instinctive appreciation of the melodic glides and nuances of Negro song, and an equally personal tendency to rich and exotic harmony, he writes a melody which is idiomatic and wholly appropriate to the subject. He also knows the voices. He is experienced in many phases of the theatre, and his work shows it. His ultimate destiny as an opera composer is yet to be seen. His native gifts won him success last night, but it appears in the light of the production that as yet he has not completely formed his style as an opera composer.

The style is at one moment of opera and another of operetta or sheer Broadway entertainment. It goes without saying that many of the songs in the score of "Porgy and Bess" will reap a quick popularity. Many of them are excellent, as we have a right to expect of Mr. Gershwin. But that is the least important thing about this work. There are elements of a more organic kind in it. Here and there flashes of real contrapuntal ingenuity combine themes in a manner apposite to the grouping and action of the characters on the stage. In ensemble pieces rhythmical and contrapuntal devices work well. Harmonic admixtures of Stravinsky and Puccini are obvious but not particularly disconcerting. Sometimes the spicy harmonies heighten felicitously the color of the music. There is effective treatment of the "spirituals." No one of the "spiritual" melodies is actually Negro in origin. They are all Mr. Gershwin's invention. He makes effective use of them, not only by harmony sometimes "modal" but by the dramatic combination of the massed voices and the wild exhortations of individual singers.

It must be admitted that in spite of cuts there are still too many set songs and "numbers" which hold back the dramatic development, and the treatment of passages of recitative is seldom significant. The songs were welcomed. Porgy's "I got plenty of nuttin'" held up the show, while all the inhabitants of Catfish Row beat time for it. Clara's lullaby, "Summer Time," sets early a melodic pace that is fairly maintained in the lyrical moments of the score. The prayer of Serena for Bess is eloquent, original and the most poetical passage in the whole work. The duets of Porgy and Bess are more obvious and savorous of Puccini.

The performance had much that was uncommonly interesting, particularly to a reviewer accustomed to the methods of the opera stage. These methods are usually as out of date as the dodo. Operatic acting and stage management have too often been fit subjects for ridicule. When it came to sheer acting last night certain operatic functionaries should have been present. If the Metropolitan chorus could ever put one-half the action into the riot scene in the second act of "Meistersinger" that the Negro cast put into the fight that followed the crap game it would be not merely refreshing but miraculous. And when did Isolde wave a scarf more rhythmically from the tower than those who shook feather dusters and sheets from the windows to accompany Porgy's song? Or Hans Sachs cobble more rhythmically to Beckmesser's Serenade than the shoemaker on the door-step? What could excel the beautiful precision of the tremolo of the shoe-shiner?

As individual and collective acting, these and many other things were admirable. There were magnificent effects of choral song and action. Other groupings were often astonishingly conventional in the operatic manner, and thus contrary to dramatic purpose. This was probably due to the sectional character of the score, but why should the pathetic and tragically helpless Porgy be given the position and the air of the strutting opera baritone?

Admitted the instinct of Negroes to dance, did the inhabitants of Catfish Row set themselves in centrifugal patterns along the floor and wiggle hands and toes like the ladies who are auxiliary to a soloist's performance in a revue? Of course this was amusing. So was the capital clogging of Sportin' Life in the forest scene. He was a rare fellow, with magnificent clothes. There were a hundred diverting details in this spectacle. What had become of the essential simplicity of the drama of "Porgy"? Let Mr. Atkinson answer.

The cast provided some excellent singing. None of the vocalists fell short of musicianship and expressiveness. The Porgy, Todd Duncan, has a manly and resonant voice, which he uses with eloquent effect. The fresh tone, admirably competent technic, and dramatic delivery of Anne Brown as Bess was a high point of interpretation. Miss Elzy's Serena was equally in key with her part, and distinguished by truly pathetic expression. Musically this was a very eloquent interpretation by soloists and chorus. Smallens conducted with superb authority and spirit.

1935 O 11

JUBILEE, a musical comedy in three acts and twenty-nine scenes. Book by Moss Hart. Music and lyrics by Cole Porter. Staged and lighted by Hassard Short; dialogue directed by Monty Woolley; costumes designed by Irene Sharaff and Connie DePinna; orchestra conducted by Frank Tours; orchestrations by Russell Bennett; dances arranged by Albertina Rasch; scenery by Jo Mielziner; produced by Sam H. Harris and Max Gordon. At the Imperial Theatre.

The King	Melville Cooper
The Queen	Mary Boland
Prince James	Charles Walters
Princess Diana	Margaret Adams
Prince Peter	Montgomery Clift
Prince Rudolph	Jackie Kelk
Lord Wyndham	Richie Ling
Eric Dare	Derek Williams
Karen O'Kane	June Knight
Eva Standing	May Boley
Charles Rausmiller (Mowgli)	Mark Plant
Mrs. Watkins	Jane Evans
Laura Fitzgerald	Olive Reeves-Smith
A Sandwich Man	Charles Brokaw
Professor Rexford	Ralph Sumpter
The Beach Widow	Dorothy Fox
Cabinet Minister	Leo Chalzell
Cabinet Minister	Charles Brokaw
Lifeguard	Don Douglas
Announcer	Albert Amato
Master of Ceremonies	Harold Murray
The Drunk	Jack Edwards
The Usher	Ted Fetter
Keeper of Zoo	Leo Chalzel

THE SATELLITES—Girls: Betty Allen, Wyn Cahoon, Jacqueline Franc, Janice Joyce, Kay Sloan, Katherine Howard, Erika Zaranov. Boys: Albert Amato, Tom Curley, Vernon Hammer, Harold Murray, Sid Salzer, Castle Williams. The Pages: Donald Brown, Evelyn Eaton, Warren Eaton, Patricia Roe, Alice Fitzsimmons, Raymond Roe, John Roemele. The Girls: Virginia Allen, Dorothy Atkins, Jeannette Bradley, Kay Cameron, Helen Cole, Miriam Curtis, Denise Denning, Rose Gale, Dorothy Graves, Marion Heemsath, Joyce Johnson, Adele Jurgens, Helene Louise, Patricia Martin, Austra Neiman, Wilma Roelof, Tanya Sanina, Peggy Seel, Rose Tyrrell, Elsa Walbridge, Finette Walker, Janice Winter. The Boys: Bruce Barclay, Robert Burns, Jack Donaldson, George Herndon, Buddy Hertelle, Jay Hunter, James Keogan, Leslie Kingdon, Robert Lewis, Jules Mann, Philip Mann, Jack Millard, John Moore, Mickey Moore, Fred Nay, Michael James, David Preston, Victor Pullman, David Arnold, Bob Schultz, Vernon Tanner, Norman Van Emburgh, Gil White, Gilbert Wilson, Jack Whitney. The Martinique Orchestra: Reuben Cohen, James Flood, Wilbur Kurz, Seymour Mann, Joseph Pergola, Jack Rosenmerkel.

By BROOKS ATKINSON.

As thousands cheer, "Jubilee" has finally hung its hat in the Imperial Theatre, where it had a tumultuous première Saturday evening. It is a rapturous masquerade. By this time every student of the theatre and of navigation must know that "Jubilee" is the musical show Moss Hart and Cole Porter wrote last Spring—or say that they wrote—while they were blandly steaming around the world in the Franconia. There is, perhaps, a hint of distant splendors in some of Mr. Porter's tunes and in one Eastern dance, "Begin the Beguine," which, according to the program, was designed right here in New York City. But "Jubilee" is no tripper's diary. It is an aristocrat of American festivals to music. It is the dome of many-colored glass that Broadway artisans know how to stretch above the raw materials of entertainment. Each of the guilds that produce our luxurious musical shows has shared equally in the general excellence of an upper-class song-and-dance arcade.

In case you have been feeling uneasy about holding the royal family of England up to ridicule, compose yourself. Although the monarchs of "Jubilee" are unmistakably acquainted with the formalities of English court life, Mr. Hart's king and queen are not victims of buffoonery, but engaging folks. His sense of humor is warm rather than impudent. Only the most apoplectic of Tories would begrudge his rulers their excursion outside the palace gates. For it is Mr. Hart's contention that even the most dutiful monarchs occasionally crave the ordinary pleasures of humanity. The king is interested in rope tricks. The queen longs to meet a famous screen hero whose swimming is beautiful and whose ululations of love in the jungle have swollen the hearts of women all over the world. The princess wants to meet the brilliant playwright, Eric Dare, who is the fashion of two continents. The prince has his eye on a night club singer. When a crisis in politics requires the government to send the royal family to a dull castle outside the city, they escape separately into anonymity and indulge themselves in commoner's joy. Having an honest love of simple pleasure, they know how to take a holiday.

For purposes of musical extravaganza it is an excellent fable—good humored, slightly romantic and eminently pragmatic. From the grandeur of court ceremonies it passes logically to bizarre scenes like public parks and beaches, the zoo, a night club and a modish ballroom. The settings that Jo Mielziner has designed for them make "Jubilee" fit company for magnificoes. The costumes and gowns by Irene Sharaff and Connie De Pinna have extraordinarily varied and stunning beauty. Saturated in Hassard Short's lustrous style of staging, "Jubilee" is a visual masterpiece. It is a light-stepping parade of splendor that never drops into humdrum theatre pageantry.

These are the places where Mr.

Porter's songs are sung, and Albertina Rasch's dances stepped out and where some of the theatres ablest performers jog your funnybone or tamper with your susceptibilities. Last year Mr. Porter wrote a brisker score than the one the Franconia brought home as cargo. But the music for "Jubilee" is jaunty, versatile and imaginative in several veins—"The Kling-Kling Bird on the Divi-Divi Tree," for patter singing; "What a Nice Municipal Park" and "Ev'rybodee Who's Anybod'ee" for general revelry; "Sunday Morning, Breakfast Time," for glee singing; "The Judgment of Paris," for ancient choristry; "When Me, Mowgli, Love," for doggerel burlesque, and "Begin the Beguine," for exotic originality.

Mary Boland is home from Hollywood. She is the queen of the book and the performance and a carnival of comic delights. For the venom she puts into her moments of shrewish indignation, the sticky unction of her philandering and the general club-lady excitability of her deportment are unconscionably sharp and funny. Melville Cooper's droll king, with its humor masked under an unperturbable manner, is likewise immensely amusing. There are Mark Plant for the cartoon of Johnny Weismuller, Derek Williams for an uppish caricature of Noel Coward, May Boley for a bustling portrait of Elsa Maxwell, Margaret Adams for a winning princess, Charles Walters for a modest prince, Jack Whitney for a flight of dancing, and an enviable dame school of singers and dancers. And June Knight as the gorgeous queen of a night club—the Franconia must have been launched for her, she is so lovely. . . . "Jubilee" is a tapestry of showshop delights.

1935 O 14

MULATTO, a "new drama" in three acts, by Langston Hughes. Setting by Ambrose & Golding; staged and produced by Martin Jones. At the Vanderbilt Theatre.
Cora Lewis................Rose McClendon
William Lewis...........Morris McKenney
Colonel Thomas Norwood.....Stuart Beebe
Sally Lewis................Jeanne Greene
Talbot ....John Boyd
Fred Higgins..............Frank Jaquet
Henry Richards...........Henry Forsberg
Grace Richards..........Gertrude Bondhill
Mary Lowell.............Connie Gilchrist
Robert Lewis.................Hurst Amyx
Storekeeper ....Clark Poth
Undertaker ....Howard Negley

By BROOKS ATKINSON.

After a season dedicated chiefly to trash it is a sobering sensation to sit in the presence of a playwright who is trying his best to tell what he has on his mind. In "Mulatto," which was acted at the Vanderbilt last evening, Langston Hughes, the Negro poet, is attempting to describe the tragic confusion of the people whose blood is half black and half white. To judge by "Mulatto" Mr. Hughes has little of the dramatic strength of mind that makes it possible for a writer to tell a coherent, driving story in the theatre. His ideas are seldom completely expressed; his play is pretty thoroughly defeated by the grim mechanics of the stage. What gives it a sobering sensation in spite of its artlessness is the very apparent earnestness of Mr. Hughes's state of mind. He is writing about the theme that lies closest to his heart.

His mulattoes are the children of Cora Lewis, Negro housekeeper, and Colonel Thomas Norwood, a widower and a wealthy planter of Georgia. Since Colonel Norwood is the immediate instrument of oppression Mr. Hughes might easily have drawn him as a white villain. As a matter of fact, the colonel is according to his code a rather decent citizen; he has always treated his field Negroes honestly and he has been generous with the illegitimate children Cora has borne him. But that merely intensifies their mental anguish and makes their race bondage the more difficult to endure. Finally one of the boys, who has been educated in the North, gets completely out of control, kills the colonel and stirs up a lynching party to conclude the play.

Obviously, Mr. Hughes is immediately concerned with the code of ethics that keeps his race in subjection—the casual begetting of illegitimate children who are denied the prerogatives of their paternity, scorned by the whites, hated by the blacks. But the writing of "Mulatto" has set Mr. Hughes so many problems that it often seems like a moral retribution drama about the misery of a white man plagued by the social misdemeanor of having illegitimate mulatto children. For Colonel Norwood is always in trouble with his neighbors and the members of his own household, and is finally killed by a boy so cocky and impudent that he seems more like an ungrateful son than a martyr to race prejudice. The sympathies evoked by Mr. Hughes's story are muddled and diffuse.

If the material the actors have to work with is taken into consideration, some of them give a pretty good account of themselves. Stuart Beebe does well by the harassed colonel's state of mind. Jeanne Greene, playing the part of a terrified mulatto girl, does an excellent job. Hurst Amyx has something to give the part of a mulatto boy when he is in flight in the last act. Morris McKenney gives a good performance as an obedient Negro servant. As for Cora Lewis, she has the honor to be played by Rose McClendon, who is an artist with a sensitive personality and a bell-like voice. Plays are not very numerous for Miss McClendon but it is always a privilege to see her adding fineness of perception to the parts she takes.

In spite of its fatal weaknesses as a drama, "Mulatto" offers the combination of Rose McClendon and a playwright who is flaming with sincerity. After a fairly shabby season a professional playgoer is grateful for at least that much relief.

1935 O 25.

DEAD END, a play in three acts, by Sidney Kingsley. Staged by the author; setting by Norman Bel Geddes; produced by Mr. Geddes. At the Belasco Theatre.

Gimpty	Theodore Newton
T B	Gabriel Dell
Tommy	Billy Halop
Dippy	Huntz Hall
Angel	Bobby Jordan
Spit	Charles R. Duncan
Doorman	George Cotton
Old Lady	Marie R. Burke
Old Gentleman	George M. Price
First Chauffeur	Charles Benjamin
"Babyface" Martin	Joseph Downing
Hunk	Martin Gabel
Philip Griswald	Charles Bellin
Governess	Sidonie Espero
Milty	Bernard Punsly
Drina	Elspeth Eric
Mr. Griswald	Carroll Ashburn
Mr. Jones	Louis Lord
Kay	Margaret Mullen
Jack Hilton	Cyril Gordon Weld
Lady With Dog	Margaret Linden
Three Small Boys	Billy Winston / Joseph Talbi / Sidney Lumet
Second Chauffeur	Richard Clark
Second Avenue Boys	David Gorcey / Leo Gorcey
Mrs. Martin	Marjorie Main
Patrolman Mulligan	Robert J. Mulligan
Francey	Sheila Trent
G.-Men	Francis de Sales / Edward P. Goodnow / Dan Duryea
Policemen	Frances G. Cleveland / William Toubin
Plainclothesman	Harry Selby
Interne	Philip Bourneuf
Medical Examiner	Lewis L. Russel
Sailor	Bernard Zaneville

Inhabitants of East River Terrace, Ambulance Men, &c.—Elizabeth Wragge, Drina Hill, Blossom MacDonald, Ethel Dell, Marc Daniels, Elizabeth Perlowin, Edith Jordan, Marie Dell, Bea Punsley, Bess

Winston, Anne Miller, Elizabeth Zabelin, George Bond, Matthew Purcell, Herman Osmond, Rose Taibi, George Buzante, Betty Rheingold, Lizzie Leonard, Catherine Kemp, Mag Davis, Nellie Ransom, Betsy Ross, Charles Larue, Paul Meacham, Tom McIntyre, George Anspecke, Jack Kellert, Elizabeth Lowe, Gene Lowe, Charlotte Salkow, Morris Chertov, Charlotte Julien, Willis Duncan.

By BROOKS ATKINSON.

By adding a little thought and art to considerable accurate observation, Sidney Kingsley has compiled an enormously stirring drama about life in New York City, "Dead End," which was produced at the Belasco last evening. Somewhere along the East River a raffish dead-end street meets the rear entrance to a fashionable apartment house where private yachts have a slip of their own. It is one of those dramatic corners on which Manhattan advertises the distance that divides poverty from riches, and it is a brilliant place to study the case history of the metropolitan gangster. Norman Bel Geddes has filled the stage of the Belasco with one of those super-realistic settings that David Belasco liked to contrive, solid down to the ring of shoes on asphalt pavement. When the curtain goes up on a scene torn out of the daily life of Manhattan you are prepared for a show. When the curtain falls you know that you have also listened to a drama.

What Mr. Kingsley has in the bottom of his mind is the social condition that breeds gangsters. One of his characters is a notorious gangster who came out of just such an environment and has slunk back to see his mother again and to meet the first girl he ever loved. Swarming around his feet is a shrill, dirty, nervous and shrewd mob of boys who are gangsters in the making. Before "Dead End" is over Mr. Kingsley shows how a celebrated gangster can come to his end in a dirty gutter, when the Federal agents find him, and how a street urchin can develop into a gangster. Once Baby-Face Martin was only a tough kid like Tommy. When Tommy serves his apprenticeship at reform school, it is Mr. Kingsley's contention that he will be like Baby-Face Martin—a cheap killer, despised by his family and feared by every one who crosses his path.

Not that Mr. Kingsley has turned "Dead End" into a public social document. In its objective photograph of one section of New York it draws inevitable comparison with "Street Scene." It is full of characters who move casually in and out of a loosely-woven story; it is strident with gutter argot. What you have seen and heard in New York, wondering and apprehensive as you trudge along our begrimed seacoast, has found lodgment in this flaring anecdote of an average day.

The boys' parts are played with such authenticity that there was a foul sidewalk canard last evening that a mob of East Side street arabs had been carted west in their street clothes. Certainly the pitch of their voices has the piercing note of the tenement streets, and their water-skater running across the stage has the rhythm of half-naked pierhead swimmers. According to the office encyclopedia, however, Billy Hallop, as the leader of the mob, is Bobby Benson of the radio, famous these many years, and the others are members of the Professional Children's School or the Madison Square Boys Club, or come from stage families.

Although they are at war with the world, they have made their peace with the professional actors who play the mature parts. Joseph Downing as the head gunman, Elspeth Eric as the sister of one of the boys, Marjorie Main as the contemptuous mother of the gangster, Sheila Trent as a cheap prostitute, Theodore Newton as the brooding artist whose constant presence binds all the bizarre elements of the drama, give excellent realistic performances.

Sometimes Mr. Geddes breaks his dramas on the wheel of stage designing. But this time he has reared up a setting that pushes the thought of the author's drama ruthlessly into the audience's face. Not only in its accuracy of detail but in its perspective and its power his setting is a practical masterpiece. Mr. Kingsley is fortunate in his association, for "Dead End" is worth the best our theatre affords. As thought it is a contribution to public knowledge. As drama it is vivid and bold. When the Pulitzer judges gave Mr. Kingsley a prize for "Men In White," they picked a first-rate man.

1935 O 29

BOY MEETS GIRL, a farce in three acts, by Bella and Samuel Spewack. Scenery by Arne Lundborg; staged and produced by George Abbott. At the Cort Theatre.

Robert Law	Allyn Joslyn
Larry Toms	Charles McClelland
J. Carlyle Benson	Jerome Cowan
Rosetti	Everett H. Sloane
Mr. Friday (C. F.)	Royal Beal
Peggy	Peggy Hart
Miss Crews	Lea Penman
Rodney Bevan	James MacColl
Green	Garson Kanin
Slade	Maurice Sommers
Susie	Joyce Arling
A Nurse	Helen Gardner
Doctor	Perry Ivins
Chauffeur	Edison Rice
Young Man	Philip Faversham
Studio Officer	George W. Smith
Cutter	Robert Foulk
Another Nurse	Marjorie Lytell
Major Thompson	John Clarke

By BROOKS ATKINSON.

By wooing the Hollywood muse with a slapstick, Bella and Samuel Spewack have succeeded in writing an extraordinarily hilarious comedy, "Boy Meets Girl," which was perfectly staged at the Cort last evening. This is the knockabout skit based on the antics of a pair of Hollywood script imps who, on the solemn word of the Spewacks, are not Hecht and MacArthur. Even if they are Hecht and MacArthur, they are gusty and original enough to enliven a comedy that combines the best features of "Once in a Lifetime" and "She Loves Me Not." George Abbott has cast it and directed it with uncommon exactitude and vitality. "Boy Meets Girl" joins the honorable tradition of madcap fooling at high speed.

The story is too crack-brained to be intelligibly recorded here. But in Hollywood the Royal Studios are sufficiently unfortunate to have under contract a pair of brilliant scribblers whose private excursions into buffoonery are funnier than anything they write. While they are reluctantly trying to throw together a hokum script for a seedy horseback star, an expectant and unchurched mother faints in the director's office. They see a great story in the career of a foundling. As soon as the baby is born the cameras begin to turn. "Boy Meets Girl" is the fantastic chronicle of studio politics, brazen schemes to put contracts on a secure basis, noble renunciations, mischief in a hospital and general skulduggery.

While the story is twisting itself into ludicrous tangles, the Spewacks take time out to conduct the usual low-comedy burlesque of Hollywood studio culture. But their chief hilarity is the inspired sophomoric prank-dance of their brilliant leading characters whose passion for practical joking exhausts the strength they should husband for their normal work.

It is the sort of fandango Mr. Abbott knows how to stage with the rarest sense of time and variety. He has cast the parts with the independent perspicacity of a theatreman who knows how to preserve a fresh point of view. Now that he has selected Jerome Cowan and Allyn Joslyn to play the twin leading parts and Joyce Arling to act the part of the nitwit parent it is easy to believe that no others could possibly be right amid such bedlamite circumstances.

The subordinate parts have been cast with an equal sense of broadfaced humor—Royal Beal for the choleric director, James MacColl for the confused scion of a titled family, Charles McClelland for the ham screen star, Garson Kanin and Maurice Sommers for the push-cart song peddlers of the studio. Under Mr. Abbott's direction they all play with so much precision of tempo that "Boy Meets Girl" fills the evening with impudent vertigo and glee.

1935 N 28

GHOSTS, a play in three acts, by Henrik Ibsen. Staged by Alla Nazimova; setting by Stewart Chaney; production lighted by A. H. Feder; revived by Luther Greene. At the Empire Theatre.

Regina	Ona Munson
Jacob Engstrand	Raymond O'Brien
Pastor Manders	McKay Morris
Mrs. Alving	Alla Nazimova
Oswald Alving	Harry Ellerbe

By BROOKS ATKINSON.

Probably Ibsen wrote "Ghosts" for Nazimova. Or, if not for her specifically, at least for a great actress, which is the measure of her Mrs. Alving in the performance that reached the Empire last evening. "Great" is a word for sparing use; it paralyzes linotype machines toward midnight. But there is no other way to characterize a transcendent performance of a tragic rôle in a drama that is not especially pertinent now. Perhaps in its day "Ghosts" was a daring drama that helped blow the stuffiness out of thought and manners. Certainly the Gradgrinds denounced it violently enough to establish it as a masterpiece. But now, apart from the acting of Nazimova and of her colleagues, it is only a temperate statement of an ugly thought with a milk-and-gruel attack upon authority and pious idealism.

Only an academician, however, would be able to look at it now apart from the performance, for Nazimova has imparted to it the aura of inspired acting. No doubt she is a mistress of her craft. If you watch her closely and divorce your emotions from what you see, you will perhaps be aware of the skill with which she puts dramatic emphasis upon the lines in the tone of her voice and in the eloquent gestures of her hands, and you will perhaps perceive craft in the positions she has assigned to herself on the stage.

But this column can give you little information of that sort this morning. For the Mrs. Alving of Nazimova is too glowing a creature to be coldly separated from the spirit of the acting. Physically she is a pale and fragile person who has bowed so long to the slings and arrows of outrageous fortune that she is all suppleness and submission. But beneath the mask there is pride that has never surrendered, mind that has not lost its edge nor humor, compassion that weeps for the sins of a careless world, and the quiet of a woman who has strength enough for suffering. Let those who are able detail the craft that evokes this imagry.

In addition to playing the leading rôle, Nazimova has directed the performance and presumably cast the parts or consented to them. At any rate, she is surrounded with players who have caught the fire of her own acting. McKay Morris can be an ornate actor and he can swallow words with relish, and sometimes, to tell the truth, he swallows a handful of them here. But his Pastor Manders is superb—resonant, authoritative, gentlemanly and full of sanctimonious convictions. Sometimes Harry Ellerbe can be a self-conscious juvenile. But his Oswald Alving is a fine and

reticent study of a doomed young man and he can go mad without an echo of maudlin heroics. Perhaps Ona Munson's Regina is on the side of showy pertness, but it is a plausible performance, nevertheless, and consistent.

Being a modern, Stewart Chaney has dispelled the gloom of Ibsen revivals by designing a capacious living room with an enormous window and a glimpse of mighty hills. He has admitted light to Ibsen. And he has chosen his occasion well. For Nazimova has flooded the whole performance with the light of exalted acting. Although the pages of the script are stark enough, they reflect light, too, and gather brightness from the wisdom of the lady who is turning them.

1935 D 13

VICTORIA REGINA, a play in three acts and ten scenes, by Laurence Housman. Settings by Rex Whistler; incidental music arranged by Walter Leigh; staged and produced by Gilbert Miller. At the Broadhurst Theatre.

A Footman .... Alfred Helton
Lord Conyngham .... E. Bellenden-Clarke
Archbishop of Canterbury .. Harry Plimmer
A Maidservant .... Mary Austin
Duchess of Kent .... Babette Feist
Victoria .... Helen Hayes
Lord Melbourne .... Lewis Casson
Prince Albert .... Vincent Price
Prince Ernest .... George Macready
Mr. Richards .... Albert Froom
Mr. Anson .... Oswald Marshall
1st Queen's Gentleman .. Arthur Gould-Porter
A Court Usher .... Edward Martin
Lady Muriel .... Mary Heberden
Lady Grace .... Renee Macready
Lady-in-Waiting .. Mary Newnham-Davis
2d Queen's Gentleman .. Fothringham Lysons
Mr. Oakley .... James Bedford
Duchess of Sutherland ...... Cherry Hardy
Lady Jane .... Helen Trenholme
General Grey .... Tom Woods
3d Queen's Gentleman ...... Edward Jones
John Brown .... James Woodburn
Lord Beaconsfield .... George Zucco
A Footman .... Robert Von Rigel
Sir Arthur Bigge ...... Herschel Martin
An Imperial Highness .... Felix Brown
His Royal Highness ...... Gilbert McKay
1st Princess .... Mary Forbes
2d Princess .... Shirley Gale
3d Princess .... Elizabeth Munn
Members of the Royal Family, Footman and Court Officials: Jean Stephenson, William Packer, Willis Duncan, Alan Bandler, Guy Moneypenny, Shirley Poirier, Buddy Buehler.

Inevitably the book gives a fuller portrait of the stubborn but resolute lady of Windsor; the book supplies more of the stateswoman gravely at work on the moral and political affairs of her nation. The episodes selected for the stage dwell on her personal character—the sudden decision to rule when she is still an innocent girl, the deeply rooted and long-enduring romance with the Prince Consort and the lonely grandeur of the old widow. Mr. Housman is aware of the rigidities of her mind that were once the joke of modern satirists. She is a tight little body of respectable prejudices. But he recognizes the strength and uprightness of her character, which set its stamp on the English spirit of her day. Being detached, his portrait is poignant, reverent and touching. In short, it is admirable.

Mr. Miller has gone about the job of production with meticulous patience, dressing it in imaginative and nostalgic scenery by Rex Whistler and in costumes that count as pageantry. For the part of Albert he has selected Vincent Price, whose personal appearance is said to be astonishingly suitable, and whose gentleness of manner as an actor is completely winning. Mr. Housman has done well by Albert, appreciating the difficulties of his position in England as well as the honor with which he served his wife, his Queen and his adopted nation; and Mr. Price plays the part in exactly that spirit. He also plays it beautifully enough to evoke all the romance that lay under the surface of a singular royal marriage.

Despite his acting and the courtly statesmen played by Lewis Casson and George Zucco, "Victoria Regina" is still a succession of literary scenes. It is deliberate, reserved, politely spectacular, and encumbered with minor actors who cannot lift a scene out of the book. To this chronicler "Victoria Regina" read is more profoundly moving than "Victoria Regina" seen on a physical stage. Mr. Housman has stirred the imagination with words that spin around memories and impressions; and for all its stage skill, the production breeds some measure of disenchantment.

And yet there is Miss Hayes's acting to reckon with—a warm, willowy expression of spirit with many disarming flashes of humility. Behind the mask of an extraordinary make-up her scenes of old age are a tour de force that still lets an unconquerable spirit through. If it were not for her presence on the stage and Mr. Price's acting, "Victoria Regina" might better gleam between covers than dutifully bask on the stage. But here she is, and she is tremulously magnificent. God save the queen!

1935 D 27

1936

ETHAN FROME, a play in a prologue, three acts and an epilogue, based on Edith Wharton's novel of the same name. Dramatization by Owen Davis and Donald Davis from a previous version made by Lowell Barrington (nom de plume for Louis B. Christ Jr.). Staged by Guthrie McClintic; scenery and costumes by Jo Mielziner; produced by Max Gordon. At the National Theatre.

Harmon Gow ....John Winthrop
A Young Man...............Oliver Barbour
Ethan Frome ....Raymond Massey
Zenobia Frome ....Pauline Lord
Dennis Eady ....Tom Ewell
Mattie Silver ....Ruth Gordon
Jotham ....Francis Pierlot
Ed Varnum ....Charles Henderson
Ned Hale ....W. Dana Hardwick
Ruth Varnum ....Sylvia Weld
Mrs. Hale ....Marie Falls

Citizens of Starkfield—Catherine Carey, Virgilia Chew, Virginia Frank, Beatrice Graham, Eddie James, Pam Lawrence, Evelyn Monte, William Morris, Ella Morrice, George Parkes, Arthur Rosen, Elmira Sessions, Tom Tempest, Jessie Wilson.

By BROOKS ATKINSON.

These must be the palmy days of acting. In order to tell the gaunt story of "Ethan Frome," which arrived at the National last evening, the management has hired Ruth Gordon, Pauline Lord and Raymond Massey, who are hereby nominated for immortality. The story of Edith Wharton's New England masterpiece is not easy to translate into the theatre, and the Davises, père et fils, have not wholly succeeded; for the theatre has put up considerable resistance. But the actors have told a story of hope, bewilderment and anguish that is likely to make your heart stand still more than once during the evening. In the tones of their voices and the apprehensive look in their eyes they have found incandescent words that no dictionary contains.

Particularly Miss Gordon, who plays the part of Mattie like an actress who is inspired. Mattie, you will remember, is the gay little wretch whom the gods torment more than they have a right to do. Taking the part as Mrs. Wharton first described it in compassionate prose, Miss Gordon has added out of her own understanding details that Mrs. Wharton would approve if she could see them, for this is a Mattie who is wholly alive. Plain, shy, awkward, restless, she is a simple person, whom youth adorns with a thousand fantastic hopes and inarticulate fears. Miss Gordon has created a remarkably vivid character, for she has become an actress with superb gifts that she knows exactly how to use.

Pauline Lord's Zenobia Frome ¢is not precisely the tight-lipped, malevolent harridan whom Mrs. Wharton described. Zenee was an unlovely object for hatred. What we have in the play is a selfish, frustrated daughter of poverty whose misfortunes engender occasional pity. It is not in Miss Lord's nature to represent cruelty without a dash of humanity as well. For she, too, is an actress of great sentient perceptions whose spirit overflows every part she takes. As Ethan Frome, the young farmer trapped between love and duty, Raymond Massey gives the best performance he has disclosed in this country—graceless, desperate yet kind withal; things happen too fast and become too wild for Ethan's powers of decision.

What faults the play of "Ethan Frome" has in the theatre are inherent in the story. Mrs. Wharton wrote it in a swift narrative against a frozen background; and the characters were tight with Yankee reticence. In order to tell the same story on the stage, Owen and Donald Davis have had to leap across the landscape and supply words and invent episodes that will be intelligible in the theatre. You cannot make a full length play of people who begrudge you a word and avoid scenes as resolutely as possible.

If you take the structural difficulties for granted, if you are prepared for a drama that has to be static occasionally, the Davises have admirably succeeded without violating the pinched mood of the story. They have given it fullness and body. Rounding out the details without cheapening them and finding words for the characters that are at once plain and expressive. Here and there they have altered the motivation for sound technical reasons. With the same aspect for the integrity of the story, Jo Mielziner has designed a dingy kitchen, a frigid, squalid bedroom, a glimpse of a snowy dooryard and a gorgeous white hilltop. With the cold light of the stars piercing the night sky.

So the bill of exceptions scarcely matters in comparison with the austere beauty of this frozen idyll. Mrs. Wharton had the grace to realize that under the dour surface of a New England community the emotions can be fierce in their in-tensity. The deepest tragedies are lonely, and the lives they blight go on wearily breathing. "Ethan Frome" was great as a novel. Although it is not great as a play, it has many great beauties and it is acted by players who have torn tragedy out by the roots and heaped the stage with it.

1936 Ja 22

SAINT JOAN, a "chronicle play" in three acts, six scenes and an epilogue, by Bernard Shaw; staged by Guthrie Mc-Clintic; settings and costumes by Jo Mielziner; incidental music by Paul Nordoff; revived by Katharine Cornell. At the Martin Beck Theatre.
Captain Robert de Baudricourt,
                            Joseph Holland
His Steward.............Arthur Chatterton
Joan ....Katharine Cornell
Bertrand de Poulengey...Tyrone Power Jr.
Monseigneur de la Tremouille,
                            Charles Dalton
The Archbishop of Rheims..Charles Waldron
Page to the Dauphin.....Robert Champlain
Gilles de Rais..................David Vivian
Captain la Hire................Barry Kelly
The Dauphin..............Maurice Evans
Duchess de la Tremouille......Ruth March
Dunois ....Kent Smith
Page to Dunois.........Edward Ryan Jr.
Richard de Beauchamp.........Brian Aherne
Master John de Stogumber.George Coulouris
Page to Warwick..........Walter Marquis
Peter Cauchon........ ....Eduardo Ciannelli
Brother John Lemaitre........Arthur Byron
Canon John d'Estivet.......Joseph Holland
Canon de Courcelles........Irving Morrow
Brother Martin Ladvenu.....John Cromwell
The Executioner...............Berry Kelly
An English Soldier..........Charles Dalton
A Gentleman of 1920.....Arthur Chatterton
Court Ladies....Hilde Albers, Anne Froelick
Courtiers and Soldiers—Richard Graham, David Orrick, William Roehrick, Hudson Shotwell, Kurt Steinbart, Fred Thompson.

By BROOKS ATKINSON.

Miss Cornell and Mr. Shaw beat us all into reverent submission last evening. Not that we were offering much resistance, for the play was "Saint Joan," which has been increasing in popular stature ever since it was first acted a dozen years ago; and Miss Cornell's pre-eminence in the rôle was virtually assured. But an occasion, if it is real, always transcends expectation. Let it be said at once that a generous share of the modern theatre's grandeur is now on display at Mr. Beck's dramatic cathedral in Forty-fifth Street. Miss Cornell, Mr. McClintic and Mr. Mielziner have seen Shaw's finest play well bestowed at the hands of many excellent actors. "Saint Joan" is acted and produced down to the last comma and coruscating phrase.

Trust the McClintics to realize

that despite the horseplay it is a religious drama that challenges man-made authority. They have drawn out of the text the profundities which Shaw, in a mood of postwar despair, saw in this legend of the warlike, voice-intoxicated maid. There are scenes no more than competent in Shaw's medieval chronicle, and in this reviewer's opinion the manner and verbosity of the epilogue snatch a fine play back into theatre tedium. Not the jokes, which are trivial enough, but the perfunctory putting together of words robs the epilogue of dramatic significance. After the Earl of Warwick's prescient "I wonder" at the close of the burning scene the literal fantasy of King Charles's dream is in the willful image of the white-bearded wit of London Town.

But if "Saint Joan" offered nothing except the solemn trial scene and the compassionate wisdom of the inquisitor's speech it would still rank with the best in the modern theatre. The present revival has molded that scene into a masterpiece. Mr. Mielziner has banked the stage with the awe and terror of it, keeping the stage levels dramatic and the lighting of the jury box shadowy and ominous. Mr. McClintic has gauged the pitch of the voices so that the rancorous, reproving and pathetic sounds of men speaking passionately, and a maid responding honestly, make your pulses beat anxiously. And in the part of the Inquisitor, Arthur Byron has wrapped a cloak of magnificence around his shoulders as an actor. It is a grand speech—sincere and thoughtful and sorrowful, an expression of honorable character. Mr. Byron speaks it not only from memory but from the heart; and he tells you emotionally what is at stake in this overwrought trial of a maid who has piqued the world by her faith.

Miss Cornell's Joan is flesh, blood and spirit, the reincarnation of a country girl and a sacred legend. In the early scenes the strength from the land and the awkwardness of country manners; in the cathedral scene the valor of a girl who recognizes her destiny amid dangers; in the trial scene the weariness of a tormented spirit, the human fear of fire and the quick defiance—Miss Cornell has caught all of it in the incandescence of her playing and added to it her respect for a girl inspired beyond the knowledge of men.

She has honored her profession by surrounding herself with actors of considerable quality—Brian Aherne for a mellifluous Warwick, Maurice Evans for a comic, fussy king, Charles Waldron for an Archbishop of eminence, George Coulouris for a stubborn Britisher with Shavian manners, Kent Smith for a resolute general and Eduardo Ciannelli for a choleric bishop which shows something of the true measure of an actor who was wasted until "Winterset" and "Saint Joan" gave him an opportunity.

In association with these actors Miss Cornell and Mr. Shaw beat us into submission last evening. They had something vital to say.

1936 Mr 10

IDIOT'S DELIGHT, a play in three acts, by Robert E. Sherwood, with incidental music. Staged by Bretaigne Windust; production conceived and supervised by Alfred Lunt and Lynn Fontanne; setting by Lee Simonson; dances arranged by Morgan Lewis; presented by the Theatre Guild as the sixth and last offering of its eighteenth subscription season. At the Shubert Theatre.

Dumptsy	George Meader
Signor Palota	Stephen Sandes
Donald Navadel	Barry Thomson
Pittaluga	S. Thomas Gomez
Auguste	Edgar Barrier
Captain Locicero	Edward Raquello
Dr. Waldersee	Sydney Greenstreet
Mr. Cherry	Bretaigne Windust
Mrs. Cherry	Jean Macintyre
Harry Van	Alfred Lunt
Shirley	Jacqueline Paige
Beulah	Connie Crowell
Edna	Frances Foley
Francine	Etna Ross
Elaine	Marjorie Baglin
Bebe	Ruth Timmons
First Officer	Alan Hewitt
Second Officer	Winston Ross
Third Officer	Gilmore Bush
Fourth Officer	Tommaso Tittoni
Quillery	Richard Whorf
Signor Rossi	Le Roi Operti
Signora Rossi	Ernestine De Becker
Major	Giorgio Monteverde
Anna	Una Val
Irene	Lynn Fontanne
Achille Weber	Francis Compton
Musicians—Gerald Kunz, Max Rich, Joseph Knopf.	

By BROOKS ATKINSON

Mr. Sherwood's love of a good time and his anxiety about world affairs result in one of his most likable entertainments, "Idiot's Delight," which the Theatre Guild put on at the Shubert last evening. Already it is widely known as the show in which Alfred Lunt plays the part of a third-rate hoofer and Lynn Fontanne wears an exotic blonde wig. That is true, and it represents Mr. Sherwood's taste for exuberance and jovial skullduggery. Having fought in the last war and having a good mind and memory, he is also acutely aware of the dangers of a relapse into bloodshed throughout the world today. His leg-show and frivolity in "Idiot's Delight" are played against a background of cannon calamity, and it concludes with a detonation of airplane bombs. At the final curtain, Mr. Sherwood shoots the works.

If this column observes that the discussion of war is inconclusive and that the mood of the play is somewhat too trivial for such a macabre subject, it is probably taking "Idiot's Delight" much too seriously. For Mr. Sherwood's new play is a robust theatre charade, not quite so heroic and ebullient as "The Petrified Forest," but well inside the same tradition.

In the cocktail lounge of a hotel in the Italian Alps, near the frontiers of Switzerland and Austria, Mr. Sherwood has gathered a few representative citizens. Among them take notice of a German scientist, a high-strung leader of the labor movement, a munitions manufacturer, an English honeymoon couple, any quantity of Italian soldiers and an American song-and-dance troupe led by a gaudy American hoofer. International relations are so incendiary that they are all being detained by the Italian Government, pending further developments. While they are unhappily waiting Mr. Sherwood has time to deliver a number of hard-fisted statements about war in general and international politics in particular and to indulge in some very pungent mountebankery, including an impromptu chorus-girl act.

As it happens, the munitions manufacturer is traveling with a fabulous blonde of many false airs whom the hoofer suspects of being a showgirl he entertained many years ago at the Governor Bryan Hotel in Omaha. This is the thread that binds the rambling piece together and permits Alfred Lunt and Lynn Fontanne to become friends once more at the final curtain.

Mr. Sherwood's talk is not conclusive, but it is interesting. In the course of the play he does manage to show that all but one of his characters are helpless victims of internationalism, drawn unwillingly into contests between fear and inferiority, jingoism and bravado. "Idiot's Delight" draws that grotesque distinction between the personal, casual lives people want to live and the roar and thunder that crackbrained governments foment. As

the hoofer says, the people are all right as individuals. They are bowled down by a headlong, angry force that is generated apart from themselves.

All this Mr. Sherwood's play suggests, though not so forcefully as perhaps he intends, for the rag, tag and bobtail mood is misleading. What you will probably enjoy more than his argument is the genial humor of his dialogue, his romantic flair for character and his relish of the incongruous and the ridiculous.

The Theatre Guild has met him more than half way. Against an amusingly ostentatious setting by Lee Simonson, Bretaigne Windust has directed a busy and versatile performance. Mr. Lunt has declared another holiday for his cheap-mannered, jaunty hoofer and metallic-voiced balladier, and his musical comedy style is recognizable honky-tonk. Mr. Lunt likes a turkey as much as Mr. Sherwood does. As the spurious Russian, Miss Fontanne also puts on the flamboyant mantle, enjoying the bombast of her accent. If it is not unmannerly to say so, perhaps she enjoys it too much, for the space she takes makes the character a little irritating and also delays the show.

In other parts Richard Whorf, Sydney Greenstreet, Edward Raquello, Francis Compton and George Meader give excellent performances. As for the chorus girls, their culture is pleasantly professional. At the close of one of the best seasons the Theatre Guild has had, Mr. Sherwood has spoken passionately about a grave subject and settled down to writing a gusty show. He and Mr. Lunt have set their hearts on a larkish time.

1936 Mr 25

MACBETH, Shakespeare's play in three acts and eight scenes, arranged and staged by Orson Welles. Costumes and settings by Nat Karson; lighting by A. H. Feder; managing producer, John Houseman; produced by the Negro Division of the Federal Theatre Project. At the Lafayette Theatre, 2,225 Seventh Avenue.

Duncan ....Service Bell
Malcolm ....Wardell Saunders
Macduff ....Maurice Ellis
Banquo ....Canada Lee
Macbeth ....Jack Carter
Ross ....Frank David
Lennox ....Thomas Anderson
Siward ....Archie Savage
First Murderer ....George Nixon
Second Murderer ....Kenneth Renwick
The Doctor ....Lawrence Chenault
The Priest ....Al Watts
First Messenger ....Philandre Thomas
Second Messenger ....J. B. Johnson
The Porter ....J. Lewis Johnson

Seyton ....Larri Lauria
A Lord ....Charles Collins
First Captain ....Lisle Grenidge
Second Captain ....Gabriel Brown
First Chamberlain ....Halle Howard
Second Chamberlain..William Cumberbatch
First Court Attendant ....Albert McCoy
Second Court Attendant.....George Thomas
First Page Boy ....Viola Dean
Second Page Boy ....Hilda French
Lady Macduff ....Marie Young
Lady Macbeth ....Edna Thomas
The Duchess ....Alma Dickson
The Nurse ....Virginia Girvin
Young Macduff ....Bertram Holmes
Daughter to Macduff ....Wanda Macy
Fleance ....Carl Crawford
Hecate ....Eric Burroughs
First Witch ....Wilhelmina Williams
Second Witch ......Josephine Williams
Third Witch ....Zola King
Witch Doctor ....Abdul

By BROOKS ATKINSON

If it is "Macbeth" that the WPA folk are staging in Harlem at the Lafayette Theatre these evenings, we shall have to wear a schoolmaster's frown. If it is a voodoo show suggested by the Macbeth legend, we can toss a sweaty night-cap in the air. For the darktown version of "Macbeth," which Orson Welles has arranged and staged, has skipped down to Haiti, chiefly in the interest of the unearthly sisters. It wears a bizarre wardrobe of costumes and screeches dire prophecy with horrid sounds that make the blood run cold. Shakespeare's play has considerably handicapped the magicians who have conjured this weird, vari-colored raree-show out of the fine stuffs of the theatre and the ferocity of Negro acting. But when the play falls in with their "Emperor Jones" caprice they have the artists and the actors who can translate supernaturalism into flaring excitement.

Perhaps we should describe it as the witches' scenes from "Macbeth." They have always worried the life out of the polite tragic stage; the grimaces of the hags and the garish make-believe of the flaming caldron have bred more disenchantment than anything else Shakespeare wrote. But ship the witches down into the rank and fever-stricken jungles of Haiti, dress them in fantastic costumes, crowd the stage with mad and gabbling throngs of evil worshipers, beat the voodoo drums, raise the voices until the jungle echoes, stuff a gleaming naked witch doctor into the caldron, hold up Negro masks in the baleful light—and there you have a witches' scene that is logical and stunning and a triumph of theatre art.

For Nat Karson, who has done the settings and costumes, has taken full advantage of the sub-tropical setting. His jungles are luxuriant and savage and ominous with shadows; his costumes are bold in color, extraordinarily imaginative in shape and pattern—an idealization of Negro extravagance. When the stage is full of them, the pageantry is a pretty heady spectacle. With an eye to the animalism of the setting, they have turned the banquet scene into a ball at a semi-barbaric court, heralded it with music and crowded it with big, rangy figures dressed in magnificent court array. Put that down in your memory-book as another scene that fills the theatre with sensuous, black-blooded vitality.

Since the program announces " 'Macbeth,' by William Shakespeare," it is fair to point out that the tragedy is written in verse and that it reveals the disintegration of a superior man who is infected with ambition. There is very little of any of that in the current Harlem festival. As Macbeth, Jack Carter is a fine figure of a Negro in tight-fitting trousers that do justice to his anatomy. He has no command of poetry or character. As Lady Macbeth, Edna Thomas has stage presence and a way with costumes, and also a considerable awareness of the character she is playing. Although she speaks the lines conscientiously, she has left the poetry out of them.

Although the staging by Orson Welles and John Houseman is uncommonly resourceful in individual scenes, it has missed the sweep and scope of a poetic tragedy. This reporter is inclined to think that in their rearrangement of the play they have been more considerate of the text than such a free-hand occasion warrants. The opening was an exciting event in Harlem last evening with an Elks band serenade and a denser mob than the Ethiopian mass-meeting drew on Lenox Avenue. As an experiment in Afro-American showmanship the "Macbeth" merited the excitement that fairly rocked the Lafayette Theatre. If is it witches you want, Harlem knows how to overwhelm you with their fury and phantom splendor.

1936 Ap 15

BURY THE DEAD, a play in one act by Irwin Shaw; preceded by PRELUDE, also a one-act play, by J. Edward Shugrue and John O'Shaughnessy, with a musical accompaniment by Fred Stewart. Staged by Worthington Miner and Walter Hart; presented by the Actors' Repertory Company; produced by Alex Yokel. At the Ethel Barrymore Theatre.

BURY THE DEAD

First Soldier.........John O'Shaughnessy
Sergeant ....Robert Williams
Second Soldier..........Robert Porterfield
Third Soldier..............Joseph Kramm
Fourth Soldier...............Joseph Wolff
Priest ....Edwin Cooper
Rabbi ....Samson Gordon
Private Driscoll..........Robert Thomsen
Private Morgan..............David Sands
Private Dean...........Douglass Parkhirst
Private Webster..........James Shelburne
Private Levy...............Bertram Thorn
Private Schelling..........Frank Tweddell
Captain ....Neill O'Malley
First General...............Aldrich Bowker
Second General...........France Bendsten
Third General............George O. Taylor
Doctor ....Erik Walz
Stenographer ....Booth Whitfield
Bevins ....Garland Smith
Charlie ....Jay Adler
Reporter ....Will Geer
Editor ....Gordon Nelson
First Whore..............Dorothy Brackett
Second Whore.............Berta Ware
Radio Announcer...............Erik Walz
Bess Schelling.............Kathryn Grill
Mrs. Dean..................Mary Perry
Joan ....Rose Keane
Julia Blake.............Lesley Stafford
Katharine Driscoll.......Norma Chambers
Martha Webster.........Paula Bauersmith
A Voice..................William Hunter

PRELUDE

"Blinky" ....Robert Thomsen
"Basket" ....Frank Tweddell
"Poppy" ....Will Geer

By BROOKS ATKINSON

After a preliminary showing about five weeks ago, Irwin Shaw's harrowing war drama, "Bury the Dead," has moved into the Ethel Barrymore Theatre, where it opened on Saturday evening, under the management of Alex Yokel. It ought to be boycotted by militarists, ammunition vendors and saber rattlers. For Mr. Shaw's grimly imaginative rebellion against warfare is a shattering bit of theatre magic that burrows under the skin of argument into the raw flesh of sensation. He is a young man, a latter-day graduate of Brooklyn College, and his knowledge of the battlefields must have come at second hand. But his moral indignation is his own, and his dramatic virtuosity is extraordinary. What "Waiting for Lefty" was to Clifford Odets, "Bury the Dead" is to Irwin Shaw. The most tormenting war play of the year has come from a new man.

Like "Miracle at Verdun," "Bury the Dead" traffics in corpses. Six privates who have been killed "in the second year of the war that is to begin tomorrow" refuse to lie down peacefully in the graves their living comrades have dug for them. They may be dead, as the medical officer carefully certifies, but they are still young, and they refuse to have their eyes packed with earth against the beauty of the world they have scarcely had time to see. The revolt of the dead alarms the generals, who do not know how to deal with it. They appeal to dead men's sense of honor. Finally, the wives, mothers and sweethearts of the dead appeal to them to lie back in their graves and let the war go on. But the dead have made up their minds, and will not be argued into cemetery submission; and in the last scene they shuffle out of the fresh-dug trench and march silently and defiantly into the world to protest against the injustice that has been done them. There is no army regulation that provides for burying dead men against their will.

If "Miracle at Verdun" had never been written, the primary assumption of "Bury the Dead" might be a more devastating stroke of imagination in the contemporary theatre. But Mr. Shaw has used the idea of dead men's rebellion resourcefully enough to make it his own. Instead of arguing he abides by the homely, heart-breaking simplicities of youth shot down, of love torn out by the roots before it has flowered, of mothers robbed of what they have brought forth in labor. He shows that nothing war achieves is worth anything so glorious as a single human life. Death is the one unpardonable crime of the battlefields. For this is a rebellion, not of reason, but of nature—of flesh, blood and bones, of the normal senses, of the dreams and hopes of wholesome young men. In the creating of character and in the tone of the dialogue, "Bury the Dead" voices the protest of youth with a poignancy that is at once touching and heartening. It is not a glib play nor is it perfectly written, but it has eloquent powers of expression.

Being supernatural, or, rather preternatural, it offers several problems in stage direction. But Worthington Miner and Walter Hart, in association with the notable "Let Freedom Ring" company, have solved the difficulties by meeting them honestly. The acting, especially of the women, is plain and fervent. At the dress rehearsal which, thanks to Mr. Yokel, this reviewer was permitted to see, the performance lacked some of the exhilaration that an audience will give it.

But this reviewer is going to make it his business to see "Bury the Dead" again under normal circumstances, for in eighty minutes of uninterrupted playing Mr. Shaw has spoken a good word for the truth.

'Prelude'

While it is no "Bury the Dead," the Barrymore's curtain raiser has the distinction of being exactly what it says—a "Prelude." Mr. Shaw's play is of the war that is to begin tomorrow, and so the Actors Repertory Company first shows a bit of what happened in the war that ended yesterday. The statesmen of 1914 sound like the statesmen of 1936, and that is the warning; the situations are alike, and "Prelude" makes possible "Bury the Dead."

It is done in the manner of the news reel style, or as the Living Newspaper down the street puts on "Triple-A." Its three main characters are the humble relics of the World War, a blind man, a soldier whose legs have been shot away, another with but one arm. They sit talking of their battles, while in the background the radio plays and the statesmen shout their speeches. "Prelude" convicts with music: "Over There" is cynical when the stage is set correctly. Through much of the play it is the music that carries all the comment that is necessary, and it is better that way. Fred Stewart, arranging the score, has done a fiercer job than the arrangers of the dialogue. It is his play.

Mr. Miner and Mr. Hart, who staged Mr. Shaw's work, also attend to "Prelude." It is put on simply and without pretense.

LEWIS NICHOLS   1936 Ap 20

HAMLET in two acts and nineteen scenes. Settings and costumes by Jo Mielziner; staged and revived by Guthrie McClintic. At the Empire Theatre.

Francisco	Murvyn Vye
Bernardo	Reed Herring
Horatio	Harry Andrews
Marcellus	Barry Kelly
Ghost, Claudius	Malcolm Keen
Cornelius	Whitner Bissell
Voltimand	James Dinan
Laertes	John Emery
Polonius	Arthur Byron
Hamlet	John Gielgud
Gertrude	Judith Anderson
Ophelia	Lillian Gish
Reynaldo	Murvyn Vye
Rosencrantz	John Cromwell
Guildenstern	William Roehrick
The Player King	Harry Mestayer
Prologue	Ivan Triessault
The Player Queen	Ruth March
Lucianus	Whitner Bissell
Fortinbras	Reed Herring
A Captain	George Vincent
A Sailor	William Stanley
First Grave-Digger	George Nash
Second Grave-Digger	Barry Kelly
Priest	Ivan Triessault
Osric	Morgan Farley

By BROOKS ATKINSON

They have seen "Hamlet" well bestowed at the Empire, where he was produced last evening. They have brought to America John Gielgud, whose Hamlet has a prodigious reputation in London, and surrounded him with a cast that includes Judith Anderson, Lillian Gish, Arthur Byron, Malcolm Keen and John Emery. Under Guthrie McClintic's direction, Jo Mielziner has been poking ominous battlements into the night air and stretching royal brocades across the king's apartments. And so the magnificoes of the modern theater, who latterly were creating a masterly "Romeo and Juliet," have come to a greater panel in the Shakespearean screen and performed honorably before it.

Although Mr. Gielgud once acted here in "The Patriot," he comes now on the clouds of glory that in the last few years have been rising around him in London. He is young, slender and handsome, with a sensitive, mobile face and blond hair, and he plays his part with extraordinary grace and winged intelligence. For this is no roaring, robustious Hamlet, lost in melancholy, but an appealing young man brimming over with grief. His suffering is that of a cultivated youth whose affections are warm and whose honor is bright. Far from being a traditional Hamlet, beating the bass notes of some mighty lines, Mr. Gielgud speaks the lines with the quick spontaneity of a modern man. His emotions are keen. He looks on tragedy with the clarity of the mind's eye.

As the results prove in the theatre, this is one mettlesome way of playing the English stage's most familiar classic—one way of modernizing the character. But it is accomplished somewhat at the expense of the full-blooded verse of Shakespeare. What Mr. Gielgud's Hamlet lacks is a solid body of overpowering emotion, the command, power and storm of Elizabethan tragedy. For it is the para-

dox of Hamlet that vigorous actors
who know a good deal less about
the character than Mr. Gielgud does
can make the horror more harrowing and the tragedy more deeply
felt.

Like Mr. Gielgud, Mr. McClintic
and his actors have studied the play
with fresh eyes. Arthur Byron's
Polonius, for example, is no doddering fool but a credible old man
with the grooved mind of a trained
statesman. Malcolm Keen's King
is physically and mentally alive.
As the Queen, Judith Anderson has
abandoned the matronly stuffiness
that usually plagues that part and
given us a woman of strong and
bewildered feeling. What any
actress can do for Ophelia Lillian
Gish has done with innocence of
perception, but that disordered
part contains some of the sorriest
interludes that ever blotted paper.
Inscribe on the credit side the
Laertes of John Emery, the first
grave-digger of George Nash and
the honest Horatio of Harry Andrews.

Mr. McClintic and Mr. Mielziner
have done better, especially in
"Romeo and Juliet." There is a
studied balance to some of Mr.
Mielziner's designs that gives them
an unpleasant rigidity, although his
costumes are vivid with beauty.
And the performance of "Hamlet"
does not proceed with the single
impetuosity of a perfectly orchestrated work of art, as most of Mr.
McClintic's do. This is an admirable "Hamlet" that requires comparison with the best. For intellectual beauty, in fact, it ranks with
the best. But there is a coarser
ferocity to Shakespeare's tragedy
that is sound theatre and that is
wanting in Mr. Gielgud's art.

1936 O 9

PRELUDE TO EXILE, a play in three
acts, by William J. McNally; staged by
Philip Moeller; settings and costumes by
Lee Simonson; production under the su-
pervision of Theresa Helburn, Mr. Moeller
and Lawrence Langner; presented by
the Theatre Guild, by arrangement with
Charles L. Wagner. At the Guild Theatre.
Countess Marie D'Agoult.....Lucile Watson
Adolph ....Roland Hogue
Cosima Liszt von Bulow...Miriam Battista
Hans von Bulow...........Manuel Bernard
Richard Wagner............Wilfrid Lawson
Mathilde Wesendonck.....Eva Le Gallienne
Otto Wesendonck..........Leo G. Carroll
Malwina Schnorr..............Beal Hober
Ludwig Schnorr.............Arthur Gerry
Minna Wagner.............Evelyn Varden
Gottfried.....................Henry Levin

By BROOKS ATKINSON

In honor of the loves and tan-
trums of Richard Wagner the Theatre Guild has produced for its second play of the season "Prelude to
Exile," which was staged at the
Guild Theatre last evening. It is
so vast an improvement upon the
first play of the season that patient
subscribers may now logically look
forward to a third play that will
be not only respectable but exciting. William McNally's composite
portrait of Wagner in the throes of
the Wesendonck affair is eminently
respectable bedecked with snatches
of the "Tristan" score both off-
stage and on, and strengthened by
the acting of a cast that includes
Wilfrid Lawson, Eva Le Gallienne
and Lucile Watson. But if the
Theatre Guild will forgive this column for saying so, the love life of
the composers usually has an egregious look in the theatre, "Prelude
to Exile" being no exception. After all, the poor man is entitled to
a primrose-treading affair if he
wants one, and without inviting the
town in to bear witness.

Possibly Mr. McNally has had to
edit history a little to give the
Wesendonck affair so much biographical scope, but no one will object to that. In the Green Hill cottage he has managed to assemble
Minna Wagner, the petulant wife;
Cosima, destined to take over the
duties of mistress and wife at some
future date; Countess Marie
d'Agoult, her mother and Liszt's
recent mistress; Mathilde Wesendonck, who is now inspiring him to
write "Tristan and Isolde"; her
gloriously bewhiskered husband,
who finds his position in the scheme
of things somewhat ambiguous--
and enough male and female singers to make a play about a composer authentic.

They are all revolving around
"The Master" with a rather painful
reverence for his genius. Even now
they might be still genuflecting before him if Frau Wagner had not
started raising the very devil about
his rapturous worship of Frau
Wesendonck, the musical blue-
stocking. By going to the mat about
it, Frau Wagner does break it up
once and for all, but, fortunately,
not before he lifts the rapture motive straight from Frau Wesendonck's inspiring lips and carries it
intact across the stage to the piano
for the second-act finale. A composer in the process of creating a
theme is always a fearful sight to
behold on the stage.

As Richard Wagner, the melo-
maniac, voluptuary, rascal and magnificent mendicant, Wilfrid Lawson
gives an accomplished performance

that one should respect more than one can. He is enormously versatile and agile without really conveying an impression of a volcanic composer. As Frau Wesendonck, Eva Le Gallienne is lucid and well-bred, worshiping Wagner with her mind rather than her body. Evelyn Varden is enjoyably tempestuous as the harassed Minna, playing the part with overtones as well as plainspeaking. Miriam Battista as Cosima and Leo G. Carroll as Herr Wesendonck give suitable performances of shadowy rôles. But it is Lucile Watson with her crinkly mind and imposing graces who gives the liveliest performance of the evening as Countess Maria d'Agoult.

All these impedimenta Philip Moeller has directed with gentlemanly ease in the midst of Lee Simonson's redolent period settings. "Prelude to Exile" is pleasant to look at. But still a disgruntled playgoer may find himself arriving at the eccentric conclusion that composers are fine folk to avoid in the home. Or perhaps it is merely that our digestion is less hearty today than in those fulsome days of the Eighteen Fifties. Too much adulation ruins the appetite.

1936 D 1

THE COUNTRY WIFE, a revival of the Restoration comedy by William Wycherley. Staged by Gilbert Miller; settings by Oliver Messel; presented by Gilbert Miller, in association with Helen Hayes. At Henry Miller's Theatre.

Mr. Horner	Roger Livesey
Quack	George Carr
A boy	Raymond Johnson
Sir Jasper Fidget	George Graham
Lady Fidget	Irene Browne
Mrs. Dainty Fidget	Edith Atwater
Mr. Harcourt	Anthony Quayle
Dr. Dorilant	Stephen Ker Appleby
Mr. Sparkish	Louis Hector
Mr. Pinchwife	Percy Waram
Mrs. Pinchwife	Ruth Gordon
Alithea	Helen Trenholme
Mrs. Squeamish	Helena Pickard
Lucy	Jane Vaughan
Old Lady Squeamish	Violet Besson
A parson	Lewis Dayton

Ladies in Exchange Scene: Frances Greet, Alice Thomson, Flora Campbell, Elizabeth Malloch, Katherine Embree, Gladys Griffith, Inge Hardison.

Footmen, Linkman, and Gentlemen in Exchange Scene: Warren Reid, Donald Stevens, Roger Blankenship, Lewis Sealy, Salo Douday, Reginald Stanborough, David Gray, William Justus.

By BROOKS ATKINSON

If a tale of literary bawdry must be told in seventeenth-century finery, it is plain that Ruth Gordon has the knack of it. After an Autumn engagement in London she is now back in New York as Mrs. Pinchwife in Wycherley's "The Country Wife," which was acted at Henry Miller's last evening. Perhaps you have not been thinking of our Ruth as the sportive heroine of a Restoration comedy, but obviously she has, and to very good purpose, for she has a refreshingly comic idea of a sin-bedizened part. She plays it with something of the artful naïveté that was so funny in "Mrs. Partridge Presents" a good many years ago.

That would not be the proper way to reanimate some of the grander ladies who tiptoe their way through the mannered middens of Restoration drama. But students who peeked into "The Country Wife" in college, when they were supposed to be reading "The Way of the World," know that the bucolic simplicity of Mrs. Pinchwife suits Miss Gordon's style down to the ground. The gaucherie of the part fits neatly into the guile of her acting. Miss Gordon is also an actress who studies a part with enough industry to give it an uncommon fullness by the time it reaches the stage. And so it is here, for her awkward and beflustered gestures, her elaborate confidences turned straight into the faces of the audience, her falling voice, her alarms and studied raptures are funny and original and resourceful, and quite the best thing in Wycherley's old trollop discursion.

By all the laws governing licentiousness on the stage "The Country Wife" ought to be as lively, say, as "Personal Appearance," which inhabited the same theatre. It is founded on the most infamous kind of scandal and it is a detailed anatomy of cuckoldry. According to the latest regulations in good taste, a play can be as obscene as it likes if it is more than two centuries and a half old and if it is written in the finely mitered prose of the day of Charles II. "Fie, fie, sir, let us not be smutty," the ladies say as they hide behind their fans, but a good wit knows that they do not mean to be rude or rebuking. So long as a wit's style is correct, his lips can be as slatternly as he chooses.

But this column regrets to report that even in the neatly pruned version now to be heard in Henry Miller's "The Country Wife" is a joke hard to keep risible all evening. The wits are pestilential fellows unless, by some sort of magic, an actor can charge them with the wit of acting. Although Gilbert Miller has housed them in gay settings by Oliver Messel, and dressed them up within an inch of their foppish lives, most of them work much too hard to be amusing. Percy Waram knows what he is about as Mr. Pinchwife; Louis Hector and George Graham have a notion of how artifice is translated into humor on the stage. The ladies, particularly Helen Trenholme, look charming in sweeping costumes that the smart shops of this town ought to imitate as soon as possible.

But the performance is so loosely woven on the one hand and so overwrought on the other, that even the smoking-room laughers are hard put to it for a lusty jest before the curtain descends. When Mrs. Pinchwife went to the theatre she was aweary of the play but she liked hugeously the actors. She was one up on most of us last evening. Excepting Miss Gordon's gleaming comedy in a modern spirit, Mr. Wycherley and his brief chroniclers are not the most spirited of companions in the theatre. Mr. Wycherley must share part of the blame.

1936 D 2

YOU CAN'T TAKE IT WITH YOU, a "farcical comedy" in three acts, by Moss Hart and George S. Kaufman. Staging by Mr. Kaufman; settings by Donald Oenslager; produced by Sam H. Harris. At the Booth Theatre.

Penelope Sycamore	Josephine Hull
Essie	Paula Trueman
Rheba	Ruth Attaway
Paul Sycamore	Frank Wilcox
Mr. De Pinna	Frank Conlan
Ed	George Heller
Donald	Oscar Polk
Martin Vanderhof	Henry Travers
Alice	Margot Stevenson
Henderson	Hugh Rennie
Tony Kirby	Jess Barker
Boris Kolenkhov	George Tobias
Gay Wellington	Mitzi Hajos
Mr. Kirby	William J. Kelly
Mrs. Kirby	Virginia Hammond
Three Men	George Leach / Ralph Holmes / Franklin Heller
Olga	Anna Lubowe

By BROOKS ATKINSON

Moss Hart and George S. Kaufman have written their most thoroughly ingratiating comedy, "You Can't Take It With You," which was put on at the Booth last evening. It is a study in vertigo about a lovable family of hobby-horse riders, funny without being shrill, sensible without being earnest. In "Once in a Lifetime" Mr. Hart and Mr. Kaufman mowed the audience down under a machine-gun barrage of low comedy satire, which was the neatest trick of the season. But you will find their current lark a much more spontaneous piece of hilarity; it is writ-

ten with a dash of affection to season the humor and played with gayety and simple good spirit. To this column, which has a fondness for amiability in the theatre, "You Can't Take It With You" is the best comedy these authors have written.

To people from the punctilious world outside, the Vanderhof and Sycamore tribes appear to be lunatics. For thirty-five years, grandfather has done nothing but hunt snakes, practice dart throwing, attend commencement exercises and avoid income tax payments. His son-in-law makes fireworks for a hobby in the cellar; various members of the family write plays, study dancing, play the xylophone and operate amateur printing presses. Being mutually loyal they live together in a state of pleasant comity in spite of their separate hobbies. If Alice Sycamore had not fallen in love with the son of a Wall Street banker there would be no reason for this comedy. The contrast between his austerely correct world and their rhymeless existence in a cluttered room supplies the heartburn and the humor. By the time of the final curtain even the banker is convinced that there is something to be said for riding hobbies and living according to impulse in the bosom of a friendly family.

Not that "You Can't Take It With You" is a moral harangue. For Mr. Hart and Mr. Kaufman are fantastic humorists with a knack for extravagances of word and episode and an eye for hilarious incongruities. Nothing this scrawny season has turned up is quite so madcap as a view of the entire Sycamore tribe working at their separate hobbies simultaneously. When Mr. Kirby of Wall Street and the Racquet Club walks into their living-room asylum his orderly head reels with anguish. The amenities look like bedlam to him. What distinguishes "You Can't Take It With You" among the Hart-Kaufman enterprises is the buoyancy of the humor. They do not bear down on it with wisecracks. Although they plan it like good comedy craftsmen, they do not exploit it like gag-men.

And they have assembled a cast of actors who are agreeable folks to sit before during a gusty evening. As grandfather, Henry Travers, the salty and reflective one, is full of improvised enjoyment. Josephine Hull totters and wheedles through the part of a demented homebody. As a ferocious-minded Moscovite, George Tobias roars through the room. Under Mr. Kaufman's direction, which can be admirably relaxed as well as guffawingly taut, every one gives a jovial performance —Paula Trueman, Frank Wilcox, George Heller, Mitzi Hajos, Margot Stevenson, Oscar Polk. Well, just read the cast. The setting is by Donald Oenslager, as usual.

When a problem of conduct raises its head for a fleeting instant in the Sycamore family, grandfather solves it with a casual nod of philosophy, "So long as she's having fun." Mr. Hart and Mr. Kaufman have been more rigidly brilliant in the past, but they have never scooped up an evening of such tickling fun.

1936 D 15

THE SHOW IS ON, a review in two acts, with sketches by the late David Freedman and Moss Hart and music and lyrics mainly by Vernon Duke and Ted Fetter, also by Carmichel and Adams, Dietz and Schwartz, the Gershwins, Harburg and Arlen, Herman Hupfeld, Irwin and Zeno and Rodgers and Hart; sketches directed by Edward Clark Lilley and dances staged by Robert Alton; the entire enterprise conceived, staged and designed by Vincente Minnelli; produced by the Shuberts at the Winter Garden.
PRINCIPALS: Beatrice Lillie, Bert Lahr, Reginald Gardiner, Mitzi Mayfair, Paul Haakon, Gracie Barrie, Charles Walters, Vera Allen, Robert Shafer, Jack McCauley, Evelyn Thawl, Ralph Riggs, Marie Carroll and Roy Campbell's Continentals.

By BROOKS ATKINSON

Thank you very much, Kris Kringle. In fact, much obliged. "The Show Is On" is on at the Winter Garden, where it opened last evening, and it is the best rowdy-dowdy that has kicked up its heels under that ancient roof. Although Vincente Minnelli's previous revues have been stunning and original, this is the finest of the lot, and Beatrice Lillie and Bert Lahr are in their top form as the chief performers. Perhaps this is no time to begin talking of intelligence and beauty in relation to a spacious show at the Winter Garden, but Mr. Minnelli and his merry-andrews have reformed that old arcade of song-and-dance pleasures. "The Show Is On" skims gayly through an evening of radiant high-jinks.

Now that the curtain has just fallen it is difficult studiously to isolate the chief pleasures of "The Show Is On." By an infallible taste in decoration and sequence Mr. Minnelli has managed to keep the flow of humor even all through the evening. You are scarcely secure in your seat before Bert Lahr, with his worried map and ornate accent, begins to save the empire by wooing the king's beloved lady to Hollywood, and before you are scarcely through with that before Miss Lillie, with a gorgeous spray of shivering orchids at her shoulder, starts singing a hot rhythm number ironically enough to destroy that music hall staple from now on.

As usual, Miss Lillie does not waste a grimace or a gleam throughout the program. She murders a performance of "Hamlet" by her upper-class manners in the audience; she condescends to sell tickets superciliously for the Theatre Guild; mimics Josephine Baker destructively and once she swings out over the audience, seated in a crescent moon, while she sings the lyrics of a dismal ballad. She is perfectly gowned, perfectly set off in the whirl of the production, and her lucid, mischievous comedy is incomparably funny. As for Mr. Lahr, they have given him the uproarious things that he can do with cartoon gusto—singing a burlesque banality in a woodsman's shirt, ruining the mannerisms of swing-music in a lethal travesty, wooing passionately in a full-dress suit. None of Mr. Lahr's stretch-mouthed talents have been wasted in "The Show Is On."

Nor do Miss Lillie and Mr. Lahr exhaust the intelligence and the humor. David Freedman wrote a whole basketful of revue sketches that make comic faces at current shows and political situations, and Moss Hart has tossed a comic balloon at the recent corner in "Hamlets." Although Reginald Gardiner has nothing to offer that can touch his concerto on the railroad business, he is still in good humor and once conducts an orchestra with an impish flourish. For dancing there are Paul Haakon, spinning through a gorgeous Casanova ballet, and Mitzi Mayfair in a portfolio of engaging antics. Gracie Barrie does most of the pert singing of serenades that Vernon Duke and Ted Fetter composed.

The credits are in the program, where you can study them in due course. They read like a roll-call of the town's bards and minnesingers. But Mr. Minnelli has transformed all the material and performers into a luminous work of art. As a designer he is never ostentatious, but the façade of "The Show Is On" is a procession of soft and winning splendors. Miss Lillie and Mr. Lahr are the most notable figures in the decoration, but when they are temporarily missing Mr. Minnelli's show is still on.

1936 D 26

THE WOMEN, a play in three acts, by Clare Boothe. Staged by Robert B. Sinclair; settings by Jo Mielziner; produced by Max Gordon. At the Ethel Barrymore

Jane	Anne Teeman
Sylvia (Mrs. Howard Fowler)	Ilka Chase
Nancy Blake	Jane Seymour
Peggy (Mrs. John Day)	Adrienne Marden
Edith (Mrs. Phelps Potter)	Phyllis Povah
Mary (Mrs. Stephen Haines)	Margalo Gillmore
Mrs. Wagstaff	Ethel Jackson
Olga	Ruth Hammond
First Hairdresser	Mary Stuart
Second Hairdresser	Jane Moore
Pedicurist	Ann Watson
Euphie	Eloise Bennett
Miss Fordyce	Eileen Burns
Little Mary	Charita Bauer
Mrs. Morehead	Jessie Busley
First Saleswoman	Doris Day
Second Saleswoman	Jean Rodney
Head Saleswoman	Lucille Fenton
First Model	Beryl Wallace
Third Saleswoman	Martina Thomas
Crystal Allen	Betty Lawford
A Fitter	Joy Hathaway
Second Model	Beatrice Cole
Princess Tamara	Arlene Francis
Exercise Instructress	Anne Hunter
Maggie	Mary Cecil
Miss Watts	Virgilia Chew
Miss Trimmerback	Mary Murray
A Nurse	Lucille Fenton
Lucy	Marjorie Main
Countess de Lage	Margaret Douglass
Miriam Aarons	Audrey Christie
Helene	Arlene Francis
Sadie	Marjorie Wood
Cigarette Girl	Lillian Norton

By BROOKS ATKINSON

Not the ladies, but "The Women" are the brew in Clare Boothe's kettle of venom which the actors set to bubbling at the Ethel Barrymore Theatre on Saturday evening. With a good deal of feline wit and without benefit of either a single or a wedded male actor, she has told the divorce story of the smart women of New York against a cyclorama of bridge clubs, permanent-wave chambers of horror, fitting-rooms, maternity wards, night-club powder rooms and one elegant bathroom where a blond trollop languishes handsomely in the suds and talks with her lover over a gilded telephone handset. Max Gordon has produced it with lustrous scenery by Jo Mielziner and brilliant costuming supervised by John Hambleton; and the acting, especially Margalo Gillmore's, is altogether first-rate. "O, 'tis a wicked, censorious world," as Mrs. Fidget says in Wycherley's companion-piece now visible elsewhere in Times Square. Perhaps theatregoers of frail constitution may be pardoned for disliking it.

Miss Boothe has her back hair down. Left to their own devices, while their men-folk are either working at the office or deceiving their wives in the evening, Miss Boothe's alley-cats scratch and spit with considerable virtuosity. For the sake of practical playmaking, she introduces as her chief character Mrs. Stephen Haines, who loves her husband and is devoted to her home and children. But Mrs. Haines discovers through a prattling manicurist that her husband has succumbed to the blandishments of an ambitious salesgirl, and she goes to Reno to divorce him. For two years she lives in heartbroken retirement with her mother and children while her former husband does his best to tolerate her successor. In the last act the first Mrs. Haines learns that the second has fallen back into the old ways of infidelity, which is the chance she has been waiting for. Virtue outwits depravity at a conclave of all the hell-hags in the powder room of a night club; and the implication of the final curtain is that the first Mrs. Haines will have her old husband back as soon as the courts have freed him again.

Mrs. Haines's tribulations and her personal character bless the play with two or three poignant scenes, which are adorned by the most graceful acting in Miss Gillmore's career and by Charita Bauer's brave and moving performance as the unhappy daughter of divorced parents. But "The Women" is chiefly a multi-scened portrait of the modern New York wife on the loose, spraying poison over the immediate landscape. Miss Boothe has chosen amusing places for the background of her school for scandal, although the bathroom is not so illuminating as had been hoped for. She has also scribbled out some cleverly spiteful dialogue, arranged a scene of hair-pulling fisticuffs between two contenders for general ignobility, and gone extensively into the physiology of the female of the species.

Under Robert B. Sinclair's able direction, some excellent actresses give stingingly detailed pictures of some of the most odious harpies ever collected in one play. As the most malignant of the lot, Ilka Chase presides over the proceedings like the mother of all vultures; playing the part as it was written, she leaves no bone unpicked. With calculated industry, Miss Boothe has thus compiled a workable play out of the withering malice of New York's unregenerate worldlings. This reviewer disliked it.

1936 D 28

1937

'Faustus' Put On by the Federal Theatre.

DOCTOR FAUSTUS, a revival of the Christopher Marlowe play; music by Paul Bowles; directed by Orson Welles; produced by "Project 891" of the Federal Theatre Project. At Maxine Elliott's.

The Pope	Charles Peyton
Cardinal of Lorrain	J. Headley
Faustus	Orson Welles
Valdes	Bernard Savage
Cornelius	Myron Paulson
Wagner, Servant to Faustus,	Arthur Spencer
First Scholar	William Hitch
Second Scholar	Joseph Wooll
Third Scholar	Huntly Weston
Clown	Harry McKee
Robin	Edgerton Paul
Ralph	Wallace Acton
Vintner	George Smithfield
Old Man	George Duthie
First Friar	Edward Hemmer
Mephistopheles	Jack Carter
Good Angel	Natalie Harris
Evil Angel	Blanche Collins
Spirit in the shape of Helen of Troy,	Paula Laurence

Seven Deadly Sins—

Pride	Elizabeth Malone
Covetousness	Jane Hale
Wrath	Helena Rapport
Envy	Cora Burlar
Gluttony	Della Ford
Sloth	Nina Salama
Lechery	Lee Molnar
Baliol	Archie Savage
Belcher	Clarence Yates

By BROOKS ATKINSON

Although the Federal Theatre has some problem children on its hands, it also has some enterprising artists on its staff. Some of them got together at Maxine Elliott's Theatre last evening and put on a brilliantly original production of Christopher Marlowe's "The Tragical History of Dr. Faustus," which dates from 1589. If that sounds like a schoolbook chore to you, be disabused, for the bigwigs of the Federal Theatre's Project 891 know how absorbing an Elizabethan play can be when it is staged according to the simple unities that obtained in the Elizabethan theatres. Every one interested in the imaginative power of the theatre will want to see how ably Orson Welles and John Houseman have cleared away all the imposing impediumenta that make most classics forbidding and how skillfully they have left "Dr. Faustus," grim and terrible, on the stage. By being sensible as well as artists, Mr. Welles and Mr. Houseman have gone a long way toward revolutionizing the staging of Elizabethan plays.

Although "Dr. Faustus" is a short play, consuming hardly more than an hour in the telling, it is not a simple play to produce. It is the story of the eminent German philosopher who sold his soul to the devil in exchange for universal knowledge. Like most Elizabethan plays, it has an irresponsible scenario; it moves rapidly from place to place, vexing the story with a great many short scenes; it includes several incidents of supernaturalism and, of course, it is written in verse.

If the directors had tried to stage "Dr. Faustus" against descriptive backgrounds it would be intolerably tedious to follow. But they have virtually stripped it of scenery and decoration, relying upon an ingenious use of lights to establish time and place. In the orchestra pit they have built an apron stage where the actors play cheek by jowl with the audience. The vision of the seven deadly sins is shown by puppets in the right-hand box. Upstage scenes are unmasked by curtained walls that can be lifted swiftly. Entrances are made not only from the wings, but from the orchestra pit and from trap doors that are bursting with light and that make small incidents uncommonly majestical.

The result is a "Dr. Faustus" that is physically and imaginatively alive, nimble, active—heady theatre stuff. As the learned doctor of damnation Orsen Welles gives a robust performance that is mobile and commanding, and he speaks verse with a deliberation that clarifies the meaning and invigorates the sound of words. There are excellent performances in most of the parts, notably Jack Carter's Mephistopheles, Bernard Savage's friend to Faustus and Arthur Spencer's impudent servant. There are clowns, church processionals and coarse brawls along the street. Paul Bowles has composed a score which is somewhat undistinguished in itself, although it helps to arouse the illusion of black magic and diabolical conjuration.

Not that Elizabethan dramas have never been staged before under conditions approximating the conventions of Elizabethan theatres. Most of those experiments have a self-conscious and ascetic look to them. But Mr. Welles and Mr. Houseman have merely looked to the script and staged it naturally. In the first place, it is easy to understand, which is no common virtue. In the second place, it is infernally interesting. "Dr. Faustus" has the vitality of a modern play, and the verse sounds like good, forceful writing. For this is a simple experiment that has succeeded on its merits as frank and sensible theatre, and a good many people will now pay their taxes in a more charitable frame of mind.

1937 Ja 9

KING RICHARD II, a revival of Shakespeare's play; costumes by David Ffolkes; directed by Margaret Webster; produced by Eddie Dowling and Robinson Smith. At the St. James Theatre.

King Richard II	Maurice Evans
John of Gaunt, Duke of Lancaster,	Augustin Duncan
Edmund of Langley, Duke of York,	Lionel Hogarth
Henry, Surnamed Bolingbroke	Ian Keith
Duke of Aumerle, Son to the Duke of York	Sherling Oliver
Thomas Mawbray, Duke of Norfolk,	William Post Jr.
Earl of Northumberland	Charles Dalton
Henry Percy, Surnamed Hotspur, His Son,	Randolph Echols
Lord Ross	Bram Nossen
Lord Willoughby	Stephen Courtleigh
Lord Marshall	Reynolds Evans
First Herald	Lawrence Murray
Second Herald	Rhys Williams
Earl of Salisbury	Lionel Ince
Captain of a Band of Welshmen,	Rhys Williams
Bishop of Carlisle	Reynolds Evans
Sir Stephen Scroop	Donald Randolph
Gardener	Whitford Kane
Second Gardener	Philip Truex
Duke of Surrey	Lawrence Murray
Sir Pierce of Exton	Donald Randolph
Servant to Exton	Robert K. Adams
A Groom	Rhys Williams
A Keeper	Lionel Ince
Queen to Richard	Olive Deering
Duchess of Gloucester	Irene Tedrow
Duchess of York	Betty Jenckes

By BROOKS ATKINSON

After winning considerable admiration during the past two years for his able acting in various parts, Maurice Evans now deserves a sort of reverence for his triumphant performance as King Richard II, which was put on at the St. James last evening. Out of one of the less familiar plays of Shakespeare he has wrought a glorious piece of characterization; his "skipping king" shines through the majesty of inspired acting. Although the play is one of the least known among the works of Elizabeth's great poet, it is bound to seem like an old, well-tried acquaintance now, for Mr. Evans and his colleagues have plucked the heart out of it in one of the most thorough, illuminating and vivid productions of Shakespeare we have had in recent memory. When the final curtain descended last evening every one realized that a play had been honestly played by one of the finest actors of our time.

And all this despite the fact that Richard II is no dominating hero.

According to Shakespeare, he had the air of a king, but he was a popinjay, with no mind for authority and no will to rule a State. "King Richard II" comes from the early period of 1593, when Shakespeare was close to 30 and still uncertainly hammering out a style of his own. In the reading it seems to be one of the minor works, but now that Mr. Evans and his company have pitched their lustrous talents into it, a theatregoer may as well revise his ideas and renovate his mind. For it is the genius of great acting to revitalize the stuff it works on and to impregnate a part with transcendent passion. Although Richard II was no hero, now we know that the anguish of his soul is heroic and has the power to make our hearts stand still.

Taking Shakespeare at his word, Mr. Evans has translated the character of Richard into devastating tragedy. The whole doleful story of weakness in a king is boldly told. Complacent and trivial when his throne is secure, callous and contemptuous in the presence of his betters, he gives way like a sheet of tissue paper at the first opposition. But it is the distinction of Richard that his mind grows keener with destruction before his enemies; although he lacks the power to rule, he has the courage to be his own confessor, and he is most kingly when the crown has been snatched from his head. The characterization is strange and progressive. Mr. Evans has met it point by point with infinite subtlety and burning emotion. There is not an unstudied corner in any part of this glowing portrait.

Not that this production of "King Richard II" has been offered as an actor's shoddy vehicle. Margaret Webster has directed it with brilliance and versatility, and it sweeps across the stage with the stormy beat and power of Shakespearean verse. For Bolingbroke, the implacable adversary, there is Ian Keith, who dominates the part as the part towers through the play. Old John of Gaunt is blessed with the valorous rectitude of Augustin Duncan's acting. The pathetic Queen is touchingly played by Olive Deering. Lionel Hogarth gives a shrewd and knowing performance as the hysterical Duke of York. If there were room, this review ought to go straight through the cast, taking time to salute Rhys Williams for a brilliantly spoken scene as a Welsh captain, Charles Dalton for his sanctimonious Northumberland and several of the others for mettlesome work.

For this is not the sort of Shakespearean revival before which one tediously equivocates. The supple staging, the musical flourishes, the imaginative costuming, the unobtrusive scenery have all been gathered up in Miss Webster's fresh-minded direction and thrust across the footlights in a vibrant performance of a stirring play. It dismisses us from the theatre with a feeling of high excitement and a conviction that there is nothing in the world so illustrious as drama and acting.

1937 F 6

SUSAN AND GOD, a play in three acts and six scenes, by Rachel Crothers. Staged by the author; settings by Jo Mielziner; produced by John Golden. At the Plymouth Theatre.
Irene Burroughs...............Vera Allen
Michael O'Hara...........Douglas Gilmore
Leeds.......................Bigelow Sayre
Charlotte Marley..........Eleanor Audley
Hutchins Stubbs..............Fred Leslie
Leonora Stubbs...........Edith Atwater
Clyde Rochester.............David Byrne
Susan Trexel.........Gertrude Lawrence
Barrie Trexel...............Paul McGrath
Blossom Trexel..............Nancy Kelly
Leontine...................Katherine Deane

By BROOKS ATKINSON

Although Rachel Crothers has been missing from our theatre for five years, all is forgiven now. "Susan and God," which was put on at the Plymouth last evening, is one of her best plays. Looking squarely at the Oxford movement, she has seen what is in it and what it lacks, for she has an enormous fund of common sense. And being a craftsman, she knows how to make her sensible notions fit the stage. In fact, they light up our morose Autumn theatre with a steady, cheerful glow of good humor and homely truth and they give the mind something friendly to lean against. More than that, they give Gertrude Lawrence the tinder for her most incandescent performance in a part that is maturely written. Miss Lawrence is all animation; she is all expression and eloquence. She and Miss Crothers have conspired to make a fairly complete use of the theatre as a place for enjoyment and mental stimulation.

If you know how Miss Crothers goes about these things you will understand the blunt way in which she tells her story. It chiefly con-

cerns Susan Trexel, a selfish, vain woman of the world, and her husband, Barrie Trexel, a hopeless dipsomaniac. During an idle tour abroad Susan has become infected with the Oxford movement in the company of some of England's best people. The public confessional mode of worshipping God by fondling the ego has given her a new social plaything. Although all her friends recognize the insincerity of her prattle, her drunken husband in a moment of abject despair thinks that perhaps she means what she says and that by faith he can pull himself up by his bootstraps. To make a long story short, he does, chiefly for the sake of their lonely adolescent daughter. But the process reforms Susan more thoroughly than him. Much to her surprise she discovers that faith comes from within and not from public exhibition and contact with influential people.

For Miss Crothers is one of our most sagacious women, not only about fundamentals in people, but about fundamentals of the theatre. By planning a play deliberately she knows how to draw her theme out of her characters, not forgetting to keep her story entertaining. There are some diverting sequences of conversation and not a few beaming lines; and at the crucial moments in her narrative there are some uncommonly moving scenes. For the Trexel family includes a schoolgirl daughter who is starved for a home and affectionate parents. Miss Crothers's play is never too genial to forget the private miseries of a human being.

Under Miss Crothers's personal direction the casting, the acting and the costuming add to the fullness of the story. As the drunken husband, Paul McGrath plays with forthright honesty that gives his part dignity in spite of its habits at the bottle. Nancy Kelly plays the school-girl daughter with poignant simplicity and unstudied charm. Among the smart profligates of Miss Crother's assembly are Vera Allen, Douglas Gilmore, Eleanor Audley, Edith Atwater and David Byrne.

But it is Miss Lawrence who keeps the drama bubbling or boiling, according to need. She bursts into it like a breath of fresh air in the first act, and never lets it down for a second. If there was ever a virtuoso performance this is it, with a spirited succession of mockeries, capricious gestures, witty intonations, sombre moods and dynamics—acting that is superlatively keen in characterization and restlessly alive. Miss Lawrence's vibrance goes through the play and through the audience, and perhaps people feel it as they walk by the theatre in the street. As long as Miss Crothers and Miss Lawrence are in the neighborhood the tempo of Times Square will be stepped up to a very exhilarating speed.

1937 O 8

AMPHITRYON 38, a comedy in a prologue and three acts, by Jean Giraudoux. Adapted from the French by S. N. Behrman. Production conceived and supervised by Alfred Lunt and Lynn Fontanne. Staged by Bretaigne Windust. Costumes designed by Valentina. Music composed and conducted by Samuel L. M. Barlow. Produced by the Theatre Guild. At the Shubert Theatre.

Jupiter......................Alfred Lunt
Mercury...................Richard Whorf
Sosie.....................George Meader
Trumpeter...........Sydney Greenstreet
Warrior......................Alan Hewitt
Alkmena..................Lynn Fontanne
Amphitryon..............Barry Thomson
Nenetza................Kathleen Roland
Kleantha..............Jacqueline Paige
Echo................Ernestine de Becker
Leda...........................Edith King

By BROOKS ATKINSON

As one of the immortals Alfred Lunt is mercifully mortal. As a fabulously faithful wife of the classical age Lynn Fontanne is deceptively modern. In other words, Jean Giraudoux's "Amphitryon 38," which the Theatre Guild put on at the Shubert last evening, may wear the robes of the time of Greek fables and talk of the gods of Olympus, but it is bedroom farce and only human. It is also the most distinguished piece of theatre the Guild has had the pleasure of presenting to the subscribers in some time. For S. N. Behrman has adapted Giraudoux's French into mettlesome prose with literary elegances. Lee Simonson, the scene draughtsman; Valentina, the costume-cutter; Bretaigne Windust, the stage director, and Samuel L. M. Barlow, the arranger of musical notes, have all seen "Amphitryon 38" well bestowed. The credits may as well be generous this morning, for the theatre is in good health.

Nearly every one knows by this time what the "38" means. For the benefit of the others, it is M. Giraudoux's rough estimate of the number of times the Amphitryon legend has been told on the stage. People familiar with M. Giraudoux's text report that Mr. Behrman's adaptation is sufficiently inventive to deserve the numerical designation of

"39." In either case, it is the story of Jupiter's infatuation with Alkmena, wife of the warrior, Amphitryon. Her one principle in life is to be faithful to her husband. Even the greatest god of them all cannot flatter her into mortal surrender. Since Jupiter is a fairly cynical fellow about his amours Alkmena's connubial integrity causes him some ungodlike embarrassment and requires uncommon nimbleness in the craftsmanship of disguises. As the lady in the adjoining seat remarked, "Amphitryon 38" is "The Guardsman" with a more imposing patrimony.

Not that it is an immortal play. Although the bedroom joke is more durable than most, it is still only one joke for the space of three acts, and it stumbles through a monotonous stretch in the middle of the evening. In several of the scenes, particularly in the sententious prologue, the authors have scribbled some coruscatingly witty dialogues between Jupiter and Mercury, contemplating from on high the strange love customs of the mortals. There is also one colloquy of vibrant irony when Alkmena belittles Jupiter's genius and politely cries down the story of creation. But "Amphitryon 38" does not dazzle the bedroom joke with inexhaustible brilliance, playing all the changes that might be gayly rung on a god's night out among the gullible mortals.

It is offered as a theatre prank. And as a prank it is one of the wonder works. When the Lunts are on a spree, as they were in "The Taming of the Shrew" a few seasons ago, they go the full distance in extravagance and stage perfection. They twist lines around their tongues until they have tasted the full savor of the humor; they wrap a play around them like a costume. With Mr. Windust's sympathetic assistance, they have surrounded themselves with capital actors this time. Richard Whorf's worldly minded Mercury is as fleet as that character. Mr. Whorf is in the top flight of the trade. Paunchy Sydney Greenstreet makes something fantastically comic out of a droll trumpeter. George Meader is a garrulous servant worth having in any play.

But since the Lunts are in it, let it pass for Lunts' gambol, exultantly outrageous, elegantly wicked, superbly acted. Mr. Lunt enjoys every second of his audacious masquerade. He towers through it like a god on a holiday, never forgetting that he is an actor and that this is make-believe. And in her distinctive style of lingering over the mischief of a part Miss Fontanne's Alkmena is excellent fooling. The bedroom joke has never had such polished telling. The wheels of the gods grind fast and exceeding merry.

1937 N 2

I'D RATHER BE RIGHT, a musical show in two acts, by George S. Kaufman and Moss Hart; music by Richard Rodgers; lyrics by Lorenz Hart; choreography by Charles Weidman; modern dances arranged by Ned McGurn; book staged by Mr. Kaufman; produced by Sam H. Harris. At the Alvin Theatre.

Peggy Jones	Joy Hodges
Phil Barker	Austin Marshall
President of the United States,	George M. Cohan
His Secretary	Ralph Glover
Postmaster General	Paul Parks
Secretary of the Treasury	Taylor Holmes
Secretary of State	Marion Greene
Secretary of Labor	Bijou Fernandez
Secretary of the Navy	David Allman
Secretary of Commerce	Al Atkins
Secretary of Agriculture	Robert Bleck
Secretary of War	Jack Mills
Secretary of the Interior,	Charles McLoughlin
Attorney General	Robert Less
Chief Justice	John Cherry
James B. Maxwell	Florenz Ames
Federal Theatre Director	Joseph Macaulay
Social Securities Messenger	Georgie Tapps
The President's Mother	Marie Louise Dana
The Judge's Girl	Mary Jane Walsh
A Butler	Joseph Allen
Sistie	Evelyn Mills
Buzzie	Warren Mills
Tony	Joseph Macaulay
Joe	Joe Verdi
Acrobats	Jack Reynolds, Sol Black

By BROOKS ATKINSON

Mr. Roosevelt should feel very happy about his part in "I'd Rather Be Right," which opened at the Alvin last evening. On the whole, George S. Kaufman and Moss Hart feel very tender about him. Apart from their affectionate treatment of him in the plot and lines of their musical comedy, they have engaged George M. Cohan to impersonate the President, which is a dispensation devoutly to be desired by any one who wants to please an audience. For Mr. Cohan is an amiable gentleman whose services to the theatre and whose personality have long held him dear in the affections of Gotham playgoers. Put him in as head man in a political garden party, and the President of the United States is bound to emerge as a buoyant, tactful man-about-town with a soft spot in his heart for young lovers and a feeling of general confusion about the government. As a matter of fact, Mr. Cohan has never been in better form. The audience was his, and lovingly his, all last evening.

If the authors had held council with Jim Farley, they could hardly have felt in better humor about our country. Although advance reports seemed to indicate that "I'd Rather Be Right" might discharge a lampoon at the follies of current politics, it turns out to be a pleasant-spoken musical comedy that leisurely ambles away the evening. There is some brisk stuff here and there—a capital object lesson in the effects of taxation, which is worthy of the Living Newspaper technique; a quip or two about the Federal Theatre, "Wherever we see three people together we are supposed to give a show"; a poke at Walter Lippmann and a few frolicsome skirmishes with the Supreme Court. But there have been Marx Brothers shows in the past that were more hilariously antic than this pastoral in Central Park, and "Of Thee I Sing" was enormously more versatile and dynamic. "I'd Rather Be Right" is playful; and, all questions of political opinion to one side, that is hardly enough for a first-rate musical show.

Richard Rodgers, the composer, and Lorenz Hart, maker of rhymes, have come closer to the spirit of the topical merry-go-round. All their political ditties are keen ones —"A Homogeneous Cabinet," "A Little Bit of Constitutional Fun," "We're Going to Balance the Budget," "Labor Is the Thing" and "Off the Record," this one for Mr. Cohan's voice. They have also written the romantic "Have You Met Miss Jones?" which Joy Hodges and Austin Marshall sing with a good deal of footlights rapture; a piece of tuneful mockery, "Spring In Vienna," which Joseph Macaulay sings with flamboyant humor, and a song or two for Mary Jane Walsh, who has the style and volume of an able chorus drum-major.

There are some varied dances for tapping and twirling, including one tedious bit of documentation entitled "American Couple." Irene Sharaff has done the costumes with her usual vivacity, and Donald Oenslager has designed a masque scene for Central Park. The cast includes Taylor Holmes and Marion Green as members of the Cabinet, a fussy Ma Perkins by Bijou Fernandez and a droll Jim Farley by Paul Parks. Florenz Ames does something lively in defense of the harassed business man. In fact, every one has conspired to make "I'd Rather Be Right" a clever and generally likable musical comedy. But it is not the keen and brilliant political satire most of us have been fondly expecting. **1937 N 3.**

GOLDEN BOY, a play in three acts and twelve scenes, by Clifford Odets. Stages by Harold Clurman; scenery by Mordecai Gorelik; produced by the Group Theatre. At the Belasco Theatre.

Tom Moody	Roman Bohnen
Lorna Moon	Frances Farmer
Joe Bonaparte	Luther Adler
Tokio	Art Smith
Mr. Carp	Leo J. Cobb
Siggie	Jules Garfield
Mr. Bonaparte	Morris Carnovsky
Anna	Phoebe Brand
Frank Bonaparte	John O'Malley
Roxy Gottlieb	Robert Lewis
Eddie Fuseli	Elia Kazan
Pepper White	Harry Bratsburg
Mickey	Michael Gordon
Call Boy	Bert Conway
Sam	Martin Ritt
Lewis	Howard Da Silva
Drake	Charles Crisp
Driscoll	Charles Niemeyer
Barker	Karl Malden

By BROOKS ATKINSON

Although Clifford Odets's "Golden Boy" has been a long time in the making, it is worth waiting for. As produced by the reunited Group Theatre at the Belasco last evening, it is a hard-fisted piece of work about a prizefighter whose personal ambition turns into hatred of the world. For the most part it is also hard-boiled theatre, although Mr. Odets is at times a tricky playwright who hopes that his free-hand sketching of the dialogue may turn out to be a prose poem with cosmic overtones. But the dialogue becomes less self-conscious as the play warms into action, and the action is melodramatically exciting. "Golden Boy" is a good show into which you can read a social message if you want to.

In the first act Joe Bonaparte, an Italian boy, makes a choice between prizefighting and music. He is already a promising young violin player, and his simple-hearted father has high hopes of his future as an artist. But Joe believes that he might have a more affluent future as a lightweight fighter. Encouraged by an able trainer and a shrewd manager, he chooses the ring as the quickest road to success. He does succeed. In due time he becomes the champion and smashes his way up until in the greatest fight of his career he kills his opponent. Although he has been callously closing his mind to the brutishness that has been steadily debasing his character, now he is horrified by what he has done and by what he has become. He and his girl complete their destruction in a fatal and deliberate automobile accident.

"Golden Boy" confirms the original convictions that Mr. Odets is an instinctive writer for the stage. He can compose dialogue with a fugue-like tossing around of themes; he can create vigorous characters; he can exploit scenes and enclose his narrative within the fullness of wholly written play. Although he writes with solemn self-confidence he is uncritical of his own talents, and particularly in the first act he takes pride in some of the most pretentiously low-life dialogue that has ever been poured out of an animated beer keg. He alternately underwrites and overwrites as though he were in love with the abundance and variety of his own genius. "Golden Boy" contains some of the worst and some of the best of the centrifugal Odets manner. The best is a pungent, flashy story of a prizefighter who knocks out his own ego.

Under Harold Clurman's direction, the Group Theatre performance is also a medley of mixed virtues. It has to fit a prize-fight play to the Procrustean bed of an earnest approach to art. Nor is the Italian accent the best accomplishment of the Group Theatre lads. Grant them certain obvious limitations in casting, however, and the performance turns out to be skillful in its planning and robust in style. Luther Adler plays the part of the headlong fighter with the speed and energy of an open-field runner. As his girl, Frances Farmer from Hollywood is sufficient to the part and excellent in the romantic scenes. Morris Carnovsky beautifully conveys the silent grief of the affectionate father who realizes that he is losing his boy. Elia Kazan's sleek racketeer and Art Smith's quiet trainer are the simplest and most effective characterizations in the cast. There are good performances by Jules Garfield and Lee J. Cobb in other parts. Mordecai Gorelik has put some of his best work into the mobile parade of scenery.

In general, the faults of both the play and the performance are an unwillingness to be simple in style or relaxed in mind and body. They are more than counterbalanced by the resourceful life Mr. Odets and the actors have brought to this shrill tale of the prize ring. After writing all around it in the first act, Mr. Odets writes his way straight through the heart of it with the strength and gusto of a genuine artisan of the theatre.

1937 N 5

Mercury Theatre

JULIUS CAESAR, the Shakespearean play in modern dress, with no intermission. Staged by Orson Welles; score by Marc Blitzstein; scenery by Samuel Leve; revived by the Mercury Theatre. At the Mercury Theatre, formerly the Comedy, 110 West Forty-first Street.

Julius Caesar	Joseph Holland
Marcus Antonius	George Coulouris
Publius	Joseph Cotten
Marcus Brutus	Orson Welles
Cassius	Martin Gabel
Casca	Hiram Sherman
Trebonius	John A. Willard
Ligarius	Grover Burgess
Decius Brutus	John Hoysradt
Metellus Cimber	Stefan Schnabel
Cinna	Ted Reid
Flavius	William Mowry
Marullus	William Alland
Artemidorus	George Duthie
Cinna	Norman Lloyd
Lucius	Arthur Anderson
Calpurnia	Evelyn Allen
Portia	Muriel Brassler

By BROOKS ATKINSON

Move over and make room for the Mercury Theatre. After a glimpse of the modern version of "Julius Caesar," which opened at the old playhouse in Forty-first Street last evening, it is plain that a place must be found for so much original acting talent. This is the theatre Orson Welles and John Houseman have modestly founded on the reputations they acquired in producing "Macbeth" and "Dr. Faustus" for the Federal Theatre. To judge by their first production, the Mercury will be a theatre where enthusiasm for acting and boldness in production are to be generously indulged by young actors with minds of their own. Mr. Welles's mind is not only his own but it is theatrically brilliant and he is an actor of remarkable cogency. Making room for the Mercury is only the first principle of common sense.

Their first production should be described as a modern variation on the theme of Shakespeare's "Julius Caesar." It is dressed in the street clothes and uniforms of a modern State. It is the story of revolution. For scenery: a few platform levels and the bare brick walls, as well as steam pipes, of the backstage. The lighting in pools, streams, floods and occasional minute designs divides the play into scenes and sets the mood for their significance. Stripped thus to the essentials of an acted performance it is honest, swift and extraordinarily vivid. What happens on the stage has an overpowering sense of tragic omnipotence. It is revolution taken out of the hands of men and driven by immortal destiny.

A Story of Action

Being interested in the look and sound of an acted performance, the demigods of the Mercury Theatre will doubtless agree that their production does not exhaust the resources of "Julius Caesar." It reduces the play and the characters to a story of action. It is sparingly eloquent. And Caesar's resemblance to Mussolini in appearance and manner defines the play so exactly that the dialogue sounds curiously restrained, as though the author could not speak the words he needs for so ominous an occasion. Furthermore, the modern mood is so literal in state politics today that the logic of "Julius Caesar" is not clear. Caesar is assassinated because he is personally ambitious; that much seems reasonable. But presently it appears that Caesar is a benevolent dictator and that his assassins have done the State a grievous wrong. The parallels should not be too closely urged, for Shakespeare was primarily interested in character. When "Julius Caesar" is presented as a play of action, Shakespeare sounds like a Fascist, and perhaps he was Fascist without knowing it.

If so, charge off his right deviation to the fortunes of war, and have the goodness to look on this version of "Julius Caesar" as an exciting excursion into stagecraft. The direction is superb. With nothing but men and lights for materials it creates scenes that are almost tongue-tied with stealth and terror, crowd scenes that overflow with savagery, columns of soldiers marching through the dim light in the distance. For the most part, the actors underplay it. As Mark Antony, George Coulouris has the one passage of declamatory eloquence in the performance; in the funeral oration, which is imaginatively staged, he dominates the multitude with sound.

A Study of Brutus

But Mr. Welles's Brutus is an admirable study in the somber tones of reverie and calm introspection; it is all kindness, reluctance and remorse. Martin Gabel plays Cassius with the casual simplicity that the production requires and Joseph Holland's Caesar is intelligibly imposing. Hiram Sherman's Casca is a shrewd piece of street-corner contemporaneousness. Norman Lloyd skillfully introduces the one humorous episode as Cinna, the poet.

In the direction the Mercurians have placed the emphasis less on character than on the swift flow of revolution swirling through the streets of Rome. With a few vibrating roars, written as a score by Marc Blitzstein, it is a headlong piece of theatre with fresh vitality behind it. Some day a modern author may use the Mercury's love of pure theatre by writing a modern epic to exploit it. In the meantime, "Julius Caesar," stripped of its footlights impedimenta, makes a turbulent show against the backstage masonry. By moving over to make a place for the Mercury Theatre it is obvious that we also move ahead. The Group Theatre, the Surry Players and the Mercury Theatre have a good many healthy ideas.

1937 N 12

PINS AND NEEDLES, a revue in two acts and nineteen scenes. Music and lyrics mostly by Harold J. Rome. Sketches by Arthur Arent. Marc Blitzstein, Emanuel Eisenberg, Charles Friedman and Mr. Rome. Directed by Mr. Friedman. Produced by Labor Stage, Inc., under the sponsorship of the International Ladies Garment Workers Union. At the Labor Stage Theatre.

A new addition to the growing list of imaginative and youthful theatrical groups which are making monkeys of the folk who think it is fashionable to say the theatre is dead, was made Saturday night at the Labor Stage in West Thirty-ninth Street. Throwing to the winds the radical stage's tradition of waxing serious over this world's more disturbing tendencies, the Players of the International Ladies Garment Workers Union, the articulate affiliate of the C. I. O., presented a musical satire, "Pins and Needles," which entertainingly spoofs boss and worker alike.

"Pins and Needles" has been in preparation for more than a year—there have been a variety of informal previews—because the garment workers, whose union labels are carefully itemized in the program, had to sandwich in rehearsals with more remunerative service to the shears and sewing machine. The finished product, however, was worth the wait, for "Pins and Needles" is a witty and tuneful morsel considerably enhanced by the infectious enthusiasm of the cast and a thoroughly workmanlike job on the technical end.

True, the I. L. G. W. U. Players,

ably directed by Charles Friedman, do not miss many plugs for the anti-fascism cause and for the working man in general, but the propaganda is deftly weaved into skits and songs more concerned with providing entertainment first. Harold J. Rome, plucked from the Summer camp circuit, emerges as a composer and lyricist worth watching, his contributions including "Sing Us a Song with Social Significance," "Doin' the Reactionary," "Four Little Angels of Peace Are We" and "One Big Union for Two."

Emanuel Eisenberg, the Group Theatre's advance man, has contributed a sketch carrying the labor play to its logical conclusion and Arthur Arent donated one about the all-Italy maternity handicap. Marc Blitzstein, of "The Cradle Will Rock" fame, dissects the Federal Theatre officials who are terrified by WPA guards. Gluck Sandor routined the dances. Benjamin Zemach did the choreography and Sointu Syrjala the settings.

Accepted in the good-natured spirit in which it is offered, "Pins and Needles" is certainly a revue out of the ordinary and one which only occasionally droops to the level of the things which it is satirizing. All in all, the left-wing theatre may take pride in this delayed descent from the usual soap box. For the present, the I. L. G. W. U. Players are giving performances Friday night and Saturday afternoon and evening. Beginning Jan. 3, it plans nightly performances, except Sunday, and a Saturday matinee.   J. G.

1937 N 29

HOORAY FOR WHAT! A musical show in two acts, conceived by E. Y. Harburg. Book by Howard Lindsay and Russel Crouse. Lyrics by Mr. Harburg. Music by Harold Arlen. Production staged and supervised by Vincente Minnelli. Book staged by Mr. Lindsay. Dances arranged by Robert Alton. Settings by Mr. Minnelli. Costumes designed by Raoul Pene Du Bois. Presented by Lee Shubert, with the cooperation of Harry Kaufman. At the Winter Garden.
PRINCIPALS—Ed Wynn, Paul Haakon, June Clyde, Vivian Vance, Roy Roberts, Leo Chalzel, Five Reillys, Robert Shafer, Ruthanna Boris, Don Popikoff, Charles Senna, Detmar Poppen, Franklyn Fox, Marcel Rousseau, Will Ferry, Arthur Kay, Al Baron, the Briants, Sue Hastings Marionettes, Al Gordon's Dogs, and others.

By BROOKS ATKINSON
"Hooray for What!" Hooray

principally for Ed Wynn. After six desperate years on the radio, the perfect fire-chief fool has returned in a Broadway carnival that opened at the Winter Garden last evening. Although this column muttered threats all the time Ed was rasping on the radio, it must confess that he comes back apparently unscratched and immediately takes front rank again as our most sociable buffoon. If you are more than six years old, you remember his tear-drop mug, buiging at the cheeks and tapering off incredibly to a tiny hat that gives him the shape of a perennial question-mark. The bone glasses still give the raised eyebrows a look of childish astonishment. The lipth thtill lithp. Yes, Ed Wynn is back, waddling through a whole costume closet of merry-andrew clothes, drooling remarkable imbecilities, and brightening the social season to a shiny polish at last.

The bookmakers of "Hooray for What!" are Howard Lindsay and Russel Crouse, who have gone to work on an idea which, the obstetrical program says, was "conceived" by E. Y. Harburg. Knocking their heads smartly together, they have presented Ed as the simple-minded inventor of gases which international diplomats covet for the putative next war. This chemical background gives Ed a chance to shoot smoke out of his ears and red fire out of a silly hat and also play a few jokes on nitro-glycerine. But if you are a disciple of Ed, the stage fool, all you need to know is that he is again telling jokes with more relish and innocence than any one else in the business, that he is giggling, looking with hopeful amazement at people he does not understand, desperately laboring at one act of horseplay, weaving his fingers eloquently around a jest and royally entertaining his audience.

After hooraying for Ed, you will probably have to content yourself with a correspondence school cheer for the rest of the show. As the result of a temperature of 102 degrees, Jack Whiting, the blond minnesinger, was unable to open the show with baritone song and dance in nearly every number; and although Roy Roberts gallantly stepped into the part on short notice and played it like a thoroughbred, "Hooray For What!" was probably not in top form last evening. But Mr. Whiting's absence is not its only infirmity. To an idea

that is funny in only the most abstract sense, it brings whimsies of dialogue and a precious literary style. Although Harold Arlen has tied his music into some stunning tangles, it lacks the simple pleasures of do-re-mi-fa-sol, etc., and we need not go into the matter of lyrics here.

Paul Haakon panicked the customers last evening with his toe arpeggios; Mr. Haakon is an artist, which is a lonely profession on Broadway. Five tap-dancing Reillys introduce a painless number or two. June Clyde and Vivian Vance sing as well as they can, which is nothing remarkable and cannot compare with the singing of Robert Shafer who, in Mr. Whiting's absence, has the only voice in the show. Since Vincente Minnelli's defection to Hollywood his scene designing has grown noisier.

But if you sit patiently in your seat and don't get cross, Ed will be back in a moment with a costume more fantastic than the last and carefully explain how he made lace curtains by crossing a silk-worm with a moth. Watch him in one abdominally hilarious sketch trying to keep an india-rubber Briant from collapsing on the stage. Listen to him warning the Geneva diplomats that if they do not pay the next two installments on the debt America will own the last war outright. In short, Hooray for Ed Wynn— that is what!

1937 D 2

'The Cradle Will Rock'

THE CRADLE WILL ROCK, an operetta in two acts. Book, music and lyrics by Marc Blitzstein. Sponsored by the Mercury Theatre as the first offering of its Worklight group. To be performed again next Sunday evening at the Mercury.

Cop	Robert Farnsworth
Dick	Guido Alexander
Moll	Olive Stanton
Gent	George Fairchild
Druggist	John Adair
Steve	Howard Bird
Sadie Polack	Marian Rudley
Gus Polack	George Fairchild
Mr. Mister	Will Geer
Mrs. Mister	Peggy Coudray
Junior Mister	Hiram Sherman
Sister Mister	Dulce Fox
Bugs	Geoffrey Powers
Larry Foreman	Howard de Silva
Editor Daily	Bert Weston
Doctor Specialist	Frank Marvel
Yasha	Edward Fuller
Dauber	John Hoysradt
President Prexy	Hansford Wilson
Ella Hammer	Blanche Collins
Rev. Salvation	Hiram Sherman
Trixie	George Smithfield
Clerk, Reporter, Prof. Mamie	Mr. Blitzstein

Chorus: Helen Carter, Lucille Schly, Robert Clark, Larry Ladria, E. Sidney, Lilia Hallums, Ralph Ramson, Billy Bodkins, Alma Dixon, Abner Dorsey.

At the Piano..................Mr. Blitzstein

By BROOKS ATKINSON

After drifting from pillar to post since last July Marc Blitzstein's "The Cradle Will Rock" had an official opening at the Mercury last evening. Written with extraordinary versatility and played with enormous gusto, it is the best thing militant labor has put into a theatre yet. Although Mr. Blitzstein's story of big industry corruption and labor union gallantry is an old one in the working-class theatre, he has transmuted it into a remarkably stirring marching song by the bitterness of his satire, the savagery of his music and the ingenuity of his craftsmanship. At last the comrades of the insurgent theatre can feel sure that they have a fully awakened artist on their side. What "Waiting for Lefty" was to the dramatic stage, "The Cradle Will Rock" is to the stage of the labor battle song.

This is the opera about steel unionization which the Federal Theatre discreetly dropped after an extensive rehearsal period last Summer. For a time it was put on al fresco without costumes or scenery at the Adelphi Theatre, where it made friends rather than money. Last week-end it had two performances at the Mercury Theatre as the first item in the projected Worklight Theatre, which is designed to give auditions to unusual pieces that are homeless. Since it was insufficiently rehearsed last week, the critics were asked to stay away—a form of charity they are always willing to extend on Sunday evenings. But last night it was sufficiently rehearsed to raise a theatregoer's basic metabolism and blow him out of the theatre on the thunder of the finale. "The Cradle Will Rock" rocked a great many things, including the audience.

One can understand the Federal Theatre's embarrassment. For the second time we have proof that a theatre supported by government funds cannot be a free agent when art has an insurgent political motive. "The Cradle Will Rock" is a summons to battle and a cry of warning, directed impartially at the steel industry. Since Big Steel has signed on the dotted line, Mr. Blitzstein's broadside is presumably directed at Little Steel, which has not yet reached for its fountain pen. Briefly, "The Cradle Will Rock" is the story of a steel magnate who unscrupulously consolidates a united front of newspapers and citizens' liberty committees against a union campaign to organize his plant.

Although "The Cradle Will Rock" has arrived at its official opening, it is still without costumes or scenery. Mr. Blitzstein sits at a piano on the rim of the stage. Behind him sit three rows of actors and singers in street clothes. They are individually introduced at the opening of the performance. As the opera progresses they come downstage to act their scenes, returning to their chairs when they are finished. To the casual playgoer this may seem like a negation of the theatre. As a matter of fact, it lays a very grave emphasis upon the deadly earnestness of this operatic pitch battle. Possibly "The Cradle Will Rock" would loose some of its direct fury in a normally accoutred performance.

If Mr. Blitzstein looks like a mild little man as he sits before his piano his work generates current like a dynamo. Most of it is caustically satiric in rhyme scheme and score.

He can write anything from tribal chant to Tin Pan Alley balladry; the piano keys scatter scorn, impishness and pathos according to the capricious mood of his story. And when Mr. Blitzstein settles down to serious business at the conclusion his music box roars with rage and his actors frighten the aged roof of the miniature Mercury Theatre.

Since most of the actors are not singers the music of "The Cradle Will Rock" gets only a noisy hearing. The voices are generally strained and some of them are harshly disagreeable. Theatregoers unhappily seated down front are entitled to ear muffs and shower curtains. But if "The Cradle Will Rock" is intended to arouse the rabble by malicious caricature and battle-line thunder it may be temperately reported as a stirring success. It is also the most versatile artistic triumph of the politically insurgent theatre.

1937 D 6

A DOLL'S HOUSE, a revival of the Henrik Ibsen play in a new acting version by Thornton Wilder. Staged and produced by Jed Harris. At the Morosco Theatre.

Nora Helmer...................Ruth Gordon
Ellen......................Jessica Rogers
Porter....................Harold Johnsrud
Thorwald Helmer.............Dennis King
Christina Linden..........Margaret Waller
Doctor Rank...................Paul Lukas
Nils Krogstad...................Sam Jaffe
Anna........................Grace Mills
Emmy...............Lorna Lynn Meyers
Ivar.....................Howard Sherman

By BROOKS ATKINSON

Ruth Gordon slammed the door on Ibsen's "A Doll's House" at the Morosco last evening. Although no one was shocked or astounded, a good many people were profoundly impressed, for Miss Gordon is a remarkable actress. Not long ago she was standing "Ethan Frome" on its ear with a richly documented and passionate performance. Last season she carried "The Country Wife" around on her comic shoulders. Although Nora, it seems to this correspondent, is a part less suited to her personal talents, she has mastered it, especially in the last act, by the extraordinary industry of her acting. Under Jed Harris's management she appears in one of the finest Ibsen revivals we have had in this neighborhood in years. None of the parts is wasted or carelessly played, and none of the play is feebly explored. After triumphing on the road for two months or more this season, and delighting Colorado last Summer, Miss Gordon is entitled to a triumph in her own city now.

If "A Doll's House" is less frequently revived than some of the other Ibsen plays it is because the revolt it chronicles is a little embarrassing now. Thornton Wilder has pruned away most of the stiff Nordic fripperies that were frequently distressing in the Archer version. But still the propriety of Helmer's little wife through the first part of the play is hard to understand in this battledore and shuttlecock interlude in history. This may account for Miss Gordon's weakness for overplaying up to the end of the second act. She has mannerisms in her acting—the frozen smile and the nervous poking at the hair. As if the part of Nora were none too credible in her own thinking, she taxes it in the first half of the evening with restlessness, artfulness and effervescences that lie on the surface of the character and underrate the earnestness of the play. In this correspondent's opinion, the first half of the evening is the least satisfactory part of her acting.

When doom begins to encircle this bird-like wife of a middle-class snob, Miss Gordon takes the part seriously. After dissipating a good deal of it on too many trivial details she goes straight to the heart of it. Nora trying to hold the world back with a desperate tarantella; Nora driven nearly out of her mind with apprehension; Nora quietly coming into her own inheritance of personal pride and taking command of the situation—these are the portions of the play that Miss Gordon has completely mastered. The motivation of the character is plagued with shibboleths today, but the moral and spiritual triumphs of Nora are still full of the fire of life. Although Miss Gordon's preparations for the big scenes are fussily planned she gives herself to them when she comes to them and concludes the play with force and her own touch of modest glory.

In every respect this is a notable revival, incisively directed by Mr. Harris. Although Dennis King may not have seemed in prospect like the right actor for Thorwald Helmer, the fact remains that he is, and this is the best thing he has done on the dramatic stage recently. It is a performance sensitive to subtleties of the character. Paul Lukas plays Dr. Rank with a fondness that is wholly above sentimentality. Sam Jaffe's Nils Krogstad and Margaret Waller's Christina are beautifully played; their one scene together is superb, subdued in tone but fervent in feeling. In the subordinate parts of the maid and nurse, Jessica Rogers and Grace Mills give excellent performances. And in designing the scenery and costumes Donald Oenslager has given Ibsen the boon of considerable unaccustomed beauty.

For this is "A Doll's House" that is devoted to the theatre as well as to a celebrated part; and if it has any fault it is overanxious to do the job thoroughly. In the last scene Miss Gordon slams the door not only on a plot but on a fine piece of theatre handiwork.

1937 D 28

1938

ONE-THIRD OF A NATION, a Living Newspaper edition (fifth of the series) about housing. Prepared by Arthur Arent and based on research compiled by the editorial staff of the Living Newspaper. Staged by Lem Ward; setting by Howard Bay; music by Lee Wainer; lighting by Moe Hack; produced by Philip Barber as an offering of the Federal Theatre Project. At the Adelphi Theatre.

By BROOKS ATKINSON

Pressing the button in its press room, The Living Newspaper of the Federal Theatre started grinding out an extra on the housing situation at the Adelphi last evening under the banner head of "One-Third of a Nation." Although it is not the most perfectly edited number in this galvanic theatre form, none of the others has been so brilliantly produced. On the huge stage of the Adelphi, Howard Bay has constructed a skeleton tenement house where fires and cholera plagues are acted with equal excitement, and on the ample forestage the editors hold housing committee investigations, court trials and examinations of the building industry and they also crack a few folksy jokes. About six months of tinkering and about eighty actors have gone into the making of something that a Broadway producer would call colossal. Even a cash customer would describe it as vivid theatre.

The Living Newspaper is no superficial sheet. Given a complete topic like the housing problem, the investigators have shaken the living daylights out of a thousand books, reports and newspaper and magazine articles and traced the real estate problem in New York from Colonial times to the present. They discover the essence of the problem in the land grants to institutions and private individuals and show in concrete form the relation between land values and wretched dwellings for the poor. Among the institutions and individuals that get unfavorable mention are Trinity Church, Rhinelander, Goelet, Wendell and Astor. About two-thirds of "One-third of a Nation" is a notable job in the simplification of New York real estate history and the ever-recurring housing

scandals that are bound up with supply and demand. Using the data compiled by his associates, Arthur Arent has written an original and fascinating dramatic lecture.

The editorial brains of the Living Newspaper work most energetically on the current situation. After investigating a rum crew of landowners, brokers, building supply men, contractors and bankers the editors conclude that housing is a government function. Incidentally, they noticeably pull their punches when they mention the effect of the building trades union scales on the high cost of housing. And although they are specifically discussing New York housing, they introduce as evidence for the plaintiff the low cost of government housing in other cities, which is incompetent, irrelevant and tricky journalism. The Living Newspaper concludes this stimulating lesson in a social problem by demanding that the New Deal stop trying to balance the budget. The Federal Theatre's Newspaper will have none of that inhuman nonsense.

In fact, the voice of The Living Newspaper, which blares across the theatre from a metallic loudspeaker, becomes more voluminous in every edition; and purely from the theatrical point of view it is tiresome. What is done in a theatre is always more important than what is said; primarily the theatre is a place for shows. And what this edition has accomplished in the way of showmanship is particularly exhilarating. Mr. Bay's vital, functional stage-setting, little scenes trenchantly acted in the foul, dark rooms of the tenement, Clarence R. Chase's good-humored playing as the inquiring citizen, the fleeting characterization of slum children, the agonizing glimpse of housing in Harlem—these are the dynamics of "One-third of a Nation." Probably some people ought to see it. Most people will want to see it because it is alive.

1938 Ja 18

SHADOW AND SUBSTANCE, a play in three acts, by Paul Vincent Carroll. Staged by Peter Godfrey; settings by David M. Twachtman; produced by Eddie Dowling. At the John Golden Theatre.
Brigid ....Julie Haydon
Dermot Francis O'Flingsley...Lloyd Gough
Thomasina Concannon......Valerie Cossart
Father Corr ....Henry Sothern

By BROOKS ATKINSON

Out of love and rebelliousness, Paul Vincent Carroll has written a beautiful play about Ireland, "Shadow and Substance," which was put on at the John Golden last evening. And out of skill and wisdom Sir Cedric Hardwicke is devoting a beautiful performance to it. Although the venerable Abbey has recently squired a number of bright bits about the darlin' folks and the quaint manners, this is a play that is passionately intended. Mr. Carroll, schoolmaster and dramatist, has dipped his pen into a bitter well.

For behind the factual surface of contemporary affairs there are forces that are crushing the lyric spirit of the Irish nature, and Mr.

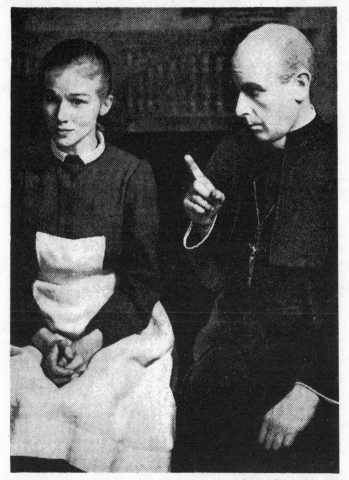

Lucas & Pritchard Studio

Julie Haydon as Brigid and Sir Cedric Hardwicke as Canon Skerritt

Carroll has represented them all in a high-minded play. It is not tidily planned nor lucidly written, which are primary virtues of the literary craft; but no matter, for it glows like a cathedral window. After some poor luck in this country, Sir Cedric shows that he is an actor of the first rank, and Julie Haydon must now be inscribed among the young actresses of uncommon talent. Out of Ireland another play has come.

The fable it tells is more properly a development of character. At the core of the play, set in a small town in County Louth, is Canon Skerritt, a classicist, an intellectual snob and a cold monarch of the church. His servant is Brigid, named in honor of St. Brigid, who disfigured her face to escape the attentions of suitors. The Canon's implacable enemy is a hot-tempered young schoolmaster, Dermot Francis O'Flingsley, who, like Mr. Carroll, cannot stand idly by and see Ireland swaddled in ignorance and vulgarity. Although the Canon and O'Flingsley are enemies, they both love Brigid for the grace and purity of her spirit; and she, in turn, worships both of them. Round about them are the "fools and boobs," impulsive, gape-mouthed and barbaric, who represent the common Irish folk of the country towns.

Thus Mr. Carroll has impersonated in his play the hostile forces that are crushing the innocent, imaginative spirit of Ireland. "Shadow and Substance" is less a drama than the evocation of a situation that slowly brings the characters into opposition. To those of us who are accustomed to look for a clear pattern of story in a play, Mr. Carroll's portrait of character is nebulous and illusive. By keeping O'Flingsley out of the play except for a moment in the first act and two appearances in the third, he has sacrificed a good deal of definition that might give the story clear dramatic force. And particularly in the first act his style lacks the singing quality of good speech for acting. Some of his sentences thicken the tongues and choke the mouths of his actors. "Be careful of the wording. Wording is an art," as the Canon says. Mr. Carroll does not always take the Canon's supercilious advice.

But the thoughts he explores, the mystical aspirations he sympathizes with, the caustic humor of his comments on character and the tragic humility of the concluding scene give "Shadow and Substance" a stature beyond any of the latter-day folk plays that come from Mr. Carroll's vexed land.

Add to the beauties of his script the glories of a fine performance under Peter Godfrey's direction, Sir Cedric's portrait of Canon Skerritt is an actor's masterpiece. The whole man is present in the severity of his acting — snobbery, learning, insouciance, sardonic contempt, formal religious devotion and personal tenderness. Sara Allgood plays the part of a country woman with the gleam and rhythm of her most animated acting. As Brigid, the maid servant with holy visions, Miss Haydon gives a deeply moving performance that is gentle and luminous with exaltation. There is an admirable fiery performance by Lloyd Gough as the schoolmaster, and Henry Sothern and Len Doyle are amusingly awkward and earnest as local curates. Gerald Buckley is more on the quaint side as a licensed teacher without portfolio, and Valerie Cossart does not give much distinction to the fluttery part of the Canon's niece.

For it is not all gold in the performance, and some of the gold of Mr. Carroll's writing is unminted. The Irish can be ambiguous as well as inspired. But the tone of "Shadow and Substance" is poetically ideal. As a writer and an Irishman, Mr. Carroll is uncorruptible.

1938 Ja 27

OUR TOWN, a play by Thornton Wilder; directed and produced by Jed Harris. At Henry Miller's Theatre.

Stage Manager	Frank Craven
Dr. Gibbs	Jay Fassett
Joe Crowell	Raymond Roe
Howie Newsome	Tom Fadden
Mrs. Gibbs	Evelyn Varden
Mrs. Webb	Helen Carew
George Gibbs	John Craven
Rebecca Gibbs	Marilyn Erskine
Wally Webb	Charles Wiley Jr.
Emily Webb	Martha Scott
Professor Pepper	Arthur Allen
Mr. Webb	Thomas W. Ross
Woman in the Balcony	Carrie Weller
Man in the Auditorium	Walter O. Hill
Lady in the Box	Aline McDermott
Simon Stimson	Philip Coolidge
Mrs. Soames	Doro Merande
Constable Warren	E. Irving Locke
Si Crowell	Billy Redfield
Baseball Players	Alfred Ryder / William Roehrick / Thomas Coley
Sam Craig	Francis G. Cleveland
Joe Stoddard	William Wadsworth

By BROOKS ATKINSON

Although Thornton Wilder is celebrated chiefly for his fiction, it will be necessary now to reckon

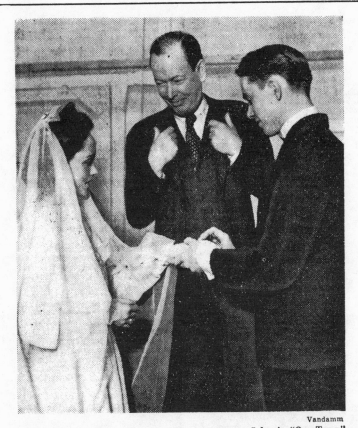

Vandamm

Martha Scott, Frank Craven and the latter's son, John, in "Our Town"

with him as a dramatist. His "Our Town," which opened at Henry Miller's last evening, is a beautifully evocative play. Taking as his material three periods in the history of a placid New Hampshire town, Mr. Wilder has transmuted the simple events of human life into universal reverie. He has given familiar facts a deeply moving, philosophical perspective. Staged without scenery and with the curtain always up, "Our Town" has escaped from the formal barrier of the modern theatre into the quintessence of acting, thought and speculation. In the staging, Jed Harris has appreciated the rare quality of Mr. Wilder's handiwork and illuminated it with a shining performance. "Our Town" is, in this column's opinion, one of the finest achievements of the current stage.

Since the form is strange, this review must attempt to explain the purpose of the play. It is as though Mr. Wilder were saying: "Now for evidence as to the way Americans were living in the early part of the century, take Grover Corners, N.H., as an average town. Mark it 'Exhibit A' in American folkways." His spokesman in New Hampshire cosmology is Frank Craven, the best pipe and pants-pocket actor in the business, who experimentally sets the stage with tables and chairs before the house lights go down and then prefaces the performance with a few general remarks about

Grover Corners. Under his benign guidance we see three periods in career of one generation of Grover Corners folks—"Life," "Love" and "Death."

* * *

Literally, they are not important. On one side of an imaginary street Dr. Gibbs and his family are attending to their humdrum affairs with relish and probity. On the opposite side Mr. Webb, the local editor, and his family are fulfilling their quiet destiny. Dr. Gibbs's boy falls in love with Mr. Webb's girl— neighbors since birth. They marry after graduating from high school; she dies several years later in childbirth and she is buried on Cemetery Hill. Nothing happens in the play that is not normal and natural and ordinary.

* * *

But by stripping the play of everything that is not essential, Mr. Wilder has given it a profound, strange, unworldly significance. This is less the portrait of a town than the sublimation of the commonplace; and in contrast with the universe that silently swims around it, it is brimming over with compassion. Most of it is a tender idyll in the kindly economy of Mr. Wilder's literary style; some of it is heartbreaking in the mute simplicity of human tragedy. For in the last act, which is entitled "Death," Mr. Wilder shows the dead of Grover Corners sitting peacefully in their graves and receiving into their quiet company a neighbor's girl whom they love. So Mr. Wilder's pathetically humble evidence of human living passes into the wise beyond. Grover Corners is a green corner of the universe.

* * *

With about the best script of his career in his hands, Mr. Harris has risen nobly to the occasion. He has reduced theatre to its lowest common denominator without resort to perverse showmanship. As chorus, preacher, drug store proprietor and finally as shepherd of the flock, Frank Craven plays with great sincerity and understanding, keeping the sublime well inside his homespun style. As the boy and girl, John Craven, who is Frank Craven's son, and Martha Scott turn youth into tremulous idealization, some of their scenes are lovely past all enduring. Jay Fassett as Dr. Gibbs, Evelyn Varden as his wife, Thomas W. Ross and Helen Carew as the Webbs play with an honesty that is enriching. There are many other good bits of acting.

* * *

Out of respect for the detached tone of Mr. Wilder's script the performance as a whole is subdued and understated. The scale is so large that the voices are never lifted. But under the leisurely monotone of the production there is a fragment of the immortal truth. "Our Town" is a microcosm. It is also a hauntingly beautiful play.

1938 F 5

HELLZAPOPPIN, described as a "screamlined revue" in two acts and twenty-five scenes, with dialogue of unannounced authorship. Songs by Sammy Fain, Charles Tobias, Earl Robinson, Alfred Hayes, Paul Mann and Stephen Weiss. Produced by Ole Olsen and Chic Johnson, with bows to Lee Shubert and Harry A. Kaufman. At the Forty-sixth Street Theatre.
Principals—Olsen and Johnson, Barto and Mann, The Radio Rogues, Hal Sherman, Ray Kinney and Aloha Maids, Bettymae and Beverly Crane, the Charioteers, Theo Hardeen, Walter Nilsson, the Starlings, Reed, Dean and Reed, Shirley Wayne, Whitey's Steppers, Bergh and Moore, Roberta and Ray, Billy Adams.

By BROOKS ATKINSON

Folks, it is going to be a little difficult to describe this one. "Hellzapoppin" is what they call it and it was discharged at the Forty-sixth Street last evening. Deciding that it might be a good idea to put on a show, Ole Olsen and Chic Johnson, a pair of vaudeville knockabouts, stood on the corner of the street and stopped every third man. Those were their actors. Taking an old broom, they went up to the attic and swept out all the gags in sight. Those were their jokes. Dropping into an ammunition store downtown, they picked up several boxes of blank cartridges. Those were to indicate that the jokes had been told and that it was time to start laughing. Then they moved everything in sight into the Forty-sixth Street Theatre, got an audience down front and set them to laughing. Anything goes in "Hellzapoppin"—noise, vulgarity, practical joking—and about every third number is foolish enough for guffawing.

* * *

Very prominent in the proceedings are Olsen and Johnson, a pair of college cut-ups now well on toward middle life without much flowering of their culture. As far as they are concerned, it is house-cleaning day in vaudeville. After a hilarious motion-picture prologue, in which some grotesque sounds and words come out of the pictures of F. D. R., the Little Flower, Hitler and Mussolini, Olsen and Johnson make their entrance in a clownish automobile and trailer and the uproar begins. It pops out of all parts of the house. Up and down the aisles of the orchestra a persistent woman keeps shouting, "Oscar, Oscar!" in a tenement voice. A ticket speculator starts hawking good seats for "I Married an Angel." Eggs and bananas are tossed out to the audience, and when the lights go out the audience is besieged with spiders and snakes in the darkness. There is no relief even in the intermission. For that is the time when a clown starts paddling up the aisle and haunting unwary customers.

* * *

Probably the entertainment ought to show a higher trace of talent. The taste of "Hellzapoppin" runs to second-rate vaudeville revue, with chorus dancing of no particular consequence and some artful warbling by a pair of damsels sweetly billed as "The Starlings." Ornithologically speaking, starlings are likely to be shot or poisoned. But you can see some mighty fine monocycling by Walter Nilsson and some roguish tap dancing by Hal Sherman, and you can hear some lymphatic fiddling by Shirley Wayne, who looks as though she were just on the point of frying a mess of doughnuts. Hardeen is there to astonish the innocent with some prodigious feats of magic.

* * *

But this is mainly a helter-skelter assembly of low-comedy gags to an ear-splitting sound accompaniment —some of it ugly, all of it fast. It is a revue concocted of what Al Graham described in yesterday's Conning Tower as "stewed fish-eyes and ragfoam." "I'll Say She Is" was funnier these many years ago because the Marx Brothers were in it. But if you can imagine a demented vaudeville brawl without the Marx Brothers, "Hellzapoppin" is it, and a good part of it is loud, low and funny.

1938 S 23

HAMLET, in its entirety (three acts and twenty scenes), presented for the first time in New York. Staged by Margaret Webster; costumes and scenery designed by David Ffolkes; incidental music by Lehman Engel; produced by Maurice Evans. At the St. James Theatre.

* * *

Francisco .... Donald Arbury
Bernardo .... Wesley Ac' ly
Marcellus .... Donald Cameron
Horatio .... Donald Randolph
Claudius .... Henry Edwards
Gertrude .... Mady Christians
Hamlet .... Maurice Evans
Polonius .... George Graham
Laertes .... Sydney Smith
Voltimand .... Reynolds Evans
Cornelius .... Emmett Rogers
A Page .... William Prince
Ophelia .... Katherine Locke
Ghost of Hamlet's Father..Augustin Duncan
Reynaldo .... Henry Jones
Rosencrantz .... Alexander Scourby
Guildenstern .... Everett Ripley
Player King .... Rhys Williams
Player Queen................... Paul Nevens
Third Player.,............... Donald Arbury
Fourth Player............... Emmett Rogers
A Lady in Waiting........... Irene Tedrow
Fortinbras .... Wesley Addy
A Captain .... Alfred Paschall
A Gentleman .... George Keane
Two Sailors .... { Richard Janaver / Emmett Rogers
A Gravedigger .... Whitford Kane
Second Gravedigger........... Henry Jones
A Priest .... Reynolds Evans
Osric .... Maury Tuckerman
Ambassadors .... { Rhys Williams / Paul Nevens
Lords, Ladies, Soldiers and Attendants: Irene Tedrow, Carmen Mathews, Constance Friend, Ruth Wilk, Richard Janaver, William Prince, Charles Bowden, Frederick Carney, Alfred Paschall.

By BROOKS ATKINSON

Word having got about that Shakespeare is a great writer, Maurice Evans has set out to prove it by producing and acting the full text of "Hamlet." He and his associates raise the curtain at 6:30; excepting for a half-hour or so for snacking they kept it raised until 11:15, making the night joint-laborer with the day. As acted at the St. James last evening before a highly expectant audience, it may be a minute or two too long, but no more than that. For the uncut "Hamlet" is a wild and whirling play of exalted sound and tragic grandeur, and Mr. Evans acts it as though it were a new text that had not been clapper-clawed by generations of actors. Out of the prompt-book he and his director, Margaret Webster, have snatched it and put it onto the modern stage. It is compact with life. Apparently Shakespeare was a great writer, because he could put lusty parts into a turbulent play; and this long, fiery tale of murder, despair and revenge is the most vivid drama in town today.

* * *

If the Elizabethans were rugged theatregoers, so are we when the drama is worth watching. We have as much time as they have when great deeds and thoughts are up for discussion. Their stage was better suited to episodic story-telling. But, using a forestage and orchestra entrances as she did in "Richard II," Miss Webster has solved the problem of covering the entire "Hamlet" landscape without letting the play drag its feet. Mr. Ffolkes, who did the "Richard" designs, has provided practicable scenic backgrounds that do not outstare the acting, and his Elizabethan costumes, unpretentiously sketched and agreeably colored, are good garments for a working actor. Although it has been the fashion for some time never to mount "Hamlet" without piling scenery on top of it, Miss Webster has had the courage to sacrifice show to action and to give the players room enough to swing a speech around their heads.

* * *

Although Hamlet is too spacious a part for any actor to exhaust, one can almost say that no one has really seen "Hamlet" until he has sat enthralled before the uncut version. Cut to the shape of an actor's vehicle, it is invariably ambiguous, especially in the second half, for that is the scrappy part as Shakespeare wrote it. It is a headlong play of vital scope in the ample text of the second quarto. That is the fresh spirit in which Mr. Evans takes it. He acts it at the top of his compass. On the negative side, he has abandoned the posturing, the school-book melancholy, the rigid acting situations and set speeches that tradition has imposed upon Hamlets, and he does not interpret the business fearfully. On the positive side, he acts a Hamlet of modern sensibilities who does not love words for their own sake but for their active meaning. This is a Hamlet of quick intellect who knows what is happening all through the play. He dominates by alertness. He is frank; and, above everything else, he is lucid. Probably the Elizabethans played Hamlet in this fashion before the scholars burdened the drama with problems. It is refreshing and exciting to see it played for sheer drama.

* * *

In so capacious a theatre night it would be fatal to stuff the cast with the battered mediocrities who often infest Shakespearean revivals.

Vandamm Studio
Maurice Evans as Hamlet

They have cast this "Hamlet" for modern values. Mady Christians acts a queen of shallow mind and nervous apprehension. Avoiding regal bombast, Henry Edwards plays the king like a man of affairs. Katherine Locke's Ophelia is touching because it is simple. Although George Graham's voice is much too small, his characterization of Polonius is immensely funny. After all these years, Whitford Kane knows how to translate the clowneries of the first gravedigger into pungent comedy. Some of the parts are only competently played. Augustin Duncan's ghost unfortunately must be put in that bracket. But the design of the performance and the swift tempo keep the story speeding down the corridors of dramatic doom.

Last night the audience was both surprised and delighted to find that the uncut "Hamlet" is no cultural chore. On the contrary, it is the grandest play ever written. In reviving it Mr. Evans has recreated it in the image of today.

Audience Stays to Cheer Evans

After the curtain fell on the American première of Maurice Evans in the full-length "Hamlet," the entire audience remained in their seats, and cheers were given which subsided only when Mr. Evans stepped forward to make a brief speech. He noted that he had been speaking a long time and that his audience were "swell listeners," but added that he was not sorry to have detained them for so long, because he wanted to show that in "Hamlet" Shakespeare had "written a play and not a study of dyspepsia."

Mr. Evans expressed the hope that the full-length "Hamlet" would lead to his goal of establishing an actor-manager's repertory theatre which might present the best of "our theatrical heritage." The sole desire of himself and his company, he concluded, was to "occupy the enviable position of being your faithful and obedient servants."

Inserted in each program at the St. James was a leaflet on which were described the details for attending the "Hamlet" that lasts from 6:30 P. M. to 11:15 P. M. For each instruction Mr. Evans has selected an appropriate quotation from Shakespeare. Two examples: "Half-hour intermission 8:15 to 8:45 ('For this relief much thanks. . .')"; "Final curtain falls at 11:15 ('But soft! Methinks I scent the morning air . . .')."

                              1938 O 13

ABE LINCOLN IN ILLINOIS, a play in two acts and twelve scenes, by Robert E. Sherwood. Staged by Elmer Rice; settings by Jo Mielziner; presented by the Playwrights' Company (comprising Maxwell Anderson, S. N. Behrman, Sidney Howard, Mr. Rice and Mr. Sherwood), as its first Broadway offering. At the Plymouth Theatre.

Mentor Graham	Frank Andrews
Abe Lincoln	Raymond Massey
Ann Rutledge	Adele Longmire
Judith	Iris Whitney
Ben Mattling	George Christie
Judge Bowling Green	Arthur Griffin
Ninian Edwards	Lewis Martin
Joshua Speed	Calvin Thomas
Trum Cogdal	Harry Levian
Jack Armstrong	Howard DaSilva
Bab	Everett Charlton
Feargus	David Clarke
Jasp	Kevin McCarthy
Seth Gale	Herbert Rudley
Nancy Green	Lillian Foster
William Herndon	Wendell K. Phillips
Elizabeth Edwards	May Collins
Mary Todd	Muriel Kirkland
The Edwards's Maid	Augusta Dabney
Jimmy Gale	Howard Sherman
Aggie Gale	Marion Rooney
Gobey	Hubert Brown
Stephen A. Douglas	Albert Phillips
Willie Lincoln	Lex Parrish
Tad Lincoln	Lloyd Barry
Robert Lincoln	John Payne
The Lincoln's Maid	Iris Whitney
Crimmin	Frank Tweddell
Barrick	John Gerard
Sturveson	Thomas F. Tracey
Jed	Harry Levian
Phil	Kevin McCarthy
Kavanagh	Glenn Coulter
Cavalry Captain	Everett Charlton

Soldiers, Railroad Men, Townspeople: Allen Shaw, Phillip Caplan, David Hewes, Dearon Darnay, Harrison Woodhull, Robert Fitzsimmons, Joseph Wiseman, Walter Kapp, George Malcolm, Bert Schorr, Bette Benfield, Ann Stevenson, Dolores Williams, Ora Alexander, Alfred Jenkins, Emory Richardson, McKinley Reeves, Elizabeth Reller.

By BROOKS ATKINSON

Mr. Sherwood has written his finest play. "Abe Lincoln in Illinois," which was staged at the Plymouth on Saturday evening, is part of the living truth of America. In the breadth and depth of its understanding it is far above the general level of commercial theatre; one hesitates to tarnish it with the familiar adjectives that announce a box-office success. For Mr. Sherwood has looked down with compassion into the lonely blackness of Lincoln's heart and seen some of the fateful things that lived there. As a craftsman he has had the humility to tell the story quietly. As a contemporary American he has had the candor to see that much of it applies to us today, and he has courageously said so. With Raymond Massey giving an exalted performance as the lanky man of destiny, "Abe Lincoln in Illinois" is an inspired play—inspired by the sorrowful grandeur of the man it portrays.

                    * * *

The facts of Lincoln's life in Illinois are good enough for Mr. Sherwood. Beginning with a rude scene in a log cabin, he has shown how the shiftless, loose-jointed youth of New Salem grows into the sad-faced man who left Springfield to become President at a dark moment in our history. The familiar people are there—Judge Green, Joshua Speed, Ann Rutledge, William Herndon, Mary Todd, Stephen Douglas. There are scenes of raw prairie life, romance, politics and rural humor. The strange story of his star-crossed marriage to Mary Todd is told with sympathetic integrity. You hear him modestly replying to Douglas in one of the debates. Toward the end you see him with solitary misgiving listening to the election returns; and at the conclusion you hear him bidding farewell to his neighbors when he departs for Washington.

Parts of this story have been told on the stage before. John Drinkwater told some of them impressively in a classical style; and more recently E. P. Conkle has been making an idyll out of them. But neither has imparted to it the high purpose that Mr. Sherwood gives it by underscoring its current significance. He keeps the principles of American liberty ringing through the concluding scenes. Sometimes Mr. Sherwood has genially tossed a brand of hokum into his plays to set them to blazing on the stage. But he is writing scrupulously this time, looking the facts squarely in the face and recording them in deadly earnest. Full of admiration for his chief character, he is also overflowing with love for the principles that Lincoln reluctantly accepted from destiny and made his own. They are Mr. Sherwood's now, and also ours; and "Abe Lincoln in Illinois" is a noble testament of our spiritual faith.

* * *

Mr. Massey has an exhaustingly long part to play. He is the center of every scene; he has a great many lines and several long speeches to deliver. An actor might be forgiven for not mastering all the details. But Mr. Massey, too, has drawn inspiration from the theme he is conveying, and he plays it with an artless honesty that is completely overwhelming at the end. Fortunately, he looks the part. But he goes deeper than surface resemblances. He has the artistic stature to measure the great things that lie beneath. From the careless, good-natured boy to the towering man of melancholy who goes on leaden feet to face his destiny, is a long road for any actor to travel in one night. But Mr. Massey tells the whole story in terms of humanity with the diffident eloquence of a man who knows what it means.

* * *

He is well supported. Under Elmer Rice's thoughtful and appreciative direction the performance is triumphant. The two principal women's parts are beautifully played— Ann Rutledge by Adele Longmire, and the nervously overwrought Mary Todd by Muriel Kirkland. Calvin Thomas acts Joshua Speed and Arthur Griffin acts Judge Green with admirable kindliness.

Wendell K. Phillips ably conveys the high-pitched fanaticism of Herndon. The rolling platform periods of Stephen A. Douglas are amusingly delivered by Albert Phillips. Although Jo Mielziner's covered wagon is no masterpiece, the rest of his scenery catches the plain fortitude of Lincoln's surroundings.

In fact, every one associated with this first production of The Playwrights Company seems to be caught up in the aura of a notable occasion. For "Abe Lincoln in Illinois" is a drama of great pith and moment, and a reviewer's only anxiety is that he may not herald it vigorously enough.

1938 O 17

KNICKERBOCKER HOLIDAY, a musical comedy in two acts. Book and lyrics by Maxwell Anderson. Music by Kurt Weill. Staged by Joshua Logan; settings by Jo Mielziner; costumes designed by Frank Bevan; dances arranged by Carl Randall and Edwin Denby; produced by the Playwrights' Company as its second offering. At the Ethel Barrymore Theatre.
Washington Irving..........Ray Middleton
Anthony Corlear............Harry Meehan
Tienhoven ....Mark Smith
Vanderbilt ....George Watts
Roosevelt....................Francis Pierlot
DePeyster ....Charles Arnt
DeVries ....John E. Young
Van Rensselaer ....James Phillips
Van Cortlandt Jr..........Richard Cowdery
Tina Tienhoven............Jeanne Madden
Brom Broeck.............Richard Kollmar
Tenpin.................Clarence Nordstrom
Schermerhorn.............Howard Freeman
Pieter Stuyvesant.........Walter Huston
General Poffenburgh.........Donald Black
Mistress Schermerhorn........Edith Angold
Citizens of New Amsterdam—Helen Carroll, Jane Brotherton, Carol Deis, Robert Arnold, Bruce Hamilton, Ruth Mamel, William Marel, Margaret MacLaren, Robert Rounseville, Rufus Smith, Margaret Stewart, Erika Zaranova, William Wahlert.
Soldiers—Albert Allen, Matthias Ammann, Dow Fonda, Warde Peters.
Fighters—The Algonquins.

By BROOKS ATKINSON

Out of the early history of Manhattan, Maxwell Anderson has written the book and lyrics for a cultivated musical comedy, "Knickerbocker Holiday," which was staged at the Ethel Barrymore last evening, and Kurt Weill has written the music. It is an antic exercise in mummery and political satire, unlike anything Mr. Anderson has attempted before. With Walter Huston giving a salty performance as Peg-Leg Stuyvesant, the first dictator of this island, "Knickerbocker Holiday" is beautifully staged by the incipient Playwrights' Company under the versatile direction of young Joshua Logan, and there is much to recommend it in the way

Ben Pinchot

Walter Huston

of intelligent showmanship to excellent music. But Mr. Anderson's style of writing leans toward the pedantic in a brisk musical setting. He cannot trip it quite gayly enough for the company he is keeping.

* * *

He is telling a fable of seventeenth century New York as Washington Irving might write it in his facetious history book. It depicts the knavery of the Dutch council government before stormy old Peg-Leg arrives and the tyranny of his personal administration when he stumps across the Battery mall. Under the conventional pattern of musical comedy making, Mr. Anderson has some general observations to make— about democracy as government by amateurs, which is superior to the practiced corruption of professionals, and about the anarchic spirit of the true American, who is constitutionally unable to take orders. At the opening of the second act Mr. Anderson takes a poke at the arbitrary economics of government by decree, which is doubtless inverted comment on the New Deal.

* * *

As a book-maker, Mr. Anderson's touch is a heavy one. He is at his best in his collaboration with Mr. Weill, whose music is lively and theatre-wise. In "How Can You Tell an American," which is the theme of this Knickerbocker festival, Mr. Anderson's rhymes have the subtlety of good lyric writing as well as the authority of a poet. Mr. Weill is a versatile fellow. He did the score for "Johnny Johnson" and "The Eternal Road." In his current work there is no style he cannot assimilate and compose. He writes dance tunes with modern gusto, romantic duets, comic pieces and a funeral march. Although it may not go far toward evoking the spirit of early America, it is vigorous composing for the modern theatre, superior to Broadway songwriting without settling in the academic groove.

* * *

As for the acting and staging of "Knickerbocker Holiday," they are both superb. Casting Walter Huston as Governor Stuyvesant is a stroke of genius. For he is an actor in the grand manner with a homely brand of native wit, bold in his gestures, commanding in his periods, yet purely sardonic and mischievous in spirit. After one of Mr. Anderson's bawdiest songs in impeccable English, Mr. Huston brings the house down with a peg-leg dance at the end of a line of Dutch chorus girls. Mr. Huston is a great fellow to have in town again.

* * *

Mr. Logan has surrounded him with new faces, fresh voices and youthful enthusiasm for the stage. As Washington Irving, a sort of commentator on the scene, Ray Middleton is a congenial actor with a good voice. Richard Kollmar and Jeanne Madden as the romantic pair are gifted young people who act and sing exuberantly. A comic chorus of obese Dutch councilors, amusingly costumed by Jo Mielziner, includes Mark Smith, whose sense of humor is out of the old theatre, and Harry Meehan, the venerable Irish thrush who can blow the top off any theatre.

* * *

Although the stage at the Barrymore is a small one to include both Mr. Mielziner's handsome view of

206

the Battery and a group of dancing Dutch maidens, Mr. Logan has discovered how to keep the performance breezy in style. But Mr. Anderson's book, which is a little arbitrary in craftsmanship, is unwieldy. The light, fantastic vein of musical comedy does not become his serious mind—or vice versa, as the case may be.

1938 O 20

THE BOYS FROM SYRACUSE, a musical comedy in two acts and nine scenes, based on Shakespeare's "The Comedy of Errors." Book by George Abbott, music by Richard Rodgers and lyrics by Lorenz Hart; Scenery and lighting by Jo Mielziner; choreography by George Balanchine; costumes designed by Irene Sharaff; staged and produced by Mr. Abbott. At the Alvin Theatre.

Singing Policeman	Bob Lawrence
Another Policeman	James Wilkinson
Antipholus of Ephesus	Ronald Graham
Dromio of Ephesus	Teddy Hart
Dancing Policeman	George Church
Tailor	Clifford Dunstan
Tailor's Apprentice	Burl Ives
Antipholus of Syracuse	Eddie Albert
Dromio of Syracuse	Jimmy Savo
Merchant of Syracuse	Byron Shores
Duke of Ephesus	Carroll Ashburn
Aegeon	John O'Shaughnessy
Luce	Wynn Murray
Adriana	Muriel Angelus
Luciana	Marcy Wescott
Sorcerer	Owen Martin
Courtezan	Betty Bruce
Secretary to Courtezan	Heidi Vosseler
Assistant Courtezan	Dolores Anderson
Angelo	John Clarke
First Maid	Florine Callahan
Second Maid	Claire Wolf
Third Maid	Alice Craig
Merchant of Ephesus	Clifford Dunstan
Seeress	Florence Fair

By BROOKS ATKINSON

Taking a swift glance at Shakespeare's "The Comedy of Errors," George Abbott, who is the jack-of-all-trades in the theatre, has written and staged an exuberant musical comedy, "The Boys From Syracuse," which was put on at the Alvin last evening. Nothing so gusty as this has come along for a week. Nothing so original has come along for a much longer period than that. For Mr. Abbott has a knack of giving everything he touches freshness, spontaneity and spinning pace. Rodgers and Hart have written him a versatile score. Jimmy Savo, who is usually lost when he strays away from his own routines, gives an immensely comic performance. And for the other parts, Mr. Abbott has again found attractive and bustling young people whose styles are never hackneyed. Add to this some volatile dancing under George Balanchine's direction, some of the most light-footed settings Jo

Mielziner has recently designed and some gorgeous costumes by Irene Sharaff, and the local theatre wakes up to a beautiful feast of rollicking mummery this morning.

* * *

As things have turned out, it was a good notion to pilfer Shakespeare's idea and leave his text alone. Against a pseudo-classical setting, which is valuable for costumes and settings, Mr. Abbott has told a knavish tale of twin brothers and twin servants who have been separated for years and are now in the same town unbeknownst to each other. Since one pair of Antipholuses and Dromios is married and the other is single, the mistaken identity results in ribald complications that suffuse this column in rosy blushes of shame. Some one will have to call out the fire department to dampen down the classical ardors of this hilarious tale.

* * *

Before rushing to the alarm box, however, consider the droll people Mr. Abbott has put to temptation. First of all, there is Savo, the pantomime genius, whose humorous gleams and fairy-tale capers have never been so delighted and disarming. As his master, Eddie Albert, whose boyishness and sparkle of comedy are altogether winning; as Luce, Wynn Murray, the fat Sapolio girl, who beams a song as much as she sings it; as the distressed wife, Muriel Angelus, who is beautiful in figure and voice; as her sister, the lovely Marcy Wescott, who has an enchanting way with a sentimental tune; as the incontinent Antipholus, Ronald Graham, who can master a song without cheapening it, and as the second Dromio, Teddy Hart, brother of the composer and an old hand with knockabout comedy—these are the principal people of the plot and they are all genial company.

* * *

Giving Shakespeare a commendable assist in the modern vernacular, Mr. Abbott has found plenty for them to do. Richard Rodgers, seated at his composing spinet, and Lorenz Hart, thumbing the rhyming dictionary, have distributed some of their gayest songs. Let us pass over their bawdries with decorous reserve, pausing only to remark that they are vastly enjoyable, and let us praise them extravagantly, for such a romantic song as "This Can't Be Love" and such gracious mischief as the "Sing for Your Sup-

ON STAGE: 1920–1970 (header)

Vandamm

Jimmy Savo in "The Boys From Syracuse"

per" trio. Not that Mr. Rodgers and Mr. Hart are averse to the down beat and the thumping of good music hall balladry. To their way of thinking, Ephesus is the home of carnival.

* * *

Nor is the dancing a clever afterthought. George Balanchine has designed and staged it. In Betty Bruce and Heidi Vosseler he has a pair of dancers who are extraordi-narily skillful and who can translate the revelry of a musical rumpus into dainty beauty. Particularly at the close of the first act Mr. Balanchine has found a way of turning the dancing into the theme of the comedy and orchestrating it in the composition of the scene. Not to put too solemn a face on it, the dancing is wholly captivating.

As the lady to the left remarked, kiss "The Boys From Syracuse" hello.   **1938 N 24**

OUTWARD BOUND, a play in three acts, by Sutton Vane. Staged by Otto L. Preminger; setting by Watson Barratt; revived by the Playhouse Company (Robinson Smith, Bramwell Fletcher and William A. Brady). At the Playhouse.

Scrubby .... Morgan Farley
Ann .... Helen Chandler
Henry .... Alexander Kirkland
Mr. Prior .... Bramwell Fletcher
Mrs. Clivedon-Banks .... Florence Reed
Rev. William Duke .... Vincent Price
Mrs. Midget .... Laurette Taylor
Mr. Lingley .... Louis Hector
Rev. Frank Thomson .... Thomas Chalmers

By BROOKS ATKINSON

After an interval of nearly fifteen years one naturally feels a little uneasy about seeing a well-loved play again. But Sutton Vane's "Outward Bound," which was revived at the Playhouse last evening, seems not to have aged nor to have lost its unearthly and compassionate magic. Even after fifteen years we still have death with us to inconvenience the certainties of life; and since Mr. Vane wrote of it once with a light, necromantic touch perhaps his play will grow old less quickly than the rest of us. In 1924 it was acted by an ideal cast that has left rapturous memories—Alfred Lunt, Leslie Howard, Dudley Digges, J. M. Kerrigan, Lyonel Watts, Margalo Gillmore, Charlotte Granville, Beryl Mercer and the late Eugene Powers, who was also a wonder. Perhaps the Playhouse company in its first production is a bit less shining in ensemble appearance, but with Laurette Taylor and Florence Reed in leading parts it recovers the beauties of Mr. Vane's fable and some of it is honest enough to break a playgoer's heart.

Unless memory is at fault it was not an immediate triumph at the box office when it was first produced. Although several fine plays have been written about death, theatregoers are inclined to raise an old taboo against them. But Mr. Vane wrote this one with such ease, good humor, common sense and kindliness that he gets his people into heaven with less pain than if they were going into Russia. They are, you remember, passengers on a comfortable steamer, unaware at first that they are dead and actually making the final crossing. They are all a bit nervous when the great fact dawns on them; some of them are, with reason, terrified. But when the inspector comes on board at the end of the voyage they are justly treated. Mr. Vane writes with judicial insight and great tenderness in the concluding scene. He even intervenes on behalf of the

Lucas & Pritchard
Laurette Taylor

lovers who have committed suicide; using an author's prerogative he comes between God and them, giving them one more chance to mold their destiny.

* * *

Although Mr. Vane wrote with decent reticence, he contrived several big scenes into which a good actor can set his teeth. Take, for instance, that scene in the third act when the sweet-souled old charwoman comes to the rescue of the drunken wretch who hardly dares face redemption without benefit of bottle. What a glorious scene that is! In the current revival it is played by Bramwell Fletcher, whose acting throughout the play is superbly winning and knowing, and Miss Taylor, whose well-remembered radiance gives a glow and a heart-beat to the old charwoman's humility and who convinces you that God is in His heaven and all's right with the celestial beyond.

* * *

As the upper-class virago with a cutting tongue, Miss Reed plays her early scenes in particular with a flair for their high amusement. She evokes the satire that lies under some brittleley worded lines. Louis Hector blesses the pompous fraud with the best performance he has given in this neighborhood in some years. Vincent Price plays the clergyman with sincerity of emotion and sufficient skill; and Thomas Chalmers's heartiness, which he keeps under control, redeems the crucial part of the inspector. In the part of the love-stricken girl who has committed suicide, Helen Chandler catches the lonely desperation of the final scene in some singularly touching acting. There are good performances by Morgan Farley as the steward and Alexander Kirkland as the unhappy lover, although perhaps both parts could do with a cleaner definition. In the direction, Otto L. Preminger has creditably arranged the scenes, and Watson Barratt has sheltered the play in a well-designed ship's smoking room that suggests without italicizing the supernatural mission of the voyage.

* * *.

In these circumstances "Outward Bound" is still a deeply moving play that is always simple in thought and narrative. Although Mr. Vane's stately ship steams through the night without pilot or side lights, she does not run into any theological fog. It is a smooth, generally amusing passage to a sunny shore.

1938 D 23

1939

Pirates of the Savoy

D'OYLY CARTE OPERA COMPANY presenting the Gilbert and Sullivan operetta TRIAL BY JURY and THE PIRATES OF PENZANCE. At the Martin Beck Theatre through tomorrow night.

TRIAL BY JURY

The Learned Judge.........William Sumner
Counsel for the Plaintiff......Leslie Rands
The Defendant............Leonard Osborn
Foreman of the Jury.....T. Penry Hughes
Usher....................Richard Walker
Associate...............C. William Morgan
The Plaintiff...............Margery Abbott
First Bridesmaid.............Maysie Dean

THE PIRATES OF PENZANCE

Major General Stanley.......Martyn Green
The Pirate King..........Darrell Fancourt
Samuel....................Richard Walker
Frederic......................John Dean
Sergeant of Police.........Sydney Granville
Mabel........................Helen Roberts
Edith.....................Marjorie Eyre
Kate........................Ivy Sanders
Isabel.....................Maysie Dean
Ruth.......................Evelyn Gardiner

Those people are back. At 8:22 last evening the red thatch of Mr. Isidore Godfrey appeared in the orchestra pit of the Martin Beck Theatre. He bowed, waved his baton once and the curtain went up on "Trial By Jury," words by W. S. Gilbert, music by Arthur Sullivan. The D'Oyly Carte Company had returned for another visit. Nor was it unappreciated. The Martin Beck is a sort of second Savoy on this side of the water—with good carpets—and last night the followers of the comic muse were out to the extent of standing room and the erasure of the false walls Mr. Beck sometimes puts in his house when the company isn't present.

They heard, first of all, "Trial By Jury" as a sort of bull-pen performance to warm up for "The Pirates of Penzance." This latter they heard in what certainly is the best version the D'Oyly Carte people have given here in recent years: and since all along they have been calling that the last word this obviously was nothing more or less than a bit beyond, or something in the nature of a paradox, a paradox, a most ingenious, etc. All the old "business" of "The Pirates" was there, all the old movements, most of the old players—with the audience waiting breathlessly to see and hear them once again.

It was, moreover, in the nature of an anniversary, for the company's present visit is celebrating the Diamond Jubilee Year of the first performance of "The Pirates," performed at the old Fifth Avenue Theatre in 1879, when Sir Arthur conducted—perhaps as well as Mr. Godfrey—and Gilbert and D'Oyly Carte were sitting in the third row. The jubilee will last nine and a half weeks, then there will be a tour before the company goes home.

Of the principal players in "The Pirates", most of the are old friends. There is Martyn Green, on whose singing of "the modern major general" the last two years have made no difference whatsoever. There is Darrell Fancourt as the pirate king. Evelyn Gardiner still remains as the unhappy Ruth and Sydney Granville still is the great sergeant of police; John Dean once again is the pirate apprentice with the unfortunate birthday. The chief change in the cast is in the part of Mabel, which now is played by Helen Roberts, who has a lovely voice, singing the "Poor Wandering One" as it has not often been sung hereabouts. Marvelous is the word they were using.

For its 1939 visit the company has new costumes—very gay—and new scenery. Tradition allows them that change and they leave the rest of it alone. Savoyards, who are suspicious people, leaned forward anxiously in several places where the company might have been tempted to write in something of history this side of 1879, but they needn't have worried. The group gives it as written, in tradition, and magnificently.   L. N.

1939 Ja 6

THE LITTLE FOXES, a play in three acts, by Lillian Hellman. Setting by Howard Bay; costumes designed by Aline Bernstein; staged and produced by Herman Shumlin. At the National Theatre.
Addie...........................Abbie Mitchell
Cal.............................John Marriott
Birdie Hubbard.............Patricia Collinge
Oscar Hubbard...........Carl Benton Reid
Leo Hubbard...................Dan Duryea
Regina Giddens.........Tallulah Bankhead
William Marshall...............Lee Baker
Benjamin Hubbard.........Charles Dingle
Alexandra Giddens......Florence Williams
Horace Giddens............Frank Conroy

By BROOKS ATKINSON

As a theatrical story-teller Lillian Hellman is biting and expert. In "The Little Foxes," which was acted at the National last evening, she thrusts a bitter story straight to the bottom of a bitter play. As compared with "The Children's Hour," which was her first notable play, "The Little Foxes" will have to take second rank. For it is a deliberate exercise in malice—melodramatic rather than tragic, none too fastidious in its manipulation of the stage and presided over by a Pinero frown of fustian morality. But out of greed in a malignant Southern family of 1900 she has put together a vibrant play that works and that bestows viable parts on all the members of the cast. None of the new plays in which Tallulah Bankhead has acted here has given her such sturdy support and such inflammable material. Under Herman Shumlin's taut direction Miss Bankhead plays with great directness and force, and Patricia Collinge also distinguishes herself

with a remarkable performance. "The Little Foxes" can act and is acted.

* * *

It would be difficult to find a more malignant gang of petty robber barons than Miss Hellman's chief characters. Two brothers and a sister in a small Southern town are consumed with a passion to exploit the earth. Forming a partnership with a Chicago capitalist, they propose to build a cotton factory in the South, where costs are cheap and profits high. The Chicago end of the deal is sound. But Miss Hellman is telling a sordid story of how the brothers and the sister destroy each other with their avarice and cold hatred. They crush the opposition set up by a brother-in-law of higher principles; they rob him and hasten his death. But they also outwit each other in sharp dealing and they bargain their mean souls away.

* * *

It is an inhuman tale. Miss Hellman takes a dextrous playwright's advantage of the abominations it contains. Her first act is a masterpiece of skillful exposition. Under the gentility of a social occasion she suggests with admirable reticence the evil of her conspirators. When she lets loose in the other two acts she writes with melodramatic abandon, plotting torture, death and thievery like the author of an old-time thriller. She has made her drama air-tight; it is a knowing job of construction, deliberate and self-contained. In the end she tosses in a speech of social significance, which is no doubt sincere. But "The Little Foxes" is so cleverly contrived that it lacks spontaneity. It is easier to accept as an adroitly designed theatre piece than as a document in the study of humanity.

* * *

One practical advantage of a theatre piece is the opportunities it supplies to the actors. In a perfectly cast performance, none of them fumbles his part. Sometimes our Tallulah walks buoyantly through a part without much feeling for the whole design. But as the malevolent lady of "The Little Foxes" she plays with superb command of the entire character—sparing of the showy side, constantly aware of the poisonous spirit within. As a neurotic victim of circumstances, Miss Collinge also drags the whole truth out of a character, and acts it with extraordinary lightness and grace. Frank

Vandamm
Tallulah Bankhead

Conroy plays the part of a tired man of the house with patient strength of character. Florence Williams is singularly touching in the part of a bewildered, apprehensive daughter of the family. There are also vivid characterizations in the other parts by Charles Dingle, Abbie Mitchell, Carl Benton Reid, Dan Duryea, Lee Baker and John Marriott.

* * *

Howard Bay has provided a setting that conveys the dark stealthiness of the story, and Aline Bernstein has designed suitable costumes for a period narrative. As for the title, it comes from the Bible: "Take us the foxes, the little foxes, that spoil the vines; for our vines have tender grapes." Out of rapacity, Miss Hellman has made an adult horror-play. Her little foxes are wolves that eat their own kind.

1939 F 16

THE PHILADELPHIA STORY, a comedy in three acts, by Phillip Barry. Staged by Robert B. Sinclair; scenery and lighting by Robert Edmond Jones; production committee, Theresa Helburn and Lawrence Langner; produced by the Theatre Guild. At the Shubert Theatre.

Dinah Lords	Lenore Lonergan
Margaret Lord	Vera Allen
Tracy Lord	Katharine Hepburn
Alexander Lord	Dan Tobin
Thomas	Owen Coll
William Tracy	Forrest Orb
Elizabeth Imbrie	Shirley Booth
Macauley Connor	Van Heflin
George Kittredge	Frank Fenton
C. K. Dexter Haven	Joseph Cotten
Edward	Philip Foster
Seth Lord	Nicholas Joy
May	Myrtle Tannahill
Elsie	Lorraine Bate
Mac	Hayden Rorke

By BROOKS ATKINSON

Considerable sustained purring ought to be audible around town this morning. For the Theatre Guild, Katharine Hepburn and Philip Barry have all come together in a gay and sagacious comedy entitled "The Philadelphia Story," put on at the Shubert last evening. None of them has been rich in luck these past few seasons. But Mr. Barry is writing now in the light vein that becomes him and about the people most congenial to his talent. Miss Hepburn plays up to him with the flexibility of a professional stage actress. As for the Theatre Guild, which has been afflicted with disaster longer than one cares to think, it has staged "The Philadelphia Story" with the taste and the sheen of better years —direction by Robert Sinclair, settings by Robert Edmond Jones. Every one should be feeling fine this morning.

* * *

Although Mr. Barry always keeps within safe distance of the drawing room, he has a moral that saves his comedy from pure frivolity. He is looking for the human being beneath the cool, arrogant virtue of a daughter of the upper classes. She ruthlessly holds every one up to the austere standards she has set for herself. Having made one bad marriage to a man unworthy of her pride, she is now on the point of trying again with a self-made man of commerce who is getting on in the world. But a number of things intervene just before the ceremony —some brutal truth-telling by her first husband and her father and a wild affair with a tough-minded magazine writer who knows the facts of life. In the end the girl with the good mind and the disciplined body also acquires the understanding heart of a woman, and the marriage hastily turns into a reunion with the husband of her first choice.

* * *

Probably it is misleading to describe "The Philadelphia Story" as a study in the moral codes of human beings. For Mr. Barry's style is buoyant; his dialogue is silken and comic and his characters are witty, worldly folks with a reticent feeling about solemn topics. By an ingenious turn of story-telling, Mr. Barry has made his narrative a full one. To give it a little contemporary scope, he introduces two magazine investigators who might be representing Fortune if Mr. Barry did not specifically call it Destiny. It is the genius of the comedy of

Vandamm Studio

Katharine Hepburn in "The Philadelphia Story."

manners to spin through the lives of recognizable characters with complete plausibility. It must be confessed that "The Philadelphia Story" is a little too convenient in its conclusion, and just a trifle arch as well. But at best that is a matter of personal opinion, and at worst it is only the ghost of a flaw in a spirited and gossamer dance of comedy with just enough idea to season it pleasantly.

* * *

Certainly Mr. Barry has written Miss Hepburn's ideal part. It has whisked away the monotony and reserve that have kept her acting

in the past within a very small compass. As the daughter of the rich she plays with grace, jauntiness and warmth—moving across the stage like one who is liberated from self-consciousness and taking a pleasure in acting that the audience can share. Mr. Sinclair has for several years been one of our wisest directors. He is very much up to the mark this time, and all the actors give beguiling performances. It would be hard to improve upon Van Heflin's honest and solid description of a tough-minded writer, and of Joseph Cotten's uphill fight with a part that looks forbidding in the early scenes. As the brat of the family, Lenore Lonergan, of a famous theatrical tribe, acts with a stout sort of humor that suits her groaning little figure. Let us also say something appreciative of Frank Fenton, Vera Allen, Shirley Booth, Forrest Orr and Nicholas Joy, who help to round out a joyful evening.

For this is an occasion that deserves appreciation. When the Theatre Guild, Miss Hepburn and Mr. Barry are in top form at the same time, all is for the best in the best of all possible Broadways. Although the comedy of manners has almost been lost in the black whirl of world affairs, it is still a source of unholy delight when experts write, act and produce it.

1939 Mr 29

THE MAN WHO CAME TO DINNER, a comedy in three acts, by Moss Hart and George S. Kaufman. Staged by Mr. Kaufman; setting by Donald Oenslager; produced by Sam H. Harris. At the Music Box.

Mrs. Ernest W. Stanley	Virginia Hammond
Miss Preen	Mary Wickes
Richard Stanley	Gordon Merrick
June Stanley	Barbara Wooddell
John	George Probert
Sarah	Mrs. Priestly Morrison
Mr. Stanley	George Lessey
Maggie Cutler	Edith Atwater
Dr. Bradley	Dudley Clements
Sheridan Whiteside	Monty Woolley
Harriet Stanley	Ruth Vivian
Bert Jefferson	Theodore Newton
Lorraine Sheldon	Carol Goodner
Beverly Carlton	John Hoysradt
Banjo	David Burns

By BROOKS ATKINSON

Whether or not it is the funniest comedy Moss Hart and George S. Kaufman have written is probably a matter of opinion. But it is a fact that "The Man Who Came to Dinner," which opened at the Music Box last evening, is the funniest comedy of this season, and is likely to remain so long after the competition has grown stiffer. Taking Alexander Woollcott in one hand, which is no mean feat, and the disorderly style of "You Can't Take It With You" in the other, Mr. Hart and Mr. Kaufman have put together a fantastic piece of nonsense, with enough plot to serve and a succession of witty rejoinders to keep it hilarious. Since Father Christmas hesitates about playing the part himself, the saturnine Monty Woolley is presiding over the comedy with wonderful aplomb and his own whiskers. Every one seemed thoroughly delighted in Times Square last evening.

* * *

Although the story is imaginary, the characterization is a chip off the old Woollcott block. As the authors tell it, a fabulous lecturer, coming unwillingly to dinner in an Ohio town, slips on the ice, fractures something or other and has to stay as an invalid on the premises. He is down, but not exactly out. For he despotically takes over the house from the indignant hosts and turns it into an asylum for his friends, his satellites and his querilous intrigue. The principal intrigue concerns an attempt to forestall his secretary's plan to marry. But that is no more than a clothesline on which this vaudeville is pinned and left hanging in the breeze.

* * *

No one would say that this is a portrait done in the oil of affection. Neither is it etched in acid. It is done out of relish for the bountiful mischief and the sharp tongue of the nation's town crier. For a rounded portrait something would have to be done for the good works that Woollcott squanders lavishly as his old juggernaut goes rolling across the country, knocking down defenseless bores and jostling the celebrities. But this chronicle of a radio publicist, turning testily on his nurse, bombing his startled doctor, match-making and match-unmaking, plotting deviously and always talking with brilliant sardonic wit, is one that theatregoers are going to relish as much as Mr. Hart and Mr. Kaufman have, and probably Woollcott will also cherish it as one of the fabulous jokes in his Dickensian career.

* * *

Having a sense of humor of his own, Mr. Woolley plays the part in the grand manner with dignity and knavery. Among other things, it is a literary part, and the Wool-

Monty Woolley in "The Man Who Came to Dinner."

ley as well as the Woollcott knows how to speak lines. Under Mr. Kaufman's direction, the comedy goes rollicking across the stage in the wake of some excellent actors. Edith Atwater plays the part of the spirited secretary with a sincerity that gives the comedy a genuine feeling. Carol Goodner is vastly amusing as a termagant actress. John Hoysradt is excellent in a Noel Coward bit, and David Burns does something amusing with a Harpo Marx item in spite of Harpo's presence in the audience last evening.

Inside a single setting by Donald Oenslager, the comedy has been pulled tautly together into an evening of astringent merry-making. It is American in its comic tone, Broadway in craftsmanship, and a roaring evening of literate hilarity into the bargain.

1939 O 17

THE TIME OF YOUR LIFE, a play in
three acts by William Saroyan. Staged
by Eddie Dowling and the author; set-
tings by Watson Barratt; produced under
the supervision of Theresa Helburn and
Lawrence Langner; presented by the The-
atre Guild in association with Mr. Dowl-
ing. At the Booth Theatre.
Newsboy...............:.....Ross Bagdasarian
Drunk.........................John Farrell
Willie.........................Will Lee
Joe...........................Eddie Dowling
Nick......................Charles De Sheim
Tom.......................Edward Andrews
Kitty Duval..................Julie Haydon
Dudley.......................Curt Conway
Harry........................Gene Kelly
Wesley......................Reginald Beane
Lorene.......................Nene Vibber
Blick.........................Grover Burgess
Arab.................Houseley Stevens Sr.
Mary L......................Celeste Holme
Krupp......................William Bendix
McCarthy.....................Tom Tully
Kit Carson......................Len Doyle
Nick's Ma.................Michelette Burani
Sailor......................Randolph Wade
Elsie.........................Cathie Bailey
A Killer........................Evelyn Geller
Her Side Kick..............Mary Cheffey
A Society Lady........Eva Leonard Boyne
A Society Gentleman.....Ainsworth Arnold
First Cop...................Randolph Wade
Second Cop...................John Farrell

By BROOKS ATKINSON

There is something very precious
about William Saroyan. Out of his
enthusiasm for all the living comes
a quality of shining beauty. His
"The Time Of Your Life," which the
Theatre Guild put on at the Booth
last evening, is only a reverie in a
bar room, without much story and
none of the nervous excitement of
the theatre. Nothing holds this
sprawling drama together except
Mr. Saroyan's affection for the
tatterdemalions who are in it. But
his affection is no casual sentiment. It has the force of a genuine
conviction about people. It is innocent at heart and creative in art.
Beautifully acted by Eddie Dowling
in a bar-fly role, "The Time of
Your Life" is something worth
cherishing—a prose poem in rag-
time with a humorous and lovable
point of view.

* * *

Taking a handful of undistinguished characters, Mr. Saroyan
lets the talk flow out of them, and
before you know it he has written
a dance in praise of life. They are
loitering in Nick's waterfront saloon
somewhere in a frowzy corner of
San Francisco. The chief one among
them is a well-heeled, steady drinker who fancies that he is a student
of life. He is quixotic and mystic
with some oddments of philosophy
rattling around in his genially be-
fuddled head. The other characters
strike a general average—a kindly
saloon-keeper, a street-walker with
dreams, a colored musician, an
aspiring tap-dancer, a fabulous

Eddie Dowling in "The Time of
Your Life."   Talbot

teller of tall tales, a worried cop,
a boy in love, a crazy Arab lounging in the corner.

* * *

What they do is hardly enough to
fill a one-act play. But what they
think interests Mr. Saroyan profoundly, and is likely to interest
you. For some of the warmest and
heartiest comedy in the modern
drama comes bubbling up through
Mr. Saroyan's pungent dialogue,
and although it is not realism it is
real. He is no logician. Facts do
not make much impression on his
exultant mind. He is not much interested in the technique of writing
drama. But his imagination is dynamic, and his sense of humor has
a vast appetite. The mood of "My
Heart's in the Highlands" was
country and lyric. The mood of
"The Time of Your Life" is city
and somber. But his saloon loung-
ers facing the world with longing
and wonder are glorious company
and as eloquent as a piece of music.

* * *

No wonder the producers had
trouble on the road shaking the

play down into some sort of stage order. Mr. Saroyan's style of impulse and inspiration fits none of the theatre's smoothest grooves. But it is difficult to see how the performance could be much truer than the one the Theatre Guild has brought to town under the dual direction of Mr. Dowling and Mr. Saroyan. In the central part Mr. Dowling gives a rich and compassionate performance in a savory vernacular that blends with the setting. Although Julie Haydon's shy, unreality of expression suits her to a play of this sort, she does not define the character of the street-walker with much insight. As a whole, the cast is excellent.' It includes some memorable scenes by William Bendix, Len Doyle, Gene Kelly, Tom Tully and Reginald Beane. Watson Barratt has given it a flavorsome setting.

* * *

Probably Mr. Saroyan will learn more about the theatre the longer he stays in it. Any one can see that "The Time of Your Life" does not use the stage efficiently. But that is no more than a pedantic reflection on the waywardness of Mr. Saroyan's genius. For he is creative, which is the most precious thing in any art, and he has rubbed his elbows in life without soiling his spirit.

1939 O 26

LIFE WITH FATHER, a play in three acts by Howard Lindsay and Russel Crouse, based on the writings of the late Clarence Day. Staged by Bretaigne Windust; settings and costumes by Stewart Chaney; produced by Oscar Serlin. At the Empire Theater.

Vinnie	Dorothy Stickney
Annie	Katherine Bard
Clarence	John Drew Devereaux
John	Richard Simon
Whitney	Raymond Roe
Harlan	Larry Robinson
Father	Howard Lindsay
Margaret	Dorothy Bernard
Cora	Ruth Hammond
Mary	Teresa Wright
Rev. Dr. Lloyd	Richard Sterling
Delia	Portia Morrow
Nora	Nellie Burt
Dr. Humphreys	A. H. Van Buren
Dr. Sommers	John C. King
Maggie	Timothy Kearse

By BROOKS ATKINSON

Sooner or later every one will have to see "Life With Father," which opened at the Empire last evening. For the late Clarence Day's vastly amusing sketches of his despotic parent have now been translated into a perfect comedy by Howard Lindsay and Russel Crouse, and must be reckoned an authentic port of our American folklore. They were as genuine as that when they first appeared in The New Yorker, and later between covers in book form. In the form of a narrative drama of family life Mr. Lindsay and Mr. Crouse have now pulled that immortal saga together, wonderfully preserving the humanity as well as the fantastic humor. Mr. Lindsay plays the part of the choleric parent with rare taste and solid heartiness, and Dorothy Stickney plays the part of the wife with enormous skill and spirit. Last evening every one was falling jubilantly in love with a minor classic in the library of American humor.

* * *

Written and acted with infinite dexterity, "Life With Father" is no cartoon out of the funny papers. Under all his rage, Father is a representative parent with a warm regard for his sons and real affection for his wife, and his portrait might come out of any family album. What makes him so hilariously amusing to us today is the violence of his temper. He is rugged individualism in full flower—passionately logical, humorless, possessive and masterful. He is the civilized male in awful grandeur. If Mr. Lindsay and Mr. Crouse were less discerning as playwrights, Father might have emerged as a cheapjack bully to be played only for the laughs. But they treat him with relish and respect against the manners of the late nineteenth century as one of the leading stalwarts of a materialistic civilization. His shouting and swearing are assertions of his importance as a responsible citizen in a hustling period in native history.

* * *

The story of "Life With Father" gives a rounded portrait of the Day's old man. At breakfast you hear him roaring at the new maid and frightening her out of her wits, stamping on the floor three times to summon the cook from the kitchen, and delivering a long, irate speech about taxes and politics that would scare the daylights out of any one who took the trouble to listen. That is the fierce part of Father. But the human side turns up in the course of the evening when his wife falls unaccountably ill and for a moment or two shatters his grand self-confidence. A good egg at heart, Father can rise to any domestic occasion.
The play is strewn with family

Howard Lindsay, in "Life With Father."   Vandamm

crises natural to a house full of growing boys and tiresome relatives, and Father punctuates the episodes with bellows of righteous anger. When he lets himself go, the other members of the family shiver a little, but their regard for the old codger never weakens. For he is the head of the house by virtue of his innate ability. No one questions his right to wear all the pants in the family.

* * *

In Mr. Lindsay's acting Father is completely defined. Although he is stiff, he is not pompous; although he is overbearing, he is not insensitive. He is the high-spirited male of middle years who expresses his vitality in business-like procedure and runs the whole gamut of passion from sulkiness to ferocity. Miss Stickney's portrait of the wife is also brilliant acting, both sweet and witty, with a supple response to the storminess of her domestic economy. Under Bretaigne Windust's knowing direction, the performance is a thorough delight. John Drew Devereaux of the House of Drew gives an excellent performance as the oldest son. As the gawky second son, Richard Simon is also completely enjoyable; and the same things should be said for the other members of a splendid cast. Stewart Chaney has dressed them in costumes touched with humor and housed them in a gay nineteenth-century living room.

* * *

Clarence Day would have been proud of this stage version of his tribute to his father. The dialogue is sparkling, the story is shrewdly told, and the acting is a treasury of appreciative humor. Life with father may have been trying at black moments on Madison Avenue, but it is overpoweringly funny in the theatre. It is also enchanting, for "Life With Father" is a darlin' play.

1939 N 9

Art
Weds Show Business:
1940-1949

By the beginning of this decade, Europe was already embroiled in the Second World War which the United States was soon to enter. Although production costs soared and, consequently, the number of productions presented annually on Broadway dropped alarmingly from the figures of the previous twenty years, the theater seemed in a healthier economic state during at least the first half of the decade. The audiences had more money to spend for entertainment and the theater, despite increased admission prices, no longer seemed a luxury. Audiences wanted to be amused; they wanted to forget for a few hours the horrors of war and the fears of death and devastation. On the other hand, audiences also wanted the theater to illuminate and clarify the complex issues of the day and to examine afresh the meaning and value of liberty, freedom, democracy, and the role of the free individual in his fight against tyranny and injustice. A new kind of reality was emerging in the theater and, for a while, the Broadway stages prospered. Escapist entertainment, topical dramas and comedies, profound works of art and, most particularly, the new musicals all attracted large and responsive audiences to the playhouses. The theater, the public was quick to realize, was there to delight, console, enlighten, and guide it through one of the darkest periods in its history.

The rise of Fascism, the battle against tyranny in any form as well as the war and its aftermath inspired a large portion of the plays written and produced during the forties. Early in the decade, prior to the entrance of the United States into the war, both Robert Sherwood in *There Shall Be No Night* (written for the Lunts) and Lillian Hellman in *Watch on the Rhine* warned of the danger and brutality of totalitarianism. Bigotry and war were intermingled in several provocative plays such as Arthur Laurents' *Home of the Brave* and James Gow and Arnaud d'Usseau's *Deep are the Roots* which focused on the plight of a black soldier returning to a Southern town. War-time profiteering was the basis of such disparate plays as Arthur Miller's *All My Sons* and Garson Kanin's brilliant comedy *Born Yesterday*. American idealism and principles were projected by three biographical plays: Sidney Kingsley's *The Patriots* (Thomas Jefferson), Howard Koch and John Huston's *In Time to Come* (Woodrow Wilson and the League of Nations), and Emmet Lavery's *The Magnificent Yankee* (Oliver Wendell Holmes). But the most inspiring play of the war years was Thornton Wilder's *The Skin of our Teeth* in which the playwright examined man throughout the ages and concluded that he could withstand fire, flood, famine, war, and devastation.

The war also served as background for a spate of comedies. Norman Krasna's *Dear Ruth* and *John Loves Mary,* Joseph Fields' *The Doughgirls,* and Ruth Gordon's witty *Over 21* were all topical and successful, but the most popular war-inspired comedy was *The Voice of the Turtle,* in which Margaret Sullavan, Elliott Nugent, and Audrey Christie enchanted New York. The public for comedy was also well-served by such uproarious works as *My Sister Eileen* and *Junior Miss* by Chodorov and Fields, the fantastical *Harvey* by Mary Chase, and *The Male Animal,* an intelligent and literate comedy by James Thurber and Elliott Nugent. Death was treated lightly in Noel Coward's *Blithe Spirit,* full of séances, ghosts, and a mad medium, as well as in another popular play of the period, *Arsenic and Old Lace* by Joseph Kesselring.

During the decade Eugene O'Neill was represented by *The Iceman Cometh,* produced by the Theatre Guild, and Clifford Odets by *Night Music* (his last play produced by The Group Theatre, which sadly disbanded in 1941), *Clash by Night,* and *The Big Knife.* In the aftermath of the war, however, the most important events in the dramatic field were the arrivals of two young American playwrights, Tennessee Williams and Arthur Miller, who would give distinction to the American theater up to the present day. *The Glass Menagerie* (in which Laurette Taylor gave one of the great performances of all time), *A Streetcar Named Desire* (with the unforgettable Jessica Tandy and Marlon Brando portrayals), and *Death of a Salesman* (superbly enacted by Lee J. Cobb, Arthur Kennedy, and Mildred Dunnock) were, along with the contributions of Wilder and O'Neill, the most distinguished American plays of the forties.

Two other events lent distinction to the decade. John Gielgud brought his productions of *The Importance of Being Earnest* and *Love for Love* to New York. Impeccably acted and staged, these productions were models of the art of high comedy.Equally impressive was the visit of the Old Vic Company, headed by Laurence Olivier and Ralph Richardson. American actors also had their triumphs during the decade. Ethel Barrymore returned to the stage with her best performance in many years in Emlyn Williams' *The Corn is Green.* Katharine Cornell gathered about her some of the finest actors for her revivals of *Candida* (Burgess Meredith, Raymond Massey, Dudley Digges, and Mildred Natwick) and *The Three Sisters* (Judith Anderson, Ruth Gordon, Dennis King, and Edmund Gwenn). In addition, Miss Anderson was especially hailed for her performances as Medea and Lady Macbeth to Maurice Evans' Macbeth. Two black actors, Paul Robeson in *Othello* and Canada Lee in *Native Son,* electrified audiences. José Ferrer's Iago, together with his performances in *Charley's Aunt* and *Cyrano de Bergerac,* placed him in the front ranks of the newer actors. Margaret Phillips in *Summer and Smoke* and *Another Part of the Forest,* Judith Evelyn in *Angel Street,* Barbara Bel Geddes in *Deep are the Roots,* and the incomparable Judy Holliday in *Born Yesterday* were the most widely acclaimed of the new actresses.

Along with a handful of plays, the decade's most cherished accomplishments were achieved in the musical theater. The new reality and seriousness extended to this genre, and a much more mature and complex form began to emerge. The usual never-never land of musical comedy disappeared in the astringent work by Rodgers and Hart, *Pal Joey,* with its anti-hero surrounded by predatory women, blackmailers, and other unsavory characters. Following the untimely death of Hart, Rodgers joined with Hammerstein to create the historic *Oklahoma!* which dispensed with the ubiquitous chorus-line and standard trappings of the conventional musical, substituting a beautifully integrated book and score and believable characters. The subject of psycho-analysis was treated in Kurt Weill's *Lady in the Dark,* in which the magnificent Gertrude Lawrence found her most gratifying role, and racial bigotry was considered in both *Finian's Rainbow* and *South Pacific,* two favorites of the period. Perhaps the most moving musical of the time was Rodgers and Hammerstein's *Carousel* (adapted from Molnár's *Liliom*), in which the accomplished John Raitt and Jan Clayton first appeared. Operas like Blitzstein's *Regina,* Menotti's *The Medium,* and *Carmen Jones,* an updating by Oscar Hammerstein of the Bizet masterpiece, shared the musical stage with the more conventional type of musical comedy, rich in fun and melody, like Irving Berlin's *Annie Get Your Gun* and Cole Porter's *Kiss Me Kate* in which Alfred Drake solidified his position as the outstanding musical star of the decade. Ethel Merman maintained her position as a top musical star in Cole Porter's *Panama Hattie* and *Something for the Boys,* in addition to her spectacular performance as Annie Oakley. Outstanding also was the inspired teaming of Mary Martin and Ezio Pinza in *South Pacific.* The emergence of two gifted leading ladies, Celeste Holm and Nanette Fabray, and three endearing new clowns, Danny Kaye, Nancy Walker, and Carol Channing, were other highlights of this most fruitful age of musical theater.

From the reviews of the forties, seventy have been selected to represent the war years and the post-war period.

1940 - 1949

THE MALE ANIMAL, a comedy in three acts, by James Thurber and Elliott Nugent. Setting by Aline Bernstein; staged and produced by Herman Shumlin. At the Cort Theatre.

Cleota ....Amanda Randolph
Ellen Turner...............Ruth Matteson
Tommy Turner..............Elliott Nugent
Patricia Stanley....... ......Gene Tierney
Wally Myers...................Don DeFore
Dean Frederick Damon...... Ivan Simpson
Michael Barnes............ Robert Scott
Joe Ferguson...................Leon Ames
Mrs. Blanche Damon........Minna Phillips
Ed Keller...................Matt Briggs
Myrtle Keller..............Regina Wallace
"Nutsy" Miller.........Richard Beckhard
Newspaper Reporter..........John Boruff

By BROOKS ATKINSON

Things having been solemn enough so far in 1940, James Thurber and Elliott Nugent have had the goodness to write "The Male Animal" and to let an audience see it at the Cort, where it opened last evening. Imagine one of Mr. Thurber's limp cartoons translated into three acts of insane hubbub and you have a fair idea of the lark Mr. Nugent and he have pushed on the stage. It dismisses you from the theatre in a spirit of dazed hilarity. For the authors have treated an ordinary uproar in a professor's domestic life in the anti-heroic style of Mr. Thurber's solemn drawings and crack-brained literary style. There is some sense mixed up in it here and there in a crisis about academic freedom. But Mr. Thurber and Mr. Nugent complicate it foolishly and the tone of the acting is as board as a dray. Put "The Male Animal" down as a fantastic beast of humorous burden.

* * *

No one will accuse the authors of being literalists. They are forever backing away from a situation into bland irrelevancies. For their central figure, Professor Turner of the English department is mentally intricate and physically inadequate. He is faced with two dilemmas. In the first place, an old football player, who was once sweet on the professor's wife, is back in town, and the wife is feeling unsteady. In the second place, the trustees of the college are Red-hunting and have forbidden the professor to read to his class Vanzetti's moving declaration of faith. Both situations demand summary and courageous action from a man of principle and intelligence. And the comedy of "The Male Animal" consists in Professor Turner's wavering and blundering attempt to play hero.

* * *

If you want to be grave about it, you can perceive under the rumble of comedy a satire on the general helplessness of the civilized man in a world dominated by primitives. That somewhat neurasthenic satire underlies Mr. Thurber's vacuous drawings of human beings and his diffuse writing. For simple enjoyment in the theatre, however, the extravagance of the fooling is enough—a roomful of serious people weaving a cloak of nonsense over their hysterical affairs. There has seldom been a funnier drunk scene than the one in which Professor Turner tries to reason himself into primitive action against a man three times his size, and nothing much funnier than the alarm of the former football player when an old sweetheart begins to take too much for granted. Mr. Thurber and Mr. Nugent are masters of the inconsequential sequence. Starting with nothing, they roll up "The Male Animal" into a mad brawl.

Fortunately, there is plenty of hokum in the performance. Mr. Shumlin has directed it like a civilized vaudeville. After a long time away from the theatre, Mr. Nugent has returned to play the professor with slightness of touch and gloominess of demeanor and considerable comic invention in the inebriated

221

Ruth Matteson in "The Male Animal."
                                    Vandamm

thought scene. Although Ruth Matteson may be overdoing the physical restlessness of the professor's distracted wife, she plays the part with intelligence and spirit. As a younger sister, Gene Tierney blazes with animation in the best performance she has yet given, and Robert Scott does particularly well as an undergraduate firebrand. Leon Ames and Matt Briggs give capital performances as the leading Philistines of the cast. Ivan Simpson is amusing as an ancient professor who deplores trouble but lives in it and Don De Fore does as well by the healthy obtuseness of a football player of today. Like all sound comedy writers, Mr. Thurber and Mr. Nugent begin their rumpus with a comic servant girl, and Amanda Randolph takes care of that very handily.

Aline Bernstein has done the professor handsome in her cheerful setting where all the trouble occurs. When the trouble gets completely out of hand after the preliminary opening act, "The Male Animal" is vastly comic. There is more than meets the funny bone in this scrawled lampoon on the civilized male at bay.

1940 Ja 10

JUNO AND THE PAYCOCK, a play in three acts, by Sean O'Casey. Staged by Arthur Shields; scenery by Robert Edmond Jones; revived by Edward Choate and Mr. Shields, in association with Mr. Jones. At the Mansfield Theatre.

Mary Boyle	Aldeen O'Connor
Juno Boyle	Sara Allgood
Johnny Boyle	Harry Young
Jerry Devine	Thomas Dillon
"Captain" Jack Boyle	Barry Fitzgerald
"Joxer" Daly	Arthur Shields
A Sewing Machine Vendor	Iris Whitney
A Coal Block Vendor	William Stone
Charlie Bentham, N. T.	Lucian Selt
Mrs. Maisie Madigan	Grania O'Malley
Mrs. Tancred	Effie Shannon
"Needle" Nugent	Hale Norcross
An Irregular Mobilizer	Charles Keenan
Furniture Removal Man	Byron Russell
Assis't Furniture Removal Man	Jack Graham
Neighbors	Nancy Grady, George O'Regan and Harry Selby.

By BROOKS ATKINSON

Although Barry Fitzgerald and Sara Allgood appeared in the original stormy performance of "Juno and the Paycock" in Dublin in 1924, they have never appeared together in New York until now. Miss Allgood played Juno in the troupe of Irish players that brought the O'Casey drama here in 1927. Barry Fitzgerald played Captain Boyle with the visiting Abbey Theatre company in 1932 and 1934. By happy chance they are now free to play together again in a revival put on at the Mansfield last evening. The performance as a whole needs considerable sharpening of mood to convey the tragic bitterness that hangs over this savage portrait of the Irish revolution. But count it as a dispensation to have two such glorious actors as Miss Allgood and Mr. Fitzgerald in immortal parts that suit them. They are both in fine fettle just now.

* * *

Probably Mr. Fitzgerald will never have a richer part. Captain Boyle can hardly be overdrawn. Mr. Fitzgerald's notion of this raffish tenement charlatan of Dublin is fantastically comic. Dressed in wrinkled rags that cling uncertainly to his portly figure, a huge belt carelessly buckled around his waist, a squalid cap at an angle on his head, Captain Boyle is stern and pompous on the surface and all bluff underneath. Mr. Fitzgerald's general unintelligibility is plainly a fault in any sort of acting. But in the light of his comic intonations it is a fault that seems less grievous than it is. For Mr. Fitzgerald's tightly-drawn face is an essential part of his portrait—querulous and alarmed by turns; and his voice plays tunes on the character. Sometimes it rises to the singsong of public speaking. Captain Boyle is a part that Mr. Fitzgerald enjoys. He has played it so long that he has filled out all the lines of O'Casey's racy drawing. It is one of the theatre's modern masterpieces.

* * *

Although the part of Juno is less spectacular, Miss Allgood's playing of it is a masterpiece also. Juno is the woman who takes all the responsibility in this harum-scarum family. She cannot preen herself as extravagantly as her shiftless husband. But Miss Allgood's hot-tempered playing reaches down all through Mr. O'Casey's drama and stirs up some of the ground swell of feeling that should be there. In Miss Allgood's acting Juno is a strong character—swift of foot and mind, with the remnants of middle-class respectability coming instinctively to life on social occasions.

A tatterdemalion in her dress and a shrew in speech, she is a mother in the protection she instinctively gives to her children, and she never forgets to straighten her hair and smooth down her apron when she answers a knock on the door. The

Sara Allgood as she appears in "Juno and the Paycock."

Vandamm

tragic scenes at the close of the play Miss Allgood acts with an anguish that gets closer to the heart of O'Casey's drama than anything else in the performance. She may well be proud of the honesty and skill of this bustling portrait of a mother against whom the black world she knows has pitilessly conspired.

* * *

As a performance of the play as a whole this revival is partly inadequate. Arthur Shields, who acts the shifty "Joxer" satisfactorily, has not succeeded in his role as director in bringing the whole play into focus. The comedy runs away with O'Casey's mordant indictment of the Dublin revolution. The black cloud of doom does not hang far enough down into the heedless life of the Boyle family. There is more pathos than bitterness in the second-act curtain. Aideen O'Connor plays a very good Mary Boyle, but the rest of the company is never better than mediocre. There is a fearless thrust of criticism in O'Casey that only partly comes through the surface of this revival. Although Mr. Shields knows the play intimately, he has staged it at top speed and has not had time to beat the performance into shape. Perhaps he can still make the rest of it more worthy of the two grand actors who are in it. What Mr. Fitzgerald and Miss Allgood are doing deserves a triumphant performance of a wonderful play.

1940 Ja 17

THERE SHALL BE NO NIGHT, a drama in three acts, by Robert E. Sherwood. Staged by Alfred Lunt; settings designed by Richard Whorf and costumes by Valentina. Produced by The Playwrights Company and The Theatre Guild. At the Alvin.

Dr. Kaarlo Valkonen	Alfred Lunt
Miranda Valkonen	Lynn Fontanne
Dave Corween	Richard Whorf
Uncle Waldemar	Sydney Greenstreet
Gus Shuman	Brooks West
Erik Valkonen	Montgomery Clift
Kaatri Alquist	Elisabeth Fraser
Dr. Ziemssen	Maurice Colbourne
Major Rutkowski	Edward Raquello
Joe Burnett	Charles Ansley
Ben Gichner	Thomas Gomez
Frank Olmstead	William Le Massena
Sergeant Gosden	Claude Horton
Lempi	Phyllis Thaxter
Ilma	Charva Chester
Photographer	Ralph Nelson
Photographer	Robert Downing

By BROOKS ATKINSON

Mr. Sherwood is speaking a good word for the truth. In "There Shall Be No Night," which was acted at the Alvin last evening, he is trying to look through the black mists of war to the spirit of man that still lives back there somewhere. Taking an attractive family of civilized Finns he has projected them, cool of head, into a doomed defense against Russian invasion and he has commented at length on the meaning of these tragic times. As a play "There Shall Be No Night" is no masterpiece; it has a shiftless second act and less continuity of story than one likes to see. It does not hang together particularly well.

But as acted by Mr. Lunt and Miss Fontanne with thoroughly awakened sincerity it is on the whole enormously impressive. There by the grace of God goes some of the spiritual agony that torments enlightened men today. For Mr. Sherwood is primarily a man of integrity. He has underwritten the play; he has eschewed the flamboyant showmanship that made "Idiot's Delight" a popular favorite. Two or three times in the new drama he has written down his private reflections about mankind in war-time in the simple, ardent prose of his best style. There is nothing cynical, cheap or shallow in his portrait of the ordeal of a brave nation. Out of the bottom of his heart he has faced the philosophy of the war today with the best counsel of which a man of principle is capable.

* * *

He is chronicling the experiences of an eminent Finnish scientist, Dr. Valkonen, who has just won the Nobel Prize for his study of the mind. He is married to an American woman; they have one son who is of military age. An uncommonly civilized person with enormous Christian faith, Dr. Valkonen is optimistic in general and immune to the common hysterias. He does not believe that the Russians will fight. Even if they did, he believes that resistance would be reckless and stupid. But the war closes in about him. His son goes into the army. Faced with a practical situation he has hardly bothered to contemplate he plunges in with his countrymen. In the last act Mr. Sherwood gives him an opportunity to justify himself and to bring his faith up to the fighting front. For men who fight barbarism, not for glory, but humbly to preserve the tradition of freedom, carry the world one step further, he says, and help to fulfill the destiny of civilization.

* * *

The topic is a big one. Moreover Mr. Sherwood plunged into it a few months ago when the story of the Finnish resistance was hot in his mind. Those are generally not the circumstances in which perfect works of art are created, and "There Shall Be No Night" is no exception. But Mr. Sherwood has admirably created the atmosphere of a wholesome family, which is the basis of the play. Part of it is humorous; all of it is affectionate. The whole thing has the feeling of modern times. When the war begins Mr. Sherwood has more difficulty in revealing character from the inside rather than by external circumstances, and the play loses the direction of the splendid first act. But the events are too poignantly true to be resisted by the usual cant of criticism. In the last act Mr. Sherwood twice pulls the whole thing together with magnificent statements of what goes on in the mind of an enlightened man confronted with the destruction of his aspirations. Although the Finnish campaign is now over, Denmark and Norway are part of the same story.

* * *

If Mr. Sherwood's craftsmanship is often uncertain, the Lunts' is unexceptionable. Aroused by the sincerity of the play, they and their associates are acting it beautifully. Mr. Lunt, who was fooling with Shakespeare a while ago, looks the part of Dr. Valkonen straight in the face and acts it with impersonal sobriety and understanding, not forgetting to speak the contemplative passages with driving precision. As Mrs. Valkonen, Miss Fontanne plays with a light touch in the early scenes and a gallantry in the later ones that round out a completely articulate character. This is one of her finest characterizations.

Richard Whorf also devotes his best acting to the part of an honest radio commentator. Sydney Greenstreet gives a fine-grained portrait of an aging Finnish patriot. Montgomery Clift has grown up to the part of the son and plays it well. Excepting a hackneyed scene of hysteria, Elisabeth Fraser gives a pleasant performance as the daughter-in-law. Maurice Colburne is excellent in the character part of a Nazi counsel.

Mr. Whorf's scene design for a gracious, well lighted living-room represents excellent cooperation with author and actors. Valentina's costumes also add life to the performance. Although "There Shall Be No Night" is uneven drama, it honors the theatre and the best parts of it speak for the truth with enkindling faith and passionate conviction.

1940 Ap 30

BIG WHITE FOG, a play by Theodore Ward. Staged by Powell Lindsay; scenery and lighting by Perry Watkins; produced by the Negro Playwrights Company. At the Lincoln Theatre, 135th Street and Lenox Avenue. No performances Monday night and Saturday afternoon.

Ella Mason	Hilda Offley
Juanita Rogers	Maude Russell
Caroline Mason	Eileen Renard
Phillip Mason	Bertram Holmes
Mrs. Brooks	Louise Jackson
Lester Mason	Kelsey Pharr
Wanda Mason	Alma Forrest
Victor Mason	Canada Lee
Percy Mason	Roburte Dorce
Claudine Adams	Muriel Cook
Dan Rogers	Edward Fraction
Count Strawder	P. J. Sidney
Count Cotton	Andrew Walker
Brother Harper	Robert Creighton
Sister Gabrella	Trixie Smith
Bertha Reubel	Almeina Green
Nathan Piszer	Jerry Grebanier
Marx	Stanley Prager
Caroline	Valerie Black
Phillip	Carl Crawford
Bailiff	Stanley Prager
Police Sergeant	Lionel Monagas
Police Lieutenant	Ted Thurston

By BROOKS ATKINSON

Another attempt is being made to establish a theatre of Negro significance in Harlem. Theodore Ward's "Big White Fog" was put on last evening by the Negro Playwrights Company at the Lincoln Theatre, Lenox Avenue at 135th Street. As a drama of social significance Mr. Ward's play has the usual ailments of the breed—monotony of tone and the regulation Communist finish. But within those boundaries "Big White Fog" is the best serious play of Negro authorship about race problems that this courier has happened to see.

* * *

For Mr. Ward has made no concessions to the white man's taste. "Big White Fog" eschews spirituals and hot dancing, which are the only two things Broadway knows about Negro theatre. In a mood of plain speaking, Mr. Ward maintains that there is no hope for the liberation of the Negro race except by alliance with the Communist party. His hero is a follower of Marcus Garvey in 1922. Against the advice of cynical and materialistic-minded friends, he throws in his lot with a leader who has a plan for the race. Garvey's troubles with the law he regards as part of the white conspiracy against the blacks. Ten years later the collapse of the

Garvey program, the loss of the fifteen hundred dollars he had invested in the movement and the withering industrial program have left him destitute. He is fatally shot in an eviction scuffle, and dies while a band of black and white comrades stand like sentinels of some rosy future in the door.

* * *

Although that is the general course of the drama, it contains many other matters. For Mr. Ward has rounded up color prejudice in all its forms, including the ugliest, which exists between members of the Negro race. And his detailed portrait of the economic problems of an intelligent Negro family is painful and unanswerable. If Mr. Ward believes that alliance of insurgent Negroes with the Communist party is the way to social and economic liberation, that is his privilege. But most of us will believe that he is moving toward a system of slavery more stifling than anything his race has yet experienced in America. For communism is no longer a mystic dream, but Soviet Russia, which is a harsh, brutal, treacherous reality.

* * *

Inside a practicable setting by Perry Watkins, who did the luxuriant settings for "Mamba's Daughters," the performance moves somewhat heavily and stiffly. Canada Lee gives an excellent performance in the leading part. He is forceful and magnetically sincere. There are good performances in other parts by Kelsey Pharr, Edward Fraction, Roburte Dorce, Alma Forrest, Maude Russell, Louise Jackson, Muriel Cook and Hilda Offley.

Although this column cannot recommend "Big White Fog" as electric and fully resolved social drama, the Negro Playwrights Company has more ability than any other serious group that has tried to become established in Harlem. Mr. Ward writes like a professional in the politically conscious genre. What he has to say is hard, bold and disturbing.

1940 O 23

CABIN IN THE SKY, a Negro fantasy in two acts and nine scenes. Book by Lynn Root. Lyrics by John Treville Latouche. Music by Vernon Duke. Entire production directed by George Balanchine; dialogue staged by Albert Lewis; settings and costumes designed by Boris Aronson; produced by Mr. Lewis, in association with Vinton Freedley. At the Martin Beck Theater.

Georgia Brown	Katherine Dunham
Dr. Jones	Louis Sharp
Brother Green	J. Rosamond Johnson
Lily	Georgia Burke
Petunia Jackson	Ethel Waters
Lucifer, Jr.	Rex Ingram
"Little Joe" Jackson	Dooley Wilson
Imps	Archie Savage / Jieno Moxzer / Rajah Chardieno / Alexander McDonald
The Lawd's General	Todd Duncan
Fleetfoot	Milton Williams
John Henry	J. Louis Johnson
Dude	Al Moore
First Henchman	Earl Sydnor
Second Henchman	Earl Edwards
Third Henchman	Maurice Ellis
Devil's Messenger	Al Stokes
Messenger Boy	Wilson Bradley
Domino Johnson	Dick Campbell

By BROOKS ATKINSON

Perhaps "Cabin in the Sky" could be better than it is, but this correspondent cannot imagine how. For the musical fantasy, which opened at the Martin Beck last evening, is original and joyous in an imaginative vein that suits the theatre's special genius. Lynn Root began it by writing an extraordinarily fresh book about heaven, hell and the common earth where black people work out their destiny. By great good fortune every one associated with him has met him on equal terms. For it would be difficult to prove that the book is happier in style than George Balanchine's lyrical direction or the excellent performance by a singularly well-chosen Negro cast.

* * *

Ethel Waters has been essential to happiness in the theatre for some time. But she has never given a performance as rich as this before. She is cast as Petunia, faithful wife of an ingratiating rascal who has the greatest difficulty in walking the narrow path to heaven. Without once stepping out of character or assuming the airs of a star performer, Miss Waters captures all the innocence and humor of a storybook character, investing it also with that rangy warmth of spirit that distinguishes her acting. At the present moment, this theatre-goer imagines that he has never heard a song better sung than "Taking a Chance on Love," music by Vernon Duke, lyrics by John Latouche and voice and acting by Ethel Waters. She stood that song on its head last evening and ought

to receive a Congressional medal by way of reward.

* * *

According to Mr. Root's dark-town fable, heaven and hell are uncommonly aroused over the fate of "Little Joe" Jackson. By strict accounting he ought to go below, for he has been running around with a flighty baggage, shooting craps and behaving outrageously. But he is a likable wastrel, and Petunia, his wife, is highly regarded in heaven. Chiefly out of respect for her, "Little Joe" has a second chance to acquire virtue on earth. Since Dooley Wilson plays the part of "Little Joe" with a kind of discouraged bewilderment and since Katherine Dunham plays the baggage at a blistering temperature, the triangular frolic is comic, disarming and incendiary by turns and "Cabin in the Sky" ranks with the best work on the American musical stage.

* * *

Negroes can act with abandon and with infectious enjoyment when the occasion is right. Rex Ingram, for example, has a gleaming magnetism that stretches the

Ethel Waters, in "Cabin in the Sky."
                    Vandamm

seams of any part he plays. As a parson and leader of the chorus, J. Rosamond Johnson has a beat and a wholesomeness that shake a show into vigorous shape. George Balanchine is artist enough to appreciate the gusto of the people he is working with in this performance. Musical shows seldom acquire dancing such as he has directed here—motion in many lines set on fire with excitement. If the rules of Equity permitted, probably the dancers in "Cabin in the Sky" would be glad to pay Mr. Balanchine something for the privilege of appearing under his direction, for he has released them from the bondage of hack dancing and ugliness.

* * *

As a matter of fact, the joy of creative work shines out of all the corners of Mr. Root's fantastic cabin. Vernon Duke has written racy music in several veins from song hits to boogie-woogie orgies. Mr. Latouche has composed crisp and jaunty lyrics. As scene and costume designer, Boris Aronson has done his finest work, giving to pure imagination many vivid shapes and flaring colors. Put "Cabin in the Sky" down as a labor of love by a group of theatre people who have enjoyed working on something that is bursting with life. Mr. Beck will need plenty of fire insurance as long as "Cabin in the Sky" remains at his theatre.

1940 O 26

THE CORN IS GREEN, a play in three acts, by Emlyn Williams. Setting by Howard Bay; costumes designed by Ernest Schrapps; staged and produced by Herman Shumlin. At the National Theatre.

John Goronwy Jones	Rhys Williams
Miss Ronberry	Mildred Dunnock
Idwal Morris	Charles S. Pursell
Sarah Pugh	Gwyneth Hughes
A Groom	George Bleasdale
The Squire	Edmond Breon
Mrs. Watty	Rosalind Ivan
Bessie Watty	Thelma Schnee
Miss Moffat	Ethel Barrymore
Robbart Robbatch	Thomas Lyons
Morgan Evans	Richard Waring
Glyn Thomas	Kenneth Clarke
John Owen	Merritt O'Duel
Will Hughes	Terence Morgan
Old Tom	Sayre Crawley

By BROOKS ATKINSON

With the first real snow of late Autumn comes the first real play of the season. It is "The Corn Is Green," and it was superlatively well played at the National last evening with Ethel Barrymore at the peak of her talents. A play of Welsh life, it is the work of Emlyn Williams, the young British actor who appeared here four years ago in "Night Must Fall," a macabre thriller of which he was also author. Almost a year before the war broke out Mr. Williams played in the original London performance of "The Corn Is Green," vastly to every one's satisfaction; and since the play means a good deal to him personally, he had hoped to act it here and supervise the performance.

As things have turned out, he need have few regrets. For Herman Shumlin has staged it with complete respect for the beauty and exaltation of a remarkable drama. There are many things for which to be devoutly thankful this morning. Not the least of them is the fact that theatre has been restored to its high estate.

* * *

Mr. Williams's theme goes straight to the heart of a glorious topic. "The Corn Is Green" shows how light can be brought into minds of rude and ignorant people. Since the story is to some extent a story of Mr. Williams's personal experience, he goes about telling it with simplicity and affection. Into a small village on a remote Welsh countryside comes a restless female with a little money of her own and a mission. She wants to educate the boys who normally go into the mines when they are 12 years old.

One of the boys turn out to have extraordinary talents as a writer. When she reads his first composition she is astonished by the imagination it discloses. She is also exhilarated, for the chance of pushing an ignorant lad over the wall into a civilized life that he can help to enrich is more than she had dared to hope for. And "The Corn Is Green" is the story of how, by faith, resolution and generosity, she passes the flame of enlightment on to a hand that will carry it further.

* * *

Since this is, at least in part, a true story that probably represents a debt Mr. Williams can never pay, he tells it with extraordinary humanity. His characters are glowing members of the human race—some of them comic, one of them supercilious, one of them slatternly, another dour but aspiring. Representing all kinds of pride, vanity, rebellion, coarseness, stubbornness and good-will, they make an uncommonly attractive lot, and Mr. Williams keeps them moving in and out of his drama with intimate understanding. But his great character is modestly heroic—the

**Ethel Barrymore, in "The Corn
Is Green."**
Vandamm

teacher, Miss Moffat, the woman
with a light in her mind. Aggressive and truculent in the opening
scenes, she grows in grace and perception as the drama moves. What
is pride and assurance in the first
act becomes a complete surrender
in the end to a cause that has overwhelmed her and become much
greater than she was when she
began.

* * *

As things go in the theatre, this
is a great part, and as things are
going in the theatre just now, Miss
Barrymore plays it magnificently.
After a long round of mediocre
parts, she knows that something of
rare quality has come her way and
she has risen nobly to the occasion.
She plays it forcefully, but she also
plays it with deep compassion, and
from now on she can wear Miss
Moffat as a jewel in her crown.
As a director, Mr. Shumlin is a
painstaking workman. He has cast
the drama with great insight and
directed it with superb skill. All

the actors appear at their best, if
not a little better. Richard Waring
has never played so well; as the
central boy in the story, he brings
the character into shape with sharp
definition. Thelma Schnee gives a
resourceful, rounded performance
as the trollop. Rosalind Ivan is
vigorously amusing as a housekeeper with religious notions. Mildred Dunnock is excellent as a
timid spinster. As a Welsh clerk
of studious inclinations Rhys Williams adds one more to a length-
ening list of admirable characterizations, and Edmond Breon catches
all the pompousness and geniality
of the squire.

All the action occurs within a
savory old living room that Howard
Bay has designed with homely appreciation. Everything about "The
Corn Is Green" reawakens enthusiasm for the theatre. For Mr. Williams has written a play of devotion
and wisdom, and the people who
have put it on the stage share his
respect for the human truth it represents.

1940 N 27

PAL JOEY, a "new" musical comedy in
two acts taken from John O'Hara's series of letters of the same name. Book
by Mr. O'Hara. Music by Richard Rodgers. Lyrics by Lorenz Hart. Dances ar-
ranged by Robert Alton; scenery and
lighting by Jo Mielziner; costumes de-
signed by John Koenig; staged and pro-
duced by George Abbott. At the Ethel
Barrymore Theatre.
Joey Evans.....................Gene Kelly
Mike Spears............Robert J. Mulligan
The Kid.....................Sondra Barrett
Gladys........................June Havoc
Agnes......................Diane Sinclair
Linda English................Leila Ernst
Valerie.....................Amarilla Morris
Albert Doane...............Stanley Donen
Vera Simpson..............Vivienne Segal
Escort..........................Edison Rice
Terry.........................Jane Fraser
Victor.........................Van Johnson
Ernest........................John Clarke
Stagehand....................Jerry Whyte
Max.........................Averell Harris
The Tenor.....................Nelson Rae
Melba Snyder..................Jean Casto
Waiter.......................Dummy Spevlin
Ludlow Lowell.................Jack Durant
Commissioner O'Brien.........James Lane
Assistant Hotel Manager.....Cliff Dunstan
   Specialty dancer: Shirley Paige.
Dancing girls: Claire Anderson, Sondra
Barrett, Alice Craig, Louise de Forrest,
Enez Early, Tilda Getze, Charlene Harkins,
Frances Krell, Janet Lavis, June Leroy,
Amarilla Morris, Olive Nicolson, Mildred
Patterson, Dorothy Poplar, Diane Sinclair,
Mildred Solly, Jeanne C. Trybom, Marie
Vanneman.
Dancing boys: Adrian Anthony, John
Benton, Milton Chisholm, Stanley Donen,
Henning Irgens, Van Johnson, Howard
Ledig, Michael Moore, Albert Ruiz.

By BROOKS ATKINSON

If it is possible to make an entertaining musical comedy out of

an odious story, "Pal Joey" is it. The situation is put tentatively here because the ugly topic that is up for discussion stands between this theatregoer and real enjoyment of a well-staged show. Taking as his hero the frowsy night club punk familiar to readers of a series of sketches in The New Yorker, John O'Hara has written a joyless book about a sulky assignation. Under George Abbott's direction some of the best workmen on Broadway have fitted it out with smart embellishments.

Rodgers and Hart have written the score with wit and skill. Robert Alton has directed the dances inventively. Scenery out of Jo Mielziner's sketchbook and costumes off the racks of John Koenig—all very high class. Some talented performers also act a book that is considerably more dramatic than most. "Pal Joey," which was put on at the Ethel Barrymore last evening, offers everything but a good time.

* * *

Whether Joey is a punk or a heel is something worth more careful thinking than time permits. Perhaps he is only a rat infested with termites. A night club dancer and singer, promoted to master of ceremonies in a Chicago dive, he lies himself into an affair with a rich married woman and opens a gilt-edged club of his own with her money. Mr. O'Hara has drawn a pitiless portrait of his small-time braggart and also of the company he keeps; and Gene Kelly, who distinguished himself as the melancholy hoofer of "The Time of Your Life," plays the part with remarkable accuracy. His cheap and flamboyant unction, his nervous cunning, his trickiness are qualities that Mr. Kelly catches without forgetting the fright and gaudiness of a petty fakir. Mr. Kelly is also a brilliant tap dancer—"makes with the feet," as it goes in his vernacular—and his performance on both scores is triumphant. If Joey must be acted, Mr. Kelly can do it.

* * *

Count among your restricted blessings Vivienne Segal who can act with personal dignity and can sing with breeding. In a singularly sweet voice she sings some scabrous lyrics by Lorenz Hart to one of Richard Rodgers's most haunting tunes—"Bewitched, Bothered and Bewildered." June Havoc applies a broad, rangy style to some funny burlesques of night-club routines and manners. Jean Casto satirizes

Gene Kelly, in "Pal Joey"
Talbot

the strip-tease with humorous condescension. As a particularly rank racketeer Jack Durant, who is a sizable brute, contributes a few amazing and dizzy acrobatics. This department's paternal heart goes out especially to Leila Ernst who is the only uncontaminated baggage in the cast.

* * *

Occasionally "Pal Joey" absents itself a little from depravity and pokes fun at the dreariness of night club frolics, and at the close of the first act it presents an admirable dream ballet and pantomime. Joey's hopeful look into a purple future is lyrically danced by Mr. Kelly. There is a kind of wry and wistful beauty to the spinning figures of Mr. Alton's dance design. But the story of "Pal Joey" keeps harking back to the drab and mirthless world of punk's progress. Although "Pal Joey" is exp rtly done, can you draw sweet water from a foul well?

1940 D 26

MY SISTER EILEEN, a play in three acts, by Joseph A. Fields and Jerome Chodorov, derived from the stories by Ruth Mc-Kenney. Staged by George S. Kaufman; setting by Donald Oenslager; produced by Max Gordon. At the Biltmore Theatre.

Mr. Appopolous	Morris Carnovsky
Ruth Sherwood	Shirley Booth
Eileen Sherwood	Jo Ann Sayers
Jensen	George Cotton
A Street Arab	Eric Roberts
A Pair of Drunks	Arthur Tell / Alva Milligan
Lonigan	Tom P. Dillon
The Wreck	Gordon Jones
Another Street Arab	Bob White
Captain Fletcher	Charles G. Martin
Helen Wade	Joan Tompkins
Frank Lippencott	Richard Quine
Chic Clark	Bruce MacFarlane
Cossack	David Macomber
Violet Shelton	Effie Afton
Mrs. Wade	Helen Ray
Robert Baker	William Post Jr.
Six Future Admirals	Michael Ames / Alan Brixey / Peter Knego / Paul Marion / Mel Roberts / Paul Seymour
Walter Sherwood	Donald Foster
A Prospective Tenant	Eda Heinemann
The Consul	Joseph Kallini

By BROOKS ATKINSON

At last—at long last, in fact—an amusing comedy has come to town. Out of Ruth McKenney's New Yorker sketches, Joseph Fields and Jerome Chodorov have devised "My Sister Eileen," which was acted at the Biltmore last evening. Under George S. Kaufman's direction, which deserves equal billing, it emerges as the antic story of two orphans of the storm from Columbus, Ohio, who expose themselves to Greenwich Village and learn about life the hard way.

To Miss McKenney this hilarious theatrical version of her bright-edged sketches must come as a mixed blessing. Her sister, Eileen, was killed in an automobile accident last Sunday on the West Coast. That extra-mural tragedy is the only somber note hovering around the appearance of the first completely gay comedy on the dramatic stage of New York this season.

* * *

What happens to the two sisters from Columbus could happen. One is a prospective writer; the other one wants to get on the stage. Like any other emigrants from America, they take a cheap apartment in New York and proceed to look for jobs. It is the virtue of "My Sister Eileen" to regard Greenwich Village as a disorderly and completely fantastic place where no one behaves sensibly, and the evidence is wholly convincing. In the Village vernacular, the basement apartment with an arched window giving onto the sidewalk becomes a studio and the Greek landlord is a frustrated

artist. An unemployed professional football player lives upstairs and for a time camps in their kitchen. And quite a variety of madmen trickles through their door—a drug-store counterman with bohemian notions, a vagrant newspaper writer, a prostitute who once did business at the same address and, finally, six cadets from the romantic Brazilian Navy.

* * *

Not being sociologists, the authors of "My Sister Eileen" have served up the adventures in the form of crack-brained comedy without much rhyme or reason. What goes on might be drab enough if Sister Ruth did not have a cutting tongue. But it is the genius of New Yorkers, who hate to be bored, to look on the normal activities of their town with disbelief, as though everything were a humorous dream. What is commonplace becomes incredible. The whole thing gradually develops into a nightmare of fabulous proportions. Thanks to Sister Ruth's acid tongue and the neatly turned dialogue that has been written for her, "My Sister Eileen" becomes a nimble-witted commentary on the humdrum foibles of Greenwich Village. Although sensible people do live there in fairly large numbers, you can forget all that in the presence of this play.

* * *

Mr. Kaufman is no rule-of-thumb director. Having his own peculiar relish for absurdities and knowing the pace and rhythms of harum-scarum stage larks, he keeps "My Sister Eileen" moving at high speed through guffawing crises. The basement window in Donald Oenslager's pungent set becomes a lively cyclorama of a musty New York street where drunks, vendors, urchins, cops and mothers airing the babies drift by. As Sister Ruth, Shirley Booth gives an admirably timed portrait of comic skepticism. As Sister Eileen, Jo Ann Sayers is attractive and plausible, though she has a good deal yet to learn about acting. Morris Carnovsky plays the Greek landlord with dry mischief, and Gordon Jones, Richard Quine, Joan Tompkins, Effie Afton, Eda Heineman and William Post Jr. play other parts as lightly as they are written.

If everyone had Ruth McKenney's sense of humor the whole town would be as hilarious as "My Sister Eileen." That is, if Mr. Kaufman were town director, which might not be a bad idea at that.

1940 D 27

1941

ARSENIC AND OLD LACE, a "new comedy" in three acts, by Joseph O. Kesselring. Staged by Bretaigne Windust; production assistant, Carmen Lewis; setting by Raymond Sovey; produced by Howard Lindsay and Russel M. Crouse. At the Fulton Theatre.

Abby Brewster	Josephine Hull
Rev. Dr. Harper	Wyrley Birch
Teddy Brewster	John Alexander
Officer Brophy	John Quigg
Officer Klein	Bruce Gordon
Martha Brewster	Jean Adair
Elaine Harper	Helen Brooks
Mortimer Brewster	Allyn Joslyn
Mr. Gibbs	Henry Herbert
Jonathan Brewster	Boris Karloff
Dr. Einstein	Edgar Stehli
Officer O'Hara	Anthony Ross
Lieutenant Rooney	Victor Sutherland
Mr. Witherspoon	William Parke

By BROOKS ATKINSON

Let's not exaggerate. At some time there may have been a funnier murder charade than "Arsenic and Old Lace," which was acted at the Fulton last evening. But the supposition is purely academic. For Joseph Kesselring has written one so funny that none of us will ever forget it and Bretaigne Windust has directed it like a man inspired.

It may not seem hilarious to report that thirteen men succumb to one of the blandest murder games ever played in Brooklyn. But Mr. Kesselring has a light style, an original approach to an old subject, and he manages to dispense with all the hocus-pocus of the crime trade. Swift, dry, satirical and exciting, "Arsenic and Old Lace" kept the first-night audience roaring with laughter. Although there have been some other good plays recently, this is the freshest invention. It is full of chuckles even when the scene is gruesome by nature.

* * *

As a matter of fact, the Brewsters of Brooklyn are homicidal maniacs. But Aunt Abby and Aunt Martha are, on the surface, two of the nicest maiden ladies who ever baked biscuits, rushed hot soup to ailing neighbors and invited the minister to tea. Part of their charitable work consists in poisoning homeless old men who have no families to look after them. Their lunatic brother, who, for no apparent reason, imagines that he is Theodore Roosevelt, buries the bodies in the cellar with military and presidential flourishes.

If their brightest nephew who, of course, is a drama critic, had not discovered a body under the window seat, the murder game might have continued indefinitely. But he is normal, although naturally more brilliant than ordinary people and he is so upset that he can only stay one act at the play he is supposed to review that evening. The riotous amusement of "Arsenic and Old Lace" consists in his attempt to keep the murders a secret and, at the same time, to commit his dear aunts to an institution where their foible will be stopped.

* * *

Nothing in Mr. Kesselring's record has prepared us for the humor and ingenuity of "Arsenic and Old Lace." He wrote "There's Wisdom in Women" in 1935 and "Cross Town" in 1937. But his murder drama is compact with plot and comic situation. In addition to the homey aunts it includes a sinister maniac who looks enough like Boris Karloff to be Boris Karloff, which as a matter of fact he is. The lines are bright. The story is mad and unhackneyed. Although the scene is always on the verge of the macabre and the atmosphere is horribly ominous, Mr. Kesselring does not have to stoop to clutching hands, pistol shots or lethal screams to get his effects. He has written a murder play as legitimate as farce-comedy.

Give Mr. Windust's direction ample credit. In the casting and in the tone of the performance it preserves the casual point of view that is so robustly entertaining. There could hardly be sweeter ladies than the two played by Josephine Hull and Jean Adair. Allyn Joslyn gives an amazingly humorous and resourceful performance as the frightened drama critic. As the evil one, Mr. Karloff moves quietly through plot and poison without resorting to trickeries, and Edgar Stehli is light footed in the part of a satellite. As the cop who wants to write a play and tell the plot to a drama critic, Anthony Ross is also amusing. Helen Brooks plays the drama critic's baffled fiancée with patience and spirit.

All the comic rag-tag and bob-tail occurs inside Raymond Sovey's setting of a decaying Brooklyn mansion. "Arsenic and Old Lace" has been produced by Howard Lindsay and Russel Crouse, who wrote the stage version of "Life With Father." Perhaps that gives you the idea.

1941 Ja 11

LADY IN THE DARK, a play with music in two acts and seven scenes, by Moss Hart. Music by Kurt Weill. Lyrics by Ira Gershwin. Play staged by Mr. Hart. Production supervised and lighted by Hassard Short. Scenery by Harry Horner. Costumes designed by Irene Sharaff and Hattie Carnegie. Choreography by Albertina Rasch. Produced by Sam H. Harris. At the Alvin Theatre.

Dr. Brooks..................Donald Randolph
Miss Bowers ....Jeanne Shelby
Liza Elliott ....Gertrude Lawrence
Miss Foster ....Evelyn Wyckoff
Miss Stevens ....Ann Lee
Maggie Grant ....Margaret Dale
Alison Du Bois.............Natalie Schafer
Russell Paxton ....Danny Kaye
Charley Johnson ....Macdonald Carey
Randy Curtis ....Victor Mature
Joe, an office boy..........Ward Tallmon
Tom, an office boy........Nelson Barclift
Kendall Nesbitt ....Bert Lytell
Helen, a model ....Virginia Peine
Ruthie, a model ....Gedda Petry
Carol, a model ....Patricia Deering
Marcia, a model.......Margaret Westberg
Ben Butler ....Dan Harden
Barbara ....Eleanor Eberle
Jack ....Davis Cunningham

THE ALBERTINA RASCH GROUP DANCERS: Dorothy Byrd, Audrey Costello, Patricia Deering, June MacLaren, Beth Nichols, Wana Wenerholm, Margaret Westberg, Jerome Andrews, Nelson Barclift, George Bockman, Andre Charise, Fred Hearn, Yaroslav Kirov, Parker Wilson.

THE SINGERS: Catherine Conrad, Jean Cumming, Carol Deis, Hazel Edwards, Gedda Petry, June Rutherford, Florence Wyman, Davis Cunningham, Max Edwards, Len Frank, Gordon Gifford, Manfred Hecht, William Marel, Larry Siegle, Harold Simmons.

THE CHILDREN: Ann Bracken, Sally Ferguson, Ellie Lawes, Joan Lawes, Jacqueline Macmillen, Lois Volkman, Kenneth Casey, Warren Mills, Robert Mills, Robert Lee, George Ward, William Welch.

By BROOKS ATKINSON

All things considered, the American stage may as well take a bow this morning. For Moss Hart's musical play, "Lady in the Dark," which was put on at the Alvin last evening, uses the resources of the theatre magnificently and tells a compassionate story triumphantly. Note the distinction between "musical play" and "musical comedy." What that means to Mr. Hart's mind is a drama in which the music and the splendors of the production rise spontaneously out of the heart of the drama, evoking rather than embellishing the main theme.

Although the idea is not new, since "Cabin in the Sky" and "Pal Joey" have been moving in that direction this year, Mr. Hart and his talented associates have carried it as close to perfection as any one except an academician can require. Eschewing for the moment his blistering style of comedy, Mr. Hart has written a dramatic story about the anguish of a human being. Kurt Weill has matched it with the finest score written for the theatre in years. Ira Gershwin's lyrics are brilliant. Harry Horner's

whirling scenery gives the narrative a transcendent loveliness. As for Gertrude Lawrence, she is a goddess: that's all.

*   *   *

What brings this about is the emotional confusion of the woman

Gertrude Lawrence, in "Lady in the Dark."   Vandamm

editor of a smart women's magazine. Up to now she has been contented, living happily with a married man whose wife would not divorce him, and absorbed in work at which she is conspicuously successful. But suddenly everything has gone awry. Frightened by the jangle of her nerves, she goes to a psychoanalyst. "Lady In the Dark" is the drama of the strange images he draws out of her memories. In the end the analyst resolves her confusion into an intelligible pattern — proving, incidentally, that you never know whom you love, which is a terrifying prospect, but that is neither here nor there.

If that sounds like a macabre theme, you can rely upon Mr.

Hart's lightness of touch and his knack for tossing in a wise-crack to keep the narrative scenes buoyant. And the long, fantastic interludes when the editor is exploring her memories carry "Lady in the Dark" into a sphere of gorgeously bedizened make-believe that will create theatrical memories for every one who sees them. Mr. Weill's score is a homogenous piece of work, breaking out into song numbers over a mood of dark evocation—nostalgic at times, bursting also into humor and swing. And Mr. Gershwin, in turn, has written his lyrics like a thoroughbred. Uproariously witty when the time is right, he also writes in impeccable taste for the meditative sequences.

* * *

To carry the burden of such a huge production, Mr. Horner has set his scenery on four revolving stages that weave naturalism and fantasy into a flowing fabric; and Hassard Short, as usual, has lighted it regally. The production is a rhapsody in blue and gold, giving reality an unreal size, shape and color, and Irene Sharaff's costumes are boldly imaginative. As the mistress of the choreography, Albertina Rasch has designed vivid lines of dance movement, and the staging is full of grace and resourcefulness.

No one but Miss Lawrence could play a virtuoso part of such length and variety. She is on stage almost at curtain-rise, and she is never off it long—leaping from melancholy to revelry with a swiftness that would be bewildering if she could not manage caprices so well. She sings, she dances. After playing a scene as a mature woman, she steps across the stage to play a scene as a schoolgirl without loss of enchantment. Sometimes Miss Lawrence has been accused of overacting, which is a venial sin at most. But no one will accuse her of being anything but superb in "Lady In the Dark." She plays with anxious sincerity in the narrative scenes and with fullness and richness in the fantasy. For good measure, she sings "The Saga of Jenny" like an inspired showgirl.

* * *

The cast, under Mr. Hart's direction, is excellent throughout. As a comic fashion photographer, Danny Kaye, who was cutting up in "The Straw Hat Revue" last year, is infectiously exuberant. Macdonald Carey, who played in the Globe Shakespeare at the World's Fair, acts the part of an aggressive magazine man with a kind of casual forthrightness. As a glamorous movie hero, Victor Mature is unobjectionably handsome and affable. Margaret Dale has an amusing part as a fashion editor and plays it with dry humor, and Natalie Schaffer has some fun with a supermodish gadabout. In the unwelcome part of the sympathetic lover, Bert Lytell gives a good performance, and Donald Randolph, as the analyst, also behaves like a gentleman.

All these actors and variegated items of a show have been pulled into place by a theatre that has been put on its mettle by an occasion. "Lady in the Dark" is a feast of plenty. Since it also has a theme to explore and express, let's call it a work of theatre art.

1941 Ja 24

'Native Son,' by Paul Green and Richard Wright, Put On by Orson Welles and John Houseman

NATIVE SON, a play in ten scenes without an intermission, dramatized by Paul Green and Richard Wright and derived from the latter's book of the same name. Staged by Orson Welles; settings by James Morcom; production supervised by Jean Rosenthal; presented by Mr. Welles and John Houseman, in association with Bern Bernard. At the St. James Theatre.

Bigger Thomas	Canada Lee
Hannah Thomas	Evelyn Ellis
Vera Thomas	Helen Martin
Buddy Thomas	Lloyd Warren
A Neighbor	Jacqueline Ghant Andre
Miss Emmett	Eileen Burns
Jack	J. Flashe Riley
Clara	Rena Mitchell
G. H. Rankin	Rodester Timmons
Gus Mitchell	Wardell Saunders
Ernie Jones	C. M. Bootsie Davis
Mr. Dalton	Erskine Sanford
Mrs Dalton	Nell Harrison
Britten	Everett Sloane
Peggy	Frances Bavier
Mary Dalton	Anne Burr
Jan Erlone	Joseph Pevney
Buckley	Philip Bourneuf
Paul Max	Ray Collins
A Reporter	Paul Stewart
Judge	William Malone
Newspaper Men	John Berry / Stephen Roberts / George Zorn / Don Roberts

By BROOKS ATKINSON

Out of Richard Wright's novel, "Native Son," Mr. Wright and Paul Green have written a powerful drama. Orson Welles has staged it with imagination and force. Those are the first things to be said about the overwhelming play that opened at the St. James last evening. But they hardly convey the excitement of the first performance of a play that represents experience of life and conviction in thought and a production that represents a dynamic use of the stage.

Mr. Wright's long and pulsing novel of a Negro boy's snarling rebellion against a white man's world was vividly subjective in expression. Particularly toward the end it poked into painful psychological details. In the drama Mr. Green and Mr. Wright work in a more objective style. Without the subjective background their defense of Bigger Thomas's ghastly crime in the court-scene sounds like generalized pleading. It lacks the stinging enlightenment of the last third of Mr. Wright's novel.

* * *

But that completes this column's bill of exceptions to the biggest American drama of the season. For Mr. Green and Mr. Wright have translated a murder story into a portrait of racial fright and hatred and given it a conclusion that brings peace to a taut, bewildered mind. Bigger Thomas is an ignorant Negro boy who hates a world that has imprisoned him with shadowy forces he does not understand. On the one side he smolders with resentment; on the other he is panicky with fright. He murders the daughter of his white employer in terror and by accident. But the murder gives him a sense of power and achievement. Now he is a man of action, fighting the enemy for his own life. He is captured, of course, in a manhunt through Chicago's rookeries, and his lawyer persuades him to plead guilty in the courts. At the trial his lawyer defends him, not on the facts of the case, which are hopeless, but on the causes of Bigger's psychological tangle. As he stands in the death cell Bigger for the first time understands that he is a member of the human race.

* * *

Roughly that is the motive which distinguishes "Native Son" from the run-of-the-mine crime play and the ordinary thriller. In staging it Mr. Welles picks up the bravura style of the Mercury Theatre where he left it two or three seasons ago. In ten savory scenes, acted on different levels with a resourceful use of the stage, he runs through the narrative, giving motion to static scenes by flares of light and putting "Native Son" into its urban

Canada Lee, in "Native Son"
Vandamm

environment by a varied use of sound accompaniment. Mr. Welles is a dramatic showman; he likes big scenes, broad sweeps of color and vigorous contrasts in tempo. He likes theatre that tingles with life. Once or twice, perhaps, the exigencies of the script drive him into a melodramatic absurdity, like the rumble of the automatic furnace stoker. If it were not for the plot Mr. Welles and the millionaire Dalton could change to a silent oil-burner. But the production as a whole represents theatre that has been released from stuffy conventions.

* * *

In Canada Lee, the authors and producers have an actor for whom they should be devoutly thankful. As Bigger Thomas, he gives a clean, honest, driving performance of remarkable versatility. Mr. Lee has already had an extraordinary career as prize-fighter, violinist, band leader and host of the "Chicken Coop" in Harlem. As an actor he is superb.

Not all of the acting measures up to the play or performance. Perhaps Mr. Welles is not sufficiently interested in the minor parts. But Ray Collins gives a straightforward, homely performance as the defense attorney, and makes his points more graphically in the acting than in the script. Everett Sloane is excellent as a nervous functionary in the Dalton household. Philip Bourneuf, Evelyn Ellis, Paul Stewart, Rena Mitchell and Frances Bavier play their parts with flavor or conviction as the case may be. "Native Son" is drama and theatre with mind and style of its own.

1941 Mr 25

WATCH ON THE RHINE, a play in three acts, by Lillian Hellman. Setting by Jo Mielziner; costumes designed by Helene Pons; song composed by Paul Bowles; staged and produced by Herman Shumlin. At the Martin Beck Theatre.

Anise ....Eda Heinemann
Fanny Farrelly...............Lucile Watson
Joseph.......................Frank Wilson
David Farrelly...............John Lodge
Marthe de Brancovis......Helen Trenholme
Teck de Brahcovis.......George Coulouris
Sara Mueller...............Mady Christians
Joshua Mueller..........Peter Fernandez
Bodo Mueller..............Eric Roberts
Babette Mueller.............Anne Blyth
Kurt Mueller...............Paul Lukas

By BROOKS ATKINSON

In "Watch on the Rhine," which was put on at the Martin Beck last evening, Lillian Hellman has brought the awful truth close to home. She has translated the death struggle between ideas in familiar terms we are bound to respect and understand. Curious how much better she has done it than anybody else by forgetting the headlines and by avoiding the obvious approaches to the great news subject of today. After the hardness and coldness of "The Children's Hour" and "The Little Foxes," it is also remarkable that she is now writing with great humanity about people whose native grace she admires.

Her two previous dramas were more perfectly put together, each scene dovetailing with the one preceding. The narrative of "Watch on the Rhine" drifts into generalities before the main action is well started. But that is carping at technicalities, and it does not destroy a general impression that "Watch

on the Rhine" is the finest thing she has written. Beautifully directed by Herman Shumlin and magnificently acted by Paul Lukas in the leading part, it is a play of pith and moment and the theatre may be proud of it.

* * *

What it says is that the death of fascism is more desirable than the lives and well-being of the people who hate it. Miss Hellman makes that familiar point without political argument and without reproducing in miniature form the struggle between fascism and democracy. In a comfortable country house near Washington a wealthy American family is offering refuge to a penniless Rumanian count and his American wife. On the day when the play opens they are also expecting to receive home their daughter, who was married to a German twenty years ago. Sara Mueller she is now, and presently she arrives, shabby and happy, with her husband and three children. As it turns out, her husband is no ordinary refugee, but a worker against fascism, deep in the intrigues of embittered Europe.

Since the power of "Watch On the Rhine" depends in large part upon the turn of the plot, it would do the theatregoer a disservice to describe it too completely here. But it gives away nothing essential to say that the struggle comes when the Rumanian count finds out Herr Mueller's secret identity and tries to blackmail him. "Watch On Rhine" has many other qualities. The characters are well drawn out of affection for people of integrity. The writing is enormously skillful—humorous, witty and also forthright when the time comes for plain speaking. Among other things, Miss Hellman draws a vivid contrast between the simple good-will of a normal American family and the dark callousness of Europeans who have grown accustomed to horror, intrigue and desperation.

* * *

Under Mr. Shumlin's direction it is acted to the hilt. The enjoyment you take in these people and the sympathy you have for their ordeal depend largely upon the high quality of the acting. As the enemy of fascism, Mr. Lukas's haggard, loving, resourceful determination becomes heroic by virtue of his sincerity and his superior abilities as an actor. George Coulouris gives a lucid and subtly repelling performance as an opportunist count with good manners and odious character. Mady Christian's Sara Mueller is

Paul Lukas, in "Watch on the Rhine."   Vandamm

full of womanly affection and a crusader's resignation to realities. As a garrulous mother, Lucile Watson is enormously witty, her conflicting emotions coming swiftly to the surface.

In his outbursts of anger, John Lodge is merely strident as a brother, and also alarmingly Bostonian for an old Washington family, but when he is under control he acts with decision. Helen Trenholme plays the part of the countess with charm and with a sharp flash of spirit in her critical scene. Little Eric Roberts is amusingly bumptious as a boy who is tingling with ideas and overflowing with language. Eda Heinemann is wryly entertaining as a temperamental companion of the house. Frank Wilson is playing a colored butler with his familiar bland humor.

As usual, Jo Mielziner has designed a drawing-room that looks inviting and makes the play feel at home. It is a well-rounded play, full of flavor and good people and the characters control its destinies. For Miss Hellman never preaches. She has given fascism a terrible ap-

pearance without introducing a uniform or a party salute. Being primarily interested in people, she has shown how deeply fascism penetrates into the hearts and minds of human beings. "Watch On the Rhine" is a compassionate drama of men, women and children.

1941 Ap 2

BLITHE SPIRIT, "an improbable farce" in three acts, by Noel Coward. Setting by Stewart Chaney; staged and produced by John C. Wilson. At the Morosco Theatre.
Edith ....Jacqueline Clark
Ruth ....Peggy Wood
Charles ....Clifton Webb
Dr. Bradman................Philip Tonge
Mrs. Bradman................Phyllis Joyce
Madame Arcati............Mildred Natwick
Elvira ....Leonora Corbett

By BROOKS ATKINSON

Probably Noel Coward ought to be feeling grave amid the anxieties of beleaguered London. But it is to be feared that the war has made him frivolous. For "Blithe Spirit," which was acted at the Morosco last evening, is a completely insane farce that is also uproarious. I hardly touches the stage as it rides a demented broomstick to hilarity. In the old days of peace the West End's Null Cahd used occasionally to have a serious thought on his mind about the iniquities of neurotic society or the grandeur of England. But "Blithe Spirit" is relaxed. It is pure entertainment. It is a travesty of ghost stories, told with the sardonic impeccability of a cafe wit.

* * *

A novelist is living with his second wife in a state of fashionable discontentment. To accumulate a little useful information about the occult for a novel he is writing he invites a spiritualist to hold a seance in his house. She does, and to such good purpose that the spirit of his first wife returns from the psychic beyond, and raises hob with his domestic arrangements. For she is not a noble spirit. She is vain and covetous. Through some eerie mischance, she even translates the second wife into a spirit. And the third act of the play finds the novelist plagued by two spirits that cannot leave him and cannot get away from each other.

That is the framework of "Blithe Spirit." But it hardly suggests the comic absurdities of Mr. Coward's high-spirited lark, which is full of droll malice and farsical insincerity. To him the mumbo-jumbo of spiritualism is an invitation to poke fun at solemn characters and write lines with a caustic stick. He skips through the exposition with witty alacrity. He picks up some vagrant laughs with the low-comedy part of fleet-footed servant drudge. As usual, he smashes crockery to point a climax. And the part of the maidenly spiritualist he has translated into a remarkably funny satire on old saws and bogus good cheer.

* * *

There is hardly enough material in "Blithe Spirit" to cover the end of your little finger. And it must be confessed that the basic joke runs thin before Mr. Coward is finished. The whole third act could be dispensed with without cheating the customers. But even the third act is brighter than any ghost story this department ever encountered before. For Mr. Coward is in a rare mood of inconsequential mischief.

Under John C. Wilson's direction, the farce is played with great vivacity. Clifton Webb can turn a line with as much neat dexterity as Mr. Coward can write it. As the second wife, Peggy Wood plays with bustle, pettiness and animation in the exact key of the part and play. Leonora Corbett's airy restlessness and spitefulness are also amusing in the haunting part of the first wife's spirit. Jacqueline Clark acts the servant girl like a startled wild hare. The most substantial part in the play is the character of the spinster spiritualist, and Mildred Natwick plays it with enormous invention and gusto. Out of all Mr. Coward's tart hocus-pocus she has created a fantastic character.

Mr. Coward's holiday charade is crack-brained and funny. It is a small thing, and unmistakably his own.

1941 N 6

MACBETH, a revival of the Shakespearean play, in two acts and nineteen scenes. Costumes by Lemuel Ayers; scenery by Samuel Leve; incidental music by Lehman Engel; staged by Margaret Webster; produced by Maurice Evans, in association with John Haggott. At the National Theatre.

First Witch...................Grace Coppin
Second Witch...................Abby Lewis
Third Witch................/...William Hansen
Duncan........................Harry Irvine
Malcolm.....................,.....Ralph Clanton
Donalbain...................William Nichols
Menteith....................Ernest Graves
Angus........................Philip Huston
Lennox......................Erford Gage
Caithness...................Walter Williams
Fleance.....................Alex Courtnay
Sergeant.....................John Ireland
Ross.........................Henry Brandon
Macbeth.....................Maurice Evans
Banquo......................Staats Cotsworth
Lady Macbeth..............Judith Anderson
A Messenger..................John Straub
Seyton......................Irving Morrow
A Porter....................William Hansen
Macduff.....................Herbert Rudley
An Old Man..................John Parrish
A Page......................Jackie Ayers
First Murderer..............John Ireland
Second Murderer............John Straub
Attendant...................Ada McFarland
Lady Macduff...............Viola Keats
Boy.........................Richard Tyler
A Doctor....................Harry Irvine
A Waiting-Gentlewoman.......Grace Coppin
A Young Soldier.............Alex Courtnay
Siward......................John Parrish

Lords, Gentlemen, Gentlewomen, Officers, Soldiers, Attendants and Messengers—Evelyn Helmore, Abby Lewis, Ada McFarland, Jackie Ayers, William Nichols, Melvin Parks, Alfred Paschall.

By BROOKS ATKINSON

None of the assorted "Macbeths" this courier has seen rank with the performance led by Maurice Evans and Judith Anderson at the National last evening. As directed by the energetic Margaret Webster, it is brimming over with the horrors and monstrosities of Shakespeare's text, and Mr. Evans and Miss Anderson play with consuming passion. Although every schoolboy knows "Macbeth," playgoers seldom make its acquaintance on the stage, for it is an unwieldy and ill-proportioned drama that refuses to make peace with the modern theatre. And even in this rational and thorough staging "Macbeth" compares unfavorably with the Evans "Hamlet," "Richard II" and "Henry IV," all of which are better suited to representational theatre.

* * *

But there are some most foul and unnatural horrors in "Macbeth," especially in the first act, when Shakespeare was writing with Elizabethan sensationalism; and there is nothing much more shocking in the theatre than the plot of the Macbeths to murder the sovereign guest in their castle. These scenes could not be acted with more excitement. Lady Macbeth's evil plotting, Macbeth's wild resolution to go through with a deed that revolts him, his shattered remorse when he returns with the bloody daggers, Lady Macbeth's cool entrance into the murder chamber to complete the false picture of betrayal and her faltering return after she has looked on horrors, her hands bathed in blood—this is the dramatic climax in "Macbeth," and it is vividly acted.

For Mr. Evans and Miss Anderson are well matched in this play. They are not a team of conspirators. They are united by something deeper than mutual advantage, and the crimes they spatter across the face of Scotland are sensual as well as political. Mr. Evans's clarity of mind and speech make Macbeth's character a lucid portrait of man in process of disintegration from the poise of nobility to the weakness of remorse and the confusion of defeat. Miss Anderson's Lady Macbeth is her most distinguished w●k in our theatre. It has a sculptured beauty in the early scenes, and a resolution that seems to be fiercer than the body that contains it. It is strong without being inhuman. And she has translated the sleep-walking scene into something memorable; the nervous washing of the hands is almost too frightful to be watched. Strange images of death haunt the magnificent acting of Mr. Evans and Miss Anderson in these macabre scenes.

*   *   *

As a drama, "Macbeth" contains a lot of undergrowth that has to be kicked out of the way before the biting scenes can be played. Although Miss Webster kicks it out of the way, the effort is apparent. Sometimes the rush of warriors is hollow motion, and short scenes essential to the narrative are not always vital parts of the drama. Apart from the hideous sounds that twice came out of a mechanical voice amplifier, the witches' scenes are staged and acted with

remarkable versatility — visually horrific, yet representative of destiny rather than the occult.

The play is well cast. Staats Cotsworth, who plays Banquo, is an actor of unusual intelligence and force; he can create character without describing it. As Macduff, Herbert Rudley is excellent also; and Harry Irvine's venerable Duncan is a creditable piece of work. Although a literal representation of "Macbeth" requires a heavy production, Samuel Leve has contrived to design a full suit of settings in baleful tones of color. Lamuel Ayres has designed the costumes in a somber key, and, it is reported, out of cotton materials ingeniously woven and blended. To provide an evocative musical accompaniment, Lehman Engel has composed another good incidental score.

*   *   *

When Shakespeare has given the actors vigorous material to work with, this "Macbeth" is compact with excitement. Mr. Evans and Miss Anderson spread a flame of acting over the highly wrought scenes. But it must be confessed that "Macbeth" as a whole is hard to adapt to the orderly rhythm of the modern theatre, and the most vivid parts of it are the central portions of the play.

1941 N 12

Patrick Hamilton's 'Angel Street' Is the New Mystery Drama at the Golden Theatre

By BROOKS ATKINSON

ANGEL STREET, a "Victorian thriller" in three acts, by Patrick Hamilton. Setting and costumes by Lemuel Ayres; staged by Shepard Traube, who produced the play in association with Alexander H. Cohen. At the John Golden Theatre.

Mrs. Manningham............Judith Evelyn
Mr. Manningham............Vincent Price
Nancy...................Elizabeth Eustis
Elizabeth................Florence Edney
Rough.....................Leo G. Carroll

Although Patrick Hamilton writes his thrillers within a small compass, he writes them with infinite craft and dexterity. "Angel Street," which sent a chill up the spine of the Golden Theatre last evening, comes off the top part of the theatre's top shelf. For Mr. Hamilton, who wrote the "Rope's End" of 1929, is telling an extremely slight tale of Victorian torture with perfect balance and suspense. He never raises his voice much higher than a shudder. And Shepard Traube, who serves as director, has matched Mr. Hamilton's skill in a tingling performance that fills the theatre with an ominous and terrifying illusion.

* * *

Probably we should take the minor witchcraft of the theatre at its own value without endowing it with the sublime qualities of art. All Mr. Hamilton and the actors aspire to is a good dose of the heebe-geebies. But they have done their jobs like a guild of master craftsmen, and it is impossible not to rejoice in their success.

Mr. Hamilton is telling the demoniac story of the Manninghams of Angel Street. Under the guise of kindliness Mr. Manningham is torturing his wife into insanity. He accuses her of petty aberrations that he has arranged himself; and since her mother died of insanity, she is more than half-convinced that she, too, is going out of her mind. While her husband is out of the house, a benign police inspector visits her and ultimately proves to her that her husband is a maniacal criminal suspected of a murder committed fifteen years ago in the same house, and that he is preparing to dispose of her. The rest of "Angel Street" is devoted to getting the evidence and proving the case.

* * *

Not very much material for a full evening in the theatre, you may be thinking. But Mr. Hamilton is a genuine writer. He understates his horrors. He never strays outside the bailiwick of dark, soft-footed nervousness. He draws his characters patiently and with some detail. The pace of the narrative is maddeningly leaden. He does not really clear away the black pall of mystery until the final curtain. And no matter how experienced a theatregoer you may be, you are never sure that the detective will not forget the hat he has left on the desk in plain view of the criminal who is just entering and you are never quite sure that the detective will not turn out to be a confederate or a crook working the same side of the street.

The performance is a triumph of skill in little things. Lemuel Ayres has designed a lugubrious Victorian living room which Feder has filled with baleful light. As the unpleasant Mr. Manningham Vincent Price is giving an excellent performance of unctuous-voiced, assured, dissembling gentleness, Judith Evelyn plays the frightened Mrs. Manningham with remarkable imagination and almost painful fidelity. As the housekeeper Florence Edney is wonderfully rigid with anxiety, and Elizabeth Eustis is amusingly chipper as squalid-tempered maid. As the benignant inspector Leo G. Carroll has the best part he has had for years. If he is glad, his votaries are with him. For he plays it with the little humors and crotchets, inflections and flourishes of a thoroughly experienced actor.

No one should play "Angel Street" less expertly than Mr. Traube's actors. If any one played it more expertly the audience would scream with fright. As a matter of fact, it did last evening when Mr. Carroll almost forgot to snatch up his hat before hiding in the next room.

1941 D 6.

1942

THE RIVALS, the comedy by Richard
Brinsley Sheridan, in two acts and eight
scenes. Prologue by Arthur Guiterman.
Lyrics and music mostly by Mr. Guiterman and Macklin Marrow. respectively.
Staged by Eva Le Gallienne; scenery and
costumes by Watson Barratt; production
under the supervision of Theresa Helburn
and Lawrence Langner; revived by the
Theatre Guild. At the Shubert Theatre.

Lydia Languish.............Haila Stoddard
Lucy...........................Helen Ford
Julia..........................Frances Reid
Mrs. Malaprop.................Mary Boland
Sir Anthony Absolute.....Walter Hampden
Fag.......................Raymond Johnson
Captain Absolute.............Donald Burr
Faulkland..................Robert Wallsten
Acres.........................Bobby Clark
Boy...........................Walt Draper
Sir Lucius O'Trigger........Philip Bourneuf
David.......................Roland Hogue
Footman......................George Boots
Footman.................William Whitehead

By BROOKS ATKINSON

If Sheridan had been lucky
enough to cast Bobby Clark as
Bobby Acres 167 years ago, "The
Rivals" would not have failed on
the first night. For Bobby is not
only the funniest clown in the
world but also a comedian of taste
and invention. Although the Theatre Guild revival of the Sheridan
war horse, which pawed the stage
of the Shubert last evening, is a
vivacious event, with Mary Boland
and Walter Hampden also in high
fettle, Mr. Clark transforms one
scene in particular into a comic
masterpiece.

It is the scene in which Sir
Lucius O'Trigger is urging Bob
Acres to fight a duel with the
mythical ensign and in which Bob
is whipping up his lagging valor
with foolish celerity. A comedian
in the grand manner, Mr. Clark
takes the whole thing at a hop,
skip and jump. He struts, whistles,
poses and runs. He plunges into
the scene with enormous gusto.
Any one of several other buffoons
might impose as funny a scene on
the ancient script as Mr. Clark
does. But it is hard to think of
any one whose boyish revelry
would also capture the spirit of
the part as Sheridan wrote it. For
all his fabulous skylarking, Mr.
Clark somehow belongs.

Nothing else in Eva Le Gallienne's high-spirited revival measures up to this one scene of
groaning merriment. But it is a
production of which she and the
Guild may be proud. Regard it not
so much as a comedy of manners
as a brawl of manners, for the
accent is on humor. And Miss
Boland's whirling Mrs. Malaprop
with a clacking voice is also enormously funny. Dressed in a billowing costume, with a bobbing headdress, she flounces through her
demented dictionary of bungled
English with a wit that is furious
and spontaneous. Mr. Hampden is
no comedian at heart. But he is an
intelligent actor, with a full knowledge of what he is playing. Especially in one choleric scene with
the young captain, his Sir Anthony
Absolute is energetic and amusing,
and his presence gives the whole
performance a useful foundation.

Mind you, not all of "The Rivals"
can be played as broadly as Miss
Le Gallienne has directed it here.
Mr. Clark's scene of challenge is
the climax of the performance.
After that, the mood of "arch irreverence," as the Guild calls it,
gets occasionally transparent when
Sheridan is trying to write mannered comedy of love. And it must
be confessed that Helen Ford, as the
mischievous maid, acts as though
she had swallowed an entire shipment of canaries. Miss Ford has
such a pretty way with a Guiterman and Marrow song that she
cannot forbear enjoying it herself.

But Haila Stoddard provides a
lovely Lydia. As Julia, Frances
Reid is demure and attractive.
Donald Burr's Captain Absolute
and Robert Wallsten's Faulkland
are both well played. Philip Bourneuf, who was giving the town a
notable Jaques last Autumn, is
playing Sir Lucius O'Trigger with
remarkable skill and understanding—strictly in the interests of the
performance as a whole.

As scene-designer, Watson Barratt has furnished the production
with some useful scenery in a light
comedy mood and some gaily caparisoned costumes. To tell the
truth, none of Macklin Marrow's
occasional songs can compare with
the "Buxom Joan" he wrote for
The Players revival of "Love For
Love" in 1940. But that may seem
to be so only because Mr. Clark
sang it then and is repeating it
here. Anything Mr. Clark puts his
hand to becomes inspired fooling.

1942 Ja 15

CANDIDA, the George Bernard Shaw play. Staged by Guthrie McClintic; setting and costumes by Woodman Thompson; revived by the American Theatre Wing War Service for the benefit of the Army Emergency Fund and the Navy Relief Society. At the Shubert Theatre. To be repeated this afternoon, Thursday and Friday afternoons and Sunday night.

Miss Proserpine Garnett	Mildred Natwick
James Mavor Morell	Raymond Massey
Alexander Mill	Stanley Bell
Mr. Burgess	Dudley Digges
Candida	Katharine Cornell
Eugene Marchbanks	Burgess Meredith

Miss Cornell's clothes were designed and made by Helene Pons Studio and Miss Natwick's by Johanna Klinge; other costumes and uniforms by Eaves Costume Company, Inc. The sets were built by the T. B. MacDonald Construction Company, and painted by Robert Bergman Studios. The electrical equipment was furnished by the Century Lighting Company. Edward P. Dimond is the stage manager.

By BROOKS ATKINSON

Although Bernard Shaw's "Candida" has been put on the stage many times, no one ever saw it until yesterday afternoon when it was really acted at the Shubert Theatre. For the Katharine Cornell revival for the Army Emergency Fund and the Navy Relief Fund is flooded with new light and is the foremost event of the theatre season. Many of us have seen Miss Cornell's Candida before. It is one of her best parts. If she had never played anything else it would be enough to distinguish her as a great actress, for it radiates from her as if it were her own nature—luminous, tender and entrancingly wise.

* * *

And now we may think of Mr. Shaw's play, not as a celebrated vehicle, but as an association of several rare people. In Burgess Meredith's matchless playing Marchbanks emerges as no whimsical half genius but as a sensitive young man wrestling with a real problem. In Raymond Massey's humane acting, Parson Morell becomes a man of superior stature who has the courage to learn the truth about his limitations. His surrender is not the humaliation of a stuffed shirt but the humility of a gentleman.

Some of us know what Prossy is like when Mildred Natwick plays the part with sharpness and edginess in a vein of comedy that does not throw self-respect away. As the curate Stanley Bell is also giving a good performance. But now we have seen Candida's father as Dudley Digges plays him, and that is a most revealing experience. Mr. Digges is an actor of rich imagination and enormous craft. He directed the memorable revival of 1926. Playing Candida's father, he has made a sentient being out of an old humbug.

For the first time in this playgoer's memory the whole of "Candida" has been played by creative actors. Although Guthrie McClintic's direction is not conspicuous, the entire performance is shot through with the sort of understanding of character that he brings to a play. He has gone instinctively to the heart of the problem and woven a shining performance out of human experience.

Not that Mr. Shaw's best-loved play needs to be recommended to any one. It has always been a popular comedy; even when it is only half-acted it is vastly enjoyable. It is no clever Shavian invention, but a humorous and at times a touching portrait of human intangibles. When Marchbanks and Morell are played from the inside by actors who are aware of life in all its tenuous perplexity, "Candida" provides an especially glowing experience in the theatre.

* * *

Let this department add a slightly bitter postscript. Why is it that we have to wait for labors of love to see the commercial theatre at its best? The five special performances of "Candida" are for Army and Navy relief, under the auspices of the American Theatre Wing. Give the theatre a cause and an opportunity to do something free and it has no trouble in solving the commercial problems that beset it. Then the art and the spirit that are pent up inside the theatre flow abundantly.

"Candida" will be played at matinees today, Thursday and Friday and next Sunday evening. Incidentally, it earned a gross of $2,615 at yesterday's performance.

1942 Ap 28,

THE SKIN OF OUR TEETH, a "new comedy" in three acts, by Thornton Wilder. Staged by Elia Kazan; settings by Albert Johnson; costumes by Mary Percy Schenck; produced by Michael Myerberg. At the Plymouth Theatre.

Announcer	Morton DaCosta
Sabina	Tallulah Bankhead
Mr. Fitzpatrick	E. G. Marshall
Mrs. Antrobus	Florence Eldridge
Dinosaur	Remo Buffano
Mammoth	Andrew Ratousheff
Telegraph Boy	Dickie Van Patten
Gladys	Frances Heflin
Henry	Montgomery Clift
Mr. Antrobus	Fredric March
Doctor	Arthur Griffin
Professor	Ralph Kellard
Judge	Joseph Smiley
Homer	Ralph Cullinan
Miss E. Muse	Edith Faversham
Miss T. Muse	Emily Lorraine
Miss M. Muse	Eva Mudge Nelson
Usher	Stanley Prager
Usher	Harry Clark
Girl	Elizabeth Scott
Girl	Patricia Riordan
Fortune Teller	Florence Reed
Chair Pusher	Earl Sydnor
Chair Pusher	Carroll Clark
Convener	Stanley Weede
Convener	Seumas Flynn
Convener	Aubrey Fassett
Convener	Stanley Prager
Convener	Harry Clark
Convener	Stephan Cole
Broadcast Official	Morton DaCosta
Defeated Candidate	Joseph Smiley
Mr. Tremayne	Ralph Kellard
Hester	Eulabelle Moore
Ivy	Viola Dean
Fred Bailey	Stanley Prager

By LEWIS NICHOLS

A few seasons ago Thornton Wilder increased the stature of the theatre with "Our Town," and now that November again lies heavy over Broadway he has done it once more. For in "The Skin of Our Teeth," which Michael Myerberg brought last evening to the Plymouth, he has written a comedy about man which is the best play the Forties have seen in many months, the best pure theatre.

Mr. Wilder is no pedantic philosopher, setting down the laws of the schoolmaster; when he is writing for the theatre he uses all of its arts. His story of man's constant struggle for survival, and his wonderment over why he so struggles, is presented with pathos and broad comedy, with gentle irony and sometimes a sly self-raillery. He does not believe the footlights should separate his players from his audience; his actors now and then step out of their characters to discuss the progress of the play, to comment on what it means or what it does not mean.

* * *

In "The Skin of Our Teeth" the scenery bounces up and down, the players carry on rehearsals, at one point there is a call to the audience to send along its chairs to keep the fire going against the advancing Ice Age. Everywhere in both the dialogue and the properties that surround it are a series of anachronisms, so beautifully blended as to make Excelsior, N. J., quite properly a hold-out against the Ice Age, and Atlantic City the point from which the ark took off against the flood.

The first act is Excelsior, and Mr. Antrobus—played by Fredric March—has had a considerable day in town: He has fixed up the alphabet by separating em from en, he has brought the multiplication table up to the hundreds, he has invented the wheel. But in August at Excelsior it is growing colder, so cold the "dogs are sticking to the sidewalk," and obviously the ice is coming down from Vermont. The neighbors come in — Homer, Moses, others—and Mr. Antrobus and his wife, after wondering if it's all worth while, begin cramming their children with knowledge, in the hope they will survive somehow and can build again on the other side.

* * *

The second act is Atlantic City, at the convention of the Ancient and Honorable Order of Mammals, Subdivision Humans, where Mr. Antrobus, pompous with power and tired of his wife, again almost falls to disaster. The third is at the end of the war — any war — when Mr. Antrobus is properly beaten, but finally decides to start off again. This time the things he sees as reasons are "the voice of the people in their confusion and need," his wife, children and home, knowledge. He goes on, having gotten by only by the skin of his teeth.

The cast Mr. Myerberg has assembled should always fill Mr. Wilder's plays. First, there is Tallulah Bankhead, in the role of Sabina, who is variously the Antrobus maid, the bathing beauty, the camp follower who has been off to the wars for seven years. Her role is the eternal Helen of Troy, Cleopatra, who wanders off on her own affairs when all is quiet, who comes home and helps out when the going is rough. Miss Bankhead is magnificent—breezy, hard, practical by turns. She can strut and posture in broad comedy, she can be calmly serene. It is she who steps out of character to discuss the play, marvelous interludes all of them.

As Mr. Antrobus, Mr. March is at first the roaring, blustering inventor and amasser of knowledge, bringing home his new wheel with a loud whoop; then the pontifical new president of the Mammals in convention assembled; finally the war-weary and discouraged soldier coming home from battle. Florence Eldridge is Mrs. Antrobus, the mother and home-builder, the steadying influence who, in the Atlantic City period, is out of place, too. Miss Eldridge can be either the steady housekeeper or a Helen Hokinson drawing. Each of the Marches has every reason to be proud of the other.

* * *

And there are others: Montgomery Clift, as Henry, the son, the Henry who used to be called Cain and has a scar on his forehead; and Frances Heflin, as Gladys, daughter of the Antrobuses. There also in Florence Reed as a cynical, surly, contemptuous fortune-teller, and Dickie Van Patten as a telegraph boy and E. G. Marshall as the stage manager, who grows more and more harassed as the evening goes on. Elia Kazan directed in the mood meant by Mr. Wilder, and Albert Johnson has provided the informal settings that tilt and slide as a perfect cover to the play.

As of last evening the theatre was looking up. Definitely.

1942 N 19

'The Three Sisters'

THE THREE SISTERS, a play in three acts by Anton Chekhov. Settings and costumes by Motley of London; staged by Guthrie McClintic; revived by Katharine Cornell. At the Ethel Barrymore Theatre.

Olga	Judith Anderson
Masha	Katharine Cornell
Irina	Gertrude Musgrove
A Maid	Patricia Calvert
Tuzenbach	Alexander Knox
Solyony	McKay Morris
Chebutykin	Edmund Gwenn
Anfisa	Alice Belmore Cliffe
Ferapont	Arthur Chatterton
An Orderly	Kirk Douglas
Vershinin	Dennis King
Andrey Prozorov	Eric Dressler
Kuligin	Tom Powers
Natasha	Ruth Gordon
Fedotik	Stanley Bell
Roddey	Tom McDermott
Another Lieutenant	Walter Craig
A Maid	Marie Paxton

By LEWIS NICHOLS

As she has done so often in the past, Katharine Cornell last evening added another distinguished production to her gallery as an actress-manager, and, what is perhaps more important, to the Broadway theatre of this Christmas week. She did so with a revival of Chekhov's "The Three Sisters," that saga of the defeated and the frustrated on a Main Street of Russia at the turn of the century. In it can be found some of the best acting of the year, for, as usual with Miss Cornell the manager, she has stinted on nothing and her cast comes from the top drawer of what would be any other manager's remote dream.

And it is as well, for "The Three Sisters," as viewed in these modern days, requires everything it can get from a cast. To Christmas week of 1942 the play seems a little remote. The descendants of Olga and Masha and Irina, writing another page in Russian history this morning, make the history of the static efforts of the sisters to return to Moscow appear a bit out of the present world. Miss Cornell's efforts, however, are quite of another order, and to the stage of the Barrymore she has brought what probably long will be referred to as the final word on this particular bit of Chekhov.

Among these things list Ruth Gordon, who is wonderful. She has the role of Natasha, the country girl who becomes the sister-in-law. Coming coyly into the Prozorov family, she eventually is a vixen and a harriden, driving them off and at the end in violent control of their lives. Miss Gordon's range from a flouncing young girl just this side of comedy to a spirit so evil it curls the hair is magnificent. The gestures are there for the first part, and a piercing voice for the second. The

Katharine Cornell

Prozorov sisters did well not to trust her even at the start.

The sisters, themselves, are played by Judith Anderson, Miss Cornell and Gertrude Musgrove. Miss Anderson is Olga, the school teacher who hates it, the ultimate head of the school who also hates that. Miss Cornell is Masha, married to a teacher and dissatisfied, who has a love affair with a soldier who then is sent away. Miss Musgrove is the youngster; working in the telegraph office, she agrees to marry and then her fiancé is killed in a duel. To their roles all three bring excellent descriptions of their various tragedies.

* * *

There are also men. One of the rich roles of "The Three Sisters" is that of Chebutykin, the army doctor who is defeated down to loneliness and drink, and in this Miss Cornell offers Edmund Gwenn, giving an excellent performance. His version of the drunken scene probably is the most realistic since Disney was at work with the pink elephants; heads must ache all through the audience this morning.

Mr. Gwenn can be kindly, cynical, sad; his role comes fully alive.

Dennis King is Vershinin, the battery commander who falls in love with Masha, and Eric Dressler is the brother Andrey. Tom Powers is excellent as Masha's husband, the high school teacher who wistfully tries to get along and is aware he doesn't amount to a great deal. Alexander Knox is the baron-fiancé of Irina, who resigns his commission in the army in order "to work" and who simply says amid all the gloom that he is quite happy. There also are nice portraits of an old nurse, by Alice Belmore Cliffe and of an old man by Arthur Chatterton. As is usual in Miss Cornell's plays, Guthrie McClintic directed, expertly as usual.

1942 D 22

1943

SOMETHING FOR THE BOYS, a musical comedy in a prologue and two acts. Songs by Cole Porter. Book by Herbert and Dorothy Fields. Entire production staged by Hassard Short; book directed by Mr. Fields; settings by Howard Bay; dances arranged by Jack Cole; costumes designed by Billy Livingston; orchestra conducted by William Parson; produced by Michael Todd. At the Alvin Theatre.

Chiquita Hart ....Paula Laurence
Roger Calhoun...................Jed Prouty
Harry Hart...................Allen Jenkins
Blossom Hart................Ethel Merman
Staff Sergeant Rocky Fulton..Bill Johnson
Sergeant Laddie Green......Stuart Langley
Mary-Francis ....Betty Garrett
Betty-Jean ....Betty Bruce
Corporal Burns ....Bill Callahan
Micheala ....Anita Alvarez
Lois }
Lucille } ....the Barnes Twins
Lieut. Col. S. D. Grubbs......Jack Hartley
Mr. Tobias Twitch...........William Lynn
Sergeant Carter ....Remi Martel
Melanie Walker.............Frances Mercer
Burke ....Walter Rinner
Mrs. Grubbs................Madeleine Clive

By LEWIS NICHOLS

All season long the world has yearned hopefully for a big, fast, glittering musical comedy. It has it now, for last evening the fabulous Mike Todd brought in "Something for the Boys," and as it danced its way across the stage of the Alvin is quite clearly was not only something pretty wonderful for the boys, but something for the girls as well. For Cole Porter has taken tunes from his topmost drawer, Herbert and Dorothy Fields have written words that are better than most, Hassard Short has directed in his usual impeccable manner and Ethel Merman gives a performance that suggests all Merman performances before last night were simply practice. In short, this is the musical comedy for which Broadway has been waiting a long, long time.

It has almost everything, this "Something for the Boys." Mr. Porter has provided songs of every description, and while none of them is as good as the best Cole Porter song on record, the average is far above the general musical show. In building his production, Mr. Todd, for whom the United States Treasury must have a friendly feeling by now, has been lavish to the point of excellent good taste. The settings by Howard Bay are superb, and the costumes designed by Billy Livingston are magnificent. Mr. Todd has thought nothing of hiring dozens of people to sing and to dance; he likes a stage full of people obviously having a good time. And with Miss Merman there, the good time is on both sides of the lights.

For she is truly immense. Ethel Merman in good voice is a raucous overtone to the trumpets of a band; it is a soft trill for a torch song, it is tinny for a parody and fast for one of Mr. Porter's complicated lyrics. Accompanying the voice are all the necessary gestures, the roll of the eye or the wave of the hand to suggest friendly ribaldries or separations forever more. In "Hey, Good Lookin' " she is loud, in "He's a Right Guy" she is soft; it is one of Mr. Porter's lines that sums it up pretty well; she is "the missing link between Lily Pons and Mae West." And a credit, of course, to the pair of them.

* * *

And there are others. Out of a few minor Broadway parts, and a few major ones in the night clubs,

has come Paula Laurence to make her professional musical comedy debut. She is an excellent foil for Miss Merman, a dead-pan comedienne of a stern and angular countenance; a duet they sing together —"By the Mississinewa"—is the funniest moment in a musical show in years. Also there is Allen Jenkins, returning to Broadway after too long an absence, to bring back that bland, faintly retarded air that should be in the foreground of all such shows from now on.

Lesser performers? They wouldn't be called that in any other musical than Mr. Todd's. Note Jed Prouty, note also Betty Bruce, who is an excellent dancer. Bill Johnson is present to sing the male part of such songs as can't be done entirely by Miss Merman; Anita Alvarez is present to lead the Spanish dance without which no musical show set in Texas would be considered legal. William Lynn, for years the Irwin of "Three Men on a Horse," is a strange little figure who bobs up throughout the proceedings, and is very comical at it. Frances Mercer has a role and Jack Hartley plays an Army colonel as though he were a major general.

* * *

The story? It is all about three folks who inherit a Texas ranch via the Court of Missing Heirs. The ranch is near Kelly Field, and when that juxtaposition doesn't completely fulfill the Fields's ideas of musical comedy, they simply stick a bit of carborundum on one of Miss Merman's teeth and she becomes a radio receiving set. The Fields read that one in the newspapers, but the papers had to get along without Mr. Porter, without Miss Merman, without dances by Jack Cole, without, in short, "Something for the Boys." And this last will be getting along by itself for some time to come.

1943 Ja 8

THEPATRIOTS, a play in a prologue and three acts by Sidney Kingsley. Staged by Shepard Traube; scenery by Howard Bay; costumes by Rose Bogdanoff and Toni Ward; incidental music arranged by Stanley Bate; produced by the Playwrights Company and Rowland Stebbins. At the National Theatre.

Captain	Byron Russell
Thomas Jefferson	Raymond E. Johnson
Patsy	Madge Evans
Martha	Frances Reid
James Madison	Ross Matthew
Alexander Hamilton	House Jameson
George Washington	Cecil Humphreys
Sergeant	Victor Southwick
Colonel Humphrey	Francis Compton
Jacob	Thomas Dillon
Ned	George Mitchell
Mat	Philip White
James Monroe	Judson Laire
Mrs. Hamilton	Peg La Centra
Henry Knox	Henry Mowbray
Butler	Robert Lance
Mr. Fenno	Ronald Alexander
Jupiter	Juano Hernandez
Mrs. Conrad	Leslie Bingham
Frontiersman	John Stephen
Thomas Jefferson Randolph	Billy Nevard
Anne Randolph	Hope Lange
George Washington Lafayette	Jack Lloyd

By LEWIS NICHOLS

In "The Patriots," Sidney Kingsley has turned to the early days of his country for the material for a truly fine play. He has written of Jefferson, of Hamilton and Washington and of a doctrine, then new, of democratic liberty. Last evening the Playwrights Company and Rowland Stebbins offered it at the National, where it quite clearly was one of the best dramas in a long while, moving and inspiring and expressing ideas that are alike of 1800 and 1943. For this is the bicentenary of the birth of Jefferson, and this also is the second year of a desperate war to preserve the doctrines he summed up as author of the Declaration of Independence. Finally, Mr. Kingsley now is a sergeant in the Army fighting for that preservation.

* * *

Although Jefferson is the leading character of "The Patriots," democracy is its hero. In the last decade of the eighteenth century freedom had fallen on dangerous days. There were monarchists here and there was a troubled Europe across the ocean. Mr. Kingsley's play begins with the return of Jefferson from France, when he wished to retire to Monticello, but was persuaded to enter Washington's Cabinet as Secretary of State. He continues with the bitter quarrel with Hamilton, through the period when it seemed only Jefferson—and the common people who had fought for it—held faith in the experiment; and he ends with Jefferson's inaugural address as President in 1800.

As a playwright, Mr. Kingsley has taken only an editor's liberty with the record. Hamiltonians may say that the first Secretary of the Treasury comes off rather badly until the end, but the title is in the plural and Mr. Kingsley agrees he was a patriot, too. As he presents the history of those terrible days when disaster was so near, the playwright need point no moral about today, although the moral is there in both the Declaration and the Inaugural Address. In writing of the past, Mr. Kingsley has written most excellently of the immediate present.

* * *

All concerned have given "The Patriots" a magnificent production. In the role of Jefferson is Raymond Edward Johnson, who is taking a step from the radio to a Broadway debut in a part such as he may never get again nor, possibly may ever play so well. Mr. Johnson has an angular, expressive face with a wide mouth and a deep voice and lanky bearing not unlike Raymond Massey. He conveys excellently the various moods of Jefferson: the idealist, the student, the man who hated politics yet always was forced to live with them, the farmer who wished himself back at his beloved Monticello. It is a portrait not unworthy of comparison with Mr. Massey's Lincoln.

* * *

House Jameson also has caught the qualities that apparently were Hamilton's—a youthful bumptiousness and an overbearing manner, prepared to go to almost any length to get his way, yet sincerely convinced that his way was the best for the country. Cecil Humphreys plays Washington, looking, incidentally, surprisingly like the Stuart portraits, and Ross Matthew and Judson Laire are Madison and Monroe. Madge Evans, who also is Mrs. Kingsley, plays the only important feminine part, that of Jefferson's daughter, Patsy. Shepard Traube, whose last Broadway directorial occupation was in the quite different mood of "Angel Street," has staged "The Patriots" so that it flows evenly and with emphasis. The settings are by Howard Bay, and they, too, are in perfect harmony.

1943 Ja 30

OKLAHOMA! a musical play in two acts and five scenes, derived from "Green Grow the Lilacs," by Lynn Riggs. Music by Richard Rodgers; book and lyrics by Oscar Hammerstein 2d. Staged by Rouben Mamoulian; choreography by Agnes de Mille; settings by Lemuel Ayers; costumes designed by Miles White; produced by the Theatre Guild. At the St. James Theatre.

Aunt Eller	Betty Garde
Curly	Alfred Drake
Laurey	Joan Roberts
Ike Skidmore	Barry Kelley
Fred	Edwin Clay
Slim	Herbert Rissman
Will Parker	Lee Dixon
Jud Fry	Howard da Silva
Ado Annie Carnes	Celeste Holm
Ali Hakim	Joseph Buloff
Gertie Cummings	Jane Lawrence
Ellen	Katharine Sergava
Kate	Ellen Love
Sylvie	Joan McCracken
Armina	Kate Friedlich
Aggie	Bambi Linn
Andrew Carnes	Ralph Riggs
Cord Elam	Owen Martin
Jess	George Church
Chalmers	Marc Platt
Mike	Paul Shierz
Joe	George Irving
Sam	Hayes Gordon

By LEWIS NICHOLS

For years they have been saying the Theatre Guild is dead, words that obviously will have to be eaten with breakfast this morning. Forsaking the sometimes somber tenor of her ways, the little lady of Fifty-second Street last evening danced off into new paths and brought to the St. James a truly delightful musical play called "Oklahoma!" Wonderful is the nearest adjective, for this excursion of the Guild combines a fresh and infectious gayety, a charm of manner, beautiful acting, singing and dancing, and a score by Richard Rodgers which doesn't do any harm either, since it is one of his best.

* * *

"Oklahoma!" is based on Lynn Riggs's saga of the Indian Territory at the turn of the century, "Green Grow the Lilacs," and, like

its predecessor, it is simple and warm. It relies not for a moment on Broadway gags to stimulate an appearance of comedy, but goes winningly on its way with Rouben Mamoulian's best direction to point up its sly humor, and with some of Agnes de Mille's most inspired dances to do so further. There is more comedy in one of Miss de Mille's gay little passages than in many of the other Broadway tom-tom beats together. The Guild has known what it is about in pursuing talent for its new departure.

Mr. Rodgers's scores never lack grace, but seldom have they been so well integrated as this for "Oklahoma!" He has turned out waltzes, love songs, comic songs and a title number which the State in question would do well to seize as an anthem forthwith. "Oh, What a Beautiful Morning," and "People Will Say" are headed for countless juke-boxes across the land, and a dirge called "Pore Jud" —in which the hero of the fable tries to persuade his rival to hang himself—is amazingly comic. "The Farmer and the Cowman" and "The Surry with the Fringe on the Top" also deserve mention only because they quite clearly approach perfection; no number of the score is out of place or badly handled. The orchestrations are by Russell Bennett, who knows his humor and has on this occasion let himself go with all the laughter he can command.

* * *

To speak and sing the words— Oscar Hammerstein 2d contributed the book and lyrics—the play has an excellent collection of players, none of whom yet is world-famous. Alfred Drake and Joan Roberts as the two leading singers are fresh and engaging; they have clear voices and the thought that the audience might also like to hear Mr. Hammerstein's poetry. Joseph Buloff is marvelous as the peddler who ambles through the evening selling wares from French cards to Asiatic perfume—and avoiding matrimony. Howard da Silva, Lee Dixon, Celeste Holm and Ralph Riggs are some of the others, and Katharine Sergava and Mark Platt are two of the important dancers.

Possibly in addition to being a musical play, "Oklahoma!" could be called a folk operetta; whatever it is, it is very good.

1943 Ap 1.

ONE TOUCH OF VENUS, a musical comedy in two acts and eleven scenes, Music by Kurt Weill, book by S. J. Perelman and Ogden Nash; suggested by F. Anstey's story, "The Tinted Venus"; lyrics by Mr. Nash; staged by Elia Kazan; choreography by Agnes de Mille; musical director, Maurice Abravanel; scenery designed by Howard Bay; costumes by Paul du Pont and Kermit Love, and those of Mary Martin by Mainbocher; presented by Cheryl Crawford; associate producer, John Wildberg. At the Imperial Theatre.

Whitelaw Savory	John Boles
Molly Grant	Paula Laurence
Taxi Black	Teddy Hart
Stanley	Harry Clark
Rodney Hatch	Kenny Baker
Venus	Mary Martin
Mrs. Moats	Florence Dunlap
Store Manager	Sam Bonnell
Bus Starter	Lou Wills, Jr.
Sam	Zachary A. Charles
Mrs. Kramer	Helen Raymond
Gloria Kramer	Ruth Bond
Police Lieutenant	Bert Freed
Rose	Jane Hoffman
Zuvetli	Harold Stone
Dr. Rook	Johnny Stearns
Anatolians	Sam Bonnell, Matthew Farrar
Premier Danseuse	Sono Osato

By LEWIS NICHOLS

As its friends were about to give it up as a wayward child, the theatre season finally reached Broadway last evening. Call this millennium "One Touch of Venus," the musical show by Kurt Weill, S. J. Perelman and Ogden Nash, which Cheryl Crawford presented at the Imperial, complete with freshness, an adult manner and lavishness of display. Once again, after what seem like long and dreary years, going to the theatre has become a pleasure.

In offering an harassed New York its first fully professional musical show in some time, Miss Crawford has gone to the best sources. Mr. Perleman and Mr. Nash are in there with a book which, while not perfect throughout, is better than those of most musicals, and Mr. Nash by himself has turned out lyrics both soft and sweet—if sometimes, perhaps, just a shade confused. Mr. Weill has offered a number of songs which are due for the juke boxes and other fame, and Agnes de Mille, who stages the dances these days, has arrived with fine choreography and Sono Osato as première danseuse.

* * *

In addition to all this, there is Mary Martin, too, the Mary Martin whose heart once belonged to daddy and who shows in "One Touch of Venus" that Hollywood has done her no harm whatsoever. In this new musical she is a statue that comes to life and falls in love with a barber; she also is a lady of high charm, an engaging quality and the ability to toss a song over the footlights, which is the only place to send a song. Her heart this morning will probably be Broadway's generally.

The two other chief players are making their first appearance on the stage, and they are good ones. The pictures yielded up John Boles, to be the proprietor of Miss Crawford's art gallery; and the radio and pictures offered Kenny Baker. Both of them are excellent, the latter giving a performance filled with good nature as the barber who suddenly finds Venus, like one of the wives of "Blithe Spirit", alive and pursuing him. Paula Laurence is present for wry wit and a couple of sinister songs, and Teddy Hart is the chief comedian.

* * *

Since music and girls are the soul of musical comedy, "One Touch of Venus" has thought of them also. There is no Rockette chorus kicking from left to right; rather Miss de Mille has gone to work with her sense of humor so that the dancing all seems new and cheerful. Miss Osato likely is to be the toast of the autumn, for she is graceful and alive as well as being beautiful and as well as giving the impression that she, herself, is having a wonderful time. She and various partners are in three numbers, including an excellent "Venus in Ozone Heights Ballet," and they seemed little enough at the time.

To turn to Mr. Weill: His "Speak Low," sung as a duet by Miss Martin and Mr. Baker, is a sure hit unless the musical world has gone mad; and "West Wind," "That's Him" and "Wooden Wedding" are also good songs in a list of about fifteen. A barber-shop quartet chants out a fine and cynical tribute under the name of "The Trouble With Woman," and Mr. Boles sings the sad story of "Dr. Crippen" in a mood and a tune not unlike that of Mr. Weill's celebrated "Saga of Jenny." The composer himself orchestrated for softness and the voices can be heard above the trumpets.

As for the rest, Elia Kazan directed for pace, and while the early part of the show is not so fast as the last, the fault there likely lay in a slow-starting book. Howard Bay designed the simple and colorful settings and Paul du Pont and Kermit Love the gay costumes. Taken altogether, "One Touch of Venus" provides one of the better evenings in the theatre.

1943 O 8

'Othello,' With Robeson in Title Role, Revived by Theatre Guild Before an Enthusiastic Audience at the Shubert

OTHELLO. Shakespearean play in two acts and eight scenes. Staged by Margaret Webster; production designed and lighted by Robert Edmond Jones; music composed by Tom Bennett; associate producer, John Haggott; revived by the Theatre Guild. At the Shubert Theatre.

Roderigo	Jack Manning
Iago	Jose Ferrer
Brabantio	Averell Harris
Othello	Paul Robeson
Cassio	James Monks
Duke	Robert E. Perry
Lodovico	Philip Huston
A Messenger	Henry Barnard
First Senator	Jack de Shay
Second Senator	Graham Velsey
Third Senator	John Ireys
Desdemona	Uta Hagen
Montano	William Woodson
First Soldier at Cyprus	Sam Banham
Second Soldier at Cyprus	Eugene Stuckmann
Third Soldier at Cyprus	Bruce Brighton
Emilia	Margaret Webster
Bianca	Edith King
Gratiano	Robert E. Perry

Senators. Soldiers. Servants. and Citizens: Martha Falconer. Timothy Lynn Kearse, David Koser. John Gerstad. Jeff Brown, Albert Hachmeister. Ronald Bishop.

By LEWIS NICHOLS

Picking up where it left off in the spring with "Oklahoma!" the Theatre Guild has given the local theatre another distinguished production. This time it is "Othello," which opened last evening at the Shubert, finally bringing to New York a Moor in the person of Paul Robeson, and in addition giving Broadway another of Margaret Webster's careful transcriptions of Shakespeare. Excellently done both in the production and in the acting, it is the best interpretation of "Othello" to be seen here in a good many years, and one that should remain on hand for a long time to come.

* * *

A production of "Othello" is not casual child's play for the drama courses, for a fair share of it in these days seems tedious, and the motivations of Iago and the unreal change of thought on the part of the Moor have been the subjects of long and bitter professorial debate. True, some of the present revival appears slow and ambling, and there is no definite attempt to stress what factors made Iago what he was, but on the whole the acting is such as to make these things unimportant. Which is what they are when Mr. Robeson is on hand, with José Ferrer as Iago.

Robeson Wins Ovation For Othello Portrayal

Not for several seasons has a play received the tumultous applause that was accorded last night's presentation of Shakespeare's "Othello," starring Paul Robeson. Cries of "Bravo!" echoed through the packed Shubert Theatre, while from the galleries higher-pitched notes of approbation were directed toward the stage.

At least ten curtain calls were demanded. The audience mostly wanted Mr. Robeson, who granted their wishes. But Uta Hagen, who played Desdemona, and her husband, José Ferrer, who had the part of Iago, and Margaret Webster, the director of the play and portrayer of Emilia, came in for their share of applause.

Miss Webster was forced to say a few words. She said that she and Paul Robeson had dreamed for many months of such a night as they had just encountered, but had never expected it to occur.

Turning to Mr. Robeson, who was standing surrounded by the entire cast, she said, "Paul, we are all very proud of you tonight." The theatre broke into cheers.

The news, of course, is Mr. Robeson's arrival back home in a part he played a few seasons ago in London and tentatively experi-

mented with in the rural playhouses the summer before last. He
looks like the part. He is a huge
man, taller by inches than anyone
on the stage, his height and
breadth accentuated by the costumes he wears. His voice, when
he is the general giving orders to
stop the street brawl, reverberates
through the house; when he is the
lover of Desdemona, he is soft. His
final speech about being a man
"who loved not wisely but too
well" is magnificent. He passes
easily along the various stages of
Othello's growing jealousy. He
can be alike a commanding figure,
accustomed to lead, a lover willing
to be led and the insane victim of
his own ill judgment.

Mr. Ferrer also is excellent as
Iago, his interpretation taking no
sides in the long quarrel as to
whether the Moor's "ancient" had
been inspired by thoughts of Cassio's gaining a position he wished,
or his wife's having yielded to the
Moor. By taking no sides, Mr. Ferrer follows the track that Iago is
unexplained evil, and he holds that
throughout. The actor has a light
walk and a light touch, and his
Iago is a sort of half dancing, half
strutting Mephistopheles, who does
what he does probably in good part
because there is pleasure in it. He
and Mr. Robeson are excellent foils
for one another.

Uta Hagen, who in private life
is Mrs. Ferrer, is Desdemona, a
very pretty, soft-spoken heroine
and victim, whose death scene is
the most moving of the play. Miss
Webster, in addition to directing in
her accustomed way, is playing
Emilia with good humor and force.
The Cassio is James Monks, who
now and then does not seem to be
the warrior Othello would trust as
his lieutenant, and Jack Manning is
Roderigo. Robert Edmond Jones
has done excellent settings and has
excellently lighted them.

1943 O 20

WINGED VICTORY, a spectacle in two
acts and seventeen scenes, by Moss Hart,
directed by Mr. Hart. Settings by Sgt.
Harry Horner; conductor and composer of
original music and arrangements, Sgt.
David Rose; costumes by Sgt. Howard
Shoup; choral direction by Second Lieut.
Leonard de Paur; lighting by Sgt. A. H.
Feder; presented by the United States
Army Air Forces for the Army Emergency
Relief. At the Forty-fourth Street Theatre.

Allan Ross	Cpl. Mark Daniels
Frankie Davis	Pvt. Dick Hogan
Danny (Pinky) Scariano	Pvt. Don Taylor
Dorothy Ross	Phyllis Avery
Mrs. Ross	Virginia Hammond
Whitey	Pvt. Red Buttons
Fred Cassidy	Pvt. Bert Hicks
Eddie Borden	Pfc. Kenneth Forbes
Tommy Gregg	Pvt. William Nash
Ronny Meade	Sgt. Kevin McCarthy
Sergeant Casey	Pvt. Elliot Sullivan
Bobby Grills	Pvt. Barry Nelson
Irving Miller	Pfc. Edmond O'Brien
Dave Anderson	Sgt. Rune Hultman
Sergeant Everett	Sgt. Edward Reardon
Major Halper	Pvt. Alan Baxter
Lieut. Jules Hudson	Pvt. Whitner Bissell
Captain Elkton	Pvt. Grant Richards
Captain Payne	Cpl. Edward Ashley
Captain Speer	Pvt. Henry Rowland
Lieutenant Johnson	1st Lieut. William Neil
Peter Clark	Pvt. Harry Lewis
Lieutenant McCarthy	Pvt. Paul Kaye
Henry Larson	Pvt. John Elliott
A. L. Simpson	Sgt. Gilbert Frye
Ed Slater	Sgt. Frank Kane
Russell Chandler	Cpl. Russell W. Drewes
Gordon Williams	Pvt. Hayes Gordon
Mark Walton	Col. Don Richards
Al Black	S/Sgt. Daniel Scholl
Gilbert Paxton	Pvt. John R. Kearney
Bob Cincomon	Pvt. Stuart Langley
Jim Gardner	Sgt. Robert Willey
Mr. Gardner	Pfc. Anthony Ross
Mrs. Gardner	Laura Pierpont
Lieutenant Stevens	Pvt. Michael Harvey
Ed Ried	Pvt. Kent Morrison
Sally	Mary Lenhardt
Jane	Jean McCoy
Captain McIntyre	Cpl. Gary Merrill
Dick Talbert	Sgt. David Colvin
Nick Bush	Pvt. Cy Perkins
Gordon Cantrell	Cpl. Ira Cirker
Hack Hall	Pfc. Edward McMahon
Sid Marshall	Sgt. David Durston
Ralph Stevens	Pvt. James Engler
Leo Nadler	Pfc. Donald Hammer
David Michaelson	Pfc. Thomas Dillon
Colonel Gibney	Pvt. Philip Bourneuf
Lieutenant Thompson	Sgt. George Reeves
Jerry Ellison	Pvt. Walter Reed
Russ Coleman	Sgt. Zeke Manners
George Morse	Pvt. Ray Merrill
Sid Green	Cpl. Jerry Hilliard Adler
Fred Kelly	Pfc. Ray McDonald
Lee	Sgt. Victor Young
Chaplain	Col. Fred Cotton
Lieut. Reynolds	2d Lieut. Gilbert Herman
Colonel Ross	Pvt. Damian O'Flynn
Lieutenant Sperry	Sgt. Ray Middleton
Lieut. Rayburn	1st Lieut. George Hoffmann
Major Burke	Pvt. William Marshall
Charles Jordan	Capt. Raye Bidwell
The Mayor	Capt. Sidney Bassler
Mr. Grills	Sgt. Joseph Meyer
Helen	Elisabeth Fraser
Mrs. Grills	Genevieve Frizzell
The Minister	Pvt. Richard Beach
Barker	Pvt. George Petrie
Milhauser	Pvt. Alfred Ryder
Adams	Pvt. Karl Molden
O'Brien	S/Sgt. Peter Lind Hayes
Gleeson	Pfc. Martin Ritt
Ruth	Olive Deering
Radio Announcer	Sgt. John Adamy
Glenn Barrows	Pvt. Archie Robbins
Paul Conway	Pvt. Jack Powell Jr.
Miguel Lopez	S/Sgt. Sascha Brastoff
Sam Preston	Pvt. Henry Slate
Harry Preston	Pvt. Jack Slate
Colonel Blakely	2d Lt. Donald Beddoe
Corporal Regan	Pvt. John Tyers
Jack Browning	Pvt. Barry Mitchell
Miss Aldridge	Mary Cooper
Doctor Baker	Pvt. Lee J. Cobb
Milton Benson	Pvt. Michael Duane

By LEWIS NICHOLS

In "Winged Victory," which
opened Saturday evening at the
Forty-fourth Street, Moss Hart

IN THE PLAY: *"I tell you one thing, and I aint fooling. If we do pass those tests, we're just the smartest guys in the world, that's all,"* Pfc. Edmond O'Brien in "Winged Victory."

has written a stirring, moving and, what is more important, a most human play about the boy next door. Being that boy next door, the Army Air Forces act it with understanding, dignity, humor and warmth. Between them, they have given the theatre a play which should remain on Broadway for the usual enlistment period—the end of the war plus six months.

* * *

Mr. Hart offers no platform speeches about the bravery of the men who fly the Fortresses and the fighters. He sees them as individuals, each with a job to do, young Americans who, according to their temperaments, are laconic, anxious, thoughtful or casual. Some of them have families, some have girls; they come from different parts of the country and have different backgrounds. On two things all of them are agreed—they like to fly and they are determined their flights over the South Pacific and Europe shall not have been taken needlessly. As is the boy next door, they are heroes unknowingly.

When it sets out to put on a show—either here or there—the Army Air Forces does a thorough job. From training camps all over the country have come some 300 members of its personnel—a captain or two, lieutenants, sergeants, corporals, privates—some of whom have been known to the theatre, others not. There are no stars, and of the principal players many have only a few lines to say. Since "Winged Victory" also tells of the feminine side of the war, it has borrowed a number of civilian players to portray the mothers, sweethearts and the young wives who follow their husbands from camp to camp and are gallant and true heroes also.

* * *

It is a huge cast and a production which in fumbling hands well might sprawl all over Broadway, but neither the Air Forces nor Mr. Hart stand for amateur nonsense. In directing the play and grouping the singing choruses which are an integral part of the play, Mr. Hart has done a masterful job. Harry Horner, now with a "Sgt." before his name, has designed perfect settings for the drama's various incidents, and David Rose—also with a "Sgt."—has made the arrangements of the music. The scenes blend easily, and the play runs along as though General Arnold were himself standing backstage with a stop watch to see there is no delay. He may have been, at that.

The basic theme of "Winged Victory" is a simple one, merely following the training of the members of a bomber's crew. But the basic theme is not all there is to the play. For Mr. Hart has realized that for every man who is a pilot there also is a family back home, on a farm in Oregon, in Texas, in Brooklyn. He has written of the Air Forces, and of the war, from their point of view, as well as from that of the members of the crew, telling of the upheaval and worry, the hours of waiting for some message from the son or husband. He likes the members of his bomber's crew, and he likes their families, and the result is most warming in a theatre.

＊　＊　＊

The opening scene of "Winged Victory" takes place in the author's favorite town of Mapleton, Ohio, a location which has come up in "The American Way," "Lady in the Dark" and "The Man Who Came to Dinner." It shows three youngsters, having joined the Air Forces, waiting for the letters which will tell them when to report. Presently they are in the barracks, beginning training along with others like themselves from various parts of the country. Some members of the group are "washed out" for physical or other reasons and the rest go on to become pilots or navigators.

In the second act the crew finally is assembled before the bomber it is to use and as its first action gives it the name of Winged Victory. There is a scene showing the wives of three members of the group, living together in Oakland and certain that, while no one had said anything about it, the bomber was about to leave. The final scene of the play is on a landing field on an island in the South Pacific when two members of the crew, battle worn and drooping with weariness, are taking their wounded gunner to the dressing station.

In telling his simple story of the impact of the war on average American people, Mr. Hart has kept it simple. He is aware that a casual air can be more effective than built-up drama and that in expressing himself the boy from the farm does not quote Plato. The play has a good many moving scenes which are moving because they are easy and filled with humor, leaving it to the audience to supply the implications. The parts of the play which are half humorous are far better than the few scenes which are outwardly serious.

The players, too, have kept their roles simple, the Air Forces obviously breeding group acting along with well coordinated bomber crews. There are some names which have been familiar to Broadway and screen audiences before they acquired the prefixes of AAF rank—Alan Baxter, Philip Bourneuf, Lee J. Cobb to mention but three—and the rest are new to the theatre but obviously should return to it after the war. Corp. Mark Daniels and Pfc. Edmond O'Brien have what are perhaps the leading roles, or, to narrow it down to just one point, Pfc. O'Brien has the leading role. He plays the part of the co-pilot from Brooklyn, a very great figure, both in the creation and acting.

＊　＊　＊

But "Winged Victory" is not a play for individual performances, since all are good, from the three men who imitate the Andrews Sisters during a Christmas party in the South Pacific to the one who plays the Mayor of the little Oregon town when one of the crew members is married just before leaving for action. In the writing, the acting, the designing, the costumes by Sgt. Howard Shoup, the Feder lighting—now with a "Sgt." before it, and the choruses trained by Second Lieut. Leonard de Paur, a great deal of talent has gone into "Winged Victory." It shows it. The Army Emergency Relief Fund receives the money, but that fact is not the reason to see the play. It is a wonderful show.

1943 N 22

CARMEN JONES, a musical comedy in two acts and five scenes, based on Meilhac and Halevy's adaptation of Prosper Merimee's "Carmen." Book and lyrics by Oscar Hammerstein 2d. Music by Georges Bizet, with new orchestral arrangements by Robert Russell Bennett. Staging, lighting and color scheme by Hassard Short; libretto directed by Charles Friedman; choreography by Eugene Loring; settings by Howard Bay; costumes designed by Raoul Pene duBois; produced by Billy Rose. At the Broadway Theatre.

Corporal Morrell	Napoleon Reed
Foreman	Robert Clarke
Cindy Lou,	
Carlotta Franzell or Elton J. Warren	
Sergeant Brown	Jack Carr
Joe	Luther Saxon or Napoleon Reed
Carmen	Muriel Smith or Muriel Rahn
Sally	Sibol Cain
T-Bone	Edward Roche
Tough Kid	William Jones
Drummer	Cosy Cole
Bartender	Melvin Howard
Walter	Edward Christopher
Frankie	June Hawkins
Myrt	Jessica Russell
Rum	Edward Lee Tyler
Dink	Dick Montgomery
Husky Miller	Glenn Bryant
Soldiers	Robert Clarke / William Woolfolk / George Willis / Elijah Hodges
Mr. Higgins	P. Jay Sidney
Miss Higgins	Fredye Marshall
Photographer	Alford Pierce
Card Players	Urylee Leonardos / Ethel White / Sibol Cain
Girl from Cuba Libra Club	Ruth Crumpton
Poncho	William Dillard
Dancing Boxers	Sheldon B. Hoskins / Randolph Sawyer
Bullett Head	Melvin Howard
Referee	Tony Fleming Jr.

Conductor: Joseph Littau
Choral director: Robert Shaw

By LEWIS NICHOLS

Billy Rose is a little man with gigantic ideas, which at suitable intervals explode over the city like a burst of fireworks. The display last evening was one of the greatest of them all, for Billy brought to the Broadway Theatre the work called "Carmen Jones," which has the Bizet music for "Carmen," an all-Negro cast and a new version of the opera's libretto by Oscar Hammerstein 2d. It is beautifully done in every way, with gay colors and gay ballets, and singers who can sing as though they meant it and were on the stage for business. Since it is an opera under discussion, just call it wonderful, quite wonderful.

Since he is not one to throw down a friend, Billy's initial attempt to set up shop alongside the Metropolitan has spared no pains. To arrange the music—not changing it, by the way—there is Russell Bennett. To design the settings there is Howard Bay, and for the costumes, which resemble nothing so much as the rainbow this side of the pot of gold, Raoul Pène duBois. Robert Shaw, who

has been spectacular as the director of the Collegiate Chorale, has directed the choruses, who sing as though their lives depended on it, as they probably do. And for general supervisor, there is Hassard Short, who in addition to everything else can make lights behave as though pressing a button started ed a major miracle.

In making his new adaptation, Mr. Hammerstein also has kept within striking distance of the original Meilhac and Halevy adaptation of Merimee's "Carmen." The original was in Spain; Mr. Hammerstein has changed that to southern United States, in a parachute factory which "use ter be a cigarette fac'ry before de war"— if the purists must have an explanation of the end of "Carmen's" cigarette factory. The opera's Don Jose now is plain Joe; Micaela has become Cindy Lou; Escamillo, the toreador, is Husky Miller, a prize fighter, and Lillas Pastia is Billy Pastor, night-club king'. But the story is the same: The flower, the cards, the death of Carmen Jones at the end. Whereas, Don Jose was in disgrace from his regiment, Joe is AWOL from his.

Mr. Hammerstein has not written a parody in any sense, but simply a parallel. Many of his lyrics are light, but there are no Broadway gags, and only one or two ultra-modern, or 1943, things have crept in. In the original, the Toreador Song describes the excitement of a bull fight; as it now is sung under the title of "Stan Up An' Fight," it describes a battle in the ring. Mr. Hammerstein has taken the plot of an opera, has matched it scene by scene, but has neither bowed down before it with diffidence nor used it as the basis for a literary prank. It is quite a libretto he has turned out.

To sing the main roles, Mr. Rose —with the assistance of John Hammond Jr., an expert on Negro singers and players—has acquired some excellent people. For Cindy Lou there are Carlotta Franzell and Elton J. Warren, who will alternate, with the former last evening singing, on the whole, charmingly. Luther Saxon was Joe at the opening performance, a Joe who has a good voice but is not a finished actor; and Muriel Smith was Carmen Jones. She looked sultry, had a fine swagger and dangerous smile and a voice that matched the part. Back of the principals were a perfect chorus, trained to the last and final degree.

* * *

But even aside from the words and the music, "Carmen Jones" is quite a show. It is dressed in the most variegated costumes of the year, as though Mr. du Bois's paints went mad in the best possible taste. There is a ballet or two contributed by Eugene Loring, with his tongue in his cheek, the dancers being cheerful and fast. There even is a night-club scene, which Billy, as the master of them, could steal for an enterprise of his own elsewhere. As Carmen and Joe sing the "Dere's a Cafe on de Corner," which used to be the Seguidilla; or as Don José's Flower Song comes out as "Dis Flower," or the Card Song as "Dat Ol' Boy," going to the theatre seems again one of the necessities of life. In cutting the cards this time, Billy did not pick the nine of spades, which spelled death to Carmen.

1943 D 3

THE VOICE OF THE TURTLE, a comedy in three acts and six scenes, by John van Druten. Staged by the author; settings by Stewart Chaney; produced by Alfred de Liagre Jr. At the Morosco Theatre.

Sally Middleton..........Margaret Sullavan
Olive Lashbrooke..........Audrey Christie
Bill Page....................Elliott Nugent

By LEWIS NICHOLS

To waste no time with dismal qualifications inspired by a Broadway winter, "The Voice of the Turtle" is the most delightful comedy of the season—and probably back a year or two as well. For John van Druten, who is happiest when his characters are few in number, has built his latest play around three of the best of them, and Margaret Sullavan, Audrey Christie and Elliott Nugent play the parts as though they were living them. "The Voice of the Turtle" has everything it needs, save that possibly it is two or three hours too short, for last night's audience, at least, would have sat there quite cheerfully until this minute, and afterward would have helped the cleaning women get ready for today.

* * *

As an exhibition of how to construct a play to amuse the world, Mr. van Druten's is very little this side of classic. His cast of three at no time seems small; probably if only one of them stayed on the stage, that would appear quite in order. For their conversation sparkles with wit, and it has the friendly grin of a high good humor. Since he is not writing a farce, the author also has given his play a quality of great tenderness. The conversation runs from love, to the Army, to food, to the theatre, and Mr. van Druten and his players have the right thing to say about all of them. Probably he has been listening to the conversation at the next table, and in the subway and the wings, for it all is very human.

The title is biblical, noting that when the turtle's voice is heard spring is upon the world—even to an apartment in the East Sixties, near Third. The apartment is Sally Middleton's, and she is an actress of smallish parts who is trying to get over a love affair with a producer. Her friend brings an Army sergeant to the apartment, and then, with a chance for a better date, leaves him there. He stays for the week-end. He wishes to have no sentiment about such things, nor does she—but the voice of the turtle carries quite an echo, which Mr. van Druten, among others, is not one to ignore.

* * *

The cast is perfect, of course. Miss Sullavan plays the role of the actress with a charm that is second to none. Her Sally Middleton is composed of a young girl, an actress who hopes some day she will get a leading part, a girl who likes to be busy around the house and whose Joplin (Mo.) upbringing makes her faintly worried about her life. Mr. Nugent is a calm sergeant on leave who has been around. He is practical and recognizes Sally's moods—and he gives a whale of a performance. The third member, Miss Christie, is on the stage for only parts of two acts, Mr. van Druten no doubt feeling three persons clutter up plays, but she is very good while there. Her role is of a cynical girl, harsh and brassy, more the type of a stock play character than are the other two.

Having written it, the author

knew what he wanted when he came to direct, and he has done an excellent job. Two or three character plays can get rather static, but not this one. There is enough unforced movement to cover the spots between brilliant lines, and those spots are few. Stewart Chaney has fallen into the spirit of the occasion by constructing a splendid set showing a bedroom, sitting room and kitchen, all apparently of normal size, perfectly appointed. The cast could live there. if the worst came to the worst, although it is not likely to. For "The Voice of the Turtle" will be heard in the spring on Broadway also.

1943 D 9

1944

ANNA LUCASTA, a play in three acts, by Philip Yordan. Staged by Harry Wagstaff Gribble, assisted by Walter Thompson Ash; scenery by Frederick Fox; costumes by Paul DuPont; produced by John Wildberg. At the Mansfield Theatre.

Katie	Theodora Smith
Stella	Rosette LeNoire
Theresa	Georgia Burke
Stanley	John Proctor
Frank	Frederick O'Neal
Joe	George Randol
Eddie	Hubert Henry
Noah	Alvin Childress
Blanche	Alice Childress
Officer	Emory Richardson
Anna	Hilda Simms
Danny	Canada Lee
Lester	John Tate
Rudolph	Earle Hyman

By LEWIS NICHOLS

Preceded by several million dollars' worth of good-will, "Anna Lucasta" moved down from Harlem last evening to prove again that it can give an exciting evening in the theatre. Between the hot June night when the American Negro Theatre gave it a first performance on 135th Street and a hot August night when John Wildberg offered it at the Mansfield, there have been a number of changes in script and cast. But the essential things have been retained—the qualities of character, and humor and pathos—and the structure of the play has been improved by editing and changes. And the acting is excellent.

* * *

Acted by a Negro cast and with a Negro setting, "Anna Lucasta" is not necessarily a Negro play as Broadway is accustomed to see them. There is none of the easy clowning which the Forties are accustomed to credit to Harlem, and

there is no particular social content. Philip Yordan wrote it originally for white players, and in the translation his mood has been retained; the characters could be either Negro or white. In the direction, Harry Wagstaff Gribble also has stayed with the script, and beyond an occasional jarring costume or so, the entire staging has been sincerely anxious to keep away from what the sages say Broadway demands from that other theatre district to the north.

The story is vaguely like O'Neill's play about the other Anna—Christie. A prostitute, who had been thrown from a Pennsylvania home by her father, goes back from the Brooklyn waterfront dives into which she had fallen. She meets and marries a nice boy from the South, she hears her past exposed and again returns to the dives until her husband comes for her. The plot is simple, but Mr. Yordan has embellished it with some wonderful characters. The girl's family and in-laws are partly dubious crooks, willing to steal anything, and partly nice, simple people. One of the Brooklyn prostitutes, with hard face and slangy, ribald tongue, probably never will be beaten on the stage. The boy is easy, casual and humorous. Mr. Yordan has a human group.

* * *

While part of the play may be a bit talky, and purists might claim certain moments of confusion, no one ever will say anything bad about the acting. Hilda Simms, who played the title role in Harlem, has come downtown with the show; a beautiful young lady who also understands what can be done with a part. Frederick O'Neal again is the ponderous, faintly philosophic brother-in-law, and he is giving a magnificent performance. Alice Childress is the Brooklyn prostitute noted above, and Earle Hyman is the boy from the South. In a small role there also is Canada Lee, normally a star in his own right but helping out his friends this time and acting in the way that had made him a star.

The American Negro Theatre has been doing honest and energetic work for many months; Broadway owes it a considerable debt of thanks for discovering "Anna Lucasta" and taking the trip down Seventh Avenue.

BLOOMER GIRL, a "new musical" in two acts and ten scenes. Music by Harold Arlen; lyrics by E. Y. Harburg; book by Sig Herzig and Fred Saidy, based on a play by Lilith and Dan James; choreography by Agnes de Mille. Musical director, Leon Leonardi; orchestrations by Russell Bennett; book directed by William Schorr; settings and lighting by Lemuel Ayers; costumes by Miles White. Production staged by Mr. Harburg. Presented by John C. Wilson, in association with Nat Goldstone. At the Shubert Theatre.

Serena	Mabel Taliaferro
Octavia	Pamela Randell
Lydia	Claudia Jordan
Julia	Toni Hart
Phoebe	Carol MacFarlane
Delia	Nancy Douglass
Daisy	Joan McCracken
Horatio	Matt Briggs
Gus	John Call
Evelina	Celeste Holm
Joshua Dingle	Robert Lyon
Herman Brasher	William Bender
Ebenezer Mimms	Joe E. Marks
Wilfred Thrush	Vaughn Trinnier
Hiram Crump	Dan Gallagher
Dolly	Margaret Douglass
Jeff Calhoun	David Brooks
Paula	Lee Barrie
Prudence	Eleanor Jones
Hetty	Arlene Anderson
Betty	Eleanor Winter
Hamilton Calhoun	Elaine Cordner
Pompey	Dooley Wilson
Sheriff Quimby	Charles Howard
1st Deputy	John Byrd
2d Deputy	Joseph Florestano
3d Deputy	Ralph Sassano
Augustus	Hubert Dilworth
Alexander	Richard Huey
State Official	John Byrd
Governor Newton	Butler Hixon

By LEWIS NICHOLS

Preceded by approximately as much fanfare as the elections, "Bloomer Girl" moved into the Shubert last evening. Let the elections be as satisfactory. Beautiful to look upon, with a good score and bright lyrics and an engaging cast to sing them, the town's newest musical show is what the town has been awaiting for some time. Nothing has been spared to make of "Bloomer Girl" one of the better evenings in the Broadway theatre and, since care calls forth its own reward, the new show is just that. It probably will be resident on Forty-fourth Street until the hoop skirts, in the usual cycle of women's fashions, come back again. That won't be tomorrow.

* * *

The careful joining of talents is "Bloomer Girl's" great asset. Harold Arlen has written a generally excellent score, with E. Y. Harburg to supply concise and witty lyrics. Celeste Holm has come forth from another fair show, "Oklahoma!", to sing some of them, and David Brooks has left the Philadelphia Opera to sing others. Joan McCracken, who is used to dancing to the steps of Agnes de Mille, is doing so once more, and in additiion has become

a comedienne of great charm and a raucous, spellbinding voice. There are one or two good ballets, a pageant, part of an Uncle Tom's Cabin" show, wonderful settings and costumes by Lemuel Ayers and Miles White—in fact, the contents of the top drawer. There also is a book, but perhaps this is not the time to go into that, since the book is not the show's most sturdy beam.

With Russell Bennett to supply the flutes and other necessities of orchestration, Mr. Arlen has turned out a score which is eminently serviceable and contains a number of items which will go on to be bothersome by radio. "Evelina," as sung by Miss Holm and Mr. Brooks, is one; "When the Boys Come Home"; "The Eagle and Me" —the property of Dooley Wilson; and "I Got a Song" are others. This last, in the form of a rapid-fire ballad, is sung by Richard Huey, who probably weighs three hundred pounds, is very dark, indeed, and makes of his own particular number the great moment in the show. Mr. Huey has songs for all occasions—trains, women, bullfrogs, freedom—and goes on through the list, to Mr. Harburg's best lyrics.

* * *

Miss McCracken's entry into the legitimate field is an important feature of "Bloomer Girl." She is all over the stage, as dancer, as harsh-shouting singer of "T'morra' T'morra,'" as Topsy in what can be called the play within a play, just like Shakespeare, and she is pretty wonderful. Miss Holm is attractive in the leading role, but sometimes cannot be fully heard when at work on the songs. Mr. Brooks has an amiable stage presence, as though he had been on Broadway always, and an easy voice. Margaret Douglass gives another of her brisk portraits as the Dolly Bloomer who is trying to free women generally, and especially to get them out of hoop skirts; and Matt Briggs is properly pompous as the manufacturer of hoops and the father of daughters.

The credit for the brave thought of dressing a whole musical comedy in hoop skirts probably goes to Sig Herzig and Fred Saidy, who wrote the book from a play by Lilith and Dan James. The story is about the youngest daughter of the hoop king, who sides with her aunt, the bloomer queen, in the pursuit of freedom. Since the time is 1861, the emancipation of women can be stretched to include the emancipation of slaves, which gives the chance for a Tom show and parade, and gives Miss de Mille the chance for a good "Civil War Ballet," the main dancers being Lidija Franklin and James Mitchell. The freedom-for-women motif supplies another dance, about what grandmother used to do, which shows Miss McCracken at her best.

And there is much more. The opening of the second act is a colorful fifteen minutes of church parade, Tom show parade, arrest and chaos under the name of "Sunday in Cicero Falls." A male group gives a song, modeled on the opera of the old barber shop quartet and having to do with the "Farmer's Daughter." Mr. Harburg shows with "Bloomer Girl" that he is not only a lyricist but an excellent director of a musical show. It has pace and rhythm, and while some sections of the dialogue in the first act are too long, it flows along smoothly. In short, "Bloomer Girl" is a good show, and if the hoops are to come back, the Shubert Theatre is the place to see the newest and best styles.

1944 O 6

HARVEY, a comedy in three acts, by Mary Chase. Staged by Antoinette Perry; settings by John Root; produced by Brock Pemberton. At the Forty-eighth Street Theatre.
Myrtle Mae Simmons............Jane Van Duser
Veta Louise Simmons............Josephine Hull
Elwood P. Dowd......................Frank Fay
Miss Johnson....................Eloise Sheldon
Mrs. Ethel Chauvenet..........Frederica Going
Ruth Kelly, R. N..................Janet Tyler
Marvin Wilson.....................Jesse White
Lyman Sanderson, M. D..........Tom Seidel
William R. Chumley, M. D...Fred Irving Lewis
Betty Chumley....................Dora Clement
Judge Omar Gaffney................John Kirk
E. J. Lofgren.....................Robert Gist

By LEWIS NICHOLS

If a rabbit, six feet one and one-half inches tall, sits down beside you at Charlie's, that will be Harvey, and you may count yourself fortunate. Harvey appears to those who are happy, and to those who have taken a drink now and then through the years and are the better for it. If Harvey does not visit Charlie's he can be found at the Forty-eighth Street Theatre, where

Mary Chase's new play opened last evening with "Harvey" in quotation marks and giving a very delightful evening to the theatre. Brock Pemberton, who hitherto has held sternly apart from plays about rabbits, is the producer and Frank Fay and Josephine Hull are providing the last word in acting. Harvey, in or out of quotation, is one of the treats of the fall theatre.

* * *

The story of "Harvey" is a little hard to explain, six-foot rabbits being unusual along Broadway by night. Elwood P. Dowd, an amiable man with a thirst for bar-rooms and people, met Harvey one day leaning against a wall, and they became friends. When Elwood began bringing Harvey home, Elwood's sister, who had respectable friends, decided it was time he had a rest. The difficulty was she had seen Harvey, too, and ultimately the psychiatrist meets up with him also—in Charlie's, of course. At the end of the play in which the title-player never appears, the sister decides that Elwood had better keep Harvey around.

A fantasy such as "Harvey" can run into fearful trouble if it is badly done, but the only objection that can be raised against Mrs. Chase's play is that some scenes are a bit slow. The first act, in particular, is far too long. But when Mr. Fay is on the stage, quietly explaining his relationship with Harvey, the theatre could ask for little more. Mr. Fay does not act. He wanders amiably about the stage, never raises his voice, and when he wants to make a full gesture he lazily lifts a finger or two. Harvey obviously is behind him all the time—and perhaps all those years of the Palace and the night clubs, where actors grow accustomed to dealing with rabbits and legitimate parts.

* * *

Josephine Hull also is no beginner on the stage, and her portrait of the woman who is trying to bring up her daughter in such a bizarre household is a masterpiece. She always is in trouble, always is misunderstood; when she takes her brother to the rest home, she herself is locked up there. Flighty and wide-eyed, Miss Hull is a perfect foil for Mr. Fay's casual ease. The rest of the cast back up the two principals, although the play is far from theirs. Janet Tyler is an attractive nurse in the rest home, Fred Irving Lewis a properly stocky psychiatrist, John Kirk the family attorney. Antoinette Perry has directed the play so that it runs easily, and John Root has designed the setting suitable for a home or rabbit hutch—whichever.

Harvey is worth knowing, either at Charlie's or on Forty-eighth Street.

1944 N 2

ON THE TOWN, a musical comedy in two acts and seventeen scenes. Book by Betty Comden and Adolph Green, based on an idea by Jerome Robbins. Music by Leonard Bernstein. Lyrics by Miss Comden, Mr. Green and Mr. Bernstein. Musical numbers and choreography staged by Mr. Robbins; scenery designed by Oliver Smith and costumes by Alvin Colt; entire production directed by George Abbott; musical director, Max Goberman; presented by Mr. Smith and Paul Feigay. At the Adelphi Theatre.

Workman	Marten Sameth
2d Workman	Frank Milton
3d Workman	Herbert Greene
Ozzie	Adolph Green
Chip	Chris Alexand
Sailor	Lyle Clark
Gabey	John Battles
Andy	Frank Westbrook
Tom	Richard D'Arcy
Flossie	Florence MacMichael
Flossie's Friend	Marion Kohler
Bill Poster	Larry Bolton
Little Old Lady	Maxine Arnold
Policeman	Lonny Jackson
S. Uperman	Milton Taubman
Hildy	Nancy Walker
Policeman	Roger Treat
Figment	Remo Bufano
Claire	Betty Comden
High School Girl	Nellie Fisher
Sailor in Blue	Richard D'Arcy
Maude P. Dilly	Susan Steell
Ivy	Sono Osato
Lucy Schmeeler	Alice Pearce
Pitkin	Robert Chisholm
Master of Ceremonies	Frank Milton
Singer	Frances Cassard
Waiter	Herbert Greene
Spanish Singer	Jeanne Gordon
The Great Lover	Ray Harrison
Conductor	Herbert Greene
Bimmy	Robert Lorenz

By LEWIS NICHOLS

There can be no mistake about it: "On the Town" is the freshest and most engaging musical show to come this way since the golden day of "Oklahoma!" Everything about it is right. It is fast and it is gay; it takes neither itself nor the world too seriously, it has wit. Its dances are well paced, its players are a pleasure to see, and its music and backgrounds are both fitting and excellent. "On the Town" even has a literate book, which for once instead of stopping the action dead speeds it merrily on its way. The Adelphi Theatre on West Fifty-fourth Street is the new Utopia.

* * *

"On the Town" is a perfect example of what a well-knit fusion of the respectable arts can provide for the theatre. Taking a book by Betty Comden and Adolph Green as a base, Leonard Bernstein has composed all manner of songs— some in Tin Pan Alley's popular style, some a bit removed. Jerome Robbins, whose idea was the basis for the show—it came from his ballet "Fancy Free"—has supplied perfect dances and found Sono Osato and others to do them. Oliver Smith's simple settings are in keeping with the spirit of the book and tunes. And finally, since the other participants were not experienced theatre people, George Abbott was invited to put the whole thing together. Mr. Abbott has done one of his perfect jobs.

"On the Town" is the story of three sailors on a twenty-four hour pass from the Brooklyn Navy Yard. In the subway they see a picture of Miss Turnstiles, and in the effort to find her in person they give Miss Comden and Mr. Green a chance to roam through New York. As half of The Revuers, those two know their city. The book they have fashioned makes cheerful fun of Miss Turnstiles, the museums, night clubs and the upper floors of Carnegie Hall, where culture learns to cult. They are serious about nothing, and oftentimes they offer only suggestions of ideas, allowing the audience to fill in the thought. It has been a long time since a musical comedy audience has been allowed to enjoy a musical comedy book.

Only last spring, Mr. Bernstein was earning the Music Critics' annual prize for the best new composition of the year; this morning he will start up the ladder of ASCAP. He has written ballet music and songs, background music and raucously tinny versions of the blues. It is possible that none of the individual numbers may spend a year on the Hit Parade, but "Lonely Town" is strict Broadway, "Lucky To Be Me" is strict torch. For a scene in Times Square he has provided the roar of that crossroads of the world. The music has humor and is unpedantic; Mr. Bernstein quite understands the spirit of "On the Town."

* * *

So does the cast, of course. Miss Osato brought down the highest rafters when she appeared a year ago in "One Touch of Venus," and there is no reason to replace any of those rafters now. Her dancing is easy and her face expressive. Any day now her picture will be in the trains as Miss Subway. Nancy Walker also is wonderful as a tough, firm, taxi driver who collects one of the sailors. She can shrill out a ballad like "Come Up to My Place" with all the harshness of a Coney Island barker and all the verve of—well, Nancy Walker. Miss Comden, in the role of another girl who likes the Navy, also is good at it; Adolph Green, Cris Alexander and John Battles are the sailors.

But the charm of "On the Town" is not so much in the individual performances as in the whole. The chorus and ballet numbers, many of them done with an edge of satire, are easy and graceful. Mr. Abbott permits no lags in his evening, and down in the pit and up on the stage everything always is in order. It is an adult musical show and a remarkably good one.

1944 D 29

TRIO, a play in three acts by Dorothy and Howard Baker based on the former's novel. Staged by Bretaigne Windust; scenery by Stewart Chaney; produced by Lee Sabinson. At the Belasco Theatre.

Janet Logan	Lois Wheeler
Pauline Maury	Lydia St. Clair
Ray Mackenzie	Richard Widmark
Ted Gordon	Kenneth Williams
Miss Hawley	Mary Alan Hokanson
Ralph Hackett	Ken Tower
Mrs. Girard	Sara Perry
Dean Harry Kennedy	Harry Irvine
House boy	Henry Goon

By LEWIS NICHOLS

At the end of a long road paved with vicissitudes, "Trio" finally reached New York, and the Belasco Theatre, last evening. For his persistence in trying to find a house for the Dorothy and Howard Baker play, Lee Sabinson, its producer, deserves the praise of the theatre. It would not have been well for the theatre had "Trio" been denied a hearing, had it been kept from Broadway because of fears over its subject-matter. Mr. Sabinson's cause was a good one, but there remains this morning the unpleasant task of saying that his play is not equally good. "Trio" has only moments that are moving or tragic; it has long stretches that

are talky, repetitious and sometimes not well acted.

* * *

The play is based upon Mrs. Baker's novel of the same name. It concerns a woman college teacher, the young girl who has been living with her and the boy the latter hopes to marry. It had been scheduled for a New York opening last November, when various local theatre owners feared that its subject-matter of lesbianism might bring down the padlock features of the Wales law. Unable to find a house, the play suspended a tour in Philadelphia and the cast and all concerned stood by until Mr. Sabinson could use the Belasco.

"Trio" is not a censorable play. It is honest and it treats its subject with dignity and restraint. The faults lie quite aside from this. The first act, a tea party which runs into a cocktail party, is interminably talky. A good deal of the second act is well written; the scene is the boy's room, when he discovers the relations between the two women. The third act goes over into melodrama, when the teacher, who had written a prize-winning book is discovered to have plagarized it. At the end she prepares to kill herself, in a rather gaudy, anticlimactic scene. The plot of "Trio" is a thin one; not enough happens. The characters of the play are not sufficiently well drawn to hold up a whole evening as character studies without action.

* * *

Lydia St. Clair, as the teacher, seems to try to give the part of Pauline Maury too many sides. Part of the time she is raging, part of the time almost whimpering; she changes mood and inflexion constantly, and the role emerges as not quite believable. Lois Wheeler is the girl. She is attractive, and in some of the passages she is very good; the emotional scenes find her wooden and a bit stilted. As the boy, Richard Widmark is excellent at the beginning. He plays easily and casually until, at the time of his discovery of the women's relationship, he overacts—a fault that may be partly the director's. Harry Irvine makes a suitable college dean, and the rest of the company, mainly tea guests, have little to do.

Because of the attention "Trio's" booking troubles earned it, Mr.

Sabinson was afraid sensation seekers might seek out the play. They will find nothing there to amuse them. "Trio" is straightforward and unsensational; it just isn't a very good play.

1944 D 30

1945

THE GLASS MENAGERIE, a play in two acts, by Tennessee Williams. Scenery by Jo Mielziner; original music composed by Paul Bowles, staged by Eddie Dowling and Margo Jones; produced by Mr. Dowling and Louis J. Singer. At the Playhouse.

The Mother...................Laurette Taylor
Her Son.......................Eddie Dowling
Her Daughter..................Julie Haydon
The Gentleman Caller...........Anthony Ross

By LEWIS NICHOLS

The theatre opened its Easter basket the night before and found it a particularly rich one. Preceded by warm and tender reports from Chicago, "The Glass Menagerie" opened at the Playhouse on Saturday, and immediately it was clear that for once the advance notes were not in error. Tennessee Williams' simple play forms the framework for some of the finest acting to be seen in many a day. "Memorable" is an overworked word, but that is the only one to describe Laurette Taylor's performance. March left the theatre like a lioness.

Miss Taylor's picture of a blowsy, impoverished woman who is living on memories of a flower-scented Southern past is completely perfect. It combines qualities of humor and human understanding. The Mother of the play is an amusing figure and a pathetic one. Aged, with two children, living in an apartment off an alley in St. Louis, she recalls her past glories, her seventeen suitors, the old and better life. She is a bit of a scold, a bit of a snob; her finery has worn threadbare, but she has kept it for occasions of state. Miss Taylor makes her a person known by any other name to everyone in her audience. That is art.

In the story the Mother is trying to do the best she can for her children. The son works in a warehouse, although he wants to go to far places. The daughter, a cripple, never has been able to finish school. She is shy, she spends her time collecting glass animals— the title comes from this—and playing old phonograph records. The Mother thinks it is time she is getting married, but there has never been a Gentleman Caller at the house. Finally the son brings home another man from the warehouse and out comes the finery and the heavy if bent candlestick. Even the Gentleman Caller fails. He is engaged to another girl.

Mr. Williams' play is not all of the same caliber. A strict perfectionist could easily find a good many flaws. There are some unconnected odds and ends which have little to do with the story: Snatches of talk about the war, bits of psychology, occasional moments of rather flowery writing. But Mr. Williams has a real ear for faintly sardonic dialogue, unexpected phrases and an affection for his characters. Miss Taylor takes these many good passages and makes them sing. She plays softly and part of the time seems to be mumbling—a mumble that can be heard at the top of the gallery. Her accents, like the author's phrases, are unexpected; her gestures are vague and fluttery. There is no doubt she was a Southern belle; there is no doubt she is a great actress.

Eddie Dowling, who is co-producer, and, with Margo Jones, co-director, has the double job of narrator and the player of The Son. The narration is like that of "Our Town" and "I Remember Mama" and it probably is not essential to "The Glass Menagerie." In the play itself Mr. Dowling gives his quiet, easy performance. Julie Haydon, very ethereal and slight, is good as the daughter, as is Anthony Ross as the Gentleman Caller. The Caller had been the hero in high school, but he, too, had been unsuccessful. Jo Mielziner's setting fits the play, as does Paul Bowles' music. In fact, everything fits. "The Glass Menagerie," like spring, is a pleasure to have in the neighborhood.

1945 Ap 2

CAROUSEL, a musical play in a prelude, two acts and eight scenes, based on Ferenc Molnar's "Liliom," as adapted by Benjamin F. Glazer. Music by Richard Rodgers; book and lyrics by Oscar Hammerstein 2d. Staged by Rouben Mamoulian; dances created by Agnes de Mille; settings by Jo Mielziner; costumes by Miles White; production supervised by Lawrence Langner and Theresa Helburn; musical director, Joseph Littau; orchestrations by Don Walker; presented by the Theatre Guild. At the Majestic Theatre.

Carrie Pipperidge	Jean Darling
Julie Jordan	Jan Clayton
Mrs. Mullin	Jean Casto
Billy Bigelow	John Raitt
Juggler	Lew Foldes
First Policeman	Robert Byrn
David Bascome	Franklyn Fox
Nettie Fowler	Christine Johnson
June Girl	Pearl Lang
Enoch Snow	Eric Mattson
Jigger Craigin	Murvyn Vye
Hannah	Annabelle Lyon
Boatswain	Peter Birch
Arminy	Connie Baxter
Penny	Marilyn Merkt
Jennie	Joan Keenan
Virginia	Ginna Moise
Susan	Suzanne Tafel
Jonathan	Richard H. Gordon
Second Policeman	Larry Evers
Captain	Blake Ritter
First Heavenly Friend (Brother Joshua)	Jay Velie
Second Heavenly Friend	Tom McDuffie
Starkeeper	Russell Collins
Enoch Snow Jr.	Ralph Linn
Louise	Bambi Linn
Carnival Boy	Robert Pagent
Principal	Lester Freedman

By LEWIS NICHOLS

Richard Rodgers and Oscar Hammerstein 2d, who can do no wrong, have continued doing no wrong in adapting "Liliom" into a musical play. Their "Carousel" is on the whole delightful. It spins and whirls across the stage of the Majestic, now fast and rousing, now nostalgic and moving. To it, the composer of the team has brought one of the most beautiful Rodgers scores, and the lyricist some of his best rhymes. The Theatre Guild, offering the play as its farewell to the season and on its twenty-sixth birthday, has given it an excellent production, with Rouben Mamoulian to direct, and Agnes de Mille for the dances. The Majestic is across the street from the St. James, where "Oklahoma!" is stationed; the pair of Rodgers-Hammerstein shows will be able to wink at one another for a long time to come.

* * *

In deciding to make a musical play of Ferenc Molnar's "Liliom," the pair automatically adopted a couple of heavy millstones. One is "Oklahoma!" and they got around that by not trying to imitate themselves. The other is the familiarity most audiences have with "Liliom." This they conquered by following the story quite closely as to incident, changing only the time and locale. "Carousel" is set on the New England coast toward the end of the nineteenth century. Its principal figure still is a barker in a carnival, he still commits suicide after an abortive holdup, he goes to heaven and comes back again to do his one good deed. There is a new ending, but one which does not violate the spirit of the original.

At the beginning of the play, where scene and mood must be established, "Carousel" moves a little slowly, but as soon as Mr. Rodgers has warmed his keyboard and Mr. Hammerstein his pen, chance complaints evaporate. The composer is offering all types of song. "June Is Bustin' Out All Over" is a cheerful, rousing number; "If I Loved You" is excellent of the type implied by its name. "What's the Use of Wond'rin'" is very good, so is "You'll Never Walk Alone." There is ballet music, soft music and sentimental, and connecting themes. Mr. Hammerstein has worked hard on his lyrics; some of them are funny, some factual, some aiming at nothing higher than to be pleasant. In the lyric to "This Was a Real Nice Clam Bake" he can make his audience hungry for an immediate shore dinner.

As lyricist, Mr. Hammerstein must have a great admiration for the cast, which sings the words audibly and well. John Raitt is Liliom under the name of Billy Bigelow. He has an excellent and powerful voice and is not afraid to use it. He perhaps is not as good an actor as singer; he lacks the easy swagger and arrogance which goes with the character. Jan Clayton is a charming Julie, and can also sing; Jean Darling is Julie's friend and Eric Mattson the latter's husband. Christine Johnson is fine in the role derived from that of the photographer with whom Julie and Liliom lived, and Jean Casto has the part of the carousel's owner.

Miss de Mille has built up two main dances. One is a hornpipe, which is light and gay; the other is a ballet which Billy sees as he looks down from heaven upon his daughter. This last is perhaps not up to Miss de Mille's final score, although Bambi Linn, late of the rival across the street, is in it. Mr. Mamoulian has directed the whole thing so as to stress the music, which is eminently proper, and to set forth every pleasant angle possible. "Carousel" lacks comedy in its usual sense, only one role—that of Billy's nemesis and played by Murvyn Vye—approaching the normal forms of musical play humor. Jo Mielziner has designed good settings, simple for a New England seacoast, whimsical for heaven, and Miles White has costumed everyone nicely. But "Carousel" remains a Rodgers-Hammerstein offering, and as such a good turn on and to the spring theatre.

1945 Ap 20

DEEP ARE THE ROOTS. a play in three acts, by Arnaud d'Usseau and James Gow. Staged by Elia Kazan; setting by Howard Bay; costumes by Emeline Roche; produced by Kermit Bloomgarden and George Heller. At the Fulton Theatre.

Honey Turner	Helen Martin
Bella Charles	Evelyn Ellis
Senator Ellsworth Langdon	Charles Waldron
Genevra Langdon	Barbara Bel Geddes
Alice Langdon	Carol Goodner
Roy Maxwell	Harold Vermilyea
Howard Merrick	Lloyd Gough
Brett Charles	Gordon Heath
Sheriff Serkin	Andrew Leigh
Chuck Warren	George Dice
Bob Izay	Douglas Rutherford

By LEWIS NICHOLS

After spending an early season fitfully dreaming, the theatre last evening decided to get in touch with the modern world again. "Deep Are the Roots" is the first work of the fall with an idea, the first not to shy away from a problem. Dealing with the Negro in the South, it has been written with deep sincerity by Arnaud d'Usseau and James Gow. Believing in it fully is an excellent cast, which plays with warmth and an equal sincerity. "Deep Are the Roots" is not only a plea for the understanding and final settlement through justice of one of America's problems, but it is, in narrower range, theatre. It offers thought—and a show; it is well worth seeing.

* * *

The story is of the present. A young Negro returns from the wars to the Southern mansion in which he grew up. He is an officer; he has been decorated, and in Europe he had run into friendliness, not prejudice. The owner of the mansion, a retired Senator, believes in keeping the Negro in his old place. One of his daughters has given lip service to equality, the other had grown up with the boy and likes him. The Negro becomes the head of a school, hoping to help in the education of his race, but before much can be done he is falsely accused of the theft of a watch and is thrown into jail. The younger daughter, his friend, realizes he is in love with her and offers to marry him. He refuses, realizing that would be the solution of nothing, that they would be just "an island."

Not all of "Deep of the Roots" is as good as its instinct; indeed, there are a great many flaws. In order to keep action going on the stage, the authors have contrived the business of the theft, which makes the play sag below its level of discussion. The matter of the love affair between the young daughter and the boy also is a theatrical trick; intermarriage is not the first step in racial equality, as the authors, themselves, concede at the conclusion. The character of the former senator is not tightly drawn; at the beginning he shows no signs of the completely warped and vicious man he becomes at the end.

The complaints probably are not of violent consequence, and about the acting there can be no complaint at all. Barbara Bel Geddes, as the younger daughter, is giving a performance which she will find difficulty beating later on. She has grace and tenderness and an honesty which breathes life into the part. Charles Waldron is the Senator and very good at it until towards the end the authors let him down. Carol Goodner is the older sister, offering forthright playing in a difficult role, and Gordon Heath is quiet and sincere as the young Negro boy. Elie Kazan has done an excellent job of direction, and Howard Bay's setting is out of the Senatorial South.

It is good to have the theatre back in New York again.

1945 S 27

HOME OF THE BRAVE, a play in three acts and eight scenes, by Arthur Laurents. Production designed and lighted by Ralph Alswang; staged by Michael Gordon; produced by Lee Sabinson, in association with William R. Katzell. At the Belasco Theatre.

Capt. Harold Bitterger	Eduard Franz
Major Dennis Robinson Jr	Kendall Clark
T. J.	Russell Hardie
Coney	Joseph Pevney
Finch	Henry Barnard
Mingo	Alan Baxter

By LEWIS NICHOLS

In "Home of the Brave," which is his first play, Arthur Laurents is making a sincere and honest effort to bring to the theatre something which is not often there. His is a serious drama, seriously produced. Lately out of the Army, he is writing of the war and about a soldier who is suffering from nerve shock. There can be no question of his motives as he discusses his case history, and he carefully keeps away from the shoddy and the easy. But unfortunately as a play to be set before an audience at the Belasco, "Home of the Brave" does not succeed in fulfilling all of the author's intentions; its aim is higher than the arrow will carry.

The history is that of a young Jewish soldier in the Pacific. Suffering from shock, he is unable to walk, and the psychiatrist says that as soon as he knows what worries him subconsciously he will recover. The scenes range from the hospital room back to the island where he and four mates are on a mapping expedition preceding invasion. His best friend is killed, and after that he cannot walk. He thinks he is different from other soldiers because he is a Jew; he has the memory of anger and says he believes his paralysis came about when his friend, in sudden rage, remarked on his faith. Another soldier, who had lost an arm, persuades him there is no distinction due to faith—all men are the same.

Mr. Laurents' best scenes are those on the island, when the mapping has been done and the men are hiding from snipers until they can get away. The talk is clipped and good, and there are suspense and excitement. The author weakens his case history by the introduction of the discussion of faith, however, since it seems to have been forced into the play rather than belonging there naturally, and it is not clearly resolved. Mr. Laurents would have had a sharper picture had he stuck to one theme.

Then, too, by the time the last act arrives, the excitement of the play has passed and there is a good deal of water-treading before the author brings down his curtain.

The acting on the whole is good, since it, too, is sincere. Joseph Pevney is the young Jewish soldier, and plays the part with restraint and dignity. Alan Baxter is a soldier who gets "the GI letter"—that his wife is leaving him; Henry Bernard is the one who is killed; Russell Hardie is a former big money-maker turned private, and Eduard Franz is the doctor. The major in command of the mapping expedition is played by Kendall Clark, who perhaps makes him a little weaker than necessary. Michael Gordon directed, and the settings—good ones—are by Ralph Alswang. Lee Sabinson, who showed his courage last year by offering "Trio," is the producer.

1945 D 28

1946

O MISTRESS MINE, a comedy in three acts, by Terence Rattigan. Staged by Alfred Lunt; settings by Robert Davison; Lynn Fontanne's gowns designed by Molyneux; produced by the Theatre Guild and John C. Wilson. At the Empire Theatre.

Olivia Brown	Lynn Fontanne
Polton	Margery Maude
Miss Dell	Esther Mitchell
Sir John Fletcher	Alfred Lunt
Michael Brown	Dick Van Patten
Diana Fletcher	Ann Lee
Miss Wentworth	Marie Paxton

By LEWIS NICHOLS

The Lunts are wonderful people, and they are back again. They came like a whirlwind to the Empire last evening, sweeping through Terence Rattigan's "O Mistress Mine." For a year or so they had been absent in London, doing this new comedy among other things, and the return of the natives obviously was one of the things for which the theatre had been waiting. The Lunts never have been better, gayer, more amusing. One swallow may not make a summer, but two Lunts can throw a great deal of weight on the credit side of what has not always been a good season. The welcome mat has been set out to good purpose this time.

* * *

"O Mistress Mine" is their show, of course. That is inevitable, and it may be said of Mr. Rattigan that he has politely stepped out of their way. He has set up a framework of a British Cabinet Minister who is contentedly living with a widow, unable to divorce his own wife because of his position. Back from Canada, aged 17, comes the widow's son with radical ideas and no high regard for either the Minister or the irregular life at home. Choosing between her two gentlemen, the lady retires to an apartment with her son until that worthy, growing up a bit and himself meeting a girl, begins to see that even the holder of a Cabinet position can be human.

As a play, Mr. Rattigan's part of the evening is inconsequential—if that is not even building it up a little. It is filled with flaws, implausibilities and occasional moments when one of the Lunts is off the stage. That means nothing for very long. Alfred Lunt and Lynn Fontanne are playing for comedy rather than thought. They build up to jokes, snap their fingers, and the jokes seem hilarious. They take part of "O Mistress Mine" as high comedy, part as farce, and they are not too high above burlesque to use that on occasion. In a curtain speech after last evening's performance, Mr. Lunt said that he thought he now was old enough to break a rule against curtain speeches; that he hoped the play had entertained a little in a troubled world. It had.

* * *

Although "O Mistress Mine" is the Lunts' play by virtue of all the virtues, there are others in it. The part of the boy is acted by Dick van Patten, who used to be Dickie as a child actor and now has grown into fierce young manhood. He is serious and intense; some of the best passages are where the minister knows the boy as a viper and the widow knows him not at all. Esther Mitchell is the secretary and Ann Lee the cabinet member's wife who will not immdiately divorce him. Mr. Lunt has directed, presumably part of the time over the breakfast table, where a family of two actors best can work out the business at hand. Playing together, the Lunts know all the shadings, at the right mannerisms, and they use them naturally and instinctively.

The theatre is cheerful again. The Lunts are back, and it will be for a long time.

1946 Ja 24

BORN YESTERDAY, a comedy in three acts, by Garson Kanin. Staged by the author; setting by Donald Oenslager; costumes supervised by Ruth Kanin Aronson; produced by Max Gordon. At the Lyceum Theatre.
Helen .... Ellen Hall
Paul Verrall .... Gary Merrill
Eddie Brock .... Frank Otto
Bellhop .... William Harmon
Bellhop .... Rex King
Harry Brock .... Paul Douglas
Assistant Manager .... Carroll Ashburn
Billie Dawn .... Judy Holliday
Ed Devery .... Otto Hulett
Barber .... Ted Mayer
Manicurist .... Mary Laslo
Bootblack .... Paris Morgan
Senator Norval Hedges .... Larry Oliver
Mrs. Hedges .... Mona Bruns
Waiter .... C. L. Burke

By LEWIS NICHOLS

If this country keeps the faith with her playwrights, the United States obviously is to be the new Utopia, and almost immediately. Following a trail set by others this season, Garson Kanin has turned a roving eye on Washington, the happy result being displayed last evening at the Lyceum under the title of "Born Yesterday." Probably Mr. Kanin is not a deep political thinker, but his heart is in the right place, and in addition he knows a funny line when he sees it on his own paper. "Born Yesterday" is one of the more amusing occasions of the season. It is light, with an undercurrent from the still waters, it is acted with enthusiasm and—well, let Washington take heed.

Mr. Kanin's bad man is a modern robber baron, one who pyramided junk yards to such an extent that he owns a Senator. Living with him in a $235 per diem room is a girl taken from the chorus of "Anything Goes!", which was a good show, too. On the dim side, she naturally must be taught book learning, so that she can mingle gracefully with Senators' wives, and so the baron hires a reporter for The New Republic to teach her. Mr. Kanin is not unaware of the inevitable ending to the Pygmalion story, and he tries to give it no twist beyond the fact the girl picks up social consciousness along with the works of Tom Paine and Sibelius. At the end, she and her teacher retire to whatever salaries The New Republic pays for a clean scoop, and the baron probably is headed for Alcatraz.

No doubt a precisionist for dramatic forms would find in the references to "Anything Goes!" more than meets the eye. Mr. Kanin has flung into "Born Yesterday" whatever his hand, being quicker than the eye, could grab. There is the lowly wisecrack, raised indeed to a high degree; there is melodrama; there are pathos, earthiness of expression and even brisk burlesque. There are times when the author could have used his red pencil less sparingly, for some of the scenes, even the funniest, are drawn out a little too long. Mr. Kanin, being no amateur, saves his best jokes to bring an end to serious moments, but now and then they are just a bit delayed. Of course, not even the government is perfect.

* * *

In that respect the chief performers run ahead of the elected officers. Judy Holliday, one time member of The Revuers, is the former member of the chorus, and she is quite wonderful. She speaks in the flat tone of utter blonde dumbness—to use the robber-baron's word for it—pantomiming some of the action, and then in her Galatea phase turning into quite a person. Paul Douglas, normally of the air, also is fine as the tough, violent junk-dealer, who thinks a good slapping around will cure most things and that money is the root of all power. Otto Hulett is the lawyer, Frank Otto the stooge for the prince of old iron, and both are good at it; Gary Merrill is extremely likable as the correspondent for The New Republic. Mr. Kanin has been expert in his direction, and Max Gordon, as producer, has seen that Donald Oenslager's setting is worth every cent of $235. a day.

1946 F 5

ANTIGONE, adapted by Lewis Galantiere from a play by Jean Anouilh; settings by Raymond Sovey; directed by Guthrie McClintic. Produced by Katherine Cornell in association with Gilbert Miller. At the Cort Theatre.
Chorus ....Horace Braham
Antigone ....Katharine Cornell
Nurse ....:...........Bertha Belmore
Ismene ....Ruth Matteson
Haemon ....Wesley Addy
Creon ....Cedric Hardwicke
First Guard ....George Mathews
Second Guard ....David J. Stewart
Third Guard ....Michael Higgins
Messenger ....Oliver Clift
Page ....Albert Biondo
Eurydice ....Merle Maddern

By LEWIS NICHOLS

As a practicing actress-manager, Katherine Cornell knows the value of an occasional experiment, of kicking aside the traces for the good of both herself and the theatre. No doubt it was this thought which prompted her to bring from Paris the script of Jean Anouilh's "Antigone," and, in an adaptation by Lewis Galantiere, to present it last evening at the Cort. Miss Cornell is entitled to respect for her experiment, and her company to credit for some excellent acting, but unhappily the story cannot conclude at that point. "Antigone" is not a full-bodied evening at the theatre. Where it should be moving and strong it too often seems empty. Too much of its length drifts away in unrationalized talk by characters who are not quite living human beings.

* * *

Although Sophocles is not mentioned, it is his tragedy which forms the basis for "Antigone". The Anouilh-Galantiere version follows the story of the daughter of Oedipus who, in burying her slain brother, defies Creon, the king. As Miss Cornell and her company offer it, the production is a mixture of the modern and classical. Physically, it is played on a stage almost bare, with three steps at the rear, and before a grey curtain. The women wear robes, the men wear dinner jackets, and the chorus is a cigarette-smoking man. The language also is of varied quality. There is poetry, there is modern slang, and homely expressions follow lyrical passages.

The anachronisms of expression, instead of bringing Sophocles to 1946, have a tendency to make him much less modern than he is. When the nurse fussily charges Antigone with having gone out "without a mouthful of breakfast," the sense of impending high tragedy is lost completely. With the one exception of Creon, the characters are badly drawn; if the authors planned to show them in current modern colors, they should have done so completely. "Antigone" opened in Paris during the Nazi occupancy, when a playwright could save his neck only by an extremely careful treatment of the state-versus-individual thesis. No doubt that fact may be responsible for some of the original weakness. But for New York and 1946 the play should be clearer.

* * *

The part of Antigone, for example, is not human; her actions lack logical motivation. Some of the time the Messrs. Anouilh and Galantiere are putting her efforts to bury her brother on the grounds of religion, some on those of personal freedom. On occasions Antigone even gives indications of plain stubbornness and the insistence that she die with or without reason. With her beauty and low, distinct voice, Miss Cornell never fails to get something out of a part, but even she cannot make Antigone as moving or as real as she should be. One scene, that with Cedric Hardwicke as Creon, finds the play and the two characters fully alive, but after that they drift again into the shadows.

Mr. Hardwicke's performance is excellent, and it does not detract from that to say Creon is the one honest role. Cynical, illusionless, the king has the theory of power making the right; and once in power, the ruler must keep his line. Mr. Hardwicke looks the tired but strong man; his voice and expressions are as logical as the even array of his thoughts and beliefs. Horace Braham is the chorus, and he tells the story, editorializes and chats with the audience, all in an easy, winning way. As the guard who captures Antigone, George Matthews is of the "dese" and "dem" school of cops, and while he does it well, the anachronism is too abrupt for comfort. Ruth Matteson is Ismene, the sister; Bertha Belmore, the nurse, and Wesley Addy, Haemon's son and Antigone's fiance. Guthrie McClintic directed.

1946 F 19

ANNIE GET YOUR GUN, a musical comedy in two acts and nine scenes. Music and lyrics by Irving Berlin. Book by Herbert and Dorothy Fields. Staged by Joshua Logan; scenery and lighting by Jo Mielziner; dances by Helen Tamiris; costumes by Lucinda Ballard; orchestra directed by Jay S. Blackton; produced by Richard Rodgers and Oscar Hammerstein 2d. At the Imperial Theatre.
Charlie Davenport ....Marty May
Yellow Foot ....Walter John
Mac ....Cliff Dunstan
Foster Wilson ....Art Barnett
Coolie ....Beau Tilden
Dolly Tate ....Lea Penman
Winnie Tate ....Betty Anne Nyman
Tommy Keeler ....Kenny Bowers
Frank Butler ....Ray Middleton
Annie Oakley ....Ethel Merman
Minnie (Annie's Sister)......Nancy Jean Raab
Jessie (Another Sister) ....Camilla de Witt
Nellie (Another Sister)....Marlene Cameron
Little Jake (Her Brother) ....Clifford Sales
Col. Wm. F. Cody (Buffalo Bill)..William O'Neal
Mrs. Little Horse ....Alma Ross
Mrs. Black Tooth ....Elizabeth Malone
Mrs. Yellow Foot ....Nellie Ranson
Trainman......................John Garth 3d
Waiter ....Leon Ribb
Porter ....Clyde Turner
Riding Mistress ....Lubov Roudenko
Maj. Gordon Lillie (Pawnee Bill).George Lipton
Chief Sitting Bull..............Harry Bellaver
The White Horse............Daniel Nagrin
Sylvia Potter-Porter........Marjorie Crossland

By LEWIS NICHOLS

The inadvertently postponed "Annie Get Your Gun" finally arrived at the Imperial last evening, and turned out to be a good professional Broadway musical. It has a pleasant score by Irving Berlin—his first since "This Is the Army"—and it has Ethel Merman to roll her eyes and to shout down the rafters. The colors are pretty, the dancing is amiable and unaffected, and Broadway by this time is well used to a book which doesn't get anywhere in particular. "Annie," in short, is an agreeable evening on the town, and it takes little gift for prophecy to add that it, and she, will chant their saga of the sharpshooting lady for many months to come.

By now, Miss Merman is regarded as heaven's gift to the musical show, and there is nothing about the new one to detract from that reputation. They have given her the part of Annie Oakley, who shot with Buffalo Bill's show, and Miss Merman is deadly with a rifle over her shoulder. She can scream out the air of a song so that the building trembles; and she can be initiated into an Indian tribe in such a way the event is singularly funny. Herbert and Dorothy Fields, as librettists, quite often have left her working in something of a void, but she has worked there before and can handle the situation adequately. Her inflections give a leering note to even sedate lyrics, and the toss of her head would be a credit to Bill's show, as it is to that of Rodgers and Hammerstein.

Mr. Berlin's return to home ground is news of high and important order. For that homecoming, he has written a good, steady score, with numbers which fit the events and the story. There is nothing like "White Christmas" or "Easter Parade" among them, but several which have a place a bracket or so below. "They Say It's Wonderful" is the love song, and that will be heard around; and "Moonshine Lullaby," "I'm an Indian Too," "Show Business" and "Sun in the Morning" all are good. Abandoning the piano for the accompanying pencil of the lyricist, Mr. Berlin has fitted gay, brisk words to his tunes, and he is blessed by singers who can enunciate them.

Although the shooting of "Annie Get Your Gun" is done most affably by Miss Merman and Mr. Berlin, there are others involved to a more or less important extent. Jo Mielziner's settings are in the style of lavish musical shows, colorful and complete. The costumes by Lucinda Ballard are summery, bright, Indian, wild West and when the time is ripe, sardonic. Helen Tamiris has designed dances which probably will not be studied at formal ballet schools but fit agreeably into the porceedings. The contributors all are professionals.

In any Merman show the other members of the acting company habitually take on the harassed air of the losing horses in a steeplechase. Ray Middleton is the Frank Butler of "Annie," Frank being the lady's rival and sweetheart, and Mr. Middleton offering a voice to Mr. Berlin and no great acting ability otherwise. William O'Neal is a dignified Buffalo Bill; Marty May is energetic as his manager; Harry Bellaver is fine as Chief Sitting Bull. The young people are played by Betty Anne Nyman and Kenny Bowers. The chorus is pleasant to look upon, the orchestrations are good, and if there are abrupt pauses with some frequency—well, Miss Merman must change costumes and Mr. Berlin is not writing continuous opera.

1946 My 17

OEDIPUS, the Sophocles play in an English version by William Butler Yeats, with music by Anthony Hopkins. Staged by Michel Saint-Denis; costumes by Marie-Helene Daste; scenery by John Piper; orchestra conducted by Herbert Menges; lighting by John Sullivan. On the same bill is THE CRITIC, Richard Brinsley Sheridan's satire. Staged by Miles Malleson; scenery and costumes by Tanya Moiseiwitsch; orchestra conducted by Mr. Menges; lighting by Mr. Sullivan; fight arranged by Peter Copley. Both offerings are revived by the Old Vic Theatre Company of London for Theatre, Incorporated. At the Century Theatre.

OEDIPUS

Oedipus	Laurence Olivier
A Priest	Cecil Winter
Creon	Harry Andrews
Tiresias	Ralph Richardson
Boy	Rudolph Cavell
Jocasta	Ena Burrill
Attendants to Jocasta	Joyce Redman
	Margaret Leighton
	Nicolette Bernard
First Messenger	Miles Malleson
Herdsman	George Relph
Second Messenger	Michael Warre
Antigone	Jane Wenham
Ismene	Dee Sparks
Chorus Leader	Nicholas Hannen

THE CRITIC

Mr. Dangle	George Relph
Mrs. Dangle	Margaret Leighton
Servant	Robin Lloyd
Mr. Sneer	Peter Copley
Sir Fretful Plagiary	Miles Malleson
Mr. Puff	Laurence Olivier
First Scene Shifter	William Squire
Under Prompter	John Garley
First Sentinel	Frank Duncan
Second Sentinel	George Cooper
Sir Christopher Hatton	George Rose
Sir Walter Raleigh	Michael Warre
Earl of Leicester	Michael Raghan
Governor of Tilbury	Nicholas Hannen
Master of the Horse	Kenneth Edwards
Tilburina	Nicolette Bernard
Confidant	Joyce Redman
Whiskerandos	Sydney Tafler
Second Scene Shifter	Max Brent
Beefeater	William Monk
Lord Burleigh	Ralph Richardson
First Niece	Diana Maddox
Second Niece	Jane Wenham
Thames	Kenneth Edwards
First Bank	Robin Lloyd
Second Bank	Joseph James
Neptune	George Cooper

By LEWIS NICHOLS

Having writ Shakespeare and Chekhov, the Old Vic's repertory finger last evening moved on to the double bill of Sophocles and Sheridan. "Oedipus" and "The Critic" are somewhat farther apart than the poles, and it obviously would take better than genius to think of putting them together. The Old Vic must have that, and from the searing tragedy and the light burlesque they have brought an excellent evening to the local theatre. It is repertory showing what it can do, and it also is Laurence Olivier showing himself as an exceptionally fine actor. Changes of style do not dismay him; he masters alike both tragedy and bubbling froth.

* * *

As Oedipus, he is the dark figure of doom. At the beginning his playing is low pitched, conversational. When Oedipus hears the prophesy that he is to kill his father and then marry his mother, there is unbelieving uncertainty, a groping for anything away from the truth. At the end, when Oedipus knows that the prophecy has been fulfilled in all its horror, Mr. Olivier rises to the highest tragic playing. The character is thought out and grows, and the actor speaks the poetry and underscores the inevitable sweeping forward of the events. Oedipus can be mangled; Mr. Olivier instead has offered a model.

Most of the other parts in the tragedy are well taken, and all of it is well staged. Harry Andrews is the Creon, a calm, easy-spoken man, and Ralph Richardson is Tiresias. Ena Burrill is Jocasta, Oedipus' mother and wife, and the two messengers are played by Miles Malleson and Michael Warre. Michel Saint-Denis has staged the production simply, with a chanting chorus and suitable and somber music by Anthony Hopkins. The scenery, also, is simple—two towering columns with a step and platform between. The Old Vic's emphasis again is right—on the play and those who play it.

* * *

Sheridan's "The Critic" is another matter. Written strictly as a burlesque about the theatre and its odd denizens, it is played accordingly. The members of the Old Vic use every wide and wild gesture at their command; they give the parody of a rehearsal performance as though it were "Hellzapoppin" —which, in an earlier manner of speaking, it is. In this one, Mr. Olivier is in tights, lace, powdered wig and a small hat—the fop become playwright. He is Mr. Puff, original gossip columnist and press agent, who allows his players to cut the script of his play as they see fit, and, with friends, watches them at it. How he changes mood while the audience has one cigarette is Mr. Olivier's business; sufficient that in the second incarnation he is as amusing as he is tragic in the first.

Since "The Critic" is a romp, the players bar no holds. Mr. Dangle, who reads plays and places them, is a misguided misfit, and Sir Fretful Plagiary, playwright, is open to insult but wants his name

spelled right. In the first part, the Old Vic offers George Relph; in the second, a very red-faced Miles Malleson. When the play moves to the rehearsal scene, most backstage misfortunes crop up, and in addition there are two wonderful studies of actresses speaking nonsense, given by Nicolette Bernard and Joyce Redman. In this afterpiece, Mr. Richardson has what definitely is a bit; as Lord Burleigh, he says not a word. Mr. Malleson directed for speed and for the prank, and he has been successful in both.

1946 My 21

CYRANO DE BERGERAC, the Brian Hooker version of the Rostand play. Staged by Melchor G. Ferrer; scenery and costumes by Lemuel Ayers; incidental music by Paul Bowles; production supervised by Arthur S. Friend; revived by Jose Ferrer. At the Alvin Theatre.

Porter	Benedict McQuarrie
A Cavalier	Samuel N. Kirkham
A Musketeer	George B. Oliver
A Lackey	Stewart Long
Another Lackey	Ralph Meeker
A Guardsman	Charles Summers
Flower Girl	Phyllis Hill
A Citizen	Wallace Widdecombe
His Son	Walter Kelly
A Cut Purse	Nick Dennis
Orange Girl	Patricia Wheel
A Marquis	John O'Connor
Brissaille	Bert Whitley
Ligniere	Robert Carroll
Christian de Neuvillette	Ernest Graves
Ragueneau	Hiram Sherman
Le Bret	William Woodson
Roxane, nee Madeleine Robin	Frances Reid
Her Duenna	Paula Laurence
Comte de Guiche	Ralph Clanton
Vicomte de Valvert	Anthony Jordan
Montfleury	Leopold Badia
Cyrano de Bergerac	Jose Ferrer
Bellrose	Howard Wierum
Jodelet	Robinson Stone
A Meddler	Francis Letton
A Soubrette	Mary Jane Kersey
A Comedienne	Jacqueline Soans
Lise	Nan McFarland
Carbon de Castel-Jaloux	Francis Compton
A Poet	Vincent Donahue
Another Poet	Leonardo Cimino
A Capuchin	Robinson Stone
A Cadet	Paul Wilson
Sister Marthe	Jacqueline Soans
Mother Marguerite	Nan McFarland
Sister Claire	Phyllis Hill
A Nun	Patricia Wheel

By BROOKS ATKINSON

José Ferrer has administered a lively draft of tonic to this ailing season by staging "Cyrano de Bergerac" as though he meant it. Acting the part of the braggart romantic, he is appearing at the Alvin in a pulsating performance that makes full use of the modern theatre. Although "Cyrano" is no longer a modern play, it is still one of the most dashing ever written, particularly in the Brian Hooker version that preserves the bravura of the Rostand text in light verse of a modern idiom. Amid all the excitement, swashbuckling and old-fashioned ham that swept across the stage of the Alvin last evening, the theatre seemed again to be something worth enjoying and cherishing.

Like people who respect the theatre, Mr. Ferrer and his associates offer everything in abundance. Inside one of Lemuel Ayers' most decorative settings, the performance begins with a gusty scene and one of the most tingling duels of a generation. For when the astonishing Gascon whips out his sword he fights with finesse and ferocity like a man inspired. Elsewhere throughout the performance the pace slackens a little; and although Mr. Ferrer has already cut the text, there is still enough left to choke a printer's alley. Even the stoutest admirer of the hero of the long nose must weary a little from the sheer volume of words that pours off the stage. But this playgoer is registering no formal complaints, for the Ferrer "Cyrano" is rattling good theatre in the cloak-and-doggerel vein.

Until Mr. Ferrer came along, this was Walter Hampden's part, as was the Brian Hooker version his text; and Mr. Hampden's Cyrano was his crowning achievement. There were times last evening when Mr. Hampden's voice seemed to be coming out of Cyrano's cloak, especially in the balcony scene. Mr. Hampden's greater height gave him a certain advantage in a part that is intended to overwhelm the play. After the first act, which is the best in this revival, Mr. Ferrer could do with a little more physical domination. The part is ham; it can stand all the ham an actor can put into it.

Apart from his mastery of costume drama, Mr. Ferrer is also an actor of keen intelligence who gets his humor, not out of the library, but out of his personal vigor and alertness. His Cyrano has a sardonic wit, a strutting style, a bombastic manner of speech and withal a shyness and modesty. For under Rostand's rodomontade this Cyrano has a streak of sadness. Without dimming the purple of Rostand's romantic scheme, Mr. Ferrer has preserved a trace of ordinary human feeling that redeems Cyrano from complete artificiality.

As a token of faith in honest theatre, Mr. Ferrer has surrounded himself with worthy associates. Frances Reid plays an enchanting Roxane with a skimming touch and daintiness of accent, as well as obvious enjoyment in the role. As the poetic pastry cook, Hiram Sherman's fussy and breathless clowneries are thoroughly enjoyable. Ernest Graves brings to the part of Christian a candor that is an improvement over the usual stuffed-shirt version. As Roxane's duenna, Paula Laurence manages to insert an impudent gleam that is comic. Ralph Clanton as the pompous Comte de Guiche is admirable; he manages to contribute an intelligible characterization to a wooden part.

Let everyone, therefore, be well bestowed—Melchor G. Ferrer for the direction, Mr. Ayers for the costumes and settings, Paul Bowles for the incidental music; and since the occasion is bountiful, say "Thank You" to the stage hands for moving the scenery. Mr. Ferrer has done "Cyrano" in the grand manner, like a man who gets fun as well as a living out of the theatre.

1946 O 9

LADY WINDERMERE'S FAN, the Oscar Wilde comedy in four acts. Staged by Jack Minster; scenery, costumes and lighting by Cecil Beaton; incidental music by Leslie Bridgewater; revived by Homer Curran, in association with Russell Lewis and Howard Young. At the Cort Theatre.

Lady Windermere	Penelope Ward
Parker	Thomas Louden
Lord Darlington	John Buckmaster
Duchess of Berwick	Estelle Winwood
Lady Agatha Carlisle	Sally Cooper
Lord Windermere	Henry Daniell
Mr. Rufford	Paul Russell
Miss Rufford	Jeri Sauvinet
Lady Paisley	Marguerite Gleason
Hon. Paulette Sonning	Tanagra Thayer
Lady Jedburgh	Elizabeth Valentine
The Bishop	Peter Keyes
Miss Graham	Pamela Wright
Sir James Royston	Jack Merivale
Lady Stutfield	Anne Curson
Mr. Dumby	Evan Thomas
Mrs. Cowper-Cowper	Leonore Elliott
Mr. Hopper	Stanley Bell
Lady Plymdale	Nan Hopkins
Lord Augustus Lorton	Rex Evans
Mr. Cecil Graham	Cecil Beaton
Mrs. Erlynne	Cornelia Otis Skinner
First Footman	Guy Blake
Second Footman	Richard Burns
Rosalie	Marjorie Wood

By BROOKS ATKINSON

At the age of 54, Oscar Wilde's "Lady Windermere's Fan" is, to tell the truth, growing a trifle seedy. It is too old to be smart, but

not old enough to be a classic like
"The School for Scandal." But at
the Cort, where it was put on last
evening, they are almost reviving
it. The scene and costume designer, who is Cecil Beaton, and
the actors, who include Cornelia
Otis Skinner, Penelope Ward, Estelle Winwood and Henry Daniell,
come as close as anyone can to
persuading you that there is a
dance or two in the old girl yet.
In fact, Mr. Beaton has contributed as much to the production as
Oscar Wilde.

* * *

For he has wrapped it up in
some of the most luxurious settings and costumes that have been
seen since the time of Louis the
Fourteenth. Years ago Mr. Beaton
used to draw rococo borders around
snobbish photographs in Vanity
Fair. To dress "Lady Windermere's Fan" properly he has added
gorgeous colors to that same extravagant style, and he has given
the actresses gowns of tremendous
magnificence. Something would
have been acted at the Cort last
evening even if the players had not
opened their mouths. To complete
his contribution Mr. Beaton plays
the part of Mr. Cecil Graham, end-
man for Oscar Wilde. Mr. Beaton
plays it well apart from occasionally overacting an epigram as
though he were on the other side
of the footlights.

Since "Lady Windermere's Fan"
is a well-built drama, it still works
in the crucial scenes. The tarnished Lady Erlynne has a moment
of imperious drama in the third
act when she boldly enters from
Lord Darlington's chamber and
quixotically claims Lady Windermere's guilty fan. The fourth act
is also a vigorous one. The affectionate scene between Lady Erlynne and Lady Windermere is
pleasantly affecting, since everyone in Manhattan except Lady
Windermere knows that Lady Erlynne is her mother. Although the
witticisms in the small talk are
mechanical, deliberately constructed out of parodox, many of them
are still very funny indeed. But
what you miss in "Lady Windermere's Fan" is the integrity of a
genuine comedy, like "The Importance of Being Earnest." The device of keeping Lady Erlynne's

identity from her daughter produces one or two effective theatre
scenes. But it is beneath the writing level of a man with Oscar
Wilde's great talents, and it makes
us well satisfied with England's
Noel Coward whose insincerity is
better sustained.

* * *

However that may be, there is
some mettlesome acting in this
performance under the direction of
Jack Minster. As Lady Erlynne,
Cornelia Otis Skinner is playing
with style and vigor, disclosing at
the proper moment a touch of
warmth under the grandeur of the
part and period. Penelope Ward
endows Lady Windermere with
her personal beauty and adds to it
force and daintiness in the acting.
In the coherently written part of a
termagant duchess, Estelle Winwood gives a perfect performance
—brittle, sharp and witty.

None of the men is quite up to
the distaff standard. But you
cannot quarrel much with the good
taste and crispness of Henry
Daniell as Lord Windermere, nor
with the accomplished good manners of John Buckmaster as Lord
Darlington. Rex Evans is amusing
in the silly part Wilde wrote for
Lord Augustus Lorton. When
there is a wit in the house, someone has to be the butt, and Lord
Augustus serves that utilitarian
purpose.

"Lady Windermere's Fan" is not
wholly delightful. The pattern is a
little threadbare now. But everyone concerned with this bright-
colored performance comes close to
conquering its infirmities.

1946 O 15.

HENRY VIII, a revival of the Shakespearean
play in two acts and thirteen scenes. Staged
by Margaret Webster; scenery and costumes
designed by David Ffolkes; music by Lehman
Engel; dances arranged by Felicia Sorel; pre-
sented by the American Repertory Theatre as
its first offering. At the International
Theatre.
The Prologue............ ...Philip Bourneuf
Duke of Buckingham..........Richard Waring
Duke of Norfolk............Raymond Greenleaf
Lord Abergavenny............Robert Rawlings
Cardinal Wolsey.....,......Walter Hampden
Cromwell ....Eli Wallach
Sir Thomas Lovell...............Emery Battis
Sergeant of the Guard...... William Windom
Henry VIII.........................Victor Jory
Duke of Suffolk......Efrem Zimbalist Jr.
Katherine of Aragon.........Eva Le Gallienne
Surveyor ....Angus Cairns
Lord Chamberlain................Ernest Truex

By BROOKS ATKINSON

Out of an indifferent play the American Repertory Theatre has fashioned a memorable performance and a notable production. The play is "Henry VIII," partly by Shakespeare, partly by Fletcher, and the whole freely edited by Margaret Webster, who directed the performance acted at the International Theatre at Columbus Circle last evening.

As a play it lacks the imagery and vitality of Shakespeare and it is hardly more than a procession of woes and reports of court political knavery. But this is enough to give the new American Repertory Theatre entrance into the life of New York with hopes of a brave career. For the "Henry VIII" that Miss Webster has managed to patch together gives Eva Le Gallienne and Walter Hampden vehicles for some of the finest acting in their careers. And David Ffolkes, who hardly more than a year ago was dreaming of the theatre in a Jap prison labor camp, has designed one of the real magnificences of the modern stage. In lieu of a great play, this superb rendering of "Henry VIII" is enough.

* * *

Nothing is actually known about the history of this play, except that cannon used in the revelry scene burned down the Globe Theatre in 1613. According to the scholars, some of it is authentic Shakespeare from the tired last years of an exhausting career; but most of it comes from other hands— Fletcher or Massinger or both. In uninflected historical forms it presents some big scenes that might have occurred in the life of England's most uxorious monarch, but it presents them without passion.

As things have worked out it is now serving the function of presenting to New York the varied talents of a repertory theatre which will open with a Barrie play on Friday and an Ibsen play next week. The presentation as accomplished last evening should be very much to the taste of New York. As Katherine of Aragon, Miss Le Gallienne is capping her career with one or two vividly acted scenes. Katherine, pleading her case fearlessly before her wayward husband and a disingenuous cardinal, gathers stature and nobility from Miss Le Gallienne's acting, and the scene of her death acquires poignancy from her neat artistic integrity.

Playing the sort of part that best becomes his talents, Mr. Hampden is wearing imposing costumes again and speaking Elizabethan verse with mastery of tone. His Cardinal Wolsey is one of his best works. Victor Jory gives an altogether admirable portrait of a vigorous, strong-headed though friendly minded Henry VIII. As the Duke of Buckingham, Richard Waring speaks triumphantly the moving charge to the people of the streets as he marches off to execution.

Unfortunately there is no time now to discuss in detail the acting of other members of an able and varied company, although something must be said in praise of Philip Bourneuf's lucid speaking voice as one of the chroniclers. If all the actors speak difficult verse uncommonly well, that is doubtless one of Miss Webster's versatile contributions. "Henry VIII" is not her best tribute to Shakespeare as a dramatist. But she has created a work of some pith and considerable moment out of the languid scenes of this routine script.

Since the dramatic narrative is tepid, Lehman Engel has almost made a dramatic concert out of his musical score. Of all the scores he has written for such occasions, this is the most complete and evocative. As designer of both scenery and costumes, Mr. Ffolkes has done work of which the whole modern theatre should be proud. It is as though he had poured into this pageant and show all the color and beauty pent up inside him during the years he was a war prisoner in the Orient.

In "Henry VIII" Shakespeare did not do half so well as some of

272 ON STAGE: 1920–197

his twentieth-century abettors in the first production of the American Repertory Theatre.

1946 N 7

NO EXIT, a play in two acts by Jean-Paul Sartre, adapted from the French by Paul Bowles. Staged by John Huston; setting and lighting by Frederick Kiesler; produced by Herman Levin and Oliver Smith. At the Biltmore Theatre.
Cradeau ....Claude Dauphin
Bellboy ....Peter Kass
Inez ....Annabella
Estelle ....Ruth Ford

By BROOKS ATKINSON

Being a person of agile mind, Jean-Paul Sartre has written a fascinating and macabre play about three lost souls in hell. "No Exit," they call it in Paul Bowles' excellent English adaptation, and it was played with horrible logic and pitiless skill by four actors at the Biltmore last evening. Since it lasts scarcely more than an hour and a half, it is a brief sensation. Short as it is, it still may be ten or fifteen minutes too long for its own good in the theatre.

But in this one hurried essay about the damned, M. Sartre has sharply dramatized the loneliness and despair of souls that are lost, imprisoned and condemned to eternal torture in each other's company. If you wish, you may accept it as a bitter and resentful comment on life by a man of intellect whose hopes have been shattered by the colossal disasters of recent experience.

* * *

On its own terms, "No Exit" is ingenious, ugly and scornful. Two women and one man are locked up together in one hideous room in hell. Their first impressions are distasteful, but not too bad. For they imagine that they can dwell at least in the privacy of their thoughts—retaining at least some private dignity in their personal "pipe dreams" about themselves. But that illusion soon passes. They wring out of each other the black secret of their squalid crimes on earth.

Each one of them fondly imagines that one of the others can save him. Each flings himself hopefully at one of the others. But in the end it turns out that none of them can escape from the acts they have committed, and must be damned by them forever. Probably this is what M. Sartre wishes to say in his flaring play about dead souls: Man is alone in this world; he is responsible to his own will and decisions; no one can save him from himself.

* * *

The picture he draws is as gruesome as the characters, who are in varying degrees unspeakable. The man has been a coward—probably a collaborator, certainly a sadistic tormentor of his wife. One of the women has been a cruel betrayer of her husband and her lover. The other is a loathsome homosexual who has poisoned and destroyed the life of a married woman of whom she had become enamored.

With such characters, "No Exit" is a grim experience to undergo in the theatre. What redeems it is the skill of M. Sartre's craftsmanship and the knife-edge dexterity of the writing, which must owe something to Mr. Bowles' idiomatic English translation. And beyond the trapped agony of the three doomed characters lies the intellectual climate in which M. Sartre is living. That has some bearing on this withered play. For M. Sartre is one of the prophets of the current vogue of a Parisian philosophy in which the individual dissociates himself from society (which has betrayed him) and acts for himself alone. Your drama courier does not understand it very clearly, and merely observes that "No Exit" proceeds out of such premises.

* * *

Under John Huston's evocative direction, the play is brilliantly acted. Frederick Kiesler, has designed a monumentally ugly room where this game of penance is played. As Cradeau, Claude Dauphin, recently from Paris, is giving a lively, pictorial performance of despair, rage and cowardice. Ruth Ford is playing the sensualist with nervous desperation; and as the homosexual, Annabella is giving a bold and calculated performance that packs one corner of hell with horror.

Not a care-free evening in the theatre, but one that gives you the creeps and also a furtive glance into the post-war state of mind of a Parisian intellectual.

1946 N 27

1947

The Cast of Characters

STREET SCENE, a dramatic musical based on Elmer Rice's Pulitzer Prize play of the same name. Book by Mr. Rice, music by Kurt Weill and lyrics by Langston Hughes. Staged by Charles Friedman; scenery and lighting by Jo Mielziner; costumes by Lucinda Ballard; dances by Anna Sokolow; musical director, Maurice Abravanel; musical arrangements and orchestrations, Mr. Weill; produced by Dwight Deere Wiman and the Playwrights Company. At the Adelphi Theatre.

Abraham Kaplan	Irving Kaufman
Greta Fiorentino	Helen Arden
Carl Olsen	Wilson Smith
Emma Jones	Hope Emerson
Olga Olsen	Ellen Repp
Shirley Kaplan	Norma Chambers
Henry Davis	Creighton Thompson
Willie Maurrant	Peter Griffith
Anna Maurrant	Polyna Stoska
Sam Kaplan	Brian Sullivan
Daniel Buchanan	Remo Lota
Frank Maurrant	Norman Cordon
George Jones	David E. Thomas
Steve Sankey	Lauren Gilbert
Lippo Fiorentino	Sydney Rayner
Rose Maurrant	Anne Jeffreys
Harry Easter	Don Saxon
Mae Jones	Sheila Bond
Dick McGann	Danny Daniels
A Music Pupil	Joyce Carrol
City Marshal James Henry	Randolph Symonette
First Nursemaid	Peggy Turnley
Second Nursemaid	Ellen Carleen

By BROOKS ATKINSON

Add to the text of Elmer Rice's "Street Scene" a fresh and eloquent score by Kurt Weill and you have a musical play of magnificence and glory. Sung by a superb cast, it opened at the Adelphi last evening. Eighteen years ago Mr. Rice's ballad of a dingy side street in New York rose high above the horizon of the theatre, and it has always remained there as a cherished masterpiece. For nothing else has recaptured so much of the anguish, romance and beauty of cosmopolis.

Now Mr. Weill, the foremost music maker in the American theatre, has found notes to express the myriad impulses of Mr. Rice's poem and transmuted it into a sidewalk opera; and Langston Hughes has set it to affectionate lyrics. Mr. Weill's record includes some notable scores for "Johnny Johnson," "Knickerbocker Holiday" and "Lady in the Dark." But obviously this is the theme he has been waiting for to make full use of his maturity as a composer.

* * *

For he has listened to the main street cries of Mr. Rice's garish fable—the hopes, anxieties and grief of people trying to beat a humane existence out of the squalor of a callous city. The main theme he has conveyed in the rueful wonder of the song Mrs. Maurrant sings in the summer moonlight—"Somehow I Never Could Believe"; in her daughter's romantic lament—"What Good Would the Moon Be?"; in the janitor's brooding song and in the horror-stricken choral entitled "The Woman Who Lived Up There." In these songs, and in the ominous orchestrations that accent the basic moods of the drama, Mr. Weill is writing serious music enkindled by the excitement of New York.

But he is a Broadway virtuoso with a love for the trivia as well as the grandeur of his theme. For relish of life in the streets there is nothing more enchanting than his tone poem to ice cream and his gay dance for the street urchins. As a poet Mr. Hughes also relishes the people whose lives spill out of packed buildings on to the pavements. His lyrics communicate in simple and honest rhymes the homely familiarities of New York people and the warmth and beauty of humanity. Acting as popular song writers, as well as artists, Mr. Weill and Mr. Hughes have tossed off one down-beat hot number, called "Moon-faced, Starry-eyed," to which Sheila Bond and Danny Daniels dance a superb American apache number that outranks any of the current show tunes on Broadway.

Not long ago the local managers were complaining that they could no longer find actors who could sing. The producers of "Street Scene" have had no such trouble. They have found superb singers who have helped to make this one of the memorable nights in theatre going. Polyna Stoska, who plays Mrs. Maurrant, has a brilliant soprano voice that contains both the sadness and sweetness of the part. As her daughter, Anne Jeffreys sings and acts with equal beauty. Norman Cordon conveys in his baritone singing the violence and sullenness of Mr. Maurrant.

* * *

There is an abundance of fine singing all through the play—Creighton Thompson as the janitor, Brian Sullivan as the restless law student, Irving Kaufman as the amusing Jewish intellectual. Hope Emerson is vastly entertaining as the garrulous old crone; and Peggy

Turnley and Ellen Carleen ably sing the tabloid lullaby.

Jo Mielziner, who designed the celebrated setting for the original production, has designed another of lighter texture—the garishness more sympathetically stated. And perhaps this is something of what the opera contributes to the old drama. With its music and dances, its chorals and lyrics, it finds the song of humanity under the argot of the New York streets.

1947 Ja 10

FINIAN'S RAINBOW, a musical in two acts and ten scenes. Book by E. Y. Harburg and Fred Saidy; lyrics by Mr. Harburg; music by Burton Lane; scenery by Jo Mielziner; choreography by Michael Kidd; costumes by Eleanor Goldsmith; orchestrations by Robert Russell Bennett and Don Walker; staged by Bretaigne Windust; produced by Lee Sabinson and William R. Latzell. At the Forty-sixth Street Theatre.

Sunny	Sonny Terry
Buzz Collins	Eddie Bruce
Sheriff	Tom McElhany
1st Sharecropper	Alan Gilbert
2nd Sharecropper	Robert Eric Carlson
Susan Mahoney	Anita Alvarez
Henry	Augustus Smith Jr
Finian McLonergan	Albert Sharpe
Sharon McLonergan	Ella Logan
Woody Mahoney	Donald Richards
3rd Sharecropper	Ralph Waldo Cummings
Og	David Wayne
Howard	William Greaves
Senator Billboard Rawkins	Robert Pitkin
1st Geologist	Lucas Aco
2nd Geologist	Nathaniel Dickerson
John	Roland Skinner
4th Sharecropper	Maude Simmons
Mr. Robust	Arthur Tell
Mr. Shears	Royal Dano

By BROOKS ATKINSON

Jettisoning most of the buncombe of the traditional musical show, E. Y. Harburg and Fred Saidy have written an original and humorous fantasy, "Finian's Rainbow," which was put on at the Forty-sixth Street last evening. Do not be terrified by the news

IN THE PLAY: *"Not immortal! You mean you've murdered him."*—Ella Logan to Albert Sharpe.

that it whirls around a leprechaun and a magic pot of gold. For Mr. Harburg and Mr. Saidy wrote "Bloomer Girl" two seasons ago, and that was no sissy show.

With some clarion music by Burton Lane and some joyous dancing by a company of inspired sprites, the authors have conjured up a raree-show of enchantment, humor and beauty, to say nothing of enough social significance to hold the franchise. It puts the American musical stage several steps forward for the imagination with which it is written and for the stunning virtuosity of the performance.

* * *

Ella Logan, with her pair of potent pipes, is bellowing some rapturous Irish songs as the daughter of a crack-brained Irish spell-maker—"How Are Things in Glocca Morra?" being her most beguiling number. As the central mischief-maker, the producers have had the good sense to import a rare Irish entertainer, Albert Sharpe. Mr. Sharpe is a high-stepping and sagacious comic who radiates merriment and who plunges into the "Finian's Rainbow" fable with the most infectious good humor.

Add to Miss Logan and Mr. Sharpe a leprechaun whose sense of humor does not destroy the purity of the fairy story, and you have an incomparable band of unhackneyed performers. The leprechaun is played by David Wayne, who has a grin just a trifle too worldly for complete innocence. His best song, sung once with Miss Logan, is entitled "Something Sort of Grandish." It and he should be inscribed in the Hall of Fame.

* * *

If the American musical stage continues to improve, it will no longer be necessary for anyone to speak dialogue on the stage. Everything essential can be said in song and dancing. Against a wide and rhapsodic setting by Jo Mielziner, the ballet dancers of "Finian's Rainbow" begin the evening with some lyrical springtime rites of real glory. If notes of music could leap across the stage, they would be no lighter or lovelier than this joyous ballet of a young and free people. Mr. Kidd has designed it with skill and enthusiasm. The leading dancer is Anita Alvarez, a

performer in a style of dancing gossamer. Mr. Kidd and his band of dancers have interpreted the theme of "Finian's Rainbow" like thoroughbreds and artists.

Not all of "Finian's Rainbow" is on the highest level. It concludes the first act with a conventional finale calculated to split your ear drums. In the second act it gives you an eyeful of tawdry musical show enticements descended from Ziegfeld. And its stubborn shotgun marriage of fairy-story and social significance is not altogether happy. The capriciousness of the invention does not last throughout the evening.

But those are minor reservations to the enjoyment of a highly original evening in the theatre in the presence of a stageful of good companions. Although the production is large and varied, Bretaigne Windust has ably put it together and set it a happy pace. Thanks for a refreshing theatre party.

1947 Ja 11

ALL MY SONS, a play in three acts, by Arthur Miller. Staged by Elia Kazan; scenery designed and lighted by Mordecai Gorelik; costumes by Paul Morrison; produced by Harold Clurman, Mr. Kazan and Walter Fried, in association with Herbert H. Harris. At the Coronet Theatre.
Joe Keller .... Ed Begley
Dr. Jim Bayliss .... John McGovern
Frank Lubey .... Dudley Sadler
Sue Bayliss .... Peggy Meredith
Lydia Lubey .... Hope Cameron
Chris Keller .... Arthur Kennedy
Bert .... Eugene Steiner
Kate Keller .... Beth Merrill
Ann Deever .... Lois Wheeler
George Deever .... Karl Malden

By BROOKS ATKINSON

With the production of "All My Sons," at the Coronet last evening, the theatre has acquired a genuine new talent. Arthur Miller, who wrote "The Man Who Had All the Luck" in 1944, brings something fresh and exciting into the drama. He has written an honest, forceful drama about a group of people caught up in a monstrous swindle that has caused the death of twenty-one Army pilots because of defectively manufactured cylinder heads.

Told against the single setting of an ordinary American backyard, it is a pitiless analysis of character that gathers momentum all evening and concludes with both logic and dramatic impact.

* * *

Mr. Miller's talent is many-sided. Writing pithy yet unselfconscious dialogue, he has created his characters vividly, plucking them out of the run of American society, but presenting them as individuals with hearts and minds of their own. He is also a skillful technician. His drama is a piece of expert dramatic construction. Mr. Miller has woven his characters into a tangle of plot that springs naturally out of the circumstances of life today. Having set the stage, he drives the play along by natural crescendo to a startling and terrifying climax.

Fortunately, "All My Sons" is produced and directed by people who value it and who have given it a taut and pulsing performance with actors of sharp and knowing intelligence. It is always gratifying to see old hands succeed in the theatre. But there is something uncommonly exhilarating in the spectacle of a new writer bringing unusual gifts to the theatre under the sponsorship of a director with taste and enthusiasm. In the present instance, the director is Elia Kazan.

* * *

"All My Sons" is the drama of one crucial day in the life of the Kellers, who live "on the outskirts of an American town." It is Sunday. Mr. Keller and his neighbors are beginning the day languidly in good humor. But their family life is swept with hidden currents of anguish and misgivings. Although Joe Keller and his son, Chris, know that the second son, Larry, will never return from the war, Mrs. Keller is neurotically convincing herself that Larry is not dead. Chris wants to marry the girl to whom Larry was engaged.

That seems to have nothing against it except loyalties that ought to be dead. But presently it develops that the great horror that is hanging over the Keller family is the suspicion that Joe Keller has escaped a jail conviction for fraudulent manufacturing by making his innocent partner the scapegoat. The suspicion develops into a fact. In some skillful dramatic construction which may, indeed, be a trifle too skillful for spontaneity, Mr. Miller involves everyone in this spiritual torture and uncertainty. He has also managed to relate the particular tragedy to the whole tragedy of the war years.

For scenery, Mordecai Gorelik has designed an attractive, sunny backyard with a life of its own. In three acts that carry the play over into the darkness of the next day, the actors are giving a brilliant performance. Beth Merrill as the neurotic and tired mother gives the impression of an inner strength that dominates at least one corner of the crisis.

As Joe Keller, Ed Begley dramatizes the whole course of the father's poignant ordeal without losing the basic coarseness of the character. As the son, Arthur Kennedy is giving a superb performance with great power for the climaxes and with insight into the progress of the character.

Lois Wheeler acts the part of the neighbor's daughter with candor, youthfulness and passion, thoroughly aware of the growth of her character. As the son of the scapegoat, Karl Malden is ably conveying the confusion and horror of a weak young man plunged into a situation he can hardly understand. There are excellent performers in other parts by John McGovern, Peggy Meredith, Dudley Sadler, Hope Cameron and Eugene Steiner.

In a performance with varying tone, rising pitch and dramatic design, they are acting an original play of superior quality by a playwright who knows his craft and has unusual understanding of the tangled loyalties of human beings.

1947 Ja 30

THE IMPORTANCE OF BEING EARNEST, a comedy in three acts, by Oscar Wilde. Staged by John Gielgud; decor by Motley; lighting by William Conway; music arranged by Leslie Bridgewater; revived by the Theatre Guild and John C. Wilson, in association with H. M. Tennent, Ltd., of London. At the Royale Theatre.

Lane .... Richard Wordsworth
Algernon Moncrieff .... Robert Flemyng
John Worthing, J. P. .... John Gielgud
Lady Bracknell .... Margaret Rutherford
Hon. Gwendolen Fairfax .... Pamela Brown
Cecily Cardew .... Jane Baxter
Miss Prism .... Jean Cadell
Rev. Canon Chasuble, D. D. .... John Kidd
Merriman .... Stringer Davis
Footman .... Donald Bain

By BROOKS ATKINSON

Owing to unavoidable circumstances, this department cannot solemnly swear that John Gielgud's performance of "The Importance of Being Earnest" is immeasurably superior to the original performance in 1895. Even Mr. Gielgud, wise though he is, cannot know that from personal observation. But traditions grow slowly, and it is highly unlikely that the original actors blessed Oscar Wilde's comedy with the knowing perfection that Mr. Gielgud and his colleagues are bestowing on it.

Having played "The Importance" triumphantly in London, Mr. Gielgud has now brought it across the Atlantic with no appreciable seachange—not, let it be said, with the entire original cast, but with superb players of artificial comedy, and they all set it meticulously on the stage of the Royale last evening. By the accuracy and uniformity of their style in acting, directing and setting they transmute a somewhat mechanical comedy into a theatre masterpiece.

* * *

Even when it was new, to judge by the records, "The Importance of Being Earnest" seemed mechanically contrived in plot and dialogue. It was a bit like Gilbert without the Sullivan music. Especially in the central parts of the second act the brilliance of the wit today shines with an effort as though Wilde were puffing a little.

That might be a point worth dwelling upon in a performance less stylized than Mr. Gielgud's. But he has approached it as if it were a score to be played for its own sake as artificial comedy without laying emphasis on the plot and without speaking the lines like jokes or deliberate rejoinders. Absurdly self-conscious, dry and arrogant, Mr. Gielgud and his associates are marvelously entertaining. In the purest meaning of the word they are "playing" Oscar Wilde. Nothing here is seriously intended except the manner of the comedy.

Notice how all the actors hold their heads high as though they were elevating themselves above vulgarity. Notice how they greet each other with dainty touches of the fingers, avoiding at all costs the heartiness of a handshake. The lines of dialogue are written elaborately; each word is carefully chosen for its satiric value; by modern standards, some of the lines are long. But notice how disdainfully these actors speak them. Instead of hammering away at the jokes, they speak dryly in an insufferable fashion, as perhaps Oscar Wilde spoke when he, too, had a large, admiring audience at some fashionable reception.

As John Worthing, who has invented a dissolute brother, Mr. Gielgud plays with an ascetic arrogance that is enormously witty quite apart from the dialogue. No play could ever match the sustained perfection of his stylized acting. But this is no exercise in star-casting. For Mr. Gielgud has surrounded himself with actors who have mastered the same attitudes. As the overbearing Lady Bracknell, Margaret Rutherford is tremendously skillful—the speaking, the walking and the wearing of costumes all gathered up into one impression of insufferability.

Pamela Brown plays Gwendolen with the same icy condescension. As the more rustic Cecily, Jane Baxter is lovely and full of merriment in a more humane style. Jean Cadell is playing the spinster Schoolma'm with an acidulously sweet and nervous virtue. Robert Flemyng's Algernon Moncrieff is an excellent foil for Mr. Gielgud's John Worthing. Without rubbing the edge off the style, Mr. Moncrieff gets a dash of well-bred revelry into his acting. As the bachelor's servant, Richard Wordsworth is also immensely expert; and John Kidd is delightfully dull and fatuous as the rector.

Especially for the two interiors Motley's settings are models of period décor; they can be played against without staring the acting out of countenance or overwhelming the performance with color. The costumes, which presumably Motley has also designed, convey the character of the parts and the satire of the comedy without sacrificing beauty. What Motley has accomplished completes Mr. Gielgud's design for artificial comedy. Like the play, it is inhuman. It sacrifices personality to style—detached, egotistical, condescending, arid, satirical and marvelously enjoyable.

1947 Mr 4

IN THE PLAY: *"Here's some lovely Scotch heather for a lovely Scotch lassie."*—David Brooks to Marion Bell.

BRIGADOON, a new musical play. Book and lyrics by Alan Jay Lerner; music by Frederick Loewe; dance and musical numbers by Agnes de Mille; production staged by Robert Lewis; scenery designed by Oliver Smith; costumes by David Ffolkes; produced by Cheryl Crawford. At the Ziegfeld Theatre.

Tommy Albright	David Brooks
Jeff Douglas	George Keane
Archie Beaton	Elliott Sullivan
Harry Beaton	James Mitchell
Fishmonger	Bunty Kelley
Angus MacGuffie	Walter Scheff
Sandy Dean	Hayes Gordon
Andrew MacLaren	Edward Cullen
Fiona MacLaren	Marion Bell
Jean MacLaren	Virginia Bosler
Meg Brockie	Pamela Britton
Charlie Dalrymple	Lee Sullivan
Maggie Anderson	Lidija Franklin
Mr. Lundie	William Hansen
Sword Dancers	Roland Guerard / George Drake
Frank	John Paul
Jane Ashton	Frances Charles
Bagpipers	James MacFadden / Arthur Horn
Stuart Dalrymple	Paul Anderson
MacGregor	Earl Redding

According to the book by Alan Jay Lerner, two American boys on a holiday stumble into a quaint Scottish village called Brigadoon on the morning of a fair and on the day of a wedding. Although Brigadoon seems pleasant and hospitable it also seems like a strange anachronism; and finally the local dominie tells them why. Brigadoon is a spectral village that comes to life one day every century; and while the rest of the world wears itself out, the villagers of Brigadoon live on from century to century in neighborly enjoyment and in a remote corner of time.

* * *

In less imaginative hands this

fable might yield nothing more than entertainment for guffawing. But the fathers of "Brigadoon" are spreading the sorcery of their village into a plastic work of art that carries dialogue into dancing and dancing into music with none of the practical compromises of the Broadway stage. There are two or three good Broadway songs in Frederick Loewe's score. "Almost Like Being in Love," sung rapturously by David Brooks and Marion Bell, is an able swing number; and "There But For You Go I," sung by Mr. Brooks, is good Broadway romance.

* * *

But most of the score, which lays the emphasis on string instruments, has a traditional background of bagpipe skirling and a melodic air. "Waitin' for My Dearie" is a lyrical romance and "I'll Go Home With Bonnie Jean" is a village festival number. Mr. Loewe has also written some lively airs for country dancing, like those for the wedding dance and the sword dance.

This is where Agnes de Mille comes in. For a kind of idyllic rhythm flows through the whole pattern of the production, and Miss de Mille has dipped again into the Pandora's box where she keeps her dance designs. Some of the dances are merely illustrations for the music. One or two of them are conventional, if lovely, maiden round dances. But some of them, like the desperate chase in the forest, are fiercely dramatic. The funeral dance to the dour tune of bag-pipes brings the footstep of doom into the forest. And the sword dance, done magnificently by James Mitchell, is tremendously exciting with its stylization of primitive ideas.

Oliver Smith's settings in low colors are commonplace and convey little of the magic common to the rest of the production. With a fresh locale to work in, David Ffolkes has designed some spirited Scotch costumes, which is probably no more than an exercise in autobiography for him. The cast has been chosen with the same taste that prevails throughout the performance. Pamela Britton for the impudence, Virginia Bosler for the innocent bride, Lee Sullivan for the tenor songs, Lidija Franklin for the solo dances, William Han-

sen for the village elder, George Keane for the ironic Yankee—these are the actors with the most conspicuous parts.

But it undermines the motive of "Brigadoon" to pick and choose among the performers. For this excursion into an imagined Scottish village is an orchestration of the theatre's myriad arts, like a singing story-book for an idealized country fair long ago.

1947 Mr 14

THE TELEPHONE AND THE MEDIUM, two musical dramas having book, music and lyrics by Gian-Carlo Menotti. Staged by the author; scenery and costumes by Horace Armstead; musical director, Emanuel Balaban; lighting by Jean Rosenthal; presented by Chandler Cowles and Efrem Zimbalist Jr., in association with Edith Lutyens. At the Ethel Barrymore Theatre.

THE TELEPHONE
Lucy .... Marilyn Cotlow
Ben .... Frank Rogier

THE MEDIUM
Monica .... Evelyn Keller
Toby, a mute .... Leo Coleman
Madame Flora (Baba) .... Marie Powers
Mrs. Gobineau .... Beverly Dame
Mr. Gobineau .... Frank Rogier
Mrs. Nolan .... Virginia Beeler

By BROOKS ATKINSON

Having been certified by the music critics as first-quality opera last February, Gian-Carlo Menotti's "The Telephone" and "The Medium" turned up at the Ethel Barrymore last evening. On the word of their public relations counselor, they are to be judged in the theatre district as music drama. Since "Street Scene," "Brigadoon" and "Finian's Rainbow" have already pushed the dramatic stage in the direction of ballet and music, there is no reason why the enterprising composer of these two brief operas should not bring music over in our direction.

* * *

The distinctions between allied arts are less trivial than might be supposed. Although "The Telephone" is a rather tedious joke, too long for the comic idea it is projecting, "The Medium" is an engrossing exercise in necromancy with a dramatic score and brilliant singing, and the orchestration is much more eloquent than the uproar that rises from most pits in the theatre. In the chief role as the obsessed medium, Marie Powers is superb as both singer and actress. Horace Armstead has designed a macabre production that imaginatively interprets the theme. As technical supervisor, Jean Rosenthal has lighted the production with a stage sorcerer's distinction.

* * *

All these are elements that the dramatic stage appreciates, also. But between opera and the dramatic stage there is a difference in emphasis that keeps the two mediums fundamentally separate. In relating his tale of the bogus medium who succumbs to her own charlatanism, Mr. Menotti has packed the drama into the music. He is not much interested in the libretto, which is undistinguished in literary style. As a story it is hardly more than a basic idea. All the development, as well as the characterizations, lie in the music. In "Street Scene" the music illustrates the drama. In "The Medium" the drama is the music.

As music it has, of course, the variety and flexibility of a primary art. Some of it is narrative, like the story of the seance; some of it is lyrical, like the daughter's love sequence with the mute Toby, and some of it is diabolically introspective, like the medium's ominous description of her obsession. But if it is true that the producers want "The Medium" judged as theatre fare, there is this very considerable distinction between opera and drama. In opera the music stands between the theatregoer and the actor, which makes for heavy and torpid expression of human emotion.

* * *

Mr. Menotti describes "The Medium" as a tragedy in two acts. From the dramatic point of view, a tragedy acquires stature from the stature of the character. Since the medium is only a coarse and vulgar faker, and since her experience in the play is only a fancied sensation, "The Medium" as a tragedy is hardly more than a superficial narrative. Miss Powers' beautiful and forceful singing; the rapturous singing of Evelyn Keller as the daughter and the mute and limpid acting of Leo Coleman as the helpless mute are admirable elements of the stage.

But the experience of bringing Mr. Menotti's modern operas downtown from the Heckscher to Broadway shows that music and drama are not interchangeable arts. Less

distinguished music than Mr. Menotti's frequently strikes brighter sparks on Broadway. For Broadway's native music is the song as in "Porgy and Bess.' In the current "Street Scene" Kurt Weill has gone about as far as a theatre musician can in extending the song in the direction of opera.

1947 My 2

THE HEIRESS, a play by Ruth and Augustus Goetz in two acts and seven scenes, suggested from Henry James' novel, "Washington Square." Directed by Jed Harris; setting by Raymond Sovey; produced by Fred F. Finklehoffe. At the Biltmore Theatre.
Maria ....Fiona O'Shiel
Dr. Austin Sloper..............Basil Rathbone
Lavinia Penniman.............Patricia Collinge
Catherine Sloper................Wendy Hiller
Elizabeth Almond..........Katharine Raht
Arthur Townsend................Craig Kelly
Marian Almond..........Augusta Roeland
Morris Townsend...............Peter Cookson
Mrs. Montgomery................Betty Linley

By BROOKS ATKINSON

With the assistance of Wendy Hiller and Basil Rathbone, a bit of Henry James came into the theatre last evening. Using "Washington Square" as their sourcebook, Ruth and Augustus Goetz call their drama "The Heiress," which is now on the stage of the Biltmore. Set in New York of a century ago, it is the tale of a dull and modest young lady who gives her heart to an idle fortune-seeker. Her father despises her for her stupidity. Her suitor jilts her when he discovers that the fortune would be less than he anticipated. In the end she has the revenge of refusing him when he comes again. But the revenge is tiny compensation for the desolation of an old maid's life.

* * *

As things have been going on Broadway recently, "The Heiress" is a refreshing excursion into intelligence and good taste. But the fact is that the authors have had a good deal of difficulty in making a play out of undramatic material. For "Washington Square" is a story of intangibles, told with an ironic reticence that scrupulously avoids big scenes. By calling their play "The Heiress," the authors indicate that they are not attempting a literal transcription of the Henry James novel. But neither have they succeeded in writing an independent work of art. For "The Heiress" begins to lose its mastery of the theme at the end of the first act when it puts the father, suitor and daughter in a gaudy scene; and it has nothing much more than well-bred flourishes of theatre to strew through the second act. It is difficult to make a stupid woman the heroine of an interesting drama. Probably that is the basic infirmity of this elusive play.

Nor has Miss Hiller succeeded in the task that has defeated the authors. She is an admirable actress, highly esteemed in America as well as England, and well-remembered for her acting in "Love on the Dole" and "Pygmalion." But in an effort to contribute some dramatic contrast to

Wendy Hiller

the plain part of Catherine Sloper, she has made her a rather painfully abnormal person in the early half of the drama, and her composure toward the end of it is not exhilarating. Nothing Miss Hiller has been able to do alters a general impression that poor Catherine is better off inside the discreet, impeccable pages of Henry James.

As Dr. Sloper, Catherine's keenly-inhuman parent, Mr. Rathbone has one of his most actable parts. He plays it perfectly with irony and arrogance. Patricia Collinge is playing Lavinia Penniman with the intolerable romanticism of a silly character, which is precisely what the part requires. As the fickle suitor, Peter Cookson is giving an attractive performance of a part that sought to be a trifle more sinister and cunning. Something should be said in praise of Betty Linley's acting of a genteel widow who behaves with pride in a scene that is stacked against her.

To house this fable of manners and a mercenary, Raymond Sovey has designed an imposing drawing-room, attractively furnished. But the nature of the materials in the Henry James novel has sorely tried the resourcefulness of Jed Harris, as the director, and of the authors as well. The heroine cannot be acted; she can only be acted against. The story cannot be dramatized.

1947 S 30

Man and Superman

By BROOKS ATKINSON

By the simple device of dipping back a half century in dramatic literature, Maurice Evans has given the season its first crackle of brilliance. He has come up with Bernard Shaw's "Man and Superman," which has been dozing on the shelf all these years, and he has had the good taste to put it on at the Alvin last evening.

Almost no one in his right mind likes to listen to two and a half hours of uninterrupted conversation, particularly if it is continuously witty. But Mr. Shaw and Mr. Evans have put every theatregoer under bond to submit to "Man and Superman" this season. For it is vastly entertaining in its anti-romantic attitude toward mating. And Mr. Evans, abetted by an excellent company, is giving it a capital performance.

* * *

Although Mr. Shaw's manner is iconoclastic, he probably means what he says. He is arguing that women are the aggressors in campaigns for marriage, and that the life force, which has a horrible sanitary sound, is more impetuous than romance. As usual, Mr. Shaw is looking behind the tribal customs of civilized people into the universal forces that govern them.

Rather than bore you with a scientific lecture, he has invented a garrulous and shameless person who serves as the quarry in the marriage hunt of the play. The person is John Tanner, a character Mr. Shaw probably invented by looking into the mirror. A frightful intellectual who talks like an inspired textbook, takes the unpopular side of every argument and throws off bright tags of socialism in the most conservative places, Tanner is the man who knows all about the fraud of marriage but finds himself caught fast in the last act. "Go on talking, John," his fiancée smugly advises just as the curtain comes down. For she knows that talk may sound big but she is the victor.

* * *

This jungle chase in fashionable clothing could be stupefying in a perfunctory performance, for after all, the talk does run on and on. But Mr. Evans has staged it as meticulously as if he were preparing a classic—giving the comedy projection, giving the lines a little sculpture to set off the wit and polish the humor. Although the performance is not stylized like

MAN AND SUPERMAN, a comedy in three acts, by George Bernard Shaw. Staged by Maurice Evans and George Schaefer; scenery designed by Frederick Stover; costumes by David Ffolkes; lighted by Mr. Schaefer; revived by Mr. Evans. At the Alvin Theatre.
Roebuck Ramsden................Malcolm Keen
Maid.........................Miriam Stovall
Octavius Robinson..........Chester Stratton
John Tanner...................Maurice Evans
Ann Whitefield.................Frances Rowe
Mrs. Whitefield.............Josephine Brown
Miss Ramsden.................Phoebe MacKay
Violet Robinson.............Carmen Mathews
Henry Straker..................Jack Manning
Hector Malone Jr................Tony Bickley
Hector Malone Sr...........Victor Sutherland

the Gielgud "Importance of Being Earnest," it is gay, dry and sunny and a good deal more radiant than life.

Take Malcolm Keen's Roebuck Ramsden, for instance. Never was there such a choleric, sanctimonious old publican, puffing with respectability. As the triumphant female, Frances Rowe's fresh, cunning, calculating style is enchanting and mischievous simultaneously. Carmen Mathews is delightful as Violet Robinson, who

ensnares her man less audaciously but cleverly enough for the purpose, and there are good performances also by Chester Stratton, Jack Manning and Josephine Brown.

* * *

As the voluble Tanner, who considerably outsmarts himself, Mr. Evans is at his best in a holiday mood. The speeches are long and the phrasing complex, but Mr. Evans keeps them refreshingly intelligible and he does not forget that "Man and Superman" is very funny stuff. To people familiar with Mr. Evans' career, there are shadows of Shakespeare chasing across the performance, particularly in the scenes between Tanner and his chauffeur. Perhaps it is only the architecture of Mr. Evans' performance which makes them seem like a Shakespearean monarch bantering words with a jester. Or perhaps this is the way Shaw conceived them. Whatever the reason, they are thoroughly enjoyable.

Although Mr. Evans has not tried to outshine nature in his production, the settings by Frederick Stover are sufficient, and the bravura costumes by David Ffolkes are splendid. After the tastelessness of most of the work this season, it is a joy to see a witty play scrupulously staged by a man who brings professional standards to the theatre. Mr. Shaw and Mr. Evans have given us the most exhilirating evening in this autumn on Broadway.

1947 O 9

Medea

By BROOKS ATKINSON

If Medea does not entirely understand every aspect of her whirling character, she would do well to consult Judith Anderson. For Miss Anderson understands the character more thoroughly than Medea, Euripides or the scholars, and it would be useless now for anyone else to attempt the part. Using a new text by Robinson Jeffers, she set a landmark in the theatre at the National last evening, where she gave a burning performance in a savage part.

Mr. Jeffers' "free adaptation,"

IN THE PLAY: *"O Jason; how you have pulled me down to this hell of vile thoughts?"*—Judith Anderson to John Gielgud.

as it is called, spares the supernatural bogeymen of the classical Greek drama and gets on briskly with the terrifying story of a woman obsessed with revenge. His verse is modern; his words are sharp and vivid, and his text does not worship gods that are dead.

* * *

Since Miss Anderson is a modern, the Jeffers text suits her perfectly and releases a torrent of acting incomparable for passion and scope. Miss Anderson's Medea is mad with the fury of a woman of rare stature. She is barbaric by inheritance, but she has heroic strength and vibrant perceptions. Animal-like in her physical reactions, she plots the doom of her enemies with the intelligence of a priestess of black magic—at once obscene and inspired. Between those two poles she fills the evening with fire, horror, rage and character. Although Miss Anderson has left some memorable marks on great women in the theatre, Medea has summoned all her powers as an actress. Now everyone realizes that she has been destined for Medea from the start.

The general performance and the production are all of a piece. As the nurse, Florence Reed is giving an eminent performance that conveys the weariness and apprehensions of a devoted servant who does not quarrel with fate. John Gielgud's Jason is a lucid,

MEDEA, freely adapted in two acts by Robinson Jeffers from the play by Euripides. Staged by John Gielgud; settings by Ben Edwards; costumes by Castillo; lighting by Peggy Clark; original music and scoring by Tibor Serly; revived by Robert Whitehead and Oliver Rea. At the National Theatre.

Nurse ....Florence Reed
Tutor ....Don McHenry
Children ....Gene Lee, Peter Moss
First Woman of Corinth..........Grace Mills
Second Woman of Corinth.......Kathryn Grill
Third Woman of Corinth........Leone Wilson
Medea ....Judith Anderson
Creon ....Albert Hecht
Jason ....John Gielgud
Aegeus ....Hugh Franklin
Jason's Slave.................Richard Hylton
Attendants to Medea,
          Martha Downes, Marian Seldes
Soldiers.....Ben Morse, Jon Dawson, Richard
          Boone, Dennis McCarthy

solemn egotist well expressed in terms of the theatre. As Creon, Albert Hecht has the commanding voice and the imperiousness of a working monarch. The chorus of women, which has been refreshingly arranged in Mr. Gielgud's unhackneyed · direction, is well acted by Grace Mills, Kathryn Grill and Leone Wilson. The parts of the two young sons are disarmingly represented in the guileless acting of Gene Lee and Peter Moss. Hugh Franklin as Aegeus and Don McHenry as the Tutor give agreeable performances, innocent of the stuffiness peculiar to most classical productions.

* * *

Ben Edwards' setting of the doorway to a Greek house is no more than pedestrian designing, although Peggy Clark has lighted it dramatically, and Castillo has dressed the characters well. Your correspondent could do very well without the conventional theatrical effects—the lightning and the surf especially, for, unlike the acting, they derive from the old-fashioned theatre of rant and ham.

Out of respect for Miss Anderson's magnificent acting in this incarnadined drama, they ought to be locked up in the lumber room. For she has freed Medea from all the old traditions as if the character had just been created. Perhaps that is exactly what has happened. Perhaps Medea was never fully created until Miss Anderson breathed immortal fire into it last evening.

1947 O 21

THE WINSLOW BOY, a play in two acts and four scenes, by Terence Rattigan. Staged by Glen Byam Shaw; decor by Michael Weight; produced by Atlantis Productions (Theatre Guild, H. M. Tennent Ltd., John C. Wilson). At the Empire Theatre.

Ronnie Wislow.................Michael Newell
Violet........................Betty Sinclair
Grace Winslow.................Madge Compton
Arthur Winslow................Alan Webb
Catherine Winslow.............Valerie White
Dickie Winslow................Owen Holder
John Watherstone..............Michael Kingsley
Desmond Curry.................George Benson
Miss Barnes...................Dorothy Hamilton
Fred..........................Leonard Michell
Sir Robert Morton,............Frank Allenby

By BROOKS ATKINSON

Terrence Rattigan's "The Winslow Boy" put on at the Empire last evening, is such a good play that one naturally wishes it could have been perfect. On the theme of a callous injustice done to a small boy, Mr. Rattigan has written a stunning first act. Glen Byam Shaw, as director, has taken the pains to see that it is stunningly acted by a talented English company. In the second act the company maintains at a high level the sort of expert acting a good English company can provide when the parts are imaginatively cast and the details of the performance are immaculately finished.

But the second act of "The Winslow Boy" fritters away the genuine emotion of the theme with some shabby theatrical devices. Since the injustice done "The Winslow Boy" by an omnipotent bureaucracy has a general moral value for today, it would be a blessing if Mr. Rattigan could finish it on its highest level. What we are getting is an admirably acted theatre piece with some deeply-moving situations.

At the age of 13 Ronnie Winslow has been sacked from a naval school for stealing money. He professes to be innocent. Although his father is a severe man, he loves and believes his son and starts legal proceedings to have his son's innocence publicly established. He is dealing, not with a private institution, but with the Government, which has a wide latitude of immunity against legal actions by individual citizens. The case of the Winslow boy becomes, first, an obsession with his father, second, a matter of debate in Parliament and, finally, a national issue involving the rights of private citizens against official despotism. Although Mr. Rattigan is no rabble-rouser, he is fully aware of the implications of his theme.

* * *

In terms of family portraiture he is a skillful and affecting writer. He knows how to contrast a frightened boy's bewilderment against the settled convictions of an English home. Since the character of the father is admirably drawn in terms of probity and compassion, these early scenes inside the Winslow home are heartbreaking in their simplicity and directness. Mr. Rattigan cheapens it a trifle with the studied flamboyance of an impromptu cross-examination by a bombastic jurist. And in the second act he gives you the standard retribution scenes as though he had been studying Pinero. This would not matter if the first act of "The Winslow Boy" did not have so much sweep and character. For it is disillusioning to discover that Mr. Rattigan is only a practicing playwright when the occasion calls for an artist.

* * *

But there will be no belittling of the performance in these columns. Meticulously directed with a fine sense of the theatre, it is superb. As the father, Alan Webb is giving a magnificent performance of severity and kindliness by turns, and in excellent taste withal. Valerie White is playing the part of a serious-minded daughter with a sincerity that puts roots down deeper as the evening progresses. As the eminent jurist, Frank Allenby plays a stuffed-shirt with the theatrical flourishes Mr. Rattigan has written into the part; and let's not pretend that they are not generally effective. Michael Newell plays the Winslow lad with a shrill-voice and a boyish pride that is altogether winning. George Benson acts a fussy little lawyer with decent humility. Madge Compton, Betty Sinclair, Owen Holder and Michael Kingsley agreeably round out the Winslow family and its appurtenances.

In its best scenes "The Winslow Boy" is a harrowing statement of a human situation, and some of the finest work of the season. But the triumph of the Winslow cause comes straight out of the journeyman theatre. Mr. Rattigan's hackneyed technique very nearly conquers his convictions in his anticlimactic conclusion.

1947 O 30

ANTONY AND CLEOPATRA, a revival of the Shakespearian play in two acts. Staged by Guthrie McClintic; settings by Leo Kerz; women's costumes by Valentina and men's by John Boyt; music by Paul Nordoff; presented by Katharine Cornell. At the Martin Beck Theatre.

Philo ....Alan Shayne
Demetrius ....Theodore Marcuse
Antony ....Godfrey Tearle
Cleopatra..................Katharine Cornell
A Messenger................David J. Stewart
Dolabella ....Robert Duke
Proculeius ....Charlton Heston
Iras ....Maureen Stapleton
Charmian ....Lenore Ulric
Alexas ....Oliver Cliff
Diomedes ....Eli Wallach
Enobarbus ....Kent Smith
Mardian ....Joseph Wiseman
Octavius Caesar.............Ralph Clanton
Lepidus ....Ivan Simpson
Agrippa ....David Orrick
Pompey ....Joseph Holland
Menas ....Martin Kingsley
Varrius ....Barnet Biro
Ventidius ....Bruce Gordon
Octavia ....Betty Low
Canidius ....Dayton Lummis
Eros ....Douglass Watson
Silius ....Charles Nolte
Thyreus ....Robert Carricart
Taurus ....Gilbert Reade
Gallus ....Rudulph Watson
An Old Soldier..............Bruce Gordon
Scarus ....Anthony Randall
Euphronius ....Ernest Rowan
Dercetas ....Martin Kingsley
A Clown......................Oliver Cliff
Slaves, Guards, Servants, Soldiers: John Russo, Peter Barno, Drummond Erskine, Milfred Hull, Orrin Redfield, Charles Holt, James Grudier, Lawrence Perron.

By BROOKS ATKINSON

In honor of Shakespeare's "Antony and Cleopatra," Katharine Cornell and her husband have staged a beautiful and respectful production, which was put on at the Martin Beck last evening. The tragedy is a difficult one with a broken story line, and few actresses have been happy in it. But believing that what is worth doing is worth doing well, Miss Cornell and Mr. McClintic have rounded up a good cast, mounted a gorgeous production and packed almost three hours with a painfully faithful transcript of Shakespeare's story.

* * *

Out of respect for the quality of their work, it is unpleasant to report that this "Antony and Cleopatra" is on the formal side and not without pedantry. Miss Cornell, our queen of tragedy, rises nobly to the tragic situations. When Antony is lost and her world has been shattered, she presides over the drama with radiant majesty. In fact, her grandest scene is the last when, attired in her reigning roles, she dies royally on the throne and outshines those who are still among the living. To one of the most memorable scenes Shakespeare ever wrote she brings the style, authority and incandescence that become her best.

But apart from being a queen, Cleopatra is also the world's most celebrated coquette—sensual as well as capricious. As a poet Shakespeare admires her, but as a man he knows she is a royal slut. The qualities of character we esteem in Miss Cornell are not those of "the Egyptian dish" that has drugged Mark Antony's will to action. That is the basic weakness of this beautifully caparisoned performance. Miss Cornell's Cleopatra is formal, good-mannered, a little fastidious. This is what well-bred people would like to think a Shakespeare tragedy is. It is pictorial, but drafty.

* * *

As Antony, Godfrey Tearle has style and force, and ably portrays the whole varying sequence of one of the great tragic parts. Tick him off a little for being no great lover in a part steeped in amour, but credit him bountifully for his intelligence and understanding.

As the witty and skeptical Enobarbus, Kent Smith gives the most successful performance of the evening. He is lucid in his reading of verse. His performance is flowing, accomplished, clearly outlined and perceptive. Lenore Ulric's Charmian is unresolved as a character and undistinguished as acting; and Ralph Clanton's Octavius Caesar is hardly more than bluster. In the affectionate part of Eros, Douglass Watson has at least one excellent scene. There are good performances in other parts in a long cast of actors.

No one will quickly forget the visual beauty of this rich production. Valentina's costumes, especially those for Miss Cornell, are vivid and overwhelming, though they also are too well-bred for Shakespeare's unscrupulous courtesan; and John Boyt's costumes for the men are also beautifully designed. Leo Kerz's settings give the production spaciousness and grandeur.

But perhaps these costly adornments are more impediment than assistance. They help to make "Antony and Cleopatra" a stately ritual which is admirable but detached and scholarly. There is more good taste than Shakespeare in this stage version of an amour that wrecked an empire. To Shakespeare, Cleopatra was passionate and dangerous, and her affair with Antony was an expensive debauch. Miss Cornell's wickedness is not very sinful.

1947 N 27

A STREETCAR NAMED DESIRE. a play in three acts, by Tennessee Williams. Staged by Elia Kazan; scenery and lighting by Jo Mielziner; costumes by Lucinda Ballard; produced by Irene M. Selznick. At the Barrymore Theatre.

Negro Woman....................Gee Gee James
Eunice Hubbel.......................Peg Hillias
Stanley Kowalski.................Marlon Brando
Harold Mitchell (Mitch)..........Karl Malden
Stella Kowalski.......................Kim Hunter
Steve Hubbel.......................Rudy Bond
Blanche du Bois.................Jessica Tandy
Pablo Gonzales.....................Nick Dennis
A Young Collector.................Vito Christi
Mexican Woman.................Edna Thomas
A Strange Woman...................Ann Dere
A Strange Man.....................Richard Garrick

By BROOKS ATKINSON

Tennessee Williams has brought us a superb drama, "A Streetcar Named Desire," which was acted at the Ethel Barrymore last evening. And Jessica Tandy gives a superb performance as rueful heroine whose misery Mr. Williams is tenderly recording. This must be one of the most perfect marriages of acting and playwriting. For the acting and playwriting are perfectly blended in a limpid performance, and it is impossible to tell where Miss Tandy begins to give form and warmth to the mood Mr. Williams has created.

Like "The Glass Menagerie," the new play is a quietly woven study of intangibles. But to this observer it shows deeper insight and represents a great step forward toward clarity. And it reveals Mr. Williams as a genuinely poetic playwright whose knowledge of people is honest and thorough and whose sympathy is profoundly human.

* * *

"A Streetcar Named Desire" is history of a gently reared Mississippi young woman who invents an artificial world to mask the hideousness of the world she has to inhabit. She comes to live with her sister, who is married to a rough-and-ready mechanic and inhabits two dreary rooms in a squalid neighborhood. Blanche—for that is her name—has delusions of grandeur, talks like an intellectual snob, buoys herself up with gaudy dreams, spends most of her time primping, covers things that are dingy with things that are bright and flees reality.

To her brother-in-law she is an unforgiveable liar. But it is soon apparent to the theatregoer that in Mr. Williams' eyes she is one of the dispossessed whose experience has unfitted her for reality; and although his attitude toward her is merciful, he does not spare her or the playgoer. For the events of "Streetcar" lead to a painful conclusion which he does not try to avoid. Although Blanche cannot face the truth, Mr. Williams does in the most imaginative and perceptive play he has written.

* * *

Since he is no literal dramatist and writes in none of the conventional forms, he presents the theatre with many problems. Under Elia Kazan's sensitive but concrete direction, the theatre has solved them admirably. Jo Mielziner has provided a beautifully lighted single setting that lightly sketches the house and the neighborhood. In this shadowy environment the performance is a work of great beauty.

Miss Tandy has a remarkably long part to play. She is hardly ever off the stage, and when she is on stage she is almost constantly talking — chattering, dreaming aloud, wondering, building enchantments out of words. Miss Tandy is a trim, agile actress with a lovely voice and quick intelligence. Her performance is almost incredibly true. For it does seem almost incredible that she could understand such an elusive part so thoroughly and that she can convey it with so many shades and impulses that are accurate, revealing and true.

* * *

The rest of the acting is also of very high quality indeed. Marlon Brando as the quick-tempered, scornful, violent mechanic; Karl Malden as a stupid but wondering suitor; Kim Hunter as the patient though troubled sister—all act not only with color and style but with insight.

By the usual Broadway standards, "A Streetcar Named Desire"

is too long; not all those words are essential. But Mr. Williams is entitled to his own independence. For he has not forgotten that human beings are the basic subject of art. Out of poetic imagination and ordinary compassion he has spun a poignant and luminous story.

1947 D 4

1948

LOOK, MA, I'M DANCIN'!, a musical conceived by Jerome Robbins. Music and lyrics by Hugh Martin; book by Jerome Lawrence and Robert E. Lee; scenery by Oliver Smith; costumes by John Pratt; musical director, Pembroke Davenport; orchestrations by Don Walker; ballet arrangements by Trudy Rittman; direction and choreography by George Abbott and Mr. Robbins; produced by Mr. Abbott. At the Adelphi Theatre. Company: Nancy Walker, Harold Lang, Janet Reed, Alice Pearce, Loren Welch, Virginia Gorski, Don Liberto, Tommy Rall, Katharine Sergava, Robert H. Harris, Alexander March, Sandra Deel, James Lane, Eddie Hodge, Raul Celada, Dean Campbell and Dan Sattler.

By BROOKS ATKINSON

For the sake of humor they have turned the folklore of the ballet into a good knockabout musical comedy, "Look, Ma, I'm Dancin'!", put on at the Adelphi last evening. Reversing the usual sex arrangement, Jerome Robbins has "conceived" it, as the program explains, and George Abbott, the carnival maestro, has staged it with the authority of the old-school style in song entertainment.

Having nothing very serious on its mind, the book offers Nancy Walker as the stage-struck backer of a ballet troupe, and this is a fine dispensation. For Miss Walker, short and pugnacious, is the most versatile young clown in the business, and thoroughly professional.

* * *

Unlike most of her colleagues of the same age, she is an actress She can move with the timing of a vaudevillian. Pushed around by the book as well as the other performers, Miss Walker is she who gets slapped. This is a very comical business, for she is constantly skipping nimbly through the book, and burlesquing vaudeville clichés when the book has nothing with which to help her.

The book is the work of Jerome Lawrence and Robert E. Lee. Taking a group of young ballet dancers, it tours them around the country and carries them amiably through the romantic crises of the business. Hugh Martin has written some cheerful music to serenade them and the most ingenious lyrics of the season.

* * *

Some people in a state that shall be nameless are not going to like "I'm Tired of Texas." But everybody ought to like "I'm Not So Bright," which Loren Welch sings beautifully, and "The Little Boy Blues," which Virginia Gorski and Don Liberto translate into a nice show-shop enchantment. Although Mr. Martin is a modish tunesmith, he is friendly enough to write one song in simple rhythm, "Shauny O'Shay," which is a jaunty bit of fooling.

Although ballet is the subject, "Look, Ma, I'm Dancin'!" comes gratifyingly close to the old musical show formula with rhapsodic dancing in familiar idioms and ballets that are either festive or comic. The show begins with a high-stepping frolic and includes one episode of wonderful sky-larking in a Pullman car.

Alice Pearce, a chinless sprite with a humming-bird mind, tosses in some refreshing lunacies. As an ambitious ballet composer, Harold Lang is light on his feet and skillful with the innocuous plot lines, and Janet Reed is equally pleasant as his partner.

* * *

Having conspicuous talent for organizing troupes of young people, Mr. Abbott has assembled a particularly beguiling group of actors and dancers; and with Mr. Robbins' assistance he has brought them on and off the stage with pace, imagination and informal high spirits. Oliver Smith has provided some of his most useful and attractive settings on train platforms, streets and rehearsal halls. John Pratt has dressed the company in costumes that agreeably suit a lively occasion.

With original material, engaging actors and expert staging, "Look, Ma, I'm Dancin'!" brings us a top-drawer Broadway show. As an incompetent ballet aspirant with flat feet and a lantern-jawed map, Miss Walker is hilarious and the best slap-stick comedian of her generation.

1948 Ja 30

MISTER ROBERTS, a play in two acts, by Thomas Heggen and Joshua Logan, based on Mr. Heggen's novel of the same name. Staged by Joshua Logan; scenery and lighting by Jo Mielziner; produced by Leland Hayward. At the Alvin Theatre.

Chief Johnson	Rusty Lane
Lieutenant (jg) Roberts	Henry Fonda
Doc	Robert Keith
Dowdy	Joe Marr
The Captain	William Harrigan
Insigna	Harvey Lembeck
Mannion	Ralph Meeker
Lindstrom	Karl Lukas
Stefanowski	Steven Hill
Wiley	Robert Baines
Schlemmer	Lee Krieger
Reber	John Campbell
Ensign Pulver	David Wayne
Dolan	Casey Walters
Gerhart	Fred Barton
Payne	James Sherwood
Lieutenant Ann Girard	Jocelyn Brando
Shore Patrolman	John Jordan
Military Policeman	Marshall Jamison
Shore Patrol Officer	Murray Hamilton

Seamen, Firemen and Others—
Tiger Andrews, Joe Bernard, Ellis Eringer, Mikel Kane, Bob Keith Jr., Walter Mullen John (Red) Kullers, Jack Pierce, Len Smith Jr., Sanders (Sandy) Turner.

By BROOKS ATKINSON

By rounding up a crew of American ruffians, Thomas Heggen and Joshua Logan have written the ideal romantic play about the war. They call it "Mister Roberts." With Henry Fonda giving a winning performance, it was wonderfully well acted at the Alvin last evening. Literate people report that the resemblance to Mr. Heggen's novel of the same title is not too exacting. On the stage in the midst of some of Jo Mielziner's sea-going scenery, "Mister Roberts" is a gusty, ribald and sentimental yarn about some brawling seamen in an American rust-bucket on the Pacific.

* * *

Although it is a war play, it is ingeniously irrelevant. For this is the blistering saga of the men on a cargo vessel who have never heard a shot fired in anger. Lieutenant Roberts, junior grade and executive officer of AK 601, is eating out his heart for a combat assignment. But his commander s a hard-bitten sea-bully who ates college men like Roberts, drives his crew in the hope of getting a promotion and spreads misery and hatred throughout the ship. What plot the play has concerns a generous sacrifice, Roberts makes to get shore liberty for his men, a misunderstanding that injustly divides him from them and a hilarious event that puts the whole ship wonderfully at ease again.

* * *

Since there is a script, it is accurate to say that "Mister Roberts" has been written. But the parts have been cast with so much relish and the direction is so spontaneous that it gives the impression of having been written on the stage during rehearsals. After a war is safely over, men can afford to recollect it joyously. The romance of "Mister Roberts" consists in recalling it in terms of comradeship, and the humor consists in giving it comic distortions so that it is outsize and overwhelming. The lines are hilarious. The humor has the irony and self-disparaging twist of Yankee jargon; it has also the habit of putting sneering and generalizing labels on ordinary things. All the men who respond to sick call, for example, are the doctors' "hypochondriacs." Dipping back into some leisurely memories, the authors have come up with an uproarious play.

* * *

Now that Mr. Fonda is back after eleven years, it would be nice to have him back for good. He has brought quite a lot of good with him this time. As Roberts he is lanky and unheroic, relaxed and genuine; he neatly skirts the maudlin when the play grows sentimental, and he skillfully underplays the bombastic scenes. As a whacky shipmate with big ideas but small accomplishments, David Wayne, the late leprechaun, also gives a darlin' performance. Robert Keith's cynically loyal doctor and man of the world is acted with sardonic perfection, and William Harrigan's tyrannical, crude master has authentic character.

For a few delirious moments the men of the AK 601 see an American girl. She is brightly played by Jocelyn Brando. But the chief pleasures of the play are the rag-tag crew of self-respecting ruffians acted by some of the brawniest members of Actors Equity.

Under Mr. Logan's idiomatic direction, the performance rolls through a thundering evening of tough humors—well-paced, well-timed and picturesque. Thanks, Mr. Heggen and Mr. Logan, for "Mister Roberts" and a royal good time. **1948 F 19**

SUMMER AND SMOKE, a play in a prologue and two acts, by Tennessee Williams, with original music and scoring by Paul Bowles. Staged and produced by Margo Jones; scenery and lighting by Jo Mielziner; costumes by Rose Bogdanoff. At the Music Box.

Alma as a Child	Arlene McQuade
John as a Child	Donald Hastings
Rev. Winemiller	Raymond Van Sickle
Mrs. Winemiller	Marga Ann Deighton
John Buchanan Jr.	Tod Andrews
A Girl	Hildy Parks
Dusty	William Layton
Dr. Buchanan	Ralph Theadore
Alma Winemiller	Margaret Phillips
Rosa Gonzales	Monica Boyar
Nellie Ewell	Ann Jackson
Roger Doremus	Earl Montgomery
Mrs. Bassett	Betty Greene Little
Vernon	Spencer James
Rosemary	Ellen James
Papa Gonzales	Sid Cassel
Mr. Kramer	Ray Walston

By BROOKS ATKINSON

Although Tennessee Williams writes a gentle style, he has a piercing eye. In "Summer and Smoke," which was put on at the Music Box last evening, he looks again into the dark corners of the human heart, and what he sees is terrifying. This is a tone poem in the genre of "The Glass Menagerie" and "A Streetcar Named Desire"—the same mystic frustration and the same languid doom. So far Mr. Williams has been writing variations on the same theme.

But again the insight into character is almost unbearably lucid. Although it derives from compassion, it is cruel in its insistence on the truth. Mr. Williams is full of scorn for the rootless people he pities. He will not raise a finger to spare them from misery. And "Summer and Smoke" has one further distinction: a memorable performance by Margaret Phillips and Tod Andrews in the central parts. Out of Mr. Williams' quiet, evocative style they have drawn immense sympathy and wonder, binding the fragments of the play into a single strand of somber, tragic emotion.

* * *

As a poet Mr. Williams is less concerned with events than with adventures of the spirit. Nothing much happens in "Summer and Smoke" except that the minister's daughter loves the physician's son next door and can never break through a shadowy wall that separates them. All her life she reaches out after him, but he pulls away. She is respectable, religious, pure-minded and idealistic. He is wild and dissipated and believes as thoroughly in gratifying the flesh as she does in worshiping the

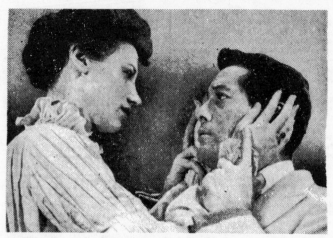

"But now I've changed my mind, or the girl who said 'no' she doesn't exist any more, she died last summer—suffocated in smoke from something on fire inside her." Margaret Phillips encourages Tod Andrews.

spirit. Halfway through the play his dissipations result in a disaster that shocks him, and now he realizes that she has always been right. He, too, now believes in the reality of the spirit. But again they pass each other. Fate stands inexplicably between them.

Like its predecessors, the play is slight in content. Mr. Williams writes brief scenes, generally for a few characters. But he is a writer of superb grace and allusiveness, always catching the shape and sound of ideas rather than their literal meaning. As its title suggests, "Summer and Smoke" deals in truths that are unsubstantial. But as Mr. Williams sees it, these are the truths that are most profound and the most painful, for they separate people who logically should be together and give life its savage whims and its wanton destructiveness. Although he is dealing in impulses that cannot be literally defined, the twin themes of his tone poem are clearly stated: spirit and flesh, order and anarchy. He has caught them in the troubled brooding of two human hearts.

If he is a poet, he is a poet of the theatre. "Summer and Smoke" is no literary exercise but a theatre

piece charged with passion and anguish. Margo Jones, who directed the original performance in Dallas, has brought it to the stage with infinite respect for its delicate qualities. On a large stage it loses some of the moving intimacy that it had in the cramped quarters of the Dallas theatre. But Jo Mielziner, who must be a genius after all, has designed a glorious setting of lightly penciled lines and curves as airy as the writing. And Paul Bowles has composed a modestly stated descriptive score. Rose Bogdanoff has designed a wardrobe of lovely, idealized costumes.

The acting is light in style and appreciative in moods that appear to be orchestrated. Raymond Van Sickle as a fussy pastor, Betty Greene Little as a cheerful gossip, Anne Jackson as an exuberant girl of the neighborhood, Monica Boyar as a tempestuous Mexican slut, Marga Ann Deighton as a demented old woman, Ralph Theadore as a responsible elderly physician give warm and neatly defined performances.

But "Summer and Smoke" rises or falls on the quality of the acting in the two chief parts; Miss Phillips and Mr. Andrews lift it to the level of a vibrant work of art. Mr. Andrews is a handsome, masculine young actor who can draw a fine line between bravado and gentle-manliness, and his portrait of the physician's son is both sensitive and sturdy. As the rueful, slightly hysterical spinster, Miss Phillips has presented the stage with a masterpiece. Behind the desperation and silliness of the character she manages to establish the pride of a woman who is essentially noble. Mr. Williams and his two principal actors have performed the miracle of translating a drab corner of life into something that is tremulous with beauty.

1948 O 7

LIGHT UP THE SKY, a comedy by Moss Hart. Staged by the author; scenery by Frederic Fox; costumes by Kiviette; produced by Joseph M. Hyman and Bernard Hart. At the Royale Theatre.

Miss Lowell	Jane Middleton
Carleton Fitzgerald	Glenn Anders
Frances Black	Audrey Christie
Owen Turner	Philip Ober
Stella Livingston	Phyllis Povah
Peter Sloan	Barry Nelson
Sidney Black	Sam Levene
Sven	Si Oakland
Irene Livingston	Virginia Field
Tyler Rayburn	Bartlett Robinson
A Shriner	John D. Seymour
William H. Gallagher	Donald McClelland
A Plainclothes Man	Ronald Alexander

By BROOKS ATKINSON

After eighteen years Moss Hart still has a good deal of "Once in a Lifetime" left in his system. In "Light Up the Sky," which opened at the Royale last evening, he has diverted it from Hollywood to Broadway in a loud, broad, tempestuous comedy that is acted at top speed by a wonderful cast. Originally it was intended as a Shavian comedy with serious overtones about the human frailties of human beings.

In the last act of the finished version there is a brief scene of introspection that is serious and, incidentally, the best job of writing in the play. But it comes toward the end of a whirlwind lampoon which is funnier than anything the dramatic stage has spawned this season. Although Mr. Hart obviously loves show-business, he has whacked it a whole series of blows with his old slap-stick and the jokes bound off the rafters in an evening of honest, merchantable laughter.

As a salute to show business Mr. Hart quotes in the program a line from "The Idle Jeste," which is unknown to this department: "Mad, sire? Ah, yes—mad indeed, but observe how they do light up the sky." They are an assembly of Broadway theatrical people running in and out of a hotel room on the occasion of an opening performance in Boston. They include a florid director, a vain leading lady, a racy-tongued producer, a handful of spiteful-minded hangers-on and an innocent, pure-hearted young author.

Before the play opens they are overflowing with flamboyant love and devotion, certain that they are about to make history in the theatre. After the first performance, they turn on each other in a furious battle of malicious invective, ashamed to be associated with a flop. But as usual the Boston 'critics' judgment is better than theirs. After the notices have appeared, they fall on each others' necks with devotion again; and after the most shattering disillusionment of his life, the young author gets down to serious work in preparation for the New York opening.

An old hand at noisy cartooning, Mr. Hart has drawn this one in a racy style of broad satire with torrents of temperament, purple patches in the dialogue and wry, malicious strokes on the wing. There are three doors in the gaily ornate setting Frederic Fox has designed, and they are never closed without a farcical bang. Knowing his characters from long years of nerve-racking drudgery on the road, Mr. Hart has caught their wildness with uproarious precision. "Light Up the Sky" works, which is the hallmark of the knockabout comedy.

But Mr. Hart's malice is professional. He respects the devotion and enthusiasm his crack-brained characters have for the theatre. In a skillfully-written interlude in the last scene he appeals to their capacity for forgiveness and common enterprise. That is the only sober scene in the whole rumpus, and it is also the best and a token of the maturity he did not have when he wrote half of "Once In a Lifetime."

Under Mr. Hart's excitable direction the performance races around the stage like a volcanic circus, everybody shouting, everybody making exits and entrances and slamming doors. The cast is superb — Audrey Christie, Sam Levene and Phyllis Povah giving particularly gusty performances. As the producer's wife, Miss

Christie is a virtuoso in sharp-tongued vulgarity. Erupting gaudy phrases like a Roman candle, Mr. Levene gives a powerful, versatile and richly comic performance. And Miss Povah's cheap, hot-tempered, babbling acting is very droll and plausible, indeed.

Runners in a comic steeplechase, all the actors are on their toes and heartily enjoyable—Glenn Anders as the supercilious director, Philip Ober as a sardonic veteran playwright, Virginia Field as an egotistical leading lady, Jane Middleton as an astonished typist new to the theatre, and Bartlett Robinson as a startled Harvard man. In the part of the innocent young author, Barry Nelson is excellent. From laconic shyness he develops into an articulate tower of strength toward the end.

The tempo is swift. The tone is boisterous. The costumes are opulent enough for professional showmanship. Again the theatre has provided Mr. Hart with the materials for a good theatre piece. This may be literary cannibalism, but it is also vastly entertaining, and it helps a lot to light up the Broadway sky.

1948 N 19

LEND AN EAR, a revue. Sketches, lyrics and music by Charles Gaynor; choreography by Gower Champion; directed by Hal Gerson; costumes, settings and lighting by Raoul Pene DuBois; musical director George Bauer; orchestration by Clare Grundman; additional sketches by Joseph Stein and Will Glickman; production staged by Gower Champion; produced by William R. Katzell, Franklin Gilbert and William Eythe. At the National Theatre.
Company: Yvonne Adair, Anne Renee Anderson, Dorothy Babbs, Carol Channing, Al Checco, Robert Dixon, William Eythe, Nancy Franklin, Antoinette Guhlke, George Hall, Gloria Hamilton, Bob Herget, Beverly Hosier, Jenny Lou Law, Arthur Maxwell, Tommy Morton, Gene Nelson, Bob Scheerer, Jeanine Smith, Lee Stacy, Larry Stewart.

By BROOKS ATKINSON

After a try-out period of about seven years "Lend an Ear" has finally come to New York where it took up residence at the National last evening. This seems to be an admirable way of getting ready for a Christmas opening. For Charles Gaynor's intimate musical revue is a model of skill and taste in this style of fooling, and it is performed by some fresh-grown youngsters whose talents have not been corrupted yet.

If "unsophisticated" is not a term of reproach, it may help to describe the direct approach of Mr. Gaynor's frolic. He is lightly satirizing some of the more palatable follies of the day, and he is so neat in his touch that he does not have to be clever. From first to last this is the most enjoyable bantam revue that has dissipated the normal boredom of Broadway for quite a long time.

Mr. Gaynor has written the sketches, lyrics and music, stopping just short of playing two pianos and acting the principal roles. As a composer he is not unbearably original. At various times you may think you can detect the styles of Kern, Rodgers and Porter. If so, they are good models. For "Lend an Ear" is full of good melodies and honest laments sung beautifully by several attractive and talented young people, and wonderfully well suited to a midwinter night's entertainment.

Although most of the numbers are bright, the distinction of "Lend an Ear" is the skill with which Mr. Gaynor and his associates can translate songs into musical sketches. Take, for example, "Friday Dancing Class," which preserves the genteel torture of going to dancing school. Beginning humorously, it acquires a kind of authentic poignancy before Bob Scheerer and Dorothy Babbs have finished their waltz and the chorus has finished its harmonic commentary. Or take "Santo Domingo," which begins as a conventional West Indian tune and broadens out into a hilarious satire on the acrimonious squalor of a modern island village. This is a vastly enjoyable caricature of stereotyped romance.

* * *

The final items in both acts are likely to be the most popular contributions "Lend an Ear" will make to the random uproariousness of the winter. At the end of the first act Mr. Gaynor offers a very funny burlesque of old-time musical comedy—"The Gladiola Girl," in which William Eythe skillfully cartoons a toothsome leading man, and Yvonne Adair, who is an uncommonly versatile performer, pops quite a few people in the aisles with her hot

"*Sharing abnormality for two.*"—William Eythe to Anne Renee Anderson in a sketch from "Lend an Ear."

dancing. At the end of the show Mr. Gaynor introduces a hackneyed opera without any music, which is a fine way of accenting the artifice of operatic acting. Carol Channing as a voluminous inamorata, and George Hall as a messy and irritable swain of purely formal passion are the good genii of this last mockery of the evening.

* * *

If there were time this column ought to report Mr. Gaynor's sketch about a modern couple's difficulties in obeying literally the admonitions of newspaper columnists, and his study of the public response to certain types of motion pictures—including a valuable parody of the English accent.

But there is time enough now to report that the cast as a whole has taste and talent equal to Mr. Gaynor's. Arthur Maxwell, Gloria Hamilton, Anne Renée Anderson and Gene Nelson are worth their weight in ticket stubs as singers, clowns and dancers. Entering enthusiastically into the spirit of the occasion, Raoul Pène DuBois has designed a simple and charming production, and a wardrobe of pleasant costumes. In fact everybody has very amiably conspired to make "Lend an Ear" an ideal band-box revue. Although it is thoroughly professional, it has not lost the genuine light-heartedness of an amateur carnival.

1948 D 17

The Cast

THE MADWOMAN OF CHAILLOT, a comedy in two acts, by Jean Giraudoux, as adapted from the French by Maurice Valency; Staged and produced by Alfred de Liagre Jr.; scenery and costumes designed by Christian Berard; music for Mazurka composed by Albert Hague and for "La Belle Polonaise" by Alexander Haas; lighting by Samuel Leve. At the Belasco Theatre.

The Waiter	Ralph Smiley
The Prospector	Vladimir Sokoloff
The President	Clarence Derwent
The Baron	Le Roi Operti
The Ragpicker	John Carradine
The Deaf Mute	Martin Kosleck
Irma	Leora Dana
The Broker	Jonathan Harris
The Street Juggler	John Behan
Dr. Jadin	Sandra Giglio
Countess Aurelia	Martita Hunt
The Doorman	William Chambers
The Policeman	Ralph Roberts
Pierre	Alan Shayne
The Sergeant	Richard Sanders
The Sewer-Man	James Westerfield
Mme Constance	Estelle Winwood
Mlle Gabrielle	Nydia Westman
Mme Josephine	Doris Rich

By BROOKS ATKINSON

Let's admit in the first place that Jean Giraudoux's "The Madwoman of Chaillot" is too long for the slight fable it has to tell. After a rapturously humorous and poetic first act, the second act grows increasingly languid, and obviously that is a fault in playmaking. But a sluggish last act is a small price to pay for the wit and whimsical loveliness of a wise fantasy by a man who had dreamed of an impossibly noble life and who criticized it with grace and compassion like a thoroughly civilized writer.

M. Giraudoux is dead, but the luster of a fine mind still shines in this original fantasy, which has been admirably adapted by Maurice Valency. Alfred de Liagre Jr. deserves a word of thanks for appreciating the quality of Giraudoux's work and for having the courage to install it on Broadway.

As a matter of fact, the madwoman of Chaillot is only a whack. Living happily in memories of a cozy past, she does not realize that the world has changed for the worse until her friends—waiters, ragmen and peddlers—tell her so. "Little by little the pimps have taken over the world," says a philosopher of the ash cans. He refers to the people who are greedy. "Men publicly worship the golden calf," she says in horror. Although the Chaillot woman is obviously a mental case she also knows the only thing that matters, which is that love is the one decent motive for living. With the assistance of Giraudoux's magic-wand, she rids the world of its parasites, and then everyone is happy.

* * *

This is the sort of impish salute to the pure in heart that Saroyan once wrote in "My Heart's in the Highlands." From Giraudoux's mind it comes with equal devotion but with greater sophistication. For he knew that his dream could never come true and that it could be expressed only in a worldly fable with a touch of "Alice in Wonderland" in the writing. An accomplished writer with a free mind, he told it enchantingly—part whimsey, part parable, lighthearted in style but sombre in thought. Someone is not sturdy enough to keep the improvisation running freely all through the evening. But perhaps it is the audience and not the author who is at fault here. For the quality of "The Madwoman of Chaillot" is priceless—pure gold with no base metal.

Having recognized the quality of the literary work, Mr. de Liagre has had the wisdom to import Christian Berard's airy and imaginative scenery and his humorously blousy costumes for the demented old crones who speak the sanest lines in the play. M. Berard's touch is as light and fanciful as Giraudoux's. Samuel Leve has lighted the production with the appreciation of an artist.

Under Mr. de Liagre's direction, the performance is not all of one piece yet, for it needs to be lived in by the actors for another week or two. Since the play is a poem the performance must be a dance. But the individual acting is nearly all superb. And Martita Hunt's kindly and droll portrait of the leading character is rich in a sort of raffish humanity—very imperious in style, very friendly in manner. As the mad woman of Passy, Estelle Winwood is incomparably fantastic and contributes a very notable piece of original acting.

* * *

The cast is a long one, but never dull or perfunctary. Vladimir Sokoloff, as a plunderer of the world on a grand scale, and Clarence Derwent, as a notable charlatan, give vastly enjoyable performances. John Carradine is excellent as a ruminative rag-picker; he has the grace to understand the part and the ability to act it lucidly. There is one especially lyric scene by Leora Dana as a romantic waitress. Sandro Giglio, Nydia Westman, Doris Rich, Le Roi Operti, James Westerfield and others weave interesting figures on the luminous screen of Giraudoux's poetic fable.

Probably "The Madwoman of Chaillot" ought to be rehearsed by a company of well-blended geniuses for a year before the curtain is raised for the public. But our theatre is not organized for such heroic enterprises. What we have is not perfect. But it is original, inspired and high-minded, and also a creative work of art. Now we know how much light went out of the world when Jean Giraudoux died.

1948 D 28

Kiss Me Kate

By BROOKS ATKINSON

Taking an obliging hint from Shakespeare, the makers of "Kiss Me, Kate" have put together a thoroughly enjoyable musical comedy, acted at the New Century last evening. Shakespeare has supplied a few bedraggled scenes from "The Taming of the Shrew." Using these as a springboard into festivity, Bella and Samuel Spewack have contrived an authentic book which is funny without the interpolation of gags.

Cole Porter has written his best score in years, together with witty lyrics. Under Hanya Holm's direction, the dancing is joyous. And Lemuel Ayers has provided carnival costumes and some interesting scenery.

The Cast

KISS ME, KATE, a musical comedy. Music and lyrics by Cole Porter; book by Bella and Samuel Spewack; choreography by Hanya Holm; scenery and costumes by Lemuel Ayers; musical director, Pembroke Davenport; orchestrations by Robert Russell Bennett; incidental ballet music arranged by Genevieve Pitot; production staged by John C. Wilson; produced by Saint Subber and Mr. Ayres. At the New Century Theatre.

Fred Graham	Alfred Drake
Harry Trevor	Thomas Hoier
Lois Lane	Lisa Kirk
Ralph (Stage Manager)	Don Mayo
Lilli Vanessi	Patricia Morison
Hattie	Annabelle Hill
Paul	Lorenzo Fuller
Bill Calhoun	Harold Lang
First Man	Harry Clark
Second Man	Jack Diamond
Stage Doorman	Bill Lilling
Harrison Howell	Denis Green
Specialty Dancers	Fred Davis, Eddie Sledge
Gremio (First Suitor)	Edwin Clay
Hortensio (Second Suitor)	Charles Wood
Haberdasher	John Castello
Tailor	Marc Breaux

Occasionally by some baffling miracle, everything seems to drop gracefully into its appointed place, in the composition of a song show, and that is the case here. No one has had to break his neck to dazzle the audience with his brilliance, and no one has had to run at frantic speed to get across the rough spots. As far as the Spewacks are concerned, "Kiss Me, Kate" is the story of a vainglorious actor and his temperamental ex-wife who are starring in a revival of "The Taming of the Shrew" in Baltimore. Although the Shakespeare circus has had some bad performances, none has been worse than the burlesque Alfred Drake and Patricia Morison have inflicted on it here.

The Italian setting has another practical advantage. It gives Mr. Porter an opportunity to poke beyond Tin Pan Alley into a romantic mood. Without losing his sense of humor, he has written a remarkable melodious score with an occasional suggestion of Puccini, who was a good composer, too. Mr. Porter has always enjoyed the luxury of rowdy tunes, and he has scribbled a few for the current festival—"Another O'p'nin', Another Show," "We Open In Venice," "Too Darn Hot" and "Brush Up Your Shakespeare," which is fresh out of the honky-tonks. All his lyrics are literate, and as usual some of them would shock the editorial staff of The Police Gazette.

But the interesting thing about the new score is the enthusiasm Mr. Porter has for romantic melodies indigenous to the soft climate of the Mediterranean. Although "Wunderbar" is probably a little north of the Mediterranean Sea, the warm breezes flow through it; and "So In Love Am I" has a very florid temperature, indeed.

The plot device concentrates the acting and singing in four people,

"Now you asked for it!" — Alfred Drake administers a spanking a la "The Taming of the Shrew," to Patricia Morison in a scene from "Kiss Me, Kate."

and fortunately they are all uncommonly talented. As a greasepaint hussy, Miss Morison is an agile and humorous actress who is not afraid of slapstick and who can sing enchantingly. She has captured perfectly the improvised tone of the comedy, and she plays it with spirit and drollery. Lisa Kirk plays a subordinate part in a style that might be described as well-bred impudence. Given a sardonic song like "Always True to You (In My Fashion)," she can translate it into pert and gleaming buffoonery.

We have all been long acquainted with Mr. Drake as headman in musical shows. In the part of the egotistical actor who plays Petruchio on stage, Mr. Drake's pleasant style of acting and his unaffected singing are the heart of the show. By hard work and through personal sincerity. Mr. Drake has be-

come about the most valuable man in his field. In the secondary male role, Harold Lang, who is principally a dancer, also gives a versatile and attractive performance.

Under the supervision of John C. Wilson there are other treasures in this humorous phantasmagoria of song — the torrid pavement dancing of Fred Davis and Eddie Sledge, the bland gunman fooling of Harry Clark and Jack Diamond, the antic dancing masquerade that serves as first scene to "The Taming of the Shrew" sequence.

All these items have been gathered up neatly into the flowing pattern of a pleasant musical comedy. To filch a good notion from The New Yorker, all you can say for "Kiss Me, Kate" is that it is terribly enjoyable.

1948 D 31

1949

DIAMOND LIL, a play in three acts, by Mae West. Staged by Charles K. Freeman: scenery by William De Forest and Ben Edwards; costumes by Paul Du Pont; revived by Albert H. Rosen and Herbert J. Freezer. At the Coronet Theatre.

Jim	Billy Van
Bill	Jack Howard
Porter	James Quinn
Ragtime	Dick Arnold
Spike	George Warren
Jerry	Harry Warren
Kitty	Harriet Nelson
Frances	Sheila Trent
Flo	Sylvia Syms
Maggie	Louise Jenkins
Flynn	Charles G. Martin
Kane	Mike Keene
Gus Jordan	Walter Petrie
Sally	Frances Arons
Rita	Miriam Goldina
Juarez	Steve Cochran
Mike	James Fallor
Diamond Lil	Mae West
Charlie	Peter Chan
Bessie	Buddy Millette
Violet	Margaret Magennis
Barbara	Marilyn Lowe
Captain Cummings	Richard Coogan
Pete the Duke	Lester Laurence
Doheney	Ralph Chambers
Jacobson	Louis Nussbaum
Chick Clark	Jeff Morrow
Sailor	Jerry Tobias
Cop	F. Ben Miller
Singer	Michael Edwards
Miss West's Accompanist	David Lapin
Bowery Pianist	Arnold New

By BROOKS ATKINSON

Gallantly supported by four or five handsome, muscular leading men, Mae West has brought "Diamond Lil" back to New York, where it began its renowned career twenty-one years ago. She wriggled through it at the Coronet on Saturday evening, attired in some of the gaudiest finery of the century—the *femme fatale* of the Bowery, bowling her leading men over one by one with her classical burlesque of a story-book strumpet.

When Miss West restored her study of society to America last November, a bus-load of the Broadway night-watch rolled out to Montclair to pay their respects to her artistry. It must be confessed that "Diamond Lil" is a tough play to see twice in one season. Any fairly observant theatregoer can penetrate its subtleties with a single visit. It does not take long to understand what Miss West has in mind.

* * *

But she is a fabulous performer and her saloon singer is an incredible creation—a triumph of nostalgic vulgarity. She is always in motion. The snaky walk, the torso wriggle, the stealthy eyes, the frozen smile, the flat, condescending voice, the queenly gestures— these are studies in slow motion, and they have to be seen to be believed. Lazy, confident of her charms, Diamond Lil does not move fast, but she never stands

Mae West

still; and Miss West paces her performance accordingly.

There is an attitude of sublime fatalism about the whole business. Miss West extends her hand to be kissed with royal assurance. Even in the clinches she is monumentally disinterested, and she concludes her love scenes with a devastating wise-crack before they are started. Although Miss West is the goddess of sex, it might reasonably be argued that she scrupulously keeps sex out of her acting by invariably withdrawing from anything but the briefest encounters. "Diamond Lil" is a play about the world of sex, but there is very little sex in it.

* * *

Like an old dime novel, it is full of crime, drink and iniquity. After beating about the bush for two sluggish acts, it settles down hospitably into an old-fashioned vaudeville show in the last act; and Miss West, billowy and swaying at the piano, sings a few sinful ballads in a small voice but with plenty of style. It is performing in the grand manner.

After thoughtfully studying her performance twice in a little over two months, this reviewer is still puzzled over one thing. Is Miss West serious or is she kidding? Not that it matters. She is obviously a good trouper, which is probably the reason she has been able to hold this ramshackle melodrama together for twenty-one years.

1949 F 7

DEATH OF A SALESMAN a play by Arthur Miller. Staged by Elia Kazan; scenery and lighting by Jo Mielziner; incidental music by Alex North; costumes by Julia Sze; produced by Kermit Bloomgarden and Walter Fried. At the Morosco Theatre.

Willy Loman	Lee J. Cobb
Linda	Mildred Dunnock
Happy	Cameron Mitchell
Biff	Arthur Kennedy
Bernard	Don Keefer
The Woman	Winnifred Cushing
Charley	Howard Smith
Uncle Ben	Thomas Chalmers
Howard Wagner	Alan Hewitt
Jenny	Ann Driscoll
Stanley	Tom Pedi
Miss Forsythe	Constance Ford
Letta	Hope Cameron

By BROOKS ATKINSON

Arthur Miller has written a superb drama. From every point of view "Death of a Salesman," which was acted at the Morosco last evening, is rich and memorable drama. It is so simple in style and so inevitable in theme that it scarcely seems like a thing that has been written and acted. For Mr. Miller has looked with compassion into the hearts of some ordinary Americans and quietly transferred their hope and anguish to the theatre. Under Elia Kazan's masterly direction, Lee J. Cobb gives a heroic performance, and every member of the cast plays like a person inspired.

* * *

Two seasons ago Mr. Miller's "All My Sons" looked like the work of an honest and able playwright. In comparison with the new drama, that seems like a contrived play now. For "Death of a Salesman" has the flow and spontaneity of a suburban epic that may not be intended as poetry but becomes poetry in spite of itself because Mr. Miller has drawn it out of so many intangible sources.

It is the story of an aging salesman who has reached the end of his usefulness on the road. There has always been something unsubstantial about his work. But suddenly the unsubstantial aspects of it overwhelm him completely. When he was young, he looked dashing; he enjoyed the comradeship of other people—the humor, the kidding, the business.

In his early sixties he knows his business as well as he ever did. But the unsubstantial things have become decisive; the spring has gone from his step, the smile from his face and the heartiness from his personality. He is through. The phantom of his life has caught up with him. As literally as Mr. Miller can say it, dust returns to dust. Suddenly there is nothing.

* * *

This is only a little of what Mr. Miller is saying. For he conveys this elusive tragedy in terms of simple things—the loyalty and understanding of his wife, the careless selfishness of his two sons, the sympathetic devotion of a neighbor, the coldness of his former boss' son—the bills, the car, the tinkering around the house. And most of all: the illusions by which he has lived—opportunities missed, wrong formulas for success, fatal misconceptions about his place in the scheme of things.

Writing like a man who understands people, Mr. Miller has no moral precepts to offer and no solutions of the salesman's problems. He is full of pity, but he brings no piety to it. Chronicler of one frowsy corner of the American scene, he evokes a wraithlike tragedy out of it that spins through the many scenes of his play and gradually envelops the audience.

* * *

As theatre "Death of a Salesman" is no less original than it is as literature. Jo Mielziner, always equal to an occasion, has designed a skeletonized set that captures the mood of the play and serves the actors brilliantly. Although Mr. Miller's text may be diffuse in form, Mr. Kazan has pulled it together into a deeply moving performance.

Mr. Cobb's tragic portrait of the defeated salesman is acting of the first rank. Although it is familiar and folksy in the details, it has something of the grand manner in the big size and the deep tone. Mildred Dunnock gives the performance of her career as the wife and mother—plain of speech but indomitable in spirit. The parts of the thoughtless sons are extremely well played by Arthur Kennedy and Cameron Mitchell, who are all youth, brag and bewilderment.

Other parts are well played by Howard Smith, Thomas Chalmers, Don Keefer, Alan Hewitt and Tom Pedi. If there were time, this report would gratefully include all the actors and fabricators of illusion. For they all realize that for once in their lives they are participating in a rare event in the theatre. Mr. Miller's elegy in a Brooklyn sidestreet is superb.

1949 F 11

SOUTH PACIFIC, a musical play. Music by Richard Rodgers; lyrics by Oscar Hammerstein 2d; book by Mr. Hammerstein and Joshua Logan, adapted from James A. Michener's Pulitzer Prize winning novel, "Tales of the South Pacific." Book and musical numbers staged by Mr. Logan; scenery and lighting by Jo Mielziner; costumes by Motley; musical director, Salvatore Dell'Isola; orchestrations by Robert Russell Bennett; produced by the Messrs. Rodgers and Hammerstein in association with Leland Hayward and Mr. Logan. At the Majestic Theatre.

Ensign Nellie Forbush.............Mary Martin
Emile de Becque.....................Ezio Pinza
Bloody Mary......................Juanita Hall
Abner ....Archie Savage
Stewpot ....Henry Slate
Luther Billis..............Myron McCormick
Professor ....Fred Sadoff
Lieut. Joseph Cable, U.S.M.C..William Tabbert
Capt. George Brackett, U.S.N...Martin Wolfson
Cmdr. Wm. Harbison, U.S.N....Harvey Stephens
Radio Oper. Bob McCaffrey.....Biff McGuire
Ensign Dinah Murphy...........Roslyn Lowe
Ensign Janet MacGregor..........Sandra Deel
Liat ....Betta St. John
Lieut. Buzz Adams ....Don Fellows

By BROOKS ATKINSON

No one will be surprised this morning to read that Richard Rodgers, Oscar Hammerstein 2d and Joshua Logan have written a magnificent musical drama. Even before they set pencil to paper and chose "South Pacific" for the title, alert theatre-goers very sensibly started to buy tickets for it. With Mary Martin and Ezio Pinza in the leading parts, the opening performance at the Majestic last evening amply confirmed preliminary expectations and brought the town a wonderfully talented show.

Although Mr. Rodgers and Mr. Hammerstein are extraordinarily gifted men, they have not forgotten how to apply the seat of the pants to the seat of the chair. One thing that makes "South Pacific" so rhapsodically enjoyable is the hard work and organization that have gone into it under Mr. Logan's spontaneous direction. They have culled the story from James Michener's "Tales of the South Pacific," which in some incredible fashion managed to retain sensitive perceptions toward the Pacific Islands and human beings in the midst of the callous misery, boredom and slaughter of war.

* * *

The perception has been preserved in this sombre romance about a French planter and an American nurse from Arkansas. Writing for Broadway, Mr. Rodgers and Mr. Hammerstein have not forgotten to entertain the customers with some exuberant antics by humorously sullen American Seabees who resent every thing they have to endure. But essentially this is a tenderly beautiful idyll of genuine people inexplicably tossed together in a strange corner of the world; and the music, the lyrics, the singing and the acting contribute to this mood.

If the country still has the taste to appreciate a masterly love song, "Some Enchanted Evening" ought to become reasonably immortal. For Mr. Rodgers' music is a romantic incantation; and, as usual, Mr. Hammerstein's verses are both fervent and simple. Mr. Pinza's bass voice is the most beautiful that has been heard on a Broadway stage for an eon or two. He sings this song with infinite delicacy of feeling and loveliness of tone. As a matter of fact, Mr. Pinza is also a fine actor; and his first appearance on the one and only legitimate stage is an occasion worth celebrating.

* * *

Since we have all been more or less in love with Miss Martin for several years, it is no surprise to find her full of quicksilver, pertness and delight as the Navy nurse. She sings some good knockabout melodies with skill and good nature, making something particularly enjoyable out of the stomping jubilee of "I'm Gonna Wash That Man Right Outa My Hair" and blowing out the walls of the theatre with the rapture of "I'm In Love With a Wonderful Guy." In the opinion of one inquiring theatregoer, there seems to be a little of Annie Oakley, the gun-girl, left in Miss Martin's attack on a song, and perhaps this should be exorcised by slow degrees. For the Navy nurse is a few cuts above Annie socially. Miss Martin is the girl who can make her captivating without deluging her in charm.

Since "South Pacific" is not an assembled show, but a thoroughly composed musical drama, you will find high standards of characterization and acting throughout. Take

Juanita Hall, for example. She plays a brassy, greedy, ugly Tonkonese woman with harsh, vigorous, authentic accuracy; and she sings one of Mr. Rodgers' finest songs, "Bali Ha'i" with rousing artistry.

* * *

After wasting his talents on stereotyped parts for several years, Myron McCormick has a good one as a braggart, scheming Seabee, and plays it with great comic gusto. "South Pacific" naturally does well by the ruffians who saved democracy amid groans of despair in the Eastern ocean, and "There Is Nothing Like a Dame" ought to go down as their theme song.

As evidence of the care that has gone into this drama take note of the part of Capt. George Brackett.

"The ladies — the wives of the planters — often go to Australia during the hot months. It can get very hot here." — Indirectly, Ezio Pinza hints at his love for Mary Martin in a scene from "South Pacific."

U. S. N. The part is written with real invention on the model of a human being, and Martin Wolfson plays him admirably.

Jo Mielziner has provided entrancing settings that presumably have a Polynesian accent. Russell Bennett has written orchestrations, especially for the overtures, that are rich and colorful in instrumental sound. For the authors and producers have a high regard for professional skill, and everything they have put their hands to is perfectly wrought. Fortunately, Mr. Rodgers and Mr. Hammerstein are also the most gifted men in the business. And "South Pacific" is as lively, warm, fresh and beautiful as we had all hoped that it would be.

1949 Ap 8

'Lost in the Stars,' the Musical Version of Alan Paton's 'Cry, the Beloved Country'

LOST IN THE STARS, a musical tragedy in two acts and twenty scenes, based on Alan Paton's novel, "Cry, the Beloved Country." Words by Maxwell Anderson and music by Kurt Weill. Staged by Rouben Mamoulian; scenery by George Jenkins; musical conductor, Maurice Levine; costumes by Anna Hill Johnstone; produced by the Playwrights Company. At the Music Box.

Leader	Frank Roane
Answerer	Joseph James
Nita	Elayne Richards
Grace Kumalo	Gertrude Jeannette
Stephen Kumalo	Todd Duncan
James Jarvis	Leslie Banks
Edward Jarvis	Judson Rees
Arthur Jarvis	John Morley
John Kumalo	Warren Coleman
William	Roy Allen
Jared	William C. Smith
Alex	Herbert Coleman
Foreman	Jerome Shaw
Mrs. Mkize	Georgette Harvey
Hlabeni	William Marshall
Eland	Charles Grunwell
Linda	Sheila Guyse
Johannes Pafuri	Van Prince
Matthew Kumalo	William Greaves
Absalom Kumalo	Julian Mayfield
Rose	Gloria Smith
Irina	Inez Matthews
Burton	John W. Stanley
The Judge	Guy Spaull

By BROOKS ATKINSON

Out of a memorable novel has come a memorable musical drama. The novel is Alan Paton's "Cry, the Beloved Country." The musical drama is "Lost in the Stars," which Maxwell Anderson and Kurt Weill have written. Under Rouben Mamoulian's direction, it opened at the Music Box last evening.

Brooding on the racial animosities of South Africa, Mr. Paton wrote a compassionate story about two old men—one black, one white —who are drawn into friendship by a grievous tragedy. The black man is a country parson whose

Todd Duncan, in character, as a South African minister in "Lost in the Stars."

simple faith is shaken by the evil in his own family. The white man is a hard British planter who acquires faith through the loss of his son in a murder.

* * *

Mr. Paton's novel is an epic in which the currents of racial hatred run deep and strong—so thoroughly a work of literary art that one might well hesitate to try transforming it into the art of the stage. Let it be said at once that Mr. Anderson and Mr. Weill have not transformed it without obvious difficulty. They have to be literal and skimming in the narrative where the novel is allusive and rich. There are spots where "Lost In the Stars" is patchy. People who have not fallen under the sublime spell of the novel may not fully appreciate the multitudinous forces that are running headlong through this tragic story.

But Mr. Anderson has the taste and integrity to know the quality of the material he is working with; and he has managed to get into the theatre the story of the parson whose son murders the white man's son and of the white man who has the manhood to recognize a noble character when he sees one. We will be lucky this season if we have another scene as profoundly moving as the last one in this drama. Being perhaps in a hurry, Mr. Anderson writes a good many of the early scenes sketchily. But when he comes to the overwhelming climax of this terrible tragedy he takes the time and has the words to write a grand and enlightening scene with unadorned beauty.

Although the novel had more detail than Mr. Anderson has space for in the theatre, the novel did not have Mr. Weill's music. And here the theatre has come bearing its most memorable gifts. In the past Mr. Weill has given the theatre some fine scores. But at the moment, which is forty minutes after the final curtain, it is difficult to remember anything out of his portfolio as eloquent as this richly orchestrated singing music. Some of it is as artless as a Broadway song. But most of it is overflowing with the same compassion that Mr. Paton brought to his novel.

Written with theatrical virtuosity, the score serves as a classical chorus, picking up and projecting the significance of the various scenes. Breaking the tragic mood of the drama, there is one light and humorous song, sung with magnetic charm by young Herbert Coleman. But most of it carries throughout the theatre the fears and hatreds, the wildness, the anguish and the heavy spiritual burdens of a big story.

* * *

Mr. Mamoulian has directed it like an epic. Without neglecting the dramatic force of the small scenes, he has given the whole work sweep and perspective. "Lost in the Stars" is beautifully sung by a Negro choir led by the rich voice of Frank Roane. As the parson,

Todd Duncan sings magnificently and captures in his acting the sincerity of a kindly old man who comes through a terrible ordeal. In the opposite part of the British planter, Leslie Banks plays with deeply felt honesty of character that provides the perfect balance.

The cast is too long, unfortunately, for the proper acknowledgments from this hurried column. But, black and white, it is of a uniform high quality well suited to a notable enterprise. In designing the settings, George Jenkins has caught the grandeur of South African scenery and the scrabble of Johannesburg; and he has also contrived to sketch in skillfully the details of the panorama of scenes.

* * *

It would not be impossible to quarrel with some of the hasty treatment the authors have applied to Mr. Paton's perfectly composed novel. Faced with the problem of getting a coherent narrative out of a many-sided story, Mr. Anderson has a heavy touch in some of his scenes. But the theme is a noble one. The music is deep, dramatic and beautiful. And the final scene, which pulls together all the strands of the tragedy, catches a fragment of the immortal truth. Probably, "Cry, the Beloved Country" should not be translated into a drama. But it has been, and into a drama that is illuminating and memorable.

1949 O 31

The Cast

REGINA, a musical drama in a prologue and two acts, adapted from Lillian Hellman's play, "The Little Foxes." Libretto, score and lyrics by Marc Blitzstein. Staged by Robert Lewis; musical director, Maurice Abravanel; scenery by Horace Armistead; costumes by Aline Bernstein; dances by Anna Sokolow; lighting by Charles Elson; presented by Cheryl Crawford in association with Clinton Wilder. At the Forty-sixth Street Theatre.

Addie .... Lillyn Brown
Cal .... William Warfield
Alexandra Giddens .... Priscilla Gillette
Chinkypin .... Philip Hepburn
Jazz .... William Dillard (trumpet)
Angel Band ..... {Bernard Addison (banjo)
                 {Buster Bailey (clarinet)
                 {Ruddy Nichols (traps)
                 {Benny Morton (trombone)
Regina Giddens .... Jane Pickens
Birdie Hubbard .... Brenda Lewis
Oscar Hubbard .... David Thomas
Leo Hubbard .... Russell Nype
Marshall .... Donald Clarke
Ben Hubbard .... George Lipton
Belle .... Clarisse Crawford
Pianist .... Marion Carley
Violinist .... Alfred Bruning
Horace Giddens .... William Wilderman
Manders .... Lee Sweetland
Ethelinda .... Peggy Turnley

By BROOKS ATKINSON

Marc Blitzstein ought to be well satisfied with the treatment the theatre has given him. In "Regina," which was sung at the Forty-sixth last evening, he has crossed the border-line between popular theatre and modern opera, and the theatre has kept step with him perfectly. Using Lillian Hellman's venomous "The Little Foxes" as his source-book, he has written a sharp-pointed opera about two greedy brothers and their greedy sister who devour each other as they move on towards devouring the earth.

Although it is a point of honor not to call opera "opera" but something less portentous, "Regina" is opera in a modern style written for lovers of music. But under Robert Lewis' direction, it is staged and acted in the cleanest theatre style inside some dramatically lighted sets by Horace Armistead and with acting costumes by Aline Bernstein.

Opera singers are not supposed to be actors also, but Mr. Blitzstein's are. As the voracious, merciless Regina, Jane Pickens acts and sings with the ferocity of a poisonous snake. Brenda Lewis' pathetically tippling Birdie is a

"What's the matter, mamma? Are you afraid?"—Priscilla Gillette, right, to Jane Pickens, in a tense maternal scene from "Regina."

masterpiece of acting and singing. These are the two memorable roles out of Miss Hellman's savage drama. Mr. Blitzstein, Mr. Lewis and the actresses have preserved the vividness of the characterizations.

* * *

And so on throughout a singularly alert and flaring performance. The compassionate Negro cook—warm and genuine in Lillyn Brown's performance; the two malevolent brothers—perfect in the performing of David Thomas and George Lipton; the tender daughter—sweet and eloquent in the person of Priscilla Gillette; William Wilderman's ailing Horace Giddens is intelligently played and sung more dynamically than his heart condition warrants. There is one point in the drama when Mr. Blitzstein comes nearer knocking him off than Regina does. As theatre, this production of "Regina" could hardly be improved upon and must certainly rank with the most enlightened stage performances of operatic works.

In "The Cradle Will Rock" and "No For an Answer" Mr. Blitzstein was writing music on group themes and for choruses. In "Regina" he is dealing with individual characters. With the virtuosity of a born composer and trained musician he has written a tart and astringent score for ferocious characters on the foundation of a stirring orchestration. A few songs and a number of arias rise out of the fierce turbulence of Mr. Blitzstein's chronicle of a cruel family; and there are some jaunty jazzband serenades and a Negro spiritual or two by way of simple contrast. Even "Street Scene" was not so thoroughly translated into the language of music, for Mr. Blitzstein has written a new work on an old theme.

* * *

By inviting the theatre reviewers to comment on Mr. Blitzstein's opera, Cheryl Crawford, the producer, has asked for theatre judgment. And here a theatre reviewer must ask himself whether Mr. Blitzstein's opera adds to the vitality of one of the theatre's keenest dramas. In this reviewer's opinion, it does not. In fact, the language of opera seems cumbersome in comparison with the compact, tensile, realistic drama that

Herman Shumlin directed with force and clarity a decade ago.

The sharp appeal to the intellect in Mr. Blitzstein's brilliant score is less impassioned than the thunderous appeal to basic emotions in Miss Hellman's more melodramatic version. In sight as well as sound, "Regina" is a remarkable achievement that finds all the theatre's workmen on their mettle —particularly Mr. Lewis, who has mastered a complicated opera and pulled it briskly together on the stage.

But to one theatregoer of long standing "Regina" has softened a hard play. What Mr. Blitzstein has added to it does not compensate for the loss in force, belligerence and directness.

1949 N 1

GENTLEMEN PREFER BLONDES, a new musical comedy. Book by Joseph Fields and Anita Loos, based on the latter's novel. Music by Jule Styne; lyrics by Leo Robin; dances and ensembles by Agnes de Mille; production designed by Oliver Smith; costumes designed by Miles White; musical direction by Milton Rosenstock; musical arrangements by Don Walker; vocal direction and arrangements by Hugh Martin; lighting by Peggy Clark; entire production staged by John C. Wilson; produced by Herman Levin and Mr. Smith. At the Ziegfeld Theatre.

Dorothy Shaw .... Yvonne Adair
A Steward ....Jerry Craig
Lorelei Lee.................... Carol Channing
Gus Esmond.................... Jack McCauley
Frank ....Robert Cooper
George ....Eddie Weston
Lady Phyllis Beekman....... Reta Shaw
Sir Francis Beekman........... Rex Evans
Mrs. Ella Spofford................ Alice Pearce
Deck Stewards................. { Bob Burkhardt
                               { Shelton Lewis
Henry Spofford................ Eric Brotherson
An Olympic.................... Curt Stafford
Josephus Gage........... George S. Irving
Pierre .... Bob Neukum
Bill ....Peter Birch
Gloria Stark..................... Anita Alvarez
Taxi Driver.................. Kazimir Kokic
Leon ....Peter Holmes
Robert Lemanteur............... Mort Marshall
Louis Lemanteur.............. Howard Morris
A Flower Girl............... Nicole France
Maitre d'Hotel............... Crandall Diehl
Zizi ... .Judy Sinclair
Fifi .... Hope Zee
Coles and Atkins................ Themselves
The Tenor.................... William Krach
Policeman .... William Diehl
Headwaiter .... Kazimir Kokic
Mr. Esmond Sr. .... Irving Mitchell

By BROOKS ATKINSON

Happy days are here again. The musical version of "Gentlemen Prefer Blondes," which lighted the Ziegfeld last evening, is a vastly enjoyable song-and-dance antic put on with humorous perfection. Millions of people doted on Anita

Loos' comic fable when it appeared as a play in 1926 with a memorable cast and the laughs pitched fairly low in the diaphragm.

Fortunately they are going to have an opportunity to enjoy it again in a thoroughly fresh treatment. For Miss Loos and Joseph Fields have now fitted it to the formula of an old-fashioned rowdydowed with Tin Pan Alley tunes by Jule Styne and some brassy and amusing lyrics by Leo Robin.

* * *

Staged expertly in a festive manner by John C. Wilson, it brings back a good many familiar delights to a street that has been adding art to the musical stage for quite a long time. But thanks to the clowning of Carol Channing, it also brings us something new and refreshing. Let's call her portrait of the aureate Lee the most fabulous comic creation of this dreary period in history.

You will recall Lorelei Lee as the flapper gold-digger who made her way through masculine society with a good deal of success in the Twenties. In Miss Channing's somewhat sturdier image, Lorelei's rapacious innocence is uproariously amusing. Made-up to resemble a John Held creature, she goes through the play like a dazed automaton—husky enough to kick in the teeth or any gentleman on the stage, but mincing coyly in high-heel shoes and looking out on a confused world through big, wide, starry eyes. There has never been anything like this before in human society.

* * *

Miss Channing can also act a

"A kiss on the hand may make you feel very good, but a diamond bracelet lasts forever."—Carol Channing, left, expounds her philosophy to Yvonne Adair in a scene from "Gentlemen Prefer Blondes."

part with skill and relish. They have given her a funny autobiographical ballad, "A Little Girl From Little Rock," which she translates into a roaringly entertaining number. She has something original and grotesque to contribute to every number. She can also speak the cock-eyed dialogue with droll inflections. Her Lorelei is a mixture of cynicism and stupidity that will keep New York in good spirits all winter.

Having good taste in general, the producers of "Gentlemen Prefer Blondes" have hired Yvonne Adair to appear with Miss Channing as Dorothy, the more cautious brunette; and Jack McCauley to play the part of Lorelei's protector. Since they are both expert performers with a sense of humor, this turns out to be very happy casting. A pleasure-mad, teetering old lady by Alice Pearce; a handsome, genteel young man from Philadelphia by Eric Brotherson; a philandering Britisher by Rex Evans, and an indecently healthy zipper manufacturer by George S. Irving—round out the principal performers of a singularly affable cast.

Although the tone of "Gentlemen Prefer Blondes" is old-fashioned, the spirit is modern and the pace is swift. Oliver Smith has provided a suite of good travelogue settings, combining the best features of New York and Paris. And Miles White has designed stunning costumes with a humorous accent.

* * *

Agnes de Mille has done the ballets with a light touch—managing somehow to combine precision dancing with gay improvisations in her pleasant folk style. Anita Alvarez sweeps in and out of the show with a whole series of impish dances, performing one of the best with Kazimir Kokic. As a matter of fact, there is a lot of entertaining and expert dancing through the many scenes of this plausible burlesque of one of the most ancient rackets of the world.

Every part of it is alive and abundantly entertaining. And above it all towers the blonde thatch of Miss Channing, who is batting her big eyes, murdering the English language and carrying the whole golden world along with her by sheer audacity. "Gentlemen Prefer Blondes" was always funny. It is even funnier, now that the lustrous Miss Channing has taken such a strangle hold on the part.

1949 D 9

Broadway
in Crisis: 1950-1959

A serious contraction of the Broadway theater began in the fifties. The steady rise in production costs, the increased admission prices, the advent of a new and frightening competitor, television, all contributed to this condition. During this period the number of productions presented on Broadway was 756, a drop of almost 100 productions from the previous decade's 842. The casual theater-goer disappeared; the films and particularly television seemed to satisfy his entertainment needs. The Broadway theater no longer had room for the "middle-of-the-road" play which could run comfortably with only a moderate-sized audience. Now the "smash-hit" syndrome gripped Broadway; the economics of the theater allowed no other. With no financial subsidies and no large and loyal audience to depend on, the Broadway theater became disoriented and cautious. As a result of the high production costs, only a brave manager would risk an untried playwright or an experimental work. The established playwright or star, the sure-fire formula comedy or lavish musical, the pre-tested English or European success — these were what the producers were seeking. To offset the Broadway decline, a new Off-Broadway movement flowered. As in the late teens and early twenties, the Off-Broadway theater provided a showcase for new playwrights, directors, and actors; for experimental works; for, in short, the seemingly non-commercial venture which Broadway, except in rare instances, could no longer welcome.

Although much that Off-Broadway presented was shoddy and amateurish, it also provided some of the more memorable events of the decade. Circle-in-the-Square rescued from early oblivion two outstanding American plays which had had disappointing Broadway engagements during the previous decade: Tennessee Williams' *Summer and Smoke* and Eugene O'Neill's *The Iceman*

Cometh. José Quintero's sensitive production of the Williams play and, especially, the performance of Geraldine Page aroused tremendous enthusiasm among the critics and the public, who now began to realize that the new Off-Broadway movement was deserving of serious attention. Quintero's later production of the O'Neill play (in which Jason Robards, Jr. distinguished himself) led to a re-awakening of interest in America's greatest playwright and to several productions of his work on Broadway. More characteristic of Off-Broadway was the opportunity it offered for the growth of new producing organizations such as the Living Theatre and the Phoenix Theatre and for the presentation of avant-garde plays by dramatists such as Eugene Ionesco and Samuel Beckett. Nor did Off-Broadway ignore the musical theater; among its happiest offerings of the decade were Kurt Weill's *The Threepenny Opera* (with Lotte Lenya) and newcomer Rick Besoyan's operetta parody *Little Mary Sunshine.*

The revival of interest in Eugene O'Neill resulted in Broadway presentations of *A Moon for the Misbegotten, A Touch of the Poet,* and the decade's most distinguished play *Long Day's Journey into Night.* Under the direction of Off-Broadway's José Quintero, O'Neill's play was flawlessly acted by Fredric March, Florence Eldridge, Bradford Dillman, and Jason Robards, Jr. as the four members of the tortured Tyrone family. Other established American playwrights were represented during the fifties: Clifford Odets by *The Country Girl* and his last play *The Flowering Peach;* Lillian Hellman by *The Autumn Garden,* among other works; Arthur Miller by *The Crucible* and *A View from the Bridge.* Tennessee Williams continued his amazing career with *The Rose Tattoo, Camino Real, Cat on a Hot Tin Roof, Orpheus Descending, Sweet Bird of Youth* and, Off-Broadway, with his long one-act play *Suddenly Last Summer.*

Several new playwrights of interest emerged during the decade: one was William Inge who, with the invaluable aid of Shirley Booth and Sidney Blackmer, achieved great success with his first production in New York, *Come Back, Little Sheba.* Inge followed this with the even more popular *Picnic, Bus Stop,* and *The Dark at the Top of the Stairs.* Television helped to nurture such playwrights as Horton Foote and Paddy Chayevsky. Two black playwrights of talent and interest appeared: Lorraine Hansberry with her prize-winning *A Raisin in the Sun* and Louis Petersen with his *Take a Giant Step*. Robert Anderson showed much promise with his first play *Tea and Sympathy,* as did William Gibson with *Two for the Seesaw* and *The Miracle Worker*. The most sensitive work by a new playwright was *The Member of the Wedding* by Carson McCullers. Under the direction of Harold Clurman, an incomparable trio of actors, Ethel Waters, Julie Harris, and young Brandon de Wilde made Mrs. McCullers' lovely play one of the most moving works of the decade.

The comic spirit which had shone so brightly in the past dimmed during the fifties although there was much public response to such conventional comedies as *The Moon is Blue* and *The Seven Year Itch*. War and its aftermath continued to furnish the settings of such comedies as *Stalag 17, No Time for Sergeants,* and *The Teahouse of the August Moon*. The most inventive comedy of the period, however, was Thornton Wilder's *The Matchmaker,* in which Ruth Gordon offered an outrageously funny performance as the indomitable Mrs. Dolly Gallagher Levi.

Foreign playwrights, actors, and directors also provided many effective productions of the decade. The verse plays of T. S. Eliot and Christopher Fry were hailed (a trifle prematurely, it would seem) as the beginning of a new golden age of playwriting. Several plays by the eminent French writers, Jean Anouilh and Jean Giraudoux, contributed merit to the Broadway theater, as did the works of John Osborne, Graham Greene, and Enid Bagnold. Samuel Beckett's *Waiting for Godot* (in which Bert Lahr rose to new heights) made its first appearance in New York, and Alfred Lunt and Lynn Fontanne had their greatest artistic triumph in recent years in Friedrich Duerrenmatt's fascinating *The Visit*. There were several superior revivals of Shaw's plays including *Misalliance* and *Captain Brassbound's Conversion* (with the captivating Edna Best) as well as the First Drama Quartet's (Charles Boyer, Charles Laughton, Cedric Hardwicke, and Agnes Moorehead) brilliant reading of the "Don Juan in

Hell" sequence of *Man and Superman*. Louis Jouvet and Jean-Louis Barrault brought their companies from France, and Katina Paxinou and Alexis Minotis, two of Greece's greatest actors, presented powerful and illuminating productions of *Electra* and *Oedipus*.

The decade was also notable for the emergence of several new players of uncommon ability and presence. Chief among them were Julie Harris, Geraldine Page, Anne Bancroft, Maureen Stapleton, Kim Stanley, and Eli Wallach while the musical theater found new stars in Gwen Verdon and Julie Andrews. Off-Broadway offered the first major acting opportunities to Colleen Dewhurst and George C. Scott during this period. Established stars, on the other hand, appeared only intermittently although from time to time actors who had left for the films returned to the stage for occasional appearances. Among these were Edward G. Robinson in Chayevsky's *Middle of the Night*, Paul Muni as Clarence Darrow in *Inherit the Wind*, Gladys Cooper in Bagnold's *The Chalk Garden*, Jean Arthur and Boris Karloff in a beguiling revival of *Peter Pan*, and Ralph Bellamy as Franklin D. Roosevelt in *Sunrise at Campobello*.

The musical theater, as usual, contributed some of the decade's happiest moments. Ethel Merman brightened the stage in Irving Berlin's *Call Me Madam* and in her most rewarding role, the indefatigable Madame Rose in *Gypsy*. The magic stage personality of Mary Martin was evident in a new musical version of *Peter Pan* (with Cyril Ritchard playing Captain Hook as a Restoration fop) and in Rodgers and Hammerstein's enormously popular *The Sound of Music*. Gian-Carlo Menotti offered two intense operas, *The Consul* and *The Saint of Bleecker Street*, while the new and immensely gifted team of Richard Adler and Jerry Ross produced two spirited musicals, *Damm Yankees* and *The Pajama Game*. The 1952 revival of *Pal Joey*, again with the wonderful Vivienne Segal in the lead, found a larger and more responsive audience than the original production which was ahead of its time. Leonard Bernstein's splendid music was heard in *Wonderful Town* (with an exultant Rosalind Russell), *Candide* (a sadly underrated work), and one of the most popular musicals of the time, *West Side Story*. Rodgers and Hammerstein also gave us the resplendent *The King and I*, in which Yul

Brynner achieved stardom and the irreplaceable Gertrude Lawrence made her final appearance. But the most notable achievements of the fifties were, undoubtedly, the two musical masterpieces: Frank Loesser's *Guys and Dolls* (with Vivian Blaine, Robert Alda, and Sam Levene) and the Alan Jay Lerner-Frederick Loewe adaptation of Shaw's *Pygmalion,* the incomparable *My Fair Lady,* in which Rex Harrison offered the decade's outstanding male performance.

Although the American theater was declining in the fifties, it should be apparent that much work of quality was still being offered during that period. Sixty-nine reviews have been selected to represent the decade of 1950-1959.

1950 - 1959

The Cast

THE MEMBER OF THE WEDDING, a play by
Carson McCullers. Staged by Harold Clur-
man; scenery, costumes and lighting by Les-
ter Polakov; produced by Robert Whitehead,
Oliver Rea and Stanley Martineau. At the
Empire Theatre.

Jarvis	James Holder
Frankie Addams	Julie Harris
Janice	Janet De Gore
Berenice Sadie Brown	Ethel Waters
Royal Addams	William Hansen
John Henry West	Brandon De Wilde
Mrs. West	Margaret Barker
Helen Fletcher	Mitzie Blake
Doris	Joan Shepard
Sis Laura	Phyllis Walker
T. T. Williams	Harry Bolden
Honey Camden Brown	Henry Scott
Barney McKean	Jimmy Dutton

By BROOKS ATKINSON

If the drama were nothing but
character sketches and acting,
"The Member of the Wedding,"
which opened at The Empire last
evening, would be a masterpiece.
For Carson McCullers' portrait of
a harum-scarum adolescent girl in
Georgia is wonderfully — almost
painfully—perceptive; and her associated sketches of a Negro mammy and a busy little boy are masterly pieces of writing, also.

Fortunately, they have fallen
into the hands of Harold Clurman,
who appreciates them. He has
staged a performance by Ethel
Waters, Julie Harris and young
Brandon De Wilde that has incomparable insight, grace and beauty.
Anyone who loves art ought to be
humbly grateful for such acting
and direction. Like Miss McCullers'
character portraiture, they are
masterly pieces of work.

* * *

Originally, "The Member of the
Wedding" was a novel. That probably has some bearing on the fact
that the play has no beginning,
middle or end and never acquires
dramatic momentum. Although
Miss McCullers has taken the material out of the novel she has not
quite got it into the form of a
play.

What she has got is an infinitely
poignant sketch of an unprepos-
sessing adolescent girl who is looking around hungrily for human
companionship and for something
that she can join. The incident of
the play concerns her brother's
wedding. Fantasy-ridden like an
overwrought adolescent, the girl
plans to join it by going away with
her brother and his bride and casting her lot with theirs permanently. Almost psychopathically imaginative, she foresees a very gaudy
future of travel, excitement and
friends.

* * *

That is about all there is to the
narrative or plot of "The Member
of the Wedding." The rest is cha-
acter analysis—the wild, whirling
impulses of a girl on tip-toe with
eagerness for a world she does not
know how to take part in; the
lumbering, elemental compassion
of the Negro cook who knows all
about life; the counterpoint activities of the little boy who is busy
about his own affairs and runs in
and out of the play like a sprite.
Miss McCullers' insight is deep and
sympathetic. Her literary style is
deft and spinning. Her characterizations of the chief people and her
sketches of them together in a
ramshackle kitchen are superb
pieces of work.

The play is acted in a casually
and imaginatively designed setting
by Lester Polakov that lets the
action spill in and out of the
kitchen and through the dooryard.
In the long, immensely complicated
part of the adolescent girl, Julie
Harris, a very gifted young actress
gives an extraordinary performance—vibrant, full of anguish and
elation by turns, rumpled, unstable,
egotistic and unconsciously cruel.

As the Negro cook and symbol

313

of maternity, Miss Waters gives one of those rich and eloquent performances that lay such a deep spell on any audience that sees her. Although the character has a physical base in Miss Waters' mountainous personality, it has exalted spirit and great warmth of sympathy.

* * *

Brandon De Wilde, who is 7½ years old, plays the neighborhood boy with amazing imperturbability. This is a vastly humorous part, and Brandon won all the hearts in the audience last evening, for he is resourceful and self-contained; and Mr. Clurman, who has a special gift for the parts of children and young people, has staged these interludes tactfully and amusingly.

None of the other parts is extensive or important, for Miss McCullers merely uses the other characters to fill out the character sketches. But the parts are well played, particularly by William Hansen, Harry Bolden and Henry Scott. In view of the rare quality of the writing and acting, the fact that "The Member of the Wedding" has practically no dramatic movement does not seem to be very important. It may not be a play, but it is art. That is the important thing.

1950 Ja 6

The Cast

THE COCKTAIL PARTY, a play in two acts and five scenes, by T. S. Eliot. Presented by Gilbert Miller, by arrangement with Sherek Players, Ltd.; staged by E. Martin Browne; lighting and settings supervised by Raymond Sovey. At Henry Miller's Theatre.

Edward Chamberlayne	Robert Flemyng
Julia (Mrs. Shuttlethwaite)	Cathleen Nesbitt
Celia Coplestone	Irene Worth
Alexander MacColgie Gibbs	Ernest Clark
Peter Quilpe	Grey Blake
An Unidentified Guest	Alec Guinness
Lavinia Chamberlayne	Eileen Peel
A Nurse-Secretary	Avril Conquest
A Caterer's Man	Donald Bain

By BROOKS ATKINSON

Being a mystic as well as a poet, T. S. Eliot has written a verbose and elusive drama that has to be respected. For it comes out of the private reverie of a man of purity, mind and character. It is "The Cocktail Party," which was wonderfully well acted by an English company at Henry Miller's on Saturday evening. Mr. Eliot is not an idiomatic theatre writer, nor an idiomatic verse writer, for that matter. But this drama about the souls of some contemporary people is closer to theatre than any of his previous plays. It comes closer to being a public expression of his private ideas.

* * *

They are religious ideas. In the first act he assembles a group of English people who have lost their way through the labyrinths of polite society. Lavinia Camberlayne has just left her husband without remembering to cancel a cocktail party she had arranged. Her husband is both annoyed and depressed. Suspecting what has happened, his mistress is elated by the expectation that he will now be free to marry her. But he finds that he wants his wife back. In the third scene of the first act she returns.

* * *

Since they are rootless and apparently on the verge of nervous breakdowns, Mr. Eliot sends them all to a psychiatrist in the second act. For the psychiatrist is the father-confessor of modern people who have no basic religion. As the play moves on, Mr. Eliot gives his psychiatrist more and more religious authority and turns over to him the spiritual destiny of his principal characters. The psychiatrist restores the husband and wife to each other by removing their illusions. All they need is psychic adjustment. But the other woman he selects for a higher destiny—for a life of dedication, selflessness and martyrdom.

* * *

Why? The reasons obviously he concealed in the figured verse to which Mr. Eliot has confided his thoughts and religious faith. No doubt they are all there for theatregoers who are in tune with him, who can invade his spiritual privacy and who have faith in metrical abstractions. But today's report is written by one theatregoer who does not understand Mr. Eliot's dogma but recognizes that it is genuine and worth understanding by means of the script, since it is too compact and too allusive to be assimilated from the stage.

No one can blame the performance. It has been directed by E. Martin Browne, who has long been thoroughly grounded in the Eliot mystique; and it is acted by some lucid and accomplished players who know how to speak the English language.

Although the theme of the play is esoteric, the performance is thoroughly intelligible and enjoyable. Robert Flemyng as the boorish husband who finds spiritual release in learning the truth of his wife's character, and Eileen Peel as the wife who learns to know her husband — both give plastic, balanced performances of sensitive quality. Irene Worth finds the lonely depths in the character of the other woman in a remarkably skillful, passionate and perceptive performance. As the psychiatrist, Alec Guinness is superb — casual and amusing in the early scenes but rising to considerable spiritual eminence in the last act.

* * *

Cathleen Nesbitt is humorously animated as a garrulous busybody who flutters in and out of the play. Ernest Clark as a somewhat enigmatic man of far-flung affairs and Grey Blake as an aspiring writer complete the cast of the principal characters by giving good performances. As scene designer, Raymond Sovey has housed the actors pleasantly in an attractive drawing room and a sober consulting room for a fashionable psychiatrist.

Although "The Cocktail Party" has a worldly title, it is the most unworldly of plays, and since the characters have no life outside the drama, they are hardly more than illustrations for Mr. Eliot's ideas. "The Cocktail Party" is Mr. Eliot's best theatre work so far— his earnestness as a man of faith sustaining it through three hours of solid thought. But it would be hard to overlook the fact that the most essential parts of it are not resolved in terms of theatre and leave a theatregoer impressed without being enlightened.

1950 Ja 23

The Cast

COME BACK, LITTLE SHEBA, a play in two acts and six scenes, by William Inge. Staged by Daniel Mann; produced by the Theatre Guild under the supervision of Lawrence Langner and Theresa Helburn; associate producer, Phyllis Anderson; setting and lighting designed by Howard Bay; costumes by Lucille Little. At the Booth Theatre.

Doc..........................Sidney Blackmer
Marie........................Joan Lorring
Lola.........................Shirley Booth
Turk.........................Lonny Chapman
Postman......................Daniel Reed
Mrs. Coffman.................Olga Fabian
Milkman......................John Randolph
Messenger....................Arnold Schulman
Bruce........................Robert Cunningham
Ed Anderson..................Wilson Brooks
Elmo Huston..................Paul Krauss

By BROOKS ATKINSON

At last the Theatre Guild has got round to doing an original play. William Inge's "Come Back, Little Sheba," which was acted at the Booth last evening, is straightforward and unhackneyed and, in its best moments, terrifyingly true. Having been a drama critic, Mr. Inge naturally knows more about more things than most people, including the sort of material worth writing about in the theatre.

In his second professionally produced drama he has poked into the agony of an alcoholic who is trying to escape the disaster of an intolerable life. Among the other useful things Mr. Inge knows is how to write two parts that Shirley Booth and Sidney Blackmer can act with a simple honesty that is pitiless and overwhelming.

* * *

"Come Back, Little Sheba," is a small play. During the first half of the evening Mr. Inge has kept it so slight that it verges on the monotonous. He is describing the dreary home life of a Middle Western chiropractor who is well along in a cure for alcoholism. Doc, which is the character's only name, lives in a messy house run by his good-natured but slovenly wife, who is sentimental, lazy and common.

Apparently Mr. Inge wants you to believe that Doc has been compensating himself through alcohol for marrying beneath his station. Since Doc is no great shakes himself, this column will reserve judgment on Mr. Inge's diagnosis pending further evidence of Doc's superiority.

* * *

Whatever the truth may be about the causes which Mr. Inge sketches very lightly and tentatively in the first act, the consequences are wild and frightening in the second act when Mr. Inge gets to work with his coat off.

For the irritations and frustrations of a squalid home and tragic memories are more than Doc can stand. He goes off the deep end and wrecks all that is left. In a last forgiving scene Doc and his wife cling desperately together, afraid of the horrible things they know. Doc is not cured. But his wife and he understand each other and love each other. They can face the future—whatever the future turns out to be.

Under the direction of Daniel Mann, the Theatre Guild and its handservants have arranged a candid production and a splendid performance. Howard Bay has designed functional scenery that catches the dreariness as well as the hominess of an old house in a run-down neighborhood. And Lucille Little has provided costumes that portray the hopelessness of the old people and the shining self-confidence of some young people who run in and out without ever realizing the horrors that surround them.

The small parts are neatly played —Daniel Reed as postman, who knows how to listen to nonsense graciously; John Randolph as an athletic milkman; Olga Fabian as a warmhearted neighbor; Lonny Chapman and Robert Cunningham as suitors for a college girl who rooms in Doc's house; Wilson Brooks and Paul Krauss as cardholders in good standing with Alcoholics Anonymous. As the blonde and self-centered college girl Joan Lorring gives a genuine and attractive performance.

But "Come Back, Little Sheba" is overweighted by the characters of Doc and his wife. Again Miss Booth is superb. She has the shuffle, the maddening garrulity and the rasping voice of the slattern, but withal she imparts to the role the warmth, generosity and valor of a loyal and affectionate woman. Mr. Blackmer gets through Doc's weak good-nature painlessly in the first act. In the

"The important thing is to forget the past and live for the present. And stay sober doing it."—Sidney Blackmer summarizes his credo to Shirley Booth in a scene from "Come Back, Little Sheba."

second act he plays the scene of disaster like a thunderbolt, leaving the Theatre Guild subscribers pretty well stunned.

Mr. Inge's play is unnecessarily bare in view of the lives he is tampering with. The first act is hardly more than an outline. There must be more to the nightmare of Doc and his wife than Mr. Inge has reported. But when he is ready to plunge into the anguish in the second act, he writes with a kind of relentless frankness and compassion that are deeply affecting. Miss Booth and Mr. Blackmer know what he means and say it with extraordinary resourcefulness and veracity.

1950 F 16

MENOTTI 'CONSUL' HAS ITS PREMIERE

Composer Also Directed Stage Presentation of Opera— Tragic Story of Europe

THE CONSUL, a "new musical drama" in three acts and six scenes, by Gian-Carlo Menotti. Staged by Mr. Menotti; produced by Chandler Cowles and Efrem Zimbalist Jr.; orchestra conductor, Lehman Engel; scenery by Horace Armistead; musical coordination by Thomas Schippers; lighting by Jean Rosenthal; costumes by Grace Houston; dream choreography by John Butler. At the Ethel Barrymore Theatre.

John Sorel	Cornell MacNeil
Magda Sorel	*Patricia Neway
The Mother	Marie Powers
Chief Police Agent	Leon Lishner
First Police Agent	Chester Watson
Second Police Agent	Donald Blackey
The Secretary	Gloria Lane
Mr. Kofner	George Jongeyans
The Foreign Woman	Maria Marlo
Anna Gomez	Maria Andreassi
Vera Boronell	Lydia Summers
Nika Magadoff	Andrew McKinley
Assan	Francis Monachino
Voice on Record	Mabel Mercer

*On Monday nights and Wednesday matinees the part will be sung by Vera Bryner.

By OLIN DOWNES

"The Consul," by Gian-Carlo Menotti, librettist and composer of the work, was given its New York première last night in the Ethel Barrymore Theatre. It had an unquestioned and overwhelming success. All rejoiced in this fresh discovery of Mr. Menotti's unequalled power of expression in the lyric theatre.

He has written, composed and directed this creation. He has produced an opera of eloquence, momentousness, and intensity of expression unequaled by any native composer. This opera is written from the heart, with a blazing sincerity and a passion of human understanding. It is as contemporary as the cold war, surrealism, television, the atom bomb. It is torn out of the life of the present-day world and poses an issue which mercilessly confronts humanity today. And this is done with a new wedding of the English language with music in a way which is singable, intensely dramatic and poetic by turns, and always of beauty.

Performance Is Superb

The performance of this work is of the highest credit to the modern-minded composer, coach and stage director that Mr. Menotti is, and the high intelligence and sincerity of a remarkable group of young American singers. They are not hardened routiners. There are, of course, ways in which they can grow as singing actors and vocal interpreters. But they have a sovereign spirit, and youth and comprehending enthusiasm for a new kind of music-drama.

And last but not least: for once, for just once in our operatic experience, an entire cast does justice to a beautiful and eminently singable English. We have more than once remarked that we are not sympathetic to opera translated into English, but most enthusiastic for opera composed in English. Mr. Menotti has a profound love and comprehension of the language, and his interpreters carried through his creative feelings. Add to this the superbly modern staging in a remarkably integrated performance.

Each act is connected by an orchestral interlude. In the second act occurs the grandmother's lullaby to the dying child; the strange dream of Magda, when her husband comes back, with a woman he describes as his loving sister, of whom Magda is somewhat terrified, and who has the face of the cold-blooded secretary, with a new malice and evil in the features. This is a dream dialogue in a kind of macabre ballad form of question and response, and fantastical orchestration.

The smash of the pane of glass announces the message from the husband. The window-mender brings it. The chief of police enters, with brutal questioning and sardonic threats. The child has died, Magda goes again to the consulate. There the Magician, Nikao Magadoff, who hypnotizes the assembled company. He makes them dream of a ball room and dancing with the beloved. The secretary tells the Magician to end that, it is irregular and produce his papers. He pulls everything from his clothes—a rabbit, bunting, gewgaws of all sorts. But the papers there are none. He apologizes. Even a great artist has to make a living.

In the third act Magda is told that she must stop John from returning by some message or the lives of all the group will be sacrificed. Her final resolve is made, but too late. The husband returns to the consulate, seeking her. He is seized by the police, as the sec-

retary, at last awakening to evil, assures him something will be done about this in the morning. The end is simplest of all. The telephone ringing repeatedly, Magda returning. I never meant to do this." And turning on the gas stove.

One would think this would be obvious and banal. It is not. It is grandly tragic. And the dying woman has visions—of her husband as he came to woo her, of her mother, wonderfully young, of the revolving dancers in the consulate, of the magician, who again commands, "Look in my eyes, look in my eyes," and ask for rest. The visions recede. The room is empty. The woman falls back unconscious. The telephone rings, the curtain falls.

The flexibility of this score, its mixture of free rhythms and realistic effects with sustained lyrical passages at the inevitable moment is thrice admirable. The concert numbers are used in the way that only the composer has at his disposal. While the secretary, for

SCENE FROM MENOTTI'S 'THE CONSUL'

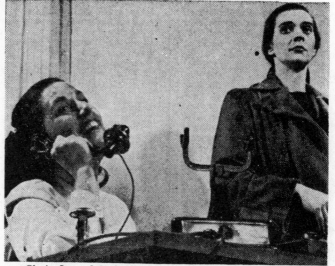

Gloria Lane, left, holds a tête-à-tête over the telephone while Patricia Neway is prevented by consular red tape from obtaining a visa to a land of freedom.

example, is assuring the lady that her papers are ready, and they sing the monotonous duet about signing them properly, Magda and Assan, the window mender, are making their last desperate resolve. While the Magician talks of his tricks the others, in a quartet, sing of their misery and their need.

Everything lends, and the dramatic structure is of the most precise and proportionate kind. And when the big moment is needed, Mr. Menotti supplies it in the superbly constructed aria of Magda, denouncing the secreteary and her bureaucratic ways, at the end of the second act. Then, after this shattering climax, comes the coup de theatre. Magda may see the Consul, says the secretary. He has a very important visitor. Their shadows are seen, saying farewell to each other, against the glass pane door. The door opens. The VIP emerges—the Chief, the terrible Chief of Police. Magda falls insensible to the ground.

Neway Tops Cast

Individually speaking, the cast was led dramatically by Patricia Neway, whose warm, brilliant voice and spirit, and feeling for her role, enabled her to give the fullest interpretive value to every note and every word, whether it was of sustained melody or graphic recitative. The climax of her nobly fashioned aria—that is what it is—at the end of the second act simply stopped the show for minutes, and overwhelmed the audience.

Marie Powers is now well known for the richness of her voice, her temperament and ability in characterization. Her cradle song was the first occasion for interrupting applause, and she had greater and less conventional moments when she made the most of shorter lyrical passages the composer has given her. Andrew McKinley is one of the finds of this cast-finds in the sense of a wholly unconventional role that he sang and interpreted with greatest skill, dexterity, vocal brilliance and imagination.

Maria Marlow, with her fine voice and style, and irresistible speech and song of the naïve, unhappy little Italian woman in her grief; Cornell MacNeil's John, excellently sung and presented with

appropriate pathos and simplicity; the excellent and affecting Kofner of George Jongeyans stood out. One of the best of them all was Gloria Lane, who has a fine voice and style, which she entirely subordinated to the representation of all the secretariat officiousness and red tape of the world. And when the secretary, awakening to the truth, saw the faces, in her imagination, peering at her from the walls, there was the breaking of the ice in a hitherto unemotional surface, that marked the unfolding of a character. One did want a more sinister Chief of Police, but all these figures blended so excellently in the dramatic ensemble that none of them was inadequate. The firm and authoritative conducting of Lehman Engel and his treatment of the score was an outstanding feature of the occasion.

And what of the inherent quality of the music per se? One cannot think of it, in the first place, as music in a category by itself. This is an opera made of inseparable strands of speech, song, action, scene. Technically, Mr. Menotti has the whole operatic vocabulary of the romantic and modern composers at his disposal. He can write in the most simple, direct, melodic manner. Or he can go contrapuntal, or use at will polytonality, cross rhythms, the most varied orchestration. He knows how to make a few strings chant requiem in the most modern way, and he knows how to rumble with kettle drumsticks on the lowest tones of the piano to make the effect of escaping gas and impending doom.

A modern, originally conceived, and wonderfully integrated opera triumphed.

1950 Mr 16

Ethel Merman as an American Envoy in 'Call Me Madam,' With Berlin's Music

The Cast

CALL ME MADAM, a musical comedy. Book by Howard Lindsay and Russel Crouse; music by Irving Berlin; staged by George Abbott;

dances and musical numbers staged by Jerome Robbins; scenery and costumes designed
by Raoul Pene du Bois; dresses by Main
Bocher; musical director, Jay Blackston;
orchestrations by Don Walker; produced by
Leland Hayward. At the Imperial Theatre.

Mrs. Sally Adams................Ethel Merman
The Secretary of State.........Geoffrey Lumb
Supreme Court Justice.............Owen Coll
Congressman Wilkins...........Pat Harrington
Henry Gibson....................William David
Kenneth Gibson................Russell Nype
Senator Gallagher............Ralph Chambers
Secretary to Mrs. Adams.........Jeanne Bal
Butler ....William Hail
Senator Brockbank..................Jay Velie
Cosmo Constantine................Paul Lukas
Pemberton Maxwell.............Alan Hewitt
Clerk ....Stowe Phelps
Hugo Tantinnin............E. A. Krumschmidt
Sebastian Sebastian.............Henry Lascoe
Princess Maria..................Galina Talva
Court Chamberlain............William David
A Maid............................Lily Paget
Grand Duchess Sophie............Lilia Skala
Grand Duke Otto..................Owen Coll
Principal Dancers: Tommy Rall, Muriel Bent-
ley, Arthur Partington, Norma Kaiser.
The "Potato Bugs": Ollie Engerbretson, Rich-
ard Fjellman.

By BROOKS ATKINSON

Despite the preliminary ballyhoo,
it is easy to enjoy "Call Me
Madam," which opened with considerable éclat at the Imperial last

evening. For the bookmakers and
the tune-smithy have put together
a good-hearted show with a very
happy manner. And Ethel Merman
is in it.

As you may have heard, she is
cast as the American Ambassador
to Lichtenburg, which, as the impish program declares, is one of the
two mythical countries—the other
being the United States of America. Our Ethel has taken a crack
at a number of parts in the last
giddy years, but this is the first
time she has represented our Government abroad.

* * *

Don't expect her to be awed, in
spite of the luxurious Mainbocher
garments. She is still lighting up
like an inspired pin-ball machine,
and still blowing the music lustily
throughout the theatre. Some of
the personages of Lichtenburg are
shocked by her vulgarity. But, as

A scene from "Call Me Madam"—Ethel Merman, Paul Lukas and
E. A. Krumschmidt, right.   Vandamm

in the case of the authors of the show, everyone can see that Ethel's heart is in the right place and that there is a streak of modesty under that drum-major's personality when a European has the audacity to reprove her. We were all eating out of Ethel's hand last evening for she was acting in the grand manner without being snobbish or pretentious.

Let's not pretend that the book is immortal. Howard Lindsay and Russel Crouse have left some dull spots in it and a few jokes that are heavy-handed. But they have had the grace to tell an ingratiating yarn about an exuberant American hostess who goes abroad full of Yankee self-confidence and learns, with a bit of a shock, that Europeans have to be respected. Among the most engaging items is a bookish Harvard graduate student, with a headful of facts and statistics, who very expeditiously falls in love with a Lichtenburg princess. Since the book constitutes a musical comedy plot, an experienced theatregoer must not admit that, in addition to being amusing, it is now and then genuinely touching.

That is where Irving Berlin comes in. This is one of his most enchanting scores, fresh, light and beguiling; and fitted to lyrics that fall out of it with grace and humor. "The Hostess With the Mostest on the Ball" turns out to be a fairly monotonous number. But "Lichtenburg" is a poignant song with a mature sense of deference toward modest people. And "It's a Lovely Day Today" is one of the most rapturous romantic song on Mr. Berlin's music-rack.

For Miss Merman he has written some jubilee ballads that have volume and authority—"The Best Thing for You Would Be Me," "Can You Use Any Money Today?" and "Washington Square Dance" being the most ringing examples. Since General Eisenhower was in the audience last night, Mr. Berlin opened the 1952 elections with a jaunty campaign song, bluntly dubbed "They Like Ike." In general, Mr. Berlin is not afraid of rhythm and melody; and Don Walker has done him the favor of arranging some appreciative orchestrations.

It is impossible to pay the prop-er respects to all the things that contribute to the pleasures of a bountiful show: Raoul Pène du Bois' carnival costumes and cheerful sets; Jerome Robbins' festive ballets; the sweet-potato arias of Ollie Engebretson and Richard Fjellman; and, of course, George Abbott's jaunty direction.

* * *

But it would be unforgivable not to express appreciation for the taste and warmth of the acting of Paul Lukas as a Lichtenburg statesman. Galina Talva is particularly attractive as a timed princess with a mind of her own. And Russell Nype made a host of friends last evening by acting with modesty and sincerity. As a timid grind fresh out of college he does not look very promising in the early scenes. But eventually it turns out that Mr. Nype can also sing. When Miss Merman and he sing "You're Just in Love," which is Mr. Berlin's top achievement for the evening, "Call Me Madam" throws a little stardust around the theatre and sets the audience to roaring.

Quite an evening on the whole.

1950 O 13

The Cast

THE LADY'S NOT FOR BURNING, a romantic comedy in three acts, by Christopher Fry. Staged by John Gielgud; decor by Oliver Messel; produced by Atlantis Productions (Theatre Guild, Tennent Productions, Ltd., John C. Wilson). At the Royale Theatre.

Richard	Richard Burton
Thomas Mendip	John Gielgud
Alizon Eliot	Penelope Munday
Nicholas Devise	David Evans
Margaret Devise	Nora Nicholson
Humphrey Devise	Richard Leech
Hebble Tyson	George Howe
Jennet Jourdemayne	Pamela Brown
The Chaplain	Eliot Makeham
Edward Tappercoom	Peter Bull
Matthew Skipps	Esme Percy

By BROOKS ATKINSON

Say a few words of welcome and appreciation, to Christopher Fry and John Gielgud. For Mr. Fry is author of "The Lady's Not for Burning," which was put on at the Royale last evening, and Mr. Gielgud leads the company that is playing it brilliantly. Little puffs of enthusiasm have been coming out of England for months over Mr. Fry's witchery with words.

The enthusiasm is not excessive. For Mr. Fry has restored the art of literature to the stage by writing a sparkling verse that also is shot with wit and humor.

* * *

He has written a whimsical fable about a misanthrope who reluctantly falls in love with an enchanting young woman sentenced to be burned as a witch. To tell the truth, the fable is not very robust or cogent; and there is no doubt at all that Mr. Fry's passion for words runs away with him. The story of "The Lady's Not for Burning" is rambling and inconsequential. And the words, pouring across the footlights in a turbid flood of imagery, can become pretty soporific now and then.

But the main thing is that the theatre has acquired an extraordinary literary writer who loves the sound of words and the embroidery of phrases. Fortunately, he is not solemn about it. He delights in irony and mischief. Like Jaques, he revels in humorous melancholy. He can turn an epigram without destroying the meter.

* * *

Some of the basic things in "The Lady's Not For Burning" are carelessly fashioned as though Mr. Fry lacked patience for the dramatic essentials. But the small things are perfectly phrased, and the minor characters are drawn with quizzical relish. Mr. Fry may be a little deficient in talent, but he has a touch of genius.

Without the most expert acting, the richness of the writing might be unbearable. For Mr. Fry is on the verge of being precocious. One suspects that he is too easily delighted with the abundance and variety of his gifts. But Mr. Gielgud has long given evidence of his mastery of style in acting; and the performance he has directed is a perfect piece of work. Mr. Gielgud and his associates have absorbed Mr. Fry's script, and they literally play with it—making a wry, mocking dance out of the fable and the characters.

* * *

For décor, Oliver Messel has designed a make-believe room of presumably the fifteenth century in England and agreeable costumes of traditional style. It takes courage in the modern theatre not to drug the audience with dazzling splendors. But Mr. Messel has intimated to the audience that "The Lady's Not for Burning" is a prank, and he has done his work with tongue-in-cheek gaiety.

Mr. Gielgud's misanthrope is sharply drawn, spoken with easy virtuosity, droll in tone and inflection. This is acting as expert as the memorable Wilde comedy he brought us several years ago. As the unhappy lady sentenced to burning, Pamela Brown gives a warm, rich and fluent performance that gleams with humorous coquetry. Both Miss Brown and Mr. Gielgud have matched Mr. Fry's writing with the lightness and bounce of their playing.

The entire company is superb. Eliot Makeham's benign and absent-minded chaplain is wonderfully ingratiating; and Nora Nicholson's silly, gabbling mother is a good joke also. As a dazed but susceptible clerk, Richard Burton gives an amusingly sober performance. A few words of appreciation should be spoken also for the acting of Richard Leech, Penelope Munday, David Evans, George Howe and Peter Bull. In the last scene, Esme Percy introduces a fresh whirl of mountebankery with his characterization of a drunken peddler.

* * *

Thanks to Mr. Fry, the literary impulse of the theatre has been revived; and since he is a sophisticated modern, it has been revived with the hard glitter of wit and skepticism. Mr. Fry ought to be very grateful to Mr. Gielgud. For it seems likely that no one else could make a dry comic antic out of so much undisciplined abundance. Mr. Gielgud has put a fine structure under it.

1950 N 9

The Cast

GUYS AND DOLLS, a musical fable of Broadway, based on a story ("The Idyll of Miss Sarah Brown") and characters by Damon Runyon. Music and lyrics by Frank Loesser. Book by Jo Swerling and Abe Burrows. Dances and musical numbers staged by Michael Kidd. Scenery and lighting by Jo Mielziner. Costumes by Alvin Colt. Musical director, Irving Actman. Orchestral arrangements, George Bassman and Ted Royal. Vocal arrangements and direction, Herbert Greene. Produced by Cy Feuer and Ernest H. Martin. At the Forty-sixth Street Theatre.
Nicely-Nicely Johnson..............Stubby Kaye
Benny Southstreet.................Johnny Silver
Rusty Charlie....................Douglas Deane
Sarah Brown......................Isabel Bigley

By BROOKS ATKINSON

Out of the pages of Damon Runyon, some able artisans have put together a musical play that Broadway can be proud of. "Guys and Dolls" they call it out of one corner of the mouth. It opened at the Forty-sixth Street last evening. With a well-written book by Jo Swerling and Abe Burrows, and a dynamic score by Frank Loesser, it is a more coherent show than some that have higher artistic pretensions.

But you can count as its highest achievement the fact that it has preserved the friendly spirit of the Runyon literature without patronizing and without any show-shop hokum. It is the story of some gamblers and their unfortunate women who try to fit into the shifty pattern of Broadway life some of the stabilizing factors of marriage and love-making.

Let one playgoer remark in passing that there is something a little disconcerting about the casual attitude this story takes toward a religious mission which is trying to save a few souls in the neighborhood. But even this intrusion on the way of life of some street-corner salvationists is redeemed by the hearty camaraderie of all the characters of the book. Although they are gamblers, showgirls, cops and adult delinquents, they have their ethics, too, and live in a gaudy, blowzy world that is somehow warm and hospitable. After all, the Broadway culture is simple and sentimental but has a better heart than some cultures that are more literate.

Sam Levene and Vivian Blaine in "Guys and Dolls"

* * *

Everyone concerned with "Guys and Dolls" has cast the show with relish and originality; and George S. Kaufman has never been in better form in the director's box. As the executive officer of the oldest floating crap game in town, Sam Levene gives an excitable and hilarious performance. Vivian Blaine makes something comic out of the lively vulgarity of a night-club leading lady, singing her honky-tonk songs in a shrill but earnest voice. Isabel Bigley does as well by a missionary sergeant who astonishes herself by falling in love with an itinerant gambler. She plays a few enticing tricks on one of Mr. Loesser's most rollicking songs—"If I Were a Bell." As the tall, dark and handsome gambler, Robert Alda keeps the romance enjoyable, tough and surly.

The Runyon milieu is rich in startling types, and "Guys and Dolls" has the most flamboyant population of any show in town. Stubby Kaye, as a rotund sidewalk emissary; Johnny Silver, as a diminutive horse philosopher; B. S. Pully, as a big gun-and-blackjack man from Chicago—are sound, racy members of hallway society; and at last Tom Pedi has got a part that runs more than five minutes as Harry The Horse, executive secretary for a thug. No one could make a more lovable salvationist than Pat Rooney Sr., who sings "More I Cannot Wish" with cordial good-will.

* * *

Everything is all of a piece in this breezy fiction which has been organized as simply and logically as a Runyon story. Michael Kidds' comic ballets of night club production numbers and crap games belong to the production as intimately as Jo Mielziner's affable settings and Alvin Colt's noisy costumes. Mr. Loesser's lyrics and songs have the same affectionate appreciation of the material as the book, which is funny without being self-conscious or mechanical.

From the technical point of view we might as well admit that "Guys and Dolls" is a work of art. It is spontaneous and has form, style and spirit. In view of the source material, that is not astonishing. For Damon Runyon captured the spirit of an idle corner of the town with sympathetic understanding and reproduced it slightly caricatured in the sketches and stories he wrote. "Guys and Dolls" is gusty and uproarious, and it is not too grand to take a friendly, personal interest in the desperate affairs of Broadway's backroom society.

1950 N 25

City Center Opens Its Winter Theatre Series With One of Shaw's Early Plays

CAPTAIN BRASSBOUND'S CONVERSION, "an adventure" in three acts, by George Bernard Shaw. Revived by the New York City Theatre Company (Maurice Evans, artistic supervisor, and George Schaefer, executive producer); staged by Morton DaCosta; scenery and lighting by Ben Edwards; costume director, Emeline Roche. At the City Center.

Rankin	Noel Leslie
Drinkwater	Ian Martin
Hassan	Walt Witcover
First Krooboy	Alfred Ruscio
Second Krooboy	Paul Steiner
Sir Howard Hallam	Clay Clement
Lady Cicely	Edna Best
Muley	Alan Cahn
Marzo	Robert Carricart
Brassbound	John Archer
Redbook	Hugh Green
Johnson	Chris Gampel
First Brassbound Man	Robert Van Hooton
Second Brassbound Man	Jack Horn
Third Brassbound Man	Walt Witcover
Osman	Wendell Whitten
Sidi El Assif	Bruce Gordon
Cadi of Kintafi	Douglas M. H. Chandler
Bluejacket	Dean Whitmore
Capt. Hamlin Kearney	Loring Smith

Sailors, Officers, and Arabs: William Ablin, Andrew Bernard, Mario Alcalde, Ted Atwood, William Bush, William Becker, Robert Burns, Alan Cahn, Edwin Christie, George Hoxie, Harvey Korman, William Leonard, Bill O'Brien, Robert O'Flaherty, Ted Sheraton, Richard Woods, Jackson Young.

By BROOKS ATKINSON

Although Bernard Shaw has now left us for a more agreeable neighborhood, his spirit is still mischievous and witty. The spirit is currently visible in "Captain Brassbound's Conversion," which opened the City Center's winter series auspiciously last evening. This is the amusing comedy that Shaw wrote for Ellen Terry out of affection, admiration and wonder in 1899.

According to the Shavian legend, she did not recognize herself in Lady Cicely when she first read the manuscript. If this is so, she must have been a modest lady, for Lady Cicely is a charming, good-hearted, altogether captivating representative of British imperialism at the turn of the century.

Not that Shaw could carry the torch romantically. For he was a sardonic admirer. And it is his contention that a fine, high-minded, sentimental, motherly lady who refuses to recognize evil is unconquerable, gets everything she wants with no effort at all and completely upsets the dignified and responsible world of men.

Lady Cicely insists on taking a dangerous journey into Moslem territory. She cheerfully puts herself in the hands of a number of scoundrels, and finds herself in a highly-perilous situation. The men wrangle and point guns at each other. But the point of "Captain Brassbound's Conversion" is that Lady Cicely, talking baby-talk and behaving innocently, sets everything to rights with no trouble at all, destroys the law, outmaneuvers the United States Navy and makes everyone love her and each other and surrender to blissful comity.

Since Shaw had to learn his craft like any other artisan, "Captain Brassbound's Conversion" begins with some of the most tedious and complicated exposition encountered in any comedy since "The Devil's Disciple." But stay with it, and it gathers lightness,

John Archer and Edna Best in a scene from "Captain Brassbound's Conversion."

satire and drollery; and, again, like "The Devil's Disciple," it turns up with a hilarious last act.

Under Morton Da Costa's direction, the City Center company performs it admirably. Edna Best, looking like one of Renoir's most adorable portraits, gives a warm, subtle and infinitely accomplished performance as Lady Cicely. Half artful, half sincere, she moves through the part with the greatest composure and good humor, making Shaw's ironic points as if they were her own. At the moment it is impossible to think of a part Miss Best has played more skillfully.

There is nothing shoddy about the casting or the performance. John Archer is an imposing though unwillingly susceptible Captain Brassbound. Clay Clement as a pompous British judge; Loring Smith as a chuckle-headed though gallant Naval captain; Noel Leslie as a wary Scottish medical missionary; Ian Martin as a loquacious lying brigand with a treacherous personality; Bruce Gordon as a romantic sheik; Robert Carricart as an affable cut-throat—give excellent performances in a buoyant comic vein.

In designing the two sets, Ben Edwards has done an especially felicitous job with a Morocco garden overlooking a harbor; and Emmeline Roche has found suitable costumes for brigands, Moslem tribesmen and U. S. Navy officers in the whites of the Spanish War period.

If you insist on being exact about it, "Captain Brassbound's Conversion" is minor Shaw. But it is gay, sly and intelligent; it is dry in style, and, since Shaw had Ellen Terry in mind when he wrote it, there is a pleasant streak of devotion running through the satire. All things considered, the City Center has begun the winter theatre series in a cheerful spirit.

1950 D 28

1951

The Rose Tattoo

By BROOKS ATKINSON

Tennessee Williams is in a good mood in "The Rose Tattoo," which opened at the Martin Beck on Saturday evening. And there is no reason now why audiences should not be in a happy mood for the rest of the season. You may grumble a little about the unevenness of the story, for not everything Mr. Williams has to say is pertinent or dramatic.

The Cast

THE ROSE TATTOO, a play in three acts by Tennessee Williams. Directed by Daniel Mann; settings by Boris Aronson; costumes by Rose Bogdanoff; incidental music by David Diamond; lighting by Charles Elson. Presented by Cheryl Crawford. At the Martin Beck Theatre.

Salvatore	Salvatore Mineo
Vivi	Judy Ratner
Bruno	Salvatore Taormina
Assunta	Ludmilla Toretzka
Rosa Delle Rose	Phyllis Love
Serafina Delle Rose	Maureen Stapleton
Estelle Hohengarten	Sonia Sorel
The Strega	Daisy Belmore
Giuseppina	Rosanna San Marco
Pepina	Augusta Merighi
Violetta	Vivian Nathan
Mariella	Penny Santon
Teresa	Nancy Franklin
Father De Leo	Robert Carricart
Doctor	Andrew Duggan
Miss Yorke	Dorrit Kelton
Flora	Jane Hoffman
Bessie	Florence Sundstrom
Jack Hunter	Don Murray
Salesman	Eddie Hyans
Alvarro Mangiacavallo	Eli Wallach
Man	David Stewart
Man	Martin Balsam

But his folk comedy about a Sicilian family living on the Gulf Coast is original, imaginative and tender. It is the loveliest idyll written for the stage in some time. For the past six years Mr. Williams has been feeling fairly hopeless about human beings, and his wretched characters have been writhing in pain.

Now he is writing about a simple-minded Sicilian woman who has known the glory of love. Although her husband, a truck-driver, is killed in a motor accident, her memory of love still sets her apart from the unloved and from the cheaters. She dedicates herself to the ideal of a great love that has enriched her life.

* * *

Unfortunately for the ideal, her husband did not love her alone. Gossip about his infidelity walls her around with a murmur of ridicule and malice. It torments the widow's spirit and turns her against the world. But another truck-driver appears off the road when she is lowest in her mind and restores her to her normal health. He is not the man her husband was, but he returns her to the warmth and comfort of human society.

As a play, "The Rose Tattoo" lacks the intensity of "The Glass Menagerie," "A Streetcar Named Desire" and "Summer and Smoke." It moves along loosely and loquaciously. But to those of us who were afraid that Mr. Williams had been imprisoned within a formula it is especially gratifying. For this is a comic play that is also compassionate and appreciative. Some of it is hilarious; those gusty and volatile Sicilians blow hot and cold at bewildering speed.

But Mr. Williams does not condescend to them. "The Rose Tattoo" is not written from the outside. Mr. Williams admires their vitality and their native understanding, and delights in their wholesomeness. The love affair between the widow and the truck driver is not far from low comedy. But there is a love affair between the widow's daughter and a sailor that has all the lyric rapture and sincerity of young poetry. As sheer writing it is one of the finest things Mr.

Williams has done. Forget the sprawling workmanship of the play as a whole. The respect for character and the quality of the writing are Mr. Williams at the top of his form.

Fortunately, the performance and the production are superb. Boris Aronson has set the play inside a livable cottage which, in turn, lies inside a warm, lazy environment. And Daniel Mann has directed a tempestuous performance that alternates between moods of anguish and excitement and also explodes now and then with comedy.

The cast includes a number of shrewish women, jeering children and local characters; and these parts are well cast and played. The chief characters are admirably acted by players who have caught the sunny freshness of the theme.

As the widow's young and eager daughter Phyllis Love gives a tremulous, darting performance that is likely to break your heart if you do not brace yourself, for she is

Maureen Stapleton and Eli Wallach in a scene from "The Rose Tattoo"

an idealization of the kind of un-spoiled love Mr. Williams is writ-ing about. As the sailor, Don Mur-ray plays opposite her with youth, honesty and principle that com-pose the perfect counterpart. Rob-ert Carricart acts a local priest with simplicity that is wholly winning.

In the part of the truck-driver, Eli Wallach gives a humorous, naïve, frustrated performance in a light, buoyant style. But "The Rose Tattoo" is a play about the widow who is always on stage and who, in the course of the evening, pretty thoroughly speaks the auto-biography of her soul. It is a long, exhausting part in a tone of con-tinuous excitement. Maureen Sta-pleton's performance is trium-phant. The widow is unlearned and superstitious and becomes some-thing of a harridan after her hus-band dies. Miss Stapleton does not evade the coarseness of the part. But neither does she miss its exal-tation. For Mr. Williams has sprinkled a little stardust over the widow's shoulders and Miss Staple-ton has kept the part sparkling through all the fury and tumult of the emotion.

Everybody deserves a little pat of appreciation—Rose Bogdanoff for the perceptive costumes, Charles Elson for the eloquent lighting and David Diamond for the evocative background music. For this is a happy occasion in the theatre. Mr. Williams can com-pose in the halcyon style as well as the somber one. Now we can be sure that he is a permanent source of enjoyment in the theatre.

1951 F 5

Billy Budd

By BROOKS ATKINSON

Nobody bothered to publish Her-man Melville's grim story of "Billy Budd" until thirty years after his death. It was easy to evade the malign implications of the sea yarn by stuffing it into a pigeon-hole. But it is going to be hard to avoid thinking about it now. For Louis O. Coxe and Robert Chap-man have made a horrifyingly can-did drama out of it, still called "Billy Budd," which opened in a superb performance at the Bilt-more on Saturday evening.

Although it has the color, savor and turbulence of a sea story, its romanticism is perverse. It is set on board H. M. S. Indomitable at sea in 1798 and it brings to life the rude and brawling ways of men on shipboard. But the brood-ing author of "Moby Dick" was really interested in the wild life of man that underlies the little cere-monies we take part in as mem-bers of society. "Billy Budd" sternly dramatizes the basic prob-lem of good and evil.

* * *

Billy Budd is a handsome, guile-less, pure-minded sailor who is im-pressed into His Majesty's service in wartime. To the author of "Billy Budd" he represents good. The master-at-arms is a malevolent sadist who hates life and repre-sents evil. He cannot let the good triumph without abandoning the whole philosophy of evil that he has developed over the years. He sets out to destroy Billy to pre-serve his own ego. In the process, Billy strikes him and accidentally kills him.

According to the laws of the Navy, he is guilty of murdering a superior officer and must be hanged. This is where the almost unbearable drama comes in. To everyone on board ship, Billy is innocent of the intent of murder. He is rather the victim of the master-at-arms' scheme to destroy him. Even the ship's court revolts at the necessity of carrying out so monstrous a sentence. But they have no discretion. Cause hurries on to the most devastating effect in the code of man-made disci-pline. Good and evil destroy each other, for neither one has made the human compromise that makes social life possible.

* * *

Mr. Coxe and Mr. Chapman have written an extraordinarily skillful play that begins casually enough below decks with the gos-sip and grumbling of the crew. But gradually it moves out of familiar things into the tension of a moral problem that tightens the whole ship and challenges the universe. The fateful reasoning in the last act is hard to follow, it wrestles with so many abstract ideas and upsets so thoroughly most human assumptions.

But there is a strong mind burrowing into Billy Budd's awful fate—a sympathetic mind that has no faith in men and is even skeptical of the goodness of God. By the time Melville wrote this story

The Cast

BILLY BUDD, a play in three acts and nine scenes, by Louis O Coxe and Robert Chapman, based on a novel by Herman Melville. Staged by Norris Houghton; scenery by Paul Morrison; costumes by Ruth Morley; production associate, Benet Segal; presented by Chandler Cowles and Anthony B. Farrell. At the Biltmore Theatre.

Jenkins	Jeff Morrow
The Dansker	George Fells
Jackson	Bertram Tanswell
John Claggart	Torin Thatcher
Talbot	James Daly
Butler	Leonard Yorr
Kincaid	Kenneth Paige
Payne	Judson Pratt
O'Daniel	Walter Burke
Messboy	Charles Hudson
Squeak	Bernard Kates
Duncan	Robert McQueeney
Surgeon	Winston Ross
Gardiner	Jack Manning
Billy Budd	Charles Nolte
Edward Fairfax Vere	Dennis King
Hallam	Lee Marvin
Rea	Henry Garrard
Philip Michael Seymour	Guy Spaull
John Ratcliffe	Preston Hanson
Bordman Wyatt	Norman Ettlinger
Stoll	Charles Carshon
Byren	Martin Brandt

Drummer	David Long
Sailor	Robert Dudley
Second Marine	Bill Froelich

he had been broiled in hellfire. He could have cited chapter and verse to account for his pessimism, for "Billy Budd" is founded on an incident in the American Navy of the nineteenth century.

Thanks to Norris Houghton, "Billy Budd" has been staged with taste, style and integrity. Paul Morrison has designed some imposing shipboard scenery, and Ruth Morley has dressed the officers and the men in interesting costumes. Dennis King plays the captain with intellectual alertness and authority, and also with decent compassion in the concluding scenes.

As the master-at-arms, Torin Thatcher plays with a combination of neatness and cold fury—the devil's advocate incarnate. Against the touching gentleness of Charles Nolte's Billy Budd, Mr. Thatcher's evil intelligence is painfully vivid. Mr. Nolte expresses Billy's artlessness without letting him ever become mawkish or cloying.

There are excellent performances

Dennis King, left, and Torin Thatcher in a scene from "Billy Budd"

by Jack Manning as a comically
supercilious midshipman, Jeff Morrow as a belligerent sailor, Bernard Kates as a treacherous pierhead jumper, Guy Spaull as the
first officer, and many others in
a long cast. On the surface "Billy
Budd" is as picturesque as "Mister
Roberts." But after the scene is
set a mind takes possession of it
and proceeds to knock against
some of the most tormenting problems of the universe. "Billy Budd"
has size and depth as well as color
and excitement.

1951 F 12

The Moon Is Blue

By BROOKS ATKINSON

Out of a hint and a grimace F.
Hugh Herbert has spun a droll romantic comedy, "The Moon Is
Blue," which opened at the Henry
Miller last evening and ought to
stay open for quite a long time. It
includes four characters, one of
whom works for only about three
minutes before he is through for
the day; and the plot is about as
extensive as a brief anecdote.

But Mr. Herbert has a very im-
impromptu attitude toward life.
And his cast includes Barbara Bel
Geddes. It is difficult on short
notice to define the relationship
between these two factors. But
some definite relationship does exist. For Mr. Herbert's attitude
seems wholly plausible and, in
fact, desirable when Miss Bel
Geddes marches through his play,
looking very much as though she
believes what she is saying.

* * *

That is manifestly impossible.
Mr. Herbert is telling the story of
an agreeable young architect
(played by Barry Nelson) who
picks up a personable young lady
(played by Miss Bel Geddes) in the
tower of the Empire State Building. In a subsequent scene, set
naturally in the architect's apartment, Mr. Herbert introduces a
middle-aged libertine (played with
an entirely fraudulent Southern
accent by Donald Cook).

There is no point in telling you
what happens. In the first place,
you would not believe it. In the
second place, the chronicler of

these proceedings does not believe
it. It is more than likely that
nothing happens after all. For Mr.
Herbert does not seem to be extraordinarily inventive; and his
dialogue leans toward the mechanical and some of it, especially in
the second act, is patently monotonous.

But while the actors are prowl-
ing around the stage, there is a
definite impression that something
delightfully crack-brained is taking place in the most normal circumstances. The architect is trying over the telephone to shake a
girl he has been inadvertently engaged to. The libertine, who is
her father, is uncertain whether he
should horse-whip the architect or
marry the Empire State young
lady. Being both naive and world-

The Cast

THE MOON IS BLUE, a new comedy by F.
Hugh Herbert. Scenery and lighting by
Stewart Chaney; staged by Otto Preminger;
produced by Aldrich & Myers and Mr.
Preminger, in association with Julius Fleisch-
mann. At Henry Miller's Theatre.
Patty O'Neill.............Barbara Bel Geddes
Donald Gresham...................Barry Nelson
David Slater....................Donald Cook
Michael O'Neill...................Ralph Dunn

ly, and also fantastically commu-
nicative, the young lady tries desperately to understand what is
going on, complicating everything
she puts her little mind to. The
whole episode is pleasantly insane.

To say that it would not be
funny if it were not acted so expertly is beside the point. For the
only fact worth mentioning is that
it is acted expertly. Otto Preminger has directed it with relish.
Stewart Chaney has given it one
of those wildly luxurious settings
that fantasticate the performance.

As the amiable young lady, Miss
Bel Geddes is radiantly beautiful
—a fact that explains quite a lot
about everything. But she also
manages to act a coherent character, looking gravely puzzled by
the behavior of the helpless male,
smiling enchantingly at the hopeful interludes in a cock-eyed manuscript and always waiting for the
right moment to speak a line. Mr.
Herbert ought to regard her as a
treasure. Everyone else inevitably
does.

* * *

She is ably abetted by Barry
Nelson, whose soft speech, creased
smile, undulating walk and theatre

sense compose the perfect comic counterpoint. And Mr. Cook's dissipated insouciance as the wealthy libertine introduces a contrast of considerable value. All Ralph Dunn has to do in the second act is to burst in belligerently, sock the architect in the eye, deliver a brief moral homily and return to the pinochle game backstage. This is not an extensive assignment, but Mr. Dunn does it satisfactorily with both biceps.

Nothing much happens in "The Moon Is Blue." But some of it is very funny, and most of it is delightful.

1951 Mr 9

Louis Jouvet and His French Company Act Moliere's 'L'Ecole des Femmes'

By BROOKS ATKINSON

In honor of International Theatre Month, Louis Jouvet and his Théatre de l'Athénée company have had the goodness to come here from Paris for a limited engagement. They opened at the Anta Playhouse last evening in Molière's "L'Ecole des Femmes," which they already have played in Europe, Egypt and South America. This is a good play for purposes of foreign travel, for it is reasonably intelligible to Americans who, like Chaucer's Prioresse, the French of Paris do unknowe.

For it is almost a masquerade as M. Jouvet plays it with a good deal of capering around the stage and grimacing. By the time Molière wrote "L'Ecole des Femmes" in 1662, he had had a long training in commedia dell' arte in the provinces. M. Jouvet's stylized acting, which is directed frankly toward the audience, is in the commedia dell' arte tradition.

* * *

"L'Ecole des Femmes" is the fable of a fatuous man of middle years who proposes to escape the chief hazard of marriage by wedding a simple girl, Agnes, who has been brought up in ignorance of the world. Although he arranges the match sagaciously, he is defeated by love which comes between him and Agnes. She falls in love with a youth who is her own age.

It is a simple, symmetrical plot, with a pat solution that Molière would have to be censured for if he were not already revered in liberal arts colleges. He could be as bad as Shakespeare when he wanted to pull down the curtain and go home. But since Molière is a classic, he must not be criticized, especially overseas, and the student of French can sit happily in the Anta Playhouse, reassured by hearing the words femme, coeur and infidélité popping cheerfully out of the dialogue.

The Cast

L'ECOLE DES FEMMES (THE SCHOOL FOR WIVES), Molière's comedy in two acts and five scenes presented in French. Staged by Louis Jouvet; scenery and costumes by Christian Berard; music by Vittorio Rieti; produced by La Compagnie Dramatique Francaise des Tournees under the auspices of the Anta Play Series (Cheryl Crawford and Robert Breen, general directors; R. L. Stevens, administrator). At the Anta Playhouse.

Horace ....Jean Richard
Arnolphe ....Louis Jouvet
Chrysalde ....Leo Lapara
Alain ....Fernand-Rene
Georgette ....Monique Melinand
Agnes ....Dominique Blanchar
Notary ....Michel Etcheverry
Notary's Clerk...................Rene Besson
Enrique ....Georges Riquier
Oronte ....Pierre Renoir

M. Jouvet has brought us a production that might be studied profitably by American scene designers or, more especially American producers, who are the ones who call the tune. Faced with the necessity of representing a street and the interior of a Parisian house, the late Christian Bérard solved it with audacious simplicity by bringing the end of a wall straight down to the footlights for the street scenes; and then dividing the wall into two mobile wings to frame a garden. Upstage rises the tower of a house with three miniature balconies.

This is a vivid set, reduced to the essentials and barely decorated; and it gives the actors both the room and the atmosphere for performing. The seventeenth-century costumes are also works of genius. Although they are beautiful, they are not stifled in splendor. Like the scenery, they are simple, sketched by a man who believed in basic design and instinctively dispensed with rich embellishment. Although M. Jouvet plays Molière's satirical prank broadly, he, too, believes in design, as though the part of Arnolphe were a figure in a dance. The French are more animated conversationalists than the Anglo-Saxons. But M. Jouvet is animated even for a Frenchman. Arnolphe blows hot and cold according to the fortunes of the plot; and M. Jouvet follows him closely, walking with a crouch, moving his cane with elation or melancholy according to the mood of the scene, giggling, guffawing, or suffering, his mouth hanging open apprehensively and his eyes laughing or sorrowing as the case may be.

* * *

It is a remarkably busy performance—sometimes so for its own sake, that it is tiresome to watch. But, like the scenery, his acting is entirely new to America, where we are disposed to imitate reality. And it obviously comes out of a long tradition — out of commedia dell'arte, in fact, which is a style that needs a solid background of heritage and study.

For contrast, there is Dominique Blanchar as Agnes. She is an adorable young lady with a symmetrical beauty straight out of the story-books. She can also act, which does not always follow. And one of the funniest scenes in the play is her simple, childlike reading of the etiquette of marital duties for wives in the book Arnolphe hands to her. Mlle. Blanchar's colorless voice and her weary sense of obedience are wonderfully comic.

* * *

The cast also includes Jean Richard as the youthful suitor,

Pierre Renoir, Louis Jouvet and Dominique Blanchar in a scene from "L'Ecole des Femmes" ("The School for Wives").

Léo Lapara as the cynical counsellor, Fernand-René and Monique Melinand as the irreverent servants and Michel Etcheverry and René Besson in a clownish scene as the notary and his clerk. Note, also, the bold make-ups of the actors in the comic parts; without being grotesque, they are humorously contrived.

"L'Ecole des Femmes" is a refreshing exercise in artificial acting by a master of the craft. For International Theatre Month, M. Jouvet has obligingly brought us the Molière tradition.

1951 Mr 19

The King And I

By BROOKS ATKINSON

Nearly two years having elapsed since they invaded the South Pacific, Richard Rodgers and Oscar Hammerstein 2d have moved over to the Gulf of Siam. "The King and I," which opened at the St. James last evening, is their musical rendering of Margaret Landon's "Anna and the King of Siam." As a matter of record, it must be reported that "The King and I" is no match for "South Pacific," which is an inspired musical drama.

But there is plenty of room for memorable music-making in the more familiar categories. Strictly on its own terms, "The King and I" is an original and beautiful excursion into the rich splendors of the Far East, done with impeccable taste by two artists and brought to life with a warm, romantic score, idiomatic lyrics and some exquisite dancing.

* * *

As the English governess who comes out from England in the Eighteen-Sixties to teach the King's children, Gertrude Lawrence looks particularly ravishing in some gorgeous costumes and acts an imposing part with spirit and an edge of mischief. Yul Brynner plays the King with a kind of fierce austerity, drawn between pride of office and eagerness to learn about the truth of the modern world from a "scientific foreigner." Apart from the pleasures of the musical theatre, there is a theme in "The King and I, and, as usual, Mr. Rodgers

and Mr. Hammerstein have developed it with tenderness as well as relish, and with respect for the human beings involved.

Part of the delight of their fable derives from the wealth of beauty in the Siamese setting; and here Jo Mielziner, the Broadway magnifico, has drawn on the riches of the East; and Irene Sharaff has designed some of her most wonderful costumes. As a spectacle, "The King and I" is a distinguished work. In the direction, John van Druten has made something fine and touching in the elaborate scene that introduces the King's charming children to their English school marm. Jerome Robbins, serving as choreographer, has put together a stunning ballet that seasons the liquid formalism of Eastern dancing with some American humor. Yuriko, the ballerina, is superb as the Siamese notion of Eliza in "Uncle Tom's Cabin."

* * *

Mr. Rodgers is in one of his most affable moods. For Miss Lawrence he has written several pleasant and ingratiating numbers which she sings brightly—"Hello, Young Lovers!" "The Royal Bangkok Academy" and "Shall I Tell You What I Think of You?" Dorothy Sarnoff does something wonderful with "Something Wonderful," which is one of Mr. Rodgers' most exultant numbers. Probably

The Cast

THE KING AND I, a musical play with music by Richard Rodgers; book and lyrics by Oscar Hammerstein 2d, based on the novel, "Anna and the King of Siam," by Margaret Landon; staged by John van Druten; scenery and lighting by Jo Mielziner; costumes designed by Irene Sharaff; choreography by Jerome Robbins; orchestrations by Robert Russell Bennett; musical director Frederick Dvonch; produced by the Messrs. Rodgers and Hammerstein. At the St. James Theatre.

Captain Orton	Charles Francis
Louis Leonowens	Sandy Kennedy
Anna Leonowens	Gertrude Lawrence
The Interpreter	Leonard Graves
The Kralahome	John Juliano
The King	Yul Brynner
Phra Alack	Len Mence
Tuptim	Doretta Morrow
Lady Thiang	Dorothy Sarnoff
Prince Chulalongkorn	Johnny Stewart
Princess Ying Yaowalak	Baayork Lee
Lun Tha	Larry Douglas
Sir Edward Ramsay	Robin Craven

the most glorious number is "I Have Dreamed," which Doretta Morrow and Larry Douglas sing as a fervent duet. Mr. Brynner is no great shakes as a singer, but he makes his way safely through a couple of meditative songs written with an agreeable suggestion of Eastern music.

Say a word of thanks to Russell Bennett for his colorful orchestrations that make a fresh use of individual instruments and that always sound not only interesting but civilized. His orchestration should be especially appreciated in the long and enchanting scene that brings on the children one by one.

Don't expect another "South Pacific" nor an "Oklahoma!" This time Mr. Rodgers and Mr. Hammerstein are not breaking any fresh trails. But they are accomplished artists of song and words in the theatre; and "The King and I" is a beautiful and lovable musical play.

1951 Mr 30

Don Juan In Hell

By BROOKS ATKINSON

Since the First Drama Quartette is composed of extraordinary actors, their reading, as they call it, of Shaw's "Don Juan in Hell" is a mighty and moving occasion. They are Charles Boyer, Charles Laughton, Cedric Hardwicke and Agnes Moorehead. Attired in evening clothes and standing before microphones they pretend that they are going to read their parts from a manuscript of the drama.

But they are actors. The reading they gave last evening at Carnegie Hall is a thrilling performance. For they have looked below the surface gabble of Shaw's lines into their meaning; and without forgetting that he has a sardonic style, they have become his advocates. This is not only a performance but an intellectual crusade, and the First Drama Quartette comes to New York bearing ideas, ideals and philosophical passion.

* * *

As far as the records of our enterprising office show, the "Don Juan in Hell" scene has never been acted professionally in New York. It is published in the texts as the third act of "Man and Superman," but generally it is shaken out of that comedy by producers who want to get their audiences home before the milkman appears. When Maurice Evans put on his hard and

glittering performance of "Man and Superman" in 1947, he considered staging the Don Juan scene for special occasions, as they are now doing in London, but nothing came of his project.

Since it was written separately,

The Cast

DON JUAN IN HELL, the dream sequence from Bernard Shaw's play, "Man and Superman." Staged by Charles Laughton; presented by Paul Gregory at Carnegie Hall for one performance.

Don Juan	Charles Boyer
Devil	Charles Laughton
Statue	Sir Cedric Hardwicke
Donna Anna	Agnes Moorehead

it is logical to play it as an independent enterprise, and since it looks almost unactable in the texts, the scheme of presenting it as a reading is not only legitimate but inspired. For it is a closely reasoned argument for the validity of Shaw's thesis of creative evolution —compact, written with unrelieved brilliance on one plane of rationalization, two of the four characters talking in the same idiom and with the same intensity of intellectual excitement.

* * *

At least to Shavians it is an immensely stimulating argument. It is paradoxical in its point of view, witty in its analysis of human manners and institutions, and alert and humorous. But there is something more stirring than that about it. It is a rousing statement of faith from a man of thought, erudition and independence. For it presents the thesis that mankind has a future, that he can keep on lifting himself up by his bootstraps, as he has done in the past.

Shaw wrote it in 1901 and it is possible that he might not have believed so passionately in the future of the race after the shattering experiences of two world wars. He is not on hand to defend or reject it now. But the drive and shining convictions of his humorous declaration of principle are mighty heartening now.

If there is any dramatic talk equal to it in New York today, it crackles out of "Saint Joan," which was written by the same genius about eighteen years later when he was not feeling quite so breezy. Shaw has been the dominant dramatist in New York ever since the last war. Apparently he is still outdazzling his juniors this year.

The two best parts are those of Don Juan and the Devil. They could hardly be played with more eloquence or understanding. As the Devil, moon-faced Mr. Laughton acts with diabolical gusto and gives dramatic weight to the whole performance. The long, closely reasoned speeches he gives with great spontaneity, putting the emphasis where it belongs, using the words carefully, pointing the meaning with gestures and movements. Call it a masterful performance and you cannot be wrong.

And Mr. Boyer's performance is masterly, also. As Don Juan, he plays the part that Shaw believed in, and he has all the constructive thought on his side. Since the prose is crisp and distinguished, it is a pity that Mr. Boyer does not speak English with more facility. There are linguistical points in the dialogue that he blunders over. But we can take him gratefully on his own terms, for he is a great actor with fire and integrity. Shaw could not speak for creative evolution with half the grandeur Mr. Boyer has put into his acting.

* * *

Cedric Hardwicke is in fine fettle as The Statue, or Shaw's professional Englishman. He plays it with grace, subtlety and wit. He was not half so skillful and amusing when he was playing "Caesar and Cleopatra" here a few years ago. As the only woman in the play, Agnes Moorehead acts the respectability and propriety with tongue-in-cheek humor, and has caught the vivacity of the whole occasion.

For this is a performance compounded of sheer skill, and it will never be forgotten by anyone in Carnegie Hall last evening. Next Thursday the First Drama Quartette will perform in the Brooklyn Academy of Music. At the end of November they will return for about a month at a theatre yet to be selected in New York. Everyone who loves great writing and great acting will want to hear this simple but inspired reading.

1951 O 23

I Am A Camera
By BROOKS ATKINSON

With the assistance of a remark-able actress, John van Druten has put together an impromptu acting piece, "I Am a Camera," which opened at the Empire last evening. The actress is Julie Harris, who was playing a restless tom-boy in the same theatre two years ago. Now she is playing a glib, brassy, temperamental woman of the world—all cleverness, all sophistication. She plays with a virtuosity and an honesty that are altogether stunning, and that renew an old impression that Miss Harris has the quicksilver and the genius we all long to discover on the stage.

* * *

The phrase "impromptu acting piece" indicates the difficulty of describing Mr. van Druten's play. It is interesting. It contains several fascinating characters. It touches on a few vital principles. It is written with the ingratiating informality of his best work. But "I Am a Camera" keeps losing its way all through the evening. Although it never is dull, it never accomplishes much.

Mr. van Druten has adapted it from some stories Christopher Isherwood wrote about life in Berlin in the first days of the Nazis. One of the two principal characters is named Christopher Isherwood. He is a young writer who, like a camera with the shutter open, is taking pictures of people and places in a period of history. He is reporting how a crucial moment in the affairs of the world looked to a bystander.

On the whole, they looked random and amusing. For "I Am a Camera" is fundamentally the character sketch of an effervescent, amoral English girl who is living a Bohemian life in Berlin and of young Christopher Isherwood, who likes her, enjoys her company and wonders about the futility of what he is doing. There are rumblings of hostility to the Jews, and a pair of young Jews **bring their problems into the play for a moment or two.**

But on the whole, Mr. Isherwood's camera shows nothing more than the harum-scarum antics of a couple of immensely likable Eng-

The Cast

I AM A CAMERA, a play in three acts and seven scenes, by John van Druten, adapted from Christopher Isherwood's "Berlin Stories." Staged by Mr. van Druten; setting and light-

ing by Boris Aronsó :; costume by Ellen
Goldeborough; presented by Gertrude Macy, in
association with Walter Starcke. At the
Empire Theatre.
Christopher Isherwood. ....William Prince
Fraulein Schneider..................Olga Fabian
Fritz Wendel....................Martin Brooks
Sally Bowles..................Julie Harris
Natalie Landauer.................Marian Winters
Clive Mortimer................Edward Andrews
Mrs. Watson-Courtneidge.....Catherine Willard

lish people, fooling around as young people were in New York. London and Paris in the previous decade.

That is why it is best to accept "I Am a Camera" as an acting piece and to be grateful for the perfection of the stage work that is in it. Out of his own memories of Berlin, Boris Aronson has designed a mouldy, dingy pension room that reeks of living and indicates the rootlessness of the fable. As his own director, Mr. van Druten has done a superb job.

* * *

In the part of the young writer, William Prince is excellent. His acting is as effortless and as engaging as the writing, and he catches all the friendliness, the ineffectualness and the vagrant misgivings of the part. Martin Brooks is also first-rate as an apprehensive young man of Berlin, and Marian Winters gives a tender, poignant performance as a Jewish girl moving toward an ominous world.

There is an immensely enjoyable performance of a sociable landlady by Olga Fabian, who is full of temperament. Catherine Willard plays the more conventional part of an English lady disturbed by her daughter's behavior; and Edward Andrews acts a flamboyant, rich American who cannot be trusted in a crisis.

Mr. van Druten has written big scenes for his important characters. The scenes ring true; the characters are searchingly observed, and the acting—particularly by Miss Harris—is illuminating and exciting. In view of the high quality of the workmanship, is it ungrateful to wish that "I Am a Camera" had more to say in the theatre? Or that the photography were a little sharper with a wider perspective?

1951 N 29

Caesar And Cleopatra

First of Olivier Portraits of Cleopatra Put On at the Ziegfeld Theatre

By BROOKS ATKINSON

Awaiting the Oliviers has been worth while. Their "Caesar and Cleopatra," which opened at the Ziegfeld last evening, is a triumph of style, and Mr. Olivier's portrait of Caesar is a masterpiece. This is Shaw's contribution to the lustrous legend of the Nile, which New York saw in 1949. Tonight the same troupe will play Shakespeare's "Antony and Cleopatra," and then we shall know the full value of the treasure the Oliviers have brought to America.

On the evidence of the first of the twin productions it is easy to speculate about the nature of their contribution. For the Oliviers and their company are stylists in acting, and they can stamp a play with a single idea. When Shaw used to jest about his similarity to Shakespeare, most of us were vastly amused.

But Shaw can be played on the heroic level; "Caesar and Cleopatra" is very impressive that way, and Shaw's lean and spare literary style seems richer than most of us had supposed. This is the transfiguration that Mr. Olivier has wrought. He plays Caesar less for wit and humor than for character, and Caesar is a memorable figure on those terms.

He is an aging hero, a little tired of so much campaigning and of the follies of the world. His face is lined; his hair is thin and he walks with a stoop of weariness. But his mind is still keen; he enjoys making quick decisions and his tenderness and clemency are the wisdom of a man who has learned from a long, full experience. Without being stately Mr. Olivier acts Caesar in the heroic vein and creates a man who is larger than life.

* * *

What Mr. Olivier achieves is a contribution to the Shaw theme. As the girlish Cleopatra, Miss Leigh's contribution is not that large. Slight and animated, she brings a quality of cameo beauty to the part. And if Lilli Palmer had not recently given it more sparkle, warmth and subtlety, we might all feel that Miss Leigh's acting were of the first rank. For her Cleopatra, ravishingly costumed, is quick-witted, adroit, disarmingly girlish and uncommonly decorative.

In comparison with the New York "Caesar and Cleopatra" of 1949, the distinction of the Olivier production is the harmony of the

The Cast

CAESAR AND CLEOPATRA, George Bernard Shaw's comedy in three acts and nine scenes, with music by Herbert Menges. Staged by Michael Benthall; settings by Roger Furse; costumes by Audrey Cruddas; sword play by Clement McCallin; orchestra conductor, Jacques Singer; revived by Gilbert Miller. At the Ziegfeld Theatre.

Belzanor ....David Greene
Persian ....Edmund Purdom
Bel Affris...................Robert Beaumont
Ftatateeta ....Pat Nye
Julius Caesar................Laurence Olivier
Cleopatra ....Vivien Leigh
Charmian ....Katharine Blake
Iras ....Mairhi Russell
Pothinus ....Harold Kasket
Theodotus ....Timothy Bateson
Ptolemy ....Dawson France
Achilles ....Dan Cunningham
Rufio ....Niall MacGinnis
Britannus ....Wilfrid Hyde White
Lucius Septimus.............Harry Andrews
Apollodorus ....Robert Helpmann
Centurion ....Anthony Pelly
Boatman ....Patrick Troughton
Musician ....Ronald Adam
Harpist ....Elizabeth Kentish
Major-Domo ....Donald Pleasence
Priest ....Terence Owen

group acting. The play has been mastered by everybody. Under Michael Benthall's direction, every actor plays in the same key; the performance has rhythm and design. Roger Furse has caught the golden splendor of Egypt in scenery that evokes the mood of the play; and Audrey Cruddas has dressed the actors brilliantly.

The cast is too long to be itemized here. But something should be said in acknowledgment of Niall MacGinnis' loyal, patient, rude-mannered Rufio, Robert Helpmann's lightly-drawn sketch of Apollodorus and Harold Kasket's obese and disingenuous Pothinus. Although "Caesar and Cleopatra" is a long, loquacious drama, Mr. Olivier and his colleagues have found theatrical structure in it, and brought exuberance to the scenes that are the liveliest.

Mr. Olivier's approach is at the expense of some of the wit and raillery. But it has struck a sound balance by discovering poetry in some of Shaw's prose. At least one Gotham playgoer never realized before how comfortably the

heroic style can rest on the shoulders of our lately-lamented ancient of letters. Like Shaw, Mr. Olivier has mastered the language.

1951 D 20

1952

The Cast

SUMMER AND SMOKE, a play by Tennessee Williams. Staged by Jose Quintero; scenery by Keith Cuerden; revived by The Circle in the Square, 5 Sheridan Square.

Rev. Winemiller...................Walter Beakel
Mrs. Winemiller.................Estelle Omens
John Buchanan Jr................Lee Richard
Alma Winemiller.............Geraldine Page
Rosa Gonzales.............Lola D'Annunzio
Nellie Ewell.............Kathleen Murray
Roger Doremus...................Bill Goodwin
Dr. John Buchanan Sr........Jason Wingreen
Mrs. Bassett.............Gloria Scott Backe
Vernon ....Duncan Bancroft
Rosemary ....Emilie Stevens
Dusty ....Robert Randall
Gonzales ....Sydney G. Stevens
Archie Kramer................Bernard Bogin

By BROOKS ATKINSON

Nothing has happened for quite a long time as admirable as the new production at the Circle in the Square—in Sheridan Square, to be precise. Tennessee Williams' "Summer and Smoke" opened there last evening in a sensitive, highly personal performance. When "Summer and Smoke" was put on at the Music Box in 1948 it looked a little detached, perhaps because the production was too intricate or because the theatre was too large.

Circle-in-the-Square is an arena style playhouse for a small audience and a simple production, and "Summer and Smoke" comes alive in that environment. It also suits the Loft Players perfectly. Geraldine Page's portrait of the lonely, panicky spinster of Glorious Hill, Mississippi, is truthful, perceptive and poignant. And Lee Richard's portrait of the wayward young doctor is the exact counterpart, assured, callous and boorish. Although "Summer and Smoke" was beautifully acted uptown four years ago, the Sheridan Square production is more intimate and penetrating. It probes as deep into the heart of the play as the play does into the heart of the lost lady of Glorious Hill.

* * *

Although "A Streetcar Named Desire" has had a conspicuous success in the theatre, you might

fairly argue that "Summer and
Smoke" is the finer piece of literature. The analysis of character is
subtler and more compassionate.
The contrasts are less brutish. For
Miss Alma, the minister's daughter, has not gone over the border-
line into madness, like Blanche du
Bois. Her torments remain inside
the familiar world of normal experience. And the young doctor is
not an animal like Stanley Kowalski, but an educated wastrel whose
dissipations are deliberate. Everything that happens in "Summer
and Smoke" is plausible and reasonable.

Perhaps that is why it illuminates a wider area of human experience and gets closer to the live
tissue of common life. Although
Mr. Williams searches Miss Alma's
soul relentlessly, he does not with-
hold his sympathy, and he knows
that she is a noble lady in terms
of the life she is compelled to live.
Blanche du Bois is insane before
she appears in "A Streetcar Named
Desire." But Miss Alma does not
go off the deep end until the heartlessness of the life swirling around
her pushes her off the deep end.
"Summer and Smoke" is a tragedy
because its heroine has a noble
spirit

* * *

The early scenes of the current
production are too deliberately
paced, as though the performance
were a refined ritual and not theatre. José Quintero's direction in
the introductory sequence is too
studied. But once the mills of the
gods start grinding away at Miss
Alma's mind and feelings, the performance is honest and deeply
moving.

Apart from Miss Page and Mr.
Richard, who respond perfectly to
the moods and impulses of the
text, the performance includes a
cool, fresh neighbor's girl by Kath-
leen Murray, a patient elderly physician by Jason Wingreen, a resolute minister by Walter Beakel and
several other able pieces of acting.

Intimacy and informality suit
"Summer and Smoke." Certain
streaks of artlessness in the acting are acceptable. For this is a
highly personal, defenseless study
of human suffering and a first-
rate piece of American literature.

1952 Ap 25

AN EVENING WITH BEATRICE LILLIE, a
revue, described as a cavalcade of songs and
sketches. Produced and directed by Edward
Duryea Dowling; scenery by Rolf Gerard;
technical supervision by Paul C. McGuire.
At the Booth Theatre.
PRINCIPALS: Beatrice Lillie, Reginald Gardiner, Xenia Bank, Florence Bray, John Philip,
Eadie and Rack.

By BROOKS ATKINSON

Beatrice Lillie is the funniest
woman in the world and her program of songs and sketches is admirable and hilarious. "An Evening With Beatrice Lillie," she
calls it, adding "with Reginald
Gardiner" to observe all the program amenities, and it opened
with a series of loud reports at the
Booth last evening.

Usually Miss Lillie is interrupted by the musical shows in which
she appears. Only Mr. Gardiner
interrupts her in this one; and
since his sense of comedy is as
mad as hers, the interruptions are
well taken. Working together
they have assembled an evening
of comic perfection. You leave
Miss Lillie's show full of laughter,
and full of admiration also. For
she is a brilliant artist and craftsman as well as an uproarious
buffoon.

* * *

At least half her material is
new to New York. Some of it derives from shows she has done in
London, and some of it she has
never done before. But the material, whatever its source, is incidental to the comic spirit she puts
into it. You know the styles—the
rowdy, impudent servant girl or
the overbearing lady of fashion,
the imposing prima donna with an
ornately feathered fan, etc. Miss
Lillie has many masquerades, all
of them funny sooner or later.
"There are Fairies at the Bottom
of My Garden" is only a variation
on "The Pain of the Wind Around
My Heart," and the insolent servant girl who is practicing tap-
dancing is only a variation on the
obtuse, egotistical society lady who
barges into a star's dressing room
after a performance.

* * *

Geniuses on the stage are always
highly individual, no matter what
part they happen to be playing.
So it is with Miss Lillie in this
show. The slender sharp-featured

lady with the polite, embarrassed smile and the dainty manner dominates the material, the stage and the theatre. She radiates satiric comedy even when she is standing still. She sits at a table and looks blank: it is funny. She pauses for a beat in a song: it is funny. It almost seems as though her thoughts were funny. For she is one of the most eloquent actresses in the theatre, and she can set the audience to laughing without saying a word, singing a note or making a gesture.

Although she has the presence of a lady—of a very jaunty lady—she is an enormously funny low comedienne. There is plenty of vulgarity in the stuff she does. She is as anatomical as Willie Howard used to be, and one of the songs she sings is bluer than the scarf she wears in her opening number. But her ribaldries somehow seem to be immaculate. For her style is always demure on the surface; the manner is dry, the gestures sharp and spare, the pace is like quicksilver and the whole thing adds up to the most brilliant comic spirit of our time.

* * *

Mr. Gardiner is up to some of his old tricks and some new ones, all of them being compounded insanity. He imitates wallpaper in sound. He makes a character analysis of the steam locomotive and impersonates marine machinery. By applying a trivial mind to profound mechanical achievements he fantastifies the machine age and devastates the audience. He sings three parts of a song simultaneously, although you may regard that as physically impossible; and he conducts an orchestra with visual appreciation of the sounds that come from the instruments. Mr. Gardiner is a very original

Reginald Gardiner and Beatrice Lillie in a scene from "An Evening With Beatrice Lillie."

mountebank, and first-rate company for a light-headed audience.

Rolf Gerard has provided some pleasantly sketched scenery and an amusing curtain with the austere Lillie profile. Eadie and Rack provide the music from two pianos. But Beatrice Lillie—the only Lady Peel currently on the stage—provides the genius. It has never been more brilliant or hilarious.

1952 O 3

The Barraults Open Season of French Repertory With a Comedy by Marivaux

The Cast

LES FAUSSES CONFIDENCES, a drama in two acts, by Marivaux, with direction by Jean-Louis Barrault, decor and costumes by Maurice Brianchon, followed by BAPTISTE, a pantomime ballet by Jacques Prevert, with music by Kosma, choreography by M. Barrault and decor by Mayo. Presented in French by Sol Hurok through Saturday night at the Ziegfeld Theatre.

LES FAUSSES CONFIDENCES

Araminte	Madeleine Renaud
Dorante	Jean Desailly
M. Remi	Pierre Bertin
Madame Argante	Marie-Helene Daste
Arlequin	Jean-Pierre Granval
Dubois	Jean-Louis Barrault
Marton	Simone Valere
Le Comte	Regis Outin
L'Orfevre	Jean-Francois Calve
Le Valet	Jacques Galland

BAPTISTE

Baptiste	Jean-Louis Barrault
La Statue	Madeleine Renaud
Le Chanteur	Jean Desailly
La Petite Fille	Elina Labourdette
Arlequin	Serge Perrault
La Gardien de Square	Jean Juillard
La Lavandiere	Simone Valere
Le Bijoutier	Jean-Pierre Granval
La Duchesse	Madeleine Renaud
Les Laquais	Jacques Galland, Pierre Sonnier
Le Marchand d'Habits	Beauchamp
Les Invitees	Simone Valere, Elina Labourdette, Anne Carrere
Les Invites	Jean-Pierre Granval, Jean-Francois Calve, Jean Juillard

By BROOKS ATKINSON

Madeleine Renaud, Jean-Louis Barrault and their Theâtre Marigny company have arrived in New York, and they are most welcome. After suitable patriotic exercises, which were also most welcome, the Barraults raised the curtain on Marivaux' "Les Fausses Confidences" (The False Secrets) at the Ziegfeld last evening, and inaugurated a month of repertory in French.

This is bound to be a merciful element in international relations, since actors are notoriously more competent than statesmen. But it is also going to be stimulating for the New York theatre. For the Barrault troupe is a repertory company, as much interested in the style of production as in the material of a play.

* * *

"Les Fausses Confidences" derives from the early eighteenth century when French comedy was developing out of Molière into a more naturalistic tradition. It is an artificial comedy involving a series of intrigues through which an impecunious suitor contrives to marry a rich widow. As a piece of literature it does not appear to be remarkably distinguished. But Marivaux wrote it for Italian actors who were still under the influence of the commedia dell' arte tradition, and this is the factor that concerns American audiences more than the text.

For the amazing plasticity of the Barrault acting is rooted in pantomime which, in turn, was the genius of commediadell' arte. From this point of view the performance of "Les Fausses Confidences" is a thorough delight, and unlike anything we have here except in ballet. It is beautifully set against a lovely, improvised setting by Maurice Brianchon that values design above construction, and it is dressed in the ornate formal costumes of the seventeenth century.

* * *

The lighting, particularly of the faces of the actors, might be more ingenious, surely; and, curiously enough, M. Barrault's costume is the only perfunctory one of the lot. But M. Brianchon's spontaneously executed décor is a real triumph of mind over matter. What we have seen of French décor in this country suggests that the French have more confidence in a designer's brains than they have in the carpenter shop.

The performance is all lightness and fluidity. These are actors who have been together so long under single management that they move around the stage as though they were in a ballet—the gestures swift and skimming, the tempo breezy, the spirit buoyantly humorous. Nothing is serious, heavy or dull. Everything's sunny and gay. The word "playing" has a specific meaning when a company of actors is accomplished enough to use a script as the theme of a performance.

Instead of playing the part of the wily suitor, which was no doubt intended originally as one of the two central roles, M. Barrault plays the intriguing servant who manuevers his master into a rich marriage. M. Barrault is a slender somewhat ascetic-looking actor with a good voice and remarkably-well co-ordinated movement. He leaps in and out of the play like a mischievous elf—the style broad and comic.

Dressed in the marvelously decorative costumes of the period and adorned with a white wig, Mme. Renaud looks every inch a lady of grace and breeding. Her wealthy widow is full of spirit—modestly coquettish, generous, quick-minded and independent.

The company is uniformly excellent. Simone Valère's susceptible though enchanting female companion; Jean Desailly's desingenuous suitor; Pierre Bertin's choleric barrister; Jean-Pierre Granval's harlequin servant are all delightful in a spirit of amiable make-believe.

Following "Les Fausses Confidences," M. Barrault and his company perform a pleasant pantomine, Jacques Prévert's "Baptiste," with a good-natured score by Kosma. Parts of this pantomine American cinema audiences have already seen in "Children of Paradise."

For a number of reasons, including a fresh point of view about the art of the theatre, the Barraults and their Marigny company are most welcome.

1952 N 13

Jean Desailly, left, Madeleine Renaud and Jean-Louis Barrault in a scene from "Les Fausses Confidences."

The Cast

THE SEVEN YEAR ITCH, a romantic comedy in three acts, by George Axelrod, with incidental music by Dana Suesse. Staged by John Gerstad; supervised by Elliott Nugent; designed and lighted by Frederick Fox; presented by Courtney Burr and Mr. Nugent. At the Fulton Theatre.

Richard Sherman ....Tom Ewell
Helen Sherman ....Neva Patterson
Ricky ....Johnny Klein
Miss Morris ....Marilyn Clark
Elaine ....Joan Donovan
Marie What-ever-her-name-was....Irene Moore
The Girl .... Vanessa Brown
Dr. Brubaker ....Robert Emhardt
Tom Mackenzie ....George Keane
Voice of Richard's Conscience......George Ives
Voice of the Girl's Conscience......Pat Fowler

By BROOKS ATKINSON

Tom Ewell and George Axelrod might begin the day by gratefully thanking each other. For Mr. Axelrod has written the sort of giddy part that a comedian can act uproariously, and Mr. Ewell has returned the favor with a superb performance. The play is called "The Seven Year Itch," and it opened at the Fulton last evening to an audience that settled down to three acts of skittish amusement.

All Mr. Axelrod has to chronicle really is a romantic episode in a summer bachelor's life. While his wife is in the country, he and the girl upstairs take a step or two down the primrose path of ordinary theatrical dalliance. Mr. Axelrod has not gone outside the Broadway bailiwick in quest of his plot.

* * *

But he has a refreshing way of telling his story. For the summer bachelor is a very nervous guy with an especially vagrant imagination. In "The Seven Year Itch," it is Mr. Axelrod's whim to let him talk to himself in irritable solilo-

Tom Ewell and Vanessa Brown in "The Seven Year Itch."

quies and also to stage some of his most frightening nightmares in the form of interpolated scenes. These are pretty funny discursions on the main theme of the evening. For the summer bachelor, who is also the publisher of paper-bound books, is both contrite and melodramatic. He frightens himself almost to death when he thinks of his wife and when he contemplates the possible consequences of infidelity.

* * *

Although Mr. Axelrod's style of humorous improvisation is most refreshing, it is hard to think of "The Seven Year Itch" without Mr. Ewell skipping through it like an apprehensive satyr. Mr. Ewell has been a happy comedian in ordinary small parts for a long time. But the part he plays here is certainly major. He is on stage all evening, contemplating morosely when he is not timidly philandering; and he gives a remarkably comic performance with every detail fondly polished. Mr. Ewell's touch is light, but his sense of invention seems to be fresh and endless. Thanks to a well-written part, we now know that Mr. Ewell is an extraordinary comedian.

Under John Gerstad's direction, with a few looney ideas contributed by Elliott Nugent, the performance as a whole is played with easy expertness. Vanessa Brown, looking very handsome, gives an attractive performance as the girl upstairs who is studying to be a trollop. The mature undertone of her naiveté is wonderfully impudent and winning.

That bulging comedian, Robert Emhardt, gives another shrewdly satirical performance as a literary psychiatrist. As the wife who is almost forgotten, Neva Patterson is delightful. And George Keane is amusingly aggressive as a professional wolf.

Faced with a familiar task of designing scenery for sin in New York, Frederick Fox has come up with a pleasant variation on the regulation fireplace, divan and bookshelves. "The Seven Year Itch" is a popular comedy written in the interests of hilarity. With Mr. Ewell giving a performance that alternates between the droll and the broad, Mr. Axelrod's play is original and funny.

1952 N 21

The Cast

OEDIPUS TYRANNUS, the Sophocles play without an intermission, translated into modern Greek by Photos Politis, with music by Katina Paxinou. Staged by Alexis Minotis; scenery by C. Clonis; costumes by Antonios Phocas; choreography by Agapi Evangelidou; orchestra conducted by George Lykoudis. Presented by the National Theatre of Greece under the sponsorship of Guthrie McClintic by arrangement with the American National Theatre and Academy. At the Mark Hellinger Theatre.

Oedipus ....Alexis Minotis
Priest ....Basil Kanakis
Creon ....N. Hadziscos
Teiresias ....J. Apostolides
Jocasta ....Katina Paxinou
Shepherd ....P. Zervos
Attendant ... .Nicos Paraskevas
Messenger ....St. Vocovitch
Chorus leader ....Thanos Cotsopoulos
    Chorus of Theban Elders: Al. Deliyannis, D. Dimopoulos, N. Papaconstantinou, D. Veakis, Th. Andriacopoulos, B. Andreopoulos, N. Betinis, St. Bogiotopoulos, E. Catsileros, Sp. Lascaridea, J. Mavroyenis, G. Moutsios, C. Naos St. Papadachis.

By BROOKS ATKINSON

Since "Oedipus Tyrannus" is a more powerful tragedy than "Electra," the second bill of the Greek National Theatre is the more impressive one. Alexis Minotis and Katina Paxinou appeared in the two chief parts in a masterly performance at the Mark Hellinger Theatre last evening where the production will remain through next Sunday's matinee.

If the entrepreneurs of the Greek visitation are happy about the reception here, they can rest assured that their audiences are happy, too. Despite the stubborn fact that the Sophocles tragedies are played in a language incomprehensible to most of us, the performances are illuminating and exalting on a high plane of formal art. Most of us have never had a chance to look so deep into the heart of a Greek classical drama.

* * *

In comparison with "Electra," "Oedipus" is more compact, and the performance is more concise and dramatic. For the story of how Oedipus learns the awful truth about his fate is told with deliberate suspense in a style that approximates the modern manner. Again, C. Clonis has filled the stage with an imposing scene depicting the steps to a royal palace. The costumes by Antonios Phocas are formal without being severe. And the musical accompaniment, composed by Miss Paxinou, lightly underscores the dramatic episodes in the performance.

/ Although Mr. Minotis and Miss

Paxinou are starred in the program (which, incidentally neglects to mention the name of the author), the performance is a completely integrated work of art, as impersonal and as majestic as the drama. The acting is in the heroic style. The pace is deliberate; the groupings are planned for dramatic symmetry; the sound of the voices has the resonance of impassioned speech about terrible things. Nothing of use in the telling of a mighty fable is wasted in this articulate performance.

* * *

It is hard to imagine how the acting could be improved. Mr. Minotis' Oedipus is royal without being aloof to the personal crises of the story. Without losing regal authority, he hangs on every word that the shepherds from the hills bring unwillingly to the palace. Although Miss Paxinou's portrait of the queen is also larger than life, it is compassionate and human. N. Hadziscos' cautious Creon who does not want to face the truth; Basil Kanakis' patriarchal priest who brings news more frightening than he imagines, and the shepherd of P. Zervos—are all played with individual flavor and with respect for the unity of the whole performance.

But, as in the case of "Electra," the staging of the chorus is the most stunning contribution of the Greek National Theatre productions. It is a male chorus for "Oedipus" — bearded, gowned in subdued colors. Under the direction of Agapi Evangelidou, the chorus both judges and participates in the action, like an idealized instrument of public opinion. Although the gestures and the movements are perfectly synchronized, they are not spectacular, but spontaneous and unobtrusive. If it is possible for acting to be natural and stately at the same time, this is it.

In mastering the function of the chorus, the Greek National Theatre has mastered the art of playing Greek classical drama as a whole. Every moment of "Oedipus Tyrannus" is alive and beautiful.

1952 N 25

1953

THE CRUCIBLE, a play in a prologue and two acts, by Arthur Miller. Staged by Jed Harris; produced by Kermit Bloomgarden; scenery by Boris Aronson; costumes by Edith Lutyens; lullaby composed by Ann Ronnell. At the Martin Beck Theatre.
Betty Parris ....Janet Alexander
Tituba ....Jacqueline Andre
Rev. Samuel Parris ....Fred Stewart
Abigail Williams ....Madeleine Sherwood
Susanna Wallcott ....Barbara Stanton
Mrs. Ann Putnam ....Jane Hoffman
Thomas Putnam ....Raymond Bramley
Mercy Lewis ....Dorothy Jolliffe
Mary Warren ....Jenny Egan
John Proctor ....Arthur Kennedy
Rebecca Nurse ....Jean Adair
Giles Corey ....Joseph Sweency
Rev. John Hale ....E. G. Marshall
Elizabeth Proctor ....Beatrice Straight
Francis Nurse ....Graham Velsey
Ezekiel Cheever ....Don McHenry
John Willard ....George Mitchell
Judge Hathorne ....Philip Coolidge
Deputy-Gov. Danforth ....Walter Hampden
Sarah Good ....Adele Fortin
Hopkins ....Donald Marye

By BROOKS ATKINSON

Arthur Miller has written another powerful play. "The Crucible," it is called, and it opened at the Martin Beck last evening in an equally powerful performance. Riffling back the pages of American history, he has written the drama of the witch trials and hangings in Salem in 1692. Neither Mr. Miller nor his audiences are unaware of certain similarities between the perversions of justice then and today.

But Mr. Miller is not pleading a cause in dramatic form. For "The Crucible," despite its current implications, is a self-contained play about a terrible period in American history. Silly accusations of witchcraft by some mischievous girls in Puritan dress gradually take possession of Salem. Before the play is over good people of pious nature and responsible temper are condemning other good people to the gallows.

Having a sure instinct for dramatic form, Mr. Miller goes bluntly to essential situations. John Proctor and his wife, farm people, are the central characters of the play. At first the idea that Goodie Proctor is a witch is only an absurd rumor. But "The Crucible" carries the Proctors through the whole ordeal—first vague suspicion, then the arrest, the implacable, highly wrought trial in the church vestry, the final opportunity for John Proctor to save his neck by confessing to something he knows is a lie, and finally the baleful roll of the drums at the foot of the gallows.

Although "The Crucible" is a powerful drama, it stands second to "Death of a Salesman" as a work of art. Mr. Miller has had more trouble with this one, perhaps because he is too conscious of its implications. The literary style is cruder. The early motivation is muffled in the uproar of the opening scene, and the theme does not develop with the simple eloquence of "Death of a Salesman."

It may be that Mr. Miller has tried to pack too much inside his drama, and that he has permitted himself to be concerned more with the technique of the witch hunt than with its humanity. For all its power generated on the surface, "The Crucible" is most moving in the simple, quiet scenes between John Proctor and his wife. By the standards of "Death of a Salesman," there is too much excitement and not enough emotion in "The Crucible."

As the director, Jed Harris has given it a driving performance in which the clashes are fierce and clamorous. Inside Boris Aronson's gaunt, pitiless sets of rude buildings, the acting is at a high pitch of bitterness, anger and fear. As the patriarchal deputy Governor, Walter Hampden gives one of his most vivid performances in which righteousness and ferocity are unctuously mated. Fred Stewart as a vindictive parson, E. G. Marshall as a parson who finally rebels at the indiscriminate ruthlessness of the trial, Jean Adair as an aging woman of God, Madeleine Sherwood as a malicious town hussy, Joseph Sweeney as an old man who has the courage to fight the court, Philip Coolidge as a sanctimonious judge—all give able performances.

As John Proctor and his wife, Arthur Kennedy and Beatrice Straight have the most attractive roles in the drama and two or three opportunities to act them together in moments of tranquillity. They are superb—Mr. Kennedy clear and resolute, full of fire, searching his own mind; Miss Straight, reserved, detached, above and beyond the contention. Like all the members of the cast, they are dressed in the chaste and love-

ly costumes Edith Lutyens has designed from old prints of early Massachusetts.

After the experience of "Death of a Salesman" we probably expect Mr. Miller to write a masterpiece every time. "The Crucible" is not of that stature and it lacks that universality. On a lower level of dramatic history with considerable pertinence for today, it is a powerful play and a genuine contribution to the season.

1953 Ja 23

Barry Jones Heads a Capital Cast in a New Staging of Shaw's 'Misalliance'

The Cast

MISALLIANCE, the Bernard Shaw comedy, in three acts. Staged by Cyril Ritchard; production supervisor, Lemuel Ayers; scenery by John Boyt; costumes by Robert Fletcher; revived by the New York City Drama Company (Albert Marre, artistic director) through March 1. At the City Center.
Bentley Summerhays..........Roddy McDowall
Johnny Tarleton.............William Redfield
Hypatia Tarleton..................Jan Farrand
Mrs. Tarleton...................Dorothy Sands
Lord Summerhays................Richard Purdy
Mr. Tarleton.......................Barry Jones
Percival ....Richard Kiley
Lina ....Tamara Geva
Gunner ....Jerome Kilty

By BROOKS ATKINSON

Thanks to the City Center, Shaw's "Misalliance" may now be graded upwards. Most of us have been foolishly assuming that it is one of those facetious conversations that get to be unbearably tedious before a long evening is over. Even Max Beerbohm, never a sober-sides, thought so when it was first produced in 1910. It is a facetious conversation. But in the version that opened at the City Center last evening, it is also vastly entertaining. From the moment the curtain goes up on an amusingly garish setting by John Boyt, "Misalliance" is sparkling and contrary in the best Shavian style.

Don't expect to discover from this column what Shaw had specifically in mind when he wrote it. Perhaps he was not adamant himself about sticking to a central point. In the early scenes there seems to be some doubt whether a marriage between a tradesman's daughter and the son of a lord is socially suitable.

* * *

But that is hardly more than the discharge of the opening gun. For "Misalliance" then starts racing through a whole evening of gay non-sequiturs, which touch in passing on a hundred vigorous ideas about social customs and prejudices. If Shaw wrote it to spite those who said he did not write plays but debates, he can now take a little wry satisfaction as he looks down or up on this angry planet. "Misalliance" is a stream of bright improvisations that contain many odds and ends from Shaw's lexicon of social principles. It is consistently funny. A theatregoer leaves it under the impression of having had a completely sardonic good time.

Say a particular word of thanks to Cyril Ritchard for having staged a breezy performance that keeps Shaw's tongue in his cheek. The tone is light; the pace is swift; the mood is dry and mocking. Barry Jones, an old hand at Shaw acrobatics, is anchor-man for the performance; there could hardly be a sounder craftsman. Cast as the garrulous, fantastically literate manufacturer of underwear, he has the bounce and gusto and the look of innocence that keep the dialogue spinning. He is the perfect Shavian by reason of the comic insincerity he can bring to a part.

But all the players are either wits or buffoons in this caper and in the order of the program are: Roddy McDowall as a cynical Marchbanks with a clever mind; William Redfield as a pompous chump; Jan Farrand as one of those deadly females who chase apprehensive Shaw heroes; Dorothy Sands as a busy, sympathetic mother whose mind is a storehouse of middle-class platitudes; Richard Purdy as a disillusioned man of the world; Richard Kiley as an unimaginative prig; Tamara Geva as a scornful circus acrobat, and Jerome Kilty as a whining, cowardly Socialist.

They talk at high speed with outrageous frankness and impudence until, toward 11 o'clock, Shaw remarks that for the moment he has nothing more to say. Since the talk is brilliantly wayward the performance gives a misleading impression of being full of action. There have been so many Shaw revivals lately that you might expect the theatre to be getting down to the bottom of his barrel. Well, the barrel seems to be lively no matter how far you dip into it. Maybe it's a barrel of what used to be known as "ardent spirits." Since "Misalliance" and "Maggie" opened simultaneously, this review is based on the dress rehearsal of Tuesday evening.

1953 F 19

The Cast

WONDERFUL TOWN, a musical comedy in two acts, based on the Joseph Fields-Jerome Chodorov comedy, "My Sister Eileen," derived from the Ruth McKenney stories. Book by Messrs. Fields and Chodorov; music by Leonard Bernstein; lyrics by Betty Comden and Adolph Green. Staged by George Abbott; dances and musical numbers arranged by Donald Saddler; sets and costumes by Raoul Pene du Bois; lighting by Peggy Clark; Rosalind Russell's clothes designed by Main Bocher; musical direction and vocal arrangements by Lehman Engel; orchestrations by Don Walker; produced by Robert Fryer. At the Winter Garden.

Guide	Warren Galjour
Appopolous	Henry Lascoe
Lonigan	Walter Kelvin
Helen	Michele Burke
Wreck	Jordan Bentley
Violet	Dody Goodman
Valenti	Ted Beniades
Eileen	Edith Adams
Ruth	Rosalind Russell
A Strange Man	Nathaniel Frey
Drunks	Albert Linville, Delbert Anderson
Robert Baker	George Gaynes
Associate Editors,	Warren Galjour, Albert Linville
Mrs. Wade	Isabella Hoopes
Frank Lippencott	Chris Alexander
Chef	Nathaniel Frey
Walter	Delbert Anderson
Delivery Boy	Alvin Bean
Chick Clark	Dort Clark
Shore Patrolman	Lee Papell
First Cadet	David Lober
Second Cadet	Ray Dorian
Ruth's Escort	Chris Robinson

By BROOKS ATKINSON

According to the Constitution, Rosalind Russell cannot run for President until 1956. But it would be wise to start preparing for her campaign at once. For she can dance and sing better than any President we have had. She is also better looking and has a more infectious sense of humor.

She can remain in residence until 1956 at the Winter Garden.

"Wonderful Town," which opened there last evening, is the most uproarious and original musical carnival we have had since "Guys and Dolls" appeared in this neighborhood. Joseph Fields and Jerome

Chodorov have founded the book on their comedy, "My Sister Eileen," which was founded in turn on Ruth McKenney's wryly comic stories. That noble lineage in laughter accounts for the humorous literacy of the story.

* * *

But everyone is more inspired than usual in the administration of "Wonderful Town." Leonard Bernstein has written it a wonderful score. Dispensing with hurdy-gurdy techniques, he has written a bright and witty score in a variety of modern styles without forgetting to endow it with at least one tender melody and a good romantic number. Orchestrated by Don Walker, conducted by Lehman Engel, the score carries forward the crack-brained comedy of the book with gaiety and excitement.

If you remember that Mr. Bernstein also wrote the music for "On the Town" a decade ago, you will be glad to know that Betty Comden and Adolph Green are associated with him again. They have written some extraordinarily inventive lyrics in a style as unhackneyed as the music. And Donald Saddler has directed the most exuberant dances of the season. Sometimes gifted people never quite get attuned to each other in the composition of a musical circus. But in "Wonderful Town" everyone seems to have settled down joyfully to the creation of a beautifully organized fandango—the book, the score and the ballets helping each other enthusiastically. George Abbott, ring-master of numberless musical shows, has put everything together in a robust, high-spirited performance.

* * *

No doubt you know already that this is the saga of two sisters from Ohio who settle down in an aguish Greenwich Village basement as the first step toward achieving careers in New York. The musical version is a little more elaborate than the prose version, and it gives Raoul Pène du Bois an opportunity to design some congenial Village scenery, to say nothing of a whole wardrobe of fantastic costumes.

Despite the elaborations of the book, the experiences the sisters have in the Village are as bizarre as they were originally. They include a festive conga line with the Brazilian sailors that brings down the first act curtain on a notable rumpus. As Sister Eileen, Edith

Adams is absolutely perfect. She is both demure and coquettish; she is simple and frank, good company and well mannered. And she sings with a sweetness that represents the character delightfully. The hill-billy lament for "Ohio" that Miss Russell and she sing early in the show is not merely funny: it tells with great skill the folk background of this sophisticated folk tale.

* * *

Everyone else is in the right key, also: George Gaynes as a magazine editor with a fine baritone voice; Dort Clark as an aggressively cynical newspaper man; Chris Alexander as a refined drugstore manager; Henry Lascoe as a combination fake painter and phony landlord; Ted Beniades as night-club charlatan. As restaurant cooks, waiters, cadets and assorted individuals, Nathaniel Frey, Delbert Anderson, David Lober and Ray Dorian are all right, too. As a husky, illiterate football player, Jordan Bentley is a very hearty buffoon. They make the Village a good deal more warmhearted and insane than it is in nature.

At the head of all this bedlam Miss Russell gives a memorably versatile comic performance. She is tall, willowy and gawky; she is droll, sardonic and incredulous. Her comedy can be broad and also subtle. For she radiates the genuine comic spirit. In "Wonderful Town" she makes the whole city wonderful; and she will make the whole country wonderful when she is elected President in 1956.

1953 F 26

Deborah Kerr Stars in 'Tea and Sympathy' at the Ethel Barrymore Playhouse

The Cast

TEA AND SYMPATHY; a drama in three acts by Robert Anderson. Staged by Elia Kazan; scenery and lighting by Jo Mielziner; clothes designed by Anna Hill Johnstone; presented by the Playwrights Company, in association with Mary K. Frank. At the Ethel Barrymore Theatre.
Laura Reynolds..................Deborah Kerr
Lilly Sears......................Florida Friebus

```
Tom Lee.........................John Kerr
David Harris...................Richard Midgley
Ralph..........................Alan Sues
Al.............................Dick York
Steve..........................Arthur Steuer
Bill Reynolds..................Leif Erickson
Phil...........................Richard Franchot
Herbert Lee....................John McGovern
Paul...........................Yale Wexler
```

By BROOKS ATKINSON

Since Robert Anderson is a sensitive writer, it is fortunate that some sensitive actors are playing his drama. He calls it "Tea and Sympathy." Deborah Kerr and John Kerr (not related despite the same name) helped to give it an infinitely sensitive performance at the Ethel Barrymore last evening. Under the direction of Elia Kazan, it restores our theatre to an art again with a fine play put on the stage with great skill and beauty.

To say that "Tea and Sympathy" is the story of a schoolboy falsely suspected of homosexuality is to place the emphasis on the motivation rather than the play. Tom Lee, a gentle, quiet boy in a New England private school, is suspected of homosexuality by the dean, the housemaster, his fellow students and even his father. But Mr. Anderson has something more than scandal in mind. For "Tea and Sympathy" is a play that catches a group of characters in a complicated web of hostilities and sympathies and looks deep into the hearts of its principal people.

* * *

Everyone in the school is heartily regular. They operate as a clan. The housemaster is a pious bully and the schoolboys are half-educated louts. They describe the boy Mr. Anderson is writing about as an "off horse." All they need is a whiff of suspicion to twist him into a complete pariah. He would be destitute of friends if it were not for the housemaster's wife, who is an "off horse" in her own right. She understands him. She defends him. Eventually she restores him to his own respect again. But not until she has turned against her husband and recognized the brutishness of the school.

As a story, "Tea and Sympathy" is not ideal. It is garrulous and rather aimless in an overlong second act. And there are some hackneyed situations in it. But as a portrait of people it is an extraordinarily illuminating piece

of work full of moods and subleties of insight. Mr. Anderson keeps changing his colors as the play moves along and new facets of character are constantly rising to the surface of a rueful story.

* * *

As theatre craftsmanship, the production and the performance are superb. Jo Mielziner's setting of the interior of the school living quarters is one of his many masterpieces—lovely and dramatic at the same time. As the wife of the housemaster, Deborah Kerr has the initial advantage of being extremely beautiful. But she adds to her beauty the luminous perceptions of an artist who is aware of everything that is happening all around her and expresses it in an effortless style.

* * *

John Kerr's portrait of the schoolboy—shy, manly, colloquial, honest — is a remarkably tender, moving piece of acting by a young man who is also an artist. Miss Kerr and Mr. Kerr create performances out of lights and shadows, out of nuances and out of unspoken ideas.

Leif Erickson's portrait of the sanctimonious, athletic housemaster is excellent, also. And the other actors are first rate—John McGovern, as the father; Dick York, as an athlete; Florida Friebus, as a gossipy faculty wife, give notably good performances.

Mr. Anderson has written a troubled idyll with a light touch and a wealth of understanding, and the actors have matched the writing in the delicacy of their playing.

1953 O 1

John Patrick's Comedy About the American Occupation of Okinawa Island

The Cast

THE TEAHOUSE OF THE AUGUST MOON, a play in three acts and ten scenes, dramatized by John Patrick from Vern Sneider's novel of the same name, with music by Dai-Keong Lee. Staged by Robert Lewis; presented by Maurice Evans, in association with George Schaefer; settings and lighting by Peter Larkin; costumes by Noel Taylor. At the Martin Beck Theatre.

```
Sakini ......................... David Wayne
Sergeant Gregovich ............. Harry Jackson
Col. Wainright Purdy 3d ........ Paul Ford
Captain Fisby .................. John Forsythe
Old Woman ...................... Naoe Kondo
Old Woman's Daughter ........... Mara Kim
Lady Astor ..................... Saki
Ancient Man .................... Kame Ishikawa
Mr. Sumata ..................... Kale Deei
Mr. Sumata's Father ............ Kikuo Hiromura
Mr. Hokaida .................... Chuck Morgan
Mr. Seiko ...................... Haim Winant
Mr. Oshira ..................... William Hansen
Mr. Omura ...................... Kuraji Seida
Mr. Keora ...................... Yuki Shimoda
Miss Higa Jiga ................. Shizu Moriya
Lotus Blossom .................. Mariko Niki
Captain McLean ................. Larry Gates
```

By BROOKS ATKINSON

John Patrick has turned some portentous ideas into a delightful comedy in "The Teahouse of the August Moon," which opened at the Martin Beck last evening. This is the story of the American occupation in Okinawa that was told originally in a novel by Vern Sneider. If Mr. Sneider and Mr. Patrick did not have a sense of humor the meeting of East and West in this play might be a bruising experience. The differences are great and fundamental.

But "The Teahouse of the August Moon" is a light and sagacious comedy. The form is inventive and familiar. The point of view is droll. And as the middleman between Okinawa and America, David Wayne gives a rich, humorous, forgiving performance that must have come straight out of heaven, it is so wise and pure. Under Robert Lewis' direction, Mr. Patrick's play is completely captivating.

The story is easily told. Captain Fisby, an amiable though bumbling American officer, sets himself up in a small town, Tobiki, to represent the army of occupation. Washington has provided him with detailed directions for introducing democracy into an Oriental village. The directions call for the erection of a schoolhouse in the shape of a pentagon.

* * *

Although Captain Fisby begins according to the rulebook, the realities of the village defeat him. Washington seems to have overlooked the cultural habits of Tobiki. Human nature keeps intruding on the plan. By natural processes of development the schoolhouse becomes a teahouse and the native industries, which the Army is supposed to foster, simmer down to a highly profitable manufacture of brandy from sweet potatoes.

If the story were told literally, it might not suffice for a whole evening in the theatre; and, in fact, it might be argued that it goes to pieces in the second act. But Mr. Patrick is also a stylist. With the connivance of Mr. Wayne as interlocutor, he presents "The Teahouse of the August Moon" as a piece of exotic make-believe in a style as intimate as a fairy story. What Mr. Patrick says is interesting. How he says it is imaginative and original. For he has contrived to break down the barrier between stage and audience and present his fable as something shared equally on both sides of the footlights.

This is just the sort of contrived improvisation that Mr. Lewis likes to fool around with, and he has done a beautiful job. Oh, there may be a little too much cuteness in the musical underscoring of the jokes, but there's nothing so precious that anyone should worry about it. Behind a striking bamboo curtain, Peter Larkin has designed a fluid production that covers the whole subject agreeably. The performance is an unalloyed delight.

Paul Ford's plain, cornfed portrait of the incredulous colonel who cannot believe what he sees is immensely funny and immensely winning. So is Larry Gates' acting of the Army psychiatrist who sheds his science and goes native the minute he becomes acquainted with Captain Fisby. And John Forsythe is as perfect in the part of the captain as Henry Fonda was in "Mister Roberts"—something of the same genial style of acting and very much of the same inflection of voice.

As the geisha girl who makes a teahouse more attractive than a school. Mariko Niki, a Tokyo actress, gives one of those lovely, mannered, liquid performances that derive from oriental art— likely a Japanese print in dance form. Mr. Wayne's leprechaun from "Finian's Rainbow" has now developed into a figure of wisdom, humor and pantomime. As the interpreter, Mr. Wayne sets the tone for the play in a preliminary scene and maintains it throughout the evening in the grace and gentleness of an imagined human being. It is wonderful work.

So is "The Teahouse of the August Moon" as a whole. Although East and West look at each

other with considerable hostility,
they can meet on friendly terms if
they keep their sense of humor.
Things that might easily make for
anger become reasonable, friendly
and sweetly comic in this ingratiating play.

1953 O 16

1954

Blitzstein's Adaptation of 'The Threepenny Opera' Given by the Theatre de Lys

For those who have been wondering whether Marc Blitzstein's
adaptation of "The Threepenny
Opera" would stand up in a dramatic performance in the theatre
as well as it did in concert form
at the Brandeis University Festival in 1952, the answer was provided last night in Greenwich
Village's Theatre de Lys. The
answer is that it does. Indeed, it
stands up beautifully and to
Mr. Blitzstein this morning this
department extends heartfelt
thanks.

The Cast

THE THREEPENNY OPERA, in a prologue
and three acts. English adaptation of
book and lyrics by Marc Blitzstein, based
on the original text of Bert Brecht. Mu-
sic by Kurt Weill. Scenery by William
Pitkin, costumes by Bolasni; musical di-
rector, Samuel Matlowsky; staged by Car-
men Capalbo, presented by Mr. Capalbo
and Stanley Chase. At the Theatre de Lys.
Streetsinger ....Gerald Price
Jenny ....Lotte Lenya
J. J. Peachum................Leon Lishner
Mrs. Peachum ....Charlotte Rae
Filch ....William Duell
MacHeath (Mack the Knife)...Scott Merrill
Polly Peachum ....Jo Sullivan
Readymoney Matt.............John Astin
Crookfinger Jake............Joseph Beruh
Bob the Saw.................Bernard Bogin
Walt Dreary...................Paul Dooley
Reverend Kimball...........Donald Elson
Tiger Brown ....George Tyne
Betty ....Marcella Markham
Molly ....Marion Selee
Dolly ....Gerrianne Raphael
Coaxer ....Gloria Sokol
Smith ....Chuck Smith
Lucy Brown................Beatrice Arthur
First Constable.............Stan Schneider
Second Constable.............Miles Dickson
Messenger ....William Duell

The score of "The Threepenny
Opera" which the late Kurt Weill
wrote to the German-language
book and lyrics of Bert Brecht is,
of course, one of the authentic
contemporary masterpieces. It is

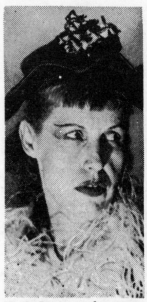

Lotte Lenya as she appears in "The Threepenny Opera."

full of beauty, of humor, of compassion and what Mr. Blitzstein
has done is to retain that score
while putting the text into English. It is a remarkable contribution.

* * *

To be sure, others have rendered the Brecht words into English, too. But this reviewer has
never heard these efforts, and
comparisons are impossible. The
important point of the moment is
what Blitzstein has done. And
what he has done is to provide
words that fit the music, words
that retain the bite, the savage
satire, the overwhelming bitterness underlying this work from
its original forebear, John Gay's
"The Beggar's Opera."

The company which has been
assembled for the present production is young, full of vigor and
goodwill. Vocally, it is entirely
satisfactory. Dramatically its
performance is somewhat rough
along the edges and there is evidence of inexperience. From
time to time it is difficult to

avoid being conscious of a lack of bite and style. But this only indicates how much lurks in this opera.

Among those who have a complete comprehension and mastery of the work, is naturally, Lotte Lenya, widow of Mr. Weill. Miss Lenya, appearing as Jenny, the part she created in the original Berlin production in 1928, delivers her role with the necessary strength and authority. Charlotte Rae as Mrs. Peachum is excellent and so are Jo Sullivan as Polly, Beatrice Arthur as Lucy and Scott Merrill as MacHeath.

An eight-piece orchestra provides the accompaniment, and within the confines of the tiny Theatre de Lys it is just right.

"The Threepenny Opera," which Bert Brecht set in Victorian England, a period Mr. Blitzstein has retained, appears to be indestructible. Its commentary on human beings and life retains a persistent vitality. To hear it rendered in language clear and comprehensible is· an added pleasure. L. F.

1954 Mr 11

The Cast

THE PAJAMA GAME, a musical comedy by George Abbott and Richard Bissell, based on the latter's novel "7¼ Cents," with music and lyrics by Richard Adler and Jerry Ross. Staged by Mr. Abbott and Jerome Robbins; scenery and costumes by Lemuel Ayers; choreography by Bob Fosse; musical director, Hal Hastings; orchestrations, Don Walker; dance music arrangements, Roger Adams; presented by Frederick Brisson, Robert E. Griffith and Harold S. Prince. At the St. James Theatre.

Hines	Eddie Foy Jr.
Prez	Stanley Prager
Joe	Ralph Farnworth
Hasler	Ralph Dunn
Gladys	Carol Haney
Sid Sorokin	John Raitt
Mabel	Reta Shaw
1st Helper	Jack Drummond
2d Helper	Buzz Miller
Charlie	Ralph Chambers
Babe Williams	Janis Paige
Mae	Thelma Pelish
Brenda	Marion Colby
Poopsie	Rae Allen
Salesman	Jack Waldron
Eddie	Jim Hutchison
Pop	William David
Worker	Peter Gennaro

By BROOKS ATKINSON

THE last new musical of the season is the best. It is "The Pajama Game," which opened at the St. James last evening with all the uproar of a George Abbott show. He and Richard Bissell put the book together out of Mr. Bissell's recent novel, "7½ Cents." Applying the good old football spirit to a strike in a pajama factory, the book is as good as most though no better.

For, like the customers who are now going to pour into the St. James, Mr. Abbott is really interested in the color, humor and revelry of a first-rate musical rumpus. "The Pajama Game" fits those specifications exactly.

Richard Adler and Jerry Ross have written an exuberant score in any number of good American idioms without self-consciousness. Beginning with an amusing satire of the work tempo in a factory, they produce love songs with more fever than is usual this year; and they manage to get through a long evening enthusiastically in other respects also. "Once a Year Day" is a jubilee number with a very rousing finish; "There Was Once a Man" takes the goo out of love expertly. Mr. Adler and Mr. Ross write like musicians with a sense of humor; and Don Walker, who has provided imaginative orchestrations, shares their high spirits.

Fortunately, the people who manufacture pajamas are wonderful company in the theatre. The head-man is John Raitt, with the deep voice and the romantic manner; and the head-woman is Janis Paige, whose voice is almost as exhilarating as her shape. Entangled in some love-and-union hokum, they make mating seem attractively normal, and they sing as though they meant it.

Eddie Foy Jr., a true clown who can strut standing still, is immensely funny as a factory time-keeper and a mighty friendly man in a dance. Reta Shaw and he contribute one amiable soft-shoe dance that made the audience explode last evening.

"The Pajama Game" has been staged by Mr. Abbott and Jerome Robbins, both of whom like motion on the stage. That may account for the lightness and friskiness of the performance. And that may also help to explain why Bob Fosse's ballets and improvised dance turns seem to come so spontaneously out of the story. This is the, place to express considerable gratitude to Carol Haney. In the cast she is the secretary to the boss of the plant.

But in fact she is a comic dancer of extraordinary versatility. Shaggy-haired and gamin-like, she suits the mode of the season except that she substitutes caricature for glamour. Her burlesque strip-tease for a funny number called "Her Is" is effortless and convulsing. With Buzz Miller and Peter Gennaro, she introduces the second act with a swift, high-pressure vaudeville that is terrific. Both as dancer and actress Miss Haney is superb.

"The Pajama Game" includes all the usual properties of a loud and ample musical carnival. The costumes and scenery are by Lemuel Ayers, who can make even a factory workroom look theatrical. There is a union picnic for purposes of festive spectacle in the first act, and a restaurant called "Hernando's Hideaway" where the second act goes pleasantly insane.

Mr. Bissell, former tow-boat skipper, and currently boss of a shirt and pajama factory, is a more original writer than you would suspect in the book of this show. Beaten into shape for Broadway, his tale of factory labor problems looks a good deal like dear old Siwash. But say this for the book: it provides an original setting. And, as usual, Mr. Abbott has provided the noise, speed, guffaws and excitement of an energetic, amusing show.

1954 My 14

The Cast

THE BOY FRIEND, a musical comedy of the 1920's. Book, lyrics and music by Sandy Wilson; staged by Vida Hope; choreography by John Heawood; scenery and costumes by Reginald Wooley; scenery and lighting by Feder; costumes by Robert Mackintosh; orchestrations by Ted Royal and Charles L. Cooke; produced by Feuer and Martin. At the Royale Theatre.

Hortense	Paulette Girard
Nancy	Millicent Martin
Maisie	Ann Wakefield
Fay	Stella Claire
Susanne	Lyn Connorty
Dulcie	Dilys Lay
Polly	Julie Andrews
Pierre	Jerry Newby
Alphonse	Buddy Schwab
Marcel	Joe Milan
Mme. Dubonnet	Ruth Altman
Bobby Van Heusen	Bob Scheerer
Percival Browne	Eric Berry
Tony	John Hewer
Phillipe	Jimmy Alex
Lord Brockhurst	Geoffrey Hibbert
Lady Brockhurst	Moyna MacGill
Gendarme	Douglas Deane
Guest	Phoebe Mackay
Guest	Marge Ellis
Waiter	Lyn Robert

By BROOKS ATKINSON

OUT of some clichés from the foolish Twenties, Sandy Wilson has written a delightful burlesque, "The Boy Friend," which opened at the Royale last evening. He wrote it originally for British audiences who have been enjoying it ever since.

There seems to be no reason why their American counterparts should not enjoy it here. For Mr. Wilson's light cartoon of the standard musical play of the Twenties is extremely well done in manuscript as well as on stage. He has written book, songs and lyrics with satirical inventiveness; and someone has directed it with great ironic skill.

For it is hard to say which is funnier: the material or the performance. With a covetous eye on the follies of the Twenties, Mr. Wilson has knocked together an old-fashioned book as maudlin as they were in those days. It tells the story of a rich little girl who falls in love with a charming messenger boy, who, fortunately, in the last act turns out to be the son of Lord and Lady Brockhurst.

Writing the music and lyrics in the same skimming, sardonic vein, Mr. Wilson has composed a tinny score in a jazzy style with amusingly innocuous lyrics.

I could be happy with you
If you could be happy with me,

his lovers sing with bogus rapture. Some other awful though plausible lines come across the footlights: "Skies will not always be blue," for example. Mr. Wilson has a knack for coating the obvious with humor.

The staging is superb. Dressed in the flapper, knee-length gowns of the Twenties, with cloche hats, and made up in the garish stage style of the period, the girls are grotesquely funny to look at before the show properly begins. But there is a lot more to the caricature than costumes. For the director has revived all the coy stage routines of the day, and they are hilarious.

The toothy charm, the girlish shrugs, the screeching laughter, the fraudulently innocent glee—they are all present or accounted for, the more horrible, the more uproarious. Was the musical stage as silly as this in the Twenties? Well, it was. We are all guilty, if only because we liked it that way.

According to the program, Vida Hope, who directed the London production, has directed the American facsimile. Since this department does not know all the details of the intramural rumpus during the rehearsal period, it will take the program at face value and give Miss Hope credit for a brisk, witty performance.

•

Many of the performers have come from England, and they are wonderful. The saucy girls who begin the festivities with squealing, grimacing and dancing are very funny. Ann Wakefield, who does a fast Charleston and flirts with all the boys, is vastly amusing. Dilys Lay, another pony soubrette, is a miniature Beatrice Lillie.

Ruth Altman, a Gothamite in good standing, plays and sings a breezy coquette of middle years. John Hewer, as a tap-dancing romantic lead, acts with the arch good nature of the period.

But it is probably Julie Andrews, as the heroine, who gives "The Boy Friend" its special quality. She burlesques the insipidity of the part. She keeps the romance very sad. Her hesitating gestures and her wistful, shy mannerisms are very comic. But, by golly, there is more than irony in her performance. There is something genuine in it, too. Sometimes her romantic sadness is almost moving. One theatregoer found himself sorry for her and just on the verge of believing "The Boy Friend"; and he was happier than she was when she found Prince Charming in the last buttery scene.

But that is obviously an illegal attitude to take towards Mr. Wilson's pastiche. "The Boy Friend" is a caricature of the hokum musical comedy of the Twenties, and a mighty good one, too.

1954 O 1

Peter Pan

Mary Martin Bows in Musical Version

By BROOKS ATKINSON

IF Mary Martin is satisfied, so are the folks out front. The musical version of "Peter Pan," which opened at the Winter Garden last evening, is a vastly amusing show.

Barrie wrote the libretto. But a lot of the exuberance of Texas has stolen into the legend now. For Miss Martin, looking trim and happy, is the liveliest Peter Pan in the record book. She has more appetite for flying and swinging than any of her more demure predecessors, and she performs as actor, dancer and singer with skill and enjoyment. Peter Pan may have been a proper Victorian originally. He is a healthy, fun-loving American now.

As the bloodthirsty Captain Hook, Cyril Ritchard gives a superb performance in the grand manner, with just a touch of burlesque. Among the other stars of the production, put Jerome Robbins' name high on the list. Mr. Robbins began as a choreographer. Without taking leave of that profession, he has directed this phantasmagoria with inventiveness and delight. The adventures of Peter Pan are marvelously enlivened in Never Never Land by any number of comic ballets for children, Indians and pirates

—rushing and winning in style, though never alien to the innocent spirit of Barrie. Mr. Robbins has done a wonderful job.

The Cast

PETER PAN, a new musical version of Sir James M. Barrie's fantasy. Music by Mark Charlap and lyrics by Carolyn Leigh; additional music by Jule Styne and additional lyrics by Betty Comden and Adolph Green; incidental music by Trude Rittman and Elmer Bernstein. Direction and choreography by Jerome Robbins; scenery by Peter Larkin; costumes by Motley; lighting by Peggy Clark; technical direction, Richard Rodda; assistant to director, Mary Hunter; conductor, Louis Adrian; orchestral arrangements, Albert Sendrey; produced by Edwin Lester under the auspices of Richard Halliday. At the Winter Garden.

Wendy .... Kathy Nolan
John .... Robert Harrington
Liza .... Heller Halliday
Michael .... Joseph Stafford
Nana .... Norman Shelly
Mrs. Darling .... Margalo Gillmore
Mr. Darling .... Cyril Ritchard
Peter Pan .... Mary Martin
Lion .... Richard Wyatt
Kangaroo .... Don Lurio
Ostrich .... Joan Tewkesbury
Slightly .... David Bean
Tootles .... Ian Tucker
Curly .... Stanley Stenner
Nibs .... Paris Theodore
Crocodile .... Norman Shelly
First Twin .... Alan Sutherland
Second Twin .... Darryl Duran
Captain Hook .... Cyril Ritchard
Smee .... Joe E. Marks
Tiger Lily .... Sondra Lee
Cecco .... Robert Tucker
Noodler .... Frank Lindsay
Jukes .... William Burke
Starkey .... Robert Vanselow
Mullins .... James White
Wendy Grown-Up .... Sallie Brophy
Jane .... Kathy Nolan

There is room for some arguments about this full-gauged show. By the time the third act comes round, it begins to look over produced. Peter Larkin's scenery is magical, as are Motley's costumes and all the other impediment of a big carnival. But a Hollywood-like lust for production for production's sake makes things look ponderous toward the end.

Nor has the music much taste. The songs and the lyrics have been contributed by many hands, and some of them are suitable. The opening nursery fugue, called "Tender . Shepherd," is a lovely piece that promises a charming evening. There is a highly comic tango for the pirates, and a sweet-tempered waltz for Liza (who is Mary Martin's daughter) in the second act. But most of the music sounds as though it had come out of Tin Pan Alley tune factories. It lacks distinction and has no audible fondness for Barrie.

Although the taste in showmanship and in music is common, the taste in performers is impeccable. Kathy Nolan's round-faced beaming Wendy is perfect—girlish without sentimentality. As the mother of the Darling children, Margalo Gillmore gives a beautiful performance. Sondra Lee, as Tiger Lily, the Indian maid, is uproarious. She dances and acts a sort of gutter Indian with a city accent that is mocking and comical.

The orphan boys are well cast, particularly in the case of one begoggled little shaver with a tooth missing who teeters gravely through the dances. Among the pirates is Joe E. Marks, a short man who looks constantly worried and more like a homebody than any pirate should. Norman Shelly's maternal - minded dog, Don Lurio's disdainful kangaroo, Richard Wyatt's scholarly lion and Joan Tewkesbury's gossip ostrich are very cheerful company.

Altogether it is a bountiful, good-natured show with a lot of disarming child's play, and Miss Martin flying through the scenery. "Peter Pan" with a Texas accent is fun.

1954 O 21

The Cast

THE RAINMAKER, a romantic play in three acts, by N. Richard Nash. Staged by Joseph Anthony; setting and lighting by Ralph Alswang; costumes by Bolasni; presented by Ethel Linder Reiner in association with Hope Abelson. At the Cort Theatre.

H. C. Curry .... Cameron Prud'homme
Noah Curry .... Joseph Sullivan
Jim Curry .... Albert Salmi
Lizzie Curry .... Geraldine Page
File .... Richard Coogan
Sheriff Thomas ... Tom Flatley Reynolds
Bill Starbuck .... Darren McGavin

By BROOKS ATKINSON

THANKS largely to Geraldine Page and an excellent cast, "The Rainmaker," acted at the Cort last evening, turns out to be an enjoyable romantic comedy. It is the work of N. Richard Nash, who was in a portentous mood last year with a cosmic piece entitled "See the Jaguar."

This year he has nothing in mind except an evening of laughter and perhaps a valuable movie scenario for the future. Last year it was a TV script. "The Rainmaker" is set during a drought in some western state, probably a quarter of a century ago. It concerns the stumbling attempts H. C. Curry and the two Curry boys make to marry off the Curry girl.

•

She is an honest girl who terrifies the men by her intelligence. Gradually she accepts the fact that she has spinster's blood in her veins. But the swashbuckling confidence man who professes to be a rainmaker persuades her to think of herself as beautiful. Before the play is over he and the deputy sheriff are competing for her hand.

The romantic sequences of "The Rainmaker" are a little sticky. Mr. Nash writes them as though he were selling a bill of goods. The ideas are mawkish; the style is ornate and the effect is a little debilitating to lovers of the true and the beautiful.

But this may be because the comedy premises of "The Rainmaker" are so fresh and funny. It is a Western without shooting and Mr. Nash's breezy sketches of the bumbling locals are uproarious. For Westerns are a fabulous convention in which all sorts of gaucheries and simplicities have values of their own. What might be hackneyed in an Eastern is pungent against the background of the West.

As a comedienne, Miss Page has some unexpected qualities. She is fresher than the play and equally funny. Looking mighty purty in dungarees that are enraptured by her long legs, she creates a saucy, spontaneous character who slides lazily through the comedy scenes, tossing off any number of quizzical ideas. Mr. Nash's humors probably do not have as much originality as her acting. A good listener as well as a fine protagonist, she improvises a genuine character out of the things Mr. Nash has provided.

Her romantic scenes don't have quite so much distinction. There seems to be too much detail in them. There are some contrived attitudes. The character she is playing begins to look like a laboratory study of romantic acting, and the buoyancy of the comic scenes begins to disappear. But when the script permits her to be free and easy without being self-conscious, Miss Page is, in her quiet way, hilarious.

Under the expert direction of Joseph Anthony, who has a genial sense of humor, the entire performance is very lively. Cameron Prud'homme as a worried though sympathetic father; Joseph Sullivan as a priggish brother; Richard Coogan as a sheepish man of the law with romantic sensibilities; Tom Flatley Reynolds as the standard sheriff—give racy performances.

Albert Salmi's coltish brother is a little better than that. Awkward, restless, rebellious, it is a vastly amusing folk character out of a country dance. And Darren McGavin's braggart rainmaker, composed of purple patches and convivial grandiloquence, is excellent theatre also. In his single setting of an open-topped ranch house on a prairie, Ralph Alswang has provided a flexible and inviting environment for Mr. Nash's tall tale.

On the whole, it is a lusty antic in a popular comedy vein. The romantic interludes will do no one any permanent harm.

1954 O 29

'The Flowering Peach' Opens at Belasco

The Cast

THE FLOWERING PEACH, a drama in two acts, eight scenes and an epilogue by Clifford Odets, with music by Alan Hovhaness. Staged by the author; scenery by Mordecai Gorelik; lighting by A. H. Feder; costumes by Ballou; produced by Robert Whitehead for the Producers Theatre. At the Belasco Theatre.

Noah .... Menasha Skulnik
Esther .... Berta Gersten
Japheth .... Mario Alcalde

Shem	Martin Ritt
Ham	Leon Janney
Leah	Osna Palmer
Rachel	Janice Rule
Goldie	Barbara Baxley
A Strange Man	Sidney Armus
Lion	
Fawns	Marjorie Barrett
	Patricia Fay
Goat	Barbara Kay
First Old Man	Ludwig Roth
Second Old Man	Sidney Kay

By BROOKS ATKINSON

MR. ODETS' new play is a beautiful one. His finest, in fact. "The Flowering Peach" he calls it. It opened at the Belasco last evening with a tender, lovely, humorous performance.

Imagine the fable of Noah's voyage told in terms of a temperamental though closely united Jewish family and there you have the plan of "The Flowering Peach." Years ago Mr. Odets came into the theatre with another play about a Jewish family. In "Awake and Sing" the members of the family were temperamental and united, too.

•

The tone of "The Flowering Peach" shows how far Mr. Odets has traveled since the cocksure days of "Awake and Sing." The brassy, ricocheting dialogue has matured into humorous, modest talk about great subjects that neither Mr. Odets nor the rest of us are likely to solve. For the new play is the story of mankind living out its destiny under the benevolent eye of God.

There were giants on the earth in those days of the Deluge. In spirit Noah was the greatest. It is Mr. Odets' mood not to put him on a pedestal but to characterize him as the worried head of a family of ordinary individuals—a peevish though loving hero who feels himself close to God. As Noah, Menasha Skulnik, previously celebrated as a low comedian, gives a memorable performance in terms of comedy, temper, pettiness and devotion. Call it a masterpiece of character acting and you cannot be far from the truth.

No doubt, the first half of "The Flowering Peach" is the more endearing. The second half is a little repetitious and garrulous. But no matter, really, for the story of how Noah persuades his skeptical family that God has given all of them a mission, how they bicker, yet do the job obediently, how God helps them solve the most prodigious problems, how they scamper into the ark when the rains fall—all this, told with sympathetic humor in the form of a folk fable, ought to be enough to delight and move any theatregoer.

•

In the second act the voyage concludes triumphantly with the grounding of the ark, the flowering of the peach and the departure of the family in their several ways to replenish and fructify the earth. It is a triumphant conclusion, but after a long series of quarrels and sorrows that symbolize the eternal questing of God's children.

Mr. Odets is every inch a theatre writer. That is probably the reason why this fantasy always seems real and human and respectful of the unseen Lord of the skies. As his own director and in association with other theatre artists, he has staged an idiomatic performance. Mordecai Gorelik has designed a whole series of settings in fable style; and Abe Feder, the lighting expert, has arranged sunshine, storms, nights and days and the final rainbow in a deeply emotional vein. Alan Hovhaness has composed an evocative musical score that serves the pulsing moods of the play admirably.

•

All honor to Mr. Skulnik for his touching, humble, virtuoso performance. But Berta Gersten also contributes a notable performance. As Noah's wife, she plays with sardonic sharpness of speech, but with fortitude, patience and forgiveness as the matriarch of the race. She has stature and homely eloquence.

The other parts are well defined individuals. Martin Ritt is a tower of strength as Shem. Nor is there anything slovenly in the other characterizations. Mario Alcaldo as a stubborn though capable Japheth, Leon Janney as a trivial-minded Ham, Osna Palmer as an industrious Leah, Janice Rule as a placid Rachel with a stone lying in her heart, Barbara Baxley as a coquettish Goldie who learns to respect some unworldly people—these are perceptive performances that grow in richness and understanding as the story tests the characters.

●

If you listen closely you can probably discover a message of hope for the sullen world of today. But Mr. Odets is not setting himself up as an oracle. He does not pretend to have the magic formula. Contemplating the long history of the race in terms of some disarming people, he is facing the world with respect and humility. "The Flowering Peach" is his testament to the endurance and native wisdom of mankind.

1954 D 29

1955

'Merchant of Venice' Is Revived Uptown

The Cast

THE MERCHANT OF VENICE, the Shakespearean play in two parts. Produced and designed by Donald H. Goldman; directed by Marjorie Hildreth; setting by Willis Knighton; incidental music by Ellen Bower; presented by the Shakespearewrights. At the Jan Hus Auditorium. 351 East Seventy-fourth Street. for Tuesday through Sunday night performances, with matinee on Saturday.
Duke of Venice ....Milton Jacobson
Prince of Morocco ....Earle Hyman
Antonio ....Robert Baines
Bassanio ....Charles Aidman
Minstrel ....} Donald Mork
Solanio ....}
Salerio ....Claude Latson
Gratiano ....Philip Lawrence
Lorenzo ....Charles Forsythe
Shylock ....Thomas Barbour
Tubal ....Milton Jacobson
Launcelot Gobbo ....Robert Cass
Old Gobbo ....John Monk
Leonardo ....Robert Miller
Stephano ....John Main

Thomas Barbour as Shylock in "Merchant of Venice."

Portia ....Laurinda Barrett
Nerissa ....,Alene Hatch
Jessica ....Laurie Vendig

By BROOKS ATKINSON

"TWELFTH NIGHT" was no accident at the Jan Hus Auditorium. "The Merchant of Venice," which opened there last evening, is also vigorous, to the point and interesting.

Some of the graces generally associated with the play are wanting, for the Shakespeare wrights, as they dub themselves, are not musicians. Against that we can set the candor of Marjorie Hildreth's direction and the youthful sincerity of the acting.

This production even faces the problem of Shylock. In Thomas Barbour's aggressive and excitable acting, he is a monster animated by the revilement of the Christians and the unfilial desertion of his daughter. However repugnant that interpretation may be to us today, it is the logic of the drama, with no equivocation. And the tension of the story is drawn tight by this pitiless, highstrung moneylender whose nerves are jangled and whose heart is dead.

What a youthful play it is! In more sophisticated productions, the youth is not so conspicuous. But as played by young people, devoted to their craft, the courtly extravagance of Shakespeare's writing the kindness and the high spirits, the passionate fervor of friendships, the mischievous humors come very much alive.

The love between Portia and Bassanio is no lyric convention in the acting of Laurinda Barrett and Charles Aidman, but youthful devotion. Robert Baines' Antonio is not a romantic fop, but a manly youth. Charles Forsythe's Lorenzo is a young man of honest address; and even Stephano, a trivial part, has a touch of self-respect in John Main's acting.

The most accomplished playing is that of Earle Hyman as the Prince of Morocco. Mr. Hyman has style as well as force. Laurie Vendig's Jessica is both lovely and rueful; and Alene Hatch's Nerissa is good,

also. Claude Latson's Salerio and Philip Lawrence's Gratiano are less skillful.

•

Let's admit that Launcelot Gobbo is an impossible part. Shakespeare must have written it with the specific drolleries of one of his fellow comedians in mind. It is a heavy-handed part in Robert Cass' acting, which is closer to the 100-yard dash than clowning.

Note that this is the troupe that plays on a platform stage without scenery. Willis Knighton is credited with the set. It consists of a few benches for Portia, the Duke of Venice and some of the other players when they get sore-footed. Unencumbered by gestures toward streets and houses, the performance is swift and compact, always bearing down on the main crisis of the court scene. Neither the director nor the actors stray away from the theme into the by-ways of interpretation or evasion. It is good work — Shakespeare's "The Merchant of Venice," in fact.

1955 F 23

Theatre: 'Bus Stop'

The Cast

BUS STOP, a play in three acts, by William Inge. Staged by Harold Clurman; scenery by Boris Aronson; costumes and lighting by Paul Morrison; produced by Robert Whitehead and Roger L. Stevens. At the Music Box.
Elma Duckworth...........Phyllis Love
Grace....................Elaine Stritch
Will Masters.................Lou Polan
Cherie...................Kim Stanley
Dr. Gerald Lyman........Anthony Ross
Carl.......................Patrick McVey
Virgil Blessing............Crahan Denton
Bo Decker.................Albert Salmi

By BROOKS ATKINSON

HAVING written a wonderful play two years ago, William Inge has now written a better. He calls it "Bus Stop." It was beautifully acted at the Music Box last evening.

To say that it records a cowboy's stormy courtship of a night club singer is to report nothing significant about the play. For "Bus Stop" is a series of character portraits of some travelers shut up in a tawdry restaurant during a snowstorm. Out of a rather ordinary situation, Mr. Inge has put together an uproarious comedy that never strays from the truth. Once it gets started it flows naturally and sympathetically through the hearts and hopes of some admirable people.

•

As a group they are common folks who don't know much except the basic principles of living. The cowboy is a blustering braggart who thinks a girl has to be lassoed into marriage. The night club singer is a vulgar girl who does not like to be bullied. In the course of the evening the cowboy learns that tenderness is more effective than bravado, and the night club singer learns that an honest boy is more lovable than a stage-door Johnny. Their courtship is riotous, violent, wild and hilarious, but in the end things turn out very well.

But Mr. Inge is no man to shackle a play with a plot. As in "Picnic," he is interested in the ordinary waywardness of simple people going about their personal affairs. There are the bus driver and the proprietress of the restaurant —a pair that gets to the main issue with a minimum of delay. There is a romantic high school girl who stands on tiptoe before life with some bookish dreams in her head.

•

There is a drunken professor with a sardonic mind and very loose habits who finds himself shamed into behaving like a gentleman. There is an amiable, level-headed sheriff.

There is a modest, fatherly cowhand with a guitar and some notes of wisdom about human behavior.

Best of all, there is some moving conversation about the nature of love and the generosity that makes it possible. For Mr. Inge has more than an evening's entertainment in mind. He has ideas and principles. While his comedy is roaring around the stage, he says a number of simple truths that give height and depth to his writing, and that bring into his play an artistic and intellectual maturity that was less conspicuous in "Picnic" or "Come Back, Little Sheba."

•

The performance is glorious. Harold Clurman's direction is both sensitive and high-spirited, and it has penetrated into every corner of the script. Boris Aronson, who has not designed a setting since night before last, has executed a vivid portrait of a slatternly diner, the wintry outdoors crowding close around the warm interior.

Kim Stanley, left, Anthony Ross, Phyllis Love in "Bus Stop"

As the night club singer, Kim Stanley is superb. Still the traveling lady, she gives a glowing performance that is full of amusing detail—cheap, ignorant, bewildered, but also radiant with personality. Albert Salmi's hulking cowboy who alternates between screaming high spirits and naïve despondency is both funny and touching. As in the case of Miss Stanley, Mr. Salmi's comic acting has plenty of human truth inside.

•

In the part of the tipsy professor, Anthony Ross gives his richest performance — sardonically witty, pathetically self-critical, always fluent in the stream of expression. Elaine Stritch's loose-jointed, tough-talking restaurant keeper is vastly amusing. And Phyllis Love's schoolgirl is innocently beautiful with quick sympathies and considerable strength of character.

There is a fond and conscientious sheriff by Lou Polan, whose homely manners are thoroughly winning. Crahan Denton plays a guitar-strumming cowboy with an unaffected gleam of humanity. Patrick McVey is the bustling, businesslike bus-driver who does not waste time on tedious formalities.

So Mr. Inge's comedy, in both the writing and the acting, is a memorable achievement. The story is uproarious. But Mr. Inge has taken a long look into the hearts of his people. Being completely human, they are the salt of the earth.

1955 Mr 3

Writer Depicts Some Restless Delta Folk

The Cast

CAT ON A HOT TIN ROOF, a drama in three acts, by Tennessee Williams. Staged by Elia Kazan; scenery and lighting by Jo Mielziner; costumes by Lucinda Ballard; production stage manager, Robert Downing; presented by the Playwrights Company. At the Morosco Theatre.

Lacey	Maxwell Glanville
Sookey	Musa Williams
Margaret	Barbara Bel Geddes
Brick	Ben Gazzara
Mae	Madeleine Sherwood
Gooper	Pat Hingle
Big Mama	Mildred Dunnock
Dixie	Pauline Hahn
Buster	Darryl Richard
Sonny	Seth Edwards
Trixie	Janice Dunn
Big Daddy	Burl Ives
Reverend Tooker	Fred Stewart
Doctor Baugh	R. G. Armstrong
Daisy	Eva Vaughan Smith
Brightie	Brownie McGhee
Small	Sonny Terry

By BROOKS ATKINSON

FOR Tennessee Williams and for the rest of us, the news could hardly be better this morning. For "Cat On a Hot Tin Roof," which opened at the Morosco last evening, is a stunning drama.

Again Mr. Williams is discussing some people of the Mississippi Delta, which he knows well. And again the people are not saints and heroes. But this time Mr. Williams has broken free from the formula or the suspicion of formula that has hovered around the edges of his plays.

•

"Cat on a Hot Tin Roof" is the work of a mature observer of men and women and a gifted craftsman. To say that it is the drama of people who refuse to face the truth of life is to suggest a whole school of problem dramatists. But one of its great achievements is the honesty and simplicity of the craftsmanship. It seems not to have been written. It is the quintessence of life. It is the basic truth. Always a seeker after honesty in his writing, Mr. Williams has not only found a solid part of the truth but found the way to say it with complete honesty. It is not only part of the truth of life: it is the absolute truth of the theatre.

In a plantation house, the members of the family are celebrating the sixty-fifth birthday of the Big Daddy, as they sentimentally dub him. The tone is gay. But the mood is somber. For a number of old evils poison the gaiety—sins of the past, greedy hopes for the future, a desperate eagerness not to believe in the truths that surround them. Most of them are living lives

Burl Ives, Barbara Bel Geddes in "Cat on a Hot Tin Roof"

as uncomfortable and insecure as the proverbial "cat on a hot tin roof."

Nothing eventful happens in the course of the evening, for Mr. Williams has now left the formulas of the theatre far to the rear. He is interested solely in exploring minds. "Cat on a Hot Tin Roof" is a delicately wrought exercise in human communication. His characters try to escape from the loneliness of their private lives into some form of understanding. The truth invariably terrifies them. That is the one thing they cannot face or speak.

They can find comfort in each other only by falling back on lies—social lies, lies about health, lies about the past, lies about the future. Not vicious lies, for the most part. The central characters want to be kind to each other. But lies are the only refuge they have from the ugly truths that possess their minds.

As the expression of a brooding point of view about life, "Cat on a Hot Tin Roof" is limpid and effortless. As theatre, it is superb. Mr. Williams and his brilliant director, Elia Kazan, have used the medium of the theatre candidly. Jo Mielziner has graphically suggested a bed-sitting room on what amounts to an apron stage that thrusts the action straight at the audience. Most of the play is written in long duologues without dramatic artifice. Occasionally the actors speak directly to the audience without reference to the other characters.

The acting is magnificent.

There is about it that "little something extra" by which the actors reveal awareness of a notable theatrical occasion. Barbara Bel Geddes, vital, lovely and frank as the young wife who cannot accept her husband's indifference; Ben Gazzara, handsome, melancholly, pensive as the husband; Burl Ives as the solid head of a family who fears no truth except his own and hates insincerity; Mildred Dunnock as the silly, empty-headed mother who has unexpected strength of character—give marvelous performances.

●

There are excellent performances also by Madeleine Sherwood, Pat Hingle, Fred Stewart, R. G. Armstrong and some other good actors. "Cat on a Hot Tin Roof" is Mr. Williams' finest drama. It faces and speaks the truth.

1955 Mr 25

'Damn Yankees' Tells Tale of Witchery

The Cast

DAMN YANKEES, a musical comedy, based on Douglass Wallop's novel "The Year the Yankees Lost the Pennant." Book by George Abbott and Mr. Wallop. Music and lyrics by Richard Adler and Jerry Ross. Directed by Mr. Abbott; dances and musical numbers staged by Bob Fosse; scenery and costumes designed by William and Jean Eckart; musical direction by Hal Hastings; orchestrations by Don Walker; dance music arrangements by Roger Adams; presented by Frederick Brisson, Robert E. Griffith and Harold S. Prince, in association with Albert D. Taylor. At the Forty-sixth Street Theatre.

Meg	Shannon Bolin
Joe Boyd	Robert Shafer
Applegate	Ray Walston
Sister	Jean Stapleton
Doris	Elizabeth Howell
Joe Hardy	Stephen Douglass
Henry	Al Lanti
Sohovik	Eddie Phillips
Smokey	Nathaniel Frey
Vernon	Albert Linville
Van Buren	Russ Brown
Rocky	Jimmie Komack
Gloria	Rae Allen
Teen-Ager	Cherry Davis
Lynch	Del Horstmann
Welch	Richard Bishop
Lola	Gwen Verdon
Miss Weston	Janie Janvier
Guard	George Marcy
Commissioner	Del Horstmann
Postmaster	Albert Linville

By LEWIS FUNKE

AS shiny as a new baseball and almost as smooth, a new musical glorifying the national pastime slid into the Forty-sixth Street Theatre last night. As far as this umpire is concerned you can count it among the healthy clouts of the campaign.

It is called "Damn Yankees" and it tells about how Casey Stengel's stalwarts are brought down to defeat by the Washington Senators in the final game of the season with the American League bunting the prize. But even the most ardent supporters of Mr. Stengel's minions should have a good time. And, as for that Dodger crowd, well you can just imagine.

●

Heading the board of strategy for this outfit is that shrewd manipulator of talent, George Abbott. He acts as general manager of the proceedings on the stage in addition to having collaborated on the book with Douglass Wallop, from whose novel, "The Year the Yankees Lost the Pennant," this merry romp was taken.

To be sure, like any other manager in the course of a long season, Mr. Abbott has not been able to iron out all the kinks in his combination. In spite of his emphasis on speed afoot and timing there is a tendency every now and then for things to settle down a bit flatly on the ground. But the story of how Joe Boyd leases his soul to the Devil in order to become Joe Hardy, champion home-run hitter and inspiration of the Washington Senators, succeeds in being a sufficiently satisfactory vehicle on which to hang some highly amusing antics and utilize some splendid performers.

●

There is for instance that enchantress, Gwen Verdon, who socked a home run two years ago in "Can-Can." Miss Verdon is the devil's handmaiden called upon to aid in sealing the fate of Joe Hardy's soul. It is difficult to understand how Joe was able to hold out for so long. For Miss Verdon

Gwen Verdon, Ray Walston and Stephen Douglass as they appear in a scene from "Damn Yankees."

is just about as alluring a she-witch as was ever bred in the nether regions. Vivacious, as sleek as a car on the show-room floor, and as nice to look at, she gives brilliance and sparkle to the evening with her exuberant dancing, her wicked, glistening eyes and her sheer delight in the foolery.

For the Devil there is the impeccable Ray Walston, a suave and sinister fellow who knows how to be disdainful of the good in man, whose pleasure, as you might expect, is to make humans squirm. Authoritative and persuasive, he does not overdo a role that easily could become irritating in less expert hands. Stephen Douglass, as Joe Hardy, is a completely believable athlete, clean-cut and earnest about his work. And, although it is impossible to spread the full credits to a large and vigorous cast, mention must be made of the effective contributions by Jean Stapleton as an autograph hound, Nathaniel Frey and Jimmy Komack as a couple of ball hawks, and Rae Allen as a nervy feminine sports writer.

In the music department Richard Adler and Jerry Ross have provided a thoroughly robust score to fit the occasion. The music has the spirit and brass that you'd expect to find out at the ball park and the lyrics are appropriate and smart. "Heart" is a humorous ode to the need for courage on the athletic field and it is done splendidly by Russ Brown, the sturdy manager of the Senators, along with the Messrs. Komack, Frey and Albert Linville. "The Game" is a humorous hymn to athletic abstinence. And "Shoeless Joe From Hannibal, Mo." sets the stage for a splendid hoedown for Robert Fosse, who attended to the choreography.

●

Mr. Fosse, with Miss Verdon's and, is one of the evening's heroes. His dance numbers are full of fun and vitality. In "Whatever Lola Wants," there is a first-class gem in which music, lyrics and dance combine to make a memorable episode of the femme fatale operating on the hapless male. "Who's Got the Pain" involves Miss Verdon and Eddie Phillips in a mambo and "Two Lost Souls" puts on a torrid and rowdy bacchanal just to prove everyone's versatility.

●

William and Jean Eckart, assigned to the scenery and costume department, have decked out the whole affair handsomely. And in the baseball sets they have imparted complete authenticity. There is a considerable amount of talent in this entertainment and it makes up for some of the wide-open spaces that pop up every now and then. Looks like Mr. Abbott has another pennant winner.

1955 My 6

French Mime Appears on the Phoenix Stage

The Cast

AN EVENING OF PANTOMIME, a program with Marcel Marceau and his partners, Pierre Verry and Alvin Epstein. Presented by T. Edward Hambleton and Norris Houghton. At the Phoenix Theatre.

By BROOKS ATKINSON

WE might as well know what many other nations have learned already: Marcel Marceau is a brilliant pantomimist. After performing last summer at the Stratford (Ont.) Festival, he has set up his props for a fortnight at the Phoenix, where he opened last evening. The props and the paraphernalia are not burdensome—a black backdrop, a box or two, a few musical recordings, a traditional pantomime costume with a variation, a couple of assistants who introduce the numbers with lettered cards and appropriate attitudes. That's about all of the baggage.

●

But it does not account for M. Marceau's most essential importation. He has also brought genius. For this Parisian mime, who was a student of Charles Dullin, is a virtuoso of the first rank in a school of art that is not especially popular because only a genius really counts in it. The comparison with Charlie Chaplin is inevitable, not only because M. Marceau has been influenced by Chaplin, but because they are geniuses of comparable stature. If he were so minded, M. Marceau could begin where Chaplin left off with his silent movies.

M. Marceau is the more conscious artist. For all its wit, humor and drollery, his evening of "Pantomime," as he calls it, is meticulously artistic in a great and ancient tradition. Notice Pierre Verry, who displays the lettered cards that introduce each number: his innocently gay costume and his wistful glow of delight are carefully designed fragments of style. A trained performer, M. Verry does not attitudinize at random.

●

There is not much point in trying to report what M. Marceau does number by number. In the first part of the program, entitled "Style Pantomimes," he portrays a man walking against the wind, a man walking up and down a staircase, a man struggling in a tug-of-war, the people in a public park, a man playing dice and another trying on merchandise at the clothier.

But those facts do not suggest the lightness, freshness and abundance of his miming. And nothing can suggest the eloquent simplicity of his brief

Marcel Marceau

life of mortal man that is entitled "Youth, Maturity, Old Age and Death." It is a masterpiece.

•

The second part is devoted to the adventures of BIP, a character M. Marceau has invented. BIP corresponds to Chaplin's little clown, although M. Marceau replaces sentimentality with wit. BIP is a pretty funny plastic image as an artist, a traveler, a skater, a dancer and a lion-tamer. He is uproarious as David warring with Goliath, M. Marceau playing both parts. As a man netting butterflies, he is tender, compassionate and beautiful. For this little exercise in purity is another master-

piece by a gifted performer who is an artist at heart.

Despite the dazzling variety of the program, he does not violate the tradition of the mime. The figure is a wistful creation — the face haggard under the white flour make-up, the eyes and mouth sad, the spirit melancholy. His adventures in imitating the follies of the human race invariably end in comic failure. He who gets slapped is silently resigned to a career of defeat and disenchantment. M. Marceau abides by the rules of an illustrious form of art.

Only a fortnight, the man says.

1955 S 21

Lovely Drama Staged From Girl's Book

The Cast

THE DIARY OF ANNE FRANK, a play in two acts by Frances Goodrich and Albert Hackett, dramatized from the book, "Anne Frank: The Diary of a Young Girl"; staged by Garson Kanin; production designed by Boris Aronson; presented by Kermit Bloomgarden; costumes by Helene Pons; lighting by Leland Watson; production manager, William Hammerstein. At the Cort Theatre.

Mr. Frank ....Joseph Schildkraut
Miep ....Gloria Jones
Mrs. Van Daan ....Dennie Moore
Mr. Van Daan ....Lou Jacobi
Peter Van Daan ....David Levin
Mrs. Frank ....Gusti Huber
Margot Frank ....Eva Rubinstein
Anne Frank ....Susan Strasberg
Mr. Kraler ....Clinton Sundberg
Mr. Dussel ....Jack Gilford

By BROOKS ATKINSON

THEY have made a lovely, tender drama out of "The Diary of Anne Frank," which opened at the Cort last evening. They have treated it with admiration and respect.

"They" are Frances Goodrich and Albert Hackett, who wrote the dramatization; Garson Kanin, who directed; Boris Aronson, who designed the setting, and a remarkable cast in which Joseph Schildkraut is the star. Strange how the shining spirit of a young girl now dead can filter down through the years and inspire a group of theatrical professionals in a foreign land.

Among them, not the least and perhaps the finest is Susan Strasberg, who plays the part of Anne. Although Miss Strasberg once appeared at the Theatre de Lys, this is her official Broadway debut, and it is worth particular notice. She is a slender, enchanting young lady with a heart-shaped face, a pair of burning eyes and the soul of an actress.

By some magic that cannot be explained, she has caught the whole character of Anne in a flowing, spontaneous, radiant performance. Anne is a girl—not the stage image of a girl—but a capricious, quick-tempered, loving maiden whose imagination is always running ahead of her experience. Whether that is Anne or Miss Strasberg it is hard to say at the moment, for they are blended into one being. It looks artless because Miss Strasberg has created it with so much purity from within.

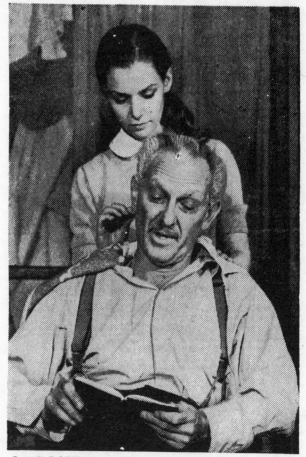

Joseph Schildkraut and Susan Strasberg as they appear in a scene from "The Diary of Anne Frank." At the Cort.

From any practical point of view the job of making a play out of the diary of Anne Frank is impossible. Perhaps that is why Mr. and Mrs. Hackett have succeeded so well. They have not contrived anything; they have left the tool-kit outside the door of their workroom. They have absorbed the story out of the diary and related it simply.

It is the story of some Jews hidden in an Amsterdam garret during the Nazi occupation, fed by some friends and successfully secreted for a couple of years. Nothing momentously dramatic happens. It is a story of stealth, boredom, bickering, searching for comfort in other people, dreams, fears, hunger, anger and joy.

It is lightly bound together by the character of an adolescent girl who is on tip-toe before life. She is amusing and vexing. But also unconquerable because she is in love with life and squeezes the bitterness and sweetness of every moment that comes her way.

•

Everyone associated with the production has caught some of her spirit and has preserved her innocence and faith.

The garret Mr. Aronson has designed glows with an elusive beauty. As Papa Frank, Mr. Schildkraut plays with taste and kindness. The members of the rather boorish Van Daan family are played with perception by Dennie Moore, Lou Jacobi and David Levin. Jock Gilford's nervous, crochety dentist is amusing and precise.

•

Gusti Huber's patient mother whose nerves are once unstrung and Eva Rubinstein's loyal, placid sister complete the closely knit Frank family. As the two people from outside, Clinton Sundberg and Gloria Jones bring into the play some of the freshness and also the anxieties of the normal world. But it is Miss Strasberg who puts the clearest print of truth on the whole enterprise. Her Anne is the Anne that won so many hearts when the book was published. Out of the truth of a human being has

come a delicate, rueful, moving drama.

1955 O 6

The Cast

THE MATCHMAKER, a comedy in two acts and four scenes, by Thornton Wilder. Staged by Tyrone Guthrie; scenery and costumes by Tanya Moiseiwitsch; presented by the Theatre Guild and David Merrick; produced under the supervision of Mr. Merrick; production stage manager, Samuel Liff. At the Royale Theatre.

Horace Vandergelder ......Loring Smith
Ambrose Kemper ......Alexander Davion
Joe Scanlon ....Philip Leeds
Gertrude ....Charity Grace
Cornelius Hackl ....Arthur Hill
Ermengarde ....Prunella Scales
Malachi Stack ....Patrick McAlinney
Mrs. Levi ....Ruth Gordon
Barnaby Tucker ....Robert Morse
Mrs. Molloy ....Eileen Herlie
Minnie Fay.......Rosamund Greenwood
A Cabman ....Peter Bayliss
Rudolf ....William Lanteau
August ....John Milligan
A Musician ....Philip Leeds
Miss Flora Van Huysen....Esme Church
Her Cook ....Christine Thomas

By BROOKS ATKINSON

AFTER convulsing the British for a season, Thornton Wilder's "The Matchmaker" has settled down at the Royale where it began convulsing New Yorkers last evening.

In 1938 it was known as "The Merchant of Yonkers" and convulsed very few, especially the backers. Since then Mr. Wilder has improved it. Now Tyrone Guthrie has directed it in the style of old-fashioned farce, and that may be the best thing that could happen to any play of theatrical proportions.

For Mr. Guthrie, who seems now to be staging plays in every country simultaneously, has enormous skill, recklessness and gusto, and believes in cramming a theatre full of vitality. Acted by a cast of highly-trained bedlamites, "The Matchmaker" is loud, vulgar, slapdash and uproarious. Some expert craftsmen have made something extraordinarily original and funny out of traditional nonsense from a lost era of theatrical history.

In London the program carried Mr. Wilder's note of acknowledgement to the German version of an English farce from which he drew the plot of "The Matchmaker." Probably it is not smart in New York to admit that a play has a record. But in this instance the record has a direct bearing on the quality of the product. For "The Matchmaker" is frankly the re-creation of the wild farce style that was profoundly loved several generations ago and is now dismissed as obsolete.

It is the fable of a rich Yonkers merchant who goes to New York to seek a wife and becomes involved in a comic volcano. There is no point in describing the plot. Nothing matters but the grotesque situations that are invented and the boldness with which Mr. Guthrie exploits them. As in traditional farce, one man hides under the table at a milliner's shop and another hides in a closet; and mistaken identities become so numerous and complex that even the actors must have trouble in remembering what part they are playing.

But every now and then "The Matchmaker" has a quality that is more surprising. Occasionally it is charming. It is suddenly charming when four of the actors harmonize "Tenting Tonight" after racing like mad people through the milliner's shop. And it switches into a new key several times during the evening when actors step up to the footlights and speak unpretentious soliloquies with thoughtful overtones. Mr. Wilder loves the ancient uses of the theatre.

So does Mr. Guthrie, a constructive iconoclast about stage forms, and so does Tanya Moiseiwitsch, the gifted designer who has made "The Matchmaker" look old-fashioned without letting it look dull or feeble.

The performance is a roar and a ripple, for Mr. Guthrie changes pace, letting up when he thinks the wildness is getting out of hand. Ruth Gordon, looking as if Hogarth had just drawn her, gives her most extravagant comedy performance — sweeping wide, growling, leering, cutting through her scenes with sharp gestures, filling in every corner with a detail or a sardonic observation. Maybe she does bear down a little too hard in the first act, but no matter, because the performance is epochally funny.

Loring Smith bustles with farcical humor as the pompous Yonkers merchant. And Eileen Herlie, a talented actress, is lady-like and exuberant at the same time as a milliner on a

Ruth Gordon and Loring Smith appearing in "Matchmaker"

tear through the town.

The cast is a long one, and there is not time at the moment to salute them all. But Arthur Hill and Robert Morse, as the innocent clerks who get infected with madness must not be ignored. Nor Prunella Scales as a whimpering niece, Patrick McAlinney as a nefarious Irishman, Rosamund Greenwood as a timid milliner's assistant, Esme Church as a pugnacious, garrulous spinster and Peter Bayliss as the most shiftless cabman you ever saw.

Put together like an insane ballet, "The Matchmaker" is fast and boisterous. No one means a word he says. But you would never suspect it from the actors. They play their parts with desperate earnestness as though their lives depended on solving the foolish situations Mr. Wilder has put them in.

1955 D 6

1956

TAMBURLAINE THE GREAT, the Christopher Marlowe melodrama, adapted by Tyrone Guthrie and Donald Wolfit. Presented by the Producers Theatre (Roger L. Stevens, Robert Whitehead and Robert W. Dowling), in association with the Stratford Festival Foundation of Canada; staged by Mr. Guthrie; scenery and costumes by Leslie Hurry; music by John Gardner; lighting and scenic supervision by Paul Morrison; musical director, Louis Applebaum; production stage manager, Sy Milbert. At the Winter Garden.

Prologue	David Gardner
Mycetes	Eric House
Cosroe	Tony Van Bridge
Meander	Robert Goodier
Theridamas	Robert Christie
Menaphon	Ted Follows
Tamburlaine	Anthony Quayle
Zenocrate	Barbara Chilcott
Agydas	Donald Davis
Techelles	William Hutt
Usumcasane	William Shatner
A Persian Messenger	Neil Vipond
Anippe	Deborah Cass
A Basso	Bruce Swerdfager
Bajazeth	Douglas Rain
Zabina	Coral Browne
Ebea	Margaret Braidwood
Soldan of Egypt	Lloyd Bochner
Amyras	Louis Negin

By BROOKS ATKINSON

CHRISTOPHER MARLOWE'S "Tamburlaine the Great" made its professional American debut at the Winter Garden last evening, 369 years late.

If Marlowe was waiting for the right director, the delay can be regarded as having been worth while. For Tyrone Guthrie is just the man to revel in the storm, blood and thunder of this mighty show-piece, which was composed out of boyish bravado by a reckless Elizabethan, and written in declamatory verse.

•

Historically, "Tamburlaine" is venerated as the great prelude to the blank verse drama in which Shakespeare triumphed in the next decade. Artistically, it is venerated because it has both the courage and the skill of its own convictions. It tells the grisly and horrifying story of "the scourge and terror of the world"—Tamburlaine, who led his bloody horde through kingdom after kingdom, slaughtering, pillaging, defying God Himself until his excesses overwhelm him.

Marlowe took two full dramas to tell this barbaric tale. Mr. Guthrie and Donald Wolfit have managed to cut it down to the normal size. Even Marlowe is not entitled to more than two-and-one-half hours of American time.

•

"Tamburlaine" is all in one key of violence and bombast. Shakespeare was the man who learned how to turn blank verse into characters and scenes. Although Marlowe did have a "mighty line" he did not know how to vary it, and "Tamburlaine" is tone-deaf in comparison with "King Lear," for example.

Little things like that do not worry Mr. Guthrie. With Anthony Quayle from Stratford-on-Avon, England, in the leading part, with Coral Browne from England as a Turkish empress, with the excellent Shakespeare company from Stratford, Ont., completing the long cast—Mr. Guthrie has plunged into the text with swagger and gusto. There are banners, fanfares, battle scenes, scenes of torture and murder, conquest and cruelty as Tamburlaine leads his gang through lands incarnadined and rides in a chariot piled high with the skulls of the victims.

•

If "Tamburlaine" remains just this side of the egregious, it is because Mr. Guthrie knows when to stop piling Ossa on Pelion. Moreover, the company has a real flair for classical acting on a big scale. It knows how to move in a sweeping style and how to speak verse with resonance, euphony and conviction. Theatregoers who have seen it in its own tent in Ontario during the summer recognize it as the soundest classical company in North America; and it's a pleasure to have a visit here during the winter.

Mr. Quayle and "Tamburlaine" are well matched in Marlowe's prize-ring. The part is bellowing and flamboyant. Made up like an Asiatic tyrant, Mr. Quayle plays with enormous agility and physical prowess, and he spends most of the evening shouting at the top of his voice. But out of the tumult a tangible character appears. An able actor, Mr. Quayle has a big part under control. The excesses are Marlowe's, not his.

•

As Zenocrate, Tamburlaine's wife, Barbara Chilcott, gives a taut performance, softened with mercy when the horde sweeps through her native country, but proud and resolute in the camp of her consort. As the wife of the defeated Emperor of the Turks, Miss Browne makes a deep impression on the story—imperious on the throne, pitiless toward herself when she and her husband become the humiliated captives of the invader.

Since Marlowe was as prodigal with parts as he was with his verse, the cast is a long one that cannot be adequately discussed at this moment. But it includes some able actors who are in thorough command of an extravagant literary medium—Donald Davis, Lloyd Bochner, David Gardner, Eric House, Douglas Rain, to mention those in conspicuous roles.

This "Tamburlaine" comes to us royally caparisoned with rudely powerful scenery and martial costumes by Leslie Hurry. There is a stirring musical score by John Gardner, with some primitive chants calculated to make your blood turn cold.

•

Marlowe and Mr. Guthrie see eye to eye. They have collaborated on a horror play in stormy blank verse and it is a triumphant theatre occasion. Some day the Ontario company may bring us Mr. Guthrie's production of "Oedipus Rex," which is equally brilliant as a production and a finer piece of literature. "Tamburlaine" appeals to Mr. Guthrie's boyish love of excitement, "Oedipus Rex" stimulates his mind and sense of artistry.

———

The famed Canadian Stratford Players, in their American debut last night, were greeted by a distinguished audience comprising representatives of the Government of Canada and Ambassadors of the United Kingdom and the United Nations.

These included Ambassadors Arnold D. P. Heeney of Canada, Sir Roger Makins of Britain, Gaganvihari Mehta of India, Sir Percy Spender of Australia, Sir Leslie Munro of New Zealand, R. S. S. Gunewardene of Ceylon, Sir Pierson Dixon, a British delegate to the United Nations, and Dr. J. E. Holloway of South Africa.

Before the performance the players were honored at a reception at the Canadian Consulate. After the première, members of the cast were guests of the American National Theatre and Academy at a supper party held at the Carlyle Hotel.

The Canadian troupe is scheduled to remain at the Winter Garden for eight weeks.

1956 Ja 20

4th St. Group Excels in Acting, Staging

The Cast

UNCLE VANYA, a drama in four acts, by Anton Chekhov, translated from the Russian by Stark Young. Staged and revived by David Ross; scenery and lighting by Zvi Geyra; costumes by Richard Mason; production manager, Frank Meottel. At the Fourth Street Theatre, 83 East Fourth Street.

Marina	Mary Perry
Astroff	Franchot Tone
Voinitsky	George Voskovec
Serebriakoff	Clarence Derwent
Sofia Alexandrovna (Sonia)	Peggy McCay
Elena Andreevna	Signe Hasso
Telegin	Gerald Hiken
Voinitskaya	Olive Templeton
A Workman	Sanford Seeger

By BROOKS ATKINSON

EACH of the Chekhov productions at the Fourth Street Theatre has been better than its predecessor. "Uncle Vanya," which opened there last evening, continues that pleasant tradition.

Of the four major Chekhov plays, "Uncle Vanya" is the least familiar. Perhaps it is inferior in design and scope. But it would take a conference of professors to settle the truth of that statement. As acted by a perfect cast, as directed and produced by David Ross, as translated by Stark Young, it is a blend of all of Chekhov's most beguiling qualities. It is the essence of life, done with so much grace and understanding that it does not seem like something written or acted.

There is no doubt of one thing about it. It is richly comic. "The normal state of man is to be odd," the doctor says. Looking through his microscope at the specimens of humanity that he has isolated for "Uncle Vanya," Chekhov was never more warily humorous in his conclusions. They are gentle folk, thrown unwillingly together in a country house. But they are egotists, possessed of illusions about themselves. They are maudlin. Sometimes they are witty.

And the scene in which Uncle Vanya twice tries to shoot a fatuous professor is hilarious. If Chekhov were writing "Uncle Vanya" today we would have to commend him for his skill in psychiatric understanding of character and personality. He dissects his aimless people with the cold detachment of a scientist, but also with the humorous warmth of a sensitive artist. That is a combination unique in the literature of the stage.

George Voskovec's Uncle Vanya is truthful and amusing at the same time—restless, impulsive and wildly futile in his big scene with the revolver. As the insufferable professor, Clarence Derwent is at the top of his form—dripping with condescension in a series of florid but empty gestures. Gerald Hiken's piously ineffectual Telegin is also comic. And in the brief part of a peasant, Sanford Seeger gives an agreeable performance.

The women are excellent also. Signe Hasso's supercilious, timid, crushed rose Elena is a merciless character portrait, despite the gentleness of its manner. As the lonely daughter, yearning to be loved, Peggy McCay gives a performance that glows with the true spirit of Chekhov. Mary Perry's patient and selfless old nurse gives the performance a solid point of reference. Olive Templeton is good in the shadowy part of the mother.

Mr. Ross has now completed three of the four major Chekhov plays, giving all of us the benefit of what he has learned. "Uncle Vanya" is sweet and touching, but also funny. Unpretentious in style, modest in accent, it is the work of a master who seems to know everything about the vagrant souls of human beings. The truth turns out to be fundamentally comic. Chekhov had no interest in reforming the world.

Thanks to the settings and the evocative lighting of Zvi Geyra and the lovely costumes of Richard Mason, this is a beautiful production. As a matter of fact, the Fourth Street Theatre is an awkward, impossible house. Bit by bit, Mr. Ross and his associates have learned how to transfigure it into a haven of art. The physical production has warmth, taste, depth and magic.

Last evening the first of the four acts seemed to be at loose ends. But once that was out of the way the performance acquired the innocently acerbic spirit of Chekhov. The acting is superb. Franchot Tone's portrait of the country doctor is the finest thing he has done, in years—perhaps in all his years on the stage. It is mature, responsive; it is wistfully alive just under the surface of a heavy-moving man of medicine

1956 F 1

The Cast

MIDDLE OF THE NIGHT, "a love story" in two acts by Paddy Chayefsky; produced and staged by Joshua Logan; settings and lighting by Jo Mielziner; costumes by Motley; incidental music by Lehman Engel; production stage manager, Neil Hartley. At the ANTA Theatre.

The Girl .... Gena Rowlands
The Mother .... June Walker
The Kid Sister .... Joan Chambers
The Manufacturer .. Edward G. Robinson
The Sister .... Nancy R. Pollock
The Widow .... Betty Walker
The Daughter .... Anne Jackson
The Neighbor .... Effie Afton
The Friend .... Janet Ward
The Husband .... Lee Philips
The Son-in-Law .... Martin Balsam

By BROOKS ATKINSON

IT seems like old times to have Edward G. Robinson back.

As a matter of fact, he is back on the stage where he used to perform before he settled down in Hollywood. For the ANTA Theatre, where "Middle of the Night" opened last evening, was the Guild Theatre when he was working for a living.

As a middle-aged garment manufacturer in Paddy Chayefsky's drama, Mr. Robinson gives a winning and skillful performance. No one could be more relaxed about a part. But no one could give the

character more warmth or tenderness, or make an undistinguished man seem so notable.

By naming all his characters "The Girl," "The Manufacturer," "The Sister," and so on, Mr. Chayefsky apparently means to suggest that they are ordinary people. So they are. Although Mr. Robinson does not make the manufacturer extraordinary, he makes him human and disarming, and very pleasant company for an evening in the theatre.

•

"Middle of the Night," which is billed as "a love story," is the tale of a widower, aged 53, who falls in love with a blonde, aged 24. Mr. Chayefsky has written it in a minor key, deliberately holding down the emotion and laying emphasis on the homeliness of the material. Everyone is intentionally average — the manufacturer and his daughter and sister; the blonde and her mother, sister and impulsive husband.

The reactions to a love affair between a middle-aged man and a girl who is younger than his daughter are average, and the dialogue is composed of average talk. Toward his material Mr. Chayefsky has a kind of O. Henry sense of familiarity. Apparently it is part of his design to underwrite the plot.

In "Marty," the celebrated screen play that Mr. Chayefsky wrote, this method resulted in a thoroughly delightful picture. The method is less successful in the theatre, where size is more important. The play that is underwritten may turn out not to be as picturesque as Mr. Chayefsky probably imagined. Without some pressure back of it the average may emerge as dullness in the theatre.

When Mr. Robinson is not on the stage, dullness is always lurking around the edges of Mr. Chayefsky's play. What we are left with is rather spiritless narrative frequently punctuated with a scene so honest and poignant that it brings the audience and the play quickly to life at the

Gena Rowlands and Edward G. Robinson as they appear in a scene from Paddy Chayefsky play "Middle of the Night."

same time. Mr. Chayefsky has a particular talent for writing about the temperament of his Jewish family. He describes the homelife of a garment manufacturer with taste and authenticity and also with sympathetic humor.

•

As both producer and director, Joshua Logan has given Mr. Chayefsky's play an inviting production and performance. Jo Mielziner has designed the two settings—one showing the grubbiness of a cheap apartment, the other showing the commonplace comforts of the manfacturer's apartment. Motley has dressed the characters suitably, and Lehman Engel has provided a score that captures the changes in the moods of the story.

Everyone acts well. Gena Rowlands is especially good as the blonde involved in a situation that she does not know how to handle. June Walker as the mother, Anne Jackson as the daughter, Nancy R. Pollock as the sister, Betty Walker as a talkative widow, Lee Philips as the husband, Martin

Balsam as the son-in-law give plausible, impeccable performances. There is never anything wrong with anything about "Middle of the Night."

•

But Mr. Chayefsky's intentional cultivation of the average and the obvious has its own limitations. It cannot wholly escape being average drama. What saves it is Mr. Robinson's quiet authority as an actor. It is good to be reminded of his easy skill and to have him back with us again.

1956 F 9

The Cast

MY FAIR LADY, a musical comedy adapted from George Bernard Shaw's "Pygmalion." Book and lyrics by Alan Jay Lerner, with music by Frederick Loewe. Production staged by Moss Hart; presented by Herman Levin; choreography by Hanya Holm; scenery by Oliver Smith; costumes by Cecil Beaton; musical arrangements by Robert Russell Bennett and Phil Lang; lighting by A. H. Feder; dance music arranged by Trude Rittman; musical director, Franz Allers; production stage manager, Samuel Liff. At the Mark Hellinger Theatre.

Mrs. Eynsford-Hill............Viola Roache
Eliza Doolittle.............Julie Andrews

Freddy Eynsford-Hill..John Michael King
Colonel Pickering............Robert Coote
Henry Higgins.............Rex Harrison.
Bartender..................David Thomas
Jamie......................Rod McLennan
Alfred P. Doolittle......Stanley Holloway
Mrs. Pearce.............Philippa Bevans
Mrs. Hopkins.........Olive Reeves-Smith
Mrs. Higgins...........Cathleen Nesbitt
Lord Boxington.........Gordon Dilworth
Zoltan Karpathy......Christopher Hewett

By BROOKS ATKINSON

BULLETINS from the road have not been misleading. "My Fair Lady," which opened at the Mark Hellinger last evening, is a wonderful show.

Alan Jay Lerner has adapted it from Shaw's "Pygmalion," one of the most literate comedies in the language. Many other workmen have built the gleaming structure of a modern musical play on the Shaw fable. They are Frederick Loewe, the composer who collaborated with Mr. Lerner on "Brigadoon" and "Paint Your Wagon"; Oliver Smith, who has designed a glorious production; Cecil Beaton, who has decorated it with ravishingly beautiful costumes; Moss Hart, who has staged it with taste and skill.

•

Although their contributions have been bountiful, they will not object if this column makes one basic observation. Shaw's

Rex Harrison and Julie Andrews in "My Fair Lady"

crackling mind is still the genius of "My Fair Lady." Mr. Lerner has retained the same ironic point of view in his crisp adaptation and his sardonic lyrics. As Professor Higgins and Eliza Doolittle, Rex Harrison and Julie Andrews play the leading parts with the light, dry touch of top-flight Shavian acting.

"My Fair Lady" is staged dramatically on a civilized plane. Probably for the first time in history a typical musical comedy audience finds itself absorbed in the art of pronunciation and passionately involved in the proper speaking of "pain," "rain" and "Spain."

•

And yet it would not be fair to imply that "My Fair Lady" is only a new look at an old comedy. For the carnival version adds a new dimension; it gives a lift to the gaiety and the romance. In his robust score, Mr. Loewe has made the Covent Garden scenes more raffish and hilarious. Not being ashamed of old forms, he has written a glee-club drinking-song, and a mock hymn for Alfred Doolittle's wedding.

Not being afraid of melody, he has written some entrancing love music, and a waltz; and he has added something to Professor Higgins' characterization in a pettish song entitled "A Hymn to Him." All this is, no doubt, implicit in "Pygmalion." But Mr. Loewe has given it heartier exuberance. Although the Old Boy had a sense of humor, he never had so much abandon. "Pygmalion" was not such a happy revel.

•

In the choreography and in the staging of the musical numbers, Hanya Holm has made a similar contribution. The "Ascot Gavotte" at the races is a laconic satire of British reserve in the midst of excitement, and very entertaining, too. "The Embassy Waltz" is both decorous and stunning. And to the rollicking tune of "Get Me to the Church on Time" there is a rowdy, festive dance that is vastly enjoyable.

Despite all the rag-tag and bobtail of a joyous musical show, Mr. Hart and his associates have never lost their respect for a penetrating comedy situation. Some things of human significance are at stake in "My Fair Lady," and some human values are involved. Thanks to the discerning casting, the values have been sensitively preserved. As Professor Higgins' sagacious mother, Cathleen Nesbitt carries off her scenes with grace and elegance.

•

As Alfred P. Doolittle, the plausible rogue, Stanley Holloway gives a breezy performance that is thoroughly enjoyable. And Robert Coote is immensely comic as the bumbling Colonel Pickering.

But it is the acting of Miss Andrews and Mr. Harrison in the central roles that makes "My Fair Lady" affecting as well as amusing. Miss Andrews does a magnificent job. The transformation from street-corner drab to lady is both touching and beautiful. Out of the muck of Covent Garden something glorious blossoms, and Miss Andrews acts her part triumphantly.

Although Mr. Harrison is no singer, you will probably imagine that he is singing when he throws himself into the anguished lyrics of "A Hymn to Him" in the last act. By that time he has made Professor Higgins' temperament so full of frenzy that something like music does come out of him. Mr. Harrison is perfect in the part—crisp, lean, complacent and condescending until at last a real flare of human emotion burns the egotism away and leaves us a bright young man in love with fair lady. Mr. Harrison acts his part triumphantly, too.

It's a wonderful show. To Shaw's agile intelligence it adds the warmth, loveliness and excitement of a memorable theatre frolic.

1956 Mr 16

Mystery Wrapped in Enigma at Golden

The Cast

WAITING FOR GODOT, a tragicomedy in two acts by Samuel Beckett; staged by Herbert Berghof; presented by Michael Myerberg, by arrangement with Independent Plays, Ltd.; scenery by Louis Kennel; costumes by Stanley Simmons; production supervisor, John Paul. At the John Golden Theatre.

Estragon (Gogo) .... Bert Lahr
Vladimir (Didi) .... E. G. Marshall
Lucky .... Alvin Epstein
Pozzo .... Kurt Kasznar
A Boy .... Luchino Solito de Solis

By BROOKS ATKINSON

DON'T expect this column to explain Samuel Beckett's "Waiting for Godot," which was acted at the John Golden last evening. It is a mystery wrapped in an enigma.

But you can expect witness to the strange power this drama has to convey the impression of some melancholy truths about the hopeless destiny of the human race. Mr. Beckett is an Irish writer who has lived in Paris for years, and once served as secretary to James Joyce.

Since "Waiting for Godot" has no simple meaning, one seizes on Mr. Beckett's experience of two worlds to account for his style and point of view. The point of view suggests Sartre—bleak, dark, disgusted. The style suggests Joyce—pungent and fabulous. Put the two together and you have some notion of Mr. Beckett's acrid cartoon of the story of mankind.

•

Literally, the play consists of four raffish characters, an innocent boy who twice arrives with a message from Godot, a naked tree, a mound or two of earth and a sky. Two of the characters are waiting for Godot, who never arrives. Two of them consist of a flamboyant lord of the earth and a broken slave whimpering and staggering at the end of a rope.

Since "Waiting for Godot" is an allegory written in a heartless modern tone, a theatregoer naturally rummages through the performance in search of a meaning. It seems fairly certain that Godot stands for God. Those who are loitering by the withered tree are waiting for salvation, which never comes.

The rest of the symbolism is more elusive. But it is not a pose. For Mr. Beckett's drama adumbrates — rather than expresses—an attitude toward man's experience on earth; the pathos, cruelty, comradeship, hope, corruption, filthiness and wonder of human existence. Faith in God has almost vanished. But there is still an illusion of faith flickering around the edges of the drama. It is as though Mr. Beckett sees very little reason for clutching at faith, but is unable to relinquish it entirely.

•

Although the drama is puzzling, the director and the actors play it as though they understand every line of it. The performance Herbert Berghof has staged against Louis Kennel's spare setting is triumphant in every respect. And Bert Lahr has never given a performance as glorious as his tatterdemalion Gogo, who seems to stand for all the stumbling, bewildered people of the earth who go on living without knowing why.

Although "Waiting for Godot" is an uneventful, maundering, loquacious drama, Mr. Lahr is an actor in the pantomime tradition who has a thousand ways to move and a hundred ways to grimace in order to make the story interesting and theatrical, and touching, too. His long experience as a bawling mountebank has equipped Mr. Lahr to represent eloquently the tragic comedy of one of the lost souls of the earth.

•

The other actors are excellent, also. E. G. Marshall as a fellow vagrant with a mind that is a bit more coherent; Kurt Kasznar as a masterful egotist reeking of power and success; Alvin Epstein as the battered slave who has one bitterly satirical polemic to deliver by rote; Luchino Solito De Solis as a disarming shepherd boy—complete the cast that gives this diffuse drama a glowing performance.

Although "Waiting for Godot" is a "puzzlement," as the King of Siam would express it, Mr. Beckett is no charlatan. He has strong feelings about the degradation of mankind, and he has given vent to them copiously. "Waiting for Godot" is all feeling. Perhaps that is why it is puzzling and convincing at the same time. Theatregoers can rail at it, but they cannot ignore it. For Mr. Beckett is a valid writer.

1956 Ap 20

'The Iceman Cometh' to Circle in Square

The Cast

THE ICEMAN COMETH, a drama in four acts, by Eugene O'Neill. Staged by José Quintero; scenery and lighting by David Hays; costumes by Deidre Cartier; stage manager, Michael Murray; revived by the Circle in the Square (Leigh Connell, Theodore Mann and Mr. Quintero). At the Circle in the Square, Seventh Avenue and West Fourth Street.

Harry Hope	Farrell Pelly
Ed Mosher	Phil Pheffer
Pat McGloin	Albert Lewis
Willie Oban	Addison Powell
Joe Mott	William Edmonson
Piet Wetjoen	Richard Abbott
Cecil Lewis	Richard Bowler
James Cameron	James Greene
Hugo Kalmar	Paul Andor
Larry Slade	Conrad Bain
Rocky Pioggi	Peter Falk
Don Parritt	Larry Robinson
Pearl	Patricia Brooks
Margie	Gloria Scott Backe
Cora	Dolly Jonah
Chuck Morello	Joe Marr
Theodore Hickman (Hickey)	Jason Robards Jr.
Moran	Mal Throne
Lieb	Charles Hamilton

By BROOKS ATKINSON

SINCE José Quintero's productions at Circle in the Square are always admirable, no one should be surprised by his latest achievement.

But it is impossible not to be excited by his production of Eugene O'Neill's "The Iceman Cometh," which opened in Mr. Quintero's theatre yesterday. It is a major production of a major theatre work. Taking a long script with a massive theme, Mr. Quintero has succeeded in bringing every part of it alive in the theatre. Although he tells the story simply and spontaneously, he leaves no doubt about the value he places on O'Neill's place in the literature of the stage. Mr. Quintero seems to take him on the level of Ibsen, Strindberg, Gorki and other modern masters of tragic writing.

•

If "The Iceman Cometh" seems to belong in Mr. Quintero's theatre, there is a good reason. For Circle in the Square was a night-club originally, and all four of the acts of the O'Neill drama are set in a saloon. The audience has the sensation of participating. The rows of seats are only an extension of David Hays' setting of the battered, blowzy waterfront saloon and flophouse that is under the fabulous proprietorship of Harry Hope. A few tables and chairs, a squalid bar, a flimsy door leading into the street, a handful of fly-blown chandeliers and a few ranks of benches for the audience—they are all part of the same setting and closely related on that account.

•

In the circumstances, it is difficult to be objective about this melancholy, sardonic drama that pulls the rug out from under the whole structure of life. It seems, not like something written, but like something that is happening. Although it is terrible in its comment on the need for illusions to maintain an interest in life, it is also comic. Some of the dialogue is pretty funny. On the surface, all the characters are comic, since they live in a world of befuddled fantasy and talk big to compensate for the puniness of their spirits.

But beneath them there is nothing more substantial than a void of blackness. These are creatures that once were men— very pungent and picturesque creatures, too, for O'Neill was a good deal of a romantic. But the tone of "The Iceman Cometh" is devastatingly tragic. Life is bearable, it seems to say, only when men contrive not to look at the truth.

The performance lasts four and three-quarter hours. For "The Iceman Cometh" is one of the O'Neill marathon dramas. No doubt it could be cut and compressed without destroying anything essential. But as a creative work by a powerful writer, it is entitled to its excesses, which, in fact, may account for the monumental feeling of doom that it pulls down over the heads of the audience.

The performance is a vital one. Mr. Quintero is a versatile conductor who knows how to vary his attack with changes in volume and rhythm; he knows how to orchestrate a performance. In one important respect, this performance surpasses the original of ten years ago. Jason Robards Jr. plays Hickey, the catalyst in the narrative, like an evangelist. His unction, condescension and piety introduce an element of moral affectation that clarifies the perspective of the drama as a whole. His heartiness, his aura of good fellowship give the character of Hickey a feeling of evil mischief it did not have before.

Although the narrative is sprawling, the acting is vibrant in every part. Conrad Bain's fanatical philosopher who sees all sides of all questions and is therefore a futile human being is especially well acted. But it would be difficult to pick and choose among the others. Farrell Pelly's crusty but soft-hearted boss of the saloon; Addison Powell's bitterly-humorous relic of culture; William Edmonson's highly emotional Negro; Richard Bowler's cashiered British Army officer; Phil Pheffer's circus con-man; Peter Falk's cocky bar-keep; Paul Andor's left-wing intellectual; James Greene's degraded war correspondent; the tarts played by Dolly Jonah, Patricia Brooks and Gloria Scott Backé—are excellent character portraits.

In both the writing and the acting, "The Iceman Cometh" is a mighty theatre work. O'Neill is a giant, and Mr. Quintero is a remarkably gifted artist.

1956 My 9

The Cast

LONG DAY'S JOURNEY INTO NIGHT, a drama in four acts by Eugene O'Neill. Staged by Jose Quintero; setting by David Hays; lighting by Tharon Musser; costumes by Motley; production stage manager, Elliott Martin; presented by Leigh Connell, Theodore Mann and Mr. Quintero. At the Helen Hayes Theatre.
James Tyrone............Fredric March
Mary Cavan Tyrone...Florence Eldridge
James Tyrone Jr.....Jason Robards Jr.
Edmund Tyrone ......Bradford Dillman
Cathleen ....Katherine Ross

By BROOKS ATKINSON

WITH the production of "Long Day's Journey Into Night" at the Helen Hayes last evening, the American theatre acquires size and stature.

The size does not refer to the length of Eugene O'Neill's autobiographical drama, although a play three and three-quarter hours long is worth remarking. The size refers to his conception of theatre as a form of epic literature.

"Long Day's Journey Into Night" is like a Dostoevsky novel in which Strindberg had written the dialogue. For this saga of the damned is horrifying and devastating in a classical tradition, and the performance under José Quintero's direction is inspired.

•

Twelve years before he died in 1953, O'Neill epitomized the life of his family in a drama that records the events of one day at their summer home in New London, Conn., in 1912. Factually it is a sordid story about a pathologically parsimonious father, a mother addicted to dope, a dissipated brother and a younger brother (representing Eugene O'Neill) who has TB and is about to be shipped off to a sanitarium.

Roughly, those are the facts. But the author has told them on the plane of an O'Neill tragedy in which the point of view transcends the material. The characters are laid bare with pitiless candor. The scenes are big. The dialogue is blunt. Scene by scene the tragedy moves along with a remorseless beat that becomes hypnotic as though this were life lived on the brink of oblivion.

"Long Day's Journey Into Night" could be pruned of some of its excesses and repetitions and static looks back to the past. But the faults come, not from tragic posturing, but from the abundance of a great theatre writer who had a spacious point of view. This summing-up of his emotional and artistic life ranks with "Mourning Becomes Electra" and "Desire Under the Elms," which this department regards as his masterpieces.

*

Like those dramas, it comes alive in the theatre. Although the text is interesting to read between covers, it does not begin to flame until the actors take hold of it. Mr. Quintero, who staged the memorable "The Iceman Cometh" in the Village, has directed "Long Day's Journey Into Night" with insight and skill. He has caught the sense of a stricken family in which the members are at once fascinated and repelled by one another. Always in control of the turbulence of the material, he has also picked out and set forth the meaning that underlies it.

The performance is stunning. As the aging actor who stands at the head of the family, Fredric March gives a masterly performance that will stand as a milestone in the acting of an O'Neill play. Petty, mean, bullying, impulsive and sharp-tongued, he also has magnificence — a man of strong passions, deep loyalties and basic humility. This is a character portrait of grandeur.

Florence Eldridge analyzes the pathetic character of the mother with tenderness and compassion. As the evil brother, Jason Robards Jr., who played Hickey in "The Iceman Cometh," gives another remarkable performance that has tremendous force and truth in the last act. Bradford Dillman is excellent as the younger brother—winning, honest, and both callow and perceptive in his relationship with the family. Katherine Ross plays the part of the household maid with freshness and taste.

•

All the action takes place inside David Hays' excellent setting of a cheerless livingroom with dingy furniture and hideous little touches of unimaginative décor. The shabby, shapeless costumes by Motley and the sepulchral lighting by Tharon Musser perfectly capture the lugubrious mood of the play.

"Long Day's Journey Into Night" has been worth waiting for. It restores the drama to literature and the theatre to art.

1956 N 8

The Cast

CANDIDE, a comic operetta in two acts, based on Voltaire's satire. Book by Lillian Hellman, score by Leonard Bernstein, lyrics by Richard Wilbur, John Latouche and Dorothy Parker. Directed by Tyrone Guthrie, assisted by Tom Brown; scenery by Oliver Smith; costumes by Irene Sharaff; lighting by Paul Morrison; musical director, Samuel Krachmalnick; orchestrations by Mr. Bernstein and Hershy Kay; hair styles by Ronald de Mann; presented by Ethel Linder Reiner, in association with Lester Osterman Jr.; production associate, Thomas Hammond; dance supervisor, Wallace Seibert; production stage manager, Peter Zeisler. At the Martin Beck Theatre.

By BROOKS ATKINSON

SINCE Voltaire was a brilliant writer, it is only right that his "Candide" should turn out to be a brilliant musical satire.

Pooling their talents, Lillian Hellman, the literary lady, and Leonard Bernstein, the music man, have composed an admirable version of Voltaire's philosophical tale, which opened t the Martin Beck on Saturday evening. Add to the honor roll Tyrone Guthrie, who has staged the production, Oliver Smith, who has designed it beautifully, and Irra Petina, Robert Rounseville, Barbara Cook and Max Adrian, who sing the chief parts gloriously. For the performance is a triumph of stage arts molded into a symmetrical whole.

Let's admit that the eighteenth century philosophical tale is not ideal material for a theatre show, for it is plotless and repetitious. And let's further concede that the Candide that Miss Hellman, Mr. Bernstein and Mr. Rounseville have created is not the blithering idiot whom Voltaire invented. He is more like a disillusioned hero.

But the authors of the musical work are quite right in supposing that Voltaire's contemptuous satire on optimism is modern in spirit, as, indeed, it must always be. Its cynical acceptance of war, greed, treachery, venery, snobbishness and mendacity as staples of civilization provokes no feeling of disbelief in the middle of the twentieth century.

Although Miss Hellman has not covered quite so much territory as Voltaire, she has transported Candide away from the mawkish idealism of Westphalia to Lisbon, Paris, Buenos Aires and back to Venice, with a return to a ruined Westphalia in the last scene.

Bit by bit, Dr. Pangloss' devotion to the best in the best of all possible worlds becomes hollow and ridiculous. Battered by their cruel travelers, Dr. Pangloss' ragged band of followers settles down in the last scene to cultivating the garden of the only kind of life that is possible.

Toward the end of a long evening, the philosophical tale that always makes the same point in a different context does lose the freshness of the opening scenes. But Candide's sorry journey has stimulated Mr. Bernstein into composing a wonderful score all the way through. None of his previous theatre music has had the joyous variety, humor and richness of this score. It begins wittily. It parodies operatic music amusingly. But it also has a wealth of melody that compensates for the intellectual austerity of Voltaire's tale. While Candide is learning about life the hard way, Mr. Bernstein is obviously having a good time.

Under Mr. Guthrie's bountiful direction, the acting and the singing are magnificent. As the raffish, ribald beldame, Miss Petina is tremendously entertaining — splendid as a singer, virtuoso as a comic performer in a happily broad style. Miss Cook is also a lustrous singer, particularly in Mr. Bernstein's own version of how a jewel song should be written. And her acting portrait of a lyrical maiden who quickly learns how to connive with the world is sketched with skill, spirit and humor.

Mr. Rounseville is a sensitive romantic singer with a captivating voice. If he gives us a more disarming Candide than Voltaire intended, no objections are raised in this corner, for the Rounseville Candide is excellent. Mr. Adrian, who plays both Dr. Pangloss, the egregious optimist, and Martin, the bitter pessimist, is a lean, ascetic actor with a chilling grin and a saturnine style. He can also sing agreeably. As a sort of Janus, he comments on Candide's journey with ironic drollery. The large cast, which is without exception a notable one, includes William Olvis, a powerful singer and a good actor as the languid Governor of Buenos Aires.

Mr. Smith's fabulous scene designs and Irene Sharaff's vigorous costumes help to make "Candide" the most stunning production of the season. Everything has been done with taste and vitality. A couple of centuries have been frittered away since Voltaire wrote "Candide." He can still put the various departments of the modern theatre on their professional toes.

1956 D 3

Popular Monologist Starts 4-Week Run

By LEWIS FUNKE

IF it were not for the fact that Ruth Draper and her Company of Characters are old friends in this precinct and consequently most welcome at this holiday season, your correspondent would being his report by announcing:

Last night Miss Draper made her appearance at the Playhouse and there cannot be any question thta she is one of the greatest if, indeed, not the greatest monologist of our time. She is a handsome woman, probably in her early seventies, with lovely gray hair, a strong face, sharp nose, a remarkable graceful carriage and a voice that is responsive to her every need.

•

Besides the fine physical endowments she has the enviable talent of being able to evoke o a bare stage, in front of a brown velvet drape and with the aid of some chairs, full-life characters.

These people—a mother at "A Children's Party," a woman working "In a Railway Station on the Western Plains," "Three Women and Mr. Clifford," and "A Scottish Immigrant at Ellis Island," which she offered

last night (as well as all the others in her repertoire) — these people have a way of becoming throbbing, entirely credible human beings.

Miss Draper, obviously, has been at her art a long time and not a detail has gone unnoted. Her ear for conversation, is pitch-perfect, her sympathy and understanding of her creations never failing. And she has a deft touch with humor.

The laughter that breaks the silence in the theatre is not the sort that stirs from the viscers and works upward into a loud guffaw. It is the daughter that comes instead from sympathetic recognition

Roy Schatt

Ruth Draper

and identification. When Miss Draper, for instance, at a chcildren's party, endures the tribulations of trying to make her brood behave, of trying to apologize for improper behavior, parents may not burst their sides but their chuckles announce that Miss Draper has hit the mark.

•

Well, all this already has
been said of Miss Draper in
one way or another, and some
time or another during her
long career and of her many
performances here and abroad.
The important point is that
she is at the Playhouse for
a limited engagement — four
weeks. Those who know her
work will not miss seeing her;
last night's audience indicated
that. Those who don't know
her work ought to make
amends.

1956 D 26

The Cast

TROILUS AND CRESSIDA, Shakespearean play in two acts. Directed
by Tyrone Guthrie; costumes and decor
by Frederick Crooke; music by Frederick Marshall; fights arranged by
Bernard Hepton and John Greenwood;
orchestra directed by Arthur Lief; revived by the Old Vic under the sponsorship of Sol Hurok. At the Winter
Garden.

Priam	Keith Taylor
Hector	Jack Gwillim
Troilus	Jeremy Brett
Paris	Ronald Allen
Aeneas	Denis Holmes
Pandarus	Paul Rogers
Cressida's groom	Aubrey Morris
Troilus' servant	John Greenwood
Helen	Coral Browne
Andromache	Jennifer Wilson
Cassandra	Margaret Courtenay
Cressida	Rosemary Harris
Agamemnon	Rupert Davies
Menelaus	Edward Harvey
Ulysses	Richard Wordsworth
Nestor	Job Stewart
Ajax	Ernest Hare
Achilles	Charles Gray
Patroclus	Derek New
Thersites	John Neville

By BROOKS ATKINSON

NO man to get into a rut,
Tyrone Guthrie has played
a few tricks on Shakespeare's
"Troilus and Cressida," which
was acted by the Old Vic
Company at the Winter Garden last evening.

He has costumed the Tro-
jans like ceremonial British
guards of about the World
War I period, and the Greeks
like Prussian officers of the
same time. Since Shake-
speare's spleenish comedy has
an anti-heroic attitude toward
Homer's illustrious fighting
men, Mr. Guthrie has all the
authority he needs to belittle
these modern warriors. Not
that Mr. Guthrie needs authority at any time. All he
needs is an opportunity to
drive boredom away.

He is very funny when he
is cartooning the bravura
ritual of warriors who regard
fighting as the cavalier's duty.
The stamping of feet when the
characters execute turns, the
fierce saluting, the pompous
mannerisms, the monocles, the
swagger sticks, the flamboyant uniforms designed by
Frederick Crooke—are vastly
entertaining and the worst
dig in the ribs that Mars has
encountered on the stage for
some time.

●

But it seems to this theatregoer that Mr. Guthrie's assault
on tradition is only successful
in part. His humor is heartier
than Shakespeare's. He is, as
always, in high spirits. But
"Troilus and Cressida" is the
comedy of a man who is in
low spirits, who has lost faith
in the world, who is full of
disgust and who is writing
liverish verse.

The difference between
Shakespeare's mood and Mr.
Guthrie's is not just a matter
of taste. It affects the relationship between his production and the dialogue. Especially in the first act, his
production makes the dialogue
sound like gibberish. What the
characters do is frequently
amusing. What they say
makes no sense at all. Mr.
Guthrie and Shakespeare are
not always on the same stage.

Since "Troilus and Cressida"
is one of Shakespeare's least
attractive plays, it is seldom
acted. On Broadway it has
been acted only once in the
last quarter-century, and then
only for a fleeting run. But it
is as good a comedy as "All's
Well That Ends Well" and
"Measure for Measure," and it
would be pleasant to have a
conventional view of it now
that the Old Vic Company is
here.

When the actors have a mo-
ment to act the drama they
are excellent. As Cressida,
Rosemary Harris is admirable.
Her slow, sensual, treacherous
strumpet is everything that
Shakespeare had in mind.
Jeremy Brett's youthful, eager
Troilus who can hardly believe
Cressida's treachery—is also a

first-rate bit of straightforward acting. Jack Gwillim's manly Hector, Charles Gray's peevish Achilles, Richard Wordsworth's perceptive Ulysses, Rupert Davies' bland Agamemnon—suggest that the Old Vic could make a considerable impression on Shakespeare's script if they could put their minds to it.

Mr. Guthrie's practical joke also has good representation in the acting. Paul Rogers' foppish, garrulous Pandarus is most entertaining. So is Ernest Hare's notion of Ajax as a military stuffed shirt, John Neville's interpretation of Thersites as a rag-bag war correspondent and Coral Browne's sketch of Helen of Troy as a night club hussy.

They fit most neatly into Mr. Guthrie's comic-book plan. But his plan is only half successful. Every now and then Shakespeare's drama has vitality enough to push it aside and rail against the world. The actors are talented, and could make "Troilus and Cressida" interesting in its own right. Mr. Guthrie's prank is not a sufficient substitute.

1956 D 27

1957

The Cast

THE WALTZ OF THE TOREADORS, a play in three acts by Jean Anouilh; English version by Lucienne Hill. Staged by Harold Clurman; designed by Ben Edwards; produced by the Producers Theatre (Robert Whitehead). At the Coronet Theatre.

Mme. St. Pe	Mildred Natwick
General St. Pe	Ralph Richardson
Gaston	John Stewart
Sidonia	Mary Grace Canfield
Estelle	Sudie Bond
Dr. Bonfant	John Abbott
First maid	Frieda Altman
Mlle. de St.-Euverte	Meriel Forbes
Mme. Dupont-Fredaine	Louise Kirtland
Father Ambrose	William Hansen
New maid	Helen Seamon

By BROOKS ATKINSON

FOR a desolate man, Jean Anouilh knows how to write a remarkably gay comedy. For a classical actor, Ralph Richardson knows better than most how to act with the gusto of a low comedian.

They have happily come together in "The Waltz of the Toreadors," which opened at the Coronet last evening, and ought to bring audiences happily together for a long time. Since M. Anouilh apparently believes in nothing, he is free to play fast and loose, not only with intellectual ideas, but also with the categories of drama.

And "The Waltz of the Toreadors" is a gallimaufry of stage entertainments—a French farce that lampoons itself by making a sensible remark now and then and that ends on a brisk note of despair. Mr. Richardson comes into the picture just about here. In his last visit to New York he was a member of the Old Vic troupe that played several of the classics. Without losing the style of a classical actor, he is now clowning exuberantly through the part of a humbug French general, giving size, depth and relish to an impish play, and making a funny skit very funny indeed.

In the first scene of the comedy, General St. Pé, formidably mustachioed, is resonantly dictating his glorious memoirs to an insipid male secretary. On a sickbed in the adjoining room, lies the general's invalid, querulous wife, suspecting him of committing infidelities in his mind even as she is dying.

Although this is not a comic situation it becomes one when it appears that her invalidism is a fake, that the general loathes her, that she is hanging on to him for the sake of comfort and security, and that for seventeen years he has been imagining himself hopelessly in love with a silly spinster.

In its guise as a French farce, "The Waltz of the Toreadors" goes through the familiar amorous motions. It concludes with a hackneyed scene in which the insipid male secretary, heretofore an orphan, is identified as the general's son by a half-forgotten illicit assignation. But the farce is on two levels. For M.

Anouilh (in Lucienne Hill's vivacious English version) keeps shifting gears from farce to cynicism or from farce to common sense, which is equally amusing. In the midst of comic extravagances, M. Anouilh suddenly brings the audience face to face with a homely fact. It is at once startling and funny.

•

One of the most useful things about a good farce is that it is pre-eminently an acting piece. Under the droll and silken direction of Harold Clurman, this one is acted to the hilt. Ben Edwards has provided an amiably fantastic set in which everything is a little too big, ornate and massive. And the performance is in a similar key. Mr. Richardson's changes of pace are

fabulous. In the midst of a military roar and posture, he suddenly drops his voice to a conversational level, and the laughter out front is probably all out of proportion to what is said. He gives a heroic performance that is just short of heroic conclusions. The disparity is as witty—wittier, perhaps—than the dialogue.

•

All through the evening, the performance is delightfully broad. Mildred Natwick's invalid wife is a torrent of vulgarities and grotesque theatrical attitudes. John Abbott's comradely physician is wonderfully bland. Meriel Forbes' rebellious spinster is a bridling, empty-headed fraud. John Stewart's male secretary is improbably innocent and bumptious.

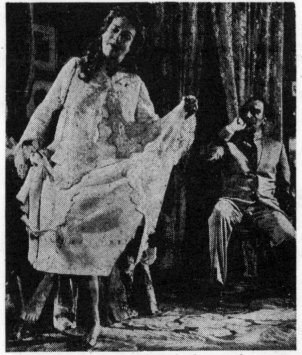

Mildred Natwick, Sir Ralph Richardson as they appear in "The Waltz of the Toreadors" at the Coronet Theatre.

At the core of "The Waltz of the Toreadors" lies the black despair of M. Anouilh's basic attitude. Understanding is the real source of unhappiness, he says at the end, and doubtless he means it. But the surface of the farce is original, bright, tart and worldly, and the acting is exuberantly comic. Between them, M. Anouilh and Mr. Richardson have brought us a remarkably civilized caper.

1957 Ja 18

'West Side Story' Is at Winter Garden

The Cast

WEST SIDE STORY, a musical comedy, based on a conception of Jerome Robbins, with book by Arthur Laurents, music by Leonard Bernstein and lyrics by Stephen Sondheim. Entire production directed and choreographed by Mr. Robbins; presented by Robert E. Griffith and Harold S. Prince, by arrangement with Roger L. Stevens; scenery by Oliver Smith; costumes by Irene Sharaff; lighting by Jean Rosenthal; co-choreographer, Peter Gennaro; production associate, Sylvia Drulie; musical direction, Max Goberman; orchestrations by Mr. Bernstein, Sid Ramin and Irwin Kostal; production stage manager, Ruth Mitchell. At the Winter Garden.

The Jets

Riff, Mickey Calin; Gee-Tar, Tommy Abbott; Tony, Larry Kert; Mouth Piece, Frank Green; Action, Eddie Roll; Tiger, Lowell Harris; A-Rab, Tony Mordente; Graziella, Wilma Curley; Baby John, David Winters; Velma, Carole D'Andrea; Snowboy, Grover Dale; Minnie, Nanette Rosen; Clarice, Marilyn D'Honau; Big Deal, Martin Charnin; Pauline, Julie Oser; Diesel, Hank Brunjes; Anybodys, Lee Becker.

The Sharks

Bernardo, Ken Le Roy; Juano, Jay Norman; Maria, Carol Lawrence; Toro, Erne Castaldo; Anita, Chita Rivera; Moose, Jack Murray; Chino, Jamie Sanchez; Rosalia, Marilyn Cooper; Pepe, George Marcy; Consuelo, Reri Grist; Indio, Noel Schwartz; Terestia, Carmen Guiterrez; Luis, Al De Sio; Francisca Elizabeth Taylor; Anxious, Gene Gavin; Estella, Lynn Ross; Nibbles, Ronie Lee; Marguerita, Liane Plane

The Adults

Doc, Art Smith; Krupke, William Bramley; Schrank, Arch Johnson; Gladhand, John Harkins.

By BROOKS ATKINSON

ALTHOUGH the material is horrifying, the workmanship is admirable.

Gang warfare is the material of "West Side Story," which opened at the Winter Garden last evening, and very little of the hideousness has been left out. But the author, composer and ballet designer are creative artists. Pooling imagination and virtuosity, they have written a profoundly moving show that is as ugly as the city jungles and also pathetic, tender and forgiving.

•

Arthur Laurents has written the story of two hostile teen-age gangs fighting for supremacy amid the tenement houses, corner stores and bridges of the West Side. The story is a powerful one, partly, no doubt, because Mr. Laurents has deliberately given it the shape of "Romeo and Juliet." In the design of "West Side Story" he has powerful allies. Leonard Bernstein has composed another one of his nervous, flaring scores that capture the shrill beat of life in the streets. And Jerome Robbins, who has directed the production, is also its choreographer.

Since the characters are kids of the streets, their speech is curt and jeering. Mr. Laurents has provided the raw material of a tragedy that occurs because none of the young people involved understands what is happening to them. And his contribution is the essential one. But it is Mr. Bernstein and Mr. Robbins who orchestrate it. Using music and movement they have given Mr. Laurents' story passion and depth and some glimpses of unattainable glory. They have pitched into it with personal conviction as well as the skill of accomplished craftsmen.

•

In its early scenes of gang skirmishes, "West Side Story" is facile and a little forbidding—the shrill music and the taut dancing movement being harsh and sinister. But once Tony of the Jets gang sees Maria of the Sharks gang, the magic of an immortal story takes hold.

Larry Kert and Carol Lawrence in "West Side Story"

As Tony, Larry Kert is perfectly cast, plain in speech and manner; and as Maria, Carol Lawrence, maidenly soft and glowing, is perfectly cast also. Their balcony scene on the firescape of a dreary tenement is tender and affecting. From that moment on, "West Side Story" is an incandescent piece of work that finds odd bits of beauty amid the rubbish of the streets.

Everything in "West Side Story," is of a piece. Everything contributes to the total impression of wildness, ecstasy and anguish. The astringent score has moments of tranquillity and rapture, and occasionally a touch of sardonic humor. And the ballets convey the things that Mr. Laurents is inhibited from saying because the charac-ters are so inarticulate. The hostility and suspicion between the gangs, the glory of the nuptials, the terror of the rumble, the devastating climax — Mr. Robbins has found the patterns of movement that express these parts of the story.

•

Most of the characters, in fact, are dancers with some images of personality lifted out of the whirlwind—characters sketched on the wing. Like everything also in "West Side Story," they are admirable. Chita Rivera in a part equivalent to the Nurse in the Shakespeare play; Ken Le Roy as leader of The Sharks; Mickey Calin as leader of The Jets; Lee Becker as a hobble-dehoy girl in one gang—give terse and vigorous performances.

Everything in "West Side Story" blends—the scenery by Oliver Smith, the costumes by Irene Sharaff, the lighting by Jean Rosenthal. For this is one of those occasions when theatre people, engrossed in an original project, are all in top form. The subject is not beautiful. But what "West Side Story" draws out of it is beautiful. For it has a searching point of view.

1957 S 27

The Cast

I KNOCK AT THE DOOR, an adaptation by Paul Shyre of the first of six autobiographical volumes by Sean O'Casey. Directed by Stuart Vaughan; presented by Lucille Lortel, Mr. Shyre and Howard Gottfried; setting and lighting supervision by Lester Polakov; flutist, Frances Blaisdell; stage manager, Robert Paschall. At the Belasco Theatre.
PRINCIPALS: Rae Allen, George Brenlin, Aline MacMahon, Paul Shyre, Roy Poole and Staats Cotsworth.

By ARTHUR GELB

THANKS to the single-minded devotion of Paul Shyre to the cause of Sean O'Casey, we now have "I Knock at the Door" on Broadway. This is where it richly deserves to be.

A staged concert reading, "I Knock at the Door" has been adapted by Mr. Shyre from the first volume in the O'Casey autobiography. The tenderness, the humor, the anguish and, above all, the poetry that sings from O'Casey's pages are being stunningly evoked on the stage of the Belasco Theatre.

Sitting on high black chairs behind lecterns, against a pure, luminously blue cyclorama, six actors bring the sad, pithy boyhood of John Casside (who stands for O'Casey) into quick and sensitive focus. His strong, resigned mother, his impetuous, groping sister, the friends and enemies of his Dublin childhood and Johnny himself are gems of truth and beauty, both in the writing and the acting.

So much feeling was generated in a brief scene where Johnny is caned by a sadistic schoolmaster that last night's audience burst into applause when the enraged boy brought an ebony ruler down on the head of his tormentor. (And all of this without props—with the merest suggestion of gestures.)

Throughout the reading, balancing pathos with humor, runs the thread of little Johnny's difficulty with his eyes. There is a ceaseless struggle between the doctor, who is treating the boy's painful cataracts, and the Protestant minister, who considers it more important for the boy to be at school.

Stuart Vaughan has directed the troupe with the ear of a musician, as well as with the sure knowledge of a theatre craftsman. All of his actors slip in and out of multiple roles with grace. The people of O'Casey's crowded youth for whom they speak flare forth—even when only briefly—with superb vividness.

•

Delicate snatches of music are woven into the reading; an offstage flute plays wistful Irish tunes and nearly all the actors at one point or other burst briefly and appropriately into a native tune.

Aline MacMahon's mother is a particularly rich and varied characterization. But it's hard to imagine how any of the others—George Brenlin as John Casside, Staats Cotsworth as the narrator and Rae Allen, Roy Poole and Mr. Shyre in a variety of roles—could be better, either. They are all intimately attuned to one another and the onrushing voice of the Green Crow.

1957 S 30

The Cast

LOOK BACK IN ANGER, a play in
three acts, by John Osborne. Staged
by Tony Richardson; presented by
David Merrick; setting by Alan Tagg;
costumes by Motley; scenery, lighting
and costumes supervised by Howard
Bay; music for songs by Tom East-
wood; stage manager, Howard Stone.
At the Lyceum Theatre.
Jimmy Porter ....Kenneth Haigh
Cliff Lewis..................Alan Bates
Alison Porter................Mary Ure
Helena Charles.....Vivienne Drummond
Colonel Redfern............Jack Livesey

By BROOKS ATKINSON

TO see "Look Back in
Anger" at the Lyceum,
where it opened last evening,
is to agree with the British
who saw the original per-
formance. John Osborne has
written the most vivid British play of the decade.

Since we have had angry
young men writing bitter
plays for a quarter of a century, "Look Back in Anger"
will not be the landmark
here that it is already in
London. But Mr. Osborne is
a fiery writer with a sharp
point of view and a sense of

theatre. Under the direction
of Tony Richardson, five British actors give his savage
morality drama the blessing
of a brilliant performance.

•

Mr. Osborne is in blind revolt against the England of
his time. In a squalid attic
somewhere in the Midlands
three young people are rail-
ing against the world. They
are Jimmy Porter, a tornado
of venomous phrases; his wife,
who is crushed by the barrenness of their life and the wildness of her husband's vocabulary, and Cliff Lewis, an

**Alan Bates, left, Mary Ure and Kenneth Haigh as they
appear in a scene from the import, "Look Back in Anger."**

unattached young man who is the friend of both.

Being in a state of rebellion, neither Mr. Osborne nor his chief character has a program or a reasonable approach to life. From any civilized point of view, they are both impossible. But Mr. Osborne has one great asset. He can write. The words come bursting out of him in a flood of satire and invective. They are cruel; they are unfair, and they leave nothing but desolation as they sweep along.

But they are vibrant and colorful; they sting the secondary characters in the play, to say nothing of the audience. You know that something is going on in the theatre, and that the British drama has for once said a long farewell to the drawing-room, the bookshelves, the fireplace and the stairway. If Mr. Osborne is disgusted with England today, he is also disgusted with the pallor of British drama.

●

Not that he does not have trouble with the form. After inveighing against everyone and his wife for two acts with a certain malevolent though tolerable logic, he switches to the craft of writing a play. At the curtain of the second act Helena, a girl who despises Jimmy and is despised by him and who has persuaded his wife to go back home to escape further torture, becomes his mistress, and takes over where the beaten wife leaves off. When the curtain goes up on the third act Helena is at the ironing-board, as the wife was in the first act. Everything has been turned upside down.

This is a bit too pat. During the first scene of the third act, Mr. Osborne finds himself more preoccupied with the job of keeping a play in motion than with hurling words at the world. But in the last scene he is in control again. He is back in top form —twisting and turning, sulking and groaning, turning civil morality inside out and doing other things he hadn't oughter. He is not the man for temperate statements.

If "Look Back in Anger" recovers its stride in the last scene, it is partly because the performance has so much pressure and passion. The acting is superb; it makes its points accurately with no waste motion. As Jimmy, Kenneth Haigh absorbs Mr. Osborne's furious literary style in an enormously skillful performance that expresses undertones of despair and frustration and gives the character a basis in humanity. This wild man is no impostor.

As the tormented wife, Mary Ure succeeds in retaining the pride of an intelligent young woman by filling her silences with unspoken vitality, by being alive and by glowing with youth in every sequence. Alan Bates gives a vigorous performance in a more fluid style as the mutual friend. Vivienne Drummond plays the more ambiguous part of the intruding female with charm and guile.

Everything occurs inside a cheerless, slatternly attic room well designed by Alan Tagg. Miserable though it is, it is sturdy enough to withstand Mr. Osborne's thunderbolts. With the lightning that goes with them, they shake quite a lot of complacency out of the theatre.

1957 O 2

Mary Stuart
By BROOKS ATKINSON

WITH "Mary Stuart," which opened last evening, the Phoenix Theatre has at last got off-center. Script, direction and acting restore to the Phoenix the high excitement and high purpose that almost vanished last season.

The script is a new adaptation of Schiller's historical drama about the two queens who maneuvered for the English throne in the sixteenth century. In the new version written by Jean Stock Goldstone and John Reich, "Mary

Eva Le Gallienne, left, Irene Worth and Douglas Campbell in adaptation of Friedrich Schiller's "Mary Stuart."

Stuart" represents at its best the power and bravura of heroic drama—big scenes, bold ventures, dreadful climaxes, melodrama and tragedy.

•

The director is Tyrone Guthrie, surely the most potent of the friends of the Phoenix. With the largeness of scale for which he is famous and faith in the legitimacy of good theatre, Mr. Guthrie has directed a tumultuous performance. In less confident hands it could be fustian.

The Cast

MARY STUART, a new adaptation in two acts and six scenes by Jean Stock Goldstone and John Reich of the Friedrich Schiller drama. Staged by Tyrone Guthrie; scenery and lighting by Donald Oenslager; costumes by Alvin Colt; incidental music by Michael Colicchio; presented by Phoenix Theatre, a project of Theatre Incorporated; managing directors, T. Edward Hambleton and Norris Houghton. At the Phoenix Theatre.

Mary Stuart	Irene Worth
Hannah Kennedy	Dorothy Sands
Sir Amyas Paulet	Robert Goodier
Sir Edward Mortimer	John Colicos
Lord Burleigh	Max Adrian
Queen Elizabeth	Eva Le Gallienne
Count L'Aubespine	James Neylin
Earl of Leicester	Douglas Campbell
Earl of Shrewsbury	William Hutt
Sir William Davison	Ellis Rabb
Sir Andrew Melvil	Michael Hogan
O'Kelly	David Ford
Captain of the Guard	Dario Barri

Guards
Dalton Dearborn, Vincent Dowling

But Mr. Guthrie has chosen an extraordinary cast. For Mary Stuart—Irene Worth; for Elizabeth—Eva Le Gallienne. In the secondary parts —such stimulating actors as Douglas Campbell, William Hutt, Max Adrian, Robert Goodier, Ellis Rabb, John Colicos, Michael Hogan, James Neylin, Dorothy Sands. Most of them have previously appeared under Mr. Guthrie's daring direction in dramas of pith and moment. Now they are with him again, caught in another swirl of big emotions and again the results are stirring.

•

Everyone knows the legend of the Queen of Scots who intrigued for the throne of Elizabeth of England. The adapters and Schiller before them improved on history, notably in a scene that brings the two rivals face to face. It is a tale of giants calculated to make a theatregoer sit on the edge of his seat. For the drama is full of confrontations, intrigues, betrayals and recklessness in general.

Give Mr. Guthrie credit for having both the courage and the skill to make full use of such gaudy material, always keeping safely on the side of logic and belief. But don't credit him at the expense of the chief actors. For Miss Le Gallienne and Miss Worth in perfect contrast of style and personality give headlong performances that are vivid in the theatre and are bound to be memorable afterwards.

This is the finest performance Miss Le Gallienne has brought to us for a long time. Her Elizabeth is an ascetic-looking woman with a wealth of passion when she is aroused by treachery or a threat to her security. Her guile with her advisers is amusing, her cautiousness and uncertainties are disarming, and her assertions of authority are brutal when she is desperate. Thin, pale, fastidious, with a small voice that can express great emotion, Miss Le Gallienne gives a big performance in a small compass.

•

Miss Worth is just the opposite as Mary. She has a resonant voice with enormous volume. She is a creature of the world. Her temper is with difficulty under control. Her mind is made up and she does not scruple. A woman of courage and poise, she goes to her doom with the measured magnificence of a queen. "Mary Stuart" is a drama that gathers into its grisly web a great many people. But it is chiefly the collision of two women who are unalike except for the fortitude of their spirits. Actors, director and authors have given it great impact in the theatre.

Everyone has conspired with everybody else on the stage to make this an occasion at the Phoenix. Donald Oenslager, the designer, has prefaced it with imposing royal curtains bearing the rival coats of arms, and Alvin Colt has caparisoned it in courtly splendor.

For great occasions do inform all men, including the audience. And particularly the friends of the Phoenix, who must be grateful to the writers, director and actors who have made the first production of the season triumphantly theatrical.

1957 O 9

The Cast

THE MUSIC MAN, a musical comedy in two acts and sixteen scenes. Book, music and lyrics by Meredith Willson, based on a story by Mr. Willson and Franklin Lacey. Staged by Morton Da Costa; choreography by Onna White; scenery and lighting by Howard Bay; costumes by Raoul Pene du Bois; orchestrations by Don Walker; dance arrangements by Laurence Rosenthal; production associate, Sylvia Drulie; musical direction and vocal arrangements by Herbert Greene; hair styles by Ronald de Mann; production stage manager, Henri Caubisens; presented by Kermit Bloomgarden, with Mr. Greene in association with Frank Productions, Inc. At the Majestic Theatre.

Charlie Cowell	Paul Reed
Conductor	Carl Nicholas
Harold Hill	Robert Preston
Mayor Shinn	David Burns
Ewart Dunlop	Al Shea
Oliver Hix	Wayne Ward
Jacey Squires	Vern Reed
Olin Britt	Bill Spangenberg
Marcellus Washburn	Iggie Wolfington
Tommy Djilas	Danny Carroll
Marian Paroo	Barbara Cook
Mrs. Paroo	Pert Kelton
Amaryllis	Marilyn Siegel
Winthrop Paroo	Eddie Hodges
Eulalie Mackecknie Shinn	Helen Raymond
Zaneeta Shinn	Dusty Worrall
Gracie Shinn	Barbara Travis
Alma Hix	Adnia Rice
Maud Dunlop	Elaine Swann
Ethel Toffelmier	Peggy Mondo
Mrs. Squires	Martha Flynn
Constable Locke	Carl Nicholas

By BROOKS ATKINSON

DOLLARS to doughnuts, Meredith Willson dotes

on brass bands.

In "The Music Man," which opened last evening at the Majestic, he has translated the thump and razzle-dazzle of brass-band lore into a warm and genial cartoon of American life. Since the style is gaudy and since David Burns plays a small town mayor with low-comedy flourishes, "The Music Man" is a cartoon and not a valentine.

But Mr. Willson's sophistication is skin-deep. His heart is in the wonderful simplicities of provincial life in Iowa in 1912, and his musical show glows with enjoyment. Mr. Willson's music is innocent; the beat is rousing and the tunes are full of gusto. The dances, improvised by Onna White, are rural and festive. Raoul Péne du Bois' country costumes are humorously hospitable. With Robert Preston in top form in the leading part, the cast is as exuberant as opening day at a county fair.

If Mark Twain could have collaborated with Vachel Lindsay, they might have devised a rhythmic lark like "The Music Man," which is as American as apple pie and a Fourth of July oration.

It is the story of a traveling-salesman charlatan who cannot read music or play any instrument, but who sells the boys of River City a brass band and gorgeous uniforms. His motives are dishonest. But during the weeks when he is mulcting the customers, he transforms a dull town into a singing and dancing community. In the last scene the law is hot on his heels. But. don't worry. Mr. Willson approves of his charlatan as thoroughly as he loves the town librarian, the barber shop quartet, the kids, the ladies, the railroad, and

Rob•rt Preston and Barbara Cook in "The Music Man"

the vitality of life in the Middle West.

In other hands, this could easily look like an assembly job, clever, smart and spurious. Serving as his own librettist, composer and lyricwriter, Mr. Willson has given it the uniformity of a well-designed crazy-quilt in which every patch blends with its neighbor. By some sort of miracle, his associates' have caught his point of view exactly. Morton Da' Costa's droll, strutting direction; Don Walker's blaring orchestrations; Howard Bay's jovial scenery, including a racing locomotive that drowns the orchestra players in steam when the curtain goes up— these aspects of the production have Mr. Willson's own kind of gaiety.

As the infectious bunko man, Mr. Preston could hardly be improved upon. His expansive energy and his concentration on the crisis of the moment are tonic. Since the music is unpretentious, he has no trouble in making it sound hearty. When the music is romantic, Barbara Cook is on hand to sing it beautifully. She is also a beguiling actress in fresh and pleasant fashions.

But the cast is attractive in every instance. Pert Kelton as a harsh-voiced Irish widow; Iggie Wolfington as a breathless conspirator; little Eddie Hodges as a lisping youth and little Marilyn Siegel as a girl who can play cross-hand on the piano, Al Shea, Wayne Ward, Vern Reed and Bill Spangleberg as close-harmonizers—are immensely entertaining.

For Mr. Willson has given them lively, artless things to do, and they keep him good company. Like Richard Bissell, another Iowa playwright, Mr Willson has a fresh slant on Americana. Although he does not take it seriously, he loves it with the pawkiness of a liberated native. "The Music Man" is a marvelous show, rooted in wholesome and comic tradition.

1957 D 20

1958

GARDEN DISTRICT, collective title for two short plays by Tennessee Williams, "Something Unspoken" and "Suddenly Last Summer." Staged by Herbert Machiz; settings by Robert Soule; costumes by Stanley Simmons; lighting by Lee Watson; incidental music by Ned Rorem; produced by John C. Wilson and Warner LeRoy. At the York Playhouse, First Avenue and Sixty-fourth Street.

SOMETHING UNSPOKEN

Cornelia Scott ....Eleanor Phelps
Grace Lancaster ....Hortense Alden

SUDDENLY LAST SUMMER

Mrs. Venable ....Hortense Alden
Dr. Cukrowicz ....Robert Lansing
Miss Foxhill ....Donna Cameron
Mrs. Holly ....Eleanor Phelps
George Holly ....Alan Mixon
Catherine Holly ....Anne Meacham
Sister Felicity ....Nanon-Kiam

By BROOKS ATKINSON

A T this late date it is no longer necessary to observe that Tennessee Williams is a writer.

But one of his two short plays, put on last evening at the York Playhouse (First Avenue and Sixty-fourth Street), is startling proof of what a man can do with words. It is called "Suddenly Last Summer," the second of the plays produced under the group title of "Garden District"; and you can be sure that it has horrifying things to say. Mr. Williams is not the man to dismiss anyone from the theatre without shocking everyone's sensibilities.

Nor is he the man to use words carelessly. "Suddenly Last Summer" is an exercise in the necromancy of writing. Out of words set down with lyrical facility, Mr. Williams constructs an infected world. He draws character out of words—even the character who died before the play opens. He creates moods, colors, shadows, manners, odors, relationships out of words. He even creates motion out of them. For once it gets going the recollected story of "Suddenly Last Summer" moves with a mad, headlong pace toward damnation, which it reaches with an explosion of words. As an exercise that is both literary and dramatic, this brief, withering play is a superb achievement.

In a luxuriant, ominous

garden, beautifully designed by Robert Soule, a tyrannical, decadent old lady in New Orleans begins the story by describing her dead son, who was a poet and sybarite. For years mother and son had traveled abroad in a state of perpetual youth, oblivious of things that were ugly or common. But when age drew its first lines on her, the son deserted her and went abroad with a female cousin. He never returned.

The core of the play is the story of that last trip abroad, its overtones and undertones of degeneracy, the harrowing details of the violent death—told almost without interruption by the cousin under the influence of a truth drug. As directed by Herbert Machiz, the performance is a dark incantation.

As the tormented cousin, Anne Meacham tells this long story with power and skill, varying the moods almost imperceptibly, relinquishing herself to compulsions and obsessions that have broken the mind of an afflicted character. It is an admirable example of dramatic recitation. Hortense Alden is also admirable as the hateful, ruthless old woman determined to make beautiful truths out of hideous illusions. Robert Lansing plays the part of a physician with mercy and reticence. The other parts are well acted, too.

"Something Unspoken," the first of the two short plays, is a trifling, inconclusive anecdote about two Southern women who have lived in the same house for fifteen years without ever facing realities. Although Eleanor Phelps, as an arrogant dowager, and Miss Alden, as her secretary, act the two parts intelligently, "Something Unspoken" is too elusive to leave an impression on the audience.

But "Suddenly Last Summer" is further evidence of Mr. Williams' genius with the language. Although his world is tainted with corruption, it is beautifully contrived. No one else can use ordinary words with so much grace, allusiveness, sorcery and power.

1958 Ja 8

'The Chairs' and 'The Lesson' at Phoenix

THE CHAIRS and THE LESSON, a program of plays by Eugene Ionesco, translated by Donald Watson and Richard Roud. Directed by Tony Richardson; scenery by Jesse Beers, with the setting for "The Chairs" based on the original design by Jocelyn Herbert; lighting by Tharon Musser; music and sound effects by John Addison; presented by the Phoenix Theatre, a project of Theatre, Inc.

THE CHAIRS

Old Man....................Eli Wallach
Old Woman.............Joan Plowright
Orator..................Kelton Garwood

THE LESSON

Maid...................Paula Bauersmith
Student..................Joan Plowright
Professor..................Max Adrian

By BROOKS ATKINSON

ARE the two Ionesco plays, put on at the Phoenix last evening, interesting pieces of theatre? In this department's opinion, the answer is "yes."

We need not take off from this point to hail them as forerunners of tomorrow's drama or to present them as comments on the mysteries of the universe or as slanders on the philosophy of existentialism. But thanks in large part to brilliant direction by Tony Richardson and to lucid acting, particularly by Joan Plowright, these odd, elliptical fantastifications are amusing and provocative.

Just the kind of thing, incidentally, that the Phoenix is in a position to produce for audiences that are willing to collaborate with the author.

The program is naturally more portentous: "Ionesco is trying to discover true theatre; to push farce, burlesque and parody to the bitter end; to push everything to the 'climax where the sources of the tragic lie.'"

The first of the two short plays, "The Chairs," is billed as a tragic farce. In a spirit of comic hyperbole, it shows a very old man and his wife of equal years about to take their departure from this earth, leaving a legacy of advice and goodwill to those who are left in the world.

Although the business of the play is wildly improbable, "The Chairs" is written with kindness and sympathy; and it does suggest the golden illusions and pleasant futilities of human existence. It is extremely well played by Miss Plowright as an old crone with sore feet, a loose plate, cracked voice and benevolent spirit; and Eli Wallach as a cheerful, garrulous, memory-ridden old codger. Both are being spirited away amiably in a mood of mutual confidence in their worldly achievements. Intentionally obscure and unintentionally overwritten, "The Chairs" is, nevertheless, a charming play.

The second play, "The Lesson," was acted last season in Tempo Playhouse, where it seemed like humorless gibberish. At the Phoenix, the greatest lesson it teaches is that a keen director and skillful actors can turn heavy facetiousness into ironic humor.

Since "The Lesson" is described as a "comic drama" it naturally comes to a macabre conclusion. It is the story of a psychopathic pedagogue who cannot resist murdering his students—obviously one of the "climaxes where the sources of the tragic lie." At the moment this department is unable to explain the cosmic significance of M. Ionesco's theme.

But no one needs a syllabus to appreciate the cherubic acting of Miss Plowright, now in the part of a schoolgirl, and the ponderous, mad pedagogue acted by Max Adrian. Miss Plowright's bright eyes, shining face and varieties of animation are very funny indeed, and Mr. Adrian's elaborate politesse, giving way gradually to fanaticism and ghastly exuberance, is funny and grisly at the same time. There is nothing in "Alice in Wonderland" more crackbrained than the long colloquy in which the teacher man-

euvers to get from his confused pupil the correct answer to 4 minus 3. By means of this comic, plausible and logical mumbo jumbo, M. Ionesco is probably foretelling the end of civilization.

But the dialogue is so droll, the direction and the acting are so disinterested that the whole episode is entertaining. Thank Jesse Beers for original settings, particularly for the first play. Thank the Phoenix for a diverting evening.

1958 Ja 10

TWO FOR THE SEESAW, a play in three acts and nine scenes, by William Gibson. Staged by Arthur Penn; produced by Fred Coe; scenery and lighting by George Jenkins; costumes by Virginia Volland; production stage manager, Porter Van Zandt. At the Booth Theatre.
Jerry Ryan .... Henry Fonda
Gittel Mosca .... Anne Bancroft

By BROOKS ATKINSON

ALTHOUGH William Gibson has only two characters in "Two for the Seesaw" he has a tender style of writing and a beautiful little story to tell. And in the production that opened at the Booth last evening, he has two extraordinarily winning actors.

Everyone knows one of them. Henry Fonda is on one end of the seesaw, playing the part of the man who is out of love with his wife in Omaha, and not sure that he is in love with a girl in New York who has wordly ideas. Mr. Fonda is a wonderfully straightforward actor who plays at low pressure. As Jerry in Mr. Gibson's play, he gives his most limpid and moving performance. What he does not say in the dialogue, he says with the silent eloquence of a fine actor.

Anne Bancroft is on the other end of the seesaw—are attractive young actress unknown to this department until last evening, but sure to be known to thousands of theatregoers before the season is over. She plays the part of Gittel, a rather ordinary New York semi-bohemian. She lives alone. She tries to believe that she is a ballet dancer. She is full of schemes and projects, none of which is worth a dime. Goodhearted, unselfish, she unwittingly lives for other people.

The part is extremely well-written in the vernacular, though never cheap or mannered. Mr. Gibson has given her a great many comic and touching things to say. But if Miss Bancroft were not a glowing young lady without a mean bone in her body, the dialogue might sound more clever than honest. She is the animated half of the cast, making a vivid contrast with Mr. Fonda's leisurely style; she explodes with gestures that are natural; she modulates the part with vocal inflections that are both funny and authentic, and she creates a gallant character who rings true.

When the curtain goes up, "Two for the Seesaw" looks like a plausible stunt. A man in a shabby room in one corner of New York is telephoning to a girl who lives in a cheap apartment decorated with a dressmaker's form and earnest art objects. In the first scene we seem to be promised one more whirl at the epic theme of two unattached people in New York. This situation has already provided us with a whole library of tasteless, squalid, prurient comedies.

But Mr. Gibson is a genuine writer. No doubt he uses the two-character form cleverly. But it is not long before "Two for the Season" turns out to be a fresh and amusing comedy that is really interested in the characters of two decent people. The talk is funny; the habits of the two characters are breezy. But Jerry has standards, and so has Gittle. They learn some illuminating truths about themselves from each other. By the time the curtain comes down, you are not so much aware that Mr. Gibson has brought off a technical stunt as that he has looked inside the hearts of two admirable people and made a charming full-length play out of them.

Everyone concerned with this miniature triumph has contributed his own kind of distinction. Arthur Penn's unobtrusive direction gets over the technical hurdles easily and goes on to help develop and analyze the characters. George Jenkins' warm and pleasant settings, against a towering skyline, bring variety into the play and help to explain the moral experience of the two people who inhabit them.

For "Two for the Seesaw" is a finely wrought cameo. Thanks to Mr. Gibson's thoughtful writing and to the soft, shining acting by Mr. Fonda and Miss Bancroft, it has style, beauty and a delightful point of view.

1958 Ja 17

Lunt, Fontanne Open 'Their' Playhouse

The Cast

THE VISIT, a drama in three acts, by Friedrich Duerrenmatt, adapted by Maurice Valency. Staged by Peter Brook; scenery by Teo Otto; Lynne Fontanne's wardrobe by Castillo; supervision and lighting by Paul Morrison; production stage manager, Frederic de Wilde; presented by Producers Theatre (Roger L. Stevens, Robert W. Dowling, Robert Whitehead and Louis Lotito). At the new Lunt-Fontanne Theatre, 205 West Forty-sixth Street.

Hofbauer	Keneth Thornett
Helmesberger	David Clarke
Wechsler	Milton Selzer
Vogel	Harrison Dowd
The painter	Clarence Nordstrom
Stationmaster	Joseph Leberman
Burgomaster	Eric Porter
Professor Muller	Peter Woodthorpe
Pastor	William Hansen
Anton Schill	Alfred Lunt
Claire Zachanassian	Lynne Fontanne
First Conductor	Jonathan Anderson
Pedro Cabral	Myles Eason
Bobby	John Wyse
Police Chief Schultz	John Randolph
First Grandchild	Lesley Hunt
Second Grandchild	Lois McKim
Mike	Stanley Erickson
Max	William Thourlby
First Blind Man	Vincent Gardenia
Second Blind Man	Alfred Hoffman
Frau Burgomaster	Frieda Altman
Frau Block	Gertrude Kinnell
Frau Schill	Daphne Newton

Ottilie Schill ....Marla Adams
Karl Schill ....Ken Walken
Dr. Nusslin ....Howard Fischer
Athlete ....James MacAaron
Truck Driver ....John Kane
Reporter ....Edward Moor
Townsman ....Robert Donley
Townsman ....Kent Montroy

By BROOKS ATKINSON

AFTER squandering their time on polite trivialities for a number of years, Alfred Lunt and Lynn Fontanne are appearing in a devastating drama, "The Visit," which opened, appropriately enough, at the Lunt-Fontanne Theatre last evening.

Whether "The Visit" suits them or they suit "The Visit" is beside the point. For when Friedrich Duerrenmatt, the author, gets seriously down to work in the savage last act, our two most gifted comic actors look like our most gifted dramatic actors. Under Peter Brook's ingenious direction, they give an unforgettable performance.

When the curtain goes up "The Visit" promises to be an amusing European drama. When the author states his premise, it seems to be settling down into a sort of Ionesco satire. The point is this: Güllen, a poverty-stricken European town, is about to welcome its richest émigré —Claire Zachanassian. Everyone hopes that she will generously endow Güllen.

She proposes to give Güllen one billion marks on one condition: that they murder their fellow townsman, Anton Schill. When she was a girl in Güllen he had seduced her and also denied the paternity of their child. All she asks now is justice.

The proposal is so fantastic that everyone rejects it, and the audience shares the attitude of the people of Güllen. But not Herr Duerrenmatt. He means it, both as an observer of life and as a dramatic craftsman. For the second half of "The Visit" consists in a slow, macabre pressing on to a ghoulish climax. Everything has its price. Put the price high enough and so-

ciety can find a way to make murder moral. Village democracy finally demands the death of Anton Schill, since village democracy is concerned with the good of the greatest number of people.

If Maurice Valency's adaptation is a faithful interpretation of the German original, Herr Duerrenmatt is a sufficiently powerful dramatist to make an unpalatable theme acceptable. He writes with wit and humor when he is setting his snares. But he writes with cold fury when he gets to the core of his theme. The slow disintegration of character, the hypocritical turning on Anton Schill by his neighbors, the community malevolence of the town meeting when the awful vote is taken—are written with a calculated cruelty that proves Herr Duerrenmatt's cruel theme.

Production and performance are superb. Teo Otto has designed a skeletonized series of settings that carry the play forward swiftly; and Paul Morrison has lighted the production vividly. The cast is long and uniformly excellent As the village burgomaster, Eric Porter gives a remarkably effective performance, his bluff good humor drifting off into sanctimonious evil at the end. As the village schoolmaster, Peter Woodthorpe is also admirable, tracing the corruption of a good man into a traitor with sensitivity and a dash of pity.

But the triumph of the evening is the acting of our two most illustrious drawing-room comedians in the harshest roles they have played in a quarter of a century. As Anton Schill, Mr. Lunt plays a haggard, futile provincial who begins the drama in a gay mood and finishes it as a corpse. Mr. Lunt manages to invest a crumpled part with dignity and character.

As the wealthy, worldly Claire Zachanassian, Miss Fontanne has a part that more closely resembles those she has latterly been playing.

She is as glamorous as ever, slow, undulating and artful. But there is hardness in the center of the character; although the manners are casual, the desire for revenge is terrifying. Miss Fontanne portrays the whole character with great insight and implacable force.

The Lunt-Fontanne Theatre, which also opened last evening, is the daintiest and most luxurious in town. It must have been shocked by the play it found on the stage when the gorgeous curtain rolled up. But it must have been proud of the actors whose name it bears. They are devoting their genius to a bold, grisly drama of negativism and genius is what they have.

1958 My 6

The Cast

ULYSSES IN NIGHTTOWN. Padraic Colum's version of the "Nighttown" section of James Joyce's "Ulysses." Conceived and directed by Burgess Meredith; stage movement by Valerie Bettis; scenery by Herman Rosse; lighting by Nikola Cernovich; music composed and selected by Arnold Black; assistant director, John Astin; stage manager, Charles T. Morrison Jr.; presented by Rooftop Productions, in association with Kelsey Marechal, Oliver M. Sayler and Marjorie Barkentin. At the Rooftop Theatre, Second Avenue and East Houston Street.

Narrators..Denis Johnston, Sean Dillon
Buck Mulligan........Carroll O'Connor
Stephen Dedalus.........Robert Brown
Coachman.................James Payton
Martin Cunningham........Tom Clancy
Leopold Bloom....o..........Zero Mostel
Simon Dedalus..Michael Clarke-Laurence
Blazes Boylan............Swen Swenson
The Idiot....................John Astin
Molly ....Pauline Flanagan
Bandy Child....................Aza Bard
Virago.....................Lucille Patton
Mrs. Breen.................Anne Meara
Zoe...........................Belita
Mrs. Thornton........Beatrice Arthur
Whore.......................Eve Beck

By BROOKS ATKINSON

IN view of the problems that Joyce's "Ulysses" presents, the performance put on at the Rooftop Theatre last evening is remarkable.

Zero Mostel is the perfect Leopold Bloom. Around him the dreams and hallucinations, the feeling of guilt, the delusions of grandeur spiral off into a mad rigadoon. But Mr. Mostel's Bloom provides a solid center of gravity—derby hat, cutaway coat, mustache, resonant voice, bulging eyes, clumsy hands, the Philistine among revelers.

Even in its original novel form, "Ulysses" is difficult enough. For it is largely composed of the debris and litter of the mind sifting through the unconscious. Although Joyce was fascinated by the stage, he wrote his novel for readers. (For writers, too, since it is a pioneer work in the science of fiction.)

The program attributes the "text supervision" to Dr. Padraic Colum. He is eager to point out, however, that most of the play comes direct from the long Nighttown chapter, which is written in the form of drama; and several other hands have been at work on the final manuscript.

•

The play version begins with a brief sketch out of the opening of the novel when Stephen Dedalus is taunted with having refused to kneel at his mother's deathbed. A crisp, lithographic scene follows in which Martin Cunningham, Simon Dedalus and Leopold Bloom ride off to the cemetery, gossiping in pungent Dublin style. Nothing else in the play captures so much of the masculine humor, music and cynicism of Joyce's vigorous literary style.

For the rest of it re-creates that haunted night in the brothel district where Bloom and young Dedalus meet in the company of prostitutes and customers. To read the Joyce text is to be convinced that no one can bring it alive on the stage. It is like a volcano of words and images.

But, by golly, they have managed to get most of it on the stage by treating it as a dance. Burgess Meredith, who has staged it, has had the foresight to persuade Valerie Bettis to direct the acting movement. She has done it brilliantly. Taking the material that Joyce put on paper, she has evoked its fantastic spirit by improvising styles of movement that define mood.

Let's ñot pretend that every part of the production is pertinent. There are sequences that never come into focus. Unfortunately, a lot of Joyce's literary phrasing is swallowed up in movement or lost in slovenly speaking. But the main panorama of Bloom's several obsessions comes into view—his timidity, his frightened respectability, his shame and his recollections of shame, his fear of judgment, his gaudy dream of being a national hero, his abasement at the feet of a sadistic brothel keeper. Here, in Joyce's view, is the human animal imprisoned in his own experience, hope and fear.

Herman Rosse, the designer, has not attempted to define any locale. The stage is a cavern with grottoes that are lighted when action takes place in them; and Nikola Cernovich has lighted the whole production dramatically.

•

Since the cast is as endless as Bloom's hallucinations, most of the actors play several parts. There is no time at the moment to recognize any except the principal players — Robert Brown as the soft, over-educated Dedalus, Swen Swenson as the cocky Blazes Boylan, Pauline Flanagan as the sensual Molly, Belita as the dancing Zoe, Beatrice Arthur as the savage brothel-keeper.

But it is Mr. Mostel who pulls the whole production together with his solid characterization of the amiable, commonplace Bloom. Joyce set the stage more problems than the stage can ever solve. But the many people who have labored on this dramatization have succeeded remarkably in visualizing the fantasy of a mind that is drenched in human expression.

1958 Je 6

Story of a Scoundrel Opens at Renata

The Cast

IVANOV, a drama in four acts by Anton Chekhov in a new translation by Elisaveta Fen. Staged by William Ball; designed and lighted by Will Steven Armstrong; costumes supervised by Poppy Lagodmos; music. Sally Breskin; additional lyrics, Alyce Finell; production stage manager, Edward Hastings; revived by Daniel Hineck, in association with Harlin Quist. At the Renata Theatre, 144 Bleecker Street.

Ivanov......................Paul Stevens
Borkin........................Jack Bittner
Anna Petrovna......Jacqueline Brookes
Shabyelsky..............Roberts Blossom
Lvov.......................Harlin Quist
Babakina................Sada Thompson
Zenaeda Saveshna .....Mary Van Fleet
Gavrila...................Ezra Howard
Kosyh................James Goldsmith
Yegorushka.............George Barry
Avdotya Nazarovna......Marian Reardon
Lyebedev.................Albert Quinton
Sasha....................Anne Fielding
Piotr......................Phil Jacobus
Grigori.................Claude Woolman
Masha.....................Yafa Lerner
Yermolal.................Hugh Whitfield
Olga.....................Vivian Neuberg
Leonid...................Robert Diehl
Irena....................Joan Kugell

By BROOKS ATKINSON

TO those who love Chekhov, even one of his second-best plays is captivating.

"Ivanov," beautifully staged at the Renata last evening, is a second-best play in comparison with the great four with which he concluded his career. The story has a coarser texture; the style is more common. But it is filled with the quiet radiance that makes Chekhov the most lovable of Russian dramatists. In 1887, when he wrote it, his point of view about men and women was already formed.

•

"Ivanov" is the story of a Russian provincial who degenerates into a scoundrel out of nothing more vicious than boredom. Although his wife is wholly devoted to him, and is also ill of the tuberculosis that eventually kills her, Ivanov lacks the energy to treat her civilly. He knows that he is a scoundrel, but he is too listless to behave in any other way. While his wife is still alive, he accepts the love of a girl who is much younger and is also the daughter of a family to whom he owes a considerable sum of money. In the last act, after his wife has died, he almost marries the girl out of inertia. He has the goodness to shoot himself before the ceremony is performed.

"Ivanov" was a popular success in Moscow and St. Petersburg. This discouraged Chekhov, who always felt uneasy when his plays succeeded, although he was devastated when they failed. There is plenty of the old claptrap theatre in "Ivanov" —tensions about money, crudeness about Jews, a big, festive wedding scene and a melodramatic shooting. When Chekhov got these conventions out of his system a decade later, he wrote "The Seagull," a masterpiece that failed. Obviously, he was right in being skeptical about the theatre.

•

But "Ivanov" also contains the attitudes that in his best plays he conjures into a half-sad, half-humorous mood. The introspection, the frantic attempts to escape boredom, the vulgar comedian, the inevitable physician, the garrulous party, the anatomy of souls, the small talk and the wistful mockery—they are all present in "Ivanov." Although the craftsmanship is less limpid, the mood is the same.

Under the direction of William Ball, the performance is sensitive and sure. Although the stage at the Renata is small, Will Steven Armstrong has succeeded in designing scenery that gives an impression of placid space. Everything else about the production is thoroughly professional.

The acting is a study in tones and half lights. Paul Stevens as the gloomy Ivanov, who nevertheless has taste and breeding; Jacqueline Brookes, lovely and touching as the rejected wife; Jack Bittner as the rowdy clown; Albert Quinton as a hearty though fearful friend and neighbor; Anne Fielding as the independent-minded daughter;

Robert Blossom as an aging wastrel; Harlin Quist as a belligerently sanctimonious physician; Sada Thompson as a voluptuous widow; Mary Van Fleet, James Goldsmith, Marian Reardon, Claude Woolman in other parts— give excellent individual performances that create a dark, fugitive mood.

"Ivanov" has never been acted in English on a professional stage in New York before. Although it is Chekhov on the second level (don't forget that there is also a third level) it contains a good deal of the sad wisdom that produced four very memorable dramas in the next eighteen years.

1958 O 8

1959

Williams' 'Sweet Bird of Youth' Opens

By BROOKS ATKINSON

STILL possessed of the demons, Tennessee Williams has written another vivid play. "Sweet Bird of Youth" he calls it with ironic pity. Under Elia Kazan's direction it is brilliantly acted at the Martin Beck, where it opened last evening.

It is a portrait of corruption and evil, which are Mr. Williams' familiar subjects. The two chief characters represent two aspects of civilized degeneracy — an aging motion-picture actress who is fleeing reality in drink, drugs and dissipation; a young gigolo who has cheap dreams of glory and means to fulfill them by cheap means.

•

Mr. Williams is not revenging himself on anyone this time. "Sweet Bird of Youth" is hardly a noble play. But it has overtones of pity for those who are damned. Although the old harridan from

Hollywood is a monster, she is no fiend; she knows what she is doing and why. Although the young man is a monster, he represents the seamy side of the American dream. He means to take whatever he can snatch; he is the perpetual adolescent, steeped in gaudy illusions of success and grandeur.

At the end, in a corrosively humorous scene, the screen star is recalled from damnation by reports of success in Hollywood, and she starts pulling herself together with professional acumen. She is never so far gone that a box-office statement cannot restore her.

But the young man—his youth gone, his abominations overwhelming him—has lost the will to go on living. He makes no attempt to escape a posse of barbarians who have announced that they are going to castrate him because he has infected a local belle with disease. He has burned out his soul with lies and depravity. When the play concludes he is accepting the horrors that await him.

The Cast

SWEET BIRD OF YOUTH, a drama by Tennessee Williams, with music by Paul Bowles. Staged by Elia Kazan; scenery and lighting by Jo Mielziner; presented by Cheryl Crawford; costumes by Anna Hill Johnstone; costumes for Geraldine Page by Theoni Vachlioti Aldredge; production stage manager, David Paroll. At the Martin Beck Theatre.

Chance Wayne .... Paul Newman
Princess Pazmezoglu ... Geraldine Page
Fly .... Milton J. Williams
Maid .... Patricia Ripley
George Scudder .... Logan Ramsey
Hatcher .... John Napier
Boss Finley .... Sidney Blackmer
Tom Junior .... Rip Torn
Aunt Nonnie .... Martine Bartlett
Heavenly Finley ...... Diana Hyland
Charles .... Earl Sydnor
Stuff .... Bruce Dern
Miss Lucy ...... Madeleine Sherwood
Heckler .... Charles Tyner
Violet .... Monica May
Edna .... Hilda Brawner
Scotty .... Charles McDaniel
Bud .... James Jeter
Men in Bar .... Duke Farley,
        Ron Harper, Kenneth Blake
Page .... Glenn Stensel

If "Sweet Bird of Youth" is less shocking than this résumé suggests, it must be because of the nature of Mr. Williams' artistry as a writer. Is is a play that ranges wide through the lower depths, touching on political violence, as well as diseases of mind and body. But it has the spontaneity of an improvisation.

Nothing seems to be planned. It begins in comic squalor in a hotel room. In the second act it moves into a private house and then a hotel lobby. But nothing seems to be arranged for theatrical sensation. Knowing his subject with chilling intimacy, Mr. Williams daintily peels off layer after layer of the skin, body and spirit of his characters and leaves their nature exposed in the hideous humor and pathos of the truth. As a writer of prose drama, Mr. Williams has the genius of a poet.

Under Mr. Kazan's limpid direction, it is beautifully performed in the mood of a black incantation. Jo Mielziner has prepared wide settings with luminous backgrounds; and Paul Bowles has contributed spidery and tinkling music of exquisite texture.

In the central roles the acting is magnificent. Geraldine Page gives a fabulous performance as the decaying movie queen. Loose-jointed, gangling, raucous of voice, crumpled, shrewd, abandoned yet sensitive about some things that live in the heart, Miss Page is at the peak of form in this raffish characterization.

And Paul Newman's young man is the perfect companion-piece. Although he has a braggart, calculating exterior, he is as immature as an adolescent; brassy outside, terrified and remorseful when he stops strutting. As a political boss, Sidney Blackmer also gives a superb performance.

Despite the acrid nature of its material, "Sweet Bird of Youth" is Mr. Williams in a relaxed mood as a writer. He seems to have made some sort of peace with himself. "Sweet Bird of Youth" is one of his finest dramas.

1959 Mr 11

A RAISIN IN THE SUN, a drama by
Lorraine Hansberry. Staged by Lloyd
Richards; presented by Philip Rose
and David J. Cogan; scenery and
lighting by Ralph Alswang; costumes
by Virginia Volland; production stage
manager, Leonard Auerbach. At the
Ethel Barrymore Theatre.

Ruth Younger	Ruby Dee
Travis Younger	Glynn Turman
Walter Lee Younger	Sidney Poitier
Beneatha Younger	Diana Sands
Lena Younger	Claudia McNeil
Joseph Asagai	Ivan Dixon
George Murchison	Louis Gossett
Bobo	Lonne Elder 3d
Karl Lindner	John Fiedler
Moving Men	Ed Hall, Douglas Turner

By BROOKS ATKINSON

IN "A Raisin in the Sun," which opened at the Ethel Barrymore last evening, Lorraine Hansberry touches on some serious problems. No doubt, her feelings about them are as strong as any one's.

But she has not tipped her play to prove one thing or another. The play is honest. She has told the inner as well as the outer truth about a Negro family in the southside of Chicago at the present time. Since the performance is also honest and since Sidney Poitier is a candid actor. "A Raisin in the Sun" has vigor as well as veracity and is likely to destroy the complacency of any one who sees it.

•

The family consists of a firm-minded widow, her daughter, her restless son and his wife and son. The mother has brought up her family in a tenement that is small, battered but personable. All the mother wants is that her children adhere to the code of honor and self-respect that she inherited from her parents.

The son is dreaming of success in a business deal. And the daughter, who is race-conscious, wants to become a physician and heal the wounds of her people. After a long delay the widow receives $10,000 as the premium on her husband's life insurance. The money projects the family into a series of situations that test their individual characters.

What the situations are does not matter at the moment. For "A Raisin in the Sun" is a play about human beings who want, on the one hand, to preserve their family pride and, on the other hand, to break out of the poverty that seems to be their fate. Not having any axe to grind, Miss Hansberry has a wide range of topics to write about —some of them hilarious, some of them painful in the extreme.

You might, in fact, regard "A Raisin in the Sun" as a Negro "The Cherry Orchard." Although the social scale of the characters is different, the knowledge of how character is controlled by environment is much the same, and the alternation of humor and pathos is similar.

If there are occasional crudities in the craftsmanship, they are redeemed by the honesty of the writing. And also by the rousing honesty of the stage work. For Lloyd Richards has selected an admirable cast and directed a bold and stirring performance.

•

Mr. Poitier is a remarkable actor with enormous power that is always under control. Cast as the restless son, he vividly communicates the tumult of a highstrung young man. He is as eloquent when he has nothing to say as when he has a pungent line to speak. He can convey devious processes of thought as graphically as he can clown and dance.

As the matriarch, Claudia McNeil gives a heroic performance. Although the character is simple, Miss McNeil gives it nobility of spirit. Diana Sands' amusing portrait of the overintellectualized daughter; Ivan Dixon's quiet, sagacious student from Nigeria; Ruby Dee's young wife burdened with problems; Louis Gossett's supercilious suitor; John Fiedler's timid white man, who speaks sanctimonious platitudes—bring variety and excitement to a first-rate performance.

All the crises and comic sequences take place inside Ralph Alswang's set, which depicts both the poverty and the taste of the family. Like the play, it is honest. That is Miss Hansberry's personal contribution to an explosive situation in which simple honesty is the most difficult thing in the world. And also the most illuminating.

1959 Mr 12

Holbrook Reads From Works of Humorist

"MARK TWAIN TONIGHT!", a program of selections from the works of Mark Twain, with Hal Holbrook as the solo performer. Presented by John Lotas in association with Bunker Jenkins. At the Forty-first Street Theatre. PROGRAM: The Dangers of Abstinence, The Italian Guide, The Genuine Mexican Plug, Advice to Youth, Encounter with an Interviewer, The Great French Duel, Accident Insurance, Poet Story, Buck Fanshaw's Funeral, The Watermelon Story and other material.

By ARTHUR GELB

AN extraordinary show called "Mark Twain Tonight!" slipped into the Forty-first Street Theatre last evening. There should have been posters up all over town to herald its arrival.

"Mark Twain Tonight!" is a reading from the works of the American humorist by a young actor named Hal Holbrook. Mr. Holbrook, who is 34 years old, has got himself up as Twain at the age of 70 and portrays him as the roaming platform entertainer, in which guise the Missourian endeared himself to the world. The result can only be described as brilliant.

Everything about the evening is perfect—the intimate theatre, Mr. Holbrook's faultless characterization and the uproariously funny selections from Twain that he has chosen. An inordinately skillful and inventive actor, Mr. Holbrook has every gesture, inflection and pause under control. Limply mustached,

Hal Holbrook as Mark Twain

fluffy white hair straying, he comes onstage with a spry shuffle, to introduce himself modestly as one of the two outstanding literary figures of his time. (The other is Kipling, who knows everything there is to know; he, Twain, knows the rest.)

Without pausing for more than a deliberate snuffle, he launches into such dissertations as "The Dangers of Abstinence," "Advice to Youth" and "Encounter With an Interviewer." This last is a hilarious account of his attempts to confuse a brash young newspaper man by a quietly insane detailing of the "facts" of his life.

Mr. Holbrook, of course, did not discover any of this delectable material. But he has shown great imagination in bringing it to the stage. After watching and listening to him for five minutes, it is impossible to doubt that he is Mark Twain or that Twain must have been one of the most enchanting men ever to go on a lecture tour.

Nothing is overdone: not the subtle, spasmodic clenching of the old man's hands; the tremulous fingering of watch chain and vest; the absent-minded holding of a lighted match, arrested in its flight to the omnipresent cigar; the twangy, cracked voice, the dry chuckle, the significant pause followed by the tag line, or the slowly gathering twinkle of the eyes as the richness of his own humor overwhelms him.

A program note states that it takes Mr. Holbrook three hours to apply his makeup for the role and that he has spent twelve years on research. No one is likely to question either of these statements, but what is far more impressive is that the whole thing looks spontaneous and effortless.

The spirit of the evening is summed up by another program note, which reads:

"While Mr. Twain's selections will come from the list below, we have been unable to pin him down as to which of them he will do. He claims this would cripple his inspiration. However, he has generously conceded to a printed programme for the benefit of those who are in distress and wish to fan themselves."

1959 Ap 7

The Cast

GYPSY, a musical fable, suggested by the memoirs of Gypsy Rose Lee. Book by Arthur Laurents, music by Jule Styne and lyrics by Stephen Sondheim. Directed and choreographed by Jerome Robbins; directorial assistant, Gerald Freedman; presented by David Merrick and Leland Hayward; sets and lighting by Jo Mielziner; costumes by Raoul Pene du Bois; musical direction, Milton Rosenstock; orchestrations by Ramin and Robert Ginzler; dance music arrangements, John Kander; additional dance music, Betty Walberg; hair styles, Ernest Adler; production stage manager, Ruth Mitchell; production associate, Michael Mindlin Jr.; assistant to Mr. Merrick, Eduard Fuller. At the Broadway Theatre.

Uncle Jocko............Mort Marshall
Baby Louise............Karen Moore
Baby June..............Jacqueline Mayro
Rose...................Ethel Merman
Pop....................Erv Harmon
Weber..................Joe Silver
Herbie.................Jack Klugman
Louise.................Sandra Church
June...................Lane Bradbury
Tulsa..................Paul Wallace
Yonkers................David Winters
Kringelein.............Loney Lewis
Miss Cratchitt.........Peg Murray
Agnes..................Marilyn Cooper
Tessie Tura............Maria Karnilova
Mazeppa................Faith Dane
Electra................Chotzi Foley

By BROOKS ATKINSON

SINCE Ethel Merman is the head woman in "Gypsy," which opened at the Broadway last evening, nothing can go wrong. She would not permit "Gypsy" to be anything less than the most satisfying musical of the season.

She is playing the indomitable mother of Gypsy Rose Lee, a stripper with a difference; and Miss Merman, her pipes resonant and her spirit syncopated, struts and bawls her way through it triumphantly.

Ever since "Annie Get Your Gun," it has been obvious that she is an actress in addition to being a singer. In the book Arthur Laurents has written for her (based on the memoirs of Gypsy Rose Lee) she is the female juggernaut who drives her two daughters into show business and keeps their noses to the grindstone until one of them is a star.

"Gypsy" is a musical tour of the hotel rooms and backstages of the seamy side of show business thirty years ago when vaudeville was surrendering to the strip-tease. Jo Mielziner has designed a savory production. Jule Styne has supplied a genuine show-business score, and Stephen Sondheim has set amusing lyrics to it.

Under the genial direction of Jerome Robbins, who is willing to take time to enjoy what he is doing, the performance is entertaining in all the acceptable styles from skulduggery to the anatomy of a termagant. There are some very funny scenes in the beginning when Jacqueline Mayro, as a baby star, makes all the clichés of juvenile performing wonderfully garish and plausible.

As Mother Rose's shoestring act sinks lower in the

profession, "Gypsy" descends into the inferno of a burlesque joint where the grind sisters—notably Maria Karnilova and Faith Dane—contribute some ludicrous exercises in vulgarity. No one could improve much on the scene Mr. Robbins and Mr. Mielziner have devised to portray one of Minsky's most elegant show pieces. It fairly explodes with rhinestone splendor.

The cast is delightful. Lane Bradbury plays with gusto the part of June, the baby star who wrecks the act by running off to be married. Jack Klugman, kindly and worried, plays Herbie, the combination boy friend and booking agent. As Gypsy, Sandra Church gives a lovely performance. A slight young lady with small features and a delicate style of acting, she conveys with equal skill the shyness of the adolescent and the tough assurance of the lady who becomes a star.

But "Gypsy" is Miss Merman's show. Mr. Styne has given her some good greased-horn music, which she delivers with earthy magnificence in her familiar manner. There are some sticky scenes toward the end when "Gypsy" abandons the sleazy grandeur of show business and threatens to become belles-lettres. It deserts the body and starts cultivating the soul. Things look ominous in the last ten minutes.

But trust Ethel. She concludes the proceedings with a song and dance of defiance. Mr. Styne's music is dramatic. Miss Merman's performance expresses her whole character —cocky and aggressive, but also sociable and good-hearted. Not for the first time in her fabulous career, her personal magnetism electrifies the whole theatre. For she is a performer of incomparable power.

"Gypsy" is a good show in the old tradition of musicals. For years Miss Merman has been the queen.

1959 My 22.

The Cast

THE CONNECTION, a drama by Jack Gelber. Staged by Judith Malina; designed by Julian Beck; lighting by Nicola Cernowich; music in the jazz idiom composed by Freddie Redd; production stage manager, Peter L. Feldman; presented by the Living Theatre, 530 Avenue of the Americas.

Jim Dunn	Leonard Hicks
Jaybird	Ira Lewis
Leach	Warren Finnerty
Solly	Jerome Raphel
Sam	John McCurry
Ernie	Garry Goodrow
First Photographer	Louis McKenzie
Second Photographer	Jamil Zakkai
Harry	Henry Proach
Cowboy	Carl Lee
Sister Salvation	Barbara Winchester
Piano	Freddie Redd
Alto	Jackie McLean
Bass	Jim Corbett
Drums	Clyde Harris

'Connection' Offered in Premiere Here

By LOUIS CALTA

JACK GELBER'S play about jazz and junk, "The Connection," which opened last night at The Living Theatre, Avenue of the Americas and Fourteenth Street, is an attempt to depict the sordid world of the narcotics addict. It also endeavors to reconcile —if that is possible—"the humor and tragedy" of the junkies' dream world.

But "The Connection" proves to be nothing more than a farrago of dirt, small-time philosophy, empty talk and extended runs of "cool" music. There is a quality of sensationalism about the work that undoubtedly will offend the squares. On the other hand, the hipsters might dig its semi-serious, semi-facetious treatment of an unhappy social situation.

•

"The Connection" opens in the dreary, baleful and shabby room of an addict. There are four musicians who play a piano, a bass fiddle, drums and an alto. They provide the music, which, according to Mr. Gelber, reflects "the emotional state of our times."

Sitting around, also, are some unshaven, unshorn and unclean characters who give the appearance of being "beatniks." But they aren't. They are waiting impatiently for some sort of a Godot. In this case, however, their Godot makes an appearance in the second half of the play amply supplied with the stuff of which dreams are made.

That "The Connection" is dead serious about this grim subject is manifest in a program note that explains that the play is dedicated to the "memory of Thelma Gadsden, dead of an overdose of heroin, at the Salvation Army, November, 1957, and to all the other junkies dead and alive in The Women's House of Detention." But instead of offering the theatregoer the pathos and terror of these sinister activities, "The Connection" fritters away its theme with inexpert and obvious stunts.

Mr. Gelber has contrived some disconcerting and distracting moments. His dramatis personae include himself (Jim Dunn) and the producer. At one point, Mr. Gelber's stage alter ego interrupts the proceedings on the stage and accuses the musicians of "lousing up the play." At another, he falls victim to the narcotics habit and bewails the fact that he will not be able to complete the scene. We prefer to believe that Mr. Gelber is a kindlier person and that he really did finish his task of script writing.

There are, too, periods of improvisations that are as frustrating as looking through a peephole into a darkened room. And when someone in the cast rhetorically screams at the audience and asks: "Why are you here, stupid? You want to watch people suffer?" Well, Mr. Gelber is not exactly going to influence people and make friends.

On the stage of the Living Theatre last night we were shown that heroin produces a condition of listless weariness. Unfortunately, some of this weariness made itself felt off stage.

1959 Jl 16

The Cast

TONIGHT WE IMPROVISE, a play by Luigi Pirandello, translated by Claude Fredericks. Staged and designed by Julian Beck; revived by the Living Theatre; music directed by Saville Clark; lighting by Nicola Cernovich; assistant director, Soren Agenoux; stage manager, Peter Feldman. At the Living Theatre, 530 Avenue of the Americas, at Fourteenth Street.
The Director................Julian Beck
Rico Verri................Alan Ansara
Palmiro La Croce......Bennes Mardenn
Signora Ignacia La Croce.....Sala Staw
Mommina................Judith Malina
Totina...................Arlyne Raines
Dorina...............Cynthia Robinson
Nene...................Ethel Manuelian
Pomarici................Melvin Brez
Sarelli...................Garry Goodrow
Nardi....................Jamil Zakkai
Magini................Joseph Chaikin
Pometti...........Warren Finnerty
Absinthe Drinker.....Margery Hollister
Chanteuse.................Jennie Davis
A Child................Bonnie Nam

By BROOKS ATKINSON

IF the indomitable people of the Living Theatre want to undertake the labor of staging Pirandello's "Tonight We Improvise," many thanks.

In the first place, they act avant-garde drama with extraordinary assurance. Being basically good actors committed to a point of view, they make the bizarre seem like a valid theatre experience. They do not pose. The staging by Julian Beck is sensible; that is, he accepts what he is doing as worth doing for its own sake. Some of his actors have first-rate talent.

•

In the second place, Pirandello's "Tonight We Improvise" (acted at the Living Theatre last evening) is the sort of script that ought to be experimented with in a theatre rather than a library, although it will probably interest only people who are fascinated with the anatomy of the theatrical process.

All his life Pirandello was obsessed with the difference between reality and illusion. Which is truth: the actor or the character? He wondered if the theatre could dispense with its own form and still be theatre. "Tonight We Improvise" is written as if it were an improvisation and as if there were no author.

It begins with sounds of quarreling backstage before

Judith Malina as Mommina

the curtains are parted. In the role of director, Mr. Beck appears before the curtains, reproves the actors and tells the audience what to expect. Impertinent people in the audience answer him rudely. Finally, the actors come before the audience like a group of sullen, bickering, unruly egotists, object to the nature of their profession, which destroys their own personality, and then begin to act a play about a volatile Sicilian family.

●

The main body of the play is negligible. Pirandello uses it as something to be tossed around in search of the nature of truth. In the second act, when the improvisations and little side games are abandoned, the main body of the play gets dull. The need for an author becomes urgent.

But in the first act, when Mr. Beck is holding the audience at bay, and the actors are wrangling in the aisles and giving him a hard time, "Tonight We Improvise" is amusing.

There is another interesting phenomenon. When

Bennes Mardenn is ostentatiously dying with red paint spattered over his shirt and streaked across his face, the circumstances are broad burlesque, but the effect is moving. In the center of a foolish farago, an improbable death scene has emotional values of its own.

And in the second act Judith Malina and Alan Ansara play a violent emotional scene that is convincing, although it has no dramatic significance. The illusion is perfect, but the truth is elusive, if it exists at all.

Presumably, that is what Pirandello wanted to find out. In the theatre, is illusion as powerful as truth? Does the author have a real function? Not many people are interested in this sort of metaphysical inquiry, and it takes a lot of work and skill for a company of actors to conduct the experiment.

But Mr. Beck and his associates in the Living Theatre have done the work well. Although the play is valueless and largely incomprehensible, the inquiry is interesting.

1959 N 7

The Cast

THE SOUND OF MUSIC, a musical play. Music by Richard Rodgers. Lyrics by Oscar Hammerstein 2d. Book by Howard Lindsay and Russel Crouse, suggested by "The Trapp Family Singers," by Maria Augusta Trapp. Staged by Vincent J. Donehue; presented by Leland Hayward, Richard Halliday, Mr. Rodgers and Mr. Hammerstein; choreographer, Joe Layton; scenery by Oliver Smith; costumes by Lucinda Ballard; Mary Martin's clothes by Mainbocher; lighting by Jean Rosenthal; musical director, Frederick Dvonch; orchestrations, Robert Russell Bennett; choral arrangements, Trude Rittman; production stage manager, Peter Zeisler. At the Lunt-Fontanne Theatre.

Maria Rainer	Mary Martin
Sister Berthe	Elizabeth Howell
Sister Margaretta	Muriel O'Malley
Mother Abbess	Patricia Neway
Sister Sophia	Karen Shepard
Capt. Georg Von Trapp	Theodore Bikel
Franz	John Randolph
Frau Schmidt	Nan McFarland
Liesl	Lauri Peters
Friedrich	William Snowden
Louisa	Kathy Dunn
Kurt	Joseph Stewart
Brigitta	Marilyn Rogers
Marta	Mary Susan Locke
Gretl	Evanna Lien
Rolf Gruber	Brian Davies
Elsa Schraeder	Marion Marlowe
Ursula	Luce Ennis
Max Detweiler	Kurt Kasznar
Herr Zeller	Stefan Gierasch

Show About a Singing Family Arrives

By BROOKS ATKINSON

FROM the Trapp Family Singers, the makers of "The Sound of Music" have acquired two valuable assets —legendary personal courage and a love of singing.

By no particular chance, those are the most winning characteristics of the bountiful musical drama that Mary Martin brought to the Lunt-Fontanne Theatre last evening. Although Miss Martin, now playing an Austrian maiden, has longer hair than she had in "South Pacific," she still has the same common touch that wins friends and influences people, the same sharp features, goodwill and glowing personality and the same plain voice that makes music sound intimate and familiar.

Using "The Trapp Family Singers" as their source book, Howard Lindsay and Russel Crouse have provided her with the libretto of an operetta. Unfortunately, it is conventional in its literary point of view. The story of the novice from the abbey who becomes governess of seven motherless children and teaches them how to sing, is an attractive one; especially when, as the wife of their father, she helps to lead them out of Austria away from the Nazis into Switzerland.

But the scenario of "The Sound of Music" has the hackneyed look of the musical theatre that Richard Rodgers and Oscar Hammerstein 2d replaced with "Oklahoma!" in 1943.

The best of "The Sound of Music" is Rodgers and Hammerstein in good form. Mr. Rodgers has not written with such freshness of style since "The King and I." Mr. Hammerstein has contributed lyrics that also have the sentiment and dexterity of his best work.

Since "The Sound of Music" opens in an Austrian abbey it begins with some religious music. Fortunately, Patricia Neway is on hand as the Mother Abbess to give the church an exalting purity of tone and feeling.

But the basic theme has had the happy effect of releasing Mr. Rodgers' endless fund of cheerful melodies—a charming, wistful song called "My Favorite Things"; a touching song for the children called "Do Re Mi" (in the friendly mood of "Getting to Know You"); an Alpine ballad entitled "The Lonely Goatherd"; an antic piece for the children, dubbed "So Long, Farewell," and the theme song, which is the most captivating of all. In the second act as well as the first, the play is rich in music.

As performance and production, "The Sound of Music" is off the top shelf. You are likely to lose your heart to the seven singing children who range from the doll-like adolescent of Lauri Peters to the chubby innocence of Evanna Lieu. In his stage direction, Vincent J. Donehue is not above being cute with the children (and coy with Miss Martin), for the direction has the stereotyped quality of the libretto. But no one could mask the natural beauty and high spirits of the Trapp boys and girls.

The cast is excellent throughout. Theodore Bikel as the serious, high-minded Baron Von Trapp, Kurt Kasznar as a witty, animated friend of the family, who accepts the Nazis, Marion Marlowe as a stunning lady of wealth who sees no point in resisting the invaders — they are all well cast and they bring taste and skill to the production.

In his settings Oliver Smith

has provided opulent décor--none of it finer than the lovely opening scene. Lucinda Ballard's costumes are up to her own standard. Russell Bennett's dainty orchestrations and Frederick Dvonch's fine conducting uphold the traditions of musical production on a high level.

It is disappointing to see the American musical stage succumbing to the clichés of operetta. The revolution of the Forties and Fifties has lost its fire. But "The Sound of Music" retains some of the treasures of those golden days —melodies, rapturous singing and Miss Martin. The sound of music is always moving. Occasionally it is also glorious.

1959 N 17

'Little Mary Sunshine' Opens at Orpheum

By LOUIS CALTA

"LITTLE MARY SUN-SHINE," a new musical that brought light and cheer last night to the Orpheum Theatre on Second Avenue and Eighth Street, is a merry and sprightly spoof of an era when "justice always triumphed," when "good meant good" and when "bad meant bad."

It is the work of Rick Besoyan, a versatile young man who might be called Off Broadway's threat to Noël Coward. With "The Boy Friend" soon scheduled to depart from town, "Little Mary Sunshine" should easily fit into that special niche long occupied by the intimate British musical caricature of the Roaring Twenties.

"Little Mary Sunshine" is an affectionate jab at the type of operetta that Rudolf Friml, Johann Strauss and Victor Herbert made popular in the early Nineteen Twenties. Its humor derives not so much from the sharp wit

Eileen Brennan

The Cast

LITTLE MARY SUNSHINE, a musical, in two acts: book, music and lyrics by Rick Besoyan; directed and choreographed by Ray Harrison; scenery and costumes by Howard Barker. Produced by Mr. Barker. Cynthia Baer and Robert Chambers. At the

Chief Brown Bear........John Aniston
Corp. Billy Jester........John McMartin
Capt. Big Jim Warington,
                          William Graham
Little Mary Sunshine...Eileen Brennan
Mme. Ernestine von Liebedich, .
                          Elizabeth Parrish
Nancy Twinkle.........Elmarie Wendel
Fleet Foot.............Robert Chambers
Yellow Feather.............Ray James
Gen. Oscar Fairfax........Mario Siletti

at the expense of an old and pleasant musical form as from the light cartoon treatment of it. The general tone is a nostalgic evocation of what appears now as a period of innocence and simple gaiety.

It is expertly performed by a group of young persons endowed with felicitous voices and with good comic sense.

The burlesque is delightful, lively and humorous. Mr. Besoyan's musical parody is tuneful, genteel and amiable. The author-composer also has a way with lyrics. "Just think what might happen to a girl?" remarks one of the young and proper ladies of the Eastchester Finishing School. "That's what I'm thinking about," replies another. Or, the fraudulent innocence of a maiden being wooed: "I do confess I burn with a young maiden's curiosity."

•

"Little Mary Sunshine" charmingly captures the formalized speech, the delicate posturing and the outrageous gentility of the old operettas. The ladies properly wring their hands, look down coyly and kick up their heels in stylized fashion. The dances, as staged and choreographed by Ray Harrison, are agile and inventive.

Another extraordinary aspect of "Little Mary Sunshine" is the plenitude of songs fashioned by Mr. Besoyan. According to the program credits there are some twenty-four, and it would be difficult to say which is the best of a good lot.

They are sung with verve and gusto by Eileen Brennan, as Mary Sunshine, the adopted daughter of the Kadota Indians of Colorado (there are only three of them left); William Graham as Capt. Jim Warington, a forest ranger; John McMartin as Cpl. Billy Jester, another forest ranger, and a group of young men and women too numerous to mention."

The musical is gaily orchestrated and colorfully designed and costumed. Jack Holmes and Gordon Munford, at twin pianos, achieve some happy results. All in all, "Little Mary Sunshine" is an extremely well done show.

1959 N 19

Change and Transition: 1960-1970

The decline of the Broadway scene was even more precipitous during these years than in the previous decade. Production and running costs mounted even higher; admission prices continued to rise; television and films became even more formidable competitors; and the Broadway district itself began to deteriorate, causing countless would-be playgoers to abandon their evenings at the theater. Legitimate theaters continued to be converted to television studios and movie-houses, and some playhouses were destroyed to make room for office buildings and parking lots. The number of Broadway productions dwindled from a high of seventy in 1960 to a pathetic low of thirty-four in 1970. The Off-Broadway picture was brighter; productions during the decade (not counting the numerous non-professional presentations) averaged approximately one hundred a season. It must be noted, however, that toward the end of the decade, Off-Broadway's production and running costs mounted so alarmingly (with a corresponding rise in admission prices) that producing there was also curtailed and attendance, as on Broadway, also dropped. Plays, both on and Off-Broadway, opened and closed with startling rapidity, unable to be nursed along until, perhaps, an audience could be found. This dark picture was partly relieved by an expanded public commitment to the stage. Non-profit theatrical institutions became increasingly stable and new physical plants were erected throughout the country. Increasingly critics reported the work of the regional playhouses and of the many cafe and street theaters that abounded in New York.

Off-Broadway served to introduce several new playwrights of interest. Chief among them, undoubtedly, was Edward Albee whose short plays *The Zoo Story, The American Dream,* and *The Death of Bessie Smith* attracted much praise and attention. His full-length *Who's Afraid of Virginia Woolf?* produced later

411

on Broadway was an enormous critical and popular success. Frank Gilroy, whose prize-winning *The Subject Was Roses* was produced on Broadway later in the decade, was first hailed for his infinitely superior play *Who'll Save the Plowboy?* produced Off-Broadway. Murray Schisgal's short comedies *The Typists* and *The Tiger* displayed an original humorous gift, realized more evidently in his subsequent play *Luv.* Jack Richardson, Oliver Hailey, Lonne Elder 3rd, Charles Gordone, Paul Zindel, John Guare, and Jean-Claude Van Itallie all displayed skill and some hope for the future of American playwriting. Mart Crowley's immensely clever *The Boys in the Band* showed impressive talent; this frank play about homosexuality reflected a new freedom and a changed morality in the contemporary theater. The regional theaters, which had recently sprung up all over the country, nurtured such productions as Howard Sackler's *The Great White Hope* and *Indians* by Arthur Kopit, who had first attracted attention Off-Broadway with his bizarre play *Oh Dad, Poor Dad, Mamma's Hung You in the Closet and I'm Feeling So Sad.* Broadway was less receptive to new playwrights, but James Goldman's *The Lion in Winter* and Herb Gardner's *A Thousand Clowns* aroused interest. In Neil Simon, Broadway found its most commercially viable playwright since George S. Kaufman. In play after play, from *Come Blow Your Horn* in 1961 to *Last of the Red Hot Lovers* in 1969, Simon seemed to have conceived a precise and infallible formula for commercial success. His detractors called him a "joke-machine"; his admirers called him America's greatest comic dramatist. Often wonderfully funny, his plays immeasurably enlivened a decade which was sadly deficient in humor.

Some of the more memorable events, both on and Off-Broadway, were plays and productions of foreign origin. Harold Pinter, the most highly-acclaimed of the new playwrights, was represented chiefly by *The Caretaker* and *The Homecoming.* The gifted Joe Orton was perhaps too alien and grotesque for American audiences, and his striking plays *Loot* and *Entertaining Mr. Sloane* had only brief runs. Samuel Beckett's *Krapp's Last Tape* and *Happy Days,* Ionesco's *Rhinoceros* and *Exit the King,* and Brecht's *Arturo Ui, Baal, Mother Courage,* and *Galileo* met with varying degrees of success with the press and the public, but all

gave depth and quality to the decade. One of the most spectacular events of the sixties was The Royal Shakespeare Company in Peter Brook's production of *Marat/Sade* by Peter Weiss.
England seemed to have an inexhaustable supply of new and
accomplished playwrights; the New York theater was introduced
to such talents as John Arden, John Whiting, David Storey,
Robert Bolt, Peter Shaffer, and Tom Stoppard, who was greatly
admired for his *Rosencrantz and Guildenstern are Dead;* nor
can one overlook Peter Nichols and his mordantly funny *Joe Egg*
or Frank Marcus who benefited by the new permissiveness with
his play about lesbian rivalry, *The Killing of Sister George.* Other
memorable events from abroad included appearances by the
thrilling Kabuki Theatre from Japan, Franco Zeffirelli's inspired
production of *Romeo and Juliet,* Paul Scofield's Lear in Peter
Brook's controversial production, and the unique presentations
of Jerzy Grotowski.

The decade also saw the formation of several adventurous
theatrical organizations. The Repertory Theater of Lincoln Center opened in a temporary structure in Greenwich Village with
Miller's *After the Fall;* after several productions downtown, the
organization moved to its new headquarters in Lincoln Center
with a production of *Danton's Death* in 1965 and has been active
there to the present day. The Actors' Studio produced notable
revivals of O'Neill's *Strange Interlude* and Chekhov's *The Three
Sisters,* in which Kim Stanley gave an outstanding performance.
The APA, under the direction of Ellis Rabb, arrived in New
York in 1962 and continued throughout the remainder of the
decade to produce worthwhile, and sometimes superlative, productions which garnered much praise; helped immeasurably by
the presence of the splendid Rosemary Harris, it became the
most successful repertory troupe to function in New York since
the days of Eva Le Gallienne's Civic Repertory Company.

During the decade other less conventional and more innovative
organizations were formed such as The Negro Ensemble Company, which introduced the promising *Ceremonies in Dark Old
Men;* Joseph Chaikin's The Open Theatre, with its novel productions of *The Serpent* and *Terminal;* Ellen Stewart's Café La
Mama, home of countless experimental works; The American
Place Theatre, which presented, among other works, Robert

Lowell's *The Old Glory* and William Alfred's *Hogan's Goat;* and the ever expanding New York Shakespeare Festival Public Theatre under the direction of Joseph Papp.

Several newcomers, in both the dramatic and musical fields, showed enormous promise and talent while the more established actors continued from time to time to enrich our stage with their ability and presence. The decade introduced to prominence such skillful and effective players as Sandy Dennis, Barbara Harris, Alan Arkin, Liza Minnelli, Brenda Vaccaro, Diana Sands, Robert Redford, Alan Alda, Zoe Caldwell, and the incredible Barbra Streisand. Unfortunately, virtually all of these promising talents soon deserted the stage for films and television. After years of work in regional theaters and Off-Broadway productions, Sada Thompson and James Earl Jones won unanimous praise for their appearances in, respectively, *The Effect of Gamma Rays on Man-in-the-Moon Marigolds* and *The Great White Hope*. In 1960, Tammy Grimes achieved stardom as the unsinkable Molly Brown, and at the end of the decade — partnered by the equally brilliant Brian Bedford — restored the art of high-comedy acting to Broadway in a revival of Noel Coward's *Private Lives*. The decade also offered many opportunities to two leading actresses of their generation, Julie Harris and Maureen Stapleton, while Katharine Cornell, one of the handful of great stars to have survived from the twenties, brought her radiance to *Dear Liar* in 1960 and then retired from the stage she had served so well.

The musical theater continued to add to the pleasures of theatre-goers. Frank Loesser's rollicking *How to Succeed in Business Without Really Trying* brought stardom to Robert Morse while Lerner and Loewe's *Camelot* introduced Robert Goulet to New York and elicited splendid performances from Richard Burton and Julie Andrews. Zero Mostel won high praise for his performances in *A Funny Thing Happened on the Way to the Forum* and as the first Tevye in the longest-run musical in New York theatrical history, *Fiddler on the Roof*. The decade also welcomed the Gower Champion production of Jerry Herman's *Hello, Dolly!* with the incomparable Carol Channing as the first of an endless stream of Dollys; later the role would also be assumed most memorably by Pearl Bailey and Ethel Merman. Richard Kiley triumphed as Don Quixote in *Man of La Mancha* as did Angela Lansbury in both *Mame* and *Dear World.* Gwen Verdon delighted her admirers in *Sweet Charity,* and Mary Martin and Robert Preston exhibited the full force and command of the star-personality in the two-character *I Do, I Do.* Two celebrated stars, Katharine Hepburn and Lauren Bacall, appeared for the first time on the musical stage and both emerged unscathed and triumphant. Harold Prince's exemplary direction of *Cabaret* (in which Joel Grey and Lotte Lenya were unforgettable) and *Company,* earned high praise; Stephen Sondheim's witty and abrasive score for *Company* was also generally lauded. To many, the musical event of the decade was the dawning of the Age of Aquarius as trumpeted in *Hair;* to others, the high spot of the period was the license and licentiousness of *Oh! Calcutta!,* heralding a new freedom on the legitimate stage.

The period of 1960-1970 was one of change and transition, a difficult and troubled time for the theater. Seventy-three reviews have been selected to represent these years.

1960 - 1970

KRAPP'S LAST TAPE and THE ZOO STORY, a bill of short plays. The former was written by Samuel Beckett and directed by Alan Schneider; the latter is the work of Edward Albee, its director is Milton Katselas and scenery and lighting were provided by William Ritman. Presented by Theatre 1960 (Richard Barr., H. B. Lutz and Harry Joe Brown Jr.); assistant to producers, Jeremiah O'Connell; stage manager, Mark Wright. At the Provincetown Playhouse, 133 Macdougal Street.

KRAPP'S LAST TAPE
Krapp ....Donald Davis
and
THE ZOO STORY
Jerry ....George Maharis
Peter ....William Daniels

By BROOKS ATKINSON

AFTER the banalities of Broadway it tones the muscles and freshens the system to examine the squalor of Off Broadway.

Donald Davis

Three actors suffice for the two short plays put on at the Provincetown Playhouse last evening. Samuel Beckett's "Krapp's Last Tape" makes do with one actor — Donald Davis from the Crest Theatre in Toronto. Edward Albee's "The Zoo Story" needs two— George Maharis and William Daniels.

Both plays are dialogues. Both plays are interesting, and both of them are well acted by intelligent professionals. Nothing of enduring value is said in either play. But each of them captures some part of the dismal mood that infects many writers today.

•

"Krapp's Last Tape" takes a wistful look back into the memories of an aging, creaking curmudgeon. All that happens really is that Krapp listens to a tape record of an idyllic day in his youth. But that is all Mr. Beckett needs. For he has a highly original sense of the grotesque comedy of life. Although Krapp looks like a Skid Row veteran he is the relic of an exultant writer; and everything Mr. Beckett says is a grim criticism of life.

•

Having once studied the sullen method of "Endgame," Alan Schneider is the perfect director for "Krapp's Last Tape." The scenery consists of a morose library table and chair, an ugly lamp and a messy array of cartons—disorder incarnate. As Krapp, Mr. Davis has very little to say and do. But he makes every movement significant and every line caustic. The whole portrait is wonderfully alive. If "Krapp's Last Tape" is a joke, the joke is not on Mr. Beckett.

•

Mr. Albee's "The Zoo Story" does not have so much literary distinction. Mr. Beckett has a terrifying sense of the mystery of life. Mr. Albee is more the reporter. There are two characters and two benches in his play set in Central Park. A cultivated, complacent publisher is reading a book. An intense, aggressive young man in shabby dress strikes up a conversation with him.

Or, to be exact, a monologue. For the intruder wants to unburden his mind of his private miseries and resentments, and they pour out of him in a flow of wild, scabrous, psychotic details. Since Mr. Albee is an excellent writer and designer of dialogue and since he apparently knows the city, "The Zoo Story" is consistently interesting and illuminating—odd and pithy. It ends melodramatically as if Mr. Albee had lost control of his material. Although the conclusion is theatrical, it lacks the sense of improvisation that characterizes the main body of the play.

•

Milton Katselas has staged "The Zoo Story" admirably; and Mr. Maharis' overwrought yet searching intruder, and Mr. Daniels' perplexed publisher are first-rate pieces of acting.

Although the Provincetown bill is hardly glamorous, it has a point of view. Both Mr. Beckett and Mr. Albee write on the assumption that the human condition is stupid and ludicrous.

1960, Ja 15

Work by Genet Opens at Circle in Square

THE BALCONY, a drama from the French of Jean Genet as translated by Bernard Frechtman. Staged by Jose Quintero; produced by Lucille Lortel and Circle in the Square; scenery and lighting by David Hays; costumes by Patricia Zipprodt; stage manager, Thomas Burrows. At Circle in the Square, 159 Bleecker Street.

The Bishop	F. M. Kimball
Irma	Nancy Marchand
Penitent	Grayson Hall
The Thief	Sylvia Miles
The Judge	Arthur Malet
The Executioner	John Perkins
The General	John S. Dodson
The Girl	Salome Jens
Carmen	Betty Miller
The Chief of Police	Roy Poole
The Envoy	Jock Livingston
Roger	Joseph Daubenas
The Slave	William Goodwin

By BROOKS ATKINSON

DON'T expect in this column a rational explanation of Jean Genet's "The Balcony," which opened last evening at the new Circle in the Square, 159 Bleecker Street. It would have to be understood to be explained.

Salome Jens as the Pony Girl, in "The Balcony."

But thanks to José Quintero's subtle and ingenious direction, it is as absorbing as a blending of a modernistic ballet and painting would be. The Balcony of the title is a brothel—the theatre's favorite institution this year. But it is a brothel that has symbolic rather than carnal significance.

•

It is a house of illusions. The patrons come there to impersonate their dreams; one to act the part of a bishop, another a judge, another a general. Since the patrons wear gigantic costumes and shoes with thick soles, they become grotesque images who tower above the level of human beings. In Mr. Quintero's staging, this part of the play is like a black masquerade of obsessed people.

After the preliminary scenes, "The Balcony" extends beyond the specific into a simile of modern life. In M. Genet's view, the whole of life is an illusion; all its people impersonate their dreams. Outside the Balcony, a revolution is going on. The sound of machine-guns comes from the streets. The Chief of Police, who represents the power of the state, visits the brothel, which is one of his perquisites, and discusses the progress of the revolution with the madame.

•

The symbolism becomes importunate in this portion of the play. Those who have been impersonating characters in the brothel now attempt to act the same parts in real life, and the madame becomes the queen of the new, unestablished state. But this is the part of "The Balcony" that becomes a riddle wrapped in an enigma. The double images acquire new significance. Everything means more than the author or the characters say.

Only a mechanical computer could absorb all the meanings and tick out the correct answers. Perhaps Mr. Quintero has already consulted the modern oracle. For his production has a certainty of outline and accent that makes everything look plausible, as if "The Balcony" were living a private life according to its own rationale.

In the first place, the stage and its décor look like a rummage sale of toys—gaudy costumes, store-window dummies hanging in a circle around the ceiling, a platform with a monstrous throne chair pushed on and off to stage M. Genet's macabre revels, spectral lighting spots, the whole paraphernalia of a ghoulish dream.

•

In the second place, the acting is an exercise in incantations—Nancy Marchant, cold and austere as the madame; Salome Jens, like a dancer of the damned as a girl who impersonates a pony; Roy Poole, brutish and shrewd as the chief of police; Betty Miller, sad and servile as madame's secretary; F. M. Kimball, Arthur Malet and John S. Dodson as weak and desperate men who impersonate men of settled affairs.

Apart from being elusive, "The Balcony" is full of a destructive sickness that infects the whole of M. Genet's empire of wraiths and demons. It also provides the materials for one of Mr. Quintero's most imaginative productions —a travesty on reality, a withering of dreams.

1960 Mr 4

THE FANTASTICKS, a musical suggested by Edmond Rostand's "Les Romantiques." Book and lyrics by Tom Jones. Music by Harvey Schmidt. Directed by Word Baker; presented by Lore Noto; associate producers, Shelly Baron, Dorothy Olim and Robert Alan Gold; musical direction and arrangements by Julian Stein; production designed by Ed Wittstein; production stage manager, Geoffry Brown. At the Sullivan Street Playhouse, 181 Sullivan Street.
Narrator.................. Jerry Orbach
Girl..................... Rita Gardner
Boy.................... Kenneth Nelson
Boy's Father...........William Larsen
Girl's Father.............Hugh Thomas
Actor.................... Thomas Bruce
Man Who Dies...........George Curley
Mute.................. Richard Stauffer
Handyman................ Jay Hampton
At the piano, Julian Stein; at the harp, Beverly Mann.

By BROOKS ATKINSON

HAVING won a lot of admirers with a short version of "The Fantasticks," Tom Jones has expanded it for the production that opened at the Sullivan Street Playhouse last evening.

Although it is ungrateful to say so, two acts are one too many to sustain the de-

Rita Gardner

lightful tone of the first. After the intermission, the mood is never quite so luminous and gay.

The remark is ungrateful because the form of a masque seems original in the modern theatre. Harvey Schmidt's simple melodies with uncomplicated orchestrations are captivating and the acting is charming. Throughout the first act "The Fantasticks" is sweet and fresh in a civilized manner.

•

According to the program, it is based on Rostand's "Les Romantiques." In the form of a dainty masque, designed in modern taste by Ed Wittstein, it is a variation on a Pierrot and Columbine theme. A boy and a girl, who are neighbors, are in love as long as a wall separates them and they believe that their fathers disapprove. Actually, their fathers want them to marry. To create an irresistible romantic mood, the fathers arrange a flamboyant abduction scene in the moonlight.

Although the story is slight, the style is entrancing in Word Baker's staging. It seems like a narlequinade in the setting of a masque. The characters are figures in a legend, acted with an artless-

ness that is winning. As the Narrator, the Girl and the Boy, Jerry Orbach, Rita Gardner and Kenneth Nelson, respectively, sing beautifully and act with spontaneity, not forgetting that they are participating in a work of make-believe.

•

After the intermission the author substitutes sunshine for moonlight. Disillusion destroys the rapture of the introductory scene. Pierrot and Columbine have combed the stardust out of their hair. But it seems to this theatregoer that the second act loses the skimming touch of the first. As an aging ham actor, Thomas Bruce is not so funny as he is in his first appearance, and the conceits of the staging become repetitious.

Perhaps "The Fantasticks" is by nature the sort of thing that loses magic the longer it endures. Any sign of effort diminishes it. But for the space of one act it is delightful. The music, played on piano and harp, has grace and humor. All the actors are thoroughbreds.

1960 My 4

GRAND KABUKI in a program of three short Japanese plays. Presented by the City Center of Music and Drama in association with the Greek Theatre (Los Angeles). Sponsored by the Society for International Cultural Relations and the Japan Society (New York). At the City Center, 131 West Fifty-fifth Street.
MUSUME DOJOJI
(The Maiden at the Dojo Temple)
The Maiden.....Nakamura Utaemon VI
Priests.Nakamura Kichijuro, Nakamura Kosanza, Nakamura Tokicho, Nakamura Senya, Nakamura Nakanosuke, Nakamura Nakasuke, Onoe Senroku, Onoe Karoku, Bando Yaenosuke.
CHUSHINGURA
(The Forty-seven Ronin)
Kono Moronao,
Oboshi Yuranosuke ..Onoe Shoroku II
Enya Hangan.Nakamura Kanzaburo XVII
Kaoyo ....Nakamura Utaemon VI
Momonoi Wakasanosuke,
Ishido Umanojo ..Nakamura Matagoro
Yakushiji Jirozaemon...Onoe Kuroemon
Oboshi Rikiya ....Nakamura Tokizo
Tadayoshi ....Ichimura Kakitsu
Sagisaka Bannai ...Nakamura Kichijuro
Kakogawa Honzo.........Kagaya Utazo
MIGAWARI ZAZEN
(The Substitute)
Yamakage...Nakamura Kanzaburo XVII
Taro ....Nakamura Matagoro
Tamanoi ....Onoe Shoroku II
Chieda ....Nakamura Tokizo
Saeda ....Ichimura Kakitsu

By BROOKS ATKINSON

GRAND KABUKI is what they call it. On the basis of the second play in last evening's bill at the City Center, they are entitled to the adjective.

The play is "Chushingura," which dramatizes a historical occurrence and derives from a puppet play of 1748. According to the Halfords' "Kabuki Handbook" it is the most popular play in the traditional repertory.

Even with the aid of the transistor simultaneous translation and the ample program notes, a theatregoer ignorant of Japanese may find himself losing his place as the story slowly unfolds. The situation is further complicated by the fact that Onoe Shoroku II plays two of the leading parts.

•

But all that probably matters is that he plays the second one with deliberate magnificence—the pace slow, the content of the scenes spare, but the quality of the acting exalted. It belongs in the royal line of theatre.

"Chushingura" appears to be a long drama in many scenes. For purposes of this visit, the Kabuki troupe has reduced it to a work of about an hour, and the central play in a bill of three. As a spectacle it is blazing with color and splendor. The costumes and the formal groups are imposing. Although Kabuki is an ancient style of theatre, the settings are elaborate in a formalized modern manner. Two of the most imposing are swung around on a revolving stage with a grandiloquent theatrical gesture.

•

In the second half of the play, one of the governor's deputies, played by Nakamura Kanzaburo XVII, is ordered to disembowel himself for having raised his sword in the palace. Our theatre could get through a scene like this in a couple of sanguinary moments. In the Kabuki play, it takes fifteen or twenty moments, most of which are statuesque and silent.

But thanks to the pride of Kanzaburo's acting and the decorum of the ritual, the scene is almost unbearably dramatic. The disemboweling consists of a few gestures amid long silences. Kabuki spares us the blood and the morbid details. But the effect is both admirable and overwhelming.

Then comes Shoroku's great scene. He is a samurai in the household of the doomed deputy. He does not arrive until the disemboweling has begun; he is too late to attend upon his leader. All he does in essence is to express in pantomime dismay, loyalty, grief and determination to secure revenge. He says almost nothing. Even that is in a language most of us do not understand. But the grandeur of his acting makes everything he does eloquent and noble. Wonderful acting!

The first play on the bill is "Musume Dojoji"—adapted from a Noh play and first performed in 1753. Essentially it is a ballet performance by Nakamura Utaemon VI, the male actor who plays the leading female roles in this troupe. To gain entrance to the courtyard of a temple, a girl dances for the priests.

It is pure fairy story, but done with extraordinary beauty. The seven costumes Utaemon wears in succession are gorgeous in color combinations and patterns beyond belief in our sedate society. And the liquefaction of Utaemon's dancing is also beyond belief—an intricate series of neck, wrist and body movements, all artifice and all beauty.

Unfortunately, your correspondent could not wait for the final play—"Migawari Zazen," derived also from Noh drama, and apparently a comedy of infidelity and intrigue. But the first two plays are distinguished enough to confirm last weeks' impression that Kabuki is grand in fact as well as title.

1960 Je 10

THE HOSTAGE, a drama by Brendan Behan. Staged by Joan Littlewood; presented by Leonard S. Field and Caroline Burke Swann; designed and lighted by Frederick Fox; costumes designed by Margaret Bury and supervised by Mr. Fox; production manager, William Ross; production stage manager, Perry Bruskin. At the Cort Theatre, 138 West Forty-eighth Street.

Pat	Maxwell Shaw
Meg Dillon	Avis Bunnage
Monsewer	Glynn Edwards
Old Ropeen	Leila Greenwood
Colette	Anita Dangler
Princess Grace	Melvita Stewart
Rio Rita	Dudley Sutton
Mr. Mulleady	Aubrey Morris
Miss Gilchrist	Patience Collier
Leslie	Alfred Lynch
Teresa	Celia Salkeld
I. R. A. Officer	Victor Spinetti
Volunteer	Michael Forrest
Russian Sailor	Metro Welles
Kate	Kathleen O'Connor

By HOWARD TAUBMAN

"THE HOSTAGE" is a grab bag of wonderful and dreadful prizes. Brendan Behan's theatrical concoction, which opened last night at the Cort, mixes irreverent hilarity with tasteless rubbish.

Organized chaos is the handiest description for "The Hostage." One calls it organized because Mr. Behan claims authorship, Joan Littlewood is identified as the director and even the improvisations are carefully encouraged, if not planned.

The evening is like a wild one in a combination saloon and bawdy house. The inmates are capable of richly amusing observations and unalleviated dullness. They sing and dance and have fun, occasionally sharing that precious commodity with the public. Vive le sport!

•

Mr. Behan is a man of immense talent, but in "The Hostage" he seems to spew on it more often than use it with purpose. If he were really not serious about anything, he might be excused for being so cavalier with his gifts. But even in this undisciplined invention, he reveals a flair for drama and a determination to communicate something.

Being an expansive Irishman—and a rebellious and imaginative one—Mr. Behan refuses to be confined within the bounds of traditional dramaturgy. That is his privilege. He wishes his stage to erupt in unexpected ways, and it does. He likes the performers to express enjoyment, and they do. But there is a limit to being uninhibited; one can overlook bad taste but not flat gibes.

There is a bit of a story in "The Hostage." It deals with an English soldier who is held in a low Dublin house as hostage for a young Irish patriot about to be executed by the British in Belfast. He is befriended by an Irish country girl. There are several scenes when, forgetting to be playful, Mr. Behan treats these two like touching human beings.

But the plot is a fragile thread on which Mr. Behan and the director string verbal jokes, sight gags, vaudeville turns and sardonic observations on politics, morals, international relations and human pretensions. If Mr. Behan gives the English a combing, he does not exactly soothe Irish sensibilities. He tries to keep the buffoonery going like a whirligig, and not even he can manage it for three acts.

There are, of course, some splendid hits in the course of this fusillade, and they are balanced by embarrassing misses. The notion of incorporating allusions to local phenomena like Tim Costello's or the IRT belong to the misses. The mock sentimentality of the songs, which break out periodically, ranks with the hits. So does the remark of Pat, a disenchanted Irish patriot, that the worst thing he encountered in prison was the other Irish heroes.

•

Any sort of foolishness goes, and some of it is funny. There is the moment when the audience is roaring at one of Mr. Behan's sallies, and the actor playing an I. R. A. officer steps forward, glares at the customers and shouts, "Silence! This is a serious play." But as you laugh you recall earlier passages devoted to obscenities that could not be amusing even to a man in his cups.

Miss Littlewood's direction seeks to capture Mr. Behan's

improvisatory mood inside Frederick Fox' diverting set. She manages the rum set of characters with a good deal of theatrical fancy. She has an abundance of fresh ideas, some excellent and some in poor taste. Like Mr. Behan's writing, her staging would not be harmed by discipline.

●

The cast is drawn largely from Miss Littlewood's Theatre Workshop in London, which has been a lively force in the British theatre. Alfred Lynch has a rough, boyish charm as the hostage, and Celia Salkeld is appealing as the country girl. Among the

Celia Salkeld and Alfred Lynch in scene from Brendan Behan's "The Hostage."

others who go through Mr. Behan's paces like cheerful troupers are Maxwell Shaw, Avis Bunnage, Glynn Edwards, Aubrey Morris, Patience Collier and Victor Spinetti.

Mr. Behan is an original, and so is "The Hostage." If you are willing to shuttle madly between delight and distaste, you might try dancing to Mr. Behan's Irish jig.

1960 S 21

Laurence Olivier Stars in Anouilh Version

The Cast

BECKET, a dramatic spectacle, by Jean Anouilh, translated by Lucienne Hill. Directed by Peter Glenville; presented by David Merrick; scenery by Oliver Smith; lighting by Jean Rosenthal; costumes by Motley; music by Laurence Rosenthal; production stage manager, Lucia Victor. At the St. James Theatre, 246 West Forty-fourth Street.

Henry II................Anthony Quinn
Thomas Becket........Laurence Olivier
Archbishop of Canterbury..Sydney Walker
Gilbert Folliot........Earl Montgomery
Bishop of York.........Victor Thorley
Saxon Peasant.............Robert Weil
His Son...........................Tom Leith
Gwendolen ....Dran Seitz
1st English Baron..........Louis Zorich
2d English Baron.......Ronald Weyand
3d English Baron.......Mel Berger
4th English Baron........Ferdi Hoffman
Queen Mother.............Marie Powers
The Queen.................Margaret Hall
Louis, King of France....Robert Eckles
The Pope..............Edward Atienza

By HOWARD TAUBMAN

LIKE so much of the serious theatre in France, the appeal of Jean Anouilh's "Becket" is to the intellect. It also allows for the splendor of pageantry. As it is being presented at the St. James, where it opened last night, the eye is diverted and the mind stimulated. But the heart is not often stirred.

M. Anouilh writes in the tradition of historical drama. Employing a diversity of scenes, he allows himself generous time to develop his story. Indeed, unless one is gravely mistaken, the version presented here in Lucienne Hill's translation is not nearly so extended as the production that was visible in Paris last spring. Even as it stands, it is long enough.

•

Mr. Anouilh is a subtle, witty, sardonic writer. "Becket" abounds in felicities of phrase. In dealing with the love-hate relationship of a king (Henry II of England) and a courtier who became Archbishop of Canterbury (Becket), he has the vast sweep of church and state on which to comment, and he makes frequent and happy use of his opportunities.

When the king's mother hears that Becket, whom she loathes, is selling his gold and wearing homespun, she observes, "I see that as ostentation." Becket himself declares that "the temptation of saintliness is one of the most insidious snares the church can lay for its priests." Later Becket, determined to leave a Cistercian retreat in France and to dare a return to England, speaks ironically of the hair shirt as "an object of so

Laurence Olivier

much vapid self-congratulation."

Being a shrewd man of the

theatre, M. Anouilh knows how to create effective scenes. There are some impressive ones in "Becket," humorous, derisive, colorful and eloquent. The last meeting of the king and Becket is one of the finest —controlled and yet cumulative in its power. The brief dialogue between the Pope and one of his Cardinals is a mordant attack on the maneuverings of Italians in the church. The encounter between Becket and King Louis of France is full of sharp observation on the art of royal politicking.

•

M. Anouilh's essential theme—the portrayal of a life that ends by championing the honor of God, no matter what the cost — has nobility and exaltation. The trouble is with a pivotal character, Becket himself. He is shown in his progress from the days of heedless life at court to his martyrdom; he is provided with stirring words. But he is not humanized; he remains a remote figure, whether charming or saintly.

The playwright may be sound in his view of Becket's psychology, as may be his estimate of this fifteen-year period of twelfth-century history. But if Mr. Anouilh's notion is right that Becket could love nothing except the honor of God, he has committed himself to a grave dramatic weakness. There is no surprise in this Becket. One always knows that this Becket will be faithful to his duty, whatever shape it takes.

•

M. Anouilh is much more successful with King Henry. At the outset he is a rough, pleasure-loving man who needs Becket as companion and counselor. He rejoices in Becket's acumen and, high spirits. And when Becket as Archbishop turns on him to serve God, the king achieves a bitter maturity.

A role like Becket has obvious attractions for an actor like Laurence Olivier, who has never stood still. He plays the part with admirable scope. The courtier is limned with elegance and spirit; the man of God has dedicated simplicity and sad, consoling wisdom. Mr. Olivier's performance almost creates the illusion that M. Anouilh has penetrated the character of Becket.

In the early sections of the play Anthony Quinn, as King Henry, is a disappointment. His voice is limited and his acting style uninflected. The King may be loutish but he is not a party to a TV Western. Fortunately, Mr. Quinn rises to the challenge of the later Henry, and his playing of the most interesting role in "Becket" becomes worthy of its possibilities.

There are good performances by Robert Eckles as the suave King Louis, Tom Leith as a peasant boy, Dran Seitz as Becket's lovely Welsh mistress, Earl Montgomery as the Norman Bishop of London, Marie Powers as the Queen Mother and Margaret Hall as the Queen.

Peter Glenville's staging takes full advantage of the intellectual sparkle as well as the opportunities for pageantry. Oliver Smith's sets, Motley's costumes, Jean Rosenthal's lighting and Laurence Rosenthal's music contribute to the picturesque production.

Out of his imagination M. Anouilh has reconstructed a vision of a stirring epoch in history. But despite his theatricalism and esprit, he has not captured its human essence.

1960 O 6

AN EVENING WITH MIKE NICHOLS and ELAINE MAY, a show with two performers, with material written by them. Staged by Arthur Penn; assistant to Mr. Penn, Gene Laske; presented by Alexander H. Cohen; associate producer, Peter S. Katz; scenery by Marvin Reiss; music by William Goldenberg; costumes by Hazel Roy; production stage manager, Joseph Brownstone; production assistant, Annette Segal. At the John Golden Theatre, 252 West Forty-fifth Street. PRINCIPALS: Mike Nichols and Elaine May.

By HOWARD TAUBMAN

CALL it the Nichols-May Law: The lower the pressure on the stage the higher the content of comfortable laughter in the audience.

"An Evening With Mike Nichols and Elaine May," which came to the John Golden on Saturday night as the second attraction of the Nine O'Clock Theatre, is one of recognition. The material derives from common problems and recurrent foibles. Without overpowering you it sneaks under your guard. It is full of casual surprises and unexpected chuckles because Miss May and Mr. Nichols combine perception with an air of genial relaxation.

•

The program is announced as it goes along. The stuff, as Miss May remarks, comes out of improvisation. It is most disarming when the small frustrations, like a man contending on the phone with an operator, supervisor and managing supervisor, reflect the maddening hazards we are all heir to. Then Miss May and Mr. Nichols hold up the mirror to nature with good-humored steadiness.

The improvisatory manner is admirable so long as one is unaware of its mechanism. In certain places, not merely those at the end where the performers frankly improvise with the help of the audience, the technique shows. Sketches are becalmed for moments as if Miss May or Mr. Nichols seem to be reaching for the next move. Such hesitations are discomfiting: they rob a scene and its characters of definition; they give professional work an amateurish vagueness.

At their best, however, the May-Nichols team is choice. Its distillation of a P.T.A. "fun night" is extensive but one would not forfeit its archest glance or most pregnant pause. Wearing a shapeless black felt hat, a matronly suit, a saccharine smile, and a huge yellow chrysanthemum that sheds leaves as if it were a bird in the moulting season, Miss May seats herself at a table flanked by flags. She is earnest and confiding, businesslike and coy;

without apparent malice, she atomizes the chairlady.

Mr. Nichols then comes on, introduced as the evening's speaker, "Mr. **Alabama** Glass," the Southern playwright. Using a high-pitched voice and a magnolia-scented accent, he explains his new play. If a certain school of writers feels its ears tingling unpleasantly this morning, it now knows why.

The preponderance of what the team does is amusing. The opening, which deserves to retain its surprise effect, sets a relaxed mood. Impressions of American, English and French couples on the verge of adultery have comic contrast. A long - distance chat between a smothering mother and a son on the defensive has an edge. So has the broadcast interview with a starlet plugging a new film and dumbly ready to help her interlocutor chat about Bernie (Baruch) and Al (Schweitzer).

A long take-off on Pirandello is the flattest number in the show. And a scene devoted to a pair of teenagers smooching in the back seat of a car is both hilarious and painful. The contortions that Miss May and Mr. Nichols go through while locked in an endless embrace during which they seek to manage the lighted cigarettes in their hands are as funny as anything on Broadway. But the sketch loses its sharpness because its pace is disturbed by those improvisatory pauses.

●

The May-Nichols duo has not relied merely on the inspiration of the moment for its Broadway appearance. Arthur Penn has helped with direction; Marvin Reiss and Hazel Roy have provided unpretentious sets and costumes. William Goldenberg has composed some music, though there is none on the stage.

In the full sense of the phrase, this is an evening with Mike Nichols and Elaine May. They are attractive comedians whose years in

night clubs have not given them a hard sheen. They are sustaining their law: You can entertain people without beating them into submission.

1960 O 10

1961

Ionesco Comedy Stars
Wallach and Mostel

RHINOCEROS, a play by Eugene Ionesco, translated by Derek Prouse. Staged by Joseph Anthony; presented by Leo Kerz, in association with Seven Arts Associates Corporation; costumes by Michael Travis; scenery and lighting by Mr. Kerz; production stage manager, Bill Ross; sound engineer d by Saki Oura. At the Longacre Theatre, 220 West Forty-eighth Street.

Waitress	Flora Elkins
Logician	Morris Carnovsky
Grocer	Dolph Sweet
Grocer's Wife	Lucille Patton
Housewife	Jane Hoffman
Berrenger	Eli Wallach
John	Zero Mostel
Old Gentleman	Leslie Barrett
Cafe Proprietor	Joseph Bernard
Daisy	Anne Jackson
Mr. Nicklebush	Philip Coolidge
Dribble	Mike Kellin
Shiftor	Michael Strong
Mrs. Ochs	Jean Stapleton
Fireman	Dolph Sweet

By HOWARD TAUBMAN

DON'T look now, but those creatures throwing up dust and trumpeting primitively may be rhinoceroses debouching from the Longacre Theatre. Or better still, look and listen, for they are comic and they are serious, too.

They come from the vivid imagination of Eugene Ionesco and they inhabit his play, "Rhinoceros," which opened here last night. It is an antic piece with overtones of gravity. And it has been staged and performed with a mad, inventive gusto that never loses sight of the important things behind the parody, horseplay and calculated illogicality.

●

In "Rhinoceros," Mr. Ionesco is telling an allegory for our time, which has been beset by various, blighting uniformities. But he is not preaching. Nor is he concerned with the conventions of routine dramatic construction. He pokes fun unremittingly at conventional ideas, established institutions and all sorts of people, including himself. He cavorts and capers. He exaggerates wildly, and lets some of his notions run on too long. But just when he seems to be losing his touch, he discovers a new vein of fun.

Thanks to the play's success in a number of cities abroad, its subject may be familiar. If you have not heard of its contents, they may be summed up quickly. Mr. Ionesco imagines a city in which first one person, then a few, then all but a feckless clerk turn into rhinoceroses. His theme is a single motive,

but he is fertile with delightful variations.

In working out his variations, Mr. Ionesco manages to say a good deal about the inconsistencies and irrationalities of human behavior. He ticks off the logician, the unionist, the straw boss, the ordinary run of men and women. He makes mincemeat of intellectual pretensions and then, of course, laughs at pompous simpletons.

●

Mr. Ionesco's mind is playful, full of quips and wanton wiles. Some of his jokes are obvious, no doubt deliberately. Others stem from a fresh view of the world. Mr. Ionesco has a fondness for the counterpoint of talk. In the first act he builds a pair of overlapping dialogues with a

Zero Mostel, left, Anne Jackson and Eli Wallach in a scene from Ionesco's "Rhinoceros" at Longacre Theatre.

clever orchestrator's ingenuity. Then he follows with a discourse by the logician that is both humorous and satirical. He is not above exchanges that are like Pat-and-Mike bits. Says one character of the office chief: "He turned into a rhinoceros." And the other responds: "He had such a good chance to become a vice president."

Is it Mr. Ionesco's final joke that his last man in a world of rhinoceroses is the weak, ineffectual clerk, Berrenger? If this is the playwright's intention, one cannot cavil. But if his moral is that the meek shall have to redeem the earth from its totalitarian follies, one would disagree violently. It requires courage, will and knowledge to hold fast to individuality—and to fight against mob psychology.

Joseph Anthony has caught Mr. Ionesco's wild, irreverent mood. To one who saw a rather stuffy, subdued version of "Rhinoceros" in London last June, this production was a joyous revelation. The staging here has the knockabout high spirits of Mack Sennett comedy. Indeed, it carries this mood too far at times, settling for noise when ideas run thin. But like Mr. Ionesco's fancy, the staging repeatedly renews itself with fresh inventions.

As Berrenger, Eli Wallach gives a sustained, varied performance that remains in a low key. As his irascible, self-righteous friend John, Zero Mostel is a superb comedian, full of bouncing movement and roaring, cooing inflections. Anne Jackson turns Daisy, the girl Berrenger admires in his modest way, into a broadly stylized ingenue; her comic signature is the familiar gesture of a leg lifted backward archly. Morris Carnovsky, Mike Kellin and Michael Strong contribute soberly droll impersonations.

There are diverting, rowdy bits by Philip Coolidge, Jean Stapleton, Leslie Barrett, Jane Hoffman, Flora Elkins, Lucille Patton, Dolph Sweet and Joseph Bernard. They help to fill Leo Kerz' oddly rakish sets with motion and turmoil.

Mr. Ionesco may be an avant-gardist, but there is nothing recherché or difficult about "Rhinoceros." Here he uses lighthearted means to remind human beings how easily they can turn beastly.

1961 Ja 10

Jean Kerr's 'Mary, Mary' in Premiere

By HOWARD TAUBMAN

IN "Mary, Mary" Jean Kerr has thrown together a confection that makes one think of sugar and spice. The sugar sums up a syrupy plot that would fit neatly into the glossy pages of a woman's magazine, and the spice is a generous sprinkling of bright, impertinent lines.

Mrs. Kerr, who has won national celebrity as a humorous writer, does not let her public down in the new comedy that opened last night at the Helen Hayes Theatre. Her mind is agile, her observation of the small frailties of people is sharp and her skill at coining a lively phrase is sure. But her people are rarely more than actors reciting amusing lines, and their problems remind one of what is described politely in publishing circles as summer reading.

●

Mrs. Kerr's story has a mild, pleasant surface quality. Its conflict is modest and its outcome predictable. It follows the formulas of polite comedy, and it even attempts to probe quietly into the forces that make several of the characters what they are. It will not grip you with excitement, and it will drift from your mind as you leave the theatre. But it will give you some occasion to smile and to laugh.

Barbara Bel Geddes as she appears in "Mary, Mary."

The Cast

MARY, MARY, a comedy by Jean Kerr. Staged by Joseph Anthony; produced by Roger L. Stevens; associate producer, Lyn Austin; scenery by Oliver Smith; costumes by Theoni V. Aldredge; lighting by Peggy Clark; general stage manager, Bill Ross; women's hair styles by Kenneth at Lilly Dache. At the Helen Hayes Theatre Forty-sixth Street west of Broadway.
Bob McKellaway .... Barry Nelson
Tiffany Richards. .Betsy von Furstenberg
Oscar Nelson............. John Cromwell
Dirk Winsten............. Michael Rennie
Mary McKellaway .Barbara Bel Geddes

You will not be overwhelmed to discover that Mary is contrary and that her trouble is basic insecurity. Seems she had an older sister, a stunner. Oh, the traumatic effect on Mary! In high school she went out for the literary monthly instead of with boys. She learned to compensate for her drabness by being clever.

When we meet her she is as witty as—well, Jean Kerr. She appears at the apartment of her former husband, Bob, because his lawyer has summoned her to help with Bob's sticky tax returns. Their marriage, it seems, foundered on the rocks of Mary's unrelenting sense of humor. The moment she arrives she gives us some excellent samples of it.

It takes Dirk Winsten, a handsome film hero whose star is in decline, to understand Mary. Dirk makes her face up to her secret. He also kisses her and offers her the kind of adoration her practical and obtuse husband has been unable to manage. Just in time, Bob, who has been on the verge of marrying a rich, young health fiend named Tiffany Richards, realizes that he still needs Mary. It will not be killing any suspense to reveal that true love triumphs.

●

Four of the five people in the play take turns at delivering a variety of Mrs. Kerr's cheerful and mocking jests. The humorous pattern is much the same for all. It is a neat pattern, and there is no reason to complain if you do not ask for humor to stem profoundly from character.

Mrs. Kerr is knowledgeable about a lot of things like books, reviewing, magazines, Hollywood. If you are in the know yourself, you will find that some of her sly jokes carry a punch. She has a special gift for making much out of tiny incidents, like the hunt for a cigarette.

She has not been kind to publishers or husbands. Bob, who represents both categories, is a singular opaque citizen. By comparison the film star is an intellectual giant. Bob may be Mrs. Kerr's explanation of what ails the book world. But as in a golden fairy tale the dull-witted prince learns at last how to be rash and gallant and Mary masters her compulsion to be contrary.

Joseph Anthony, who seems to have cornered a large share of Broadway's business, has staged "Mary, Mary" in relaxed, amusing fashion. He makes no effort to turn it into a loud, knockabout affair, which it is not, but he and the actors contrive to make all the humorous points.

Barbara Bel Geddes plays Mary with an agreeably light touch; her quirk of pausing for quick intakes of breath in the midst of phrases, whether a habit or not, seems felicitous here. Michael Rennie gives Dirk suavity and fine timing. Barry Nelson as Bob handles a dense role valiantly. Betsy von Furstenberg as Tiffany and John Cromwell as the lawyer are in the spirit of the piece.

The spirit of "Mary, Mary" is placidly contrary, like the world of nursery rhymes, with a gleaming Broadway packaging to make it modish.

1961 Mr 9

Judy Garland
Attracts Cheering Fans to Carnegie Hall

By LEWIS FUNKE

THE religious ritual of greeting, watching and listening to Judy Garland took place last night in Carnegie Hall. Indeed, what actually was to have been a concert—and was—also turned into something not too remote from a revival meeting.

From the moment Miss Garland came on the stage, a stage, incidentally, on which have trod before her the immortals of music, the cultists were beside themselves. What Rev. Dr. Billy Graham would have given for such a welcome from the faithful!

They were on their feet even before the goddess grabbed the microphone, and by the time she had bestowed the first of those warm smiles, they were applauding

Judy Garland

The Program

JUDY GARLAND in a solo offering. Presented by Freddie Fields and David Begelman; orchestra directed by Mort Lindsay; production stage manager, Verne Alves. At Carnegie Hall, 154 West Fifty-seventh Street.

and screaming "Bravo!" Miss Garland could have probably ended the concert right there and they would still be cheering. The fact is that at least a half dozen times more during the evening the standing ovation, plus the screaming, took place.

Whether or not this sort of unadulterated adulation was warranted is a matter a non-cultist had better not discuss in public. And whether or not so professional a performer as Miss Garland requires the ritual to put her on her mettle is questionable. But on her mettle she was last night as she went through a repertoire of favorites.

Looking trimmer and a good deal more youthful than she has in years, Miss Garland was always in control of herself. She soothed the tender songs as only she knows how to soothe tender songs, and she projected the loud ones with all the vigor at her command. With "Alone To-gether" or "The Man That Got Away" she wove en-chantment. With "San Fran-cisco," "Come Rain or Come Shine" or "I Can't Give You Anything But Love" she whipped the adherents into frenzies of exaltation.

It was, to be truthful, sur-prising that this audience was able to muster the pande-monium it let loose when Miss Garland wound up with "The Trolley Song," "Rock a Bye" and included among her encores "Over the Rainbow" and "Swanee."

Through it all she was the usual Judy, perspiring pro-fusely ("sweat," she said candidly and more earthily), taking the usual sip of water, standing frequently in front of the microphone letting her voice convey her emotions with a minimum of gesture or movement; other times she skipped a bit, sort of dancing lightly with the rhythm, always making her audience feel—as one listener remarked—"as if she's sing-ing just to you."

In any case, one thing is certain: old Carnegie Hall can take it and by this morning everything undoubtedly is serene again on West Fifty-seventh Street.

1961 Ap 24

Play From the French at the St. Marks

THE BLACKS, a play by Jean Genet,
translated by Bernard Frechtman.
Staged by Gene Frankel; presented by
Sidney Bernstein, George Edgar and
Andre Gregory, by arrangement with
Geraldine Lust; scenery by Kim E.
Swados; lighting by Lee Watson;
costumes and masks by Patricia Zip-
prodt; movement by Talley Beatty;
music supervised by Charles Gross;
production associate, Alfred Manacher;
production stage manager, Maxwell
Glanville. At the St. Marks Play-
house, Second Avenue and Eighth
Street.
Archibald Wellington.Roscoe Lee Browne
Deodatus Village.......James Earl Jones
Adelaide Bobo........Cynthia Belgrave
Edgar Alas Newport News..Louis Gossett
Augustus Snow.............Ethel Ayler
Felicity Trollop Pardon....Helen Martin
Stephanie Virtue Diop.....Cicely Tyson
Diouf.........Godfrey M. Cambridge
Missionary.................Lex Monson
Judge...........Raymond St. Jacques
Governor...................Jay J. Riley
Queen.............Maya Angelou Make
Valet................Charles Gordone
Drummer............Charles Campbell

By HOWARD TAUBMAN

IN writing and performance, Jean Genet's "The Blacks" at the St. Marks Playhouse is a brilliantly sardonic and lyrical tone poem for the theatre.

In form, it flows as freely as an improvisation, with fantasy, allegory and intima-tions of reality mingled into a weird, stirring unity. If you like your drama plain and naturalistic, "The Blacks" will leave you unsettled and disoriented. But if you are willing to venture into the diabolical chambers in which the French playwright con-jures up his demons of the imagination, you will encoun-ter one of the most original and stimulating evenings Broadway or Off Broadway has to offer.

If you wish an inkling of what M. Genet is up to, you must know the three sen-tences with which he prefaces his script. In the English of Bernard Frechtman, who has made the excellent transla-tion of "The Blacks," these sentences are:

"One evening an actor asked me to write a play for an all-black cast. But what exactly is a black? First of all, what's his color?"

M. Genet's investigation of the color of black begins where most plays on this burning theme of our time leave off. Using the device of performances within a per-formance, he evokes a group of players involved in a cere-mony. On an upper level of the stage there is a court composed of a queen, valet, missionary, judge and gover-nor. Below them is a group of ordinary mortals who weave in and out of a variety of impersonations that shift subtly and often abruptly.

All the players are dark-skinned. Those of the court wear white masks and for the greater part of the evening they represent the whites, the colonial masters, the domi-nant, superior race. While they roar, preen themselves and ultimately cringe, the illusion of their whiteness is meant to be transparent. By using Negro players in these roles M. Genet adds another level of bitter comment.

The ceremony is a trial for a murder that you eventually discover has not taken place. It occurs before a catafalque that turns out in the end to be merely a white sheet over a pair of chairs that the valet and missionary had complained about missing. But there is no mistaking the fierce motif that courses through M. Genet's furious flights of language encompassing obscenity and purity, violence and tenderness, hatred and love.

•

That motif is the meaning, in all its burden of the past and in the determination that shapes the future, of being a color that happens to be black. "Invent hatred," cries a character early in the drama. A little later comes an invocation to Africa and darkness and the hatred they have engendered. There is a ferociously satirical scene in which the Negroes below recite a "litany of the livid" as the devout in a church might intone the litanies of the Blessed Virgin.

In its conception "The Blacks" calls for an interpretation that summons most of the magic of the theatre but abjures its literalisms. Music including the minuet from "Don Giovanni" and the Dies Irae, the dance from the tribal movements of Africa to the sinuosities the Western world has grafted on it, architectural forms like platforms and curving ramps, acting and speaking that are formal and rhapsodic by turns—all these elements are required by M. Genet.

Gene Frankel has staged a performance that paces M. Genet's theatrical tone poem with humor and passion. The craftsmen and artists who have contributed to this interpretation deserve their meed of credit. So do the actors, who bring vibrancy and intensity to their performances. Read the names of all in the cast with respect, and remember with special warmth Roscoe Lee Browne, James Earl Jones, Cynthia Belgrave, Ethel Ayler, Helen Martin, Cicely Tyson and Godfrey M. Cambridge.

•

Theatregoers acquainted with M. Genet's "The Balcony" know that this vastly gifted Frenchman uses shock-

Ethel Ayler, left, Godfrey Cambridge, wearing the mask, and Cynthia Belgrave in "The Blacks," play by Jean Genet.

ing words and images to cry out at the pretensions and injustices of our world. In "The Blacks" he is not only a moralist of high indignation but also a prophet of rage and compassion.

"Everything is changing," says Felicity, who speaks often like a high priestess. "Whatever is gentle and kind and good and tender will be black." So M. Genet has a Negro declare as if in a vision, but surely he looks for the day when these things will be all colors and no color.

1961 My 5

Ossie Davis Stars in His Play at Cort

PURLIE VICTORIOUS, a comedy by Ossie Davis. Staged by Howard Da Silva; presented by Philip Rose; scenery and lighting by Ben Edwards; costumes by Ann Roth; stage manager, Leonard Auerbach. At the Cort Theatre, 138 West Forty-eighth Street.

Purlie Victorious Judson	Ossie Davis
Lutiebelle Gussie Mae Jenkins	Ruby Dee
Missy Judson	Helen Martin
Gitlow Judson	Godfrey M. Cambridge
Charley Cotchipee	Alan Alda
Idella Landy	Beah Richards
Ol' Cap'n Cotchipee	Sorrell Booke
The Sheriff	Ci Herzog
The Deputy	Roger C. Carmel

By HOWARD TAUBMAN

IT is marvelously exhilarating to hear the Negro speak for himself, especially when he does so in the fullness of his native gusto and the enveloping heartiness of his overflowing laughter.

Ossie Davis, actor and author, has passed this miracle of uninhibited and jovial speaking out in his new play, "Purlie Victorious," which bounced and whooped into the Cort Theatre last night. Although his good humor never falters, he has made his play the vehicle for a powerful and passionate sermon. While "Purlie Victorious" keeps you chuckling and guffawing, it unrelentingly forces you to feel how it is to inhabit a dark skin in a hostile or, at best, grudgingly benevolent world.

For his plot Mr. Davis has used a simple scaffolding. Over it he has poured a bubbling mixture of gibes, jokes and wry and uproarious variations of clichés about whites and blacks. The ingredients seem superficially to be too wildly stirred to fit the framework of the dramatic structure. But they have a strange and wonderful way of becoming as firm as concrete—and hitting as hard.

The play tells the story of Purlie Victorious Judson, a joyous, robust Negro with the gift of tongues, who sounds like Ecclesiastes, Jeremiah and a possessed gospel singer rolled into one. Purlie has come back to his old plantation village in South Georgia. His ambition is to acquire Big Bethel and convert it into an integrated church.

His antagonist is Ol' Cap'n Cotchipee, an irascible, apoplectic, white - suited gray-haired, bullwhip-toting exponent of the unreconstructed old South. Ol' Cap'n, of course, is the very stereotype of Confederate villainy. He isn't much of an opponent to Purlie Victorious and isn't meant to be. He is another of Mr. Davis' explosive jokes.

•

Mr. Davis is turning the tables. How long have Negroes had to endure the white versions of Negroes, good and bad? His evil white man could walk right out of "Uncle Tom's Cabin." As if to compound the irony, Mr. Davis has created Gitlow Judson, a fat, smiling old Negro who carries out the ritual of being an Uncle Tom with a sly and hilarious obsequiousness.

There is a wonderful scene in which Ol' Cap'n, outraged because his son, Charley, is "too friendly to the Supreme Court," decides to prove that his darkies love the way they are treated. He causes Gitlow to stand and raise his right hand, and he fires a series of rhetorical questions at the beaming Negro, who agrees with everyone of the Cap'n's convictions about

Ruby Dee and Ossie Davis, appearing in "Purlie Victorious"

race relations. Then the two join in a tender duet of "Ol' Black Joe," as Ol' Cap'n nods blissfully and Gitlow smirks like a child caught with his fist in the cookie jar.

It is the Negro characters whom Mr. Davis has brought to life with freshness and vitality as if for the first time they were being presented from the inside. He has turned this trick with another feat of writing legerdemain. For he has started, even in their case, with stereotypes — the Bible-spouting spellbinder, the Mammy, the slow-witted, drawling drudge and the Uncle Tom. But these figures increasingly take on the warmth of individuality, until you hate to leave their company.

In Purlie Victorious Mr. Davis has written himself as

fat a part as any actor could wish. He struts and chants his incantations to the coming of freedom with irresistible excitement. In the third act he has a long account of a supposed encounter with Ol' Cap'n that is like hellfire and brimstone preaching. And his final scene, when he stands at his own pulpit in Big Bethel, he sums up the heart of the Negro's desire to live and let live with a glowing and touching humanity.

Ruby Dee, who is Mr. Davis' wife, has also been treated generously. As Lutiebelle, the seemingly backward girl, she has enough charm and humor to make one envy Purlie Victorious that she is his eager disciple. Godfrey M. Cambridge brings a genial shrewdness to the scraping, bowing Gitlow. Sorrell Booke as Ol' Cap'n roars and rants with delightful fury. Helen Martin does the Mammy bit with a knowing comic touch.

•

Ben Edwards' sets depict—and comment—on this corner of the South. Howard Da Silva has staged the play with the fluidity and vigor of an expansive folk tale.

And rambunctious folk tale it is. The Negro laughs at himself. "Whatsa matter with running?" demands Gitlow. "Running emancipated more Negroes than Abe Lincoln." The Negro also shouts his insistence on his rights. "We want our cut of the Constitution," cries Purlie, "not in a teaspoon but with a shovel."

"Purlie Victorious" will do as much to bring that about as a grim oration, and it won't let you wipe that grin off your face.

1961 S 29

Harold Pinter's 'The Caretaker' Opens

By HOWARD TAUBMAN

OUT of a scabrous derelict and two mentally unbalanced brothers Harold Pinter has woven a play of strangely compelling beauty and passion. "The Caretaker," which opened last night at the Lyceum, proclaims its young English author as one of the important playwrights of our day.

At first glance the materials of this play could hardly be less promising. Two of the characters are just this side of articulate, and the third spins a glib, wild line about real estate, leases, interior decoration and other common concerns. Yet Mr. Pinter finds comedy, tenderness and heartbreak in all three. He builds his spare elements into powerful drama with a climax that tears at the heart.

•

"The Caretaker" begins as if it will turn into sardonic comedy, beatnik style. An old bum receives shelter in a cluttered room of an abandoned house. His samaritan is a gentle young man whose kindness is so casual that he seems almost indifferent. Dirty, tattered, unkempt, itching and scratching, the tramp is by turns wheedling, truculent and full of bravado.

This human jetsam, Davies or Jenkins or whatever his name may be, begins as a grossly comic figure. He speaks the proud lingo of those who have untold resources awaiting them at near-by havens. He pronounces his meager phrases with the exaggerated precision of one unaccustomed to being heeded. He flails a fist into a palm or into the air with the belligerence of a

The Cast

THE CARETAKER, a comedy-drama by Harold Pinter. Staged by Donald Mc-Whinnie; presented by Roger L. Stevens, Frederick Brisson and Gilbert Miller; scenery by Brian Currah; supervision and lighting by Paul Morrison; production stage manager, Fred Hebert. At the Lyceum Theatre, 149 West Forty-fifth Street.
Mick......................Alan Bates
Aston......................Robert Shaw
Davies..................Donald Pleasence

fighter no one will ever corner. He associates himself with fastidious practices like soap as if they were his daily habit. He is very funny—at first.

•

But the laughter shades increasingly into pity. Like a cornered animal, he cannot believe anyone means to be kind to him. He complains about the hospitality he receives, and although it is impoverished, it clearly exceeds any recent comfort he has known. He looks down on the blacks who live in an adjacent abandoned house and is fearful that they will share his lavatory. He hates foreigners. He trusts no one, and fears everyone.

•

He alienates the two brothers who separately have offered him a job as caretaker of the premises. Their offers and the job itself become themes with subtle overtones.

For Aston, the samáritan, lives in personal and emotional isolation, tinkering with gadgets and dreaming of building a shed out in the yard. And Mick, who carries on like a man of affairs, inhabits a dream world that resembles an extrovert's nightmares.

•

Mr. Pinter has been vehement in his assertions that his play is no more than the story it tells. But he cannot prevent his audiences from finding in it a modern parable of derisive scorn and bitter sorrow. Who will take care of Davies, the caretaker? Even the demented cannot endure the scrofulous old vagrant. If it is possible for one such as Davies to have a Gethsemane, this play at last brings him to it.

Donald Pleasence gives an unforgettable performance as Davies. He exudes a sense of degradation. He speaks in a strangled voice and then shouts with the anger of the frightened. He is comic and pathetic and, in his facing up to what seems his last agony, shattering. A very distinguished actor.

Robert Shaw is enormously touching as Aston, particularly in a long soliloquy at the end of the second act.

Donald Pleasence, left, and Robert Shaw in a scene from "The Caretaker," the drama by Harold Pinter of Britain.

Alan Bates brilliantly manages the eager geniality and the mad intensity of Mick. Donald McWhinnie's staging in Brian Currah's imaginatively cluttered set has the strength of character to begin patiently and to build with cumulative force.

A work of rare originality, "The Caretaker" will tease and cling to the mind. No matter what happens in the months to come, it will lend luster to this Broadway season.

1961 O 5

Musical Comedy Seen at 46th St. Theatre

HOW TO SUCCEED IN BUSINESS WITHOUT REALLY TRYING, a musical comedy, based on Shepherd Mead's book. Adaptation by Abe Burrows, Jack Weinstock and Willie Gilbert. Music and lyrics by Frank Loesser. Directed by Mr. Burrows; presented by Cy Feuer and Ernest Martin, in association with Frank Productions, Inc.; musical staging, Bob Fosse; choreography, Hugh Lambert; scenery and lighting, Robert Randolph; costumes, Robert Fletcher; musical direction, Elliot Lawrence; orchestrations, Robert Ginzler; production stage manager, Phil Friedman. At the 46th Street Theatre, 226 West Forty-sixth Street.

Finch	Robert Morse
Gatch	Ray Mason
J. B. Biggley	Rudy Vallee
Rosemary	Bonnie Scott
Bratt	Paul Reed
Smitty	Claudette Sutherland
Frump	Charles Nelson Reilly
Miss Jones	Ruth Kobart
Mr. Twimble	Sammy Smith
Hedy	Virginia Martin
Miss Krumholtz	Mara Landi

By HOWARD TAUBMAN

IT'S an open question whether big business in America should be warier of trust busters than of the new musical that frolicked into the Forty-sixth Street Theatre Saturday night.

The antitrust watchdogs can crack a mean whip, but "How to Succeed in Business Without Really Trying" applies a gigantic hotfoot. It stings mischievously and laughs uproariously.

Big business is not likely to be the same again. If it isn't guarding self-defensively against invoking the old team try and the sanctified corporate image, it will be so busy chuckling at its reflection in this impish mirror of a musical that it won't have time to do big business. But you can bet that this show will. It belongs to the blue chips among modern musicals.

●

"How to Succeed" is as impudent as a competitor who grabs off a fat contract and as cheerful as the tax collector who gets his cut no matter who makes the deal. Its irreverence is as bracing as a growth stock that matures into a nice capital gain.

Not a bypath in the honored folkways of big business avoids a going over. The mailroom, plans and system, personnel, advertising, the president, chairman of the board, the executive conference, secretaries, stenographers, cleaning women, the coffee break and even the executive washroom are sources of anything but innocent merriment. Not even love is sacred, but being shrewd showmen, the authors don't knock it.

"How to Succeed" arrives bearing precious gifts of an adult viewpoint and consistency of style. Abe Burrows, sly and robust magician of the musical theatre, has directed brilliantly as well as helped Jack Weinstock and Willie Gilbert in drawing the story from Shepherd Mead's book. Frank Loesser has written lyrics with an edge and tunes with a grin. Bob Fosse's staging, like the dances, sets and costumes, is gaily in the spirit of the production.

There are dividends of diverting comment everywhere, even in extra musical touches. When boy and girl meet in a long, tender kiss, the orchestra in the pit, as if rebuking Mr. Loesser's song for not feeling the moment keenly enough, breaks into a lush theme from a piano concerto of the romantic school. As the executives solemnly march into the conference room for a fateful meeting, an organ plays a soulful voluntary as if to fix a fitting mood for the highest meditations.

Imagine a collaboration between Horatio Alger and Machiavelli and you have Finch, the intrepid hero of this sortie into the canyons of commerce. As played with unfaltering bravura and wit by Robert Morse, he is a rumpled, dimpled angel with a streak of Lucifer. Butter couldn't melt in his mouth because he is so occupied spreading it on anyone who can help him up a rung of that ladder you've heard about.

Finch starts his climb to glory by bumping into J. B. Biggley, president of World Wide Wickets Company, Inc., and being knocked down by him. J. B. is played with admirable shortness of patience and temper by Rudy Vallee, looking austere behind a pince-nez. Only a few things melt J. B.—flattery, a luscious dish named Hedy and the enduring joy of being an alumnus — therefore, a Groundhog — of dear, old Ivy.

When J. B. and his Hedy (Virginia Martin looking like come-hither alabaster poured into garments that cling and caress) join in a heartrending ballad, "Love from a Heart of Gold," and Hedy belts out the top tones like a Valkyrie sopping with emotion, you know that passion has had it. When J. B. and Finch strut through "Grand Old Ivy," you know that the rousing heartfelt tributes to Alma Mater have had it, too. And when Mr. Vallee cups his hands to his mouth like a megaphone, for a moment the years roll back on our youth when we listened to him sing the "Maine Stein Song" with as much sentiment as he poured into it.

On his painless way up Finch meets Rosemary, charmingly played by Bonnie Scott, who loves him instantly and forever. With gentle forbearance he crosses swords with J. B.'s nephew, Frump. Charles Nelson Reilly plays the villain with a wonderful sneaky relish. As he lays his dark plans and chortles fiendishly, "I shall return," you realize that the machinations in the towers of industry have more melodrama

Friedman-Abeles

Rudy Vallee, at left, with Robert Morse in a scene from "How to Succeed in Business Without Really Trying."

than the Westerns they sponsor.

When you enter the Park Avenue office building of World Wide Wickets and find the staff in frozen attitudes, like manikins in a store window, you know that "How to Succeed" is bent on fun with a helping of malice. It never lets up; indeed, it becomes livelier and funnier as it moves up the ladder with Finch.

•

A coffee break without coffee undermines free enterprise. An ingenious dance celebrating the point that a stenographer is not a toy keeps a tongue in cheek. The authors pay their good-humored and biting respects to Paris originals that aren't, to a Madison Avenue presentation full of sound, fury, and maybe a lot of truth, to the in-fighting that flows over into the executive washroom and to the sort of entertainment big business concocts for television.

•

As in modern musicals of quality, the songs in "How to Succeed" sharpen the ridicule. "Cinderella, Darling" is a hymn sung by grateful—and hopeful—secretaries to the occasional bosses who make them honest women. "I Believe in You" is a torch song to self-esteem. And "Brotherhood of Man" is a jubilant, twinkling ode that will leave you as happy as if you owned a piece of the show.

Let Wall Street and Madison Avenue tremble as the rest of us rejoice.

1961 O 16

A Man For All Seasons
Drama Based on Life of Thomas More Opens

By HOWARD TAUBMAN

IN "A Man for All Seasons" Robert Bolt has written a play that is luminous with intelligence and steely with conviction.

The central figure of this work, which arrived last night at the ANTA Theatre, is Sir Thomas More, the lawyer and scholar, who would not yield to the expediency required by his sovereign, Henry VIII. The theme of the play is the pressure that a community of friends and foes brings to bear on a man who can do no other but listen to the still, small voice of his conscience.

•

"A Man for All Seasons" is written with distinction. It combines in equal measure the dancing, ironic wit of detachment and the steady blue flame of commitment. With its commingling of literary grace, intellectual subtlety and human simplicity, it challenges the mind and, in the end, touches the heart. For it is not only about a man for all seasons but also about an aspiration for all time.

Mr. Bolt, a young English playwright, has written a chronicle play, using the fluid structure of the Elizabethan narratives and adding to it a chorus in the tradition of the Greek dramas. This chorus is The Common Man. It is his proposition that "the sixteenth century is the century of the common man, as are all centuries."

This Common Man, who serves at one time or another as servant, boatman, jailer, foreman of a jury and executioner, is an engaging rogue. Played with wonderful sharpness, humor and familiarity by George Rose, he is the shrewd, nimble comic fellow who knows how to adapt to his environment and look after himself. Not a bad fellow at heart, not even heedless, he is merely cautious. Who except the Sir Thomas Mores can cast the first stone at him?

Mr. Bolt sports with The Common Man, using him not only for sharp-witted, disenchanted comment but also for a helping hand with changes of scene. With Sir

Thomas the author does not trifle. His steadfastness is rooted in wisdom, and his words are the warm, mellow, penetrating expression of a sad, knowing observer of the world and its ways.

By the standards of neatly plotted drama, there is a basic weakness in the con-

The Cast

A MAN FOR ALL SEASONS, a play by Robert Bolt. Staged by Noel Willman; presented for the American National Theatre and Academy by Robert Whitehead and Roger L. Stevens; scenery and costumes by Motley; lighting by Paul Morrison; production stage manager, Fredric de Wilde. At the ANTA Theatre, 245 West Fifty-second Street.

The Common Man..........George Rose
Sir Thomas More...........Paul Scofield
Richard Rich...........William Redfield

Duke of Norfolk...........Albert Dekker
Alice More................Carol Goodner
Margaret More.............Olga Bellin
Cardinal Wolsey............Jack Creley
Thomas Cromwell............Leo McKern
Signor Chapuys........David J. Stewart
His Attendant............John Colenback
William Roper.........P ter Brandon
King Henry VIII...........Keith Baxter
The Woman................Sarah Burton
Cranmer.................Lester Rawlins

ception of Sir Thomas. For when we meet him, years before his end, his character seems to be fixed in its perception and courage. As he moves down the inevitable road to destruction, the early traits are re-enforced. There is no fatal flaw in him.

But one feels that Mr. Bolt's intention is to use Sir Thomas More's fate as the gauge of man's desperate,

Paul Scofield, left, and Leo McKern as they appear in a scene from "A Man for All Seasons" at Anta Theatre.

ever-renewing predicament. Mr. Bolt is not writing a tragedy in the conventional sense but recalling history with pungency, letting us draw whatever contemporary lessons we may. And he is careful to observe that there are many, that the cap may be worn where it fits.

•

Because the nature of Sir Thomas More deepens rather than alters and because his emotions are merely suggested in the quiet sparkle of his mind, the role is enormously exacting. Paul Scofield brings dignity and reserve to it. The crinkle of an eye emphasizes the pithiness of a phrase; the droop of a shoulder sums up the weight of an unbending conscience. Mr. Scofield is so fine an actor that he can permit himself the repose that lets others shine in crucial scenes. Keith Baxter's glittering headstrong, restless King, Leo McKern's unctuous, ruthless Thomas Cromwell, Albert Dekker's bluff yet morally frail Norfolk are admirably aided by Mr. Scofield's mask of calm. Yet this Sir Thomas can reveal his agony as he says farewell to his wife and daughter and his pride as a man in his final declaration in court.

The other performances, notably those by William Redfield, Carol Goodner, David J. Stewart and Olga Bellin, deserve mention. Noel Willman has staged the play with a grasp of its fluidity, its humor and its strength. Motley's sets and costumes evoke the color of the Tudor epoch.

"We are dealing with an age less fastidious than ours," says one of Mr. Bolt's characters. Well, are we? This fine, meaty play will stir you and cause you to ask further questions of your own.

1961 N 23

1962

The Cast

BRECHT ON BRECHT, a program of songs, plays, poems and events written by or about the German playwright, Bertolt Brecht. Material arranged by George Tabori and staged by Gene Frankel. Produced by Cheryl Crawford and designed by Wolfgang Roth; presented by the Greater New York Chapter of the American National Theatre and Academy (Lucille Lortel, artistic director); Lotte Lenya's piano accompaniment by Lys Bert Symonette; production stage manager, Don Gilliland. At the Theatre de Lys, 121 Christopher Street.
PRINCIPALS: Dane Clark, Anne Jackson, Lotte Lenya, Viveca Lindfors, George Voskovec and Michael Wager.

By HOWARD TAUBMAN

AN overflowing abundance of observation and emotion marks the wonderful world of Bertolt Brecht as revealed in "Brecht on Brecht."

This living anthology, which began a run last night at the Theatre de Lys, is merely a glimpse into the heart and workshop of the poet and playwright. Yet it illuminates the richness of Brecht's sympathies, the edge in his humor, the acuteness of his mind, his disarming gift for self-deprecation and, above all, his cool and flaming command of the theatre.

•

Depend on theatre people to serve their art. "Brecht on Brecht" grew out of their zeal to pay homage to a writer whose fame in this country grows but whose work rarely receives attention on Broadway. Drawing on Brecht's sayings, poems, songs and fragments from his letters, essays and plays, George Tabori arranged a program. A devoted group joined to perform it, and Lucille Lortel presented it in her matinee series for the Greater New York Chapter of ANTA in mid-November.

With changes of cast and modifications in material, the

new version of "Brecht on Brecht" is filled with wry and slashing comments on the foibles of individuals and the organized insanities of nations. Its compassion for the unfortunate and the oppressed is never far from the surface, and it offers moments of searing poignancy.

Because he cared so passionately about so many things, Bertolt Brecht could allow himself the luxury of laughter. When he is most scathing, as in his observations on the peculiarities of that common bit of paper called a passport, he chuckles a little. His remarks on tidiness and sloppiness snap as they smile. Irony is his milieu.

How astutely and lovingly he describes the intensity of a young actor who gets a chance to play a bit part in "The Threepenny Opera." The agony of this dedicated performer as he deliberates over which of two battered old hats to choose for his role is irradiated by unforgettable tenderness. It is as if the whole universe depends on the young man's decision. It is as if Brecht has reached deeply into the heart not merely of one unsung actor but all the ardent spirits who burn to devote themselves to a craft or a cause.

As the evening begins on an almost bare stage with some high stools and a bench —only a few props are added later—an enlarged photograph of Brecht looks down on the audience. The searching eye and the lips turned up slightly give him a quizzical, sardonic look. A sound track carries his voice, struggling with the English language. During the evening this voice recalls autobiographical facts haltingly and sings a familiar tune from "The Threepenny Opera."

•

The six performers appear, and take seats in attractive

patterns arranged by Gene Frankel, the evening's sensitive director. Since they all perform with modesty and conviction, they are, to follow the program's alphabetical order, Dane Clark, Anne Jackson, Lotte Lenya, Viveca Lindfors, George Voskovec and Michael Wager. They take turns speaking the swiftly paced and provocatively contrasted excerpts from Brecht's observations on himself and the world around him.

Much as the songs sung by Miss Lenya, the ironic shafts and the brooding insights spoken by all the performers communicate the measure of Brecht and the scope of his interests, it is the second half, with its emphasis on his theatre, that builds to a memorable climax.

The flashes of Brecht's theatre glow brilliantly. Miss Lenya's singing of the song of Mother Courage, with the pride of a marcher in the ranks, has a grim vitality. Mr. Wager, Mr. Clark and Mr. Voskovec join in a sad, wise moment from "Galileo." Miss Jackson, depending in part on pantomime, does a touching excerpt from "The Good Woman of Setzuan." And Miss Lindfors, with a finely controlled disclosure of the hysteria and heartbreak of a Jewish wife as she prepares to leave her home and husband in Nazi Germany, turns a playlet into a scorching experience.

Until we can have Brecht's finest plays in New York, "Brecht on Brecht" will do. For these fragments from his life and works merge into a warm and sardonic portrait that assumes haunting immediacy on the stage.

1962 Ja 4

Romeo And Juliet

Zeffirelli's Production at the City Center

By HOWARD TAUBMAN

GRAFT the tempestuous realism of Italy on the headstrong beauty of Shakespeare and you have the turbulent, youthful and ardent "Romeo and Juliet" of the Old Vic.

Rarely will you see a "Romeo" with the slashing vigor and wild passion of the one that the London Company unveiled last night at the City Center. For Franco Zeffirelli's staging has the brightness, the gusto and the cutting clarity of the Mediterranean lands, and he has framed it against his own sets with the stately structures and dark hues of ancient Italy.

Signor Zeffirelli's realism is in the contemporary Italian style called neo-realism. Like Shakespeare's cascading images, it is not afraid of abundance, even superabundance. The young blades roister and brawl with violence. Mercutio can no more restrain the nervous vitality of his movements than he can contain his exuberant wit. Romeo and Juliet meet and kiss and plight their troth with an eagerness and fire that are the very anatomy of young love.

This "Romeo" is never content with half measures. The comic scenes are so broad that their point would not be lost on the dullest brain in the pit of an Elizabethan theatre. The sword play surges with naturalistic fury. Signor Zeffirelli is not above letting his Mercutio pick up Tybalt's lost blade and, before returning it to him, brush it arrogantly with his sleeve, like a young fire-eater in a modern romance. For effete tastes this "Romeo" may be too earthy and too emotional.

●

But Signor Zeffirelli is nearer Shakespeare's mark than the delicate, overrefined "Romeos." For this tragedy imprisons the overflowing richness and vitality of a young poet who suddenly has full command of the stage. In its mood and pace, if not its realistic sets of Verona's street and palaces, this production reflects the tumult and fervor of the playwright's unbuttoned epoch.

Nowhere is Signor Zeffirelli's approach more enhancing than in the balcony scene. Romeo paces the ground under the Capulet wall set back deep on the stage, invoking his fair one's felicities. Then she appears as he hovers at the side and she sighs at the harsh misfortune of his name.

He makes his presence known with a leap and a shout. He climbs a tree and stands precariously on the wall's ledge. They embrace, part, embrace again. The action has the unpremeditated

The Cast

ROMEO AND JULIET, a revival of William Shakespeare's tragedy by the Old Vic Company of London. Directed by Franco Zeffirelli; presented by the City Center of Music and Drama, Old Vic Trust, Ltd., and the Arts Council of Great Britain under the management of S. Hurok; scenery by Mr. Zeffirelli; costumes by Peter Hall; incidental music by Nino Rota; dances arranged by Pirmin Trecu; fight scenes arranged by William Hobbs; stage director, Robert Gaston. At the City Center, 131 West Fifty-fifth Street.

Benvolio	Job Stewart
Tybalt	Michael Meacham
Montague	Andre Van Gyseghem
Capulet	Peter Forest
Lady Montague	Diana Scougall
Lady Capulet	Irene Sutcliffe
Romeo	John Stride
Paris	John Quentin
Nurse to Juliet	Rosalind Atkinson
Juliet	Joanna Dunham
Mercutio	Edward Atienza
Friar Laurence	Gerald James

ecstasy that finds expression in their enchanted words.

In John Stride and Joanna Dunham the Old Vic has a Romeo and Juliet who fulfill the director's design and add a glowing emotion of their own. They bring to the balcony scene a sense of the wonder of consuming young love with its desire, sweetness and uncontainable rashness.

Mr. Stride is unmistakably a young actor on the rise. He speaks the radiant lines as if poetry glorified rather than shamed a modern player. He has verve, humor and romantic fervor. He knows how to modulate the voice, and he can even tear into a passion and make it believable rather than an old-fashioned, tattered thing.

•

Miss Dunham's Juliet appears almost as young as Shakespeare would have her. Pretty and fragile, she might well drive Rosalind from the fickle Romeo's mind. But as she reveals the constancy and warmth of her nature, she grows in maturity and womanliness, and Miss Dunham conveys the sense of her loyalty and devotion. She, too, reads Shakespeare with relish, and she manages the big emotional scenes without strain.

Edward Atienza's Mercutio is quicksilver in movement and brilliant in speech. Rosalind Atkinson's nurse is divertingly bawdy and warmhearted. Gerald James' compassionate Friar Laurence, Michael Meacham's dashing Tybalt and Job Stewart's likable Benvolio are among the valuable contributions in a neatly fused cast.

The colorful costumes are by Peter Hall, who heads the Royal Stratford Theatre. Signor Zeffirelli calls the magic of sight and sound to his aid. Besides the graceful music of Nino Rota, with its organ and choral phrases, he employs crowd noises, bells, clanking of gates as counterpoints to the action. Was that a recorded voice of a lark that heralded the dawn?

The touches of literalism are not out of place. They are part of a neo-realistic frame that shows off but does not enclose a young poet's intoxicated, stormy drama of young love.

1962 F 14

Producing Artists Give 'School for Scandal'

By LEWIS FUNKE

THE Association of Producing Artists, a repertory group that has been slowly but steadily building itself a company and a repertoire in various sections of the country during the last year and a half, is making its first New York appearance, having begun a stand at the Folksbiene Playhouse on East Broadway over the week-end. For its initial rendition it

Rosemary Harris

The Cast

THE SCHOOL FOR SCANDAL, a revival of Richard Brinsley Sheridan's comedy. Staged by Ellis Rabb; presented by The Association of Producing Artists, Inc.; designed by Lloyd Burlingame; music by Conrad Susa; production stage manager, Geoffry Brown. At the Folksbiene Playhouse, 175 East Broadway.

Lady Sneerwell..........Nancy Marchand
Snake....................Page Johnson
Joseph Surface...........George Grizzard
Maria.......................Ellen Geer
Mrs. Candour............Joanna Roos
Crabtree................Tucker Ashworth
Sir Benjamin Backbite....Nicholas Martin

Sir Peter Teazle...............Will Geer
Rowley...................William Larsen
Lady Teazle.........Rosemary Harris
Sir Oliver Surface.........David Hooks
Charles Surface..........Clayton Corzatte

has selected Richard Brinsley Sheridan's "The School for Scandal," and if there are those who would choose to quibble about style, finesse and the like and be also impolite enough to suggest that native English actors might do it better, they undoubtedly could find support.

But judging by the reactions of a group of early teen-agers who happened to make up the major portion of yesterday's matinee audience, director Ellis Rabb's approach to one of the greatest comedies of manners in English literature has the right youthfulness and vivacity to turn Sheridan into a revelation for those unacquainted with his work beyond the library or the classroom.

Grant that the production is lacking in the opulence and elegance one would desire in a play about society in the London of the eighteenth century. But the Association of Producing Artists has not been blessed yet by wealthy patrons, and since it moves around the country, its scenery must be more on the modest and utilitarian side. The costumes vary from plain to fancy, again within the bounds of budgetary limitations.

But, as for exuberance, that being a quality not to be purchased in the market place, the company can afford plenty of it. The result is a jolly performance that overrides diversity of acting styles and occasional lapses of common accent. There is an infectious spirit in the players that helps to underscore what a wonderfully bright comedy Sheridan wrote.

For the gossipmongers and reputation despoilers of the eighteenth century have their living counterparts today, and if yesterday's youngsters left the playhouse pondering the evils of tale bearing, insincer-

ity, hypocrisy and intrigue the theatre has done its job well.

Among the pleasures of this revival is Rosemary Harris, playing Lady Teazle. Miss Harris is lovely to look at and what's more an expert actress. She gives the role a mischievous charm, conveying delightfully her petulance and arrogance, her disrespect for her aging husband, her acquisition of the traits of high society into which her marriage has taken her, a lass from the country. She is affectingly contrite when she discovers the sincerity of her husband and the duplicity of the circle into which he has moved. There is roguery in her smile and honesty in her repentance.

Nancy Marchand is a wily, sinister Lady Sneerwell, a ringleader in the destruction of her friends. George Grizzard's Joseph Surface is correctly repelling in its cant and false sentiment. Ellen Geer is a dainty Maria and her father, the veteran Will Geer, is a blustery and touching Sir Peter Teazle. Clayton Corzatte is a real gay blade as Charles Surface, while David Hooks' Sir Oliver is sound.

"The School for Scandal" may not receive the stylishness desired, but it has something else to appreciate—buoyancy and bounce.

1962 Mr 19

The Tempest

Stratford Production Is Given an Ovation

By LEWIS FUNKE
Special to The New York Times.

STRATFORD, Ont., June 21 —"The Tempest," one of Shakespeare's most beautifully poetic plays, has been

given a most regal and enticing production on the
Stratford Festival stage.

The third and last addition
to the Shakespearean repertory that will be performed
here this season, it was offered last night with meticulous devotion and care. The
standing ovation at its conclusion was a justified tribute
from an audience that had
sat spellbound, enveloped by
the magic of Prospero's haunted isle.

"The Tempest" was created
by the master of English
verse at the end of his career,
after he, too, had passed
through his own violent
storms. He had reached his
own serenity and there is a
strong belief that in the play
he reflected the peace he had
found after contemplation of
the world's good and evil.
The speech to Ariel at the
end, in which Prospero grants
him the freedom to soar as
and where he will, has been
regarded as Shakespeare's
own farewell to the London
stage, his laying down of his
immortal pen.

Because it is a reflective
piece, and because it is virtually without plot, it is not
an easy play to capture on
the stage. There are long
stretches of inaction. It is
never truly possible to become
involved in its conflicts. Prospero, with his magic staff,
lurks always in the back-
ground to wield his powers,
to offset or to provide the
conductor for all machinations. This is a fairy tale, a
dream, full of lovely poetry
and music. Evocation of mood
is essential to its fullest appreciation. Only expert minds
and expert acting can lift it
into its proper realm.

It is possible to argue that
George McCowan's direction
is almost too deliberate. But
to this reviewer that would
come under the category of
quibbling. For though the
pace is slow and occasionally
tedium takes over, the over-
all effect cannot be denied.
From each scene the essence
is wrung, and with actors who
can deliver the verse with

The Cast

THE TEMPEST by William Shakespeare.
Staged by George McCowan; presented
by the Stratford Shakespearean Festival Foundation of Canada; production
designed by Desmond Heeley; music
by John Cook; dances arranged by Alan
and Blanche Lund. At the Stratford
Shakespearean Festival, Stratford, Conn.

Boatswain	Bernard Behrens
Master	Nelson Phillips
Alonso	Max Helpmann
Ferdinand	Peter Donat
Gonzalo	William Needles
Antonio	Leo Ciceri
Sebastian	John Horton
Francisco	Al Kozlik
Adrian	Leh Birman
Stephano	Norman Welsh
Trinculo	Hugh Webster
Prospero	William Hutt
Miranda	Martha Henry
Ariel	Bruno Gerussi
Caliban	John Colicos
Iris	Pat Galloway
Ceres	Dinah Christie
Juno	Amelia Hall

appreciation for its cadences
and beauty, the cumulative
effect is enchanting.

Nor are the actors and director alone responsible for
the felicitous results. Desmond Heeley, as designer of
the costumes, has seized every
opportunity for lavishness and
color. He has flashed scenes
in whites, reds, golds and
blacks, captured the elegance
of royalty in satins and brocades against the stage's deep
gray. Especially vivid and
breathtaking are the creations for the mask, that airy,
delicate entertainment of music and dance. Credit also goes
to John Cook whose accom-
panying score contributes
much to supporting the filmy
texture of the action itself.

●

Among the players, first
attention, of course, must be
given to William Hutt's Prospero who, as the deposed
Duke of Milan shipwrecked
on the island has conjured up
the tempest by which he has
brought his enemies to his
shores. Mr. Hutt, stately in
his magic robes, his face
framed in a gray beard, his
head topped by full and flowing gray hair, delivers a portrait that provides the needed
core and sparkle of the play.

He is stern and determined
as he sets tasks for Ferdinand
lest the young man find life
on the island idyllic, especially after he has beheld the
fragile beauty of Miranda; he
is full of controlled wrath as

he sets out to thwart the evil Caliban's plot against him and when he is finally ready to confront the King of Naples and others of the Court who helped depose him. For one brief moment the prospect seems to unsettle him, as all the pent up grievance is ready to be unharnessed. But in that pivotal momen the knows that forgiveness though it be a difficult virtue, is the great one. Mr. Hutt is excellent and touching as he grants mercy to his erstwhile tormentors. Throughout he speaks with grace and regard for his lines.

John Colicos' Caliban is an unforgettable creation. Made up as a black monster, in a hornylike forbidding garb, bold and powerful he is gruesome to behold in his semi-animalism. Growling when crossed, his red tongue wig-wagging like a serpent's fangs, he brings terror and a tension to his scenes. Nowhere, indeed, is he more frightening than when he finds companions who will aid him in the destruction of Prospero, whom he has come to regard as torturer and ursurper of his island. He commences a rhythmic tattoo with his feet, a wail of hysterical joy in a sort of song, his eyes wide and glaring.

•

In the difficult role of Ariel, Bruno Gerussi is first rate. Agile as he needs to be he presents a picture of a spirit restive in his servitude to Prospero, often a bit scornful and mocking. Anxious for his freedom, he is sometimes like a truculent youngster going through outward manifestations of rebellion yet knowing always that he cannot gain release until he fulfills his assigned chores.

As Ferdinand, Peter Donat possesses virility and romantic ardor. His love for Miranda is tender and worshipful. He speaks with feeling and grace. And little wonder either. For Martha Henry's Miranda is a vision of young beauty. Her wonder at the sight of other mortals is full of a child's open-eyed innocence.

Norman Welsh as the drunken butler, Stephano, and Hugh Webster as the terrified, dimuntive court jester, give their low comedy scenes their fullest flavor, offering a relieving counterpoint to the mysteries of the ambience in which they discover themselves.

For a change "The Tempest" has found a company equal to its challenge. The result will be cherished by all who relish a lovely fairy tale and find inspiration in wisdom distilled by a mature mind.

1962 Je 22

Who's Afraid of Virginia Woolf?

Dramatist's First Play on Broadway Opens

By HOWARD TAUBMAN

THANKS to Edward Albee's furious skill as a writer, Alan Schneider's charged staging and a brilliant performance by a cast of four, "Who's Afraid of Virginia Woolf?" is a wry and electric evening in the theater.

You may not be able to swallow Mr. Albee's characters whole, as I cannot. You may feel, as I do, that a pillar of the plot is too flimsy to support the climax. Nevertheless, you are urged to hasten to the Billy Rose Theater, where Mr. Albee's first full-length play opened Saturday night.

For "Who's Afraid of Virginia Woolf?" is possessed by raging demons. It is punctuated by comedy, and its laughter is shot through with savage irony. At its core is a bitter, keening lament over man's incapacity to arrange his environment or private life so as to inhibit his self-destructive compulsions.

•

Moving onto from off Broadway, Mr. Albee carries

along the burning intensity and icy wrath that informed "The Zoo Story" and "The American Dream." He has written a full-length play that runs almost three and a half hours and that brims over with howling furies that do not drown out a fierce compassion. After the fumes stirred by his witches' caldron are spent, he lets in, not sunlight and fresh air, but only an agonized prayer.

Although Mr. Albee's vision is grim and sardonic, he is never solemn. With the instincts of a born dramatist and the shrewdness of one whose gifts have been tempered in the theater, he knows how to fill the stage with vitality and excitement.

Sympathize with them or not, you will find the characters in this new play vibrant with dramatic urgency. In their anger and terror they are pitiful as well as corrosive, but they are also wildly and humanly hilarious. Mr. Albee's dialogue is dipped in

acid, yet ripples with a relish of the ludicrous. His controlled, allusive style grows in mastery.

In "Who's Afraid of Virginia Woolf?" he is concerned with Martha and George, a couple living in mordant, uproarious antagonism. The daughter of the president of the college where he teaches she cannot forgive his failure to be a success like her father. He cannot abide her brutal bluntness and drive. Married for more than 20 years, they claw each other like jungle beasts.

In the dark hours after a Saturday midnight they entertain a young married pair new to the campus, introducing them to a funny and cruel brand of fun and games. Before the liquor-sodden night is over, there are lacerating self-revelations for all.

On the surface the action seems to be mostly biting talk. Underneath is a witches'

Uta Hagen and George Grizzard, standing, and Melinda Dillon and Arthur Hill make up the cast of the new play.

revel, and Mr. Albee is justified in calling his second act "Walpurgisnacht." But the means employed to lead to the denouement of the third act, called "The Exorcism," seem spurious.

Mr. Albee would have us believe that for 21 years his older couple have nurtured a fiction that they have a son, that his imaginary existence is a secret that violently binds and sunders them and that George's pronouncing him dead may be a turning point. This part of the story does not ring true, and its falsity impairs the credibility of his central characters.

●

If the drama falters, the acting of Uta Hagen and Arthur Hill does not. As the vulgar, scornful, desperate Martha, Miss Hagen makes a tormented harridan horrifyingly believable. As the quieter, tortured and diabolical George, Mr. Hill gives a superbly modulated per-

The Cast

WHO'S AFRAID OF VIRGINIA WOOLF?, a play by Edward Albee. Staged by Alan Schneider; presented by Richard Barr and Clinton Wilder; production designed by William Ritman; stage manager, Mark Wright. At the Billy Rose Theater, 208 West 41st Street.
Martha .... Uta Hagen
George .... Arthur Hill
Honey .... Melinda Dillon
Nick .... George Grizzard

formance built on restraint as a foil to Miss Hagen's explosiveness.

George Grizzard as a young biologist on the make shades from geniality to intensity with shattering rightness. And Melinda Dillon as his mousy, troubled bride is amusing and touching in her vulnerable wistfulness.

Directing like a man accustomed to fusing sardonic humor and seething tension, Mr. Schneider has found a meaningful pace for long—some too long—passages of seemingly idle talk, and has staged vividly the crises of action.

●

"Who's Afraid of Virginia Woolf?" (the phrase is sung

at odd moments as a bitter joke to the tune of the children's play song, "Mulberry Bush") is a modern variant on the theme of the war between the sexes. Like Strindberg, Mr. Albee treats his women remorselessly, but he is not much gentler with his men. If he grieves for the human predicament, he does not spare those lost in its psychological and emotional mazes.

His new work, flawed though it is, towers over the common run of contemporary plays. It marks a further gain for a young writer becoming a major figure of our stage.

1962 O 15

1963

A Brilliant Production of Gargantuan Drama

The Cast

STRANGE INTERLUDE, a revival of Eugene O'Neill's drama. Staged by José Quintero; presented by Actors Studio, Inc., by arrangement with the Circle in the Square; scenery and lighting by David Hays; costumes by Noel Taylor; Miss Page's costumes by Pheoni V. Aldredge; production stage manager, Richard Blosson. At the Hudson Theater, 141 West 44th Street.
Charles Marsden .... William Prince
Professor Henry Leeds .... Franchot Tone
Nina Leeds .... Geraldine Page
Edmund Darrell .... Ben Gazzara
Sam Evans .... Pat Hingle
Mrs. Amos Evans .... Betty Field
Gordon Evans (as a child) ... Richard Thomas
Madeline Arnold .... Jane Fonda
Gordon Evans .... Geoffrey Horne

By HOWARD TAUBMAN

Special to The New York Times.

NEW YORK.

With a brilliant revival of Eugene O'Neill's "Strange Interlude" the Actors Studio has taken a step forward. It may turn out to be a giant step forward for the good of the theater in America.

For this revival, introduced Monday at the Hudson Theater, is the first production by the Actors Studio Theater, the newly established arm of the Actors Studio. Its success or failure, praise be, will not determine the existence of the Actors Studio Theater.

The new unit has the funds for at least 10 productions; it has the enthusiastic cooperation of a group of actors and other dedicated theater people; it has a purpose and a vision. One can only wish that it can come close to living up to its high ideals.

●

On balance the first production deserves public support. Thirty-five years after its unveiling in New York, O'Neill's gargantua of a drama seems to be shot through with flaws and absurdities hard to credit in America's foremost dramatist. But it is also full of flashes that illuminate its character; it abounds in dramatic moments that make the stage a place of magic; and it reflects an honest and aching view of man in relation to the huge world he inhabits.

If you have forgotten "Strange Interlude" as it was 35 years ago or if you are too young to remember, this is the first of O'Neill's massive efforts. It runs to nine acts, and in its performances at the Hudson, there will be an hour interval for dinner after the fifth. It is the play in which O'Neill returned to a device as ancient as the soliloquy and also attempted to r e v e a l his characters' thoughts by frequent asides.

The soliloquies still have occasional validity, but the asides none. Indeed, the thoughts expressed are so often commonplace and predictable that they become an unplanned source of laughter. It probably would be regarded sacrilege if any producer had the temerity to eliminate the silly and pretentious asides. On the other hand, it may be argued that O'Neill need not be saved from himself; let the new generation see him as he was, with his pretentions as well as his courage to be audacious.

Forgetting the absurd asides and the soliloquies that don't function, one can find more serious faults in "Strange Interlude." At the core it is a remorseless portrait of a spoiled and self-indulgent woman. This central character, Nina Leeds, does not have the human size to sustain a drama of such ambitious scope. One finds on revisiting the play 35 years later that Nina Leeds is a bit of a bore; O'Neill does not prove her right to dominate the lives she is meant to.

Yet Nina Leeds offers wonderful opportunities to an actress. Geraldine Page has seized them in her own way just as Lynn Fontanne did 35 years ago. With the slightly quavering girlish voice of her first entrance, Miss Page suggests the young woman whose preoccupation is largely with herself. If O'Neill's insistence on her irresistibility is not credible, Miss Page subdues this belief. As Nina ages, Miss Page discovers subtleties of gestures that convey both the brittleness of her emotions and the emptiness of her heart.

●

In one of O'Neill's finest moments — and the production's, as staged imaginatively by Jose Quintero—Miss Page joins Ben Gazzara, William Prince and Pat Hingle for an unforgettable curtain at the end of the sixth act. Here Nina reaches her highest triumph. Her three men—Mr. Hingle as her good, foolish husband, Mr. Gazzara as her intense, yet honorable lover and Mr. Prince as her spinsterish, father-substitute of a friend—are with her. All is momentary peace. And the fourth man, her new son, waits for her. O'Neill, Mr. Quintero and the actors create the scene of incandescent stagecraft.

There are five fine performances in briefer roles by Franchot Tone as Nina's gently exacting father, Betty Field as a candid, tender mother of a foolish husband, Richard Thomas as Nina's sensitive

11-year-old son, Geoffrey Horne as the sturdy son grown into m a n h o o d and Jane Fonda as his adoring friend.

David Hays has provided simple and graceful sets on the Hudson's revolving stage. What a pleasant theater the Hudson and what a pity that it seems destined sooner or later to be torn down and converted into another garage.

1963 Mr 13,

Neil Simon's 'Barefoot in the Park' Opens

The Cast

BAREFOOT IN THE PARK, a comedy by Neil Simon. Staged by Mike Nichols; presented by Saint Subber; scenery by Oliver Smith; costumes by Donald Brooks; lighting by Jean Rosenthal; production stage manager, Harvey Medlinsky. At the Biltmore Theater, 261 West 47th Street.

Corie Bratter.............Elizabeth Ashley
Telephone Man...........Herbert Edelman
Delivery Man..............Joseph Keating
Paul Bratter................Robert Redford
Mrs. Banks..............Mildred Natwick
Victor Velasco...............Kurt Kasznar

By HOWARD TAUBMAN

NEIL SIMON is a droll fellow, and not only has he spun "Barefoot in the Park" into a bubbling, rib-tickling comedy, but has also brought off the neat trick of a running gag about walking.

Not ordinary walking, you understand; climbing. Everyone in the cast of this lark, that swooped into the Biltmore Theater last night, must at some time or other walk up a stoop and five flights of stairs to reach the door of the skylight pad of a pair of newlyweds played by Elizabeth Ashley and Robert Redford.

There are only six in the cast, and some must scale the height more than once. Mr. Redford, for example, has to do it twice in the first act. Each performer must find a new way to convey the impression of breathlessness,

Friedman-Abeles

Mildred Natwick, left, Elizabeth Ashley, Kurt Kasznar and Robert Redford as they appear in "Barefoot in the Park."

exhaustion and imminent debility. Each arrival must be a diverting variation, if not a topper, of the last.

Herbert Edelman, who has come to install the telephone, is gaspingly astonished but resigned, like a man who knows he must follow his vocation wherever it calls; his best hope is that in case of trouble another repairman will get the assignment. Joseph Keating, a delivery man, just writhes in pain, drops his packages and oozes out without a word.

●

Mr. Redford improves on the short breath and staggers with each try. Mildred Natwick as his mother-in-law dodders in with stunned weariness. Miss Ashley floats in, but she's just enjoyed a party. And Kurt Kasznar as a worldly neighbor has several debonair entrances, the last with a stick and a broken big toe. The smasher is the one in which Mr. Redford carries in Miss Natwick after the big bash, and they both collapse like veterans of Iwo Jima.

This sort of thing is duck soup for actors, and this group has had the benefit of Mike Nichols's guidance in the staging. Mr. Nichols, you may remember, is a comic chap in his own right, and his invention is as resourceful as his author's flair for humorous twists in rapid-fire dialogue. Those entrances could become classics of a kind as exercises for students of advanced acting.

The basic materials of Mr. Simon's comedy are not notably fresh; it is his manipulation that makes them funny. If you broke down the main theme into its fundamental elements, you would have this formula:

After six days of marriage husband loves bride, though bride is a happy kookie who thinks it's fun to walk barefoot in the park when its snowing and who's leased this uncomfortable aerie at an exorbitant rent; and bride is smoochingly enamored of husband.

After 10 days of wedded bliss bride and bridegroom have a noisy falling out, and Mr. Simon's muse here loses some of its ingenuity.

On the 11th day the couple prepares once again to live happily ever after.

●

For a subtheme there are Miss Natwick as a careful middle-aged woman who lives alone in New Jersey and sleeps on a board, and Mr. Kasznar, a charming deadbeat who sleeps on a rug, is a connoisseur of a rare appetizer like knichi and a special drink like ouzo and knows of a remarkable Albanian restaurant somewhere on Staten Island.

Mr. Simon evidently has no aspirations except to be diverting, and he achieves those with the dash of a highly skilled professional writer. His modest plot is nearly always ready with a surprise turn, and his lines, while they crackle as unexpectedly as in "Come Blow Your Horn," are not often simply wisecracks here but natural to character and situation.

Oliver Smith's walkup hideaway is amusing in its own right, unfurnished as well as furnished, and the players fill it with conviviality. Miss Ashley's bride is a delectable, ardent scatterbrain. Mr. Redford's husband is gallant in happiness and sorrow and only needs babying when he gets the sniffles. Mr. Kasznar is delightfully adept as the old-world roué who's really, as he admits, a nice chap. Miss Natwick's mother-in-law is the kind you laugh with, not at. And don't forget Mr. Edelman if you need a telephone man with a sympathetic heart.

Broadway tosses off such a fable with a laughing grace that makes you almost credit every mood and action. I say almost because Mr. Simon would have me believe that all a new telephone customer has to do is to ask for an extra long cord and he gets it as easily as his monthly bill. Maybe Miss Ashley can manage it that smoothly. But remind me to tell you a long story about a long cord that took longer to get than a tax cut through Congress.

1963 O 24

Euripides Play Opens at Circle in Square

The Cast

"THE TROJAN WOMEN" by Euripides, translated by Edith Hamilton. Staged by Michael Cacoyannis. Music by Jean Prodromides. Costumes by Theoni V. Aldredge; lighting by Jules Fisher; choreography by Mr. Cacoyannis; chorus master, Erin Martin. Presented by the Circle in the Square and Theodore Mann. At the Circle in the Square, 159 Bleecker Street.

Hecuba ....Mildred Dunnock
Talthybius ....Alan Mixon
Cassandra ....Carrie Nye
Andromache ....Joyce Ebert
Astynax ....Chris Man
Helen ....Jane White
Menelaus ....Robert Mandan
Trojan Women ....Kay Chevalier,
        Carolyn Coates, Elaine Kerr,
Karen Ludwig, Erin Martin, Linda Martin,
Dixie Marquis, Dimitra Steris, Maria Tucci

By HOWARD TAUBMAN

WHAT if the world listened to the poets for a change? What if it had taken eternally to heart the searing words Euripides set down in "The Trojan Women" in 416 B.C.?

The thought overwhelms the imagination. Let's think more modestly and let's propose that we pay attention to "The Trojan Women" here and now. For this great tragic canvas of Euripides is as pertinent as ever, and it can be studied in a large-voiced, passionate display, which opened last night at the Circle in the Square.

●

Michael Cacoyannis, the Greek director, has staged Euripides's masterwork with the boldness of a man who

Bert Andrews

Dimitra Steris, left, Mildred Dunnock and Carolyn Coates

knows in his own bloodstream that this is drama meant not for the dusty archives but for any place and time where fear and cruelty are perils. He has not hesitated to let it roar and keen and sing out as it laments man's fury and hymns his power to endure.

This production is in the mainstream of the style used for modern productions of the Greek classics in Greece — with a difference. Mr. Cacoyannis has toughened the fiber of the approach, which, on the basis of performances I saw in 1962 in the amphitheater of Herod Atticus under the brow of the Acropolis, has become arty and flaccid.

He uses his own choreographed movement for the chorus of Trojan women, and it is flexible and intense. He has obtained a score from Jean Prodromides that heightens the ominous mood, and he has let the chorus break into chanting in the odes that brood over the story's final section.

Mr. Cacoyannis is not afraid to demand a wide vocal range from his actors. At first it is somewhat startling to hear a performer let out all the stops within his power, for our theater tends to be neat, precise and narrow in its bounds.

But these Trojan women are torn by wrenching griefs. They mourn the loss of everything they hold dear. And through them Euripides is indicting his own Greece, which could besiege, capture and sack a neutral island like Melos, murder its adult males and enslave its women and children.

While this production does not shy away from largeness of utterance, it also knows how to be heart-rending in restraint. Thus Mildred Dunnock as Hecuba, the gray queen, can denounce with a grim, towering rage, she can thunder at Menelaus and she can say farewell to her slain grandson, Astynax, lying on his father's shield, with subdued tenderness.

Carrie Nye as the crazed Cassandra has full scope for her painful visions. Joyce Ebert as Andromache expresses her anguish at the loss of husband and country in great, wrenching cries and then, when she hears that her boy, Astyanax, will be flung from the tower, she says good-by in hushed incantatory phrases that affirm the preciousness of life.

Jane White's Helen is crafty in her self-esteem and shrewd in her effort to save herself. Alan Mixon's Talthybius is dutiful, yet sympathetic. Robert Mandan's Menelaus hovers on the edge of renewed frailty. The women in the chorus speak and move well.

Mr. Cacoyannis uses the long, rectangular playing space and a broad flight of steps leading to a platform with a white luminous screen as a background with a fluidity that is both natural and dramatic. The theater in which he staged "The Trojan Women" at the Spoleto Festival last July surely had no such layout.

The translation, the late distinguished Edith Hamilton's, is direct and sinewy, all the better because it eschews floweriness. Mr. Cacoyannis, like Miss Hamilton, treats Euripides as if a great dramatic poet of two milleniums ago were still worth attending. And curiously enough, he is.

1963 D 24

1964

Hello, Dolly!

By HOWARD TAUBMAN

AS a play Thornton Wilder's "The Matchmaker" vibrated with unheard melodies and unseen dances. Michael Stewart, Jerry Herman and Gower Champion apparently heard and saw them, and they have conspired ingeniously to bring them to shining life in a musical shot through with enchantment.

"Hello, Dolly!," which blew happily into the St. James Theater last night, has qualities of freshness and imagination that are rare in the run of our machine-made musicals. It transmutes the broadly stylized mood of a mettlesome farce into the gusto and colors of the musical stage. What was larger and droller than life has been puffed up and gaily tinted without being blown apart. "Hello, Dolly!" is the best musical of the season thus far.

It could have been more than that. Were it not for lapses of taste, it could have been one of the notable ones. But Mr. Champion, whose staging and choreography abound in wit and invention, has tolerated certain cheapnesses, like the vulgar accent of a milliner's clerk, like the irritating wail of a teen-ager crying for her beau, like the muddled chase in the midst of a series of tableaux vivants.

Mr. Stewart's book has settled for some dull and cheap lines the musical would not miss.

It is a pity because "Hello, Dolly!" does not need such crutches. One can understand, of course, why offenses against taste creep into an essentially imaginative musical. The stakes are so high that there is a tendency to whip things up, as if the public could not be trusted. But only musicals without ideas or talent must resort to desperate measures, which don't help anyhow.

But enough of peevishness. Let us rejoice in the blessings "Hello Dolly!" bestows.

The Cast

HELLO DOLLY—, a new musical comedy suggested by Thornton Wilder's "The Matchmaker." Book by Michael Stewart; music and lyrics by Jerry Herman; scenery by Oliver Smith; costumes by Freddy Wittop; lighting by Jean Rosenthal; musical direction and vocal arrangements by Shepard Coleman; orchestrations by Philip Lang; dance and incidental music arranged by Peter Howard; directed and choreographed by Gower Champion, assisted by Lucia Victor; presented by David Merrick. At the St. James Theater,

246 West 44th Street.

Mrs. Dolly Gallagher Levi	Carol Channing
Ernestina	Mary Jo Catlett
Ambrose Kemper	Igors Gavon
Horse	Jan LaPrade, Bonnie Mathis
Horace Vandergelder	David Burns
Ermengarde	Alice Playten
Cornelius Hackl	Charles Nelson Reilly
Barnaby Tucker	Jerry Dodge
Irene Molloy	Eileen Brennan
Minnie Fay	Sondra Lee
Mrs. Rose	Amelia Haas
Rudolph	David Hartman
Judge	Gordon Connell
Court Clerk	Ken Ayers

The conception as a whole, despite an occasional excess of exuberance that turns into turbulence, is faithful to the spirit of Mr. Wilder's broad, chuckling jest. Mr. Stewart's book holds fast to Mr. Wilder's atmosphere and style even if it trots off into Broadwayese now and then. Mr. Herman's songs are brisk and pointed and always tuneful.

Mr. Champion's direction at its happiest darts and floats on stylized, yet airborne patterns of choreography. Oliver Smith's sets with their back-drops that unroll like screens have the elegance of pen-and-ink drawings and the insouciance of a rejuvenated old New York. Freddy Wittop's costumes join Mr. Smith's designs in an extravagance of period styles and colors.

The basic story, deliberately calculating in its simplicity, is unchanged. Here in a shrewdly mischievous performance by Carol Channing is the endlessly resourceful widow, Mrs. Dolly Gallagher Levi, matchmaker and lady-of-all-trades, who sets her enormous bonnet crested by a huge pink bird for the half-millionaire, Vandergelder, and lands him on her pleasure-loving terms.

Miss Channing's Dolly is all benevolent guile. She can talk faster than a con man without losing her big-eyed innocent gleam. She can lead Vandergelder to the widow Molloy and manage to rub noses with him enticingly.

She can teach "Dancing" to Mr. Herman's gliding three-four muse. Resplendent in scarlet gown embroidered with jewels and a feathered headdress, and looking like a gorgeous, animated kewpie doll, she sings the rousing title song with earthy zest and leads a male chorus of waiters and chefs in a joyous promenade around the walk that circles the top of the pit.

Here is David Burns as the curmudgeon Vandergelder, bellowing nasally like W. C. Fields redivivus. His intransigence in the face of warmth and kindness is a comfort in a Pollyanna world. When he roars that he is "rich, friendless and mean, which in Yonkers is as far as you can go," you are bound to share his pride. And when, standing on a dismantled parade float that is being pulled out of sight, he roars, "Where are you taking me?", he has the righteous wrath of a Horatius defending a sinking bridge.

•

Charles Nelson Reilly and Jerry Dodge as two of Vandergelder's oppressed clerks loose on the town sing and dance agreeably, and their buffoonery would be funnier if it were toned down. Eileen Brennan is as pretty and desirable a Widow Molloy as one could wish—with a voice, too. Igors Gavon is another performer with a big, resonant voice.

What gives "Hello, Dolly!" its special glow is its amalgamation of the lively theater arts in the musical numbers. Mr. Champion has provided fragments of dance for the overture-less opening that are all the more attractive because they are spare and unexpectedly spaced.

When he fills the stage for the ebullient "Put on Your Sunday Clothes" at the Yonkers Depot and has his lavishly garbed cast promenading along the oval runway out front, the theater throbs with vitality. As if to put a cherry on the sundae, the stage magicians have provided a railroad car pulled by an engine that spits smoke and ashes.

For a 14th Street parade Mr. Champion has deployed his forces in a cheerful old New York version of medieval guilds. To a bouncing

gallop by Mr. Herman, Mr. Champion has set a corps of waiters with trays, spits and jeroboams at the ready, dancing a wild, vertiginous rout. To Mr. Herman's lightly satirical "Elegance," Mr. Champion has fashioned a delightfully mannered routine for his quartet of singers—Miss Brennan, Sondra Lee, Mr. Reilly and Mr. Dodge.

Making the necessary reservations for the unnecessary vulgar and frenzied touches, one is glad to welcome "Hello, Dolly!" for its warmth, color and high spirits.

1964 Ja 17

After The Fall
Arthur Miller's Play
Opens Repertory

By HOWARD TAUBMAN

WHICH to celebrate first? The return of Arthur Miller to the theater with a new play after too long an absence? Or the arrival of the new Repertory Theater of Lincoln Center with its high promise for a consecration to drama of aspiration and significance?

Celebrate the conjunction of events, for together they may mark a turning point in the American drama. There have been discomfiting years of shrinkage and decline. The new company proclaims a fresh affirmation. The new play, though unsparing in its search for one man's truth, also ends on a note of hope.

•

In the beginning are the playright and his vision. "After the Fall," which opened officially last night in the newly built and impressively utilitarian ANTA Washington Square Theater, is Mr. Miller's distillation of the remembrance of things past.

Autobiographical, as the scuttlebutt has intimated with a wicked leer? Obviously, as even a fool would know. But is that the play's central truth? Unmistakably not. Like all writers who matter and who inevitably write about what they have felt, sensed and learned, Mr. Miller is probing into his own life and those near and dear to him and seeking answers to the eternal riddles that confront human beings on this earth.

What is love? What are its limits? Is there any difference in those limits in proportion to the nature of the beloved? Does anyone, however hard he tries to save those he loves, do more than mourn their loss and secretly rejoice at one's own survival? If living itself is filled with peril, should one go on?

The Cast

AFTER THE FALL, by Arthur Miller. Staged by Elia Kazan; presented by the Repertory Theater of Lincoln Center for the Performing Arts (Elia Kazan and Robert Whitehead, producing directors); production designed and lighted by Jo Mielziner; music by David Amram; costumes by Anna Hill Johnstone; production stage managers, Robert Downing and Frederick De Wilde. At the ANTA Washington Square Theater, 40 West Fourth Street.

Quentin	Jason Robards Jr.
Felice	Zohra Lampert
Holga	Salome Jens
Mother	Virginia Kaye
Dan	Michael Strong
Father	Paul Mann
Nurses	Faye Dunaway
	Diane Shalet
Doctor	Scott Cunningham
Maggie	Barbara Loden
Elsie	Patricia Roe
Louise	Mariclare Costello
Lou	David J. Stewart
Mickey	Ralph Meeker
Man in the park	Stanley Beck
Carrie	Ruth Attaway
Chairman	David Wayne
Rev. Harley Barnes	Hal Holbrook
Porter	Jack Waltzer
Secretary	Crystal Field

Inge Morath, Magnum

Jason Robards Jr. and Barbara Loden in Arthur Miller play

Lucas .... Harold Scott
Clergyman .... James Greene
Others: Stanley Beck, Scott Cunningham,
Faye Dunaway, Crystal Field,
Lou Frizzell, James Greene,
Clinton Kimbrough, John Phillip
Law, Barry Primus, Harold
Scott, Diane Shalet, Jack Waltzer

After three hours of turning and searching, "After the Fall" offers a firm, though quiet yes to the last question. For Quentin, the protagonist, is on a pilgrimage for self-knowledge as he harrowingly reviews his past and fearfully contemplates a future. He is not simply the mouthpiece of an author wishing to shrive himself of what is gone and dead. He represents any and all courageous enough to hunt for order in the painful and joyous chaos of living.

Quentin's pilgrimage traverses his mind filled with its mingling of thoughts and events. Like the simple set of many levels on the outthrust stage in the amphitheater of classic design, Quentin's quest covers terraces of memory. Time seems vagrant, like the mind itself. Scenes from childhood, first marriage, second marriage, new love, work and play years apart flow and ebb like overlapping waves.

●

At the outset Quentin emerges, moves forward and seats himself on the edge of the stage and begins to talk, like a man confiding in a friend. In the background are key figures in his life, and they move in and out of his narrative. The narration shades into scenes, little and big. They are revelations and illuminations.

They remind Quentin of an awkward young girl whom he made proud of herself. They bring back the tortured image of his mother's death and another of his mother's fury with his father, who lost all in trying to save a foundering business. They crisscross through his relations with a number of women—the first wife who wanted to be a separate person, the second who drove him into separateness and a possible third who knew, as a German raised

in a furnace of concentration camps, that "survival can be hard to bear."

These intertwining images bring back the memories of inquisition when men were asked to name names of those who had joined with them in a communism that they mistook for a better future. And they recall those who would name names and those who wouldn't and destroyed themselves as they lost everything.

"After the Fall" seeks to understand, not to judge. The bitter gulf that appears between Quentin and Louise, his first wife, is not blamed exclusively on one. The long, searing relation between Quentin and Maggie, the sexy, popular entertainer, who inescapably will be equated with Marilyn Monroe, is described with the tenderness and anguish it meant for both.

"After the Fall" is a pain-wracked drama; it is also Mr. Miller's maturest. Quentin's long, tormenting struggle with Maggie's devouring demands and her self-destructive drive is too extended for the point it makes in Quentin's pilgrimage. But even these scenes are gripping in their own way. For to sit in Mr. Miller's theater is to be in an adult world concerned with a search that cuts to the bone.

The production staged by Elia Kazan, who also has been absent too long from our stage, is unfaltering in its perception and orchestration. Quentin's pilgrimage into his memories is like the fine threads spun into a glistening web that encompasses all tension. The images flow into one another as imperceptibly as chords in a musical work. There is motion but no clutter, intensity but no shrillness.

How can one commend Jason Robards Jr. adequately for a performance that keeps him onstage for the entire three hours of the play and that never loses its fluidity? His shading from intimate confidences to flashes of action through a delicately grained variety of emotions is beyond praise. He is Quentin, his blue eyes contemplating his past and moving in and out of its frames as if instant changes of mood were as natural as the air he breathes.

And what about the stunning performance of Barbara Loden as Maggie? Virtually a newcomer, Miss Loden all but enkindles the stage, in her early scenes as the warm, childlike enchantress and in her later ones as the sick, frenzied demon of allure bent on self-destruction.

No performance is less than compelling in this company, which gives every indication of becoming a true ensemble. But a word should be said for Mariclare Costello as Louise, Salome Jens as the third woman, Virginia Kaye and Paul Mann as Quentin's parents and David J. Stewart and Ralph Meeker as the men who are asked to name names.

Rejoice that Arthur Miller is back with a play worthy of his mettle. Rejoice also that a new company has been born committed to theater of consequence, not only the new but the old that New York so scandalously neglects.

1964 Ja 24

'Deputy'

Drama About Pius XII at the Brooks Atkinson

By HOWARD TAUBMAN

AS a play "The Deputy" is flawed. As a polemic it is fierce and compelling. Since it wrestles with one of the most important moral issues of this or any time, it deserves to be seen, debated and taken to heart.

As it is being performed at the Brooks Atkinson Theater, where it opened last night, "The Deputy" has been shrunk drastically from its original five-act length, which would take something like eight hours to perform. In the version condensed by Rolf Hochhuth, the young German author, with the advice of Herman Shumlin, the director and co-producer, and adapted into English by Jerome Rothenberg, the playing time here is a little more than the normal two and a half hours.

Compared with the full text as published in England, this version sharpens the play's incendiary thesis. More intensely than in the uncut version, the play is a remorseless, furious "J'accuse" flung directly at the person and policy of Pope Pius XII.

The gravamen of the play is that the Pope was wanting as God's vicar on earth when he failed to denounce the Nazi extermination of the Jews in the hideous death factories.

To mount this charge against the Pope, Mr. Hochhuth has imagined a young Jesuit priest, Father Riccardo Fontana, who expresses the harrowed conscience of those in the faith who wished to protest openly. Being wellborn—his father is a member of the Roman nobility and an economic adviser to the Vatican—Father Fontana has the protection of a cardinal, is sent on delicate missions and has access to the Pope.

With interesting, complex strands in the play's structure eliminated, the story line is now straight as a long lance and as sharply pointed. It introduces the young priest as he reports for duty to the Papal Nuncio in Berlin in December, 1942. Here he meets an intense, distraught S.S. (élite guard) lieutenant, Kurt Gerstein, who has virtually forced his way into the Papal Legation.

●

Gerstein, whom Mr. Hochhuth based on a real-life figure who infiltrated the S.S. to fight Hitlerism, has just come from Poland. He has proof of the mass murders being committed at Treblinka and Belzec. He pleads with the Papal Nuncio for a protest from the Holy See. Thus Father Fontana learns for the first time of the monstrous crimes that the Nazis are committing.

Thereafter the play follows Father Fontana as he discovers more of the nature of the Nazi evil and as he seeks to persuade his father and a practical, realistic cardinal of the urgency of the situation. As the Nazis, after the overthrow of the Mussolini Government in 1943, begin to round up Jews for deportation, gathering them virtually under the shadow of St. Peter's, Father Fontana gets a final chance to state his case directly before the Pope. When Pius refuses to alter his policy of silence, the young priest pins a yellow star on his soutane and joins the miserable passengers to Auschwitz.

Leaving no possible doubt about his contempt for the Pope's position, Mr. Hochhuth has brought him onto the stage in a long scene. And here "The Deputy," though most inflammatory is weakest.

For Mr. Hochhuth has been guilty of a grave oversight in a dramatist. He has not allowed the Pope to be the kind of strong adversary needed for a powerful confrontation. In the historical sidelights he has appended to the printed version of the play, Mr. Hochhuth argues that the facts bear him out in his presentation of Pius XII.

Emlyn Williams, left, Fred Stewart, center, and Jeremy Brett in one of the scenes from the Rolf Hochhuth drama.

Maybe they do, but his Pope is not convincing. Mr. Hoch-huth insists that Pius XII was much preoccupied with Vatican investments and that his chief wish was to be a mediator between the Germans and the Allies. But it is hard to believe that Pius could have been as cold, sanctimonius and insipid a caricature as he is made to be. If he was, the dramatist should have made more of an antagonist of him.

The Cast

THE DEPUTY, a drama by Rolf Hochhuth, adapted by Jerome Rothenberg. Staged by Herman Shumlin; presented by Mr. Shumlin, Alfred Crown and Zvi Kolitz; production designed by Rouben Ter-Arutunian; lighting by John Harvey; costumes by Edith Lutyens Bel Geddes; stage manager, Howard Whitfield. At the Brooks Atkinson Theater, 256 West 47th Street.

Papal Nuncio	Reynolds Evans
Father Riccardo Fontana	Jeremy Brett
Monk	David Thomas
Lieut. Kurt Gerstein	Philip Bruns
Jacobson	Stefan Gierasch
Doctor	James Mitchell
Vittorio	Idwa Bowen
Photographer	Guy Repp
Count Fontana	Carl Low
Cardinal	Fred Stewart
Officer of the Pope's Guard	Gerald E. McGonagill
Brother Irenaeus	Richard Bengal
Father General	Ian Wolfe
Captain Salzer	Ron Leibman
Sergeant Witzel	Jack Livingston
First Italian Militiaman	Victor Arnold
Second Italian Militiaman	Ion Berger
Girl	Maria Tucci
Prisoners	Ben Hammer, Albert M. Ottenheimer
Pope Pius XII	Emlyn Williams
Officer of the Papal Guard	Guy Repp
Scribe	Gerald E. McGonagill
Woman	Pepa Kanter
Guards	Roger Hamilton, Victor Arnold, Ion Berger, Paul Flores
Little Girl	Denise Joyce

But the defects in this characterization do not vitiate what Mr. Hochhuth is saying. He himself is haunted by the fiendish crimes the Germans committed, as all Germans ought to be.

But all of us, he is crying, share in the burden of the guilt—the countries that did not open their doors in time to save lives, the Jews themselves who submitted passively or who tried to save their skins by collaborating and the good, law-abiding citizens in Germany and out of it who averted their eyes and ears and saw and heard no evil.

In broad, slashing strokes "The Deputy" dramatizes the agony of those who were per-secuted and those who, like Father Fontana and Gerstein, were moved to active compassion. The counterpointing of German guilt has been diminished by the excision of scenes, but it is still there in the figure of the diabolical Doctor modeled after the infamous Mengele and in the nasty Nazi officer in Rome, Captain Salzer.

Against Rouben Ter-Arutunian's stark suggestions of sets with bits of furniture, walls, portals and barbed wire, Mr. Shumlin has staged "The Deputy" with intensity. The scene with the Pope, played coldly and shrewdly by Emlyn Williams made up to look like Pius, is as glaring as a poster, but it is too easy a theatrical victory for the playwright and the production.

Jeremy Brett brings fire and dedication to the role of Father Fontana. Fred Stewart's crafty Cardinal, James Mitchell's darkly sleek Doctor, Philip Bruns's impassioned Gerstein, Carl Low's troubled father of the young priest, Stefan Gierasch's terrified hidden Jew and Ron Leibman's irritable Captain Salzer are among the vivid figures in "The Deputy."

Now that "The Deputy," which has stirred Europe for the last year, is here, the debate, already begun, will be intensified. Our theater rarely touches on moral issues of this magnitude. For this is a play about choice. Every man, no less than the Pope, must make choices, and the avoidance of choosing is an act of choice in itself. "The Deputy" poses a universal problem in a sensational way.

1964 F 27

'Funny Girl'

Musical Based on Life of Fanny Brice

By HOWARD TAUBMAN

WHO wouldn't want to resurrect Fanny Brice? She was a wonderful entertainer.

Since Fanny herself cannot be brought back, the next best thing is to get Barbra Streisand to sing and strut and go through comic routines à la Brice. Miss Streisand is well on her way to becoming a splendid entertainer in her own right, and in "Funny Girl" she goes as far as any performer can toward recalling the laughter and joy that were Fanny Brice.

If the new musical that arrived last night at the Winter Garden were dedicated entirely to the gusto and buffoonery of Fanny Brice, all would be well nigh perfect this morning. But "Funny Girl" also is intent on telling the story of how Fanny loved and lost Nick Arnstein, and part of the time it oozes with a thick helping of sticky sentimentality.

But that's show-business sagas for you. They rarely can untrack themselves from the hokum and schmaltz that authors and, for all one knows, show people consider standard operating procedure. As for the public, it often is a pushover for the glamour of the stage and the romances of show folk. Say for "Funny Girl" that it has not reached to be neck deep in show business. It has every right to be there.

"Funny Girl" is most fun when it is reveling in Fanny's preoccupation with show business. Miss Steisand as a young Brice bursting with energy and eagerness to improve her

Henry Grossman

Barbra Streisand and Sydney Chaplin in the new musical

routines is an impudent dancing doll who refuses to run down. Miss Streisand imagining herself in a radiant future in "I'm the Greatest Star," an appealingly quirky song, is not only Fanny Brice but all young performers believing in their destinies.

The Cast

FUNNY GIRL, a musical. Book by Isobel Lennart. Music by Jule Styne. Lyrics by Bob Merrill. Staged by Garson Kanin; presented by Ray Stark, in association with Seven Arts Productions; associate producer, Al Goldin; production supervised by Jerome Robbins; associate director, Lawrence Kasha; choreographed by Carol Haney; scenery and lighting by Robert Randolph; costumes by Irene Sharaff; musical director, Milton Rosenstock; orchestrations by Ralph Burns; vocal arrangements by Buster Davis; dance orchestrations by Luther Henderson; production stage manager, Richard Evans. At the Winter Garden, Broadway and 51st Street.

Fanny Brice	Barbra Streisand
Emma	Royce Wallace
Mrs. Brice	Kay Medford
Mrs. Strakosh	Jean Stapleton
Mrs. Meeker	Lydia S. Fredericks
Mrs. O'Malley	Joyce O'Neil
Tom Keeney	Joseph Macaulay
Eddie Ryan	Danny Meehan
Snub Taylor	Buzz Miller
Trombone Smitty	Blair Hammond
Five Finger Finney	Alan E. Weeks
Nick Arnstein	Sydney Chaplin
Florenz Ziegfeld Jr.	Roger De Koven
Mimsie	Sharon Vaughn
Ziegfeld Tenor	John Lankston
Ziegfeld Lead Dancer	George Reeder
Mr. Renaldi	Marc Jordan

Then there are the production numbers that recall the theater before World War I. Miss Streisand and a wildly agitated chorus, set loose in a pattern designed by Carol Haney, do the explosive "Cornet Man" in a way that would startle the music halls of old but does not betray their spirit.

For an evocation of the stately Ziegfeld Follies, which Miss Brice brightened with her exuberance, there are two big nostalgic numbers. One glorifies the bride, with beautiful girls, draped and undraped, fixed in the scenery and rippling on a lofty flight of stairs topped by candelabra, and with Miss Streisand turning the overblown "His Love Makes Me Beautiful" into a spoof. The other, using the same stairway, shoots soldiers and soldierettes into a furious drill to a military "Rat-Tat-Tat-Tat," with Miss Streisand doing her bit as a comic veteran.

Fanny's friends making merry with a block party on Henry Street after her debut in the Follies are festive company. And Miss Streisand as Fanny hamming it up in her first rendezvous with Sydney Chaplin in a private room in a swank restaurant is almost as funny as the funny girl herself might have been. She uses a fan with mock coyness; she arranges herself on a chair like a rachitic femme fatale; she walks across the room with a wiggle Mae West would envy.

These maneuvers nevertheless to a Brice or a Streisand are the small tricks of the clown's trade. What makes Miss Streisand's manipulation of them in this scene particularly impressive is that she conveys a note of honest emotion underneath the clowning. Indeed, at this point the romance of Fanny and Nicky is as charming as young love.

Isobel Lennart's book skirts sentimentality reasonably well until Fanny and Nick turn serious, get married and run into troubles. By the end "Funny Girl" is drenched in tears.

Fortunately, Miss Streisand can make a virtue out of suffering, if she is allowed to sing about it. Jule Styne, who has written one of his best scores, has provided her with bluesy tunes like "Who Are You Now?" and she turn them into lyrical laments.

Miss Streisand can also draw rapture from the yearning "People." For a change of pace she makes her raffish share of "You Are Woman," for which Bob Merrill has done smiling lyrics, worthy of the performer she impersonates.

●

Mr. Chaplin is a tall, elegant figure as Nick, gallant in courting and doing his best when he must be noble. Kay Medford, who seems to be a stage mother every time you see her in a musical, is dry and diverting as Fanny's shrewd parent. Danny Meehan is agreeable as a hoofer who befriends the young

Fanny.

Garson Kanin gets credit for being the director and Jerome Robbins for being the production supervisor, and only they and the company know what their contributions were. Say for both of them that "Funny Girl" behaves as if it takes its hokum seriously and that its show-business sequences framed in Robert Randolph's cheerful sets move at a pace hard to resist.

It's the authentic aura of show business arising out of Fanny Brice's luminous career that lights up "Funny Girl." Much of the spoken humor is homespun—that is, East Side homespun. The true laughter in this musical comes from the sense of truth it communicates of Fanny Brice's stage world. And Fanny's personality and style are remarkably evoked by Miss Streisand. Fanny and Barbra make the evening. Who says the past cannot be recaptured?

1964 Mr 27

King Lear

Scofield in Title Role of British Production

By HOWARD TAUBMAN

ALTHOUGH Paul Scofield is a Lear you will not forget, he is not merely a star around whom an ad hoc production has been reared with faulty underpinning. The "King Lear" that brought the reverberations of great tragedy for the first time last night into the New York State Theater at the Lincoln Center for the Performing Arts is a proud, unified company achievement.

The Royal Shakespeare Company from Stratford-on-Avon and the Aldwych Theater in London has sent us a great masterpiece produced with regard for the noble arch of its structure, and all the parts are like stones fitted into their niches and carrying their share, however large or modest, of the mighty burden.

Peter Brook has staged this "Lear" with a kind of elemental spareness and simplicity. It is said that he was influenced by the analysis of Jan Kott, the Polish scholar, whose "Shakespeare Our Contemporary" is to be published here in September. In an essay on "King Lear or Endgame," Mr. Kott has attempted to show the parallels between Shakespeare's tragedy and Samuel Beckett's play.

It is Mr. Kott's contention that both plays deal with the disintegration of established values. The theme of "Lear," he insists, is an inquiry into man's journey from the cradle to the grave "into the existence of nonexistence of Heaven and Hell." The theme, he adds, is nothing less than "the decay and fall of the world."

The Cast

KING LEAR, Shakespeare's drama. Staged and designed by Peter Brook; presented by Bonard Productions and Donald Seawell, by arrangement with the governors of the Royal Shakespeare Theater, Stratford-on-Avon; the Royal Shakespeare Company (Peter Hall, managing director); costumes in collaboration with Kegan Smith; assistant designer, Adele Hankey; assistant director, Charles Marowitz; fight arranged by John Barton; music by Guy Woolfenden; Royal Shakespeare Wind Band, Mr. Woolfenden, music director; stage manager for Bonard Productions, Fred Heberl; repertory stage manager for the Royal Shakespeare Company, David Brierley. At the New York State Theater of Lincoln Center for the Performing Arts, Broadway and 65th Street.

Earl of Kent..............Tom Fleming
Earl of Gloucester.........John Laurie
Edmund ....Ian Richardson
Lear, King of Britain.......Paul Scofield
Goneril ....Irene Worth
Duke of Albany..........Clifford Rose
Regan ....Pauline Jameson
Duke of Cornwall........Tony Church
Cordelia ....Diana Rigg
Duke of Burgundy.......Michael Murray
King of France ....Barry MacGregor
Edgar ....Brian Murray
Oswald ....Michael Williams
Knight ....Michael Murray
Fool ....Alec McCowen
Curan ....John Harwood
Servant ....John Cobner
Old Man..................Ken Wynne
Doctor ....Michael Burrell
Messenger ....Ian Lindsay
Captain ....John Church
Herald ....Peter Blythe
British Captain ....Leslie Southwick
British Captain ....Peter Tory

It does not matter whether one accepts Mr. Kott's view. The important point is that it apparently has led Mr. Brook to conceive of a "Lear" stripped of the panoply of old-fashioned Shakespearean staging. This is a "Lear" whose pertinence to man's predicament yesterday, today and probably always is inescapable.

Mr. Brook's design is based on a couple of enormous gray rectangular panels that, standing diagonally at the sides, frame a similar, unornamented gray rear wall. In several places rectangular sheets of metal, looking like copper, are lowered from above; for several scenes two rough-hewn fences, are lowered from the sides, and early in the play Lear and his retinue dine at great, rough tables. Otherwise, there is hardly any furniture. The huge stage is like a vast, empty, heartless earth.

The clothes are equally evocative. The dresses and tunics look as if they were made of homespun fabrics and leather. They bring to mind the far past; yet they are simplified and stylized so that they could be of any period.

●

Mr. Brook has composed his scenes in the framework of the open spaces of his deep stage so that man, though often in the foreground, is a small figure against the thick rotundity of the world. Mr. Scofield as the mad, spent Lear and the blind Gloucester of John Laurie, consoling each other, form a sculptured pietà in an unfeeling plain. Mr. Laurie, seated alone on the bare stage, his body contorted yet limp, while the battle rages unseen, is a harrowing vision.

Mr. Scofield's Lear has size, but it remains within the proportions of modern man's sensibility. In his first scene he allows himself the signs of old age—a cracked, quavering voice and a trembling arm—as he exhorts his daughters to expatiate on the extent of their love. When Goneril later crosses him, he can overturn the table and set his knights roaring in anger. And in the tempest his powerful voice

can contend with the elements without resort to ranting.

Although Mr. Scofield commands the grand manner, he is at his noblest and most moving as his anguish increases and his mind turns inward and cracks. His scene, after the storm with the Fool, played with poignant lightness by Alec McCowen, with Brian Murray's tender madman of an Edgar and with Tom Fleming's manly, honest Kent has a haunting sense of pity. Mr. Brook uses long silences here and elsewhere with remarkable effect.

Mr. Scofield finds subtleties of movement, expression and speech to convey the deepening of his awareness and humility. Awakening from his long sleep, he recognizes Cordelia, played with pride and purity by Diana Rigg, with a sense of bewilderment and shame. At the end when he carries in the slain Cordelia, he is like a man who has summoned up unexpected reserves of physical strength and moral courage.

Villainy is stark and brutal in this "Lear." Irene Worth's Goneril is as stony of voice as she is marble of heart. Pauline Jameson's Regan is vicious and vengeful. Ian Richardson's Edmund has bitterness as well as evil and at the end the necessary touch of gallantry. Tony Church's Cornwall is an eye-gouger to the brutal manner born. Michael Williams's Oswald is foppish and meanly servile.

With this visit the Royal Shakespeare Theater helps us to honor Shakespeare worthily on this anniversary year. For it brings us a memorable Lear in an integrated, searching and illuminating "Lear."

1964 My 19

'The Subject Was Roses'

Play by Frank Gilroy at the Royale Theater

By HOWARD TAUBMAN

FRANK D. GILROY has made good on the promise of "Who'll Save the Plowboy?" His new play, "The Subject Was Roses," which opened last night at the Royale Theater, is not only an impressive stride forward but also an honest and touching work in its own right.

Mr. Gilroy has not resorted to gimmicks, razzle-dazzle or advanced techniques to be in fashion. He has written a straightforward, realistic play that wears no airs. With simplicity, humor and integrity he has looked into the hearts of three decent people and discovered, by letting them discover, the feelings that divide and join them.

The Cast

THE SUBJECT WAS ROSES, a play by Frank D. Gilroy. Staged by Ulu Grosbard; presented and designed by Edgar Lansbury; lighting by Jules Fisher; costumes by Donald Foote; production-stage manager, Paul Leaf. At the Royale Theater, 242 West 45th Street.

John Cleary ....Jack Albertson
Nettie Cleary ....Irene Dailey
Timmy Cleary ....Martin Sheen

In "Who'll Save the Plowboy?," which was produced by the Phoenix Theater in 1962, Mr. Gilroy revealed that he had a refreshing awareness of the way ordinary-seeming

Irene Dailey and Jack Albertson with Martin Sheen, in uniform, in the play that opened at the Royale Theater.

men and women talk, think and feel but had not yet sharpened his dramatic style. "The Subject Was Roses" is evidence of marked progress, for it is written with economy and precision.

Although it is deceptively quiet in its reserve, "The Subject Was Roses" never loses a beat in its building of mood and conflict. It knows where it's going. It makes every line and gesture work and convey meaning. And at the end it has reached its destination, which, though no mountain peak, is at a raised plateau of perception.

It would have been easy to descend into bathos in this story of Timmy Cleary, a 21-year-old veteran, and his parents, to whose middle-class Bronx apartment he returns in 1946 after three years in the Army. But Mr. Gilroy knows the difference between sentiment and sentimentality, and he is not betrayed into the latter.

When the curtain rises on a Saturday morning, Jack Albertson as John Cleary is in the kitchen admiring his son's Eisenhower jacket with its corporal's stripes, its hash marks for overseas service and the infantryman's combat medal. There is a crude streamer on the adjoining living room wall welcoming Timmy home, and an up-turned beer keg, draped in bunting, bears witness to the previous night's celebration for the returned warrior.

Irene Dailey as Nettie Cleary joins her husband in the kitchen, and there is an intimation that their relations are edgy. Mr. Gilroy does not labor his points. His touch is light; and he relies on his director, Ulu Grosbard, and his actors to flesh out the characters and to establish the atmosphere.

Miss Dailey's effort to make her son's favorite breakfast of waffles runs into trouble. Martin Sheen as the son who seems suddenly to hear and see everything afresh realizes that he has wounded her by not noting her concern. He coaxes his mother into dancing with him, and the taste of Miss Dailey's and Mr. Sheen's playing and of Mr. Grosbard's direction shed a glow on this scene.

The events of the 48 hours covering the play's action are not flashy. If one were to detail them, they would provide a bare outline. But each scene is another step in the education of the Clearys as they learn to face and accept truths about themselves.

Miss Dailey's Nettie is a luminous creation. She can suggest hurt and desiccation with a stricken glance. Wearing a plain hat and coat and holding her purse, she can turn to walk out of her apartment so that her back conveys her utter defeat and despair. In the one interlude that does not quite ring true —her recollection of her happy youth—her tender reminiscence resolves all doubts in favor of the character.

Mr. Albertson plays the contrary and sentimental Irishman of a father with a fine mixture of truculence and self-pity. He has a tendency to slur his words, which made him difficult to follow early in the play, but when he speaks out, he is not only understandable but also vibrant.

Mr. Sheen's Timmy communicates an alert, attractive sense of newly won maturity. He knows how to listen to his parents so that he seems to reappraise their familiar phrases and attitudes before our very eyes. He has the skill to suggest independence without arrogance.

Credit Mr. Grosbard's sensitive, unobtrusive staging and Edgar Lansbury's scrupulously commonplace set as well as Mr. Gilroy for the dignity and warmth of this modest, truthful play. Don't these people know that it's flying in the face of tradition to bring in an honest work this late in May?

1964 My 26

Maria Karnilova and Zero Mostel in musical comedy based on Sholem Aleichem's storie

Fiddler On The Roof
Sholem Aleichem Tales Made Into a Musical

By HOWARD TAUBMAN

IT has been prophesied that the Broadway musical theater would take up the mantle of meaningfulness worn so carelessly by the American drama in recent years. "Fiddler on the Roof" does its bit to make good on this prophecy.

The new musical, which opened last night at the Imperial Theater, is filled with laughter and tenderness. It catches the essence of a moment in history with sentiment and radiance. Compounded of the familiar materials of the musical theater —popular song, vivid dance movement, comedy and emotion — it combines and transcends them to arrive at an integrated achievement of uncommon quality.

The essential distinction of "Fiddler on the Roof" must be kept in mind even as one cavils at a point here or a detail there. For criticism of a work of this caliber, it must be remembered, is relative. If I wish that several of the musical numbers soared indigenously, if I find fault with a gesture that is Broadway rather than the world of Sholem Aleichem, if I deplore a conventional scene, it is because "Fiddler on the Roof" is so fine that it deserves counsels toward perfection.

The Cast

FIDDLER ON THE ROOF, a musical based on Sholem Aleichem's stories. Book by Joseph Stein. Music by Jerry Bock. Lyrics by Sheldon Harnick. Staged and choreographed by Jerome Robbins; presented by Harold Prince; scenery by Boris Aronson; costumes by Patricia Zipprodt; lighting by Jean Rosenthal; orchestrations by Don Walker; musical direction and vocal arrangements by Milton Greene; dance music arranged by Betty Walberg; production stage manager, Ruth Mitchell. At the Imperial Theater, 249 West 45th Street.

Tevye	Zero Mostel
Golde	Maria Karnilova
Tzeitel	Joanna Merlin
Hodel	Julia Migenes
Chava	Tanya Everett
Shprintze	Marilyn Rogers
Bielke	Linda Ross
Motel	Austin Pendleton
Perchik	Bert Convy
Yente	Beatrice Arthur
Lazar Wolf	Michael Granger
Morche	Zvee Scooler

Rabbi .... Gluck Sandor
Mendel .... Leonard Frey
Avram .... Paul Lipson
Nachum .... Maurice Edwards
Grandma Tzeitel............ Sue Babel
Fruma-Sarah .... Carol Sawyer
Constable ....Joseph Sullivan
Fyedka .... Joe Ponazecki
Shandel .... Helen Verbit
Bottle Dancers.......Louis Genevrino,
   Mitch Thomas, Duane Bodin, John C. Attle
Fiddler .... Gino Conforti

But first to the things that are marvelously right. The book that Joseph Stein has drawn from the richly humorous and humane tales of Sholem Aleichem, the warmhearted spokesman of the poor Jews in the Russian villages at the turn of the century, is faithful to its origins.

It touches honestly on the customs of the Jewish community in such a Russian village. Indeed, it goes beyond local color and lays bare in quick, moving strokes the sorrow of a people subject to sudden tempests of vandalism and, in the end, to eviction and exile from a place that had been home.

Although there is no time in a musical for a fully developed gallery of human portraits, "Fiddler on the Roof" manages to display several that have authentic character. The most arresting, of course, is that of Tevye, the humble dairyman whose blessings included a hardworking, if sharp-tongued, wife, five daughters and a native philosophical bent.

If Sholem Aleichem had known Zero Mostel, he would have chosen him, one is sure, for Tevye. Some years ago Mr. Mostel bestowed his imagination and incandescence on Tevye in an Off-Broadway and television version of Sholem Aleichem's stories. Now he has a whole evening for Tevye, and Tevye for him. They were ordained to be one.

Mr. Mostel looks as Tevye should. His full beard is a pious aureole for his shining countenance. The stringy ends of his prayer shawl hang from under his vest; the knees of his breeches are patched, and his boots are scuffed. On festive occasions he wears a skull cap and kaftan that give him an appearance of bourgeois solidity. But he is too humble to put on airs.

A man of goodwill, Mr. Mostel often pauses to carry on a dialogue with himself, arguing both sides of a case with equal logic. He holds long conversations with God. Although his observations never are disrespectful, they call a spade a spade. "Send us the cure," he warns the Lord, "we got the sickness already."

●

When Maria Karnilova as his steadfast but blunt wife breaks in on one of these communions with a dry greeting, "Finally home, my breadwinner!", he is polite enough for a parting word to God, "I'll talk to You later."

Mr. Mostel does not keep his acting and singing or his walking and dancing in separate compartments. His Tevye is a unified, lyrical conception. With the exception of a grimace or a gesture several times that score easy laughs, Tevye stays in character.

The scope of this performance is summed up best in moments made eloquent through music and movement. When Mr. Mostel sings "If I Were a Rich Man," interpolating passages of cantillation in the manner of prayer, his Tevye is both devout and pungently realistic. When Tevye chants a prayer as the good Golde tries to convey an item of vital news, Mr. Mostel is not only comic but evocative of an old way of life. When Tevye hears the horrifying word that his third daughter has run away with a gentile, Mr. Mostel dances his anguish in a flash of savage emotion.

The score by Jerry Bock and the lyrics by Sheldon Harnick at their best move the story along, enrich the mood and intensify the emotions. "Sabbath Prayer" is as hushed as a community at its devotions. "Sunrise, Sunset" is in the spirit of a traditional wedding under a canopy. When Tevye and Golde after 25 years of marriage ask themselves, "Do You Love Me?", the song has a touching angularity. But several of the other romantic tunes are merely routine.

Jerome Robbins has staged "Fiddler on the Roof" with sensitivity and fire. As his own choreographer, he weaves dance into action with subtlety and flaring theatricalism. The opening dance to a nostalgic song, "Tradition," has a ritual sweep. The dances at the wedding burst with vitality. A dream sequence is full of humor. And the choreographed farewells of the Jews leaving their Russian village have a poignancy that adds depth to "Fiddler on the Roof."

Boris Aronson's sets provide a background that rings true; they give the work an unexpected dimension of beauty in scenes like "Sabbath Prayer," the wedding and the epilogue.

●

Joanna Merlin, Julia Migenes, Tanya Everett as three of the daughters, Beatrice Arthur as a busybody of a matchmaker, Austin Pendleton as a poor tailor, Bert Convy as a young radical, Michael Granger as a well-to-do butcher and Joe Ponazecki as the gentile suitor are among those who sing and act with flavor.

Richness of flavor marks "Fiddler on the Roof." Although it does not entirely eschew the stigmata of routine Broadway, it has an honest feeling for another place, time and people. And in Mr. Mostel's Tevye it has one of the most glowing creations in the history of the musical theater.

1964 S 23

The Cast

LUV, a comedy by Murray Schisgal. Staged by Mike Nichols; presented by Claire Nichtern; production designed by Oliver Smith; lighting by Jean Rosenthal; costumes by Theoni V. Aldredge; song by Irving Joseph; production stage manager, Harvey Medlinsky. At the Booth Theater, 222 West 45th Street.

Harry Berlin.................Alan Arkin
Milt Manville..............Eli Wallach
Ellen Manville ....Anne Jackson

By HOWARD TAUBMAN

WHATEVER the truth of the old saw that misery loves company, the chances are excellent that you'll love the company of the three recurrently miserable characters who make up the cast of "Luv."

Murray Schisgal's comedy, which opened last night at the Booth Theater, is a delicious spoof on a multitude of matters: love, marriage, loneliness, lost identity, homosexuality, suicide, housekeeping—you name it, Mr. Schisgal probably has a guffaw at its expense.

●

"Luv" combines a number of styles into what may come to be known as the Schisgal manner. It employs the irrelevancies of the theater of the absurd and skips cheerfully over preoccupations that this style often contemplates bitterly and somberly. Farce constantly rises to the surface and takes over. Comedy of manners in a raffish, bizarre way is invoked. So are the techniques of vaudeville and low comedy.

Mr. Schisgal's impish fancy is beautifully complemented by Mike Nichols's staging, which is so full of inventive high spirits that it introduces drolleries as irrelevant as some of the playwright's lines. The requirements of writer and director are handsomely met in the performance of Anne Jackson, Eli Wallach and Alan Arkin, who do and say delightfully foolish things with an earnestness that compounds the comic interest.

The action of "Luv" takes place on a bridge, and Oliver Smith has designed a lean, graceful setting seen through an arched false proscenium that detaches the story from reality. If you choose to find recognizable traits and foibles in the daft characters involved in the unrealistic occurrences on this bridge, Mr.

Schisgal certainly won't mind, for he planted them there. But you are free to enjoy "Luv" as unalloyed comic fiction, and there is plenty to relish on that level.

●

The fun is largely in misery —present troubles, memories of suffering, the tribulations of love past, current and future. When the play begins there is Alan Arkin as Harry Berlin, looking like a shaved, mustachioed beatnik who has sunk so low that honest beatniks would disown him. He has no future except to jump off the bridge and is about to do so when Eli Wallach as Milt Manville comes along and intervenes.

Milt and Harry turn out to be college classmates. As Harry, in his rags, slowly drops hints of his tale of woe, Milt, a picture of prosperity, is all sympathy. But "Luv" has ample place in its bosom for more than one miserable fellow. Milt is also full of frustration, for his wife won't release him and let him marry the girl he loves.

Presently Anne Jackson as Milt's wife, Ellen, appears. As she stands under a lamppost, her expression congealed and her fur-coated body rigid, it is clear that she,

too, is torn by anguish. Now we have a triangle matched in misery.

Milt has had an inspiration. Why not bring Ellen and Harry together and thus win the freedom to marry the other girl? But Ellen looks despairing; she needs sprucing up.

Under Mr. Nichols's tutelage, Mr. Wallach and Miss Jackson develop a wonderful comic bit. He tidies her dress and slip, combs her hair, rouges her lips, powders her cheeks, delicately touches up her eyelashes and sprays her with perfume. Could a husband be more tender with a wife he hopes to palm off?

The events that follow need not be detailed. All you will wish to know is that whatever marriages are made and unmade, Milt, Ellen and Harry end up in sorrow and agony, and the greater their misunderstandings and problems, the more you laugh.

●

Mr. Schisgal has mastered the trick of using stereotyped gag lines in freshly humorous contexts. After four months of living with Harry, Ellen turns to Milt, and with the perplexity of a vaudevillian

Henry Grossman

Eli Wallach, left, Alan Arkin and Anne Jackson in play

setting up a big laugh, she demands, "Who is he?" When she later tells Harry that she finds him the most obnoxious person in the world, he replies, again in the fashion of ancient comic routine, "That's a good beginning."

There are times when Mr. Schisgal strains a little, and there are places where his comic muse falters and stutters. But his director and actors often fill the tenuous spots with laughter.

Miss Jackson is a treasure of womanhood eager for love, however you spell it, and the joys of motherhood. She is also credible as a girl with such astonishing brain power that she can recall which states were carried by Al Smith in 1928.

Mr. Wallach has a flair for enduring indignities, whether of poverty or affluence, marriage or divorce. It is his destiny to tumble off the bridge twice, throwing up geysers of water in his wake, and to return each time in more outlandish costumes and in magnified outrage.

Mr. Arkin, the Dostoevsky-to-be of his college class, tends to etherealize miseries. In love, he moos like a strangulated cow. In annoyance he is shrilly petulant. He is the first sufferer we meet, and at the end he still suffers the most. Poor Harry; funny Arkin.

Poor Schisgal, doesn't even know how to spell "Luv." If he wants to call them laffs, that's his privilege. After all, that's what "Luv" really spells.

1964 N 12

'Slave' and 'Toilet' by LeRoi Jones Open

By HOWARD TAUBMAN

LEROI JONES is one of the angriest writers to storm the theater—and one of the most gifted. On the evidence of his new one-acters, "The Slave" and "The Toilet," one wonders whether his rage is not at war with his instincts as an artist.

In both halves of the double bill, which opened last night at the St. Marks Playhouse, Mr. Jones has exciting and moving things to say. Once again, as in "Dutchman," he discloses a sure grasp of the theatrical image.

But he cannot resist the urge to shock by invoking violence and all the obscenities he can think of. There are times when these shock tactics perform no useful dramatic function, when they clarify no meaning, when they merely set up needless resistance to what the play is saying.

When Mr. Jones sets out to be literal, he is about as unsubtle as the law will allow. "The Toilet" occurs in a toilet of a boys' high school. Larry Rivers has obliged the author by designing a retreat with all the equipment you would find in a men's room. Leo Garen has staged the opening moments of the play to indicate realistic use of the equipment. Mr. Jones and his colleagues apparently assume that nothing can be left to an audience's imagination.

●

The students, nearly all of them Negro, drift into the toilet. Again Mr. Jones, his director and his actors are nothing if not realistic. The talk is latrine language. The boys are ugly, mindless, full of bravado and violence. They are waiting for a fight to be fought between two boys. Meanwhile, the Negroes assail each other and are particularly vicious to a white boy who has drifted into the room.

Karolis, apparently a Puerto Rican, is finally hauled in, already bloodied from a beating he has received en route to the arena. Foots, a bright boy, whom a teacher has called "a credit to his race," is waiting to take on Karolis. Foots is angry because Karolis has sent him a love letter. Though badly hurt,

Karolis rises to fight, and as he is getting the better of Foots, the other Negroes savage him.

For all its violence and "ritual filth," to use Mr. Jones's phrase, "The Toilet" ends on a note of tenderness. The denouement of the play is moving as only a natural dramatist can make it, and underneath its coarseness there runs a strong sense of the needless debasement of human beings. One is sure, however, that Mr. Jones could have made his points without the shock tactics.

In "The Slave" Mr. Jones widens his frame of reference. He imagines what he calls "a fable" sometime in the future when open war for domination is being fought in the

The Casts

THE SLAVE and THE TOILET, short plays by LeRoi Jones. Staged yb Leo Garen; presented by Mr. Garen and Stan Swerdlow in association with Gene Persson and Rita Fredricks and Theater Vanguard; production designed by Larry Rivers; associate designer and lighting by Harold Baldridge; sound by Art Wolff; production stage manager, Ed Cambridge. At the St. Marks Playhouse, Second Avenue and Eighth Street.

Ora ....James Spruill
Willie Love................Gary Bolling
Hines ....D'Urville Martin
Johnny Holmes ....Boslic Van Felton
Perry ....Norman Bush
George Davis ....Antonio Fargas
Donald Farrell ....Gary Haynes
Knowles ....Walter Jones
Skippy ....Tony Hudson
Karolis ....Jaime Sanchez
Foots ....Hampton Clanton
        THE SLAVE
Walker Vessels......:.....Al Freeman Jr.
Grace Easely...............Nan Martin
Bradford Easely..........Jerome Raphel

streets of many cities between black and white. The setting is a college professor's home, but the sound of shooting punctuates the dialogue so insistently that at times one cannot hear every word spoken by Nan Martin, even though this is a small theater.

Walker Vessels, a poet and obviously a leader of the embattled blacks, appears at the home of his former wife, a white woman now married to a white man, a professor. Vessels reviles the professor for his liberalism and for his defense of minority causes. He threatens him with a gun, slugs him, heaps obscene abuse on him and his wife.

Much of "The Slave" is debate. Whatever Mr. Jones's personal views may be, he attempts to play fair with all his characters. There is no mistaking the fact, however, that Vessels is the violent, uncompromising voice of the Negro in furious rebellion, and that this rebellion is what the play is all about. Here again, at the end Mr. Jones remembers to be a dramatist as well as a platform orator.

He ends with a shooting and with a bomb bursting in the professor's home and Mr. Rivers has worked up an ingenious set that all but collapses into rubble. But the explosions and the cries of the wounded and dying become something more than theatrical effects. They sum up a vision of what might happen if the patience of the neglected and scorned gave out.

●

Al Freeman Jr. is brilliant as Vessels; as an old man he reads a long, poetic soliloquy at the outset with taut intelligence. Miss Martin brings horrified intensity to the wife, and Jerome Raphel is solid in a role that turns eventually into a straw man. Hampton Clanton, Jaime Sanchez and James Spruill stand out in the impressive and enormously athletic cast of "The Toilet."

Despite its larger scope, "The Slave" is not so welldesigned a play as "The Toilet," which has a lot more gamey language and a lot less rhetoric. People with delicate ears and easily shocked minds will find Mr. Jones's latest efforts hard to take. But he is a writer who cannot be ignored. Indeed, he is so full of talent and fire that he does not need to thumb his nose at his audience.

1964 D 17

1965

Carney, Matthau Under Direction of Nichols

THE ODD COUPLE, a comedy by Neil
Simon. Staged by Mike Nichols; presented by Saint Subber; scenery by
Oliver Smith; lighting by Jean Rosenthal; costumes by Ann Roth; production stage manager, Harvey Medlinsky.
At the Plymouth Theater, 236 West
45th Street.

Speed .... Paul Dooley
Murray .... Nathaniel Frey
Vinnie .... John Fiedler
Vinnie .... John Fiedler
Oscar Madison .... Walter Matthau
Felix Unger .... Art Carney
Gwendolyn Pigeon ...... Carole Shelley
Cecily Pigeon .... Monica Evans

By HOWARD TAUBMAN

THE opening scene in "The
Odd Couple," of the boys
in their regular Friday night
poker game, is one of the
funniest card sessions ever
held on a stage.

If you are worried that
there is nothing Neil Simon,
the author, or Mike Nichols,
his director, can think of to
top that scene, relax. The
main business of the new comedy, which opened last night
at the Plymouth Theater, has
scarcely begun, and Mr. Simon, Mr. Nichols and their
excellent cast, headed by Art
Carney and Walter Matthau,
have scores of unexpected
ways prepared to keep you
smiling, chuckling and guffawing.

Mr. Simon has hit upon an
idea that could occur to any
playwright. His odd couple
are two men, one divorced
and living in dejected and
disheveled splendor in an

Friedman-Abeles

Walter Matthau, left, and Art Carney in scene in comedy

eight-room apartment and the other about to be divorced and taken in as a roommate.

One could predict the course of this odd union from its formation in misery and compassion through its disagreements to its ultimate rupture. Mr. Simon's way of writing comedy is not to reach for gimmicks of plot; he probably doesn't mind your knowing the bare outline of his idea.

His skill—and it is not only great but constantly growing —lies in his gift for the deliciously surprising line and attitude. His instinct for incongruity is faultless. It nearly always operates on a basis of character.

Begin with that poker game. Mr. Matthau, the slovenly host, is off stage in the kitchen fixing a snack while Nathaniel Frey, John Fiedler, Sidney Armus and Paul Dooley are sitting around the table on a hot summer night, sweating and grousing at the luck of the cards. The burly Mr. Frey is shuffling awkwardly, "for accuracy, not speed," and the querulous Mr. Fiedler, the big winner, talks of quitting early.

●

The cards are dealt. Mr. Matthau walks in with a tray of beer and white and brown sandwiches. They're brown in his scheme of housekeeping because they're either new cheese or very old meat. As he opens the beer cans, sending sprays of lager over his guests (surely a Nichols touch), the dealer inquires whether he intends to look at his cards. "What for," Mr. Matthau, the big loser, grumbles, "I'm gonna bluff anyhow."

The sixth member of the Friday night regulars, Mr. Carney, is missing. Evidently he has been away from his known haunts for 24 hours, and a phone call from his wife informs his friends that she hopes he never turns up. Since they know that he is a man who takes such blows seriously, they fear that he will do something violent to himself.

With Mr. Carney's arrival as Felix, the discarded husband, the principal action begins. Mr. Carney is truly bereaved, a man of sorrows. His eyes are stricken, his lips quiver, his shoulders sag. Even poker gives way before his desolation. The players are too concerned about possible moves by Felix toward self-destruction. When at last they go home, they depart softly and gravely like chaps leaving a sick room.

Mr. Matthau as Oscar, the host, consoles Felix, massaging away the spasms in his neck and enduring the moose calls with which the unfortunate fellow clears ears beset by allergies. Nothing much happens during the rest of the act except that these two inevitably blunder into a domestic alliance, but there is scarcely a moment that is not hilarious.

The unflagging comedy in the remainder of the play depends on the fundamental switch—of the odd couple. Felix is a compulsive house keeper, bent on cleaning, purifying the air and cooking. When the gang assembles for its poker game, Felix has special treats ready for snacks.

Mr Carney handles the housewifely duties with a nice, delicate, yet manly verve. But he is strict. When he serves a drink to Mr. Frey, he wants to know where the coaster is. The answer—and this is Mr. Simon, the marksman at firing droll lines—is, "I think I bet it."

Mr. Matthau for his part is wonderfully comic as a man who finds his companion's fussy habits increasingly irksome. He walks about with a bearish crouch that grows more belligerent as his domestic situation becomes both familiar and oppressive. There is a marvelous scene in which he and Mr. Carney circle each other in mutual distaste—Mr. Matthau looking like an aroused animal about to spring and Mr. Carney resembling a paper tiger suddenly turned neurotic and dangerous.

To vary the humors of the

domestic differences, Mr. Simon brings on two English sisters named Pigeon — yes, Pigeon, Gwendolyn and Cecily — for a date with Oscar and Felix. The girls induce more laughter than their names promise. Carole Shelley and Monica Evans are a delight as the veddy British and dumb Pigeons.

Mr. Nichols's comic invention, like Mr. Simon's, shines through this production and the comfortable Riverside Drive apartment invoked by Oliver Smith's set. Just a sample: Mr. Carney left alone with the Pigeons is as nervous as a lad on his first date. When one of the girls takes out a cigarette, he hastens to her with his lighter and comes away with the cigarette clamped in its mechanism. "The Odd Couple" has it made. Women are bound to adore the sight of a man carrying on like a little homemaker. Men are sure to snicker at a male in domestic bondage to a man. Kids will love it because it's funny. Homosexuals will enjoy it— for obvious reasons. Doesn't that take care of everyone?

1965 Mr 11

Zoe Caldwell Excels in Minnesota Play

THE WAY OF THE WORLD, a play by William Congreve. Staged by Douglas Campbell; presented by the Minnesota Theater Company; production designed by Tanya Moiselwitsch; music by Henry Purcell, arranged by Eric Stokes and Herbert Pilhofer. At the Tyrone Guthrie Theater, Minneapolis.

Prologue	Ann Whiteside
Mirabell	Robert Milli
Fainall	Robert Pastene
Witwoud	Ken Ruta
Sir Willful Witwoud	Paul Ballantyne
Petulant	Ed Flanders
Waitwell	Graham Brown
Lady Wishfort	Jessica Tandy
Mistress Millamant	Zoe Caldwell
Mistress Marwood	Nancy Wickwire
Mrs. Fainall	Ellen Geer
Foible	Helen Harrelson
Mincing	Krinstina Callahan
Betty	Evie McElroy
Peg	Niki Flacks
Coachman	Earl Boen
Servant to Sir Willful	James Lineberger
John	James J. Lawless
Lady in the park	Ann Whiteside
Chocolate House Keeper	John Cappalletti
Grenadier	Donald West
Musicians	Bruce Allard, Edouard Blitz, Dave Karr

By HOWARD TAUBMAN
Special to The New York Times

MINNEAPOLIS, June 1— There are many good reasons to justify going out of one's way for the Minnesota Theater Company's "The Way of the World," and hardly the least of them is Congreve himself. But an excellent one is to enjoy the impeccable high-comedy playing of Zoe Caldwell as Millamant.

Jessica Tandy brings a raf fish gusto to Lady Wishfort. Nancy Wickwire is a cool, suave intriguer as Marwood. Robert Pastene is all showy manners and hard bargainer as Fainall. Robert Milli conveys the shrewd charm of Mirabell. But it is Miss Caldwell who is unfaltering in every velvet thrust.

●

Not an inflection or a gesture is out of place in this handsomely composed portrait of a wise and witty young woman of the London world of 1700. In Tanya Moiseiwitch's modish clothes, with their headdresses and trains, Miss Caldwell moves with the poised self-knowledge of one who has stepped out of a Restoration drawing room.

Her face with its pale make-up, obviously the careful concern of a young woman of breeding who will not look vulgarly outdoorsy, rarely betrays an emotion. The eyes are detached but brighten occasionally with mischief. The voice is silken, but what humor there is in the phrasing—not catchpenny humor but the sense of fun that sparkles in a civilized mind.

When Miss Caldwell talks of being persecuted by letters, there is amusement in the weariness of her tone.

When she reads the poems of Sir John Suckling to confuse addle-brained Sir Willful, it is as if only she and we were privy to the dry jesting.

When she sets forth the conditions on which she will agree to marry Mirabell, she does so with a mingling of seriousness and laughter that suits perfectly Congreve's milieu and style. And Mr. Milli's response in kind gives the necessary fillip to a scene that has not lost its edge in 265 years.

Douglas Campbell has directed "The Way of the World" with a relish of its manners and mannerisms. Miss Moiseiwitch's designs with their suggestion of colorful elegancies turn the open stage of the Tyrone Guthrie Theater into a garden or boudoir with equal felicity.

The over-all tone of the production, with its occasional background of Purcell music and with its ingratiating concluding dance, is admirable. But the Minnesota Theater Company would be deluding itself if it thought that it had met all the challenges implicit in a Congreve revival.

The balance of the performance is not always right. One or two players handle the Restoration extravagances self-consciously, making their points too obviously. Several others lack the flexibility of movement and diction needed for this kind of work.

And what is to be done about the mélange of accents with which Congreve's glittering English is spoken?

●

Consider Miss Tandy, Miss Wickwire and Miss Caldwell, all of whom know their business and speak well. Miss Wickwire's speech has the flatness of the American timbre. Miss Tandy's seems now to be an accommodation

Zoe Caldwell and Robert Milli in Minneapolis production

between her native English and the American approach. Miss Caldwell's enunciation and rhythm have the ring of authenticity. As for some of the company's younger members, they are struggling in deep, unfamiliar waters.

But if we are going to wait for perfection, we will never attempt revivals of the classics. It is better to do Congreve with forces not equal in all the parts than not to do him at all, provided, of course, you have such delightful exemplars as Miss Caldwell to show the irresistible way.

1965 Je 2

Shakespeare Tragedy Back at Stratford

Actor Continues Search to Plumb Character

KING LEAR, Shakespeare's drama. Staged by Allen Fletcher; presented by the American Shakespeare Festival Theater and Academy; scenery and costumes by Will Steven Armstrong; lighting by Tharon Musser; music by Conrad Susa; musical director, Jose Serebrier; duels staged by Christopher Tanner; production stage manager, John Seig. At the American Shakespeare Festival, Stratford, Conn.

Earl of Kent	Roy Poole
Earl of Glocester	Patrick Hines
Edmund	John Cunningham
King Lear	Morris Carnovsky
Goneril	Patricia Hamilton
Regan	Mary Hara
Cordelia	Ruby Dee
Duke of Albany	Josef Sommer
Duke of Cornwall	Theodore Sorel
Duke of Burgundy	DeVeren Bookwalter
King of France	Robert Benedict
Edgar	Stephen Joyce
Oswald	Ted Graeber
Knight	Dennis Jones
Other Knights	Richard Kuss
	Richard Morse
	John Carpenter
Fool	Richard Mathews
Servant to Cornwall	David Grimm
Old Man	Thomas Ruisinger
Knight to Regan	Edwin Owens
French captain	Todd Drexel
Officer	Nick Smith
Herald	Richard Kuss

By HOWARD TAUBMAN

Special to The New York Times

STRATFORD, Conn., June 24—There is no end to "King Lear." Ask Morris Carnovsky; he knows.

Two years ago Mr. Carnovsky undertook Shakespeare's most challenging and most profound tragic role at the American Shakespeare Festival Theater here and achieved moments of greatness. Then he went on to play the role in other cities, including Los Angeles. Now he is grappling with Lear again in Connecticut's Stratford, where the production returned last night.

●

To one who has watched Mr. Carnovsky cope with Lear in Connecticut, in California and again in Connecticut, it is clear that he keeps searching for new ways to plumb the overwhelming tragedy's depths. In his latest try he has arrived at his most coherent and sustained realization.

Surely and steadily Mr. Carnovsky has moved toward a performance that reminds one of a secret of the greatest musicians—their capacity to manage a wealth of subtle inflections within a carefully controlled compass. Mr. Carnovsky's current Lear is masterly in the delicacy and penetration of its nuances.

Indeed, it is more poignant than ever because it is so vulnerably and sadly human. But it is no less heroic than before, even if grandeur is not sought for in thunder. For its heroism is firmly rooted in an awareness and acceptance of the human condition.

In Connecticut two years ago Mr. Carnovsky managed scenes of surging passion, particularly in the storm, and of ineffable tenderness, particularly in his pathetic encounters with the Fool, Edgar feigning madness, and the blinded Gloucester. But the early scenes were not of the same order, possibly because Mr. Carnovsky was saving something for the big one to come.

In Los Angeles last summer Mr. Carnovsky succeeded in raising the pitch of the early scenes and maintaining it throughout the play. The result was an interpretation of greater consistency and impressive potency.

For this revival Mr. Carnovsky has refined his entire performance. He no longer needs to roar at the extremity of his vocal powers, even in the storm sequence. Because he begins with more restraint, he gets the effects he wants without bellowing.

The risk of this kind of regulated attack is that Lear might become diminished and self-conscious. Nothing of the sort has happened. The reason is simple; Mr. Carnovsky's control is not a virtuoso actor's stunt but organic to his conception.

Watch him now as he divides his kingdom. He is old, deliberate and abstracted; the warrants of love he wants from his daughters are routine contracts he expected them to deliver, signed and sealed. The latent fire in the sovereign smolders as he turns on Kent and as he snarls at Cordelia's suitors. It flares up as he cries out his curse on Goneril. But this is the fierce eruption of a man who is still vain and proud.

As Lear teeters on the edge of madness, there is a delicate balancing between bitterness and tenderness, expressed most movingly in the dialogues with the Fool. The last effort to believe in his stable world is reflected in his desperate embrace of Regan when he hopes that she will be dutiful. The cry, "Reason not the need," becomes a supplication, helpless and grief-stricken.

●

Like Mr. Carnovsky, Allen Fletcher, the director, has subtilized and simplified his production. There is less scenery and there are fewer props than two years ago. The storm scene is played on a bare stage with only a crash of thunder and rays of ominous light to support Mr. Carnovsky's defiance of the elements.

Mr. Carnovsky's madness is not a performer's effect. It is a release of inhibitions, and it is achingly, piteously gallant. The awakening to sanity and to humility in the final scenes have a wrenching and healing truth.

In the fallible and costly world of the theater it would probably be too much to expect the company to match the maturity and perception of a Carnovsky. Those who come nearest to what one would like are Patrick Hines as Gloucester, Roy Poole as Kent and Richard Mathews as the Fool.

John Cunningham plays Edmund with intelligence but the note of commanding authority is not yet there. Patricia Hamilton is a venomous Goneril. Ruby Dee as Cordelia brings warmth to the final scenes. Stephen Joyce as Edgar is pathetic when he feigns madness but needs size at the end.

But "King Lear" as always takes upon itself the mystery of things, and Mr. Carnovsky perseveres imaginatively and eloquently in his search for an ultimate Lear, knowing, as we do, that there is triumph in the seeking.

1965 Je 25

DANTON'S DEATH, play by Georg Buchner, staged by Herbert Blau; setting and lighting, Jo Mielziner; costumes, James Hart Stearns; electronic music and songs by Morton Subotnick. Presented by the Repertory Theater of Lincoln Center, under the direction of Mr. Blau and Jules Irving. At the Vivian Beaumont Theater, Broadway and 64th Street.

Herault-Sechelles ....Michael Granger
George Danton ....Alan Bergmann
Julie, Danton's wife ....Claudette Nevins
Philippeau ....James Earl Jones
Camille Desmoulins ......Robert Stattel
Lacroix ....David J. Stewart
Simon ....Ray Fray
Simon's wife ....Shirley Jac Wagner
Billaud ....Louis Zorich
Robespierre ....Robert Symonds
Legendre ....Ronald Weyand
Collot d'Herbois ....Paul Mann
Marion ....Marcie Hubert
St. Just...........Roscoe Lee Browne
Lucille, Camille's wife .....Gail Fisher
Fouquier ....Glenn Mazen
General Dillon ....Robert Haswell
Barere ....Tom Rosqui

By HOWARD TAUBMAN

THE new Vivian Beaumont Theater is a beauty in red and black. The new leadership of the Repertory Theater of Lincoln Center has plunged into its task with energy and boldness. The first production, "Danton's Death," which marked the official baptism of new theater and leadership last night, is a memorable occasion, bearing promise of a significant enhancement of the city's dramatic culture.

The importance of this event, which is bound to be historic, is not diminished by one's reservations about the company's present capacity to cope with this remarkable work by Georg Büchner, a first play by a genius of 21 who did not live to be 24. Herbert Blau and Jules Irving, the new directors, have not hesitated to launch their regime daringly, and Mr. Blau has had the hardihood to put himself and his colleague on the block by beginning with his own version and staging of a play full of pitfalls.

Mr. Blau's adaptation, to begin with, is pungent and idiomatic without sacrificing the somber, bitter poetry that darkens Büchner's vision. Mr. Blau's staging, for all its efforts to make free, full use of the vast stage and its dazzlingly swift modern equipment, concentrates on the business of Büchner's drama, which tells the pain-racked story of how the French Revolution destroyed those who helped to make it.

Mr. Blau and his company have not made good every scene and point in "Danton's Death." The early crowd scenes carry no conviction. There is a commotion caused by people screaming and racing hither and yon, but instead of the illusion of the mobs in bloody, feverish Paris, one has the impression of actors going through their paces.

Mr. Blau knows this simple truth as well as anyone. But he cannot help being stimulated by the possibilities of this new stage. He has not

Alan Bergmann, left, and Robert Stattel in scene from play

been afraid to employ its resources.

He has been abetted by Jo Mielziner's designs, which use great thrusting lines to achieve perspective in depth and which evoke the streets and gardens of the surging city. The imposing benches of the Deputies roll out from the rear of the stage, and they are backed in an instant by a black curtain bearing the words of "The Rights of Man." At the end the guillotine stands tall and ominous down forward, and the blade descends with a sickening thud. Doesn't this realism become a species of Schadenfreude?

Well, Mr. Blau is intent on underscoring Büchner's irony that terror is the child of virtue. He wants Büchner's anguished question, put into Danton's mouth, to reverberate: "What is it within us that lies, whores, steals and murders?" He takes care to emphasize the tormented query asked by a Deputy who goes along with Robespierre and the ruthless St. Just: "Am I a murderer or a prisoner?"

These are searching questions, still pertinent. It is the measure of the new theater's and leadership's sense of responsibility that they begin with a play that asks them.

Not all the problems of "Danton's Death" — some, indeed, are an outcome of the play's episodic structure and its noncombatant hero—have been solved, nor all the problems of forming a strong company and using this impressive new stage.

But there are heartening signs of a viewpoint and a commitment. One could not ask for more this early in the game.

The acting company is wildly uneven. At its most brilliant it gleams furiously through the seething, thin-lipped intensity of Robert Symonds's Robespierre. At its worst it offers the inept mouthings of performers who know not what they say or how to say it.

It is true that "Danton's Death" requires a huge cast, and not even a repertory company whose board of directors accepts the fact that a deficit is inevitable has the means to recruit a host of impeccable performers. But Mr. Blau and Mr. Irving elected not to play it safe. By choosing a big work, they took risks that turned out to be serious.

To Alan Bergmann falls the most difficult and challenging role, that of Danton. For Büchner, writing well over a century ago, created a hero who is a forerunner of the alienated man who broods so disenchantedly through so much contemporary drama.

His Danton is a hero who is weary. He does not contend with his antagonists or his fate, except in a brief flare-up of the old passion for action, and even this outburst seems to come from memory rather than conviction. Profound pessimist and obsessive pleasure-seeker, Danton is eager for the abyss. As a result, he makes things tough for actor and director.

Mr. Bergmann's Danton is not quite at ease in the early scenes. His tenderness with his wife, Julie, is too distracted, and his night with the prostitute, Marion, does not even suggest weary sensuality. The obligation to be passive, almost recessive, is a test for the subtlest acting, and Mr. Bergmann is still struggling to meet it.

When he takes the tribune in his own defense, however, Mr. Bergmann is more commanding. With his proud cry at the end of the scene, "Now you know Danton!" Mr. Bergmann catches at last the man's flaming pride and the bottomless despair in his heart.

The prison scene near the end is Mr. Bergmann's—and Mr. Blau's—best. Here Danton and the four comrades who are facing the guillotine spend their last night with wrenching fear and brave dignity.

Mr. Bergmann and Robert Stattel as the ardent young Desmoulins are immensely affecting in their farewell. David J. Stewart, James Earl Jones and Michael Granger join in discovering the savage, compassionate poetry of this great scene.

It is played entirely on the forward section of the thrust stage. It demands no rich panoply, no huge spaces, no magic from electronically speeded curtains, revolves or traveling sections of set. All that is needed is the play of light as if filtered through barred windows, capable actors and the fierce, probing words of a poet.

1965 O 22

'Man of La Mancha' Has Kiley in Title Role

The Cast

MAN OF LA MANCHA, a musical, suggested by the life and works of Miguel de Cervantes y Saavedra. Book by Dale Wasserman. Music by Mitch Leigh. Lyrics by Joe Darion. Staged by Albert Marre; presented by Albert W. Selden and Hal James; choreography by Jack Cole; scenery and lighting by Howard Bay; costumes by Mr. Bay and Patton Campbell; musical direction by Neil Warner; musical arrangements by Music Makers, Inc.; production stage manager, Marnel Sumner. At the ANTA Washington Square Theater, 40 West Fourth Street.

Don Quixote (Cervantes)	Richard Kiley
Sancho	Irving Jacobson
Aldonza	Joan Diener
Innkeeper	Ray Middleton
Padre	Robert Rounseville
Dr. Carrasco	Jon Cypher
Antonia	Mimi Turque
Barber	Gino Conforti
Pedro	Shev Rodgers
Anselmo	Harry Theyard
Jose	Eddie Roll
Juan	John Aristedes
Paco	Anthony de Vecchi
Tenorio	Fernando Grahal
Maria	Marceline Decker
Fermina	Gerianne Raphael
Captain of the Inquisition	Renato Cibelli
Guitarist	David Serva

By HOWARD TAUBMAN

AND now Cervantes and his ineffable Don Quixote have been transported to the popular musical theater. With the exception of a few vulgarities and some triteness, they have made the transition in "Man of La Mancha" with remarkable spirit and affection.

Virtually every medium of communication has attempted to seize Don Quixote in its own language and imagery. The fond and foolish knight, his quest and his adventures have been turned into film, opera, symphonic tone poem, what you will. The results, sometimes distinguished and often not, depended on the genius of the new form and the capacities of the transformers.

The dire peril to Don Quixote if cheap, rude hands were laid on him are readily apparent. But no such fate befalls the Don himself in "Man of La Mancha," which opened last night at the ANTA Washington Square Theater. As Dale Wasserman has written him, Albert Marre directed him and Richard Kiley plays him, he is admirably credible—a mad, gallant, affecting figure who has honestly materialized from the pages of Cervantes.

One can quibble about other aspects of "Man of La Mancha." Irving Jacobson is a sympathetic, gentle Sancho, but it is difficult to shake the uneasy feeling that he is a Spaniard with a Jewish accent.

Mitch Leigh and Joe Darion have made every conscientious effort to integrate their songs into the texture of action and character. Indeed, the program eschews the usual list of numbers. But their muse, though it aspires, does not always soar in the imaginative vein of Cervantes and Quixote.

Yet "Man of La Mancha" rates far more plusses than minuses. At its best it is audacious in conception and tasteful in execution. Many of the familiar adventures of Don Quixote are caught in evocative scenes. Howard Bay's use of the thrust stage, where the Lincoln Center Repertory Theater endured its first struggles, is sparing in its furniture and props and, thanks to the employment of light, rich in illusion. Mr. Marre and his choreographer, Jack Cole, have conjured up some impressive pictures in action and repose.

Best of all is Mr. Kiley, who has never given a finer performance. We meet him at the beginning as Cervantes being led down a huge stairway, which has been lowered from on high, into a large prison cell.

After the guards are gone, he is attacked by his fellow inmates, who rob him, find his immortal manuscript and prepare to cast it into the flames. To save it, Cervantes goes on trial before this jury of the condemned, and he tells them the story of Don Quixote.

Seated on a box before a crude mirror, Cervantes turns himself into Don Quixote, as he pastes on mustache, pointed beard and thick eyebrows, dons a battered cuirass and arms himself with a lance. As the musical play progresses, Mr. Kiley shuttles back and forth between Cervantes and Don Quixote, and the transformation always is amazingly apt.

As Cervantes he is a man of spirit with a quizzical humor and a keen flexible intelligence. Shading into Quixote, he becomes the amiable visionary, childlike in his pretensions and oddly, touchingly gallant. His eyes take on a wild, proud, otherworldly look. His posture is preternaturally erect. His folly becomes a kind of humbling wisdom.

Richard Kiley, left, and Irving Jacobson during a scene

Watch him as he and Mr. Jacobson sit on their wooden mounts, pulled by actors wearing delicious masks of horses' heads. This is the innocent, radiant knight errant ready for any derring-do. Mr. Kiley also can sing, and he delivers the confident "I am Don Quixote of La Mancha" with a marchlike stride.

Watch Mr. Kiley as he arrives at the inn, which he imagines to be the castle where he is to be dubbed a knight. With a blossom in his plumed helmet and a green sprig in his lance, he appears with the delicate pride and conviction of a lighthearted soul about to meet its destiny. Listen to him serenade Joan Diener as the strumpet of a servant, who is to become his dream Dulcinea. The song itself is ordinary, but the Quixote has endearing credibility.

Mr. Kiley defends his Dulcinea against the muleteers in stout combat that is a little too stagy for comfort, but how true, disarming and amusing he is when he sends the bewildered girl to bind up the enemy's wounds. The binding up of the wounds, by the way, is turned in a blistering, orgiastic dance for the muleteers and the shapely, mobile Miss Diener, who is dragged and hauled as violently as any performer in town.

Mr. Kiley's finest scene is at the end. Now an old man, feeble and dying, he has forgotten his days of knighthood. But his Dulcinea comes to his bedside. She whispers the words of the song he once sang, "To Dream the Impossible Dream." The memory of Quixote floods the old man's consciousness. He rouses himself, stands up: he is for a last precious moment Don Quixote again.

●

One could dispense with the added bit where Mr. Kiley, with arms around Mr. Jacobson and Miss Diener, belts out a chorus in operetta style. One wishes Mr. Kiley did not mutter a banal, modern "Yeah" in an earlier scene as he glances at a pot on the fire. One could do without other reminders of show biz here and there that traduce the essential atmosphere.

Ray Middleton as a fellow inmate and as innkeeper plays and sings with sturdy forthrightness. Robert Rounseville, who used to sing tenor leads in opera, reminds us how exhilerating it is to hear a real voice in the popular musical theater, and he has a tender, moving "De Profundis" to sing for the departed Don Quixote.

Whatever concessions "Man of La Mancha" has made to easy popularity, it has not filled the stage with an extraneous chorus line or turned Don Quixote into an oafish clown. One does not expect complete fidelity to Cervantes outside his pages—who reads him these days?—but there are charm, gallantry and a delicacy of spirit in this reincarnation of Quixote.

1965 N 23

The Cast

THE PERSECUTION AND ASSASSINATION OF MARAT AS PERFORMED BY THE INMATES OF THE ASYLUM OF CHARENTON UNDER THE DIRECTION OF THE MARQUIS DE SADE, a play by Peter Weiss. Staged by Peter Brook; presented by the David Merrick Arts Foundation, by arrangement with the Governors of the Royal Shakespeare Theatre, Stratford-on-Avon; English version by Geoffrey Skelton; verse adaptation by Adrian Mitchell; scenery and properties by Sally Jacobs; costumes by Gunilla Palmstierna-Weiss; choreography by Malcolm Goddard; lighting and design supervision by Lloyd Burlingame; music by Richard Peaslee; assistant to the director, Ian Richardson; stage manager, Christine Staley. At the Martin Beck Theater, 302 West 45th Street.

Coulmier	Clifford Rose
Mrs. Coulmier	Brenda Kempner
Miss Coulmier	Ruth Baker
Herald	Michael Williams
Cucurucu	Freddie Jones
Kokol	Hugh Sullivan
Polooch	Jonathan Burn
Rossignol	Jeanette Landis
Jacques Roux	Robert Lloyd
Charlotte Corday	Glenda Jackson
Jean-Paul Marat	Ian Richardson
Simonne Evrard	Susan Williamson
Marquis de Sade	Patrick Magee
Duperret	John Steiner
Abbott	Mark Jones
Mad animal	Morgan Sheppard
Schoolmaster	James Mellor
Military representative	Ian Hogg
Mother	Mark Jones
Father	Henry Woolf
Newly rich lady	John Hussey
Voltaire	John Harwood
Lavoisier	Leon Lissek

By HOWARD TAUBMAN

IMAGINATION has not vanished from the stage. Nor intelligence. For proof see Peter Weiss's play, which opened last night at the Martin Beck Theater.

The exceptional length of the play's title is not caprice. The play reverberates with overtones even as its name is crowded with words and syllables: "The Persecution and Assassination of Marat as Performed by the Inmates of the Asylum of Charenton Under the Direction of the Marquis de Sade."

Mr. Weiss has written a play within a play, and in both there are unexpected resonances of comment and meaning. He has used the techniques of Brechts, invoking verse, music and speeches to the audience to produce an effect of standing apart, but has orchestrated them in his own way. In the end one is involved as one stands apart; one thinks when one should feel and feels when one should think.

There is hardly anything conventional about the play. But Mr. Weiss's novel devices are not employed for the sake of novelty. His primary purpose, if one may dare to isolate one aim as the chief one, is to examine the conflict between individualism carried to extreme lengths and the idea of a political and social upheaval.

●

Spokesman for this sort of individualism is Sade; the voice of upheaval is Marat. But Mr. Weiss has gone beyond a simple confrontation. He has achieved a remarkable density of impression and impact by locating his conflict, in the course of his play within a play, in a mental institution.

The result is a vivid work that vibrates on wild, intense, murmurous and furious levels. It is sardonic and impassioned, pitiful and explosive. It may put you off at times with its apparent absurdity, or it may shock you with its allusions to violence and naked emotions. But it will not leave you untouched.

As the play begins on the wide, lofty uncurtained stage, furnished with a few planks, benches and several pits, the inmates of Charenton wander in. They wear rough, tattered rags, and some are twisted in body and limbs as well in mind. The director of the asylum and two of his ladies in their elegant clothes arrive, and he explains that he has encouraged Sade to direct the inmates in this play for its therapeutic value.

Mr. Weiss has not invented this point. Sade, who was an inmate at Charenton, did write and stage plays there in the early years of the 19th century. What Mr. Weiss has invented is the play that Sade has chosen to write and direct, though certain details of the Marat story used in Sade's play are facts of history.

The play unfolds in a series of episodes. The basic action involves the events leading up to the slaying of Marat by Charlotte Corday. But the episodes do not follow an ordinary continuity. Songs, scenes that at first view seem irrelevant, the unpredictable movements and sounds of the patients, weave around the main action to provide a remarkable richness of texture.

●

Marat, his body angry and blotched with a feverish ailment, sits in his bathtub, a bandage on his head and a sheet over his shoulders, but the tormenting pains and memories cannot be appeased. Since Marat is played by a Charenton paranoiac, his fierce outbursts have a deepened anguish. Sade, of course, is Sade, but despite his worn, faded finery, he is also an inmate, and the fury of his worship of self becomes both heightened and oddly pathetic.

They are both rebels. Sade is in revolt against accepted

notions because he needs to believe in and explore himself. Marat is the social revolutionary. Their ideas clash, but Mr. Weiss does not choose between them.

He lets passionate, burning truths emerge from their feverish preoccupations. Out of the mouths and actions of other inmates in this madhouse come other insights.

Mr. Weiss, a German who fled Nazism and who now lives in Sweden, has written in a kind of singsong vernacular, which rises often to eloquence. Geoffrey Skelton's English version and Adrian Mitchell's verse adaptation establish the flavor of the playwright's style.

•

This is a work, that demands all the theater's arts and artifices, and this production by Great Britain's Royal Shakespeare Company, staged with savage brilliance by Peter Brook, translates Mr. Weiss's writing into throbbing theatrical terms.

The images of life in a mental institution are weird and moving. An inmate who raves like a mad animal and utters searing truths is not an oddity; he freezes the blood. Inmates going through a make-believe guillotining and falling pell mell into a pit are horrifying and piteous. A quartet of inmates done up as clowns caper and cavort amusingly and piercingly. Even the whipping of Sade by Charlotte Corday with her long hair, though not literally painful, stings.

Mr. Brook has used sound like a conjurer. There is not only Richard Peaslee's evocative, simple music for the songs and for the band, dressed like inmates and seated in boxes on opposite sides of the house. There are also the clanging of chains, the pounding of boards, the eerie moans of the inmates.

•

The visitors from Britain are performing Mr. Weiss's play with conviction and intensity, in taut, colorful ensemble. The entire company deserves to be noticed, but there is time only to speak admiringly of Ian Richardson's flaming Marat, Patrick Magee's cold, sinuous Sade, Glenda Jackson's wild Corday, Clifford Rose's elegantly superficial asylum director, and Michael Williams's subtle Herald.

Mr. Weiss's play expresses a fresh, probing sensibility in original stage terms. Like its title, it will give you original stage terms. Like its title it will give you pause, stir your imagination and provoke your mind. It is good to encounter a playwright who dares to challenge the theater and its audience to full participation.

1965 D 28

1966
Angela Lansbury Stars as the Zesty Aunt

The Cast

MAME, a musical, based on the novel by Patrick Dennis and the play, "Auntie Mame," by Jerome Lawrence and Robert E. Lee. Book by the Messrs. Lawrence and Lee. Music and lyrics by Jerry Herman. Staged by Gene Saks; presented by Robert Fryer, Lawrence Carr and Joseph P. Harris; associate producer, John Bowab; choreography by Onna White; scenery by William and Jean Eckart; costumes by Robert Mackintosh; lighting by Tharon Musser; musical direction and vocal arrangements by Donald Pippin; orchestrations by Philip J. Lang; dance music arranged by Roger Adams; assistant choreographer, Tom Panko; hair styles by Ronald DeMann; production stage manager, Terence Little. At the Winter Garden, Broadway and 51st Street.
Patrick Dennis, age 10..Frankie Michaels
Agnes Gooch...............Jane Connell
Vera Charles...........Beatrice Arthur
Mame Dennis...........Angela Lansbury
Ralph Devine.................Ron Young
Bishop ....Jack Davison
M. Lindsay Woolsey.......George Coe
Ito ....Sab Shimono
Doorman ....Art Matthews
Elevator Boy................Stan Page
Messenger ....Bill Stanton
Dwight Babcock.....Willard Waterman
Art Model.....................Jo Tract
Dance Teacher.........Johanna Douglas
Leading Man...............Jack Davison
Stage Manager...........Art Matthews
Madame Branislowski....Charlotte Jones
Gregor ....John Tallaferro
Beauregard Jackson Picket
  Burnside ....Charles Braswell
Cousin Fan..............Ruth Ramsey
Uncle Jeff.............Clifford Fearl
Sally Cato................Margaret Hall

Mother Burnside.........Charlotte Jones
Junior Babcock.............Randy Kirby
Patrick Dennis, age 19 to 29,
                          Jerry Lanning
Gloria Upson..............Diana Walker
Mrs. Upson.............Johanna Douglas
Mr. Upson.............John C. Becher
Pegeen Ryan............Diana Coupe
Peter Dennis..........Michael Maitland

By STANLEY KAUFFMANN

"MAME" is back, with music — probably to stay as long as last time when it was "Auntie Mame," without music. As show biz goes, this is good news. It opened last night at the Winter Garden (I saw the last preview), replete with lively song and dance, an exceptionally able cast, and a splendidly splashy production. Even the scenery is entertaining.

There may be a few benighted Eskimos who still need to be told that the story comes, originally, from Patrick Dennis's novel; was dramatized by Jerome Lawrence and Robert E. Lee and was then filmed. It concerns (dear Eskimo readers) a zesty Manhattan lady of the nineteen-twenties, wealthy and ingratiatingly wild, who inherits a young nephew from her deceased brother and shortly afterward inherits the Depression.

●

Through thick and several thins, the large-minded lady and the adoring boy make their difficult ways, until she marries a rich Southerner. After some years of honeymooning abroad, she returns to find Patrick grown and in the grip of a blond suburban bore.

Mame knocks the stuffing out of the prospective stuffy marriage and steers Patrick into a more likely one. At the end, she works her world-opening wiles on Patrick's young son, preparing to Mame him happily for life.

This star vehicle deserves its star, and vice is very much versa. No one can be surprised to learn that Angela Lansbury is an accomplished actress, but not all of us may know that she has an adequate singing voice, can dance trimly, and can combine all these matters into musical *performance*.

●

In short, Miss Lansbury is a singing-dancing actress, not a singer or dancer who also acts. (Somewhat surprisingly, there is even more character color in her singing than in her spoken dialogue.) In this marathon role she has wit, poise, warmth, and a very taking coolth. The visceral test, I suppose, is whether one is jealous of little Patrick growing up with an aunt like that. I was green.

Then there is little Patrick himself. Child actors in important roles are the chanciest of theater chances. (Two musicals in a row have taken this chance.) Frankie Michaels, as Patrick, is fine: no saccharin, complete conviction, a good enough singer, and he even dances a little (a tango!). The hazard with young performers is that either they look coached or, if they are gifted, are show-offs. Young Mr. Michaels is neither. He is simply a competent member of the cast, and I'm sure that Miss Lansbury would be the first to assert how difficult her job would be with a lesser nephew.

●

But grown-ups can be crackerjack professionals, too. Beatrice Arthur plays a sodden stage star, the bosom pal of Mame and a viper in her bosom. Miss Arthur gives a caustic musical-comedy performance that is fluent in skill and superb in timing. There is a particularly long pause that Miss Arthur takes —a very risky moment—that she judges to fine-hair exactness and crowns with a perfect payoff.

Jane Connell is Agnes Gooch, the comic secretary,

and this part, as written, is still too broad for me, particularly in the change from chastity to chase. But Miss Connell, another singing actress, plays it better than it deserves, with the caricature rather than character that it asks.

The mature Patrick is firm-jawed Jerry Lanning. Special praise for Diane Coupe in the small role of the girl he eventually marries. With a very few lines Miss Coupe establishes swiftly and sweetly that Patrick is making the right move at last.

Messrs. Lawrence and Lee have applied a neat distilling touch to their original play-script, allowing for what is supplied by songs and dances. In fact, the accidental death of Mame's husband is handled better here than it was in play or film—it is slipped less bumpily into the comic proceedings.

Jerry Herman's score has music that is strongly rhythmic and sufficiently tuneful, and lyrics that are generally deft. I could have done with one less cheer-up number in the first act ("We Need a Little Christmas"). And although the duet between Mame and Patrick after her stage flop is essential, "My Best Girl" has a bit more goo than is good for it.

●

Still "The Man in the Moon" is the best of the many recent parodies of old-fashioned operettas, "Bosom Buddies" (Mame and her actress friend) is a sharp duelling duet, and the show's title song is a foursquare twenties-type number that whams us into grinning submission. My own favorite, however, is Mame's solo, "If He Walked Into My Life," in which she wonders whether she is responsible for the grown Patrick's mistakes—a good song well done by an *actress*.

"Gene Saks has directed with inventiveness and an unstrained sense of pace. Onna White's choreography is not startlingly original (after all, she had to do a lot of nineteen-twenties numbers) but it is always spirited. The scenery by William and Jean Eckart is not only pretty but mobile (most of it changes interestingly before your eyes), and the costumes by Robert Mackintosh are gorgeously exaggerated.

●

Like some other recent musicals, "Mame" is a bit too long, particularly in the first act — which puts an extra burden on the second act. Like most others, it comes to our ears through an amplifying system of which we are never unaware. Like most others, it is, fundamentally, one more trip through material that most of us know very well already; and this is not necessarily a cheery comment on the State of the Theater or the State of Us.

But, whatever those truths may be, the present truth is that "Mame" does its job well with plenty of effective theatrical sentiment, laughs and vitality.

And with Miss Lansbury.

1966 My 25

'America Hurrah' Puts U.S. in Eerie Focus

The Casts

AMERICA HURRAH, three one-act plays, by Jean-Claude van Itallie. Staged by Jacques Levy and Joseph Chaikin; incidental music: Marianne du Pury; lighting by James Dwyer and Ken Glickfeld; costumes by Tania Leontov, assisted by Beckie Cunningham; slides and poster design, Francisca Duran-Reynals. Presented by Stephanie Sills Productions. At the Pocket Theater, 100 Third Avenue, at 13th Street.

INTERVIEW

First Interviewer.........Cynthia Harris
First Applicant ....Conard Fowkes
Second Interviewer.......James Barbosa
Second Applicant.........Ronnie Gilbert
Third Interviewer........Brenda Smiley
Third Applicant..........Henry Calvert
Fourth Interviewer............Bill Macy
Fourth Applicant.............Joyce Aaron

TV

Hal ....Conard Fowkes
Susan ....Brenda Smiley
George ....Bill Macy
Television people............Joyce Aaron,
James Barbosa, Henry Calvert,
Ronnie Gilbert and Cynthia Harris

MOTEL

Dolls played by Conard Fowkes, James
Barbosa and Brenda Smiley.
Motel Keeper's Voice: Ruth White

By WALTER KERR

I THINK you'll be neglecting a whisper in the wind if you don't look in on "America Hurrah."

There's something afoot here. And it's nothing so simple as the subtitle on the program — "3 Views of the U. S. A." — suggests. That suggests a montage of sorts, perhaps documentary in flavor, and the hint is rather depressingly reinforced by the fact that you notice, as you wander into the lobby of the Off Broadway Pocket Theater, a plastered-up assortment of photographs ranging from Louisa May Alcott to Wilbur and Orville Wright.

Forget the photographs. What is going on inside the blindingly white tile walls that enclose the raked stage of the Pocket is a great deal more complex, more elusive, and more promising than that.

●

Take a slippery, and in the end rather chilling, moment in the first "view." We've watched a handful of unemployed persons sit wistfully on square blocks while bland masked interviewers, sugared with smiles, hurl impertinent questions at them. We've watched the stage dissolve into the city streets, the players dissolve into wailing sirens, whispered folk songs, the jumpy cacophony of marionettes rattling through a recording tape at the wrong speed. We've noticed that the lurching through sound and space has an interior urgency about it that is odd indeed, especially since there isn't the least trace of obvious narrative to lure us on. We lurch along willingly, bidden

to do so by something original and personal in playwright Jean-Claude van Itallie's restrained voice.

Now a moment comes when a full-throated siren alerts us to a corner accident. Someone's been killed. The labored inhale-exhale of artificial respiration, made into a musical continuum by the same malleable actors who are saying all the lines, fails.

A pretty girl—a girl with a strong sense of obligation— leaves the accident to go on to a party. She would like to tell everyone at the party about the accident, though no one will listen. Above all, she would like to apologize for being late. No accident is enough to make a person late for a party.

Slowly, subtly and with a sense of having been slapped in the face, we do grasp that it is the girl herself who has been killed and that she is apologizing for having been killed at so inopportune a moment. The dead must never be inconveniently dead. Not in America, not just now.

In his second and third bits of spying on the way it *feels* to be on this continent these days, the playwright offers us two strong, plain contrasts that are quietly, and deftly kept from turning obvious.

In a television studio, three very normal workers glance at the monitor now and then, where busy performers with striped faces—they look like so many up-ended zebras— go through all of the violent, cloying, synthetic motions that pass for companionable entertainment on the national airwaves. But there is no relation between the workers and the work: a yawning gulf, big enough to drown us all, has opened between the real concerns of real people and the imaginary concerns of our imaginary archetypes.

One of the real workers nearly strangles to death on a bone in his chicken-salad sandwich. But the burly chanteuse who pours affection across the land as though she were an open fire hydrant of boundless goodwill goes right on beaming her thousand good nights. Disaster is irrelevant in a time of eternal delight.

In a "respectable, decent, and homey" motel—we are in the last playlet now—a massive Mother Hubbard made of very clammy clay revolves and revolves, like a warming beacon, welcoming the transient to a haven filled with the books of John Galsworthy and "toilets that flush of their own accord." Meantime, two oversize grotesques, male and female, enter a paid-for room to strip to their flesh-tinted Band-Aid bodies and then to destroy the room wantonly, book by book, toilet by toilet.

●

None of this is didactic. It is simply observant. None of it is labored. For the most part, Mr. van Itallie treads gently across the sorrowing, inattentive earth. If some of the evening sounds as though the verse of E. E. Cummings had been rearranged by Kenneth Fearing and then set to the intrusive rhythm of "Turkey in the Straw," it's no mistake. For one of the things the theater is trying to discover at the moment is a means of approaching poetic effect on the stage without reverting to echoing forms. And these deliberate "primitives" come to seem a valid, perhaps necessary, first try—almost as though we were Greeks again, searching out a right sound for the stage. Perhaps that is why there are so many garish Greek masks, and even elevated Greek boots, puffing up the players at the Pocket.

The players are, one and all, first-rate, though the program identifies them so rarely that I won't risk individual comment. Joseph Chaikin and Jacques Levy have directed, in general, with a casual grace. And the author is someone to be watched, and wished well.

1966 N 7

Musical by Masteroff, Kander and Ebb

The Cast

CABARET, a musical based on the play by John van Druten and stories by Christopher Isherwood. Book by Joe Masteroff; music by John Kander; lyrics by Fred Ebb; dances and cabaret numbers by Ronald Field; settings by Boris Aronson; costumes by Patricia Zipprodt; lighting by Jean Rosenthal; musical direction by Harold Hastings; orchestrations by Don Walker; dance arrangements by David Baker; directed by Harold Prince. Presented by Mr. Prince, in association with Ruth Mitchell. At the Broadhurst Theater, 235 West 44th Street.

Master of Ceremonies	Joel Grey
Clifford Bradshaw	Bert Convy
Ernst Ludwig	Edward Winter
Custom Official	Howard Kahl
Fraulein Schneider	Lotte Lenya
Herr Schultz	Jack Gilford
Fraulein Kost	Peg Murray
Telephone Girl	Tresha Kelly
Kit Kat Band	Maryann Burns, Janice Mink, Nancy Powers, Viola Smith
Maitre D'	Frank Bouley
Max	John Herbert
Bartender	Ray Baron
Sally Bowles	Jill Haworth
Two Ladies	Mary Ehara, Rita O'Connor
German Sailors	Bruce Becker, Steven Boockvor, Roger Briant, Edward Nolfi
Frau Wendel	Mara Landi
Herr Wendel	Eugene Morgan
Frau Kruger	Miriam Lehmann-Haupt
Herr Erdmann	Sol Frieder
Kit Kat Girls:	
Maria	Pat Gosling
Lulu	Lynn Winn
Rosie	Bonnie Walker
Fritzie	Marianne Seibert
Texas	Kathie Dalton
Frenchie	Barbara Alston
Bobby	Jere Admire
Victor	Bert Michaels
Greta	Jayme Mylroie
Felix	Robert Sharp

By WALTER KERR

"CABARET" is a stunning musical with one wild wrong note. I think you'd be wise to go to it first and argue about that startling slip later.

The first thing you see as you enter the Broadhurst is yourself. Designer Boris Aronson, whose scenery is so imaginative that even a gray green fruit store comes up like a warm summer dawn, has sent converging strings of frosted lamps swinging toward a vanishing point at upstage center. Occupying the vanishing point is a great geometric mirror, and in the mirror the gathering audience is reflected. We have come for the floor show, we are all at tables tonight, and anything we learn of life during the evening is going to be learned through the tipsy, tinkling, angular vision of sleek rouged-up clowns, who inhabit a world that rains silver.

●

This marionette's-eye view of a time and place in our lives that was brassy, wanton, carefree and doomed to crumble is brilliantly conceived. The place is Berlin, the time the late 20's when Americans still went there and Hitler could be shrugged off as a passing noise that needn't disturb dedicated dancers. Adapted by Joe Masteroff from the Christopher Isherwood-John van Druten materials that first took dramatic form as "I Am a Camera," the story line is willing to embrace everything from Jew baiting to abortion. But it has elected to wrap its arms around all that was troubling and all that was intolerable with a demonic grin, an insidious slink, and the painted-on charm that keeps revelers up until midnight making false faces at the hangman.

Master of Ceremonies Joel Grey bursts from the darkness like a tracer bullet, singing us a welcome that has something of the old "Blue Angel" in it, something of Kurt Weill, and something of all the patent-leather nightclub tunes that ever seduced us into feeling friendly toward sleek entertainers who twirled canes as they worked. Mr. Grey is cheerful, charming, soulless and conspiratorially wicked. In a pink vest, with sunburst eyes gleaming out of a cold-cream face, he is the silencer of bad dreams, the gleeful puppet of pretended joy, sin on a string.

No matter what is happening during the evening, he is available to make light of it, make sport of it, make macabre gaiety of it.

Perhaps an amoral chanteuse with the mind of a lightning bug ("I guess I am a really strange and extraordinary person") is installing herself without warning in the rented apartment of an American writer, ready to share bed and bread but not for long. Perhaps the landlady is shyly and ruefully succumbing to a proposal of marriage from a Jewish grocer (she is rueful because she is old now, singing "When you're as old as I—is anyone as old as I?") and perhaps the Jewish grocer is beginning to feel the bite of things to come. Precisely as a brick is hurled through her suitor's shop window, Mr. Grey comes bouncing from the portals to grab a gorilla in rose tulle. The two spin into a hesitation waltz with the prim and stately delicacy of partners well-met. Let the world lose its mind, let the waltz go on.

●

Under choreographer Ronald Field's beautifully malicious management, Mr. Grey is superb, as are the dancers, the four girls who bang at instruments and call themselves the Kit Kat Klub Kittens (even the piano seems to wear feathers), and the unending supply of tenors to give an Irish lilt ("Tomorrow Belongs to Me") to a contrapuntal pause in the tacky, rattling, bizarre and bankrupt goings-on. With the exception of an unlucky last song for landlady Lotte Lenya, the John Kander-Fred Ebb tunes snatch up the melodic desperation of an era and make new, sprightly, high-voltage energy of it, providing the men of the company with a table-to-table telephone song that comes to seem rhythm in a state of shock, and offering Miss Lenya several enchantingly throaty plaints, notably a winning acceptance of the way things are, called "So What?"

Miss Lenya has never been better, or if she has been, I don't believe it. Suitor Jack Gilford, with just enough hair left to cross his forehead with spitcurls and gamely spinning his partner in spite of clear signs of vertigo, makes his first-act wrap-up, a rapid-fire comic turn called "Meeskite," one of the treasures of the occasion. Bert Convy, as the American with a small whirlwind on his hands, not only acts well but opens his throat for "Why Should I Wake Up?" with the belief and the urgency of a singer who'd never given acting a second thought.

•

We are left now with the evening's single, and all too obvious, mistake. One of the cabaret tables is empty, the table reserved for heroine Sally Bowles. Sally Bowles, as the narrative has it, is a fey, fetching, far-out lassie with a head full of driftwood and a heart she'd rather break than shackle. She is a temperament, and she needs a temperament to play her.

Producer - director Harold Prince, in a totally uncharacteristic lapse of judgment, has miscast a pretty but essentially flavorless ingenue, Jill Haworth, in the role. Miss Haworth has certain skills and may be able to use them in other ways. Wrapped like a snowball in white fur and sporting that pancake tam that girls of the 20's used to wear whenever they were going to be photographed having snowball fights, she succeeds—at some angles—in looking astonishingly like Clara Bow. But her usefulness to this particular project ends there. She is trim but neutral, a profile rather than a person, and given the difficult things "Cabaret" is trying to do, she is a damaging presence, worth no more to the show than her weight in mascara.

The damage is deeply serious and must be stressed. With the kooky heroine canceled out, the tangled love story vanishes. Its disappearance is scarcely noticed during the striking first half, because Miss Lenya and Mr. Gilford are there to take over. But the second act must account for a botched romance and build to a disillusion ending on it and that's a bad time to watch the emotional air being steadily drained from a show that takes its style and its subject matter seriously. The style is there, though, driven like glistening nails into the musical numbers, and

I think you'll find they make up for what's missing.

1966 N 21.

Robert Preston Stars With Mary Martin

The Cast

I. DO! I DO!, musical based on "The Fourposter" by Jan de Hartog. Book and lyrics by Tom Jones; music by Harvey Schmidt; settings by Oliver Smith; costumes by Freddy Wittop; lighting by Jean Rosenthal; musical direction by John Lesko; orchestrations by Philip J. Lang; staged by Gower Champion; stage manager, Wade Miller. Presented by David Merrick. At the 46th Street Theater, 226 West 46th Street.

She (Agnes) .... Mary Martin
He (Michael) .... Robert Preston

By WALTER KERR

FOR the purposes of "I Do! I Do!" at the 46th Street Theater, a Santa Claus who shall here be known as David Merrick has hitched a very high-powered Donner and a very high-powered Blitzen to a very low-powered One Horse Shay. The show that comes out of the teamwork will still do for Christmas, though your passion for it is going to depend heavily upon the depth of your devotion to two of the fastest-starting sprinters the contemporary stage knows.

Donner, let's say, is Mary Martin, and a demon on a bright blue bicycle—it belongs to one of the children, really—as she curves and curves about Oliver Smith's simple, tasteful, balustrade-shaped bedroom while hubby Robert Preston tries to get a little work done.

Miss Martin's aim with a popgun is absolutely unerring as she perseveres in unnerving her mate, who is trying to be a writer, and when at last she decides to tuck all of the toys away so that ordinary life can go forward she does it with a wink and a whisk of skirts that is mysteriously enchanting. She simply walks into an upright guardhouse complete with painted Grenadier on the door, slips the door shut behind her, and waltzes off, guardhouse and all, like the friendliest possible turtle with the world on its back.

•

What else does she do while librettist Tom Jones and composer Harvey Schmidt are busy cooking up folksy songs to adorn Jan de Hartog's two-character play, "The Fourposter?" Well, she has several funny little vocal tricks that she sneaks in just once or twice — I wish she'd done them more often last evening, because I wanted to learn to whistle them—and while I can't exactly describe the way she breaks a single word down into four husky swoops that sound like Bojangles Robinson negotiating a staircase, I can tell you that she does it in a very brisk little tune called "Nobody's Perfect." You just listen for it.

Otherwise, she imitates— most spectacularly — Mr. Preston chewing in his sleep, she pretends—quite prettily —to be a decidedly scarlet woman while wearing a Bird of Paradise hat that is so big she could take it off and raise crops on it, and—as married life begins to wane a bit—she pouts up a storm worrying that she's turned into Little Nell behin da kitchen stove. And, always, always with that mellow sound that comes from her throat like red wine at room temperature.

Mr. Preston is Blitzen or her husband, however you want to look at it, and he's in the race to stay. The role is straighter, perhaps, intentionally stodgier. But that's a gain for Mr. Preston because he can play the gray striped pants off it.

He is at his untouchable best when the show asks him to be pompous, and blissfully obtuse. Miss Martin, now pregnant, mourns that their carefree days are over and that diapers and all that sort of thing are hereafter going to take up a great deal of time.

"Well I'll find something to do," he murmurs, cheerfully.

And do wait for a number called "A Well Known Fact" in which the male star of the occasion discovers fresh plumage at 40. Comfortably explaining to his spouse why men hold up so much better than women do and why, in fact, he is utterly irresistible' to those about him, he manages to describe himself as "a late October rose." The toss of the profile is perfect, the strut delicious.

Then, courtesy of director Gower Champion, there are all those engaging things the two do together when their hearts are high. One of them is literally the soft-shoe to end all soft-shoes, because it is done with no shoes at all. Barefoot, you see, in nightgowns, hand in hand about the alarm-clock, happy as only newlyweds can be ("I Love My Wife," its called).

Of course, they're cutting up didoes pretty constantly together, because there are only the two of them in the whole show (we do get a flash of the orchestra behind a scrim just to get the second half under way) and I suppose their New Year's Eve dido, in which they try their itching fingers at ukuleles, fiddles and saxophones, may prove as memorable—if carefully rigged—as any. My own preference is for the sight of Mr. Preston's putting Harry Richman to shame in a blazing green dressing-gown, slithering one patent-leather shoe along the floor as he whirls time with a walking-stick and a high silk hat.

There now, the stars. They're great. What about the material? It's on the whole barely passable, a sort of carefully condensed time capsule of all the clichás that have ever been spawned by people married and/or single. Not that the familiarity (labor pains, waiting at the hospital, the first spat, Mr. Preston's outraged cry that "my daughter is marrying an idiot!") would matter so much if the lines were fresh from the mint and the lyrics gleaming with new wit.

Though the lines and lyrics serve as bridges that the principals can manage to get across, they're never anything much more than that, with the result that the weather is sometimes unseasonably mild. Miss Martin, when pregnant, soothes Mr. Preston's palpitating heart by insisting that "After all, this has been going on for millions and millions of years," to which Mr. Preston replies, "I don't see how the men lived through it." Pretty easy going, there.

•

And the lyrics are for the most part remarkably plain-spoken. (I don't mean outspoken, just plain and four-square.) "It's a strange new world that you enter when you say 'I do,'" is where we begin, and "That's why a woman is only alive when in love" is pretty nearly where we end, stating the case factually and without much in the way of engaging fooling. When husband and wife get to finding fault with each other and some comedy is called for, we must make do at the level of "When I get to where the joke should be, you tell it just ahead of me." True enough, you see. But not too neatly turned. Generally, you can do the rhyming right along with the folks on stage.

But, of course, there are those folks on stage to reckon with. They make a handsome couple. I even see what he sees in her.

1966 D 6

1967

The Homecoming

By WALTER KERR

HAROLD PINTER'S "The Homecoming" consists of a single situation that the author refuses to dramatize until he has dragged us all, aching, through a half-drugged dream.

The Cast

"THE HOMECOMING," The Royal Shakespeare Company's production of Harold Pinter's play. Staged by Peter Hall; setting by John Bury; production stage manager, Jake Hamilton. Presented by Alexander H. Cohen in association with Gerry Geraldo. At the Music Box, 239 West 45th Street.

Max	Paul Rogers
Lenny	Ian Holm
Sam	John Normington
Joey	Terence Rigby
Teddy	Michael Craig
Ruth	Vivien Merchant

The situation, when it *is* arrived at, is interesting in the way that Pinter's numbed fantasies are almost always interesting. A Doctor of Philosophy who actually teaches philosophy returns with his wife to the family home in North London, a home that looks like an emptied-out wing of the British Museum gone thoroughly to seed. (The few pieces of furniture are lonely in this cavern, the molding along the walls breaks off and gives up before it can reach the doorways, the carpet could be made of cement.)

•

A father and two brothers take one look at the wife and mistake (or do not mistake) her for a whore. She is silent, poised, leggy, self-contained. In due time the family decides that they would rather like to have a whore around, whatever about her husband and about the three children she has left behind in America. She might very well be kept available in a room at the top of the steep, forbidding staircase, and she could always pay her own keep by renting herself out a few nights a week.

They put the proposition to her, matter-of-factly, after she has obliged them by moving into trance-like dance with one of the brothers, brushing unfinished kisses across his lips and then obligingly draping herself to another brother's needs across a cold and impersonal sofa.

It is at this point that Mr. Pinter's most curious and most characteristic abilities as a diviner of unspecified demons come effectively into play. We are in an unconventional situation, and of course we know that. But our habits of mind—our compulsive attempts to try to deal with the world by slide rule—still continue to function, stubbornly. We expect even so bizarre a crisis to provoke logical responses: the husband will be humiliated or outraged, the wife will prove herself either a genuine wife or a genuine whore, and so on. We have the probabilities all ready in our heads.

But Mr. Pinter is not interested in the rational probabilities of the moment. He is interested in what *might* happen if our controlling expectations were suddenly junked, if flesh and heart and moving bone were freed from preconditioning and allowed simply to behave, existentially. The world might go another way—a surprising and ultimately unexplained way—if it went its own way, indifferent to philosophers.

Just how the tangle at the Music Box rearranges itself I won't say, because saving nails down what is meant to continue as movement. It's enough to report that for approximately 20 minutes during the final third of "The Homecoming" the erratic energies onstage display their own naked authority by forcing us to accept the unpredictable as though it were the natural shape of things.

During this time Vivien Merchant, as the wife who is as hard-headed as she is enigmatic, coolly and with great reserve points out that her legs move, her underwear moves with her, her lips move. ("Perhaps the fact that they move is more significant than the words that come through them.") Husband Michael Craig draws on his donnish pipe with opaque detachment ("I won't be lost in it"), father Paul Rogers leers through sucked-in teeth that seem to have been borrowed from Bert Lahr, and poltergeist Ian Holm grins maliciously at the thought of all the tables that can be turned. The performing is cagey, studied,

bristling with overtones. (A good half of Mr. Pinter's suspense invariably comes from the question that sticks in our heads: "What are these people *not* mentioning?").

Until the final moments of the evening, however, the playwright is simply cheating us, draining away our interest with his deliberate delay. He has no more vital material to offer here then he had, say, in the very much shorter "A Slight Ache," to which "The Homecoming" bears a strong resemblance.

But he is determined that we shall have two hours worth of improvisational feinting, and it leads him into a good bit of coy teasing giggly echoes of Ionesco ("You liked Venice, didn't you? You had a good week. I mean, I took you there. I can speak Italian") and calculated incidental violence that is without cumulative effect (the father spits at one son, rams another in the gut, canes his own paraffin-coated dullard of a brother).

Because none of this is of any growing importance to the ultimate confrontation, *everything* must seem to have its own arbitrary and artificial importance: the clink of a sugar lump on a saucer, the stiff, ritual crossing of trousered legs, the huddled lighting of four cigars, the effortful pronunciation of so much as a single word.

Holding too much back for too long, the play comes to seem afflicted by an arthritic mind and tongue, and while Peter Hall has directed the visiting members of England's Royal Shakespeare Company to make sleep-walking and strangled speech constitute a theatrical effect in and for itself, we are not engrossed by the eternal hesitation waltz but seriously put off by it. The play agonizes over finding its starting point, and we share the prolonged agony without being certain that the conundrum is approaching a real core.

Mr. Pinter is one of the most naturally gifted dramatists to have come out of

England since the war. I think he is making the mistake, just now, of supposing that the elusive kernel of impulse that will do for a 40-minute play will serve just as handily, and just as suspensefully, for an all-day outing. "The Homecoming," to put the matter as simply as possible, needs a second situation: We could easily take an additional act if the author would only scrap the interminable first. The tide must come in at least twice if we are to be fascinated so long by the shoreline.

1967 Ja 6

Galileo

By WALTER KERR

WHILE Galileo is waiting to be picked up by the Inquisition, in the new mounting of Bertolt Brecht's historical lecture - cum - pageant at the Vivian Beaumont, a friendly industrialist who has made a fortune in iron claps the badgered scientist on the shoulder and lets him know he still has friends. Anthony Quayle, the Galileo of the occasion, is grateful, but with reservations. "I don't know why he's got to be so friendly in public," he frets. "His voice carries."

The Cast

GALILEO, the Bertolt Brecht play. English version by Charles Laughton. Staged by John Hirsch; settings by Robin Wagner; costumes by James Hart Stearns; masks by Ralph Lee; lighting by Martin Aronstein; music by Hanns Eisler; additional music by Stanley Silverman; conductor and vocal director, Roland Gagnon; stage managers, Timothy Ward and James Kershaw. Presented by the Repertory Theater of Lincoln Center, Jules Irving, director. At the Vivian Beaumont Theater, 150 West 65th Street.
Ballad singer .... George S. Irving
Ballad singer's wife ...... Kate Hurney
Ballad singer's child .... Robert Puleo
Galileo Galilei .... Anthony Quayle
Mrs. Sarti .... Aline McMahon
Andrea Sarti as boy .... Alan Cabal
Ludovico Marsilli ...... Charles Siebert
Priuli .... Fred Stewart
Virginia .... Estelle Parsons
Sagredo .... Philip Bosco
Federzoni .... Robert Symonds
Matti .... John Carpenter
The Doge .... Glenn Mazen
Prince Cosimo de Medici. .Charles Abruzzo

Philosopher .... Ronald Weyand
Mathematician .... Earl Montgomery
Furious Monk .... Robert Phalen
Old Cardinal .... Edgar Daniels
Christopher Clavius, papal astronomer
                            Warren Wade
Little Monk .... Frank Bayer
Cardinal Bellarmine ......
                    Ted van Griethuysen
Cardinal Barberini .... George Voskovec
Cardinal Inquisitor....Shepperd Strudwick
Andrea Sarti as a man.....Stephen Joyce
Informer .... Earl Montgomery

The very best thing about John Hirsch's staging of the piece is that its voice does carry. More than anything that has yet been done at the Beaumont, the production walks the stage unafraid, confident that it will be listened to, conscious of its vocal and visual authority.

The key is set instantly by Mr. Quayle's playful, but very precise, treatment of a lad who is fascinated by science but pretty certain that the earth he's standing on is dutifully standing still. With a sharp clap of laughter and a wonderfully generous patience, Mr. Quayle turns the sun around for the boy simply by spinning a chair, then spears an apple with a knife to show him that knives—like people—don't necessarily fall off a sphere when the sphere is spun around.

With an alert mind, attentive eyes, and a kindly care for the sound of words, Mr. Quayle establishes the classroom tone that is going to mark the whole occasion, but establishes it with geniality as well as with precision. From his other principal players, Mr. Hirsch has got much the same insistence on minding thought, sound and energy.

Visually, the production is not only handsome but open in its use of the available forward spaces of the Beaumont stage. The vast mottled floor is crossed and recrossed endlessly, by masked-ball fantastics with griffin's heads for faces, by salmon-colored cardinals, hurried cowled monks, Venetian doges riding sedan-chairs ablaze with gilded lions.

Lackeys climb twin scaffolds that spiral to the top of the auditorium, lighted candelabra in hand, to suggest the fires that are being lighted by the force of one man's mind. An edgy Pope, determined not to "set himself against the mathematical tables" but succumbing to the conservative pressures around him nonetheless, attires himself in a great gold jewel-encrusted cape and stalks into the upstage darkness, turning his back on light.

Robin Wagner's settings are fluid and functional, James Hart Stearns's costumes are judiciously monochromatic until the forceful thrust of a primary color is called for—at which point the spectrum lets rip.

There is very little production for production's sake—when the stage moves, it is escorting the play. The play, as it happens, can use the discreet help it gets. Brecht's "Galileo" occupies a curious and somewhat awkward middle-ground between the world of "epic" theater and the much more mundane world of commonplace historical melodrama. There are, in the experimental Brecht manner, brief and sometimes ironic sung introductions to the evening's 13 scenes, accompanied by train-station announcements of the content that is to come.

On the other—and rather feebly conventional — hand, there are the standard domestic crises and foreseeable sentimental stage effects of anybody else's accounting of The Scientist at Home or The Scientist at Bay. At the very moment that Galileo is defying the Inquisition by resuming his study of sun-spots, his daughter bursts into the laboratory freshly pallid from the loss of a lover. "I must know the truth!" the scientist thunders, ignoring her.

While friends and co-workers wait in horror for the toll of a bell that will say Galileo has recanted, we are offered standard suspense that cannot work as suspense. The bell doesn't ring at the promised time. Those waiting are ecstatic. As they sound their most triumphant note, the bell of course rings. But the scene is plain cardboard because we have seen its familiar mechanics coming; we could give the backstage cue for the bell with our own ready hand.

And the language, adapted by Charles Laughton, belongs for the most part to the "Bring me something to discover" school. Perfectly able actors struggle to find human and fresh inflections for "Yes, a new age has dawned, a great age," "Why, those are stars, countless stars!" and "Galileo, you're setting out on a fearful road." There's some Hollywooditis in all of this, and the play sacrifices a good bit of its natural intellectual interest in its determination to make certain that the Common Man—nay, the babe in arms—will understand.

●

Fortunately, the calculated repetitions and the scientific and ecclesiastical baby-talk are made tolerable by the fact that the material *is* interesting, the mounting colorful, and the performing (in general) respectable. Although the supers on the fringes still seem unable to put foot on the Beaumont stage without announcing that they are acting, there are controlled and clearly spoken vignettes from John Carpenter as a loyal industrialist, Aline MacMahon as a housekeeper who shudders every time she hears scientists laugh, Frank Bayer as a monk with a passion for physics, Philip Bosco in a brief appearance as a man who learns to believe his own eyes, and from George Voskovec, Ted van Griethuysen, and Shepperd Strudwick as an assortment of stubborn and/or grieving clerics.

On the whole, better than average work for the house.

1967 Ap 14.

Shakespeare Is Well Served in the Park

The Cast

THE COMEDY OF ERRORS, by William Shakespeare. Staged by Gerald Freedman; setting by Ming Cho Lee; lighting by Martin Aronstein; costumes by Theoni V. Aldredge; music by John Morris; production stage manager, Russell McGrath. Presented by the New York Shakespeare Festival. Produced by Joseph Papp; associate producer, Bernard Gersten. At the Delacorte Theater, West 81st Street and Central Park West.

Egeon	Ralph Driscoll
Solinus	Jonathan Reynolds
First Merchant	Joseph R. Sicari
Antipholus of Syracuse	David Birney
Antipholus of Ephesus	Josep Bova
Dromio of Syracuse	John Call
Dromio of Ephesus	Charles Durning
Adriana	Julienne Marie
Luciana	Elizabeth Eis
Angelo	Robert Ronan
Balthazar	Jack Hollander
Luce (Nell)	Zoe Kamitses
Second Merchant	Albert Quinton
Dr. Pinch	Joseph R. Sicari
Emilia	Eve Collyer
Clockworks	
Steven Shaw, Donald K. Warfield	

By DAN SULLIVAN

OF all the nice things that have happened in Central Park since Thomas P. F. Hoving reclaimed it—so to speak—for the natives, the New York Shakespeare Festival's "Comedy of Errors" is one of the nicest.

The most welcome aspect of Gerald Freedman's trim new production, which opened Tuesday night under such stars as were available at the Delacorte Theater, is its faith in its script.

Mr. Freedman avoids two current pitfalls in staging Shakespearean comedy. He does not try to make the play "relevant to a contemporary audience" by imposing an eccentric point of view on it. And he does not clutter up the stage with so much extracurricular horseplay as to suggest that the story would bore us to tears if we really had to pay attention to it.

●

Mr. Freedman knows, of course, that certain passages in "The Comedy of Errors" would ossify anyone but a specialist in Elizabethan bawdry. At such moments he has a pocketful of sight gags (including a running one about two batty bellringers) to keep us attentive until the narrative clears. But his sight gags know their helpful place —and generally stay there.

The director also has a nice ear for the play's tone and keeps things tongue-in-cheek, but not conspicuously so. Caught in an impossible tangle of mixed identities and long-lost relatives, the characters are all the funnier for taking their predicament so seriously.

What *do* you do when some woman you've never seen in your life starts calling you "husband"? What happens when your wife won't let you through the front door on the grounds that you're already in the living room?

●

David Birney, as the twin from Syracuse, faces his identity crisis with the uncomplicated instincts of a teen-age idol. When somebody calls you "husband," you give her the old niceboy grin and go along with the gag.

Joseph Bova, as the twin from Ephesus, faces his moment of truth with the resources of a secret swinger. When your wife locks you out, you knock the door down. If it won't budge, you have supper with another lady.

The twin slaves, John Call and Charles Durning, share their masters' troubles and a further problem peculiar to their trade: how to avoid getting beaten. Mr. Call distracts Mr. Birney by turning him into a straight man for a Henny Youngman routine known today as "My girl is so ugly. . . ." Mr. Durning deals with Mr. Bova's blows by turning off his pain receptors and thinking about something else

It's interesting that Mr. Birney looks no more like Mr. Bova than Mr. Call resembles Mr. Durning, yet we accept them as dead ringers with no trouble at all. This is partly because of Theoni Aldredge's carbon-copy costumes but mostly because the rest of the cast is so stunned by the resemblance that it would be impolite for us to doubt it. Consensus thus breeds illusion.

●

The other players are uniformly excellent: Julienne Marie as the yappy wife, Ralph Drischell as the doddering sire, Robert Ronan as the somewhat limp - wristed goldsmith (the only campy touch in the show), Eve Collyer as the nun (in a hilarious Minnie-Mouse coif) and Joseph R. Sicari as that fraudulent old necromancer, Dr. Pinch.

One also could mention Elizabeth Eis as the sensible sister-in-law and Jonathan Reynolds, who portrays, not the Duke of Ephesus, but a naive Cockney actor playing the Duke of Ephesus — an amusing conceit that does no harm to the play's lightly held credibility.

Ming Cho Lee's setting is playful and efficient: three towers that look like giant toys left on the lawn too long. The Delacorte's sound system is playful, too: According to its whim, it sends the actors' voices to you in high fidelity, low fidelity and no fidelity.

1967 Je 15.

25 Musicians Support 21-Song Performance

The Program

MARLENE DIETRICH, one-woman show, for six weeks. Musical arrangements and orchestra conducted by Burt Bacharach; lighting by Joe Davis. Presented by Alexander H. Cohen of the Nine O'Clock Theater production. At the Lunt-Fontanne Theater, 205 West 46th Street, at 9.

By VINCENT CANBY

MRS. RUDOLF SIEBER, a German - born grandmother who is officially 62 years old, slunk out onto the stage of the Lunt-Fon-

tanne Theater last night wearing $30,000 worth of bugle beads and looking for all the world like Marlene Dietrich.

It was probably one of the most remarkable impersonations ever to be seen in the New York theater.

The fact that Mrs. Sieber is Marlene Dietrich does not minimize the accomplishment. For this, her first New York stage appearance, the star succeeded in projecting her familiar glamour image through a combination of nostalgia, iron will, technique and perhaps even a little hypnosis.

Not the least of her talents is the manner in which she persuades the audience to bring to her all those things she does not bring to it, particularly a kind of exuberant zest that makes a theater glow.

In this one-woman show, Miss Dietrich, backed by 25 musicians, sings—or perhaps recites is a better word—no fewer than 21 songs, and there are times when one would think he were listening to Marian Anderson. Not, good heavens, because of the quality of the husky, often harsh voice, but because of the magic with which Miss Dietrich spellbinds her listeners.

Picture, if you will, Miss Dietrich in a center stage spotlight, clinging, sparkling gown, one foot slightly forward, hands at her sides (rather like a still from "Desire"), working up a tear as she croons "I Wish You Love"; or better yet, reeking with chic as she goes through such a humble line as "Just Molly and me, and baby makes three . . ." in some strange Blue Heaven.

It's difficult to tell in this performance where self-caricature begins, but there are many times when it seems to be totally absent.

The star is at her best as she seems to mock the very image she has so carefully nurtured, in numbers such as "The Boys in the Back Room" or "The Laziest Girl in Town." She is also persuasive doing her "Lola-Lola" number from "The Blue Angel" and the still haunting "Lili Marlene."

But when she sings—apparently with her heart—of hammocks, lying in the hay and of the games we used to play, the technique wears as thin and the voice is essentially uninteresting.

Miss Dietrich is not so much a performer as a one-woman environment, assaulting the senses in all manner of means. She looks unreal, as one lady in the audience observed, like a life-size Marlene Dietrich doll. But she is so completely in control of herself, and the audience, we are helpless to be anything but cheerfully amazed.

She is certainly not the laziest girl in town, but she doesn't waste a gesture—an upturned hand turns off the applause—just as a not too modest, deadpan gaze at the floor, concludes a number and signals the bravos.

This star is a cool, self-possessed cookie, and anyone who wants a lesson in thought control had better get over to the Lunt-Fontanne sometime in the next six weeks.

1967 O 10

Play by Tom Stoppard Opens at the Alvin

The Cast

ROSENCRANTZ AND GUILDENSTERN ARE DEAD, play by Tom Stoppard; staged by Derek Goldby; setting and costumes by Desmond Heeley; lighting by Richard Pilbrow; music by Marc Wilkinson; production stage manager, Mitchell Erickson. Presented by David Merrick Arts Foundation by arrangement with the National Theater of Great Britain; associate producer, Samuel Liff. At the Alvin Theater, 250 West 52d Street.

Rosencrantz	Brian Murray
Guildenstern	John Wood
The Player	Paul Hecht
Alfred	Douglas Norwick
Tragedians	Roger Kemp, Dino Laudicina, B. J. DeSimone, Roy Lozano
Hamlet	Noel Craig
Ophelia	Patricia McAneny
Claudius	Roger Hamilton
Gertrude	Anne Meacham
Polonius	Ralph Drischell
Soldier	Alexander Courtney
Ambassador	Carl Jacobs
Horatio	Michael Holmes

By CLIVE BARNES

IT IS not only Hamlet who dies in "Hamlet." They also serve who only stand and wait. Tom Stoppard's play "Rosencrantz and Guildenstern are Dead," which opened last night at the Alvin Theater, is a very funny play about death. Very funny, very brilliant, very chilling; it has the dust of thought about it and the particles glitter excitingly in the theatrical air.

Mr. Stoppard uses as the basis for his play a very simple yet telling proposition; namely that although to Hamlet those twin-stemmed courtiers Rosencrantz and Guildenstern are of slight importance, and that to an audience of Shakespeare's play they are little but functionaries lent some color by a fairly dilatory playwright, Rosencrantz and Guildenstern are very important indeed to Rosencrantz and Guildenstern.

This then is the play of "Hamlet" not seen through the eyes of Hamlet, or Claudius, or Ophelia or Gertrude, but a worm's-eye view of tragedy seen from the bewildered standpoint of Rosencrantz and Guildenstern.

●

We first see them on a deserted highway. They have been summoned to the King's palace; they do not understand why. They are tossing coins to pass the time of day. The ordinary laws of chance appear to have been suspended. Perhaps they have been. Destiny that has already marked out Hamlet for such a splendid, purple satin death, is keeping a skimpy little piece of mauve bunting for poor Guildenstern and gentle Rosencrantz. They are about to get caught up in the action of a play.

Their conversation, full of Elizabethan school logic and flashes of metaphysical wit, is amusing but deliberately fatuous. Rosencrantz and Guildenstern are fools. When you come to think of it, they would have to be. Otherwise they might have been Hamlet.

As they talk, the suspicion crosses the mind (it is a play where you are encouraged to stand outside the action and let suspicions, thoughts, glimmers and insights criss-cross your understanding) that Mr. Stoppard is not only paraphrasing "Hamlet," but also throwing in a paraphrase of Samuel Beckett's "Waiting for Godot" for good measure. For this is antic lunacy with a sad, wry purpose.

Like Beckett's tramps, these two silly, rather likable Elizabethan courtiers are trying to get through life with a little human dignity and perhaps here and there a splinter of comprehension. They play games with each other and constantly question not their past (probably only heroes can afford that luxury) but their present and their future. Especially their future.

On the road they meet the strolling players, also, of course, for the plot is a mousetrap seen from the other side of the cheese, on the road to Elsinore. The leading Player, a charming, honest and sinister man, invites the two to participate in a strolling play. They, with scruples, refuse, but in fact they cannot refuse—because in life this precisely is what they have done.

Mr. Stoppard seems to see the action of his play unfolding like a juicy onion with strange layers of existence protectively wrapped around one another. There are plays here within plays—and Mr. Stoppard never lets us forget that his courtiers are not only characters in a life, but also characters in a play. They are modest—they admit that they are only supporting players. But they do want to see something of the script everyone else is working from.

It is one of Mr. Stoppard's cleverest conceits of stagecraft that the actors re-enacting the performance of "Hamlet" that is, in effect, dovetailed into the main section of the play, use only Shakespeare's words. Thus while they are waiting in the tattered, drafty antechamber of the palace for something to happen, we in the audience know what is happening on the other side of the stage. As one of them says, "Every exit is an entry somewhere else."

Finally reduced to the terminal shrifts of unbelief, it seems that Rosenkrantz and Guildenstern realize that the only way they can find their identity is in their "little deaths." Although on the final, fateful boat they discover the letter committing them to summary execution in England, they go forward to death, glad, even relieved.

•

It is impossible to re-create the fascinating verbal tension of the play — Mr. Stoppard takes an Elizabethan pleasure in the sound of his own actors—or the ideas, suggestive, tantalizing that erupt through its texture. Nor, even most unfortunately, can I suggest the happy, zany humor or even the lovely figures of speech, such as calling something "like two blind men looting a bazaar for their own portraits." All this is something you must see and hear for yourself.

When the play had its first professional production in London in April of this year it was staged by the British National Theater, and to an extent this version has been reproduced here by its original and brilliant director, Derek Goldby. Helped by the tatterdemalion glories of Desmond Heeley's setting, the richness of his costumes, and Richard Pilbrow's tactfully imaginative lighting, the play looks very similar. But whereas the supporting players in London—the Hamlet, Claudius and the rest—could well have played their roles in Shakespeare as well as in Stoppard, here there is understandably less strength.

However, the mime roles of the players (expertly devised by Claude Chagrin) are superbly done, Paul Hecht is remarkably good as the chief Player (although I would have welcomed a touch more menace) and Brian Murray and John Wood provide virtuoso portrayals as Rosencrantz and Guildenstern.

●

Mr. Murray, blandly exuding a supreme lack of confidence, and Mr. Wood, disturbed, perhaps more intellectually than viscerally, play against each other like tennis singles champions. And luckily this is a game where neither needs to win and both can share the trophy.

This is a most remarkable and thrilling play. In one bound Mr. Stoppard is asking to be considered as among the finest English-speaking writers of our stage, for this is a work of fascinating distinction. Rosencrantz and Guildenstern LIVE!

1967 O 17

Pearl Bailey Captures Audience From Start

HELLO, DOLLY! Musical, book by Michael Stewart; music and lyrics by Jerry Herman, based on the play by

Thornton Wilder; settings by Oliver Smith; costumes by Freddy Wittop; lighting by Jean Rosenthal; dance and incidental music arrangements by Peter Howard; musical direction by Saul Schechtman; orchestrations by Philip J. Lang; original production staged and choreographed by Gower Champion; restaged by Lucia Victor; dance assistant, Jack Craig; stage manager, Toni Manzi. Presented by David Merrick. At the St. James Theater, 246 West 44th Street.

Mrs. Dolly Gallagher Levi	Pearl Bailey
Ernestina	Mabel King
Ambrose Kemper	Roger Lawson
Horse	Dianne Conway, Barbara Harper
Horace Vandergelder	Cab Calloway
Ermengarde	Sherri Peaches Brewer
Cornelius Hackl	Jack Crowder
Barnaby Tucker	Winston DeWitt Hemsley
Irene Molloy	Emily Yancy
Minnie Fay	Chris Calloway
Mrs. Rose	Marie Bryant
Rudolph	Morgan Freeman
Judge	Walter P. Brown
Court Clerk	James Kennon-Wilson

By CLIVE BARNES

WITH the endearing modesty that has already made him the toast of one continent, David Merrick, the impresario, has himself described in all his programs as "the most vital force in the theater today." Well, now, some people might dispute that—suggesting, say, Bertolt Brecht, or Antonin Artaud, or Soupy Sales. But one thing is certain about Mr. Merrick: He has showmanship running out of his ears.

Who else would have thought of bringing Pearl Bailey, Cab Calloway and a whole Negro cast to the St. James Theater to revive the fortunes of the musical "Hello, Dolly!" which has only been running 68 years or so and will now, I swear it, run for 168 years or so more? The answer is rhetorical.

Before saying that I adored this new "Dolly!", let me admit that I went prejudiced. I had not been bowled over by it earlier, and frankly my sensitive white liberal conscience was offended at the idea of a nonintegrated Negro show. It sounded too much like "Blackbirds of 1967," and all too patronizing for words. But believe me, from the first to the last I was overwhelmed. Maybe Black Power is what some of the other musicals need.

For Miss Bailey this was a Broadway triumph for the history books. She had no trouble at all in stopping the show—her problem was getting it started again. On her entrance the audience wouldn't even let her begin. After about a minute's applause, she cleared her throat, grinned amiably and with those gargling gurgles that have been hers ever since she lost it at the Astor, murmured: "I've a few more words to say in this show . . ." She had, and a few more to sing.

She took the whole musical in her hands and swung it around her neck as easily as if it were a feather boa. Her timing was exquisite, with asides tossed away as languidly as one might tap ash from a cigarette and her singing had that deep throaty rumble that is, at least to me, always so oddly stirring. It had that touch of the blues tone, warm and soulful, overlaid with the authentic Broadway heart-vibrato, and yet made as personal, as ironically appealing, as Miss Bailey in cabaret.

By the second act the audience was not merely eating out of Miss Bailey's hand, it had started to chew at her fingernails. When she came to the actual "Hello, Dolly!" number with that entrance into the Harmonia Gardens down the red carpet, the curtains at the top parted just slightly, she slipped in, paused and then, while the audience roared, came down the steps like a motherly debutante. Through this whole number, with a gesture here and a grind there, she kept the crowd roaring. As she pranced, hips wagging and eyes a'joy, around on the runway in front of the orchestra, waving cheerfully to the original Dolly, Carol Channing, sitting there center front in a blaze of platinum hair, the audience would have elected her Governor if she'd only named the state.

So far I've done something I never thought I could —I've overlooked Cab Calloway. The gorgeous Mr. Calloway, as the mean and respectable Horace Vandergelder who is Dolly's perfect match, amply shared his Dolly's triumph. His acting was polished, and his singing was so stylish that right from the start anyone who knew the show—and is anyone left who doesn't? —must have been regretting that he had so little to sing.

But even apart from Miss Bailey and Mr. Calloway, a great face job has been done on the whole show, which now goes like a rocket in a shower of sparks. Jerry Herman's songs are belted out with a Fourth of July gusto, and Gower Champion's direction has been most zestfully restaged by Lucia Victor. Mr. Champion's choreography has never looked so good. When he saw it, I hope he had the grace to be as surprised as I was.

The new cast is strong in length, breadth and depth. There were kids in the chorus singing and dancing their hearts out, looking great in Freddy Wittop's costumes while parading in front of Oliver Smith's elegant simulation of old New York engravings.

As for the junior leads, they all deserve a mention, but let me confine myself to Emily Yancy and Jack Crowder (two of the best-voiced and personable young lovers to be heard hereabouts for some time), and the bubblingly spontaneous comedy of Winston DeWitt Hemsley and Chris Calloway—yes, she is, a daughter.

Oh dear, I've forgotten to tell the story. Oh well, go to the library and get out Thornton Wilder's play "The Matchmaker." Most of "Hello, Dolly!" is based on it. Then go and see Miss Bailey, Mr. Calloway and company.

1967 N 13

Circle in Square Offers 'Iphigenia in Aulis'

By CLIVE BARNES

THE strength of Euripides is his humanity—he always saw the man beneath the crown and would inveigh at the immorality of wilful gods and an errant fate. It is this humanity and spirit that is so heartbreakingly caught in a most moving production of "Iphigenia in Aulis," which last night opened at the Circle in the Square. Here is great theater and an adornment to the New York stage.

Although Euripides's sole authorship of "Iphigenia in Aulis" is often questioned, the usual ending being particularly suspect, the play undoubtedly has one of the most pathetic and touching themes in Greek tragedy. And because of its very human motivation, despite a crucial command of an oracle, there are no shafts from the gods to deflect interest from a situation that is not without its contemporary significance. For one of the things "Iphigenia in Aulis" is about—or, rather, now seems to be about—is a person's duty toward a nation pursuing a war he feels to be worthless.

●

The worthless war is the battle to retrieve Helen from Troy. Is it a war over a whore? Euripides at times suggests it is. Or is it rather

a war to protect Greece from the barbarians? As his heroine goes with glory to her death, Euripides also suggests that it is even that. Against this background of waiting armies, a strange domestic tragedy is played out.

Friedman-Abeles

Irene Papas in the role of Clytemnestra with Jenny Leigh, who plays Iphigenia.

The Cast

IPHIGENIA IN AULIS, an English version of Euripides's drama by Minos Volanakis. Staged by Michael Cacoyannis; scenery and costumes by Michael Annals; music by Marvin David Levy; lighting by Jules Fisher. Produced by Circle in the Square, Inc. (Theodore Mann, artistic director; Paul Libin, managing director, and Gillian Walker, associate director). Associate producer, Sheldon Soffer. At the Circle in the Square, 159 Bleecker Street.

Agamemnon .... Mitchell Ryan

Old Man .... Tom Klunis
Menelaus .... Alan Mixon
Messenger .... Robert Stattell
Clytemnestra .... Irene Papas
The Child .... John Marks
Iphigenia .... Jenny Leigh
Achilles .... Christopher Walken
Chorus Leader .... Erin Martin

Menelaus, anxious to get back his faithless wife Helen, persuades Greece to launch a thousand ships on her behalf. Agamemnon is the commander of this force, but the ships are becalmed in harbor at Aulis. With no wind they cannot sail. The high priest consults the oracle—Agamemnon must kill his first-born, his daughter Iphigenia, and then, and only then, will the ships sail and Troy fall.

What follows is the agony of four people: Agamemnon, his daughter, his wife Clytemnestra and Achilles, the young hero used as a bait to bring Iphigenia to Aulis. It is the agony of people faced with a sacrifice they cannot believe is necessary, faced with a directive from the gods that they know to be unjust.

Using an impressively fluent and understatedly poetic English version by Minos Volanakis, Michael Cacoyannis has directed this Euripides with a forceful feel for its contemporary relevance. At first the direction seems uncertain—wavering between a ritualistic view of tragedy, to an extent unavoidable in the Greek classic theater, and the naturalistic approach to which the play lends itself.

As a result, the heroes occasionally lurch around the stage like stylized giants, while the chorus is treated with an almost idiomatic freedom. Yet as the tragedy approaches its climax, such inequalities fade away, and Mr. Cacoyannis presses toward the end with his actors unveiled by any artifice and pouring out their lives with a noble simplicity.

It is in keeping with Mr.

Cacoyannis's view of the play (a view that the ancient Greeks themselves might have found sentimental) that he rejects the play's disputed happy ending. He prefers to finish with Iphigenia's being led to sacrifice and Clytemnestra, caught in a spotlight that is tantamount to a cinematic close-up, in an ashenblaze of grief.

The cast is exceptionally strong. That fine Greek actress Irene Papas is a Clytemnestra of the most noble passion, with a wine-dark voice that rolls like distant thunder, bold eyes, and a cry of anguish that echoes in the soul. She plays Clytemnestra as a wife and mother more than a tragedy queen, and not once could one forget that here was a woman giving up her child. As she stood, hopelessly aghast, while Iphigenia calmly argued all the fine reasons why she should go to her death like a girl embracing a lover, this Clytemnestra, still yet tortured, wrenched the heart with her electric impassivity.

Jenny Leigh was almost as impressive as Iphigenia, superbly expressing first the girl's swift surge of youth, then her fear of boundless death, and finally the resignation that comes to her by choosing death as if it were by her own will.

●

The men perhaps get the worst of it, but they also provide performances of solid merit. Mitchell Ryan's Agamemnon, part politician, part hero, part father, provided a subtly judged performance of a man of patchy conscience who wants to do the right thing, but hasn't truly got the moral equipment to know what the right thing is.

Against such a detailed portrayal, Christopher Walken's heroically spoken and finely ardent Achilles and Alan Mixon's not-all-villainous Menelaus, lost something in the comparison, just as their roles had already lost something in the playwright's original insight. The chorus was led sharp intensity by Erin Martin. '

The staging looked beautifully convincing, and with a simple setting and well-designed costumes, all by Michael Annals, it had a great deal of atmosphere, which was also helped by Marvin David Levy's somberly, lambently elegiac music.

1967 N 22

Flemish Writer Given Broadway Debut

PANTAGLEIZE, play by Michel de Ghelderode, translated by George Hauser. Staged by John Houseman and Ellis Rabb; assistant director, Jack O'Brien; music and organized sound by Bob James; incidental lyrics by Jack O'Brien; setting and lighting by James Tilton; costumes by Nancy Potts. The A.P.A. Repertory Company presented by A.P.A.-Phoenix, Ellis Rabb, artistic director, Norman Kean, general manager. At the Lyceum Theater, 149 West 45th Street.

Pantagleize.................Ellis Rabb
Bamboola...................Nat Simmons
Innocenti..................Sydney Walker
Poet.......................Nicholas Martin
Policeman..................Richard Easton
Anarchist..................Keene Curtis
Rachel Silbershatz.........Patricia Conolly
General MacBoom............Joseph Bird
Bank Managers.......George Addis and
                          Kermit Brown
First Soldier..............George Pentecost
Second Soldier.............James Whittle
Distinguished Counsel.....Richard Woods
Generalissimo..............Gordon Gould
Officer....................Alan Fudge
Soldiers, Waiters, Jurymen..George Addis,
     Dan Bly, Kermit Brown,
     Alan Fudge, Reuben Green,
     Gil Michaels, Gastone Rossilli

By CLIVE BARNES

OUR most serious repertory, the A.P.A., is back at its home at the Lyceum Theater, with its first production of a crowded season, Michel de Ghelderode's "Pantagleize." As I saw the play at one of its final previews, it struck me that the company has never looked so good. A theatrical institution is like a body—it is growing or with-

ering. The A.P.A. is growing, and growing most promisingly.

Even its confident choice of an opening play offers some circumstantial evidence of this growth. Michel de Ghelderode is one of the best-known, little-known playwrights of this century, and no one could accuse a company that offers this now dead Flemish playwright a belated Broadway debut of playing safe.

Having read some of Ghelderode's plays I must confess I went expecting little but bombast and a kind of self-pitying intellectualism. I was surprised, ambushed, confounded and, most important, deprejudiced. "Pantagleize'" is a marvelous play, the production is excellent, and the whole thing is funny, thoughtful, stimulating and entertaining.

Much of what is interesting in modern drama is simply man's quest for his own identity. Never before has the question "Who am I?" meant either so much or so little. Who are we indeed? In "Pantagleize" Ghelderode seems to be suggesting that we are nothing but the focus of our environment. We are what we believe in, what happens to us. We are the channel through which experience becomes personalized—just as one might embroider initials on a shirt, or engrave a pathetically private name on a mass-produced cigarette lighter. We are not what we are, but what happens to us. We are not what we think, but what people think about us.

One morning—May 1, that symbolically red day of revolution—Pantagleize is awakened by his Negro servant, Bamboola. It is Pantagleize's 40th birthday. He has achieved nothing, tried nothing. He is a man without a destiny—a man with an undistinguished past, a boring present and an arbitrary future. This is Pantagleize, bewildered, flustered, a Chaplinesque everyman profoundly aware of his limitations and yet chirpily cheerful.

"What a lovely day!" Pantagleize remarks, "What a lovely day!" It is the password to a revolution. The country, poised ineptly between one war and its successor, is waiting for the password to set the torch to the uprising. Pantagleize, wandering around like a warm-hearted automaton, unwittingly presses a button he never dreamed existed.

Pantagleize discovers a destiny. He finds himself on a wall addressing the people. He finds himself in love and embracing a leather-suited girl revolutionary. He finds himself in a bank stealing the crown jewels. Finally, for this is what Ghelderode describes as "a farce to make you sad," he finds himself in front of a firing squad, dying like a surprised butterfly with his comrades of the moment.

Identity brings involvement, and involvement may bring a firing squad. I suppose you could think of Ghelderode's play as a political parable with a universal message, but you would have to be a very dull fellow to cherish such thoughts. For the first thing that strikes one about "Pantagleize" is not how enlightening it is, but simply how funny it is. The farce buzzes on with the hazy hum of a bee, and only afterward do you realize you have been stung.

The staging is exemplary. It is stylized—often in the expressionist manner of the 1930's that seems very right for Ghelderode, who was politically a child of that time —and yet has admirable fluency. The direction by John Houseman and Ellis Rabb uses obvious expressionist devices, such as masks or a military tribunal in which the judges are puppets suspended from the ceiling by motivated string, yet uses them with a happy zest.

It is as though everyone responsible for the staging had taken a pledge to stress the theatricality of the piece. This is to be seen in the finely imagined and realized scenery and lighting by James Tilton, which puts the whole play in shades of black and white (apart from a few defiantly red flags) offering a superb effect that is almost calculatedly dramatic.

This is the force of the whole staging — its unashamed theatricality. A parade brilliantly suggested by waving flags countermarching behind a high wall, or a group of firing-squad victims, posed eloquently in their deaths, that has the pictorial value of a painting.

Painting is, in fact, the clue to Ghelderode. He was much inspired by Breughel and Bosch, and to an extent it was the Flemish painters' vision of life and hell (they knew no heaven), that he was trying to express in his plays. There is a painterly vigor here, and an unliterary consistence, a stress on image rather than incident, that chime in well with times that are taking a new look at drama's strict linear development.

The performances are polished. Mr. Rabb himself, a virtuoso of the off-hand voice and the glazed middle-distance gaze, is more Jacques Tati than Charlie Chaplin as Pantagleize. Yet this is a performance of sweetly contrived style, beautifully calculated and including a death scene that in its sheer athleticism might win the envy even of Laurence Olivier.

The rest of the company supports Mr. Rabb with notable, but unnoticeable. smoothness. The A.P.A. still lacks the cohesive yet individually virtuoso teamwork that marks out the great repertory company. But certainly I have never seen the troupe look better than in this. Patricia Conolly, Richard Easton (a valuable newcomer to the company). Sydney Walker and Joseph Bird (leading a very properly Keystone Kops army) all excelled.

●

Finally, what impressed was not only a very entertaining play very entertainingly done, but also a sense that the company's resources, both in simple material and in far from simple goodwill of the regular audience, have reached a point where its future could be fascinating. How else, for example, would we ever have got "Pantagleize" on Broadway? Now it is there, do go and see it.

1967 D 1

The Show-Off
George Kelly's Comedy of '20's Given by A.P.A.

By CLIVE BARNES

WITH the unerring skill in the selection of plays that has always done the A.P.A. Repertory Company credit, it came up with a beautifully timed—in every sense—revival of George Kelly's "The Show-Off" last night at the Lyceum Theater. This is unquestionably the best American play seen on Broadway for some seasons, and the A.P.A. company gives it with exquisitely judged style.

Forty or so years is a tricky age for a play, for while in one sense it is a period piece, its ideas and concepts are not yet historically frozen. As a result, such a play can seem merely old-fashioned in its thinking, or in its style, and the risk of this is magnified in a realistic play such as "The Show-Off."

"The Show-Off" survives magnificently, partly because it is a good, well-written play, but much more because Mr. Kelly's dramatic situations—and even more his characters—are timeless and, in that sense, classic.

Van Williams
Helen Hayes

The Cast
THE SHOW-OFF, A.P.A.-Phoenix revival of the George Kelly comedy. Staged by Stephen Porter; setting and lighting by James Tilton; costumes by Nancy Potts; artistic director, Ellis Rabb; general manager, Norman Kean. Presented by the A.P.A.-Phoenix Repertory Company, managing director, T. Edward Hambleton. At the Lyceum Theater, 149 West 45th Street.

Clara .... Gwyda DonHowe
Mrs. Fisher .... Helen Hayes
Amy .... Pamela Payton-Wright
Frank Hyland .... Alan Fudge
Mr. Fisher .... Joseph Bird
Joe .... George Pentecost

Aubrey Piper..............Clayton Corzatte
Mr. Gill..................James Greene
Mr. Rodgers...............Gordon Gould

As can be learned in one of the excellent program supplements that the A.P.A. is selling, when Mr. Kelly wrote his play in 1924 he thought he was writing about "the problem of marriage among the young and the poor," and presumably he was. But this is not what survives. The staying power of "The Show-Off" is to be found in two splendid characters—the vinegary, sweet-and-sour, quince-jam mother, and the big-mouthed compulsive liar—and best of all in the confrontation of those two.

Few loves even in plays seem to have been as blind as the one Amy Fisher has for Aubrey Piper, a $32-a-week railroad clerk who not only dreams of riches but actually invents, wears a carnation and a toupee, and has a hyena-like braying laugh. But love him she does, and marry him she does, even against her mother's advice. The feud between the show-off and the mother is of course totally one-sided. He has no wish to give offense; indeed, affability is his deadliest virtue. But he is monstrous, a boaster, braggart and buffoon.

The play is handsomely developed, with the story emerging and building with an unobtrusive craftsmanship that would be good to watch if Mr. Kelly were not too clever to let you see it. For naturalism is Mr. Kelly's aim, and unlike so many lesser well-made plays earlier in this century that gloried in their technical devices, Mr. Kelly's art is largely to conceal art.

What is partly so satisfying is the manner in which it catches people speaking—not so much what they say, but the flutterings and hesitations of the way they say it. There is a fine honesty to this writing. Also there is the way in which Mr. Kelly has captured two archetypal American figures, almost as emblematically recognizable as Uncle Sam himself.

The mother, narrow, blinkered, clucking like a hen protecting her brood, with a no-nonsense, warm-hearted waspishness and a skeptical nonconformity, has been seen many times, but rarely I think with such affection and authority. As for the show-off, that romanticist charlatan, here Mr. Kelly has excelled himself by showing the man's essential likability that makes him credible.

The scenery of James Tilton and the costumes of Nancy Potts show a very proper sensibility toward the period, never exaggerating yet very slightly heightening the reality, and even the hair styles have been created with the same care. For this depth of detail credit goes to Stephen Porter, who has directed his ensemble with an easy care.

I have left till last the acting, but this is an actor's play, not in the sense that it demands great acting (I imagine it would be still effective enough if played by amateurs) but simply that it must be a very gratifying play to act.

There are no stars in a repertory company, but there will always—thank heavens — be star performances. Helen Hayes as Mrs. Fisher is a miracle of sweetly calculated charm; it is a performance without a hair out of place. It is acting that is aimed at the impeccable rather than the spontaneous, but of its type it is bewitching. Miss Hayes can make a phrase such as "Everybody will have trouble if they live long enough" seem to echo with a timeless wisdom, and she can invest the two words "That's it," when a door is slammed, with a comic finality uncanny in its accuracy.

●

Miss Hayes's radiantly crabapple face and indomitably perky presence dot not have it all their own way, nor does she stand apart from the ensemble as she so sadly did last season when she moved into "You Can't Take It With You" as if she imagined she could. It is Miss Hayes's biggest triumph here that she is coordinated into a team.

Clayton Corzatte's flamboyant Aubrey Piper is very sensitively done, almost deliberately exaggerated at first, but then, as the playwright explores more this all-American wheeler-dealer, toned down so that the audience feels first pity and then a kind of friendship for the unlikable popinjay.

Of the others, I admired most the girls, Pamela Payton-Wright, touching in her love, and Gwyda DonHowe, who gave a well-balanced study of the unloved elder sister learning tolerance.

The A.P.A. has done American drama a service. What other plays by Mr. Kelly might be worth dusting down from the shelves and given another chance in an American repertory?

1967 D 6

1968

YOUR OWN THING, rock musical. Book by Donald Driver; music and lyrics by Hal Hester and Danny Apolinar; settings by Robert Guerra; visual projection effects by Des Pro Studios, Inc.; lighting by Tom Skelton; costumes by Albert Wolsky; orchestration by Hayward Morris; musical direction and dance arrangements by Charles Schneider; technical direction by Richard Thayer; sound by Port-O-Vox; entire production staged by Donald Driver. Presented by Zev Bufman and Dorothy Love, associate producer, Walter Gidaly. At the Orpheum Theater, 126 Second Avenue.
Danny .... Danny Apolinar
John .... John Kuhner
Michael .... Michael Valenti
Orson .... Marian Mercer
Viola .... Leland Palmer
Sebastian .... Rusty Thacker
Purser .... Igors Gavon
Nurse .... Imogene Bliss
Stage Manager .... Igor Gavon

By Clive Barnes

THE prospect of not one but two musicals based on Shakespeare's "Twelfth Night," within the space of two weeks, offered, at least momentarily, a grim Noah's Ark-like prospect of New York theatergoing, where everything was going to come in twos, just like those troubles that never come singly. After "Love and Let Love," the second of the "Twelfth Night" musicals, which is called "Your Own Thing," arrived Saturday night at the Orpheum Theater on Second Avenue. It is, however, cheerful, joyful and blissfully irreverent to Shakespeare and everything else.

Hal Hester and Danny Apolinar, who devised the show and wrote the music and lyrics, and Donald Driver, who was responsible for the book, clearly have no Shakespeare hang-up. Malvolio, Toby and all the rest of that gang have gone, so only the lovers are left. Of these Orsino (Orson) here runs a rock group, and Olivia owns a discothèque.

One of the members of the rock group the Apocalypse has been drafted, so Viola, shipwrecked in Illyria (a place that has John Lindsay for Mayor and looks like New York) fills in for the draftee. Sebastian, Viola's twin brother, also saved from the shipwreck, turns up and with the proper Shakespearean complications—and then some—and falls in love with Olivia.

Shakespeare is occasionally quoted — haphazardly yet pleasantly—and a couple of songs, "Come Away Death" and "She Never Told Her Love," have the benefit of Shakespearean lyrics. Yet the work is as modern as today, and Mr. Driver's zestful staging reinforces the good impression he made

with last season's "Marat/
Sade" on Broadway.

•

Here, with a blank white
stage and rostrums, Mr.
Driver makes full use of
visuals and movie material,
and he has a number of
slide-projected commentators
on the show, including John
Wayne, Humphrey Bogart
(cast as kind of bad and
good angels respectively),
the Pope, Shirley Temple,
Shakespeare, Queen Eliza-
beth and God.

The humor of the show is
light-fingered and light-hearted, and its vitality and charm
are terrific. The music is
always engaging, and far
from consistently strident.
People who like "The Sound
of Music" rather than the
sound of music do not have
to stay away — indeed one
number has a ground bass
taken from Beethoven's
"Moonlight" Sonata, and
even the pop group on occasion plays Corelli on kazoos.

Perhaps the show's hap-
piest characteristic is its
freshness and unexpected-
ness. Where else, for example, in "Twelfth Night" would
you find Orson so disturbed
by his feelings for Viola,
whom he thinks to be a boy,
that he starts searching in
psychology books for information on latent homosexuality? Where else would you
get Olivia musing on the wisdom of falling in love with
a boy 10 years younger than
herself?

The zip of the show itself
comes also from the per-
formers, who are that rare
thing in a musical these days
—singers. Genuine honest-to-
goodness singers with honest-
to-goodness voices. Leland
Palmer, kooky and appealing
as Viola, has a leprechaun's
face, a glowing smile and
sweetly belting voice, and
Rusty Thacker, grinning as
if he had just discovered
the world, is equally as
charming as Sebastian.

•

Marian Mercer, full of a
sad and worldly wisdom as
Olivia, also scores, as does
Tom Ligon as Orson (desperately trying to recall that
somewhat shady aspect of
the glory that was Greece in
an effort to rationalize his
love), and two pleasant re-
fugees from squaresville,
Igors Gavin and Imogene
Bliss. And as for the Apocalypse, Danny Apolinar,
John Kuhner and Michael
Valenti, all individually talented, they would be worth
a place in any discothèque.

1968 Ja 15

The Cast

JOE EGG, comedy by Peter Nichols. Staged
by Michael Blakemore; setting by Robin
Pidcock; music by Andy Park; lighting
and set supervision by Lloyd Burlingame; production stage manager, Ben
Janney. Presented by Joseph Cates and
Henry Fownes and by Michael Medwin
for Memorial, Ltd. At the Brooks Atkinson Theater, 256 West 47th Street.

Bri ....Albert Finney
Sheila ....Zena Walker
Joe ....Susan Alpern
Pam ....Elizabeth Hubbard
Freddie ....John Carson
Grace ....Joan Hickson

By Clive Barnes

A STRANGE thing hap-
pened to me leaving
the theater last night. I
passed a lady wrapped round
in what I perhaps generously
imagined to be musquash,
saying to her escort: "It's not
funny, it's not tragic, it's not
meaningful — it's nothing."
The good lady was referring
to Peter Nichols's comedy "A
Day in the Death of Joe
Egg," which had just opened
at the Brooks Atkinson
Theater.

To an extent I suppose the
lady was right—ladies in
even pretend musquash usually are. The play's humor,
its tragedy and its meaning
might seem less to musquash
than to humanity, and Mr.
Nichols's command of playwriting skills, for all his
beautiful ear for speech, and
his daring willingness to try

anything, is, on occasion, rough around the edges. Yet "Joe Egg" (to use its shortened title) is an immensely moving, even profound play about love and marriage. No it's not funny—it has wit, a bitter, excoriating wit. No it's not tragic—it is ironic, as ironic as the uncalled-for domestic accident, the unexpected death in incongruity. And, certainly, no, it's not meaningful — only critics, poor devils, have to be meaningful, not playwrights.

What "Joe Egg" attempts, and I think, to a surprising extent achieves, is the analysis of a relationship, the dissection of human feeling, the laying bare of people. The people are commonplace enough. Because Mr. Nichols is English and lives in Bristol, his people are English and live in Bristol—but they could just as well be American. The hero, Bri, is a schoolteacher. Spoiled by his mother, he depends upon a self-defensive, antic jokyness to get by in life. Sheila, his wife, is a kind of earth mother, bestowing her love promiscuously upon tame fish, cats, budgerigars, and, of course, Bri. And their 10-year-old child, Josephine, the Joe Egg of the title.

A normal enough couple— but with an abnormal child. Joe is a spastic, subject to fits, virtually unable to move, to see, to talk. As a Viennese doctor who sees Joe says: "She is a vegetable." This is the vegetable love between Bri and Sheila, the thing they have to live with, equate to and, somehow, cope with. "It would have been a good enough marriage," as Bri says toward the end, "except . . ."

How do you face a child that is a vegetable? It is not a nice subject, is it? More like a skeleton in the back of people's minds, lurking unspoken, than a fit subject for entertainment? Bri accepts it with bitter, corrosive laughter. To be himself he

has to be outrageous.

With his wife he taunts God (whom he characterizes as "a manic-depressive rugby footballer") in a series of jokes. Between themselves they act out absurd playlets, self-searching exposés of their relationship with their "living parsnip." Here is the wife taking Joe to the family doctor at their first hint of disturbance, or with the Viennese specialist who first diagnoses the neurological damage, or with the pipe-smoking curate, who in some medieval way wants to exorcise the demon.

The wife plays these games because their self-inflicted, mocking lacerations soothe Bri. Nothing is so bad if you can laugh at it. But beneath the fabric of the marriage, its workings are wrecked. Sex is something they share, but even this has the undertones of their failure to conceive more children, other than Joe.

Mr. Nichols handles this part of the play with considerable imagination. He uses both the direct, vaudeville-style soliloquy (complete with band combo to introduce it, isolating it from the conventional narrative of the rest) and a technique of exaggerated revue sketches to map out the child's life. In all this the audience is used as a kind of mass marriage counselor, where Bri expounds his problems, and Sheila, with much less self-pity, tries to help.

Sheila, you see, is happy. To Sheila, Joe Egg is just another animate object to be loved and nurtured. When a successful school friend of Bri, and his wife, come to visit them, it is Bri who constantly tries to shock them, and Sheila who, with total understanding, smooths them down. Finally it is Bri who is compelled to do something about Joe Egg, and eventually something about the marriage.

It is an aspect of the play worth noting perhaps that its dialogue has more the pure naturalism of a screenplay than the heightened manner of dramatic dialogue — lines are tossed away as if to a camera. Partly as a result, the play seems more episodic than might a theater work more carefully shaped, and at times the play has the totally honest inconsequentiality of dialogue that all but demands a camera to keep it company and give it depth.

There are flaws here, but then we live in a fascinating era of the un-well-made play. Certainly I think few plays this season will prove as provocative or as moving.

●

It is, also, a grateful play for actors. Albert Finney now takes the part of Bri in place of the perhaps more vaudevillianly brilliant Joe Melia who played the role in the London production. Mr. Finney, mildly but gamely miscast, is superb, running the gamut of manic immaturity with a raw-nerved semi-hysteria. As in London, Zena Walker, concerned, just slightly shopworn yet as beautiful as Lilith, totally convincing, totally touching and totally lovely, makes a marvelous thing of Sheila.

Of the rest, the exquisite playing of both John Carson as the rich school friend and Joan Hickson as the doting mother are retained from the London production, and Elizabeth Hubbard, a newcomer, matches their skill as the snooty, yet not inhuman, rich wife. Michael Blakemore directed with a smooth unobtrusiveness that provides its own high praise.

"Joe Egg" is not a comfortable evening, and definitely not a perfect evening, but it is very much worthwhile.

1968 F 2

Loot

Black Comedy Attacks Church and Police

By CLIVE BARNES

THERE is something for everyone to detest in Joe Orton's outrageous play, "Loot," which opened last night at the Biltmore Theater. To like it I think you might have to have a twisted sense of humor. I liked it. But I do trust it's not for you, for you would be a far nicer person if it were not.

Before the curtain rises we hear the Roman Catholic mass for the dead, but this is broken into by some extraordinarily cheap and tawdry rock 'n' roll. Such irreverence is all too sadly typical of a play that leaves no stone unthrown and no avenue undefiled.

The quite deplorable story is about death, religion, money and the police, and it is soon apparent that the late Mr. Orton held sadly unconventional views about all four of these highly regarded human institutions. The work is sacrilegious and blasphemous, and, indeed, some of it is also distasteful. The fashionable thing to say of it will be: "No, I was not shocked, but merely bored." Nothing is such a fine defense against the shocking as a plea of boredom, as it sounds so agreeably worldly.

●

The play is in fact a kind of artificial drawing room comedy—in some respects not unlike those of Oscar Wilde — although the drawing room has been replaced by a front parlor, the principal object in which is a coffin. A freshly bereaved husband is mourning his wife, assisted by a pretty nurse who attended the good lady to the end. The scene of mourning is joined by the dead woman's son. He is preoccupied to some extent because, together with his best friend, an undertaker's assistant, he has just robbed a bank.

The two accomplices are also disturbed by the presence of a sinister pipe-smoking gentleman who is snooping around the house and claims to be an official of the Metropolitan Water Board. Since they have both had the misfortune to have been beaten up by him in the police station, they suspect him of being a police officer. Where then to hide the loot? They decide to put it in the coffin—first, of course, removing the corpse, which is placed, upside down, in a convenient closet.

Orton's comedy is not merely voguishly black. It is distinctly dirty. Its attacks on the Catholic Church and the police have a touch of madness in them; yet there is method in it.

Mr. Orton—and for this some will never forgive him—is being deadly serious. He clearly hated the Catholic Church and all it stands for, and this hatred gives the play an uncomfortable cutting edge. It wounds even to think that an author could have so much bile in him. The bitter, jeering wit is all the more corrosive because at times it snakes out like a serpent in pointless anger. Here Mr. Orton is like a little boy trying to shock his elders but—here's the rub — wielding, albeit clumsily, a real knife.

•

His attacks on the police, coming at a time when both Britain and America might well use a little skepticism concerning the police's fulfillment of their traditional function, have a light-hearted anger beneath a sometimes heavy handed humor. The police officer trying to get a confession out of a suspect knocks him down, twists his arm and kicks him viciously.

"Under any other political system I'd have you on the floor in tears," he shouts.

The victim replies: "You've got me on the floor in tears."

Mr. Orton's style of writing varies between the ornately polished, with all the bedeviled and devastating comedy of statements taken beyond logic, and strange carelessness, where the director has had to make good the gaps in the text.

Orton was a tragic loss to the English-speaking theater because of his lively sense of the absurd. Almost any conventional sentiment he turns inside out to shock. The boy, for example, does not worry about using his mother's coffin to hide the loot, but is horrified at having to bury her naked.

"It's a Freudian nightmare," he murmurs. And the beautifully contrived farcical situations Orton managed: Here the corpse and the money go in and out of doors with the precision of the participants of a bedroom farce.

Strangely, Orton's savage disgust never affects a kind of sunny and stylish good humor that occasionally lights up his darkest powers: Touches such as the bit when the nurse, with murder in her heart and a red smile on her lips, drops a book on the corpse, with the words: "Here, the Ten Commandments. She was a great believer in some of them."

That is a comic line that few playwrights could aspire to, for it is not a slick wisecrack but offers an insight.

Had Orton ever acquired more polish, had he disciplined his talent with technique, he might have written a comedy masterpiece. "Loot" is not that, and does make severe demands upon the director, which Derek Goldby, much helped by a superior cast, sustains better than did the London production last season.

•

Mr. Goldby keeps the mannered, staccato dialogue stabbing across the scene like machine-gun fire, and the sheerly mechanical farce business is adroitly handled. The play, moreover, in William Ritman's authentic seeming set, looks better than it did'in London.

The Cast

LOOT, a play by Joe Orton. Staged by Derek Goldby; setting and lighting by William Ritman; costumes by Patton Campbell; production stage manager, Warren Crane. Presented by Losal Productions, by arrangement with Oscar Lewenstein and Michael White. At the Biltmore Theater, 261 West 47th Street.
McLeavy ....Liam Redmond
Fay ....Carole Shelley
Hal ....Kenneth Cranham
Dennis ....James Hunter
Truscott ....George Rose
Meadows ....Norman Barrs
A Policeman...........William MacAdam

Of the actors, George Rose, as the mad Scotland Yard inspector, as corrupt as he is foolish, is superlative, doubletaking on his double-takes, mugging like a vaudeville comic, and never losing his matchless comic authority.

Carole Shelley, all deadly composure, was acid-sweet as the nurse, Liam Redmond piously apoplectic as the father, while Kenneth Cranham and James Hunter had a kind of terrible mod poetry as the ruthless boys who would do anything for money or a laugh.

You will either hate "Loot" or like it a lot. But don't take your Aunt Mildred—especially if she has just died.

1968 Mr 19

The Boys In The Band

Mart Crowley Drama Is at Theater Fair

By CLIVE BARNES

AS the conventional thing to say about Mart Crowley's "The Boys in the Band" will be something to the ef-

fect that it makes Edward Albee's "Who's Afraid of Virginia Woolf?" seem like a vicarage tea party, let me at least take the opportunity of saying it first.

The play, which opened last night at Theater Four, is by far the frankest treatment of homosexuality I have ever seen on the stage. We are a long way from "Tea and Sympathy" here. The point is that this is not a play about a homosexual, but a play that takes the homosexual milieu, and the homosexual way of life, totally for granted and uses this as a valid basis of human experience. Thus it is a homosexual play, not a play about homosexuality.

Just as you do not have to be Negro to appreciate a play about the Negro experience, you do not have to be homosexual to appreciate "The Boys in the Band." On the other hand, it would be equally idle to pretend that, just as a Negro will see the plays of LeRoi Jones differently from the way I do, so some of my best friends (as Alan Brien wrote in The Sunday Times of London the other week, "some of the best homosexuals are my friends") will be able to identify with its specifics more closely than I can myself.

•

Yet wherever we stand, sit or lie on the sliding scale of human sexuality, I have a feeling that most of us will find "The Boys in the Band" a gripping, if painful, experience. I know I did. It is about a long, bloody and alcoholic party; but only the superficial (and perhaps the suspiciously easily shocked) will see it as a pack of youngish middle-aged fairy queens shouting bitchicisms at one another down the long night.

The similarity between Albee's "Virginia Woolf" and "The Boys in the Band" is striking. Both are concerned with the breaking down of pretences, with the acceptance of reality. Both plays achieve that purpose by using the flame throwers of a cruel, excoriating wit. The victims are flayed alive, and even the persecutors are victims.

"The Boys in the Band" starts out as a birthday party for Harold, an ugly, pockmarked queer. Michael, a man of 30 with no visible means of support but the possessor of a handsome duplex apartment, is g ving the party, and all Harold's friends, homosexual to the last, are there to eat, drink

The Cast

THE BOYS IN THE BAND, play by Mart Crowley. Staged by Robert Moore; setting by Peter Harvey; stage manager, Charles Kindl. Presented by Richard Barr and Charles Woodward Jr. At Theater Four, 424 West 55th Street.

Michael .... Kenneth Nelson
Donald .... Frederick Combs
Emory .... Cliff Gorman
Larry .... Keith Prentice
Hank .... Laurence Luckinbill
Bernard .... Reuben Greene
Cowboy .... Robert La Tourneaux
Alan .... Peter White
Harold .... Leonard Frey

and be gay, if not merry.

The preparations for the party are disturbed slightly when a friend of Michael's, an old college friends named Alan, telephones in distress and asks to see him at once. Alan is straight (married, and with a couple of kids) and would clearly be out of place with the boys of the band.

He arrives anyway, and at first Michael and his friends try to pretend that everything is normal; but the truth soon emerges. What also soon emerges is a strong doubt about the heterosexuality of Alan.

●

As the party proceeds, Michael, getting drunker all the time, seems impelled to play crueler and crueler jokes on his companions until he introduces a game in which all the contestants have to telephone the person they most love in the world and

tell them they love them. The results are rather different from those Michael envisaged, but to a greater or lesser extent everyone is wounded—even a $20 contemptuously mocked dumb-ox of a hustler who has been bought for $20 as a special birthday gift for Harold.

Friedman-Abeles
Reuben Greene

This is Mr. Crowley's first play, and here and there it betrays signs of inexperience. The opening exposition of theme, for example, when Michael gratuitously has to explain who and what he is to one of his closest friends, is a little clumsily contrived, and some of the dialogue is certainly overwritten.

The special self-dramatization and the frightening self-pity—true I suppose of all minorities, but I think especially true of homosexuals—is all the same laid on too thick at times.

There is also the question of camp or homosexual humor. Like Jewish humor, it is an acquired taste; and in both instances every adult New Yorker I know has acquired them. (Indeed, the

New York wit, famous the world over, is little more than a mixture of Jewish humor and homosexual humor seen through the bottom of a dry martini glass.) But camp humor — relentless, over-polished and heartless—can after a time prove a little too much.

The play is often scream-ingly funny as well as screamingly fag, but this camp, always-be-prepared wit is too personally vitupera-tive, too lacking in a sense of pure fun or even a sense of comic perspective, not to pall after a time. The bitter jokes lose their savor—but perhaps they are meant to.

•

The power of the play, which I saw at one of its press previews, is the way in which it remorselessly peels away the pretensions of its characters and reveals a pes-simism so uncompromising in its honesty that it becomes in itself an affirmation of life.

The best thing I can say of both the acting and Robert Moore's almost invisible but clearly most effective direc-tion is that, not only were they completely at one with the play, but also there were times when I all but expected the audience to answer back to the actors. It would be unfair to mention individual members of the cast—all nine names are listed above, and they all have my praise. This is one of the best acted plays of the season.

It is also a very attractive production visually. With the bold use of photo-montages, the designer, Peter Harvey, has precisely con-veyed in black and white a slightly flashy, yet believ-able, New York apartment.

A couple of years ago, my colleague Stanley Kauffmann, in a perceptive but widely misunderstood essay, pleaded for a more honest homo-sexual drama, one where

homosexual experience was not translated into false, pseudoheterosexual terms. This I think "The Boys in the Band," with all its faults, achieves. It is quite an achievement.

1968 Ap 15

Hair

Likable Rock Musical Moves to Broadway

By CLIVE BARNES

WHAT is so likable about "Hair," that tribal-rock musical that last night com-pleted its trek from down-town, via a discothèque, and landed, positively panting with love and smelling of sweat and flowers, at the Biltmore Theater? I think it is simply that it is so likable. So new, so fresh and so un-assuming, even in its pre-tensions.

When "Hair" started its long-term joust against Broadway's world of Sig-mund Romberg it was at Joseph Papp's Public Thea-ter. Then its music came across with a kind of acid-rock, powerhouse lyricism, but the book, concerning the life and times of hippie pro-test was as rickety as a knock-kneed centipede.

•

Now the authors of the dowdy book—and brilliant lyrics—have done a very brave thing. They have in effect done away with it altogether. "Hair" is now a musical with a theme, not with a story. Nor is this all that has been done in this totally new, all lit-up, gas-fired, speed-marketed Broad-way version. For one thing it has been made a great deal franker. In fact it has been made into the frankest show in town—and this has been a season not noticeable for its verbal or visual reti-cence.

Since I have had a number of letters from people who have seen previews asking me to warn readers, and, in the urbanely quaint words of one correspondent, "Spell out what is happening on stage," this I had better do. Well, almost, for spell it out I cannot, for this remains a family newspaper. However, a great many four-letter words, such as "love," are used very freely. At one point — in what is later affectionately referred to as "the nude scene" — a number of men and women (I should have counted) are seen totally nude and full, as it were, face.

Frequent references — frequent approving references— are made to the expanding benefits of drugs. Homosexuality is not frowned upon— one boy announces that he is in love with Mick Jagger, in terms unusually frank. The American flag is not desecrated—that would be a Federal offense, wouldn't it? — but it is used in a manner that not everyone would call respectful. Christian ritual also comes in for a bad time, the authors approve enthusiastically of miscegenation, and one enterprising lyric catalogues somewhat arcane sexual practices more familiar to the pages of the "Kama Sutra" than The New York Times. So there—you have been warned. Oh yes, they also hand out flowers.

●

The show has also had to be adapted to its new proscenium form—and a number of new songs have been written, apparently to fill in the gaps where the old book used to be. By and large these new numbers are not quite the equal of the old, but the old ones — a few of them sounding like classics by now —are still there, and this is a happy show musically. Galt MacDermot's music is merely pop-rock, with strong soothing overtones of Broadway

melody, but it precisely serves its purpose, and its noisy and cheerful conservatism is just right for an audience that might wince at "Sergeant Pepper's Lonely Hearts Club Band," while the Stones would certainly gather no pop moss.

Yet with the sweet and subtle lyrics of Gerome Ragni and James Rado, the show is the first Brodway musical in some time to have the authentic voice of today rather than the day before yesterday. It even looks different. Robin Wagner's beautiful junk-art setting (a blank stage replete with brokendown truck, papie-maché Santa Claus, juke box, neon signs) is as masterly as Nancy Potts's cleverly tattered and colorful, turned-on costumes. And then there is Tom O'Horgan's always irreverent, occasionally irrelevant staging—which is sheer fun.

Mr. O'Horgan has worked wonders. He makes the show vibrate from the first slow-burn opening — with half-naked hippies statuesquely slow-parading down the center isle — to the all-hands-together, anti-patriotic finale. Mr. O'Horgan is that rare thing: a frenetic director who comes off almost as frequently as he comes on. Some of his more outlandish ideas were once in a while too much, but basically, after so many musicals that have been too little, too much makes a change for the good.

But the essential likability of the show is to be found in its attitudes and in its cast. You probably don't have to be a supporter of Eugene McCarthy to love it, but I wouldn't give it much chance among the adherents of Governor Reagan. The theme, such as it is, concerns a dropout who freaks in, but the attitudes are those of protest and alienation. As the hero says at one point: "I want to eat mushrooms. I want to sleep in the sun."

These attitudes will annoy many people, but as long as Thoreau is part of America's heritage, others will respond to this musical that marches to a different drummer.

The Cast

HAIR, love-rock musical. Book and lyrics by Gerome Ragni and James Rado; music by Galt MacDermot. Staged by Tom O'Horgan; dance director, Julie Arenal; musical director, Galt Mac-Dermot. Costumes by Nancy Potts; setting by Robin Wagner; lighting by Jules Fisher; sound by Robert Kiernan; production stage manager, Fred Reinglas. Presented by Michael Butler; Bertrand Castelli, executive producer. At the Biltmore Theater, 261 West 47th Street.

Ron ....Ronald Dyson
Claude ....James Rado
Berger ....Gerome Ragni
Woof ....Steve Curry
Hud ....Lamont Washington
Sheila ....Lynn Kellogg
Jeanie ....Sally Eaton
Dionne ....Melba Moore
Crissy ....Shelley Plimpton
Mother....Sally Eaton, Jonathan Kramer, Paul Jabara
Father......Robert I. Rubinsky, Suzannah Norstrand, Lamont Washington
Tourist Couple ....Jonathan Kramer Robert I. Rubinsky
General Grant................Paul Jabara
Young Recruit ....Jonathan Kramer
Sergeant ....Donnie Burks
Parents ....Diane Keaton Robert I. Rubinsky

You don't have to approve of the Yip-Yip-Hooray roaring boys to enjoy "Hair," any more than you have to approve of the Royal Canadian Mounted Police to enjoy "Rose Marie," and these hard-working and talented actors are in reality about as hippie as Mayor Lindsay—no less. But the actors are beguiling. It would be impossible to mention them all, so let me content myself with Mr. Rado and Mr. Ragni, actors and perpetrators both, Lynn Kellogg and Shelley Plimpton—one of the comparatively few holdovers from the original production —who does marvels with a lovely Lennon and McCartney-like ballad, "Frank Mills."

Incidentally, the cast washes. It also has a delightful sense of self-mockery.

1968 Ap 30

PARADISE NOW, creation collective. Performed by the Living Theater Company. Presented by the Brooklyn Academy of Music, 30 Lafayette Avenue.

By CLIVE BARNES

THE black flag of anarchy fluttered gamely, if symbolically, over the Brooklyn Academy of Music, where last night the Living Theater gave the first New York performance of its collective creation, "Paradise Now." To ensure that it would not be also "jail tomorrow," the company, by arrangement with the police, did not lead its revolution onto the streets, as it did in New Haven, but at the end remained only at the portals of Paradise.

Nothing would be easier than to mock this quest for a group theatrical experience, and some members in the audience availed themselves of just this opportunity. Indeed, the quality of the wisecracks that the audience— hippie, groovy and brainy— shouted at the performers, were funnier than those to be found in most Broadway comedies. This was the comic-relief to an experience that combined involvement, an almost mystical sense of tedium and an exciting new insight into the theater of action, or the theater of cooperation.

Of course, the tedium was the most obvious element— rather as in church or temple. The proceedings open with the cast walking or running down the aisles and stating, rhetorically but plaintively, such remarks as: "I cannot travel wtihout a passport" or "I am not allowed to smoke marijuana." The climax here comes when they chant, "I am not allowed to take my clothes off," whereupon they promptly do.

In fact, they strip down only to skimpy yet adequate bikini-like covering. Interestingly, the cast was preceded in its strip by a drama critic, Richard Schechner, who—to the everlasting glory of his profession — stripped completely in his seat, an action I had never previously observed from any of my other colleagues, although Mr. Schechner was, in fairness, wearing a mustache.

Many of the audience went on stage and mingled. The atmosphere was friendly and relaxed. From here on the rituals—all of them directed at involving the audience in the confrontation of direct political assertions—proceed with an air of gingerly planned improvisation.

At times, when the talk was of racial hatred or revolution, hostilities are simulated. Love itself is simulated, and in what it described as "the rite of universal intercourse," the company staged a gently rocking but perfectly proper love-in.

Eventually it is the very properness the realization that for all its rejection of the stricality it was really only a new, hand-crafted and instant form of make-believe that slightly disappointed.

Also, the very limitation of the medium — its necessary amateurism — at times annoyed. Someone shouted out, "Peter Brook does it better?" And the shouter was right. In his staging of Seneca's "Oedipus" the Britain's National Theater, Peter Brook certainly makes the theater of ritual work magnificently. Mr. Brook, however, was not concerned with political protest, as are Julian Beck, Judith Malina and the Living Theater. It is the necessity to think in repetitious slogans placed upon the piece by the ritualization that leads both to the blatency of the political comment—the thoughts are sincere but not intellectually provocative—and the slight air of demagogue haranguing that emerges in performance.

It was all for this an experience that I would not have missed, even though it did last nearly four and a half hours without an intermission, which is rather longer than "Parsifal."

This is not the main path the theater will take in the future. Playwrights can sleep snugly in their beds, content that the world will always be safe for their typewriters. Yet it is one development, one possible digression that the theater might take. We are often wondering how to get young people to come into the theater. One answer, judging from last night, might be to invite them up on stage.

1968 O 15

'Dames at Sea' Opens at Bouwerie Lane

The Cast

DAMES AT SEA, musical. Book and lyrics by George Haimsohn and Robin Miller; music by Jim Wise; staged and choreographed by Neal Kenyon; settings and costumes by Peter Harvey; lighting by Martin Aronstein; musical director, Richard J. Leonard; assistant choreographer, Bonnie Ano; production stage manager, T. L. Boston. Presented by Jordan Hott and Jack Millstein, associate producer, Robert S. Mankin. At the Bouwerie Lane Theater, 330 The Bowery.

Mona Kent .... Tamara Long
Joan .... Sally Stark
Hennessey .... Steve Elmore
Ruby .... Bernadette Peters
Dick .... David Christmas
Lucky .... Joseph R. Sicari
The Captain .... Steve Elmore

By CLIVE BARNES

OFFHAND I can think of few play titles less liable to attract me to a theater than that of the musical "Dames at Sea," which opened last night at the Bouwerie Lane Theater. And when I noted it was coyly subtitled "the new-30's musical" I remembered that we were now living in the 60's and felt slightly, mildly squeamish. It could have been the start of seasickness.

I suppose the show, which I saw at a preview, took about five minutes to lull my suspicions, and about ten for me to accept the unexpected fact that I was thoroughly enjoying myself. "Dames at Sea" is a real winner, a little gem of a musical.

It is, of course, a pastiche of all those Busby Berkeley Hollywood following-the-fleet extravaganzas, plus the backstage on 42d Street understudy bit. It is, equally of course, knowing and cute. But not repulsively knowing and not disgustingly cute. "Dames at Sea" tries to do for the 30's what "The Boy Friend" tried for the 20's. But it is much better than "The Boy Friend," because it is informed by a genuine love and knowledge for the period. It is perhaps this above all that makes it such a delight.

●

Someone — Susan Sontag, perhaps—should do a sociological essay on the manner in which the movies have developed a new kind of instant nostalgia. Today you do not have to have lived through the 30's to have loved them. In fact it is probably better not to have. For the real lovers of the 30's are the people who have absorbed them through that new time machine called the late-night movie on television. Even a kid of 20 can hear "Cheek to Cheek" and think to himself, without any sense of incongruity, "Ah, those were the days!"

It is this kind of blithe nostalgia for the glimpse rather than the remembrance of things past that informs "Dames at Sea," giving a youthful air, making a pastiche without a middle-aged sag. (Having said that, I just

know that in tomorrow's mail I shall get an anonymous letter from some rejected lover informing me that all three of the musical's collaborators are uncomfortably in their 40's—such is life. Oh well, they write young, so who's counting?)

The book and lyrics by George Haimsohn and Robin Miller, and the music by Jim Wise, hardly seem to put a foot wrong. All the right period references are here— not only Roosevelt, for example, but Coué.

Sometimes you get a straightforward parody of a number such as "The Man I Love," but more often the authors catch just the essence of what they need. To compare a girl to "a sketch by El Greco, the bubbles in vintage champagne," is simply Cole Porter at his toppest. And production details — the dresses are modified 30's but the marcelled hairstyles seem accurate enough —are fine.

And since when did you see a green pack of Luckies? Neal Kenyon has directed and choreographed his cast of six with great resourcefulness. Without resourcefulness you wouldn't get far in a Hollywood-style musical with a cast of six. Just as with the book, lyrics and music, the staging shows a great love for the period, even when it is mocking it. He has the cast leaning back in what now seems to have been a characteristic 30's movie post — no one ever seemed to make a point without producing a split-second impersonation of the leaning tower of Pisa—and now and again, such as in a rain number with circling umbrellas, he lightly guys the old show-biz styles. But the show not only guys the 30's. In a strange way it captures them.

The show is wonderfully helped by its cast. The star I

suppose is Bernadette Peters as the wholly sweetly silly small-town chorine who taps her way from the bus station to stardom in 24 hours. Miss Peters is adorable.

•

The rest of the cast also has great quality. Tamara Long as the Broadway star gives a new life to the word blasé, Sally Stark, good nature and bunions, excels as the confidante of the chorus line, David Christmas as the sailor who is really a songwriter (such a change from songwriters who are really sailors) is just right, as is Joseph R. Sicari as his friend, a gob with a look of minor pain on his face as if he had just swallowed the Bronx subway. Finally, in two rôles as a hardbitten Broadway director and naval captain, Steve Elmore sings well and acts happily distraught.

"Dames at Sea" is a fun musical. It should remain afloat for some time.

1968 D 21

1969

'Ceremonies in Dark Old Men' at the St. Marks

The Cast

CEREMONIES IN DARK OLD MEN, play by Lonne Elder 3d. Staged by Edmund Cambridge; settings by Whitney Lee Blanc; costumes by Gertha Brock; lighting by Shirley Pendergast; stage manager, James S. Lucas Jr. Presented by the Negro Ensemble Company. At the St. Marks Playhouse, 133 Second Avenue.

Russell B. Parker ....:.Douglas Turner
William Jenkins .... Arthur French
Theopolis Parker .... William Jay
Bobby Parker ......David Downing
Adele Eloise Parker ... Rosalind Cash
Blue Haven .... Samuel Blue, Jr.
Young Girl .... Judyann Jonsson

By CLIVE BARNES

WE have known for decades that Negroes were natural actors; we are now busy discovering that they are also natural playwrights. Black writers are nothing new, but the existence of a developing black theater has provided them with totally new possibilities.

A case in point is "Ceremonies in Dark Old Men," by Lonne Elder 3d, which was given by the Negro Ensemble Company at St. Marks Playhouse last night.

Although this was its first professional production, "Ceremonies" is not a new play, and it has been given a number of times by amateur groups. Nor is Mr. Elder a particularly young playwright, but through lack of opportunity he has had to wait for the Negro Ensemble Company to see his work properly produced. I hope he feels the wait was worthwhile, for this is a magnificent, breathtaking performance of a remarkable play.

The play reminded me almost irresistibly of O'Casey's "Juno and the Paycock." Its mood, poised between comedy and tragedy, is identical, its intensity of feeling and love of language are similar, and there is common cause in its undercurrents of rebellion.

•

A onetime vaudeville hoofer, Russell B. Parker, finds himself conned, by family and friends, into using his monstrously unsuccessful, Harlem barber shop for storing illicit corn liquor. The tragic results of this action provide the backbone of the play.

Parker is a good man—battered down by the failure of his dancing talent, the death of his wife, and his instinctive realization that not every good black man works for a living. In conditions of oppression, to work is to submit.

His life is surrounded by his family—a daughter who tries, nose in air and spirit flying, to replace his dead wife, and two sons, sharp with ghetto understanding and nonconformist wit.

Mr. Elder's play straggles a great deal—comes to indeterminate conclusions, changes directions, and loses the thread of its thought. Yet beneath these failings, these tergiversations of dramatic purpose, the play still survives. His theme of a man struggling for honesty in a world where honesty is not so much a luxury as an incongruity, works wonderfully. It is moving, and realistic. And it is no less moving because the honesty has an ironic, bitter aftertaste.

The white view of the black ghetto has a kind of hope tinged onto it. The black view of the black ghetto is less cheerful, even though it is full of sad laughter.

The Negro Ensemble Company is on the point of appearing this season in the World Theater Season organized by the Royal Shakespeare Theater in London, probably the most prestigi-

Bert Andrews

William Jay and Rosalind Cash in Lonne Elder 3d's play

ous drama festival in the world. Quite simply, we could send no better troupe. This is a marvelous company.

In "Ceremonies in Dark Old Men" there are so many wonderful performances that it is almost an embarrassment to start singling people out. Douglas Turner, as the former vaudeville dancer, had a tragic range and power, with just the right comic under-current the author demanded. It was a perfectly judged performance, and if the company at St. Marks Playhouse had given us nothing else I would have exulted in it.

But the play was full of glorious performances. In fact I think it difficult to think of any play—on Broadway or off—that by over-all standards is better acted. Every single person in the cast acts as if his life depended on it. If I mention William Jay as the shiftless elder brother, or Rosalind Cash as the swish-kid sister, I am already aware that I am doing an injustice to the rest. This is an ensemble company —and ensemble acting is both its ideal and its achievement.

●

The staging by Edmund Cambridge seemed as smooth as silk, perfectly catching the play's idiom. I was enormously impressed by this play and its performance. It was easy to see that the Negro Ensemble Company would go far and in a very short time. But how far it would go, and in how short a time, still seems remarkable. This is a marvelous company. Go, see and enjoy. And, maybe, learn a little.

1969 F 6

Founding Fathers' Tale
Is a Happy Musical
The Cast

1776, a musical. Music and lyrics by Sherman Edwards; book by Peter Stone; based on a conception of Sherman Edwards; setting and lighting by Jo Mielziner; costumes by Patricia Zipprodt; musical direction by Peter Howard; orchestrations by Eddie Sauter; musical numbers staged by Onna White; associate to Miss White, Martin Allen; hairstyles by Ernest Adler; staged by Peter Hunt; production stage manager, Peter Stern. Presented by Stuart Ostrow. At the 46th Street Theater.

John Hancock .... David Ford
Dr. Josiah Bartlett .... Dal Richards
John Adams .... William Daniels
Stephen Hopkins .... Roy Poole
Roger Sherman .... David Vosburgh
Lewis Morris .... Ronald Kross
Robert Livingston .... Henry Le Clair
Rev. Jonathan Witherspoon
 .... Edmund Lyndeck
Benjamin Franklin ...... Howard Da Silva
John Dickinson .... Paul Hecht
James Wilson .... Emory Bass
Caesar Rodney .... Robert Gaus
Col. Thomas McKean .... Bruce Mac Kay
George Read .... Duane Bodin
Samuel Chase .... Philip Polito
Richard Henry Lee ...... Ronald Holgate
Thomas Jefferson .... Ken Howard
Joseph Hewes .... Charles Rule
Edward Rutledge .... Clifford David
Dr. Lyman Hall .... Jonathan Moore
Charles Thomson .... Ralston Hill
Andrew McNair .... William Duell
A Leather Apron .... B. J. Slater
Courier .... Scott Jarvis
Abigail Adams .... Virginia Vestoff
Martha Jefferson .... Betty Buckley

By CLIVE BARNES

ON the face of it, few historic incidents seem more unlikely to spawn a Broadway musical than that solemn moment in the history of mankind, the signing of the Declaration of Independence. Yet "1776," which opened last night at the 46th Street Theater, most handsomely demonstrated that people who merely go "on the face of it" are occasionally outrageously wrong. Come to think of it, that was also what the Declaration of Independence demonstrated, so there is a ready precedent at hand.

"1776," which I saw at one of its critics' previews on Saturday afternoon, is a most striking, most gripping musical. I recommend it without reservation. It makes even an Englishman's heart beat a little bit faster. This is a musical with style, humanity, wit and passion.

The credit for the idea of the musical belongs to Sherman Edwards, who has also contributed the music and lyrics. The book is by Peter Stone, best known as a Hollywood screenwriter. The two of them have done a fine job.

●

Mr. Edwards and Mr. Stone have found a wonderful story for themselves in the birth pangs of a nation. Here is John Adams ("obnoxious and disliked," as everyone is agreed) fighting for his dream of freedom, the avuncular Franklin, full of aphorisms plagued by gout and confident of the good report of history, and then the laconic Virginian, Thomas Jefferson,

Martha Swope

Howard Da Silva

the great drafter of independence, who, even though he sometimes plagiarized John Locke, wrote with the eloquence of justice. It is a great cast and a great story.

In fairness, my personal comprehension of American history is probably as profound as was that of General Burgoyne. However, it should perhaps be noted that the authors have, on occasion, bent history just a little. The general thrust of their story is undoubtedly honest, but here and there one or two parries have been perhaps exaggerated in the interest of histrionic accuracy.

As even a European schoolboy knows, there were 56 signatures to the Declaration of Independence, not the dozen or so represented here. Assuredly the economics of the theater are to blame, and this is a license, if not poetic at least practical.

●

Then again—my memory could be wrong here—I believe that historians consider that Congress's resolution of July 2—all signatures, amendments and holidays to the contrary—was the really vital event. Also I wonder about the authors' treatment of Richard Henry Lee, the Virginia patriarch. They present him as a charming fool, and the pawn of Franklin who sends him, in May, back to Virginia to get a resolution through the Virginia Legislature proposing independence. In fairness to the reputation of Mr. Lee, I think it is true that even a month before that he had already written to Patrick Henry suggesting that independence was absolutely essential.

What only is important however, is that the authors have really captured the Spirit of '76. The characterizations are most unusually full for a musical, and even though the outcome of the story is never in any very serious doubt, "1776" is consistently exciting and entertaining, for Mr. Stone's book is literate, urbane and, on occasion, very amusing.

For the music it would have been easy for Mr. Edwards to have produced a pastiche of Revolutionary tunes, but this he has studiously avoided. There is admittedly a flavor here, but the music is absolutely modern in its sound, and it is apt, convincing and enjoyable.

•

The authors have, bravely perhaps although in the event it seems perfectly natural, omitted any chorus, so that absolutely everyone in the cast has a significant part to play. This offers a great challenge to the actors and to the people responsible for the staging. In almost every respect this is excellent, although personally I felt that the settings by Jo Mielziner were very disappointing and old-fashioned. Here, with such an adventurous musical, was an opportunity for some outstanding design, but it was an opportunity missed.

Fortunately the costumes by Patricia Zipprodt were stylishly appropriate — although, as a matter of accuracy, virtually everyone should have been in white wigs, certainly at the signing—and the direction by Peter Hunt and the musical staging by Onna White were both faultless. Mr. Hunt has encouraged his actors to behave precisely as if they were in a play rather than a musical, and Miss White has most adroitly done the rest. Both are helped by a great cast.

William Daniels has given many persuasive performances in the past, but nothing, I think, can have been so effective as his John Adams here. This is a beautiful mixture of pride, ambition, an almost priggish sense of justice and yet — the saving grace in the character — an ironic self-awareness. Mr. Stone and Mr. Edwards provided Mr. Daniels with the character to play, but Mr. Daniels plays it to the hilt. Also, notably, he still remains perfectly in character when he sings.

•

The other star performance is provided by Howard Da Silva as Ben Franklin. Mr. Da Silva has a voice as sweet as molasses and as mellow as rum, and his humor and good nature are a constant delight. But this is a cast without a weak link. I must mention Clifford David's rapier-sharp arrogance as the Southern Edward Rutledge, Paul Hecht's aristocratic elegance as the loyalist John Dickinson—the Pennsylvanian who, though unable to vote for Independence, did join the Continental Army as a private—Ronald Holgate's brilliantly extrovert and show-stopping performance of Richard Henry Lee, and the aptly clumsy poise of Ken Howard as Thomas Jefferson. And then there were the ladies, the beautiful Virginia Vestoff as Abigail Adams, and Betty Buckley as the spirited Martha Jefferson.

But enough. I cannot mention all 26 of the actors, and yet utter fairness would demand no less. The musical will, I suspect, prove to be the sleeper of the season. Who knows, it might even run until the celebration of the bicentenary in 1976. I rather hope so. Certainly you don't have to be a historian to love "1776."

1969 Mr 17

Story of Racial Conflict and Gangsterism

Charles Gordone Play Is on 'Other Stage'

NO PLACE TO BE SOMEBODY, a play by Charles Gordone. Staged by Ted Cornell; setting and lighting by Michael Davidson; stage manager, Adam Perl. Presented by the New York Shakespeare Festival Public Theater, Joseph Papp, producer; Gerald Freedman, artistic dirctor; Bernard Gersten, associate producer. At the Public Theater, 425 Lafayette Street.

Gabe Gabriel	Ron O'Neal
Shanty Mulligan	Ronnie Thompson
Johnny Williams	Nathan George
De Jacobson	Susan Pearson
Evie Ames	Lynda Westcott
Cora Beasely	Marge Eliot
Melvin Smeltz	Henry Baker
Machine Dog	Paul Benjamin
Mary Lou Bolton	Laurie Crews
Ellen	Iris Gemma
Sweets Crane	Walter Jones
Mike Maffucci	Nick Lewis
Judge Bolton	Ed VanNuys
Sergeant Cappaletti	Charles Seals
Harry	Malcolm Hurd
Louie	Martin Shakar

By CLIVE BARNES

THE New York Shakespeare Festival Public Theater is more than just a complex name—it is a complex complex. Apart from Shakespeare in the Park and all that, a new theater in preparation in the Lafayette Street home, where, of course, the Florence Anspacher Theater is situated, there is also the Other Stage.

This, at the bottom of the Lafayette Street building, is the experimental wing of the Shakespeare Festival, and, with the help of a grant from the Rockefeller Foundation, it tries out new plays on weekends. The Other Stage has now discovered "No Place to Be Somebody," a play by the black playwright Charles Gordone and the first to move from workshop status to a regular run as part of the Public Theater's programing.

Rather too long and certainly too episodic for its own good, I found that "No Place to Be Somebody," despite a few flagging patches, was an engrossing play. In form and style it is a 30's gangster play. Then it would have been about the Lower East Side, it would have been made into

a movie by Warner Bros. and the movie would have starred James Cagney and Pat O'Brien.

But now the hero, Johnny, is black—and he is in the rackets, or so it seems, for reasons of political activism. This is the best way he can get back at the whites. In the 30's such motivation would have seemed farfetched, but now it is merely tragic.

Ron O'Neal, Nathan George

In fact, Johnny is only a small-time crook — a little pimping for the most part— and his activities are seriously curtailed by the Mafia. He dreams of the day when an old gangster, Sweets Crane, a father figure to him, will be released from the pen, so

that they can make bad together on the big time.
Sweets is released, but the
old spirit has gone, and he is
reduced to a little token
pickpocketing.

But Johnny perseveres and
decides to take on the Mafia
alone. Eventually he is put
down by bad luck, a crooked
judge, police corruption and
Mafia hoodlums. The same
kind of thing used to happen
to Bogart, Robinson and Muni
in the good old days.

The play holds the interest,
but what is really rewarding
is the vigor of the writing
and language. Witty, salty
and convincing, the dialogue
brings Johnny's West Village
bar to vivid life, and Mr. Gordone can create characters.

Johnny — played superbly
well by Nathan George as an
object study in uptight relaxation and unflinchingly
tragic destiny—emerges as
someone completely credible,
and so does Gabe Gabriel, the
narrator and link-man of the
story. Gabe is the nearly
white actor and playwright
who finds himself becoming
blacker than black in his
search for identity. But he is
also the spokesman for black
moderation, and together with
a white barman who eventually realizes that he will achieve
nothing by making himself
into a pretend-black out of
guilt, the only hopeful aspect
of a play full of bleak action.

The construction of the play
is a little weird. Not only is
the playwright-narrator given
soliloquies on the black position—and like the entire role
these are done brilliantly by
Ron O'Neal, another remarkably powerful actor — but a
figure called Machine Dog, a
black militant, occasionally
wanders through the action
like the ghost of Hamlet's
father. However, Ted Cornell's
staging is so firm and precise
that this matters less than
it might have.

What I especially liked
about the staging was its phy-

sical preciseness. When a
man drank in one draft an
almost full tumbler of bour-
bon, his eyes almost popped
out with the effort, and when
a man was knocked down or
shot, the realism of the acting was most commendable.
I admired also Mr. Cornell's
use of Michael Davidson's
persuasive setting of a seedy
Village bar. In the intermission one was almost tempted
to sit down at one of the
tables and order a drink.

The acting was taut and
punchy. I have already mentioned Mr. George and Mr.
O'Neal. Other performances
of real quality came from
Susan Pearson as a white
hooker, Ronnie Thompson as
the pathetic little bartender,
Marge Eliot as the black girl
who loves him, Walter Jones
as the broken-down gangster
and Paul Benjamin as the
black militant. There are few
better casts than this on or
off Broadway. If Mr. Gordone
has got another play in him,
it will awaited with interest.
1969 My 5

The Cast

INDIANS, a play by Arthur Kopit.
Staged by Gene Frankel; settings by Kert
Lundell; costumes by Marjorie Slaiman;
lighting by William Eggleston; music
by Richard Peaslee; choreography by
Virginia Freeman; production manager,
Hugh Lester; stage manager, Albert L.
Gibson. Presented by Arena Stage,
Thomas C. Fichandler, executive director;
Zelda Fichandler, producing director. At
Arena Stage, Washington.

Buffalo Bill Cody..........Stacy Keach
Sitting Bull................Manu Tupou
John Grass.................Barry Primus
Interpreter ....Yusef Bulos
Spotted Tail...............Howard Witt
Grand Duke Alexis.........Raul Julia
Ned Buntine...............Robert Prosky
Uncas.......................Raul Julia
Wild Bill Hickok........Barton Heyman
Chief Joseph..............Richard Bauer
Jesse James................Ronny Cox
Oglethorpe ....Jack Malarkey
Colonel Forsythe..........Peter MacLean

By CLIVE BARNES
Special to The New York Times

WASHINGTON, May 26—
There will always be a
particular fascination about

Stacy Keach

seeing a work in progress. Last July I saw Arthur Kopit's play "Indians" at its world premiere in London, given by the Royal Shakespeare Company. Last evening I saw a new version at Washington's Arena Stage, and the play, with a completely different staging and a largely new cast, is due for Broadway next fall.

In the light of this I would not normally have come to Washington if only for fear of seeing something in an unfinished state. But Mr. Kopit, I was told, raised no objection, and one or two other New York critics had written about it, so I came to see it. I am glad I did, and this partly because of the Arena Stage itself.

When a regional theater makes national news with a major premiere, it deserves national attention. Without this attention our regional theaters will always be regarded as second-class citizens, a kind of Off-off-off-Broadway wasteland. But the play itself has been reshaped and rewritten—almost unrecognizably from the London version — and is markedly better.

Mr. Kopit's play charges that the United States Government toward the end of the last century was guilty of genocide—that in effect, whether by definite design or casual error, it wiped out most of the Indian people, denying them both land and food. The destruction of the buffalo, to provide food for the railway workers pushing westward, removed the Indians' food and shelter. Eventually, sometimes by deception, sometimes by force, the Government cheated on Thomas Jefferson's pledge: "It may be regarded as certain that not a foot of land will ever be taken from the Indians without their consent."

Mr. Kopit makes those charges in a play of considerable originality. For the London staging, he based it all around Buffalo Bill's Wild West Show. To an extent this framework is maintained, but now the author finds a second dramatic focus in the commission sent by the President in 1886 to investigate Indian grievances at the Standing Rock reservation. Interestingly, the play cuts between the show and the commission, emphasizing the contrast between the two.

There is still an odd strain of facetiousness in the play, although not nearly so much as before. In addition to that occasional stylistic unevenness, there remains the occasional irrelevancy, so that the play is not quite well-organized enough. But the more I think about it the more impressive an achievement it seems. I suppose that from the beginning Mr. Kopit had a startlingly good concept, which went slightly but disastrously awry.

Now it is coming round into excellent shape. It was also very sensible to try again in the creative but comparatively relaxed atmosphere of the Arena Stage, rather than trying to fix the Broadway production on the road. That is just the way the regional theater should be used.

In Buffalo Bill Mr. Kopit has found a genuine tragic hero—the first white liberal. Blundering, blustering, misguided and lost, Buffalo Bill is trying to do the right thing, yet infallibly doing the wrong, pathetically reduced at the end yet still having the courage to face up to an impossible situation, where simple compassion was not enough. If you want to take it so, I think you may find "Indians" extraordinarily relevant to the black/white confrontation, but Mr. Kopit never draws a specific parallel. He just leaves you to make your own choices.

•

The Arena Stage is one of the liveliest companies in the country. But of the productions I have seen therein—cluding last season's "The Great White Hope"— nothing can match this "Indians." Admittedly the director, Gene Frankel, has virtually an entirely different play to work on, but the staging itself is a vast improvement over the London version. It uses the Arena Stage with such virtuosity that I wonder how this can be repeated in a proscenium theater on Broadway. This is destined to be a major problem, for from the opening to the close Mr. Kopit and Mr. Frankel seek—usually successfully – to catch up the audience in a total experience. I do not believe I have ever seen more persuasive advocacy for theater in the round.

In many respects—no, in most respects—the acting is not as polished as that of the Royal Shakespeare, which after all is one of the two great English-speaking thea-ter companies. But it has better material, a better director, and more identification with and understanding of the subject. London's Buffalo Bill, Barrie Ingham, produced a brilliantly detached performance, amusing, touching, elegant. But Stacy Keach is infinitely more convincing, partly because he is a better, very different kind of actor, but much more because the role is torn out of his own experience.

•

Mr. Keach, smiling too widely, with always the guilty break in his voice, reveals a man fooling himself yet still maintaining a kind of baffled, battered honesty. This, I think, is integral to Mr. Kopit's character, whereas the dazzling charlatan offered by Mr. Ingham, remarkable as it was, lacked the same relevance to the play.

The other great performance at the Arena is that of Manu Tupou as Sitting Bull, who has the strange beauty of comprehended pain, and a nobility all the more impressive for its humanity. The rest of the cast is very fine. Barry Primus is poignant and passionate as the half-Westernized John Grass. Richard Bauer has the right, stumbling dignity for Chief Joseph. Raul Julia does some most attractive stage conjuring tricks in a variety of roles. Peter MacLean impresses particularly as Colonel Forsythe, the officer in charge of the final Indian massacre, and Barton Heyman makes a boisterously effective Wild Bill Hickok.

There are still things that I think could be done with the play, and it also has to be adapted for the proscenium. But I think it will be one of the more interesting Broadway openings next season, and I hope the producers take along for the trip the excellent Washington designers, Kert Lundell and Marjorie Slaiman, as well as the composer, Richard Peaslee, and the choreographer, Virginia Freeman.

1969 My 27

Kenneth Tynan's Revue Opens at the Eden

OH! CALCUTTA! an entertainment with music. Devised by Kenneth Tynan; conceived and staged by Jacques Levy; contributors: Samuel Beckett, Jules Feiffer, Dan Greenburg, John Lennon, Mr. Levy, Leonard Melfi, David Newman and Robert Benton, Sam Shepard, Kenneth Tynan, Sherman Yellen; music and lyrics by the Open Window; choreography by Margo Sappington; setting by James Tilton; lighting by David Segal; costumes by Fred Voelpel; projected media designed by Gardner Compton and Emile Ardolino; still photography by Michael Childers; audio design by Robert Liftin; production supervisor, Michael Thoma; stage manager, John Actman. Presented by Hillard Elkins in association with Michael White and Gordon Crowe, associate producer, George Platt. At the Eden Theater, 189 Second Avenue (at 12th Street).
PRINCIPALS: Raina Barrett, Mark Dempsey, Katie Drew-Wilkinson, Boni Enten, Bill Macy, Alan Rachins, Leon Russom, Margo Sappington, Nancy Tribush, George Welbes; and the Open Window: Robert Dennis, Peter Schickele, Stanley Walden.

By CLIVE BARNES

VOYEURS of the city unite, you have nothing to lose but your brains. During "Oh! Calcutta!," which I saw at the final preview and which opened last night at the Eden Theater, a member of the cast—barebacked as it were —announces with a simple but euphoric pride: "Gee, this makes 'Hair' seem like 'The Sound of Music.'"

On the contrary my friend. I assure you "Oh! Calcutta!" makes "The Sound of Music" seem like "Hair." There is no more innocent show in town —and certainly none more witless—than this silly little diversion, devised by Kenneth Tynan, produced by Hillard Elkins and destined to make the shrewd entrepreneurs the crock of gold

that lies there somewhere over the rainbow.

Innocent it is, completely. It is childlike when they strip —and the stripping, dancing and staging are the only tolerable parts of the evening for the "mature audiences" to whom the producers are somewhat foolhardily addressing their sales pitch— and childish when they talk. The sketches are unbelievably weak. The sex joke, I must protest, has not in reality sunk so low. This is the kind of show to give pornography a dirty name.

●

I have enormous respect for Ken Tynan, as critic, social observer and man of the theater. But what a nice dirty-minded boy like him is doing in a place like this I fail to understand.

I thought we were to be offered a little pleasant erotic dramatic literature and a few neatly turned bawdy jokes. It was, I imagined, not to be the kind of evening for everyone, but for those who wanted it, a diverting place not to take your maiden aunt to.

The authors, gathered together (although their individual contributions remain unidentified) are formidable. Listen to them — Samuel Beckett, Jules Feiffer, Dan Greenburg, John Lennon, Jacques Levy, Leonard Melfi, David Newman and Robert Benton (they wrote "Bonnie and Clyde" although which wrote which I am not sure), Sam Shepard, Mr. Tynan himself and Sherman Yellen. But personally I think the butler did it, and that none of these fine and worthy men are really guilty.

It is curious how anti-erotic public nudity, as opposed to private nudity, is. There is a clinical lack of mystery about it that, speaking for myself, makes me disconcertingly think pure and beautiful thoughts. Other people of course may have other reactions. For students of form, I should point out that while Margo Sappington (an ex-Joffrey dancer of great promise I always expected to see more of, although hardly as much as this) has devised pleasant choreography, it is not very original. The San Francisco Dance Workshop does the nude bit better and prettier.

In sum, "Oh! Calcutta!" is likely to disappoint different people in different ways, but disappointment is the order of the right. To be honest, I think I can recommend the show with any vigor only to people who are extraordinarily underprivileged either sexually, socially or emotionally. Now is your chance to stand up and be counted.

●

Etymological Note

Perhaps the only witty joke of the evening is the title "Oh! Calcutta!" This is not a reference to the black hole of Indian mutiny fame, but is the title of a painting by the contemporary French artist Clovis Trouille that shows the tattooed behind of a well-endowed young lady.

The title is a pun. It suggests in French: "Oh! Quelle ——— t'as!" The dashes represeit a three-letter French argot word that Le Monde would not dream of publishing. Or, freely translated: "What a lovely ——— you have!" The dashes represent a slightly longer Anglo-Saxon word the English language edittion of Le Monde would not dream of publishing. Yes, Virginia, that really was the best joke.

For the humor is so doggedly sophomoric and soporific that from internal evidence alone I would go to court and testify that in my opinion such highly literate men could not have been responsible. Luckily at the

preview I saw the audience appeared to be moderately unsophisticated, and modestly grateful for anything.

●

The jokes are prissy and silly—depending for their effectiveness, such as it is, on their naive attempts at being daring. My 7-year-old son recently went through a phase where he kept on trying to shock my young daughter with one of the more vital and active Anglo-Saxon swear words. For a day or so he succeeded—but I hasten to add that my daughter is only 5, and was not really a "mature audience" for him. Eventually he failed to shock, and now seems to have accepted the advisibility of restricting such language to private moments of considerable stress.

But, I hear you asking yourself, is all the written material stale, flat and merely profitable. The answer is no. One sketch—called "Delicious Indignities"—was very funny indeed and had a genuine literary feel to it. Wait till they do it on television—you'll scream. I also admit I was very amused by a burlesque-style skit, a few years after Dr. Kronkheit, on human sexual response. It wasn't witty, it wasn't clever, but it made me laugh immoderately.

The failure here is almost exclusively a failure of the writers and the producers. The director, Jacques Levy, has done his best with the weak material at hand. The opening—a group-spoof striptease—has just the right touch of erotic sophistication, but regrettably it is a touch never again repeated in the show.

However, the nude scenes, while derivative, are attractive enough. The best effects —including the rather sweet grope-in immediately after the intermission—have been taken from Robert Joffrey's ballet "Astarte," and the show uses the same projected media designers, Gardner Compton and Emile Ardolino, and, of course, rock music, here provided by the Open Window. The Joffrey Ballet version was not only better but also far, far sexier.

1969 Je 18

The Cast

ACROPOLIS, based on the text of Stanislaw Wyspianski. Staged by Jerzy Grotowski; co-realization, properties, costumes by Jozef Szajna; architecture by Jerszy Gurawski; literary adviser, Ludwik Flaszen. Performed by the Institute of Actor's Research Laboratory Theater of Wroclaw, Poland. Presented by the Brooklyn Academy of Music, in association with Ninon Tallon Karlweis and the Committee to Welcome the Polish Lab Theater, Ellen Stewart, co-chairman. At the Washington Square Methodist Church, 133 West 4th Street.

Jacob-Priam ....Zygmunt Molik
Rebecca-Cassandra ....Rena Mirecka
Isaac-Troyan Guardian.Antoni Jaholkowski
Esau-Hector ....Ryszard Cieslak
Angel-Paris ....Zbigniew Cynkutis
Leah-Helen of Troy ....Stanislaw Scierski
and Andrzej Paluchiewicz

By CLIVE BARNES

IT is a room, except it isn't a room, it's a church. And inside the room, which is the concentration camp Auschwitz, are prisoners. And inside the church are spectators. The spectators are mixed up with the prisoners, so that the actors and the audience are in a constant position of emotional confrontation.

The scene is provided by Jerzy Grotowski's Polish Laboratory Theater, brought by the Brooklyn Academy of Music for its first American season. Last night at the Washington Square Methodist Church, it gave the first American performance—only the Polish Laboratory Theater would give a premiere on

Election Night — of Grotowski's most remarkable staging of "Acropolis."

•

Grotowski believes that the theatrical environment should have relevance to the theatrical experience—or, if you prefer it, that the physical conditions of the theater should be shaped to the play, not the play shaped to the physical conditions of the theater.

Thus in "Acropolis" the audience is · grouped all around the central playing area and the actors move around and by them. To an extent, your fellow members of the audience become lay actors—not exactly invisible, but rather like the black-garbed puppeteers in the Japanese Bunraku theater. You see them, but you don't see them. Yet their presence, their common civilian status with yourself, actually adds to the immediacy of the actors.

Grotowski's purpose in "Acropolis" is to challenge the audience to see itself in the context of Auschwitz. To accept some iota, a scintilla of that horror, to be involved in that web of human choices and squalid heroism.

The staging is based upon the Polish play "Acropolis," written in 1904 by Stanislaw Wyspianski. It is apparently a symbolic play, set in the Royal Castle of Gracow (the Polish "Acropolis" in the sense of a fortified citadel) where figures from the tapestries come down from the walls and re-enact the great mythic scenes of Western civilization.

The playwright — I have never encountered the actual play, so I depend for my information on the program note—described this Royal Castle as "the Necropolis of tribes." What would be a meaningful contemporary realization of this? Grotowski settled on Auschwitz, where, as Ludwik Flaszen, Grotowski's literary adviser, puts it, "the European civilization of the 20th century was put on trial."

The Laboratory Theater works on a text to provide a style and manner of performance. Grotowski is said to feel that in his first American notices too much attention was paid to him, and too little to his actors. He is probably right there, for director and cast clearly work together in a collaboration that must have something of the atmosphere of choreographic creation to it.

•

In "Acropolis" the Laboratory Theater has devised both this environmental setting, with the actors responding antiphonally to one another, across the audience, and a stylized playing style in which simple sculptural-like objects, or even day-to-day things like wheelbarrows, involve the spectator by familiarity into a sense of participation.

The style of the acting is singular. The actors use their face muscles to provide mask-like images of misery and acceptance, their voices are dehumanized, their entire manner represents humanity in such a condition of degradation that the humanity itself is flickering like a guttering candle.

Now they re-enact certain Biblical and Homeric myths. Without any knowledge of Polish I couldn't identify these myths specifically, although the mood is clearly enough evoked, and the graven images of suffering are portrayed with a scalding yet piteous vitality. (Incidentally, I am far from certain whether a knowledge of Polish would offer any more enlightenment — I have a suspicion that many of the guttural and

sonorous sounds and songs that the actors offer are gibberish.)

To say something must be seen when all the seats for the entire engagement are sold is something in the manner of gibberish itself. However, as with Grotowski's earlier "A Constant Prince," this "Acropolis" offers a strange, challenging and vibrantly beautiful experience. Grotowski really does make us look once more at what basic theater is.

•

Grotowski's actors are all dazzling technicians, with masterly discipline and control. They aim in technique to remove the shadow line between appearance and reality, and to take us with them on a new theatrical journey.

It is a fascinating experience. It has changed my basic thinking about the theater, and I think it will change many others also. I would stress though that this is a "laboratory" as well as a "theater." I think the importance of Grotowski is to be seen as much in his disciples as in his own work—and ultimately it may well be his role as a maverick theatrical catalyst that will be his final significance.

In the last couple of years, few things have impressed me in the theater so much as Peter Brook's staging of Seneca's "Oedipus Rex" for Britain's National Theater and Jerome Robbins's "Dances at a Gathering" for the New York City Ballet. I suspect that neither would have been the same without Grotowski.

1969 N 5

PRIVATE LIVES, revival of the Noel Coward comedy, in the APA production. Staged by Stephen Porter; settings and lighting by James Tilton; costumes by Joe Eura; Miss Grimes's costumes by Barbara Matera Ltd.; stage manager, Lo Hardin. Presented by David Merrick. At the Billy Rose Theater, 208 West 41st Street.

Sibyl Chase............Suzanne Grossmann
Elyot Chase...............Brian Bedford
Victor Prynne.............David Glover
Amanda Prynne...........Tammy Grimes
Louise......................J. J. Lewis

By CLIVE BARNES

GORGEOUS—that would be one word for Stephen Porter's restaging of "Private Lives," which arrived at the Billy Rose Theater last night. Delicate might be another word, dazzling if you want a third.

Noël Coward, who, surprisingly enough, will be 70 on Dec. 16, devoted much of his career to writing entertaining—and often somewhat less than entertaining—material that was presumably intended to be as disposable as a paper tissue and hardly more valuable. But in the 1929 "Private Lives," he came up with a little masterpiece, indeed the only classic English comedy of manners since Oscar Wilde.

It was an excellent idea of the A.P.A. to revive it, and even more excellent to get Mr. Porter to stage it, and Tammy Grimes and Brian Bedford to star in it. It makes a funny and, yes, touching evening. Coward has a name for flippancy, even heartlessness, but the emotions in "Private Lives" are very real, and the human situation completely convincing.

●

Amanda and Elyot love each other passionately but cannot stand the sight of each other. And that is what the entire play is about. Divorced for five years, Amanda and Elyot have at last remarried. And chance has it that, unbeknown to both they are starting their respective honeymoons on the same moonlit night, in the same town in the south of France, in the same hotel, on the same floor. Indeed, chance just has it that they are even sharing the same balcony.

They meet, gasp, fall in love all over again over the champagne cocktails and elope together to Paris and sin. Their new sobersided and unconsummated mates chase them like private eyes with a public mission.

Some people say that Coward is witty. Absolute nonsense. Coward has hardly written a witty line in his life. Coward, at least in "Private Lives," is simply and fantastically funny. There is nothing cerebral in his humor, which is derived from an antic sense of the ridiculous and a shrewd observation of human behavior.

Coward should be heard and not read. Even his funniest lines are not clever—which is why he is one of those rare humorists a critic can quote without thieving his jokes.

For example, Elyot has been telling Amanda that he met his wife at a houseparty in Norfolk. With acidulated precision, Amanda comments: "Very flat Norfolk." Nothing else is needed. To read it is as flat as Norfolk; to hear on the stage it comes over like an Oscar Wilde bon mot.

Oddly enough, when Coward tries the occasional epigram or aphorism — "Women are like gongs. They should be struck regularly"— they sound more nostalgic than clever. The lines that truly matter, truly linger, are simple, deceptive, perfectly planned and executed phrases such as. You really are . . . very . . .sweet."

●

"Private Lives" is, of course, a great test of style for both director and actors. Originally, when it first played Broadway in 1930, with Coward himself, Gertrude Lawrence and a young mustached Laurence Olivier as the dull-dog husband, it could have been no such thing. But distance demands enchantment, and what was once a contemporary comedy —and a somewhat daring, racy one at the time—is now period quadrille for four stylish actors.

Tammy Grimes as Amanda is outrageously appealing. She plays every cheap trick in the histrionic book with supreme aplomb and adorable confidence. Her voice moans, purrs, splutters; she gesticulates with her eyes, almost shouts with her hair. She is all campy, impossible woman, a lovable phony with the hint of tigress about her, so ridiculously artificial that she just has to be for real. This is beautiful.

Miss Grimes plays the role in mid-Atlantic twang, which sounds just right and terribly, terribly twenties. Brian Bedford has a more difficult vocal problem — whether or not to unclip those specially clipped vowels always associated with Coward himself and, by common inference and long-selling records, with the actual role of Elyot. Sensibly, Mr. Bedford compromises—giving not an imitation of Coward yet never forgetting quite the echoes of that quite unforgettable voice. "Strange how potent cheap music is!"

Mr. Bedford, impeccable, with his flippancy well-groomed, his anxieties well-bred, and his life-style as dead as a dinosaur's skeleton, is a delight as Elyot. He plops words into space with the diffident deliberateness of a man tossing pebbles into a pool, for his speech is so clearly more articulated than articulate.

The other two roles in this matrimonial pas de quatre are less obvious and less appealing than Amanda and Elyot, but they also are rewarding opportunities that are gratefully and effectively grabbed by Suzanne Grossmann as the piteously put-upon and flatter-than-Norfolk Sibyl and David Glover as the pompous Victor.

Mr. Porter's staging is sweetly elegant, lingering over the period affectionately yet without affectation, and the performances of the cast are themselves their own testimony to his skill. I admired also the setting by James Tilton and the costumes by Joe Eula.

Everything came together to make me at least realize that "Private Lives" is not a revival but a classic. Who would have thought it?

1969 D 5

1970

"Hello, Dolly!"
By LEWIS FUNKE

BROADWAY hasn't had much to cheer about this hapless season, but on Saturday night at the St. James Theater it more than made up for it by giving Ethel Merman three standing ovations as she took over the role of Dolly Gallagher Levi, in "Hello, Dolly!"

The first explosion came, as might have been expected, the moment Miss Merman came out from behind the newspaper she was reading on the horse trolley that had just pulled on stage. Applause, cheers, whistles weren't enough.

•

Young gallants who still were taking their spinach strained when the incomparable Ethel was bowling them over in "Girl Crazy" back in 1930 leaped to their feet. Others followed, and in no time the house was giving Miss Merman a performer's dream reception.

The second standing ovation arrived early in the second half. There was Ethel in that red outfit and tremendous hat coming down the staircase at the Harmonia Gardens singing the title song. And when she sang, "It's nice to be home where I belong," and the other line in the same song, "Dolly will never go away again," you can imagine the excitement.

The third standing ovation at the finale topped everything, with Miss Merman standing there beaming and bowing. It was like being at Madison Square Garden for the Knicks or in Shea Stadium the day the Mets clinched the pennant.

Even those who never had been able to "see" Miss Merman as the star she is—and yes, there have been those over the years—may have been persuaded to join the tribute. For truly she is one of the great ladies of the musical stage of a vanishing musical genre that does nothing more than try to entertain the customers.

•

As Dolly, of course, she is Merman to the core, a bit brassy and raffish, a performer schooled in vaudeville and loaded with all the little tricks of that all-but-forgotten trade. Her voice hasn't lost any of that wonderful gravelly, earthy quality. At 61 she still can bounce notes off the rafters without the aid of the chest mike so essential for so many latter-day entertainers.

Jerry Herman, composer and lyricist, has given her two new songs, "World, Take Me Back" and "Love, Look in My Window." You're bound to hear them again and again in the coming months and what she does with "Hello, Dolly!", the title tune, has to be seen as well as heard. She knows how to give each word its value, and with its musical lilt and swing it seems to have been made just for her.

Indeed, the show actually would have been made for her from the beginning had she accepted the importuning of those involved in its creation. But she was in the long-running "Gypsy" at the time and apparently could not see herself getting caught up in another musical immediately. So she turned down the offer, Carol Channing took the assignment and, to be sure, was delightful in it, launching the musical on its way to fortune. When Miss Channing departed, Mr. Merrick began pulling out aces from every sleeve to keep the show going. First there was Ginger Rogers, and then came Martha Raye, Betty Grable, Pearl Bailey and Phyllis Diller. Call Miss Merman his lucky seventh.

Joining the company with Miss Merman are Russell Nype as Cornelius Hackl and Jack Goode as Horace Vandergelder—two sound selections. In the absence of Gower Champion, choreographer and director who was prevented by illness from working with the cast, his wife, Marge, and his assistant Lucia Victor have done splendidly in giving the production the verve and spirit it had on opening night.

•

"Hello, Dolly!" is, inevitably, the "new" hit in town, and if David Merrick can hold onto Miss Merman for longer than the three months to which she has agreed, he's going to make good his boast that the show would break the longevity mark for a musical set by "My Fair Lady" at 2,717. At 2,532, "Hello, Dolly!" certainly is within shooting distance now.

1970 Mr 30

Tale of Rise to Stardom Opens at the Palace

APPLAUSE, a musical based on the film "All About Eve" and the story by Mar Orr. Book by Betty Comden and Adolph Green; music by Charles Strouse; lyrics by Lee Adams; setting by Robert Randolph; costumes by Ray Aghayan; lighting by Tharon Musser; musical direction and vocal arrangements by Donal Pippin; orchestrations by Philip J. Lang; dance and incidental music arranged by Mel Marvin;

production associate, Phyllis Dukore;
directorial assistant; Otto Pirchner;
choreographic assistant; Tom Rolla;
production stage manager, Terence
Little; directed and choreographed by
Ron Field. Presented by Joseph Kip-
ness and Lawrence Kasha, in association with Nederlander Productions and
George M. Steinbrenner 3d. At the
Palace Theater, Broadway at 47th
Street.

Tony Announcer	John Anania
Tony Host	Alan King
Margo Channing	Lauren Bacall
Eve Harrington	Penny Fuller
Howard Benedict	Robert Mandan
Bert	Tom Urich
Buzz Richards	Brandon Maggart
Bill Sampson	Len Cariou
Duane Fox	Lee Roy Reams
Karen Richards	Ann Williams
Bartender	Jerry Wyatt
Peter	John Anania
Bob	Howard Kahl
Piano Player	Orrin Reiley
Stan Harding	Ray Becker
Danny	Bill Allsbrook
Bonnie	Bonnie Franklin
Carol	Carol Petri
Joey	Mike Misita
Musicians	Gene Kelton, Nat Horne, David Anderson
TV Director	Orrin Reiley
Autograph Seeker	Carol Petri

By CLIVE BARNES

WHATEVER it is Miss Lauren Bacall possesses she throws it around most beautifully, most exquisitely and most excitingly in a musical called "Applause" (it's really all about someone called Eve), which last night reclaimed the Palace Theater once more from the always invidious threat of moving pictures.

Miss Bacall is a honey, and the book is among the best in years—so who is going to care too much about the second-rate music? Not, I am sure, the public. We have little enough—why should we now be choosy?

Seriously, Miss Bacall is a sensation. She sings with all the misty beauty of an on-tune foghorn. She never misses a note—she is not one of your all-talking musical dramatics—and although her voice is not pretty, it does have the true beauty of un-forgettability. Her dancing is more conventional—she is av-eragely, if beautifully groovy. Her acting is her own thing. Miss Bacall is probably going to be the Marlene Dietrich of the 1980's—she

has that same enchantingly cool asexual sexuality. She has that same well-bred air of experience hard-won and the sensibility of well-trimmed honesty. She is the kind of girl everyone would be proud to have as a sister; but she is also a bright, bright star, fascinating but unmenacing.

●

The story is that classic of Broadway, the understudy who moves over and comes out on top. It was once an original (or at least the pro-gram calls it "original") story by Mary Orr, and later the film, "All About Eve," which Bette Davis fans still call one another about—I am told—when it is on one of the later of the Late, Late Shows.

Lauren Bacall

As a theme it has a certain guts to it, if only because it is the rags to riches Cin-derella story told from the viewpoint of the lady who was the princess when Cin-derella was still barefooted.

And it is not too kind about the way Cinderella got her crystal slipper up there to the top. It has a welcome, lovely cynicism about show business, and this cynicism the present book by Betty Comden and Adolph Green has preserved in the most astringent aspic. This is a musical play that is bright, witty, direct and nicely punchy.

It is, after all, a heaven-sent opportunity to write bitchily inspired show-biz wisecracks—the kind of lines you wake up in morning wishing you said the night before, and not quite remembering whether you did. The whole show is sharp and fun —everyone's idealized version of what show business ought to be.

Even potential hit shows are entitled to a few weaknesses (why not, hit women claim that privilege!) and with "Applause" it is the music, which while never unpleasant, has a kind of "here-we-go-round-again" sound to it that is more soothing than stimulating. I got the impression that the Lee Adams lyrics were a lot more lively than was the score by Charles Strouse. Even so Mr. Strouse never actually does anything wrong. But then he never does such a great amount that is actually right.

The direction and choreography are by Ron Field and both are sweetly unnoticeable and swinging. Mr. Field does a very nice job keeping the show moving, Miss Bacall in the spotlight, and giving credit to the quite serious dramatic soap opera being happily unfolded before the expectant public.

And, I suspect, to keep all three aspects in focus at one and the same time is no easy mission to accomplish. But Mr. Field has done a lovely job with coherent dances and neatly dovetailed dramas. He is helped by the handsome scenery by Robert Randolph and the very stylish costumes by Ray Aghayan.

To challenge memories of "All About Eve" you need a very strong cast, and the producers have assembled one, even apart from the totally if strangely adorable Miss Bacall.

Len Cariou as the wonderboy director, straight as an arrow and as fast as Mike Nichols, is a bluff, tough delight: just the kind of person that no one in audience would mind carrying off Miss Bacall. I always knew Mr. Cariou could act very well indeed, yet I was surprised he could sing. (Yet I was not surprised about Miss Bacall being able to sing; I would even expect her to be great at chess.)

As Eve, Penny Fuller had all the brassy, pushy, belty quality a young girl needs to make good in show business. As Miss Bacall's rival she was fine, not only in being acceptable in any juvenile-anonymous way, but also in one great and hungry explosion of ambition, exposing just the kind of talent that any star, however secure, might look insecurely twice at.

The cast as a whole was superior, the look of the show proved sweet and glossy, but it was Miss Bacall's night. She is a good lady, and New York is going to love her and love her—we take her to our brittle hearts.

You know what upset me? George Sanders! In the movie George Sanders played the role of a critic who was so smooth that I found him quite inspiring as a way of life. In the musical they have made him into a producer. If I had known that, I would have completely revised my career! I always thought it was the critic who was supposed to have all the fun.

1970 Mr 31

Paul Zindel Melodrama at Mercer-O'Casey

The Cast

THE EFFECT OF GAMMA RAYS ON MAN-IN-THE-MOON MARIGOLDS, a play by Paul Zindel. Directed by Melvin Bernhardt; music and sound by James Reichert; setting by Fred Voelpel; lighting by Martin Aronstein; costumes by Sara Brook; production stage manager, Bud Coffey. Presented by Orin Lehman, associate producer Julie Hughes. At the Mercer-O'Casey Theater, 240 Mercer Street.

Tillie .... Pamela Payton-Wright
Beatrice .... Sada Thompson
Ruth .... Amy Levitt
Nanny .... Judith Lowry
Janice Vickery .... Swoosie Kurtz

By CLIVE BARNES

OFF BROADWAY is at last warming up again. At the weekend we had the engaging "Dear Janet Rosenberg, Dear Mr. Kooning," and now I can also most warmly recommended a new domestic drama that arrived last night at the Mercer-O'Casey Theater. It is a new play by Paul Zindel and it is one of the best of the season so far.

It has, I must admit, one of the most discouraging titles yet devised by man. It is called "The Effect of Gamma Rays on Man-in-the-Moon Marigolds," which sounds as if Arthur Kopit might have taken up science fiction. Yet curiously enough you realize at the end of the play that the title is valid—valid but stupid.

•

The play is about a mother bringing up two daughters. The mother is an acid-tongued slut, wears a dressing gown all day, smokes too much, doesn't approve of housework and drinks whisky from a tooth mug. She scrapes up a living by giving home to a human wreck whose relations are prepared

to pay money for the privilege of not having to look after her. Her house is the last top before the graveyard.

Her name is Beatrice, and at first you think she is all bad. She stands in the way of her daughters' schooling, she attacks life itself without offering any alternative to it. And yet she is a victim.

Her older daughter, Ruth, is also a victim. She has already had one mental seizure and she is even now narrowly balanced. And the second daughter? She, Tillie, is vague—an indeterminate girl, loves her white angora rabbit and is interested in science.

A high school science teacher encourages the young girl—encourages her to the point of an experiment with the effect of atomic energy, gamma rays on marigold seeds. The results are either interesting mutants or genetic disasters. Most are disasters.

Mr. Zindel, who writes alarmingly well, contrasts the fate of the poor marigolds with the fate of this tortured family. We are all the product of our environment, all the product of our particular "gamma-rays," but some survive and some are destroyed.

"Marigolds," if Mr. Zindel will forgive the contraction, is precisely one of those plays that seems easy enough to write, even though the history of dramatic literature unnoticeably rides upon the fossil-remains of so many writers who have tried to write them. This is the kind of true-life melodrama that fascinates Arthur Miller, and rather like Mr. Miller it is extremely successful. My heart was held by it. And, unlike most of its genre, the ending is unusually satisfying.

Melvin Bernhardt's staging is unemphatic and most successfully naturalistic. You really become involved with these people—sad that Beatrice and Ruth are bitterly unsalvageable, glad that Tillie—the new and tentative mutant—is going to survive. I admired also the squalid and cluttered setting provided by Fred Voepel, the cleverly apt costumes by Sara Brook, and the impeccable acting of the cast.

•

Sada Thompson's Beatrice, embittered, beleaguered, cynical and yet, despite herself, supremely pitiable, is among the best things in the current New York theater. Pamela Payton-Wright's Tillie is a delicate portrayal of shadings for circumstances, and Amy Levitt's abrasive yet poignant Ruth is another performance to remember. Also there is Judith Lowry, silent yet eloquent, as Nanny, Beatrice's geriatric boarder, insensate yet poignant. See this play— it has a compassion that is all to its own.

1970 Ap 8

Alvin May Have a Hit in a Lean Season

The Cast

COMPANY, a musical comedy. Music and lyrics by Stephen Sondheim; book by George Furth; settings and projections designed by Boris Aronson; costumes by Sara Brook; lighting by Robert Ornbo; musical direction by Harold Hastings; orchestrations by Jonathan Tunick; dance music arrangements by Wally Harper; musical numbers staged by Michael Bennett; production directed by Harold Prince; production stage manager, James Bronson. Presented by Harold Prince in association with Ruth Mitchell. At the Alvin Theater, 250 West 52d Street.

Robert	Dean Jones
Sarah	Barbara Barrie
Harry	Charles Kimbrough
Susan	Merle Louise
Peter	John Cunningham
Jenny	Teri Ralston
David	George Coe
Amy	Beth Howland
Paul	Steve Elmore
Joanne	Elaine Stritch
Larry	Charles Braswell
Marta	Pamela Myers
Kathy	Donna McKechnie
April	Susan Browning
The Vocal Minority	Cathy Corkill, Carol Gelfand, Marilyn Saunders and Dona D. Vaughn.

By CLIVE BARNES

WITH the always possible exception of Vladivostok, Manhatan must surely be the most masochistic village in the world. We expect visitors to our grubby canyons to come to us, exhausted by our pollution, soused by our martinis, maimed by our muggers, and to say: "This is hell on earth. How do you stand it?"

We agree, feel a little bit prouder, like some survivors from a natoinal catastrophe, and straighten out shoulders for the next day's battle in the streets, in the offices and in the bedroom of the place that calls us home.

"Company," a show that opened last night at the Alvin Theater, and about which I have some personal reservations, deserves to be a hit in a lean season. It is a very New York show and will be particularly popular with tourists— especially those from Vladivostok and Westchester— who will get the kind of insight into New York's jungle that you perceive in the survival-kit information provided by New York magazine. Indeed, if you like New York magazine you will probably love "Company."

•

The musical, directed and produced by Harold Prince, with music and lyrics by Stephen Sondheim and book by George Furth, is about the joys and pains of married love in New York City. Particularly the pains.

Five apparently childless and seemingly unemployed couples are visited by their friend Robert, a Peter-Pannish young man of 35 and a bachelor of fascinating eligibility. Robert seems the only worthwhile thing in these uncertain marriages. He flirts with the principals, introduces a couple of them to pot, watches a karate demonstration between another couple, watches one couple get divorced (they stay together, of course, as man and mistress) and another couple (who had, of course, been living together) get married. He proposes to one girl, is propositioned by another.

In case you had any doubts about his sexual inclinations —and I am not sure that I did—he has three girls on the side. One of them is vulgar enough actually to work for a living. She is an airline stewardess, but luckily takes her hat off in bed.

•

Creatively Mr. Sondheim's lyrics are way above the rest of the show; they have a lyric suppleness, sparse, elegant wit, and range from the virtuosity of a patter song to a kind of sweetly laconic cynicism in a modern love song. The music is academically very interesting. Mr. Sondheim must be one of the most sophisticated composers ever to write Broadway musicals, yet the result is slick, clever and eclectic rather than exciting. It is the kind of music that makes me say: "Oh, yeah?" rather than "Gee whiz!" but I readily concede that many people will consider its sheer musical literacy as off setting all other considerations.

Mr. Furth's book is a strange mixture of lines almost witty enough to be memorable and other phrases that more decorously might have been left on the road. The dialogue is starched with a brittle facetiousness that with luck might be confused with a barbed and savage humor. Still, it never talks down to us; indeed, it rises to talk up.

The conception has two difficulties. In the first place these people are just the kind of people you expend hours each day trying to escape from. They are, virtually without exception—perhaps the airline stewardess wasn't

too bad—trivial, shallow, worthless and horrid.

•

Go to a cocktail party before the show, and when you get to the theater you can have masochistic fun in meeting all the lovely, beautiful people you had spent the previous two hours avoiding. You might enjoy it. At least this lot goes away with the curtain, and doesn't know your telephone number.

The second fault is a structural one. Here is a series of linked scenes, all basically similar to one another, and it is left to the director to find a variety of pace and character, and to impose a satisfactory unity on the show. This Mr. Prince has not done. It may not be his fault. The odds were against him.

The setting by Boris Aronson is admirable—a mixture between an East Side multiplex, Alcatraz and an exhibition display of some 20 years ago demonstrating the versatility of elevators. It is all in a tasteful shade of perspex, and looks better than it sounds.

Michael Bennett is one of those artists who carry the past into the future, and stylizes his view of it into a signature. Of course you can see the influence of Gower Champion, and all the other champions, yet his choreography has genuine vitality, and it is one of the major joys of the show.

The cast, apart from the leading man, Dean Jones, is excellent. In a role that needed a mixture of Dean Martin and Tom Jones, Dean Jones might be thought to have something going for him. He is very amiable, but in this role, at least, he needs more charisma. He needs to be the cynosure of all eyes, the aspiration of all hearts.

He comes over as the kind of guy you would be delighted to encounter in a carbaret.

●

The others are all fine

1970 Ap 27

'Me Nobody Knows,' a Musical, Bows

THE ME NOBODY KNOWS, a musical. Music by Gary William Friedman; lyrics by Will Holt. Based on the book "The Me Nobody Knows," edited by Stephen M. Joseph, and an original idea by Herbert Schapiro. Setting and lighting by Clarke Dunham; costumes by Patricia Quinn Stuart; media design and photography by Stan Golberg and Mopsy; additional lyrics by Herbert Schapiro; orchestrations by Gary William Friedman; musical director, Edward Strauss; musical numbers staged by Patricia Birch; directed by Robert H. Livingston; production stage manager, Martha Knight. Presented by Jeff Britton, in association with Sagittarius Productions, Inc., a One Star, Ltd. production, Erlinda Zetlin, assistant to producer. At the Orpheum Theater, 126 Second Avenue.

Rhoda .... Melanie Henderson
Lillian .... Laura Michaels
Carlos .... Jose Fernandez
Lillie Mae .... Irene Cara
Beniamin .... Douglas Grant
Catherine .... Beverly Ann Bremers
Melba .... Gerri Dean
Donald .... Paul Mace
Lloyd .... Northern J. Calloway
Clorox .... Carl Thoma
William .... Kevin Lindsay
Neil .... Hattie Winston

By CLIVE BARNES

What is poverty? What is a ghetto? What is a slum? Garbage in the strets, rats on the sidewalk, death in the heart? Yes, of course. It is also a certain awareness of life, a certain sensibility, a certain knowing, half-knowing gamble between survival and disaster. And in New York City, it is mostly black and soulful.

"The Me Nobody Knows" is a new musical at the Orpheum Theater. It opened last night. I loved it. I loved its understanding and compassion, and I felt its pain and yet also its unsentimental determination for hope.

●

Many musicals have arrived with the tag of being characteristic of New York City attached to them like a gold medal—musicals such as "West Side Story" or even "Company." But "The Me Nobody Knows" is New York, it is the New York nobody wants to remember.

Does this sound depressing? Perhaps, but as I left the audience was cheering, and it was not cheering gloom, but the victory of the human spirit over circumstances. For the slums these kids find themselves in may be squalid, but the kids are beautiful. And the show, assertive and passionate, reflects that beauty.

This dark and lovely rock-folk musical has a strange genesis. Stephen M. Joseph is a teacher. He teaches in New York, in the ghetto. A year ago he collected some writings from his classes and the classes of friends. The result was a published anthology of children's voices from the ghetto—200 of them. Uncensored, this writing from a young, underprivileged America, aged from about 7 to 18, largely black or Puerto Rican, is enormously vivid and honest. It sees the world with the cold-eyed stare of skepticism, yet at the same time hugs to itself a hope, like a child clinging to a skinny kitten.

It was Herb Schapiro who, according to the program, had the idea to transform this anthology into a musical, and with the help of Gary William Friedman's eloquent music and Will Holt's tersely apt yet poetic lyrics, the emergent work is somehow both bitter and joyous.

There is no story, of course —rather, it is a picture of a place and a time. There are 12 children—old children, rich in poverty, only just winning over life—and they talk and sing about this and that. About birds, about drugs, about being black. Mostly they talk and sing about being alone and trying

Bert Andrews
Beverly Ann Bremers

to reach not just the world outside but also the world inside. The language is plain and blunt—the music bluesey and attractive.

The direction by Robert H. Livingston, much helped by Patricia Birch's musical staging, is as simple and as effective as the subject matter. It uses the various levels of Clarke Dunham's archetypally slum setting with enormous resource, offering that continual variety the eye needs in a non-narrative show.

It also never loses sight of the musical's purpose. Just as is "Hair," this show is an excursion into a way of life. There is no story, but there are dozens of stories. There is the story of the 13-year-old boy first taking heroin; the story of the little kid in a drug store shocked to find a white boy order some "milk and a nigger"; or a boy watching an alcoholic black man being picked up by an ambulance on Broad-

way and 90th after a street accident.

●

The stories have a validity, a feel of truth to them. (They reminded me of those Studs Terkel documentary tape recordings of America, in their frighteningly pertinent inconsequentiality.) And they are given by the cast with just the right unblinking honesty. There are 12 of them — eight black, four white — and I enjoyed them so much, thought they were so transparently good people, that I have no wish to differentiate between them. They acted and sang from their hearts, and it was good.

One last word for the media designing of Stan Goldberg. With its very clever projections always essisting Mr. Dunham's lighting, this is not only one of the most meaningful and ultimately joyful shows of the season, it is also technically one of the more advanced. "Hair" at its climax borrows from Hamlet's "What a piece of work is man." It could also stand as a motto for "The Me Nobody Knows."

1970 My 19

'The Serpent' Offered by Open Theater

The Cast

THE SERPENT: A CEREMONY, a play, created by the Open Theater Ensemble; words and structure by Jean-Claude Van Itallie, under the direction of Joseph Chaikin; associate director, Roberta Sklar; bruitage, Richard Peaslee and Stanley Walden, associate, Patricia Cooper; lighting, Will Mott; production supervisor, Dale Whitt; administrative director, Marianne de Pury. Presented by the Open Theater, Inc. At the Washington Square Methodist Church, 137 West Fourth Street. The Ensemble: James Barbosa, Raymond Barry, Shami Chaikin, Brenda Dixon, Ron Faber, Jayne Haynes, Ralph Lee, Peter Maloney, Mark Samuels, Ellen Schindler, Tina Shepard, Barbara Vann, Lee Worley, Paul Zimet.

From the middle of life, "a stop between open and closed," Joseph Chaikin's Open Theater reflects on our beginnings. "The Serpent" is the group's eloquent re-examination of Genesis:

What does "The Serpent" say about Genesis? That man created God to set limits on himself. That Cain meant to kill Abel, but not to cause his death. That events in Genesis will be re-enacted until the end. That no one *really* knows what happened in the beginning.

Mostly "The Serpent" doesn't say; it shows. This is "a ceremony," but the actor-authors are not high priests. They are superbly disciplined artists who are very aware of their own mortality. What is sometimes overlooked about the Open Theater is its lack of artistic pretension and its extraordinary playfulness.

"The Serpent" will be presented tonight and June 11 as part of the Open Theater two-week repertory season at the Washington Square Methodist Church. The play begins in the audience. Actors sit silently in the aisles, then delicately begin rubbing sandpaper blocks together, clacking wood rods, blowing whistles. Slowly the sound becomes more insistent, pervasive, rhythmic, and finally musical — until the entire church is filled.

One is engaged and entertained, then realizes that this is not only the beginning of the ceremony, but perhaps also a metaphorica representation of the creation of the world. The most provocative thing about "The Serpent" is that its many levels of approach and meaning are enticing and open-minded.

●

Three actors carry a dead girl on stage (there is, by the way, no scenery). The first word spoken is "Autopsy"—one indication, I believe, that the Open Theater's later

"Terminal" had its origins within "The Serpent." Death is one of the many themes in "The Serpent"—also, love, hate, revenge—all of which could give birth to individual ensemble works.

Having achieved verbalization the actors retrace themselves (as they do repeatedly), returning to sounds, then back to words, until they appear to have created their own language, sometimes identifiable, sometimes not.

There is more "language" in "The Serpent" than in "Terminal." "Words and structure" are by Jean-Claude van Itallie. There are scenes and, one might say, even a plot. There are commentaries and dialogue, and much of it is startling, such as a counterpointed conversation between two women in which each follows every statement, (some prophetic, some outrageous) with a fixed grin.

First the primordial ooze, then crawling creatures. Slithering snakes become a tree of serpents. There are only five actor-snakes; they seem like hundreds. As they enmesh themselves, they dart their tongues and shower Eve with temptations. They are not so much evil, as tempting—and maliciously amusing.

When Adam bites the apple, it sticks in his craw. He looks dumbstruck, as if to say, what have I wrought.

Suddenly the victorious snakes dump crates of shiny red apples on stage. The stage rolls and bumps with apples. Actors grab them and gobble them. The scene is wild, farcical, and hilarious. Then actors dash into the audience, sneaking apples to the customers.

The temptation is so delightful and exuberant that the banishment from Eden seems, in contrast, even more horrible, more terrifying than one might imagine. Not fire and smoke, but a rising chant of "Accused! Accused! Accused!"

●

Abel's death is staged as a ritual with Cain reflexively going through the motions (almost slow motion: down comes the arm, up goes the elbow) until the murder itself. Cain himself is the most surprised at the finality of the act.

While the "begats" are being recited, the Open Theater performs a mass orgy, ending in mass orgasm. In "Zabriskie Point," a quite similar (although naked) Open Theater display of carnal passion seemed merely ridiculous, here it is intentionally ironic and absurd, as if to say, isn't copulation what was really behind all those begats?

There is more—much more —in "The Serpent." In fact, it is amazing that the evening is so short (about 80 minutes), because it is filled with so much imagination, theatricality and perception.

"The Serpent" is the most fully formed piece in the Open Theater's current repertory. Although it is complex, it is also the most accessible and the most entertaining. "Terminal," which by contrast seems serial and somewhat rough-edged, has images that I found even more haunting. But I hesitate to rate one work over the other. Each in its own way is a unique and enormous theatrical experience. Beckett's "Endgame," the third piece in the repertory, proves that the ensemble is capable not only of creating its own masterpieces, but also of performing someone else's.

If you intend to witness the Open Theater before it disappears again, a word of caution: The crowds at Washington Square Methodist are thick and clamorous, and the seating is very limited.

MEL GUSSOW.

1970 Je 2

THE GOLDEN STREETS, a play by Piri Thomas. Directed by Miriam Colon; setting and visuals by John Braden; costumes by Maria Ferreira; sound by Richard Logothetis; project coordinator, Allen Davis 3d; production stage manager, Bob Volin. Presented by the Puerto Rican Travelling Theater and Mayor Lindsay's Urban Action Task Force with the Parks Recreation and Cultural Affairs Administration, August Heckscher, Administrator, Dore Schary, Commissioner. At theaters throughout Greater New York.

Luis Perez	Robert Burgos
Anibal	Reinaldo Arana
Raul Perez	Alex Colon
Susana Perez	Carmen Maya
Mariano Perez	Art Vasil
Myrna	Maria de Landa
Chino	Shelly Desai
Child	Christopher Medina
Cathy Donalds	Kathleen Scarlett
Priest	Tomy Vargas
Young Girl	Kitty-Alice Snead
Young Man	Jeffrey Grimes

By MEL GUSSOW

This is the fourth year in which Miriam Colon and her Puerto Rican Travelling Theater have been fulfilling their purpose "to bring the living theater to the people, also to acquaint the citizens of this great city with the cultural and artistic values of one of its largest minority groups."

As a highly vocal, participatory audience watched from a slope in Riverside Park, the troupe performed Piri Thomas's new play, "The Golden Streets" on Wednesday night. The equipment will be moved to Tompkins Park tonight. Almost every other night this month, Thomas's play will be staged in a park or playground in one of the city's boroughs.

At the premiere, whole families were in attendance, even some wailing babies (which embellished the naturalistic atmosphere of the play). Unescorted youngsters crouched on the grass, popping bubble gum, sipping soda and gluing their eyes to the stage.

●

The audience was full of unscreened emotions. They booed the villain (a junkie), loudly cheered the actress who chased the villain away from her boy friend, encouraged stage romance ("Hot

Dog, don't you have nobody to dance with?"), laughed when things got too melodramatic, applauded the author's well-chosen slang and seemed warmed by ethnic references, particularly the humorous ones.

The play talks right to the audience with a message that bears constant repeating — and offers little reassurance: These people are forgotten, pushed aside, often forced into drugs and delinquency.

"We are going to make it one way or another," asserts Raul Perez at the end. Then he asks: "God, *porqué no?*"

"The Golden Streets," although fictionalized, seems like a continuation of Thomas's autobiography, "Down These Mean Streets." It begins with a young Puerto Rican's release from prison and return to El Barrio, where he works—as Thomas himself did—in a rehabilitation center. The title of the play is meant ironically — these are "gray streets," not golden streets—just as the title of the book was meant literally, although it is also clear that Thomas loves those mean streets. He runs away to them.

The book was an impassioned, subjective cry from the ghetto, full of poetry and conviction. Thomas is not only Puerto Rican but dark-skinned, which created a special, extraordinarily moving identity crisis. The book revealed a great deal about its author and his various worlds: streets, junkies, thieves, prison.

There is more than enough material in that book to fill a dozen stages. Thomas's picture of prison life for example, is far more evocative and disturbing than any prison play in recent memory.

•

Thomas's play is another matter entirely. Unlike his heartbreakingly sensitive book, the play is unsubtle in its emotions, and has many stock characters and situations. It is also heavy-handed in its polemics.

"I have treated you as the very best," says the father.

"No one can do more," says the mother.

"I think it's beautiful," says Paul's WASP girl. "I never heard my mother and father talk like that."

I never heard anybody talk like that either, except on soap operas, but I remember that indelible portrait of the father in Thomas's book — that self-deceptive, unapproachable man, so removed from reality that he is not even aware when his son runs away from home.

There are several scenes in "The Golden Streets" (which runs about 90 minutes without intermission) that make one realize what the play could be, and what a playwright Thomas could be. In one, the white liberal girl volunteers her services in Raul's ghetto storefront. He, as expected, derides her. She, as expected, refuses to be typecast.

The scene, in one form or another, occurs with almost ritualistic frequency in protest plays, but this time there is something about the level of writing and performance (by Alex Colon as Raul) that makes it rise far above banality.

•

"What do you know about our stick of living?" Raul challenges the girl, and begins cataloging the deprivations: "They only time we had meat was when a cockroach fell off the ceiling into the rice and beans," and then carries it further into a complete emotional assault. The author gives the story book encounter a new feeling of urgency.

But there are not enough such moments to give the play urgency or cohesion. With "The Golden Streets," it is the entire event, that is more important than the play. The event has much to say of value, to, and about, El Barrio.

1970 Ag 14

THE HAPPINESS CAGE, a play by Dennis J. Reardon. Directed by Tom Aldredge; settings by Marjorie Kellogg; costumes by Theoni V. Aldredge; lighting by Martin Aronstein; music by Ronny Cox; stage manager, Jane Neufeld. Presented by the New York Shakespeare Festival Public Theater, produced by Joseph Papp; Bernard Gersten, associate producer. At the Public Theater, 425 Lafayette Street.

Reese .... Lewis J. Stadlen
Orderly .... Charles Durning
Miles .... Ronny Cox
Rhodes .... James De Marse
Dr. Freytag .... Henderson Forsythe
General .... Paul Sparer
Aide .... George Loros
Visitors .... John Benson, Walter
   De Lano, Alice Merton Benson
Nurse .... Pamela Grey
Assistant .... Jason Miller
Anna Ames .... Bette Henritze
The Press ... Alice Merton Benson, John Benson, Walter De Lano, Jason Miller

By CLIVE BARNES

Joseph Papp and the New York Shakespeare Festival have gotten themselves a most beautiful new theater, and New York this morning is a better place. The theater is the Estelle R. Newman Theater, and it is in the same building as the company's Anspacher Theater, the old Astor Library on Lafayette Street.

The new theater is a beauty. It has been designed by Giorgio Cavaglieri, the architect, with the help of Ming Cho Lee and Martin Aronstein. What has emerged is a splendid theater, with great sightlines and atmosphere. Although there is no proscenium, the new theater is conventionally shaped, quite different from the Anspacher on the floor above. Each holds about 300 people.

The festival launched the Anspacher with "Hair," and while it has nothing quite so sensational this time, it does have a new playwright with a new play, "The Happiness Cage," very much worth seeing.

First a word of welcome to the playwright, Dennis J.

Zodiac

Ronny Cox and Bette Henritze at the Newman Theater.

Reardon, who is almost as young and probably quite as promising as the new theater itself. Mr. Reardon has written a play that is by turn gripping, entertaining and, oddly enough, not infrequently amusing. It is a pleasurably well-crafted work, although it is perhaps too long, the ending is weak, and Mr. Reardon seems in two minds about precisely what he wants to tell us. The faults of the play matter a great deal less than its virtues, which emerge very clearly.

A man, discharged from the Army but in a veterans hospital, finds himself transferred to a ward with two other patients. They both have terminal cancers, but he has merely a broken arm. Where, he wonders, does he fit in, and how soon can he get out? One of the patients is said to have a stomach cancer. But the doctors have operated on his brain. Why?

Also, why is the hospital constantly under the surveillance of a non-medical General and observers, who flit around as if watching some special project? Reese, the young man with a broken arm and a neurosis on his shoulder where other people wear a chip, is at first suspicious and then terrified. What are they trying to do to his mind?

They are trying to make him happy. They are trying to make everybody happy—especially soldiers. The Army, it seems, is very anxious for happy soldiers. Now, happiness is clearly a state of mind. It is induced by the mind's reaction to favorable sensory stimuli. But the mind could be placed into a state of permanent euphoria. No more pain, no more trouble—simple, blissful happiness.

This is the hospital's project. And the inmates of this cancer ward are persuaded to offer themselves as human rats for experimentation, all to the good of mankind and the greater glory of the General, and the Surgeon, who can just see a Nobel Prize lurking around the next scalpel.

There is a lot of tension and mystery to the play, and it would be unfair to disclose the story in any detail. It is to the point perhaps that Mr. Reardon's philosophic purpose—for although the play has all the trappings of realistic melodrama there is clearly a deeper theme—does, at the end, appear blunted.

●

He appears to be attempting two themes, and as a result not expressing either with the power he clearly possesses. His first theme is the godlike propensities of medical scientists, perhaps giving a heart to this man, a liver to that and perhaps experimenting on human specimens for their own greater prestige.

His other perhaps more serious theme is that man is born unique simply because he is disaffected and that suffering as much as happiness is inextricable from the nobility of man. A man is defined by pain as much as by happiness. However, certain totalitarian forces in the world might like to use bovine happiness as an instrument of suppression.

At a time when few plays have any serious theme, perhaps it might seem carping to complain of a play having two. Yet a play can rarely carry more than one basic idea at a time. The writing is good—taut, tough and funny — and the characterizations run more convincingly when it is accepted that the situation, said to be based on a real incident, is really a melodramatic fantasy.

●

The staging by Tom Aldredge kept up the suspense, and showed a certain expertise in the way that hospitals are run, as did Marjorie Kellogg's setting, which is so real that you feel you ought to be able to get the price of your seat back from Blue Cross. The performances were at a high level, with Lewis J. Stadlen most impressive as the tortured Reese, Charles Durning as a zonked-out Orderly who believes happiness is just a pill, and Ronny Cox as the coarse-mouthed Miles, Reese's fellow guinea pig. In the two stereotyped roles of the General and the Surgeon, Paul Sparer and Henderson Forsythe did their talented best to emerge. There were faults, but I was never bored.

1970 O 5

INDEX

Author Index

Title Index